W9-ASO-410

Law in the Schools

SECOND EDITION

William D. Valente
Professor of Law
Villanova University School of Law
Adjunct Professor of Education
Villanova University Graduate School of Education

MERRILL PUBLISHING COMPANY
A Bell & Howell Company
Columbus Toronto London Melbourne

For Joseph, Christina, Andrew, and Claire, who taught their father much about education

Published by Merrill Publishing Company
A Bell & Howell Company
Columbus, Ohio 43216

This book was set in Goudy Old Style.

Administrative Editor: Beverly Kolz
Production Coordinator: Anne Daly
Cover Designer: Cathy Watterson

Library of Congress Catalog Card Number: 86–61189
International Standard Book Number: 0–675–20399–6
Printed in the United States of America

1 2 3 4 5 6 7 8 9 — 91 90 89 88 87

PREFACE

Six years is usually an insubstantial period for changes in law, but in that interval since the first edition of this book, the pace of school law developments has been not normal, but hectic. Since 1980 the United States Supreme Court decisions alone account for major shifts in the legal relations and obligations of public and private schools. This much is evident from the listing of new Supreme Court cases in the case outlines at the beginning of each chapter. Of equal importance is the stream of new federal and state statutes and case decisions affecting every group in the school community, especially with reference to religion in the schools, affirmative action minority preference programs, claims of students and teachers regarding discrimination based upon gender or handicap, and management-union rights under new public sector bargaining laws.

The second edition undertakes to update the rapid developments of law across the entire range of the chapter topics, through the 1985–86 Supreme Court term. Even as this edition goes to press, however, new cases arise and are pending as evidence that evolution of school law is still in a burgeoning state. While this second edition maintains the general organization and approach of the first edition, the emergence of new issues and controversies has required some modification in the stress and coverage given to particular topics. Those changes are also evident in the topical outline introducing each chapter. The index has also been extended and revised to serve the revised text more closely.

For their material support and research assistance in the preparation of this second edition, I remain continually grateful to Dean John Murray, the director and staff of the Villanova Law Library, and students too numerous to list here. My special thanks go to my secretary, Joan DeLong, and to Anne Daly, Associate Production Editor at Merrill Publishing Co., for their patience and skill in preparing and editing the manuscript for publication.

W. D. V.

PREFACE TO THE FIRST EDITION

Anyone interested in school law must be impressed, if not overwhelmed, by the flood of new statutes, bureaucratic regulations, and court decisions that constantly affect the operations of schools. This inundation has been caused by the complex demands imposed on schools and other institutions, which necessitate ever increasing governmental involvement in all phases of education. The consequent reexamination of institutional policies and relationships places heavy burdens upon educators and their legal advisors. Keeping up with "the law", and revising practices to satisfy that law, was far more challenging in the seventies than in the sixties and promises to be more demanding in the decade ahead. This text is intended to assist professionals in the school community to meet these challenges.

Given the proliferating welter of laws, careful organization of legal materials becomes critical to a practical understanding of the dominant policies and themes of school law. Without an organized foundation and rational framework, the elements of constitutional, statutory, regulatory, and case law become, in the words of Holmes, a "ragbag of details."

This book can be used as a basic reference for graduate studies and as a practical desk reference for school administrators and counselors. In the interest of economy, the contents are primarily narrative discussion, supplemented by illustrative excerpts from leading court opinions. The book contains quick reference compendiums of major federal statutes and individual state school codes (as prepared by the National Institute of Education). Collections of case authorities on given topics in the annotations of the American Law Reports and special studies of scholars are also features.

Emphasis is placed upon current and emerging issues, with most of the legal authorities dating from 1965 to the present. The topical breakdown of text materials allows for a variety of study and research techniques and permits users to concentrate on areas of special interest, where the reader's time or interest indicates selective rather than total review of the law.

A few words about the specific content organization may be helpful. Each chapter opens with a detailed outline of the subjects covered, usually amplified by an introductory comment providing an overview of the materials that follow. Chapters 1 and 2 outline the basic structure and processes of the federal and state legal systems as they bear upon the rights and obligations of various school authorities and groups.

Chapter 3 covers the basic legal requirements of managing the public school, its programs, teachers, and students. Chapter 4 deals with the issues of religion and public education. Chapters 5 and 6 focus upon the legal status and rights of the major school groups, i.e., teachers and students. Special attention is given in Chapter 5 to the developing state laws governing teacher-labor relations.

Chapter 7 gives special attention to the expanding group discrimination law, particularly as it affects the civil rights of various teacher and student groups. Under the unifying policy of equal opportunity in education, the material stresses the special classification problems relating to race, sex, age, handicap, and poverty. Chapter 8 surveys the traditional rules of tort liability and their special application to different school settings, as modified by state and federal statutes. Separate treatment is given to new tort remedies that have emerged under modern civil rights statutes.

Chapter 9 outlines the principal legal methods that control the raising and expenditure of school revenues, both for school districts and for individual schools. Foundation principles of public budgeting, accounting, taxation, school fees, borrowing, and public contracting, followed by specific examples, set the framework for analyzing school finance problems.

Chapter 10 addresses only those areas of law that are unique to nonpublic schools and notes important distinctions between sectarian and nonsectarian private schools. In the many instances where public school law is common to private schools, cross references are made to the preceding chapters. Chapter 10 is pertinent not only to private school administrators, but also to their counterparts in public education who have occasion to interact with them, particularly under government-sponsored programs that require intersystem administration and cooperation. The need for administrators in both systems to understand the rights and duties of their counterparts in the other system, in order to avoid unnecessary misunderstandings of particular school practices, is evident in today's complex interaction of public and private education.

I have stressed relevant opinions from the United States Supreme Court (through March, 1979), and from the highest appellate courts of individual states wherever possible.

However, where a point of law is not covered by higher authority, I have included lower court opinions. Differences among the courts have been indicated by discussion of cases from different states, which also helps to ensure representative national coverage. Comparisons of divergent state laws are made possible by the data tables throughout the book that summarize the statute law in each state on selected features of school organization.

The footnotes to the text are cited to regional case reporters, since these are more accessible across the land than the official case reports of individual states.

Regarding reproduced court opinions, I have, with few exceptions, omitted the court's footnotes and the dissenting opinions. In those instances where an important decision was made by a closely divided court, that fact has been reported and discussed in the narrative text.

Finally, I still hold the view that a good index is indispensable to the practical and efficient use of the text. Accordingly, I have personally prepared a detailed index to allow quick reference to text discussions on specific points of interest.

W. D. V.

CONTENTS*

State Law Comparisons and Federal Statutes (Tables/Figures) viii
Excerpts—United States Constitution x

1 Education Under the American Legal System—An Overview 2
2 Public Education in the Legal Structure 18
3 The Law Governing School Organization 66
4 Religion and Public Education 122
5 Professional Personnel 180

Part I Employment Eligibility 180
Part II Employment Rights and Duties 191
Part III Collective Labor-Management Relations 240

6 Student Rights and Discipline 302
7 Equal Opportunity in Public Education 356
8 Tort Liability 424
9 Financing Public Education 478
10 Private Education 534

Glossary 627

Table of Cases 633

Index 655

Addendum 659

---

*Detailed outlines of contents are presented at the beginning of each chapter.

STATE LAW COMPARISONS AND FEDERAL STATUTES (TABLES/FIGURES)*

No.	Subject	Page
1–1	Summary of Individual State School Laws	9
2–1	Summary of State Standards—Admission Requirements	25
2–2	Summary of State Standards—Attendance Requirements	26
2–3	Summary of State Standards—School Calendar	28
2–4	State Level Agencies	40
3–1	Summary of State Standards—Grade Organization	80
3–2	Summary of State Standards—Curriculum	84
3–3	Summary of State Standards—Textbook Control	87
3–4	Summary of State Standards—Extracurricular Activities	91
3–5	Summary of State Standards—Promotion Requirements	94
3–6	Summary of State Standards—High School Graduation Requirements	96
5–1	Summary of State Standards—Teacher Personnel Policies	176
5–2	Summary of State Laws—Teacher Bargaining	242
6–1	Summary of State Laws—Student Records	332
7–A	**Appendix:** Principal Federal Laws Affecting Equal Opportunity in Schools	418
	A 42 U.S.C. §1981—Civil Rights Acts of 1866, 1870	419
	B 42 U.S.C. §1983—The Civil Rights Act of 1871	419
	C 42 U.S.C. §§1985 and 1986—The Civil Rights Act of 1871	419
	D 42 U.S.C. §1988—Civil Rights Acts of 1866, 1870	420
	E 42 U.S.C. §2000(d)—Civil Rights Act of 1964, Title VI	420

*Since the National Institute of Education has not recently updated the information in the summary tables, readers must check for possible changes in each state since 1979.

No.		Subject	Page
	F	42 U.S.C. §2000(e)—Civil Rights Act of 1964, Title VII	420
	G	20 U.S.C. §1681—Education Amendements of 1972, Title IX	421
	H	29 U.S.C. §206(d)—Equal Pay Act	421
	I	29 U.S.C. §621—Age Discrimination Act (§623)	422
	J	20 U.S.C. §1703—Equal Education Opportunities Act	422
	K	29 U.S.C. §794—Rehabilitation Act of 1973 (§504)	423
	L	20 U.S.C. §1401—The Education of the Handicapped Act (§1412)	423
9–1		Federal, State and Local Expenditures for Education	480
9–2		Per-Pupil Revenue for Elementary and Secondary Education by Source	481
10–1		State Statutes on Qualifications for Teachers in Private Schools	541
10–2		Nonpublic School Participation in Federal Assistance Programs	574

SELECTED PROVISIONS OF THE CONSTITUTION OF THE UNITED STATES OF AMERICA

We the People of the United States, in Order to form a more perfect Union, establish Justice, insure domestic Tranquility, provide for the common defence, promote the general Welfare, and secure the Blessings of Liberty to ourselves and our Posterity, do ordain and establish this Constitution for the United States of America.

Article I

• • •

Section 8. [1] The Congress shall have Power to lay and collect Taxes, Duties, Imposts and Excises, to pay the Debts and provide for the common Defence and general Welfare of the United States; . . .

[3] To Regulate Commerce with foreign Nations, and among the several States, and within the Indian Tribes; . . .

[18] To make all Laws which shall be necessary and proper for carrying into Execution the foregoing Powers, and all other Powers vested by this Constitution in the Government of the United States, or in any Department or Officer thereof . . .

Section 10. [1] No State shall . . . pass any . . . Law impairing the Obligation of Contracts, . . .

Article III

Section 1. The judicial Power of the United States, shall be vested in one supreme Court, and in such inferior Courts as the Congress may from time to time ordain and establish. The Judges, both of the supreme and inferior Courts, shall hold their Offices during good Behaviour, and shall, at stated Times, receive for their Services a Compensation, which shall not be diminished during their Continuance in Office. . . .

Section 2. [1] The judicial Power shall extend to all Cases, in Law and Equity, arising under this Constitution, the Laws of the United States and Treaties made, or which shall be made, under their Authority; . . . to Controversies to which the United States shall be a Party; — to Controversies between two or more States; — between a State and Citizens of another State; — between Citizens of different States; — between Citizens of the same State claiming Lands under the Grants of different States, and between a State, or the Citizens thereof, and foreign States, Citizens or Subjects. . . .

Article VI

[2] This Constitution, and the Laws of the United States which shall be made in Pursuance thereof; and all Treaties made, or which shall be made, under the Authority of the United States, shall be the supreme Law of the Land; and the Judges in every State shall be bound thereby, any Thing in the Constitution or Laws of any State to the Contrary notwithstanding.

* * *

AMENDMENT I [1791]

Congress shall make no law respecting an establishment of religion, or prohibiting the free exercise thereof; or abridging the freedom of speech, or of the press; or the right of the people peaceably to assemble, and to petition the Government for a redress of grievances.

* * *

AMENDMENT IV [1791]

The right of the people to be secure in their persons, houses, papers, and effects, against unreasonable searches and seizures, shall not be violated, and no Warrants shall issue, but upon probable cause, supported by Oath or affirmation, and particularly describing the place to be searched, and the persons or things to be seized.

AMENDMENT V [1791]

No person shall be . . . compelled in any criminal case to be a witness against himself, nor be deprived of life, liberty, or property, without due process of law; nor shall private property be taken for public use, without just compensation.

* * *

AMENDMENT IX [1791]

The enumeration in the Constitution, of certain rights, shall not be construed to deny or disparage others retained by the people.

AMENDMENT X [1791]

The powers not delegated to the United States by the Constitution, nor prohibited by it to the States, are reserved to the States respectively, or to the people.

* * *

AMENDMENT XIII [1865]

Section 1. Neither slavery nor involuntary servitude, except as a punishment for crime whereof the party shall have been duly convicted, shall exist within the United States, or any place subject to their jurisdiction.

Section 2. Congress shall have power to enforce this article by appropriate legislation.

AMENDMENT XIV [1868]

Section 1. All persons born or naturalized in the United States, and subject to the jurisdiction thereof, are citizens of the United States and of the State wherein they reside. No State shall make or enforce any law which shall abridge the privileges or immunities of citizens of the United States; nor shall any State deprive any person of life, liberty, or property, without due process of law; nor deny to any person within its jurisdiction the equal protection of the laws.

* * *

AMENDMENT XXVII [Proposed]*

Section 1. Equality of rights under the law shall not be denied or abridged by the United States or by any State on account of sex.

Section 2. The Congress shall have the power to enforce, by appropriate legislation, the provisions of this article.

Section 3. This amendment shall take effect two years after the date of ratification.

---

*Submitted by Congress for ratification on March 22, 1972. The amendment was neither ratified nor adopted.

Law in the Schools

CHAPTER 1

CHAPTER OUTLINE

A. The relation of law, politics, and education
B. Parents' interest in education
C. The state interest in education
D. The federal interest in education
   1. Civil Liberties
   2. Curriculum
E. The American legal system
   1. Sources and levels of law
      a. Written constitutions
      b. Statutes
      c. Judge-made law
      d. Administrative law
      e. The role of courts in law application
   2. The relation of federal to state law
F. Structure and functions of courts
   1. The federal court system
   2. State court systems

Education Under the American Legal System —An Overview

A. The Relation of Law, Politics, and Education

Education, politics, and law are inextricably interrelated.

> "Education is inherently subject to a struggle for control. . . . Parents may well have different interests in their child's education. . . . But when education moves outside the home, . . . this intrafamily conflict is overshadowed by that which occurs between the family and the community which operates the school. In more recent years, a second shift . . . has occurred; a shift from family versus school, or family versus community, to local community versus the state . . . or local community versus the national government,"[1]

> "Most people don't know who controls American education because little attention has been given the question by either educators or the public. The field of education, even though it consumes a giant's share of the nation's resources, has until recently received little political analysis. . . . People in and out of education are not at all happy with the traditional methods by which decisions get made. . . . Public interest in the politics of education has also grown out of the frustration of people who want to see reforms . . . but who see them constantly blocked by the rigidities of a well-entrenched bureaucracy. So they turn their attention to the problem of how to gain political leverage in education and of how radical change can be made in the schools. . . . As most people know by now, the distribution of governmental power in the United States is undergoing some fundamental changes. On the one hand, the federal government is exercising much more authority over state and local government . . . ; on the other there is much talk of decentralization and many efforts to make state and local governments stronger than ever before. The result is called Creative Federalism by some and chaos by others."[2]

The foregoing statement reflects the basic fact that school law is not static, but is part of a continuing political process of revising educational policy. This process explains why school law varies among the states with respect to different facets of public education. In some instances primary legal control vests in central state education agencies; in others, in local school districts; and in still others in local municipalities. This allocation of educational control represents practical accommodations of individual and institutional claims. For example, curriculum control is generally vested in the state, but in special circumstances, parental and student demands supersede agency authority. The broad discretion of school officials to determine whether or how to exercise their legal authority also allows each local school board to adjust its programs to prevailing conditions in its respective district.

B. Parents' Interest in Education

Parents have substantial interests in public education—as citizen-taxpayers, as guardians of their children, and as holders of constitutionally protected parental rights. These

---

1. Coleman, The Struggle for Control of Education, Education and Social Policy: Local Control of Education 64 (1970).

2. Koerner, Who Controls American Education? vii-viii, 3–4, 166 (1968).

interests provide the basis for legal standing to sue school authorities on challenges to the validity of school laws and regulations. Without essaying the details of "standing" law, it is important to recognize that courts will not hear a case unless the suing party has a legally recognized interest and stake in the subject matter and in the outcome of the particular case. For example, state and federal taxpayers have standing to sue on matters affecting their taxes and tax spending, but they generally lack standing to challenge official decisions in which they have no personal stake, such as a decision to suspend a student who is unrelated to them.[3] Parents have standing to challenge any educational decision that adversely affects the legal rights of their children, whether they relate to religion, curricular needs, racial or sexual equality, or health and safety. But a parent whose child or taxes are not affected by a particular school activity generally lacks standing to challenge its legality.[4]

The parental right to control the upbringing of children exists independently of the rights of other citizens. For example, parents have legal standing to oppose forced enrollment of their children in public schools; to challenge state law outlawing foreign languages from private schools; and to oppose school indoctrination contrary to their religious beliefs. A perennial issue in education law, which will be evident in the later chapters, is how to accommodate or balance the interests of governments and of parents when those interests collide.

The identification of the legal interests of parents regarding public education, though obvious in most instances, is a threshold requirement for litigation by parents. Without parental standing to sue, the legality of many public school actions could not be put to judicial trial. Thus, standing is needed to get a case tried, but it does not resolve the ultimate question whether a parent's suit has merit and is justified under the law.

The legal recognition of parental rights takes education law beyond the political task of assigning jurisdiction to various agencies of government, to the legal task of defining individual rights in the school scene.

C. The State Interest in Education

Public education in the United States has always been primarily the responsibility of individual states. The Federal Constitution makes no mention of education, and the Tenth Amendment (see p. xi) operates to reserve that power to the states. All state constitutions, on the other hand, expressly provide for the creation of a state system of public education.[5]

In addition to the specific powers enumerated in state constitutions, state legislatures also exercise general police power to promote the public welfare. This broad

---

3. *See* Flast v. Cohen, 392 U.S. 83 (1968).

4. Muka v. Cornell,370 N.Y.S.2d 909 (1975), appeal dismissed, 331 N.E.2d 688 (1975).

5. Some state constitutions mandate a "thorough and/or efficient" System of public education; while others call for a "general and/or universal" system. Most of the remaining states have broader clauses, e.g.,"a system of common schools." HEW, *State Constitutional Provisions and Selected Legal Materials Relating to Public School Finances* (L. Perle ed. 1973). See also U. Columbia, CONSTITUTIONS OF THE UNITED STATES, NATIONAL & STATE (1974).

police power, for example, legitimates compulsory attendance laws to ensure minimal education of its residents in a qualified public or private school or in special circumstances, in approved programs of at-home or custodial instruction.

> "It is, therefore, recognized by the authorities, without exception, so far as we can find, that to accomplish this end the state may resort to what is generally referred to as compulsory education or school attendance of children." *Rice* v. *Commonwealth,* 49 S.E.2d 342, 348 (Va. 1948).

States have the predominant role and responsibility for citizen education, but their interest is not exclusive. They are bound by federal constitutional commands:

> "By and large, public education in our Nation is committed to the control of state and local authorities. Courts do not and cannot intervene in the resolution of conflicts which arise in the daily operation of school systems and which do not directly and sharply implicate basic constitutional values." *Epperson* v. *Arkansas,* 393 U.S. 97, 104 (1968).

Federal statutes also affect educational activity. This interaction of federal and state law is continually expanding and accounts for many of the complexities in contemporary school law.

D. The Federal Interest in Education

Although the subject of education is not specifically delegated to the national government, there are two major avenues by which it acquires some jurisdiction over schools.

1. Civil Liberties

The first is provided by federal constitutional law and civil rights statutes that prohibit actions that abridge civil liberties and contract rights of individuals, whether in school or out of school. These include First and Fourteenth Amendment freedoms of speech, press, association, and religious liberty; and immunity from racial or sexual discrimination. Increasingly, the United States Supreme Court influences educational policy by interpreting the constitutionality of school practices and by defining what a school may *not* do in its day-to-day operations. Congress also has far-reaching authority to protect these interests both by direct regulation and by economic incentives (i.e. federal financial aid based upon compliance with terms and conditions specified by the federal government). These restraints extend in many cases to private schools that receive government assistance. Recently, the denial of federal income tax exemptions has been used to impose national policy on private schools.[6]

6. See discussion of Bob Jones University v. United States, ch. 10 at n. 178 *infra.*

2. Curriculum

The second channel of federal influence is less direct; that is, federal regulation of subjects that affect and are affected by education. Thus, the federal government may spend funds to promote the following:

1. Foreign language training to carry out international affairs;
2. Physical science studies, research and development in order to improve our military security;
3. Health care and research under its power to spend for the general welfare. (See Article I of the U.S. Constitution.)

Since education affects these and many other federal interests, the federal jurisdiction to regulate and control many aspects of education, though indirect, is still very broad. Between the carrot of federal funds, which currently amount to about 8 percent of all school revenues, and the stick of federal enforcement of federal law, federal influence is substantial.[7] For good or ill, the camel's head is in the tent, and it is a very large head with very sharp bristles.

Once federal jurisdiction attaches, the federal law supersedes any inconsistent state law by reason of the supremacy clause of the Constitution:

> "This Constitution, and the laws of the United States which shall be made in pursuance thereof; and all treaties made, or which shall be made, under the authority of the United States, shall be the supreme law of the land; and the judges in every state shall be bound thereby, anything in the Constitution or laws of any state to the contrary notwithstanding." U.S. Constitution, Article VI, §2.

It is a peculiar irony that in reserving primary jurisdiction over education to the states, the Constitution also subjects that state jurisdiction to displacement by indirect education legislation by the national government.

E. The American Legal System

The allocation of control in education, through law, is expressed by the term *jurisdiction.* This term means *authority that is legitimated through law.* The exercise of power without legal authority is unlawful; hence the concept of *jurisdiction* is central to distinguishing between lawful and lawless acts of school administrators. In our system, the hierarchy of legal jurisdiction is determined in two ways: (1) by the source or level of law and (2) by the authority of different government agencies. Since school law is an outgrowth of the

---

7. See HEW, *Statistical Report of National Center for Education Statistics,* vol. 3, part 1, The Condition of Education (1977 ed.) p. 125.

basic scheme of the entire legal system, its place in that system must be understood in terms of universal principles that determine legal jurisdiction.

1. Sources and Levels of Law

The law draws upon four principal sources of official direction. They are written constitutions, statutes, administrative rules and regulations, and court decisions. These Sources are not all of equal authority, and when they come into conflict, an understanding of their relative weight and interaction becomes crucial.

a. Written Constitutions. Constitutions are the highest form of law. They are written charters adopted by the people to establish the basic structure and powers of their state and federal governments. Constitutions, intended to apply to changing circumstances over long periods of time, are broadly worded, and require continuing judicial interpretation for their application to new social conditions. Because the process of constitutional amendment is burdensome, the public seldom resorts to this process to solve specific and immediate problems. Thus, the courts have great power in updating the meaning and application of constitutional principles.

b. Statutes. The written enactments of Congress and of state legislatures are the next highest level of law after federal and state constitutions. Statutes establish the specifics of government organization and policy. For example, a state constitution generally provides for the creation of a public school system; the specific structure, design and operation of that system are decided by the enactment of education statutes. These statutes are continually revised or supplemented by successive legislatures and are all subject to review by the courts to determine their meaning and constitutionality. So long as a statute does not violate constitutional limitations, it is binding on all citizens and government agencies.

Most states compile education statutes into a *school code* for ease of reference. Educational administrators should familiarize themselves with the contents of their home-state codes. (See the state-by-state summary of educational laws, Table 1–1.) Helpful summaries of state school laws are also published by many state educational agencies, and by professional organizations like the state school boards and teacher associations.

c. Judge-made Law. Legislatures enact law designed to affect the entire citizenry; courts decide individual disputes between particular parties. In the decisional process, the courts also fashion legal principles of wide application by interpreting the general meaning of constitutions and statutes and by supplying judicial principles to fill in the gaps left by enacted law. In the Anglo-American family of laws, judges created two bodies of case law independently of written Constitutions and statutes: the common law and the law of equity.

Development of the Common Law. The *common law* grew by looking to customs and principles that prevailed in the community, including prior court decisions (called

TABLE 1-1. Summary of individual state school laws *

State	Laws
ALABAMA	Public School Laws of Alabama Annotated, Michie Co. (1970).
ALASKA	Compiled School Laws of Alaska, Dept. of Education (1974); Alaska Administrative Code, State Dept. of Education (1973).
ARIZONA	School Laws and Pocket Supplement (1973); (various rules and regulations State Dept. of Education, State Board of Education).
ARKANSAS	School Laws of Arkansas (1973).
CALIFORNIA	West's Annotated California Codes, West Publishing Co. (1969); California Administrative Code, Office of Administrative Hearings (1973).
COLORADO	Colorado School Laws of 1971, Department of Education. Handbook for Colorado School Board Members, Department of Education (1964).
CONNECTICUT	General Statutes of Connecticut, Revision of 1958, Volume 11, Published by Authority of the State (1973).
DELAWARE	A Compilation of School Laws of the State of Delaware, State Department of Public Instruction (1971). Handbook for Secondary Schools, State Department of Public Instruction (1970). Handbook for Elementary Schools, State Department of Public Instruction (1973).
FLORIDA	Florida School Laws, State Department of Education (1972). Elementary and Secondary Standards, State Department of Education (1971).
GEORGIA	Georgia School Laws, Office of the State Superintendent of Schools, Department of Education (1972). Teacher Certification in Georgia, Office of Instructional Services, Department of Education (1971).
HAWAII	Laws Relating to the Department of Education, State of Hawaii (1969). Policies and Regulations, Department of Education (1970).
IDAHO	Idaho School Code and 1973 Pocket Supplement. Standards and Recommendations for Elementary Schools, Department of Education (1962). Accreditation Standards and Procedures for Secondary Schools, Department of Education (1970).
ILLINOIS	School Code of Illinois, State Superintendent of Public Instruction (1973). The Certification of Educational Personnel, Superintendent of Public Instruction (1972).
INDIANA	Indiana Code of 1971, Bobbs-Merrill Co., Inc. (1971). The Education of Indiana Teachers, State Superintendent of Public Instruction (1969). Administrative Handbook for Indiana Schools, State Superintendent of Public Instruction (1973).

SOURCE: Adapted from National Institute of Education.

*All data tables must be updated for possible changes in each state since 1979.

TABLE 1-1. Summary of individual state school laws (*cont.*)

State	Laws
IOWA	School Laws of Iowa (1972). Rules and Policies of Iowa State Board of Education, State Board of Education (1972).
KANSAS	School Laws of Kansas, State Department of Education (1968). Regulations, State Board of Education, Agency 91 (1974 Supp.)
KENTUCKY	School Laws of Kentucky, Annotated, Department of Education (1972). Kentucky Administrative Regulations, Legislative Research Commission (1972).
LOUISIANA	Laws of Louisiana. Louisiana Standards for State Certification of School Personnel, Superintendent of Public Education (1971). Handbook for School Administration, Department of Public Education (1974).
MAINE	State of Maine Laws Relating to Public Schools, State Department of Education and Cultural Services (1972). Procedures and Standards for Basic Approval of Schools Public and Private, Grades K-12 and Schools for Exceptional Children, State Department of Education and Cultural Services (1973).
MARYLAND	Public School Laws of Maryland, Department of Education, The Michie Company (1970). Principles and Standards, Public Secondary Education in Maryland, Department of Education, Maryland School Bulletin, Volume XL, No. 3 (May 1964).
MASSACHUSETTS	Massachusetts General Laws Annotated. Regulations of the Board of Education.
MICHIGAN	School Laws of Michigan and Pocket Supplement (1973). Educational Accountability, Department of Education (1972).
MINNESOTA	Minnesota School Laws, Department of Education (1971). Minnesota Administrative Rules and Regulations, State Board of Education (1967).
MISSISSIPPI	Mississippi Code 1972 Annotated, Harrison Company (1973). Handbook for Superintendent, Mississippi State Department of Education (1971). Standards for Accreditation of Elementary and Secondary Schools, State Board of Education (1972).
MISSOURI	Missouri School Laws, State Department of Education (1970). The School Administrator's Handbook, Publication No. 20-H, Commissioner of Education (1969).
MONTANA	School Laws of Montana, Allen Smith Company (1971); Pocket Supplement (1973). Standards for Accreditation of Montana Schools, Department of Education (1973).
NEBRASKA	Nebraska School Laws, Stephenson School Supply Co. (1973). Rules and Regulations for the Accreditation of Public and Non-Public School Systems, Department of Education (1971).

TABLE 1-1. Summary of individual state school laws (*cont.*)

State	Laws
NEVADA	Nevada School Laws, Superintendent of Public Instruction (1972). Nevada High School Graduation Requirements, Division of Educational Services (1973).
NEW HAMPSHIRE	New Hampshire Revised Statutes Annotated (1974). State Board of Education Policies, State Department of Education (August 1969). Minimum Standards and Recommended Practices for Elementary and Secondary Schools in New Hampshire, Department of Education (1970).
NEW JERSEY	New Jersey Statutes Annotated, West Publishing Company (1968), Cumulative Pocket Part (1974). New Jersey Administrative Code, Division of Administrative Procedure, Department of State (1973).
NEW MEXICO	School Laws of New Mexico Public School Code, Constitutional Provisions, State Board Regulations (1973). Minimum Standards for New Mexico Schools, State Department of Education (1973).
NEW YORK	McKinney's Consolidated Laws of New York Annotated, West Publishing Co. (1969); Cumulative Annual Pocket Part (1974). Minimum Requirements for Schools in New York State, State Education Department (1973). Regulations of the Commissioner of Education (1971–1973). Rules of the Board of Regents.
NORTH CAROLINA	School Laws of North Carolina. Public School Laws of North Carolina, State Board of Education (1971). State Accreditation, Curriculum/Administration Series, Department of Public Instruction, No. 454 (1973).
NORTH DAKOTA	North Dakota Century School Code, Department of Public Instruction (1971). Administrative Manual for North Dakota Schools, Department of Public Instruction (1973).
OHIO	School Laws of Ohio Minimum Standards for Ohio Elementary Schools, Department of Education (1970). Minimum Standards for Ohio Junior High Schools, Department of Education (1968). Minimum Standards for Ohio High Schools, Department of Education (1968). Laws and Regulations Governing Teacher Education and Certification, Department of Education (1972).
OKLAHOMA	School Laws of Oklahoma, State Superintendent of Public Instruction (1971). Annual Bulletin for Elementary and Secondary Schools (Administrator's Handbook), State Superintendent of Public Instruction (1973). Teacher Education, Certification and Assignment Handbook, State Board of Education (1971).

TABLE 1-1. Summary of individual state school laws (*cont.*)

State	Laws
OREGON	Oregon Revised Standards (1972) Oregon Administrative Rules Oregon Board of Education Policies
PENNSYLVANIA	Purdon's Pennsylvania Statutes Annotated, West Publishing Co. (1962); Cumulative Annual Pocket Part (1974-1975). Pennsylvania Regulations of the State Board of Education, State Board of Education (1974).
RHODE ISLAND	Education Laws of Rhode Island, Department of Education. Regulations of the State Board of Regents Governing the Special Education of Handicapped Children, State Board of Regents.
SOUTH CAROLINA	School Laws of South Carolina and Pocket Supplement (1973). Defined Minimum Programs for South Carolina School Districts, State Department of Education (1973).
SOUTH DAKOTA	Education Laws of South Dakota, Department of Public Instruction (1968).
TENNESSEE	Tennessee Statutes and Pocket Supplement (1973). Rules, Regulations and Minimum Standards, Tennessee State Board of Education (1973).
TEXAS	Texas Education Code, Bulletin 721, Texas Education Agency (1971). Policies of the Texas State Board of Education, Texas Education Agency.
UTAH	School Laws of the State of Utah, State Board of Education (1971).
VERMONT	Vermont School Laws and Supplement (1973). Certification Regulations, Department of Education (1972). Supervisory and Administrative Regulations, Department of Education (1967). Requirements and Minimum Standards for School Districts Providing Elementary Education, Department of Education.
VIRGINIA	Virginia School Laws. Regulations of the Board of Education of Virginia, Board of Education (1973). Standards for Accrediting Secondary Schools, State Department of Education (1970). Standards for Accrediting Elementary Schools, State Department of Education (1970).
WASHINGTON	Revised Code of Washington and Pocket Supplement (1973). Washington Administrative Code (1970).
WEST VIRGINIA	West Virginia School Laws, Michie Co. (1971), with 1972 Supplement.
WISCONSIN	Laws of Wisconsin Relating to Public Schools, Department of Public Instruction (1972). Wisconsin Administrative Code, Department of Public Instruction (1973).
WYOMING	Wyoming Education Code of 1969, State Department of Education.

precedents). The laws of contracts and of tort liability are products of the common law. Under the doctrine of *stare decisis* (let the past decision stand), courts incline to follow precedent cases, but they are not unalterably locked to every precedent. A precedent may be avoided by showing that the earlier case was significantly different from the current one. Or, it may be rejected outright as ill-reasoned. Finally, constitutional or legislative change may override a precedent case.

Development of the Law of Equity. In spite of their power to avoid precedent decisions, the early English courts tended to petrify the common law, even where it produced unjust results. To cure inadequacies in the common law, a second court system, sometimes known as *courts of chancery* or *courts of equity*, was developed to fashion a body of flexible rules to supervene the restrictions of the common law. Rather than looking to precedent or custom, equity courts looked to precepts of conscience and principles of justice as applied to the individual parties. They drew upon maxims of ecclesiastical and Roman law such as "He Who comes into equity must come with clean hands," and "Equity looks upon that as done which ought to have been done."

While modern courts combine the functions of the common law and equity law, they still apply common law and equity law as distinct principles of judge-made law. Equity law has a limited field of operation—only where the judge sees a need for extraordinary relief because the common law does not provide an adequate remedy.[8] Further, the use of equity powers is discretionary with the court, and relief may be denied even though the common law produces a less than ideal result. Each court must decide whether a particular claim is sufficiently strong to justify special relief.

The remedies provided in equity law were unknown to the common law, which only afforded monetary compensation to injured parties. Equity acts by coercive orders to force a wrongdoer, under penalty of contempt of court, to take corrective action and to avoid continuing injuries. The court injunction, as a product of equity, remains a potent legal tool to prevent or terminate unlawful work stoppages or racial, sex, or employment discrimination; and to force affirmative action in public schools to redress past discrimination. Since equity judges have discretion to decide what cases involve noncompensable or irreparable harm, and since there is no right to a jury trial in equity proceedings, the equity courts play a very significant role in the resolution of school legal disputes.

d. Administrative Law. The largest, most detailed mass of law is created by administrative rules and regulations of agencies that are authorized by statute to regulate public activities. The "administrative law" of education agencies, boards, and officers has the full force of law so long as it complies with governing constitutions, statutes, and court decisions.

The hierarchy of the foregoing sources of law is observed in the respective legal systems of each state and of the federal government. As the voice of the sovereign people, the constitution prevails over any inconsistent statute, decision, or administrative ruling.

---

8. *E.g.*, "Estopping" a party from pleading a valid legal defense that would defeat a just claim. Stahelin v. Bd. of Education, 230 N.E.2d 465 (Ill. 1967).

Similarly, enacted laws and court decisions supersede and nullify any inconsistent administrative decision. The practical results of this interaction will become more evident in later chapters, but it is well to stress here that *school administrators must act in conformity with the three higher levels of law if their administrative decisions are to withstand legal challenge.*

e. Role of Courts in Law Application. As the forum of last resort in any legal dispute, courts have the final say on how law operates in a given case. Through the power of *judicial review,* courts clarify, supplement, reconcile, and nullify prior law. Their broad power cannot be discounted by any student of American law. To cite a few examples, courts make the following decisions:

1. What is or is not *due process* in constitutional disputes;
2. Whether requisite *reasonable* guidelines are provided by a statute that delegates power to school administrators;
3. Whether administrative decisions are *reasonable or arbitrary*
4. Whether given facts justify avoidance of common law on grounds of equity;
5. Whether a school decision falls within or outside the scope of an authorizing statute;
6. Whether a particular act or omission should be classified as prudent or negligent, as in tort claim cases.

Given their broad tasks in dealing with varied elements of law in each state, courts in different states often render decisions on similar school situations that are not parallel or even consistent with each other. Since law is not an exact science, they may reasonably differ on many value judgments that underly the development of legal policy.

2. The Relation of Federal to State Law

The difficulty in understanding the four levels of lawmaking is compounded by the dual system of federal and state laws. For the most part, federal and state laws operate concurrently and without conflict; but where they come into conflict on a common subject, the choice of applicable (federal or state) law is dictated by the supremacy clause of the Constitution (quoted at p. 7). Pertinent federal law will, therefore, displace inconsistent state law, including the state constitution.

Differences that arise between the law of sister states present no choice of law problems since each state's legal powers are independent of other states'. The experience and law of sister states, however, often provide guidance on novel legal questions. Hence the development of legal trends in one state often influences lawmaking in other states.

F. Structure and Functions of Courts

In the process of resolving individual disputes, courts maintain the "rule of law":

"The supremacy of law demands that there shall be opportunity to have some court decide whether an erroneous rule of law was applied; and whether the proceeding in which facts were adjudicated was conducted regularly." *St. Joseph Stockyards Co.* v. *United States,* 298 U.S. 38, 84 (1936).

Court decisions guide future official conduct, but to ascertain the scope of a particular decision, one must know both the territorial and the subject matter jurisdiction of the deciding court. This can only be discerned in the total structure of the federal and state court systems.

1. The Federal Court System

There are three basic tiers of federal courts, excluding special-purpose tribunals (military, patent, and customs courts). The United States Supreme Court is the court of final appeal on federal law questions, and is the only court whose decisions bind all territorial regions of the country. It is also the only court that is created directly by the federal constitution. Below the Supreme Court, Congress has established thirteen Circuit Courts of Appeal as courts of intermediate appeal. The territories governed by each circuit court are shown by the map in Figure 1–1.

Until the United States Supreme Court rules on a given question, the decision of each circuit court is binding upon schools within that particular circuit. Hence a different rule may apply in different circuits until the Supreme Court resolves the conflict. An illustration of such conflicts among federal circuits is provided by the male hair length regulation cases reported at p. 322.

Within each of the federal circuits, Congress has also established trial courts, called district courts (about 92 in all). Disgruntled parties may appeal district court decisions to the proper circuit court of appeals, and thereafter to the Supreme Court. In limited instances, appeals may be taken directly from district courts to the Supreme Court.

Federal courts may generally take only two types of cases: those in which *diversity jurisdiction* is present—where suits involve citizens of different states; and those that present federal questions—questions arising under federal law. When a case gives rise to both federal and state law questions, federal courts must decide the state question according to the court rules of the affected states.[9] Conversely, state courts presented with federal questions follow the rules of law laid down by the governing federal court. In the absence of a federal decision, state courts are free to determine the federal law, subject to future change by later federal decision on the same point.

2. State Court Systems

The great majority of cases involving schools are decided by state courts. Court structure varies from state to state, but many states have a three-tier pattern similar to the federal system. Trial courts, often organized along county lines, form the base of the system;

9. Erie R. Co. v. Tompkins, 204 U.S. 64 (1938).

FIGURE 1-1. Federal Courts of Appeal

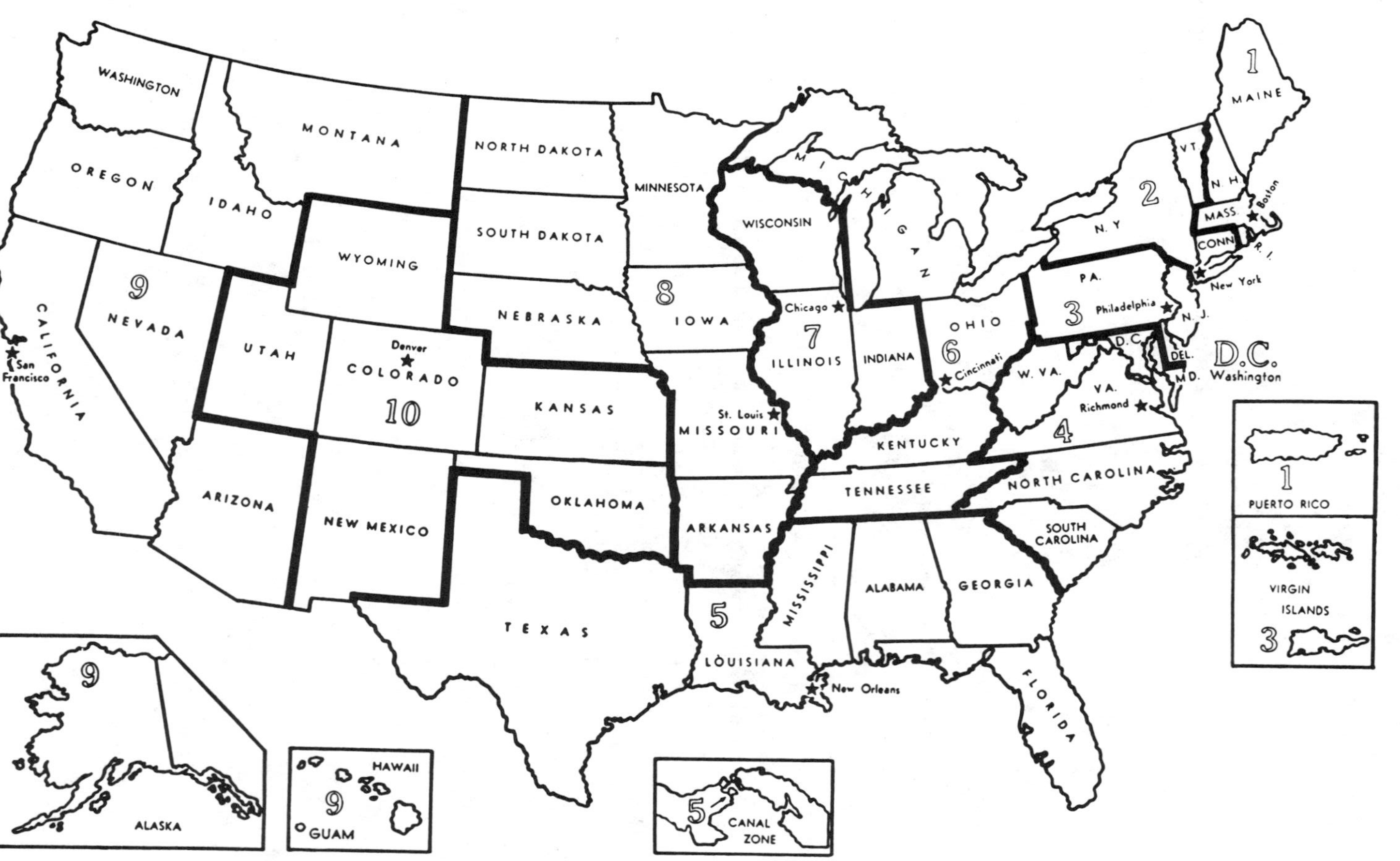

intermediate and final courts of appeal exercise statewide territorial jurisdiction. Titles given by each state to its courts at trial and appeal levels are not uniform.

The United States Supreme Court may review state court decisions only on questions of federal law and only after the highest court of the state has rendered its judgment.

Although appellate courts speak with greater authority and geographic jurisdiction than trial courts, they review only questions that the attorneys choose to raise on appeal. They will neither reconsider the fact findings of the trial court nor consider legal arguments that were not presented at trial.[10] The failure of an appellate opinion to address points that could have substantially affected a case often indicates that legal counsel did not properly present them on appeal, and not that such points were considered irrelevant by the court. This limiting process explains why a particular problem situation in school administration may have to be litigated several times before all critical issues involved in that situation are fully clarified in the law.

10. *See, e.g.*, part B of Channel 10 opinion, at the end of Chapter 2.

CHAPTER 2

CHAPTER OUTLINE

- A. State legislative control
  - 1. Direct and indirect legislative controls: ministerial and discretionary powers and duties
- B. Administrative agencies' control: Delegation doctrines
  - 1. Determining what powers are delegable
    - a. Redelegation
  - 2. Determining what powers are delegated
    - a. Expressed and implied powers
  - 3. Determining what powers are abused
  - 4. Court review of administrative decisions
    - a. Exhaustion of administrative remedies
    - b. Standing to sue
  - 5. Defective execution of statutory duties
  - 6. Ratification of past actions
- C. Administrative structure of public education
  - 1. State-level agencies
    - a. State boards of education
    - b. Chief state school officers
    - c. State departments of education
  - 2. Regional agencies
  - 3. Local agencies
    - a. School districts
    - b. School boards
- D. Other constitutional restrictions

Public Education in the Legal Structure

TABLE OF CASES FOR CHAPTER 2

Gann v. Harrisburg Community Unit School District, 218 N.E.2d 833 (Ill. 1966), 55.
Mullen v. Board of School Directors of DuBois Area S. Dist., 259A.2d 877 (Pa. 1969), 56.
Channel 10, Incorporated v. Independent School District No. 709, St. Louis County, 215 N.W.2d 817 (Minn. 1974), 58.
Conover v. Board of Education of Nebo School District, 267 P.2d 768 (Utah 1954), 63.

While all states have a public education system, their scheme of administration and allocation of authority to state-level, regional and local educational agencies varies. Most states divide administrative authority between state-wide and local school boards, but it is possible for a state to vest control solely in the local board, as in Virginia.[1] In looking to the law of other states for guidance, therefore, administrators must determine whether legal arrangements in the sister states are sufficiently similar to their own to be comparable.

A. State Legislative Control

The sweep of state legislature control over public education is indicated by the following judicial pronouncement:

> "The legislature has entire control over the schools of the state. . . . The division of the territory of the state into districts, the conduct of the school, the qualifications of teachers, the subjects to be taught therein, are all within its control. . . . " *Child Welfare Society of Flint* v. *Kennedy School Dist.*, 189 N.W. 1002, 1004 (Mich. 1922).[2]

School districts, like municipalities, are wholly dependent upon the state from which all their powers are delegated. This local subordination to the ultimate state control was forcefully described by the United States Supreme Court in *Hunter* v. *Pittsburgh*, 207 U.S. 161, 177–79 (1907):

> " . . . This court has many times had occasion to consider and decide the nature of municipal corporations, their rights and duties, and the rights of their citizens and creditors. [Citations omitted] . . . Municipal corporations are political subdivisions of the State, created as convenient agencies for exercising such of the governmental powers of the State as may be entrusted to them. For the purpose of executing these powers properly and efficiently they usually are given the power to acquire, hold, and manage personal and real property. The number, nature and duration of the powers conferred upon these corporations and the territory over which they shall be exercised rests in the absolute discretion of the State. . . .
>
> The State, therefore, at its pleasure may modify or withdraw all such powers, may take without compensation such property, hold it itself, or vest it in other agencies, expand or contract the territorial area, unite the whole or a part of it with another municipality, repeal the charter and destroy the corporation. . . .

---

1. *Compare* School Board v. Parham, 243 S.E.2d 468 (Va. 1978) *with* Robinson v. Cahill,287 A.2d 187 (N.J. 1972).

2. "Essentially and intrinsically, the schools . . . are matters of State,and not local jurisdiction. In such matters, the State is the unit, and the Legislature the source of power. The authority over schools and school affairs is not necessarily a distributive one to be exercised by local instrumentalities; but on the contrary, it is a central power residing in the Legislature of the State. It is for the law-making power to determine whether the authority shall be exercised by a state board of education, or distributed to county, township, or city organization throughout the state. . . . " State v. Haworth,23 N.E. 946, 947 (Ind. 1890). For a recent restatement of these principles, *see* Sch. District 12 v. Hughes, 552 P.2d 328, 332-333 (Mont. 1976).

Although the inhabitants and property owners may by such changes suffer inconvenience, and their property may be lessened in value by the burden of increased taxation, or for any other reason, they have no right by contract or otherwise in the unaltered or continued existence of the corporation or its powers, and there is nothing in the Federal Constitution which protects them from these injurious consequences."

A typical authority on school district reorganization reflects the same view:

"We have repeatedly held that '[a] School District is a creature or agency of the Legislature and has only the powers that are granted by statute.' *Barth* v. *Philadelphia School Dist.*, 393 Pa. 557, 562, 143 A.2d 909, 911 (1958). . . . The continued ability to alter the organization of the school system throughout the Commonwealth is a prerequisite to the fulfillment of the Legislature's constitutional duty to provide for the maintenance of a thorough and efficient system of public schools.

"It is clear beyond doubt that statutes enacted under the Legislature's duty to provide for education in the Commonwealth and administrative acts fixing school districts pursuant to that legislation are subject to change and revision thereafter." *Chartiers Valley Jt. School* v. *County Bd. of Sch. Dir.*, 211 A.2d 487, 500 (Pa. 1965).

Courts have recognized that the plenary power of state legislatures includes authority to (1) direct or authorize the creation, modification, and abolition of school districts; (2) alter the structure and powers of school boards; (3) remove incumbent school board members and abolish their offices; (4) prescribe the school calendar and curriculum; (5) determine the sources and procedures for raising school revenues and school spending; (6) fix the appointment, term, and qualifications of teachers; (7) require local schools to admit children of nontaxpayers; and (8) revoke charters of public schools for noncompliance with state regulations.[3]

Because its power is plenary, each legislature is free to modify prior legislation. "As the power over schools is a legislative one, it is not exhausted by exercise. The legislature, having tried one plan, is not precluded from trying another. It . . . may change its plans as often as it deems necessary or expedient." *State* v. *Haworth*, 23 N.E. 946, 948 (Ind. 1890).

Despite repeated attempts to assert autonomy, educational agencies have no inherent powers, but only those that the state legislature delegates to them from time to time. Of course, educational agencies are additionally constrained by conditions of federal aid.[4]

---

3. (1) Kosmicki v. Kowalski, 171 N.W.2d 172 (Neb. 1969). (2) Dobrovolny v. Reinhart, 173 N.W.2d 837 (Iowa 1970); Cohen v. State, 52 Misc. 2d 324, 275 N.Y.S. 2d 719 (1966). (3) Lanza v. Wagner, 183 N.E. 2d 670 (N.Y. 1962). (4) Sturgis v. Allegan County, 72 N.W. 2d 56 (Mich. 1955). (5) San Antonio Ind. School Dist. v. Rodriguez, 411 U.S. 1 (1973); In re Advisory Opinion, 211 N.W. 2d 28 (Mich. 1973). (6) See Chapter 5 *infra.* (7) Child Welfare Society of Flint v. Kennedy School Dist., 189 N.W. 1002 (Mich. 1922). (8) Board of Education v. State Board of Education, 189 N.E. 2d 81 (Ohio 1962).

4. *See* Yellow Springs, etc. School District Board of Education v. Ohio H.S. Athletic Association, 647 F.2d 651 (6th Cir. 1981).

1. Direct and Indirect Legislative Controls: Ministerial and Discretionary Powers and Duties

The degree of control exercised by legislatures depends upon practical consideratons. If direct legislative specification is feasible, lawmakers may leave little discretion to school administrators. For example, many statutes directly fix admissions and attendance requirements, school calendars, and school election dates (see Tables 2–1, 2–2, and 2–3). Duties that are largely mechanical are described in law as *ministerial duties.* In most instances, however, legislative imposition of explicit ministerial duties is impractical. The educational bureaucracy and the welter of educational programs are too complex to direct from the legislative center. More commonly, therefore, state legislatures confine themselves to promulgating educational goals and policies, while delegating broad *discretionary duties* to school officials and administrators, to determine whether, when, and how specific action shall be taken to achieve legislated policy. The manner and scope of delegation is itself controlled by law; hence the legality of an educational decision, as shown in the following section, is often measured by legal standards of proper and improper delegation of authority.

B. Administrative Agencies' Control: Delegation Doctrines

The general law on the delegation of authority is summarized as follows:

> "The legislature may delegate these legislative controls to an administrative agency . . . provided, in so doing, it defines what is to be done; the instrumentality which is to accomplish it; and the scope of the instrumentality's authority in so doing by prescribing reasonable administrative standards." *State* v. *Kinnear,* 423 P.2d 937, 940 (Wash. 1967), citing *Keeling* v. *Public Utility* Dist. No. 1 of Clapham Cy., 306 P.2d 762 (Wash. 1957).

The foregoing statement embraces *three independent rules:*

1. *The conferred power must be one that is legally delegable.* Delegability is primarily a question of *constitutional law,* for if a legislature attempts to transfer a nondelegable power, the statute itself is unconstitutional, and no legal authority can be derived therefrom.
2. *The power that is challenged must have been actually delegated,* that is, it must fall within the limits of power conferred by the delegating statute. The scope of delegated authority is primarily a question of legislative intent and *statutory interpretation,* for if an administrator's action is beyond legislative authorization, it also lacks legal foundation and validity.
3. *The power,* though delegable and actually delegated by statute, *may not be exercised in a bad faith, unreasonable, or arbitrary manner.* This "abuse of

discretion" test is *judge-made law,* and turns on the facts of each case as viewed by a court.[5]

These simple propositions are more easily stated than applied. Each rule calls for separate analysis, even though courts often strike down an administrative decision in language that seems to cover more than one of the rules.[6]

1. Determining What Powers Are Delegable

The law is settled that a legislature may by statute delegate *administrative* powers to the agencies in the executive branch of government but may not delegate *lawmaking* powers. The legal distinction between these powers is best understood in terms of constitutional theory. Transfer, or delegation, of lawmaking power from the legislature to administrative agencies would violate the constitutional purposes of separation of powers and the system of checks and balances. Further, lawmaking by persons who were not duly elected by the populace and who were not accountable to the electorate would defeat citizen control of their government. Elected legislators may not abdicate their lawmaking responsibilities to appointed administrators, because state and federal constitutions vest the lawmaking power *exclusively* in the elected legislatures.[7]

While the ban against delegation of *legislative* power is a constitutional necessity, the delegation or transfer of *administrative* power is a practical necessity. No legislative body has the resources to exercise direct central management over vast educational systems. Therefore, courts have forged a legal test to serve both needs: delegable administrative power is distinguished from nondelegable lawmaking power by the presence in enabling statutes of *reasonably adequate guidelines* that (1) establish the policy of the legislature and/or (2) guide the administrator's discretion as to *how* the legislative goal is to be achieved. In legal theory, statutory guidelines are adequate if they reasonably direct and confine the discretion of administrators to execute the legislative will and to prevent them from substituting their own will for that of elected lawmakers.[8] Powers delegated under legally adequate guidelines are labeled as valid administrative power, while powers delegated without such guidelines are labeled as invalid attempts to transfer lawmaking power.

> "The legislature cannot delegate legislative authority to an individual. It can prescribe the terms and conditions which may bring into operation a dissolution or consolidation of school districts. This is the legislative act. It then can authorize the county superintendent to determine if the facts exist which call the law into operation." *Bierman* v. *Campbell*, 124 N.W.2d 918, 921 (Neb. 1963).

---

5. *See* Bunger v. Iowa H.S. Ath. Asso., 197 N.W.2d 555 (Iowa 1972).
6. *Ibid.*
7. *Ibid.*
8. An exception to the general rule arises where the state constitution directly delegated specified powers to designated agencies, or where it authorized the enactment of laws by popular vote in a referendum. Guthrie v. Taylor, 185 S.E.2d 193 (N. Car. 1971); Tecumseh Sch. District No. 7 v. Throckmorton, 403 P.2d 102 (Kan. 1965). A referendum cannot be characterized as unconstitutional delegation where the state constitution submits the legislative decision to popular referendum. City of Eastlake v. Forest City Enterprises, Inc., 426 U.S. 668 (1976).

TABLE 2-1. Summary of state standards—admission requirements *

States	Statute	Regulation	Kindergarten			First Grade			Medical Examination Immunization
			Age	By What Date	Exceptions	Age	By What Date	Exceptions	
ALABAMA	S					6	Oct. 1	Yes	
ALASKA	S		5	Nov. 2	Yes	6	Nov. 2	Yes	D
ARIZONA		R				6	Jan. 1	Yes	
ARKANSAS	S		5	Oct. 1		6	Oct. 1		M
CALIFORNIA	S		5	Jan. 1	Yes	6	Jan. 1	Yes	
COLORADO	S		5			6	Sept. 1		M
CONNECTICUT	S		5	Jan. 1	Yes	6	Jan. 1	Yes	
DELAWARE		R	5	Jan. 1	Yes	6	Jan. 1	Yes	
FLORIDA	S		5	Jan. 1		6	Jan. 1		M
GEORGIA	S								M
HAWAII	S		5	Dec. 31	Yes	6	Dec. 31	Yes	
IDAHO	S					6	Oct. 16		
ILLINOIS	S					6	Dec. 1		
INDIANA	S		5			6			M
IOWA	S		5			6			
KANSAS	S		5	Sept. 1		6	Sept. 1	Yes	M
KENTUCKY	S					6			M
LOUISIANA	S					6	Jan. 1	Yes	M
MAINE	S					6	Oct. 15		
MARYLAND	S	R	5	Dec. 31		6	Dec. 31		M
MASSACHUSETTS		R				6	Dec. 31		
MICHIGAN	S		5	Dec. 31	Yes	6	Dec. 1	Yes	
MINNESOTA	S		5	Sept. 1	Yes	6	Sept. 1	Yes	M
MISSISSIPPI	S		5			6			
MISSOURI	S		5	Oct. 1	Yes	6	Oct. 1	Yes	M
MONTANA	S					6			
NEBRASKA	S					6	Oct. 15	Yes	M
NEVADA	S					6	Sept. 30		M
NEW HAMPSHIRE	S					6	Sept. 12	Yes	
NEW JERSEY	S		5	Oct. 1	Yes	6			M

TABLE 2-1. Summary of state standards—admission requirements (*cont.*)

States	Statute	Regulation	Kindergarten Age	Kindergarten By What Date	Kindergarten Exceptions	First Grade Age	First Grade By What Date	First Grade Exceptions	Medical Examination Immunization
NEW MEXICO	S					6	Sept. 1	Yes	
NEW YORK	S		5						
NORTH CAROLINA	S		5	Oct. 15		6	Oct. 1	Yes	M
NORTH DAKOTA	S					6	Oct. 30		
OHIO	S								
OKLAHOMA	S	R	5	Nov. 1	Yes	6	Nov. 1		M
OREGON	S					6			
PENNSYLVANIA	S					6	Feb. 1	Yes	
RHODE ISLAND	S		5	Dec. 31		6	Dec. 31		
SOUTH CAROLINA	S					6	Nov. 1		M
SOUTH DAKOTA	S		5	Nov. 1		6	Nov. 1		
TENNESSEE	S	R	5	Oct. 31		6	Sept. 30	Yes	M
TEXAS	S					6	Sept. 1		M
UTAH	S		5			6			D
VERMONT	S								
VIRGINIA	S		5	Sept. 30		6	Sept. 30	Yes	M
WASHINGTON			4-6			6			
WEST VIRGINIA	S					6	Nov.1		
WISCONSIN	S					6	Dec. 1		
WYOMING	S		5	Sept. 15		6	Sept. 15		

SOURCE: National Institute of Education.

*All data tables must be updated for possible changes in each state since 1979.

NOTE: Some states allow pupils previously enrolled in another state to transfer regardless of age. As with the kindergarten programs, several states allow their local boards to grant exceptions to the minimum age requirements: others permit their state education agency to promulgate guidelines for granting exceptions. . . . What these various alternatives illustrate is a greater tendency for states to grant exceptions for children entering first grade than for those entering kindergarten. An attendance statute usually places the responsibility on the parent or guardian; that is, the parent must cause his child to attend school if he is between 7 and 16. By contrast, the responsibility for carrying out the admission statute is with the state, or in some cases, delegated to the local board. But the common admission statute vests no such discretion to the state agency, local board or school; a child who reaches the minimum age must be admitted if his parent decides to send him. *Medical examination and/or immunization*—The state either requires (M) or grants the district board the discretion to require (D) that a child be examined and or immunized before he can enroll in school.

TABLE 2-2. Summary of state standards—attendance requirements *

STATES	COMPULSORY ATTENDANCE	ATTENDANCE PERMITTED	BASIS FOR EXEMPTION												FINES FOR VIOLATION		
			Employment At Age	Grade Completed	Local Decision	A	B	C	D	E	F	G	H	I	Jail (Days)	1st Offense	2nd Offense
ALABAMA	7–16				X	X	X					X	X			to $100	
ALASKA	7–16		14		X	X	X	X		X	X	X		X		$50-$200	
ARIZONA	8–16	6–21			X	X	X			X				X		Yes	
ARKANSAS	7–16	6–21			X	X	X				X						
CALIFORNIA	6–16					X	X		X		X			X	5	$125	$125-250
COLORADO	7–16		14			X	X			X						$20-100	
CONNECTICUT	7–16	5–21	14	8						X						$5	$5
DELAWARE	6–16	6–21	16				X			X				X		$25	$35
FLORIDA	7–16	7–21	14				X	X		X	X	X		X		$10	$15
GEORGIA	7–16				X	X	X				X			X		to $100	to $100
HAWAII	6–18		15			X	X			X				X	80	$5-50	
IDAHO	7–16	6–21				X	X				X			X			
ILLINOIS	7–16					X	X			X	X			X	5	$5-20	
INDIANA	7–16					X	X				X				60	$10-200	
IOWA	8–15		14	8		X	X	X		X						$5-25	
KANSAS	7–16					X	X			X							
KENTUCKY	7–16					X	X			X							
LOUISIANA	7–16					X	X					X		X	10	$100	
MAINE	7–17	6–20	15			X	X										
MARYLAND	6–16					X	X	X		X				X		$50	$50
MASSACHUSETTS			14	6		X	X									to $20	
MICHIGAN	6–16					X	X			X		X		X			
MINNESOTA	7–16	6–21		10						X	X		X		30	$50	
MISSISSIPPI																	
MISSOURI	7–16		14			X	X								2-10	$10-20	
MONTANA	7–15	6–20		8		X	X			X						$5-20	
NEBRASKA	7–16		14	8		X	X			X							
NEVADA	7–17		14	8	X	X	X	X				X		X			
NEW HAMPSHIRE	6–16		14			X								X			

NEW JERSEY	6–16		14			X	X									$5-25	
NEW MEXICO	8–17		14				X		X		X			X			
NEW YORK	6–16						X				X			X			
NORTH CAROLINA	7–16						X										
NORTH DAKOTA	7–16		14	8	X	X	X			X						to $100	to $200
OHIO	6–18	5–21	14		X		X			X	X			X		$100	
OKLAHOMA	7–18					X		X			X			X	10	$50	
OREGON	7–18		16	8	X	X	X		X	X			X				
PENNSLYVANIA	8–17	6–21	16			X	X				X			X			
RHODE ISLAND	7–16															$20	
SOUTH CAROLINA	7–16	6–21		8		X	X			X	X		X	X	30	to $50	
SOUTH DAKOTA	7–16	5–21	16	8	X	X	X			X						to $50	
TENNESSEE	7–16	6–21															
TEXAS	7–17	7–21	17	9	X	X	X									$5-25	$10-50
UTAH	6–18		16	8	X	X	X			X		X				$5-50	
VERMONT	7–16		15	6	X	X	X				X			X			
VIRGINIA	6–17	5–20					X			X		X	X	X			
WASHINGTON	8–15	6–21	15			X	X			X							
WEST VIRGINIA	7–16	6–21	Yes			X	X			X		X				$3-20	
WISCONSIN	7–16	6–20			X	X	X	X						X	90	$5-50	
WYOMING	7–16	6–21				X	X							X	10	$5-25	

SOURCE: National Institute of Education

*All data tables must be updated for possible changes in each state since 1979.

NOTES:

Local Decision—The district board or other local authority has some discretionary latitude in choosing to exempt certain pupils who might not be exempt under state guidelines.

A, B) *Mental Condition, Handicapped*—Exemptions where mental or physical condition prevents placement in regular or special education programs. Usually granted only after a licensed physician or qualified psychologist certifies the child would not benefit from any state educational program.

C) *Court Decision*—A decision by a juvenile court can exempt a child.

D) *Academic Equivalency Test*—A child is exempt if he achieves a certain score on a standard test.

E) *Alternate Equivalent Education*—Education in private or parochial schools or by a private tutor.

F) *Chronic Ill Health*—Ill health could exempt a child from meeting the minimum annual attendance requirements, or it could exempt him for attendance altogether.

G) *Great Distance*—If a child must walk a great distance to the nearest school or bus route and no other transportation is available, then the child is exempt. Walking distance can be as short as a mile and a half. In some states, applies only to children in elementary school.

H) *Parental Objection*—If approved by the district board or superintendent.

I) *Other*—General exemptions.

Almost all states will exempt a child if he has completed satisfactory work at a certain grade level (usually the eighth) and reached a certain age or he is legally employed under the state's child labor laws. . . . In a few states there are statutes enabling the district board to admit persons over twenty-one. Special education, adult education or vocational education may have different age requirements.

TABLE 2-3. Summary of state standards—school calendar *

STATES	PUPIL INSTRUCTION DAYS					LENGTH OF DAY (in hours) BY GRADE LEVEL				MINIMUM CLASS LENGTH		MINIMUM LAB COURSE LENGTH		CALENDAR PROHIBITIONS	
	Statute	Regulation	Minimum	Maximum	Sanction For Violation					Daily min.)	Annual (hrs.)	Daily (min.)	Annual (hrs.)	Year Round Sch.	Satur-day Sch.
ALABAMA	X		175			K-12, 6				50					
ALASKA	X		180			K-3, 4	4-12, 5								
ARIZONA	X					1-3, 4	4-6, 5	7-8, 6							
ARKANSAS						K-12, 5									
CALIFORNIA	X		175		A	K, 4	1-3, 5 1/2	4-8, 6							
COLORADO	X		172			1-12, 5 1/2									
CONNECTICUT	X		180			K-2 1/2	1-12, 4								
DELAWARE	X		180			K-2 1/2	1-2, 5	3-12, 6			120				
FLORIDA	X		180			K, 3	1-3, 4	4-12, 5							
GEORGIA	X					1-3, 4 1/2	4-12, 6								
HAWAII	X		180							40					
IDAHO	X		180			Pri., 4 1/2	above 5				120		145		
ILLINOIS	X		180	185		K, 2	1, 4	2-12, 5							
INDIANA		X	175			1-2, 4 1/2	3-4, 5	5-6, 5 1/2	7-12, 6	50		55			
IOWA	X		180			K-3, 4	4-12, 5 1/2			55					
KANSAS		X	180				9-12, 6			40		55		X	
KENTUCKY	X		185			K, 3	1-12, 6			45					
LOUISIANA	X		180			K-12, 5				55					
MAINE	X		180		A										
MARYLAND	X		180			K-12, 6									X
MASSACHUSETTS		X			A	Ele., 5	Sec., 5 1/2								
MICHIGAN	X		180											X	
MINNESOTA	X		175		A	K, 2 1/2	1-3, 5	4-8, 5 1/2	9-12, 6	50		55			
MISSISSIPPI	X		155			K-12, 5								X	
MISSOURI	X		174		A	K-12, 6					116		145		
MONTANA	X		180		A	K, 2	1-3, 4	4-12, 6		45		55			
NEBRASKA	X		175							40		55			

STATES	PUPIL INSTRUCTION DAYS					LENGTH OF DAY (in hours) BY GRADE LEVEL				MINIMUM CLASS LENGTH		MINIMUM LAB COURSE LENGTH		CALENDAR PROHIBITIONS	
	Statute	Regulation	Minimum	Maximum	Sanction For Violation					Daily min.)	Annual (hrs.)	Daily (min.)	Annual (hrs.)	Year Round Sch.	Saturday Sch.
NEVADA		X	180		A						120				
NEW HAMPSHIRE	X		180			1, 4 1/2	2-8, 5 1/4	7-12, 5 1/2							
NEW JERSEY		X	180							(h)					
NEW MEXICO		X				1-3, 4 1/2	4-6, 5	7-12, 5 1/2			120		165		
NEW YORK	X		180		A					40					
NORTH CAROLINA	X		180			K-12, 6									X
NORTH DAKOTA	X		180			K-12, 6				40		55			
OHIO	X		180			K, 2 1/2	1-6, 5	7-12, 6							
OKLAHOMA	X	X	180			K, 2 1/2	1-12, 6			55					X
OREGON		X	175			1-2, 3 1/2	4-6, 5	7-8, 5 1/2	9-12, 6						X
PENNSYLVANIA	X		180		A	K, 2 1/2	1-6, 5	7-12, 5 1/2							X
RHODE ISLAND	X		170												
SOUTH CAROLINA	X		180		A	K, 2 1/2	1, 5	2-12, 6		50	120				
SOUTH DAKOTA	X		180	190		K-12, 5									
TENNESSEE	X		175			K-12, 7									
TEXAS	X		180			K-12, 7								X	
UTAH	X		180											X	
VERMONT	X		175			1-12, 5 1/2									
VIRGINIA	X		180		A	K-8, 5	9-12, 6			55					
WASHINGTON	X		180			K, 2 1/2	1-3, 5				120				
WEST VIRGINIA	X		180	185											
WISCONSIN	X		180		A										
WYOMING	X		175												

SOURCE: National Institute of Education.

*All data tables must be updated for possible changes in each state since 1979.

NOTES: A = Loss of state aid.

About one-third of the states provide that schools or local boards which violate the statutory minimum suffer a loss of state aid. It should be noted that many states calculate state aid on the basis of average daily membership (ADM), so that a school does not lose aid because of the temporary absence of its students for less than the statutory minimum.

Frequently a state statute specifies the length of the school day. The length of the school day usually varies according to grade level.

There is no universal formula to measure adequacy of legislative standards for all circumstances, but the following quotations provide some index for determining the legal sufficiency of statutory standards:

> "The difference between a delegation of legislative power and the delegation of authority to an administrative agency to carry out the expressed intent of the Legislature, . . . has long been a difficult and important question. Increased complexity of our social order, and the multitude of details that necessarily follow, has led to a relaxation of the specific standards in the delegating statute in favor of more general ones where a specialized state agency is concerned." *School Dist. No. 8* v. *Bd. of Education,* 127 N.W.2d 458, 461 (Neb. 1964), *citing, Bluemer* v. *Turner,* 137 S.W.2d 387 (Ky. 1939).

> "The line separating that which is purely regulation, and that which is purely legislation, is necessarily indistinct, and becomes more so as the line separating such authority is approached. Therefore, courts . . . will resolve the doubt in favor of the validity of the [delegating] act rather than holding it invalid . . . which is especially true when the [administrative] act is essential and necessary for carrying out the broad purpose and intent of the Legislature." *Dicken* v. *Kentucky State Board of Education,* 199 S.W.2d 977, 981 (Ky. 1947).

School reorganization statutes are favorite targets of challenge as standardless delegations of lawmaking power. Courts generally uphold broad reorganization guidelines as reasonable and adequate because the subject calls for expert administrative opinion addressed to varied local circumstances.[9]

A second index appears where the asserted power impinges upon important citizen rights. In such instances, courts require greater clarity and explicitness in the enabling statute. For example, the power to limit or censor student or teacher speech must be clearly stated in statutory standards. These standards limit administrative interference to cases of necessity. A law that gave school boards discretion to excuse students from immunization vaccinations but did not provide adequate legislative guidelines as to which students should or should not be excused was, therefore, declared void.[10]

The power to impose substantial penalties is also one for which many courts require more explicit legislative expression. For example, a commissioner's statutory power to require racial census reports was held not to authorize him to punish noncomplying school districts by withholding state aid funds.[11] To prevent harsh penalties, many statutes, particularly those on student transportation, specify standards for the imposition of penalties.[12]

a. Redelegation. When may an educational agency redelegate its administrative

---

9. Board of Education v. Presque Island County Bd. of Education, 364 Mich. 605,111 N.W. 2d 853 (1961).

10. Avard v. Dupuis, 376 F. Supp. 479 (D. N.H. 1974).

11. Sch. Comm. of New Bedford v. Commissioner of Education, 208 N.E.2d 814 (Mass. 1965). *See also* Austin, Ind., Sch. District v. Morris, 41 S.W.2d 9(Tex. 1931). Authority to assess School district for expenses does not confer authority to withhold state funds for nonpayment of assessments.

12. Bd. of Education Sch. District No. V v. Bakalis, 299 N.E.2d 737 (Ill. 1973).

powers to another body or to a subordinate employee? The law is summarized in the following text:

> "[A] board of education, or of directors, trustees, or the like, of a school district or other local school organization cannot lawfully delegate to others, whether to one or more of its members, or to any school officer, or to any other board, the exercise of any *discretionary* power conferred on it by law." 78 C.J.S., Schools and School District §122, p. 910 (Emphasis supplied).

A delegated agency may always direct others to perform purely *ministerial*, or mechanical, duties since it does not thereby give away any of its discretion. Therefore, hiring employees to carry out ministerial orders under continuing administrative guidelines and supervision does not constitute a redelegation of authority. Nor does adoption by a school board of a subordinate's recommendation constitute a delegation of discretion.[13]

The legislature may authorize redelegation of discretionary powers expressly or by implication. Whether a particular statute authorizes redelegation of discretionary powers is a question of law, but the separate question whether a particular subassignment involves a transfer of administrative power or merely a ministerial direction is a mixed question of fact and of law.[14] The athletic association cases at the end of Chapter 3 and board authority cases at the end of this chapter provide some concrete examples of how courts differentiate between permissible directives and impermissible abdication of discretion.

The redelegation power is particularly significant in determining what areas of school governance a school board may lawfully submit to the controls of collective bargaining agreements. The redelegation barrier prevented recovery by a teacher for breach of contract when a school district refused to reemploy the teacher who invoked the prior promise of the director of curriculum that the teacher would be employed, even if his course were dropped. The promise was held to have no legal force because the statutory authority to make teacher contracts vested *only* in the school board.[15] A board agreement to submit to grievance procedures on teacher promotions was likewise held to be an unauthorized redelegation of exclusive board responsibility.[16]

2. Determining What Powers Are Delegated

However delegable in nature, a claimed power must be actually conferred by, and founded on, the express or implied intent of a statute. Any exercise of power beyond the statutory authorization is *ultra vires* and legally void. The scope of administrative

---

13. Boyd v. Mary E. Dill School District, 631 P.2d 577 (Ariz. 1981).

14. *See, e.g.*, Tyska v. Board of Education, 453 N.E.2d 134 (Ill. 1983); Peck v. Board of Education, 612 P.2d 1076 (Ariz. 1980).

15. Boyce v. Alexis I. duPont Sch. District, 341 F. Supp. 678 (D. Del. 1972).

16. Bd. of Education v. Rockford Education Assn., 280 N.E.2d 286 (Ill. 1972); Dayton Classroom Teachers Assn. v. Dayton Bd. of Education,323 N.E.2d 714 (Ohio 1975). See also Noe v. Edmonds Sch. District, 515 P.2d 977 (Wash. 1973) (power to fine teachers held not delegable); Bd. of Education v. Rockaway Twp. Educ. Assn., 295 A.2d 380 (N.J. 1972) (class discussion subjects held not delegable).

authority thus depends upon judicial construction of statutory terms.[17] In construing a labor statute that authorized a school board to negotiate a teachers' agreement, a court concluded that the statute did not intend to authorize the board to agree that the teachers' union would allocate negotiated benefits among its members. The agreement was held to be unauthorized and void.[18] The *ultra vires* doctrine applies to all levels of school administration, including state-level agencies. For example, a state education commission's authority to supervise the creation of independent school districts does not confer authority to order territorial annexation from an existing district.[19] Other illustrations of *ultra vires* actions appear in later discussions on board revision of school programs and imposition of school fees.

a. Expressed and Implied Powers. Knowing what acts are authorized would be simple if administrators were confined to powers expressly articulated in statutory language, but a complete specification of powers to cover all contingencies is neither possible nor desirable. A vast range of implied powers is assumed by administrators and by courts to achieve necessary flexibility in advancing legislated policy over changing times and conditions. Education codes generally adopt the common law rule that any power that is *reasonably necessary or incidental to* carrying out *express statutory powers* will fall within the scope of delegated authority as an implied power. Codes usually specify that school authorities shall have all powers reasonably necessary for the proper and efficient management of public education.

Judicial recognition of implied power depends on how closely the regulated subject is related to educational needs. Legislatures can always clarify such questions by expressly granting or revoking disputed powers.[20] However, until they do so, the scope of implied powers is ultimately decided by a court. As the general concept of education expands, so does the range of powers implied. Administrators often take the initiative in claiming implied powers. Since relatively few implied powers are challenged, they emerge largely as a matter of accepted practice and custom.

Powers that are inconsistent with, or contrary to, the manifest language or intent of a statute may not be implied. For example, the authority to construct school buildings was held not to support an implied authority to lease a building for school purposes.[21] Nor may a board imply from its powers to employ personnel the additional power to limit areas of tenure, when state law expressly defines tenure qualifications.[22]

---

17. Brandon Valley Ind. Sch. District v. Minnehaha County Bd. of Education, 181 N.W,2d 96 (S.D. 1970).

18. Chatham Assn. of Educators v. Bd. of Public Education, 204 S.E. 2d 138 (Ga. 1974).

19. State ex rel Dix v. Bd. of Education, 578 P.2d 692(Kan. 1978); Elk Pt. Ind. Sch. District v. State Comm. of Elem'ry and Secondary Ed., 187 N.W. 2d 666 (S.D.1971).

20. *Compare* Matter of Siegel, 255 N.Y.S.2d 336(1965), in which the Court implied power in the State Commissioner to refuse to register a school *with* Carter v. Allen,250 N.E. 2d 30(N.Y. 1969), where a subsequent statute was held to expressly negate the implication of that power.

21. Haschke v. Sch. District, 167 N.W.2d 79 (Neb. 1969). *See also* Elroy Kendall Witton Schools v. Coop Educational Service Agency Dist. 12, 302 N.W.2d 89 (Wis. 1981) (authority to acquire space did not include authority to purchase real estate).

22. Baer v. Nyquist, 357 N.Y.S. 442 (1974).

3. Determining What Powers Are Abused

The exercise of administrative power, albeit lawfully delegated, is always subject to reversal by a court for *abuse of discretion.*[23] Not given to precise judicial definition, abuse of discretion may describe a multitude of sins such as manifest unfairness,[24] error in judgment, findings not based in facts, inconsistent application of procedures or policy, or failure to follow previously announced standards on which a party is entitled to rely.[25]

In reviewing discretionary decisions, courts have distinguished between two classes of administrative decisions—the quasi-legislative and the quasi-judicial. Decisions pertaining to general school management, such as adoption of rules for system-wide application, are kindred to legislation and are called *quasi-legislative.* Decisions resolving disputes between specific parties, such as the resolution of teacher disciplinary charges, are more kindred to adjudication and are called *quasi-judicial.* As indicated in the following section, the degree to which courts will scrutinize or defer to administrative discretion depends in part on whether the administrator's judgment is more quasi-legislative or more quasi-judicial. Since few administrative decisions are exclusively legal or educational (and not a little of both), the classification is heavily litigated, and courts can only resolve the question case by case.

4. Court Review of Administrative Decisions

On appeal from an administrative decision, the first question is whether the court will provide only limited review (an examination of the record of proceedings before the agency board or commission) or whether it will reconsider the entire case, independently of the administrative proceeding. Unless a statute authorizes a new trial or authorizes the court to hear new evidence that was not presented at an administrative hearing, the parties are normally entitled only to a review of the evidence recorded before the administrative tribunal. The *rule of limited review,* which applies in most cases, is summarized by the following case excerpt:

> "Our scope of review in these cases is limited. . . . We are required to affirm the action of the local agency unless we find a violation of applicant's constitutional rights, an error of law or manifest abuse of discretion by the local agency, or that any necessary finding of fact made by the agency is not supported by substantial evidence." *Gabriel* v. *Trinity Area Sch. District,* 350 A.2d 203, 205 (Pa. 1976).

Thus, in limited review a party is restricted to the administrative record and cannot ask the court to make an independent judgment as to the wisdom of the decision

---

23. In teacher and student disciplinary cases, courts have often reduced penalties which they considered excessive on the grounds of abuse of discretion. *See* Bott v. Bd. of Education,379 N.Y.S.2d 172(1976); Beverlin v. Bd. of Education, 216 S.E.2d 554(W. Va. 1975); Wright v. Superintending Committee, 331 A.2d 640 (Me. 1975). All reversed teacher dismissals as excessive penalty.

24. *See, e.g.* Bott v. Board of Education, 379 N.Y.S. 2d 172 (1976); Beverlin v. Board of Education, 216 S.E. 2d 554 (W. Va. (1975); Wright v. Superintending Committee, 331 A.2d 640 (Me. 1975). In all of the foregoing, dismissal of a teacher was found to be an excessive penalty and therefore an abuse of discretion.

25. Tyska v. Board of Education, 453 N.E. 2d 134 (Ill. 1983).

or as to findings that are supported by substantial evidence. A fact is supported by *substantial evidence* if the weight of the evidence in the record supports that fact. An *abuse of discretion* is not shown merely because the court disagrees with the administrator's decision. Rather, the court must conclude that the decision was made irrationally, arbitrarily, or capriciously. It is more difficult under limited review to overturn an administrative decision than when the court conducts an independent review of the case.

Therefore, it is important to determine whether the applicable statute provides for limited or independent judicial review. In any case; courts will more closely scrutinize a quasi-judicial decision than a quasi-legislative decision because courts consider quasi-legislative decisions *primarily* educational. Since such judgments are entrusted by the legislature to its delegated agencies, courts refuse to reconsider their wisdom and pass only upon their legality:

> "In the absence of fraud, abuse of discretion, arbitrariness or unreasonableness . . . this court will not interfere with that authority nor substitute its judgment for that of defendant board upon matters delegated to it to decide in conducting the affairs of its schools." *Dworken* v. *Cleveland Bd. of Education,* 108 N.E.2d 103 (Ohio 1951).

School decisions that deal primarily with individual rights and discipline and with disputed facts or law rather than educational matters are considered quasi-judicial, however, and judges rather than educators are considered the primary experts. For example, the suspension of a teacher or student will normally be more closely scrutinized for legal justification than a decision to modify the curriculum.[26] Where important individual rights are at stake, courts scrutinize school decisions to ensure that school authorities observed those legal safeguards required by the due process clause of the Fourteenth Amendment or by state statutes.[27]

When school decisions involve both quasi-legislative and quasi-judicial issues, different review standards may be applied to separate elements of the same case. If a particular point involves no dispute on the facts, but only opinions or conclusions, a court will normally pass only upon their legality, and not their wisdom, but if another point turns on contested facts, the courts will decide if the fact findings are supported by substantial evidence. In overturning administrative decisions for lack of substantial evidence,[28] courts do not substitute their own appraisal of specific evidence or of witness credibility. Rather, they look to see if there is "such relevant evidence as a reasonable mind might accept as adequate to support a conclusion."[29]

Errors of law are always reversible, however innocently or reasonably made, if

---

26. State of Missouri v. Schoenlaub, 507 S.W.2d 354 (Mo. 1974); Older v. Bd. of Education, 266 N.E.2d 812 (N.Y. 1971).

27. Smith v. Siders, 183 S.E.2d 433 (W.Va. 1971). The constitutional law on procedural due process is taken up in Chapters 5 and 6.

28. On the question of what state statutory rights are protected by constitutional due process, *see* Bishop v. Wood, 426 U.S. 341 (1976).

29. *See* Tarbox v. Greensburgh Central Sch. District, 375 N.Y.S.2d 610 (1975); Sherefield v. Sheridan County Sch. District, 544 P.2d 870 (Wyo. 1976). See Gerry v. Bd. of Education, 376 N.Y.S.2d 737 (1975). See also Wilson v. Bd. of Education, 411 S.W. 2d 551 (Tex. 1974); Sch. Committee of Boston v. Bd. of Education, 292 N.E.2d 870 (Mass. 1973).

they are incurable and substantial. This is especially true in teacher dismissal cases in which a board's failure to follow procedures mandated by law is fatal.[30] As will be seen shortly, some errors of law are so insubstantial that courts will treat them as harmless error, insufficient to invalidate the result.

a. Exhaustion of Administrative Remedies. Apart from statutory restriction, the courts have formulated judicial rules that limit appeals from administrative decisions. Prominent among these is the "exhaustion" doctrine, which requires grievants to pursue and exhaust all available appeals to administrative agencies before seeking relief in court. The rationale of the exhaustion doctrine has been summarized by the United States Supreme Court as follows:

> "Exhaustion is generally required as a matter of preventing premature interference with agency processes, so that the agency may function efficiently and so that it may have an opportunity to correct its own errors, to afford the parties and the courts the benefit of its experience and expertise, and to compile a record which is adequate for judicial review." *Weinberger* v. *Salfi*, 422 U.S. 749, 756–66 (1975).

The foregoing rationale and doctrine are followed by state courts.[31]

As with most rules of law, there are several exceptions to the exhaustion rule. The rule does not apply where administrative hearings would serve no special purpose. For example, where the presumed expertise of the administrative fact finder is not needed, the dispute would involve only a pure question of law.[32] Nor will the courts block appeal on exhaustion grounds where the appellant would be irrevocably harmed by delays.[33] A student excluded from an athletic program could seek immediate court relief, since reference to an administrative hearing would result in his loss of participation for the long period required by that hearing.[34] The strongest exception arises when a person is claiming interference with constitutional rights.[35] Most courts are not inclined to delay relief in constitutional claims cases, but some hold that once a party elects to test his or her rights by administrative proceedings, the party must raise all issues therein, including constitutional issues, or be barred from raising those issues in a later appeal to the courts.

The exhaustion of administrative relief can be required by statutes that provide special remedies, such as certain of the federal civil rights statutes, but even in such cases,

---

30. Flowing Wells Sch. District v. Stewart, 499 P.2d 750 (Ariz. 1972); McKelvey v. Colonial Sch. District 348 A.2d 445 (Pa. Cmwth 1975); Hill v. Dayton Sch. District, 517 P.2d 223 (Wash.1974). Reversals of teacher dismissals.

31. *See, e.g.*, Emerson v. Bible, 271 S.E.2d 382 (Ga. 1981); Dawson v. Iowa Merit Employment Commission, 303 N.W.2d 158 (Iowa 1981); Merritt v. West Mifflin Area School District, 424 A.2d 572 (Pa. 1981); Brooks v. School Board of Brevard County, 382 S.E. 422 (Fla. 1980); Martin v. Harrah Ind. Sch. District, 543 P.2d 1370 (Okla. 1976); Griswold v. Mt. Diablo Un. Sch. District, 135 Cal. Rptr. 3 (1976).

32. *See* Hector County Ind. Sch. District v. Hopkins, 518 S.W.2d 576 (Tex. 1975).

33. Middough v. Bd. of Trustees, 119 Cal. Rptr. 826 (1975); State Bd. of Education v. Anthony, 389 So.2d 279, 284 (La. 1974); Franks v. Bowman Trans. Co. Inc., 424 U.S. 747 (1976); Hickey v. Bd. of School Directors, 328 A.2d 549 (Pa. 1975).

34. Indiana High School Athletic Assn. v. Blanche, 329 N.E.2d 66 (Ind. 1975).

35. Hayes v. Cape Henlopen Sch. District, 341 F.supp. 823 (D. Del. 1972).

exemptions are allowed where delays incident to administrative appeals would unreasonably prejudice a party.[36]

b. Standing to Sue. The doctrine of standing to sue is a judicial device to avoid suits by parties that are not sufficiently affected by a particular dispute. The person bringing suit must have a sufficient legal interest, sometimes described as a *personal stake* in the outcome, rather than a general citizen's interest in the dispute. Thus, homeowners and taxpayers who are unaffected by a school decision that they seek to challenge would lack standing to do so, even though other parties may be adversely affected by the decision.[37] There are many refinements to the standing doctrine, but they are beyond the scope of this text (see *Channel 10 Case,* p. 58).

5. Defective Execution of Statutory Duties

The question whether noncompliance with a statutory duty nullifies a particular action may hinge upon the legal classification of the ignored duty. The legal rule is simply stated: Noncompliance with "mandatory" duties invalidates the action, while noncompliance with "directory" duties does not. The question whether a particular duty is "mandatory" or merely "directory" should be a matter of statutory interpretation and legislative intent. The answer depends on whether the legislature meant to insist that compliance was a prerequisite to legality or whether it meant merely to provide general directions. Courts candidly acknowledge that their "interpretation" is often influenced more by the predicted outcome of each alternative interpretation than by ambiguous statutory language. The *Gann* and *Mullen* cases, reported at the end of this chapter, starkly illustrate this result-oriented stance. The finding of mandatory or directory intent turns principally upon the gravity of the statutory error; upon the magnitude of public cost or disruption that would follow nullification of official action; and upon the presence or absence of official fault or bad faith. The issue is particularly critical in challenges to public elections affecting public school bond proposals and other school questions. Courts are loathe to overturn such elections in the absence of evidence that performance of the defaulted duty would have affected the outcome of the election.[38]

6. Ratification of Past Actions

The *law of agency* supplies another method, known as *ratification,* to cure official errors. The ratification doctrine permits an educational agency or board, in proper circumstances, to adopt retroactively a past action that was not properly authorized. Ratification thus retrospectively supplies the legal authorization that was originally missing but needed for the action in question.

---

36. Beattie v. Roberts, 436 F.2d 747 (1st Cir. 1971); Fuentes v. Rohr, 519 F.2d 379 (2nd Cir.1975); and Gonzales v. Shenker, 399 F.Supp. 858 (S.D. N.Y. 1975).

37. Coughlin v. Seattle School District, 621 P.2d 183 (Wash. 1980); Muka v. Cornell, 370 N.Y.S. 2d 909, 331 N.E. 2d 688 (1975).

38. Butsche v. Coon Rapids Comm. Sch. District, 255 N.W.2d 337 (Iowa 1977); Little v. Alto Ind. Sch District, 513 S.W.2d 626 (Tex. 1974) (school bond election).

A detailed explanation of the law on ratification must be left to specialized texts, but the following list summarizes the essential elements that limit ratifications:

1. A board can only ratify such actions that it was legally empowered to authorize when the ratified action was taken.
2. The board cannot ratify accidentally. It must specifically intend to affirm and be bound by the action in question, and it must do so with full knowledge of all material facts pertaining to the transaction that is affirmed.
3. The board must ratify the entire action or none of it. It may not approve some parts and reject other parts of actions taken on behalf of the school.
4. Notwithstanding the presence of the foregoing elements, the law prohibits ratification in circumstances when retroactive legalization would result in fraud or unfair consequences to third parties.
5. The ratification must be made by the same procedures and formalities as would have been required initially to authorize the action.
6. The action must also be legally authorizable at the time of ratification.
7. A board may only ratify action by a party who had purported to act on behalf of or pursuant to authority of the board.[39]

Within the foregoing limits, a board may ratify past transactions either by affirmative conduct or, in some circumstances, by failure to object to the transaction, that is, receiving the benefits with full knowledge of the transaction.[40] The effectiveness of ratification does not depend upon notice to third parties, except where the lack of notice would be unfair and inequitable to those parties. Since the operation of the ratification doctrine often requires complex legal analysis, school authorities should not rely upon the ratification doctrine without the benefit of legal counsel.

C. Administrative Structure of Public Education

The formal organization of state education agencies falls into three basic patterns. The least typical is the single echelon system of statewide education that exists only in Hawaii. In 17 states a two-echelon (state-local) system existed as of 1971; the predominant three-echelon system (state-intermediate-local agencies) prevailed in the remaining states.[41]

---

39. See AMERICAN LAW INSTITUTE, RESTATEMENT OF THE LAW, Agency 2d, Sections 82-104. (1) Dept. of Education v. Jersey Shore Area Sch. District, 353 A.2d 91 (Pa. 1976); Comeaux v. Sch. Emp'ees Retirement System, 241 So.2d 298 (La. 1970) (board could not ratify an *ultra vires* contract). Accord: Zevin v. Sch. District No. 11, 12 N.W.2d 634 (Neb. 1944). (2) Grippo v. Dunmore School Bd.,365 A.2d 678 (Pa. 1976).

40. Sabin v. La. State Bd. of Education, 289 So. 2d 554 (La. 1974). Holding board to have ratified lease, though not expressly.

41. State-local: Alabama, Alaska, Connecticut, Delaware, Florida, Georgia, Idaho, Kentucky, Louisiana, Maryland, Nevada, New Mexico, North Carolina, Tennessee, Utah, Virginia, and West Virginia. See "Survey of State Administrative Structures" in Pa. Dept. of Education, PREP Report No. 23, pp. 3, 4 (1971).

With the rapid growth of intermediate units to service groups of local school districts on an area-wide basis, the trend toward a three-level system is likely to grow. In addition to official structures created by law there are numerous, informal, voluntary agencies, such as regional school councils.

1. State-Level Agencies

States exercise statewide regulation and allocate assistance through a number of central state agencies.

"State education agencies vary in terms of structure and organization, size, duties, powers, relationship with other agencies, and general competence of staff."[42] The most typical state agencies are a state board of education, a chief state school officer, a state department of education, and special divisions of other departments, such as labor and welfare, whose duties affect some segment of the school community. While administrative organization varies from state to state, certain organizational features predominate.

a. State Boards of Education. As of 1973, 48 of the 50 states were reported to have state boards of education. Of these, 22 were established by the state constitution and 26 by statute.[43] In 31 states, board members were appointed by the governor. State boards vary in size, with most states employing 7, 9, or 11 members. The details of state board organization in the individual states are set forth in Table 2–4.

State boards may exercise indirect control over local educational decision-making through statutorily authorized predecision regulation or postdecision review. Such authorization is usually limited to decisions of major importance, however, such as school district reorganizations, school closings and contested reductions, or dismissals of professional staff.[44]

b. Chief State School Officers. All states have a chief state school officer who is designated as commissioner, superintendent, or secretary of public instruction or of education. The office is created by a state constitution or statute. Within the limits of designated authority, the chief state school officer often acts as executive director of the state educational program, either as a member of the governor's cabinet, of the state board of education, or of the state department of education. As of 1973, this office was still filled by election in 21 states, but the trend toward selection and appointment by the state board of education is favored by educators in the interest of promoting merit appointments. The term of the chief school officer is fixed by law in 31 states (ranging from one to six years) and largely runs at the pleasure of the appointing authority in the

---

42. U.S. Department of Health, Education and Welfare, State Departments of Education, State Boards of Education, and Chief State School Officers, DHEW Publication No. (OE) 73-07400 (1973), p. iii. Presents state- by-state narrative and tabular summaries of data on state education agencies and an extensive bibliography.

43. E. Bolmeier, School and the State Structure 116 (2d ed., 1973); Campbell, Cunningham and McPhee, The Organization and Control of American Schools 56 (1965).

44. Walker v. Board of Education of Olean City School District, 433 N.Y.S. 2d 660 (1980).

other states.[45] Whether through the exercise of delegated powers or influence upon legislative policy and upon the state administrative staff, the chief state school officer plays a substantial role in setting educational policy.

c. State Departments of Education. "The State Department of Education is the professional arm of the chief state school officer and of the State Board of Education. . . . Ordinarily, these people are organized into divisions such as administration and finance, teacher certification, instructional services . . . vocational and adult education. . . ."[46] Such departments commonly provide statewide research and statistical report services that are indispensable to educational planning.

Central state agencies perform numerous supervisory, regulatory, enforcement, research, and supportive functions that affect the structure, staffing, pupils, and programs in public schools. Their most important functions relate to setting minimum educational standards. Unfortunately, until 1974 there had been no comprehensive study of existing minimum educational standards.[47]

2. Regional Agencies

Midlevel regional agencies administer special services and coordinate area-wide functions for local school districts within their territories. In about 16 states, county educational units serve as the midlevel structure, but an increasing number of states (Colorado, Illinois, Iowa, Michigan, Nebraska, New York, Pennsylvania, Washington, and Wisconsin) have developed new multidistrict or multicounty structures known as *intermediate units* that largely displace or absorb county school agencies. Intermediate units are not coterminous with county lines in all states. Several New England states (Connecticut, Maine, New Hampshire, and Vermont) pursue midlevel administration through units that are called *supervisory unions.*

Intermediate units may control state-mandated educational services and may also provide optional services elected and supported by member local districts. Thus, for some purposes, these units may exercise authority over local school districts, while for other purposes they are subject to the decisions of local districts.[48]

3. Local Agencies

a. School Districts. The local school district is a special unit or subdivision of state government created by law for the special purpose of exercising local powers over the construction, maintenance, and direct operation of public schools within its territorial bounds. Inasmuch as school districts are limited to special-purpose functions, as

---

45. BOLMEIER, op. cit. *supra,* 123 (1973).

46. CAMPBELL, et al., op. cit. ORGANIZATION AND CONTROL, p. 57.

47. See *A Study of State Legal Standards for the Provision of Public Education,* National Institute of Education, U.S. Department of Health, Education and Welfare (1979).

48. Detailed data on the general and state-by-state operation of "formal" regional agencies and of other "informal" regional cooperatives, plus a specialized bibliography, are reported in Pa. Dept Education, PREP Reports No. 23, 23A through 23I (1971).

TABLE 2-4. State-level agencies *

States having a SBE for the State system of education	Chief method of selecting members: Elected by the people or representatives of the people (type of election)	Appointed by the Governor	Ex officio (by virtue of office or position held)	Number of members	Term of elected or appointed members in years
Total	17	35	2	514 + 48 ex officio	--
Alabama	Partisan	-	-	8 + 2 ex officio	4
Alaska	-	X	-	7	5
Arizona	-	X	-	8 + 1 ex officio	4
Arkansas	-	X	-	9 + 1 ex officio	9
California	-	X	-	10	4
Colorado	Partisan	-	-	5	6
Connecticut	-	X	-	9 + 1 ex officio	6
Delaware	-	X	-	6 + 2 ex officio	3
District of Columbia	Nonpartisan	-	-	11 + 1 ex officio	4
Florida	-	-	X	7 ex officio	4
Georgia	-	X	-	10	7
Hawaii	Partisan	-	-	11	4
Idaho	-	X	-	7 + 1 ex officio	5
Illinois	Undetermined - to be decided by Illinois General Assembly			Undetermined	Undet.
Indiana	-	X	-	18 + 1 ex officio	4
Iowa	-	X	-	9	5
Kansas	Partisan	-	-	10	4
Kentucky	-	X	-	7 + 1 ex officio	4
Louisiana	Partisan	-	-	11 + 1 ex officio	6, 8
Maine	-	X	-	9	5
Maryland	-	X	-	7	5
Massachusetts	-	X	-	11 + 3 ex officio	5
Michigan	Partisan	-	-	8 + 2 ex officio	8
Minnesota	-	X	-	9	5
Mississippi	-	-	X	3 ex officio	-
Missouri	-	X	-	8	6
Montana	-	X	-	8 + 3 ex officio	8
Nebraska	Nonpartisan	-	-	8	4
Nevada	Nonpartisan	-	-	9	4
New Hampshire	-	X	-	7	5
New Jersey	-	X	-	12 + 2 ex officio	6
New Mexico	Partisan	-	-	10	6
New York	Legislature	-	-	15	15
North Carolina	-	X	-	11 + 2 ex officio	8
North Dakota	-	X	-	7 + 1 ex officio	6
Ohio	Nonpartisan	-	-	23	6
Oklahoma	-	X	-	6 + 1 ex officio	6
Oregon	-	X	-	7	7
Pennsylvania	-	X	-	17	6
Rhode Island	-	X	-	9	4
South Carolina	Legislative delegations	-	-	16	4

TABLE 2-4. State-level agencies (*cont.*)

States having a SBE for the State system of education	Chief method of selecting members: Elected by the people or representatives of the people (type of election)	Appointed by the Governor	Ex officio (by virtue of office or position held)	Number of members	Term of elected or appointed members in years
South Dakota	-	X	-	7	5
Tennessee	-	X	-	12 + 3 ex officio	9
Texas	Partisan	-	-	24	6
Utah	Nonpartisan	-	-	11	4
Vermont	-	X	-	7	6
Virginia	-	X	-	9	4
Washington	-	-	-	14 + 1 ex officio	6
West Virginia	-	X	-	9 + 2 ex officio	9
Wisconsin	No State board for public elementary and secondary education				
Wyoming	-	X	-	9 + 1 ex officio	6
American Samoa	-	X	-	9 + 1 ex officio	2, 3
Guam	-	X	-	7	3
Puerto Rico	-	X	-	8 + 2 ex officio	6
Trust Territory of the Pacific Islands	-	High Comm.	-	6 + 1 ex officio	3
Virgin Islands	At large basis	-	-	9 + 1 ex officio	2

SOURCE: U.S. Office of Education, State Boards of Education (OE 73-07400) pp. 60-61.

*All data tables must be updated for possible changes in each state since 1979.

NOTE: Board members in all states except Florida, Hawaii, and Mississippi serve overlapping terms.

distinguished from general-purpose "municipal" governments, they are classified as *quasi-municipal* in nature. Unlike state level departments, school districts have a legal identity somewhat similar to private corporations. They can sue and be sued, make contracts, adopt rules and regulations, and receive grants from sources other than the state. Hence, they are also classified as quasi-corporations. The dual nature of school districts—as government units on the one hand and as separate legal corporations on the other—complicates education law because school districts derive legal powers from different branches of public (government) and private (corporation) law. They incur obligations as well as rights under these separate branches of law, and the implication of their powers and duties as government entities is not the same as the implication of their powers as corporate entities. For example, whether a school district may impose particular charges or fees often depends upon whether the particular fees are classifed as governmental or proprietary in nature. Further, school districts remain immune from tort liability for their governmental actions, but not so immune for their proprietary actions under the tort law of many states. In the absence of governing statutes, the courts of each state decide which acts are governmental or proprietary.

Organization and Classification. Every state organizes school districts as it deems best. There is no common pattern. A number of states create several classes of school districts, with separate laws governing each class.[49] Most school districts are "unified"—they manage schools at both elementary and high school levels—but some school districts are restricted by law to specialized levels or areas of education. Most school districts have the same territorial boundaries as municipalities or counties, but this is not a universal condition. Another classification is based upon the presence of local municipal controls. Districts subject to such controls are "dependent"; those free of local government regulation are "independent" districts. Educational administrators must be aware of the laws and educational structure of their home state regarding this relationship.

School District Alteration. As previously noted, the legislature may create, abolish, or alter school districts by direct enactment or by delegation of authority to education agencies or to the local electorate. Lawsuits to halt such reorganizations are usually unsuccessful. School districts generally lack legal standing to challenge reorganization even where they lose territory to a newly formed district. They may have legal standing to challenge under the following conditions: (1) the state legislature or constitution provides special grounds for suit; (2) since reorganization decisions are quasi-legislative, courts will not interfere without a showing of bad faith or abuse of discretion; (3) the abuse of discretion test is avoided where reorganization is attacked on the purely legal ground that it has not been authorized by state law.[50] Objections that the reorganization statute provides inadequate standards to guide redistricting usually fail because courts recognize that school officials must have broad discretion to exercise their educational expertise in such matters.[51]

It is not unusual, therefore, for reorganization opponents to attack district reorganization on all conceivable grounds—that it is unconstitutional, or *ultra vires*, or an abuse of discretion. Some typical objections are considered in the following sections.

State Constitutional Limits. Two principles are regularly invoked to oppose district changes: state constitutional prohibitions (1) against government taking of property without compensation and (2) against laws that infringe the obligation of contracts. Similar provisions are found in the federal constitution.

Other provisions that are peculiar to certain states also qualify legislative power over district organization. For example, a state constitution may forbid the transfer of debts from one government subdivision to another, so that the merger of school districts that resulted in such a debt transfer was nullified.[52] Where district reorganization merely

---

49. The Pennsylvania School Code covers five classes of school district, based upon the residential population of each district. 24 Pa. Stat. Ann. §202. See also N.Y, Educ. Law §1501 (McKinney); Cal. Educ. Code §35500 (West); Ill Ann. Stat. ch. 122, §3A-a (Smith-Hurd); Ky. Rev. State. §160.010.

50. (1) Special grounds: Unified Sch. District v. State Bd. of Education, 478 P.2d 201 (Kan. 1970); Minn. Assn. of Public Schools v. Hanson, 178 N.W. 2d 846 (Minn. 1970). (2) Abuse of discretion: Ballard v. Gregory, 530 P.2d 1163 (Mont. 1975). (3) Not authorized: Elk Point Ind. Sch. District No. 3 v. State Commission, 187 N.W. 2d 666 (So. Dak. 1971).

51. *See* Hamilton v. State Board of Education, 172 Cal. Rptr. 748 (1981).

52. Protest of Mo. Keno-Tex. R. Co., 73 P.2d 173 (Okla. 1937).

effected an interdistrict transfer of territory, however, without any transfer of debts, the reorganization was upheld.[53] Reorganization law thus turns upon the particular wording of each state's constitution. Challenges to reorganization on state constitutional grounds seldom succeed unless the constitution speaks directly to the feature of reorganization that is challenged.

Federal Constitutional Limits to Alteration.

Deprivation of Property. Interdistrict transfers of territory and school property in reorganizations commonly raise the complaint that property is being taken without compensation in violation of condemnation clauses of state and federal constitutions. (See Amendment V to U.S. Constitution, p. xi.) While such takings may be unfair, they are not unconstitutional. As previously noted, school district property is *state* property, not property of local districts or of local residents. Accordingly, a Washington statute that transferred school district property (without compensation) to a state board for community college education was upheld,[54] and a similar result occurred recently in Delaware.[55] Although not constitutionally compelled to do so, many states have enacted measures to compensate school districts for property transferred in reorganization as a matter of legislative discretion.

Compensation may be *constitutionally* required, however, if the property taken or transferred was held and used by the school district in its "proprietary" capacity. Where, for example, the property was granted to the district under a specific trust, the state may be required to provide direct compensation or other benefits to preserve the interest of the district citizens, in their capacity as the trust beneficiaries.[56]

Impairment of Contract Obligations. The Contracts Clause of the federal constitution (Art. I, §10, cl. 1) provides that: "No State shall . . . pass any . . . law impairing the obligation of contracts. . . . " Similar clauses are found in many state constitutions. Since most reorganizations have some impact upon the value or performance of existing school district contracts, these clauses are often invoked. In law, however, the bare fact of contract frustration is not always an "impairment."

> "If the legislature of the State has the power to create and alter school districts, no contract can arise, no property of a district can be said to be taken, and the action of the legislature is compatible with a republican form of government." *Kies* v. *Lowry*, 199 U.S. 233, 239 (1905).

The foregoing principle was applied to sustain a reorganizational dissolution of a district that, as a consequence, could not honor its contracts with other school districts:

---

53. Excise Board of Lincoln County v. St. Louis-S.F. Ry., 93 P.2d 1085 (Okla. 1939); *but see* Southern Pacific Co. v. Maricopa County, 129 P. 2d 312 Ariz. 1942.

54. Moses Lake Sch. District No. 161 v. Big Bend Community College, 503 P.2d 86 (1972), appeal dismissed, 412 U.S. 934 (1973).

55. New Castle County School District v. State, 424 A.2d 15 (Del. 1980).

56. Town of Winchester v. Cox, 26 A.2d 592 (Conn. 1942).

> "The jointure agreement involved here was made pursuant to the authority given to school districts . . . with the concomitant condition inherent in such legislative authority that actions taken pursuant thereto are subject to later change by the Legislature. . . . Obviously, the Public School Code . . . did not intend to create vested rights in the administrative districts . . . but merely authorized the formation of school districts which would exist until changed . . . by future legislative direction. . . . We have no doubt that the School Reorganization Act of 1963 does not violate the constitutional prohibition against impairing the obligation of contracts." *Chartiers Valley Jt. Schools* v. *County Bd. of School Directors*, 211 A.2d 487, 500–01 (Pa. 1965).

Although school districts may not claim constitutional rights against their sovereign states, private creditors of a reorganized district may do so in certain circumstances. Not every contract disappointment, even of district creditors, amounts to an *impairment* in the constitutional sense. The reorganization must effect a substantial loss or threat of loss that the creditor did not assume in the original contract.[57] Thus a creditor who lent money or advanced services or materials on the *general* credit of the district incurs no impairment so long as the debtor district remains in existence. By not demanding specific security beyond the district's promise to pay, the creditor took the risk of later reduction in district assets.[58]

However, where a creditor bargained for and received a contract commitment that the district would reserve certain funds or sources of repayment to secure the debt, the elimination or substantial diminution of that security through district reorganization could impair the contract. In one instance bondholders had a contract right to attach and liquidate property within the district to collect their loans. A reorganizational detachment of large territory from the debtor district was nullified as an unconstitutional impairment of the bondholders' contracts.[59] Similarly, a detachment of taxable territory, where the district's existing tax base was specifically pledged to repay its creditors, was held unconstitutional in Michigan.[60]

The contract impairment challenge has been avoided by several courts through strained rulings that preserve contract rights while sustaining the reorganization. A New York court held that the preexisting school district, though totally absorbed by a central school district, was deemed to continue to exist for the purpose of paying all of its prior debts.[61] The Supreme Court of South Carolina also upheld the consolidation of several districts into a single district where a statute required the new district to assume the indebtedness of the absorbed districts. It reasoned that the creditors could still look for payment from the prior districts, which were their original debtors.[62]

Where the reorganization statute provides for another source of debt repayment in substitution of the security destroyed by reorganization, a court may find no impairment

---

57. For an authoritative exposition of the fuzzy Contracts Clause, *see* U.S. Trust Co. of New York v. New Jersey, 431 U.S. 1(1977). See also Camardo v. Bd. of Education of City School Dist., 434 N.Y.S. 2d 514 (1980).

58. *See* Opinion of the Justices, 246 A.2d 90 (Del. 1968).

59. Canal National Bank v. School Administrative District, 203 A.2d 634 (Me. 1964).

60. Bd. of Education of City of Lincoln Park v. Bd. of Education of Detroit, 222 N.W. 763 (Mich. 1929).

61. Leone v. Hunter, 191 N.Y.S.2d 334 (1959).

62. Tindall v. Byers, 59 S.E.2d 337 (So. Car. 1950).

if the substituted security and the ease of debt collection is reasonably equivalent to the original contract security.[63]

Courts may also protect vested contract rights of employees, such as teachers. Where a district was totally absorbed by another district, the court applied the common law rule that the absorbing district succeeds to the contract obligations of the absorbed district and accordingly required the consolidated district to either retain or to pay the teachers who were under contract with the absorbed district.[64]

Referendum Limitations. Where the state legislature decides to submit questions on school district reorganization to local referendum, the elections must comply with the one-person, one-vote requirements of the equal protection clause of the Fourteenth Amendment.[65] The Supreme Court decisions in this area are very complex and can only be generalized in a text of this scope. The following summary is neither complete nor precise:

1. If the electoral candidate or question involves only *administrative* and not policy-making *governmental* functions, the election does not fall within the constitutional rule.
2. If the election involves governmental functions, it may not exclude citizens merely because they do not own property that is taxed by the school district or because they are not parents of public school children.
3. Where the electorate is divided into separate voting districts, the registered population (not registered voters) in each electoral district must be substantially equal in number to ensure that the votes in each district receive substantially equal weight and representation.[66]

Thus, a school district reorganization effected pursuant to a local election that violates the constitutional standards of voter apportionment may be nullified at the suit of an aggrieved local resident. The restrictions imposed by the Voting Rights Act must also be observed.

Adjustment of Assets and Obligations. The allocation of assets and obligations of reorganized school districts varies from state to state. In some states the common law has been superseded by special statutes, and in a few others, by state constitutions. Different legal criteria may apply to different kinds of organization such as total merger, partial detachment, or annexation of district territory. Where the common law prevails, a reorganization that transfers the assets or territory of a district will also automatically transfer the district's obligations. In the absence of statutory authorization, any attempts by school administrators to avoid the transfer of obligations to the new district will be

63. See footnote 17 of the opinion of the United States Supreme Court in U.S. Trust Co. v. New Jersey, 431 U.S. 1 (1977).

64. Shirley v. School Board, 332 P.2d 267 (Kan. 1958).

65. Phoenix v. Kolodziejski, 399 U.S. 204 (1970) (school bond issue).

66. (1) Sailors v. Bd. of Education, 387 U.S. 105(1967). (2) Kramer v. Union Free Sch. District, No. 15, 395 U.S. 621 (1969). (3) DeLozier v. Tyrone Area School Bd., 247 F.2d 30 (W.D. Pa. 1965).

invalidated by a court as *ultra vires,* although in extraordinary cases a court may invoke its equitable powers to avoid an unjust allocation of assets and liabilities between reorganized districts.[67]

The authority of state legislatures to prescribe their own rules for interdistrict allocation of assets and obligations is well settled.[68] Many statutes provide broad authority to reorganization agencies to avoid unfair burdens or windfalls upon affected communities. These statutes are binding on school authorities and have been held to impose mandatory duties that are enforceable by citizen suit.[69]

One type of statute permits administrative or judicial allocation under the guideline of "fairness"—"to allocate equitably the assets and debts of the districts affected by the plan of reorganization." Such provisions have been upheld.[70] Broad guidelines allow officials to employ a wide range of adjustment techniques to fit specific circumstances. For example, two newly created districts in Kansas were ordered by the court to pay specified sums to the school district whose facilities were absorbed by the new district.[71] Specific rules for interdistrict adjustments may also be imposed by statute, as in Wisconsin.[72]

b. School Boards. The management of school districts is vested by state laws in local school boards. They have no powers, other than those expressed by or implied from delegating statutes. Board organization and powers vary in detail from state to state, and within many states, according to the size and class of the school district.

School boards operate under mandatory statutes (such as budget and tax laws) and under delegating statutes that confer wide discretion upon them (viz."to equip, furnish and maintain . . . public schools"). The large scope of discretionary authority accorded to school boards is indicated by statutes that authorize "other schools or educational departments as the directors, in their wisdom, may see proper to establish" and empower boards to "make . . . such reasonable rules and regulations as it may deem necessary and proper, regarding the management of its school affairs."[73] These broadly worded delegations support implied powers far beyond those expressed; however, the board's discretion is limited where a statute fixes a particular *method* of operation. For example, a board may not retain its own attorney where a statute provides that legal assistance is

---

67. *Transfer of assets or territory:* Rapp v. Bethel Tate Cons. Sch. District, 16 N.E.2d 224 (Ohio 1937); State ex rel. Bilby v. Brooks, 249 S.W.73 (Mo. 1923). *Ultra vires*: Sch. Dist. 14 v. Sch. Dist. 21, 67 P.2d 137 (Wyo. 1937). *Equitable powers:* See discussion of equity in chapter 1. *Avoiding unjust allocation: See* Unified Sch. District No. 255 v. Unified Sch. District No. 254, 463 P.2d 499, 503 (Kan. 1969). The various allocation rules used by sister states are reported in Lund v. Schrader, 492 P.2d 202 (Wyo. 1971).

68. Sch. District No. 47 of Hall County v. Sch. District of City of Grand Island, 186 N.W.2d485 (Neb, 1971).

69. State ex rel. Taylor v. Lease, 153 N.W.2d 205 (Ohio 1957).

70. Unified Sch. District No. 255 *v.* Unified Sch. District No. 254, *supra*; Sch. District of City of Lansing v. State Bd. of Education, 116 N.W.2d 866 (Mich. 1962).

71. Un. Sch. District No. 255 v. Un. Sch. District No. 254, 463 P.2d 499 (Kan. 1969).

72. Joint Sch. District No. 1 of Village of Cedar Grove v. Unified Sch. District No. 1 of the Village of Belgium and Fredonia, 163 N.W.2d 132 (Wis. 1969).

73. See e.g., Pa, School Code Sections 501, 502, 510; Pa. Stat. Ann., Tit. 24, sections 5-501,to 5-526, 21-2103.

to be provided by the county attorney.[74] When a statute requires written notification for certain procedures, oral notice may render the proceeding *ultra vires* and legally void.[75] Similarly, a board may not execute a teacher's contract for a period longer than the statutory contract period.[76] Nor may a local board redelegate to third persons powers vested by statute exclusively in the board.[77] Since school boards exercise the powers of the school district and are subject to legislative control, many of their powers may be subjected by statute to review by other state agencies or subdivisions. The interaction of local boards with other government units is illustrated by several recent cases. In Kansas the court upheld the authority of the state board to issue rules governing the conduct of all persons employed by or attending public schools over the objection of the local school board.[78]

Board Membership. Although they operate and are elected or appointed at the local level, school board members are state officers, carrying out a state function. They remain subject to ongoing state legislative control of both their incidents of office and their powers and duties. The composition, method of selection, term of office, and qualifications for board membership are specified by statutes in each state. Eligibility to serve on school boards is commonly restricted by statute or common law to certain categories of persons. Minors, nonresidents, persons convicted of specified misconduct, persons related by blood or marriage to district officers or employees, persons in a conflict-of-interest position (such as one who is doing business with the district), and persons holding positions whose duties are incompatible with duties of board membership (teachers employed by the board) are generally disqualified from serving on that school board.[79] Candidates for school boards may not, of course, be subjected to unconstitutional eligibility conditions or requirements.[80]

Board Proceedings. As a general rule, school directors must act as a board, by action

---

74. School District No. 1 v. Lohr, 498 P.2d 512 (Ariz. 1972).

75. Wecherly v. Board of Education, 202 N.W.2d 777 (Mich. 1972).

76. Nethercutt v. Pulaski County Spec. School District, 475 S.W.2d 517 (Ark. 1972). *See also* Savino v. Bradford Central School Dist. Bd. of Education, 429 N.Y.S.2d 108 (1980) (multiyear contract for school principal held contrary to limited period provided in statute).

77. Bd. of Education v. Rockaway Twp. Educational Assn., 295 A.2d 380 (N.J. 1972); Bd. of Education v. Rockford Assn. 280 N.E.2d 286 (Ill. 1972). *See* discussion on Redelegation, p. 29.

78. State ex rel. Miller v. Bd. of Education, 511 P.2d 705 (Kan. 1973). Accord: Sch. District 12 v. Hughes, 552 P.2d 328 (Mont. 1976).

79. *Age Requirements:* Human Rights Party v. Secretary of State, 370 F.Supp. 921 (E.D. Mich. 1973). *Residency requirements*: Brown v. Patterson, 609 S.W.2d 287 (Tex. 1980); State v. Thomas, 293 So.2d 40 (Fla. 1974). *Misconduct disqualifications:* Pa. Stat. Ann. tit. 24, §3-323. *Family relationships:* Rosenstock v. Scaringe, 357 N.E.2d 347 (N.Y. 1976). *District employees:* Pa. Stat. Ann. tit. 24, §3- 324. The variations among states on board conflicts of interest are illustrated by the following decisions: State v. Hensel, 206 N.E.2d 563 (Ohio 1965); Comm. v. Coatney, 396 S.W.2d 72 (Ky. 1965); Stroud v. Pulaski Co. Special Sch. District, 424 S.W.2d 141 (Ark. 1968); Comm. v. Collins, 379 S.W.2d 436 (Ky. 1964); Ayres v. Junek, 247 N.W.2d 489 (S.D. 1976), *Conflict of interest or incompatible dual office holding:* 16 McKinney's Cons. Laws of N.Y. §2103; Commonwealth v. Ressler, 13 D. & C.2d 175 (Pa. 1958); Ramirez v. Flores, 505 S.W.2d 406 (Tex. 1974). *See* Annotations: *Teacher as a Member of School Board,* 70 A.L.R. 3d 1188 (1976); Haskins v. State, 516 P.2d 1171 (Wyo. 1973).

80. Socialist Workers Party v. Hardy, 607 F. 2d 704 (5th Cir. 1977); Communist Party of Indiana v. Whitcomb, 414 U.S. 441 (1974); Col. v. Davidson, 117 Cal. Rptr. 630 (1975).

at a meeting duly assembled, in the manner prescribed by law, and by a present quorum of the membership required by law for particular business. In law, the board is a single legal entity, not an aggregation of individuals, and its official acts and obligations are those of the district, and not of the individual board members. Its existence is continuous and independent of the survival of individual members. Decisional authority, therefore, rests in the board *as a whole* and not in its individual members.[81]

Thus individual members of a board cannot, without a proper meeting, hire or dismiss a teacher, even when they constitute a majority of the number of board members.[82] Board actions based upon reports by appointed committees at a duly convened meeting constituted lawful board action, as did board authorization to the president to exchange documents to complete land purchase.[83] The authorization to the president involved only ministerial action and not the exercise of his discretion. Conversely, a board may not delegate its discretionary powers and duties to hire teachers by directing the school superintendent to do so.[84]

As in other areas of law, the existence of an emergency may allow for variation from the normal law. "If [an emergency] ever does arise, the board will be justified in passing over such of the requirements as cannot be fully met, but not in ignoring the Code altogether."[85]

In appropriate cases, a court of equity may also reject the lack of board action as a defense to a just claim. Thus, where a board unfairly induced a teacher into believing that the board approved his appointment and it thereafter accepted his services, the court ordered the board to retain and compensate the teacher. (See the Mullen case at the end of Chapter 2.)

In the absence of constitutional or statutory requirements to the contrary, local boards may make reasonable rules and regulations for the conduct of their business. But in many respects, state school codes impose specific requirements. The extent to which local boards may depart from statutory requirements without rendering their actions unlawful and void will depend upon the construction of the governing statute as mandatory or directory. As later examples will show, noncompliance with statutory standards may expose both the district and board members to legal losses or liabilities. The more typical statutory controls over board proceedings relate to notice, time, and place of meetings; quorum and voting requirements; public access to official proceedings and records; and maintenance of official records of board actions.

---

81. State v. Cons. Sch. District No. 3, 281 S.W.2d 511 (Mo. 1955).

82. Sch. Bd. v. Goodson, 335 So.2d 308 (Fla. 1976); Konovalchik v. Sch. Comm. of Salem, 226 N.E.2d 222 (Mass. 1967) (teacher hiring without action by school board in official meeting, held void).

83. Whalen v. Minn. Special Sch. District, 245 N.W. 2nd 440 (Minn. 1976); Dugan v. Bollman, 502 P.2d 113 (Colo. 1972) (board action on hearing panel's findings); Kraft v. Bd. of Education; 51 A.2d 483 (N.J. 1902) (supply contract on formal board approval, after discussion of committee recommendation). *But see* Sch. District No. 50 v. Witthaus, 490 P.2d 315 (Colo. 1971) (board acceptance of committee recommendations, without considering evidence or findings held of no legal effect).

84. Looney v. Cons. Sch. District, 204 N.W. 328 (Iowa 1925) (ministerial delegation upheld); Big Sandy Sch. District v. Carroll, 433 P.2d 325 (Colo. 1967) (discretionary delegation, void).

85. *See* Chester Sch. District's Audit, 151 A. 801 (Pa. 1930); Smith Lab. v. Chester Co. Sch. Bd., 33 Dela. Co. Rep. 97 (Pa. C.P. 1944).

Notice, Time, and Place of Meetings. As a general rule, a board meeting cannot be lawfully convened unless each member receives legally appropriate notice of the meeting.[86] In the absence of a statutory notice standard, appropriate notice is one that would afford a reasonable opportunity to each member to prepare for and attend the meeting under normal circumstances. School codes often prescribe a minimum number and schedule of meetings. Where advance notice of meetings is announced by statute or by prior board action, the requirement of notice to individual board members is met constructively, and further individual communication to them is not required. Many state open meeting laws require publication of notice of board meetings to inform the public. Whether the failure of the board to comply with the public notice requirement nullifies the proceedings or merely subjects board members to individual sanctions depends upon the terms of individual statutes. The appointment of a superintendent at a board meeting that was called without proper notice was invalidated in New Jersey.[87]

The general requirement of meeting notices may be excused in special cases. The emergency exception previously noted is one example, excuse for harmless error is another, and a waiver of notice in limited circumstances is still another.

Where legal notice could not have affected a member's attendance, due to his or her great distance or condition of health, a court may hold that the lack of notice was harmless error, and, therefore, would not affect the legality of the meeting.[88] The question as to what facts show harmless error is determined by the courts.

Some courts have excused nonnotification to board members who waived the notice, but the case law on waiver of notice is not uniform among the states. The application of waiver rules depends upon special facts, and upon the form of waiver presented in each case. Finally, the question whether notice waivers will serve or defeat the public interest depends upon a court's views of the purposes of notice requirements. The following cases indicate some bases for excusing lack of notice, but the law of each state must be consulted on notice waivers and exemptions.

A board member who was not notified, but appeared at a meeting to protest the same was held not to waive the defect.[89] However, a nonnotified member who appears and participates in the meeting without protesting its validity may be held to waive the objection. An agreement among board members that any two of the three members may act for all, without prior notice of meetings, is not a lawful waiver and violates both the rules on notice and on the need for action as a board.[90]

Legal distinctions are drawn between notice requirements for an original meeting and notice concerning a postponed or adjourned meeting. Where a lawful meeting is *continued* to another day, one court has found it unnecessary to send notice of the continuance, even to absent board members.[91] But where the board *postponed* its meeting

86. *Appropriate notice:* Mead Sch. District v. Mead Educ. Assn., 530 P.2d 302 (Wash. 1975). *Reasonable opportunity to attend:* News & Observer Pub. v. Interim Bd. of Ed., 223 S.E.2d 580 (N.C. 1976). *Number and schedule:* 16 McKinney's Cons. Laws of New York §§1708, 2504; Pa. Stat. Ann. Tit. 24,§ 4-421. *Publication of notice:* Calif. Education Code §96.

87. Cullum v. Bd. of Education, 99 A.2d 323 (N.J. 1953).

88. Cons. Sch. District of Glidden v. Griffin, 206 N.W. 86 (Iowa 1925).

89. Comm. v. Doran, 70 D. & C. 17 (Pa. 1950).

90. Sch. District No. 22 v. Castell, 150 S.W. 407 (Ark. 1912).

91. Barnhardt Ind. Sch. District v. Mertzon Ind. Sch. District, 464 S.W.2d 197 (Tex. 1971).

from a scheduled date to another date, another court ruled that the notice of the postponed meeting must be given to the absent board members.[92]

Statutes may specify a required time and/or place for school board meetings. Without such specification, the board may fix any time or place for its meetings that is reasonable. Where open meeting statutes are in force, the time or place of a meeting must not defeat the intent of the law to promote local participation. Selection of a meeting place that is inconvenient, very distant, or outside the district territory may be considered unreasonable and an abuse of discretion or *ultra vires* act. Thus, a board meeting held outside the district was held to be void notwithstanding the absence of any statutory requirement that meetings be held inside the district boundaries.[93]

Quorum and Voting Requirements. In common law, a quorum of a majority of the board members must be present to convene a lawful meeting, and a majority vote of the members present suffices for official board action. At a minimum, a majority vote of a majority of all board members, constituting a quorum, would be legally binding. To the question whether a school board may alter the common law rules, in the absence of express legislative authority, as part of its general authority to control its own proceedings, one court has answered that it may not.[94] While many school codes adopt the common law rule for most board actions, it is not uncommon for legislatures to require a higher quorum and a higher minimum percentage of affirmative votes for special transactions, such as votes affecting teacher dismissals or budget adoptions. In such cases, the statute criteria must be satisfied to make legally binding decisions.[95]

In the absence of express statutory requirement, the *form* in which votes are cast and recorded (i.e., voice or written ballot, open or secret ballot, and general count or recorded roll call) would also rest with the board's discretion. School codes often impose specific procedures for special transactions, however, most notably in teacher dismissal cases. Specific statutory procedures as well as statutory voting percentages are strictly enforced as mandatory, so that any failure to comply will void the board decision. Thus, in many states, teachers may not be dismissed or demoted unless a specified supermajority vote is taken by recorded roll call and affirmatively cast by the board.[96]

Where a board member casts a blank ballot or abstains from voting, the legal effect of such action will depend upon the wording of governing statutes. If only a parliamentary quorum and majority vote are required, some authorities follow the rule that failure to vote constitutes agreement with the voting majority. If the court finds a *duty* in the board member to vote on *every* issue, abstention has also been regarded as a vote with the majority. But where the pertinent statute requires a majority of those *voting*, abstention by a board member will not be counted as a vote for the majority.[97]

---

92. Keyes v. Class B Sch. District, 261 P. 2d 811 (Idaho 1953).

93. Quast v. Knudson, 150 N.W.2d 199 (Minn. 1967).

94. Endeavor-Oxford Union Free H.S. Dist. v. Walters, 72 N.W.2d 535 (Wis. 1955).

95. *See* Jacob v. Bd. of Regents, 365 A.2d 430 (R.I. 1976); Wesley v. Bd. of Education, 403 S.W.2d 28 (Ky. 1966).

96. Robb v. Sch. District No. RE 50 (J), supra; Oldham v. Drummond Bd. of Education, 542 P.2d 1309 (Okla. 1975).

97. *Failure to vote constituting agreement:* Edwards v. Mettler, 129 N.W.2d 805 (Minn. 1964). *Abstention—a vote with majority:* Mullins v. Eveland, 234 S.W.2d 639 (Mo. 1950). *Majority of those voting:* Bunsen v. County

A more difficult question arises where board members seek to thwart a meeting by withdrawing in sufficient numbers to remove the required quorum of members present and attending. One court has indicated that true withdrawal may destroy the necessary quorum, but that mere removal from the board table to the public audience area did not represent a withdrawal from the meeting or effect a change in the quorum.[98]

Where the law requires that a specified number or percentage of the *total* board membership be cast affirmatively for specially designated decisions or resolutions, a member's absence or abstention would have the same effect as a negative vote.[99]

Public Access to Board Meetings and Records. Under the statutes of most states (some of which apply generally to public agencies, and some of which refer specifically to school districts), school boards must conduct official business at meetings that are open to the public, except when discussing certain expressly exempted subjects.[100]

Open Meeting Requirements. The more typical exemptions from the open meeting requirement involve hearings where confidentiality is required to protect individual reputations or the public interest; for example, hearings on charges against teachers or students who request a closed hearing, board discussions concerning labor negotiations, or proposals to condemn property needed for school purposes. Where a need for confidentiality is not evident, however, a closed meeting may be disapproved.[101]

State laws vary in their particulars.[102] They often require judicial interpretation as to what constitutes a "public meeting" and as to what sanctions may follow noncompliance. For example, meetings of a board committee may not fall within the provisions of an open meeting law.[103] A good discussion of the legal problems concerning the construction of open meeting laws and the remedies courts may impose for their violation is contained in *Channel No. 10, Inc.*, v. *Ind. Sch. District No. 709,* which is reported at the end of this chapter.

Although boards must take official action in open meetings, they are generally permitted to meet informally or in closed sessions to discuss official business, so long as their official action is later taken before the public.[104] Courts differ on the question of

---

Bd. of Sch. Trustee, 198 N.E.2d 735 (Ill. 1964).

98. State v. Vanosdal, 31 N.E. 79 (Ind. 1892).

99. Wesley v. Bd. of Education, 403 S.W.2d 28 (Ky. 1966).

100. Dobrovolny v. Reinhardt, 173 N.W.2d 837 (Iowa 1970); Oldham v. Drummond Bd. of Education, 542P. 2d 1309 (Okla. 1975) (rev'g nonrenewal of teacher contract not done at an open meeting). Case authorities are collected in Annotation: *Statutes—Proceedings Open to Public,* 38 A.L.R.3d 1070 (1971).

101. Ridenour v. Bd. of Education, City of Dearborn, 314 N. W. 2d 760 (Mich. 1981); Orford Teachers Association v. Watson, 427 A. 2d 21 (N. H. 1981).

102. *See* Sch. District for City of Royal Oak v. Schulman, 243 N.W.2d 673 (Mich. 1976) (teacher discharge); Racine Union School Dist. v. Thompson, 321 N. W. 2d 334 Wis. 1982) (student discipline); Bassett v. Braddock, 262 So.2d 425 (Fla. 1972) (board meeting on labor negotiations); Collinsville Comm'y Unit Sch. District No. 10 v. White, 283 N.E.2d 718 (Ill. 1972) (board meeting to discuss land acquisition); McCown v. Patagonia Union School Dist. 629 P.2d 94 (Ariz. 1981) (employment matters).

103. Daily Gazette Co. v. North Colonie Bd. of Education, 412 N.Y.S.2d 494 (1979); Henderson v. Los Angeles City Bd. of Education, 144 Cal. Rptr. 568 (1978); Wash. Sch. District v. Superior Ct., 541 P.2d 1132 (Ariz. 1975). *But see* Puglisi v. School Committee of Whitman, 414 N. E. 2d (Mass. 1981).

104. *See* Dryden v. Marcellus Comm'y Schools, 257 N.W.2d 79 (Mich. 1977); Jewell v. Bd. of Education, 312 N.E.2d 659 (Ill. 1974); Reeves v. Orleans Parish Sch. Bd., 264 So.2d 243 (La.1972); Schults v. Bd. of

whether an open meeting vote, taken without discussion and following an executive-session discussion and agreement on how to vote in the open meeting, violates the open meeting law. A private meeting called in advance to discuss a fixed agenda and to take a poll that would predetermine the board vote at a subsequent public meeting was held to be governed by the open meeting statute, but a contrasting stance was taken by another court in ruling that an open meeting statute did not bar secret balloting at a public meeting or require the board to announce the votes to those present.[105] The disparity in judicial construction of legislative intent explains in part the diversity of case law on open meeting statutes.

The consequences of board actions that do not satisfy open meeting laws also vary from state to state. Nullification is the strongest remedy. It has been applied in New York, Oklahoma, and Texas but denied elsewhere, especially if action taken in reliance on a board resolution could not be reversed without great cost to the public.[106] In Minnesota, Pennsylvania, and California, courts held that the only legal remedy for violation of the open meeting requirement are suits against individual board members with sanctions of fines, suspensions, or removal from office, but not nullification of the board action.[107]

Where circumstances permit a timely remand to the board for consideration in conformity with open meeting law requirements, extreme consequences of noncompliance may be avoided.[108] Some courts have also granted injunctive relief in cases of continued or threatened violation of open meeting laws.[109]

Right to Know. "Right to know" statutes governing school board records also vary from state to state. If the statute does not require the board to keep a record of its official actions, then the lack of official minutes does not invalidate an otherwise provable board action. The more typical statute does require the keeping of board records and public access thereto.[110]

What constitutes an official or public record is more often a subject of judicial interpretation than of statutory specification. While there is little doubt that the official minutes of board meetings are both official and public records, a question can arise as to when and how such minutes become official in form.

The cases illustrate the open-endedness of judicial construction in this area. An Ohio court held that although board minutes were not prepared by the person specified

---

Education, 205 A.2d 762 (N.J. 1964).

105. *Compare* Reeves v. Orleans Parish Sch. Bd., 281 S.2d 719 (La. 1973); *with* Bd. of Education v. State Bd. of Education, 443 P.2d 502 (N.M. 1968).

106. White v. Battaglia, 434 N.Y.S.2d 537 (1980); Matter of Order Declaring Annexation, 637 P.2d 1270 (Okla. 1981); Toyah Ind. Sch. District v. Pecos-Barstow Ind. Sch, District, 466 S.W.2d 377 (Tex. 1971); Dobrovolny v. Reinhardt, 173 N.W.2d 837(Iowa 1970).

107. *See* Griswold v. Mt. Diabio Un. Sch. District, 134 Cal. Rptr, 3 (1976); Pa. Stat. Ann. tit.65 §268. See Channel 10 case at the end of this chapter.

108. Puglisi v. School Committee of Whitman, 414 N.E.2d 612 (Mass. 1981).

109. Belcher v. Mansi, 569 F. Supp. 379 (D.R.I. 1983); Maurice River Township Board of Education v. Maurice River Township Teachers Association, 455 A.2d 463 (N.J. 1982); Nevens v. City of Chino, 44 Cal. Rptr. 50 (1965).

110. Elliot v. School Dist. No. 64-JT, 425 P.2d 826 (Mont. 1967); 23 McKinney's New York Consolidated Laws §51.

in state law, the minutes and proceedings were valid, and a court of Iowa upheld board action, even though it failed to record the action in its minutes,[111] as prescribed by statute. In effect it ruled that the record-keeping provision was merely directory.

Similar variations are found in decisions regarding the sufficiency of board records. One view is that records showing the board's intention are sufficient, notwithstanding technical defects or irregularities.[112] In surveying the law of sister states, one court has suggested that the widespread decisional variations on school board records are better explained by judicial attempts to support the public interest depending on the particular matter in dispute, than upon any rigid rules regarding the form and content of public records. (See the *Conover* opinion, which is reproduced at the end of this chapter.) One must, therefore, look to factually similar precedents in the governing state. Boards best minimize risks of legal miscalculation by meticulous and complete recordation of official actions.

The point at which board minutes become "public" and subject to inspection is also subject to a conflict of authority. Do they become public upon transcription or only after formal approval by the board? This issue is also reviewed in the *Conover* case. But even where the minutes are deemed public *prior* to approval and adoption by the board, they generally remain subject to board correction for errors and omissions at a later meeting. Once adopted, however, board minutes are conclusive evidence of its proceedings in the absence of fraud or bad faith.[113] The law draws a fine distinction between oral testimony changing the written record, which is prohibited, and oral testimony merely explaining or clarifying it, which is permitted.[114]

The "Right to Know" laws of many states permit copying and reproduction of board minutes as public records as well as inspection, at reasonable times and places, often at the cost of the citizen seeking the same. Recent federal legislation has expanded rights of inspection for parents and students with respect to student records. (See discussion of student records in Chapter 6.)

Access to the records of the school board may not be limited to official board minutes. One court recently held that minutes of the board's executive session are official records open to public inspection, even though no law required the board to keep minutes of executive sessions.[115] Statutes permitting access to public records may be so worded to require board disclosure of file data other than board communications, such as payroll records and the names of applicants and candidates for appointment to professional positions, including that of superintendent, in the absence of any special privilege of confidentiality.[116]

---

111. Crabtree v. Board of Educ., Wellston City School Dist., 270 N.E.2d 668 (Ohio 1970); Sch. District v. Moeller, 73 N.W.2d 43 (Iowa 1955).

112. Linden School District v. Porter, 130 N.W.2d 76 (N.D. 1964).

113. State v. Board of Educ. of Bath-Richfield Local School Dist., 218 N.E.2d 616 (Ohio 1966); Del Prete v. Board of Selectmen, 220 N.E.2d 912 (Mass. 1966).

114. *Compare* Lewis v. Board of Educ. of Johnson County, 348 S.W.2d 921 (Ky. 1961) *with* Spann v. Joint Boards of School Directors, 113 A.2d 281 (Pa. 1955) (oral testimony admitted to clarify, but not to contradict, board minutes).

115. Orford Teachers Association v. Watson, 427 A.2d 21 (N.H. 1981).

116. Attorney General v. Sch. Committee of Northampton, 375 N.E.2d 1188 (Mass. 1978) (names of appointive candidates); Mans v. Lebanon School Board, 290 A.2d 866 (N.H. 1972) (payroll records).

D. Other Constitutional Restrictions

Public education is a state function performed by state officers and employees. Hence all public school activity qualifies as "state action" within the meaning of the Fourteenth Amendment to the Constitution, which forbids any form of state action, whether legislative, executive, or administrative, that abridges the civil rights secured by the Constitution. As construed by the United States Supreme Court, these civil rights include due process, substantive civil liberties (freedom of speech, press, association, and privacy), and rights of equal protection of the laws (freedom from government discrimination in the classification and treatment of individuals and of groups).

The sweep of federal and state constitutional limitations on school actions, as expanded by remedial civil rights statutes, is both vast and specialized. These controls will be reviewed in the context of the particular school activities covered in later chapters. While the basic powers to create and define public education are the province of state governments, the states and public schools are limited by the federal Constitution, the supreme law of the land.

Cases

Gann v. Harrisburg, Community Unit School District

218 N.E.2d 833 (Ill. 1966)

GEORGE J. MORAN, *Justice.*

[Appeal from dismissal of suit to void a special election that authorized the creation of a school district, on the grounds that one of the polling places was located outside the territory of the proposed school district, in violation of the governing election statute.] . . . The statute . . . expressly provides that the polling place for a particular precinct must lie within the boundaries of the precinct. . . .

Generally, an election should be held at the time and in the place provided by law in order that it have validity. . . . However, a distinction has been drawn between directory and mandatory provisions. . . . The failure to follow a mandatory provision will invalidate an otherwise valid election, while the failure to follow a directory provision will not. People ex rel. v. Graham, supra. This is not to say, however, that a directory provision may or should be disregarded, but only that an entire election will not be invalidated for the failure to follow such a provision. . . . This analysis has been used not only for general elections, but also for special school elections. . . .

The determination whether a statutory provision is mandatory or directory has depended upon the following criteria: (1) Whether the statutory scheme expressly or impliedly provides that the failure to follow the provision shall render an election void; (2) whether the failure interfered in any way with the result of the election; (3) whether any person legally entitled to vote was not permitted to do so; (4) whether any person voted who was not a resident or the territory sought to be organized; (5) whether the polling place was chosen for any improper motive; and (6) whether any fraud occurred in or as a result of the selection of the polling place. People ex rel. v. Green, 265 I11.39, 106 N.E. 504. . . . Generally, "statutory provisions regulating the conduct of an election are deemed directory after an election in which no improper voting has occurred." People ex rel. Elder v. Quilici, supra, 309 Ill. App. at 472, 33 N.E.2d at 495.

In this case, the statutory scheme does not expressly or impliedly provide that a failure to follow the provision shall render an election void. In addition, none of the adverse effects mentioned above were alleged to have occurred as a result of the failure. Nor was there any fraud alleged. Hence, the provision is directory, not mandatory, and the election need not be voided.

For the foregoing reasons, the judgment of the lower court is affirmed.

Judgment affirmed.

Mullen v. Board of School Directors of DuBois Area S. Dist.

259 A.2d 877 (Pa. 1969)

ROBERTS, Justice.

. . . Mullen was abruptly dismissed by appellant Board of School Directors [Board] from his position as a temporary professional employee of the DuBois Area School District. . . . Mullen brought an action in mandamus seeking reinstatement to his position . . . and related economic damages. . . . Mullen alleged that his dismissal was arbitrary and capricious and that he had no other adequate remedy because his dismissal had made it impossible for him to obtain employment as a teacher in any other school district.

The Board answered that . . . he had no valid and enforceable contract with the Board, and that he had other adequate remedies.

The trial court resolved all of the issues in favor of Mullen and ordered both reinstatement and payment of damages. We affirm. . . .

The second issue in the case involves the validity of the contract between Mullen and the Board. The Public School Code requires that the hiring of a professional employee be effected by an affirmative vote of a majority of the members of the hiring board duly recorded in its minutes. The Board takes the position that there is no valid and enforceable contract covering Mullen's employment because there is no recorded vote of the Board with regard to that contract.

The facts concerning Mullen's hiring bear narration at this point. On January 22, 1966, while still a student, Mullen was interviewed by the superintendent of the DuBois Area School District. At the close of this interview Mullen signed a document which proclaimed itself to be a contract of employment. The instrument was subsequently signed by the President and Secretary of the Board. The exact nature of the authority given by the Board to the superintendent in hiring teachers is unclear, and their records are less than complete. However, we agree with the trial court's finding that "[i]t is quite clear that the Board did approve the appointment and accepted it. Further, its prior approval was followed by further acceptance of the contract." The Board clearly acquiesced in Mullen's appointment for over a year; at one point he was personally feted at a Board meeting for having received a favorable commendation from the Pennsylvania Department of Public Instruction on the handling of one of his courses. . . .

We are aware that there is a line of cases giving this statute a very strict construction. To the extent that they interpret the requirement that there be a formal vote recorded in the minutes as being mandatory we overrule them. In a way we are only returning to the interpretation given the predecessor of this statute in the first case which dealt with it. . . .

Neither are we inclined to eviscerate the force of the statute. However, it is clear beyond doubt that the expression of the board members' approval required by the statute can be evidenced in ways other than by a formal vote recorded in the minutes. To allow this does no violence to the purpose of the statute. . . . To hold that the lack of a formal vote recorded in the minutes, the presence or absence of which is entirely within the control of the Board, renders this contract null and void, would be to exalt form over substance. What possible value can there be in establishing rigid civil service requirements to protect public employees, if such legislation can be defeated by school board mistakes in the appointive process? We hold the requirement of a formal recorded vote to be directory only, although with the caveat that the proof from which Board approval can be inferred must be solid.

Any result other than the one we reach today would arm every school board in the Commonwealth with a tool by which they could regularly avoid otherwise valid contracts. All they would need do is fail to specifically record in their minutes the required vote; then at their whim, as in this case, a contract could be voided by acknowledgement of the failure. . . .

The third and final question in this appeal is whether mandamus is proper. "Mandamus is an extraordinary writ which lies to compel the performance of a ministerial act or mandatory duty where there is a *clear* legal right in the plaintiff, a corresponding duty in the defendant, and a want of any other appropriate and adequate remedy." *Travis* v. *Teter*, 370 Pa. 326, 330, 87 A.2d 177, 179 (1952). This is such a case. The existence of a right in Mullen and a corresponding duty in the Board has been established. The only other condition is the absence of an adequate alternative remedy. None exists. Mullen has not been able to secure other satisfactory employment since his dismissal. We have concluded, as did the trial court, that he is entitled to restoration to his position, damages for lost salary . . . and a certification which would result in his becoming a "permanent professional employee. . . . "

POMEROY, J. files a dissenting opinion in which *JONES, J.*, joins.

POMEROY, Justice (dissenting). I cannot agree with the conclusion of the majority that mandamus will lie in the present case . . . As the majority recognizes, mandamus will lie only to compel performance of a ministerial act or a mandatory duty where there is a clear right-duty relationship between plaintiff and defendant. . . .

Thus, the existence or such a contract is the crucial issue.

The standards for making a valid employment contract between a teacher and a school district are not the usual common law standards; they have been set forth in meticulous fashion by the legislature. The relevant statute is clear and unequivocal: "the affirmative vote of a majority of all the members of the board of school directors in every school district, duly recorded, showing how each member voted, *shall be required* in order to take action on the following subjects:— . . . Appointing or dismissing . . . teachers. . . . *Failure to comply with the provisions of this section shall render such acts of the board of school directors void and unenforceable.*" Act of September 28, 1951, P.L. 1546 § 1, 24 P.S. § 5-508. . . . Accordingly, the employment contract in question is void and unenforceable unless the quoted provision is, as the majority concludes, directory in nature.

Whether a particular statutory provision is mandatory or directory is determined by the intent of the legislature as ascertained by a consideration of the statute as a whole. . . . In the present case, the legislature has prescribed that failure of a board to adhere to the statutory procedures for the appointment of teachers shall render such acts void and unenforceable. I can imagine no way in which the legislature could have better or more categorically expressed its intent that these procedures were to be considered mandatory. . . .

Finally, it should be noted that the statutory requirement of a recorded affirmative vote applies not only to the appointment of teachers but also to a wide variety of other school board actions. . . . Cases holding the present provision to be mandatory as to these other actions by school boards are numerous. . . .

I see no ground upon which we could logically find the affirmative recorded vote requirement mandatory as to some board actions and directory only as to other actions. While this case is decided on its own facts, it seems inevitable that the decision may have unwanted consequences in other areas.

Nothing I have here said is intended to condone in any way the negligent, or even improper, conduct of the School Board in the situation before us. Moreover, I recognize that certain problems of policy are inherent in a statute which subjects the substantive rights of one party to a second party's faithful observance of procedural requirements. But the choice of such a procedure is within the province of the legislature, and the legislature . . . spoke with unmistakable clarity. For this Court to hold that the words "void and unenforceable" mean "valid and enforceable" is, in my view, judicial legislation unwarranted by even the hard facts of this case.

Channel 10, Incorporated v. Independent School District No. 709, St. Louis County

215 N.W.2d 817 (Minn. 1974)

KELLY, Justice.

This action was brought by Channel 10, Inc., a Duluth television station, and Richard E. Gottschald, its news director, as resident taxpayers within defendant school district, seeking a permanent injunction to restrain defendant's school board from holding meetings in violation of the Minnesota Open Meeting Law, Minn. St. 1971, §471.705. . . .

The plaintiffs detail a number of instances in which meetings were held, at some places other than at the regular meeting room of the board, without prior notice to the public. These instances of allegedly improper board meetings are, in substance, as follows: (1) On June 6, 1968, the board met at a closed meeting without prior notice to the public . . . and formally adopted a fact finding panel's report relating to teachers' salary increases. (2) In September 1969, the school board met secretly and agreed upon a proposed budget and tax levy for the upcoming school year. (3) On February 10, 1970, a majority (six of nine) of the board members held informal discussions in a coffee room immediately before a previously announced meeting in the regular meeting room. . . . (4) An unannounced gathering of eight out of nine members of the board was held in June 1971 in the board chairman's home, at which time discussion and expression of views occurred on at least two topics of major interest—construction of a walkway over a highway to a new high school and offering a new contract to the superintendent of schools—and an informal vote was taken on the latter topic. (5) On June 29, 1971, a majority met in the regular meeting room to discuss the highway overpass. (6) At 5:30 p.m. on August 9, 1971, prior to the regularly scheduled meeting of August 10, 1971, the board held a session not announced to the public and discussed, among other things, rural busing, the closing of an elementary school, a special education program at a new high school, and the present lawsuit. (7) At an informal school board session on August 24, 1971, without notice to the public, a proposed budget was presented to the school board. (8) On October 6, 1971, a majority of the board met at a Duluth nightclub and voted not to rehire the superintendent of schools, which decision was to be conveyed to him on October 11. (9) On October 11, 1971, the board held a closed meeting, expressly barring the press. The chairman stated after the meeting that its purpose was to discuss "personnel matters." (10) A realtor was retained, apparently at a closed and unannounced meeting, to act as agent for acquiring a site for a new high school prior to any public and official action by the board to hire him. . . .

1. *The Issue of Plaintiffs' Standing.* . . . The Minnesota Open Meeting Law was obviously designed to assure the public's right to be informed. All meetings of the governing body of a school district, in the language of the statute, "shall be open to the public." . . . The plaintiffs are within the group of persons whom this statute was designed to assure that meetings of school boards would be open to the public. Thus, a right to attend open public meetings having been given to the general public, impliedly they should have standing to enforce that right. . . .

We sustain the trial court's decision that these plaintiffs had standing, basing our holding on the implications from the statute, i.e., the right of the people to be informed in a practical way by the news media, and in keeping with the trend of broadening the standing rights of litigants, particularly where the facts and issues will be vigorously, fairly, and adequately presented in an adversary setting.

2. *Injunctive Relief and Exceptions.* There were no penal provisions in the open meeting law at the time this case was decided in the lower court. However, Minn. St. 645.241 makes it a misdemeanor to perform any act prohibited by statute where no penalty for that violation is imposed in any statute. . . . The open meeting law did not authorize the courts to issue injunctions or writs of mandamus as some states do. See, e.g., Iowa Code Ann. § 28A.7 (1967).

No question was directly raised on this appeal as to the adequacy of the remedy provided by Minn. St. 645.241. The trial court did point out that it might have dismissed this action in its discretion on the grounds propounded by the defendant but did not because using its equitable powers to resolve the dispute was in the public interest. . . .

Similarly, although the law did not require any notice of meetings called by the Board, the court again used its equity power by requiring that the Board give notice to the local news media of any meeting open to the public. . . .

The trial court, having decided to use an equitable remedy not directed nor even authorized by the open meeting law, could also decide that it was within its discretion to determine the extent of the injunctive relief to be granted, provided such limitation was not contrary to the plain policy and purpose of that law. The open meeting law did not provide that certain meetings could be closed if it was in the public interest to do so. The court nonetheless looked to the public interest as an equitable and fair guideline in fashioning the relief granted. . . .

Plaintiffs complain that the trial court after enjoining secret meetings engrafted exceptions upon the open meeting law to protect what it considered the public interest.

The open meeting law was devoid of any authorization or directions for injunctive relief, and the court engrafted an equitable remedy thereon, to which it in turn engrafted exceptions based on what it considered to be equitable principles. . . .

Whether or not injunctive relief should have been granted at all in this case may be open to some question. . . .

We hold that injunctive relief is an appropriate remedy in this case but have misgivings about the extent of the relief and some of the exceptions.

Plaintiffs in effect assert that the trial court should have issued its broad order enjoining the defendants from violating the open meeting law without adding the exceptions it did. . . .

We generally concur with the trial court's decision to enjoin the board from holding secret or closed meetings but are troubled by the exceptions and will discuss them separately.

A. Committee meetings of the board where less than a quorum of the board is present. . . .

The trial court could and should state that the question of the validity of such closed committee meetings was not litigated and that they are neither prohibited nor permitted.

B. Hearings for the discharge, suspension, or termination of employment of tenured teachers, if so requested by the teacher pursuant to Minn. St. 125.17, subd. 7. . . .

At least one case from another state court suggests that closed meetings in violation of an open meeting law can be enjoined without an enabling provision in the statute. *State ex. rel. Adams* v. *Rockwell,* 167 Ohio St. 15, 145 N.E.2d 665 (1957). . . . The court below should, as with Exception A, point out that because this issue was not litigated, such closed meetings are neither prohibited nor permitted by the court's order and no decision is made as to whether they are or are not prohibited by the open meeting law. . . .

D. Meetings for the purpose of interviewing prospective employees for administrative or other sensitive positions. . . .

This exception is apparently based entirely on the theory that it is in the public interest that such meetings be closed. The legislature not having made such meetings an exception, we must conclude that it has decided that it is in the public interest that such meetings be open and that this was not an appropriate exception.

E. Meetings with the board's attorney or attorneys to discuss pending litigation by reason of the confidentiality thereof.

The only factual information that the trial court had concerning this exception was that the present lawsuit was discussed at a closed meeting of seven or eight members. Under the circumstances we hesitate to make a precedent-setting decision adopting either the rule, adopted by a majority of the courts, favoring recognition of this exception or the minority rule refusing to recognize it, or possibly some modification of either. . . .

In some instances, the best protection for the public might be a full public disclosure of any conference between a school board and its attorney. Where tort claims against the school district are being discussed by and between the school board and its attorney, disclosure might not be in the best interests of the public nor in the best interests of the administration of justice.

Another basis cited for favoring this exception is the legislative policy underlying the statutory attorney-client privilege. . . . California has an open meeting law somewhat similar to that of Minnesota. A California court recognized this exception to its open meeting law in these words:

> " . . . Neither the attorney's presence nor the happenstance of some kind of lawsuit may serve as the pretext for secret consultations whose revelation will not injure the public interest." *Sacramento Newspaper Guild* v. *Sacramento County Bd. of Supervisors,* 263 Cal. App. 2d 41, 58, 69 Cal. Rptr. 480, 492 (1968).

Arkansas has an open meeting law quite similar to that of Minnesota and has refused to recognize an exception based on the attorney-client relationship. *Laman* v. *Mccord,* 245 Ark. 401, 432 S.W.2d 753 (1968). Plaintiffs would have to adopt the minority rule espoused by the Arkansas court, or in the alternative, pass upon this exception "when the case is appropriately raised and argued before the court."

Open meeting laws and their exceptions are a developing field of law and at this stage we are inclined to employ judicial restraint. We think this exception is too broad and that if any exceptions are to be made because of an attorney-client relationship, it should be done on a case-by-case basis or at least in a case with a more detailed factual setting than is presented by this record.

F. Meetings of the board with its labor negotiators to discuss proposals relating to terms and conditions of employment and instructions to its negotiators as to their authority. This does not extend to any meeting involving the approval of any final negotiated agreement.

At the time of the trial court's decision in this case there was no express statutory exception of labor negotiations from the open meeting law. We conclude that this was not an exception and is contrary to the policy of the open meeting law.

G. Meetings at which communications are considered made to the board in official confidence by other public agencies or the school districts staff where the disclosure of such information to the public is forbidden by law.

The basis for this exception apparently is Minn. St. 595.02(5) which provides:

> " . . . (5) A public officer shall not be allowed to disclose communications made to him in official confidence when the public interest would suffer by the disclosure."

. . . It is not claimed here that any of the school board meetings were closed because of any communications made in official confidence when the public interest would suffer by the disclosure. One of plaintiffs' objections to this exception is that it was not presented in the evidence nor litigated. We concur in this view as we would prefer to pass upon this exception in some case in which there is some clamed communication made in official confidence and the public's interest in nondisclosure is ventilated.

H. Social gatherings at which no school board business is conducted.

The plaintiffs's main objection to this exception is that the board will consider that discussion, debate, and all steps preliminary to voting are not "conducting business." . . . We think the fears of the plaintiffs are groundless, considered in the light of the court's memorandum and order. On the other hand, a "strict social get-together" at which there is no discussion or consideration of "any matter proper to a public meeting" is so obviously not the kind of meeting that is to be prohibited by the open meeting law that it need not have been set forth as an exception.

Now that we have determined that the eight trial court exceptions are not appropriate, should we affirm the remaining parts of the injunction? We think not because fundamental fairness, . . . requires that the injunction be so tailored that the defendant knows with some reasonable degree of certainty what it is restrained from doing. We have set out in substance the subject matter of a number of closed meetings. None of these meetings should have been closed under the open meeting law with the possible exception of that portion of meeting (6) of August 9, 1971, at which the present lawsuit was discussed. The trial court should make findings as to all of the closed meetings held in violation of the open meeting law and as to the subject matters thereof and enjoin the defendants from holding such meetings in secret. . . .

3. *The Bylaws Issue.* Plaintiffs contend that the trial court should have expressly held those bylaws of the school board that are repugnant to the open meeting law void. . . .

The open meeting statute has been amended since this case was heard and has a penal provision imposing a civil penalty not to exceed $100 for violation of the statute and forfeiture of office for a specified period of time upon a third violation. L. 1973, c. 680, § 1, subd. 2. In addition, two other changes were made in the open meeting law that may have some effect on the future relief to be granted in this case. First, committee and subcommittees have been added to the entities whose meetings shall be open to the public and, second, the statute as amended will not apply to any board "when exercising quasi-judicial functions involving disciplinary proceedings." L. 1973, c. 680, § 1, subd. 1.

Affirmed in part and reversed in part with directions for further proceedings consistent with this opinion. . . .

Conover v. Board of Education of Nebo School District

267 P.2d 768 (Utah 1954)

HENRIOD, *Justice.*

Appeal from a judgment holding that the minutes of a local board of education meeting, transcribed by its Clerk, were not a public writing subject to inspection under Titles 78-26-1, 2 U.C.A. 1953. Reversed. . . .

On Feb. 16, 1953, in answer to the Clerk's inquiry, the State Superintendent of Public Instruction, legal adviser to boards under the terms of an unusual statute, . . . advised the Clerk that minutes of local board meetings were not official until approved by the board, which body should determine its own policy with reference to releasing such minutes to persons other than board members. On Feb. 18, the board held a meeting which was open to the public. The Clerk took notes of what transpired, and transcribed them into minutes for board approval and placement in his Journal. On Feb. 19 the plaintiffs asked permission to examine and copy the minutes so transcribed, but the Clerk, partly because of the Superintendent's letter, advised that they would not be available for inspection until the board approved them at its next meeting. The minutes, as transcribed, later were approved by the board unchanged, and were placed in the Journal which, by statute, the Clerk must keep. . . .

Plaintiffs urge that the notes of the Clerk, or at least the transcribed minutes, prepared for Journal entry, subject only to board approval, were a public writing under our statute and should have been open to inspection immediately after preparation, and that preparation immediately should have followed the meeting. Defendants say this might lead to public misinformation and embarrassment to board members because of possible inaccuracies in what they claim were tentative minutes, unofficial until approved and placed in the Journal.

The statutes and cases relating to public writings are divergent as the shading of the spectrum. There appears to be no formula for determining what is or is not a public writing, except by defining the terms, looking at the facts, and relying on court decisions for determination and settlement. The contentions of opposing counsel, however, point up what frequently is true, that between two extremes, not necessarily midway, there is a point where reason shows brightest, dimming as the point shifts in one direction or the other. To hold that a public writing includes the unexpurgated scribbled notes of a Clerk, legible, perhaps, to him alone, would be unreasonable, we think, and even might deify doodling. It would be unreasonable also to hold that any record made by the Clerk short of approval by a board and placement in a Journal, is not a public writing. Such conclusion might deify dawdling. We hold, therefore, that the Clerk's untranscribed notes reasonably are not classifiable as a public writing under the statute, whereas the transcribed minutes, in final form, but awaiting only approval and placement in the Journal, are a public writing in contemplation of the statute. In so holding, we are aware of those authorities stating that not every memorandum of a public officer is a public record. We believe, however, that the more pertinent cases are found in a long line holding that whenever a written record of a transaction of a public officer in his office is a *convenient and appropriate* mode of discharging the duties of his office, and is kept by him as such, whether required by express provision of law or not, such a record is a public record. To hold that the minutes in this case were not, but the Journal was, a public writing, would attach a magic significance to the word "journal," and might repose in boards a power to act on matters of great public moment without opportunity for public scrutiny.

Here the Clerk did everything he intended to do by way of recording the meeting. Under the statute he could have placed the minutes in the Journal as soon as prepared. The board's policy of having him refrain from doing so until approval was had cannot justify circumvention of a statute requiring him to prepare the minutes, nor the withholding of information from the public for an unreasonable length of time. It is no answer to our conclusions to say that the meeting was open to the public. We cannot blind ourselves to the facts that many such meetings go unattended by the public, that no newspaper can have its agents at all of such meetings, and that no country editor can be in two towns or counties at once.

The parties here have requested that we address ourselves also to the matter of when the minutes should be available for public inspection. . . . We believe that what is a reasonable time to prepare a record of a public board meeting depends entirely on the facts of each case. If the board action called for the purchase of textbooks advocating communism, the record reasonably should be prepared for public release at once after the meeting, while a resolution to dismiss school on Washington's Birthday perhaps need never be documented—at least so far as one very important segment of the public is concerned—the children. It seems to us that the reasonable time when the record of such meetings should be made available to the public, may vary with the exigencies of the particular case, and the time for preparation and dissemination would be directly proportional to the importance of the action taken.

Both sides concede that the public is entitled to know what happened at school board meetings within a reasonable time. Competent authority supports this proposition. We believe further, that a reasonable time after the meeting for making available the record of actions taken there would be some time *before* any important action was to take place. If available only *after* action taken, such information would have little or no news value, except as it might be the basis for criticism of injudicious action. The people would be precluded from indulging their traditionally democratic practice and privilege of complaining of or approving the actions of their elected servants.

There is the further problem as to when *information* of what transpired at the meeting should be made available to the public, quite apart from documentation in a public writing. It would seem that, unless matters were of such a delicate nature or of the type where public policy dictates nondissemination, the meeting itself should be open to the public and press, and information concerning what transpired there should be made available at least in a general way, to both at any time thereafter, by him whose duties require its recordation. There is nothing unreasonable in that under our free and democratic way of life. . . . Any attempt to withhold information after a meeting, itself should be a subject for a wide publicity, irrespective of the fact that withholding it might prevent someone's embarrassment because of inaccuracy. Such inaccuracy may be reason enough to replace him responsible therefor, but most certainly is no reason for withholding information to which the public is entitled, nor to prevent the embarrassment of anyone; nor to perpetuate anyone in public office. We believe and hold that although the Clerk's action in refusing permission to inspect his minutes, was reasonable for the purpose of obtaining an adjudication of correlative rights and duties, it would be unreasonable in preventing the public and press from obtaining information as to what happened at the meeting. . . .

CHAPTER 3

CHAPTER OUTLINE

A. Providing the school plant
   1. Site selection
   2. Acquisition of property
   3. School construction
B. Student transportation
   1. Statutory construction of authority to transport
   2. Minimum distance standards
   3. Bus routes
   4. Special arrangements
C. School studies program
   1. Compulsory education and attendance laws
   2. Admission standards
   3. School assignments
   4. Grade and course placement
   5. Curriculum
      a. Prescribed courses and activities
      b. Textbooks
   6. Extracurricular activities
      a. Interscholastic athletic associations
   7. Promotion and graduation
   8. Special education
D. Nonschool uses and disposition of school property
   1. Community uses
      a. Statutory patterns
      b. Constitutional restrictions
   2. Lease and sale of school property

The Law Governing School Organization

TABLE OF CASES FOR CHAPTER 3

Port Arthur Independent School District v. City of Groves, 376 S. W. 2d 330 (Tex. 1964), 102.
State v. Stojack, 330 P.2d 567 (Wash. 1958), 105.
Wisconsin v. Yoder, 406 U.S. 205 (1972), 106.
In re U.S. Ex Rel. Missouri State High School etc., 682 F.2d 147 (5th CIR 1982), 111.
Board of Education v. Pico, 457 U.S. 853 (1982), 115.

The organization of public education involves a network of laws and regulations that radiate to and from state, regional, and local administrative agencies. For example, teachers' certification standards are normally set by state level agencies, and job specifications for particular positions in each district are set by local school boards. The topics in this chapter also involve intersecting laws regarding school finance and civil rights. Although each segment of these laws forms one "seamless web," practical study can only be undertaken strand by strand. This chapter identifies the more prominent legal problems that recur in organizing the public schools.

A. Providing the School Plant

The manner in which school authorities locate, acquire, construct, and operate school property is determined by state enactments. Disparity of laws regarding land use and construction for school purposes is indicated by the cases in the footnotes.[1] Any generalization on school board authority over the school plant must be qualified by the specifics of land-use regulation in each state. School districts hold school property as trustees, and not as owners.

> "School property is held in trust for school purposes by the . . . corporations authorized for the time being by statute to control the same. It is in the power of the legislature, at any time, to change the trustee." *Carson* v. *State,* 27 Ind. 465,469 (1967).

1. Site Selection

The *initial* selection of school sites is generally entrusted by law to the discretion of local boards, and courts will not interfere with their judgments in the absence of an error of law or abuse of discretion.[2] The fact that students in more remote areas must travel far greater distances to school than most students in the district does not give rise to any burden of which they can legally complain, so long as school locations are reasonable in the light of the district's resources.[3]

It is clear that a municipality may not exclude all public schools from its boundaries by ordinance,[4] but state courts have split three ways on the extent to which local zoning laws may limit the locations of schools. A majority of state courts have held school districts to be immune from all local zoning controls,[5] but a contrary view has been

1. Board of Education v. Common Council, 376 N.Y.S.2d 314 (1975) (school location decision in School board, but subject to veto by municipal council; Federated Conservationists v. Reed, 377 N.Y.S.2d 380 (1975) (school board required to cooperate with environmental control agencies in making location decisions).

2. It is unlawful to employ school sites that foster or perpetuate racial segregation. *See* Chapter 7. Baker v. Un. Sch. District No. 346, 480 P.2d 409 (Kan. 1971): Spann v. Jt. Bd. of Sch. Directors, 113 A.2d 281 (Pa. 1955).

3. Hootch v. Alaska State Operated Sch. System, 536 P.2d 793 (Alaska 1975).

4. Union Free School Dist. v. Hewlett Bay Park, 107 N.Y.S.2d 858, app. den., 109 N.Y.S.2d 175 (1951).

5. City of Addison v. Dallas Ind. School District, 632 S. W. 2d 711 (Tex. 1982); Austin Independent School Dist. v. Sunset Valley, 502 S.W.2d 670 (Tex. 1973); Durand v. Board of Cooperative Educational Services, 334 N.Y.S.2d 670, 341 N.Y.S,2d 884 (N.Y. 1972); Atherton v. Superior Court of San Mateo

taken by others.[6] The reasoning of these conflicting cases is expressed in the following excerpts.

"The underlying logic of some of these authorities is, in substance, that the legislature could not have intended, in the absence of clear expression to the contrary, to give municipalities authority to thwart the state, or any of its agencies in performing a duty imposed upon it by statute." *City of Bloomfield* v. *Davis County Community School Dist.*, 119 N.W.2d 908, 911–12 (Iowa 1963).

"We therefore find that the City of Philadelphia has been empowered to prescribe reasonable ordinances for the protection of safety, health and the general welfare, which, in regard to municipal functions, shall have the force of legislative enactment. . . . The School District is not immune from such ordinances and it must comply therewith." *Sch. District of Phila.* v. *Zoning Bd. of Adjustment*, 207 A.2d 864, 871 (Pa. 1965).[7]

A third, more flexible, view recognizes but limits zoning immunity by public welfare considerations. As one Court put it:

"It is, however, most important to stress that such immunity is not completely unbridled. Even where it is found to exist, it must not . . . be exercised in an unreasonable fashion so as to arbitrarily override all important legitimate local interests. This rule must apply to the state and its instrumentalities as well as to lesser governmental entities entitled to immunity." *Rutgers State University* v. *Piluso*, 286 A.2d 697, 703 (N.J. 1972).

Taking this balancing-of-interest approach, a Court may immunize a school district from some regulations while subjecting it to others. After holding school construction materials to be subject to municipal building regulation, the Courts of Iowa and Pennsylvania held districts to be immune from zoning codes.[8] The *Port Arthur* opinion, at the end of this chapter, deals with building sites.

2. Acquisition of Property

School board authority to acquire property for school purposes, raises the question—what are school purposes? Acquisition of property to provide parking for district employees has been held to be a school purpose, as has the borrowing of capital funds to construct an athletic stadium.[9] The issue is particularly pertinent where school authorities seek to

---

County 324 P.2d 328 (Cal. 1958).

6. Denville v. Board of Education, 279 A.2d 846 (N.J. 1971). Cf. Santa Clara v. Santa Clara Unified School Dist., 99 Cal Rptr 212 (Cal. 1971).

7. To like effect *see* Village of Blaine v. Independent School Dist. No. 12, 138 N.W.2d 32 (Minn. 1965).

8. *Compare* Cedar Rapids Comm. Sch. District v. City of Cedar Rapids, 106 N.W.2d 655 (Iowa 1960) (building requirements) *with* City of Bloomfieid v. Davis County Comm. Sch. District, 119 N.W.2d 909 (Iowa 1963) (zoning immunity); Sch. District v. Zoning Board, 207 A.2d 864 (Pa. 1965) (building requirements) *with* Appeal of Radnor Twp., 252 A.2d 597 (Pa. 1969) (zoning immunity). See Annotation: *Zoning Regulations as Applied to Public Elementary and High Schools,* 74 A.L.R.3d 136 (1976).

9. *In re* Sch. District of Pittsburgh, 244 A.2d 42 (Pa. 1962); Wayman v. Bd. of Education, 215 N.E.2d 394 (Ohio 1966) (parking lot); Alexander v. Philiips, 254 P. 1056 (Ariz. 1927) (stadium).

condemn property of an unwilling owner through the power of *eminent domain.*

a. Eminent Domain. When a district cannot negotiate a voluntary sale of private property, it may compel a sale only if state law expressly vested the district with the sovereign power of eminent domain. Condemnation statutes are strictly construed, and school district condemnations are limited to the conditions and the areas set down by enabling laws. The condemnation power is further restricted by the federal and state constitutions, which oblige public authorities to pay fair compensation for condemned property. The parameters of condemnation law are indicated in *State* v. *Stojack,* which is reported at the end of this chapter. School districts are generally not authorized to condemn property beyond their boundaries.[10]

Intergovernmental condemnations (one government unit condemns the property of other government units) may be regulated by legislation, but it often happens that statutes do not cover them. In such cases, courts have developed conflicting views. Some cases favor a rule that immunizes political subdivisions from condemnations by other political subdivisions. Others modify the rule by permitting intergovernmentai condemnations where the condemned tracts will be put to a higher or more necessary public use than its existing use. This "relative use test" raises interesting fact questions and requires judgments on which individual courts may easily disagree. For instance, school use was held to be a higher use than park use, to support school district condemnation of park land.[11] Public road use was deemed a higher use than public education to sustain condemnations of a school for a roadway.[12] The problem of ranking public uses may be resolved by legislation that expressly authorizes one substate unit of government to condemn the property of other government agencies, including school property. Condemnation statutes seldom authorize a substate unit to redelegate its condemning power, but a legislature may authorize such a transfer. For example, a town might be permitted to transfer its eminent domain authority to a board of education upon referendum approval of the town citizens.[13] Periodic research to summarize these variations in state law is helpful, but incomplete.[14] Intergovernmental condemnations must be investigated by careful research into the laws of each state.

3. School Construction

Government controls over school design, cost, materials, and specifications are not uniformly assigned to state-level or local agencies in the states.[15] State-level agencies may exert indirect control through denial of certifications that are necessary for building, for example, refusal to accredit a proposed school or refusal to certify that the new school will

---

10. Clear Creek School District RE-1 v. Holmes, 628 P. 2d 154 (Colo. 1981)
11. Board of Education v. Park District of Minot, 70 N.W.2d 99 (N. Dak. 1955).
12. Easthampton v. County Commissioners of Hampshire, 28 N.E. 298 (N.H. 1891).
13. Cheney v. Strasburger, 357 A.2d 905 (Conn. 1975).
14. Dau, *Problems in Condemnation of Property Devoted to Public Use,* 44 Tex. L.Rev. 1517 (1966); Annotation: *Condemnation—Of Public Entity's Land,* 35 A.L.R. 3d 1293 (1971).
15. See Pa. Stat. Ann., Tit. 24, §731; New York Education Law §408, (McKinney Supp. 1975).

not impede district reorganization.[16] Where state laws vest broad discretion in school boards regarding the cost and financing of school buildings, courts have refused to question the board's decisions without factually supported complaints of abuse. Courts have dismissed complaints about cost levels, without hearing or trial.[17]

Municipal regulation of school construction is diverse. In California and Arizona, courts held school districts to be immune from municipal building codes; those of Pennsylvania, Texas, and Washington held school districts to be subject to such codes.[18] Where local building control is not settled by a general rule, courts must determine if state statutes are intended to preempt, and thus exclude, local building regulation. The Wisconsin Supreme Court recently ruled that a school district was bound by the municipal building regulations, even though the state had adopted a building code that covered construction of public buildings.[19]

B. Student Transportation

All but a few states have statutes that authorize or require school districts to provide pupil transportation to public schools.[20] State legislatures, however, are continually enacting new laws and amendments on student transportation.

The following excerpt summarizes the national pattern of pupil transportation laws:

> "In almost all states the responsibility for providing pupil transportation rests with the local school districts. However, the districts are almost equally divided between having mandatory and discretionary provisions, if the provision is mandatory, the state either unconditionally requires that the district provide pupil transportation or requires that the district provide transportation to pupils if they live a certain number of miles from school. Similarly, if the provision is discretionary, the district may either have total discretion in providing pupil transportation or it may have discretion to provide transportation only to pupils if they live a certain number of miles from school. A state usually will not reimburse the district for the cost of transporting students who live within the discretionary distance outlined by the state.
>
> Transportation distances vary considerably from state to state. California districts must provide transportation to primary school students who live 3/4 mile from school; whereas Missouri districts must provide transportation to students only if they live 3 1/2 miles from school. A few states, such as New York and Delaware, set different distance

16. Du Pont-Fort Lewis Sch. District v. Bruno, 489 P.2d 171 (Wash. 1971); Siegel v. Allen, 225 N.Y.S.2d 336 (1965).

17. Dixon v. Carroll County Bd. of Education,217 A.3d 364 (Md. 1966); Bd. of Education v. Phillips, 96 So.2d 96 (Ala. 1956).

18. *Compare* Hall v. City of Taft, 302 P.2d 574 (Cal. 1956); Bd. of Regents v. City of Tempe, 356 P.2d 399 (Ariz. 1960), *with* Sch. District of Phila. v. Zoning Bd.,207 A.2d 864 (Pa. 1965); Edmonds Sch. District v. City of Mountain Lake Terrace, 465 P.2d 177 (Wash. 1970). The law of various states is reviewed in Note, *Municipal Power to Regulate Building, Construction, and Land Use by Other State Agencies*, 49 MINN. L. REV. 284 (1964).

19. Hartford Union H.S. v. City of Hartford, 187 N.W.2d 849 (Wis. 1971).

20. State transportation statutes are reviewed in Annotation: School Transportation—Statutory Requisites, 52 A.L.R.3d 1036(1973).

standards for elementary and secondary schools. In this situation secondary school students must live farther from school than elementary school students before the district must provide transportation.

A few states require that district provide transportation but do not prescribe any specific distance requirements; instead they establish a standard which allows the district a certain amount of discretion. In Kentucky and Vermont, for example, a district must provide transportation to a student who does not live within a "reasonable walking distance" of school. In Rhode Island a district must provide transportation to students whose attendance would otherwise be impractical.

In all states the routing of school buses is a task left to the local districts, although half the state education agencies have established regulations concerning bus routes. A few state education agencies have passed regulations which not only guide the district in drawing the routes but also require that the district submit the route plans to the State agency for final approval.

In most instances state education agencies have developed thorough regulations concerning bus equipment. Some states have assembled their regulations for bus and safety equipment into booklets which have more than a hundred pages.

About half the states have requirements for school bus inspections in the school code; however, it is probable that the remaining states have provisions elsewhere in the state code. Only a few states have requirements for bus driver's qualifications such as a certificate or a special license. Again, it is likely that these provisions appear elsewhere in the State code." *A Study of State Legal Standards for the Provision of Public Education,* p. 57 (National Institute of Education 1974).

1. Statutory Construction of Authority to Transport

In the few states that lack transportation statutes, the question arises whether school boards have implied powers to provide such transportation. The courts of several states have refused to imply such power.[21] Transportation issues usually revolve around judicial construction. Whether a particular court will interpret a statute strictly or loosely usually depends upon its evaluation of the cost-benefit relationships between the urgency of student need for transportation, and the financial burden upon the district. In striking that balance, a court may be affected more by the facts than by any abstract preference for strict or liberal construction. Similar factors of practicality affect judicial decisions where parents challenge school board transportation decisions. The following cases illustrate the role of the courts in determining the scope and the reasonableness of board discretion.

School transportation for extracurricular activity participants, such as athletic teams and bands, finds support in some cases, but an Iowa court decided that statutory authority to transport students "to and from school" did not authorize the board to transfer pupils to school sponsored events outside the district.[22] The Utah court drew a distinction between district transportation after school hours for students who participated in extracurricular activities, which it upheld; and school transportation for student

21. Conecuh County Bd. of Education v. Campbell, 162 So.2d 233 (Ala. 1964).

22. *Compare* State v. McKinnon, 118 S.E.2d 134 (N.Car. 1961), *with* Schmidt v. Blair,213 N.W. 593 (Iowa 1927).

patrons or spectators at such school extracurricular activities, which it disallowed.[23] In a Rhode Island case, the statutory phrase "to and from school" was held not to authorize transportation of resident private school students as far as the town line on their journey to a school outside the district boundaries. However, such transportation has been authorized and provided under a Pennsylvania statute, which was upheld.[24]

2. Minimum Distance Standards

Many disputes involve the minimum distance that a school board may or must transport students from their homes to the school. Where no distance guideline is set by statute, such as where a statute authorizes "reasonable" transportation, board rulings must be tested on the facts of each case. Although courts defer to school board discretion, they tend to scrutinize board decisions more closely where student safety is involved. Accordingly, a Connecticut court upheld a state agency order that the local district ensure student safety by furnishing school transportation.[25]

Similarly, a California court overturned, as an abuse of discretion, a board refusal to transport a small number of students from an inaccessible part of the district. The board pleaded excessive costs. After finding that the students' families were very poor, and could not get them to school without such transportation, the court overruled the board decision.[26]

Safety considerations sometimes support a denial of busing services. In Illinois and Washington, courts upheld board rulings that barred school buses from roads that were unsafe or presented traffic hazards, such as a short, dead-end road.[27] However, where a school board became excessively meticulous in measuring minimum distance for bus transportation, that is, by measuring the distance from the student's driveway, rather than from his front door, a court ruled that the board misread the statute.[28]

School boards that are not compelled by statute to provide transportation may refuse it[29] or may discontinue existing transportation,[30] so long as all similarly situated students are treated equally.[31]

3. Bus Routes

Board decisions that establish school bus routes and pickup points are often questioned

---

23. Beard v. Board of Education, 16 P.2d 900 (Utah 1932).

24. *Compare* Chaves v. Sch. Committee of Town of Middletown, 211 A.2d 639 (R.I. 1965); *with* School Dist. of Pittsburgh v. Commonwealth, 382 A.2d 772 (Pa. 1978).

25. *Compare* Flowers v. Ind. Sch. District of Tama, 16 N.W.2d 570 (Iowa 1944) (board discretion upheld under wartime conditions) *with* People *ex rel.* Schuldt v. Schimanski,266 N.E.2d 409 (Ill. 1971) (disapproved shuttle bus arrangement that required student to walk great distance to the pickup point). *See also* Town of Waterford v. Connecticut State Board of Education, 169 A.2d 891 (Conn.1961).

26. Manjares v. Newton, 411 P.2d 901 (Cal. 1966).

27. State v. Grand Coulee Dam Sch. District, 536 P.2d 614 (Wash. 1975); Randolph v. Sch. Unit 201, 270 N.E.2d 50 (Ill. 1971).

28. Madison County Board of Education v. Grantham, 168 So.2d 515 (Miss. 1964).

29. Plesnicer v. Kovach, 430 N.E.2d 648 (Ill. 1981).

30. Abraham v. Wallenpaupak Area Sch. Dist., 422 A.2d 1201 (Pa. 1980).

31. Shrewsbury et al. v. Board of Education, 265 S.E.2d 767 (W.Va. 1980).

in the context of walking burdens placed on students. A board may not arbitrarily require pupils to walk unreasonable distances from their homes to pickup points.[32]

Where the transportation statute does not expressly provide exemptions from minimum distance limits (as in the case of unsafe walking conditions) or does not expressly allow the board to make such exemptions, a court could strictly enforce statutory distance requirements, even in hazardous circumstances, on the theory that the legislature did not intend to allow special arrangements for hazardous crossings.[33] A number of states have express statutory exemptions from minimum distance and bus route restrictions for students who lack safe walking paths either to the school or to bus pickup points.[34] Where statutes refer to unreasonable distance, hazardous conditions could be a factor in the determination of reasonable distance.[35] The determination of what crossings are hazardous for such purposes may be delegated to traffic authorities rather than to the school district board.

District reimbursement of students for costs of private transportation in lieu of school transportation has not been widely litigated. In a recent case, the court upheld the practice as reasonable, where roads were unsafe for buses, even though parents disputed the reasonableness of the amount of reimbursement tendered by the district.[36]

4. Special Arrangements

Parents may not demand bus transportation to a school other than that regularly assigned by the school board, provided the transportation was reasonable.[37] Nor may a parent, in the absence of supporting statute, demand transportation outside the district.[38]

The law regarding individualized transportation to specialized learning centers is disuniform among the states. Some states provide transportation, often door to door, for handicapped children, regardless of distance, but in the absence of statutory authorization, the legality of such transportation will depend upon a court's willingness to imply school authority to provide the same. A New York education law authorizing special education at public expense (including board, lodging, and tuition for deaf children), without mention of transportation, was interpreted by the court as not authorizing free public transportation to and from such schools.[39]

Constitutional considerations may also govern student transportation. Bus transportation for special student groups only must be rationally based, and may not be discriminatory.[40] Nor may the state grant or withhold student transportation privileges where such action would impede judicially ordered desegregation.

---

32. Fn. 28, supra.

33. Studley v. Allen, 261 N.Y.S.2d 138 (1965); *cf.* Hoefer v. Hardin County Bd. of Education, 441 S.W.2d 418 (Ky. 1969).

34. *See* Pa. Stat. Ann. Tit. 24 §13-1362; *cf.* Cartwright v. Sharpe, 162 N.W.2d 5 (Wis. 1968).

35. Schmidt v. Payne, 199 S.W.2d 990 (Ky. 1947).

36. *See* State v. Grand Coulee Dam School District, 536 P.2d 614 (Wash. 1975).

37. Davis v. Fentress County Bd. of Education, 402 S.W.2d 873 (Tenn. 1966). *See also* Hatch v. Board of Education, Ithaca City Sch. Dist., 439 N.Y.S.2d 466 (1981) (transportation denied to student attending nonneighborhood schools under open enrollment program).

38. O'Neil v. School District No. 15, 451 P.2d 791 (Wyo. 1969).

39. Knauff v. Bd. of Education, 293 N.Y.S.2d 133 (1968).

40. Morrisette v. DeZonia, 217 N.W.2d 377 (Wis. 1974); Sparrow v. Gill, 304 F. Supp. 86 (M.D. No. Car. 1969)

C. School Studies Program

1. Compulsory Education and Attendance Laws

The right of each state to compel parents, under penalty of law, to have their children attend a qualified public or private school or to provide an otherwise acceptable education is well settled.[41] However, the extent of state authority in relation to parental authority is subject to both constitutional law and to the policy set by state statutes. These limits are discussed in detail in Chapter 10, but may be summarized as follows. The general "liberty" of parents protected by the Fourteenth Amendment includes their fundamental right to direct the upbringing of their children, and this right prohibits the state from requiring that all children be educated only in public schools. Second, the religious liberty guarantee of the free exercise clause of the First Amendment further limits the state from imposing educational requirements that force parents to act against their religion, unless the state can prove an overriding public necessity to justify such infringement. Subject to these constitutional limits, however, the state may establish reasonable standards of public and private education. For violation of valid compulsory education standards, parents may not only be prosecuted criminally, they may also be deprived of their child's custody in case of serious neglect.[42]

The United States Supreme Court, however, has recently imposed a greater burden to prove child neglect by "clear and convincing evidence" before the state may interfere with "fundamental liberty interest of natural parents in the care, custody, and management of their child," thus making enforcement of compulsory attendance laws through prosecution for child neglect more difficult.[43]

Sanctions against truant children range from legally declaring the child a delinquent, or in need of supervision by a social service agency, to placement in institutions. Academic penalties such as expulsion or lengthy suspension are generally frowned upon by the courts as counterproductive.[44] In a severe case, the court's contempt authority may be invoked, but only if children are fully advised and aware of the consequences of their actions.[45] Penalty against the child will often be tempered when the parent has acquiesced in or encouraged the truancy, and the severity of the punishment will turn on the circumstances in each case. Many states' laws providing penalties for habitually truant children are being reformed and modernized.[46]

States may also require school attendance up to a specified age, but here also exemptions are provided by statute, and in limited situations, by constitutional law.

---

41. *See, e.g.*, State v. M. M. 407 So.2d 987 (Fla. 1981); Concerned Citizens For Neighborhood Schools v. Bd. of Education 379 F. Supp. 1233 (E.D. Tenn. 1974).

42. Shoreline Sch. District v. Superior Ct., 346 P.2d 999 (Wash. 1959); Scoma v. Illinois, 391 F. Supp. 452 (N.D. Ill. 1974); Matter of McMillan, 226 S.E. 2d 693 (N.C. 1976).

43. Santosky v. Kremer, 450 U.S. 993, 102 S. Ct. 1388 (1982).

44. Matter of King v. Farmer, 424 N.Y.S.2d 86 (1979).

45. *Re* T. V. P., 414 N.E.2d 209 (Ill. 1980).

46. See generally, Annotation: *Truancy as Indicative of Delinquency or Incorrigibility*, 5 A.L.R. 4th 1212 (1981).

Typical statutory exemptions include children who are legally emancipated, lawfully employed, or so severely disabled as not to be capable of benefiting from formal schooling.

Of increasing concern is the question whether parents may defy public school attendance authorities by refusing to send their children to assigned public schools on the ground that the children will be exposed to unreasonable risks of physical and emotional harm due to unruly school conditions. Three recent cases from Pennsylvania and New York evoked judicial statements that child safety could constitute a good defense against prosecution under the compulsory education laws, but two of the cases found that the parents did not meet their heavy burden of proving the facts required for that defense.[47] In the first Pennsylvania case, evidence of extortion, threats, physical assault, and emotional harm was found sufficient ground for a parent to demand reassignment of the child to another school. In the later Pennsylvania case, the fact that one child was thrown against a corridor wall and another child cut by a scissors-wielding student was held insufficient proof of grave danger to excuse nonattendance. In the New York case, the parent's evidence of her child's alleged mistreatment was also held insufficient. A sympathetic judicial attitude was also expressed in an earlier New York prosecution where parents elected not to send their child to the assigned school and employed a fictitious address to enroll the child in another public school. In dismissing the prosecution, the court found that the district was obliged to permit the enrollment in the second school and ordered the district to do so, stating: "While the court cannot and will not condone this trickery [false address] it cannot prejudice the right of the children to have this court act to protect their best interests." A similar sentiment was voiced in a Kansas decision where the parent refused to send a child to a school whose location made it very hazardous for that child to reach.[48]

Refusal to comply with compulsory attendance laws for religious reasons has met with mixed success. In a landmark case, the Supreme Court found enforcement of a state's law against the Amish to infringe their free exercise of religion unconstitutionally (see *Wisconsin* v. *Yoder* reproduced at the end of this chapter). Religious justification is not an automatic defense for noncompliance with attendance laws, however. Where parents, because of religious objection to a particular class activity, removed a child totally from school, as opposed to seeking exemption of the child from the objectionable activity, charges of delinquency and parental neglect were sustained.[49] Courts have been even less sympathetic to parents raising cultural reasons for noncompliance. One court found that an American Indian's desire to inculcate Indian heritage in his children did not justify his withdrawal of the children from schools that did not teach Indian culture.[50] Similarly, a federal court rejected the objection that a school's hair-length regulation conflicted with Indian custom, tradition, and religious belief.[51]

---

47. *Compare* School District of Pittsburgh v. Zebra, 325 A.2d 330 (Pa. 1974) *with* Comm. ex. rel. Sch. District v. Ross, 330 A.2d 290 (Pa. 1975); Matter of Baum, 382 N.Y.S. 2d 672 (1976).

48. Foster, 330 N.Y.S.2d 8, 10 (1972); Williams v. Bd. of Education, 99 P. 216 (Kan. 1908).

49. State *ex rel* Shoreline School District v. Superior Court, 346 P.2d 999 (Wash. 1959).

50. Matter of McMillan, 226 S.E.2d 693 (N.C. 1976).

51. Hatch v. Goerke, 502 F.2d 1189 (10th Cir. 1974).

2. Admission Standards

> "The difference between an admission and an attendance requirement should be noted. An attendance statute usually places the responsibility on the parent or guardian; that is, the parent must cause his child to attend school . . . By contrast, the responsibility for carrying out the admission statute is with the state, or in some cases, delegated to the local board." *Study of State Legal Standards for the Provision of Public Education,* p. 15 (National Institute of Education).

Pupil admission standards are established directly by statute in most states with respect to certain qualifications—age, residence, and immunization (see Table 2–2), but discretion is often left to local authorities regarding admission to schools, programs, and grade placement. Parents may not insist on admission without meeting admission requirements.[52]

Admission to public schools in a given school district is generally limited to students who reside within the district. Without statutory authorization, a district may not admit nonresident students to its schools, but most states permit admission of nonresidents under specified circumstances. Some grant discretion to the admitting districts; some allow nonresident admission only if both the admitting district and the resident district agree.[53] Special rules of admission often apply to students in special circumstances (e.g., handicapped, lacking parental care) or when sending districts lack certain facilities (e.g., high school or special education facilities), but there is no uniformity among the states.[54]

Generally, a student's residence is governed by the residence of the parent or legal guardian.[55] Legally emancipated students may acquire an independent residence and may not be denied admission on the basis of their parents' residence.[56] Where the student is not emancipated and is living apart from the parents, state laws typically require proof that the child's residency in the district is not taken for the primary purpose of attending, without charge, the district's schools.[57] Each case will be determined on its particular facts,[58] and the burden of proof lies with the party seeking exceptional residency status.[59]

The residence of the child is not always fixed by the residence of the child's legal custodian. For example, a child for whom a nonparent guardian had been appointed, but who continued to live with the parent, was deemed to retain the residence of the natural

---

52. *See* Hammond v. Marx, 406 F. Supp. 853 (D. Me. 1975), which affirmed the constitutionality of minimum age requirements for admission to public school; O'Leary v. Wisecup, 364 A.2d 770 (Pa. 1976)

53. *Compare* Jones v. Grand Ledge Public Schools, 84 N.W.2d 327 (Mich. 1957) *with* Cord-Charlotte School District v. Independence County Board of Education, 608 S.W.2d 12 (Ark. 1980).

54. *See* School District of Chester Twp. v. School District of City of Chester, 210 A.2d 501 (Pa. 1965); *contra* Jones v. Grand Ledge Public Schools, 84 N.W.2d 327 (Mich. 1957).

55. Matter of Montcrieffe, 467 N.Y.S. 2d 812 (1983); DeLeon v. Harlingen Consolidated Ind. Sch. Dist., 552 S.W.2d 922 (Tex. 1977).

56. Street v. Cobb Co. School Dist., 520 F.Supp. 1170 (N.D.Ga. 1981).

57. *See, e.g., Tex. Educ. Code Ann. tit.* 2 § 21.031(d) (Vernon Supp. 1982).

58. Luoma v. Union School District of Keene, 214 A.2d 120 (N.H. 1965).

59. Herscher Community Unit School District v. Kankakee School District, 422 N.E.2d 273 (Ill. 1981).

parent.[60] Where parents are divorced or separated, the residence of the child generally becomes that of the parent who has legal custody,[61] unless special circumstances justify temporary placement with the noncustodial parent.[62]

The residence of a nonparent custodian determines the child's residence only if the child resides with the custodian and the custody has not been arranged to gain free admission to the district's schools.[63]

In deciding the primary motivation for nonparental custody, courts look to the specific needs of the child and the parents' ability to meet those needs. Factors such as parents' financial resources[64] and the child's physical or mental health[65] are considered. State statutes are often liberally construed to uphold informal custodial arrangements as to the source of the child's residence,[66] especially where circumstances such as parental abandonment or death leave no choice but to place the child with others.[67]

Immunization and health requirements vary from state to state (see Table 2–1), but the state interest of protecting students from communicable disease has been deemed sufficiently compelling to overcome challenges that such requirements violate religious tenets.[68] A number of states accommodate religious objections to immunization requirements, but they do so as a matter of policy and not of constitutional necessity. Such accommodation raises other constitutional considerations, such as whether exempting students for religious reasons violates equal protection[69] or constitutes government preference of religion in violation of the Constitution's establishment clause.[70]

Minimum age requirements for admission also vary among the states. They may be set by statute or by regulation, and may apply to entry into kindergarten as well as first grade. Some states permit exception to age requirements at the discretion of the local school board, and courts tend to defer to such local decisions.[71] Admission of part-time students under dual-enrollment programs is discussed in Chapter 10.

3. School Assignments

Subject to statutory and constitutional limits, school authorities have discretion to assign students to particular schools and school hours. Student needs and preferences may be

---

60. School District No. 3 of Maricopa County v. Dailey, 471 P.2d 736 (Ariz. 1970); Matter of Proios, 443 N.Y.S.2d 828 (1981).

61. State ex rel. Frasier v. Whaley, 234 N.W.2d 909 (Neb. 1975).

62. Luoma v. Union School District of Keene, 214 A.2d 120 (N.H. 1965).

63. *See* School District No. 3 of Maricopa County v. Dailey, 471 P.2d 736 (Ariz. 1970); Matter of Proios, 443 N.Y.S.2d 828 (1981).

64. See Mich. Op. Atty. Gen. 1976, No. 5004, p. 457.

65. University Center, Inc. v. Ann Arbor Public Schools, 191 N.W.2d 302 (Mich. 1971); *but see* Nelson v. Tuscarora Intermediate Unit, 426 A.2d 1234 (Pa. 1981).

66. *See, e.g.*, Luoma v. Union School District of Keene, 214 A.2d 120 (N.H. 1965).

67. *See, e.g.*, Simms v. Roosevelt Union Free School District 420 N.Y.S.2d. 96 (1976).

68. Zucht v. King, 260 U.S. 174 (1922); Jacobson v. Commonwealth of Massachusetts, 197 U.S. 11 (1905); Brown v. Stone, 378 So.2d 218 (Miss. 1979), cert. denied, 449 U.S. 887 (1980); Syska v. Montgomery County Board of Education, 415 A.2d 301 (Md. 1980), app. dism'd., 450 U.S. 961 (1981). *See also In re* Clark, 185 N.E.2d 128 (Ohio 1962).

69. Brown v. Stone, 378 So.2d 218 (Miss. 1979).

70. *See* Welsh v. United States, 398 U.S. 333 (1970) (Harlan, J., concurring).

71. *See* Zweifel v. Joint District No. 1, Belleville, 251 N.W.2d 822 (Wis. 1977).

subordinated to the needs of the overall student population. Shortened hours, half-day sessions, and school transfers that are reasonably indicated by district resources will be upheld, even though alternative arrangements might have been considered reasonable by a court.[72] Although the burden of proving an error of law or abuse of discretion in these matters rests on the party attacking the school decision,[73] and courts are slow to interfere with educational decisions, they will overturn decisions based on manifest errors. A decision to close a high school that was based on gross mistake of fact, and school assignments that were racially discriminatory, were overturned.[74] The transfer of a talented student from a school that offered music and language studies required to develop that talent to a school that did not provide such studies is an example of abusive discretion that courts will reverse.[75]

Where statutes expressly limit school transfers to certain conditions, such as only for emergencies, the local board cannot make transfers for any other reasons, no matter how beneficent in nature.[76] Nor can legislative control be defeated by interdistrict contracts that call for elective attendance zones contrary to a statutory plan.[77]

The authority to transfer students is further affected by school closing statutes that prescribe the conditions under which districts may or must close schools. The problem arises where classes from different schools are consolidated in one school, but less than the entire school is closed. Courts must decide how much reduction amounts to a school closing. In North Dakota, the court ruled that partial grade elimination at one school did not constitute a "closing." The school closing statute, if applicable, would have required citizen electoral approval before student transfer.[78]

The assignment of students based upon exceptional group characteristics, for instance, by handicap, sex, or race, implicates overriding principles of constitutional and civil rights law, and requires separate discussion. The law affecting such students is considered in Chapter 7.

4. Grade and Course Placement

As a general rule, state laws entrust to various central and local agencies the responsibility of promulgating standards for placement and promotion at different grade or course levels. (See Table 3–1.) Thus, a board can require even a child with outside advance training to register for kindergarten before affording tests for advance placement and may refuse to admit any child below a specified age.[79] Generally, courts will defer to

72. Bronestine v. Geinsendorfer, 613 S.W.2d 465 (Mo. 1981) (transfer of certain grades to nonneighborhood school) Welling v. Bd. of Education, 171 N.W.2d 545(Mich.1969)(half-day sessions); Zoll v. Anker, 414 F. Supp. 1024 (S.D.N.Y. 1976)(shortening of school hours) Hiers v. Brownell,136 N.W.2d 10(Mich.1965); Potter v. School Directors, *supra;* Kuntz v. Benz 187 N.W.2d 65 (N.D. 1971).

73. Kinsel v. Rettinger, 277 N.E.2d 913 (Ind. 1972).

74. See race discrimination cases, Chapter 7. Bartlett v. Bd. of Trustees, 550 P.2d 416 (Nev. 1976).

75. *In re* Reassignment of Hayes, 135 S.E.2d 645 (N.C. 1964)

76. Board of Education v. Oklahoma Sch. Bd. of Education, 521 P.2d 390 (Okla. 1974).

77. Bd. of Sch. Directors v. Dock, 318 A.2d 370 (Pa. 1974).

78. Choal v. Lyman Ind. Sch. District, 214 N.W.2d 3 (N. Dak. 1974).

79. Silverberg v. Bd. of Education, 303 N.Y.S.2d 816 (1969); Frost v. Yerozunis, 385 N.Y.S.2d 181 1976); Rosenstein v. North Penn Sch. District, 392 A.2d 788 (Pa. 1975).

TABLE 3-1. Summary of state standards—grade organization *

STATES	STATUTE AND/OR REGULATION	STATE DECISION	LOCAL DECISION			No Provisions
			Within State Guidelines	Upon State Approval	No State Restrictions	
ALABAMA	R			X		
ALASKA	R		X			
ARIZONA						X
ARKANSAS						X
CALIFORNIA	S		X			
COLORADO						X
CONNECTICUT						X
DELAWARE	R		X			
FLORIDA	S		X	X		
GEORGIA	S				X	
HAWAII						X
IDAHO	R		X	X		
ILLINOIS	S				X	
INDIANA	S		X			
IOWA	R		X			
KANSAS	R		X			
KENTUCKY	S		X			
LOUISIANA	S			X		
MAINE	S		X			
MARYLAND	R			X		
MASSACHUSETTS	S		X			
MICHIGAN	S		X			
MINNESOTA	S		X			
MISSISSIPPI	R	X				
MISSOURI	S		X			

SOURCE: National Institute of Education.

*All data tables must be updated for possible changes in each state since 1979.

NOTE: Only Virginia has no state supervision over or restrictions on the local boards decision in grade organization.

a school board's evaluation of academic achievement in making placement decisions.[80]

Judicial deference to school board discretion is also illustrated by a Montana case that upheld a board decision to exclude a child who attained the requisite age of six only three days after the deadline fixed by board regulation.[81]

School placement decisions beyond the kindergarten will also prevail against parental wishes if the decisions are not arbitrary, and authority to establish nongraded programs has also been vested in local officials.[82] A decision to exclude a previously

80. *See* Sandlin v. Johnson, 643 F.2d 1027 (4th Cir. 1981); Hoffman v. Board of Education, City of N.Y., 424 N.Y.S.2d 376 (N.Y. 1979).

81. State ex rel Ronish v. Sch. District, 348 P. 2d 797 (Mont. 1960).

82. *See* State v. Gloist, 270 N.W. 2d 376 (Iowa 1936); Schwan, etc. v. Bd. of Education, etc., 183 N.W. 2d 594 (Mich. 1971).

STATES	STATUTE AND/OR REGULATION	STATE DECISION	LOCAL DECISION			No Provisions
			Within State Guidelines	Upon State Approval	No State Restrictions	
MONTANA						X
NEBRASKA	R		X			
NEVADA	S	X				
NEW HAMPSHIRE	S		X			
NEW JERSEY	R		X			
NEW MEXICO	S,R		X	X		
NEW YORK	R		X			
NORTH CAROLINA	S		X			
NORTH DAKOTA	R		X			
OHIO						X
OKLAHOMA	R		X			
OREGON	R		X			
PENNSYLVANIA	S		X			
RHODE ISLAND						X
SOUTH CAROLINA	R		X			
SOUTH DAKOTA						X
TENNESSEE	S		X			
TEXAS						X
UTAH						X
VERMONT	S		X			
VIRGINIA	R				X	
WASHINGTON	S		X			
WEST VIRGINIA						X
WISCONSIN			X			
WYOMING						X

accelerated youngster from a special progress class, notwithstanding the student's admitted academic qualifications, was upheld with the following observation:

> "Certainly, the court may not hold as arbitrary or capricious the respondent's determination that chronologically determined physical, social, and emotional maturity are vital and proper factors to be considered in the development and education of a child. To thrust a youngster into an environment where all his classmates are older may well result in the consequent impairment of the necessary social integration of the child with his classmates"[83]

Courts generally defer to administrative judgment, but they will not uphold dual standards. A policy of admitting new students to grades beyond kindergarten on the basis of age, while requiring achievement tests to advance students already enrolled in kindergarten, was overturned as discriminatory.[84]

---

83. Ackerman v. Rubin, 231 N.Y.S.2d 112 (1962).
84. Morgan v. Bd. of Education, 317 N.E.2d 393 (Ill. 1974).

5. Curriculum

A recent study summarizes the law on public school curriculum as follows:

> "In all states the local district must offer a curriculum that the state prescribes. The degree of control exercised by the education agency differs from state to state. In about half the states the local district must offer the curriculum prescribed by the state. . . . Even in those states where districts retain some discretion, course offerings must still be chosen within state guidelines. . . . For example, all schools must offer courses in American history and government. The statutes of nearly all states contain such requirements. In addition, the choice of the district is often limited by state board guidelines regulating the number, content or quality of the courses. Some states provide that a district must offer a specified number of courses. Some also enforce the dictates . . . by making the district's choice of curriculum a requirement for accreditation. Sanctions for noncompliance would include . . . loss of state aid. . . . The local district selects its curriculum offerings on the basis of the extent of authority delegated by the State." National Institute for Education, *Study of State Legal Standards for the Provision of Public Education*, p. 28 (1974).

The state-by-state breakdown on curriculum statutes is presented in Table 3–2.

Courts liberally imply authority in state and local agencies to add new activities that are deemed necessary or incidental to the ever-expanding concept of "education." Authority to institute physical education programs, health inspection programs, and medical treatment programs where treatment cannot reasonably await private medical care has been implied.[85]

With respect to course requirements for individual students, local school authorities also have broad discretion. District residents cannot, through legal action, force the board either to add or delete a particular course from the curriculum, unless there is a special duty to do so under state statute or under constitutional law. In Massachusetts, however, parents were empowered by state statute to compel the local school committee to offer courses not included in the regular curriculum.[86] (Other examples of special legal duties are discussed in Chapter 7 with relation to minority groups.)

a. Prescribed Courses and Activities

> "As government pressure towards unity becomes greater, so strife becomes more bitter as to whose unity it shall be." *West Virginia Bd. of Education* v. *Barnette*, 319 U.S. 624, 641 (1943).

The authority to establish a school's curriculum raises the threshold question, what subjects other than those prescribed by statute fall within the nebulous concept of curriculum? Educators are not in agreement on this point. Viewed narrowly, *curriculum*

---

85. Alexander v. Phillips, 254 P. 1056 (Ariz. 1927); City of Dallas v. Mosely, 286 S.W.497 (Tex. 1926); Jarrett v. Good 11, 168 S.E.2d 763 (W. Va. 1933).

86. Johnson v. School Committee, 356 N.E.2d 820 (Mass. 1977) (driver training course).

pertains only to courses given regularly for credit. Viewed broadly, it embraces all life experiences offered students in the schools. Under these polar and other intermediate opinions, the demarcation between curricular and extracurricular activity remains blurred.[87] Courts bypass such controversy when deciding curriculum authority by accepting the judgment of local school authorities as to what subject matter is appropriate to public education. Legal conflict is not so easily avoided where school activities expand into areas formerly reserved to family control. The conflict was forecast by the above quotation from the landmark flag-salute case. Three sources compete for control over what is taught to children—the parent, the school management, and the individual teacher who claims academic freedom. These sources produce different legal alliances, which shift according to the subject matter of a particular lawsuit. The *Mercer* opinion (at the end of Chapter 4) illustrates how law attempts to reconcile these competing interests. This section focuses upon the parent/administration conflict, and the problem of ranking their relative authority. Here also, the subject matter is often the determining factor. For example, school requirements of English courses could not be seriously challenged by a parent, but sex education courses, unless carefully structured, may infringe parental interests.

School/parent conflicts also surface over nonconstitutional decisions on course elections. Courts do not agree on which party has the initial right of choice and which party has the burden of defeating the other's choice. The theory of *primary parental initiative* is that the parent should initially have the opportunity to make a reasonable selection for the prescribed studies for his child to pursue, as superior to that of the trustees and of the teachers. This theory was voiced in an early case that upheld the parent's desire to roster his child for musical studies, rather than for domestic science.[88] A similar view was taken in Oklahoma:

> "We think it would be a reversal of the natural order of things to presume that a parent would arbitrarily, without cause or reason, insist on dictating a course of study for his child in opposition to the course established by the school authorities. A better rule, we think, would be to presume, in the absence of proof to the contrary, that the request of the parent was reasonable and just, to the best interest of the child, and not detrimental to the discipline and efficiency of the school."[89]

The opposing view was noted in a decision sustaining a school requirement of musical studies over parental objection that the course was not in the best interest of the child:

> "The arbitrary wishes of the relator . . . must yield . . . to the governing authorities of the school . . . and their reasonable rules and regulations. . . . This is the doctrine of the cases decided by the courts . . . in many of our sister states, and . . . we think it is better doctrine. [Citing decisions from Massachusetts, Vermont, Ohio, Maine, and New Hamp

87. E. Bolmeier, School in the Legal Structure 281 (1973).
88. State v. Ferguson, 144 N.W. 1039 (Neb. 1914).
89. School Bd. Dist. No. 18 v. Thompson, 103 P. 578 (Okla. 1909).

TABLE 3-2. Summary of state standards—curriculum*

STATES	LOCAL SELECTION OF CURRICULUM			SECONDARY SCHOOLS PROGRAM SPECIFICATIONS				SANCTIONS FOR NON COMPLIANCE
	Determined by State							
	Executive Agency	Independent	Within State Guidelines	Minimum No. of Req'd Courses	Maximum No. of Electives	Req'mnt for Accredit.	Bilingual Educ.	
ALABAMA		X(a)						
ALASKA	X						M	
ARIZONA	X			7 1/2 credits	8 1/2 credits		M	
ARKANSAS	X							
CALIFORNIA			X				D	
COLORADO			X				D	
CONNECTICUT	X							
DELAWARE	X							
FLORIDA	X		X	36 courses	(b)	X		
GEORGIA	X							
HAWAII	X							
IDAHO			X					
ILLINOIS			X				M	
INDIANA			X					
IOWA			X					
KANSAS	X			30 units		X	D	
KENTUCKY	X		X					
LOUISIANA	X						M	
MAINE			X				D	
MARYLAND			X					
MASSACHUSETTS	X		X				M	
MICHIGAN			P					
MINNESOTA				1950 hours	1200 hours	X	M	X
MISSISSIPPI		X		12		X		
MISSOURI			X	(d)		X		
MONTANA			X	16 units				
NEBRASKA			X	18 courses		X		
NEVADA	X			(e)		X		

STATES	LOCAL SELECTION OF CURRICULUM			SECONDARY SCHOOLS PROGRAM SPECIFICATIONS				SANCTIONS FOR NON COMPLIANCE
	Determined by State							
	Executive Agency	Independent	Within State Guidelines	Minimum No. of Req'd Courses	Maximum No. of Electives	Req'mnt for Accredit.	Bilingual Educ.	
NEW HAMPSHIRE			X	16 units		X		X
NEW JERSEY	X							
NEW MEXICO			X	30		X		X
NEW YORK	X					X	D	X
NORTH CAROLINA	X		X					
NORTH DAKOTA			X			X		
OHIO			X	55	(b)			
OKLAHOMA			X	36 units				
OREGON	X		X			X		X
PENNSYLVANIA	X						M	
RHODE ISLAND			X				M(f)	
SOUTH CAROLINA	X		X	40	(b)			
SOUTH DAKOTA	X							
TENNESSEE			X(a)					
TEXAS			X				M(f)	
UTAH		X						
VERMONT	X			26				
VIRGINIA			X	18 units	24 units	X		
WASHINGTON	X		X	38 units	(b)	X		
WEST VIRGINIA			X					
WISCONSIN	X							
WYOMING	X							

SOURCE: National Institute of Education.

*All data tables must be updated for possible changes in each state since 1979.

NOTES: S—State; D—Discretionary; P—Partial; L—Local; M—Mandatory. In all states the local district must offer a curriculum that the state prescribes. The degree of control exercised by the education agency differs from state to state. In about half the states a local district must offer the curriculum devised by the state. . . . Even in those states where districts retain some discretion, course offerings must still be chosen within state guidelines. . . .

Local Selection of Curriculum: The local district selects its curriculum offerings on the basis of the extent of authority delegated by the state.

shire.] On the other hand, it is not denied that the decisions of the supreme courts of Illinois and Wisconsin are in apparent conflict . . . with what we here decide."[90]

Under either view, it is clear that the school authorities may not arbitrarily disregard the student's welfare.[91]

School officials have discretion to eliminate courses or activities not mandated by the state. Students' rights are not violated simply because their district does not offer courses or subjects available in other school districts.[92] Reductions in services are generally not overruled unless found to be arbitrary or capricious.[93] Declining enrollment is a common justification for elimination of course[94] and even for reductions in mandated courses if the statutory minimums are still met.[95]

The increasing population of preschool children and the growing number of working mothers have created a significant demand for preprimary programs.[96] Reinforcing that demand are reports that kindergarten and other preprimary experience have a significant positive effect on the progress of the child entering first grade. Some states require local school districts to offer kindergarten, while others leave its provision to the discretion of the district, or in some cases to the resident electorate. Compulsory education laws do not generally require attendance at kindergarten. School districts may not, therefore, require completion of kindergarten as a condition for admission into first grade, although satisfactory completion of kindergarten may be conclusive evidence that a child of appropriate age is qualified for admission to first grade.[97]

b. Textbooks and Reading Materials. As indicated by Table 3–3, most states permit local school districts to select their own books from state-approved lists. Some states authorize local districts to adopt supplementary texts that are not on the state list, within general state guidelines. A minority provide recommended book lists, without restricting local districts to that list, and a few, such as New York, place no restriction whatsoever on local district textbook selection, other than a general prohibition against subversive books. Table 3–3 also shows that most states require public school textbooks to be supplied free to the students, with some variations on this general pattern.

In recent years, increasing challenges have arisen to the use of particular books. Blacks and other minorities have decried the lack of fair coverage of their history. Ethnic groups complain of texts that tend to portray or stereotype their group unfavorably. Still others object to text content as subversive of social morality and civic responsibility.

---

90. State v. Weber, 8 N.E. 708, 713 (Ind. 1886).

91. *In re* Reassignment of Hayes, 135 S.E.2d 645 (N.C. 1964).

92. Board of Education of Okay Independent School District v. Carrol, 513 P.2d 872 (Okla. 1973).

93. *See* Borough v. Governing Board of El Segundo Unified School District, 173 Cal. Rptr. 729 (1981).

94. *See* Chambers v. Board of Education, Lisbon Cent. Sch. Dist., 397 N.Y.S.2d 436, appeal after remand, 404 N.Y.S.2d 400, aff'd, 418 N.Y.S. 291 (N.Y.A.D. 1977); Cooper v. Fair Dismissal Appeals Board, 570 P.2d 1005 (Ore. 1977); Penzenstadler v. Avonworth School District, 403 A.2d 621 (Pa. Cmwlth 1979).

95. Campbell Elementary Teachers Assn., Inc. v. Abbott, 143 Cal. Rptr. 281 (Cal. App. 1978). *See also* Worchester Vocational Teachers' Assn. v. City of Worchester, 429 N.E.2d 718 (Mass. App. 1982); Sharp v. Huron Valley Board of Education, 314 N.W.2d 785 (Mich. App. 1981).

96. *The Condition of Education—1982 Edition* p. 4 (National Center for Education Statistics, U.S. Dept. of Education).

97. *See, e.g.*, Morgan v. Board of Education, 317 N.E.2d 393 (Ill. 1974).

TABLE 3-3. Summary of state standards—textbook control †

STATES	TEXTBOOKS SUPPLIED FREE	LOCAL SELECTION			PERIODIC REVIEW OF STATE LIST (in years)	STATE REGULATION OF TEXTBOOK CONTRACTS
		Without State Approval	From State Approved List	Within State Standards*		
ALABAMA			X		4	X
ALASKA			X			
ARIZONA	X	P	P		5	X
ARKANSAS	X		X			
CALIFORNIA	X		X		2	X
COLORADO	P	X				
CONNECTICUT	X	X			5	
DELAWARE	X			P		X
FLORIDA	X		P	P		X
GEORGIA	X		X			
HAWAII						
IDAHO	X		X			
ILLINOIS	X		X			
INDIANA	X		X		5	X
IOWA	X	X				
KANSAS			X			
KENTUCKY	X		P	P	4	X
LOUISIANA	X		X		5	
MAINE	X	X				
MARYLAND	X	X				X
MASSACHUSETTS	X	X				X
MICHIGAN	X		P	P		
MINNESOTA	X	P		P		X
MISSISSIPPI	X		X			X
MISSOURI	X		X		5	X
MONTANA	X		X		10	
NEBRASKA	X	X			5	
NEVADA	X		X			
NEW HAMPSHIRE	X					
NEW JERSEY	X			P		
NEW MEXICO	X	P	P	P		X
NEW YORK	X	X				
NORTH CAROLINA	X		X			
NORTH DAKOTA	X	P	P			X
OHIO	X	P	P			X

SOURCE: National Institute of Education.

†All data tables must be updated for possible changes in each state since 1979.

NOTES: X—All; P—Partial; *—From state approved list or with approval of specific books.

The adoption of textbooks occurs at the local level and the decision process is usually subject to some state restrictions. In most states the district board selects its textbooks from a list prepared by the state education agency. This state approved list contains recommendations for several books for each course rather than a specific book for each course that must be adopted. . . .

In several states, the state education agency does not oversee the local selection process and a district board may adopt any textbook. Even in these states, however, the state agency, as a service, will generally provide the district with a recommended list. In New York, the state places no restrictions on a district's selection process other than a general prohibition against subversive texts. . . .

Most states require that textbooks be supplied free to all students. Some states refine that requirement to account for years when the state may have alloted insufficient money to provide free textbooks to all students. Under these circumstances, these states require that elementary grades be provided with free textbooks before secondary grades. In some states the district board must provide free textbooks to all indigent pupils, but for all remaining pupils the district board retains the discretion of providing free books. It should be noted that the absence of a provision for free textbooks does not necessarily mean that they are not free since the state constitution may require it.

TABLE 3-3. Summary of state standards—textbook control (*cont.*)

STATES	TEXTBOOKS SUPPLIED FREE	LOCAL SELECTION			PERIODIC REVIEW OF STATE LIST(in years)	STATE REGULATION OF TEXTBOOK CONTRACTS
		Without State Approval	From State Approved List	Within State Standards*		
OKLAHOMA	X	P	P		4	X
OREGON	X		P	P	6	X
PENNSYLVANIA	X	X				
RHODE ISLAND	X		X		3	
SOUTH CAROLINA	X		X			X
SOUTH DAKOTA	X			X	3	
TENNESSEE	X		X		3–5	X
TEXAS			X			X
UTAH	X		X		4	X
VERMONT						
VIRGINIA	X		P	P		
WASHINGTON			P	P		
WEST VIRGINIA	P		X		5	X
WISCONSIN	P		X			
WYOMING	X	X				

These challenges go to particular selections, not to the general power of school authorities to select textbooks.

Challenges to school board text selections have largely failed, even when the text allegedly engendered hostility to a group or religious beliefs.[98]

Constitutional challenges to school board control of reading materials, based on students' First Amendment rights to have access to information, and of teachers to exercise academic freedom have generated conflicting doctrine among the federal circuits and state courts.[99] Uncertainty was also evident regarding possible distinctions to be drawn between classroom texts and library texts, between initial selection and retention or removal of books, and between the control over required (as opposed to elective) reading materials.

The Supreme Court's recent pronouncement in this area highlights the confusion. In *Board of Education, Island Tree Union Free District No. 26* v. *Pico* (reprinted at page 115 *infra*), the Supreme Court considered a constitutional challenge to the school board's removal of library books that the board deemed objectionable on numerous

98. Rosenberg v. Bd. of Educ., 92 N.Y.S.2d 344 (1949) (*Oliver Twist*); Williams v. Bd. of Educ.,388 F. Supp. 93 (S.D. W.Va. 1975), aff'd, 530 F.2d 972 (4th Cir. 1975) (materials offensive to parents' beliefs).

99. *See* Pratt v. Independent School District No. 831, 670 F.2d 771 (8th Cir. 1982); Bicknell v. Verginnes Union H.S. Board, 638 F.2d 438 (2d Cir. 1980); Zykan v. Warsaw Community School Corp., 631 F.2d 1300 (7th Cir. 1980); Cary v. Board of Education, 598 F.2d 535 (10th Cir. 1979); Minarcini v. Strongsville City School District, 541 F.2d 577 (6th Cir. 1976); Sheck v. Baileyville School Committee, 530 F.Supp. 679 (D. Me. 1982); Loewen v. Turnipseed, 488 F.Supp. 1138 (N.D. Miss. 1980); Salvail v. Nassua Board of Education, 469 F.Supp. 1269 (D. N.H. 1979); Right to Read Defense Committee v. School Committee, 545 F.Supp. 703 (D. Mass. 1978); Davis v. Page, 385 F.Supp. 395 (D. N.H. 1974).

grounds. Seven of the nine justices authored separate opinions. Four justices found no constitutional grounds to reverse the school board's removal of the books, while four other justices found some constitutional limitation on the board's discretion and remanded the case for trial on a charge of unconstitutional "motive." The remaining "swing" justice refused to vote on the constitutional issue *and* voted to remand to determine whether the removal of books resulted from unlawful motives. Of the four justices finding constitutional limitations on board authority to remove school library books, three recognized a First Amendment student right to receive ideas and information through school books, while the fourth stopped short of that position, and ruled only that the Constitution prohibited school officials from removing books solely because of political disagreement with the views expressed therein.

The future implications of *Pico* remain obscure. The four plurality justices expressly limited their decision to *removal* of *library* books, and they agreed with the dissenting justices that school boards would not be so constitutionally confined on initial selection of reading materials or on their control of classroom and curriculum materials. The justices also appeared to agree that school boards could constitutionally seek (1) to promote reading materials reflective of community values, and (2) to remove *any* material that they deemed "educationally" unsuitable. The difficulty, of course, is how to decide when a given school board decision represents its independent "educational" judgment, and when it acts solely from a political or censorial motive. Readers may draw their own conclusions after reading the excerpted opinions of the various justices at the end of this chapter.

The heavy burden facing parents in challenging school board selection of textbooks is indicated by the following comments:

> "[D]eference to local control . . . is a recognition of the varying wants and needs of the Nation's diverse and varied communities, each with its unique character, standards and sense of social importance of a variety of values."[100]
>
> "Careful consideration, evaluation and analysis of plaintiffs' complaint and testimony compel the conclusion that materials in some of the controversial textbooks . . . are offensive to plaintiffs' beliefs, choices of language, and code of conduct. However, the Court cannot find in the defendant's actions in placing the textbooks and supplemental materials in the Kanawha County schools any establishment of religion. . . . Further, the Court finds nothing in defendant's conduct or acts which constitutes an inhibition on or prohibition of the free exercise of religion. These rights are guaranteed by the First Amendment, but the Amendment does not guarantee . . . that nothing offensive to any religion will be taught in the schools. . . .
>
> "In the absence of bases for relief in the courts, . . . plaintiffs and parties similarly situated, with reference to books and materials found offensive to and objectionable by them, may find administrative remedies through board of education proceedings or ultimately at the polls on election day."[101]

---

100. Mercer v. Michigan State Bd. of Educ., 379 F.Supp. 580, 585 (E.D. Mich.), aff'd, 419 U.S. 1081 (1974).

101. *See* Williams v. Bd. of Educ., 388 F.Supp. 93 at 96 (S.D.W.Va. 1975).

Parent/teacher conflicts on readings selected by teachers, but not required by the school administration, raise the distinct issues of the balance of parental rights with academic freedom. These issues are discussed in Chapter 5.

School board authority to control dissemination of nonschool literature has not been extensively considered by the courts. One case voided the school board's policy against distribution of a weekly newspaper to high school students for lack of proof that the policy was necessary to prevent disruption of school activities. The court concluded that the policy interfered with students' First Amendment freedoms.[102] Cases involving similar issues under state constitutions and college campuses also recognized legal constraints on official control of distribution of outside literature.[103] Literature distribution by teachers, students, and school-related groups are discussed in Chapters 5 and 6. Distribution of religious literature is discussed in Chapter 4.

6. Extracurricular Activities

> "Along with entrusting the education of our children to teachers and administrators, we also entrust the control and supervision of the extra-curricular activities incident to that education. Implicit in the responsibility for these activities is the power to make reasonable rules and regulations. . . . A court should not interfere with the enactment of those regulations as long as they are reasonable and do not infringe on public policy or law." *Art Gaines Baseball Camp, Inc.* v. *Houston,* 500 S.W.2d 735, 740, 741 (Mo. App. 1973).

Nonacademic pursuits, such as club activities and athletic programs, are normally classified as extracurricular. As Table 3–4 shows, there is no dominant pattern of extracurricular organization. Some states require their school districts to provide extracurricular activities in specified forms. Others, through state education agencies, merely encourage or permit local districts to initiate such programs. In the absence of state law or regulations, most local districts could probably claim the implied power to establish relevant extracurricular activities in fostering quality education.

School rules on extracurricular activities raise two questions. The first involves school board authority to establish eligibility standards. The second is whether a school's submission to regulation by interscholastic athletic associations is an unauthorized redelegation of school board responsibility to an outside source.

School board authority to control student clubs and associations is widely recognized. The courts of most states have upheld school board prohibitions against "secret" or "oath bound" organizations[104] and have also upheld bans on fraternities or sororities that admit new members solely on the basis of existing members' preference.[105] Student objections to such bans as inimical to First Amendment freedom of association have generally been rejected.[106] The constitutional rights of public school students to free

102. Peterson v. Board of Education, 370 F. Supp. 1208 (D. Neb. 1973).

103. Cf. Princeton University v. Schmid, 423 A.2d 615 (N. J. 1981), dismissed for want of jurisdiction, 102 S.Ct. 867 (1982); Commonwealth v. Tate, 432 A.2d 1382 (Pa. 1981).

104. *See* Bradford v. Board of Education, 121 P.929 (Cal. 1912).

105. Robinson v. Sacramento City Unified School District, 53 Cal. Rptr. 771 (1966).

106. *Idem* at 788–789; *see also* Passel v. Ft. Worth Ind. Sch. Dist., 453 S.W.2d 888 (Tex. 1970).

TABLE 3-4. Summary of state standards—extracurricular activities *

STATES	DISTRICT MUST PROVIDE	PROGRAM SPECIFICATIONS					
		No Provisions	Detailed State Regulations	State Approval Required	Regulations for Athletic Competition	Secret Societies Prohibited	District Must Provide Facilities for Public Use
ALABAMA					X		
ALASKA		X					
ARIZONA		X					
ARKANSAS		X					
CALIFORNIA			X			X	
COLORADO					X	X	
CONNECTICUT		X					
DELAWARE				X	X		
FLORIDA		X					
GEORGIA		X					
HAWAII	ES		X		X		
IDAHO		X					
ILLINOIS	ES					X	
INDIANA	ES						
IOWA	S		X	X			
KANSAS						X	
KENTUCKY		X					
LOUISIANA	S				X(a)		
MAINE	S					X	
MARYLAND						X	
MASSACHUSETTS					X		
MICHIGAN					X	X	
MINNESOTA	S					X	
MISSISSIPPI						X	
MISSOURI					X		
MONTANA						X	
NEBRASKA	ES					X	
NEVADA	S		X				
NEW HAMPSHIRE		X					
NEW JERSEY	ES					X	
NEW MEXICO	ES		X	X			
NEW YORK		X					
NORTH CAROLINA					X		
NORTH DAKOTA	ES				X(b)		
OHIO				X			
OKLAHOMA			X		X	X	
OREGON		X					
PENNSYLVANIA	ES		X		X		
RHODE ISLAND		X					
SOUTH CAROLINA					X		
SOUTH DAKOTA	S		X				
TENNESSEE		X					
TEXAS		X					
UTAH	ES						X
VERMONT		X					
VIRGINIA	S		X				
WASHINGTON		X					
WEST VIRGINIA					X		
WISCONSIN		X					
WYOMING		X					

SOURCE: National Institute of Education. NOTE: E—Elementary; S—Secondary.

*All data tables must be updated for possible changes in each state since 1979.

association cannot, of course, be equated with those of college or private school students.[107] The right of public school students to participate in nonschool associations is discussed in Chapter 6. The special problems posed by religious association in the public school context are taken up in Chapter 4.

a. Interscholastic Athletic Associations. To promote fair and wholesome interscholastic competition, athletic associations make and enforce regulations on institutional and student conduct, such as recruitment, independent team rules, and use of transfer students. Such regulations raise delegation issues; and their validity with respect to student athletes raises issues of student rights. The resolution of questions that arise in the context of school athletics may also have applicability to other extracurricular activity.[108]

On the delegation issue, there is some conflict of authority. The majority of states have ruled that school boards may lawfully join and subject themselves to the regulations of interscholastic athletic associations.[109] In upholding the suspension of a member school and two of its students on a charge of talent raiding, an Ohio court held that the affected school was lawfully empowered to join and to bind itself to the rules of the association. The fact that the suspension prevented the school from honoring its game contracts with other schools was held *not determinative* because such contracts were subject to the governing rules of the athletic association.[110] A contrary view was taken in Iowa where the court held that the school board could not lawfully delegate its authority to the athletic association. Hence the school was not bound by association rules.[111] The conflict turns essentially upon legislative intent—to grant or to deny school boards the power to redelegate managerial discretion to outside bodies. The Iowa court stressed that school authorities could authorize third parties or private associations to perform purely ministerial duties, so long as regulatory discretion remained with the school board. The majority of state courts avoided the delegation issue by limiting review to the question whether association rules were reasonable or arbitrary, and by treating the dispute as involving purely voluntary associations.[112] Once the delegation barrier is overcome, courts uphold association eligibility rules that disqualify certain students from interscholastic competition and rules against unfair practices by the member schools. Thus, courts have upheld student residency rules,[113] rules against outside training,[114]

---

107. *See* Robinson v. Sacramento City Unified School District, 53 Cal. Rptr. 771 (1966).

108. *See, e.g.*, Kite v. Marshall, 661 F.2d 1027 (5th Cir. 1981) (interscholastic regulation of speech, journalism, literature, drama, and music as well as athletics); Dennis J. O'Connell H.S. v. Virginia H.S. League, 581 F.2d 81 (4th Cir. 1978), cert. denied, 449 U.S. 936 (1979) (regulation of literary and debating competition as well as athletics); ABC League v. Missouri State H.S. Activities Association, 530 F.Supp. 1033 (E.D. Mo. 1982) (statewide regulation of speech, debate, and music competition as well as athletics).

109. *See* Anderson v. So. Dakota H.S. Activities, 247 N.W.2d 481 (S.D. 1976); Indiana H.S. Athletic Assn. v. Raike, 329 N.W.2d 66 (Ind. 1975); Marino v. Waters, 220 So.2d 802 (La. 1969).

110. State v. Judges of the Court of Common Pleas, 181 N.E.2d 261 (Ohio 1962).

111. Bunger v. Iowa High School Athletic Association, 197 N.W.2d 555 (Iowa 1972).

112. Crandell v. Dak.H.S.Activities Ass'n.,261 N.W.2d 21 (N.D. 1978); Dumez v. La. H.S. Athletic Assn., 334 So.2d 494 (La. 1976).

113. Menke v. Ohio H.S. Athletic Assn., 2 Ohio App. 3d 244 (1981).

114. Kite v. Marshall, 661 F.2d 1027 (5th Cir. 1981).

rules against participation by academically deficient students,[115] rules against delay of student promotions for athletic reasons,[116] and disqualifying rules for participation on independent teams.[117]

Public school athletic associations involve a form of "state action" and are thus subject to the requirements of the Fourteenth Amendment and Federal Civil Rights Statutes (§ 1983).[118] They may not discriminate among students on the basis of race, sex, or marriage; or among schools.[119] Since state action is involved, student athletes may demand due process in association proceedings that could affect their constitutionally protected interests.[120] The nature of that interest was recently discussed by the Eighth Circuit in the *Missouri State High School* case reprinted at the end of this chapter.[121] Whether participation in interscholastic athletics is deemed a "right," and "expectation," or a mere "privilege," some procedural due process is due.[122]

The impact of state equal rights amendments on sex discrimination remains to be fully developed, but association rules that barred sports competition or practice between students of different sexes have been nullified under such amendments in at least two states.[123]

In parochial school challenges to state athletic association rules, courts have upheld exclusion of such schools from association participation[124] and also upheld uniform admission rules that had greater exclusionary impact on parochial school students than on public school students.[125]

7. Promotion and Graduation

Subject to statewide legal guidelines, local boards may establish promotion and

115. Adamek v. Pennsylvania Interscholastic Athletic Assn., 426 A.2d 1206 (Pa. 1981).

116. Burtt v. Nausau County Athletic Assn., 421 N.Y.S.2d 172 (1979).

117. Kubriszyn v. Alabama H.S. Athletic Assn., 374 So.2d 256 (Ala. 1979).

118. Clark v. Arizona Interscholastic Assn., 695 F.2d 1126 (9th Cir. 1982); *In re* U.S. ex rel. Missouri State High School, 682 F.2d 147 (8th Cir. 1982). *See also* Leffel v. Wisconsin Int. Athletic Assn., 398 F.Supp. 749 (E.D. Wis. 1975).

119. Rogers v. Bd. of Education, 281 F.Supp. 39 (E.D. Ark. 1968) (race); Clark v. Arizona Interscholastic Assn., 695 F.2d 1126 (9th Cir. 1982); Brenden v. Ind. Sch. Dist. 742, 477 F.2d 1292 (8th Cir. 1973; Dobson v. Arkansas Activities Assn., 469 F.Supp. 394 (E.D. Ark. 1979) Haas v. So. Bend Community Corp., 289 N.E.2d 495 (1972) (sex); Baltic Ind. Sch. District v. So. Dakota H.S. Activities Assn., 362 F.Supp. 780 (D. S.D. 1973) (schools). *See also* Mahan v. Agee, 652 P.2d 765 (Okla. 1982) (age).

120. On procedural due process, *compare* Regents U. Minn. v. NCAA, 422 F. Supp. 1158 (D. Minn. 1976); and Kelly v. Metropolitan County Bd. of Education, 293 F Supp. 485 (M.D. Tenn. 1968) *with* Tennessee Secondary Sch. Athletic Assn. v. Cox, 425 S.W.2d 597 (Tenn. 1968) (finding that student has no "right" but only a privilege, and therefore is not entitled to a hearing on his suspension from interscholastic athletics).

121. *In re* U.S. ex rel. Missouri State High School, 682 F.2d 147 (8th Cir. 1982).

122. Duffley v. New Hampshire Interscholastic Athletic Assn., 446 A.2d 462 (N.H. 1982).

123. Commonwealth v. Pa. Interscholastic Athletic Assn., 334 A.2d 839 (Pa. Cmwlth. 1975); Opinion of the Justices, 371 N.E.2d 426 (Mass. 1977).

124. *See* Windsor Park Baptist Church, Inc. v. Arkansas Activities Assn., 658 F.2d 618 (8th Cir. 1981); Dennis J. O'Connell H.S. v. Virginia H.S. League, 581 F.2d 81 (4th Cir. 1978), cert. denied, 440 U.S. 936 (1979); Valencio v. Blue Hen Conference, 476 F.Supp. 809 (D. Del. 1979); Christian Brothers Institute v. Northern New Jersey Int. League, 432 A.2d 26 (N.J. 1981).

125. Walsh v. Louisanna H.S. Athletic Association, 616 F.2d 152 (5th Cir. 1980).

TABLE 3-5. Summary of state standards—promotion requirements*

STATES	STATUTE OR REGULATION	NO PROVISIONS	MINIMUM ATTENDANCE (in days) per year	PASS STANDARDIZED TEST	OTHER
ALABAMA	R		155		X
ALASKA		X			
ARIZONA					X
ARKANSAS		X			
CALIFORNIA		X			
COLORADO		X			
CONNECTICUT		X			
DELAWARE		X			
FLORIDA	S, R				X
GEORGIA		X			
HAWAII	R				X
IDAHO	R		153		
ILLINOIS		X			
INDIANA		X			
IOWA		X			
KANSAS		X			
KENTUCKY		X			
LOUISIANA		X			
MAINE		X			
MARYLAND		X			
MASSACHUSETTS		X			
MICHIGAN		X			
MINNESOTA		X			
MISSISSIPPI	R				X
MISSOURI		X			

SOURCE: National Institute of Education.

*All data tables must be updated for possible changes in each state since 1979.

NOTES: Very few states have developed promotion requirements. In those that have requirements, most are found in regulations rather than statutes. Of the dozen states that have requirements half have quantifiable criteria for promotion. . . .

In half a dozen other states the promotion requirements are based on a more subjective standard. For example in Alabama a pupil is promoted if he progressed "within the limits of his ability." Similarly, in Hawaii, promotion is based on a teacher's evaluation of a pupil's performance in relation to his ability.

graduation requirements.[126] Other than minimal attendance standards, very few state statutes deal with promotion questions. (See Tables 3–5 and 3–6.) Many states have enacted legislation requiring administration of a minimum competency test prior to graduation. (See Table 3–6.) Some states require all students to pass the test to receive a diploma.[127] Others let the local board decide whether such test results should determine

126. Bernerd v. Shelburne, 102 N.E. 1095 (Mass. 1913), Cf. Johnson v. Sullivan, 571 P.2d 798 (Mont. 1977).

127. See, e.g., 16 Ala. Code §§ 16-4-14, 16-8-10; 15 Ariz. Rev. Stat. § 15-741 to 15-744 (1981 Supp.); Cal. Educ. Code §§ 51215, 51217; 14 Del. Code Ann. § 121; Fla. Stat. § 232-246 (1) (b); Md. Ann. Code §§ 7-203 to 7-205; 34 Nev. Rev. Stat. § 389.015; Vol. 3A pt. II N.C. Gen. Stat. §§ 115C-175 to 115C-184 (1981 Supp.); Or. Rev. Stat. § 326.051; 9 Tenn. Code Ann. §§ 49-1901, 1902; 5B Utah Code Ann. §§

STATES	STATUTE OR REGULATION	NO PROVISIONS	MINIMUM ATTENDANCE (in days) per year	PASS STANDARDIZED TEST	OTHER
MONTANA		X			
NEBRASKA		X			
NEVADA		X			
NEW HAMPSHIRE		X			
NEW JERSEY		X			
NEW MEXICO		X			
NEW YORK		X			
NORTH CAROLINA		X			
NORTH DAKOTA		X			
OHIO		X			
OKLAHOMA		X			
OREGON		X			
PENNSYLVANIA		X			
RHODE ISLAND		X			
SOUTH CAROLINA	R		150		
SOUTH DAKOTA		X			
TENNESSEE		X			
TEXAS		X			
UTAH		X			
VERMONT		X			
VIRGINIA	R		160	X	
WASHINGTON		X			
WEST VIRGINIA		X			
WISCONSIN		X			
WYOMING		X			

the receipt of a diploma.[128] A few states allow tests to be developed at the local level.[129] Generally, courts have upheld the requirement that students pass a minimum competency test to graduate—provided the testing is not discriminatory or otherwise unconstitutional.[130]

The trend is toward upholding the right to graduate once a student satisfies the academic requirements, notwithstanding student defaults of a nonacademic nature.[131] The courts have, for example, ordered school districts to award diplomas to students who met academic requirements, but who failed to pay school fees.[132] Even where a student was charged with academic violations (i.e.,cheating), one court ordered the award of a

53-14-1 (1981 Supp.); 16 Vt. Stat. Ann. § 906 (1982 Supp.); 22 Va. Code §§ 22.1-201, 22.1-18 (1980 Supp.).

128. See Mass. Dept of Educ., *Proposed Regulations: Basic Skills Improvement* (1978); Conn. Pub. Acts. 258, Pub. L. No. 78-194 (1978); R.I. Gen. Laws § 16-21-9 (1956) (reenactment of 1981); N.H. Dept. of Educ., *Guidelines for the Implementation of New Hampshire Accountability Plan.*

129. *See* Brookhart v. Illinois State Board, 697 F.2d 179 (7th Cir. 1983).

130. *Idem;* Debra P. v. Turlington, 644 F.2d 397 (5th Cir. 1981); Anderson v. Banks, 520 F.Supp. 472 (S.D. Ga. 1981); Board of Education v. Ambach, 436 N.Y.S.2d 564 (1981), aff'd, 458 N.Y.S.2d 680 (1982).

131. United States v. Choctaw County Bd. of Education, 310 F. Supp. 804 (S. Dak. 1969);Ladsen v. Bd. of Education, 323 N.Y.S.2d 545 (1971)(student striking school principal); Sageser v. Ledbetter, 559 S.W. 2d 230 (Mo.1977) (student chronic absence).

132. State v. Wilson, 297 S.W. 419 (Mo. App. 1927) (failure to pay school expenses).

TABLE 3-6. Summary of state standards—high school graduation requirements †

STATES	Total Credits Required	Total Electives	Pass Standardized Test (not current)	Local Requirements Option	No Provisions
ALABAMA	20	7			
ALASKA	16	6 1/2		Yes	
ARIZONA	16	8 1/2			
ARKANSAS					X
CALIFORNIA			Yes*	Yes	
COLORADO					X
CONNECTICUT					X
DELAWARE	18	10 1/2			
FLORIDA	15	7			
GEORGIA	18	9	Yes		
HAWAII	18	6			
IDAHO	18	6			
ILLINOIS	16				
INDIANA	16	8			
IOWA				Yes	
KANSAS	17	8			
KENTUCKY	18	10			
LOUISIANA	20	10			
MAINE					X
MARYLAND	18	8		Yes	
MASSACHUSETTS					X
MICHIGAN					X
MINNESOTA	12	7		Yes	
MISSISSIPPI	16	4			
MISSOURI	16	6		Yes	
MONTANA	16	6 1/2		Yes	
NEBRASKA	160				
NEVADA	19	9 1/2			
NEW HAMPSHIRE	16	8			
NEW JERSEY	92-100			Yes	
NEW MEXICO	18	9			
NEW YORK	16	7 1/2	Yes		
NORTH CAROLINA					X
NORTH DAKOTA	16	6		Yes	
OHIO	17	9			
OKLAHOMA	18	10 1/2			
OREGON	21	10			
PENNSYLVANIA	13(b)	4	Yes		
RHODE ISLAND					X
SOUTH CAROLINA	18	8			
SOUTH DAKOTA					X
TENNESSEE	18	9		Yes	
TEXAS	16	6 1/2			
UTAH					X
VERMONT	16	8			
VIRGINIA	18	3	Yes		
WASHINGTON	16	7 1/2			
WEST VIRGINIA					X
WISCONSIN					X
WYOMING					X

SOURCE: National Institute of Education.

†All data tables must be updated for possible changes in each state since 1979.

* A student in California who is over 18 and who has not completed high school may earn a diploma by passing a high school equivalency test. In some other states students must pass a standardized test in addition to achieving the required credits.

diploma because the evidence (possession of unauthorized materials) was insufficient in its view to justify the strong sanction of denial of graduation.[133]

However, distinctions are drawn between awarding the diploma and permitting or refusing a student to participate in graduation ceremonies. Awarding of the diploma once earned may be seen as a mandatory duty; denial of the privilege to participate in graduation ceremonies may be viewed as discretionary power to maintain discipline within the school. Even where that distinction applies, some courts consider this form of discipline unreasonable. A New York court overturned a superintendent's order to bar from the graduation ceremony (while awarding the diploma privately) a student who struck the school principal.[134] The court held that the power to discipline students did not embrace the power to exclude the student unless her presence would be disruptive. Other state courts ruled that a student who refused to wear the cap and gown at the ceremony could be excluded.[135]

B. Special Education

The expanding field of special education covers a wide range of physical, mental, emotional, and cultural disabilities that obstruct adequate study and learning. These handicaps require special resources and curriculum. The discretionary power of school boards to provide programs to overcome such handicaps has long been recognized, but is no longer the sole basis for special education. School boards are being *required* to provide special education for various classes of handicapped children, partly under constitutional requirements and partly under statutes that mandate specialized services for specified classes of handicapped children. These statutory requirements often penalize noncompliance by withdrawal of federal or state subsidies. While the courts, Congress, and state legislatures leave many particulars to the discretion of school boards, supervision of district performance has increased substantially under modern legislation.

D. Nonschool Uses and Disposition of School Property

1. Community Uses

a. Statutory Patterns As previously noted, school property is state property, subject to the will of the legislature. Many state enactments permit outside use of school property. For example, some western states open school buildings and grounds to public use as community centers when not required for school purposes. Others permit, but do not require, local boards to open school facilities to community groups for designated purposes; still others do not designate the permissible uses, but merely empower local boards to open the schools for such lawful purposes as the board in its discretion deems

---

133. Ryan v. Bd. of Education, 257 P. 945 (Kan. 1927). See fuller discussion of academic penalties, chapter 6, p. 271.

134. See Ladsen v. Bd. of Education, 323 N.Y.S. 2d 545 (1971).

135. Fowler v. Williamson, 251 S.E.2d 889 (N. Car. 1979); Accord: 448 F. Supp. 497 (W.D.N.C. 1978).

appropriate.[136] The board's authority as to outside use is subject to local voter approval or veto in two states.[137] Most states authorize the use of school buildings as polling places for official elections.

When the statutory authority as to particular uses is questioned, courts must determine whether the board's allowance or restriction of such uses falls within the terms of the statute. A recent study concludes that courts tend to favor interpretations that expand community access and use of school facilities.[138] Under the California Civic Center Act, requiring school boards to permit community use of school property free of charge, the court ruled that the school board lacked authority to require a user to take out insurance, or to pay any fee.[139] The California Education Code has been interpreted to allow free use of public school facilities for a private summer school program.[140] Courts have also sustained private use of school facilities for events that involved incidental competition to private businesses (such as entertainment shows, lectures, and food services) and for which charges were made by the sponsors.[141] Such activities were not considered commercial enterprises if they served nonprofit civic goals or school objectives, such as student convenience and raising funds for student activities.[142] Courts have disapproved uses for pure commercial benefit to private business, such as the use of athletic fields for professional baseball games.[143] But they are not likely to question decisions where state law vests broad discretion in the board.[144]

b. Constitutional Restrictions. Federal constitutional restrictions against uses of government property that aid religion or disadvantageously discriminate against particular kinds of students will be considered in later chapters. The Constitution also prohibits public school authorities from denying the use of school facilities *solely* for censorial reasons (because the ideas of petitioning individuals or organizations are unpopular and distasteful). Explaining the protection of free speech and assembly in a case that struck down a law barring picketing at public schools, the Supreme Court declared:

> "Once a forum is opened up to assembly or speaking by some groups, government may not prohibit others from assembling or speaking on the basis of what they intend to say. Selective exclusions from a public forum may not be based on content alone, and may not be justified by reference to content alone." *Police Dept. of Chicago* v. *Mosley*, 408 U.S. 92, 96 (1972).

In describing the constitutional right to associate to advance beliefs and ideas, the Court further observed:

---

136. See Cal. Ed. Code, 16556;Hawaii Rev.Stat., 298.23;Laws of Utah, 4551 (1917) (good community use); Fla Stat., 235.02 (designated purposes); Colo.Rev.Stat.,123-10-19(26) (broad discretion).

137. Ind. Stat., 28-4302; Iowa Code, 278.1

138. See P. Piele and J. Forsberg, School Property: The Legality of Its Use and Disposition (Nat'l. Organization on Legal Prob. of Educ. 1974).

139. Ellis v. Bd. of Education, 164 P.2d 1 (Cal. 1946).

140. California Teachers Assn. v. Board of Education, 167 Cal. Rptr. 429 (1980).

141. Beard v. Bd. of Education, 16 P.2d 900 (Utah, 1932).

142. Hall v. Shelby County Bd. of Education, 472 S.W.2d 489 (Ky. 1971) (lease to civic organization); Hempel v. Sch. District No. 329, 59 P.2d 729 (Wash. 1936).

143. Canter v. Lake City Baseball Club, 62 S.E.2d 470 (S.C. 1950).

144. E.g., Delaware Code 124.

" . . . it is immaterial, whether the beliefs sought to be advanced by association pertain to political, economic, religious, or cultural matters." *NAACP* v. *Alabama,* 357 U.S. 449 (1958).

Courts have accordingly overturned selective denials of school facilities and have insisted that public uses be administered in a nondiscriminatory manner.[145] Speaker bans based on fears of violence are unconstitutional unless school authorities can show a manifest and imminent danger of material disorder.[146]

One board denied use of a school for meetings of a Parent Teachers Association that it considered unsupportive of the school, although it permitted other outside organizations to use the school for nonacademic meetings. The court held such action to be arbitrary and an unconstitutional denial both of freedom of expression and of the equal protection of the law.[147] For like reasons, courts disapproved denial by the board of its mailing lists and of its internal communication facilities to some groups with views not favored by the board where it provided the same school resources to groups whose viewpoints were favored by the board.[148] An Oregon court invalidated a rule that was adopted under community pressure for the immediate purpose of excluding a specific individual.[149] It found that the board not only violated the civil rights of the excluded speaker, but also interfered with the civil rights of teachers and students to arrange the event. A questionable ruling in Virginia extended the foregoing principles to a school board exclusion of an allegedly racist political party from its school auditorium. Under the board's practice of renting the auditorium to civic groups at nominal rental, the court held that it must grant equal privileges to the National Socialist White People's Party.[150] The board argued that it could not constitutionally accommodate that party as this would involve the state in supporting unconstitutional discrimination. The court ruled that the party's practice of private discrimination could not be imputed to the state through the rental of state property. The Virginia decision is open to question in view of the Supreme Court's prior decision that racial discrimination by a tenant of a government-financed facility is unconstitutional.[151]

Just as school authorities may not favor or disfavor particular ideas, neither may they throw their official weight behind particular ideas by affirmative sponsorship of particular political uses. A New York court thus found that public school officials are forbidden to express sympathy for student victims and their antiwar protest (Kent State killings) by flying the school flag at half-mast.[152]

---

145. Lawrence U. Bicentenial Comm. v. City of Appleton, 409 F. Supp. 1319 (E.D. Wis. 1976); East Meadow Comm. Concerts Assn. v. Bd. of Ed., 219 N.E.2d 172 (N.Y. 1966).

146. Ibid., Pickings v. Bruce, 430 F.2d 595 (8th Cir. 1970); Goodman v. Bd. of Education, 120 P.2d 665 (Cal. 1941).

147. Hennessey v. Ind. Sch. District No. 4, Lincoln County, 552 P.2d 1141 (Okla. 1976).

148. Wood v. Sch. Dist. No. 65,309 N.E.2d 408 (Ill. 1974); Bonner v. Lyons School Committee,480 Fed. 2d 442 (1st Cir. 1973).

149. Wilson v. Chancellor, 418 F. Supp. 1358 (D. Oregon 1976).

150. National Socialist White People's Party v. Ringers, 473 F. 2d 1011 (4th Cir. 1973).

151. Burton v. Wilmington Parking Authority, 365 U.S. 715 (1961).

152. Lapolla v. Dullaghan, 311 N.Y.S.2d 435 (1970); cf. Nistad v. Bd. of Education, 304 N.Y.S.2d 971 (1969) (Enjoined dismissal of teachers and students from regular classes to allow them to attend anti-war demonstration.)

Properly drawn regulations that aim at preservation of property,[153] school order, and the rights of persons are lawful, even though they have the indirect effect of limiting citizen expression. The Supreme Court upheld an ordinance barring noise at school sites that interfered with the peace and order of classes in session because the ordinance justifiably regulated the time, place, and manner of expression but did not prohibit it.[154] (Regulation of speech-connected activities to preserve substantial state interests is considered in greater detail in later chapters.)

In attempting to extract advance assurances from outside users that the premises will not be employed for unlawful purposes, school authorities must carefully regulate only conduct and not speech or beliefs. To suppress political expression itself, the government must establish a grave danger of *action to* achieve violent overthrow. Hence, a school board may not extract, as a condition of using its property, an oath denying that the petitioners *believe* in violent overthrow.[155] The school board may require a pledge that users will not put the property to any use prohibited by law as such a condition was held to be a constitutional regulation of conduct and not censorship of speech or belief.[156]

2. Lease and Sale of School Property

Disposition, by lease or sale, of school property that is no longer needed or fit for school use falls within the powers delegated to school boards, subject to special restrictions.

Statutory provisions for the sale of school property vary from state to state. Delaware law, for example, requires the school district to transfer unused school property to the state.[157] California gives former owners (but not their estates) a right of first refusal to repurchase the property unless it is transferred to another government body.[158] In Oregon, a school board cannot sell school property without voter approval;[159] in New York, voter approval is also required for the sale of a school within a certain number of years of the school's closing.[160]

In leasing property for a continuous term, as distinguished from a license or permission for occasional use, the school board has a duty to limit the lessee to lawful uses. A lease that contained no such restriction was held to be void, even though the lessee's actual use would have been lawful.[161] A school board may not (in the guise of a lease at nominal rental) make a gift of school property without statutory authorization.

---

153. School Directors v. Toll, 149 Ill. App. 541 (1909).

154. Grayned v. City of Rockford 408 U.S. 104 (1972). *See also* Dunkle v. Elkins, 325 F. Supp. 1235(D. Md. 1971); Payroll Guarantee Assn. Inc. v. Bd. of Education of San Francisco Un. Sch. District, 163 P.2d 433 (Cal. 1945) (denial of use of school during school hours, as interfering with school activities).

155. Danskin v. San Diego Un. Sch. District, 171 P.2d 885 (Cal. 1946); American Civil Liberties Union of So. California v. Bd. of Education of City of Los Angeles, 359 P.2d 45 (Cal. 1961).

156. American Civil Liberties Union of So. California v. Bd. of Education of City of Los Angeles, 379 P.2d 4(Cal. 1963). *See also* Healy v. James, 408 U.S. 169, 193 (1972).

157. New Castle County School District v. State, 424 A.2d 15 (Del. 1980).

158. Cal. Educ. Code § 39369.5; Don Wilson Builders v. City of Torrence, 178 Cal. Rptr. 690 (1980); Al J. Vela & Assoc., Inc. v. Glendora Unified School District, 166 Cal. Rptr. 732 (1980).

159. Seloover v. Columbia County Admin. Sch. Dist. No. 5, 600 P.2d 931 (Ore. App. 1979).

160. W. Haging, School Law § 9534 (N.Y. School Board Assn. Handbook for School Board Members).

161. Presley v. Vernon Parish Bd. of Education, 139 So.2d 692 (La. 1932).

This is true even though the recipient is a nonprofit hospital whose use will benefit the community.[162] Nor may the board exceed its authority by fixing rental rates different from those specified in the statute.[163]

While the law on *occasional* uses often bars purely commercial use of school property, school codes commonly authorize term leasing of unused school property at fair charges to commercial tenants. Competitors of such tenants have been held to have no legal complaint because business has no constitutional right to protection from competition.[164]

Rental of unused school property to increase school funds is clearly consistent with sound management of school resources. Constitutional obligations to desegregate public schools may not be avoided by lease or sale of public schools to private segregated academies, but school closings based on fiscal necessity or safety considerations have been sustained, even where such closings would have some impact on the progress of school desegregation.[165] In the area of desegregation, however, courts hold school boards to a higher standard than mere good faith in making sales of school property that might frustrate desegregation orders. Thus the defense that the board did not know the buyer would operate a segregated private academy was rejected. In the circumstances of desegregation, the board had an affirmative duty to ascertain the purchaser's intentions.[166]

162. Prescott Community Hospital Commission v. Prescott Sch. Dist. #1, 115 P.2d 160 (Ariz. 1941).

163. Henry George Sch. of Social Science v. San Diego Un. Sch. District, 6 Cal. Rptr. 661 (1960).

164. Hall v. Shelby Cty. Bd. of Education, 472 S.W.2d 489 (Ky. 1971).

165. United States v. State of Mississippi,499 F.2d 425 (5th Cir. 1974); Ellis v. Bd. Of Education,465 F.2d 878 (5th Cir. 1972).

166. McNeal v. Tate County Sch. District, 460 F.2d 568 (5th Cir. 1972).

Cases

Port Arthur Independent School District v. City of Groves

376 S.W.2d 330 (Tex. 1964)

HAMILTON, *Justice*. . . .

Petitioner owns certain real property located within the geographical confines of the respondent city, and . . . ascertained the necessity for the construction of an elementary school on such property. When such construction project began, the respondent asserted that the petitioner must abide by and conform to certain building ordinances passed by the respondent city making provision for the standards of construction, the obtaining of building permits, and the inspection of the construction work while in progress by officials of the respondent city. Petitioner took the position that as an independent governmental subdivision, such ordinances of respondent were not applicable to it, and when respondent notified petitioner that the penal provisions of such ordinances would be enforced, . . . petitioner filed suit in the trial court seeking a declaratory judgment to the effect that such ordinances were invalid and inapplicable as to petitioner. . . .

To narrow the question, it should be stated that there is no question here as to validity of the ordinances as being a proper exercise of the police powers of the city. It is not contended that they are unreasonable or arbitrary. The school's contention is simply that they do not apply to it because the operation of public schools is a function of the State, against which the police power of a municipality cannot be exercised unless the statutes clearly show that such was the intention of the Legislature and that the Legislature has, in fact, given school districts exclusive control of schools. . . .

It is the city's position that Article 1175, Section 34, V.A.C.S., empowers it in the exercise of its police powers to enforce its ordinances against the school district. . . .

There appears to be no case in this state which has passed on the question before us. There are some out of state cases which have been cited that deal with the question. It appears from an analysis of these cases that the police powers of a municipality are not applicable to the state itself, or its property. *Hall* v. *City of Taft*, 47 Cal.2d 177, 302 P.2d 574; *Salt Lake City* v. *Board of Education of Salt Lake City*, 52 Utah 540, 175 P. 654; *Kentucky Institution for Education of Blind* v. *City of Louisville*, 123 Ky. 767, 97 S.W. 402, 8 L.R.A., N.S., 553; *City of Milwaukee* v. *McGregor*, 140 Wis. 35, 121 N.W. 642. Neither are police powers applicable to any political subdivision where the Legislature of the state has legislated with reference to the particular matter covered by the ordinance sought to be enforced. *Hall* v. *City of Taft, supra; Board of Education of City of St. Louis* v. *City of St. Louis*, 267 Mo. 356, 184 S.W. 975. The police power of a municipality is applicable to the buildings of a political subdivision unless the Legislature has by statute occupied the particular field covered by the ordinance under attack. *Kansas City* v. *School District of Kansas City*, 356 Mo. 364, 201 S.W.2d 930; *Cook County* v. *City of Chicago* 311 Ill. 234 142 N.E. 512 31 A.L.R. 442; *Pasadena School District* v. *City of Pasadena*, 166 Cal. 7, 134 P. 985, 47 L.R.A., N.S., 892, Anno. Cas. 1915B, 1039.

One of the first courts to write on the question was the *Supreme Court of California* in *Pasadena School District* v. *City of Pasadena,* 166 Cal. 7, 134 P. 985, 47 L.R.A., N.S., 892. . . . It was there held that the constitution gave the municipality the authority to make and enforce within its limits police, sanitary and other regulations not in conflict with the general law. . . .

The California Supreme Court has subsequently written on the subject in the case of *Hall* v. *City of Taft,* 47 Cal.2d 177, 302 P.2d 574. However, the facts in that case were quite different from the facts of the Pasadena case. By general statute there had been set up an elaborate system whereby the state itself controlled all building of schools in the state. It provided that the state department of education should establish standards for school buildings, review and approve all plans and specifications for buildings and disapprove those not meeting the standards, furnish plans, specifications and building codes, and make rules and regulations to carry out those activities. Another provision of the general law, which we quote from the court's opinion, was:

> "The Division of Architecture of the Department of Public Works under the police power of the State shall supervise the construction of any school building or, if the estimated cost exceed four thousand dollars ($4,000), the reconstruction or alteration of or addition to any school building, for the protection of life and property."

. . . The State of California itself preempted the field covered by the ordinance of the City of Taft. This case differed from the *Pasadena* case because in *Pasadena* the state had not provided for standards and regulations of school buildings by general law. However, the court in *City of Taft* also held that under the Legislature's method of providing for public education, the public local boards of trustees of school districts were holding school property in trust for the state; that since police powers of a city are not applicable to the state itself that the ordinance regulating buildings was not applicable to the school district; and that the *Pasadena* case was overruled insofar as it was inconsistent with their holding in the *City of Taft* case.

We do not agree with the reasoning of the California court in *Hall* v. *City of Taft* as applied to the organization of public schools in Texas. . . .

Although our independent school districts are creatures of the state and receive substantial funds for their operation from the state, they are independent political entities and we will not classify their property as state property. The Legislature in its wisdom has vested the local school board with broad powers and we know of no state which allows more control of its local schools to the local people than does the State of Texas. . . .

The Supreme Court of Missouri has written twice on this subject in the cases of *Board of Education of City of St. Louis* v. *City of St. Louis,* 184 S.W. 975, and *Kansas City* v. *School District of Kansas City,* 201 S.W.2d 930. We believe that the reasoning and holdings of that court are persuasive because of the similarity between the constitutional and statutory provisions of Missouri and Texas.

Board of Education of City of St. Louis v. *City of St. Louis,* supra, involved the applicability of the city building ordinances to a system of vents from the water closets in a school building. The contract for the building provided for a certain type of venting while the city ordinances required another. By statute, school officials were charged with the responsibility for ventilation, warming, sanitary conditions and proper repair thereof and were authorized to appoint assistants, one who was to be an engineer, to design and construct such apparatus for the public school buildings. The court merely held that the general charter powers of the city must yield to the provisions of a law having special application to particular matters.

In the later case of *Kansas City* v. *School District of Kansas City*, supra, the question was whether the city could collect inspection fees for the school district for inspection of boilers, smokestacks, fuel-burning facilities and elevators pursuant to city ordinances passed under the police power. In passing on collection of such fees, the court found it necessary to pass on the applicability of the ordinance itself as applied to a school district and held that the school district was subject to the regulations in question. The Missouri court recognized that the state could have delegated to the school district the full responsibility of taking particular measures in relation to school buildings which would otherwise be within the scope of the city's police power, but stated:

> ". . . Since the State itself has taken no precautionary measures, and City has been vested with the regulatory and supervisory responsibilities of the exercise of the police power, and School District (having no police power) has not been expressly and specifically given full duty to attend to these responsibilities, we think the Legislature is content in the thought the measures to be taken are within the police power vested in City." 201 S.W.2d at 934.

The *Kansas City* case is not inconsistent with the earlier *St. Louis* case, that decision only holding that the Legislature had in fact placed responsibility in the School District as to the building requirements in question. . . .

In *Salt Lake City* v. *Board of Education of Salt Lake City*, 175 P. 654, the Supreme Court of Utah held the ordinances of the city requiring construction with fireproof materials not applicable to school buildings. The holding appears to be based partially on peculiar statutory provisions of Utah and partially on the lack of necessity of such provisions as applied to school buildings. It should be noted, however, that the court did uphold the city ordinance requiring the school buildings to be connected by telephone or otherwise to the fire department. . . .

We believe the better rule to be that the school buildings of an independent school district are subject to the reasonable ordinances of the city. . . . The city, in performing its duties does not usurp the authority and responsibility of the school district requiring the school buildings to meet certain minimum standards of construction any more than it usurps the control and management of individuals and private corporations over their property and affairs by making them meet those same standards.

To hold otherwise would be to leave a hiatus in regulation necessary to the health and safety of the community. . . .

We adopt the language of the Supreme Court of Missouri in *Kansas City* v. *School District of Kansas City*, quoted above:

> ". . . we think the Legislature is content in the thought the measures to be taken are within the police power vested in City." 201 S.W.2d at 934.

The judgment of the Court of Civil Appeals is affirmed.

State v. Stojack

330 P.2d 567 (Wash. 1958)

WEAVER, Justice. . . .

A municipal corporation does not have an inherent power of eminent domain. It may exercise such power only when it is expressly authorized to do so by the state legislature. . . .

Of course, by statute, the state may delegate the power of eminent domain to one of its political subdivisions, but such statutes are strictly construed. . . .

The trial court erred when it concluded that the school district was not entitled to condemn defendant's property because the district already owned 73 acres of land. . . .

Public education is a public use for which private property may be appropriated under the power of eminent domain. If an attempt is made to take more property than is reasonably necessary to accomplish the purpose, then the taking of excess property is no longer a public use, and a certificate of public use and necessity must be denied.

In the selection of a site, the board of directors had the authority to determine the area of land reasonably necessary to accommodate suitable buildings, playgrounds (*Sorenson* v. *Perkins & Co.*, 1913, 72 Wash. 16, 129 P. 577, and cases cited), student activity areas, and related facilities to establish an adequate senior high school in accordance with present day educational requirements. The board considered, as disclosed by the evidence, present, as well as possible and probable future needs; population increase and shift; school attendance areas; the increased cost of acquiring additional land, once a community has consolidated around a school house site; the present day concept of one-story school buildings to minimize cost and fire hazard; and the need and extent of student activity areas. The superintendent and the assistant superintendent of the Tacoma school district testified that, in their opinion, the entire tract, including defendant's land, was necessary to accomplish the purpose set forth in resolution No. 175 of the board, even though it be admitted that no buildings would be erected on defendant's land because of the nature of the terrain.

Generally, the action of a public agency or a municipal corporation having the right of eminent domain in selecting land for a public use will not be controlled by the courts, except for a manifest abuse of discretion, violation of law, fraud, improper motives, or collusion. This court has frequently held that, in eminent domain proceedings, selection of land to be condemned by the proper public agency is conclusive in the absence of bad faith, or arbitrary, capricious, or fraudulent actions. . . .

It is true that the statute authorizes the court to " . . . set the hearing of such petition [for eminent domain] down for trial by a jury . . . " to determine value only after the court " . . . shall further find that such real estate sought to be taken is required and necessary for the purposes of a schoolhouse site. . . . " RCW 8.16.050.

In resolving this issue, however, the court is governed by the rule applicable to other public agencies and municipal corporations, as set forth above.

Defendant introduced no evidence. There is nothing to indicate a manifest abuse of discretion by the school board, nor that its determination was arbitrary, capricious, fraudulent, or collusive. If the court's conclusion, quoted supra, is to be sustained, it must be on the theory that acquisition of defendant's property is in violation of law, a theory which we have demonstrated to be erroneous; hence, the court's conclusion cannot stand. . . .

Wisconsin v. Yoder

406 U.S. 205 (1972)

Mr. *Chief Justice BURGER* delivered the opinion of the Court.

On petition of the State of Wisconsin, we. . . . review a decision of the Wisconsin Supreme Court holding that respondents' convictions for violating the State's compulsory school-attendance law were invalid under the Free Exercise Clause of the first Amendment to the United States Constitution made applicable to the States by the Fourteenth Amendment. For the reasons hereafter stated we affirm the judgment of the Supreme Court of Wisconsin.

Respondents Jonas Yoder and Wallace Miller are members of the Old Order Amish religion, and respondent Adin Yutzy is a member of the Conservative Amish Mennonite Church. . . .

Wisconsin's compulsory school-attendance law required them to cause their children to attend public or private school until reaching age 16 but the respondents declined to send their children, ages 14 and 15, to public school after they complete the eighth grade. The children were not enrolled in any private school, or within any recognized exception to the compulsory-attendance law, and they are conceded to be subject to the Wisconsin statute.

On complaint of the school district administrator for the public schools, respondents were charged, tried, and convicted of violating the compulsory-attendance law in Green County Court and were fined the sum of $5 each. . . .

The trial testimony showed that respondents believed, in accordance with the tenets of Old Order Amish communities generally, that their children's attendance at high school, public or private, was contrary to the Amish religion and way of life. They believed that by sending their children to high school, they would not only expose themselves to the danger of the censure of the church community, but, as found by the county court, also endanger their own salvation and that of their children. The State stipulated that respondents' religious beliefs were sincere.

In support of their position, respondents presented as expert witnesses scholars on religion and education whose testimony is uncontradicted. They expressed their opinions on the relationship of the Amish belief concerning school attendance to the more general tenets of their religion, and described the impact that compulsory high school attendance could have on the continued survival of Amish communities as they exist in the United States today. . . .

As a result of their common heritage, Old Order Amish communities today are characterized by a fundamental belief that salvation requires life in a church community separate and apart from the world and worldly influence. This concept of life aloof from the world and its values is central to their faith. . . .

Amish beliefs require members of the community to make their living by farming or closely related activities. Broadly speaking, the Old Order Amish religion pervades and determines the entire mode of life of its adherents. Their conduct is regulated in great detail by the *Ordnung*, or rules, of the church community. Adult baptism, which occurs in late adolescence, is the time at which Amish young people voluntarily undertake heavy obligations, not unlike the Bar Mitzvah of the Jews, to abide by the rules of the church community.

Amish objection to formal education beyond the eighth grade is firmly grounded in these central religious concepts. They object to the high school, and higher education generally, because the values they teach are in marked variance with Amish values and the Amish way of life; they view secondary school education as an impermissible exposure of their children to a "worldly" influence in conflict with their beliefs. . . .

Formal high school education beyond the eighth grade is contrary to Amish beliefs, not only because it places Amish children in an environment hostile to Amish beliefs . . . but also because it takes them away from their community, physically and emotionally, during the crucial and formative adolescent period of life. During this period, the children must acquire Amish attitudes favoring manual work and self reliance and the specific skills needed to perform the adult role of an Amish farmer or housewife. They must learn to enjoy physical labor. Once a child has learned basic reading, writing, and elementary mathematics, these traits, skills, and attitudes admittedly fall within the category of those best learned through example and "doing" rather than in a classroom. And, at this time in life, the Amish child must also grow in his faith and his relationship to the Amish community if he is to be prepared to accept the heavy obligations imposed by adult baptism. . . .

The Amish do not object to elementary education through the first eight grades as a general proposition because they agree that their children must have basic skills in the "three R's" in order to read the Bible, to be good farmers and citizens, and to be able to deal with non-Amish people when necessary in the course of daily affairs. . . .

On the basis of such considerations, Dr. Hostetler testified that compulsory high school attendance could not only result in great psychological harm to Amish children, because of the conflicts it would produce, but would also, in his opinion, ultimately result in the destruction of the Old Order Amish church community as it exists in the United States today. The testimony of Dr. Donald A. Erickson, an expert witness on education, also showed that the Amish succeed in preparing their high school age children to be productive members of the Amish community. . . . The evidence also showed that the Amish have an excellent record as law-abiding and generally self-sufficient members of society. . . .

There is no doubt as to the power of a State, having a high responsibility for education of its citizens, to impose reasonable regulations for the control and duration of basic education. . . . Yet even this paramount responsibility was . . . made to yield to the right of parents to provide an equivalent education in a privately operated system. . . .

Thus, a State's interest in universal education, however highly we rank it, is not totally free from a balancing process when it impinges on fundamental rights and interests, such as those specifically protected by the free Exercise Clause of the First Amendment, and the traditional interest of parents with respect to the religious upbringing of their children so long as they, in the words of *Pierce,* "prepare [them] for additional obligations." 268 U.S., at 535, 45 S. Ct., at 573.

It follows that in order for Wisconsin to compel school attendance beyond the eighth grade . . . it must appear either that the State does not deny the free exercise of religious belief by its requirement, or that there is a state interest of sufficient magnitude to override the interest claiming protection under the Free Exercise Clause. . . . We can accept it as settled, therefore, that, however strong the State's interest in universal compulsory education, it is by no means absolute to the exclusion or subordination of all other interests. . . .

We come then to the quality of the claims of the respondents. . . . In evaluating those claims, we must be careful to determine whether the Amish religious faith and their mode of life are, as they claim, inseparable and interdependent. A way of life, however virtuous and admirable, may not be interposed as a barrier to reasonable state regulation of education if it is based on purely secular considerations; to have the protection of the Religion Clauses, the claims must be rooted in religious belief. . . . Thus, if the Amish asserted their claims because of their subjective evaluation and rejection of the contemporary secular values . . . much as Thoreau rejected the social values of his time and isolated himself at Walden Pond, their claims would not rest on a religious basis. . . .

Giving no weight to such secular considerations, however, we see that the record in this case abundantly supports the claim that the traditional way of life of the Amish is not merely a matter of personal preference, but one of deep religious conviction, shared by an organized group, and intimately related to daily living. That the Old Order Amish daily life and religious practice stem from their faith is shown by the fact that it is in response to their literal interpretation of the Biblical injunction from the Epistle of Paul to the Romans, "be not conformed to this world. . . . " This command is fundamental to the Amish faith. . . .

The impact of the compulsory-attendance law on respondents' practice of the Amish religion is not only severe, but inescapable, for the Wisconsin law affirmatively compels them, under threat of criminal sanction, to perform acts undeniably at odds with fundamental tenets of their religious beliefs. . . .

Wisconsin concedes that under the Religion Clauses religious beliefs are absolutely free from the State's control, but it argues that "actions," even though religiously grounded, are outside the protection of the first Amendment. But our decisions have rejected the idea that religiously grounded conduct is always outside the protection of the Free Exercise Clause. It is true that activities of individuals, even when religiously based, are often subject to regulation by the States [to] . . . promote the health, safety, and general welfare, or the Federal Government in the exercise of its delegated powers. . . . This case, therefore, does not become easier because respondents were convicted for their "actions". . . . Nor can this case be disposed of on the grounds that Wisconsin's requirement for school attendance to age 16 applies uniformly to all citizens of the State and does not, on its face, discriminate against religions or a particular religion, or that it is motivated by legitimate secular concerns. A regulation neutral on its face may, in its application, nonetheless offend the constitutional requirement for governmental neutrality if it unduly burdens the free exercise of religion. . . .

We turn, then, to the State's broader contention that its interest in its system of compulsory education is so compelling that even the established religious practices of the Amish must give way. Where fundamental claims of religious freedom are at stake, however, we cannot accept such a sweeping claim; . . . recognizing the claimed Amish exemption. . . .

The State advances two primary arguments . . . that some degree of education is necessary to prepare citizens to participate effectively and intelligently in our open political system if we are to preserve freedom and independence. Further, education prepares individuals to be self-reliant and self-sufficient participants in society. We accept these propositions.

However, the evidence adduced by the Amish in this case is persuasively to the effect that an additional one or two years of formal high school for Amish children . . . would do little to serve those interests. . . . It is one thing to say that compulsory education for a year or two beyond the eighth grade may be necessary when its goal is the preparation of the child for life in modern society as the majority live, but it is quite another if the goal of education be viewed as the preparation of the child for life in the separated agrarian community that is the keystone of the Amish faith. . . .

The State attacks respondents' position as one fostering "ignorance" from which the child must be protected by the State, . . . but this argument does not square with the facts disclosed in the record. Whatever their idiosyncrasies as seen by the majority, this record strongly shows that the Amish community has been a highly successful social unit within our society even if apart from the conventional "mainstream." Its members are productive and very law-abiding members of society; they reject public welfare in any of its usual modern forms. The Congress itself recognized their self-sufficiency by authorizing exemption of such groups as the Amish from the obligation to pay social security taxes. . . . A way of life that is odd or even erratic but interferes with no rights or interests of others is not to be condemned because it is different.

The State, however, supports its interest . . . because of the possibility that some such children will choose to leave the Amish community, and that if this occurs they will be ill-equipped for life. . . . However, on this record, that argument is highly speculative. There is no specific evidence of the loss of Amish adherents by attrition, nor is there any showing that upon leaving the Amish community Amish children, with their practical agricultural training and habits of industry and self-reliance, would become burdens on society because of educational shortcomings. . . . Absent some contrary evidence supporting the State's position, we are unwilling to assume that persons possessing such valuable vocational skills and habits are doomed to become burdens on society should they determine to leave the Amish faith, nor is there any basis in the record to warrant a finding that an additional one or two years of formal school education beyond the eighth grade would serve to eliminate any such problem that might exist. . . .

The requirement for compulsory education beyond the eighth grade is a relatively recent development in our history. . . .

The requirement of compulsory schooling to age 16 must therefore be viewed as aimed not merely at providing educational opportunities for children, but as an alternative to the equally undesirable consequence of unhealthful child labor displacing adult workers, or, on the other hand, forced idleness. The two kinds of statutes—compulsory school attendance and child labor laws—tend to keep children of certain ages off the labor market and in school; this regimen in turn provides opportunity to prepare for a livelihood of a higher order than that which children could pursue without education and protects their health in adolescence.

In these terms, Wisconsin's interest in compelling the school attendance of Amish children to age 16 emerges as somewhat less substantial than requiring such attendance for children generally. . . .

Finally, the State, . . . argues that a decision exempting Amish children from the State's requirement fails to recognize the substantive right of the Amish child to a secondary education, and fails to give due regard to the power of the State as *parens patriae* to extend the benefit of secondary education to children regardless of the wishes of their parents. . . .

This case, of course, is not one in which any harm to the physical or mental health of the child or to the public safety, peace, order, or welfare has been demonstrated or may be properly inferred. . . .

Contrary to the suggestion of the dissenting opinion of Mr. *Justice* DOUGLAS, our holding today in no degree depends on the assertion of the religious interest of the child as contrasted with that of the parents. It is the parents who are subject to prosecution here for failing to cause their children to attend school, and it is their right of free exercise, not that of their children, that must determine Wisconsin's power to impose criminal penalities on the parent. . . .

Our holding in no way determines the proper resolution of possible competing interests of parents, children, and the State in an appropriate state court proceeding in which the power of the State is asserted on the theory that Amish parents are preventing their minor children from attending high school despite their expressed desires to the contrary. Recognition of the claim of the State in such a proceeding would, of course, call into question traditional concepts of parental control over the religious upbringing and education of their minor children recognized in this Court's past decisions. It is clear that such an intrusion by a State into family decisions in the area of religious training would give rise to grave questions of religious freedom comparable to those raised here and those presented in *Pierce* v. *Society of Sisters,* 268 U.S. 510, 45 S.Ct. 571,69 L.Ed. 1070 (1925). On this record we neither reach nor decide those issues. . . .

Indeed it seems clear that if the State is empowered, as *parens patriae,* to "save" a child from himself or his Amish parents, . . . the State will in large measure influence, if not determine, the religious future of the child. . . . This primary role of the parents in the upbringing of their children is now established beyond debate as an enduring American tradition. . . .

However read, the Court's holding in *Pierce* stands as a charter of the rights of parents to direct the religious upbringing of their children. And, when the interests of parenthood are combined with a free exercise claim of the nature revealed by this record, more than merely a "reasonable relation to some purpose within the competency of the State" is required to sustain the validity of the State's requirement under the first Amendment. To be sure, the power of the parent, even when linked to a free exercise claim, may be subject to limitation under *Prince* if it appears that parental decisions will jeopardize the health or safety of the child, or have a potential for significant social burdens. . . .

For the reasons stated we hold with the Supreme Court of Wisconsin, that the First and Fourteenth Amendments prevent the State from compelling respondents to cause their children to attend formal high school to age 16. . . .

It cannot be overemphasized that we are not dealing with a way of life and mode of education by a group claiming to have recently discovered some "progressive" or more enlightened process for rearing children for modern life.

Nothing we hold is intended to undermine the general applicability of the State's compulsory school-attendance statutes or to limit the power of the State to promulgate reasonable standards that, while not impairing the free exercise of religion, provide for continuing agricultural vocational education under parental and church guidance by the Old Order Amish or others similarly situated. The States have had a long history of amicable and effective relationships with church-sponsored schools, and there is no basis for assuming that, in this related context, reasonable standards cannot be established concerning the content of the continuing vocational education of Amish children under parental guidance, provided always that state regulations are not inconsistent with what we have said in this opinion.

Affirmed.

In re U.S. Ex Rel. Missouri State High Sch., etc.

682 F.2d 147 (5th Cir. 1982)

LAY, Chief Judge

The basic question presented is whether a rule of the Missouri State High School Activities Association (MSHSAA) barring a student's participation in interscholastic athletics for a period of one year after the student transfers from one high school to another violates the federal Constitution. We hold that it does not. . . .

The Missouri State High School Activities Association is a voluntary, nonprofit unincorporated association of high schools whose purpose is the regulation of interscholastic activities including sports, speech, debate, and music. MSHSAA is comprised primarily of public schools although many parochial and nonsectarian private schools are also members of the association. . . .

The ABC League is an association of private schools in the St. Louis area containing four denominational and two nondenominational schools. The six schools schedule sports competition among themselves on three levels determined by grade, age, height, and weight of the athletes. Because several of the ABC League schools have no physical education program and require all their students to participate in interscholastic athletics and because the League had traditionally been self-regulating, the League was granted a partial exemption from the transfer rule. However, during the course of this litigation, MSHSAA repealed this exemption effective July 1, 1981.

Three actions are consolidated in this appeal. In *Zander* v. *Missouri State High School Activities Association,* No. 81–0369– C(1) (E.D.Mo April 7, 1981), Chief Judge H. Kenneth Wangelin enjoined MSHSAA from preventing William A. Zander, III, from participating in interscholastic tennis competition during the spring of 1981 after Zander transferred to a Missouri high school from a school in Florida. . . .

The parties concede that his individual claim is moot.

In *Barnhorst* v. *Missouri State High School Activities Association,* 504 F.Supp. 449 (W.D.Mo.1980), Judge Russell G. Clark refused to issue a preliminary injunction barring application of the transfer rule to prevent Julie Ann Barnhorst from participating in athletics during the 1980–81 school year. The court held the rule did not violate the due process or equal protection clauses of the fourteenth amendment.

Barnhorst subsequently conducted additional discovery and amended her complaint to claim that the transfer rule as modified by the ABC League exemption deprived her of equal protection of the law (Barnhorst did not transfer to or from an ABC League school). The court held that the exemption created discrimination between students which had no rational basis and thus violated the equal protection clause. However, the court found that the proper remedy was not the invalidation of the transfer rule, but rather the striking of the exemption. The court held the exemption unconstitutional and enjoined its application. *Barnhorst* v. *Missouri State High School Activities Association,* No. 80–1036–CV–W–4–3 (W.D.Mo. April 8, 1981). MSHSAA appealed (No. 81–1526).

On May 4, 1981, the ABC League moved to intervene in the *Barnhorst* case. . . .

Because of the subsequent repeal of the ABC exemption, the court's ruling as to the constitutionality of the exemption is moot. . . .

The final case consolidated in this appeal is *ABC League* v. *Missouri State High School Activities Association,* 530 F.Supp. 1033 (E.D.Mo.1981). In this case, the ABC League and Andrew T. Nelson, a transferee to an ABC League school interested in participating in interscholastic sports throughout the 1981–82 school year, filed suit against MSHSAA alleging that repeal of the ABC exemption and the transfer rule itself were unconstitutional. Judge Wangelin enjoined enforcement of the repeal and declared the transfer rule unconstitutional. . . .

The issues presented on appeal concern the constitutionality of the transfer rule, the constitutionality of the application of the transfer rule to those schools formerly exempt under the ABC exemption, and the legality of the district court's decision to enjoin repeal of the ABC exemption. . . .

Because MSHSAA is an association comprised primarily of public schools, its rules are state action governed by the fourteenth amendment. However, federal courts have uniformly upheld comparable rules governing transfers against challenges based on both the due process and equal protection clauses. *See Walsh* v. *Louisiana High School Athletic Association,* 616 F.2d 152, 159–61 (5th Cir. 1980), *cert. denied,* 449 U.S. 1124, 101 S.Ct. 939, 67 L.Ed.2d 109 (1981); *Moreland* v. *Western Pennsylvania Interscholastic Athletic League,* 572 F.2d 121 (3d Cir. 1978); *Hamilton* v. *Tennessee Secondary School Athletic Association,* 552 F.2d 681 (6th Cir. 1976); *Albach* v. *Odle,* 531 F.2d 983 (10th Cir. 1976) (New Mexico); *Oklahoma High School Athletic Association* v. *Bray,* 321 F.2d 269 (10th Cir. 1963) (residency requirement); *Kulovitz* v. *Illinois High School Association,* 462 F.Supp. 875 (N.D.Ill. 1978); *Dallam* v. *Cumberland Valley School District,* 391 F.Supp. 358 (M.D.Pa.1975); *Paschal* v. *Perdue,* 320 F.Supp. 1274 (S.D.Fla.1970). . . .

Participation in interscholastic athletics is an important part of the educational process. Nonetheless, education has not been deemed a fundamental right under the fourteenth amendment requiring application of strict judicial scrutiny. *San Antonio*

Independent School District v. *Rodriquez,* 411 U.S. 1, 29–39, 93 S.Ct. 1278, 1294–1300, 36 L.Ed.2d 16 (1973).

Plaintiffs argue that the transfer rule burdens their exercise of the fundamental right to travel interstate and restricts their freedom to associate. When a student alters his or her place of residence from one state to another without an accompanying change by his or her parents (as did Zander), the rule prohibits the student from participating in interscholastic athletics for one year. Classifications which penalize the exercise of the right to travel are subject to strict scrutiny. *Shapiro* v. *Thompson,* 394 U.S. 618, 634, 89 S.Ct 1322, 1331, 22 L.Ed.2d 600 (1969). But most cases which implicate the rule's sanction do not involve interstate travel and, those which do, implicate the sanction because they involve school transfers and not because they involve interstate travel. The rule's minimal impact on interstate travel does not require strict scrutiny.

Plaintiffs also argue the rule burdens the exercise of the right to freely associate by penalizing students' choice to change schools and thus to alter the body of people with which they associate. Students have no indefensible right to associate through choice of school. Mandatory assignment to public schools based on place of residence or other factors is clearly permissible. The transfer rule does not prevent association through private schooling nor discriminate against such association. Thus no right is burdened and the rule is not thereby subject to strict scrutiny.

Finally, plaintiff ABC League argues the rule burdens students' and parents' exercise of their right to choose and devise a nonpublic education. As discussed below, the rule does not impinge on this limited right.

Plaintiffs challenge the transfer rule as being both under-inclusive and over-inclusive. The rule is claimed to be under-inclusive because it does not apply to nonathletic activities. Since athletes are not a suspect class and no fundamental right is impinged by applying the rule to athletics and not to other school activities, the standard of judicial scrutiny which should be applied is the rational relationship test. *Dandridge* v. *Williams,* 397 U.S. 471, 485– 87, 90 S.Ct. 1153, 1161–1162, 25 L.Ed.2d 491 (1970); *Williamson* v. *Lee Optical Co.*, 348 U.S. 483, 75 S.Ct. 461, 99 L.Ed. 563 (1955). A rational basis clearly exists for believing that the danger of incurring the harms involved in transfers motivated by athletics and attempts to induce such transfers is greater than the danger of parallel harms in other areas.

The transfer rule is claimed to be over-inclusive because it reaches many transfers which do not involve the harms it is designed to prevent. The rule does not, however, create an inherently suspect classification. Thus, as indicated, the rule need only be rationally related to a legitimate state purpose. The clear purpose of the rule is to prevent the evils associated with recruiting of high school athletes and transfers motivated by athletics. School officials urge the administrative difficulties and political pressures encountered in determining, on an individual basis, which transfers involve the feared evils justify the rule's prophylactic nature. *Weinberger* v. *Salfi,* 422 U.S. 749, 784–85, 95 S.Ct. 2457, 2476, 45 L.Ed.2d 522 (1975). We must agree. . . .

Once a rational relationship exists, and it exists here, judicial scrutiny must cease. Whether the rule is wise or creates undue individual hardship are policy decisions better left to legislative and administrative bodies. Schools themselves are by far the better agencies to devise rules and restrictions governing extracurricular activities. Judicial intervention in school policy should always be reduced to a minimum. . . .

Plaintiffs also argue the rule violates the due process clause. Our equal protection analysis reveals that the rule is not arbitrary. The Association's bylaws, section 10.1, provide for notice and hearings before both the executive secretary and the Board of Control concerning eligibility determinations. The specified procedures combined with the availability of application under the hardship exception satisfy any procedural due process requirements.

As noted above, the constitutionality of the ABC League exemption is no longer before this court. After repeal of the exemption, the League may only argue that the transfer rule cannot constitutionally be applied to students transferring to or between its schools. The League argues that individuals have a constitutional right—derived from the first and fourteenth amendments—to choose to educate their children in private schools and to devise the curriculum of those schools without state interference. . . .

The fourteenth amendment prevents states from prohibiting attendance of nonpublic schools, but it does not preclude reasonable, nondiscriminatory regulation designed to advance legitimate, secular interests. . . .

The transfer rule is a reasonable and neutral regulation. It does not burden the choice of private education, but merely attaches a restriction to all transfers whether to private or public schools schools except those falling into a specified exception. The ABC League argues that participation in interscholastic sports is an integral element of its vision of private education. The League makes no claim that this philosophy is rooted in religious practices and thus its claim is not cognizable under *Yoder,* 406 U.S. 205, 92 S.Ct. 1526, 32 L.Ed.2d 15, nor can the League demonstrate that the rule represents a fundamental restriction of liberty as was the compulsion of public education in *Pierce,* 268 U.S. 510, 45 S.Ct. 571, 69 L.Ed. 1070, and the ban of instruction in a foreign language involved in *Meyer,* 262 U.S. 390, 43 S.Ct. 625, 67 L.Ed. 1042. The League may constitutionally be required to choose between conforming to the transfer rule or foregoing athletic competition with the members of MSHSAA. We find the rule may constitutionally be applied to students transferring to schools in the ABC League.

Board of Education *v.* Pico

457 U.S. 853 (1982)

[Suit by students against school board and its members, alleging violation of student First Amendment rights by removal of nine books from school libraries,* despite protests and recommendation for restoration of some of the books by an advisory "Book Review

*The nine books in the high school library were: *Slaughterhouse Five,* by Kurt Vonnegut, Jr.; *The Naked Ape,* by Desmond Morris; *Down These Mean Streets,* by Piri Thomas; *Best Short Stories of Negro Writers,* edited by Langston Hughes; *Go Ask Alice,* of anonymous authorship; *Laughing Boy,* by Oliver LaFarge; *Black Boy,* by Richard Wright; *A Hero Ain't Nothin' But A Sandwich,* by Alice Childress; and *Soul On Ice,* by Eldridge Cleaver. The book in the Junior High School library was *A Reader for Writers,* edited by Jerome Archer. Still another listed book, *The Fixer,* by Bernard Malamud, was found to be included in the curriculum of a twelfth grade literature course. 474 F.Supp. 387, 389 and nn. 2–4.

Committee." The trial court dismissed the action on pretrial motion for summary judgment, but was reversed by the Second Circuit Court of Appeals which ordered a trial to determine whether the board was acting from unconstitutional motives in removing the books. The Supreme Court affirmed the order for trial on the issue of board motivation, by a five to four vote, with the majority Justices not agreeing on the precise ground of the Court's decision. The following excerpts from the opinions of the various Justices indicate their different rationales.]

We emphasize at the outset the limited nature of the substantive question presented by the case before us. Our precedents have long recognized certain constitutional limits upon the power of the State to control even the curriculum and classroom . . . For as this case is presented to us, it does not involve textbooks, or indeed any books that Island Trees students would be required to read. Respondents do not seek . . . to impose limitations upon their school board's discretion to prescribe the curricula of the Island Trees schools. On the contrary, the only books at issue in this case are *library* books, books that by their nature are optional rather than required reading. Our adjudication of the present case thus does not intrude into the classroom, or into the compulsory courses taught there. Furthermore, even as to library books, the action before us does not involve the *acquisition* of books. Respondents have not sought to compel their school board to add to the school library shelves any books that students desire to read. Rather, the only action challenged in this case is the *removal* from school libraries of books originally placed there by the school authorities, or without objection from them. . . .

The substantive question before us is still further constrained by the procedural posture of this case. . . . We can reverse the judgment of the Court of Appeals, and grant petitioners' request . . . only if we determine that "there is no genuine issue as to any material fact," . . .

In sum, the issue before us in this case is a narrow one, both substantively and procedurally. It may best be restated as two distinct questions. First, does the First Amendment impose *any* limitations upon the discretion of petitioners to remove library books from the Island Trees High School and Junior High School? Second, if so, do the . . . evidentiary materials before the District Court . . . raise a genuine issue of fact whether petitioners might have exceeded those limitations? . . .

The Court has long recognized that local school boards have broad discretion in the management of school affairs . . . and that federal courts should not ordinarily "intervene in the resolution of conflicts which arise in the daily operation of school systems. . . . "

We are therefore in full agreement with petitioners that local school boards must be permitted "to establish and apply their curriculum in such a way as to transmit community values," and that "there is a legitimate and substantial community interest in promoting respect for authority and traditional values be they social, moral, or political."

At the same time, however, we have necessarily recognized that the discretion of the States and local school boards in matters of education must be exercised in manner that comports with the transcendent imperatives of the First Amendment. . . . In short, "First Amendment rights, applied in light of the special characteristics of the school environment, are available to . . . students."

Of course, courts should not "intervene in the resolution of conflicts which arise in the daily operation of school systems" unless "basic constitutional values" are "directly and sharply implicated[d] in those conflicts. *Epperson* v. *Arkansas,* 393 U.S., at 104. But we think that the First Amendment rights of students may be directly and sharply implicated by the removal of books from the shelves of a school library. Our precedents have focused "not only on the role of the First Amendment in fostering individual self-expression but also on its role in affording the public access to discussion, debate, and the dissemination of information and ideas." *First National Bank of Boston* v. *Bellotti,* 435 U.S. 765, 783 (1978). And we have recognized that "the State may not, consistently with the spirit of the First Amendment, contract the spectrum of available knowledge." . . . In keeping with this principle, we have held that in a variety of contexts "the Constitution protects the right to receive information and ideas. . . . "

This right is an inherent corollary of the rights of free speech and press that are explicitly guaranteed by the Constitution, in two senses. First, the right to receive ideas follows ineluctably from the *sender's* First Amendment right to send them. . . .

More importantly, the right to receive ideas is a necessary predicate to the *recipient's* meaningful exercise of his own rights of speech, press, and political freedom. . . .

In sum, just as access to ideas makes it possible for citizens generally to exercise their rights of free speech and press in a meaningful manner, such access prepares students for active and effective participation in the pluralistic, often contentious society in which they will soon be adult members. Of course all First Amendment rights accorded to students must be construed "in light of the special characteristics of the school environment." *Tinker* v. *Des Moines School Dist.*, 393 U.S., at 506. But the special characteristics of the school *library* make that environment especially appropriate for the recognition of the First Amendment rights of students. . . .

The school library is the principal locus of such freedom. As one District Court has well put it, in the school library

> "a student can literally explore the unknown, and discover areas of interest and thought not covered by the prescribed curriculum. . . . Th[e] student learns that a library is a place to test or expand upon ideas presented to him, in or out of the classroom." *Right to Read Defense Committee* v. *School Committee,* 454 F.Supp. 703, 715 (Mass. 1978).

Petitioners emphasize the inculcative function of secondary education, and argue that they must be allowed *unfettered* discretion to "transmit community values" through the Island Trees schools. But that sweeping claim overlooks the unique role of the school library. It appears from the record that use of the Island Trees school libraries is completely voluntary on the part of students. Their selection of books from these libraries is entirely a matter of free choice; the libraries afford them an opportunity at self-education and individual enrichment that is wholly optional. Petitioners might well defend their claim of absolute discretion in matters of *curriculum* by reliance upon their duty to inculcate community values. But we think that petitioners' reliance upon that duty is misplaced where, as here, they attempt to extend their claim of absolute discretion beyond the compulsory environment of the classroom, into the school library and the regime of voluntary inquiry that there holds sway.

In rejecting petitioners' claim of absolute discretion to remove books from their school libraries, we do not deny that local school boards have a substantial legitimate role to play in the determination of school library content. We thus must turn to the question of the extent to which the First Amendment places limitations upon the discretion of petitioners to remove books from their libraries. In this inquiry we enjoy the guidance of several precedents. *West Virginia Board of Education* v. *Barnette,* stated:

> "If there is any fixed star in our constitutional constellation, it is that no official, high or petty, can prescribe what shall be orthodox in politics, nationalism, religion, or other matters of opinion. . . . If there are any circumstances which permit an exception, they do not now occur to us." 319 U.S., at 642.

This doctrine has been reaffirmed in later cases involving education. . . .

With respect to the present case, the message of these precedents is clear. Petitioners rightly possess significant discretion to determine the content of their school libraries. But that discretion may not be exercised in a narrowly partisan or political manner. If a Democratic school board, motivated by party affiliation, ordered the removal of all books written by or in favor of Republicans, few would doubt that the order violated the constitutional rights of the students denied access to those books. The same conclusion would surely apply if an all-white school board, motivated by racial animus, decided to remove all books authored by blacks or advocating racial equality and integration. Our Constitution does not permit the official suppression of *ideas.* Thus whether petitioner's removal of books from their school libraries denied respondents their First Amendment rights depends upon the motivation behind petitioners' actions. If petitioners *intended* by their removal decision to deny respondents access to ideas with which petitioners disagreed, and if this intent was the decisive factor in petitioners' decision, then petitioners have exercised their discretion in violation of the Constitution. . . . On the other hand, respondents implicitly concede that an unconstitutional motivation would *not* be demonstrated if it were shown that petitioners had decided to remove the books at issue because those books were pervasively vulgar. . . . And again, respondents concede that if it were demonstrated that the removal decision was based solely upon the "educational suitability" of the books in question, then their removal would be "perfectly permissible. . . . " In other words, in respondent's view such motivations, if decisive of petitioners' actions, would not carry the danger of an official suppression of ideas, and thus would not violate respondents' First Amendment rights.

As noted earlier, nothing in our decision today affects in any way the discretion of a local school board to choose books to *add* to the libraries of their schools. Because we are concerned in this case with the suppression of ideas, our holding today affects only the discretion to *remove* books. In brief, we hold that local school boards may not remove books from school library shelves simply because they dislike the ideas contained in those books and seek by their removal to "prescribe what shall be orthodox in politics, nationalism, religion, or other matters of opinion." *West Virginia Board of Education* v. *Barnette,* 319 U.S., at 642. . . .

We now turn to the remaining question presented by this case: Do the evidentiary materials that were before the District Court, when construed most favorably to respondents, raise a genuine issue of material fact whether petitioners exceeded constitutional limitations in exercising their discretion to remove the books from the school libraries? We conclude that the materials do raise such a question, which forecloses summary judgment in favor of petitioners. . . .

Justice BLACKMUN, concurring in part and concurring in the judgment.

To my mind, this case presents a particularly complex problem because it involves two competing principles of constitutional stature. On the one hand, as the dissenting opinions demonstrate, and as we all can agree, the Court has acknowledged the importance of the public schools "in the preparation of individuals for participation as citizens, and in the preservation of the values on which our society rests." *Ambach* v. *Norwick,* 441 U.S. 68, 76 (1979). . . . Because of the essential socializing function of schools, local education officials may attempt "to promote civic virtues," *Ambach* v. *Norwick,* 441 U.S., at 80, and to "awake[n] the child to cultural values." . . . It therefore seems entirely appropriate that the State use "public schools [to] . . . inculcat[e] fundamental values necessary to the maintenance of a democratic political system." *Ambach* v. *Norwick,* 441 U.S., at 77.

On the other hand, as the plurality demonstrates, it is beyond dispute that schools and school boards must operate within the confines of the First Amendment. . . .

In combination with more generally applicable First Amendment rules, most particularly the central proscription of content-based regulations of speech, . . . the cases outlined above yield a general principle: the State may not suppress exposure to ideas—for the sole *purpose* of suppressing exposure to those ideas—absent sufficiently compelling reasons. . . .

In my view, then, the principle involved here is both narrower and more basic than the "right to receive information" identified by the plurality. I do not suggest that the State has any affirmative obligation to provide students with information or ideas, something that may well be associated with a "right to receive." See *post,* at 887 (*BURGER, C.J.*, dissenting); *post,* at 915–918 (*REHNQUIST, J.*, dissenting). And I do not believe, as the plurality suggests, that the right at issue here is somehow associated with the peculiar nature of the school library, see *ante,* at 868–869; if schools may be used to inculcate ideas, surely libraries may play a role in that process. Instead, I suggest that certain forms of state discrimination *between* ideas are improper.

Certainly, the unique environment of the school places substantial limits on the extent to which official decisions may be restrained by First Amendment values. But that environment also makes it particularly important that *some* limits be imposed. . . . In starker terms, we must reconcile the schools' "inculcative" function with the First Amendment's bar on "prescriptions of orthodoxy."

In my view, we strike a proper balance here by holding that school officials may not remove books for the *purpose* of restricting access to the political ideas or social perspectives discussed in them, when that action is motivated simply by the officials' disapproval of the ideas involved. . . .

As I view it, this is a narrow principle. School officials must be able to choose one book over another, without outside interference, when the first book is deemed more relevant to the curriculum, or better written, or when one of a host of other politically neutral reasons is present. These decisions obviously will not implicate First Amendment values. And even absent space or financial limitations, First Amendment principles would allow a school board to refuse to make a book available to students because it contains offensive language, cf. *FCC* v. *Pacifica Foundation,* 438 U.S. 726, 757 (1978) (*POWELL, J.*, concurring), or because it is psychologically or intellectually inappropriate for the age group, or even, perhaps, because the ideas it advances are "manifestly inimical to the public welfare." *Pierce* v. *Society of Sisters,* 268 U.S. 510, 534 (1925). And, of course, school officials may choose one book over another because they believe that one subject is more important, or is more deserving of emphasis.

[Concurring opinion of *Justice WHITE* omitted.]

Chief Justice BURGER, with whom *Justice POWELL, Justice REHNQUIST,* and *Justice O'CONNOR* join, dissenting.

In an attempt to deal with a problem in an area traditionally left to the states, a plurality of the Court, in a lavish expansion going beyond any prior holding under the First Amendment, expresses its view that a school board's decision concerning what books are to be in the school library is subject to federal-court review . . . would come perilously close to becoming a "super censor" of school board library decisions. Stripped to its essentials, the issue comes down to two important propositions: *first,* whether local schools are to be administered by elected school boards, or by federal judges and teenage pupils; and *second,* whether the values of morality, good taste, and relevance to education are valid reasons for school board decisions concerning the contents of a school library. In an attempt to place this case within the protection of the First Amendment, the plurality suggests a new "right" that, when shorn of the plurality's rhetoric, allows this Court to impose its own views. . . .

I agree with the fundamental proposition that "students do not "'shed their constitutional rights to freedom of speech or expression at the schoolhouse gate.'" . . . Here, however, no restraints of any kind are placed on the students. They are free to read the books in question, which are available at public libraries and bookstores; they are free to discuss them in the classroom or elsewhere. Despite this absence of any direct external control on the student's ability to express themselves, the plurality suggests that there is a new First Amendment "entitlement" to have access to particular books in a school library. . . .

The apparent underlying basis of the plurality's view seems to be that students have an enforceable "right" to receive the information and ideas that are contained in junior and senior high school library books. *Ante,* at 866. This "right" purportedly follows "ineluctably" from the sender's First Amendment right to freedom of speech and as a "necessary predicate" to the recipient's meaningful exercise of his own rights of speech, press, and political freedom. *Ante,* at 866–867. No such right, however, has previously been recognized. . . .

Never before today has the Court indicated that the government has an *obligation* to aid a speaker or author in reaching an audience.

Second, the plurality concludes that "the right to receive ideas is a necessary predicate to the *recipient's* meaningful exercise of his own rights of speech, press, and political freedom." *Ante,* at 867 (emphasis in original). However, the "right to receive information and ideas," *Stanley* v. *Georgia,* 394 U.S. 557, 564 (1969), cited *ante,* at 867, does not carry with it the concomitant right to have those ideas affirmatively provided at a particular place by the government. . . .

In short, even assuming the desirability of the policy expressed by the plurality, there is not a hint in the First Amendment, or in any holding of this Court, of a "right" to have the government provide continuing access to certain books. . . .

The plurality distinguishes library books from textbooks because library books "by their nature are optional rather than required reading." *Ante,* at 862. It is not clear, however, why this distinction requires *greater* scrutiny before "optional" reading materials may be removed. It would appear that required reading and textbooks have a greater likelihood of imposing a "'pall of orthodoxy'" over the educational process than do optional reading. *Ante,* at 870. . . .

Today the plurality suggests that the *Constitution* distinguishes between school libraries and school classrooms, between *removing* unwanted books and *acquiring* books. Even more extreme, the plurality concludes that the Constitution *requires* school boards to justify to its teenage pupils the decision to remove a particular book from a school library. I categorically reject this notion that the Constitution dictates that judges, rather than parents, teachers, and local school boards, must determine how the standards of morality and vulgarity are to be treated in the classroom.

Justice POWELL, dissenting

The plurality opinion today rejects a basic concept of public school education in our country. . . .

I therefore view today's decision with genuine dismay. Whatever the final outcome of this suit and suits like it, the resolution of educational policy decisions through litigation, and the exposure of school board members to liability for such decisions, can be expected to corrode the school board's authority and effectiveness. . . . Judges rarely are as competent as school authorities to make this decision; nor are judges responsive to the parents and people of the school district.

Justice O'CONNOR, dissenting.

If the school board can set the curriculum, select teachers, and determine initially what books to purchase for the school library, it surely can decide which books to discontinue or remove from the school library so long as it does not also interfere with the right of students to read the material and to discuss it. As *Justice REHNQUIST* persuasively argues, the plurality's analysis overlooks the fact that in this case the government is acting in its special role as educator.

I do not personally agree with the Board's action with respect to some of the books in question here, but it is not the function of the courts to make the decisions that have been properly relegated to the elected members of school boards. It is the school board that must determine educational suitability, and it has done so in this case. I therefore join *The Chief Justice's* dissent.

[Dissenting opinion of *Justice REHNQUIST* omitted.]

CHAPTER 4

CHAPTER OUTLINE

A. The establishment clause
   1. Excuse from school sessions for religious purposes
   2. School prayer, Bible reading, and religious literature
   3. Religion-related curriculum subjects
      a. Study of the Bible and religious history
      b. Sex education
   4. Religion-related pageants and displays
   5. Invocations and baccalaureate services
   6. Religious teachers and religious garb
   7. Dual enrollment and special services to church-school students
      a. Federally funded programs
      b. State-funded programs
   8. Leasing of church property for public school use
   9. Use of public school buildings by church groups
B. Free exercise of religion
   1. School conduct requirements
   2. School curriculum requirements

Religion and Public Education

TABLE OF CASES FOR CHAPTER 4

Wallace v. Jaffree (II) _______U.S. _______(1985), _______, 140.
Mercer v. Michigan State Board of Education, 379 F.Supp. 580 (E.D. Mich. 1974), 145.
Citizens for Parental Rights v. San Mateo County Board of Education, 124 Cal. Rptr. 68 (1975), 148.
Lynch v. Donnelly, 465 U.S. 668 (1984), ____, 156.
Bender v. Williamsport Area School District, 741 F.2d 538 (3d Cir. 1984), 162.
Widmar v. Vincent, 454 U.S. 263 (1981), 168.

> "As government pressure towards unity becomes greater, so strife becomes more bitter as to whose unity it shall be." *W.Va. Bd. of Education* v. *Barnette,* 319 U.S. 624, 641 (1943).

This prophetic observation from the landmark flag-salute case, which prohibited a state from compelling public school students to salute the flag in violation of their religious beliefs, is evident today. Given the many sects in American society, and the interface of religion and education in the development of youth, public school management is fraught with religious concerns and conflicts. Those conflicts revolve around disputed interpretation and applications of the religious clauses of the First Amendment:

> "Congress shall make no law respecting an establishment of religion, or prohibiting the free exercise thereof. . . . "[1]

As repeatedly noted by the Supreme Court, the twin clauses tend to run in counter directions:

> "The Court has struggled to find a neutral course between the two Religion Clauses, both of which are cast in absolute terms, and either of which, if expanded to a logical extreme, would tend to clash with the other." *Lemon* v. *Kurtzman,* 397 U.S. 664, 668–69 (1970).

In its attempt to reconcile the demands that government neither favor nor abridge the practice of religion, the court has subjected challenged practices to independent analysis under each clause and has adopted separate constitutional tests for each clause:

> "Hence it is necessary in a free exercise case for one to show the coercive effect . . . against him in the practice of his religion. The distinction between the two clauses is apparent—a violation of the Free Exercise Clause is predicated on coercion, while the Establishment Clause violation need not be so predicated." *School District* v. *Schempp,* 374 U.S. 203, 222–23 (1963).

The difficulties posed by the interpretation and application of the religion clauses to public school contexts will be illustrated shortly.

In addition to the federal constitution, most state constitutions contain provisions regarding antiestablishment and free exercise of religion, but the state courts are free to interpret their respective state constitutions independently of the meaning ascribed to the religion clauses of the federal constitution.[2]

A. The Establishment Clause

The tortuous course of Supreme Court development of establishment clause doctrine is best stated in that Court's latest opinions in *Wallace* v. *Jaffree,* regarding the constitu-

---

1. The First Amendment, originally addressed only to Congress, has been held to apply to public schools, by judicial incorporation of its principles into the Fourteenth Amendment. Cantwell v. Connecticut, 310 U.S. 296 (1940).

2. *E.g.,* Springfield Sch. Dist. v. Dept. of Ed., 397 A.2d 1154 (Pa. 1979).

tionality of voluntary prayer and meditation in public schools. They are reported at the end of this chapter and should be read carefully as the best exposition of current, somewhat unstable, constitutional doctrine regarding government-religion relationships in the schools. Those opinions underscore the difficulty of the educator's task to identify practices that, in constitutional contemplation, do or do not amount to impermissible aids to religion. As each of the following sections illustrates, the particularized determination of what constitutes an establishment of religion often depends more on particular circumstances and the degree of government-religion contract than on any intrinsic conceptual test.

While the majority opinion in *Wallace* purports to adhere to the three-pronged test of constitutionality under the establishment clause—namely, that the law must have a secular purpose, a primary effect that does not advance or inhibit religion, and avoid excessive entanglement of government with religion—several opinions in *Wallace* indicate that this test is not a rigid rule, but is subject to considerable qualification and refinement. A few Justices apparently would reject that test altogether.

1. Excuse from School Sessions for Religious Purposes

In 1948 the Supreme Court struck down the public school program that excused students from regular classes to permit them to attend private religious instruction, at their parents' election, in other parts of the public school building.[3] The Court ruled that the program constituted an aid to religion in violation of the establishment clause. Four years later, the same Court held that *dismissal* of students from school, on parental request, to permit them to pursue religious studies outside the school was constitutional and not an aid or establishment of religion.[4] The Court distinguished the later decision (*Zorach*) from the former decision (*McCollum*) because the use of public school property was not involved in the later case. In reasoning that the Constitution permitted government accommodation of religious interests, the *Zorach* decision revealed a basic tension (separation versus accommodation) in the constitutional theory of Establishment.

The courts continue to apply the *Zorach/McCollum* distinction to uphold *dismissals* from school for religious accommodation purposes.[5] A school board policy prohibiting extracurricular activities and programs on Friday evenings, during the day on Saturday, and on Sunday mornings was upheld as an accommodation of religion.[6] The Court found the policy to be secular, not religious, and designed to equalize opportunities for students with different Sabbaths. It concluded that the prohibition did not, in primary effect, aid religion or involve excessive entanglement of government with religion. Yet courts have

---

3. McCollum v. Bd. of Education, 333 U.S. 203 (1948). *See also* Moore v. Bd. of Education, 212 N.E.2d 833 (Ohio 1965).

4. Zorach v. Clauson, 343 U.S. 306 (1952).

5. *See* Lanner v. Wimmer, 662 F.2d 1349 (10th Cir. 1981) (dismissal for instruction at nearby seminary sustained, but grant of academic credit for studies there held unconstitutional); Smith v. Smith, 523 F.2d 121 (4th Cir. 1975), *cert. denied,* 423 U.S. 1058 (1976); State v. Thompson, 225 N.W.2d 678 (Wis. 1975).

6. Student Members of the Playcrafters v. Board of Education of the Township of Teaneck, 424 A.2d 1192 (N.J. 1981).

denied exemption of students from compulsory attendance for weekly Sabbaths that fall during the normal school week.[7]

The closing of schools on major religious holidays is not extensively litigated, and may be viewed as accommodation of religious expression if significant numbers of students or teachers are involved, but state courts have divided on the question whether Good Friday may be made a paid holiday under teacher contracts.[8]

The disallowance or limitation of excused absences for religious purposes (when schools remain open) has been tested in recent litigation. A student of Worldwide Church of God successfully challenged a limitation of two days' excused absences for religious purposes as an unconstitutional abridgment of religious freedom when his religion required observance of seven annual holy days.[9] A teacher practicing the same faith successfully overturned a similar limitation on teacher leaves for religious holy days.[10] Teacher claims of religious accommodation, such as for religion-dictated absences or leave, have also been upheld under the antidiscrimination mandates of Title VII of the federal Civil Rights Act of 1964 and under a state constitution and state civil rights statutes.[11]

2. School Prayer, Bible Reading, and Religious Literature

Recitation of a public school-sponsored prayer, though voluntary and non-denominational, has been held to be a religious exercise and unconstitutional under the establishment clause.[12] On the same grounds, the Supreme Court also nullified state statutes that provided for voluntary reading of verses from the Bible, without comment, at the opening session of the school day and the voluntary recitation of the Lord's Prayer.[13] The Supreme Court insisted that these decisions were neutral and not hostile toward religion and added that public schools could constitutionally teach *about* religion and employ the Bible for secular educational purposes.

Lower courts have applied the Supreme Court rulings on overt prayer and Bible recitations[14] to invalidate school-supervised voluntary prayer, whether conducted by

---

7. Commonwealth v. Bey, 70 A.2d 693 (Pa. 1953) (Mohammedan Friday sabbath); *In re* Currence, 248 N.Y.S.2d 251 (1963) (Wednesday and Thursday sabbath).

8. *Compare* California School Employees Assn. v. Sequoia Union H.S. District, 136 Cal. Rptr. 594 (1977) (contracted-for paid holiday upheld) *with* Hunterden Central H.S. Board of Education v. Hunterden Central H.S. Teachers Assn., 416 A.2d 980 (N.J. 1980) (similar contract term voided). *See also* Mandel v. Hodges, 127 Cal. Rptr. 244 (1976) (Governor's designation of noon–3:00 p.m. on Good Friday as paid holiday period voided).

9. Church of God Worldwide Texas Region v. Amarillo, 511 F.Supp. 613 (N.D. Tex. 1981).

10. Niederhuber v. Camden County Vocational Technical School District Board of Education, 495 F.Supp. 273 (D.N.J. 1980).

11. Edwards v. School Board, 483 F.Supp. 620 (W.D.Va. 1980); accord; Philbrook v. Ansonia Board of Education, 757 F.2d 476 (10th Cir. 1985) (Title VII); Rankin v. Commission on Professional Competence, 593 P.2d 852 (Cal. 1979) (state constitution); *cf.* Wondzell v. Alaska Wood Products Inc., 583 P.2d 860 (Alaska 1978); Olin v. Fair Empt. Practices Comm'n., 367 N.E.2d 1267 (Ill. 1977) (state statutes).

12. Engle v. Vitale, 370 U.S. 421 (1962). The promotion of civic virtue and public morality remains a goal of public education, but the Supreme Court has not ventured suggestions as to how public schools can either teach *about* religion or promote civic morality, without reference to or reliance upon religion.

13. School District of Abington Twp. v. Schempp, 374 U.S. 203 (1963).

14. Meltzer v. Bd. of Pub. Instruction, etc. 548 F.2d 559 (5th Cir. 1977); Mangold v. Albert Gallatin Sch. District, 438 F.2d 1194 (3rd Cir. 1971).

teachers or students,[15] requested by students,[16] or conducted before, during, or after school hours.[17] Recitations, without the word "God" ("We thank You for the flowers so sweet; we thank You for the food we eat; we thank You for the birds that sing, we thank You for everything") have also been banned as unconstitutional religious exercises.[18] Thus, the presence of school-sponsored religious activity, regardless of form, has to date been prohibited as an establishment of religion.[19]

Two other issues of religious significance that do not involve official school sponsorship have recently surfaced. The first is the demand by students, or the grant to them by statute, of a right of equal access to use school facilities during nonclass hours for the pursuit of voluntary prayer or religious discussion without school supervision. The second is the official provision of a moment of silence at the opening of classes for student meditation, on whatever subject they choose to pursue, including silent prayer. The few recent decisions on these questions provide some guidance, but not final answers.

With respect to the right of student access to public school facilities for optional religious activity during nonclass hours, two Circuit Courts of Appeal upheld the denial of access for such purposes by local school authorities, on the ground that allowance of such access, even without formal school approval, would nevertheless amount to unconstitutional religious sponsorship or entanglement by government with religion. After agreeing to review the second of those cases (Bender), the Supreme Court ascertained that the Circuit Court in *Bender* lacked jurisdiction to hear the case because the party appealing lacked "standing" to take the appeal. Accordingly, the Supreme Court vacated the decision of the Circuit Court, without ruling on the substantive issue, with the result that the original decision of the District Court was left in force. The District Court had ruled in favor of the students' claim to assemble for optional religious purposes as a matter of freedom of speech. With the current split between the Circuit Court of Appeal and the district court of the Third Circuit,[20] it remains unclear how the law will delineate right of access claims; and whether it will sustain or overturn the new federal Equal Access Act of 1984,[21] which requires access to public school facilities before and after school hours for religious meetings, equal to that accorded other civic meetings. The reason for uncertainty is twofold: (1) the Supreme Court of the United States has not spoken to that issue at the public school level, and (2) equal access claims have

---

15. Karen B. v. Treen, 653 F.2d 897 (5th Cir. 1981), aff'd without opinion, 102 S.Ct. 1267 (1982); Kent v. Commissioner of Education, 402 N.E.2d 1340 (Mass. 1980).

16. Collins v. Chandler Union School District, 644 F.2d 759 (9th Cir. 1981), cert. denied, 102 S.Ct. 322 (1981); Goodwin v. Cross Country School District No. 7, 394 F.Supp 417 (E.D.Ark. 1973); Hunt v. Board of Education, 321 F.Supp. 1263 (S.D.W.Va. 1971).

17. Lubbock Civil Liberties Union v. Lubbock Ind. School Dist., 669 F.2d 1038 (5th Cir. 1982); Brandon v. Board of Education of Guiderland Central School District, 635 F.2d 971 (2nd Cir. 1980), cert. denied, 102 S.Ct. 970 (1981).

18. DeSpain v. DeKalb Co. Comm. School Dist. 348 F.2d 836 (7th Cir. 1967), cert. denied, 390 U.S. 906 (1968); see also Stein v. Oshinsky 348 F.2d 999 (2d Cir. 1967), cert. denied, 384 U.S. 957 (1965).

19. Pertinent cases are collected in Annotation: 79 A.L.R.2d 1148 (1961).

20. Brandon v. Board of Education of Guiderland Central School District, 635 F.2d 971 (2nd Cir. 1980), cert denied, 102 S.Ct. 970 (1981); Bender v. Williamsport Area School Dist., 741 F.2d 538 (3rd Cir. 1984), vacated and remanded, 103 S. Ct. 1326(1986).

21. 98 Stat. 1302 (approved Aug. 11, 1984).

potentially different constitutional dimensions, depending upon whether the school considers each access request separately or has created an open period for optional student discussion as part of its own educational program, as was done in the *Bender* case. The Court of Appeals' majority and dissenting opinions in *Bender* are reproduced at the end of this chapter and set forth the opposing arguments to be resolved by the Supreme Court. Briefly stated, the Court will have to choose between the conclusion that even "permission" to use school facilities for religious meetings is official sponsorship or entanglement with religion, on one hand; and the argument that denial of such permission unconstitutionally denies students either the free exercise of religion or freedom of speech.

With respect to moment-of-silence statutes, the recent Supreme Court decision in *Wallace* v. *Jaffree,* which is also reproduced at the end of this chapter, provides somewhat firmer guidance. Following enactment of such statutes in some 25 states, some mentioning of "prayer" and others mentioning only "meditation"; and following case conflicts between lower state and federal courts regarding moment-of-silence statutes,[22] the majority of the Justices ruled: (1) that if the official *purpose* of a moment of silence is to promote prayer in public schools, the law is unconstitutional, without regard to the presence or absence of the word "prayer"; and (2) if the purpose of such a statute is educational and secular, and does not expressly mention and avow "prayer", then it is constitutional, even though it permits students to elect to pray silently during the silence period.

The cases on religious literature distribution in public schools clearly tend to prohibit such activities, even where the distribution is undertaken at private expense.[23] Certainly a public school teacher can be punished for proselytizing his or her religious beliefs.[24]

3. Religion-Related Curriculum Subjects

Public school curriculum is also limited by the religion clauses. In *Epperson* v. *Arkansas,* the United States Supreme Court nullified a state law that prohibited instruction on the theory that human beings evolved from a lower order of animals because that law advanced or preferred a particular religious view as to human creation.[25] The *Epperson* decision was later interpreted by lower courts to invalidate statutes that required public school texts on evolution to include equal discussion of Biblical and non-Biblical versions of human development, with a statement that the non-Biblical view was based on a

---

22. *Compare, e.g.,* Opinion of the Justices, 307 A.2d 558 (N.H. 1973); Gaines v. Anderson, 421 F.Supp. 337 (D. Mass. 1976) (upholding meditation sessions); *with* Kent v. Commissioner of Education, 402 N.E.2d 1340 (Mass. 1980) (voiding meditation statute that included "prayer"); Karen B. v. Treen, 653 F.2d 897 (5th Cir. 1981), *aff'd without opinion,* 102 S.Ct. 1267 (1982) (voiding "prayer" section of meditation statute); Malnak v. Yogi, 440 F.Supp. 1284 (D.N.J. 1977) (voiding meditation exercise of a specific sect as religious practice).

23. Meltzer v. Bd. of Pub. Inst., 548 F.2d 559 (5th Cir. 1977); Goodwin v. Cross County Sch. District, 394 F.Supp. 417 (E.D.Ark. 1973) Tudor v. Bd. of Education, 100 A. 2d 857 (N.J. 1953) (Gideon Bibles); Miller v. Cooper, 244 P.2d 520 (N.M. 1952) (religious magazine).

24. La Rocca v. Bd. of Education, 406 N.Y.S.2d 348 (1978).

25. 393 U.S. 97 (1968).

theory and not upon scientific fact.[26] The neutrality of these decisions is debatable. Absolute neutrality between religious and scientific viewpoints also eluded the Fifth Circuit Court of Appeals where parents objected to the teaching of a purely materialist version of evolution.[27] The court reasoned that teaching a subject in a way that is offensive to some religions does not offend the establishment clause, because the connection between religion and scientific evolution theory was too tenuous, notwithstanding the parties' insistence that the scientific theory violated their religious beliefs. Ignoring the Supreme Court's dictum that even secular humanism is a form of religion,[28] the court held that the parties could only complain about free exercise of religion and that subjection to the materialist view of evolution did not coerce students into acting contrary to their religion. Since the Texas statute there considered also permitted students to be excused from the evolution classes the court elected to treat the case solely in terms of Free Exercise rather than of state neutrality to religion under the establishment clause.

Further evidence of the neutrality dilemma (protecting students against instruction that favors religious belief, but not against instruction that offends religious belief) is found in other cases where courts refuse to enjoin school use of courses or texts on the view that "the [First] Amendment does not guarantee that nothing about religion will be taught in the schools, nor that nothing offensive to any religion will be taught in the schools.[29] The Michigan high court reversed a decision against the use of a novel (*Slaughterhouse Five*) in a literature course, notwithstanding parents' objections that the book's religious references were derogatory of Christianity.[30] The Court concluded that the novel's use of religious materials was appropriate literature and not anti-Christian and that teacher neutrality in handling the book would cure the book's potential offensiveness.

Parental complaints against allegedly harmful instruction have also been shunted aside by procedural rulings (e.g., by dismissing a case on procedural grounds, rather than reviewing the alleged injuriousness of an "outside" book that had not been approved by the board).[31] Such uses of judicial discretion present formidable barriers to relief against religiously offensive material in public schools.

Until the Supreme Court supplies further clarification, the following bifocal view of religion-related constitutional objections will probably prevail. Where the objector complains of instructions that favors a religious viewpoint, courts will forbid it under the establishment clause, which cannot be satisfied by exemption of objecting students from

---

26. McClean v. Arkansas Bd. of Education, 529 F.Supp. 1255 (E.D.Ark. 1982); Daniel v. Waters, 515 F.2d 485 (6th Cir. 1975); Steele v. Waters, 527 S.W.2d 72 (Tenn. 1975) and following footnote.

27. Wright v. Houston Ind. Sch. District, 486 F.2d 137 (5th Cir. 1973), cert. denied, Brown v. Houston Ind. Sch. District, 417 U.S. 969 (1974).

28. "Among religions in this country which do not teach . . . a belief in the existence of God . . . [are] Ethical Culture, Secular Humanism, and others." See Torcaso v. Watkins, 376 U.S. 488, 495, n.11 (1961).

29. Williams v. Board of Education, 388 F.Supp. 93, aff'd, 530 F.2d 972 (4th Cir. 1975). See also Davis v. Page, 385 F.Supp. 395 (D.N.H. 1974).

30. Todd v. Rochester Comm. Schools, 200 N.W.2d 90 (Mich. 1972). See authorities reviewed in the Minarcini opinion, end of Chapter 3.

31. Carroll v. Lucas, 313 N.E.2d 864 (Ohio 1974).

the course.[32] Where, however, the objector complains that government courses favor an antireligious viewpoint, courts do not invoke the establishment clause, but meet the objection as rising only under the free exercise clause, which is satisfied by exemption of objecting students from the course. The difficulties inherent in this split approach to the twin religion clauses were further compounded in an unusual case in which parents objected to the use of audio-visual equipment by their children as being contrary to their religious convictions. The court held that the Constitution did not require that the children be excused from such use unless the equipment were used only for entertainment, rather than education, in which event the children should be excused.[33] The court did not explain why government coercion of antireligious practice is constitutional in education, but not in entertainment.

a. Study of the Bible and Religious History. The Supreme Court dicta in the bible reading cases[34] strongly indicate that the Bible could be used in public schools to teach students about religion or to study the Bible as a source of literature and historical reference. Comparative study of various religions in the study of world cultures is also apparently consititutional. Similarly, the study of religion in the context of political history does not offend the establishment clause. The study of the parables of Jesus in the study of fables and parables as methods of teaching was permitted.[35] Study of the biblical account of the rise of the kingdom of Israel to contrast with the history of modern Israel to contrast with the history of modern Israel was also allowed.[36] But study of the prophecies of Daniel, accounts of God's anger over the worship of the golden calf, and the fall of Sodom and Gommorah were disapproved as carrying a religious message.[37] Courts will not permit use of the Bible in curriculum if it advances particular religious precepts.[38]

b. Sex Education. Courts have upheld the general power of state legislatures to control public school curriculum, including sensitive, such as sex-related, subjects whether by forbidding or by authorizing sex education courses. Compare the Mercer opinion with the Citizens For Parental Rights opinion at the end of this chapter.[39] Religiously based objections to content of "sex education" courses (those dealing with veneral disease, contraception, and abortion) have met with scant success in the courts. Since the legal aspects of each course depend upon particular content, method of presentation, and elective or compulsory attendance requirements; and since the form and scope of such courses continue to evolve, the decided cases provide only limited evidence where their particular facts fit later cases. Three lines of decisions have emerged. The first denies that such complainants raise any substantial constitutional

---

32. See the Schempp case at the end of this chapter.
33. Davis v. Page, 385 F.Supp. 395 (D.N.H. 1974).
34. School District of Abington Twp. v. Schempp, 374 U.S. 203, 225 (1963).
35. Wiley v. Franklin, 475 F.Supp. 390 (D.Tex. 1980).
36. *Id.*
37. *Id.*
38. Crockett v. Sorensen, 568 F.Supp. 1422 (W.D.Va. 1983).
39. *See also* Hopkins v. Bd. of Education, 289 A.2d 914 (Conn. 1971) affd. 305 A.2d 536 (Conn. 1973).

question.[40] A second line would recognize a substantial constitutional question that justifies judicial consideration.[41] The third and most representative line arose where statutes expressly exempt students whose parents raise religious objections from taking the course. In those instances, courts uniformly held that the statutory exemption obviated any unconstitutional interference with free exercise of religion.[42] They either ignored the establishment clause claim or, as in California, refused to acknowledge that sex education courses involved conflicting sexual moralities of different religions. The latter position is well illustrated by the foot-stamping opinion of the California court in *Citizens for Parental Rights* v. *San Mateo County Board of Education.*[43]

Objections to sex-oriented materials in student publications also raise distinct constitutional issues regarding speech and the press. These are discussed in Chapter 6. The dilemma posed by variable standards of religious neutrality is expressed in the following excerpt:

> "First, the mere fact that certain students are permitted to leave makes the court question whether students are being indoctrinated to religion rather than being taught within the permissible boundaries. If the course is taught within constitutional limits, every student should be required to attend. If the course is necessary to the education of one child, it is equally necessary to the education of all students. The controversial nature of a course should not be grounds for dismissing a student from its study. . . . While permitting non-attendance does not ordinarily raise constitutional questions, it does indicate that a constitutionally questionable course is being taught in this situation. If the course is being properly taught within the constitutional limits, there is no reason for nonattendance by any student." *Vaughn* v. *Reed,* 313 F.Supp. 431, 433–34 (W.D.W.Va. 1970).

Prevailing cases on controversial public school courses do not govern noncourse school activities. The following materials show that judicial evaluation of religious offensiveness varies with the subject matter in dispute.

4. Religion-Related Pageants and Displays

The overlap of religious and secular elements in historic commemorations also fuels constitutional litigation. Whether Christmas or Chanukkah pageants are primarily educational and cultural or religious in nature depends upon variables too numerous and subtle to capture in one legal formula.

In a recent series of rulings, the United States Supreme Court refused to prohibit religion-related holiday displays as a matter of course. After declining to consider a

---

40. Cornwell v. State Bd. of Education, 314 F.Supp. 340 (D.Md. 1969); affd. 428 F.2d 471 (4th Cir. 1970), cert. denied, 400 U.S. 942 (1970).

41. Valent v. New Jersey State Bd. of Educ., 274 A.2d 832 (N.J. 1971), later dismissed on procedural grounds.

42. Hobolth v. Greenway, 218 N.W.2d 98 (Mich. 1974); Medeiros v. Kyosaki, 478 P.2d 314 (Hawaii 1970).

43. Citizens for Parental Rights v. San Mateo Co. Bd. of Education, 124 Cal. Rptr. 68 (1975). *See also* Smith v. Ricci, 446 A.2d 501 (N.J. 1982).

decision that allowed the singing of Christmas carols in public school classes,[44] it upheld the constitutionality of placing nativity scenes in municipal park Christmas holiday displays. In *Lynch* v. *Donnelly*, which is reproduced at the end of this chapter,[45] the Court reasoned that such displays, at modest public expense, were primarily secular and were only incidentally religious. These park cases are not squarely controlling of public school creches, but the court's many references in the *Lynch* opinion to permitted religious displays in government buildings (including the Supreme Court chamber) may deter further litigation on this perennial controversy.

If, however, a Court finds that public officials are employing religious material for the *purpose* of advancing religious principles, rather than cultural or educational objectives, such action would be unconstitutional. Prior to upholding the above-mentioned creche cases, the Supreme Court voided a state statute that authorized the placement, at private expenses, of plaques containing the decalogue in public schools, on the ground that the 10 commandments promoted religion.[46] The Court rejected the state's claim that the use of the plaques was purely secular (to show the historic background of contemporary secular ideals of honesty and respect for fellow humans). It noted that the initial commandments relate only to man's relationship to God, a clearly religious message. This decision distinguished employment of religious sources or symbols in secular studies, such as the study of bible as history. It further avoided comment on the installation in public places of other public memorials that might contain religious symbols, such as monuments to fallen patriots. On the latter question, the older cases are mixed and turn on special case facts.[47] But, as above noted, the latest opinion in *Lynch* lends support to incidental religious content in public monuments. Here also the issue may turn on matters of degree.

5. Invocations and Baccalaureate Services

The cases on the constitutionality of invocations, benedictions, and religious services at public school meetings and graduation ceremonies are also mixed. In *Wiest* v. *Mt. Lebanon Sch. District*,[48] 54 plaintiffs sued to enjoin the school district from authorizing a clergyman to give an invocation and benediction at the high school graduation exercises.

---

44. Florey v. Sioux Falls School District, 619 F.2d 1311 (8th Cir. 1980) cert. denied, 449 U.S. 987 (1980).

45. Lynch v. Donnelly, 465 U.S. 668 (1984); semble: McCreary v. Stone, ________105 S.Ct. 1859.

46. Stone v. Graham, 449 U.S. 39 (1980). See also Ring v. Grand Forks, 483 F.Supp. 272 (D.N.Dak. 1980).

47. *Compare, e.g.*, Anderson v. Salt Lake City, Corp., 475 F.2d 29 (10th Cir. 1973) (Public monument with Ten Commandments—upheld); Opinion of the Justices, 228 A.2d 161 (N.H. 1967) (public school plaque with motto, "In God We Trust," upheld; Meyer v. Oklahoma, 496 P.2d 789 (Okla. 1972), cert denied, 409 U.S. 980 (1972); Paul v. Dade County, 202 So.2d 833 (Fla. 1967); cert denied, 207 So.2d 690 (Fla. 1967), cert. den., 390 U.S. 1041 1968). *But see contra:* Fox v. City of Los Angeles, 587 P.2d 663 (Cal. 1978) (city Display of Lighted Cross); Eugene Sand & Gravel Inc. v. City of Eugene 558 P.2d 338 (Ore. 1976) (city display of Latin Cross). Older case authorities on religious displays on public property are collected in Annotation: Religious Freedom—Public Symbols, 36 A.L.R.3d 1256 (1971). Laurence v. Buckmueller, 253 N.Y.S.2d 87 (1958); Borg v. Kolmorgen, 181 N.Y.S.2d 230 (1958); Allen v. Hickel, 424 F.2d 944 (D.C. Cir. 1970); Allen v. Morton, 495 F.2d 65 (D.C.Cir. 1973).

48. 320 A.2d 362 (Pa. 1974), cert. denied, 419 U.S. 967 (1974).

The state court dismissed the complaint, and found the traditional practice to be a permissible accommodation of religion, not unlike other occasional public ceremonies. It reasoned that, in degree, the practice did not threaten undue interdependence between religion and the state. Although the issue was religious establishment, and not solely free exercise, the *Wiest* opinion stressed that student attendance was optional and was not a requirement for graduation. Invocations at graduation ceremonies in public schools were also upheld in other states,[49] but the Supreme Court has not directly considered this question. Its refusal to review the *Wiest* case and a similar decision from Florida leaves the question open to independent rulings in other states.[50] The dicta in the *Wallace* and *Lynch* cases, which appear at the end of this chapter, may be argued to support such activity as falling within exceptions recognized by the Supreme Court for ceremonial occasions that are primarily secular in nature. Whether that argument will prevail in the public school convocation context, however, must await further court decisions.

Where graduation exercises were conducted inside a church, the church-state involvement was too direct to survive constitutional challenge, even though students organized the program for optional attendance.[51]

6. Religious Teachers and Religious Garb

A member of a religious order cannot be constitutionally excluded from employment as a public school teacher solely by reason of religious belief and association.[52] The fact that a minister- or nun-teacher is committed to donate his or her wages to a religious institution was deemed not constitutionally relevant, and a private, rather than government, concern.[53]

The wearing of religious garb by public school teachers raises the question whether such garb introduces religious influence into public education. In the absence of a statute or regulation to the contrary, few cases ruled that clergymen and nuns, no less than other teachers, could dress as they pleased.[54] But at least one court upheld a superintendent's order forbidding the use of such garb by public school teachers to be a reasonable regulation.[55] Legislation in several states expressly prohibits teacher use of religious garb in public schools, and the question has not reached the United States Supreme Court. The balance between the teacher's constitutional choice of dress and the state's right to exclude sectarian influence will turn on the determined impact of such garb. Few citizens would litigate or complain about individual use of small insignia, such as crosses or stars of David; or about the small caps of female Mennonites or the occasional use of a fez by muslims. Such questions are rarely litigated, but one court has

---

49. Grossburg v. Deusebio, 380 F.Supp. 285 (E.D.Va. 1974); Goodwin v. Cross County Sch. District, 394 F.Supp. 417 (E.D. Ark. 1973); Lincoln v. Page, 241 A.2d 799 (N.H. 1968).

50. See concurring opinion in Chamberlin v. Dade County Bd. of Public Instruction, 377 U.S. 402 (1964).

51. Lemke v. Black, 376 F.Supp. 87 (E.D.Wis. 1974).

52. Buford v. Southeast Dubois County Sch. Corp.,472 F.2d 890 (7th Cir. 1972) *See, e.g.*, McDaniel v. Patty, 435 U.S. 618 (1978); Civil Rights Act of 1964, 42 U.S.C. §2000(e).

53. Hysong v. Sch. District, 30A2d 482 (Pa. 1894); Rawlings v. Butler, 290 S.W.3d 801 (Ky. 1956).

54. See Hysong and Rawlings cases; Moore v. Bd. of Education, 212 N.E.2d 833 (Ohio 1965).

55. O'Connor v. Hendrich, 77 N.E. 612 (N.Y. 1906).

focused the issue in terms of what is *distinctively* religious garb and not in terms of any religious symbol, however unobtrusive.[56]

7. Dual Enrollment and Special Services to Church-School Students

Government assistance to private school children is often channeled through state agencies, including local school districts. Chapter 10 discusses forms of aid that involve public school administration and use of public school employees. The legality of such programs depends upon a variety of factors, including the nature of different services (health, welfare, or educational), the sources of funding, and their location and duration. The one general observation that may be ventured is that public schools and public school districts may not be organized, controlled by, or turned over to any church or sectarian body.[57]

a. Federally Funded Programs. Federal laws that fund benefits to children in both public and nonpublic schools typically require public authorities to administer such benefits. Public school authorities may not disregard federal conditions on the use of federal funds because state laws prohibit what the federal law commands. In *Wheeler* v. *Barrera* the United States Supreme Court held that Missouri school authorities could not receive and hold funds provided by federal law for nonpublic as well as public school children, while refusing to spend the funds for religious school students.[58] The Court noted that Congress could not force state officials to violate their state laws, but it insisted that Congress could limit each state to complying with federal legislation or returning the aid. Many states have avoided such conflicts by interpreting state law restrictions to control only state and not federal funds. Missouri is one of the few states (if not the only) whose courts have held that state law bars dual enrollment and public educational services to private school children.[59]

The constitutionality of various forms of federal and state financial assistance to private church-sponsored education is considered in Chapter 10. The Supreme Court has indicated that the Constitution does not bar public school authorities from administering federal benefits to church-school students if the particular benefit is itself constitutional.

b. State-funded Programs. State laws differentiate between admitting students to special sessions and activities that are not part of the regular public school day such as summer and evening schools special training courses, community recreation programs, and part-time enrollment in the regular daily classes, on one hand; and admission to the regular full-time school on the other. Special or supplementary public educational services open to all members of the community are not seriously challenged.

States have enacted laws to authorize part-time enrollment of nonpublic school

---

56. *See, e.g.*, O'Connor v. Hendrick, 77 N.E. 612 (N.Y. 1906). Other relevant cases are collected in Annotation: 60 A.L.R.2d 300 (1958).

57. See Ch. 10, *infra*; Americans United for Separation of Church & State v. Paire, 348 F.Supp. 506 (D.N.H. 1972); Zellers v. Huff, 236 P.2d 949 (N.M. 1951); State v. Taylor, 240 N.W. 573 (Neb. 1932).

58. 417 U.S. 402 (1974).

59. Mallory v. Barrera, 544 S.W.2d 556 (Mo. 1976).

students in regular public school classes.[60] Without a statutory mandate,[61] however, there is no obligation to open public school classes to private school students. This practice of "dual enrollment" or "shared time" has been upheld in several states as meeting the three requirements of the establishment clause; namely, a secular educational purpose, no primary effect in aid of religion, and no excessive entanglement of government and religion.[62]

Where dual enrollment courses are given within the public school, by public school personnel, and jointly attended by public and nonpublic school students, little dispute has arisen. Where public school courses are given in church-school facilities, even though controlled and administered by public school personnel and even though religious artifacts are removed from the classroom, more serious constitutional issues arise.

The Oregon and Michigan courts prohibited such programs under their state constitutions.[63] With respect to the federal constitution, the lower courts were divided on the question whether shared time classes located in religious schools violated the establishment clause.[64] The conflict appears to have been resolved by two decisions of the United States Supreme Court: *Felton* v. *Aquilar*[65] and *City of Grand Rapids* v. *Ball*,[66] which are discussed more fully in Chapter 10, and reproduced at the end of that chapter. The *Felton* decision prohibits even remedial instruction by public school personnel on the premises of operating religious schools, while the *Grand Rapids* decision prohibits location of shared time programs in church schools. While the Court was closely divided, these twin decisions appear to foreclose any location of shared times within an operating religious school. They do not, however, outlaw the use of public school professionals or the location of shared time programs in nonreligious private schools. It therefore remains necessary to distinguish between the permissibility of dual enrollments as a matter of educational policy and the legality of the particular means adopted to pursue that policy.

To be distinguished from dual enrollment is the complete takeover and operation of facilities for total public school use or for total private school use. The latter situation is discussed in the following sections.

8. Leasing of Church Property for Public School Use

The authority of school districts to lease private property for public school needs is qualified by the establishment clause. Such leases must exclude terms that aid religion or

60. See, e.g., 24 Pa. Stat. Ann. §5–502.

61. Citizens to Advance Public Education v. Porter, 237 N.W.2d 232 (Mich. 1976); Morton v. Bd. of Education, 216 N.E.2d 305 (Ill. 1966); *In re* Proposal C, 185 N.W.2d 9 (Mich. 1971).

62. Snyder v. Charlotte Public School Dist., 333 N.W.2d 542 (Mich. 1983).

63. Fisher v. Clackamas Cty. Sch. District, 507 P.2d 839 (Ore. 1973); State v. Sch. District No. 10,472 P.2d 1013 (Mont. 1970).

64. *Compare, e.g.,* Americans United For Separation of Church & State v. Paire, 348 F.Supp. 506 (D.N.H. 1972), *with* Citizens to Advance Pub. Education v. Porter, fn. 61, *supra.* See also State v. Neb. State Bd. of Education 195 N.W.2d 161 (Neb. 1972) cert. denied, 409 U.S. 921 (1972); Thomas v. Schmidt, 397 F. Supp. 203 (D.R.I. 1975).

65. ________ U.S. ________; 105 S.Ct. 3232 (1985).

66. ________ U.S. ________; 105 S.Ct. 3216 (1985).

create "excessive" entanglement. Courts have disapproved leases of parochial school buildings for public school use where the religious furnishings and garb of religious teachers were maintained in the leased facilities.[67] But leases of church-owned buildings that were fully staffed and controlled by public school authorities, without religious symbols furnishings or instruction, were sustained.[68]

Courts are more reluctant to uphold leases of only a part of an entire church-related building. The close proximity of religious and secular functions engenders concern over possible church-state entanglement. Nevertheless, a Rhode Island court upheld the part-time lease of a Catholic school by public school authorities though the facility was used at other times by the Catholic school. The court found that the school-church contacts were sufficiently minimal to satisfy the constitution.[69]

9. Use of Public School Buildings by Church Groups

As already noted, the use of public school facilities for nonsectarian community purposes during nonschool hours is authorized in many states. Older cases have upheld usage by religious groups where there is no substantial support for religion.[70] On the critical question—what uses involve support of religion—the later cases stress such factors as the nature, frequency, and duration of the religious groups' use and the relative gain or cost to the school district. For example, a lease at full fair-market rental of a state college stadium to Reverend Billy Graham for religious meetings, for periods when the stadium was not needed for college purposes, was upheld as a purely commercial transaction, involving no state aid to religion,[71] and the lease of a public school building for use as a Catholic mission was upheld in Florida.[72] Several older state cases have upheld occasional accommodation of church groups seeking to use school buildings for Sunday services in exigent circumstances.[73]

Whether such decisions will survive challenge under Supreme Court decisions that require separation of public religious school activities (discussed above) is uncertain. On the other hand, occasional uses of school facilities and arm's length lease transactions do not involve the degree of government subsidy and involvement presented in the above-discussed *Felton* and *Grand Rapids* cases; but on the other hand, the Supreme Court has not indicated whether it would extend its strict separation thesis to occasional uses or to market value leases of government property for religious uses. The issue is complicated by the impact of different uses by religious associations. For example, a board regulation that permitted use of public schools by civic associations, but barred access to

---

67. Fisher v. Clackamas Cty. Sch. District, 507 P.2d 839 (Ore. 1973); State v. Taylor, 240 N.W. 573 (Neb. 1932); *see also* Zellers v. Huff, 236 P.2d 949 (N.M. 1951).

68. Brown v. Heller, 273 N.Y.S.2d 713 (1966); State v. Neb. State Bd. of Education, fn. 64, *supra*.

69. Thomas v. Schmidt, 397 F.Supp. 203 (D.R.I. 1975). A good analysis of the entanglement issue is contained in Buford v. S.E. DuBois Co. Sch. Corp., 472 F.2d 890 (7th Cir. 1973).

70. See D. FELLMAN, RELIGION IN AMERICAN PUBLIC LAW, p. 74, fn. 418 (1965); 79 A.L.R.2d 1148 (1961).

71. Pratt v. Arizona Bd. of Regents, 520 P.2d 514 (Ariz. 1974).

72. Cooper v. County School Bd., Fla.Sup.Ct.No. 81–3625 (11-2-82).

73. Resnick v. E. Brunswick Twp. Bd. of Education, 389 A.2d 944 (N.J. 1978); South Side Estates Baptist Church v. Board of Trustees Tax District No. 1, 115 So.2d 697 (Fla. 1959); See also Lewis v. Mandeville, 107 N.Y.S.2d 865 (1950).

a religious group for a lecture on world conditions "from a Bible viewpoint" was upheld,[74] before the United States Supreme Court held that denial of access to a state college campus based upon the religious content of the group's expression violated the First Amendment freedom of speech.[75] The *Widmar* case, which is digested at the end of this chapter, points up the potential clash between the free speech and the establishment clause of the First Amendment in the school facilities access cases. It would seem, therefore, that the particular use, rather than the user's religious affiliation, is the proper determinant of legality. The letting of public school buildings to religious groups for civic or cultural activities was found not to infringe the state constitution in New York.[76] Conversely, discrimination in favoring of religious groups (e.g., by more lenient rates of charge) in comparison to other user groups will also violate the establishment clause.[77]

B. Free Exercise of Religion

1. School Conduct Requirements

The Supreme Court has repeatedly stressed that while freedom to *believe* is absolute, that freedom to *act* upon religious belief is not. Nevertheless, constitutional protection of freedom to practice one's religion is substantial. The state must demonstrate a "compelling" official interest to enforce conduct regulations that violate the actor's religious precepts. That burden of proof on "compelling" interest is very heavy. Thus the state's interest in fostering patriotism was held not sufficient to abridge free exercise of religion by compelling students or teachers whose religion decries such action to salute the flag or recite the pledge of allegiance.[78] Similarly, regulations requiring unwilling students to stand or leave the classroom during the pledge of allegiance were also held unconstitutional infringements of student liberty.[79] The state's substantial interest in adequate citizen education was also held not sufficiently compelling to force Amish children to attend high school against their religious conscience, since proof was lacking that such children could not become responsible citizens without such schooling.[80]

Religion-based objections to school-prescribed gym costumes or to school dancing exercises were also held to be constitutional grounds to protect the recalcitrant students from school punishments.[81] The state's interest in class regularity and discipline was not

---

74. McKnight v. Bd. of Education, 76 A.2d 207 (Pa. 1950).

75. Widmar v. Vincent, 454 U.S. 263 (1981). Accord: County Hills Christian Church v. Un. School District, 560 F.Supp. 1207 (D.Kan. 1983).

76. Lewis v. Bd. of Education, 285 N.Y.S. 164 (1935).

77. Resnick v. E. Brunswick Twp Bd. of Education, 343 A.2d 127 (N.J. 1975). See the cases collected in Annotation: *Schools—Use for Religious Purposes,* 79 A.L.R.2d 1148 (1961).

78. *See* W.Va. Bd. of Education v. Barnette, 319 U.S. 624 (1943); Russo v. Central Sch. District, 469 F.2d 623 (2d Cir. 1972); Hanover v. Northrup, 325 F.Supp. 170 (D.Conn. 1970). *But see* discussion in Palmer v. Bd. of Education 603 F.2d 1271 (7th Cir. 1979), *infra,* for special circumstances where teacher cannot reject curriculum directives on religious grounds.

79. Lipp v. Morris, 579 F.2d 834 (3d Cir. 1978); Frain v. Barron, 307 F.Supp. 27 (E.D.N.Y. 1969).

80. Wisconsin v. Yoder, 406 U.S. 205 (1972).

81. Mitchell v. McCall, 143 So.2d 629 (Ala. 1962); Hardwick v. Bd. of Sch. Trustees, 205 P. 49 (Calif. 1921).

sufficiently compelling to burden religious practice. In their endeavor to describe conduct that directly contravenes religious belief, the courts have not developed sure guides. A court that excused the student from wearing religiously offensive (immodest) attire also refused to excuse her presence from the class when other students wore the religiously offensive attire. The argument that enforced attendance forced the child into a religiously offensive situation and subjected her to embarrassment because of her conspicuously different attire was rejected. Whether such reasoning would be followed in other states is an open question.

Examples of compelling state interests that justifiably burden religious practice are seen in cases of serious health and safety hazards. Statutes requiring students to be immunized against communicable diseases have been uniformly enforced and upheld against students whose religious tenets were thereby violated.[82] Where parents refused to have their children vaccinated, an Arkansas court upheld the state's authority to appoint a substitute guardian for the purpose of achieving compliance with immunization and compulsory school laws. The court expressed the dominant view that "a person's right to exhibit religious freedom ceases where it . . . transgresses the rights of others."[83] In recent years, some states have exempted conscientious objectors from immunization laws. Such statutes raise fact questions as to whether an exemption claim is based on good faith religious beliefs or only on personal opinions that are not truly religious.[84] Selective exemptions also raise discrimination problems. A Massachusetts statute that limited the immunization exemption to members of *recognized* churches was held unconstitutional, but similar statutes were sustained in New York and Kentucky.[85] The broad conception of "religion" adopted by the United States Supreme Court under the draft laws compounds the problem of distinguishing between religious and nonreligious beliefs.[86] The definition of "religion" under the Constitution has not been squarely resolved.

Free exercise claims are increasingly litigated. While there is no *universal* constitutional duty on school authorities to accommodate *all* religious interests of teachers and students,[87] the cases reviewed in section 1 of this chapter (on excusal of teachers and students to observe their mandatory religious holy days) confirm that in special circumstances such as *constitutional* duty may arise.[88] With respect to teachers and

---

82. Jacobson v. Massachusetts, 197 U.S. 11 (1905); *In re* Clark, 185 N.E.2d 128 (Ohio 1962). Bd. of Education of Mountain Lakes v. Maas, 158 A.2d 330 (N.J. 1959), cert. den. 363 U.S. 843 (1960); Mosier v. Barron County Bd. of Health, 215 S.W.2d 967 (Ky. 1948).

83. Cude v. State, 377 S.W.2d 816, 819 (Ark. 1964).

84. *Compare* State v. Miday, 140 S.E.2d 325 (N.C. 1965); *with* McCartney v. Austin, 293 N.Y.S.2d 188 (1968).

85. Dalli v. Bd. of Education, 267 N.E.2d 219 (Mass. 1971). Kleid v. Bd. of Education, 406 F.Supp. 902 (Ky. 1976); Maier v. Besser, 341 N.Y.S.2d 411 (1972); *cf.* Avard v. DuPuis, 376 F.Supp. 479 (D.N.H. 1974) (exemption provision held unconstitutionally vague).

86. See United States v. Seeger, 380 U.S. 163, 165-66 (1965) where the Court said: "We believe that under this [draft statute], the test of belief 'in a relation to a Supreme Being' is whether a given belief that is sincere and meaningful occupies a place in the life of its possessor parallel to that filled by the orthodox belief in God of one who clearly qualifies for the exemption."

87. California Teachers Assn. v. Board of Trustees, 138 Cal.Rptr. 817 (1977).

88. *See* Rankins v. Comm'n. on Prof. Competence, 593 P.2d 852 (Cal. 1979) (unauthorized absence for religious holy days held nonpunishable where substitute teachers were available). *Cf.* Sherbert v. Verner, 374 U.S. 398 (1963) (state law denying unemployment compensation to Sabbatarian who refused Saturday work as violating his religion—held unconstitutional).

employees, a statutory duty of accommodation is also required in certain circumstances by Title VII of the Civil Rights Act, that is, where such an accommodation would not impose an undue business hardship or violate the seniority rights of other employees.[89]

2. School Curriculum Requirements

The *Davis* case (discussed on p. 130) involved religion-grounded objections to required courses and materials, but the court in finding no constitutional barrier to the school requirements accepted the state's need to avoid excessive patchwork religious exemptions that could disrupt public education.

While the United States Supreme Court under the free exercise clause has condemned enforced conformity, the lower courts have tended to avoid free exercise attacks on public school course contents by insisting that challenged courses and materials were "nonsectarian." The conclusion avoids, but does not resolve, the paradox discerned by the Supreme Court long ago:

> "There is no right in a state or an instrumentality thereof to determine that a cause is not a religious one. Such a censorship of religion as the means of determining its right to survive is a denial of liberty protected by the First Amendment and included in the liberty which is within the protection of the Fourteenth Amendment." *Cantwell* v. *Connecticut,* 310 U.S. 296, 60 S.Ct. 900, 84 L.Ed. 1213 (1940).

---

89. Trans World Airlines v. Hardison, 432 U.S. 63 (1977).

Cases

Wallace v. Jaffree (II)

_______ U.S. _______; 105 S.Ct. 2479 (1985)

[*STEVENS, J.*, delivered the opinion of the Court, in which *BRENNAN, MARSHALL, BLACKMUN*, and *POWELL, JJ.*, joined. *POWELL, J.*, filed a concurring opinion. *O'CONNOR, J.*, filed an opinion concurring in the judgment. *BURGER, C.J.*, and *WHITE* and *REHNQUIST, JJ.*, filed dissenting opinions.]

Justice STEVENS delivered the opinion of the Court.

At an early stage in this litigation, the constitutionality of three Alabama statutes was questioned: (1) § 16–1–20, enacted in 1978, which authorized a one-minute period of silence in all public schools "for meditation"; (2) § 16–1–20.1, enacted in 1981, which authorized a period of silence "for meditation or voluntary prayer"; and (3) § 16–1–20.2, enacted in 1982, which authorized teachers to lead "willing students" in a prescribed prayer to "Almighty God . . . the Creator and Supreme Judge of the world."

The Court of Appeals agreed with the District Court's initial interpretation of the purpose of both §§ 16–1–20.1 and 16–1–20.2. Moreover, appellees have not questioned the holding that § 16–1–20 is valid. Thus, the narrow question for decision is whether § 16–1–20.1, which authorizes a period of silence for "meditation or voluntary prayer," is a law respecting the establishment of religion within the meaning of the First Amendment. . . .

As is plain from its text, the First Amendment was adopted to curtail the power of Congress to interfere with the individual's freedom to believe, to worship, and to express himself in accordance with the dictates of his own conscience. Until the Fourteenth Amendment was added to the Constitution, the First Amendment's restraints on the exercise of federal power simply did not apply to the States. But when the Constitution was amended to prohibit any State from depriving any personal liberty without due process of law, that Amendment imposed the same substantive limitations on the States' power to legislate that the First Amendment has always imposed on the Congress' power. . . .

When the Court has been called upon to construe the breadth of the Establishment Clause, it has examined the criteria developed over a period of many years. Thus, in *Lemon* v. *Kurtzman*, 403 U.S. 602, 612–613 (1971), we wrote:

> "Every analysis in this area must begin with consideration of the cumulative criteria developed by the Court over many years. Three such tests may be gleaned from our cases. First, the statute must have a secular legislative purpose; second, its principal or primary effect must be one that neither advances nor inhibits religion, *Board of Education* v. *Allen*, 392 U.S. 236, 243 (1968); finally, the statute must not foster 'an excessive government entanglement with religion.' [*Walz* v. *Tax Commission*, 397 U.S. 664, 674 (1970)]."

It is the first of these three criteria that is most plainly implicated by this case.

In applying the purpose test, it is appropriate to ask "whether government's actual purpose is to endorse or disapprove of religion." In this case, the answer to that question is dispositive. For the record not only provides us with an unambiguous affirmative answer, but it also reveals that the enactment of § 16–1–20.1 was not motivated by any clearly secular purpose—indeed, the statute had *no* secular purpose.

The unrebutted evidence of legislative intent contained in the legislative record and in the testimony of the sponsor of § 16–1–20.1 is confirmed by the consideration of the relationship between this statute and the two other measures that were considered in this case.

The legislative intent to return prayer to the public schools is, of course, quite different from merely protecting every student's right to engage in voluntary prayer during an appropriate moment of silence during the school day. The Legislature enacted § 16–1–20.1 despite the existence of § 16–1–20 for the sole purpose of expressing the State's endorsement of prayer activities for one minute at the beginning of each school day. The addition of "or voluntary prayer" indicates that the State intended to characterize prayer as a favored practice. Such an endorsement is not consistent with the established principle that the Government must pursue a course of complete neutrality toward religion.

Justice POWELL, concurring.
I concur in the Court's opinion and judgment that Ala. Code § 16–1–20.1 violates the Establishment Clause of the First Amendment. . . . I agree fully with *Justice O'CONNOR'S* assertion that some moment-of-silence statutes may be constitutional, a suggestion set forth in the Court's opinion as well. *Ante,* at 20.

I write separately to express additional views and to respond to criticism of the three-pronged *Lemon* test. . . . *Lemon, supra,* has not been overruled or its test modified. Yet, continued criticism of it could encourage other courts to feel free to decide Establishment Clause cases on an *ad hoc* basis. . . .

Although we do not reach the other two prongs of the *Lemon* test, I note that the "effect" of a straightforward moment-of-silence statute is unlikely to "advanc[e] or inhibi[t] religion." See *Board of Education* v. *Allen,* 392 U.S. 236, 243 (1968). Nor would such a statute "foster 'an excessive government entanglement with religion.'" *Lemon* v. *Kurtzman, supra,* at 612–613, quoting *Walz* v. *Tax Commissioner,* 397 U.S. 664, 674 (1970).

I join the opinion and judgment of the Court.

Justice O'CONNOR, concurring in the judgment.
Nothing in the United States Constitution as interpreted by this Court or in the laws of the State of Alabama prohibits public school students from voluntarily praying at any time before, during, or after the school day. Alabama has facilitated voluntary silent prayers of students who are so inclined by enacting Ala. Code § 16–1–20, which provides a moment of silence in appellees' schools each day. The parties to these proceedings concede the validity of this enactment. . . . In my view, there can be little doubt that the purpose and likely effect of this subsequent enactment is to endorse and sponsor voluntary prayer in the public schools. . . . Despite its initial promise, the *Lemon* test has

proven problematic. The required inquiry into "entanglement" has been modified and questioned, see *Mueller* v. *Allen,* 463 U.S. 388, 403 n. 11 (1983), and in one case we have upheld state action against an Establishment Clause challenge without applying the *Lemon* test at all. *Marsh* v. *Chambers,* 463 U.S. 783 (1983). The author of *Lemon* himself apparently questions the test's general applicability. See *Lynch* v. *Donnelly,* 465 U.S. ____, ____(1984). *Justice REHNQUIST* today suggests that we abandon *Lemon* entirely, and in the process limit the reach of the Establishment Clause to state discrimination between sects and government designation of a particular church as a "state" or "national" one. *Post,* at ____.

Perhaps because I am new to the struggle, I am not ready to abandon all aspects of the *Lemon* test. I do believe, however, that the standards announced in *Lemon* should be reexamined and refined in order to make them more useful in achieving the underlying purpose of the First Amendment. We must strive to do more than erect a constitutional "signpost," *Hunt* v. *McNair,* 413 U.S. 734, 741 (1973), to be followed or ignored in a particular case as our predilections may dictate. . . . Last Term, I proposed a refinement of the *Lemon* test with this goal in mind. *Lynch* v. *Donnelly,* 465 U.S., at ____(concurring opinion).

The *Lynch* concurrence suggested that the religious liberty protected by the Establishment Clause is infringed when the government makes adherence to religion relevant to a person's standing in the political community. . . .

The endorsement test does not preclude government from acknowledging religion or from taking religion into account in making law and policy. It does preclude government from conveying or attempting to convey a message that religion or a particular religious belief is favored or preferred. . . .

Twenty-five states permit or require public school teachers to have students observe a moment of silence in their classrooms.[1] A few statutes provide that the moment of silence is for the purpose of meditation alone. See Ariz. Rev. Stat. Ann. § 15–522 (1984); Conn. Gen. Stat. § 10–16a (1983); R.I. Gen. Laws § 16–12–3.1 (1981). The typical statute, however, calls for a moment of silence at the beginning of the school day during which students may meditate, pray, or reflect on the activities of the day. See *e.g.*, Ark. Stat. Ann. § 80–1607.1 (1980); Ga. Code Ann. § 20–2–1050 (1982); II Rev. Stat. ch. 122, § 771 (1983); Ind. Code § 20–10.1–7–1 (1982); Kan. Stat. Ann. § 72–5308a (1980); Pa. Stat. Ann., Tit. 24, § 15–1516.1 (Purdon Supp. 1984). Federal trial court have divided on the constitutionality of these moment of silence laws. Compare *Gaines*

---

1. See Ala. Code §§ 16–1–20, 16–1–20.1 (Supp. 1984): Ariz. Rev. Stat. Ann. § 15-522 (1984); Ark. Stat. Ann. § 80–1607.1 (1980); Conn. Gen. Stat. § 10–16a (1983); Del. Code Ann., Tit. 14, § 4101 (1981) (as interpreted in Del. Op. Atty. Gen. 79–I011 (1979)); Fla. Stat. § 233.062 (1983); Ga. Code Ann. § 20–2–1050 (1982); Ill. Rev. Stat., ch. 122, ¶ 771 (1983); Ind. Code § 20–10.1–7–11 (1982); Kan. Stat. Ann. § 72.5308a (1980); La. Rev. Stat. Ann. § 17:2115(A) (West 1982); Me. Rev. Stat. Ann., Tit. 20-A, § 4805 (1983); Md. Educ. Code Ann. § 7–104 (1985); Mass. Gen. Laws Ann., ch. 71, § 1A (1982); Mich. Comp. Laws Ann. § 380.1565 (Supp. 1984–1985); N.J. Stat. Ann. § 18A:36–4 (West Supp. 1984–1985); N.M. Stat. Ann. § 22–5–4.1 (1981); N.Y. Educ. Law § 3029–a (McKinney 1981); N.D. Cent. Code § 15–47–30.1 (1981); Ohio Rev. Code Ann. § 3313.60.1 (1980); Pa. Stat. Ann., Tit. 24, § 15.1516.1 (Purdon Supp. 1984–1985); R.I. Gen. Laws § 16–12–3.1 (1981); Tenn. Code Ann. § 49–6–1004 (1983); Va. Code § 22.1–203 (1980); W.Va. Const., Art. III, § 15-a. For a useful comparison of the provisions of many of these statutes, see Note, Daily Moments of Silence in Public Schools: A Constitutional Analysis, 58 N.Y.U.L. Rev. 364, 407–408 (1983).

v. *Anderson,* 421 F. Supp. 337 (Mass. 1976) (upholding statute) with *May* v. *Cooperman,* 572 F. Supp. 1561 (NJ 1983) (striking down statute); *Duffy* v. *Las Cruces Public Schools,* 557 F. Supp. 1013 (NM 1983) (same); and *Beck* v. *McElrath,* 548 F. Supp. 1161 (MD Tenn. 1982) (same). See also *Walter* v. *West Virginia Board of Education,* Civ. Action No. 84–5366 (SD W. Va., Mar. 14, 1985) (striking down state constitutional amendment). Relying on this Court's decisions disapproving vocal prayer and Bible reading in the public schools, see *Abington School District* v. *Schempp,* 374 U.S. 203 (1963), *Engle* v. *Vitale, supra,* the courts that have struck down the moment of silence statutes generally conclude that their purpose and effect is to encourage prayer in public schools.

The *Engle* and *Abington* decisions are not dispositive on the constitutionality of moment of silence laws. . . .

A state sponsored moment of silence in the public schools is different from state sponsored vocal prayer or Bible reading. First, a moment of silence is not inherently religious. Silence, unlike prayer or Bible reading, need not be associated with a religious exercise. Second, a pupil who participates in a moment of silence need not compromise his or her beliefs. . . . Scholars and at least one member of this Court have recognized the distinction and suggested that a moment of silence in public schools would be constitutional. . . .

By mandating a moment of silence, a State does not necessarily endorse any activity that might occur during the period. Cf. *Widmar* v. *Vincent,* 454 U.S. 263, 272, n. 11.

Chief Justice BURGER, dissenting.

Some who trouble to read the opinions in this case will find it ironic—perhaps even bizarre—that on the very day we heard arguments in this case, the Court's session opened with an invocation for Divine protection. Across the park a few hundred yards away, the House of Representatives and the Senate regularly open each session with a prayer. These legislative prayers are not just one minute in duration, but are extended, thoughtful invocations and prayers for Divine guidance. They are given, as they have been since 1789, by clergy appointed as official Chaplains and paid from the Treasury of the United States. Congress has also provided chapels in the Capitol, at public expense, where Members and others may pause for prayer, meditation—or a moment of silence.

Inevitably some wag is bound to say that the Court's holding today reflects a belief that the historic practice of the Congress and this Court is justified because members of the Judiciary and Congress are more in need of Divine guidance than are schoolchildren. . . .

I make several points about today's curious holding.

(a) It makes no sense to say that Alabama has "endorsed prayer" by merely enacting a new statute "to specify expressly that voluntary prayer is *one* of the authorized activities during a moment of silence," *ante,* at 12 (O'CONNOR, *J.,* concurring in the judgment) (emphasis added). . . .

(c) The Court's extended treatment of the "test" of *Lemon* v. *Kurtzman,* 403 U.S. 602 (1971), suggests a naive preoccupation with an easy, bright-line approach for addressing constitutional issues. We have repeatedly cautioned that *Lemon* did not establish a rigid caliper capable of resolving every Establishment Clause issue, but that it sought only to provide "signposts." . . . In any event, our responsibility is not to apply tidy formulas by rote; our duty is to determine whether the statute or practice at issue is a step toward establishing a state religion.

Justice WHITE, dissenting.
For the most part agreeing with the opinion of the Chief Justice, I dissent from the Court's judgment invalidating Alabama Code § 16–1–20.1. . . .

As I read the filed opinions, a majority of the Court would approve statutes that provided for a moment of silence but did not mention prayer. But if a student asked whether he could pray during that moment, it is difficult to believe that the teacher could answer in the affirmative. If that is the case, I would not invalidate a statute that at the outset provided the legislative answer to the question "May I pray?" This is so even if the Alabama statute is infirm, which I do not believe it is . . .

Justice REHNQUIST, dissenting.
The "wall of separation between church and State" is a metaphor based on bad history, a metaphor which has proved useless as a guide to judging. It should be frankly and explicitly abandoned.

The Court has more recently attempted to add some mortar to *Everson's* wall through the three-part test of *Lemon* v. *Kurtzman, supra,* at 614–615, which served at first to offer a more useful test for purposes of the Establishment Clause that did the "wall" metaphor. Generally stated, the *Lemon* test proscribes state action that has a sectarian purpose or effect, or causes an impermissible governmental entanglement with religion. *E.g., Lemon, supra.* . . .

The secular purpose prong has proven mercurial in application because it has never been fully defined, and we have never fully stated how the test is to operate. . . .

The entanglement prong of the *Lemon* test came from *Walz* v. *Tax Commission,* 397 U.S. 664, 674 (1970). *Walz* involved a constitutional challenge to New York's time-honored practice of providing state property tax exemptions to church property used in worship. The *Walz* opinion . . . upheld tax exemption. . . . One of the difficulties with the entanglement prong is that, when divorced from the logic of *Walz,* it creates an "insoluable paradox" in school aid cases: we have required aid to parochial schools to be closely watched lest it be put to sectarian use, yet this close supervision itself will create an entanglement. . . .

These difficulties arise because the *Lemon* test has no more grounding in the history of the First Amendment than does the wall theory upon which it rests. . . . The results from our school services cases show the difficulty we have encountered in making the *Lemon* test yield principled results.

For example, a State may lend to parochial school children geography textbooks[2] that contain maps of the United States, but the State may not lend maps of the United States for use in geography class.[3] A State may lend textbooks on American colonial

2. *Board of Education* v. *Allen,* 392 U.S. 236 (1968).

3. *Meek,* 421 U.S., at 362–366. A science book is permissible, a science kit is not. See *Wolman,*

history, but it may not lend a film on George Washington, or a film projector to show it in history class. A State may lend classroom workbooks, but may not lend workbooks in which the parochial school children write, thus rendering them nonreusable.[4] A State may pay for bus transportation to religious schools[5] but may not pay for bus transportation from the parochial school to the public zoo or natural history museum for a field trip.[6] A State may pay for diagnostic services conducted in the parochial school but therapeutic services must be given in a different building; speech and hearing "services" conducted by the State inside the sectarian school are forbidden, *Meek* v. *Pittenger,* 421 U.S. 349, 367, 371 (1975), but the State may conduct speech and hearing diagnostic testing inside the sectarian school, *Wolman,* 433 U.S., at 241. Exceptional parochial school students may receive counseling, but it must take place outside of the parochial school,[7] such as in a trailer parked down the street. *Id.*, at 245. A State may give cash to a parochial school to pay for the administration of State-written tests and state-ordered reporting services,[8] but it may not provide funds for teacher-prepared tests on secular subjects.[9] Religious instruction may not be given in public school,[10] but the public school may release students during the day for religion classes elsewhere, and may enforce attendance at those clases with its truancy laws.[11]

These results violate the historically sound principle "that the Establishment Clause does not forbid governments . . . to [provide] general welfare under which benefits are distributed to private individuals, even though many of those individuals may elect to use those benefits in ways that 'aid' religious instruction or worship." *Committee for Public Education* v. *Nyquist,* 413 U.S. 756, 799 (1973) (*BURGER, C.J.*, concurring in part and dissenting in part). It is not surprising in the light of this record that our most recent opinions have expressed doubt on the usefulness of the *Lemon* test. . . .

Mercer v. Michigan State Board of Education

379 F.Supp. 580 (E.D. Mich. 1974)

MEMORANDUM OPINION AND ORDER

JOINER, District Judge.

I. Background

. . . Plaintiffs seek declaratory relief and preliminary and permanent injunctions prohibiting enforcement of Michigan Statutes Annotated, §§ 15.3782 and 15.3789(3), M.C.L.A. §§ 340.782 and 340.789c, which prohibit instruction, advice or information

433 U.S., at 249.

4. See *Meek, supra,* at 354–355, nn. 3, 4, 362–366.
5. *Everson* v. *Board of Education,* 330 U.S. 1 (1947).
6. *Wolman, supra,* at 252–255.
7. *Wolman, supra,* at 241–248; *Meek, supra,* at 352, n. 2, 367–373.
8. *Regan,* 444 U.S., at 648, 657–659.
9. *Levitt,* 413 U.S., at 479–482.
10. *Illinois ex rel.* v. *McCollum* v. *Board of Education,* 333 U.S. 203 (1948).
11. *Zorach* v. *Clauson,* 343 U.S. 306 (1952).

on the subject of birth control in the course of sex and health education classes in the Michigan schools, and further involve parents withdrawing a student for no reason, other than the parents' own from classes on sex education, hygiene, or the symptoms of disease. The plaintiff Richard Goldfine is a physician, and the plaintiff Alexander Mercer is a teacher in the Detroit school systems. . . .

III. The Constitutional Issues

Mercer's basic contention is that his First Amendment rights are being infringed by the statutory prohibition against teaching birth control. Mercer's contention is in essence a question of who controls the school's curriculum and to what extent.

The Supreme Court has answered the question in part by recognizing the undoubted right of the State to establish the curriculum. *Epperson* v. *Arkansas,* 393 U.S. 97, 107, 89 S.Ct. 266, 21 L.Ed. 2d 228 (1968). The Supreme Court has also recognized that the right of the State is not absolute. *Meyer* v. *Nebraska,* 262 U.S. 390, 43 S.Ct. 625, 67 L.Ed. 1042 (1923), and *Epperson* v. *Arkansas, supra.* It is the duty of this court to sift the law and the facts and determine whether or not the State has overstepped its boundaries in prohibiting the teaching of birth control.

The State may establish its curriculum either by law or by delegation of its authority to the local school boards and communities. This is a long recognized system of operation within our Nation. . . .

The statutes under attack represent both forms of curriculum establishment. *Michigan Statutes Annotated* § 15.3782 forbids the teaching of birth control. Other statutes authorize the communities to establish a sex education program. The statute neither commands that such a program be established nor forbids its establishment. Thus the wants and needs of a tiny rural community wherein sex education might be vehemently opposed, and the wants and needs of the cosmopolitan university-oriented community that might be overwhelmingly in favor of sex education are both accommodated. The statute permits individual community members to be accommodated still further by permitting withdrawal of children from any sex education programs.

Among other things, teachers are engaged to impart to the students the various bodies of knowledge and learning contained in and offered by the curriculum. There is nothing in the First Amendment that gives a person employed to teach the Constitutional right to teach beyond the scope of the established curriculum. Nor are there any judicial decisions giving the teacher the right to teach beyond an established curriculum.

There are cases which touch on curriculum control. The Supreme Court struck down a law which " . . . sought to prevent . . . teachers from discussing the theory of evolution because it is contrary . . . " to the Book of Genesis, *Epperson, supra,* p. 107, 89 S.Ct. p. 272. The law was struck down on First Amendment Anti-establishment grounds.

Meyer v. *Nebraska,* 262 U.S. 390, 43 S.Ct. 625, 67 L.Ed, 1042 (1923), involved a teacher in a private school who was criminally prosecuted for teaching the German language. The statute there was struck down because it unconstitutionally interfered with the right of the individual guaranteed by the Due Process Clause to engage in any of the common occupations of life. The present case does not involve any of those three factors, to wit: a private school teacher, a statute including criminal sanctions or a common occupation of life.

On the other hand, courts have realized that certain limitations on what is to be taught are necessary. In *Goldwasser* v. *Brown,* 135 U.S.App.D.C. 222, 417 F.2d 1169 (1969), a teacher had been fired for what he had said in the classroom. The court sustained the firing despite protestations of suppression of First Amendment rights. The teacher had been hired to teach English and not to express his views on the Nation's Viet Nam policies and Anti-Semitism. There is a balancing test: the State's interest in heightening the level of the public services it offers by assuring the efficiency of its employees in the performance of their tasks on the one hand, and the teachers' free speech interest on the other hand. In *Goldwasser* the employer thought English was best taught by omitting controversial and politically explosive issues; here, the State apparently believes its educational goals are best accomplished by omitting any discussion of birth control.

The application of *Goldwasser* to the present case is not an inappropriate decision. The whole range of knowledge and ideas cannot be taught in the limited time available in public school. This is especially true as to any given year or to any given course. Additionally, it is important that a student's program fit together and it therefore becomes necessary to make certain choices. The authorities must choose which portions of the world's knowledge will be included in the curriculum's programs and courses, and which portions will be left for grasping from other sources, such as the family, peers or other institutions.

Parents are not compelled to send their children to public schools. They are presented with a choice. They may opt to send their children to either public or private schools. This is a choice which is protected by the Constitution, *Pierce* v. *Society of Sisters,* 268 U.S. 510, 45 S.Ct. 571, 69 L.Ed. 1070 (1925). This gives the parents a degree of authority concomitant with the State and the local authorities in molding, shaping and selecting the type of education to which their children are exposed. Often the most obvious reason for choosing one over the other is a desire for sectarian or nonsectarian educations.

The parents who send their children to public schools accept the curriculum which is offered with certain limited exceptions. Parents may and often times do work at local and state levels in an effort to add to or delete from the curriculum certain material. Part of this state's curriculum is a further option for the parents; whether or not to permit their children to receive the benefits, if any, of a sex education program implemented by the local school boards. Other such options exist perhaps in choosing whether or not to take a certain course or courses. No teacher has the right to demand that his particular specialty be imparted to each and every student. The legislature has seen fit to insure a particularly sensitive subject be left to the wisdom of parents. *See Goldwasser* v. *Brown, supra.*

The statutes which have been presented for the court's scrutiny are not overly broad nor do they violate the first Amendment Anti-establishment Clause. The State has the power to establish the curriculum or to delegate some of its authority to local agencies for the final shaping of the curriculum. It also has the power to permit the parents to make the final decision as to exactly which courses the child should take. Implicit in such a state of the law is the observation that a teacher does not have a right, Constitutional or otherwise, to teach what he sees fit, or to overrule the parents' decision as to which courses their children will take unless, of course, the State has in some manner delegated this responsibility to the teacher which is not the case here.

There is no question but that a Constitutional statute may be applied in an unconstitutional manner, but the plaintiffs' contention that the statute is vague or overbroad to the point of causing the plaintiffs to refrain from certain constitutionally protected conduct to avoid the possibility of penalty cannot be decided in this case.

There is no indication that there have been any threats or reprisals against any teacher for conduct or speech in connection with family planning courses. Problems of abuse of this sort cannot be solved in the abstract pronouncements found in declaratory judgments, but can be reached and solved only in connection with concrete problems presented after the facts have been fully defined. Solutions to this type of problem are best left until there is an ability to define specifically the acts and words that are asserted to offend, in other words, the acts and words that do not involve the teaching, advising, etc., on birth control but do fall within the overall concept of family planning or sex education.

The thrust of this suit is to obtain an abstract determination of the invalidity of the statute on its face at a time when there are no concrete problems before the court. . . . The statute on its face is valid. . . .

There is no indication there have been efforts to apply improperly the statute or that its application is causing any problems in connection with attempting to teach matters directed and authorized by the state. . . .

The defendants' motion to dismiss as to both statutes is granted. . . .

So ordered.

Citizens for Parental Rights v. San Mateo Board of Education

124 Cal. Rptr. 68 (1975)

TAYLOR, Presiding Justice.

This is an appeal by Citizens for Parental Rights, et al. (an unincorporated association of parents and as individual parents, hereafter parents), from a judgment of dismissal entered to their seventh amended class action complaint for declaratory and injunctive relief. The basic substantive question is whether the implementation of family life and sex education programs by the five respondent school districts in the jurisdiction of respondent, San Mateo County violates the constitutional rights of the individual parents and their children under the First, Ninth, Tenth and Fourteenth Amendments of the U.S. Constitution, and the parallel provisions of the California Constitution. The case also presents a question of first impression as to the constitutionality of Education Code, sections 8506 and 8701. We have concluded that the family life and sex education programs, adoption of the resource guides, and the statutes are constitutional for the reasons set forth below. . . .

In each district, the respective programs were taught by specially selected teachers who had received special training.

The exhibits filed by each of the districts consist of the Teachers' Program Guides. The guides are substantially similar in content but the level of the program, discussion tapes and reading materials increase in detail and complexity for the upper grades. . . .

Under the concept of training and guidance of children, the program also suggests for discussion a debate on "Spare the Rod and Spoil the Child" and "Children Should be Seen and not Heard." Also included are topics such as citizenship, financial responsibility, and the roles and responsibilities of children in the family. . . .

As to roles and responsibilities, it is suggested that students write a story: "My parents expect too much of me" or "My parents don't expect enough of me." Among the concepts and understandings included is that most teenagers have problems with parents and most parents have problems with teenagers. The guide suggests that the absence of problems indicate that no growth is occurring past preadolescence.

On the unit relating to normal sexual development from infancy to adulthood, the guide indicates that the teachers should not indicate that certain kinds of a behavior are good or bad, right or wrong, but indicates simply various kinds of normal behavior patterns. As to an area entitled "Unusual Behavior" which includes such topics as child molestation, exhibitionism, homosexuality and prostitution, the guide indicates that this unit is to be withheld until the background material written by the consultants is prepared. Under the concept of the family and home as the basic unit in American life, suggested for brainstorming, are topics such as what changes are taking place in family units, and include such readings as the *History of the American Family* by Kenney.

In the version used at all of the grade levels, the program clearly indicates that there are many kinds of families and that family composition may change from time to time. Among the suggested experiences are: a story describing the family and all of the significant changes that occurred in the family since the student was born; and a family scrapbook. . . .

In the unit on human reproduction, the concepts and understandings to be reviewed are the male and female reproductive systems. As to sexual intercourse, there is a special note to the teachers indicating that it should be explained as a natural sequence of studying the reproductive process, and the physiological facts should be dealt with within the framework of human love of husband and wife and the means of producing new life. As to sexual behavior, the concepts and understandings cover a broad range of behavior and emphasize that curiosity and interest about one's own body are normal and acceptable, including infantile masturbation. The teacher is told to answer questions honestly and sincerely and not to interpret the material and when covering topics, such as masturbation, contraception, abortion and divorce, to indicate that there are many different points of view concerning them, that it is important that each person live within the framework of his religion or moral code of behavior. The section on learning experiences, expressly states:

> "*Masturbation:* Excessive or prolonged masturbation is thought by psychologists to be a symptom of other emotional problems. Some religions regard masturbation (when it is consciously performed as a substitute for sexual intercourse) as an immoral act to be discouraged.
>
> "The teacher should not say that it is 'bad' or 'good' or 'right' or 'wrong' but should give the above as facts."

Under the concept heading of value of sex within the marriage are covered the legal consequences of sexual intercourse outside of marriage. The learning experience section suggests a discussion of the legal, emotional, social and spiritual consequences of sexual intercourse outside of marriage. In the concept entitled family planning, the outline lists the various factors relating to family planning. . . . The means of limiting family size include abstinence, rhythm, and contraceptives. The remaining experiences section contains the following note to the teachers: "If questions arise, pupils may be told that there are contraceptives, but that there are varying viewpoints concerning their use. . . .

"Teacher background information related to contraceptives is being prepared by the sub-committee from the Medical Society and the sub-committee on Moral & Ethical Values and will be distributed as soon as completed and approved by the Family Life Education Committee."

The allegations of the many pleadings . . . may be summarized as follows: 1) the county's Family Life Education Program . . . interfered with the parents' and the students' free exercise of religion; 2) the program was not neutral but, in fact, established a new and different religion; 3) the excusal system, pursuant to Education Code sections 8506 and 8701 did not, in fact, exist and even if an excusal system were in force, it is unconstitutional as it is discriminatory and deprives the parents and students of equal protection and due process; 4) the excusal system . . . had elements of coercion that violate the Free Establishment Clause; 5) as the program interfered with the right of parental control, it deprived the parents and students of life, liberty and the pursuit of happiness; 6) as to the right of privacy . . . the program deprived the parents of their right to control the education of their children in matters relating to marriage, the family, marriage and sex, and also deprived the students of privacy of mind as they were forced to reveal their innermost personal and private feelings and the intimate details of family life to teachers and fellow students; and 7) the program also deprived both the parents and students of equal protection, as well as procedural and substantive due process. . . . The major thrust of each of the parents' contentions on appeal is that they have alleged sufficient facts or raised factual questions as to the constitutional issues raised, so that they were at least entitled to a trial on the merits and entitled to prove the allegedly disputed questions of fact. . . .

I Contentions Relating to Freedom of Religion

The parents and amicus curiae first assert that since they have alleged violations of the Free Exercise and Establishment of Religion Clauses they have stated several causes of action. However, not all infringements of religious beliefs are constitutionally impermissible. A state may require vaccinations against disease of those who object on grounds of transgression of religious beliefs (*Jacobson* v. *Massachusetts,* 197 U.S. 11, 25 S.Ct. 358, 49 L.Ed. 643), prohibit polygamy (*Reynolds* v. *United States,* 98 U.S. 145, 25 L.Ed. 244), or require the observance of child labor laws (*Prince* v. *Massachusetts,* 321 U.S. 158, 64 S.Ct. 438, 88 L.Ed. 645). The issue, properly framed, therefore, is not whether the parents' objections to the program are a matter of religious belief, but whether the program violates the Free Exercise and Establishment Clauses of the First Amendment, as construed by the United States Supreme Court. While we recognize that the individual rights guaranteed by the Free Exercise and Establishment Clauses of the First Amendment (and the state Constitution) interface and overlap, we think a separate discussion of these two clauses is more helpful here to clarify the complex issues presented in this "extraordinarily sensitive area of constitutional law" (*Lemon* v. *Kurtzman,* 403 U.S. 602, 612, 91 S.Ct. 2105, 2111, 29 L.Ed.2d 745).

A The Free Exercise Clause

The Supreme Court of Hawaii in *Medeiros* v. *Kiyosaki* (1970) 52 Haw. 436, 478 P.2d 314, faced an identical question with an excusal system substantially like that provided by Education Code sections 8506 and 8701. . . .

In *Medeiros,* as here, the parties based their "free exercise" argument on *Abington* v. *Schempp,* 374 U.S. 203, 83 S.Ct. 1560, 10 L.Ed.2d 844. . . . As the court pointed out at page 223, 83 S.Ct. at page 1572: "The distinction between the two clauses is apparent—*a violation of the Free Exercise Clause is predicated on coercion* while the Establishment Clause violation need not be so attended." (Emphasis supplied.)

The Hawaiian court then concluded that there was no violation of the Free Exercise Clause. An identical conclusion on the same grounds was reached by the court in *Cornwell* v. *State Board of Education* (D.C.Md. 1969) 314 F.Supp. 340 (cert. den. 400 U.S. 942, 91 S.Ct. 240, 27 L.Ed.2d 246), in granting motions to dismiss for failure to present a substantial federal question. The court said at page 344: " . . . the purpose and primary effect of the bylaw here is not to establish any particular religious dogma or precept, and that the bylaw does not directly or substantially involve the state in religious exercises or in the favoring of religion or any particular religion. The bylaw may be considered quite simply as a public health measure. . . . "

The parents and amicus curiae also urge that since Education Code sections 8506 and 8701 (set forth in full below) require the affirmative election of an exemption from the program or any of its parts, an informal pressure is exerted on the students to forego the exercise of their religious beliefs. . . .

While we recognize that the U.S. Supreme Court has held in cases arising under the Establishment Clause that informal social pressures can constitute compulsion (*Abington School Dist.* v. *Schempp,* 374 U.S. 203, 83 S.Ct. 1560, 10 L.Ed.2d 844; *Engel* v. *Vitale,* 370 U.S. 421, 82 S.Ct. 1261, 8 L.Ed.2d 601), the court has never applied that reasoning to the Free Exercise Clause: for example, an express dictum in *Abington* (374 U.S. at 233, 83 S.Ct. 1560) indicating that indirect social pressures are not sufficient to cause a violation of the Free Exercise Clause. . . .

Neither *Engel* nor *Abington,* supra, support the parents' contention that the instant excusal statutes subject the students to sufficient pressure to amount to compulsion. In both *Engel* and *Abington,* the students had the option of either leaving the classroom or remaining during the religious exercises. The court's finding of compulsion was based on the fact that the students, by exercising either option, were in direct and immediate contact with their peers when they exercised their beliefs. There is simply not the same degree of pressure where, as here, pursuant to Education Code sections 8506 and 8701, the parents and the students can choose not to enroll in the program or any part of it that is objectionable. We suggest that if, in accordance with the request for an injunctive relief, the trial court had enjoined the program because it incidentally offended the religious beliefs of certain parents and students, the court would have acted in violation of the Establishment Clause. . . . . . . In sum then, the direct answer to the parents' contentions concerning free exercise is that the program against which the parents seek a permanent injunction is not compulsory as Education Code sections 8506 and 8701 provide that the student may be excused from any part that conflicts with the parents' religious beliefs or that uses materials to which the parents object. However, even assuming an infringement for the sake of argument, the incidental burden is justified by the compelling state interest in education, (*Medeiros* v. *Kiyosaki,* supra, 478 P.2d at 318; cf. *Hopkins* v. *Hamden Board of Education,* 29 Conn.Sup. 397, 289 A.2d 914).

B The Establishment of Religion Clause

. . . Although the pleadings are lacking in specificity, we glean from the exhibits and the briefs that the parents' complaint refers to the fact that, among others, the program deals with subjects such as abortion, birth control, divorce and masturbation. Our examination of these documents indicates that most of these sensitive areas are carefully delineated with cautionary instructions to the teachers to indicate that a variety of beliefs and practices exist. The teachers are also instructed to refer their students to their parents and religious counselors for guidance and information as to specifics. For example, under the subject of birth control, all present day methods are listed, Thus, there is evidence of neutrality in the religious sphere and ample support as a matter of law for the trial court's finding that the subjects are not covered from a religious point of view, but simply as public health matters. . . .

Nor can we find any indication in the guidelines that the program affirmatively espouses the view that religious beliefs are irrelevant to matters of family life and sex. To the contrary, the program encompasses a wide variety of family life styles and in careful recognition of the diversity of religions and points of view that enhance and enrich the diverse culture and population of the country and the Bay Area, directs the instructors to refer students to their parents or religious advisors for specific instruction. . . . . . . The fact that the parents possess certain ideas or views concerning family life relationships and sex which are based on moral standards that are the outgrowth of their religious principles does not make the teaching of sex education and family life religious in nature, nor does it constitute the establishment of a religion in the public schools. Thus, the trial court properly concluded that the complaint alleged no triable factual issues as to these matters. . . . "We agree of course that the State may not establish a 'religion of secularism' in the sense of affirmatively opposing or showing hostility to religion, thus 'preferring those who believe in no religion over those who do believe.' *Zorach* v. *Clauson,* supra, 343 U.S. at 314, 72 S.Ct. [679] at 684, 96 L.Ed. 954. We do not agree, however, that this decision in any sense has that effect. . . .

II Equal Protection and Substantive Due Process

We turn next to the contention that the program deprives them of equal protection and due process under the U.S. Constitution. As the program on its face applies to all students equally and is taught to all students of mixed religious beliefs without discrimination, there is no denial of equal protection . . .

As to substantive due process, we find persuasive the following from *Cornwell* v. *State Board of Education,* supra, 314 F.Supp. 342:

> "*There is first no denial of substantive due process to the plaintiffs.* Under Section 6 of Article 77 of the Maryland Code (as amended and re-codified by Chapter 405 of the Acts of 1969), the State Board is directed to determine the educational policies of the state and to enact bylaws for the administration of the public school system, which when enacted and published shall have the force of law. Assuredly *it cannot be said that the bylaw here is an arbitrary or unreasonable exercise of the authority vested* in the State Board to determine a teaching curriculum, nor *that there is no basis in fact for the legislative policy expressed in the bylaw.*" (Emphasis added; cf. *Medeiros* v. *Kiyosaki,* 478 P.2d 314, at 319–320.) . . .

III Privacy, "Parental Authority" and the Asserted Exclusive Constitutional Right to Teach Family Life and Sex Education Only at Home

. . . "[A]lthough the right of privacy is *not specifically* afforded in the First Amendment of the United States Constitution, the Supreme Court of the United States has held that the Amendment ' . . . has a penumbra where privacy is protected from governmental intrusion'." *Griswold* v. *Connecticut,* 381 U.S. 479, 483, 85 S.Ct. 1678, 1681, 14 L.Ed.2d 510(1968). . . .

The county in formulating policies for the adoption of the program anticipated possible objections by parents and guardians to the program. The Legislature, pursuant to Education Code sections 8506 and 8701, therefore, *established an "excusal system" whereby parents and guardians had the option of withholding or withdrawing their children from the program by submitting a written excuse to the school.*

We view the dual statutory "excusal system" as an effort by the county and state to allow those parents or guardians who might object to the program or any part of it on moral or religious grounds to have their children excused. *The program was in no way compulsory,* and, therefore, we cannot see how the state by "unnecessarily broad means" contravened the parents' right of privacy. . . .

The parents and amicus curiae also contend that the program invades the students' right of privacy by requiring them to reveal their innermost thoughts, conversations and facts relating to the personal and intimate lives of their families and invade the privacy of mind of the parents and students. We cannot agree that the subject matter discussed by the program compels the disclosures mentioned by the parents. The same applies to the asserted right of exclusive parental control and authority. . . .

Finally, the parents and amicus curiae contend that they have an exclusive constitutional right to teach their children about family life and *sexual matters in their own homes, and that such exclusive right would prohibit the teaching of these matters in the schools.* No authority is cited in support of this novel proposition, and this court knows of no such constitutional right (cf. *Cornwell* v. *State Board of Education,* 314 F.Supp. 340, 342). . . .

We conclude, therefore that the trial court properly concluded . . . the parents have failed to raise any substantial constitutional issues or any factual issues that would entitle them to the declaratory or injunctive relief sought. . . .

KANE, Associate Justice (dissenting).

I dissent. Notwithstanding the fact that the fundamental question in this appeal is a procedural one, the proper resolution of which renders any discussion of the substantive constitutional issues premature, the majority reaches the latter by a cavalier disposal of the former in a footnote.

In doing so, the majority has reached a conclusion which is contrary to both the spirit and the law of pleading in this state and, in my opinion, has countenanced the unsavory practice of "judge-shopping" which is specifically prohibited by Code of Civil Procedure, section 1008.

The results of the court's holding are (1) an unnecessary treatise on constitutional principles which are discussed in the abstract for the simple reason that the issues raised by the pleadings have not been filled in with evidentiary support and amplification, and (2) a denial of the right of the plaintiffs to attempt to factually prove their bases for relief. . . .

Having traveled a very tortuous route of demurrers, motions for judgment on the pleadings and summary judgment, followed by a detailed pretrial conference, plaintiffs finally reached the threshold of trial only to be frustrated by a "motion to dismiss". . . .

Except for the first demurrer to the original complaint, defendants' repetitive attack on plaintiffs' pleadings was the single contention that the complaint failed to state a cause of action. . . . . . . [O]nce the exhibits were included in the complaint, defendants asserted no further objection as to uncertainty or lack of particularity in the complaint, choosing rather to assert a bare, general demurrer. The demurrer to the first amended complaint was heard by Judge Reisch, who sustained it . . . as to 12 counts . . . overruled it as to eight other counts.

Following that ruling, the defendants answered the first amended complaint. . . .

Next, defendants moved for summary judgment "on the ground that the action has no merit, and that there is no triable issue of fact". . . .

The motion for summary judgment was denied by Judge Scott. . . .

Next, pursuant to stipulation, plaintiffs filed amendments to their first amended complaint to which defendants both answered and demurred generally. The general demurrer was overruled by Judge Blum.

Next, a second motion for judgment on the pleadings "on the ground that the Complaint . . . fails to state facts sufficient to constitute a cause of action" was filed, heard, and denied by Judge Branson.

Thus, four different superior court judges concluded that plaintiffs' complaint did indeed state a cause of action on which they were entitled to go to trial. . . .

In ruling upon a general demurrer (or a motion to dismiss) the allegations of the complaint must be regarded as true. It is assumed that plaintiffs can prove all facts as alleged; defects in the complaint which do not affect the substantial rights of the parties are disregarded. . . .

In the case at bench, even a cursory reading of plaintiffs' final complaint, as amended and including the exhibits, demonstrates that a cause of action has been alleged. For example, in paragraph II of Count Eleven of the First Amended Complaint, it is alleged that

> "Portions or the content and subject matter of the Family Life Education course of study and subject matter interfere with and are contradictory to certain of plaintiffs' personal religious beliefs, and therefore are an infringement of, in contradiction to, and in violation of Amendment I of the Constitution of the United States, in that they are designed to question, affect, prohibit and interfere with the free exercise of existing religious and spiritual practices and beliefs, and to establish new or different religious and spiritual practices and beliefs that are promulgated by the State through its public school system, as illustrated by items contained in Exhibit 'E', which exhibit is attached hereto and is incorporated herein by this reference."

. . . The rule of liberal construction of pleadings has also been enhanced by the adoption of the rules for discovery whereby any uncertainty as to the factual basis of plaintiffs' cause of action can be efficiently discovered. Such was the holding in *Dahlquist v. State of California* (1966) 243 Cal.App.2d 208, 52 Cal.Rptr. 324. . . . Thus, in the case at bench if defendants were truly in doubt or uncertain as to how or in what manner plaintiffs' constitutional rights were claimed to be violated by the Family Life Education course, a simple interrogatory would have resolved any such doubt. But the record discloses that defendants engaged in no discovery whatever. It is therefore apparent that after the original demurrer defendants' one and only objection to plaintiffs' pleadings was that they failed to state a cause of action, an objection consistently rejected by four different superior court judges.

This background brings us, then, to the next logical inquiry: How, and by what authority, was a fifth judge empowered to render a decision completely contrary to his predecessors on precisely the same issue? The short answer is that he was not so empowered and that the granting of the motion to dismiss was an abuse of discretion for noncompliance with Code of Civil Procedure, section 1008. . . .

Consequently, as a matter of true substance the motion to dismiss was a "subsequent application" for the same orders previously made to each of the preceding four judges. . . .

The fact that defendants at pretrial received the right to file a motion to dismiss is of no significance whatever. Likewise, the fact that after the filing of the first amended complaint on September 11, 1968 the Legislature enacted Education Code, section 8506, is of no moment, either. . . .

First of all, section 8506 was enacted in 1969. The ruling by Judge Blum, overruling the general demurrer to the first amended complaint and amendments thereto, was filed on April 15, 1971. . . . Judge Branson's ruling was filed February 24, 1972.

Thus, it is manifestly clear that the motion to dismiss was and is nothing more than another general demurrer presented to a different judge. Code of Civil Procedure, section 1008, is a sound and essential mandate for efficient judicial administration. The fact that the sanction of contempt for a violation of the statute is expressly provided is strong evidence of its importance and the need for maintaining its integrity.

Respondents do not contend that they attempted to comply with section 1008 at all. Their argument is simply that the motion to dismiss was a new motion unrelated to the prior demurrers and motions. As we have shown, however, this contention is totally groundless since each and every prior motion or demurrer—save and except the very first demurrer—raised but one issue: Did the complaint state a cause of action? Having received the rulings of four judges that the complaint did state a cause of action, it was incumbent upon defendants in presenting their motion to dismiss to show "by affidavit what application was before made, when and to what judge, what order or decision was made thereon and *what new facts are claimed to be shown.*" (Code Civ. Proc., § 1008; emphasis added).

The record shows that plaintiffs promptly brought the provisions of section 1008 to the attention of the court by seeking to have the order granting the motion to dismiss vacated.

The pleadings filed by the plaintiffs are technically sufficient. The issues between the parties have been framed and the pretrial order provides an excellent framework in which the case can be tried on its merits. Having arduously and successfully taken their case over nearly every procedural obstacle in the civil advocates' arsenal, plaintiffs should not be denied that right. I would reverse the judgment.

Lynch v. Donnelly

465 U.S. 668 (1984)

[Suit challenging the erection of a nativity scene in the city's Christmas display in a park owned by a nonprofit organization and located in the heart of the shopping district. The United States Supreme Court held that the city's inclusion of the nativity scene or crèche in its annual Christmas display did not violate the First Amendment's establishment clause, because the city had a secular purpose for including the crèche, the city had not impermissibly advanced religion, and including the crèche did not create excessive entanglement between religion and government.]

The crèche, which has been included in the display for 40 or more years, consists of the traditional figures, including the Infant Jesus, Mary and Joseph, angels, shepherds, kings, and animals, all ranging in height from 5[mM] to 5[mN]. In 1973, when the present crèche was acquired, it cost the City $1365; it now is valued at $200. The erection and dismantling of the crèche costs the City about $20 per year; nominal expenses are incurred in lighting the crèche. No money has been expended on its maintenance for the past 10 years.

This Court has explained that the purpose of the Establishment and Free Exercise Clauses of the First Amendment is

> "to prevent, as far as possible, the intrusion of either [the church or the state] into the precincts of the other."

At the same time, however, the Court has recognized that

> "total separation is not possible in an absolute sense. Some relationship between government and religious organizations is inevitable."

There is an unbroken history of official acknowledgment by all three branches of government of the role of religion in American life from at least 1789. . . .

Beginning in the early colonial period long before Independence, a day of Thanksgiving was celebrated as a religious holiday to give thanks for the bounties of Nature as gifts from God. President Washington and his successors proclaimed Thanksgiving, with all its religious overtones, a day of national celebration and Congress made it a National Holiday more than a century ago. . . . That holiday has not lost its theme of expressing thanks for Divine aid any more than has Christmas lost its religious significance. . . .

Other examples of reference to our religious heritage are found in the statutorily prescribed national motto "In God We Trust," 36 USC § 186 [36 USCS § 186], which Congress and the President mandated for our currency, see 31 USC § 324 [31 USCS § 324], and in the language "One nation under God," as part of the Pledge of Allegiance to the American flag. That pledge is recited by thousands of public school children—and adults—every day.

Art galleries supported by public revenues display religious paintings of the 15th and 16th centuries, predominantly inspired by one religious faith. The National Gallery in Washington, maintained with Government support, for example, has long exhibited masterpieces with religious messages, notably the Last Supper, paintings depicting the Birth of Christ, the Crucifixion, and the Resurrection, among many others with explicit Christian themes and messages. The very chamber in which oral arguments on this case were heard is decorated with a notable and permanent—not seasonal—symbol of religion: Moses with Ten Commandments. Congress has long provided chapels in the Capitol for religious worship and meditation. . . .

> "The real object of the [First] Amendment was . . . to prevent any national ecclesiastical establishment, which should give to an hierarchy the exclusive patronage of the national government." 3 Story, Commentaries on the Constitution of the United States 728 (1833).

In each case, the inquiry calls for line drawing; no fixed, per se rule can be framed. The Establishment Clause like the Due Process Clauses is not a precise, detailed provision in a legal code capable of ready application. The purpose of the Establishment Clause "was to state an objective, not to write a statute." *Walz, supra,* at 668, 25 L Ed 2d 697, 90 S Ct 1409. The line between permissible relationships and those barred by the Clause can no more be straight and unwavering than due process can be defined in a single stroke or phrase or test. The Clause erects a "blurred, indistinct, and variable barrier depending on all the circumstances of a particular relationship." *Lemon, supra,* at 614, 29 L Ed 2d 745, 91 S Ct 2105.

In the line-drawing process we have often found it useful to inquire whether the challenged law or conduct has a secular purpose, whether its principal or primary effect is to advance or inhibit religion, and whether it creates an excessive entanglement of government with religion. *Lemon, supra.* But, we have repeatedly emphasized our unwillingness to be confined to any single test or criterion in this sensitive area. . . .

In two cases, the Court did not even apply the *Lemon* "test." We did not, for example, consider that analysis relevant in Marsh, supra. Nor did we find *Lemon* useful in *Larson* v. *Valente*, 456 US 228, 72 L Ed 2d 33, 102 S Ct 1673 (1982), where there was substantial evidence of overt discrimination against a particular church.

In this case, the focus of our inquiry must be on the crèche in the context of the Christmas season. See, e.g., *Stone* v. *Graham*, 449 US 39, 66 L Ed 2d 199, 101 S Ct 192 (1980) (per curiam); *Abington School District* v. *Schempp, supra.* In *Stone*, for example, we invalidated a state statute requiring the posting of a copy of the Ten Commandments on public classroom walls. But the Court carefully pointed out that the Commandments were posted purely as a religious admonition, not "integrated into the school curriculum, where the Bible may constitutionally be used in an appropriate study of history, civilization, ethics, comparative religion, or the like," 449 US, at 42, 66 L Ed 2d 199, 101 S Ct 192. Similarly, in *Abington*, although the Court struck down the practices in two States requiring daily Bible readings in public schools, it specially noted that nothing in the Court's holding was intended to "indicat[e] that such study of the Bible or of religion, when presented objectively as part of a secular program of education, may not be effected consistently with the First Amendment," 374 US, at 225, 10 L Ed 2d 844, 83 S Ct 1560. Focus exclusively on the religious component of any activity would inevitably lead to its invalidation under the Establishment Clause. . . .

The Court has invalidated legislation or governmental action on the ground that a secular purpose was lacking, but only when it has concluded there was no question that the statute or activity was motivated wholly by religious considerations. See, e.g., *Stone* v. *Graham, supra* at 41, 66 L Ed 2d 199, 101 S Ct 192; *Epperson* v. *Arkansas*, 393 US 97, 107–109, 21 L Ed 2d 228, 89 S Ct 266 (1968); *Abington School District* v. *Schempp, supra,* at 223–224, 10 L Ed 2d 844, 83 S Ct 1560; *Engel* v. *Vitale*, 370 US 421, 424–425, 8 L Ed 2d 601, 82 S Ct 1261, 86 ALR2d 1285 (1962). Even where the benefits to religion were substantial, as in *Everson, supra; Board of Education* v. *Allen*, 392 US 236, 20 L Ed 2d 1060, 88 S Ct 1923 (1968), *Walz, supra,* and *Tilton, supra* we saw a secular purpose and no conflict with the Establishment Clause. . . .

The narrow question is whether there is a secular purpose for Pawtucket's display of the crèche. The display is sponsored by the City to celebrate the Holiday and to depict the origins of that Holiday. These are legitimate secular purposes. The District Court's inference, drawn from the religious nature of the crèche, that the City has no secular purpose was, on this record, clearly erroneous.

The District Court found that the primary effect of including the crèche is to confer a substantial and impermissible benefit on religion in general and on the Christian faith in particular. . . .

But to conclude that the primary effect of including the crèche is to advance religion in violation of the Establishment Clause would require that we view it as more beneficial to and more an endorsement of religion, for example, than expenditure of large sums of public money for textbooks supplied throughout the country to students attending church-sponsored schools. . . . . . . It would also require that we view it as more of an endorsement of religion than the Sunday Closing Laws upheld in *McGowan* v. *Maryland*, 366 US 420, 6 L Ed 2d 393, 81 S Ct 1101 (1961); the release time program for religious training in *Zorach, supra;* and the legislative prayers upheld in *March, supra.*

We are unable to discern a greater aid to religion deriving from inclusion of the crèche than from these benefits and endorsements previously held not violative of the Establishment Clause. . . .

The dissent asserts some observers may perceive that the City has aligned itself with the Christian faith by including a Christian symbol in its display and this serves to advance religion. We can assume, arguendo, that the display advances religion in a sense; but our precedents plainly contemplate that on occasion some advancement of religion will result from governmental action. The Court has made it abundantly clear, however, that "not every law that confers an 'indirect,' 'remote,' or 'incidental' benefit upon [religion] is, for that reason alone, constitutionally invalid." *Nyquist, supra,* at 771, 37 L Ed 2d 948, 93 S Ct 2955; see also *Widmar* v. *Vincent,* 454 US 263, 273, 70 L Ed 2d 440, 102 S Ct 269 (1981). Here, whatever benefit to one faith or religion or to all religions, is indirect, remote and incidental; display of the crèche is no more an advancement or endorsement of religion than the Congressional and Executive recognition of the origins of the Holiday itself as "Christ's Mass," or the exhibition of hundreds of religious paintings in governmentally supported museums.

The District Court found . . . no administrative entanglement between religion and state. . . . But it went on to hold that some political divisiveness was engendered by this litigation. . . . Entanglement is a question of kind and degree. . . .

There is no evidence of contact with church authorities concerning the content or design of the exhibit prior to or since Pawtucket's purchase of the crèche. No expenditures for maintenance of the crèche have been necessary; and since the City owns the crèche, now valued at $200, the tangible material it contributes is de minimis. . . .

The Court of Appeals correctly observed that this Court has not held that political divisiveness alone can serve to invalidate otherwise permissible conduct. And we decline to so hold today. This case does not involve a direct subsidy to church-sponsored schools or colleges, or other religious institutions, and hence no inquiry into potential political divisiveness is even called for. . . . The District Court stated that the inclusion of the crèche for the 40 years has been "marked by no apparent dissension". . . .

Curiously, it went on to hold that the political divisiveness engendered by this lawsuit was evidence of excessive entanglement. A litigant cannot, by the very act of commencing a lawsuit, however, create the appearance of divisiveness and then exploit it as evidence of entanglement.

We are satisfied that the City has a secular purpose for including the crèche, that the City has not impermissibly advanced religion, and that including the crèche does not create excessive entanglement between religion and government. . . .

We hold that, notwithstanding the religious significance of the crèche, the City of Pawtucket has not violated the Establishment Clause of the First Amendment. Accordingly, the judgment of the Court of Appeals is reversed.

Justice O'CONNOR, concurring.

I concur in the opinion of the Court. I write separately to suggest a clarification of our Establishment Clause doctrine. . . .

The Establishment Clause prohibits government from making adherence to a religion relevant in any way to a person's standing in the political community.

Government can run afoul of that prohibition in two principal ways. One is excessive entanglement with religious institutions, which may interfere with the independence of the institutions, give the institutions access to government or governmental powers not fully shared by nonadherents of the religion, and foster the creation of political constituencies defined along religious lines. . . .

The second and more direct infringement is government endorsement or disapproval of religion. Endorsement sends a message to nonadherents that they are outsiders, not full members of the political community, and an accompanying message to adherents that they are insiders, favored members of the political community. Disapproval sends the opposite message. . . .

Our prior cases have used the three-part test articulated in *Lemon* v. *Kurtzman*, 403 US 602, 612–613, 29 L Ed 2d 745, 91 S Ct 2105 (1970), as a guide to detecting these two forms of unconstitutional government action. It has never been entirely clear, however, how the three parts of the test relate to the principles enshrined in the Establishment Clause. Focusing on institutional entanglement and on endorsement or disapproval of religion clarifies the Lemon test as an analytical device. . . .

Although several of our cases have discussed political divisiveness under the entanglement prong of *Lemon*, see, e.g., *Committee for Public Education* v. *Nyquist*, 413 US 756, 796, 37 L Ed 2d 948, 93 S Ct 2955 (1973); *Lemon* v. *Kurtzman, supra* at 623, 29 L Ed 2d 745, 91 S Ct 2105, we have never relied on divisiveness as an independent ground for holding a government practice unconstitutional. Guessing the potential for political divisiveness inherent in a government practice is simply too speculative an enterprise, in part because the existence of the litigation, as this case illustrates, itself may affect the political response to the government practice. Political divisiveness is admittedly an evil addressed by the Establishment Clause. Its existence may be evidence that institutional entanglement is excessive or that a government practice is perceived as endorsement of religion. But the constitutional inquiry should focus ultimately on the character of the government activity that might cause such divisiveness, not on the divisiveness itself. The entanglement prong of the *Lemon* test is properly limited to institutional entanglement. . . .

The purpose prong of the *Lemon* test asks whether government's actual purpose is to endorse or disapprove of religion. The effect prong asks whether, irrespective of government's actual purpose, the practice under review in fact conveys a message of endorsement or disapproval. An affirmative answer to either question should render the challenged practice invalid. . . .

Applying that formulation to this case, I would find that Pawtucket did not intend to convey any message of endorsement of Christianity or disapproval of nonChristian religions. . . .

Celebration of public holidays, which have cultural significance even if they also have religious aspects, is a legitimate secular purpose. . . .

Focusing on the evil of government endorsement or disapproval of religion makes clear that the effect prong of the Lemon test is properly interpreted not to require invalidation of a government practice merely because it in fact causes, even as a primary effect, advancement or inhibition of religion. The laws upheld in *Walz* v. *Tax Commission*, 397 US 664, 25 L Ed 2d 697, 90 S Ct 1409 (1970) (tax exemption for religious, educational, and charitable organizations), in *McGowan* v. *Maryland,* 366 US 420, 6 L Ed 2d 393, 81 S Ct 1101 (1960) (mandatory Sunday closing law), and in *Zorach* v. *Clauson,* 343 US 306, 96 L Ed 954, 72 S Ct 679 (1952) (released time from school for off-campus religious instruction), had such effects, but they did not violate the Establishment Clause. What is crucial is that a government practice not have the effect of communicating a message of government endorsement or disapproval of religion. . . .

Pawtucket's display of its crèche, I believe, does not communicate a message that the government intends to endorse Christian beliefs represented by the crèche. . . . The display celebrates a public holiday, and no one contends that declaration of that holiday is understood to be an endorsement of religion.

These features combine to make the government's display of the crèche . . . no more an endorsement of religion than such governmental "acknowledgments" of religion as legislative prayers of the type approved in *Marsh* v. *Chambers,* 463 US _____, 77 L Ed 2d 1019, 103 S Ct 3330 (1983), government declaration of Thanksgiving as a public holiday, printing of "In God We Trust" on coins, and opening court sessions with "God save the United States and this honorable court." Those government acknowledgments of religion serve, in the only ways reasonably possible in our culture, the legitimate secular purposes of solemnizing public occasions. . . .

Justice BRENNAN, with whom *Justice* MARSHALL, *Justice* BLACKMUN and *Justice* STEVENS join, dissenting.

The "primary effect" of including a nativity scene in the City's display is, as the District Court found, to place the government's imprimatur of approval on the particular religious beliefs exemplified by the crèche. . . .

For many, the City's decision to include the crèche as part of its extensive and costly efforts to celebrate Christmas can only mean that the prestige of the government has been conferred on the beliefs associated with the crèche, thereby providing "a significant symbolic benefit to religion. . . . " *Larkin* v. *Grendel's Den, Inc., supra,* US, at _____, 74 L Ed 2d 297, 103 S Ct 505. . . .

Finally, it is evident that Pawtucket's inclusion of a crèche as part of its annual Christmas display does pose a significant threat of fostering "excessive entanglement." As the Court notes, ante, at _____79 L Ed 2d 616, the District Court found no administrative entanglement in this case. . . .

Of course, there is no reason to disturb that finding, but it is worth noting that after today's decision, administrative entanglements may well develop. . . .

More importantly, although no political divisiveness was apparent in Pawtucket prior to the filing of respondents' lawsuit, that act, as the District Court found, unleashed powerful emotional reactions which divided the City along religious lines. 525 F Supp, at 1180. The fact that calm had prevailed prior to this suit does not immediately suggest the absence of any division on the point for, as the District Court observed, the quiescence of those opposed to the crèche may have reflected nothing more than their sense of futility in opposing the majority. Id., at 1179. Of course, the Court is correct to note that we have never held that the potential for divisiveness alone is sufficient to invalidate a challenged governmental practice; we have, nevertheless, repeatedly emphasized that "too close a proximity" between religious and civil authorities . . . may represent a "warning signal" that the values embodied in the Establishment Clause are at risk. *Committee for Public Education* v. *Nyquist, supra* at 798, 37 L Ed 2d 948, 93 S Ct 2955. Furthermore, the Court should not blind itself to the fact that because communities differ in religious composition, the controversy over whether local governments may adopt religious symbols will continue to fester. In many communities, nonChristian groups can be expected to combat practices similar to Pawtucket's; this will be so especially in areas where there are substantial non-Christian minorities.

In sum, considering the District Court's careful findings of fact under the three-part analysis called for by our prior cases, I have no difficulty concluding that Pawtucket's display of the crèche is unconstitutional.

Bender v. Williamsport Area School Dist.

741 F.2d 538 (3d Cir. 1984)

Opinion of the Court

GARTH, *Circuit Judge:*
This appeal requires us to resolve the tension between the first amendment free speech claim of high school students meeting in an activity devoted to prayer, and a school district's claim that the Establishment Clause—also found in the first amendment—overrides free speech guarantees in the context of a "limited forum." . . .

Plaintiffs-Appellees Lisa Bender, et al., are or were students at the Williamsport Area High School. It was their desire to form a student organization within the high school, which would be devoted to prayer and other religious activities, and which would meet during the regularly scheduled student activity period. The school officials, fearing violation of the Establishment Clause of the first amendment, denied the students permission to meet.

The students brought this suit for declaratory and injunctive relief under 42 U.S.C. § 1983, alleging violation of their constitutional rights of free speech and free exercise of religion. . . . the district court granted summary judgment in favor of the school district and against the students on the free exercise claim. Relying, however, on *Widmar* v. *Vincent,* 454 U.S. 263, 102 S.Ct. 269, 70 L.Ed.2d 440 (1981), the district court agreed with the students that their free speech rights had been abridged, and that, under these circumstances, the Establishment Clause did not provide a compelling state interest to justify that abridgement. The court therefore granted summary judgment in favor of the students and against the school district on the free speech claim. . . . We conclude that the Establishment Clause concerns expressed by the school district must prevail. We therefore reverse. . . .

Proposal for a New Student Organization

NAME OF THE ORGANIZATION

πετρα [sic] (the Rock)

NATURE OF THE ORGANIZATION

The organization will be a non-denominational prayer fellowship. Participation will be voluntary and open to all students.

PURPOSE OF THE ORGANIZATION

The purpose of the organization will be to promote spiritual growth and positive attitudes in the lives of its members.

LEADERSHIP

Selection of leaders will be by democratic election. The leaders will be responsible for directing the meetings and coordinating activities in a manner that will carry out the purpose of the organization.

MEETINGS

Regular meetings of the organization will be held on school premises during the Tuesday and Thursday morning activity periods. They will include Scripture reading, discussion, prayer and other activities which may be of interest to the group.

SUPERVISION

Meetings of the organization will be supervised by a faculty advisor. Student attendance may be verified by the signing of a roster.

. . . The students asked permission to meet during the school's regularly scheduled activity period. They agreed that they would not use the bulletin boards, newspaper, or public address systems to promote their meetings. App. at 401 (Affidavit of Lisa Bender).

Petros was allowed to hold one organizational meeting, at which approximately forty-five students were present. During the meeting, passages of scripture were read, and students who wished to do so, prayed. After this first session, however, the school administration withheld permission for further meetings pending investigation as to their legality. After consultation with the school's attorney, the Williamsport School Board denied the student's request for permission to meet. The President of the School Board wrote to Bender, stating:

> The solicitor [has] advised the Board that to approve your proposal would be a violation of existing case law and therefore, an improper action. The Board decided, therefore, to deny your appeal. . . . Present law simply does not permit public schools to authorize or support religious activities on school property. App. at 235 (Letter of R.F. Eberhart).

The activity period at Williamsport Area High School is held during a thirty minute time slot regularly provided on Tuesdays and Thursdays, during which student groups may conduct meetings. The school day begins at 7:45 a.m. when all students must be in their homerooms. School supervision of students begins the moment they enter the school premises. App. at 356 (Affidavit of Principal Wayne Newton). The activity period starts at 7:57 a.m., after attendance has been taken in homeroom and the school day has begun. Those students who do not participate in a club may study in the library, visit the school's computer station, examine career or college placement materials, or simply remain in their home rooms until the next class period begins. Participation in activities is completely voluntary, although each student must be on school grounds and accounted for during the activity period. . . .

In memory of the current principal, who has served since 1974, no proposed student club or activity has ever been denied school sponsorship, other than Petros. The only articulated qualification as to the nature of the activity allowed during this period is that it "*contribute to the intellectual, physical or social development of the students and is otherwise considered legal and constitutionally proper.*" App. at 367 (Affidavit of Principal Wayne Newton).

It is the policy of the school that each student club have an adult advisor, who is usually a member of the faculty, but may be another school employee or a parent. App. at 404 (Stipulation of Parties). There is no written policy "concerning the role of adult advisors of . . . clubs or who those adult advisors must be," *id.*, although an advisor or monitor must be present at each student meeting. App. at 366 (Affidavit of Principal W. Newton). The principal has final approval over who the advisor will be. At the first meeting of Petros, a monitor was present, but used the time to grade papers and took no part on the meeting. App. at 228, 402 (Affidavits of L. Bender).

Our analysis will proceed along these lines:

First, did the student members of Petros have a free speech right guaranteed by the first amendment? To answer this inquiry, we will have to examine whether the school district created a forum, and if so, what kind, i.e. was it "public" or "limited," and if "limited," in what manner?

Second, if, as we conclude, the Williamsport school district did create a forum, limited to accommodating student activities which would promote the intellectual and social development of its students as part of the secondary school educational process, then did the students in the Petros program come within the prescribed parameters of that limited forum so created?

Third, assuming an affirmative answer to the preceding inquiries, may the school district validly object to the presence of Petros within the school, based on the potential violation of the Establishment Clause? The answer to this question, in turn, depends on an analysis of the three pronged *Lemon* tests: (1) would permitting the activity within the school day have a secular purpose; (2) would permitting the activity have the primary effect neither of advancing nor inhibiting religion; and (3) would permitting the activity avoid excessive government entanglement with religion? *See Lemon* v. *Kurtzman,* 403 U.S. 602, 612–613, 91 S.Ct. 2105, 2111, 29 L.Ed.2d 447 (1971) and *infra* note 20.

Lastly, if we conclude, as we do, that allowing Petros to meet within the school would violate the Establishment Clause, then which of the two provisions of the first amendment should control, where the students, on the one hand, have a free speech right, but the school district, on the other hand, would be in violation of the Establishment Clause if it permitted the religious activity and speech of Petros? The last stage of our analysis, therefore, requires a balancing process, which, when given effect, we believe sustains the action taken by the Williamsport school district. . . .

In determining the nature of the free speech protections which exist within the school, we of course take note of the general axiom that students do not shed their rights to freedom of speech or expression at the schoolhouse gate. . . .

On the other hand, the mere fact that speech is involved and the free speech clause of the first amendment is invoked does not require the government to open the use of its facilities as a public forum to anyone desiring to use them. *See Perry Educational*

Association v. *Perry Local Educators Association,* 460 U.S. 37, 103 S.Ct. 948, 954, 74 L.Ed.2d 794 (1983). . . .

The Supreme Court, however, has held that, when the state decides, albeit on its own motion, to open its facilities for use as a "limited forum," for particular purposes, it assumes a responsibility to explain its exclusion of a qualified group under applicable constitutional criteria. "Although a state is not required to indefinitely retain the open character of the facility, as long as it does so it is bound by the same standards as apply in a traditional public forum." . . .

Although the State may create a "limited forum" for particular groups or specific activities, . . . it may not exclude expression that falls within whatever objective parameters it has set . . . In *Widmar,* students at the University of Missouri sought permission, as did the students in Williamsport, to use school facilities for religious activities. They formed a group known as "Cornerstone," and for a time were allowed to hold meetings on school premises. The university withdrew that permission, however, citing school regulations against use of its facilities "for purposes of religious worship or religious teaching."

In a suit brought by members of Cornerstone, the Supreme Court held that, by opening its facilities for general use by campus groups, the university *had* created a forum for its students, and thus it could not make content-based discriminations against particular groups absent in a compelling state interest. . . .

The fact that *Widmar* involved a *university,* while we here are concerned with a *high school,* does not mean that we are free to ignore the nature of the free speech rights enjoyed by the students. As is discussed below, however, the opportunity to exercise those rights is not necessarily coextensive with that which exists in an adult environment. . . .

Since elementary and secondary schools, unlike universities, are not the academic battleground for clashes among contending lines of thought, particularly since the level of student maturity rarely reaches the more advanced level of those attending college, it is unlikely that school authorities would seek to create a truly open forum in a high school environment for unregulated dialogue and inquiry. Because of the inherent nature of a secondary school, any forum created has purposes which are narrower, and uses more exclusive than a forum such as in *Widmar* or one open generally to all forms of communication by the public. In detemining the type of forum, if any, created by secondary school authorities such as the Williamsport Area School District, therefore, we must take into account, among other things, the level of maturity of the students and the nature of the academic program involved. . . .

. . . The record therefore reveals that the activity period at Williamsport Area High School provides a forum for self-expression, by which students exercise their own discretion in deciding which organization, if any, to support. Indeed, unlike compulsory instructional classes, which are created and designed by the school authorities, the very existence of such organizations depends entirely upon voluntary student participation and interest. . . . Thus, the latitude allowed to student groups, and the manner in which it encourages students to exercise independent judgment, supports the conclusion that the Williamsport Area School District did indeed create a forum—albeit a limited one—restricted to high school students at Williamsport and also restricted to the extent that the proposed activity promote the intellectual, physical, or social development of the students. . . . . . .

It is clear to us that religious discussion, religious study, and even prayer, fall within the articulated qualification that student organizations promote the intellectual and social welfare of students. . . .

Having found that a limited open forum was created within the high school, such that the students' free speech rights were implicated, we must now determine whether the school may constitutionally impose restrictions on those rights. . . . Moreover, because the restriction imposed by the school district in denying permission for Petros to meet is content-based, Williamsport ("the State") must demonstrate that it is narrowly drawn to meet a compelling state interest. *E.g.*, *Widmar*, 454 U.S. at 270, 102 S.Ct. at 274. The sole justification advanced by Williamsport for denying Petros permission to organize is that such permission might violate the Establishment Clause. As noted in *Widmar*, "the interest of [the school] is complying with its constitutional obligations *may* be characterized as compelling." . . .

In the present case, no assertion has been made that the Williamsport School District *created the activity period* for anything other than valid educational purposes.

We therefore conclude that, in establishing a general activity program of the type disclosed by the record, Williamsport had no religious objective or nonsecular purpose. . . .

We encounter greater difficulty in considering whether the second *Lemon* test has been satisfied, i.e. whether the policy of allowing religious groups access to an otherwise open forum would have the effect of advancing religion. Justice O'Connor, in her concurring opinion in *Lynch* v. *Donnelly*, ____U.S. ____, 104 S.Ct. 1355, 1368, 79 L.Ed.2d 604 (1984) states the issue thus: "[w]hat is crucial is that a government practice not have the effect of communicating a message of government endorsement or disapproval of religion." . . . In Justice O'Connor's terms, as expressed in *Lynch*, allowing a religious group to meet on a public university campus would not have the effect of communicating a message of government endorsement of religion. *See Lynch*, 104 S.Ct. at 1368.

In the matter before us, however, different considerations present a more serious question of state advancement or endorsement of religion than was present in *Widmar*. . . .

As the *Widmar* Court itself noted, high school students stand in a very different position than university students in terms of maturity and impressionability. . . . Thus, the possible perception by adolescent students that government is communicating a message of endorsement of religion if it permitted a religious group to meet would be vastly different in a high school setting than the perception of such action by college students in a college setting. . . .

Moreover, the record here discloses that such activity was to be monitored by a teacher, parent, or other adult. It is true that the monitor was not required to participate in the program's activities, although many adult supervisors did so. . . . While the students in their affidavits characterized the monitor's activities as benign and neutral, designed only to maintain order, it is readily apparent that a school teacher or someone associated with the school necessarily must impart the impression to students that the school's authority and that the school's endorsement is implicated in the relevant activity, since every monitor must be approved by the school. . . . When the monitor factor is added to the other considerations which we have discussed under the "effects" test of *Lemon,* it becomes evident that, if Petros were allowed to meet under these circumstances, Williamsport would be perceived as endorsing and encouraging religious practice. . . .

. . . [W]e are therefore left with the conclusion that the presence of religious groups within the school during the curricular day has the effect of advancing religion, in that it communicates a message of government endorsement of such activity. . . .

Since we have already determined that the primary or direct effect of permitting Petros to meet would be to advance religion, we need not dwell overly long on consideration of the third prong of the test, i.e. whether permitting Petros to meet would engender "excessive entanglement" with religion. . . . "[I]f the state must engage in continuing administrative supervision of nonsecular activity, church and state are excessively intertwined." *Brandon,* 635 F.2d at 979.

We reach this conclusion with the knowledge that, in the context of a *university,* the *Widmar* Court has suggested that prohibition of religious meetings may actually exacerbate entanglement.

. . . We have doubts, however, that *Widmar* dictates that the prohibition of religious activity from a public high school itself creates an excessive entanglement. . . .

In considering the entanglement feature of the *Lemon* tests, moreover, at least as applied to the Williamsport school district situation, our unease stems not so much from the metaphysical concerns which we have just recited, but more from the fact that the activities in which Petros intends to engage will be conducted during school hours, on school premises, and under official school supervision. . . .

We have already concluded that the students of Petros enjoy a free speech right to engage in religious activity. We have also held, however, that allowing such religious activity would violate the mandate of the Establishment Clause. We are thus faced with a constitutional conflict of the highest order. Moreover, in deciding *Widmar,* the Supreme Court explicitly declined to "reach the questions that would arise if state accommodation of free exercise and free speech should, in a particular instance, conflict with the prohibitions of the Establishment Clause." 454 U.S. at 273 n. 13, 102 S.Ct. at 276 n. 13. We are therefore left with no definitive guidance from the Court as to the proper direction to take in this unique circumstance.

Two other courts of appeals have addressed circumstances comparable to those presented here, but for various reasons did not reach the ultimate question raised in this case of how to reconcile free speech with the proscriptions of the Establishment Clause. . . .

In those cases in which there is a true and uncontrived conflict between the free speech clause on the one hand, and the Establishment Clause on the other, we believe that the appropriate analysis requires weighing the competing interests protected by each constitutional provision. . . .

. . . The facts of this case concededly present a close question. In sum, however, we conclude that the interest in protecting free speech within the context of the activity period as it exists at Williamsport Area High School is outweighed by the Establishment

Clause concerns described earlier. . . . To this extent, therefore, it can be said that the interest of Williamsport in complying with its constitutional obligations provides a compelling state interest. *See Widmar,* 454 U.S. at 271, 102 S.Ct. at 275. Under other circumstances, of course, this same analysis could work to override the Establishment Clause, if a sufficiently compelling interest were shown. We need not address those circumstances here, however, since the record in this case does not lend itself to such a conclusion.

ADAMS, Circuit Judge, dissenting.

. . . Nothing in the record, the briefs, or the oral argument suggests that the high school sought by this policy to promote religious activity, or that a teacher or other school employee sponsored Petros, or that the activity period in any way encouraged attendance at Petros. Nonetheless, the majority holds that Petros must be excluded. Given the high school's conceded neutrality toward all student activities and the unquestioned voluntariness of an individual student's decision to attend any particular activity, the majority's conclusion essentially rests on the view that collective religious speech simply may not take place within the walls of a public secondary school without violating the Constitution. . . . While I agree that the case before us is not completely free from doubt, I cannot join the majority's conclusion that the Establishment Clause, as construed by the Supreme Court, requires exclusion of Petros solely because of the religious content of its speech. In particular, I do not believe that Petros can be meaningfully distinguished from the student religious group permitted to meet in a public university by *Widmar* v. *Vincent,* 454 U.S. 263, 102 S.Ct. 269, 70 L.Ed.2d 440 (1981). Because I cannot subscribe to the majority's wooden reading of the First Amendment, and because I believe the result reached today is at variance with controlling precendent, I respectfully dissent.

Widmar v. Vincent

454 U.S. 263 (1981)

Justice POWELL delivered the opinion of the court.

This case presents the question whether a state university, which makes its facilities generally available for the activities of registered student groups, may close its facilities to a registered student group desiring to use the facilities for religious worship and religious discussion.

It is the stated policy of the University of Missouri at Kansas City to encourage the activities of student organizations. The University officially recognizes over 100 student groups. It routinely provides University facilities for the meetings of registered organizations. Students pay an activity fee of $41 per semester (1978–1979) to help defray the costs to the University.

From 1973 until 1977 a registered religious group named Cornerstone regularly sought and received permission to conduct its meetings in University facilities. In 1977, however, the University informed the group that it could no longer meet in University buildings. The exclusion was based on a regulation, adopted by the Board of Curators in

1972, that prohibits the use of University buildings or grounds "for purposes of religious worship or religious teaching."

Eleven University students, all members of Cornerstone, brought suit to challenge the regulation in Federal District Court for the Western District of Missouri. They alleged that the University's discrimination against religious activity and discussion violated their rights to free exercise of religion, equal protection, and freedom of speech under the First and Fourteenth Amendments to the Constitution of the United States. . . .

Through its policy of accommodating their meetings, the University has created a forum generally open for use by student groups. Having done so, the University has assumed an obligation to justify its discriminations and exclusions under applicable constitutional norms. . . .

Here the University of Missouri has discriminated against student groups and speakers based on their desire to use a generally open forum to engage in religious worship and discussion. These are forms of speech and association protected by the First Amendment.

. . . In order to justify discriminatory exclusion from a public forum based on the religious content of a group's intended speech, the University must therefore satisfy the standard of review appropriate to content-based exclusions. It must show that its regulation is necessary to serve a compelling state interest and that it is narrowly drawn to achieve that end. See *Carey* v. *Brown,* 447 U.S. 455, 461, 464–465, 100 S.Ct. 2286, 2290, 2292, 65 L.Ed.2d 263 (1980).

In this case the University claims a compelling interest in maintaining strict separation of church and State. It derives this interest from the "Establishment Clauses" of both the Federal and Missouri Constitutions. . . .

. . . We agree that the interest of the University in complying with its constitutional obligations may be characterized as compelling. It does not follow, however, that an "equal access" policy would be incompatible with this Court's Establishment Clause cases. Those cases hold that a policy will not offend the Establishment Clause if it can pass a three-pronged test. . . .

. . . In this case two prongs of this test are clearly met. Both the District Court and the Court of Appeals held that an open-forum policy, including nondiscrimination against religious speech, would have a secular purpose and would avoid entanglement with religion. But the District Court concluded, the University argues here, that allowing religious groups to share the limited public forum would have the "primary effect" of advancing religion.

The University's argument misconceives the nature of this case. The question is not whether the creation of a religious forum would violate the Establishment Clause. The University has opened its facilities for use by student groups, and the question is whether it can now exclude groups because of the content of their speech. See *Healy* v. *James,* 408 U.S. 169, 92 S.Ct. 2338, 33 L.Ed.2d 266 (1972). In this context we are unpersuaded that the primary effect of the public forum, open to all forms of discourse, would be to advance religion.

We are not oblivious to the range of an open forum's likely effects. It is possible—perhaps even foreseeable—that religious groups will benefit from access to University facilities. But this Court has explained that a religious organization's enjoyment of merely "incidental" benefits does not violate the prohibition against the "primary advancement" of religion. . . .

We are satisfied that any religious benefits of an open forum at UMKC would be "incidental" within the meaning of our cases. Two factors are especially relevant.

First, an open forum in a public university does not confer any imprimatur of State approval on religious sects or practices. As the Court of Appeals quite aptly stated, such a policy "would no more commit the University . . . to religious goals," than it is "now committed to the goals of the Students for a Democratic Society, the Young Socialist Alliance," or any other group eligible to use its facilities. *Chess* v. *Widmar, supra,* at 1317.

Second, the forum is available to a broad class of non-religious as well as religious speakers; there are over 100 recognized student groups at UMKC. The provision of benefits to so broad a spectrum of groups is an important index of secular effect. . . .

At least in the absence of empirical evidence that religious groups will dominate UMKC's open forum, we agree with the Court of Appeals that the advancement of religion would not be the forum's "primary effect."

Arguing that the State of Missouri has gone further than the Federal Constitution in proscribing indirect State support for religion, the University claims a compelling interest in complying with the applicable provisions of the Missouri Constitution.

The Missouri courts have not ruled whether a general policy of accommodating student groups, applied equally to those wishing to gather to engage in religious and non-religious speech, would offend the State Constitution. We need not, however, determine how the Missouri courts would decide the issue. It is also unnecessary for us to decide whether, under the Supremacy Clause, a state interest, derived from its own constitution, could ever outweigh free speech interests protected by the First Amendment. We limit our holding to the case before us. . . .

In this constitutional context, we are unable to recognize the State's interest as sufficient as "compelling" to justify content-based discrimination against respondents' religious speech.

Our holding in this case in no way undermines the capacity of the University to establish reasonable time, place, and manner regulations. . . .

The basis for our decision is narrow. . . .

Its exclusionary policy violates the fundamental principle that a state regulation of speech should be content-neutral, and the University is unable to justify this violation under applicable constitutional standards.

CHAPTER 5

CHAPTER OUTLINE

Introduction: Teachers' legal status
PART I: Employment eligibility
A. Certification
  1. Time deadlines
  2. Legal controls on denial or revocation
    a. Grounds for noncertification and decertification
B. Teacher loyalty
C. Residency
D. Other general requirements
  1. Health
  2. Dual allegiance–conflicts of interest and duties
    a. Employment of close relatives
    b. Outside employment
PART II: Employment rights and duties
A. Nonteaching duties
B. Tenure status
  1. Tenure by official default
C. Teacher placement
  1. Assignment and transfer
  2. Performance ratings
  3. Demotion
    a. Requisite procedures
    b. Lawful and unlawful demotion
D. Termination and suspension
  1. Excess teachers
  2. Position abolition
    a. Order of release
    b. Order of recall
  3. Contract renewal
    a. Notice
    b. Challenging nonrenewal

Professional Personnel

4. Discharge for cause
    a. Grounds for discharge
    b. Remedies for wrongful discharge
5. Resignation and abandonment

E. Teachers' rights
1. Procedural due process
    a. Property interests
    b. Liberty interests
    c. Due process criteria
2. Statutory due process
3. Substantive rights
    a. Constitutional rights
    b. Freedom of expression
    c. Associational expression
    d. Teacher appearance and dress
    e. Academic freedom
    f. Privacy interests

PART III: Collective labor-management relations

A. Informal bargaining

B. Formal bargaining
1. The bargaining unit and representative
2. The scope of collective bargaining
    a. Statutory restrictions
3. Union security

C. Dispute resolution
1. Mediation
2. Arbitration
3. The right to strike
    a. Limitations on statutory right to strike
4. Strike sanctions

D. Labor-related speech activities

TABLE OF CASES FOR CHAPTER 5

McGrath v. Burkhard, 280 P.2d 865 (Cal. 1955), 259.
Hawkins v. Linn County School District No. 14, 517 P.2d 330 (Ore. 1973), 263.
Ryan v. Aurora City Board of Education, 540 F.2d 222 (6th Cir. 1976), 266.
Commonwealth of Pennsylvania v. Charleroi Area Sch. Dist., 347 A.2d 736 (Pa. 1975), 271.
James v. Board of Education of Central District No. 1 of the Towns of Addison, et al., 461 F.2d 566 (2d Cir. 1972), 274.
Connick v. Myers, 461 U.S. 138 (1983), 280.
Perry Ed. Assn. v. Perry Local Educators Assn., 460 U.S. 37 (1983), 286.
Ellis v. Railway Clerks, 466 U.S. 85 (1984), 289.
Chicago Teachers Union v. Hudson, ___U.S. ___, 106 S.Ct. 1066, 89 L Ed2d 232(1986), 293.
Board of Education of Long Beach Unified School District of Los Angeles County v. Jack M., 566 P.2d 602 (Cal. 1977), 294.
Hortonville Dist. v. Hortonville Ed. Asso., 426 U.S. 482 (1976), 298.

Introduction: Teachers' Legal Status

The rights and duties of teachers are defined by many federal and state statutes as well as by constitutional law. These layers of law often operate independently of each other. For example, a teacher's claim that finds little or no support in constitutional, statutory, or common law (or even in the individual contract) may be sustained by the terms of a lawful union agreement that supplements the other sources of law. The following divisions of materials should, therefore, be viewed as parts of a connected series of legal controls. Since teachers and administrators are (with few exceptions) classified as employees and not as officers, all references in this chapter to *employees* apply as well to professional employees who are engaged in administrative or special service positions.

The legal positions of teachers are determined partly by official rules and partly by their individual and collectively bargained contracts. Although contracts must comply with statutory terms, they often expand teacher rights and duties so long as those terms do not conflict with written law.[1] Thus, statutes authorize employment of different classes of teachers (viz. substitutes, temporary, probationary, and permanent teachers) and provide different protections to each such class, but local boards often determine by individual contracts to which class each teacher is appointed.

Where the terms of a statute, individual contract, or collectively bargained agreement are alleged to be inconsistent or in conflict with each other, courts must decide whether a conflict exists and if so, which source of law governs. A teacher hired as a substitute could not claim to become a probationary teacher merely because duties and length of service would have qualified him or her as a probationer had the board so employed him or her.[2] Since the statute authorized the board to employ substitutes as well as probationary teachers, no inconsistency existed.

In the occasional case where courts cannot reconcile the public law and individual contract requirements, they may supply a special rule. For example, a person under contract as a teacher who accepted temporary duty as a principal at a principal's salary scale could not later seek to recover overtime pay under the teacher's contract for extra time worked as temporary principal. The duties of the accepted temporary position governed employment status, rather than the original contract.[3] (A graphic summary and comparison of state laws on teacher personnel policies is presented in Table 5–1.)

1. Howard v. Bogart, 575 S.W.2d 281 (Tenn. 1979) (state requirements for state-funded positions did not prevent board from ignoring state standards for positions funded by federal government); Matthews v. Bd. Of Education, 18 Cal. Rptr. 101, 102 (1962); Bd. of Education v. Messer, 79 S.W.2d 225 (1935).

2. See the Matthews case, prior footnote; Paolus v. Bd. of Trustees, 134 Cal. Rptr. 220 (1976).

3. Taggart v. Bd. of Directors of Cannon-MacMillan Jt. School System, 185 A.2d 332 (Pa. 1962).

TABLE 5-1. Summary of state standards—Teacher personnel policies †

STATES	SALARY		PROBATIONARY PERIOD				TEACHER'S FILE		HEALTH STANDARDS		
			TERMINATION OF EMPLOYMENT								
	State	Local	Length (in yrs.)	Notice	Hearing	Appeal	Personnel Evaluations	Access Of Teacher	Prior Certification	Periodic Re-exams	Suspension For Ill Health
ALABAMA	X		3	X					(a)	X	
ALASKA	X		2	X	X						
ARIZONA									X	X	
ARKANSAS	X			X	X				X		
CALIFORNIA	X		4	X	X	X			X	X	
COLORADO		X	3	X							
CONNECTICUT		X		X	X		X	X			
DELAWARE	X		3								
FLORIDA		X	3				X	X			
GEORGIA	X		3								
HAWAII	X		2								
IDAHO	X		3	X	X						
ILLINOIS	X		2(c)	X					X	X	
INDIANA	X		5								
IOWA		X		X	X					X	
KANSAS		X	3	X			X	X	X	X	
KENTUCKY	X		3								
LOUISIANA	X		3	X							
MAINE	X										
MARYLAND	X		2						X	X	
MASSACHUSETTS	X		3	X					X	X	X
MICHIGAN		X	2	X				X			
MINNESOTA		X	3	X	X		X	X			X
MISSISSIPPI	X								X	X	
MISSOURI		X	5(e)	X			X		X		
MONTANA			3	X							

STATES	SALARY		PROBATIONARY PERIOD				TEACHER'S FILE		HEALTH STANDARDS		
			TERMINATION OF EMPLOYMENT								
	State	Local	Length (in yrs.)	Notice	Hearing	Appeal	Personnel Evaluations	Access Of Teacher	Prior Certification	Periodic Re-exams	Suspension For Ill Health
NEBRASKA		X	3				X	X			
NEVADA		X	3	X							
NEW HAMPSHIRE	X			X	X	X					
NEW JERSEY	X		3	X							
NEW MEXICO	X		3	X			X		X	X	
NEW YORK	X		3	X							
NORTH CAROLINA		X(f)	3	X			X	X	X	X	
NORTH DAKOTA	X			X	X						
OHIO	X		3	X	X	X					
OKLAHOMA		X									
OREGON	X		3	X			X	X	X		X
PENNSYLVANIA	X		2						X		X
RHODE ISLAND		X	3	X	X	X					
SOUTH CAROLINA	X(g)										
SOUTH DAKOTA		X	2	X					X	X	X
TENNESSEE	X		3							X	
TEXAS	X			X	X				X		
UTAH	X		(h)	X	X				(i)		
VERMONT	X								X		
VIRGINIA	X		3	X							
WASHINGTON		X		X	X	X(j)			X		
WEST VIRGINIA	X		3								
WISCONSIN	X		3	X	(k)				X		
WYOMING		X	3								

TABLE 5-1. Teacher personnel policies (*cont.*)

STATES	TENURED TEACHERS					PROFESSIONAL ETHICS		
		DISCHARGE OR DEMOTION FOR CAUSE						
	Automatic Status	Notice	Hearing	Appeal*	Sabbatical Leave	Name of Agency ‡	Advisory	Regulatory
ALABAMA	X	X	X	STC	X			
ALASKA	X	X	X	Court	X	1		X
ARIZONA		X	X	Court				
ARKANSAS		X	X					
CALIFORNIA		X	X		X	2		X
COLORADO	X	X	X	Court		3		
CONNECTICUT	X	X	X	Court				
DELAWARE		X	X	Court	X			
FLORIDA		X	X	SDE	X	3		X
GEORGIA						3	X	
HAWAII	X	X	X		X			
IDAHO	(b)	X	X			4		X
ILLINOIS	X	X	X	Court	X			
INDIANA	X	X	X	Court				
IOWA						1		X
KANSAS		X	X					
KENTUCKY	X							
LOUISIANA		X	X	Court	X			
MAINE								
MARYLAND	X	X	X	SBE				
MASSACHUSETTS		X	X	Court	X			
MICHIGAN	X	X	X	STC	X			
MINNESOTA	X	X	X	Court	X	1	X	
MISSISSIPPI		X	X	Court				
MISSOURI		X	X	Court				
MONTANA	X	X	X	CS	X			
NEBRASKA	X					3	X	
NEVADA	X	X	X			5	X	
NEW HAMPSHIRE								
NEW JERSEY		X	X	SBE	X			
NEW MEXICO	X	X	X	SBE	X			
NEW YORK		X	X	CE	X			
NORTH CAROLINA		X	X					
NORTH DAKOTA				Court		6		X
OHIO	X	X	X	Court	X			
OKLAHOMA		X	X	SBE		3		X
OREGON		X	X	Court		7	X	

TABLE 5-1. Teacher personnel policies (*cont.*)

STATES	TENURED TEACHERS					PROFESSIONAL ETHICS		
		DISCHARGE OR DEMOTION FOR CAUSE						
	Automatic Status	Notice	Hearing	Appeal*	Sabbatical Leave	Name of Agency‡	Advisory	Regulatory
PENNSYLVANIA		X	X	SPI	X	4	X	
RHODE ISLAND		X	X	SDE				
SOUTH CAROLINA				Court				
SOUTH DAKOTA		X	X			3		X
TENNESSEE		X	x	Court	X			
TEXAS		X	X	SBE		6		X
UTAH		X	X			3	X	
VERMONT		X	X	BSD				
VIRGINIA	X	X	X					
WASHINGTON								
WEST VIRGINIA		X	X		X			
WISCONSIN	X	X	X					
WYOMING		X	X					

* Abbreviations

STC—State Tenure Commission
SDE—State Department of Education
SBE—State Board of Education
CS—County Superintendent
CE—Commissioner of Education
SPI—Superintendent of Public Instruction
BSD—Board of School Directors
D—Discretion

‡ Legend

1. Professional Teaching Practices Commission
2. Teachers' Professional Standards Commission
3. Professional Practices Commission
4. Professional Standards Commission
5. Professional Review Commission
6. Teachers' Professional Practices Commission
7. Teacher Standards and Practices Commission

SOURCE: National Institute of Education.

†All data tables must be updated for possible changes in each state since 1979.

NOTES: Every state requires that a teacher possess a certificate in order to teach in its school system. The chart refers only to full-time instructors, not to student or substitute teachers, for whom certification is often unnecessary. When a certified teacher enters into a contract, the amount of his salary is usually specified therein. In most states a legal minimum salary is established, sometimes far below the actual salary earned. In others a state salary schedule, promulgated by statute or regulation, specifies the contract salary of every teacher in the state. Both these categories are illustrated in the chart as determined by the state. If there is no mention in the laws or regulations of a minimum or schedule, or if the laws specifically allow the local board to fix the salary, the chart indicates that the control is local.

A teacher's employment may also be interrupted if he catches a contagious disease. The right of a school board to suspend a teacher with ill health is made an implied term of contracts in some states; in others, the power probably exists though not specified in the laws or regulations.

After the teacher finishes his service for the probationary period, he may achieve tenure or career status. In many states a teacher reaches tenure when the local board fails to cancel his contract after the probationary period.

PART I

Employment Eligibility

Applicants for teaching employment must meet *eligibility* standards that are set by state certification statutes and administered by state and local agencies. In addition, they must satisfy the job *qualifications* that are set for particular positions, primarily by local school boards and occasionally by other agencies. *Eligibility* herein indicates that the applicant has the necessary license status to serve as a teacher while *qualifications* refer to the experience or special training a licensed professional is required to have for a designated position.

A. Certification

Practically every state requires certification of public school teachers.[4] The number, types, areas, and nomenclature of educator certificates vary from state to state, as do the standards and procedures for obtaining different certificates. Professional eligibility is usually limited to the area of competency that is covered by the employee's certificate.[5] A teacher who has only a certificate for foreign language instruction, may not be assigned to an English class, irrespective of tenure or length of service.[6] Certification, therefore, affects placement and assignment as well as original access to teacher employment. In the absence of explicit statutory exception (viz. for urgent or emergency needs), the prerequisite of certification cannot be waived by a local board or cured by the board's knowing employment of an uncertified teacher, despite the teacher's reliance on assurances that the lack of certification was not critical.[7]

---

4. See *Study of State Legal Standards for the Provision of Public Education,* pp. 66–70 (National Institute of Education 1974). Certification may not be required in some states for instructional employees who are not deemed to be part of the public school system, i.e., in nonclass functions that are federally funded for exclusive minority groups. *See, e.g.,* Phila. Fed'n of Teachers v. Bd. of Education, 414 A.2d 424 (Pa. 1980).

5. Krolopp v.So. Range Local Sch. District Bd. of Education, 353 N.E.2d 642 (Ohio 1974).

6. Steele v. Bd. of Valhalla Union Free Sch. District,384 N.Y.S.2d 860 (1976). *See also* Giowacki v. Ambach,385 N.Y.S.2d 819 (1976) (teacher tenured and certified in Latin. Disqualified from position of guidance counsellor that was subject to separate certification).

7. Bradford Cent. Sch. District v. Ambach, 436 N.E. 2d 1256 (N.Y. 1982); Grams v. Melrose-Mindoro Jt. Sch. District, 254 N.W.2d 730 (Wis. 1977) (teacher discharges upheld for noncertification). *Re* emergencies, see, e.g., Pa. Stat. Ann., tit. 24, § 12-1214 (Purdon Supp. 1982); Cranston Teachers Assn. v. Cranston School Com'ee, 424 A.2d 648 (R.I. 1982); Panlillio v. Dallas Ind. Sch. District., 643 F.2d 317 (5th Cir. 1981); Golanka v. State Bd. of Ed., 308 N.W.2d 425 (Mich. 1981).

Certification law serves several purposes. It fosters adequate professional training to ensure competence in the licensed area;[8] maintains registration of teachers with state and district agencies to ensure compliance with certification law and enforce certification guidelines; and protects certified teachers to some degree against unfair displacement.

Unless an error of law or arbitrary action is proven, courts will not interfere with the discretion of certification authorities.[9] Although a certificate establishes an element of eligibility, it does not entitle its holder to particular employment.[10] Nor does it guarantee retention or renewal of the certificate. The state's authority over certificate issuance, renewal, and retention is continuing in nature. The state may alter requirements, from time to time, as to new certificates and as to renewal or revocation of outstanding certificates.[11] Most laws vest certification authority in central state agencies, but the state legislature may delegate that authority directly to a local school district, as is the case with the District for the city of New York.[12]

The authority of certifying agencies to set the grounds for new or renewal certificates includes the power to suspend or revoke certificates for cause (e.g., disabling mental illness or drug addiction)[13] if the administrative regulations are fair in content and fairly applied. Therefore, where an agency finding of illness was not supported by substantial evidence, its denial of certificate reinstatement was overturned.[14] Nor could public authorities require a teacher to submit to a psychiatric examination in the absence of reasonable proof to suspect mental illness.[15] The validity of a certificate issued (at the request of a school board) without the teacher's prior knowledge or consent was considered in a case where the teacher refused transfer to the area covered by the new certificate. The court ruled that she could not refuse reassignment since the certificate was primafacie valid and that the teacher had the burden of having the certificate withdrawn as invalidly issued.[16]

---

8. Lack of certification has been held to be sufficient evidence of incompetence to justify teacher dismissal; Slattery v. Comm. of Cranston, 354 A.2d 741 (R.I. 1976); Kobylski v. Bd. of Education, 304 N.Y.S.2d 459 (1969).

9. Application of Bay v. State Bd. of Education, 378 P.2d 558 (Ore. 1963) (upheld denial of certificate to paroled felony convict); *compare* Parolisi v. Bd. of Education, 285 N.Y.S.2d 936 (1967) (denial of substitute teaching license on basis of petitioner's excessive weight, overturned as abuse of discretion).

10. Coe v. Bogart, 519 F.2d 10 (6th Cir. 1975); Wheeler v. School District No. 20, 535 P.2d 206 (Colo. 1975) (transfer of tenured principal to teaching position—upheld).

11. Guthrie v. Taylor 185 S.E.2d 193 (N.C. 1971); Last v. Bd. of Education, 185 N.E.2d 282 (Ill. 1962). *See* Moser v. State Bd. of Education, 101 Cal. Rptr. 86 (1972), and revocation cases discussed at p. 183.

12. *See* Chavick v. Bd. of Examiners, 258 N.Y.S.2d 677 (1965) (holding that the city certifying board could lawfully set higher requirements for its certificates than those set by the state agency). Johnson v. Bd. of Elementary and Secondary Ed., 414 So.2d 352 (La. 1982) (state constitution vested control over teachers discharge in local boards; preventing state agency decertification of teachers, except for fraud or misrepresentation).

13. Alford v. Dept. of Education, 91 Cal. Rptr. 843 (1971); Anonymous v. Bd. of Education, 318 N.Y.S.2d 163 (1970).

14. Conover v. Bd. of Examiners, 298 N.Y.S.2d 757 (1968) (heart disease) similarly if suspension only rather than dismissal is reasonable, the dismissal may be overturned. Bd. of Trustees v. Perini, 70 Cal. Rptr. 73 (1968).

15. Stewart v. Pearce, 484 F.2d 1031 (9th Cir. 1973).

16. Harrisburg R-VIII Sch. District v. O'Brien, 540 S.W.2d 945 (Mo. 1976).

1. Time Deadlines for Certificate Registration

Many states require teachers to file their certificates with their employing district before the commencement of the contract term. In some states, the filing deadline and the signing of the employment contract coincide, but in others certificates may be filed any time before the commencement of actual work.[17] The effect of failure to file the required certificate by the proper time depends upon the interpretation of each certification statute, and in some cases on the fault or excusability of the teacher. Where proper filing was not made, courts of several states took the strict view that failure to file voids the entire employment contract, upheld dismissal, and denied wages, even for the period taught.[18] In other states, late filing of certificates was held to void the contract and wage claim only partially (i.e., for the period of work preceding perfection of the certification process).[19] Forfeiture of position and salary was avoided in some states by interpreting the statutory filing requirement to be merely directory and not mandatory and by court ruling that a short delay in obtaining a renewal certificate did not justify board dismissal.[20]

Where government agencies contributed to the certification or registry default, a few courts relieved teachers from any penalty. Tardy issuance of a renewal certificate through bureaucratic delays could not suspend the teacher's probationary period or postpone acquisition of tenure in Pennsylvania, but an official letter that an unfiled, backdated certificate should have been issued was not considered sufficient to overturn denial of employment in Wyoming.[21] In Pennsylvania, the grant of maternity leave was also held to extend the expiration date of the teacher's certificate and to prevent her dismissal for lack of certificate renewal before the normal expiration date.[22]

Even where teacher contracts are void for lack of certification, courts have the equity power to authorize compensation for the period worked or to permit the teacher to retain payments received for that work in order to prevent unjust enrichment. The courts have split, however, on whether it is more important to protect the policy against uncertified teachers by denying any recovery or to allow compensation in the interest of justice, even though such allowance undercuts the deterrent to use of uncertified teachers.[23]

---

17. See the Akers case, fn. 19.

18. Luz v. Sch. Committee of Lowell, 313 N.E.2d 925 (Mass. 1974) (summary discharge despite long years of service, for failure to obtain certificate within statutory time limitation—upheld); Riley v. Sch. District 24, 221 N.E.2d 424 (Ill. 1966); State v. Bd. of Education, 156 N.E.2d 924 (Ohio 1958) (teacher misfiled his certificate); Zevin v. Sch. District No. 11, 12 N.W.2d 634 (Neb. 1944). For a contrary view, *see* Bates v. Hinds,324 F. Supp.528 (D.C. Tex. 1971). See also Floyd County Bd. of Education v. Slone, fn. 23.

19. Bd. of Education v. Akers,47 S.W.2d 1046 (Ky. 1932); Johnson v. Sch. Dist. No. 3,96 N.W.2d 623 (Neb. 1959); *compare* Mass v. Bd. of Education of San Francisco Unified School District, 394 P.2d 579 (Cal. 1964) (teacher held entitled to pay during period of improper suspension up to but not beyond, expiration of his certificate).

20. *See* Woracheck v. Stephenson Town Sch. District, 70 N.W.2d 657, 660, 661 (Wis. 1955); Ball v. Bunch, 324 S.W.2d 828 (Ky. 1959). *See also* Woodrum v. Rolling Hills Bd. of Education, 421 N.E.2d 859 (Ohio 1981) (harmless error).

21. Commonwealth Department of Education v. Great Valley Sch. District,352 A.2d 252 (Pa. 1976); Sorenson v. Sch. District No. 28, 418 P.2d 1004 (Wyo. 1966).

22. Pointek v. Elk Lake Sch. District, 360 A.2d 804 (Pa. 1976).

23. *Compare* Luz v. Sch. Committee of Lowell, 313 N.E.2d 925 (Mass. 1974); Floyd County Bd. of Education v. Slone, 307 S.W.2d 912 (Ky. 1957); *with* Sorenson v. Sch. District No.28,418 P.2d 1004 (Wyo.

2. Legal Controls on Denial or Revocation of Certificates

Individuals have no "right" to certificates independently of conditions established by state law and no right, even if certified, to public employment.[24] Yet the law does protect a person's "interest" in pursuit of a livelihood. After satisfying all legal requirements for a certificate, the applicant's interest ripens into a right to compel issuance of the certificate. Courts will, therefore, overturn unauthorized and capricious denials of certificates.[25] Protective procedures are mandated by many state laws and in certain circumstances by constitutional doctrines of procedural due process.[26] Denial or revocation of certificates without complying with statutory procedures (viz. as to rating, notice, and hearings) have been reversed.[27] However, where a teacher is charged with an offense that indicates potential serious harm to public education, a court may allow *suspension* of the certificate, even prior to a pending hearing on revocation.[28]

a. Grounds for Noncertification and Decertification. State laws generally provide greater protections to a teacher with acquired status than to new applicants, hence a distinction may be drawn between an initial refusal to certify a first-time applicant and withdrawal of an outstanding certificate. For example, legislatures may authorize denial of initial certificates without prior hearings to persons with specified illness, disabilities, or criminal records.[29] Or they may authorize denial upon administrative findings of unfitness of original applicants (e.g., for moral character).[30] But, for terminating *acquired* certification status, hearings on charges of adequate cause are usually required by constitutional law and by many state statutes. Exception to the hearing requirement has been made by a few courts where the legislature specified particular grounds, such as conviction of certain crimes, for dismissal.[31] In the absence of statutory specification, the bare fact of conviction was not considered sufficient in some states to dispense with a termination hearing, either under the state statute or under constitutional due process.[32] The burden of proving cause for decertification lies with the school authorities. Several states, led by California, insist that the proven charge must be job related. In deciding

---

1966); *cf.* Bates v. Hinds, 334 F.Supp. 528 (D.C. Tex. 1971).

24. *See* Perry v. Sindermann, 408 U.S. 593, 597 (1972).

25. Commonwealth Dept. of Education v. Great Valley Sch. District, 352 A.2d 252 (Pa. 1976).

26. *Re* statutory procedures, see Neal case, fn. 27. *Re* constitutional due process, *see* Huntley v. No. Car. State Bd. of Education,493 F.2d 1016 (4th Cir. 1974). *Cf.* Schwartz v. Bogen,281 N.Y.S.2d 279 (1967) (unsuccessful examinee entitled to see model answers to examination in aid of his challenge to his grade.)

27. Lehman v. Bd. of Education, 439 N.Y.S.2d 670 (1981); Leetham v. McGinn, 524 P.2d 323 (Utah 1974); Meliti v. Nyquist, 385 N.Y.S.2d 407 (1976); Neal v. Bryant, 149 So.2d 529 (Fla. 1962); Lerner v. L.A. City Bd. of Education, 380 P.2d 97 (Cal. 1963).

28. Pordom v. Bd. of Regents of State of New York, 491 F.2d 1381 (2d Cir. 1974), cert. denied, 419 U.S. 843 (1974).

29. See Iowa Code Ann. § 260.2, Pa. Stat. Ann. Tit. 12 § 1209.

30. Application of Bay v. State Bd. of Education, 378 P.2d 558 (Ore. 1963).

31. Vogulkin v. State Bd. of Education, 15 Cal. Rptr. 335 (1961) (decertification mandated by statute for specified convictions).

32. Carl S. v. Comm. for Teacher Preparation, 178 Cal. Rptr. 753 (1981) (decertification of teacher accused of rape-reserved where heresay report of accuser's statements provided sole evidence contra teacher denial); Steward v. E. Baton Rouge Parish Sch. Bd. 251 So.2d 487 (La. App. 1971) (discharge of female school bus driver for "immorality" following divorce by her husband for adultery).

what conduct is job related, however, courts may well disagree, even in California. (See, e.g., the opinion in *Bd. of Education of Long Beach* v. *Jack* M at the end of this chapter.)

The factors for judging fitness to be certified closely parallel those governing teacher dismissal that are discussed under *Termination and Suspension* in Part II of this chapter. For present purposes, adequate illustrations are provided by two California cases that were decided together in one court opinion. The first involved decertification, and the other involved dismissal from employment. Both involved teachers who had been convicted of possession of marijuana. In one case, the court found that the teacher was shown to be unfit but not in the other. It explained the conclusions in terms of the different circumstances in each case.[33]

As previously noted, the *abuse of discretion* doctrine provides protection independent of statutes or constitutional terms. A New York court overturned denial of a teacher's license renewal for obesity, notwithstanding an earlier New York decision that obesity could support a finding of physical unfitness.[34] Much will depend, therefore, on case circumstances and the relationship of specific conditions to the duties of the particular position.

The fact that certification is needed to obtain and retain a teaching position tends to blur important differences between certification laws and other laws affecting job security. Certification does not guarantee tenure.[35] Tenure is controlled exclusively by separate tenure statutes, even though a ground for terminating tenure may also be ground for decertification. A school board may dismiss a tenured teacher where it abolished positions in his or hertenure area, but it may not decertify the teacher on that ground.[36] In like vein, nonrenewal of a probationary teacher is discretionary and requires no hearing in many states, but it does not justify automatic certification revocation.[37] In establishing the order of layoff in staff reductions, tenure seniority rather than certificate seniority is usually controlling. In reviewing teacher status, therefore, the legislation and decisions directed to each of these different aspects of professional standing and security must be separately analyzed lest the law on related, but distinct, topics be confused.

B. Teacher Loyalty

The right of the government to exclude dangerous subversives from public positions is acknowledged, but the means used to avoid actual subversion must not be vague or excessively overbroad as to suppress individual rights.

The Supreme Court recently voted 5 to 4 that the State of New York could, by statute, constitutionally disqualify from public school teaching positions noncitizens who

---

33. Comings v. State Bd. of Education, 100 Cal. Rptr. 73 (1972). *Compare* Walton v. Turlington, 444 So.2d 1082 (Fla. 1984) (revocation upheld on facts underlying criminal charges).

34. Parolisi v. Bd. of Examiners, 285 N.Y.S.2d 936 (1967); Tripp v. Bd. of Examiners, 255 N.Y.S.2d 526 (1964).

35. Bloomburg-Dubin v. Bd. of Education, 43 N.Y.S.2d 956 (1981); Steele v. Bd. of Education of City of N.Y., 354 N.E.2d 807 (N.Y.1976); Matter of Baer, 351 N.Y.S.2d 447 (1974).

36. *See* Steele v. Bd. of Education of City of N.Y., 354 N.E.2d 807 (N.Y. 1976).

37. Ambrose v. Comm'y. Sch. Board, 367 N.Y.S.2d 550 (1975).

were not eligible for and seeking United States citizenship.[38] The citizenship disqualification has nothing to do with the loyalty problems that follow, since the New York statute barred even aliens who were willing to take the state's loyalty oath.

The use of loyalty oaths as prerequisites of public employment involve primarily a question of the means used, i.e. the form of the loyalty oath, rather than the legality of excluding subversives from government positions. Since the federal constitution limits the government to prevention of dangerous action, and forbids government compulsion of any declaration concerning beliefs themselves, however dangerous they may seem, the wording of loyalty oaths is crucial.[39] While no one has a right to a government job, neither does the government have the right to place unconstitutional conditions, even upon public benefits or privileges.

The Supreme Court of the United States has upheld loyalty oaths whose language is taken to indicate no more than disavowal of unlawful action, such as the attempt to use unlawful force that would constitute a clear and present danger to the state.[40] But oaths requiring a disclaimer of association with "subversive organizations" have been overturned because their meaning is too vague for a teacher to safely swear to, and because innocent membership in an actually dangerous group without knowledge or intent to further its designs cannot be constitutionally punished by job disqualification.[41] In short, the state may by oath require the teacher to disavow intent to act for violent overthrow, but may not require disavowal of revolutionary principles. A person who refused to take a lawfully worded oath was thus constitutionally denied employment as a teacher.[42]

C. Residency

School boards, particularly in urbanized school districts, increasingly require district employees to reside within the territory of the school district. Constitutional attacks against such regulations have been made in other public employment fields on the ground that the restriction interferes with individual liberty and the right to travel. The United States Supreme Court and a majority of federal and state cases upheld employment residency regulations, and the few cases to the contrary either preceded these later decisions and are of doubtful authority or are based exclusively upon state court readings of their own state constitution.[43]

---

38. Ambach v. Norwick, 441 U.S. 68, 99 S.Ct. 1589 (1979).

39. Connell v. Higginbotham, 403 U.S. 207 (1971).

40. Cole v. Richardson, 405 U.S. 676 (1972). For other case authorities, *see* Annotation: *Oath of Allegiance or Loyalty,* 18 A.L.R.2d 268, 314 (1951).

41. Elfbrandt v. Russell, 384 U.S. 11 (1966); Wieman v. Updegraff, 344 U.S. 183 (1952).

42. Biklen v. Syracuse Bd. of Education, 333 F. Supp. 902 (N.D.N.Y. 1971). Religious objection was not involved since an affirmation would have satisfied the oath requirement.

43. *Residency regulations upheld:* Meyers v. Newport Cons. School Dist., 639 P.2d 853 (Wash. 1982); Mogle v. Sevier Co. Sch. District, 540 F.2d 478 (10th Cir. 1976) (School Solicitor), cert. den. 429 U.S. 1121 (1977); Wardwell v. Board of Education,529 F.2d 625 (6th Cir. 1976) (teachers); Park v. Lansing, 233 N.W.2d 592 (Mich. 1975) (teacher), cert. denied 425 U.S.904 (1976); McCarthy v. Philadelphia Civil Service Commission,424 U.S. 645 (1976) (fire fighter). See Review of Authorities in O'Melia v. Sweetwater

While the constitution forbids a state, or its agencies, from *unreasonably* burdening citizen movement, the United States Supreme Court has expressly noted that the bare requirement of current residence within the employing municipality serves a rational purpose of the employer.[44] The majority of cases have upheld in-district teacher residence requirement on the view that it improves teacher-administrator identification with, and personal interest in, the problems of the district and its students; whether as taxpayers, instructors, employees, or as members of the local community.[45]

Where district regulations exempt employees who acquired outside residence prior to the effective date of the residency regulation, the new residency requirement has been challenged as unconstitutional discrimination between covered and exempted employees. These challenges were also rejected on the ground that "grandfather" type exemptions are not unreasonable and that new regulations need only be uniform in prospective operation.[46] Teacher associations are seeking to overcome the residency employment barrier through adoption of state statutes that would supersede board regulations and require boards to hire teachers without reference to their location within the state. Where in-district residence policy is not dictated by law, but by local board discretion, the question also becomes a lively issue for collective bargaining. (Bargaining problems are discussed in Part III of this chapter.)

A different issue arises when in-district residence is the basis for employment *preference* rather than eligibility. Preference for *natives* of the employing district has been held unconstitutional discrimination.[47]

D. Other General Requirements

1. Health

The majority of states have adopted universal health standards for all teachers (e.g., an affidavit or physician's certificate as proof of good health) and periodic medical examinations.[48] Accordingly, courts have upheld suspensions and dismissals of employees whose condition would endanger the health and well-being of pupils and associates.[49] This power is independent of the question whether, and for what periods of time, a

---

County Sch. District,497 P.2d 540 (Wyo. 1972). *Contra:* Hanson v. Unified School District No. 500, 364 F. Supp 330 (D. Kan. 1973) (school teachers); Krzewinski v. Kuger, 338 F. Supp 492 (D. N.J. 1972) (police officer); Donnelly v. City of Manchester,274A.2d 789 (N.H.1971) (school teacher). *Re:* State Constitution, *see* Angwin v. City of Manchester, 386 A.2d 1272 (N.H. 1978).

44. *See* Shapiro v. Thompson, 394 U.S. 618 at 638 n.21; Detroit Police Officers Association v. City of Detroit, 190 N.W.2d 97 (Mich. 1971), dismissed for want of a substantial federal question,405 U.S. 950 (1972).

45. See Rensselear Co. Ed. Local v. Newman, 448 N.Y.S. 2d 883 (1982); Board of Education v. Phila. Federation of Teachers 397 A.2d 1273 (Pa. 1979); Wardwell and Park cases, fn. 43. For a contra minority view, *see* Hanson v. Un. Sch. District, 364 F. Supp. 330 (D. Kan. 1973).

46. See prior footnote; Pittsburgh Fed'n. of Teachers v. Aaron,417 F. Supp. 94 (W.D. Pa. 1976).

47. Johnson v. Dixon,501 S.W.2d 256 (Ky. 1973) (board expectation of less teacher turnover held not sufficient justification).

48. See Table 5–1.

49. *See, e.g.,* King-Smith v. Aaron,455 F.2d 378 (3d Cir.1972); Bd. of Trustees v. Perini,70 Cal. Rptr. 73. (1968).

teacher so suspended is entitled to regular or special compensation. That question will depend upon particular state law and the policies adopted by each school district.

As with other legal standards, health standards may not be applied in an arbitrary or unlawful manner. Where a teacher was suspended for mental illness to provide an opportunity of rehabilitation, subsequent proceedings to dismiss her on that ground were overturned because the school authorities failed to establish by substantial evidence that she remained disabled, but relied on stale medical opinion that had been rendered more than a year before the dismissal hearing.[50] But where a certificated teacher resigned after being stricken with polio, the certifying board could limit her later application to a temporary, rather than regular, teaching certificate since she was still partially disabled. The board could further condition that certificate upon passing annual medical examinations, even though such action subjected her to lower salary rates and prevented her acquisition of tenure under state law.[51]

2. Dual Allegiance—Conflicts of Interest and of Duties

Persons whose business, political, or family relationships would undermine or conflict with their employment duties may be denied teacher employment, but legal opinion and authority is unsettled as to the kinds and degrees of dual allegiance that render a teacher ineligible for school district employment. The list of relationships giving rise to dual allegiance is not fixed. The principal targets include nepotism (i.e., close kinship by blood or marriage between school board member and administrators and teachers), concurrent holding of dual public offices or dual employments, and business interests or connections that may be adverse to school district interests (viz. insiders doing business with the employer district). Many relationships are not automatically disqualifying, but depend upon the intensity of conflicts of interest.

The law in the several states is widely divergent as to (1) whether *potential* conflict of interests without proof of *actual* conflict of interest is a sufficient ground for exclusion; (2) whether any given potential or actual conflict is sufficiently *substantial* to warrant disqualification from school district employment; and (3) whether even serious dual allegiance situations require total *exclusion* or dismissal, or merely *temporary suspension* of participation by school personnel in the particular transaction that gives rise to such conflicts.

a. Employment of Close Relatives. Even the employment of close relatives of board members is subject to different treatment among the states. Pennsylvania and New York, by statute, permit such employment upon special vote of the board, excluding that of the related board member.[52] The courts of other states are divided on the general question and on the interpretation of their respective school codes.[53] The law on

50. See the Perini case, previous footnote.

51. Crofts v. Bd. of Education, 245 N.E.2d 87 (N.Y. 1969).

52. N.Y. Education Law § 3016 (McKinney's), Pa. Stat Ann. Tit.24 § 11-1111; Lach v. Defigio,9 D&C 2d 326 (Pa. Co. Court 1958).

53. *Compare, e.g.*, Hollister v. North, 365 N.E.2d 658 (Ill. 1977); Gambese v. Bd. of Education, (N.J. Commr. of Education, Dec. 1976) (permitting employment of board member relatives); *with* Corbin and Whateley cases, fn. 55, *infra.*

nepotism may affect the board member differently since separate statutes deal with board member eligibility. Where the state undertook to force the resignation of a board member whose wife was a teacher and a teacher union negotiator in his school district, a federal court found that no constitutional rights were violated by the disqualifying statutes.[54]

Even in the absence of statute, courts in a few states have upheld board regulations barring the employment of spouses of high-level administrators.[55] A California court, however, refused to void the wife's contract on conflict of interest grounds and noted that her husband board member did not participate in the teachers' salary vote.[56] A similar abstention by board members was considered adequate to avoid disqualifying conflicts in New Jersey, but in Illinois the court found that a teacher's wife who became a member of the employing school board presented a conflict of interest that was not cured by her nonparticipation in board approval of teachers' contracts.[57] Thus it rests with each state court to decide what relationships (other than those specified by statute) create a sufficiently serious conflict of interest and whether such conflicts are curable by abstention or other special arrangements.

The rule against concurrent employment of spouses as teachers was upheld by the Eighth Circuit Court of Appeal where a school principal whose wife worked as a teacher in the same school was dismissed, even though their employment in the district long preceded their marriage. The argument that the disqualification rule unconstitutionally abridged the right to marry was turned aside.[58] In larger school districts or where spouses are not placed in direct superior-subordinate relationships, the rule might well be viewed differently. The courts are in conflict on the power of a board, over the objections of spouses, to prohibit teacher spouses from teaching in the same school.[59] Still another approach was taken under North Dakota and Utah statutes that prohibited school district employment of certain relatives of board members. These were construed to apply only to "first hirings" and not to postemployment elections to the district school board.[60]

An ingenious challenge was recently made to a board regulation that prohibited full-time employment of a second member of an immediate family. The plaintiff, whose father was the district's supervisor of buildings and grounds, argued that the regulation violated the state law that barred employment discrimination based on ancestry, but the court ruled otherwise.[61]

---

54. Shoresman v. Burgess,412 F.Supp. 831 (E.D. Ill. 1976). It is not clear whether later changes in the Illinois statutes will change the Shoresman decision. *Accord:* State ex rel. McKittrick v. Whittle, 63 S.W.2d 100 (Mo. 1933) (board membership forefeited upon appointment of the member's relative as a teacher).

55. Corbin v. Special Sch. District of Fort Smith,465 S.W.2d 342 (Ark. 1971); Whateley v. Leonia Bd. of Education, 358 A.2d 826 (N.J. 1976).

56. Coulter v. Board of Education, 114 Cal. Rptr. 271 (1974).

57. *Compare* In the Matter of the Election of Dorothy Bayless to the Board of Education of Lawrence Twp. School District (N.J. Comm. of Ed. decision, Oct. 1974); *with* People v. Willard, Circuit Court of Lee County, Ill. 74-MR-269 (1975). *Cf.* Hoskins v. Walker, 315 N.E.2d 25 (Ill. 1974).

58. Keckeisen v. Independent School District 612, 509 F.2d 1062 (8th Cir. 1975).

59. *Compare* Meier v. Evansville-Vanderburgh School Corp.,416 F.Supp.748 (S.D. Ind. 1975,affd. 539 F.2d 713 (7th Cir. 1976); *with* Bromley v. Wilks, D.C. Ariz. Civ, No.79-657 (1979) (transfer held to infringe right to marry).

60. Hinek v. Bowman Public Sch. District No.1, 232 N.W.2d 72 (N.D. 1975); Backman v. Bateman,263 P.2d 561 (Utah 1953) (no nepotism found where one of two brother teachers elected to school board long after their original employment).

61. Whateley v. Leonia Bd. of Education, 358 A.2d 826 (N.J. 1976).

b. Outside Employment. When a teacher or administrator holds outside political employment, two possible objections may be raised. If the outside position is *inherently* incompatible with school district duties, he or she may be required to surrender one of the positions.[62] If the jobs are not *inherently* incompatible, but still prevent efficient performance of school district duties, a court may still uphold disqualification. In the absence of a controlling statute, the determination of incompatibility and efficiency rests with the courts, but many courts have been fairly insensitive to the potential risks in dual employment. New Jersey courts ruled that a city council member could also act as a school district guidance counselor, even though the local city council might, in certain circumstances, be required to approve the general school budget.[63] In like vein, a Pennsylvania court ruled that a supervisor of special classes in an intermediate unit was technically not a supervisor of any of the school districts served by the unit and, therefore, was not disqualified from election to the board of a district that was part of the intermediate unit.[64]

Courts are split on the question whether a teacher could be excluded from membership on the state board of education although the state board exercised jurisdiction over the teacher's certificate. A New Mexico court thought the potential conflict of interests insufficient to justify the rule of exclusion, while an Illinois court upheld such exclusion.[65]

Where school personnel hold outside positions, the dual allegiance issue is complicated by still other considerations. In Oregon and Alaska the courts found that a public school teacher works in the executive branch of state government and could not concurrently act as a legislator in the legislative branch without violating the separation of powers provision of their state constitutions.[66] The mere potential for merging the powers of different branches rendered the concurrent positions unlawful, even though no misconduct was alleged or charged. The Oregon court noted that the wording of constitutions and statutes of different states vary, so that judicial interpretations of the separation doctrine in other jurisdictions were not binding on it.

The question whether school boards may, as a matter of administrative discretion, restrict their personnel from outside public positions has seldom arisen. In Mississippi and Indiana, board regulations forcing teacher candidates for elective office to take a leave of absence, without pay, were upheld.[67] A Wisconsin statute forbidding public employment to persons running for partisan political office was upheld.[68] The Supreme Court has recently ruled, however, that any school board regulation forcing employees to take

---

62. La Buhn v. White, 133 N.W.2d 903 (Iowa 1965).

63. Kaufman v. Pannuccio, 295 A.2d 642 (N.J. 1972).

64. Commonwealth v. Tekavec, 319 A.2d 1 (Pa. 1975); *cf.* Dobler v. Mincemoyer, 285 A.2d 159 (Pa. 1971)

65. Amador v. New Mexico State Bd. of Education,455 P.2d 840 (N.M. 1969); Hoskins v. Walker,315 N.E.2d 25 (Ill. 1974).

66. Monaghan v. Sch. District No.1,315 P.2d 797 (Ore. 1957); Begich v. Jefferson,441 P.2d 27 (Alaska 1968).

67. Chatham v. Johnson, 195 So.2d 62 (Miss. 1967); Sch. City of E. Chicago v. Sigler, 36 N.E.2d 760 (Ind. 1941).

68. Wisconsin State Employees Assn. v. Wisconsin Natural Resources Board, 298 F.Supp. 339 (W.D. Wis. 1969) *see generally* Civil Service Comm. v. National Assn. of Letter Carriers, 413 U.S. 548 (1973).

unpaid leave of absence while campaigning for elective office must, to be lawfully effective, be approved by the Attorney General or federal court in accordance with the federal Voting Rights Act.[69]

While the state may prohibit plural employments, it may not penalize employees merely because of their political party affiliations. The Supreme Court has ruled that state officials may no longer constitutionally dismiss nonpolicy-making employees as a matter of political patronage and that to justify patronage dismissals, the hiring authority must prove that party affiliation is an appropriate requirement for the effective performance of the public position involved.[70] A distinction must be made between permissible restriction against exercising outside public functions and restraining expression of political opinions outside the school that are made as a citizen and not as a public officer or employee. The constitutional doctrines on personal political expression are taken up later.

---

69. Dougherty County v. White, 435 U.S. 921 (1978).
70. Branti v. Finkel, 445 U.S. 507 (1980).

PART II

Employment Rights and Duties

Employment *rights,* in contrast to *eligibility,* rest upon the terms of one's contract—both individual and collective (union) agreements. In most states, a statutory contract *in writing* is required before any teacher can assert professional employment rights.[71] The form of contract is critical, and it must conform in many respects to statutory prescriptions. For example, a board could not require a tenured teacher to execute a contract that would alter rights fixed by the tenure statute; nor may a board by contract, intentionally or accidentally, confer tenure where the employee has not qualified with statutory requirements for tenure.[72] In the absence of such errors, however, the school board decides by its contracts how to classify and place an individual (i.e., as a substitute, temporary, or probationary teacher).[73]

> "It has been repeatedly recognized that unless statutory mandate compels otherwise, the position of the teacher is created and fixed by the terms of the contract of employment. As was said in Richardson v. Board of Education, 6 Cal.2d 583, 586 [2-3], 58 P.2d 1285, 1287, "The relation between the teacher and the school district is one that is created by contract. (Cita.) . . . Plaintiff's rights are governed by the contract in all matters in which the law leaves the parties free to contract. . . . The provisions of the contract, therefore, are controlling. . . . "It is, of course, true that the terms of the contract may be and often are controlled by mandatory provision of statute. . . . But no statute has been called to our attention and we have found none that requires the classification of the substitute teacher as probationary." *Matthews* v. *Bd. of Education,* 18 Cal. Rptr. 101, 104 (1962).

The terms of the contract determine both the compensation and the job-security status of the employee. For instance, probationary teachers may earn service credits toward tenure and enjoy certain statutory protections regarding dismissal, whereas teachers under contract as substitutes may not do so in many states.[74]

---

71. Dept.of Education v. Jersey Shore Area Sch. District,353 A.2d 91 (Pa. 1976), Heine v. Sch. District No. 271, 481 P.2d 316 (Idaho 1971). On the requirements for valid execution of contracts, see p. 496.

72. Halsey v. Bd. of Education, 331 A.2d 306 (Md. 1975); George v. Comm. Dept. of Education,325 A.2d 819 (Pa. 1974); Cipu v. No. Haven Bd. of Education, 351 A.2d 76 (Conn. 1974).

73. Hopp v. Oroville Sch. District, 639 P.2d 872 (Wash. 1982) (provisional employee not entitled to statutory tenure); Poulus v. Bd. of Trustees, 134 Cal. Rptr. 220 (1976) (temporary teacher cannot claim status of probationary teacher); Harrison Cent. Sch. Dist. v. Nyquist, 373 N.Y.S.2d 796 (1975) (school attorney appointed without contract is removable at any time at the pleasure of the board).

74. Poulus v. Bd. of Trustees, 134 Cal. Rptr. 220 (1976) (teacher under contract as "temporary teacher"

The laws of most states directly set standards of professional competence and fitness that must be met by all teachers and further require compliance by teachers with employment regulations of state and local school authorities. Hence the obligations of teachers are drawn partly from their employment contracts and partly from general laws and regulations, which are made part of those contracts either by explicit reference in the contract language or by operation of law as a matter of public policy.[75] This "reading in" of other duties, despite the teacher's plea of ignorance or lack of notice of any statute or regulation has been approved, not only as to rules in effect before contract signing, but also as to postcontract regulations, so long as later regulations do not impair previously vested contract rights.[76]

Another source of contract duties is the collectively bargained union agreement. The subject of collective agreements requires special discussion later, but all of the observations in this section are subject to the qualification that, to the extent they are authorized, collective bargaining agreements are also determinative of employment rights. In dovetailing these various sources, the essential problem is to ascertain which source will prevail when they are inconsistent with each other. (This problem is also explored in the later section on collective bargaining.)

The duties of public school teachers fall into several categories. The acquisition and maintenance of technical skills and knowledge is but one standard of "fitness" to teach. Fitness involves other relationships, in and out of school. In school, the teacher must obey and cooperate with lawful authority and avoid disruption of school work, whether dealing with students, professional colleagues, school boards, or parents. The teacher must meet minimal personal conduct standards in private life where such conduct relates to his or her influence on, and interaction with, the school community. In tracing the bounds of these general duties, courts must also determine when a teacher's civil rights prevail over public interests that tend to limit such rights. The large subject of "fitness", therefore, becomes meaningful only in terms of identifiable lines of cases.

A. Nonteaching Duties

Many of the duties derived from written contracts and laws are sometimes referred to as "implied duties." It may be helpful, however, to distinguish between duties that are inferred from the language of a written document on one hand and duties that are implied from the very nature of the teaching function, without reference to written terms. While the inference of duties from contract language often rests upon the same kinds of considerations that support duties implied in law (namely, what is reasonably expected of public school teachers), implication of work duties in the absence of express agreement

---

cannot claim status of "probationary teacher" or the job-security protections governing probationary teachers); Tyrone Area Ed. Assn. v. Tyrone Area Sch. District, 356 A.2d 871 (Pa 1976) (teacher hired as substitute cannot claim status as probationary teacher to work toward tenure).

75. *See* McGrath v. Burkhard, 280 P.2d 864, 867 (Cal. 1955); Pa. Stat. Annot. Titl 24, § 11-1121 (statutory formal contract).

76. *See* Arlington Ind. Sch. District v. Weekley,313 S.W.2d 929, (Tex. 1958) and case authorities there cited from other states.

involves the intent of the law and not of the parties. No court will imply a duty that contradicts the express agreement of the parties or express requirements of written law. For this reason, many previously disputed work duties are increasingly being defined or excluded by express stipulation in collectively bargained agreements.

As to open items, the only legal guideline is whether designated work is reasonably related to the teacher's function in a particular school. "There is no necessity that all the rules orders and regulations for the discipline, government and management of the school shall be made a matter of record by the school board, or that every act, order or direction affecting the conduct of such schools shall be authorized or confirmed by a formal vote."[77] Therefore, much is left to the judgment of school authorities and courts. As one court recently noted, "Naturally the courts have differed in the interpretation of what is 'reasonable' in various similar situations."[78] It is to the problem of implying work obligations, independently of document interpretation, that the following discussion is directed.

Lead cases from Illinois, California, and New York indicate that any duties, including nonteaching assignments, that are reasonable adjuncts to the normal school activities may be required of teachers, provided such duties are not demeaning to professional status, unreasonably burdensome, or discriminatory in the manner of their distribution among teachers.[79] Among the extracurricular duties implied by courts are supervision of study halls, cafeterias, school-sponsored events (social or athletic), attendance at open house, and teacher workshops.[80] A good discussion of the legal guidelines for specific implied duties is set forth in the much cited lead case of *McGrath v. Burkhard*, which is reported at the end of this chapter.

Where school authorities required teachers to do work not reasonably related to their employment duties, courts have disapproved such action. Thus, a directive to a teacher to supervise off-campus, after-school bowling by an independent student group not sponsored by the school was held to be beyond the teacher's obligations.[81] Conversely, physical education teachers have normally been assigned to team coaching duties as reasonably within their competence and sphere of work.[82] Yet a New York court indicated that a coaching assignment could not fall within the implied duties of a mathematics teacher and disapproved the same as unreasonable.[83] Since the rulings on implied powers are contingent and tied to the circumstances in each school, the issue of what is unrelated or unprofessional work may turn more upon the circumstances in any school than upon the labels applied to the teacher or the assignment. The language of the above-cited *McGrath* opinion is certainly broad enough to accommodate a finding that, in appropriate circumstances, the math teacher who is qualified to coach might be under

---

77. McGrath v. Burkhard, fn. 75, at p. 868.

78. District 300 Education Assn. v. Bd. of Education, 334 N.E.2d 165, 167 (Ill. 1975).

79. District 300 Education Assn. v. Bd. of Education, prior fn.; McGrath v. Burkhard, fn. 75 supra; Parrish v. Moss, 106 N.Y.S.2d 577 (1951). *Accord:* Thomas v. Bd. of Education, 453 N.E.2d 151 (Ill. 1983).

80. Blair v. Robstown Ind. Sch. District, 556 F.2d 1331 (5th Cir. 1977) (high school football game); Fox v. Bd. of Education,236 S.E.2d 243 (W. Va. 1977) (parent conference); *See* cases in prior fn.; Johnson v. United Sch. District Jt. Sch. Bd., 191 A.2d 897 (Pa. 1963).

81. Pease v. Millcreek Twp. Sch. District, 195 A.2d 104 (Pa. 1963).

82. Appeal of Ganaposki, 2 A.2d 742 (Pa. 1938).

83. Parrish v. Moss, fn. 79.

an implied duty to take such an assignment (viz. as to intramural games in a small rural school).

The generous scope afforded by courts to board discretion is indicated by an Illinois case in which teachers resisted assignments to nonacademic school-sponsored activities on the ground that the school code expressly permitted the school board to employ voluntary or paid nonprofessional persons to supervise the same activities. The court ruled that, while the law gave school boards the option of assigning nonprofessionals to such duties, it did not deprive them of discretion to assign teachers to that work. Since the duties assigned were found not to be onerous, time-consuming, or discriminatory, the court held the board's position to be legally enforceable.[84] In distinguishing between statutory options and the reasonableness of board discretion under one of those options, the court stressed that the burden of proving abuse of board discretion lay with the teachers. The case also raised the question whether nonteaching duties could be implied as to Saturday assignments where state law prohibited teaching assignments on Saturdays. The court held that the statute applied only to teaching and did not bar nonteaching assignments on Saturdays.

B. Tenure Status

Tenure and continuing contract laws exist in practically every state (see Table 5–1). They invest teachers with statutory rights that may not be removed merely at the discretion of school authorities. The primary aim of tenure law is to attract and hold good teachers by protecting them from political abuse or arbitrary interference.[85] The purpose is achieved principally by legislative provisions regarding tenured contract renewals, order of teacher layoff, disciplinary suspension, and termination of employment. Tenure rights qualify for constitutional procedural protections as a species of "property" interest under the Fourteenth Amendment, whereas such protections do not ordinarily extend to nontenured teachers. State legislatures can always modify tenure laws, but the trend has been toward increasing, rather than weakening, tenure protection.

There is no universally adopted description of tenure, but one author well described tenure as "the right of employment for a continuing or indefinite period of time, subject to removal only for a cause prescribed by . . . law." (viz. by mandatory retirement, professional unfitness, or necessary reductions in school staff).[86] Courts view tenure as creating a presumption of teacher fitness, and therefore exercise stricter review of administrative decisions that affect tenured teachers.

Not every class of teacher is given an opportunity to acquire tenure. A recent Minnesota decision construed the state's tenure statute as not covering a basketball coach.[87] Most statutes expressly exclude certain appointees (e.g., those who are hired as

---

84. District 300 Education Assn. v. Bd. of Education, fn. 78 *supra.*
85. Rockwell v. Crestwood Sch. District Bd. of Education, 227 N.W.2d 736 (Mich. 1975).
86. BOLMEIER, SCHOOL IN THE LEGAL STRUCTURE, 192 (1973).
87. Strong v. Ind. Sch. District, 256 N.W.2d 82 (Minn. 1977).

temporary or substitute personnel) from the class of (probationary) teachers who may acquire tenure.[88]

Teachers employed as probationers acquire tenure only by satisfactory performance over the period fixed by each state's tenure law, usually three years. Administrative agencies may not ignore or modify (by waiver or extension) the statutory probationary period.[89]

To qualify for tenure credit (and for seniority status), teachers must be in regular and continuous service. Continuous part-time teaching has been held to be probationary service counting toward tenure in Alaska, New York, and Oklahoma, but not in Louisiana.[90] In several states probation time will count for tenure credit only if the teacher devotes at least half of the work time to the area for which tenure is sought.[91]

The intent of the tenure statutes is also unclear where a teacher's salary is partially funded by outside sources. Teachers in federally funded positions were held to be eligible for tenure under Massachusetts law, but not in Louisiana, and reimbursement by the state to the school district for part-time consultation services of a full-time district teacher did not affect her probationary service in Oregon.[92] Courts must also decide what kinds of work interruptions discontinue the probationary period.[93] A year's leave of absence without pay was recently held to interrupt employment for seniority calculation in a staff reduction suit.[94]

There is division among the states as to whether probationary service in one school district can be carried over to another school district of the same state. Tacking on of such service is prohibited in some states, but permitted in others.[95]

The scope of teacher tenure also varies with state law. Tenure may be as broad as the holder's certification area, as in Pennsylvania.[96] Or it may be only as broad as the area of actual service under the employment contract, as in Colorado and New York.[97] Where

---

88. *See* Biancardi v. Waldwick Bd. of Education, 353 A.2d 123 (N.J. 1976); Paulus v. Bd. of Trustees, 134 Cal. Rptr. 220 (1976); Hudson v. Ind. Sch. District, 258 N.W. 2d 594 (Minn. 1977).

89. Halsey v. Bd. of Education of Garrett County,331 A.2d 306 (Md.1975); *cf.* City University v. Bd. of Higher Education, 330 N.Y.S.2d 688 (1972) (tenure acquisition could not be determined by a labor arbitrator).

90. District v. Lollar,547 P.2d 1324 (Okla. 1976); State v. Redman,491 P.2d 157 (Alaska 1971); People v. Kapp, 389 N.Y.S.2d 645 (1976) (kindergarten teacher on half-day sessions); *cf.* Brodie v. Sch. Committee, 324 N.E.2d 922 (Mass. 1975). Brown v. Bd. of Education, 347 N.E.2d 791 (Ill. 1976); Rosenberg v. Bd. of Education,378 N.Y.S.2d 433 (1976). *But see* Thompson v. E. Baton Rouge Parish Sch. Board, 303 So.2d 855 (La. 1974).

91. Copella v. Bd. of Education,367 A.2d 444 (N.J.1976); Rhee v. Allegheny Intermediate Unit No.3, 315 A.2d 644 (Pa. 1974); cf. Stang v. Ind. Sch. District,256 N.W.2d 82 (Minn.1977) (special assignment—coaching—not basis for added tenure claim).

92. *Compare* Brophy v. School Committee, 383 N.E.2d 521 (Mass. 1978) *with* Hayes v. Orleans Parish Sch. Bd., 237 So.2d 681 (La. 1970); *with* Thompson v. Sch. District, 548 P. 2d 161 (Ore. 1976).

93. See the case authorities collected in Annotation: *Teachers—Service Period—Computation,* 2 A.L.R.2d 1033 (1948).

94. Dreyfuss v. Bd. of Education, 339 N.Y.S.2d 547 (1972).

95. *Prohibited:* see e. g. Nagy v. Bd. of Education, 500 P.2d 987 (Colo. 1972); Pa. Stat. Ann. Tit. 24, § 1108. *Permitted: cf.* Oak Harbor Sch. Dist. v. Oak Harbor Ed. Assn., 545 P.2d 1197 (Wash. 1976) (seniority determined by total service in the state, and not only in the district); Harbe v. Hazelwood Sch. District, 532 S.W.2d 848 (Mo. 1975) (strict measurement of statutory period).

96. See fn. 91, *supra.*

97. See the Nagy case, fn. 95, *supra;* Coates v. Ambach, 383 N.Y.S. 2d 672 (1976); Prekindergarten teachers were held to be within elementary tenure area. McNamara v. Bd. of Education, 389 N.Y.S.2d 682 (1976).

tenure extends only to subject area and teacher works in two or more areas, seniority in each may (in some states) be measured only by the time worked in the claimed tenure area. One who served as both guidance counsellor and guidance coordinator, but spent more time in counselling, was entitled to seniority placement as guidance counsellor following abolition of the guidance coordinator position.[98] In "tenure area" states, courts must also decide which positions are sufficiently similar to fall within a designated tenure area. For example, a determination that a part-time psychologist position is similar to that of full-time psychologist entitles a psychologist to seniority tenure preference in either position.[99]

Many states do not extend tenure to administrative positions as such, but only to the general class of "professional employee," so that principals cannot claim tenure in that position, but others extend separate tenure to administrative positions, but rarely to the highest administrative posts.[100]

1. Tenure by Official Default

The general rule that tenure will vest only when the probationer has met all statutory conditions may not apply where the district culpably fails to observe its own obligations to the teacher. For example, a Michigan court held that the district's failure to give timely notice of performance ratings in the final year of probationary service effected a completion of satisfactory probation and a vesting of tenure.[101] Official failure to complete removal proceedings instituted prior to expiration of the teacher's probationary period until several months thereafter was also held to stop the board from denying tenure to the teacher.[102] Such a use of the *equitable estoppel* is, however, wholly within a court's discretion—as to whether particular circumstances require judicial intervention "in the interest of justice."[103] In a Florida case, a preliminary school board approval of a teacher for tenure was not deemed to estop the board from revoking its decision, due to probationer's later arrest, and consequent failure to complete his probationary contract.[104]

In Louisiana and New York, tenure was denied despite the board's failure to give timely notice of nonrenewal in the probationer's final probationary year. The courts held that the boards had under the presented facts acted with reasonable dispatch in making

---

98. Griffith v. Bd. of Education, 352 N.Y.S.2d 214 (1974).

99. Abrams v. Ambach, 351 N.Y.S.2d 750 (1974).

100. Compare, e.g., cases from jurisdictions with separate tenure for administrators; Wooten v. Alabama Tenure Commission, 421 So.2d 1288 (Ala. 1982); Paqua v. LaForche Paris Sch. Bd., 408 So.2d 438 (La. 1981); *with* sample cases from jurisdictions where administrators hold tenure as teachers; Snipes v. McAndrew, 313 S.E.2d 294 (S.Car. 1984); Waltz v. Bd. of Education, 329 N.W.2d 131 (S. Dak. 1983); Fuller v. N. Kansas City Sch. Dist., 629 S.W.2d 404 (Mo. 1982).

101. Hyde v. Willpinit Sch. Dist., 648 P.2d 892 (Wash. 1982); *cf.* Wilt v. Flannigan, 294 S.E.2d 189 (W.Va. 1982) (board policy violated); Morse v. Wozniak, 398 F.Supp. 597 (E.D. Mich. 1975). But see *contra:* fn. 102 below.

102. Elisofon v. Bd. of Education, 379 N.Y.S.2d 145 (1976); but cf. LaBarr v. Bd. of Education, 425 F. Supp. 219 (D. N.Y. 1977).

103. See the discussion of equity law in Chapter 1.

104. Williams v. Bd. of Public Instruction, 311 So.2d 812 (Fla. 1975).

the tenure denial decision.[105] A court could grant a common law remedy for contract damages and still deny the remedy of ordering a grant of tenure. Such was done in Tennessee.[106]

C. Teacher Placement

So long as school boards act reasonably, upon substantial evidence and do not violate lawful contracts, statutes, and constitutional rights, their employment decisions will prevail.[107] The burden of proving errors of law or abuse of discretion is upon the complaining teacher, but the nature of proofs to meet that burden will depend upon the subject matter in particular cases.

Courts regularly uphold local requirements for initial or in-service physical and medical examinations (e.g., with respect to communicable disease, minimum vision levels, and psychiatric evaluations).[108] Local requirements of educational training and experience (e.g., merit examinations and performance ratings) are upheld, save where they abridge statutory entitlements or constitutional rights.[109] Local boards may require professional growth, and adaptation to new teaching methods as conditions for contract renewal. Even for tenured teachers, the failure to meet such requirements may constitute cause for termination of their contract.[110] However, where board rules prescribe a specific penalty for failure to achieve professional growth (i.e., by a freeze on salary) the board may not ignore its own rule to impose the greater penalty of dismissal.[111]

1. Assignment and Transfer

Except for limited instances of direct statutory controls, teacher placement is generally delegated to school board discretion. So long as no error of law(e.g., illegal demotion) is committed, courts uphold administrative discretion on assignments and transfers.[112] Professional personnel normally have no right to hold particular posts within the district, and they may not reject an assignment, so long as it falls within their certification and

---

105. School Dist. v. Norwood, 644 P.2d 13 (Colo. 1984) (automatic renewal of tenure status held ineffective notwithstanding school board failure to meet statutory deadline); LaBorde v. Franklin Parish Sch. Bd.,510 F.2d 590 (5th Cir.1975); Mugavin v. Nyquist,367 N.Y.S.2d 604 (1975).

106. Snell v. Brothers, 527 S.W.2d 114 (Tenn. 1975).

107. Lee v. Macon County Bd. of Education, 463 F.2d 1174 (5th Cir. 1972); State v. Bd. of School Directors, 274 N.W. 301 (Wis. 1937).

108. School Dist. No. 1 Multnomah Cty. v. Teachers' Retirement Fund Ass'n.,95 P.2d 720 (Ore. 1939); *cf.* Chavich v. Bd. of Education of City of New York, 258 N.Y.S.2d 677 (1965); Gish v. Bd. of Education, 366 A. 2d 1337 (N.J. 1976).

109. Bd. of Education v. Nyquist,293 N.E.2d 819 (1973); Placerville Un. Sch. Dist. v. Porini, 70 Cal. Rptr. 73 (1968); King-Smith v. Aaron,317 F.Supp. 164 (W.D. Pa. 1970), reversed on other grounds 455 F.2d 738 (3rd Cir. 1972).

110. Jennings v. Caddo Parish Sch. Board,276 So.2d 386 (La.1973); Last v. Bd. of Education,185 N.E.2d 282 (Ill. 1962); Rible v. Hughes, 150 P.2d 455 (Cal. 1944).

111. Heifner v. Bd. of Education, 335 N.E.2d 600 (Ill. 1975).

112. Goodwin v. Bennett County H.S. Ind. Sch. District, 226 N.W.2d 166 (S.D. 1976).

tenure area.[113] Teachers who refuse lawful assignments may be discharged for insubordination.[114]

The employing board has no obligation to afford a hearing on its placement decisions[115] unless state law so requires,[116] but where the board has adopted assignment rules, it may not ignore them.[117] Nor may it use the transfer power for improper purposes, for instance, as punishment for conduct of which the board disapproves, but that is constitutionally protected. Disciplinary transfers in such cases have been overturned and the teacher reinstated to his former position. Some examples include teacher refusal to shave his beard, teacher off-school political support of a school board candidate, and teacher criticism of school policies at an open forum that was sponsored by the school to discuss such matters.[118]

The law does not forbid all disciplinary transfers, only those that are capricious or that violate legal rights. For example, a board may punish, by transfer, a teacher who wrongfully disobeys a lawful order to attend a workshop, and may punish his or her refusal to accept such transfer by discharge for insubordination.[119] In sum, courts will uphold transfers unless the teacher meets the burden of proving that the board acted arbitrarily or contrary to statute or constitutional limits on its authority.[120]

Teachers often seek to avoid the school board's authority by alleging that a particular assignment is an illegal "demotion" or violates vested teacher rights. The law on demotions will be taken up shortly, but a teacher must prove more than a distasteful transfer to nullify board assignments. A teacher returning from sabbatical leave could not demand reinstatement in her former position, nor could a teacher assigned to guidance counselling refuse transfer to class duties, if the reassignment also fell within the terms of her contract.[121] Similarly, a teacher certified to teach seventh and eighth grades could not refuse assignment to those grades merely because she had taught fourth grade for 18 years.[122]

---

113. Coe v. Bogart, 519 F.2d 10 (6th Cir. 1975); State v. Wilson,481 S.W.2d 760 (Tenn. 1972); Rosenthal v. Orleans Parish Sch. Bd., 214 So.2d 203 (La. 1968); Bd. of Education v. Williams 403 P.2d 324 (Ariz. 1965); Collins v. Wakonda Ind. Sch. District, 252 N.W.2d 646 (S.D. 1977).

114. Harrisburg R-VIII Sch. District v. O'Brian, 540 S.W.2d 945 (Miss. 1976); Matthews v. Bd. of Education, 18 Cal. Rptr. 101 (1962).

115. Wheeler v. Sch. District No. 20, 535 P.2d 206 (Colo. 1975); Hentschke v. Sink, 109 Cal. Rptr. 549 (1973); Mccoy v. Mcconnell, 461 S.W.2d 948 (Tenn. 1970).

116. State v. Berger, 314 So.2d 700 (Ala. 1975) (transferred principal had right to prior hearing under Alabama statute); Tenure Comm. v. Anniston City Bd. of Education, 326 So.2d 760 (Ala. 1976).

117. Rockey v. Sch. District No. 11, 508 P.2d 796 (Colo. 1973); American Federation of Teachers v. Oakland Unified Sch. District, 59 Cal. Rptr. 85 (1967).

118. Finot v. Pasadena City Bd. of Education, 58 Cal. Rptr. 520 (1967), Calhoun v. Cassidy, 534 S.W.2d 806 (Ky. 1976); Adcock v. Bd. of Education, 513 P.2d 900 (Cal. 1973). See also Givhan v. Western Line Cons. Sch. District, 439 U.S. 410 (1979) (discussed in *Connick v. Myers* case at the end of the chapter).

119. Brough v. Bd. of Education, 463 P.2d 567 (Utah 1970).

120. State v. Wilson, 481 S.W.2d 760 (Tenn. 1972).

121. Adelt v. Richmond Sch. District, 58 Cal. Rptr. 151 (1967) (postsabbatical reassignment); State v. Bd. of Education, 229 N.E.2d 663 (Ohio 1966); *cf.* Scottsdale Sch. District v. Clark, 512 P.2d 853 (Ariz. 1973).

122. Collins v. Wakonda Ind. Sch. District, 252 N.W.2d 646 (S.D. 1977).

2. Performance Ratings

Performance and efficiency ranking in teaching skills are crucial to employment decisions. They affect assignments, job security, tenure, contract renewals, order of layoff, and the discipline of teachers by transfer, demotion, suspension or dismissal. The validation of performance ratings is, therefore, essential.[123] Table 5–1 lists nine states in which formal rating systems are set by statute, but administratively designed performance ratings are authorized in many other states.[124] The importance of performance ratings leads courts to insist upon strict compliance with procedures that are established by statute for the rating process.

The failure to rate a teacher within the legal time deadline has been held to amount in law to a satisfactory rating.[125] The failure to give notice of an unsatisfactory rating, where required by law, is also ground to nullify the rating. This is true even though such rating, if properly given, would have resulted in denial of tenure or dismissal from probationary employment.[126] An unsatisfactory rating that was given without following applicable by-laws of the employing district has also been overturned.[127] The harmless error doctrine applies in some states to deny relief where board failure to rate a teacher was considered nonprejudicial (i.e., where the teacher's position was abolished and where no positions within her professional competence remained open in the district).[128]

Where an unsatisfactory rating is given, some state laws require a hearing upon request of the affected teacher. In such cases, the board must present evidence to support its unsatisfactory rating. If it merely presents a conclusion, the court may order it to withdraw the unsatisfactory rating.[129]

Rating methods vary considerably from state to state and within those states where districts are permitted by law to select one of several legal rating methods. Thus a rating system may be very primitive (i.e., using only the alternatives of "satisfactory" or "unsatisfactory") or refined to use a number of factors that are then weighted to arrive at different levels of numerical or verbal efficiency ranks.

The law on performance rating has been supplemented by collective bargaining agreements that specify specific methods and procedures for establishing ratings and resolving employee grievances on ratings. Therefore, in states that authorize such collective bargaining, the terms of the union agreements must be consulted.

---

123. Banks v. Comm'y Sch. Bd. No. 29, 364 N.Y.S.3d 379 (1975) (denial of renewal based upon valid unsatisfactory performance rating).

124. *See, e.g.*, Lipan v. Board of Education, 295 S.E.2d 44 (W.Va. 1982); Amato v. Oxford Area Comm. Sch. District, 245 N.W.2d 728 (Mich. 1976); and cases in the following footnotes.

125. Tyler v. Jefferson City-DuBoise Area Voc. Tec., 359 A.2d 761 (Pa 1976); Matteson v. State Bd. of Education, 136 P.2d 120 (Cal. 1900).

126. Holland v. Bd. of Education, 327 S.E.2d 155 (W.Va. 1985); Morse v. Wozniak, 398 F.Supp. 597 (E.D. Mich. 1975); George v. Union Area Sch., 350 A.2d 918 (Pa. 1976).

127. Longarzo v. Anker, 578 F.2d 469 (2d Cir. 1978).

128. Smith v. Bd. of Sch. Directors, 328 A.2d 883 (Pa. 1974).

129. Kudasik v. Bd. of Directors, 350 A.2d 887 (Pa. 1976).

3. Demotion

The power to transfer and reassign professional employees is qualified in most states if the transfer involves a "demotion." While the term *demotion* has different meanings in different states, it is clear that not every distasteful transfer involves a demotion, and not every demotion is unlawful. These two issues—what is a demotion and what demotions are legal—are separate and distinct. A teacher must first prove that the transfer was a demotion and then must show that the demotion was unlawful.[130]

The legal tests for demotion vary. In many states a transfer that results either in a reduction in salary or salary class *or* in the loss of professional rank, reputation, and prestige constitutes a demotion.[131] Thus, the loss of professional rank with diminished authority, responsibility, or prestige (viz. by transfer from principal to classroom teacher) was held a demotion.[132] Such a measure includes community reactions and impact upon the teacher's reputation. Reduction from a full- to a half-time position with lesser salary was also held to be a demotion.[133]

These alternating tests are not universally adopted. In Michigan the loss of professional ranking does not effect a demotion, and the indispensible element for demotion is reduction of compensation.[134] In other states, notably Illinois and California, demotion is determined solely by reference to the change, if any, in statutory classification of the teacher's certification or tenure area. Thus any assignment or reassignment that falls within the employee's certification or tenure area, albeit at a reduced salary, and at some loss of professional image or dignity, would not constitute a demotion in those states.[135]

The tenure laws of several states prohibit transfers of tenured teachers at reduced compensation unless there are sufficient grounds to "dismiss" the tenured teacher. Under some school codes, similar statutory protections may apply to particularly costly teachers reassignments.

a. Requisite Procedures. A number of state laws require that notice and hearing be afforded to teachers on any transfer that they claim is a "demotion." With narrow exception, such laws are considered mandatory, so that failure to provide proper notice and hearings will result in reversal of the board.[136] Such reversals do not automatically

---

130. Lee v. Pickens County Sch. System, 563 F.2d 143 (5th Cir. 1977); Dept. of Education v. Kauffman, 343 A.2d 391 (Pa. 1975).

131. *Cf.* Bd. of Education v. Williams, 403 P.2d 324 (Ariz. 1965); Mccoy v. Tangipahoa Parish Sch. Bd., 308 So.2d 382 (La. 1975); Kenaston v. Sch. Adm've District No. 40, 317 A.2d 7 (Me. 1974); Lee v. Macon County Bd. of Education, 453 F.2d 1104 (5th Cir. 1971); Mccoy v. Mcconnell, 461 S.W.2d 948 (Tenn. 1970); *cf.* Rosenthal v. Orleans Parish Sch. Bd., 214 So.2d 203 (La. 1968). In re Santee's Appeal, 156 A.2d 830 (Pa. 1959).

132. *Idem;* Glennon v. Sch. Comm'ee of Boston, 378 N.E.2d 1372 (Mass. 1978).

133. Norwin Sch. District v. Chlodney, 390 A.2d 328 (Pa. 1978).

134. Street v. Bd. of Education, 104 N.W.2d 748 (Mich. 1960); Dodge v. Bd. of Education, 170 N.W.2d 290 (Mich. 1959).

135. Preuss v. Bd of Education, 667 S.W.2d 391 (Ky. 1984); Lane v. Bd. of Education, 348 N.E.2d 470 (Ill. 1976); Council of Directors and Supervisors v. Los Angeles Un. Sch. District, 110 Cal. Rptr. 624 (1973) (mass demotions for fiscal reasons).

136. White v. Banks, 614 S.W.2d 331 (Tenn. 1981); Candelari v. Bd. of Education, 428 A.2d 331

prohibit transfers, but only require that a proper hearing be provided on the demotion issue. Statutory procedures are equally binding on teachers, and a teacher's failure to follow the statutory appeal procedure is ground to deny any relief.[137] A teacher's failure to make timely demand for a hearing was also held to have waived the right to hearing.[138]

But acceptance of a new assignment without consent to the demotion pending a hearing on the issue has been held not to constitute such a waiver.[139] Nor is a teacher barred from legal redress where the teacher resigned rather than accept the challenged reassignment.[140] On the issue of rights, pending a full hearing, one court held that the teacher is not entitled to retain his former position pending the hearing decision.[141] In the absence of a clear statute, the latter case is consistent with the general rule that a school board's assignment decisions are prima facie valid, until proven otherwise.

Whether violations on statutory procedure are curable or avoidable as harmless error will depend on the strictness with which state courts interpret their respective statutes.

A Massachusetts court rejected a teacher's complaint that a required hearing was not held, where that hearing would only cover a legally insignificant issue.[142] Legally deficient notices have also been held to be curable by adequate later notifications, even at the hearing or trial.[143] In one state the notice statute was interpreted as requiring only notice of certain action to be taken, without specification of reasons for a teacher transfer.[144]

The rationale that notice requirements may be satisfied by alternate procedures that fairly advise the teacher has not been followed by all courts.[145] Where a school district reorganization resulted in position eliminations, the well-publicized formal resolution to eliminate the plaintiff's position was itself held to be sufficient notice of his impending demotional transfer.[146] A contrary view requiring strict compliance with statutory notice prevailed in Louisiana, where the court voided reorganizational demotions for lack of proper statutory notice.[147]

Demotion decisions, like hiring decisions, must be made by the school board and cannot be delegated to any individual.[148] But the board may delegate the ministerial function of carrying out its directive to subordinate individuals.[149]

(Conn. 1980); Barton v. Governing Bd. of Middletown Un. Sch. District, 131 Cal. Rptr. 455 (1976); Black v. Wyalusing Area School Dist., 365 A.2d 1352 (Pa. 1976).

137. Greene v. County Bd. of Education, 197 So.2d 771 (Ala. 1967).

138. Williams v. Cody, 545 P.2d 905 (Ore. 1976); Clark v. Mt. Greylock Regional H.S. District, 336 N.E.2d 750 (Mass. 1975).

139. Bd. of Sch. Directors v. Pittinger, 305 A.2d 382 (Pa. 1973).

140. Calhoun v. Cassady, 534 S.W.2d 806 (Ky. 1976).

141. Dept. of Education v. Charleroi Area Sch. District, 347 A.2d 736 (Pa. 1975).

142. Jantzen v. Sch. Comm'ee of Chelmsford, 124 N.E.2d 534 (Mass. 1955).

143. Potts v. Gibson, 469 S.W.2d 130 (Tenn. 1971).

144. State v. Bd. of Education, 172 S.E.2d 796 (W.Va. 1970).

145. Wilks v. Bd. of Education, 383 N.Y.S.2d 64 (1976) (defective notice of hearing held not cured by subsequent acts).

146. Clark v. Mt. Greylock Regional Sch. District, 336 N.E.2d 750 (Mass. 1975).

147. Palone v. Jefferson Parish Sch. Bd., 306 So. 2d 679 (La. 1975).

148. Bd. Of Sch. Directors v. Pittinger, 305 A.2d 382 (Pa. 1973).

149. Frank v. Arapahoe County Sch. District, 506 P.2d 373 (Colo. 1972).

b. Lawful and Unlawful Demotion. Demotions may be lawfully effected for two distinct purposes, namely, efficient management of available resources and the discipline of particular individuals. Demotions necessitated by position and salary revisions to meet school needs are usually lawful, and courts sustain such decisions where there is no abuse of discretion or error of law.[150]

In states where tenure is held only as a teacher and not as a principal or administrator, transfers between principal and teaching positions necessitated by job eliminations are not necessarily illegal demotions.[151] In states where principals hold tenure as principals and their position is abolished, they are entitled to placement in a comparable position, if one is held by someone of lesser tenure rank.[152] Where no comparable position remains open for transfer of a tenured principal or teacher, the legal result varies in different states. In Pennsylvania and Massachusetts, reorganizational position abolitions justify transfers to lower ranks and pay positions if there is no position of similar rank, but in California such a transfer was treated as dismissal under that state's tenure law.[153] In Kentucky and Louisiana, a transfer from an abolished to a lesser position is lawful, but the district may not reduce the transferee's salary for the work in the lesser position.[154]

The good faith of a board's decision is always subject to legal challenge. A board may not use its transfer authority solely to avoid a teacher's contract that specifies a given position and salary.[155]

Federal courts may override transfer decisions to achieve school desegregation and may require preferential assignments or promotion for minority teachers, even though such action is contrary to general state law.[156]

Disciplinary transfers to lesser positions (i.e., for teacher deficiency in performance or in professional conduct) are allowed in many states, provided proper procedures are followed and the findings justifying demotions are based upon sufficient evidence.[157] Many of the above-discussed legal principles noted in this section are reviewed in the opinion in *Comm. of Pennsylvania* v. *Charleroi Area Sch. District,* which is reproduced at the end of this chapter.

Since demotional decisions arguably involve working terms and conditions, they may also be subjected to collectively bargained contract provisions in states that

---

150. Steiler v. Spokane Sch. District, 558 P.2d 198 (Wash. 1977); McMullen v. Dist. Sch. Bd.,533 P.2d 812 (Ore. 1975). *See* Mohr v. Dade County Sch. Bd., 287 So.2d 337 (Fla. 1973).

151. *Compare, e.g.,* McCoy v. Tangipahoa Parish Sch. Bd., fn. 131, *supra,* with the Lane case, fn. 135, *supra.*

152. *See, e.g.,* Jadick v. Bd. of Education, 204 N.E.2d 202 (N.Y. 1964).

153. Kaplan v. Sch. Comm'ee of Melrose, 294 N.E.2d 209 (Mass. 1973); Downey v. Sch Comm'ee of Lowell, 25 N.E.2d 738 (Mass. 1940); Brownsville Area Sch. District v. Lucostic, 297 A.2d 516 (Pa. 1972); Mitchell v. Bd. of Trustees, 42 P.2d 397 (Cal. 1935).

154. *See, e.g.,* Huff v. Harlan County Bd. of Education,408 S.W. 2d 457 (Ky. 1966); Verrett v. Calcasieu Parish Sch. Bd. 103 So.2d 560 (La. 1958); *cf.* Mitchell v. Garrett, 510 S.W.2d 894 (Tenn. 1974).

155. Kotan v. Sch. District No. 110C, 509 P. 2d 452 (Ore. 1973); Bd. of Education v. Williams,403 P.2d 324 (Ariz. 1965); *but see* Mouras v. Jefferson Parish Sch. Bd., 300 So.2d 540 (La. 1974).

156. Lee v. Macon County Bd. of Education,463 F.2d 1174 (5th Cir. 1972); Singleton v. Jackson Mun. Sep. Sch. District, 425 F.2d 1211 (5th Cir. 1970).

157. Sullivan v. Brown, 544 F.2d 279 (6th Cir. 1976); Wheeler v. Sch. District No. 20,535 P.2d 206 (Colo. 1974) (principal demoted for failure to maintain proper discipline); *cf.* Bates v. Dause, 502 F.2d 865, (6th Cir. 1974) (principal demoted for supporting illegal teacher strike).

recognize that subject as bargainable. To the extent that union agreements are pertinent, therefore, they must be consulted.

D. Termination and Suspension

Shrinking teacher employment and expansion of teachers' rights have encouraged lawsuits to prevent teacher dismissals. Different laws apply to different forms of dismissal (e.g., nonrenewal of contract, layoff, suspension, or discharge for cause) and vary with the status (tenured or not) of the affected teachers and with the grounds for dismissal. The following sections cover the more typical termination situations.

1. Excess Teachers

Reduced enrollments, fiscal shortfalls, school consolidations, and curriculum revisions often require professional staff reductions and consequent release of excess teachers. Employees who challenge their release usually focus on two major issues, namely, that their position was not lawfully abolished and that persons other than themselves should have been selected for release from employment.

2. Position Abolition

The power of school boards to operate an efficient system includes the power to abolish positions in the absence of any contravening statute. Abolition decisions will be upheld so long as the asserted grounds are reasonable and supported by substantial evidence.[158]

Position abolition must be real. Teachers who disproved that any true abolition was made obtained reinstatement. Thus filling the same position with another employee, under a new job title, does not qualify as a position abolition to justify release.[159] However, the elimination of a distinct position, with redistribution of its duties as additional tasks to holders of different positions, is lawful.[160] Such eliminations leave only the independent question of priority in the bumping order among surplus teachers.

While economic necessity is a strong basis for abolishing positions, it is not always sufficient. A number of abolitions have been reversed or reduced as excessive, notwithstanding fiscal pressures, where the abolished positions were deemed necessary to maintain quality education or to carry out state mandated duties.[161] Abolition of all

---

158. Baer v. Nyquist,338 N.Y.S.745 (1972) (single position abolition); E. Detroit Fed. of Teachers v. Bd. of Education, 223 N.W.2d 9 (Mich. 1974) (probationary teachers in large staff reduction); Lacy v. Richmond Un. Sch. District, 119 Cal. Rptr. 1 (1975). For explanation of interrelated, and confusing, California statutes bearing upon excess teachers, *see* Gassman v. Gov'g Bd. of Rincon Valley Sch. District, 128 Cal. Rptr. 273 (1976). *See also* Works v. Abrahamson Union High School District Bd. of Directors, 483 A.2d 258 (Vt. 1984).

159. Baron v. Mackreth, 260 N.E. 2d 554 (N.Y. 1970); Viemeister v. Bd. of Education, 68 A.2d 768 (N.J. 1949).

160. Young v. Bd. of Education, 315 N.E.2d 768 (N.Y. 1974); Jordahl v. Ind. Sch. Dist. No. 129, 225 N.W.2d 224 (Minn. 1974).

161. Palone v. Jefferson Parish Sch. Bd., 297 So.2d 208 (La. 1974); Karbach v. Bd. of Education, 114 Cal. Rptr. 84 (1974).

attendance teacher positions, without reassignment of their duties to ensure compliance with attendance laws, was, therefore, overturned.[162]

Released teachers are normally not entitled to demand a hearing on the abolition decision, be they nontenured or tenured, unless state legislation so requires.[163] Courts are inclined to consider abolition dismissals as falling outside teacher termination statutes because releases pursuant to position abolition are impersonal and in no way impugn the released teacher personally.[164]

a. Order of Release. Tenure status provides job security, but not job insurance. In staff reduction, tenured teachers are entitled to retention preference in the "bumping order" over nontenured teachers. A tenured teacher is entitled to a position until all nontenured teachers holding positions for which the tenured teacher is qualified have been released.[165] This preference applies as well to tenured teachers who are on leave when the staff reduction takes place, and probationers may be released to make way for future returning tenured teachers.[166]

Between tenured teachers holding like positions, seniority is the predominant, but not exclusive, factor on order of release.[167] Since seniority rights did not exist at common law, they must be found in a governing statute or in the terms of a teacher's contract. Even in staff reductions, a teacher's contract requiring notice of termination was held to prevent dismissal.[168]

Under prevailing statutes, tenured teachers with higher seniority rights usually are entitled to priority of retention only with respect to positions that they are qualified to fill: "the law does not require a school district to retain unneeded teachers in one area of education at the expense of not hiring needed teachers in another."[169] Seniority standards have been qualified by other factors under the statutes of some states. A substantial difference in the recorded performance ratings among teachers competing for the same position is one example.[170] However, even there seniority has largely prevailed.

---

162. Geduldig v. Bd. of Education, 351 N.Y.S.2d 167 (1974).

163. *Nontenured*: Phillippi v. Sch. District, 367 A.2d 1133 (Pa. 1977); Boyce v. Bd. of Ed. 257 N.W.2d 153 (Mich. Ct. App. 1977); Palone v. Jefferson Parish School Bd., 297 So.2d 208 (La. 1974). *Tenured:* Mitchell v. Bd. of Education, 389 N.Y.S.2d 354 (1976); Johnson v. Bd. of Education, District of Riveredge, (case no. 75-1958) (D.C. N.J. 1975); statutory hearing provision: Fatscher v. Bd. of Sch. Directors, 367 A.2d 1130 (Pa. 1977) (applicable to tenured teachers only).

164. *See* Palone, fn. 163.

165. Sto-Rox Sch. District v. Horgan, 449 A.2d 796 (Pa. 1982); Coates v. Bd. of Ed., 662 P.2d 1279 (Kan. 1983); Fedele v. Board of Education of Town of Branford, 394 A.2d 737 (Conn. 1977); State v. Ind. Sch. District No. 695, 217 N.W.2d 212 (Minn. 1974); Bd. of School Trustees v. O'Brien, 190 A.2d 23 (Del. 1963).

166. McManus v. Ind. Sch. District, 321 N.W.2d 891 (Minn. 1982). *See* E. Detroit Fed. of Teachers v. Bd. of Education, fn. 157.

167. *Idem.; Mitchell v. Bd. of Education, 389 N.Y.S.2d 354 (1976); cf.* Karbach v. Bd. of Education, 114 Cal. Rptr. 84 (1974).

168. *Cf.* Zimmerman v. Minot State College 198 N.W.2d 108 (N.J. 1972).

169. See Smith v. Bd. of Sch. Directors, 328 A.2d 883, p. 885 (Pa. 1974); *accord:* Ward v. Nyquist, 389 N.Y.S.2d 638 (1976); Young v. Bd. of Education, fn. 159, supra; Evans v. Mount View School, 525 P.2d 1172 (Colo. 1974); *cf.* Foesch v. Ind. Sch. District No. 646, 223 N.W. 2d 371 (Minn. 1974).

170. Pa. Stat. Ann. titl 24 § 11-1125(a) (pkt. part 1976); superceded by Pa. Stat. Ann. titl 24 § 11-1125.1 (marking seniority the sole priority test).

To assure good faith application of statutory seniority, courts may require school boards to realign the entire teaching staff, following staff reduction, to ensure senior tenured teachers proper access to the remaining positions.[171] Courts have, however, divided on the question whether the board or the complaining teacher has the burden of proving that proper realignment was or was not made.[172]

When professional employees of two districts are absorbed into a single merged district, their seniority rankings will depend upon their particular state statutes. In New Mexico the court read the state law to require recognition of the prior seniority of teachers in the absorbed, as well as the absorbing, system.[173] However, where a regional school was created directly by statute in Maine, the court interpreted that statute to authorize hiring probationers for the new school without preference to tenured teachers in other area schools. The separate statute vested discretion on staffing in the new school board without reference to the general tenure laws.[174]

As noted previously, tenured teachers have no legal claim to particular teaching assignments. There is, however, a conflict of authority on the questions whether a displaced principal with seniority is entitled to preferential placement in comparable principalship or whether he or she may be placed in a lower level principalship while less-senior principals remain in comparable principalships.[175]

Nontenured Personnel. Seniority preference is not commonly provided to nontenured personnel, but some states have statutes that establish seniority ranking among the nontenured staff.[176] Absent such special protections, the retention of nontenured employees generally remains within the school board's discretion unless seniority rights are created by contract.[177]

b. Order of Recall. The job security afforded tenured teachers extends to the order of recall after layoffs. When released as excess personnel, tenured teachers are not truly discharged, but merely furloughed, laid off, or, as described in some states, suspended, until another suitable position becomes available. Furloughed tenured teachers are generally given recall preference in the order of seniority rank.[178]

---

171. *See* Peters v. Bd. of Education, 435 N.E.2d 814 (11. 1982); Smith v. Bd. of Sch. Directors, 328 A.2d 883 (Pa. 1974).

172. Compare Smith case, *ibid.*, with Penasco Ind. Sch. District No. 4 v. Lucero, 526 P.2d 825 (N.M 1974).

173. Gill v. Duchess County Bd. of Coop. Educ. Services, 472 N.Y.S.2d 435 (1984); Hensley v. State Bd. of Education, 376 P.2d 968 (N.M. 1962).

174. Beckett v. Roderick, 251 A.2d 427 (Me. 1969).

175. *Compare* Jadick v. Bd. of Education, 204 N.E.2d 202 (N.Y. 1964) *with* Jantzen v. Sch. Comm'ee. 124 N.E. 2d 534 (Mass. 1955).

176. *See* Lezette v. Bd. of Education, 319 N.E.2d 189 (N.Y. 1974).

177. See the discussion of contract renewal in the next section.

178. *See* Walker v. Bd. of Ed. 442 N.E.2d 870 (Ill. 1982); Portage Area Sch. District v. Portage Area Sch. Assn., 368 A.2d 864 (Pa. 1977).

3. Contract Renewal

Tenured teachers are entitled to automatic contract renewal unless they are discharged for cause or laid off as excess teachers.[179] Nontenured teachers generally have no such right, and their contract renewal is a matter of school board discretion. (The exceptional laws in minority states are noted in the following discussion.) Nonrenewal terminates a probationer's legal ties with the district, without any contingent rights regarding recall. Within rather narrow limits probationers may contest their nonrenewal, but their claims to renewal must usually rest upon factors other than the bare status of probationer. Nonrenewals based on misconduct charges are more like dismissals for cause, which are discussed in a later section.[180] This section deals with discretionary nonrenewals based upon factors other than a teacher's personal deficiencies.

a. Notice. Where individual rights are not implicated, the board is not required to provide *advance* hearings, or statements of its reasons for probationer nonrenewal.[181] The summary of state laws in Table 5–1 reveals, however, that most state codes require some notice of *intention* not to renew prior to a statutory time deadline, only to afford the probationer a reasonable opportunity to seek substitute employment, but not to empower the teacher to challenge the board's decision.[182] Even where the statute gave a right to notice and hearing, a Rhode Island court found that it did not confer any right to a statement of reasons for nonrenewal.[183] Table 5–1 also indicates the few states that permit probationers to request a hearing and appeal the board's decision. A few states also protect probationers with satisfactory ratings by procedures normally reserved to tenured teachers, namely, that probationers receive an advance statement of reasons and a hearing on the nonrenewal decision and that satisfactory probationers be furloughed (subject to recall) but not discharged.[184] School board by-laws may also limit the process, and courts have invalidated nonrenewals not effected in compliance with board by-1aws.[185]

---

179. Minn. Assn. Public Schools v. Hanson, 178 N.W.2d 846 (Minn. 1970) (tenure cannot freeze school organization and is always subject to police power arrangements of public schools by the state).

180. On the denial of renewal for unconstitutional reasons, *see* Lusk v. Estes 361 F. Supp 653 (N.D. Tex. 1973).

181. Ryan v. Aurora City Bd. of Education, 540 F.2d 222 (6th Cir. 1976), cert. denied 429 U.S. 1041 (1977); Buhr v. Buffalo P. Sch. Dist., 509 F.2d 1196 (8th Cir. 1974); Satterfield v. Edenton-Chowan Bd. of Education, 530 F.2d 567 (4th Cir. 1975); Moore v. Knowles, 512 F.2d 72 (5th Cir. 1975); Miller v. Sch, District No. 167, 500 F.2d 711 (7th Cir. 1974); Newman v. Bd. of Education, 325 A.2d 387 (Del. 1974); Blackmore v. Jasper City Comm. Un. Sch. District No. 1,314 N.E. 2d 677 (Ill. 1974); Gibson v. Butler,484 S.W.2d 356 (Tenn. 1972); Munro v. Elk Rapids Schools,178 N.W.2d 450 (Mich.1970). *But see* states that are *contra,* fn. 184, *infra.*

182. Fisher v. Ind. School Dist. No. 118, 215 N.W.2d 65 (Minn. 1974). But where only board policy established notice deadline, board delay beyond deadline to give teacher opportunity to convince board to renew, held no ground to overturn late nonrenewal. Carl v. So. San Antonio Ind. Sch. District, 561 S.W. 2d 560 (Tex. 1978).

183. Jacob v. Board of Regents, 365 A.2d 430 (R.I. 1976).

184. *Advance statement or hearing:* McKelvey v. Colonial Sch. District, 348 A.2d 445 (Pa. 1975); Cronacher v. Scribner, 369 N.Y.S.2d 780 (1975); Kruse v. Bd. of Directors, 231 N.W.2d 626 (Iowa 1975); California Education Code. 13443. *Furlough:* Gabriel v. Trinity Area Sch. District,350 A.2d 203 (Pa. 1976).

185. Cronacher v. Scribner, fn. 183. *But see contra,* Carl v. So. San Antonio Ind. Sch. District, fn. 182.

Different state courts have not been equally strict in enforcing renewal notice deadlines. Some hold the statutory notice deadline to be mandatory and nullify nonrenewal decisions that violate such statutes,[186] even though the notice defect was not shown to materially prejudice or harm the teacher.[187] Despite the absence of statutory notice, courts in other states upheld nonrenewal decisions under the harmless error doctrine.[188] Under that doctrine, technical failures will not void employment decisions where the teacher is not prejudiced by the error. Thus, an improperly posted and misaddressed nonrenewal notice that actually reached the teacher within the same time as a properly mailed notice was held harmless error and insufficient to overturn the nonrenewal.[189] Courts that view statutory notice provisions as a rule of reason, rather than a rigid mandate, will also disfavor teachers who willfully attempt to avoid or frustrate timely delivery of a nonrenewal notice.[190] Courts also allow boards to cure notice errors by giving a proper substitute notice and hearing, if such can be provided within the time deadlines set by law.[191]

b. Challenging Nonrenewal. Probationers who challenge a nonrenewal on abuse of discretion grounds have a heavy burden of proof, since courts will not presume to second guess board discretion. Courts decline to weigh evidence anew or question the wisdom of board decisions unless state statutes expressly call for a new trial.[192] Nor will they question the board's good faith unless proof of bad faith is first provided by the teacher.[193] The board itself, however, may reverse its prior renewal decision at a later meeting if its action is otherwise timely under state law.[194]

Probationers have in recent years resorted to labor grievance procedures under state labor laws and to constitutional litigation in seeking to avoid nonrenewal decisions. The emerging body of law on teacher labor relations requires separate study in later sections, but union agreements that define subjects of grievance or nonrenewal procedures will prevail only if they are held to be consistent with education statutes.[195]

The Fourteenth Amendment does not protect a probationer unless he or she can show a *property* or *liberty* interest in the job, as those terms are conceived in constitutional law. Except in very limited circumstances that will be reviewed later, the United States

---

186. Bessler v. Bd. of Chartered Sch. District, 296 N.E.2d 89 (Ill. 1973); Dryden v. Marcellus Comm. Schools, 250 N.W.2d 782 (Mich. 1977); Hill v. Dayton Sch. District, 517 P.2d 223 (Wash. 1973).

187. Tsakiris v. Phoenix Union High School System, 502 P.2d 1093 (Ariz. 1972) (nonrenewal notice two days beyond deadline, held to result in automatic contract renewal).

188. Joanou v. Bd. of Education, 345 A.2d 46 (Conn. 1974).

189. Governing Bd. of Palo Verde Peninsula Un. Sch. District v. Felt, 127 Cal. Rptr. 381 (1976). But in Oregon, timely mailing of notice was held insufficient if received after the statutory deadline. Welo v. District Sch. Bd., 545 P.2d 921 (Ore. 1976).

190. Conte v. Sch. Comm'ee, 356 N.E.2d 261 (Mass. 1976).

191. Hunter v. Bd. of Dir. of Inchelium Sch. District, 536 P.2d 1209 (Wash. 1975); Snider v. Kit Carson Sch. Dist., 442 P.2d 429 (Colo. 1968).

192. Turner v. Bd. of Trustees, 535 P.2d 1171 (Cal. 1975). *See* the discussion on judicial review in Chapter 1.

193. Jinkerson v. Lane City Sch. District No. 19, 531 P.2d 289 (Ore. 1975).

194. Venes v. Comm'y. Sch. Bd., 373 N.E.2d 387 (N.Y. 1978).

195. *See* Newman v. Bd. of Education, 325 A.2d 387 (Del. 1974) (grievance provision held unenforceable); Lockport Area Sp. Ed. Coop. v. Lockport Area Sp. Ed. Coop. Assn.,338 N.E.2d 463 (Ill. 1975) (nonrenewal provision held unenforceable).

Supreme Court has affirmed the view of the majority of courts that, as a class, probationers have no cognizable property or liberty interests in continued school employment.[196] Probationers have had a poor success rate on establishing the special facts required to obtain a constitutional hearing. Nevertheless, the nonrenewal litigation in a shrinking job market has been heavy and the cases that do succeed encourage new efforts to find constitutional protection.

A prime constitutional ground for reversing nonrenewals is board motivation to punish the teacher for the exercise of constitutionally protected rights. For example, school board denial of contract renewal in retribution for a teacher's union activities violates the teacher's civil right to freedom of association and cannot be sustained as a lawful exercise of discretion.[197] But if a teacher cannot prove that charge, nonrenewal will be upheld on such grounds as lack of cooperation or a personality conflict between the superintendent and the probationer.[198] Thus, cases involving union activist teachers often turn upon the resolution of fact issues.

A convenient discussion of the limited constitutional procedural and substantive rights of nontenured teachers under federal constitutional law is contained in *Hawkins* v. *Linn County School District No. 14* (reproduced at the end of this chapter).

A decision not to renew a probationer's expired contract must be distinguished from a decision to terminate employment during the unexpired contract period. While the board has unilateral discretion on signing new contracts, it cannot violate a teacher's existing contract (property) rights or cut them off without a hearing. Otherwise, the board will be liable for its own breach.[199] In such situations, constitutional as well as statutory hearings are required. The general law of contracts is beyond the scope of this text, but the termination of nontenured as well as tenured teachers must normally be justified by grounds that amount to a teacher breach of contract.

4. Discharge for Cause

At common law, either party to a contract may end it upon substantial breach by the other party, but the state legislature may limit the power to discharge a teacher to grounds specified by statute. School statutes commonly allow school boards to discipline teachers by less severe sanctions (e.g., suspension), though the violation might also justify discharge.[200] As previously noted, courts may always reduce disciplinary penalties that they find to be unreasonably excessive.[201]

---

196. Roth v. Bd. of Regents,408 U.S. 564 (1972); Perry v. Sindermann,408 U.S.593 (1972); Weathers v. W. Yuma County Sch. District, 530 F.2d 1335 (10th Cir. 1976).

197. Hanover Twp. Fed. of Teachers v. Hanover Comm., 318 F.Supp. 757 (D. Ind. 1970).

198. See Givhan case fn. 118, *supra*, Mt. Healthy City Bd. of Ed. v. Doyle,429 U.S. 274 (1977), Simcox v. Bd. of Education, 443 F.2d 40 (7th Cir. 1971) (lack of cooperation); Petersburg Ed. Assn. v. Petersburg Sch. District No. 14, 543 P.2d 35 (Ore. 1975) (personality conflicts).

199. Wertz v. Southern Cloud Unified Sch. Dist., 542 P.2d 339 (Kan. 1975) (probationer's property interest in existing contract and stigma from midyear discharge held to require termination hearing as matter of constitutional due process); *accord:* Indian Oasis Sch. District No. 40 v. Zambrano, 526 P.2d 408 (Ariz. 1974); *cf.* McKelvey v. Colonial Sch. District, 348 A.2d 445 (Pa. 1975) (termination of probationer during the contract period requires hearing under state statute).

200. Goldsmith v. Bd. of Education, 225 P. 783 (Cal. 1924).

201. Sarro v. N.Y.C. Bd. of Education, 405 N.Y.S.2d 777 (1978).

With regard to nontenured teachers, a board has alternative remedies for defaults, namely, immediate discharge or nonrenewal following expiration of the current contract term. As previously noted, nonrenewal normally places no burden of justification on the board, but midterm contract terminations do require a hearing and justification by the board. For wrongful midterm discharge, the board may be ordered to reinstate the teacher and be held liable for loss of contract earnings and possibly for injury to the teacher's reputation.[202]

All grounds for teacher discharge relate to the core concept of teacher "fitness," which encompasses a broad range of factors.[203] The state has a recognized interest in maintaining a proper moral as well as intellectual environment in public schools:[204]

> "The calling of a teacher is so intimate, its duties so delicate, the things in which a teacher might prove unworthy or would fail are so numerous that they are incapable of enumeration in any legislative enactment. . . . His habits, his speech, his good name, his cleanliness, the wisdom and propriety of his unofficial utterances, his associations, all are involved. His ability to inspire children and to govern them, his power as a teacher, and the *character* for which he stands are matters of major concern in a teacher's selection and retention." (Emphasis supplied)[205]

Therefore, fitness has a double focus—the first looking to capability to teach or administer and the second looking to personal conduct and character, in or out of school, that may harm the school, its students, and personnel. State statutes implement these goals by specifying broad grounds for discharge, such as *incompetency, incapacity, insubordination, unprofessional conduct, immorality, intemperance, sufficient cause,* and so on.[206] These grounds often overlap in coverage, so that the same conduct may be subject to multiple charges, or may be prosecuted under different labels in different states. For example, grossly offensive language by a teacher may fall under a charge of incompetency, immorality, or insubordination.[207]

The foregoing standards can mean different things to different courts and permit evolving interpretations to track changes in educational standards and social mores over long periods.[208] Teacher discharge law is, therefore, a matter of case development.

Notwithstanding their imprecision, discharge standards are generally sustained in the face of claims that they are unconstitutionally vague.[209] Most discharge disputes raise

---

202. See the case authorities collected in Annotation: *Employment Contract Terminable at Will,* 62 A.L.R.3d 371 (1975); *Damages—Teacher's Wrongful Discharge,* 22 A.L.R.3d 1047 (1968).

203. *See* Beilan v. Bd. of Public Education, 357 U.S. 399, 406 (1958).

204. Andrews v. Drew Mun. Separate Sch. District, 507 F.2d 611 (5th Cir. 1975); Purifoy v. State Bd. of Education, 106 Cal. Rptr. 201 (1974).

205. Bd. of Trustees v. Stubblefield, 94 Cal. Rptr. 318, 321 (1971); see also Sanders v. Bd. of Education. 263 N.W.2d 461 (Neb. 1978).

206. Chicago Bd. of Ed. v. Payne, 430 N.E.2d 310 (Ill. 1981); Wishart v. McDonald, 500 F.2d 1110 (1st Cir. 1974); Denton v. South Kitsap Sch. District, 516 P.2d 1080 (Wash. 1973).

207. *Multiple charges:* Clayton v. Bd. of Education, 375 N.Y.S. 2d 169 (1975). *Incompetency: cf.* de Groat, fn. 250. *Immorality:* Bovino v. Bd. of Sch. Directors, 377 A.2d 1284 (Pa. 1977) (calling student a "slut" said to constitute "immorality" and "cruelty").

208. *See* Burton v. Cascade Sch. District Union H.S. No. 5., 353 F.Supp. 254, 255 (D. Ore. 1973).

209. See the discussion of vagueness beginning on p. 227.

two related issues: Did the teacher's alleged misconduct qualify as a ground for discharge and did school authorities establish and prove the necessary facts to sustain the charge? The separation of these related issues is somewhat artificial, but necessary to obtain a clear outline of legal doctrine. Teachers may also avoid, without disproving, misconduct charges where there is a violation of civil rights. (That subject is taken up in a later section.)

a. Grounds for Discharge. Where statutory grounds are exclusive, any attempt to discharge a teacher for other reasons will be legally impermissible.[210] The most typical statutory grounds are as follows.

Incompetence. This term is broad enough to encompass every other statutory basis for discharge. It may embrace inefficiency or some personal defect that precludes effective teaching or administration.[211] The following have, in one state or another, been held to justify termination on the ground of incompetence:[212] (1) physical or mental incapacity, (2) lack of knowledge or ability to impart knowledge, (3) failure to adapt to new teaching methods, (4) physical mistreatment of students, (5) violation of school rules, (6) violation of duties to superiors or coworkers, (7) lack of cooperation, (8) persistent negligence, (9) failure to maintain discipline, and (10) personal misconduct, in or out of school.

Dismissal charges often involve a pattern of past behavior that indicates present incompetence.[213] Isolated incidents of inefficiency that are not substantial have been held insufficient to sustain discharge for incompetence.[214] Illinois has a unique rule

---

210. Spencer v. Laconia Sch. District, 218 A.2d 437 (N.H. 1966).

211. For an extensive collection of cases covering varied aspects of competency, see Annotation: *Teachers-Incompetency-Inefficiency* 4 A.L.R.3d 1090 (1965).

212. **(1)** E. G. Singleton v. Iberville Parish Sch. Bd., 136 So.2d 809 (La. 1961); **(2)** Celestine v. Lafayette Parish School Board, 284 So.2d 650 (La. 1973); Blunt v. State Board of Ed., 275 So.2d 303 (Fla. 1973); **(3)** *See* Mortweet v. Ethan Bd. of Education, 241 N.W. 2d 580 (S.D. 1976) **(4)** Fender v. Sch. District No. 25, 347 N.E.2d 270 (Ill. 1976); Powell v. Young 74 N.E.2d 261 (Ohio 1947); **(5)** Tichenor v. Orleans Parish Sch. Bd., 144 So.2d 603 (La. 1962); **(6)** Spano v. Sch. District of Brentwood, 316 A.2d 162 (Pa. 1974) (refusal to consult superiors and others on curriculum program); **(7)** Hyland v. Smollack,349 A.2d541 (N.J. 1975) (refusal to testify under court subpoena); State v. Bd. of Education, 222 N.W.2d 277 (Minn. 1974) (refusal to testify at board hearing); Cooley v. Bd. of Education, 327 F.Supp. 454 (E.D. Ark. 1971); *cf.* Brown v. Portsmouth Sch. District,451 F.2d 1106 (1st Cir. 1971); Simcox v. Bd. of Education,443 F.2d 40 (7th Cir. 1971) (both cases sustaining nonrenewal of nontenured personnel for lack of cooperating); Beilan v. Bd. of Education, 357 U.S. 399 (1958). The Beilan holding was followed in Bd. of Pub. Instruction v. Soler, 176 A.2d 653 (Pa. 1962), cert. denied, 370 U.S. 919 (1962). **(8)** Mortweet v. Ethan Bd. of Education, 241 N.W.2d 580 (S.D. 1976) (insensitivity to needs and feelings of students; lack of energy; reluctance to try new teaching methods); di Leo v. Greenfield, 541 F.2d 949 (2nd Cir.1976) (neglect of professional duties). **(9)** Phillips v. Bd. of Education, 330 A.2d 151 (Del. 1975); Mims v. W. Baton Rouge Parish Sch. District,315 So.2d 349 (La. 1975) Potter v. Richland Sch. District, 534 P.2d 577 (Wash. 1975); Guthrie v. Bd. of Education, 298 S.W.2d 691 (Ky. 1975); Tucker v. San Francisco Un. Sch. District, 245 P.2d 597 (Cal. 1952). **(10)** Hankla v. Governing Bd. of Roseland Sch. District, 120 Cal. Rptr 827 (1975) (dismissal for sexual misconduct though acquitted of criminal charge); Celestine v. Lafayette Parish Sch. Bd., 284 So.2d 650 (La. 1973) (ordering students to write vulgar words repeatedly).

213. Redcay v. State Bd. of Education,33 A.2d 120 (N.J. 1943); State v. Peterson, 294 N.W. 203 (Minn. 1940), but see the following cases where courts did not find circumstances to justify reference to past incompetence to support charges of present incompetence: Roller v. Young, 67 N.E.2d 710 (Ohio 1946). Hebert v. Lafayette Parish Sch. Bd., 146 So.2d 848 (La. 1962).

214. New Castle Area Sch. District v. Bair, 368 A.2d 345 (Pa. 1977) (single unsatisfactory rating).

requiring substantial evidence that a teacher's personal or professional delinquency is irremediable before the teacher can be discharged. This rule appears to be confined to Illinois. It may be met under either of two tests, namely, that damage to the school is irremediable or that the teacher's rehabilitation is not likely.[215]

Incapacity. Physical, mental, or emotional illness or disability that is permanent and incurable and that incapacitates the employee from performing educational tasks is an indisputable ground for discharge.[216] Questions regarding degree and permanence of disability must be resolved adversely to the teachers before this ground may be invoked. New legal obligations have been introduced by federal laws that prohibit employment discrimination against, and require reasonable accommodation for, handicapped persons who are "otherwise qualified." (See the discussion on the handicapped in Chapter 7.) The federal rehabilitation statutes introduce standards of proof that boards of education must meet to justify discharge of a handicapped employee.

Insubordination. A single insubordinate incident, if sufficiently serious, supports discharge.[217] Teachers are often charged with insubordination for persistent and willful violations of laws or direct orders.[218] Some examples are taking time off from work without official authority, encouraging students to disobey or disrespect school authorities, inflicting corporal punishment in violation of school regulations, and disrupting school harmony by untoward criticism of school superiors.[219] Insubordination was found

---

215. Gilliland v. Bd. of Education,343 N.E.2d 704 (Ill. 1976); Aulwurm v. Bd. of Education, 357 N.E.2d 1215 (Ill. 1976) (long course of defiant attitude); Roland v. Sch. Directors,358 N.E.2d 945 (Ill.1976) (use of cattle prod on students as irremediable cruelty).

216. Dusanek v. Hannon, 677 F.2d 538 (7th Cir. 1982); Fitzpatrick Sch. Administrative Dist., 465 N.Y.S.2d 240 (1983); Anonymous v. Bd. of Examiners, 318 N.Y.S.2d 163 (1970) (decertification of drug addict); Hoffman v. Jannarone, 401 F.Supp. 1095 (D. N.J. 1975) (upholding board directive to submit to psychiatric examination); *cf.* Oneal v. Colton Cons. Sch. District No. 396, 557 P.2d 11 (Wash. 1976) (failing eyesight).

217. State v. Bd. of Education, 222 N.W.2d 277 (Minn. 1974) (refusing to submit to cross-examination at school board hearing); Gilbertson v. McAlister, 403 F.Supp. 1 (D. Conn. 1975) (distribution of commercial advertising in violation of board policy and refusal to report to principal's office, as ordered); Petition of Davenport, 283 A.2d 452 (Vt. 1971) (leaving building against orders).

218. Siglin v. Kayenta Un. Sch. Dist., 655 P.2d 353 (Ariz. 1982) (refusing principal's directive to remain at meeting); *semble:* Harris v. Mechanicsville Central Sch. Dist., 380 N.E.2d 213 (N.Y. 1978). Sutherby v. Bd. of Education, 252 N.W.2d 503 (Mich. 1977); Hickey v. Bd. of Sch. Directors, 328 A.2d 549 (Pa. 1974). For a recent collection of case authorities on insubordination, see Annotation: 78 A.L.R. 3d 83 (1977).

219. *Unauthorized absence:* Christopherson v. Spring Valley Elem. Sch. District, 413 N.E.2d 199 (Ill. 1980); Anderson v. Independent Sch. Dist., 292 N.W.2d 562 (Minn. 1980); Willis v. Sch. District, 606 S.W.2d 189 (Mo. 1980); Lucciola v. Comm. of Pa.,360 A.2d 310 (Pa. 1976) (using leave allowance for vacation with a student); Evans v. Page, 516 F. 2d 18 (8th Cir. 1975) (absent against orders to serve as election clerk); Pell v. Bd. of Education, 373 N.E.2d 321 (N.Y. 1974) (absent without permission to attend state senate meetings); Ferndale v. City of Ellsworth Sup'g Sch. District, 342 A.2d 704 (Me. 1975). For a recent collection of cases on unauthorized absences, see Annotation: 78 A.L.R. 3d 117 (1977). *Encouraging disrespect:* Whitsel v. Southeast Local Sch. District, 484 F.2d 1222 (6th Cir. 1973); Birdwell v. Hazelwood Sch. District,491 F.2d 490 (8th Cir. 1973) (inciting students to "get the R.O.T.C. off campus"); Ahern v. Bd. of Education, 327 F.Supp. 1391 (D. Neb. 1971) (class comments regarding fellow teacher). *Corporal punishment:* Barnes v. Fair Dismissal Bd., 548 P.2d 988 (Ore. 1976); Bd. of Education v. Shank, 542 S.W.2d 779 (Mo. 1976). *See also* Jerry v. Bd. of Education,376 N.Y.S.2d 737 1975). *Criticism:* Reed v. Bd. of Education, 333 F.Supp. 816 (E.D. Mo. 1971).

where a teacher failed to report suspicious student conduct as required by school policy and initiated a federal narcotics investigation without the knowledge or approval of his superiors.[220]

Courts have excused and reinstated employees where the actions were not willful, persistent, or very serious. A superintendent who refused to follow board directives was reinstated on a finding that he sincerely misunderstood his authority vis à vis the board.[221] A teacher who was late the first day of the school term due to her registration for graduate studies at a nearby university was held not to be willfully insubordinate, but a court upheld dismissal of a principal who left his school a few days early to register for summer programs, where his absence left students unsupervised and necessary work undone.[222]

Unprofessional Conduct. The standard of conduct unbecoming a teacher is almost as broad and elastic as that of incompetence. It has been held to include actions that fall under several other grounds of discharge, such as (1) offensive language and abuse of corporal punishment in dealing with students; (2) threatening and insulting fellow teachers in presence of students; (3) taking time off without permission of superiors; (4) involvement in shoplifting incidents.[223] Any conduct that violates ethical standards of the teaching profession could conceivably fall under this ground. Some examples are (1) use of classroom time to promote partisan political causes; (2) distributing poems that proclaim the joys of marijuana; (3) beckoning students to throw off family morals and enter a new world of freedom; and (4) inspiring disloyalty to school superiors.[224]

Interpretations of unprofessional conduct vary. New York cases held that a teacher could not be dismissed for unprofessional conduct because he engaged in a fight with a rowdy student and that a teacher was not dischargeable for private consensual sexual relations with a former student.[225] But a teacher who dressed and undressed a mannequin in a lewd and suggestive manner at his home, but in public view, was held dischargeable in another circuit for unprofessional conduct.[226]

---

220. Calvin v. Rupp, 334 F. Supp. 358 (N.D. Mo. 1971).

221. Rumora v. Bd. of Education, 335 N.E.2d 378 (Ohio 1973).

222. *Compare* Beverlin v. Bd. of Education, 216 S.E.2d 544 (W.Va. 1975); *with* Howell v. Winn Parish Sch. Bd., 321 So.2d 420 (La. 1975).

223. Myers v. Orleans Par. Sch. Bd., 423 So.2d 1030 (La. 1983); (1) Wood v. Goodman, 381 F.Supp. 413 (D. Mass. 1974); (2) Kurlander v. School Committee, 451 N.E.2d 138 (Mass. 1983); Amburgey v. Cassady, 507 F.2d 728 (6th Cir. 1974); (3) Fernald v. City of Ellsworth Sup'g. Sch. Comm'ee,342 A.2d 704 (Me. 1975). (4) See the Caravello case, fn. 230, which also involved several charges, including conduct unbecoming a teacher.

224. (1) See the Cooley and Branch cases discussed in Chapter 3; (2) Goldsmith v. Bd. of Education,225 P. 783 (Cal. 1924). (3) Brubaker v. Bd. of Education, 502 F.2d 973 (7th Cir. 1974). (4) Morelli v. Bd. of Education, 356 N.E.2d 438 (Ill. 1976) (enrolling police informant under false pretenses); Toups v. Authement,496 F.2d 700 (5th Cir. 1974) (unprofessional attitude toward superiors); Washington v. Bd. of Education, 408 F.2d 11 (7th Cir. 1974).

225. Clayton v. Bd. of Education, 375 N.Y.S.2d 169 (1975); Goldin v. Bd. of Education,359 N.Y.S.2d 384 (1973). *But see* Carrao v. Bd. of Education,360 N.E.2d 536 (Ill. 1977) (dismissal for indecent liberties with minor student away from school).

226. Wishart v. McDonald, 500 F.2d 110 (1st Cir. 1974).

Immorality. Immorality remains a significant ground for discharge, and usually involves dishonesty, sexual misconduct, or criminal action.[227] The Supreme Court recently recognized the state's long-recognized authority to consider moral fitness of public school professionals, stating: "We are, therefore, in full agreement . . . that there is a legitimate and substantial interest in promoting . . . traditional values, be they social, moral, or political."[228] There are, however, considerable differences of opinions as to the kinds, levels, durations, and notoriety of conduct that justifies teacher discharge. For example, immorality is not considered unconstitutionally vague in most jurisdictions, but if standing alone and unconnected to job fitness it is considered irrelevant in several states.[229] It is, therefore, necessary to consult the case law of each state and, in certain states, how regional standards of immorality in a particular school district influence the courts.

With respect to crime, the law may turn on the specifics of the crime. For example, a conviction for leaving the scene of a minor traffic accident and for falsely denying involvement in the accident was held insufficient to support teacher discharge in Ohio, but conviction for other nonfelonious crimes sustained discharge for immorality in other states.[230] Misappropriation of school funds sustained discharge in Pennsylvania while negligent mishandling of funds did not in South Carolina.[231]

Variations abound in cases dealing with sexual and drug misconduct.[232] Less difficulty arises where the teacher's activity directly involves the school or persons in the school, as the teacher cannot sustain any claim of privacy in such circumstances.[233] But the question of what private immoral conduct is job-related is much disputed, since public authorities must show a rational connection between private, out-of-school conduct and school purposes to justify official punishments as a matter of constitutional law.[234]

The various views on proof of immorality were well expressed in a long line of California decisions which arose under changing California statutes. They are summarized in the latest decision of the California Supreme Court (*Bd. of Education of Long*

---

227. Burton v. Cascade Sch. District, 512 F.2d 850 (Ore. 1975); Weissman v. Bd. of Education,547 P.2d 1267 (Colo. 1976); Morrison v. State Bd. of Education, 461 P.2d 375 (Cal. 1969).

228. See Board of Education v. Pico, 457 U.S. 853 (1982).

229. *Compare* Penn Delco Sch. District v. URSO,382 A.2d 162 (Pa.1978) *with* Bd. of Education of Long Beach Un Sch. District v. Jack M. 566 P.2d 602 (Cal. 1977).

230. Leslie v. Oxford Area Sch. District, 420 A.2d 764 (Pa. 1980) (discharge for shoplifting); Adams v. State Professional Practices Council, 406 So.2d 1170 (Fla. 1980) (possession of marijuana plant); Bethel Park Sch. District v. Karl, 405 A.2d 1377 (Pa. 1982) (false report of illness to cover unauthorized leave); Hale v. Bd. of Education,234 N.E.2d 583 (Ohio 1968). *See* Gary Teachers Union v. School City,332 N.E.2d 256 (Ind. 1975) (conviction for disorderly conduct, fleeing arrest and assault). Scott v. Bd. of Education, 156 N.E.2d 1 (Ill. 1959) (arrests for drunkenness that were publicized); to like effect, *see* Bradford v. Sch. District No. 20, 364 F.Supp. 185 (4th Cir. 1966); *cf.* Caravello v. Bd. of Education, 369 N.Y.S.2d 829 (1975).

231. Appeal of Flannery, 178 A.2d 751 (Pa. 1963); Betterson v. Stewart, 140 S.E. 2d 482 (S.C. 1965).

232. See cases collected in Annotation: *Dismissal of Teachers— Sexual Conduct,* 78 A.L.R.3d 19 (1977); *Dismissal of Teachers—Illegal Drugs,* 47 A.L.R.3d 754 (1973).

233. Teacher-student sexual relations: Yang v. Special Charter Sch. District, 295 N.E.2d 74 (Ill. 1973); Denton v. So. Kitsap Sch. District No.402,516 P.2d 1080 (Wash. 1973); *cf.* Bd. of Trustees v. Stubblefield, 94 Cal. Rptr.318 (1971); Teacher molestation of students; Lombardo v. Bd. of Education,241 N.E.2d 495 (Ill. 1968); Weissman v. Bd. of Education, fn. 227.

234. The rational connection test is a constitutional requirement of due process. *See* Schware v. Bd. of Bar Examiners, 353 U.S. 232 (1957).

Beach, reproduced at the end of this chapter). Where the California statute authorized automatic dismissal for specified crimes, the court upheld discharge without proof of job impact, apparently on the view that the legislative presumption of unfitness was conclusive: "The law implies a threat. The state through its legislation, has mandated that where such outrageous criminal conduct as that present here has taken place, the elementary school children need not hazard a risk of any kind whatever with the presence of such a person in the classroom . . . The teacher's ability to serve as an exemplar is compromised."[235]

But where the statute merely authorizes discharge under a general norm of immorality, the courts split on the measure of required proof.[236] Dismissal may thus hinge upon one of two inconsistent tests, namely, that a teacher who acts immorally is unfit because immorality destroys the basis for student respect; or because he or she is no longer a suitable role model and exemplar for students, irrespective of proof of actual job impact.[237]

In its much-cited *Morrison* decision, the California Supreme Court attempted to reconcile these tests together under one set of eight factors. In most cases these factors can be reduced to five considerations: potential for misconduct *with* students, potential adverse impact *on* students (e.g., psycho-sexual development and discipline), notoriety and public notice, criminal nature of the conduct, and impact on working relationships in school and with parents.[238] The following cases indicate how these factors have operated in different settings.

Consensual sexual acts between a teacher and her former student at her home were held insufficient to discharge a New York teacher in the absence of evidence that they were a continuation or outcome of her conduct while he was a student.[239] The court, nevertheless, sustained the discharge because she lied in denying the affair. Another court sustained discharge of a teacher whose open cohabitation with an unmarried man in a small rural school district was considered a public scandal. The court ruled that no showing of actual sexual misconduct was required to infer impropriety.[240]

The sex revolution and new constitutional rights of privacy have generated changes in the law regarding unmarried teachers who have children or are pregnant. Some courts have overturned dismissals in the absence of proof of adverse job consequences, on the view that the state's interest in having exemplary teachers to promote sexual restraint is, without more, insufficient to override privacy claims or to

---

235. Bd. of Education v. Millette, 133 Cal. Rptr.275 (1976) (conviction for homosexual solicitation in a public restroom). Cf. Long Beach Case, p. 294, infra.

236. See the Penn Delco and Long Beach cases, fn. 229; Wishart v. McDonald, fn. 235; Gaylord v. Tacoma Sch. District, fn. 246, *infra;* Bd. of Education v. Millette, fn. 235.

237. *E.g.,* Morrison v. State Bd. of Education, 461 P.2d 375 (Cal. 1969).

238. See Morrison, prior footnote, at p. 386; Thompson v. Southwest Sch. Dist., 438 F.Supp. 1170 (W.D. Mo. 1980); Gov'g. Bd. of Nicasio Sch. District, 96 Cal. Rptr. 712 (1971) (dismissal for publicized court testimony in praise of marijuana and attacking drug laws).

239. Goldin v. Bd. of Central Sch. District No. 1, 359 N.Y.S.2d 384 (1973).

240. Sullivan v. Meade County Ind. Sch. District No. 101,387 F.Supp. 1237 (D. So. Dak. 1975); affd. 530 F.2d 799 (8th Cir. 1976). *Accord:* Sedule v. Capitol Sch. District, 425 F. Supp. 552 (D.D.C. 1976); *cf.* Hollenbaugh v. Carnegie Free Library, 436 F. Supp. 1328 (W.D. Pa. 1977). *But see* Bd. of Ed. v. Jennings, 651 P.2d 1037 (N.Mex. 1982) (reinstatement of discharged principal for adulterous affair with school secretary, held not unreasonable).

demonstrate unfitness for immorality.[241] Episodic adultery was also held insufficient in a case where the teacher had overwhelming community support.[242] While the absence of hostile reaction was noted in these cases, the courts stressed the need for concrete proof of job-relatedness of the teacher's immoral acts.

The rule against abuse of discretion may prevent discharge in circumstances where the board itself did not act in a consistent manner (viz. where it discharged some but not other pregnant, unmarried teachers and where it dismissed a divorced teacher who rented an extra bedroom in her home to males, at the suggestion of a board member, to relieve a housing shortage).[243]

The authorities on discharge or other punishments against homosexual teaching professionals in public schools are even more mixed than those dealing with heterosexual immorality. The lower courts have not agreed on the significance of the "notoriety" of the individual's sex preference or life-style, or on the relevance between verbally espousing homosexuality, on one hand, and engaging in homosexual conduct, on the other. For example, the Tenth Circuit Court of Appeals in a case summarily affirmed by tie vote in the Supreme Court recently upheld one portion of a state law that authorized discharge of a teacher for public homosexual conduct, while striking down another part of the same law (as overbroad) authorizing discharge for "advocacy" of homosexuality.[244] In a still later case, which the Supreme Court has declined to review, and thus let stand, the Sixth Circuit Court of Appeals held that the discharge of a female public school counsellor who disclosed to her colleagues and administrators that she was bisexual and happily in love with another woman did not violate her constitutional right.[245] To the date of this writing, however, the refusal by the United States Supreme Court to rule upon the constitutional claims regarding homosexual advocacy or conduct leaves the constitutional issues unsettled and subject to conflicting disposition in different lower courts.[246]

Cases upholding dismissals have rested on several grounds: (1) that homosexuality

---

241. Avery v. Homewood City Bd. of Ed., 674 F.2d 337 (5th Cir. 1982) (unwed pregnancy not per se "cause", especially when school has retained other unwed pregnant teachers); Andrews v. Drew Mun. Sep. Sch. District 507 F.2d 611 (5th Cir. 1975); *cf.* Drake v. Covington County Bd. of Education,371 F.Supp.974 (M.D. Ala. 1974). *See also* Reinhardt v. Bd. of Education, 311 N.E.2d 710 (Ill. 1974). *But see* Brown v. Bathke, 566 F.2d 588 (8th Cir. 1977); Doherty v. Wilson,356 F. Supp. 35 (M.D. Ga. 1973) (teacher living on communal farm).

242. Erb v. Iowa State Bd. of Public Instruction, 216 N.W.2d 339 (Iowa 1974). For a contrary view, *see* Stewart v. E. Baton Rouge Parish Sch. Bd., 251 So.2d 487 (La. 1971) (school bus driver).

243. New Mexico St. Bd. of Education v. Stoudt, 571 P.2d 1186 (N.M. 1977); Fisher v. Snyder,476 F.2d 375 (8th Cir. 1973).

244. Board of Education v. National Gay Task Force, 729 F.2d 1270 (10th Cir. 1984), affirmed, 105 S.Ct. 1858 (1985).

245. Rowland v. Mad River Sch. Dist., 730 F.2d 444 (6th Cir. 1984), cert. denied, ________U.S. , 105 S.Ct. 1373 (1985).

246. *Compare, e.g.*, Rowland v. Mad River Sch. Dist., *supra;* Gaylord v. Tacoma Sch. District, 559 P.2d 1340 (Wash. 1977) (upholding discharge of disclosed homosexual teacher); *cf.* Doe v. Commonwealth's Attorney, 425 U.S. 901 (1976) (summary affirmance of sodomy criminal conviction) *with* Bd. of Ed. v. National Gay Task Force, *supra;* Ratchford v. Gay Lib, 558 F.2d 848 (8th Cir. 1977) and the cases in the following footnotes. See generally Annot: *Validity of Statute Making Sodomy a Criminal Offense,* 20 A.L.R. 4th 1009 (1983); Note, Homosexuality and the Law: An Overview, 13 N.Y.L.F. 273 (1971). Teacher molestation of children, whether homosexual or heterosexual, definitely presents a different case. *Cf.* Tomerlin v. Dade County Sch. Bd., 318 So.2d 159 (Fla. 1975) (teacher discharge for out-of-school sexual molestation of his minor stepdaughter). See Addendum on p. 662.

alone justified discharge, (2) that the teacher failed to disclose his or her homosexuality in applying for school employment, or (3) that the teacher publicized and flaunted unconventional sexual conduct.[247] Potential emotional harm to students was held sufficient to dismiss a teacher who underwent sex-reassignment surgery.[248] Even while disapproving discharge for homosexuality without proof of job impairment, the California courts noted that a school district might initially have reason not to hire a homosexual and that homosexual acts in public buildings might justify discharge.[249] Going "public" on "swinger" conduct or posing nude for a magazine photograph resulted in approved dismissals and in loss of any claim of invasion of privacy.[250]

The hesitation to immunize unconventional sex behavior from school restrictions undoubtedly stems from the absence of any clear consensus on the nature and social effects of different kinds of homosexuality (i.e., transitory, confirmed, biologically rooted, psychically rooted) or inability to predict with assurances how the tendency will affect conduct and attitudes in the schools.

The use of grossly vulgar language may support a charge of immorality, as well as of unprofessional conduct.[251] Here also there is no firm test. Courts can easily modulate any test by loose or strict application and by exemptions for "extenuating circumstances." Two reversals of teacher discharges illustrate this pervasive judicial power. In one, the mother of a recent graduate received, read, and disclosed to school authorities, a grossly vulgar letter written to her son by his former teacher. In overturning the consequent discharge, the court argued that the letter might not have been so offensive to the son as it was to his mother and that the teacher was not responsible for its disclosure.[252] In the other reversal, the court reinstated a teacher who failed to halt a school presentation that exposed students to profane, obscene, immoral, distasteful, and inappropriate language with regard to the human reproductive organs and their functions.[253] The court found extenuating circumstances in the failure of other school authorities to interrupt the program, the improbability of a repetition, and the lack of proof of illicit motive or adverse impact on teaching ability.

Other Grounds. Many actions that justify discharge under grounds previously discussed are also encompassed by other grounds found in the laws of some states, to wit: disloyalty, intemperance, cruelty, willful misconduct, good and sufficient cause, evident unfitness, and neglect of duty.[254]

---

247. (1) Burton v. Cascade Sch. District, 512 F.2d 850 (9th Cir. 1975); *cf.* Gaylord v Tacoma Sch. District, *supra.* (2) Acanfora v. Bd. of Education, 491 F.2d 498 (4th Cir. 1974); (3) McConnell v. Anderson, 451 F.2d 193 (8th Cir. 1971) (publicized attempt by avowed homosexual for license to marry another male).

248. In re Grossman, 316 A.2d 39 (N.J. 1974).

249. Gov'g Bd. of Mountain View Sch. Dist. v. Metcalf, 111 Cal. Rptr. 724 (1974) (homosexual act in dept. store restroom). But see the Long Beach (California) case at end of this chapter.

250. Pettit v. State Bd. of Education, 513 P.2d 889 (Cal. 1973); Weissbaum v. Hannon, 439 F. Supp. 873 (N.D. Ill. 1977); *cf.* Wishart v. McDonald, 500 F.2d 1110 (1st Cir. 1974); (lewd gestures with mannequin in public view), compare Acanfora case, fn. 247. (Maryland homosexual teacher who discussed homosexuality on television could not be discharged on that ground).

251. Compare the offensive language cases at pp. 212 and 237.

252. Jarvella v. Willoughby-Eastlake City Sch. Dist. Bd. of Education, 233 N.E.2d 143 (Ohio 1967).

253. de Groat v. Newark Un. Sch. District, 133 Cal. Rptr. 225 (1976).

254. *See* Roland v. Sch. Directors, 358 N.E.2d 945 (Ill. 1976); Caffas v. Bd. of Sch. Directors, 353 A.2d

The ground of "disloyalty" has been severely narrowed by constitutional considerations. A teacher, like any other citizen, has a constitutional right to believe in and discuss any ideas outside of school, however revolutionary they might be, so long as he or she does not attempt to carry those ideas into action that presents a "clear and present danger."[255] A teacher may not be punished for belonging to a subversive organization unless the authorities can prove that the teacher knew of the subversive purposes and joined with the specific intent to activate those purposes—as distinguished from an intent to advance ideology, without subversive action.[256]

The immunity to advocate ideas does not justify a refusal to cooperate in lawful official investigation of subversion unless the teacher can show some abridgement of his or her own personal rights.[257] There are many constitutional refinements affecting disloyalty charges that are not of major current interest, and these are, therefore, passed over in this text.

b. Remedies for Wrongful Discharge. The law provides several remedies for unlawful discharge. Under contract law, the teacher is entitled to receive compensation for the breach—the contract price unpaid less any substitute earnings that the teacher made or reasonably could have made following the breach.[258] Although the teacher has a duty to mitigate contract damages following breach, the school district has the burden of proving that the teacher had a reasonable opportunity and failed to do so.[259] The duty to mitigate extends only to similar employment that is reasonably available.

A teacher is not required to accept employment of a different or inferior kind, nor incur unreasonable burdens in seeking the same, such as by seeking work in a distant region.[260] Where breach of contract cannot be adequately remedied by compensatory damages (viz. where tenure is involved), courts of equity have discretion to order reinstatement, even in the unusual case when state school statutes do not expressly provide that remedy. Finally, a wrongful discharge arising out of a violation of the teacher's civil rights will sustain a tort action under state and federal laws to recover for injuries that are not covered by contract damages (e.g., interference with civil rights, emotional distress, and damage to professional reputation). (The latter type damages are considered in the section on federal torts in Chapter 8.)

5. Resignation and Abandonment

A teacher or administrator may surrender or abandon employment. Resignation may be accomplished in different ways: (1) on forms supplied by the administration, (2) by

---

898 (Pa. 1976) (cruelty); Simon v. Jefferson Davis Parish Sch. Bd. 289 So.2d 511 (La. 1974) (willfull misconduct); Bradford v. Sch. District, 364 F.2d 185 (4th Cir. 1966); Gary Teachers Un. v. School City, 332 N.E.2d 256 (Ind. 1975) (good and sufficient cause); Miller v. BC. of Education, 452 F.2d 894 (6th Cir. 1971) (neglect of duty).

255. Keyishian v. Bd. of Regents, 385 U.S. 589 (1967); Dennis v. United States, 341 U.S.494 (1951); *See also* discussion of loyalty oaths, p. 184.

256. Scales v. United States, 367 U.S. 203 (1961).

257. Beilan v. Bd. of Education, 357 U.S. 399 (1958).

258. Bd. of Education v. Metskas, 436 N.E.2d 587 (ILL. 1982); See generally Annotation: *Damages—Teacher's Wrongful Discharge,* 22 A.L.R.3d 1047 (1968).

259. *Ibid.* at 1052.

260. *Ibid.* at 1051.

statements of intent to retire, or (3) by notice of inability to complete the contract.[261] The resignation must be accepted as tendered, and a change in the effective date without the consent of the resigning teacher rendered such resignation invalid.[262]

To be effective, a resignation must be voluntary. A resignation obtained by threats may be voided on the grounds of undue influence.[263] A letter to the superintendent stating availability to work full time, part time, or not at all and inviting the superintendent to use his judgment in assigning the author-teacher was held not to show any intent to resign and thereby relinquish tenure status.[264] The authorities are not in agreement where a resignation is submitted for a purpose other than to relinquish employment and tenure status. In New York, a resignation submitted to thwart the operation of the tenure laws was, nevertheless, held to be voluntary and effective and not void as against public policy. It resulted in the loss of tenure as a principal.[265] In an earlier Minnesota case, however, the court held that a teacher's resignation at the end of her probationary period in order to circumvent tenure laws was ineffective to waive protection of the tenure laws where she had no intention of ending employment.[266] Where a resignation was submitted only for the purpose of establishing illness for disability benefits and was so understood by all parties,the intent to resign was lacking. Hence, the court ruled that the submission should be treated as a request for a leave of absence.[267] Intent to resign may be implied from taking indefinite leave of absence without permission of the board.[268]

Inasmuch as a teacher's contract is with the school board and not with any subordinate party, many jurisdictions hold that the written resignation becomes final and irrevocable only when formally accepted by the board. Hence, a teacher could withdraw a letter of resignation before board acceptance thereof, even though it was accepted by a superintendent or principal.[269]

The same effect as a resignation may be accomplished by operation of law where the teacher is deemed to abandon or reject employment. Refusal to accept altered teaching contracts that increased extracurricular duties was held to be an abandonment because the addition of extra duties was considered reasonable.[270] The intent to abandon must, however, be clear. Even though a teacher was equivocal about her new assignment,

---

261. (1) Gardner v. Hollifield, 533 P.2d, 730 (Idaho 1975); (2) Schwartz v. Bd. of Education, 358 N.Y.S.2d 49 (1974); (3) Cords v. Window Rock Sch. District, No. 8, 526 P.2d 757 (Ariz. 1974) (inability to keep sabbatical leave contract held a resignation); *compare* Rumph v. Wayne Community Sch. District, 188 N.W.2d 71 (Mich. 1971) (failure to fulfill sabbatical contract held not to discontinue teacher's services).

262. Wiljamaa v. Bd. of Education, 213 N.W.2d 830 (Mich. 1975).

263. *See also* Ledew v. Schl. Bd., 578 F.Supp. 202 (M.D.Fla. 1984); Marland v. Ambach, 463 N.Y.S.2d 422 (1983); Piper v. Bd. of Trustees, 426 N.E.2d 262 (Ill. 1981); Odorizzi v. Bloomfield Sch. District, 54 Cal. Rptr. 533 (1966).

264. Brown v. Bd. of Education, 347 N.E.2d 791 (Ill. 1976).

265. Herbert v. Nyquist, 384 N.Y.S.2d 541 (1976).

266. Hosford v. Bd. of Education, 275 N.W. 81 (Minn. 1937).

267. State v. Hatley, 450 P.2d 624 (N.M. 1969).

268. Miller v. Noe, 432 S.W.2d 818 (Ky. 1968).

269. Sherman v. Bd. of Education, 389 N.Y.S.2d 515 (1976); Hart v. Sch. Bd. of Wakalla County, 340 So.2d 121 (Fla. 1976).

270. Mccullough v. Cashmere Sch. District, 551 P.2d 104 (Wash. 1976).

her call to the school that she could not attend the first day because of illness could not be considered an abandonment.[271] An interesting question is raised where teachers strike in violation of state law. In Michigan such action was held not to effect an abandonment or discontinuance of their employment status.[272]

A noncoercive agreement between the teacher and the school district whereby the teacher resigned in exchange for a lump sum consideration was upheld as effecting a waiver of tenure rights.[273] An oral resignation may be effected, but an attempted oral resignation without agreement as to the effective date was held ineffective.[274] Disputes sometimes arise as to whether a resignation operates to terminate appointment to a particular position only or to terminate all employment with the district. The submission and acceptance of a generally worded resignation has been construed as a resignation from all employment with the school district.[275] The court reasoned that any other construction would tie the hands of the managing board of the district.

A lawfully effected resignation is held by a majority of courts to cut off tenure rights, but in a minority of states, tenure status is preserved following resignation, by special statutory provision.[276]

E. Teachers' Rights

The explosion of civil rights law greatly strengthened the security of teachers and administrators. As a professional class, they are shielded by state codes, but as individuals, they have constitutional rights that have been buttressed by civil rights statutes. As discussed previously, the due process clause of the Fourteenth Amendment vests substantive rights in persons, and this coverage of the clause is often referred to as *substantive due process.* The clause also vests procedural protections against unlawful deprivation of substantive rights, and this aspect of the clause is referred to as *procedural due process.* These distinct categories of due process form the major frames of reference for board discipline of teachers.

1. Procedural Due Process

> "Due process of law is susceptible of no simple definition. . . . What is due process depends on circumstances. It varies with the subject matter and the necessities of the situation. . . .

---

271. Pennel v. Pond Un. Sch. District, 105 Cal. Rptr. 817 (1973). *But see* Kearns v. Lower Merion Sch. District, 346 A.2d 875 (Pa. 1975) (where failure to report for work, even if due to physical problems, could be considered an abandonment of the contract).

272. Rockwell v. Bd. of Education, 226 N.W.2d 596 (Mich. 1975); Shiffen v. Bd. of Education, 206 N.W.2d 250 (Mich. 1973). See the discussion of teachers' strikes in Part 3 of this chapter.

273. Cedar v. Commissioner of Education, 279 N.Y.S.2d 661 (1967).

274. Luse v. Waco Community Sch. District, 141 N.W.2d 607 (Iowa 1966).

275. Leithliter v. Bd. of Trustees, 91 Cal. Rptr. 215 (1971).

276. The courts of California, Florida, Idaho, Indiana, Kentucky, Louisiana, Nevada, New Jersey, Ohio, and Pennsylvania uphold the majority view terminating tenure by resignation, notwithstanding later reemployment of the claimant. See Annot: *Termination of Teacher Tenure—Resignation,* 9 A.L.R.4th 729 (1981); Norwitz v. Bd. of Education, 23 A.2d 914 (N.J. 1942).

Its content is a function of many variables, including the nature of the right affected, the degree of danger caused by the proscribed condition or activity, and the availability of prompt remedial measures. . . . "[277]

In the words of the Supreme Court, procedural due process rules are meant to protect persons not from any deprivation, but from the mistaken or *unjustified* deprivation of substantive rights. The following excerpts from leading Supreme Court opinions explain the operation of constitutional due process in public schools: "Application of this prohibition requires the familiar two stage analysis: we must first ask whether the asserted individual interests are encompassed within the Fourteenth Amendment's protection of 'life, liberty or property'; if protected interests are implicated, we then must decide what procedures constitute 'due process of law'."[278] Unless a teacher can show the requisite interest in *liberty* or *property* (life usually not being threatened in school proceedings) the procedural requirements of the constitution do not apply.[279] "The range of interests protected by procedural due process is not infinite." These alternative bases of 'liberty' and 'property' interests have different legal sources and require separate analysis.

a. Property Interests. A person who seeks a hearing on the basis of an alleged property interest under the Fourteenth Amendment has the burden of establishing a property interest. Unlike liberty interests, which are created directly by the constitution itself, property interests in public school employment must be found in some "legal entitlement" under the laws, rules, regulations, and contracts of the employing state.[280] "[A] state employee who, under state law or rules promulgated by state officials, has a legitimate claim of entitlement to continued employment absent sufficient cause for discharge may demand the procedural protection of due process."[281] The specific benefits given to tenured teachers by state laws constitute a property interest that entitles them to pretermination hearings. Similarly, professional certification involves a property interest that cannot be revoked without constitutional due process.[282] Nontenured public employees enjoy no *general* right to continued employment.[283] Hence the mere succession of contract renewals does not alone create any property interest in school employment.[284] "To have property interest in a benefit, a person clearly must have more than an abstract need or desire for it. . . . He must, instead, have a legitimate claim or

---

277. *See* S. v. Bd. of Education, 97 Cal. Rptr.422,425 (1971); Hannah v. Larche,360 U.S.420,442 (1960).

278. Ingraham v. Wright, 430 U.S. 651, 672 (1977).

279. *See* Bd. of Regents v. Roth, 408 U.S. 564, 570 (1972).

280. *See* Bd. of Regents v. Roth, *supra. Accord:* Ryan v. Aurora City Bd. of Education,540 F.2d 222 (6th Cir. 1976); Skidmore v. Shamrock Ind. Sch. District, 464 F.2d 605 (5th Cir. 1972); Miller v. Sch. District, 500 F.2d 711 (7th Cir. 1974).

281. *See* Goss v. Lopez,419 U.S. 565,573 (1975): Since tenure is a legislated and not contract status, it may be legislatively conditioned to permit position abolitions, or general salary reductions, without notice and hearing. *See* Johnson v. Bd. of Education, Dist. Ct. N.J. Civil Action #75-1958 (1975).

282. Huntley v. No. Carolina State Bd. of Education, 493 F.2d 1016 (4th Cir. 1974).

283. Bd. of Regents v. Roth, *supra; cf.* Bishop v. Wood, 426 U.S. 341 (1976) (denying right to pretermination hearing for nontenured police officers).

284. Meyr v. Bd. of Education, 572 F.2d 1229 (8th Cir. 1978); Bertot v. Sch. District, 522 F.2d 1171 (10th Cir. 1975); Siler v. Brady Ind. Sch. District,393 F.Supp. 1143 (W.D. Tex. 1975); Lukac v. Acocks,466 F.2d 577 (6th Cir. 1972).

entitlement to it. . . . [T]he respondent surely had an abstract concern in being rehired, but he did not have a property interest sufficient to require . . . a hearing when they [university authorities] declined to renew his appointment."[285]

Although nontenured teachers do not generally possess property interest in continued employment, they may acquire a property interest in special circumstances. Three such situations have been noted by the courts. First, in a minority of states education statutes give probationers a right to hearing on nonrenewal decisions. Such a statutory benefit represents a constitutionally protected property interest.[286] Second, a probationer's rights under an unexpired contract or under contract terms that commit the school district to renewal are property interests.[287] Third, unless a statutory (de jure) tenure system precludes any implied understandings, a state employee may acquire the property interest if officially fostered customs, rules, understandings, and practices *imply* a contract promise to grant continuing contract status and thus establish a "de facto" tenure system.[288] Courts will not lightly imply a contract expectancy of retention.[289] If by long customary practice a board applied a penalty other than dismissal for violation of a professional development regulation and such was relied upon, the penalty of dismissal may be reversed as excessive and unfair.[290]

Although nontenured teachers have a poor success rate in trying to establish a "property interest," some have succeeded in special cases. For example, a school board's handbook that indicated that probationers with three years' service would be terminable only for cause was held to create a constitutionally protected property interest requiring a termination hearing.[291] An implied "entitlement" was also achieved by a discharged professor because (1) he was recommended for tenure on the sole condition that he achieve American citizenship, (2) he was permitted to participate in the meetings of tenured faculty, and (3) he was permitted to vote on tenure status of other faculty members.[292] As previously indicated, however, tenure will not vest merely because the superintendant recommended tenure or because of the board's *reasonable* delay in formal denial of tenure. A good summary of the foregoing principles is presented in the *Ryan* opinion reproduced at the end of this chapter.

---

285. Bd. of Regents v. Roth, 408 U.S. at 577, 578.

286. Kruse v. Bd. of Directors, 231 N.W.2d 626 (Iowa 1975); Fogel v. Bd. of Education, 369 N.Y.S.2d 517 (1975); Ajluni v. Bd. of Education, 229 N.W.2d 385 (Mich. 1975).

287. *See* Wertz v. So. Cloud Un. Sch. District, 542 P.2d 339 (Kan. 1975); Roane v. Callisburg Ind. Sch. District, 511 F.2d 633 (5th Cir. 1975); Bates v. Hinds, 334 F.Supp. 528 (N.D. Tex. 1971). *See* Thomas v. Ward, fn. 291, *infra.*

288. Perry v. Sinderman, 408 U.S. 593 (1972). Several lower courts have confined implied tenure to the facts of the Perry case. "We hold . . . that a nontenured teacher has no 'expectancy' of continued employment, whatever may be the policies of the institution, where there exists a statutory tenure system." Ryan v. Aurora City Bd. of Education, 540 F.2d 222, 227 (6th Cir. 1976). *Accord:* Meyr v. Bd. of Education, fn. 284.

289. Newcastle-Gunning Bedford Educ. Assn. v. Bd. of Education, 421 F. Supp. 960 (D. Del. 1976) (union agreement calling for informal hearing held not to create a property interest); Abbott v. Bd. of Educ., 558 P.2d 1307 (Utah 1976); Stapp v. Awoyelles Par. Sch. Bd., 545 F.2d 527 (5th Cir. 1977); Siler v. Brady Ind. Sch. District 393 F. Supp. 1143 (W.D. Tex. 1975); Bertot v. Sch. District No. 1, fn. 284.

290. Martin v. Harrah Ind. Sch. District, 579 F.2d 1192 (10th Cir. 1978), Reversed on other grounds 440 U.S. 194, 99 S.Ct, 1062 (1979).

291. Thomas v. Ward, 529 F.2d 916 (4th Cir. 1975).

292. Soni v. Bd. of Trustees, 376 F.Supp. 289 (E.D. Tenn. 1974).

b. Liberty Interests. Nontenured as well as tenured teachers may demand due process where a school decision abridges their "liberty". The government, including public school officials, "may not deny a benefit to a person on a basis that infringes his constitutionally protected interests . . . even though a person has no [property right] to a . . . governmental benefit."[293] The Supreme Court has expressly declined to define "with exactness" what interests are encompassed by the constitutional concept of "liberty". "Liberty" includes rights specified in the Bill of Rights and also those unspecified fundamental rights and privileges that the Court has found to be "essential to the orderly pursuit of happiness by free men." A fuller exploration of these substantive rights appears later, but for purposes of procedural due process, it may be said that liberty interests are implicated whenever government action threatens either to penalize or deter the exercise of constutional rights or impair one's freedom to seek a livelihood (e.g., by stigmatizing the employee's honor, integrity, or reputation sufficiently to foreclose his opportunities to obtain employment).[294]

Stigmatization will not be inferred from the bare fact of nonrenewal even though nonretention makes the teacher less attractive to other employers.[295] "Because the hearing required where a nontenured employee has been stigmatized . . . is solely 'to provide the person an opportunity to clear his name,'"[296] an employee is not constitutionally entitled to a dismissal hearing where the truth or fairness of the charge is not challenged by the employee. Even when the reasons for discharge are stigmatizing or false, a nontenured employee has been held to suffer no injury to a protected liberty interest if those reasons are kept confidential and not made public.[297]

The issue of what charges are sufficiently prejudicial to require a hearing is very broad and often depends upon particular circumstances and the opinion of individual courts. Most courts have not considered uncomplimentary charges regarding work habits as stigmatizing per se.[298] For example, courts found no injury to a teacher's "liberty" interest from the following charges: (1) noncooperation; (2) tardiness, absence, and failure to maintain discipline; (3) unsatisfactory performance of work duties; (4) advising a retarded student to obtain an abortion, contrary to welfare department regulations; and (5) insubordination and aggressive behavior.[299] On the other hand, one court found that dismissal for insubordination so stigmatized the teacher's professional reputation as to

---

293. *See* Perry v. Sindermann, *supra,* at p. 597; Mt. Healthy City Sch. District Bd. of Ed. v. Doyle,429 U.S. 274 (1977).

294. *See* Board of Regents v. Roth, 408 U.S. at 573,574; Bishop v. Wood,426 U.S. 341 (1976); Pelisek v. Trevor State Graded Sch. Dist. 371 F. Supp. 1964 (E.D. Wis. 1974); Berg v. Berger, 570 F.2d 348 (7th Cir. 1978), *cert. denied,* 439 U.S. 992 (1978).

295. Bd. of Regents v. Roth, supra, at p. 575; Lavin v. Bd. of Education, 317 N.E.2d 717 (Ill. 1974).

296. *See* Codd v. Velger, 429 U.S.624 (1977). *See also* Carpenter v. City of Greenfield Sch. District, 358 F.Supp. 220 (E.D. Wis. 1973).

297. Buhr v. Buffalo Pub. Sch. District No. 38, 509 F.2d 1196 (8th Cir. 1974).

298. "Such matters as the competence of teachers, and the standards of its measurement are not, without more, matters of constitutional dimensions. They are peculiarly appropriate to state and local administration." *See* Scheelhaase v. Woodbury Central Comm. Sch. District,488 F.2d 237,244 (8th Cir. 1973); See Huntley fn. 282 (charge of fraud against probationer, held to affect a liberty interest).

299. (1) Irby v. McGowan, 380 F.Supp. 1024 (S.D. Ala. 1974) (teacher later allowed to resign and have dismissal charges expunged from her record). (2) Cooper v. Curry, 399 F.Supp. 372 (S.D. Miss. 1975). (3) Coen v. Boulder Valley Sch. District, 402 F.Supp. 1335 (D. Colo. 1975). (4) and (5) Gray v. Union County Int. Education District, 520 F.2d 803 (9th Cir. 1975).

require a due process hearing.[300] A clearer case of personal stigma was raised by a charge that a teacher was emotionally disturbed.[301]

Midyear dismissals, for any cause, are much more damaging than year-end nonrenewal. For this reason, midyear dismissals, even of probationers, have been held to affect a protected liberty interest as well as a contract (property) interest.[302]

c. Due Process Criteria. "Once it is determined that due process applies, the question remains—what process is due?"[303] There is no fixed formula. "'Due process', unlike some legal rules, is not a technical conception with a fixed content unrelated to time, place and circumstances. . . . Representing a profound attitude of fairness . . . 'due process' is compounded of history, reason, the past course of decisions,. . . . "[304] "The very nature of due process negates any concept of inflexible procedures universally applicable to every imaginable situation."[305] Nevertheless, certain basic elements have been stressed by the courts, though each element is not required in all cases.

The following procedures are traditionally associated with constitutional due process:

1. The affected party must be given fair and reasonable *notice* of the charges.
2. The affected party must be accorded a *hearing.*
3. The hearing should be set promptly but sufficiently in advance to afford a fair opportunity to prepare for the hearing.
4. The party is accorded the right to be represented by legal *counsel.*
5. The party is permitted to present oral and written evidence at the hearing.
6. The party and his or her counsel is allowed to confront and challenge all evidence against him or her, including written documents and testimony of adverse witnesses.
7. The hearing must be conducted by an *impartial tribunal.*
8. The party is entitled to have an *official* record, usually by stenographic transcript, of the hearing.
9. The party should be allowed *appeal* to higher legal authority, including access to courts to redress legal errors.[306]

At a *minimum,* the affected party is entitled to notice and hearing in *every* case before *final* decision unless the hearing would be pointless (e.g., where the facts are undisputed and the board has no discretion but to take action on those facts in a manner

300. Morris v. Bd. of Education, 401 F.Supp. 188 (D. Del. 1975).

301. Lombard v. Bd. of Education, 502 F.2d 631 (2d Cir. 1974); *See also* Hoffman v. Jannarone, 401 F.Supp. 1095 (D.N.J. 1975)

302. See Wertz case, fn. 287; Cooley v. Bd. of Education, 453 F.2d 282 (8th Cir. 1972); McKelvey v. Colonial Sch. District, 348 A.2d 445 (Pa. 1975).

303. *See* Goss v. Lopez, 419 U.S. at 577 (1975).

304. *See* Ingraham v. Wright, 430 U.S. 651, 675 (1977).

305. Goss v. Lopez, 419 U.S. at 578.

306. *See* S. v. Bd. of Education, 97 Cal. Rptr. 422, 425 (1971); Fielder v. Bd. of Education, 346 F.Supp. 722 (D. Neb. 1972). The laws in most states allow appeals to the courts.

prescribed by statute).[307] The standard as to what notice is fair and timely will vary with the nature of the case. An impartial tribunal is also required in all cases, but an impartial tribunal for administrative hearings is not strictly defined. Whether fairness requires any additional elements is, according to the Supreme Court, a matter for each court to decide by analyzing and "balancing" the following factors:

> "First, the private interest that will be affected . . . ; second, the risk of erroneous deprivation of such interest, . . . and the probable value, if any, of additional or substitute procedural safeguards; and, finally, the [state] interests, including the functions involved and the fiscal or administrative burdens that the additional or substitute procedural requirements would entail."[308]

While procedural requirements of state law often parallel constitutional standards, the two systems do not and are not required to track each other.[309] In some cases the constitutional requirements are more stringent, and they must be met. Where state procedural requirements are more stringent, they also must be met.

A party may by voluntary action abandon any or all of his due process rights.[310] Further, school authorities may cure procedural defaults where substitute correct notices and new hearings may be provided without undue prejudice to the affected teacher.[311]

The foregoing general principles indicate the nature of due process, but do not provide concrete guidelines for specific cases. Those guidelines must be sought in pertinent cases of which the following are illustrative.

Notice of Charges. Failure to give notice will invalidate a dismissal where constitutional interests are implicated.[312] The notice must include the bases for termination in sufficient detail to enable the teacher to determine and to contest any errors that might exist. Courts do not require minute specification or unsolicited advance presentation of all the evidence. They require only enough information to provide a fair opportunity to refute the charges.[313] Where the board gives unreasonably vague notice of charges or

---

307. Biklan v. Bd. of Education, 333 F.Supp. 902 (N.D. N.Y.1971) (teacher dismissed for refusal to take qualifying loyalty oath).

308. Mathews v. Eldridge, 424 U.S. 319, 335 (1976).

309. *See* Rost v. Horky, 422 F.Supp. 615 (D. Neb. 1976); Groopman v. Community Sch. Bd.,374 N.Y.S.2d. 27 (1975) (Constitutional right to counsel not applicable to state statutory hearing).

310. *See, e.g.*, Ferguson v. Bd. of Trustees,564 P.2d 971 (Idaho 1977) (waiver of hearing by intentionally walking out of hearing); McDonough v. Kelly, fn. 320, *infra* (waiver of right to counsel); Hickey v. Bd. of Sch. Directors, 328 A.2d 529 (Pa. 1974) (waiver of right to have witnesses testify); Fleming v. Concordia Parish Sch. Bd., 275 So.2d 795 (La. 1973); Hayes v. Cape Henlopen Sch. District, 341 F.Supp. 823 (Del. 1972) (waiver of right to hearing); Cords v. Window Rock Sch. District,526 P.2d 757 (Ariz.1974) (waiver by resignation or abandonment); Pyle v. Wash. Co. Sch. Bd.,238 So.2d 121 (Fla. 1970) (waiver of right to have hearings transcribed); Mullally v. Bd. of Education, 164 N.W.2d 742 (Mich. 1968) (waiver prior notice); Williams v. Cody, 545 P.2d 905 (Ore. 1976) (waiver of right of appeal).

311. Board of Education of Charles County v. Crawford,395 A.2d 835 (Md. 1979); Oliveri v. Carlstadt-E. Rutherford Reg. Sch. Bd. of Education,388 A.2d 1324 (N.J. 1978); Alexander v. Sch. District No. 17,248 N.W.2d 335 (Neb. 1976); Hunter v. Bd. Dir. of Inchelium Sch. District, 536 P.2d 1209 (Wash. 1975)

312. Pelisek v. Trevor State Graded Sch. District, fn. 294, *supra; cf.* Karstetter v. Evans,350 F.Supp.209 (N.D. Tex. 1971) (notice to counsel held sufficient).

313. Buck v. Bd. of Education, 553 F.2d 315 (2d Cir. 1978); Parker v. Letson, 380 F.Supp. 280 (N.D. Ga. 1974); Potts v. Gibson, 469 S.W.2d 130 (Tenn. 1971).

refuses a request to make the evidence accessible to teacher review, the proceedings may be voided as a denial of due process.[314]

Hearing Requirements. The hearing must be set at a reasonable time and a reasonable place.[315] Hence notice given one day or several hours before the hearing was unreasonable and led to a reinstatement order.[316] Where the time of notice and place of hearing is fixed reasonably by statute or regulation, it will govern.[317]

All of the elements of a "formal" hearing are not required for every case.[318] The need for more formalities increases with the seriousness of the charges and penalties. It is settled, however, that administrative hearings are not required to apply the strict rules of procedure and of evidence that obtain in courts of law.[319]

A fair hearing cannot be said to exist where an absent board member later cast the vote that broke a tie vote of the members who *did* participate in the hearing.[320] A proceeding at which the board refuses to allow the respondent teacher to present evidence on his or her own behalf is not a hearing in the legal sense and will be nullified.

Prehearing Suspensions. An important question, which admits of no single answer, is whether a person may be suspended from employment *before* the hearing required for final decision. To resolve this question, the Supreme Court has approved the same flexible standard as it employed to determine what process is due. Where "the nature of the private interest is not so great" or where "the risk of an erroneous deprivation in the absence of a prior hearing is not great," the Court has found that "something less than an evidentiary hearing is sufficient prior to adverse administrative action" especially where "the substantial public interest would be impeded by the availability of a pretermination hearing in every case."[321] This flexible balancing standard permits a court to weigh the factors in each case and to determine whether the state's interest in immediate suspension or the teacher's interest in the hearing prior to suspension should prevail. New York courts approved prehearing suspension, provided the hearing was promptly arranged.[322] Where the teacher may recover back pay if successful at the later hearing and suffers no irreparable harm to reputation, or where school safety may be threatened by continued presence of the teacher, or where the teacher's presence would seriously disrupt school operations, such factors support prehearing suspension, as

---

314. Blackburn v. Bd. of Education, 564 S.W.2d 35 (Ky. 1978); Bd. of Trustees v. Spiegel, 549 P.2d 1161 (Wyo. 1976).

315. Wagner v. Little Rock Sch. District, 373 F.Supp. 876 (E.D. Ark. 1973).

316. Bates v. Hinds, fn. 287, *supra.*

317. Barrett v. E. Iowa Community College District, 221 N.W.2d 781 (Iowa 1975); Hayes v. Cape Henlopen Sch. District, 341 F.Supp. 823 (D. Del. 1972).

318. Goss v. Lopez, fn. 281, at p. 578-579.

319. Knox County Bd. of Education v. Willis, 405 SW 2d 952 (Ky.1966); *see* Dixon v. Love, 431 U.S. 105, 115 (1977).

320. McDonough v. Kelly, 329 F.Supp. 144 (D. N.H. 1971).

321. The quoted language is from Dixon v. Love, 431 U.S. 105 (1977). *See also* Matthews v. Eldridge, 424 U.S. 319 (1976).

322. Myers v. Bd. of Education, 391 N.Y.S.2d 323 (1977); Pordum v. Bd. of Regents, 491 F.2d 1281, (2d Cir. 1974) cert. denied, 419 U.S. 843 (1974).

consistent with due process.[323] Conversely, courts have prohibited prehearing action where the action itself or the mere public announcement of the charges would damage the employee's reputation and opportunities for future employment.[324] Thus the legality of prehearing disciplinary actions turns essentially upon the facts in each case. While due process normally requires a hearing *before* termination, it may be satisfied by a prompt posttermination hearing if rendered sufficiently timely to avoid any unfairness to the affected teacher.[325]

Right to Counsel and Confrontation. The right to legal counsel is hardly disputed in serious cases, but it does not attach to all cases. The party's right to confront and refute adverse evidence carries with it the right to ascertain the nature and sources of such evidence and testimony. Board refusal to supply such information or exclusion of a respondent and his or her attorney from the hearing when such evidence is presented has been found to deny due process.[326] The reliance by a school board on hearsay evidence that cannot be tested by the defending teacher is often a denial of the right of confrontation and cross-examination.[327] Similarly, the refusal of a board to subpoena an examining doctor to appear to testify, as requested by the respondent teacher, was held to nullify the proceedings.[328] Legislation that would authorize a board to make decisions on evidence not challengeable by the affected teacher would be equally unconstitutional.[329]

Impartial Tribunal. The concept of fair decision making is predicated on hearing and judgment by an impartial body. Since school boards and state agencies make and enforce rules and later judge and punish alleged violators, their impartiality has been challenged in many discharge and discipline cases. In 1976, the Supreme Court of the United States first considered the issue of school board impartiality; it held the school board to be presumptively impartial for constitutional purposes. The board discharged teachers who admittedly conducted an illegal strike following unsuccessful labor negotiations between the board and the striking teacher union. The Court thus recognized that in appropriate circumstances school boards may combine the functions of prosecutor, judge, and jury. Other courts had recognized this.[330] Nevertheless, the party alleging bias has the burden of proving actual, and not mere potential bias. (See the *Hortonville* opinion at the end of this chapter.) The Court rejected the suggestion of conflict of interest, since the board

---

323. Hodgkins v. Central Sch. District No. 1, 368 N.Y.S.2d 891 (1975); *See, e.g.*, Brubaker v. Bd. of Education, 502 F.2d 973, at 988,989 (7th Cir. 1974); Ott v. Bd. of Education of Hamilton Twp., 389 A.2d 1001 (N.J. 1978).

324. Huntley v. Comm. Sch. Bd. of Brooklyn, 543 F.2d 979 (2d Cir. 1976); *cf.* Embrey v. Hampton,470 F.2d 146 (4th Cir. 1972) (discharge for arrest, prior to conviction); State v. Jefferson Parish Sch. Bd., 188 So.2d 143 (La. 1966).

325. Blair v. Robstown Ind. Sch. District, 556 F.2d 1331 (5th Cir. 1977).

326. Springfield Sch. District v. Shellem, 328 A.2d 535 (Pa. 1974); *cf.* Ayers v. Lincoln County Sch. District, 432 P.2d 170 (Ore. 1967) (statutory right of confrontation).

327. Pounder v. Harper Woods Bd. of Education, 250 N.W.2d 504 (Mich 1977).

328. Doran v. Bd. of Education, 285 N.E.2d 825 (Ind. 1972).

329. Kinsella v. Bd. of Education, 378 F.Supp 54 (W.D. N.Y. 1974).

330. Aubuchon v. Gasconade County R-1 Sch. District, 541 S.W.2d 322 (Mo. 1976); Leach v. Bd. of Education, 295 A.2d 582 (Del. 1972); Withrow v. Larkin, 421 U.S. 35 (1975).

members acting in an official capacity have no individual personal stake in the hearing outcome. The Supreme Court also refused to infer any bias from the board's familiarity with and participation in the background labor negotiations, even though that process might have produced some irritation between the parties, and even though the board had taken a public stand on the negotiations.[331] In the absence of proof of personal interest, malice, or final prejudgment of disputed facts, the Supreme Court held that bias could not be inferred.[332]

The issue of fact prejudgment was not involved in the Hortonville case since there *were* no material fact disputes. However, boards must often make managerial judgments involving a teacher's personal condition or performance, and courts have been reluctant to consider prehearing investigations or opinions by the board sufficient to establish bias or prejudgment at later hearings.[333] Thus a teacher who was entitled to a hearing on a board order to undergo a psychiatric examination could not, on such facts alone, disqualify the board from conducting the hearing. The court reasoned that the board members were not shown to have unchangeable opinions with respect to evidence that might be offered for their final judgment.[334]

Where a teacher meets the heavy burden of proving that board members prejudged the defending party, the teacher can disqualify the board decision.[335] Instances of bias include participation by school officials as both judge and witness against the teacher and school solicitor participation as both prosecutor and board counsel or hearing officer.[336] But the participation of board counsel as an advocate against a teacher does not alone destroy the requisite impartiality.[337] The question of an impartial tribunal, therefore, is primarily a matter of proving facts and circumstances that disable the board from acting as an unbiased decision maker.

Vagueness and Overbreadth. The fair notice ingredient of constitutional due process requires that statutes and regulations governing teacher conduct be sufficiently clear to permit persons of ordinary intelligence to determine what conduct is permissible and

---

331. *Accord:* Farrelly v. Timberlane Reg. Sch. District,324 A.2d 723 (N.H. 1974); Simard v. Groton, 473 F.2d 988 (2d Cir. 1973) (board members involved in heated labor negotiations with nonrenewed teacher held not disqualified from voting on nonrenewal recommendation of superintendent).

332. *Accord:* Duke v. No. Texas St. Univ., 469 F.2d 829 (4th Cir. 1972); White v. Bd. of Education, 501 P.2d 358 (Hawaii 1972); Bates v. Hinds, 334 F.Supp 528 (N.D. Tex. 1971). But see Kamjathy v. Bd. of Education, 348 N.Y.S.2d 28 (1973) (board members personally involved in assault incident by teacher—held disqualified from the hearing tribunal).

333. Penn-Delco Sch. District v. Urso, 382 A.2d 162 (Pa. 1978); Weissman v. Bd. of Education,547 P.2d 1267 (Colo. 1976); Bd. of Education v. Burkett, 525 S.W.2d 747 (Ky. 1975); King v. Caesar Rodney Sch. District, 380 F.Supp. 1112 (D. Del. 1974). The law is reviewed in Withrow v. Larkin 421 U.S. 35 (1975).

334. Hoffman v. Jannarone,401 F.Supp. 1095, 1101 (D.N.J. 1975). *Accord:* Petitions of Davenport, 283 A.2d 452 (Vt. 1971) (board participation in prehearing suspension).

335. Staton v. Mayes, 552 F.2d 908 (10th Cir. 1977); Sigmon v. Poe, 528 F.2d 311 (4th Cir.1975); King v. Caesar Rodney Sch. District, 380 F.Supp. 1112 (D. Del. 1974).

336. Commonwealth Dept. of Education v. Oxford Area Sch. District,356 A.2d 857 (Pa. 1976); Keith v. Community Sch. District, 262 N.W.2d 249 (Iowa 1978) English v. Northeast Bd. of Education, 348 A.2d 494 (Pa. 1975) (solicitor as hearing officer); Miller v. Bd. of Education,200 N.E.2d 838 (Ill. 1964) (solicitor as prosecutor and counsel to board on admissibility of evidence). *See* Staton v. Mayes, 552 F.2d 908 (10th Cir. 1977) for example of board member bias.

337. Yuen v. Bd. of Education, 222 N.E.2d 570 (Ill. 1966).

what is proscribed. Statutes that are excessively vague or overbroad in their coverage (i.e., embrace conduct that may be protected) will be struck down not only for lack of fair notice, but also because of their tendency to chill freedom of action by leaving a person uncertain of his or her rights and obligations.

Courts particularly disfavor excessive vagueness or overbreadth in the area of First Amendment freedoms.[338] As previously noted, vagueness challenges to statutory grounds have been rejected in the great majority of cases, while those dealing with loyalty oaths and with forced disclosure of past teacher associations were strictly scrutinized for vagueness and overbreadth.[339] Administrative regulations governing teacher expression have also been strictly construed and overturned where found to be unconstitutionally vague.[340]

2. Statutory Due Process

The procedures required by state statutes are especially significant in cases that do not qualify for constitutional due process and in many cases provide greater safeguards than those required by constitutional due process. For example, some state statutes require notice and hearings for probationer dismissal and impose extraordinary requirements that board votes be cast publicly and recorded.[341] Different procedures are often specified for different kinds of decisions (e.g., those pertaining to nonrenewal, to demotion, and to midterm dismissals, certificate revocation, or termination of tenure). Legislative requirements for each category vary widely from state to state, as do the judicial construction of whether particular procedural statutes are mandatory or directory. Generalizations about state statutory due process, therefore, only supply an orientation.

Probationary personnel are given a statutory right to notice and hearings in a fair number of states regarding decisions on performance ratings, nonrenewal, or dismissal.[342] The failure to allow hearings in such instances may entitle the teacher to reinstatement, money damages, or to reconsideration by the board under proper statutory procedures.

State statutes usually require greater formalities and protections for weightier teacher interests. For example, statutes governing discharge of tenured teachers may call for a supermajority vote of the board, on recorded roll call.[343] Only a majority vote is normally required for board decisions. Rights of appeal are not uniform under state statutes, but the *scope* of an appeal is often critical. If, on appeal, the court is limited to review of the administrative record, it is more difficult to overturn the decision than if

---

338. *See, e.g.*, Whitehill v. Elkins, 389 U.S. 54 (1967); Keyishian v. Bd. of Regents, 385 U.S. 589 (1967).

339. *Statutory grounds:* Kirkpatrick v. Wright, 437 F.Supp. 397 (M.D. Ala. 1977) ("immorality" held not vague); Aubuchon v. Gasconade, R-1 Sch. District, 541 S.W.2d 322 (Mo. 1976). Cf. Arnett v. Kennedy, 416 U.S. 134 (1974) (upholding federal employee discharge for "such cause as will promote the efficiency of the service"). *Loyalty oaths*: See above section on teacher loyalty. *Past associations:* Shelton v. Tucker, 346 U.S. 479 (1960).

340. Webb v. Lake Mills Sch. District, 344 F.Supp. 791 (N.D. Iowa 1971).

341. See Pa. Stat. Annot., Tit. 24, § 11-1127, § 11-1129 (Purdons).

342. *See* Fogel v. Bd. of Education, 369 N.Y.S.2d 517 (1975); Kruse v. Bd. of Directors, 231 N.W.2d 626 (Iowa 1975).

343. *See, e.g.*, Nutter v. Sch. Com. of Lowell, 359 N.E.2d 962 (Mass. 1977).

the law authorizes the reviewing court to conduct a new trial or to hear new evidence.[344] In the exceptional cases where facts are not disputed, a statute may even deny any right of appeal, except for clear errors of law.[345]

3. Substantive Rights

School regulations cannot abridge substantive rights conferred by the higher law of federal and state constitutions. Civil rights statutes impose civil liability upon school superiors who interfere with teacher rights and provide additional reason for caution in dealing with substantive rights. Federal and state laws on teacher rights are cumulative:

> "Not every civil right is a right derived or secured by the constitution or laws of the United States. . . . Only those rights, privileges or immunities that are secured by the Constitution, . . . or some act of Congress are within the protection of the federal courts. Rights, privileges and immunities not derived from the federal Constitution . . . are left exclusively to the protection of the states."[346]

It is, therefore, necessary to canvass the federal and state laws separately to determine the full range of substantive rights.

a. Constitutional Rights. The Fourteenth Amendment provides antidiscrimination guarantees through the equal protection clause (Chapter 7) as well as procedural protections. The due process clause "likewise protects substantive aspects of liberty against unconstitutional restriction by the State." Fourteenth Amendment "liberty" includes both rights enumerated in the Constitution and rights that are not specified in the Bill of Rights.[347] Among the unspecified rights are those dealing with freedom of choice in marriage, family life, and procreation. Under the specific guarantees of the First, Fourth, and Fifth Amendments, public school employees are entitled to freedom of religion and of expression (whether by speech, press, association, or petition to government), to freedom from unreasonable search and seizure by government authority, and to freedom from compelled self-incrimination. Since state employment of teachers may not be conditioned upon the surrender of constitutional rights, teachers may not be punished for exercising such rights.[348] In acknowledging these points, however, the Supreme Court also noted that the exercise of such rights by teachers may be more restricted than those of ordinary citizens: "[A]t the same time it cannot be gainsaid that

---

344. Review of administrative record only: Turner v. Bd. of Trustees, 548 P.2d 1115 (Cal. 1976) (dismissal of probationer sustained). New evidence: *See, e.g.*, County Sch. Bd. of Spottsylvania County v. McConnell, 212 S.E.2d 264 (Va. 1975); Francisco v. Bd. of Directors, 537 P.2d 789 (Wash. 1975); Osborne v. Bullitt County Bd. of Education, 415 S.W.2d 607 (Ky. 1967).

345. Turner v. Bd. of Trustees, 121 Cal. Rptr. 715 (1975). *But see* 68 *Am. Jur.* 2d 530 for conflicting authorities.

346. *See* Scheelhouse v. Woodbury Cent. Comm'y. Sch. District,488 F.2d 237, 243 (8th Cir. 1973).

347. The Constitution operates differently in private schools. See Chapter 10.

348. *Re* unlawful punishment of protected speech, *see, e.g.*, Columbus Education Assn. v. Columbus School System, 623 F.2d 1155 (6th Cir. 1980). *Re* unlawful discharge of teacher who invoked Fifth Amendment against self-incrimination, *see, e.g.*, Bd. of Public Education v. Intille, 163 A.2d 420 (Pa.1960). *Re* fundamental privacy defense, see decisions on unwed pregnant teachers. p. 215.

the State has interests as an employer in regulating the speech of its employees that differ significantly from those it possesses in connection with regulation of speech of the citizenry in general."[349]

As repeatedly stated by the Supreme Court, civil rights are not abstract absolutes, but are measured according to specific needs in the context of teacher-government relationships. Teacher freedoms and the needs of the school must be balanced, and the interests of each set limits to the other's. This balancing can only proceed on a case-by-case basis because different combinations of balancing factors come into play in different case lines. For example, cases involving pupil safety implicate greater concern than cases involving business efficiency, and cases involving political speech raise weightier teacher interests than cases involving choice of dress or hair style. Other factors, such as the nature and level of the teacher's position, the particular school environment, and the grounds for discipline, also weight the scales in striking the balance of individual and public interests. A good discussion of the foregoing process is contained in the *James* opinion, which is reported at the end of this chapter.

Before 1977, courts were in conflict on the validity of teacher terminations that were based in part on valid grounds and in part upon board disapproval of constitutionally protected teacher speech.[350] In 1977, the United States Supreme Court resolved the conflict by ruling that, to overturn a board decision, the teacher must prove that the challenged decision would not have been made *but* for the "motivating purpose" to punish the exercise of free speech.[351] In that case, the teacher released nonconfidential information to a radio station, to the displeasure of the board, but did not prove that his discharge would not have occurred anyway on other grounds.

The decision permits courts to ignore allegations of constitutional infringement unless the teacher proves a "direct causal link" between the alleged infringement of constitutional rights and the decision to dismiss the teacher. The fact that the foregoing decision involved nonrenewal of a probationary teacher, rather than termination of a tenured teacher, does not seem to be constitutionally significant since the Supreme Court recognized that probationers, as well as other teachers, are protected by the First Amendment right of free speech.

b. Freedom of Expression. The cases on freedom of expression in public schools voice a consistent underlying theme, namely, that no teacher or student may press constitutional rights to the point of disrupting the operation of schools. Short of actual or *serious threat* of a *material disruption* of a *substantial* educational interest, teacher rights are protected; but beyond that point, they do not exist. The *disruption* test is broad and encompasses tangible and intangible injury to, or interference with, the rights of others, school property, school activities, and school discipline. The United States Supreme Court declined to adopt a universal constitutional measure for disruption:

---

349. *See* Pickering v. Bd. of Education, 391 U.S. 563, 568 (1968).

350. *Compare* Gray v. Union County Int. Ed. District, 520 F.2d 803 (9th Cir. 1975) and cases cited therein at p. 806, *with* Bertot v. Sch. District No. 1, 522 F.2d 1171 (10th Cir. 1975).

351. Mt. Healthy City Sch. District Bd. of Education v. Doyle,429 U.S.274 (1977). *Accord:* Bryant v. St. Helena Par. Sch. Bd., 561 F.Supp. 239 (M.D.La. 1983); Smith v. Harris, 560 F.Supp. 677 (D.R.I. 1983); Busker v. Bd. of Education, 295 N.W.2d 1 (So.Dak. 1980).

"[B]ecause of the enormous variety of fact situations in which critical statements by teachers . . . may be thought by their superiors . . . to furnish grounds for dismissal, we do not deem it either appropriate or feasible to attempt to lay down a general standard against which all statements may be judged."[352]

More recently, however, the Supreme Court, by closely divided vote, placed a restrictive gloss on its general disruption test. In *Connick* v. *Myers,* which is reported at the end of this chapter, the majority justices ruled that the level of constitutional protection and judicial scrutiny of public employee speech are significantly lower where the employee speaks on a matter of personal interest regarding employment conditions, than where he or she speaks out as a "citizen" on matter of "public concern." In the latter case, the public employer could not prohibit or punish employee expression without meeting a heavy burden of satisfying the court that the sanctions on public-interest civic speech is required by an overriding state interest. In the case of personal interest speech, however, the Court held that the Constitution does not require any such proof, and that courts should not interfere with administrative employment decisions to disfavor speech that would undermine worker discipline and efficiency. The difficulties posed by the distinction between personal interest and public interest speech can be discerned from a reading of the *Connick* opinion, *supra,* and from the dissent of four out of nine justices on the Court.

Official coercion of expression is as unconstitutional as official suppression of expression: "It is our conclusion that the right to remain silent in the face of an illegitimate demand for speech is as much a part of First Amendment protections as the right to speak out in the face of an illegitimate demand for silence."[353] A school board may not, therefore, suspend regularly scheduled classes to allow teachers and students to attend an outside war protest rally. Such action would force individuals to manifest their support or opposition to the war through staying in school or going to the rally.[354]

More difficult issues appear where a teacher asserts a First Amendment right to opt out of an official school exercise (e.g., refusal to join in classroom flag-salute exercises). On the one hand, the teacher's refusal undercuts the school's purposes in conducting the flag salute; on the other, coerced teacher participation would burden his or her freedom of belief and expression. Courts resolved this dilemma in favor of the teacher's right of expression, whether it is politically motivated (i.e., that American life does not truly provide "liberty and justice for all") or merely grammatical (i.e., the pledge is very poor grammar).[355] In so holding, the courts were required to conclude that the teacher's expressive silence did not disrupt or undermine the acknowledged state interest in promoting patriotism. In these cases, the courts noted that the teacher stood respectfully aside and did not positively invite the students to undermine the exercise. Whether the teacher's silence in other circumstances would substantially undermine

---

352. Pickering v. Bd. of Education, 391 U.S. 563, 569 (1968).

353. *See* Russo v. Central Sch. District No. 1, 469 F.2d 623, 634 (2d Cir. 1972) (teacher refusal to participate in flag salute).

354. Nistad v. Bd. of Education, 304 N.Y.S. 971 (1969). The right to refrain from political expression extends to union dues collection. See the *Ellis* case at end of this chapter.

355. *Political:* Russo v. Central Sch. District No. 1, *supra. Grammatical:* Hanover v. Northrup, 325 F. Supp. 170 (D. Conn. 1970). *But see* Palmer v. Bd. of Education, 603 F.2d 1271 (7th Cir. 1979).

school goals and discipline obviously calls for judgments on which courts remain free to agree or disagree.

Censorship of Expression. As previously noted, school authorities cannot selectively exclude speech or speakers based solely on disfavored opinion. Nor can they avoid a charge of censorship by banning *all* political speech and literature from the school.[356] In-class partisan political expression may be prohibited not because of content, but as a diversion and interference with organized studies or as a violation of school neutrality. A teacher could no more impose his or her political viewpoints upon the school than could the school authorities. Hence, the use of class time to promote teacher-union activity or to organize civil rights groups, albeit under a mistaken belief of constitutional right, is grounds for teacher discharge.[357] Class discussion of course-related political or social issues may be conducted in an objective and neutral fashion because such expression would be educational, rather than disruptive. Further, a teacher could not be punished for petitioning school authorities for permission to sponsor an outside political symposium. However misguided, inconvenient, and irritating it might be, the petition did not instigate rebellion or school disorder. It was not disruptive and hence was protected.[358] Even the power to ban partisan teacher political expression from school classes was qualified for matters of large public concern. As with the flag-salute cases, courts extend constitutional protection to in-school passive, symbolic, political expression. In the *James* case the court held that a teacher could not be disciplined for wearing an armband to express opposition to the Vietnam War. In upholding such actions, however, courts explicitly rejected any fixed ranking of school authority and teacher constitutional rights. They only insisted that school authorities meet the burden of proving disruptive impact as a necessary predicate to barring such expression: "Teachers cannot be allowed to patrol the precinct of radical thought with the unrelenting goal of indoctrination, a goal compatible with totalitarianism and not democracy. . . . Lest the decision be misunderstood, . . . we disclaim any intent to condone partisan political activities in the public schools which reasonably may be expected to interfere with the educational process."[359] The same court that upheld a teacher's right to petition his superiors for leave to attend an outside antiwar rally also upheld the punishment of two fellow teachers who left the school for the same purpose in defiance of superiors' orders.[360]

Critical Expression. Teacher criticism of school superiors, policies, or personnel loses constitutional protection when it disrupts the school. Although the disruption potential is greater when uttered within the school, the same rule applies to out-of-school expression.

---

356. *See* Wilson v. Chancellor, 418 F.Supp. 1358 (D. Oreg. 1976); Friedman v. Union Free School Dist., 314 F.Supp. 233 (E.D. N.Y. 1970) (prohibition of distribution of all literature by teachers in all areas of the school violated constitutional rights of teachers).

357. *Teacher-union:* Knarr v. Bd. of Sch. Trustees, 317 F.Supp. 832 (N.D. Ind. 1970). *Civil rights:* Cooley v. Bd. of Education, 327 F.Supp 454 (E.D. Ark. 1971); *cf.* Johnson v. Branch 364 F.2d 177 (4th Cir. 1966).

358. Petition of Davenport, 283 A.2d 452 (Vt. 1971).

359. James v. Bd. of Education 481 F.2d 566, 573 and 576 (2nd Cir. 1972).

360. Petition of Davenport, fn 358.

In 1968, the Supreme Court held (1) that a teacher's public criticism of school board management of a public bond proposal was constitutionally protected speech and (2) that a teacher could not be disciplined for such speech unless the board proved that the speech resulted or was likely to result in material disruption or interference with the work of the school or the working relationships of the teacher with others in the school. In 1979, the Court extended this ruling to private face-to-face criticisms by a teacher to her principal. In 1982, as reported above, the Supreme Court adopted a two-level test of expression by public employees, namely, that involving matters of public concern, and that confined to the speaker's personal employment interests. (See *Connick* case at the end of this chapter.)

Obviously, the publishing of known falsehoods or unwarranted personal attacks on school superiors or colleagues may so undermine school discipline and harmony as to justify teacher punishment, but the Supreme Court has made clear that not every disagreement or protest is enough to show a *reasonable* likelihood of *substantial* interference with the work of the school. A leader's remark at his union's meeting that the board was attempting to buy off teachers with little concessions was held insufficient ground to deny contract renewal.[361] Nor can a teacher be punished for expressing political views outside the school, even in elections of the school board.[362] But hostile and harassing personal criticism of superiors or fellow teachers with whom the speaker must work in regular and close relationship, was held to lack constitutional protection and to support terminations of employment.[363]

The difficulty of differentiating between protected expression and unprotected disruptive speech is illustrated by a pair of recent cases in the 9th Circuit Court of Appeals. The first involved a teacher who was also an official of the American Civil Liberties Union. In school and out, he vigorously criticized invocations at school graduations and banquets, he espoused legalization of marijuana, and distributed literature to students that portrayed teacher-student relations as a form of slavery. The latter two actions could easily have supported dismissal, but the board's action was overturned on the court's finding that the board acted solely to punish unacceptable ideas.[364] In the second case, the Court overturned an involuntary transfer of a counselor who criticized the school's testing policy of Mexican-Americans, advised their parents to seek legal assistance to avoid harmful assignment to special education courses, and refused her principal's orders to obtain parental consents for certain testing. The Court sustained findings that the transfer was made on the basis of the counselor's sincere criticism of school testing policies, which were lawful, and not upon insubordination or

---

361. Roberts v. Lake Central Sch. District 317 F.Supp. 63 (N.D. Ind. 1970); Gieringer v. Central Sch. District, 477 F.2d 1164 (8th Cir. 1973).

362. Calhoun v. Cassidy, 534 F.2d 806 (Ky. 1976); Guerra v. Roma Ind. Sch. District, 444 F.Supp. 812 (S.D. Tex. 1977).

363. Gray v. Union Co. Intermediate Ed. Dist.,520 F.2d 803 (8th Cir. 1975) (agitating criticism against superiors ban on teacher's advising student to obtain elective abortion); Watts v. Seward Sch. Bd.,454 P.2d 732 (Alaska 1969) cert. denied 397 U.S.921 (1970) (hostile incitement against school superintendent); *Semble:* Moffett v. Calcasieu Parish Sch. Bd., 179 So.2d 537 (La. 1965); see also the following teacher discharge cases: in the table of cases—Knarr, Amburgey, Whitsell, Birdwell, Ahern, Reed, McAlester, and Davenport. For a minority view, *see* Fuentes v. Bd. of Education, 250 N.E.2d 232 (N.Y. 1969).

364. Wagle v. Murray, 546 F.2d 1329 (9th Cir. 1976).

harassment, which would have been punishable.[365] The foregoing decisions will obviously have to be reassessed in the light of the later *Connick* decision by the Supreme Court, which is discussed above.

The foregoing examples suggest that disruption may be tested two ways, namely, by the impact of the message itself or by the impact of the *manner* of uttering the message. The influence of each varies with the occasion. Where the school sponsors a forum to discuss school issues and invites students', parents', and teachers' participation, orderly criticism of school policies by teachers is protected expression and cannot be punished.[366] But a teacher invited to address a school board meeting could not claim constitutional protection to deliver abusive and defamatory remarks toward his superiors, including a patent suggestion that his superintendent was a liar. His subsequent nonrenewal was sustained and found not to violate freedom of speech.[367] A teacher who helped to distribute in school a pamphlet containing false accusations against a school principal was held subject to discharge, though she did not author the pamphlet.[368] A teacher who encouraged students to print an underground newspaper, without reference to its content, was reinstated after discharge. The court found no adverse connection between the encouragement of student publications and the performance of her teaching duties.[369]

Distinctions must be drawn, therefore, between criticism that instigates disorder and disharmony and criticism that seeks changes in a reasonably tolerable manner. Criticism of school stress on athletics in a professional journal was held not disruptive.[370] A teacher's tolerant display of student cartoons that twitted the school administration on the delays in repairing a classroom water fountain was also held not disruptive.[371]

c. Associational Expression. The First Amendment protects group expression, and an individual may not be deterred from or punished for joining or forming associations—be they political, labor related, or purely social in nature.[372] The right of association is subject to the same limitations as those governing individual speech. Nondisruptive criticism of school policies in union meetings is constitutionally protected, but not abusive attacks on school policy or personnel that incite disharmony in the school.[373] Associational activity that conflicts with professional duties loses constitutional protection. Accordingly, courts upheld dismissals of teachers who took time off to

---

365. Idem. *See also* Zoll v. Eastern Allamakee Comm. Sch. Dist., 588 F.2d 246 (8th Cir.1978) (teacher ordered reinstated with back pay when school board declined to renew her contract in retaliation for her criticism in local newspaper of school authorities and a decline in academic excellence); Bernasconi v. Tempe Elementary School Dist. No. 3, 548 F.2d 357 (9th Cir. 1977), cert. denied 434 U.S. 825 (1977). *But see* contra: Swilley v. Alexander, 448 F.Supp. 702 (S.D.Ala. 1978).

366. Adcock v. Bd. of Education, 513 P.2d 900 (Cal. 1973); *cf.* Washington v. Bd. of Education, 498 F.2d 11 (7th Cir. 1974).

367. Jones v. Battles, 315 F.Supp. 601 (D. Conn. 1970).

368. See the Gilbertson case, fn. 217.

369. See the Bertot case, fn. 350.

370. Williams v. Sch. District of Springfield, 447 S.W.2d 256 (Mo. 1969).

371. Downs v. Conway Sch. District, 328 F.Supp. 338 (E.D.Ark. 1971).

372. See Branti v. Finkel, 445 U.S. 507 (1980)

373. *Criticism:* See the Roberts and Gieringer cases, fn. 361. *Abusive attacks: See* Amburgey v. Cassady, 370 F.Supp. 571 (E.D. Ken. 1974); Pietrunti v. Bd. of Education, 319 A.2d 262 (N.J. 1974).

conduct an illegal strike, and sustained the demotion of a principal who sought to negotiate on behalf of teachers in collective bargaining with the district.[374]

Purely private association is also covered by the First Amendment; hence a school board could not discipline a teacher because she married a civil rights activist.[375] Without furnishing proof of immorality, a board could not discipline a teacher for entertaining male guests for prolonged periods in her apartment, but when a teacher's publicly known associations are detrimental to the school (e.g., open and avowed extramarital cohabitation), the right of privacy did not shield her from sanctions by the school board.[376] An interesting collision of private associational rights with school needs appeared where a board refused to rehire a teacher who sent his child to a segregated private school. The court upheld the nonrenewal on the ground that the school's duty to promote racial desegregation superseded the teacher's freedom of association. That view was later modified by the same court and another federal court to hold that a school board could not abridge a teacher parent's constitutional right to control the education of his or her children without showing that enrollment of the child in a private school would substantially interfere with the teacher's effectiveness in the public school.[377]

d. Teacher Appearance and Dress. General authority to regulate teacher appearance insofar as it may distract or disrupt the educational process is not disputed, but specific controls of hair styles and dress raise fact issues that are seriously disputed. The courts have neither agreed on the scope of constitutional protection of teacher appearance nor on the proofs that must be supplied to sustain or overturn appearance regulations.

With respect to male hair grooming, some courts hold that teachers do not have a sufficiently substantial constitutional interest in appearance to limit school hair regulations to situations where the teacher's hair style would disrupt school operations. Termination of teachers for refusing to trim or remove disapproved hair styles, beards, and sideburns was held not to abridge any constitutional right.[378] A second line of authority prohibits regulation or punishment of hair styles unless the school meets the burden of proving the necessity for grooming restriction (i.e., to avoid material disruption).[379]

Further judicial disagreement surfaced on the question whether, even in the absence of a specific right to control one's appearance, the Constitution forbids any

---

374. *Time off to strike:* See Hortonville at end of this chapter; National Education Assn. v. Lee County Bd. of Instruction, 467 F.2d 447 (5th Cir. 1972). *Principal seeking to negotiate:* Norbeck v. Davenport Comm. Sch. District, 545 F.2d 63 (8th Cir. 1976).

375. Randle v. Indianola Sep. Sch. District, 373 F.Supp. 766 (N.D. Miss. 1974).

376. *Compare* Fisher v. Snyder, 346 F.Supp. 396 (D. Neb. 1972) (prolonged entertainment), *with* Hollenbaugh v. Carnegie Free Library, 578 F.2d 1374 (3d Cir. 1978) (open adulterous cohabitation).

377. *Compare* Cook v. Hudson, 511 F.2d 744 (5th Cir. 1975); rehearing den. 515 F.2d 762 (5th Cir. 1975), cert. dismissed as improvidently granted, 429 U.S. 165 (1976), *with* Brantley v. Surles, 718 F.2d 1354 (5th Cir. 1983); Stough v. Crenshaw County Bd. of Education, 744 F.2d 1479 (11th Cir. 1984)

378. Domico v. Rapides Par. School Bd., 675 F.2d 100 (5th Cir. 1982); Morrison v. Hamilton County Bd. of Education, 494 S.W.2d 770 (Tenn. 1973); Miller v. Sch. District No. 167, 495 F.2d 658 (7th Cir. 1974).

379. Finot v. Pasadena City Bd. of Education, 58 Cal. Rptr. 520 (1967); Conard v. Goolsby, 350 F.Supp. 713 (N.D. Miss. 1972); *cf.* Braxton v. Bd. of Public Instruction, 303 F.Supp. 958 (M.D.Fla. 1969).

government restriction not rationally related to the state's purpose.[380] Some courts rejected this view on the premise that board regulations are prima facie valid and that the burden should not lay with the board to justify its action, but should lay upon the individual to supply substantial evidence that the regulations are clearly arbitrary and capricious.[381] The rational relation test of due process has had erratic acceptance and rejection by the United States Supreme Court, but a recent grooming decision of that Court regarding police officers appears to adopt the rational relationship approach while rejecting the more strict proof of disruption test. In upholding the department's grooming standards for male officers, the Court stated:

> "We believe, however, that the hair length regulation cannot be viewed in isolation, but must rather be considered in the context of the county's chosen mode of organization for its police force. . . . Thus the question is not, . . . whether the State can establish a genuine public need for the specific regulation. It is whether respondent can demonstrate that there is no rational connection between the regulation . . . and the promotion of safety of persons and property. . . . The constitutional issue to be decided . . . is whether the petitioner's determination that such regulation should be enacted is so irrational that it may be branded 'arbitrary,' and therefore a deprivation of respondent's 'liberty' interest in freedom to choose his own hair style."[382]

Punishments for disapproved grooming have been reversed on procedural grounds. Dismissal of a teacher who refused to shave his beard was reversed when the teacher was not given prior warning that his refusal would result in dismissal.[383] Thus, teacher hair style cannot be punished in the absence of any officially stated warning, policy, or regulation on the subject.[384]

Teachers' rights on modes of dress is also "not free from doubt." The few decided cases indicate that, like grooming, a teacher's choice of dress is a generalized rather than "elemental" liberty interest and is entitled only to minimal constitutional protection.[385] Nonrenewal of a teacher based on her refusal to lengthen her miniskirt was upheld as a reasonable employer demand, and dress code regulations requiring jackets and ties to be worn by male teachers in school have also been upheld as reasonable and constitutional.[386] In deciding that the teacher's liberty interest in dress was subordinate to the state educational interest, the Seventh Circuit Court of Appeal held that the proof of disruption test for speech regulation did not apply to dress regulations.[387]

---

380. *See* Conard v. Goolsby, prior fn.; Ball v. Kerriville Ind. Sch. District, 529 S.W.2d 792 (Tex. 1975) (refusal to shave beard not ground for dismissal).

381. Compare the Morrison and Miller cases, fn. 378.

382. *See* Kelley v. Johnson, 425 U.S. 238, 247-248 (1976).

383. Lucia v. Duggan, 303 F.Supp. 112 (D.C. Mass. 1969).

384. Ramsey v. Hopkins, 320 F.Supp. 477, remanded on other grounds, 447 F.2d 128 (5th Cir. 1970).

385. The cases are collected in annotation: Teacher Dress, 58 A.L.R.3d 1227 (1974).

386. Tardif v. Quinn, 545 F.2d 761 (1st Cir. 1976). *cf.* E. Hartford Ed. Assn. v. Bd. of Education, 405 F. Supp. 94 (D. Conn. 1975) (upholding teacher dress code); E. Hartford Educational Assn. v. Bd. of Education, 562 F.2d 838, (1st Cir. 1977) (dismissal of teacher for refusing to wear necktie); Blanchet v. Vermilion Parish Sch. Bd., 220 So.2d 534 (La. 1969).

387. Miller v. Sch. District No. 167, 495 F.2d 658 (7th Cir. 1974).

e. Academic Freedom. The concept of academic freedom originated as a higher education ideal. It has only recently received some legal recognition in public schools.[388] Unlike university scholars who stress independent research on frontiers of knowledge, public school teachers are primarily dedicated to instruct impressionable children in a preset curriculum. Unlike university students, school children are often incapable of distinguishing fact from value or opinion. Nevertheless, a few courts have, by analogy to higher education cases, treated academic freedom in public schools as a "special subset" of constitutionally protected speech.[389] Neither the courts, nor the commentators, however, have developed any consistent guidelines to reconcile the independence of the teacher with the state's right to ensure teacher neutrality in instruction and to compel teacher observance of official curricular directives. Few recent cases do suggest, however, that any protection of teacher academic freedom is subordinate to managerial control where the control has to do with the curriculum and course content, or with the obligations of administrative as distinguished from classroom duties.[390]

Three cases decided in a short interval by the First Circuit Court of Appeals indicate the unsettled state of the law on academic freedom.[391] In the first case (*Keefe*), an English teacher of a coed high school class assigned a reading from the *Atlantic Monthly* that employed and explored the uses of a highly offensive, vulgar epithet. The court itself declined to insert the epithet into its opinion text and resorted to a footnote to identify the term (which it described as "a vulgar term for an incestuous son"). Despite parent protests and orders of the school board, the teacher refused to agree not to use the term again in his class. He brought suit to enjoin the board from carrying out a threat to discharge him for noncompliance. In an ambivalent opinion, the First Circuit preliminarily enjoined the board, noting that the same term was in current usage and could be found in some volumes in the library.

One year later, a university professor who had been invited by university officials to display his art on the campus sued to enjoin the university from shutting down his art show, which the university considered to be tasteless and accompanied by vulgar captions.[392] In upholding the university's finding that the display was inappropriate, the same court rejected the professor's academic freedom claim and made reference to the fact that women and children customarily passed through the campus and should not be exposed to the art.

Still later, the same Court reviewed dismissal of a public high school teacher for making a transitory reference on the blackboard to a vulgar word (for sexual intercourse) that came up in connection with a general discussion of taboo words. Protesting that it

---

388. *See* Cary v. Bd. of Education, 427 F. Supp. 945, 950 (1977); Developments in the Law of Academic Freedom, 81 Harv. L. Rev. 1045, 1050, 1051 (1968). See generally Goldstein, *The Asserted Constitutional Right of Public School Teachers to Determine What They Teach,* 124 U. Pa. L. Rev. 1236 (1976).

389. See the Keyishian case, fn. 255, and the Epperson case, p. 000. Hostrop v. Bd. of Jr. College District No. 515, 337 F. Supp. 977, 980 (N.D.Ill. 1972).

390. Milliken v. Bd. of Directors, 611 P.2d 414 (Wash. 1980) (teaching method may not detract from the scope of intended history course); Russ v. White, 541 F.Supp. 888, aff'd 680 F.2d 47 (8th Cir. 1981) (administrator claim not as strong as that of teacher).

391. Keefe v. Geanakos, 418 F.2d 359 (1st Cir. 1969); Close v. Lederle, 424 F.2d 988 (1st Cir. 1970); Mailloux v. Kiley, 436 F.2d 565 (1st Cir. 1970).

392. *See* Close, *supra.*

"in no way regrets its decision" in *Keefe (supra)* the Court hypothesized distinctions between serious pieces of writing, on one hand, and serious, relevant discussion of "social mores and the use of language with the chalking of a socially taboo word on the blackboard." It did not comment on the transitory exposure of the single taboo word as contrasted with the saturation impact of the much more offensive reading in *Keefe*. Recognizing the dilemma of ruling either way, the Court sent the case back for a prompt trial and ordered that the teacher refrain from similar conduct pending the trial.[393] When, after trial, the case was appealed a second time, the First Circuit judges candidly stated: "We confess that we are not of one mind as to whether the plaintiff's conduct fell within the protection of the First Amendment" and sidestepped the academic freedom question on procedural grounds, namely, that the regulations authorizing teacher discipline were unconstitutionally vague and, therefore, an improper basis for punishment.

This remarkable progression in the First Circuit Court of Appeal prompted the Second Circuit Court of Appeal to quip: "While the First Circuit has indicated that it does not 'regret' its decision in *Keefe* v. *Geanakos, supra,* its enthusiasm for intrusion into academic issues seems to be lessening."[394]

Another case *(Parducci)* that is often cited to support teacher immunity on selection of class materials arose in Alabama.[395] There the court reinstated an English teacher who was discharged for refusing to refrain from assigning a book disapproved by her superiors as "literary garbage" (Kurt Vonnegut's *Welcome to the Monkey House*).[396]

The discussion in Chapter 3 of the various authorities touching upon textbook control by school boards is pertinent as well to teacher claims to control in-class text selections. As the *Pico* decision of the Supreme Court (which is also discussed in Chapter 3 and partially reproduced at the end of that chapter) demonstrates, board control of regular course texts receives the most weight, although board control over elective readings and library texts, especially at the initial selection stage, is also acknowledged by the courts as a legitimate managerial interest. The difficulty arises from the attempt to balance those interests against student or teacher claims of constitutional right of access to particular literature. As the materials in Chapter 3 demonstrate, the cases have not drawn any bright line answers as to how that balance should be struck.[397]

Where teachers undertake discussions in class not proximately related to course material or assigned readings, the defense of academic freedom has not fared well.[398] Extemporaneous discussions of sex matters in class, especially of a vulgar or insensitive

---

393. See Mailloux, *supra.*

394. See footnote 7 to opinion in President's Council v. Community School Board, 457 F.2d 289 (2d Cir 1972).

395. *Accord:* Parducci v. Rutland, 316 F. Supp. 352 (N.D. Ala. 1970). Harris v. Mechanicsville Cent. Sch. District, 382 N.Y.S.2d 251 (1976).

396. *See* Parker v. Bd. of Education, 237 F.Supp. 222 (D. Md.), affd. 348 3F.2d 464 (4th Cir. 1966) (teacher dismissal upheld for assignment of BRAVE NEW WORLD as class reading).

397. See *e.g.*, cases cited at fn. 99 of Chapter 3 and related text discussion; Cary v. Bd. of Education, 427 F. Supp. 948 (D. Colo. 1977) (sustaining board refusal to approve certain texts for elective courses, including THE EXORCIST and A CLOCKWORK ORANGE).

398. *See* Pietrunti v. Bd. of Education, 319 A.2d 266 (N.J. 1974) and previously cited cases upholding teaching discharge for in-class criticism of school superiors. *Compare* Sterzing v. Ft. Bend Ind. Sch. District, 496 F.2d 92 (5th Cir. 1974).

nature, have not been considered protected exercises of academic freedom.[399] Nor has poor judgment in administering discipline. A teacher punished 11-year-old girls for using a vulgar term during the recess period by having them write the same word 1000 times. He was discharged despite his objections that this form of punishment was a standard procedure in his school and that he had received no fair warning that his conduct would be grounds for discharge. The court upheld the discharge, observing that it was based upon "extremely poor judgment" in forcing children, in the presence of classmates, to write vulgar words repeatedly.[400]

f. Privacy Interests. Official intrusion into private conduct of teachers, as previously indicated, must be limited to conduct that affects school operations. The Fifth Amendment's protection against compelled self-incrimination also creates a zone of privacy immunity, as does the Fourth Amendment's prohibition against warrantless and unreasonable searches and seizures of a citizen's person or effects. Very few cases involving search of public school teachers have been adjudicated, but a recent case of first impression held that an after-school search of a counsellor's desk by a school board member who had no warrant was unlawful under the Fourth Amendment.[401] While there is a sparsity of precedents on the ability of school districts to use evidence that was unconstitutionally searched by third parties (i.e., the police), another case of first impression held that illegally seized evidence could be used in a school disciplinary proceeding against the teacher, as noted in Chapter 6, even though such evidence would have been inadmissible in a criminal trial.[402] Student search cases are also less protective than other searches. They offer little guidance for teacher searches because the rights and responsibilities of students cannot be equated with those of teachers.

The claim of privilege to withhold, as confidential, student communication and information is not constitutional in nature, but springs from norms of professional ethics and claims of student privacy. Confidentiality claims are also limited by considerations of student welfare. (These claims will be reviewed in Chapter 6.)

---

399. *See* Moore v. School Bd. of Gulf County, 364 F.Supp 355 (N.D. Fla. 1973) (biology teacher's flagrant reference to personal sexual attitudes, and to student sexual development); State v. Bd. of Directors, 111 N.W.2d 198 (Wis. 1961) (teacher discussion of sex in class). *Cf.* Simon v. Jefferson Davis Par. Sch. Bd., 289 So.2d 511 (La. 1974). *Compare* Palo Verde Un. Sch. Dist. v. Hensey, 9 Cal. App.2d 967 (1970) *with* Lindros v. Gov'g Bd. of Torrance Un. Sch. District, 9 Cal.3d 524 (1973).

400. Celestine v. Lafayette Parish Sch. Bd., 284 So.2d 650 (La. 1973).

401. Gillard v. Schmidt, 579 F.2d 825 (3d Cir. 1978).

402. Governing Bd. of Mountainview Sch. District v. Metcalf, 36 Cal. App. 3rd 551 (1974).

PART III

Collective Labor-Management Relations

Teachers have a constitutional right to form and join labor organizations as part of the right of association. This right, however, does not confer any right to strike[403] or oblige school districts to confer or bargain with teacher organizations.[404] For this reason, a growing number of states have enacted the statutes that are needed to permit or require school boards to negotiate with teacher associations. The first such law was enacted in Wisconsin in 1959. Many questions remain to be clarified under these statutes, and as one authority put it: "there is not as yet anything approaching a common law of public sector public relations."[405]

As of 1975, more than 40 states had some form of public employee labor law. Of these, 29 authorized collective negotiations by public school teachers. The law varies widely on such important topics as unit composition, the subjects of bargaining, methods of dispute settlement, union security, and the right to strike. (A comparison of state labor laws appears in Table 5–2.[406]) Public sector bargaining made its greatest impact in public education, where the rate of unionization, wage gains, and work stoppages has far exceeded that of any other governmental units.[407] An extensive review of bargaining laws must be left to specialized texts, but the following overview covers the more prominent issues and trends.

---

403. Atkins v. City of Charlotte, 296 F.Supp. 1068 (W.D. N.C. 1969). See also the cases on associational freedom: Orr v. Thorpe, 427 F.2d 1129 (5th Cir. 1970); AFSCME, AFL-CIO v. Woodward, 406 F.2d 137 (8th Cir. 1969); McLaughlin v. Tilendis, 398 F.2d 287 (7th Cir. 1968).

404. City of San Diego v. AFSCME, Local 127, 87 Cal. Rptr. 258 (1970); Zeluck v. Bd. of Education, 307 N.Y.S.2d 329 (1970). Winston-Salem/ Forsythe Co. Unit, No. Car. Assn. of Educ'rs v. Phillips, 381 F.Supp 644 (M.D. N.C. 1974); Beaudeof v. State Bd. of Education, 428 F.2d 470 (4th Cir. 1970); Atkins v. City of Charlotte, *supra.* For a contrary, minority view, see Richmond Ed. Assn. v. Crocksford, 55 F.R.D. 362 (E.D. Va. 1962).

405. Grodin and Wollett, Collective Bargaining and Public Employment xiv (B.N.A. Labor Relations and Social Problems, Unit 4, 1975). The labor relations laws governing teachers in private schools are reviewed in Chapter 10.

406. See J. Weitzman, The Scope of Bargaining in Public Employment, pp. 50, 327 (1975); *Developments in the Law, Public Employment,* 97 HARV. L. REV. 1611 (1984).

407. See the comparison data in U.S. Bureau of the Census, *Labor-Management Relations in State and Local Governments: 1974* (Series G.S.S. #75) pp. 1-2, 5-6.

A. Informal Bargaining

In the absence of enabling legislation, the courts disagree on the legality and enforceability of collective agreements. Without express legislative authority, they are split on the questions whether a board has implied powers to enter collective negotiations and whether a collective agreement violates the rule against redelegation of board managerial powers.[408] The permissible scope of collective negotiations is also uncertain where not indicated by statute. Prior to adoption of a teacher-bargaining statute, Illinois courts held that school boards could enter into collective bargaining agreements with one union as an exclusive bargaining representative and could lawfully prefer its teachers in filling job openings and agree to submit "minor" disputes to binding arbitration.[409] But other Illinois courts also nullified, as ultra vires or as unlawful redelegations of responsibility, board-union agreements to follow contract evaluation procedures (in addition to those specified in the state school code) and to submit to binding arbitration disputes concerning teacher transfers or reassignment and disputes regarding hiring of administrators.[410] Kentucky follows the strict common law view that school boards have no obligation to negotiate with their employees and that they retain exclusive control over teacher working terms and conditions.[411] In other states, informal bargaining under extralegal guidelines has proceeded by tacit agreements between public school authorities and teacher associations. When ripened into custom, such informal practices may well be formally incorporated into law.[412]

B. Formal Bargaining

Most teacher-bargaining statutes adopt the pattern, but not the full content, of federal labor laws. Their principal topics are selection of bargaining units and representatives, identification of bargainable subjects, methods of dispute resolution, union rights and security, control of unfair labor practices, and the creation of state agencies to administer the labor statute.

---

408. *Implied powers: Compare* Fayette Co. Ed. Assn. v. Hardy, 628 S.W.2d 217 (Ky. 1980); Chicago Div. Ill. Ed. Assn. v. Bd. of Education, 222 N.E.2d 243 (Ill. 1966) (finding implied power) *with* Commonwealth v. County Bd. of Arlington County, 232 S.E.2d 30 (Va. 1977) (denying implied power). *Rule against redelegation:* Peters V. Health & Hospital Gov'g. Comm., 430 N.E.2d 1128 (Ill. 1981). The conflicting lines of state decision surveyed in Nichols v. Bolding,277 SO.2d 868, at 870 (Ala. 1973); *see also* Bd. of Regents v. U.P.W.A., 175 N.W.2d 110 (Iowa 1970).

409. Chicago Division, Ill. Ed. Assn. v. Bd. of Education, 222 N.E.2d 243 (111.1966); see also Libertyville Ed. Assn. v. Libertyville Bd. of Education, 371 N.E.2d 676 (Ill. 1977) (power to make multiyear labor agreement); *accord:* Rockey v. School Dist. No. 11, 508 P.2d 796 (Colo. 1973); Bd. of Education v. Johnson, 315 N.E.2d 634 (Ill. 1976) (submit "minor" disputes to arbitration).

410. *Evaluation procedures:* Davis v. Bd. of Education, 340 N.E.2d 7 (Ill, 1975); Wesclin Education Asso. v. Bd. of Education,331 N.E.2d 335 (Ill. 1975). *Transfers:* See Bd. of Education v. Johnson,fn.409. Hiring: Bd. of Education v. Rockford Education Asso., 280 N.E.2d 286 (Ill. 1972).

411. Ky. Atty. Gen. Op. 75-126 (1975).

412. See Grodin and Wollett, fn. 405, 1:7-1:8.

TABLE 5-2. Summary of state laws on teacher bargaining*

STATE	AUTHORITY	RECOGNITION	BARGAINING OBLIGATION	STRIKES	UNION SECURITY	
					REQUIRED MEMBERSHIP	CHECK-OFF
Alabama	(S)	Exc.	Meet & Discuss	—	—	**
Alaska	(S) §14.20.550	Exc.	Comp.	Qualified right	—	—
Arizona	Case Law	—	Perm.	—	—	Perm.
Arkansas	Case Law	—	Perm.	Prohibited	—	Emp'ee. Auth'n.
California	(S) Ed. Code §13080	Proportional where more than 1 union	Meet & Discuss	Prohibited	Agency shop prohibited	—
Colorado		General	Meet & Discuss	—	—	—
Connecticut	(S) Gen. Stat. Ann. §10-153a	Exc.	Comp.	Prohibited	—	—
Delaware	(S) Del. Code tit. 14 §4001	Exc.	Comp.	Prohibited	Union Shop Prohibited	Emp'ee. Auth'n.
D. of Col.	De Facto Practice	—	—	—	—	—
Florida	(S) Fla. Ann. §230.22.	Exc.	Comp.	Prohibited	—	Emp'ee. Auth'n.
Georgia	Atty. Gen. Op.	—	Perm.	—	—	—
Hawaii	Haw. Rev. Stat. 89-1 et seq.	Exc.	Comp.	Qualified Right	Agency Shop Comp.	Emp'ee. Auth'n.
Idaho	(S) Id. Code §33-1271 et seq.	Exc.	Comp.	—	—	—
Illinois	Case Law	—	Perm.	Prohibited	—	—
Indiana	Ind. Code Ann. §20-7.5-1-1	Exc.	Comp.	Prohibited	—	Perm.
Iowa	Iowa Code Ann. 90.15 et seq.	Exc.	Comp.	Prohibited	Perm.	Emp'ee. Auth'n.
Kansas	Kans. Stat. Ann. §72-5413	Exc.	Comp.	Prohibited	No provision	No provision
Kentucky	Atty. Gen. Op.	—	Perm.	Case Law	No provision	No provision
Louisiana			Perm.	No provision	No provision	Emp'ee. Auth'n.
Maine	Me. Rev. Stat. tit. 26 §961	Exc.	Comp.	Prohibited	No provision	No provision
Maryland	Md. Educ. Code Ann. Art. 77 §160	Exc.	Comp.	Prohibited	No provision	No provision
Mass.	Mass. Gen. Laws Ann. ch. 149 §178G (West)	Exc.	Comp.	Prohibited	Agency Shop Perm.	Emp'ee. Auth'n.
Michigan	Stat. Mich. Comp. Laws Ann. §423.201	Exc.	Comp.	Prohibited	Agency Shop Perm.	—
Minn.	Stat. Minn. Stat. Ann. §179.61 (West)	Exc.	Comp.	Prohibited	Agency Shop Perm.	Emp'ee. Auth'n.
Miss.	—	—	—	—	—	—
Missouri	Atty. Gen. Op.	—	Meet & Discuss	No provision	No provision	No provision
Montana	Stat. (S) Mont. Rev. Code tit. 75 §6115 et seq.	Exc.	Comp.	Qualified Right	No provision	No provision
Nebraska	Stat. (S) Neb. Rev. Stat. §79-1287	Members only	Meet & Discuss	Prohibited	No provision	No provision
Nevada	Nev. Rev. Stat. 238.010	Exc.	Comp.	Prohibited	No provision	No provision
New Hampshire	Stat. N.H. Rev. Stat. Ann. §31-3	Perm.	Perm.	Qualified rights	—	—

TABLE 5-2. Summary of state laws on teacher bargaining (*cont.*)

STATE	AUTHORITY	RECOGNITION	BARGAINING OBLIGATION	STRIKES	UNION SECURITY: REQUIRED MEMBERSHIP	UNION SECURITY: CHECK-OFF
New Jersey	N.J. Stat. Ann. §34:13A-1	Exc.	Comp.		Agency shop Prohibited	—
New Mexico	Atty. Gen. Op.& Case Law	—	Perm.	—	—	—
N. Y. State	N. Y. Civil Service Law §200 (McKinney)	Exc.	Comp.	Prohibited	Agency Shop Perm.	Emp'ee. Auth'n.
N. Y. City						
N. Carolina	Stat.	—	Prohibited	—		—
N. Dakota	Stat. (S) N. Dak. Cent. Code §15-38.1	Exc.	Comp.	Prohibited	No provision	No provision
Ohio	Stat. Ohio Rev. Code	Stat.	—	Prohibited		Perm.
Oklahoma	Stat. (S) Okla. Stat. Ann. tit. 70 §509	Exc.	Comp.	Prohibited	No provision	No provision
Oregon	Stat. Or. Rev. Stat. §342.440	Exc.	Comp.	Qualified Right	Union & Agency Shop Perm.	—
Penna.	Stat. Pa. Stat. Ann. tit. 43 §1101. 101 (Purdon)	Exc.	Partially comp. Part. Meet & Discuss	Qualified Right		Perm.
Rhode Island	Stat. (S) R.I. Gen. Laws §28-9.3-1	Exc.	Comp.	Prohibited	Agency Shop Perm.	Perm.
S. Carolina	Atty. Gen. Op. only So. Car. Code L.1962 1-66	—	Prohibited		—	—
S. Dakota	Stat. S.D. Compiled Laws Ann. §3-18-1	Exc.	Comp.	Prohibited	—	Perm.
Tennessee	Case Law	—	Prohibited	Prohibited	—	—
Texas	Stat. Tex. Educ. Code Ann. §21.905	Prohibited	Prohibited	Prohibited	—	—
Utah	Atty. Gen. Op.	—	Perm.	—	—	—
Vermont	Vt. Stat. Ann. tit. 16 §1981	Exc.	Comp.	Qualified Right	—	No provision
Virginia	Stat.	—	Perm. (Atty. Gen. Op.)	Prohibited	—	—
Washington	Stat. (S) Wash. Rev. Code Ann. §28.72.010	Exc.	Meet & Discuss	No provision	Perm.	Perm.
W. Virginia	Atty. Gen. Ops. & Case Law	Perm.	Meet & Discuss	Prohibited	—	—
Wisconsin	Stat. Wis. Stat. Ann. §111.70 (West)	Exc.	Comp.	Prohibited	Agency Shop Perm.	Emp'ee. Auth'n.
Wyoming	—	—	—	—	—	—

* This Summary must be updated in light of continuing annual revision of public employee labor relations laws by state legislatures.

** Prohibited in Ala. counties having populations of 10,900 to 11,500.

Key Symbols:

S = Statute
Exc. = Exclusive.
Perm. = Permissible, but not required.
Comp. = Made compulsory by law.
Emp'ee. Auth'n. = Individual employee authorization is required to make dues deductions.
"Qualified" means that statutory proceedings must be exhausted before strike can commence or strike is terminable by court order.

1. The Bargaining Unit and Bargaining Representative

The employee group to be represented in any single negotiation (i.e., the bargaining unit) must be established before a particular union or association can be certified to negotiate for the members of that unit. Statutory guidelines to determine the "appropriate bargaining unit" vary from state to state. Two criteria generally dominate official certification of the size and composition of different bargaining units: (1) Membership should be divided into as few units as possible, and (2) they should include only members who have a "community of interest" in the same collective labor negotiation.[413] To combine in the same unit employees whose interests and duties are adverse to or in conflict with each other would create incurable conflicts of duties for the bargaining representative and defeat the goal of fair representation for all employees.

Most statutes allow labor boards large discretion in determining the appropriate bargaining unit, but some legislatures have enacted specific restrictions on unit composition. For example, Minnesota law requires all teachers to be placed in a single unit; Connecticut, Delaware, and Hawaii require separation of professional employees according to certification classes or administrative duties.[414] Pennsylvania and Wisconsin empower teachers to veto inclusion of nonprofessionals in their bargaining unit, while Rhode Island and Wisconsin prohibit any representation of supervisors by any labor organization.[415] Pennsylvania and New Jersey law places them in units limited to supervisors but New York leaves inclusion of such supervisors in a teachers' unit to the discretion of labor boards.[416]

Determination of the most appropriate unit for collective bargaining under these guidelines often turns on facts and practices that are peculiar to a particular locality or school district. Expert legal counsel may therefore be required to appraise a unit determination problem in doubtful cases.

Once the bargaining unit is established, its representative must be selected and certified in the manner provided by law. Most states authorize the organization receiving a majority vote of unit members to act as the *exclusive* bargaining agent for all unit members, including nonunion members. Very few states provide for proportional (union-members-only) representation.[417]

The grant of exclusive bargaining rights to a certified union or association, by statute, was found to be constitutional by the Supreme Court, notwithstanding the incidental restrictions that exclusive representation places upon a teacher's freedom of

---

413. Pa. Stat. Ann., tit. 43 § 1101.604; Wis. Stat. Ann. § 111.70(4)(d)2. *See generally*, Annot: *Who are Supervisors for Purposes of Bargaining Unit Determination*, 96 A.L.R.3d 723 (1980); Charles County Supp. Services Employees Local Union 301 v. Bd. of Education, 472 A.2d 1025 (Md. 1981) (denial to some employees of bargaining rights given to other employee groups does not violate equal protection, where there is a rational basis for the classification).

414. Minn. Stat. Ann. § 179.63, subd. 17; Conn. Gen. Stat. Ann. § 10-153b; Del. Code Ann., tit. 14, § 4001 (5); Haw. Rev'd Stat. 89-6(a)(5-8).

415. See Pa. and Wis. statutes fn. 413. R.I. Gen Laws, § 28-9.3-2; Wis. Stat. Ann. § 111.81(12).

416. 34 NJSA 34:13A-1; Pa. Stat. Ann. tit. 43 § 1101.604(15); N.Y. Civil Service Laws § 207(1).

417. See GRODIN AND WOLLETT, fn. 405, at pp. 58–59; Fayette Co. Ed. Assn. v. Hardy, 626 S.W.2d 217 (Ky. 1980); Minnesota State Bd. of Community Colleges v. Knight, 465 U.S. 271 (1984).

association.[418] In so deciding, the Court reasoned that the state's interest in stable and peaceful labor relations, as promoted by exclusive unit representation, outweighed the adverse effect upon dissident teachers who did not wish to be associated with or represented by the certified unit representative.

2. The Scope of Collective Bargaining

Several basic questions are encountered in negotiating a collective agreement:

1. What subject matter can or must a board refuse to negotiate?[419]
2. What matters *must* be "bargained" until both sides agree?
3. What matters need only be discussed (meet and discuss), leaving ultimate unilateral decision solely with the board?

In many states, these questions are neither anticipated nor addressed by laws or by new labor statutes, and they may be affected by how earlier general education statutes are interpreted in the light of overlapping special labor relations statutes. For example, how do statutes and regulations dealing with budget law, professional standards, and educational policies affect rights to bargain employment conditions that in turn affect those statutory and regulatory policies?

The courts and administrative bodies have taken different approaches to these questions. The most favored approach is "incremental"—to decide only narrow points, item by item, rather than fashion a general rule of bargainability for all contested items.

a. Statutory Restrictions. Eight states, by statute, restrict all negotiations to a "meet and discuss" consultation, but the effect of agreements so made is not the same in each of those states. (See Table 5–2.) The majority of state bargaining statutes mandates mutual bargaining by the board, but most of these also carve out from mandatory bargaining certain subjects that are classified as *exclusive management rights.* The exclusions vary from blanket references to managerial powers to itemized specifications of particular subjects.[420] Table 5–2 identifies states that use the broad standard of nonnegotiability (inherent managerial rights) and those that specify particular items as nonbargainable (e.g., tenure determination, pension rights, or budgets).

---

418. *See* Abood v. Detroit Bd. of Education, 431 U.S. 209 (1977). *See also* Ohio Assn. of Public School Employees v. Bexley City School District Bd. of Education, 440 N.E.2d 622 (Ohio 1982) and Reynolds School District v. Oregon School Employment Assn., 650 P.2d 119 (Ore. 1982) (voiding voluntary unit-composition and representation agreements between school board and one employee group as a device to exclude organization that the majority of employees supported).

419. For a recent collection of authorities on *Negotiable Issues in Public Employment,* see Annotation, 84 A.L.R.3d 242 (1978).

420. See Pa. Stat. Ann. tit. 43 § 1101.702 (excluding matters of inherent managerial policy); Mont. Rev. Code Ann. § 75-6119 (1971) (excluding, inter alia, matters of curriculum); the Nevada statute, fn. 427, *infra.* For annual updates of state-by-state legislative activity affecting public school labor relations, see *Special Reports, Labor Relations in Secondary and Elementary Education* (Issues for 1982, 1981, 1980) (Government Employee Relations Reporter, Bureau of National Affairs, Inc.).

In deciding how new labor statutes operate with relation to preexisting school codes, the courts have not developed a fixed pattern. A few courts have attempted specification of subjects that are bargainable and nonbargainable, but most courts declined to define fixed categories of bargainable or nonbargainable items.[421] The case-by-case approach weighs the element of board policy control in each case, setting against its effect on teacher working terms and conditions, to arrive at a limited decision.[422] This balancing standard enlarges the discretion of labor boards, since they presumably have special competence and their judgments will not be lightly overturned by the courts.

None of the current approaches to bargainability has produced consistent results. For instance, many courts remain divided on the bargainability of class size.[423] The softness of court decisions on class size bargaining is indicated by New York cases, which first ruled that it was not mandatory, but later concluded that teacher workloads, when affected by class size decisions, were bargainable.[424] Similar distinctions were made in Connecticut between class size (held to be bargainable) and scheduling of working hours and length of the school day (held not to be bargainable).[425] School calendar was considered bargainable in Wisconsin, but with dictum hinting that curriculum matters were not bargainable.[426] Court interpretations of labor statutes may always be reversed by legislative amendments. The legislature in Nevada, in reaction to court decisions to the contrary, amended the labor laws to exclude from mandatory bargaining such items as class size, school calendar, work load, and teacher selection.[427]

Board decisions concerning promotional and supervisory appointments, teacher transfers, tenure, and nonrenewal of contracts have generally been held to be not bargainable.[428] Several courts have also ruled that boards could not bargain away

---

421. *Specification given:* Kenai Pen. Borough Sch. District v. Kenai Pen. Ed. Assn., 572 P.2d 416 (Alaska 1977); Aberdeen Ed. Assn. v. Aberdeen Bd. of Ed., 215 N.W.2d 837 (S.D. 1974).

422. Sutherland Educ. Assn. v. Sutherland Sch. District, 548 P.2d 647 (Ore. 1976); Pa. Labor Relations Bd. v. State College Area Sch. Dist.,337 A.2d 263 (Pa. 1975); Nat'l Ed. Assn. of Shawnee Mission, Inc. v. Bd. of Education, 512 P.2d 426, 534 (Kans. 1970).

423. *Held bargainable:* W. Hartford Ed. Assn. v. deCourcey, 295 A.2d 536 (Conn. 1972); Matter of Washoe Co. Sch. Dist. and Washoe Co. Teachers' Assn., Nev. (L. Govt. Emp.-Mgmt. Rel. Bd., Item 3, Oct. 1971); Hawaii Public Employee Relations Bd. decision (in Govt. Emp. Relations Rptr. E-1 (1972)). *Held not bargainable:* Aberdeen Ed. Assn. v. Aberdeen Bd. of Ed.,215 N.W.2d 837 (S.D. 1974); Nat'l Ed. Assn. of Shawnee Mission v. Bd. of Ed. of Shawnee Mission, fn. 422. *See* Kenai Pen. Borough Sch. District v. Kenai Pen. Ed. Assn., fn. 421.

424. *Compare* matter of W. Irandequoit Teachers Assn. v. Helsby, 35 N.Y.2d 46 (1974); *with* Yorktown Faculty Ann. v. Yorktown Central Sch. Dist., 7 N.Y.P.E.R.B. 3030 (1974). But see Susq. Valley C. Sch. District v. Susq. Valley Teachers Assn., 358 N.Y.S.2d 235 (1974).

425. *See* W. Hartford Ed. Assn. v. deCourcey, fn. 423.

426. Jt. Sch. Dist. No. 8 v. Wis. Employees' Relation Bd., 155 N.W.2d 78 (Wis. 1967). *Compare* Hillsborough Classroom Teachers Assn. v. School Bd., 423 So.2d 969 (Fla. 1982), *with* Eastbrook Community School Corp. v. Indiana Ed. Employment Relations Board, 446 N.E.2d 1007 (Ind. 1983).

427. Compare Nev. Rev. Stat. § 228.150 with Clark City Sch. District v. Loc. Govt. Rel'ns. Bd.,530 P.2d 114 (Nev.1975).

428. Marsh v. St. Vrain Sch. District, 644 P.2d 41 (Colo. 1981); Heneoye Falls-Lime Central School Dist., 402 N.E.2d 1165 (N.Y. 1980); Camden Cty. Voc. v. Cam/Voc Teachers, 443 A.2d 756 (N.J. 1982); Minn. Fed. of Teachers v. Minn. Sp. Sch. District, 258 N.W.2d 802 (Minn. 1977); In Matter of Cohoes City Sch. Dist. v. Cohoes Teachers' Assn., N.Y.2d 774 (1976); Bd. of Ed. v. N. Bergen Fed. of Teachers, 357 A.2d 302 (N.J. 1976); Newman v. Bd. of Education,325 A.2d 387 (Del. 1974); Dunellen Bd. of Educ. v. Dunellen Educ. Assn., 311 A.2d 737 (N.J. 1973); School Dist. of Seward Educ. Assn. v. School Dist., 199 N.W.2d 753 (Neb. 1972).

decisions regarding budget reductions and job eliminations.[429] Nevertheless, there is a growing line of decisions that distinguish between the right to decide and the method of executing a decision. Thus, decisions on management rights may still require bargaining or arbitration as to the *procedures* for implementing them when they affect teacher work.[430] It may thus be necessary to discuss the board's policy decision before negotiating the procedures of implementation, to avoid time-consuming bargaining that only results in procedures and grievance mechanisms that make it almost impossible to carry out the management policy.

In addition to mandatory bargaining, a board may expand the scope of negotiations to include items of "permissive" bargaining, which includes subjects it could legally refuse to bargain, but on which it is not legally prohibited from bargaining. Unless elective bargaining is ultra vires or contrary to public policy, agreements are legal and enforceable.[431] The cases from industrial states indicate a trend toward extending permissive bargaining to any item that is not "explicitly and definitely prohibited by statute," but the trend is by no means universal.[432]

The explosive issue of whether school boards must bargain their decision to contract to outside sources, work that would otherwise be performable by employees in house, remains largely untested in public education. A California statute authorizing school districts to contract pupil driver training instruction to private contractors was upheld, but courts in Michigan and Wisconsin held that board decisions to contract bus and food services so affected employee "working terms and conditions" that they were subject to mandatory negotiation with the bargaining agent of affected employees.[433]

The scope of bargaining is also affected by alleged conflicts between the provisions of new labor statutes and those of older education statutes regarding school management.

---

429. See Sch. Comm'ee of Hanover v. Curry, 325 N.E.2d 282 (Mass. 1975); City of New Rochelle v. New Rochelle Federation of Teachers,4 PERB 3060 (N.Y. 1971); Pa. Labor Rel'ns Bd. v. Mars Area Sch. District, 344 A.2d 284 (Pa. 1975); *cf.* Bd. of Ed. of W. Orange v. W. Orange Ed. Assn., 319 A.2d 776 (N.J. 1974). But see *contra:* Barrington Sch. Committee v. Rhode Island State Labor Relations Bd., 388 A.2d 1369 (R.I. 1978).

430. Bd. of Education v. Poughkeepsie P.S. Teachers Assn., 436 N.Y.S.2d 50 (1981); *See* Minn. Fed. Teachers v. Minn. Sp. Sch. District, 258 N.W.2d 802 (Minn. 1977); Canon-McMillan Sch. Bd. v. Cmw'lth, 316 A.2d 114 (Pa. 1974); Bd. of Ed. of W. Orange v. W. Orange Ed. Assn., fn. 429. *Contra:* Ridgefield Park Ed. Assn. v. Ridgefield Park Bd. of Education,393 A.2d 278 (N.J. 1978).

431. *See* Bd. of Education v. Yonkers Fed. of Teachers, 383 N.E.2d 569 (N.Y. 1976) (upholding no layoff provision as subject of permissive bargaining). *Contra:* the Kenai case, fn. 421; Westtown Ed. Assn. v. Westtown Pub. Sch. Bd. of Education, 337 N.W.2d 533 (Mich. 1983); Fortney v. Sch. Dist. of W. Salem, 321 N.W.2d 225, 230-31 (Wisc. 1981).

432. See prior footnote; City of Beloit v. WERC and Beloit Ed. Assn., 242 N.W.2d 231 (Wis. 1976); Scranton Sch. Bd. v. Scranton Fed. of Teachers, 364 A.2d 1339 (Pa. 1976). On the permissibility of agreements that subjects teacher dismissal decisions to arbitration, *compare* Moravek v. Davenport Community Sch. District, 262 N.W.2d 797 (Iowa 1978) (held impermissible); *with* Denville Bd. of Sch. Directors v. Fifield, 315 A.2d 473 (Vt. 1974) (held permissible). *Compare* Illinois Ed. Assn. v. Bd. of Education, 320 N.W.2d 240 (Ill. 1974); *with* Westlin Area Spec. Edu. Coop. v. Lockport Spec. Ed. Coop. A, 338 N.E.2d 463 (Ill. 1975). Court conflicts in other states remain to be resolved.

433. Calif. Teachers Assn. v. Bd. of Trustees, 146 Cal. Rptr. 859 (1978). See Southwestern Vermont Educational Ass'n, 396 A.2d 123 (Vt. 1978) (school Board contract for outside janitorial services in the midst of a labor dispute held to be an unfair labor practice). Van Buren P. Sch. District v. Wayne Cty. Cir. Judge,232 N.W.2d 278 (Mich. 1975); Unified Sch. District v. Wisconsin Empt. Relations Comm., 259 N.W.2d 724 (Wis. 1977).

Unless both statutes can be harmonized by statutory construction, courts must decide which statute was intended to prevail. Since the legislative history of statutes varies with each state, the state courts can be expected to arrive at diverse results. For example, in Connecticut the terms of a lawfully bargained agreement "shall prevail" over any conflicting law or regulation, but in Massachusetts, the terms of prior laws prevailed over later inconsistent labor laws.[434] Most states lack a clear rule; their courts can either read the labor laws narrowly and interpret general education laws to restrict the scope of bargaining (as in South Dakota) or read the labor statutes broadly as intended to control in doubtful cases.[435] The tendency to uphold bargained terms under labor statutes has not been uniform. For instance, where the labor agreement provides *less* protection for teachers than education statutes, courts may nullify the agreement as contrary to public policy. Statutory provisions on teacher dismissal and maternity leave were held to supersede bargained terms in New York, and an arbitrator's order upholding teacher dismissal pursuant to labor agreement was voided as contrary to general education statutes in Pennsylvania.[436] Statutory regulation of teacher layoff and seniority credit were also held controlling over inconsistent labor agreements in Washington.[437]

The uneven results on the interaction of labor statutes and education statutes are best explained by the fact that judicial reasoning in labor disputes is much more pragmatic than in other areas of law. New York courts would not permit a "back door" grant of tenure via a bargained agreement procedure, even though it favors the teacher, nor would a Georgia court permit a teacher union, through a bargained agreement, to decide how a package of negotiated wage benefits should be distributed among different classes of teachers.[438] Similarly, Pennsylvania and Wyoming courts held that school boards could not surrender, by agreement, managerial control over teacher transfers. A board agreement prohibiting board member access to teacher files was held unlawful and unenforceable in New York.[439]

Perhaps the most telling long run influence on issues of bargainability will be the development of accepted labor practices. When experience reveals what subjects can be effectively bargained without harm to school management and the general public, legislatures and courts are likely to adopt them into formal law. As with the common law, lawmakers prefer to seek and follow proven custom in difficult areas.

---

434. Conn. Gen. Stat. Ann. § 7-474 (f)(Supp. 1969). Mass. Gen. Laws ch. 150E, § 7. See fn. 406, *supra.*

435. Compare the Aberdeen case, fn. 421 with the Scranton case, fn. 432; Wayne County Civil Service Comm. v. Bd. of Supervisors, 184 N.W.2d 201 (Mich. 1971). *Compare also* Botson Teacher's Union v. School Committee, 434 N.E.2d 1258, 1266 (Mass. 1982), *with* Niagara Wheatfield Cent. Sch. District, 375 N.E.2d 37 (N.Y. 1978).

436. Johnson v. Nyquist, 361 N.Y.S.2d 531 (1974) (probationer dismissal, contrary to education statutes, held void); Union Free Sch. Dist. No. 6 v. N.Y. Human Rights App. Bd.,320 N.E.2d 859 (N.Y. 1974) (bargained maternity leave provisions contrary to later statute, held void); Dauphin Co. Tech. Sch. Education Assn. v. Sch. Bd., 357 A.2d 721 (Pa. 1976) (dismissal for failure to pay union dues held void).

437. Oak Harbor Sch. Dist. v. Oak Harbor Ed. Assn., 545 P.2d 1197 (Wash. 1976).

438. *See* Chatam Assn. of Educators v. Bd. of Public Education, 204 S.E.2d 138 (Ga. 1974).

439. Diefenderfer v. Budd, 563 P.2d 1355 (Wyo. 1977); Newkirk v. Sch. District of Phila., 261 A.2d 305 (Pa. 1970); Bd. of Education v. Areman, 362 N.E.2d 943 (N.Y. 1977),

3. Union Security

Labor associations endeavor to maintain their organizational strength by collectively bargained terms on union rights. Of primary interest are those that strengthen union finances and membership. Table 5–2 indicates the prevailing state-by-state variations on union security questions.[440]

One goal of union security is the "agency shop" in which all employees in the bargaining unit must, as a condition of continued employment, either pay union dues as union members, or pay as nonmembers a service charge for union representation. A Michigan statute authorizing agency shop clauses in teacher labor agreements was recently upheld by the United States Supreme Court against the charge that compelled payments by nonunion members infringed upon their freedom to oppose causes espoused by the union.[441] While the Supreme Court agreed that dissident employees have a constitutional right not to be forced to support political causes unrelated to representation services rendered to them by the union, it held that the state's interest in efficient labor relations nevertheless justified the law that required employees to contribute a reasonable fee for representation services to the union (i.e. expenses of union bargaining, contract administration, and grievance adjustment).

In holding that nonmember payments could not exceed reasonable representation costs and that any fee amounts exceeding those costs are recoverable by such employees, the decision raised a number of important related issues, to wit: with what party would the burden of making demands and of proving union representation costs lie? The Court later answered that question by requiring challenging employees to make the necessary demand, but then placing upon the union the burden of coming forward with the information concerning its expenditures. The question of proper *procedures* concerning notice, demand, and proof regarding alleged excess fees was also resolved by placing upon the union the burden of establishing necessary procedures to adjust fee disputes. Since such disputes would not arise until after fees were assessed and deducted from an employee's paycheck, the proper disposition of fee funds in the interval between deduction challenge and final settlement had to be resolved.

The latter questions were directedly addressed in the subsequent Supreme Court decisions in *Ellis* v. *Brotherhood of Railway, Airline & Steamships Clerks* and in *Chicago Teachers Union* v. *Hudson,* which are reported at the end of this chapter. The *Ellis* and *Chicago* opinions should be read as the best response to all of the foregoing questions. But briefly summarized, the Court there ruled that unions could consider as reasonable representation expenses certain activities only indirectly related to their bargaining with specific employers, but that enhance their ability to achieve better representation results. Examples of such costs include expenses of attending national union conventions, union social activities to which nonmembers are invited, litigation expenses relating to bargaining unit contract negotiation and administration, and costs of publication content that related to employee representation.

---

440. For a summary of individual state statutes governing union security as of 1973, see WOLLETT AND CHANIN, THE LAW AND PRACTICE OF TEACHER NEGOTIATIONS, p. 3:524m (1973).

441. Abood v. Detroit Bd. of Education, 431 U.S. 209, (1977).

Ellis made it equally clear, however, that expenses that redounded more to the union's organizational interest rather than to employee benefits, or to union political activities, could not be included in the costs to be recovered by representation fees. Such items that the court noted included union organizing expenses and political activities not related to representation goals.

With respect to union accounting for funds collected, the *Ellis* and *Chicago* cases ruled that merely refunding excess collections would not avoid the constitutional defect of forced contributions, either with respect to the union's use of the said funds, or with respect to the fact that a straight refund would amount to an interest-free loan to the union during the period between the employee's challenge and its final return. The Supreme Court therefore suggested that while employees could not resist payroll deductions for agency shop fees, unions must provide prompt and effective procedures to settle fee-level disputes and to sequester disputed amounts to avoid their being used for impermissible purposes, possibly by placing such sequestered funds into interest-bearing accounts to avoid unnecessary loss to employees who claim their right thereto.

While the Supreme Court in the above two cases endeavored to provide guidelines and suggestions to accommodate both the legitimate interests of the union and the constitutional rights of dissidents, the Ellis opinion still invited conflicting interpretations by lower court judges with respect to refund mechanisms. In *Robinson* v. *State of New Jersey*,[442] the court upheld a state statute that set up a refund system formula as reasonable, while the dissenter argued that the Constitution required more—a system, not satisfied by the state statute, that *insured* that no nonmember payments would be used at any time for impermissible union purpose. The dissenting position was later vindicated by the Supreme Court 1986 decision involving the Chicago Teachers Union (see excerpt at end of this chapter), where it held that (1) placing funds in escrow pending settlement of fee disputes was not enough; (2) the union must inform nonmembers of its representation cost calculations that justify the fee, as a matter of fair notice and opportunity for the payees to determine the fairness of the fee; and (3) the union must provide a procedure for prompt decision by an impartial party to determine any fee challenges raised by nonmembers.

It should be emphasized that the Supreme Court cases on agency shop fees only hold the proposition that a state *may*, with proper procedural safeguards, constitutionally authorize and require all represented employees to pay union service fees. Those cases do not hold that a state *must* impose a fee requirement. It remains possible, therefore, for individual states to forbid agency shops (i.e., by certain versions of "rights to work" laws), and for courts, in the absense of authorizing legislation, to find that compelled union service fees violate the First Amendment rights of the association and political freedoms of dissident employees.[443]

---

442. 741 F.2d 599 (3d Cir. 1984). See also Bd. of Education v. Cahokia Sch. District, 417 N.E.2d 151 (Ill. 1981).

443. NEA v. Unified School Dist., 608 P.2d 415 (Kans. 1980); Sch. Bd. of Escombia County v. PERB, 350 So.2d 819 (Fla. 1978) (checkoff as mandatory subject of bargaining); Kentucky Ed. Public Affairs Council v. Kentucky Registry of Finance, 667 F.2d 1125 (6th Cir. 1982) (checkoff prohibited without individual employee consent).

Another valuable security provision in collective bargaining agreements is the check-off clause whereby the employer agrees to collect through payroll deductions, and transmit to the bargaining representative, payments that are currently due to the union by the employee. Check-off provisions are lawful in a majority of states, but there is no dominant view as to whether such clauses are a mandatory or merely a permissive bargaining subject, or whether individual written authorization by the employee is required to effectuate the payroll deduction (see Table 5–2.)

The majority of courts have sustained the allowance of check-off privileges exclusively to the certified bargaining agent, notwithstanding minority unions' claims that such practices were discriminatory and unconstitutional.[444] Interunion conflicts also arise where bargained agreements give other exclusive privileges to the bargaining union for the conduct of union business.

With respect to granting the representing union of exclusive rights to use school facilities, while excluding minority unions and their members from like privileges, the Supreme Court's recent decision in *Perry Education Association* v. *Perry Local Educators Association,* which is reproduced at the end of this chapter, answered some, but not all, of the questions that have heretofore divided the lower courts. In *Perry,* the court held that a school board could, by bargaining agreement, give to the representing union the exclusive right to use certain school mail facilities not made available to the minority union. In doing so, however, the court stressed that the school board had not totally excluded the minority union or its members from access to other school channels of communications (viz. bulletin boards). *Perry,* therefore, merely holds that some limitation of access to school facilities is constitutionally justified by state labor relations policy,[445] but it carefully avoided any suggestion that a school board and a union could constitutionally exclude minority unions and teachers from all channels of communication in a school. Thus, *Perry* leaves intact those minority jurisdictions that have struck down blanket exclusion of all use of school communication channels by dissenting employees. It remains to be seen, however, whether the *Perry* decision will later be extended to undermine the majority cases that have heretofore favored school board agreements that excluded minority unions from school facilities for labor related communication. New York and Wisconsin decisions support the opposite view that blanket exclusion unlawfully and unconstitutionally discriminates against minority organizations and First Amendment rights.[446] Although uncertified minority groups have no right to participate in collective negotiations, the United States Supreme Court has decided that a school board may not go so far as to deprive dissident teachers from

---

444. San Lorenzo Ed. Assn. v. Wilson, 32 Cal.3d 841 (1983); Memphis A.F.T. v. Bd. of Education, 534 F.2d 699 (6th Cir. 1976); Conn. State Fed. Teachers v. Bd. of Education Members, 538 F.2d 471 (2d Cir. 1976); Bauch v. City of New York, 237 N.E.2d 211 (N.Y. 1968), cert. denied 393 U.S. 834 (1968). *Contra:* Bd. of Sch. Directors v. Wisconsin Empt. Rel'ns. Comm. 168 N.W.2d 92 (Wis. 1969).

445. Accord: Memphis AFT v. Bd. of Education, *supra;* Conn. State Fed. Teachers v. Bd. of Education Members, *supra;* Clark Co. Classroom Teachers Assn. v. Clark Co. Sch. District, 532 P.2d 1032 (Nev. 1975); Federation of Delaware Teachers v. DeLaWarr Bd. of Education,335 F.Supp. 385 (D. Del.1971); Local 858 of A.F.T. v. Sch. District No. 1, 314 F.Supp. 1069 (D. Colo. 1970).

446. Friedman v. Union Free Sch. District No.1, 314 F.Supp. 223 (E.D. N.Y.1970) (prohibition of school facilities except for purely internal school purposes); Bd. of Education v. Wisconsin Empt. Rel'ns. Comm., 191 N.W.2d 242 (Wis. 1971) (paid time off to majority union officers only).

petitioning the school board at public meetings on matters of general interest where such meetings are not directly connected with the collective bargaining process.[447]

C. Dispute Resolution

Three major types of disputes recur in collective labor relations:

1. *Organizing and recognition disputes,* in which the organizational status of teacher associations are contested either by the school districts or by other unions;
2. *Interest disputes,* in which a school district and the certified bargaining representative are unable to agree upon employment matters by collective bargaining; and
3. *Grievance disputes,* in which the school district and bargaining agent disagree upon the meaning or performance of a collectively bargained contract.

Public employee labor relations statutes generally specify means for resolving such disputes, primarily through third-party intervention. Organizing and recognition disputes are largely controlled by state labor boards and commissions, subject to judicial review. The following discussion covers the principle methods of dispute resolution for bargaining deadlocks (interest disputes) and for performance conflicts (grievance disputes).

1. Mediation

In mediation a neutral third party enters the negotiations in an attempt to bring the parties into agreement. Mediation efforts may involve conciliation and "fact finding" to clarify the matters in dispute, with or without recommendations by the fact finder. In some cases these findings are publicized in a further effort to induce the parties to reach agreement.

2. Arbitration

In arbitration the negotiating parties refer disputed issues to an arbitrator or panel of arbitrators for decision. Arbitration takes several forms.[448] The legal problems in arbitration directly parallel those affecting bargaining rights. Questions arise as to what labor disputes are arbitrable, when arbitration is mandatory or permissive, whether the arbitrator's decision is binding or merely advisory, and whether arbitration decisions violate other laws.

---

447. City of Madison Joint School Dist. No. 8 v. Wisconsin Employment Relations Commission, 429 U.S. 167 (1976).

448. "Final-offer" arbitration, a recent innovation, not common to teacher negotiations, is not covered in this text. For an explanation, *see* Long and Fuelle, *Final-Offer Arbitration: Sudden Death in Eugene,* IND. AND LAB. REL. REV. 186 (1974).

Most labor statutes employ some form of arbitration as a technique of dispute resolution, but the forms vary from state to state and within any one state on particular subject matter. For example, a number of state laws mandate arbitration of grievances over the meaning and performance of outstanding bargained agreements, whereas the arbitration of negotiation issues on new contracts is permissive in some states—at the election of the parties.[449] As with bargaining problems, most courts have eschewed broad general tests and have confined arbitration rulings to the circumstances at hand. While mandatory and permissive arbitration decisions have for the most part withstood legal challenges, the nature of the particular dispute is often crucial to the outcome.[450]

Several states adopt the view that arbitration awards made under a bargained agreement are presumptively valid, that is, unless and until a challenger meets the burden of showing their illegality.[451] However, courts will not uphold arbitrations prohibited by statutes or by superior principles of judge-made law, such as the rule against delegating away discretionary duties that are vested exclusively in the school boards. Hence an agreement to arbitrate board decisions on selecting promotion candidates was held unenforceable as was an agreement to pay sabbatical salaries greater than that specified in the education statutes.[452] Arbitration may also be defeated where the labor agreement itself makes the matter either nonarbitrable or subjects it to some exclusive settlement procedure other than arbitration.[453]

Where the law excludes certain board responsibilities from the scope of bargaining, courts will also prohibit arbitration of that area. Thus courts nullified grievance arbitration of decisions on position elimination, on board examination of teachers' files, and on teacher nonrenewal.[454] Similarly, where the matter in dispute (school work-day) is restricted to "meet and discuss" negotiation, arbitration was held impermissible and contrary to the policy of the law.[455] Courts differ, however, in the classification of what matters are subject to arbitration. Three state courts held that once school boards agree

---

449. Annotation: *Unfair Labor Practices—State Acts,* 9 A.L.R.4th 20 (1981); *see also* Bd. of Ed. v. Chicago Teachers Union, 412 N.E.2d 587 (Ill. 1980); Pa. Stat. Ann., tit. 43 §§ 1101.804, 1101.903.

450. *See* Dayton Classroom Teachers Assn. v. Dayton Bd. of Ed.,323 N.E.2d 714 (Ohio 1975); Danville Bd. of Sch. Directors v. Fifield, 315 A.2d 473 (Vt. 1974); Bd. of Ed., Town of Huntington v. Assoc. Teachers of Huntington, 30 N.Y.2d 122 (1972); City of Biddeford v. Biddeford Teachers Assn., 304A.2d 387 (Mo. 1973); Sch. Dist. of Seward Ed. Assn. v. School Dist. of Seward, 199 N.W.2d 752 (Nev. 1972); Annotation: *Statutory Arbitration for Public Employees* 68 A.L.R.3d 885 (1976).

451. *See* Kaleva-Norman-Dickson Sch. Dist. No. 6 v. Kaleva-Norman-Dickson Sch. Teachers Assn., 227 S.W. 2d 500 (Mich. 1975); Internat'l Bd. of Firemen v. Sch. Dist. of Phila., 350 A.2d 804 (Pa. 1976); Fredericks v. Sch. Bd. of Monroe Co., 307 So.2d 463 (Fla. 1975). *See also* Annotation: *Bias of Arbitrations,* 56 A.L.R.3d 679 (1974).

452. *See* Port Jefferson Station Tchrs' Ass'n. v. Brookhaven Comsewogue Union Free Sch. Dist. 411 N.Y.S.2d 345 (App.Div. 1978) (award in agreement to retain teaching specialists in absence of enrollment fall off); Bd. of Education v. No. Bergen Ed. Assn., 357 A.2d 302 (N.J. 1976); Cumberland Valley Ed. Assn., v. Cumberland Valley Sch. District, 354 A.2d 265 (Pa. 1976).

453. Sup. Sch. Committee v. Portland Teachers Assn., 338 A.2d 155 (Me. 1975); Rylke v. Portage Area Sch. District, 341 A.2d 233 (Pa. 1975).

454. Sch. Comm. of Hanover v. Curry, 325 N.E.2d 282 (Mass. 1975) (Position elimination); Bd. of Education v. Areman, 363 N.Y.S.2d 437 (1975) (teacher files); Newman v. Bd. of Education, 325 A.2d 387 (Del. 1975) (teacher nonrenewal).

455. Sup. Sch. Comm. v. Portland Teachers Assn., 338 A.2d 155 (Me. 1975).

to arbitrate teacher evaluations, teacher ratings are subject to grievance arbitration.[456] Several states, including New York, held that teacher termination was subject to grievance arbitration where the bargained agreement limited termination to "just cause," but one New York court declined to enforce an arbitration under an agreement limiting nonrenewal to "just cause."[457] While denying arbitrators the power to order nonrenewal for violation of agreed evaluation procedures, New York and Massachusetts did allow the arbitrator to award the teacher other (monetary) forms of relief.[458]

The legality of arbitration awards turns ultimately upon a court's interpretation of whether the award is consistent with related state statutes. New Jersey courts upheld arbitration on changes of teacher duties, but voided arbitration of class schedule changes on the ground that the former item was bargainable, but that the latter item was not.[459] Bargained agreements on class size and seniority credits were held enforceable in arbitration in New York.[460]

State courts differ on the arbitrability of disputes concerning supervisory positions, but one upheld an arbitration order that a grievant be promoted.[461] Courts are however loathe to sustain arbitration orders that require a school district to grant tenure, even to an improperly dismissed teacher.[462] The narrowness of arbitration scope rulings is indicated by decisions that upheld arbitration awards for the payment of sick leave and for reinstatement of an improperly abolished position.[463] New Jersey law gives the Public Employees Relations Commission discretionary power to suspend arbitration proceedings and provides an exception to the general rule that valid arbitration agreements will be enforced.[464]

3. The Right to Strike

Employee strikes are the ultimate and most potent weapons to obtain concessions in collective negotiations. Hence, labor organizations have strenuously pressed for legislation to permit public employee strikes. Such strikes remain illegal in the great majority

---

456. *Teacher ratings:* Central Pt. Sch. District v. Emp. Rel. Bd., 555 P.2d 1269 (Ore. 1976); Bd. of Education v. Harrison Assn. of Teachers,360 N.Y.S.2d 49 (1974); Milberry v. Bd. of Ed.,345 A.2d 559 (Pa. 1976).

457. *Termination:* Bd. of Directors v. Merrymeeting Ed. Assn., 354 A.2d 169 (Me. 1976); Bd. of Education v. Niagara Wheatfield Teachers, 388 N.Y.S.2d 459 (1976); Bd. of Ed. v. Phila. Fed. of Teachers, 346 A.2d 35 (Pa. 1975); Danville Bd. of Sch. Directors v. Fifield, 315 A.2d 473 (Vt.1975) Kaleva-Norman Dickson Sch. Dist. No. 6, fn. 451; Morris Cent. Sch. District v. Morris Ed. Assn., 388 N.Y.S.2d 371 (1976) (nonrenewal).

458. *Other relief:* Bd. of Education v. Bellemore-Merrick Soc. Teachers, 347 N.E.2d 603 (N.Y. 1976); Sch. Comm. of Danvers v. Tyman, 360 N.E.2d 877 (Mass. 1977).

459. Red Bank Bd. of Ed. v. Warrington 351 A.2d 778 (N.J. 1976); Ridgefield Park Ed. Assn. v. Ridgefield Bd. of Education, 393 A.2d 278 (N.J. 1978).

460. Bd. of Education v. Greenburgh Teachers Fed. 381 N.Y.S.2d 517 (1976).

461. *Supervisory disputes:* compare Sch. Committee of W. Springfield v. Korbut, 358 N.E.2d 831 (Mass. 1976) (denying arbitrability); *with* Scranton Sch. Bd. v. Scranton Fed. of Teachers, 365 A.2d 1339 (Pa. 1976) (enforcing arbitration). *Upheld grievant promotion:* Belanger v. Matteson, 346 A.2d 124 (R.I. 1975).

462. Bd. of Trustees v. Cook Cty. College Teachers Union, 318 N.E.2d 202 (Ill. 1974).

463. Chippewa Valley Schools v. Hill, 233 N.W.2d 208 (Mich. 1975) (grant of sick leave); Rockville Centre Teachers Assn. v. Bd. of Education, 368 N.Y.S. 240 (1975) (improperly abolished position).

464. Bd. of Education v. Englewood Teachers Assn., 342 A.2d 866 (N.J. 1975).

of states, either as a matter of common law or by express statutory prohibition.[465] The minority states that have legalized teacher strikes do so with many restrictions.[466]

A strike is a concerted refusal to work by large employee groups to induce employer bargaining concessions, but not all concerted refusals to work are unlawful. Courts must decide, therefore, when teacher refusals to work amount to an unlawful strike. The mass refusal of teachers to sign new individual contracts for the following year (contract-stacking with union representatives) has been held to be a lawful means of expressing collective demands. Mass teacher resignations, if tendered unconditionally and in proper form to effect a termination of employment, are also lawful since terminated employees are no longer involved in labor bargaining. But mass resignations that are submitted only conditionally—upon failure of their union to achieve a satisfactory labor settlement—have been condemned as an illegal strike.[467] In like vein, sanction orders by teacher organization (pressing their members to refuse work in a particular district under threat of organizational disciplinary action) were held illegal in New Jersey, as an incitement to illegal strike, but a union letter advising teachers of poor professional conditions in a given New York district, and counselling against accepting employment in that district, without any threat of union reprisal against member employees, has been held to be constitutionally protected speech.[468]

Other forms of concerted work interruption (viz. slowdowns, "going-by-the book," and massive absence from work), if used as a negotiation weapon, run the risk of being held a disguised form of strike pressure. Some statutes cover these possibilities by defining a strike very broadly:

> "Strike means concerted action in failing to report for duty, the willful absence from one's position, the stoppage of work, slowdown, or the absence in whole or in part from the full, faithful and proper performance of the duties of employment for the purpose of inducing, influencing or coercing a change in the conditions or compensation for the rights, privileges, or obligations of employment."[469]

Massive unauthorized absence from work was held to constitute a strike in situations where the teachers took time off to petition or protest to the state legislature on issues affecting their welfare.[470]

One of the hazards of "going by the book" (i.e., refusing to perform duties not specified in written contracts) arises from the fact that courts have held teachers to be in

---

465. The antistrike authorities in the various states are collected in Annotation: *Public employees—right to strike,* 37 A.L.R.3d 1147 (1971).

466. *See* Hortonville Ed. Assn. v. Hortonville Sch. Dist. p. 000 *infra;* Alaska Stat. 23.40.200 (1972); Hawaii Rev. Stat. § 89-12 (Supp. 1975); Mont. Rev. Code § 59-1603 (Supp. 1975); Or. Rev. Stat. § 243.726 (1958); 43 Pa. Stat. § 1101.1001 *et seq.*; Vt. Stat. Ann. tit. 21 § 1730 (Supp. 1973).

467. Bd. of Education v. Shanker, 283 N.Y.S.2d 548; aff'd. 386 N.Y.S.2d 543 (1967); *see also* Bd. of Education, Borough of Union Beach v. N.J. Ed. Assn., 247 A.2d 867, 872 (N.J. 1968).

468. *Compare* Bd. of Education, Borough of Union Beach v. N.J. Ed. Assn., prior fn.; *with* Bd. of Education, Union Free School Dist. No. 3 v. N.E.A., 30 N.Y.2d 938 (1972).

469. Pa. Stat. Ann. tit. 46, § 215.1. Similar provisions are found in Mass. Gen. Laws Ann. ch. 150E § 1; Ohio Rev. Code Ann. § 4117.01; Wisc. Stat. Ann. § 111.81.

470. Pruzan v. Bd. of Ed., 209 N.Y.S.2d 966 (1960); Bd. of Education v. Sinclair,373 A.2d 572 (Del. 1977).

breach of contract, and therefore subject to dismissal, for failure to perform implied duties that are not reduced to writing.

Illegal concerted activities are subject to injunction and penalty, irrespective of the label placed thereon.[471]

The legality of picketing by teachers depends upon the form and purpose of the picketing. Purely informational picketing is constitutionally protected as freedom of speech, but picketing action that trespasses upon the rights of others or incites a breach of contract or illegal work stoppages has been held to be unlawful conduct and not constitutionally protected speech.[472]

a. Limitations on Statutory Right to Strike. The states that permit teacher strikes also impose a number of significant qualifications. For example, strikes are permitted where negotiations reach an impasse, but not to protest work grievances or unfair labor practices or to further labor goals of employees in other bargaining units (refusing to cross picket lines of other striking employees).[473] Most statutes that permit impasse strikes require the parties to exhaust statutory settlement procedures, such as mediation and fact finding, before a strike action can legally begin.[474]

The labor statutes also provide that legally commenced strikes may be lawfully terminated by court injunction on public interest grounds (viz. in circumstances where the court finds that the strike poses a clear and present danger or threat to public health, safety, and welfare or imminent threat of irreparable harm to public welfare).[475] The kinds and degrees of dangers to public welfare that satisfy these statutes are largely left to court determination, and thus call for individual case evaluation. It is clear, however, that mere inconvenience will not justify injunctive relief.[476] Under Pennsylvania law, courts lack jurisdiction to entertain injunction petitions where there is no strike actually in progress, but injunction of a threatened strike was upheld in New Jersey.[477] Since injunctive relief is discretionary, a court may refuse to enjoin even a harmful strike if it finds that the public interest in promoting good faith use of third-party procedures is of greater importance than the temporary interruption of public education.[478]

---

471. Warren Ed. Assn. v. Adams, 226 N.W.2d 536 (Mich. 1975).

472. City of Rockford v. Local 113, 1AF, 240 N.E.2d 705 (1968) (speech); Bd. of Education v. Ohio Ed. Assn., 235 N.E.2d 538 (Ohio 1967); Bd. of Education v. Kankakee Fed. of Teachers, 264 N.E.2d 18 (Ill. 1970) (conduct). *See also* Pa. Stat. Ann. tit. 43 § 1101.1101.

473. *Unfair labor:* See, e.g., Pa. Stat. Ann. tit. 43, §§ 1101.1003, 1101.1004; 1101.903. *Crossing picket lines:* Pa. Stat. Ann.tit.43 § 1101.1101; Hawaii Rev. Stat. § 89-12(a)(1); Or. Rev. Stat. § 243.732; Vt. Stat. Ann.-tit. 21 § 1730(3).

474. Pa. Stat. Ann. tit.43 § 1101.1003; Alaska Stat § 23.40.200; Haw. Rev. Stat. § 89-12(b); Or. Rev. Stat. § 243.726; Vt. Stat. Ann. tit. 21 § 1730(1).

475. *See* Bristol Twp. Ed. Assn. v. Sch. District of Bristol Twp., 322 A.2d 767 (Pa. 1974); PERB v. Hawaii St. Teachers Assn., 511 P.2d 1080 (Haw. 1973); Jt. School Dist. No. 1 v. Wisconsin Rapids Ed. Assn.,234 N.W.2d 289 (Wis. 1975); Rockwell v. Bd. of Education, 226 N.W.2d 596 (Mich. 1976).

476. State v. Delaware Ed. Assn., 326 A.2d 868 (Del. 1974).

477. *Compare* Commonwealth v. Ryan, 327 A.2d 351 (Pa. 1974); *cf.* Bd. of Education v. Peoria Ed. Assn., 330 N.E.2d 235 (Ill. 1975); *with* Bd. of Education v. Newark Teachers Union, 296 A.2d 175 (N.J. 1971). See also PERB v. Hawaii St. Teachers Assn, fn. 475.

478. Timberlane Regional Sch. District v. Timberlane Regional Ed. Assn., 317 A.2d 555 (N.H. 1974).

4. Strike Sanctions

When teachers or labor organizations wilfully disobey a court injunction, it may punish violators for contempt of court either under its own enforcement powers or pursuant to penalty provisions of governing labor statutes. Contempt punishments generally take the form of individual or union fines or imprisonment of dissident individuals.[479] Fines may be made cumulative and imprisonment continuous as long as the parties remain in contempt of court. Some statutes also impose or authorize specific sanctions, such as loss of back pay, disqualification for pay increases, and pay deductions measured by each day's disobedience to the court injunction.[480] The severity of contempt penalties and their danger of hardening group defiance leads most courts to employ contempt sanctions sparingly and to require unequivocal proofs of willful injunction violations before any finding of contempt will be made. Absent actual proofs of contempt, sanctions have been denied.[481] Courts are in conflict on the question whether teachers or union representatives may avoid contempt sanction by challenging the validity of the disobeyed injunction order.[482]

The ultimate sanction for unlawful work stoppage is discharge for cause. It may be imposed by school boards independently of court orders. Whether cast in terms of breach of contract, unauthorized absence, insubordination, or statutory penalty, such sanctions have been upheld.[483] A school principal who supported an illegal teacher strike was lawfully demoted, and an officer of a teacher organization who took time off to attend a teacher convention without school permission was held subject to discharge.[484]

Whether teachers who engaged in illegal strike action retain a sufficient interest in job retention to require due process hearings before they may be disciplined or terminated has not been widely litigated. The question may turn on whether individual state statutes are interpreted to preserve or deny job entitlements to striking teachers. To date, the few decided cases have favored the view that teachers may be dismissed without pretermination hearings where the facts on illegal strike activity are not in dispute. Even without constitutional compulsion, however, a school district may voluntarily grant such hearings.

---

479. *See* Annotation: *Damage Liability of Public Employee Union or Union Officials for Unlawful Work Stoppage,* 84 A.L.R.3d 336 (1978).

480. Head v. Spec. Sch. District No. 1, 182 N.W.2d 887 (Minn. 1970); N.Y. Civil Service Law § 210 (McKinney); *see also* Plainview Old Bethpage Cong. of Teachers v. Bd. of Education, 359 N.Y.S.2d 136 (1973).

481. Bd. of Education v. Detroit Fed. of Teachers,223 N.W.2d 23 (Mich.1974); Jt. School District No. 1 v. Wisconsin Rapids Ed. Assn., fn. 475.

482. *Compare* Mead Sch. District v. Mead Ed. Assn., 534 P.2d 561 (Wash. 1975) (contempt order upheld, notwithstanding improprieties in the prior injunction proceedings); *with* Commonwealth v. Ryan, fn. 477 (contempt order reversed where the injunction order was improperly issued).

483. Hortonville Jt. Sch. District No. 1 v. Hortonville Ed. Assn., 426 U.S. 481 (1976); Skeim v. Ind. Sch. District, 234 N.W.2d 806 (Minn. 1975); Farrelly v. Timberlane Regional Sch. District, 324 A.2d 723 (N.H. 1974); Rockwell v. Bd. of Education, 227 N.W.2d 736 (Mich. 1975); Lake Mich. College Federation of Teachers v. Lake Mich. Community College, 518 F.2d 1091 (6th Cir. 1975).

484. *Principal demoted:* Bates v. Dause, 502 F.2d 865 (6th Cir. 1974). *Teacher discharged:* Yuen v. Bd. of Education, 222 N.E.2d 570 (Ill. 1966).

D. Labor-Related Speech Activities

Most disputes on school regulation of labor-related communications fall between the clear extremes of First Amendment violations, such as blanket bans on all use of school facilities for union communications, and reasonable limitations on group activities, such as exclusive dealing with certified bargaining representatives. As previously noted, teachers may not be disfavored solely because of their associational activities so long as such activity does not disrupt school operations. It is equally clear, however, that teacher speech gains no special constitutional immunity merely because it is labor related. If it is bracketed with illegal conduct, such as unauthorized absence, insubordination, illegal work stoppage, or incitement to disruptive conduct, the element of disruption will deprive the teacher of First Amendment protection.

CASES

McGrath v. Burkhard

280 P.2d 865 (Cal. 1955)

SCHOTTKY, *Justice*. . . .

Plaintiff asked the court to declare the rights and duties under the contract of employment; that the non-classroom work was not within the scope of employment; that plaintiff should not be assigned duties on a teaching day which required more than eight hours per day to perform competently; that if more than eight hours may be assigned the court should declare the number of hours per day plaintiff is obligated to perform under the contract; that no duties be assigned on days for which he is not paid, i,e., Saturdays, holidays and most non-teaching days.

Defendants denied the material allegations of the complaint and following a trial the trial court concluded (1) that the respondent board has the right to assign to appellant any teaching duties within the scope of his credential, provided that such assignment does not reduce the rank and grade of his position below the rank and grade of the position held by him during his probationary service with the Sacramento City Unified School District, (2) that the board has the right to assign appellant to assist in the supervision of athletic and social activities conducted under the name or auspices of the Sacramento Senior High School, provided the assignments are made impartially and without discrimination, and (3) that since appellant's employment is professional in nature the services cannot be arbitrarily measured, but depend upon the reasonable needs of the school program; however, the hours of such services must be reasonable. . . .

Appellant is a teacher in the Sacramento Senior High School. . . .

During his course of employment by respondents, appellant and other male teachers have been required to attend certain non-classroom activities and act in a supervisory capacity. The activities are school football and basketball games, which are under the auspices and control of the school authorities. These games may be held at places other than on the school grounds. Six of these athletic assignments are made to each male member of the faculty during each school year, three football games and three basketball games. At the beginning of the school year each male teacher selects the three football games at which he would prefer to supervise; at the end of such season he then selects the three basketball games at which he would prefer to attend in a supervisory capacity. To the extent possible the requests of the teachers are complied with in the scheduling of these assignments, but at times a teacher receives an assignment on a date other than the one he had selected. The teachers are selected impartially and without discrimination. . . .

Appellant did not object to these assignments during the time he served as a long term substitute teacher or during the three years he served as a probationary teacher, but after he attained the status of permanent teacher appellant objected to these assignments and failed to cooperate in the performance of such duties. Effective July 1, 1950, the respondent Board of Education transferred appellant from Chairman of the Social Studies

Department to a full time teacher of English. In lieu of the non-classroom assignments appellant was assigned an extra class to teach, so that he and an industrial arts teacher are the only ones who teach six class hours per day. This is in accordance with a rule of the school and apparently is the first time in several years that it has been used. Since this time appellant has not received any athletic assignments.

Appellant first contends that he is under no contractual obligation in regard to the athletic assignments and that if so obligated, the required duties are unreasonable and not within the scope of teaching duties. He states that such obligation is nowhere set forth in the contract, the rules of the Board of Education, nor in the laws of the state of California. While it is true that this specific duty is not set forth, a study of the evidence and the provisions set forth in the Education Code and the Administrative Code reveals that the assignment complained of by appellant is and was within the contemplation of the parties when the contract of employment was entered into. Relevant portions of each are set out below:

> Education Code, section 2204. "The governing board of any school district shall: (a) Prescribe and enforce rules not inconsistent with law or with the rules prescribed by the State Board of Education, for its own government, and for the government of the schools under its jurisdiction."
>
> Education Code, section 13201. "The governing board or each school district shall fix and prescribe the duties to be performed by all persons in public school service in the school district."

These sections provide for the delegation of rule making authority, so that the correct body can prescribe exactly what the duties are. In connection with this, certain rules promulgated by the State Board of Education must be considered. The following excerpts are taken from the California Administrative Code, Title 5, Article 3, which is entitled "Duties of Principals and Teachers."

> "Section 16. Responsibility or Principal. The principal is responsible for the supervision and administration of his school."
>
> "Section 18. Playground supervision. Where playground supervision is not otherwise provided, the principal of each school shall provide for the supervision, by teachers, of the conduct and direction of the play of the pupils of the school or on the school grounds during recesses and other intermissions and before and after school. All athletic or social activities wherever held, when conducted under the name or auspices of any public school, or any class or organization thereof, shall be under the direct supervision of the authorities or the district."

. . . Appellant's contract expressly set forth that it was subject to the laws of California, the rules of the State Board of Education and of the local governing board. The trial court found that the rule of the Sacramento City Unified School District with reference to the athletic assignments was a part of appellant's contract. The code provisions relating to the duties of teachers do not set forth the particular duty which is the subject of this controversy. The rules promulgated by the State Board of Education do not set forth such specific duty. However, the rules in Article 3 of Title 5 of the

Administrative Code do show that the principals and teachers are charged with certain duties, for example, sections 16, 18 . . . quoted supra. . . . To carry out this responsibility, respondent Board requires teachers to attend certain athletic and social activities in a supervisory capacity. . . . Section 18 clearly places upon the authorities of the district the duty to supervise these activities. This section does not expressly place the particular duty in controversy upon the teachers, but such duty is placed upon the district authorities who in turn have properly delegated it to their representatives and agents. One of the published rules by respondent board in regard to matters of supervision requires teachers to cooperate with their superiors. This is absolutely necessary to carry out the proper administration of the district.

While it is true that the rule requiring teachers to fulfill the athletic assignments is not expressly set forth in the printed booklet of rules and regulations of the Board of Education of the Sacramento City Unified School District, it is also true that none of the non-classroom duties required of the teachers are set forth therein and yet the teachers are fully aware of such duties as cafeteria assignments, variety shows, club sponsors and duties at commencements, etc. All of these duties are supervisory in nature and a minute detailing of them is quite unnecessary, notwithstanding appellant's contention that they should be specifically set forth. These duties are so interrelated with the other duties of the teacher and his position that it is not necessary that each one of them be specifically stated. The booklet of rules and regulations does state that "in matters of supervision teachers shall work cooperatively with special supervisors, the Principal of the school and the Assistant Superintendent in charge." And it is clear from the evidence that appellant was fully aware of the rule and practice as to these athletic assignments when he entered into the contract with the respondent district, and that it was within the contemplation of the parties to the contract.

Furthermore, the general rule is, as stated in 24 Ruling Case Law, at page 574:

> "There is no necessity that all the rules, orders and regulations for the discipline, government and management of the schools shall be made a matter of record by the school board, or that every act, order or direction affecting the conduct of such schools shall be authorized or confirmed by a formal vote."

Appellant's next major contention is that even though the Board has the authority to make the athletic assignments, the specific duties performed by the teachers at the games are unreasonable and not within the scope of their teaching duties. Appellant cites the case of *Parrish* v. *Moss,* 200 Misc. 375, 106 N.Y.S.2d 577, 580, in support of this contention, and the same case is cited and relied upon by respondents. In that case some teachers were seeking to set aside a board regulation which stated that: " . . . 1. Every teacher is required to give service outside of regular classroom instruction in the performance of functions which are the essential duties of every teacher. 2. There is an area of teacher service which is important to the well rounded educational program of the students, but in which teachers participate in varied ways according to their interests, capabilities and school programs. The principal has the responsibility and duty to see to it that these activities are carried on. The principal may assign a teacher to reasonable amounts of such service beyond the specified hours of classroom instruction, and the teacher is required to render such service. . . . " One ground of attack was that this unlawfully delegated to the principals the power to fix the duties and hours of the teachers without providing for adequate protection of the teachers. The court held that such position was not tenable, and upheld the regulation as valid. . . . The court also said in the course of its opinion, 106 N.Y.S.2d at page 584:

> "The hours established in any case must be reasonable. 'The board grant of authority to fix "duties" of teachers is not restricted to classroom instruction. Any teaching duty within the scope of the license held by a teacher may properly be imposed. The day in which the concept was held that teaching duty was limited to classroom instruction has long since passed. Children are being trained for citizenship and the inspiration and leadership in such training is the teacher. Of course, it is recognized that any bylaw of a board outlining teachers' duties must stand the test of reasonableness.'"

Appellant seeks to apply the language of *Parrish* v. *Moss,* supra, to the instant case and asserts that the trial court should be reversed since the duties at the athletic contests were (1) in the nature of police work, (2) unprofessional, (3) foreign to the field of instruction, and (4) imposed unreasonable hours, and therefore were not within the scope of the teaching duties required by the contract. However, the record does not sustain appellant's contention in this regard. The teachers have no authority to act as police officers; in fact, they are expressly informed that their duties are supervisory only. At no time is a teacher to exert police powers. The teachers are to act in a supervisory capacity, much as they do at school assembly meetings, etc. They are acting to protect the welfare of the students. Appellant asserts that he has received no training for this type of work and that the evidence suggests, since women are not assigned this type of duty, that physical strength is a requisite and that the motivating reason for the assignments is to quell and put down disturbances, which is in the nature of police duty. The record refutes appellant's statement. From the deposition of Dr. Murphy, the principal at Sacramento Senior High School, it appears that he was asked questions directly on this point and he replied that the duties did not relate to physical strength or power and stated that he thought many of the female teachers could perform the duties at the games. He stated that he thought that a man's presence at the games was more effectual on the students than a woman's and that it just seemed to be more of a man's job. In explaining this he stated that the work in cafeteria supervision seemed to be more in line with a woman's presence than a man's. Appellant states that the duties were degrading, humiliating and unprofessional. Certain instances are cited. Dr. Murphy admitted that the duty was disagreeable to some, but he felt that it was the same with some women with the cafeteria assignments, or with anyone when they have to perform a task which they do not like, and apparently this is especially so with some teachers when they are faced with these types of supervisory duties. . . . Viewing the duties at the games in light of the above, it is apparent that they are not of an unprofessional nature. . . .

Appellant's final contention is that the duties here involved impose unreasonable hours. The record shows that six of these assignments are made in a school year from September to the following June. Generally, the hours are evening ones, from about six or seven o'clock to ten o'clock. Some assignments fall on Saturday evenings or on

Thanksgiving Day. Appellant also claims that the Saturday or legal holiday on which an assignment occasionally occurs is a day of duty for which he is not paid. However, appellant is not paid on a basis of so much per hour worked. Teachers are engaged in a professional employment. Their salaries and hours of employment are fixed with due regard to their professional status and are not fixed upon the same basis as those of day laborers. . . . A teacher expects to and does perform a service. If that service from time to time requires additional hours of work, a teacher expects to and does perform it. . . . All of his duties are taken into consideration in his contract for employment at the annual salary. All of this is, of course, subject to the test of reasonableness. It does not appear that six of these athletic assignments in an entire school year are unreasonable, nor that the hours of such assignments are unreasonable under the circumstances. What is reasonable must necessarily depend upon the facts of the situation and the teachers are protected in that regard by the appropriate administrative and judicial procedure. Supervising the students and being present to protect their welfare at school athletic and social activities, conducted under the name and auspices of the school, is within the scope of the contract and such assignments are proper so long as they are distributed impartially, they are reasonable in number and hours of duty and each teacher has his share of such duty.

In view of the foregoing we are convinced that the court correctly determined that respondent school board had "the right to assign Plaintiff to assist in the supervision of any and all athletic or social activities, wherever held, when conducted under the name or auspices of the Sacramento Senior High School, or any class or organization thereof, provided such assignment is made impartially and without discrimination against Plaintiff with relation to the other teachers employed at said Sacramento Senior High School."

. . . We find nothing unreasonable in the assignments objected to by appellant. We must presume that the school authorities were acting for what they considered the best interest of the students and the people of the district. To quote again from *Parrish v. Moss*, supra [200 Misc. 375, 106 N.Y.S.2d 585]: "Our courts have repeatedly enunciated the principle that they will not lightly interfere with the exercise of the functions intrusted by law to the school authorities."

The judgment is affirmed. . . .

Hawkins v. Linn County School District No. 14

517 P.2d 330 (Ore. 1973)

SCHWAB, *Chief Judge*. . . .

Plaintiffs complaint alleged that she had been employed as a nontenured teacher by defendants for a period of nearly 14 years under annual contracts. In March of 1972 she was notified by defendants that she would not be re-employed for the following year. As permitted by ORS 342.513 plaintiff requested that defendants spread upon their records the reason for the nonrenewal. They complied, stating:

"'Mrs. Mildred Hawkins was not offered a contract for the 1972-1973 school year because of:

1. Failure in general to communicate with and cooperate with the Principal and Staff of the school in her field of responsibility.
2. Altering of the classroom schedules and use of the building facilities without prior agreement with the classroom teacher and permission of the Principal.'"

The complaint concluded with a prayer for a decree directing defendants to hold a pre-discharge hearing and to reinstate plaintiff as a teacher with back pay pending the hearing. Plaintiff contends that by virtue of *Board of Regents* v. *Roth,* 408 U.S. 564, 92 S.Ct. 2701, 33 L.Ed.2d 548 (1972), and *Perry* v. *Sindermann,* 408 U.S. 593, 92 S.Ct. 2694, 33 L.Ed.2d 570, 578 (1972), she is constitutionally entitled to the relief she seeks because: (1) the reasons for her discharge as spread upon the record of defendant district deprived her of "liberty" and, separately; (2) her 14 years of continuous employment with defendants gave her a property right which could not be terminated without a pretermination hearing.

Pretermination hearings for nontenured teachers are not required by statute, and thus are required only in situations contemplated by *Board of Regents* v. *Roth,* supra, and *Perry* v. *Sindermann,* supra:

> " . . . [T]he Constitution does not require opportunity for a hearing before the nonrenewal of a nontenured teacher's contract, unless he can show that the decision not to rehire him somehow deprived him of an interest in 'liberty' or that he had a 'property' interest in continued employment, despite the lack of tenure or a formal contract. . . . " *Perry* v. *Sindermann,* supra, 92 S.Ct. at 2698, 33 L.Ed.2d at 578.

For the reasons which follow we find that the facts set forth in plaintiffs complaint do not constitute a case of deprivation of either "liberty" or "property."

A. Deprivation of Liberty

While not precisely defining the meaning of the term "liberty," the court in *Roth* attempted to describe it:

> "'Without doubt [the word "liberty"] . . . denotes not merely freedom from bodily restraint but also the right of the individual to contract, to engage in any of the common occupations of life, to acquire useful knowledge, to marry, establish a home and bring up children, to worship God according to the dictates of his own conscience, and generally to enjoy those privileges long recognized . . . as essential to the orderly pursuit or happiness by free men.' . . .
>
> "The State, in declining to rehire the respondent, did not make any charge against him that might seriously damage his standing and associations in his community. It did not base the nonrenewal of his contract on a charge, for example, that he had been guilty of dishonesty, or immorality. Had it done so, this would be a different case. For '[w]here a person's good name, reputation, honor, or integrity is at stake because of what the government is doing to him, notice and an opportunity to be heard are essential.' . . . In such a case, due process would accord an opportunity to refute the charge before University officials, . . .
>
> "Similarly, there is no suggestion that the State, in declining to re-employ the

> respondent, imposed on him a stigma or other disability that foreclosed his freedom to take advantage of other employment opportunities. . . . Had it done so, this, again, would be a different case. . . . The Court has held . . . that a State . . . cannot foreclose a range of opportunities 'in a manner . . . that contravene[s] . . . Due Process' . . . and . . . in a manner that denies the right to a full prior hearing. . . . " *Board of Regents* v. *Roth,* supra, 92 S. Ct. at 2706, 33 L.Ed.2d at 558-559.

The only statements about the plaintiff in the case at bar were that she was uncooperative and uncommunicative and that she altered classroom schedules and used the building facilities without prior agreement.

A review of cases from other jurisdictions considering the question indicates that the charges made against plaintiff here are generally not considered to result in such an injury to reputation or employment opportunities as to constitute a deprivation of liberty requiring a pretermination hearing. For example, it has been held that charges alleging complaints of inadequate attention to students, hostility to colleagues, indifference to rules and regulations, and failure to evidence potential for professional growth do not entitle a nontenured teacher to a hearing.*Berry* v. *Hamblin,* 356 E.Supp. 306, 308 (M.D.Pa. 1973). Nor do allegations of difficulty in relating to pupils and parents, weakness in class control and inadequate motivation of pupils. *Miller* v. *School District Number 167,* Cook County, 111., 354 F. Supp. 922, 925 (N.D.Ill.1973). For other cases holding that similar language did not create a right to a pretermination hearing, *see, Jenkins* v. *United States Post Office,* 475 F.2d 1256, 1257 (9th Cir. 1973); *Lipp* v. *Board of Education of City of Chicago,* 470 F.2d 802 (7th Cir. 1972), and *Russell* v. *Hodges,* 470 F.2d 212 (2d Cir. 1972). The only published opinion we have found which holds language analogous to that in the case at bar required a pretermination hearing is *Whitney* v. *Board of Regents of University of Wis.*, 355 F.Supp. 321 (E.D.Wis. 1973), in which the court held that a statement that a teacher was immature and inadequate was sufficient. It is contra to other authority, and we do not agree with it.

B. Deprivation of Property

. . . The only factual contention that could establish such a property interest in her job is the statement that she had been employed by defendant school district since 1958. This, standing alone, is not enough to support a claim of a deprivation of property under *Roth* and *Sindermann.* She must allege the existence of rules or understandings promulgated or fostered by state officials which would justify a legitimate claim of entitlement to job tenure; mere statements of continuous employment will not suffice. *Board of Regents* v. *Roth,* supra, 92 S.Ct, 2701, 33 L.Ed.2d at 561; *Skidmore* v. *Shamrock Independent School District,* 464 F.2d 605, 606 (5th Cir. 1972). In the absence of such allegations plaintiff has not pleaded any basis for a property interest in her job sufficient to require a pretermination hearing.

Since the actions of defendants deprived plaintiff of neither "liberty" nor "property," the judgment of the court below was proper., and no pretermination hearing was required.

Affirmed.

Ryan v. Aurora City Board of Education

540 F.2d 222 (6th Cir. 1976)

PHILLIPS, Chief Judge

This appeal presents the recurring problem of non-tenured teachers whose contracts of employment are not renewed and who claim due process rights under *Board of Regents* v. *Roth,* 408 U.S. 564, 92 S.Ct. 2701, 33 L.Ed.2d 548 (1972), and *Perry* v. *Sindermann,* 408 U.S. 593, 92 S.Ct. 2694, 33 L.Ed.2d 570 (1972). Plaintiffs Ryan, Miller, Felber and Touby were non-tenured public school teachers employed by the Aurora, Ohio, school system under limited contracts of varying duration, all of which expired at the end of the 1972-73 school year. On April 25, 1973, the Aurora City Board of Education . . . voted not to renew their contracts. . . .

[T]he Board did not provide plaintiffs a hearing, nor did it give any reasons for its action. District Judge William K. Thomas concluded that the Board's regulations, which provided for written reasons to be given to the teachers whose contracts were not renewed, does not create an "expectancy of continued employment" where the teachers are nontenured under Ohio law. We hold that a teacher who is non-tenured under state law does not have a "legitimate claim of entitlement" to continued employment within the meaning of *Roth* and *Sindermann.* Accordingly, we affirm the District Court.

I

Plaintiff Steven Ryan had been employed in 1967 as a science teacher . . . on a one year contract. In 1968, he was re-employed on a five year limited contract. Plaintiff Joan Felver had been first employed to teach home economics in 1966 . . . under a one year limited contract. Thereafter, she had been re-employed to teach the same subject on additional limited contracts for one year, two years, three years and one year. Plaintiff James Miller, hired first in 1968, had taught mathematics . . . under five successive one year limited contracts. Plaintiff Clair R. Touby had been employed in 1971 to teach music . . . He had two one year contracts.

During a specially scheduled public meeting on April 25, 1973, the Board took up the subject of the non-renewal of the plaintiffs' contracts. . . . At the conclusion of the discussion the Board unanimously adopted the following resolution: "[It is moved that] consistent with section 3319.11 of the Ohio Revised Code, the [designated] teachers be notified that their contracts which expire at the conclusion of the 72/73 school year, not be renewed." In voting not to renew these contracts, the Board followed the recommendation of Superintendent of Schools Paul Snyder. Pursuant to § 3319.11 of the Ohio Revised Code, each plaintiff was given written notification before the 30th day of April, 1973. . . .

Ohio, like many other states, has enacted statutes under which tenure rights may be conferred upon teachers after a period of probationary employment. In *Orr* v. *Trinter,* 444 F.2d 128 (6th Cir. 1971), cert. denied, 408 U.S.943, 92 S.Ct. 2847, 33 L.Ed.2d 767 (1972), in construing the same Ohio statutes that are before us in the present case, this court said:

> [W]e emphasize that an essential feature of State teacher tenure laws is to require a teacher to serve a probationary period before attaining the rights of tenure. State statutes prescribe the rights of tenured teachers to written charges, public hearings and judicial review. The determination as to whether the quality of services of a particular teacher entitles him to continued employment beyond the probationary period, thereby qualifying him for tenure status, or whether his contract of employment should not be renewed prior to attainment of tenure status, is the prerogative of the employer, the Board or Education. 444 F.2d at 135.

Under Ohio Rev. Code § 3319.08, contracts for the employment of teachers are of two types, limited contracts (non-tenured) and continuing contracts (tenured). . . . Section 3319.16 makes termination of any contract during its term subject to cause. Accordingly, since "continuing contracts" are of indefinite duration, this provision has the effect of conferring tenure on teachers with "continuing contracts."

Section 3319.11 defines requirements and procedures for renewal and non-renewal of limited contracts and for initially acquiring continuing contract status. The statute delineates only three situations recognized by Ohio law in which a teacher whose limited contract is about to expire can acquire a right to re-employment without action by the Board to offer continued employment. Limited contract teachers who meet eligibility requirements (e.g., years of service, appropriate teaching certification) for continuing contracts, have a right to re-employment on a continuing contract if: (1) the superintendent recommends a continuing contract and the Board fails to reject this recommendation by a three-fourths vote and to notify the teacher to that effect by April 30; or (2) the Board fails to send notice with reasons by April 30 of its action on a recommendation by the superintendent that the teacher be offered another limited contract rather than a continuing contract. A teacher employed under a limited contract, and not eligible to be considered for a continuing contract, can acquire a right of re-employment on a limited contract only if the Board fails to send written notice by April 30 (without reasons) of its decision not to renew the teacher's limited contract. (Section 3319.11 quoted in n. 1.)

Appellants do not claim the above specific statutory tenure scheme confers rights on them. They assert, however, that the Board's regulations contained in a 1965 Policy Manual gave them a "property" interest in their jobs. Appellants rely on the following provisions of the Policy Manual to support their allegation of implied tenure:

Chapter II. Instructional Personnel.
A. Administrative Organization

. . . . .

2. Principals

. . . . .

(b) General Duties

. . . . .

(c) Specific Duties

. . . . .

(11) Hold at least one conference and *one classroom visit each year with teacher*

personnel, in regard to their individual growth contribution to the educational program and making such suggestions for continuous improvement as necessary and reporting such conferences in writing to the conferees. *If a person's work is unsatisfactory, specific suggestions for improvement shall be made in the conference report.* Subsequent written reports shall confirm progress made and *provide a basis for reappointment:* The superintendent shall receive "The Teacher Evaluation Sheet" from the evaluation report for each teacher with the principal's recommendation for reappointment or dismissal by March 1 of each year. Any teacher recommended for dismissal must have been clearly informed of his status by the superintendent and completely aware that such a *recommendation is being made with definite reasons for same.*

Chapter III. Duties and Responsibilities of Instructional Staff.

. . . . .

4. Contracts

. . . . .

> (e) Teachers who are *not to be reappointed shall be given the reasons* and notified in writing by the clerk-treasurer of the school district as confirmed by the board of education on or before April 30. Such written notice to the teacher on non-reemployment shall not be necessary provided that the teacher, after having consulted with the superintendent of the schools, shall give to the board of education before April 30 a letter asking that he not be reappointed. All teachers not so notified shall be considered reappointed (emphasis added).

In *Orr* this court recognized that a due process hearing must be accorded a non-tenured teacher if his contract is not renewed because he exercised his rights of free speech as guaranteed by the first amendment; or if the non-renewal is in violation of the self-incrimination clause of the fifth amendment, the due process clause of the fifth or fourteenth amendment, or the equal protection clause of the fourteenth amendment. *Accord: Hatton* v. *County Board of Education,* 422 F.2d 457 (6th Cir. 1970); *Rolfe* v. *County Board of Education,* 391 F.2d 77 (6th Cir. 1968). We said: "These are constitutionally impermissible reasons for refusal to rehire a teacher." 444 F.2d at 134.

The present case, however, does not invoke a question of free speech, self-incrimination, or equal protection. Rather, the appellants are alleging a fourteenth amendment procedural due process violation on the argument that the Board's regulations have created a "property" interest in their employment under the authority of *Roth* and *Sindermann.* In particular, they argue the regulations of the board contain a clearly implied promise under *Roth,* 408 U.S. at 577, 92 S.Ct. 2701, that limited-contract teachers would be renewed unless there are valid reasons for nonrenewal, thereby creating a "property" interest in continued employment.

Section 1983 was never intended as a catch-all statute under which myriads of suits, traditionally within the exclusive jurisdiction of state courts, may be filed in the federal courts in the absence of a showing of deprivation of a constitutional right.

It is the rule of this Circuit that judicial review in actions of school authorities involving the administration of State Teacher Tenure Laws is in the State courts, not the federal courts, with the exception of cases involving deprivation of rights delineated by this court in *Orr,* as summarized above. . . .

In *Bates* v. *Dause,* 502 F.2d 865, 867 (6th Cir. 1974), we said:

> An action was brought against the Superintendent of Schools and certain members of the Board of Education in their individual capacities under 42 U.S.C. § 1983 and 28 U.S.C. § 1343. By amendments to the pleadings, plaintiffs also asserted that their claims under the State Teachers' Tenure Statute were cognizable in federal court on the theory or pendent jurisdiction. The District Court assumed pendent jurisdiction and rendered judgments of $5,948 in favor of one principal and $8,175 in favor of the other, against the Superintendent of Schools and four members of the Board of Education, all in their individual capacities.
>
> We reverse on the ground that the record shows no deprivation of any rights, privileges or immunities of appellees secured by the Constitution and laws of the United States so as to support an action under § 1983; and that, since the federal claim does not have substance sufficient to confer subject matter jurisdiction on the District Court, that court erred in assuming pendent jurisdiction under the Kentucky Teachers' Tenure Act and the common law of Kentucky. . . .
>
> This statute should be administered by Courts of the Commonwealth of Kentucky, and not by the federal judiciary. Transfer of jurisdiction to federal courts cannot be accomplished by the procedural device of filing an unsubstantial action under § 1983, coupled with a prayer for exercise or pendent jurisdiction. (Footnote omitted.)

A non-tenured teacher may acquire an "expectancy" of continued employment where "the policies and practices of the institution" rise to the level of implied tenure. . . .

We hold, however, that a non-tenured teacher has no "expectancy" of continued employment, whatever may be the policies of the institution, where there exists a statutory tenure system. . . .

Since property interests are created by state law and not the Constitution, *Roth* at 577, 92 S.Ct. 2701, the fact that the State limits the guarantee to only tenured teachers, necessarily negatives any property interest.

This conclusion is supported by the Supreme Court's decision in *Sindermann.* There the Court stated the effects of a state law tenure system upon a claim of entitlement to implied job tenure:

> We do not now hold that the respondent has any such legitimate claim of entitlement to job tenure. For "[p]roperty interests . . . are not created by the Constitution. Rather, they are created and their dimensions are defined by existing rules or understandings that stem from an independent source *such as state law.* . . . " *Board of Regents* v. *Roth,* supra, 408 U.S., at 577 [92 S.Ct. 2701, at 2709]. *If it is the law of Texas that a teacher in the respondent's position has no contractual or other claim to job tenure, the respondent's claim would be defeated.* 408 U.S. at 602 n. 7,92 S.Ct. at 2700. (Emphasis added.)

The fact that Ohio already has an explicit tenure policy obviates the need, which existed in *Sindermann,* to supply one by implication.

The Supreme Court recently stated in *Bishop* v. *Wood,* ______U.S.______, 96 S.Ct. 2074, 48 L.Ed.2d 684 (1976), that the sufficiency of a claim of entitlement to a property interest in employment must be decided by a reference to state law even if the entitlement is based on an implied contract theory. _______U.S._______, 96 S.Ct. 2075. . . .

II

Plaintiffs contend that even if they are not entitled to a hearing under the authority of *Roth* and *Sindermann,* they at least are entitled to the protections prescribed by the Board's own regulations. They complain that the Board did not adopt any statement of "reasons" for its action, and did not give any "reasons" in its notice of non-renewal, as required by its rules.

In an opinion by Circuit Judge John Paul Stevens in *Jeffries* v. *Turkey Run Consolidated School District,* 492 F.2d 1 (7th Cir. 1974), the court held that a non-tenured teacher can be dismissed for no stated reasons, or for voluntarily offered reasons unsupported by factual evidence, without violating due process: . . . *Accord, Buhr* v. *Buffalo Public School District No. 38,* 509 F.2d 1196 (8th Cir. 1974). We agree with the reasoning of the Seventh Circuit. The fact that the Board may voluntarily offer "reasons" by its policies does not in itself create a federal right that does not otherwise exist. No matter what provision may have been contained in the Board's regulations with respect to "reasons" for non-renewal of the contracts of plaintiffs there would be no right to substantive due process under the *Jeffries* decision.

We agree with the opinion of Judge Thomas in the present case that:

> A school board may not limit its exercise of its admitted statutory power under section 3319.11 not to re-employ a teacher on limited contract, by self-imposing a requirement that it give written reasons for nonrenewal in addition to the sole statutory requirement that the board give written notice of nonrenewal before April 30. To condition the Board's exercise of its power under section § 3319.11 on the giving of reasons in effect would make the termination of a teacher, employed under a limited contract, subject io cause. But only teachers who have tenure are entitled to an expectancy or employment terminable only for cause. As earlier explicated the first paragraph of Ohio Rev. Code § 3319.11 fixes the tenure procedures for teachers in Ohio's public schools. Patently no board of education has the authority or power to enlarge the limits of teacher tenure beyond those limits. Indeed, the Aurora School District policy book, on which plaintiffs rely, frankly and correctly concedes.
>
> In developing rules and regulations, it cannot adopt standards which enlarge its authority or that of its employees beyond the statutory limits.

This is in accord with the decision of this court in *Orr,* where we said:

> In the present case Orr seeks to persuade this court to render a decision which would confer certain tenure privileges upon non-tenured teachers—in effect to amend the Ohio statute by judicial decree. This we decline to do. 444 F.2d at 135.

As stated in *Jeffries,* the statement of reasons and their adequacy or accuracy are matters of state law, not federal constitutional law. *See also, Coe* v. *Bogart,* 519 F.2d 10, 13 (6th Cir. 1975); *Manchester* v. *Lewis,* 507 F.2d 289, 291 (6th Cir. 1974); *Bates* v. *Dause,* 502 F.2d 865, 867 (6th Cir. 1974).

Accordingly, the decision of the District Court is affirmed.

Commonwealth of Pennsylvania v. Charleroi Area Sch. Dist.

347 A.2d 736 (Pa. 1975)

MENCER, *Judge.*

This is an appeal from an order of the Secretary of Education (Secretary), requiring the Board of School Directors (Board) of the Charleroi Area School District to reinstate Eleanor McCormick to the position of remedial reading supervisor without loss of pay.

The facts in this case are not in dispute. Eleanor McCormick had been a teacher in the Charleroi Area School District for five years when, on August 26, 1966, she was appointed to the newly created position of reading specialist and remedial reading supervisor. She held this position until June 29, 1973, when she was advised that the position was being abolished and that she was being reassigned to a classroom as a teacher. The Board offered, and Miss McCormick requested, an opportunity to be heard pursuant to the provisions of the Public School Code of 1949 (School Code) on her claim that her reassignment constituted a demotion. . . .

At the July 25, 1973 meeting, Miss McCormick claimed that the reassignment constituted a demotion in type of position. Her counsel then asked that a full hearing, with an impartial public stenographer, be held. His request was denied by the Board, which offered instead that a summary of the meeting would be prepared by a board member. Neither side would relinquish its position, and the meeting was adjourned without the presenting of any testimony by either side.

Miss McCormick appealed the denial of a hearing by the Board to the Secretary. The Secretary found against the Board, and the Board appeals to this Court.

The precise question here is whether a professional employee who claims that she has been demoted in type of position without her consent is entitled to a hearing recorded by an impartial public stenographer. We find that she is entitled to such a hearing.

The law in this regard is clear: If Miss McCormick is a professional employee within the meaning of the School Code, then she is entitled to a hearing if she is demoted in either salary or type of position. Section 1151 of the School Code provides:

> "[T]here shall be no demotion of any professional employe either in salary or in type of position, except as otherwise provided in this act, without the consent of the employe, or, if such consent is not received, then such demotion shall be subject to the right to a hearing before the board of school directors and an appeal in the same manner as herein before provided in the case of the dismissal of a professional employe."

One of the safeguards in such a hearing is provided in Section 1127 of the School Code:

> "[A]ll testimony offered . . . shall be recorded by a competent disinterested public stenographer whose services shall be furnished by the school district at its expense."

This the School Board admittedly failed to do in this case. The Board argues, however, that Miss McCormick is not a professional employee in her capacity as reading supervisor, although they admit that she is a professional employee as a teacher and reading specialist. Since Miss McCormick was, at all times pertinent to this appeal, designated as a reading specialist, it would follow that she was and is a professional employee. We find no authority for the proposition that one can be partially a professional employee.

At first glance, then, this question seems squarely within the holding of the Supreme Court of Pennsylvania in *Smith* v. *Darby School District,* 388 Pa. 301, 319, 130 A.2d 661, 671 (1957), that "[w]hen a professional employee *claims* that he has been demoted it is the school board's duty to grant him a hearing. At that hearing two questions are before the school board: (1) *whether or not the Professional employee has been demoted either in type of position or salary,* and, (2) in the event the professional employee has been demoted, the reason for such demotion must be made clear and apparent." (Emphasis added, footnote omitted.)

However, in that case the demotion complained of was clearly from a so-called "mandated" position to one of lower rank. In this case, we must examine whether, if we accept the Board's contention that the position of reading supervisor was "nonmandated," the result should change.

> "[T]he criterion for determining whether a position or office is or is not 'mandated' depends upon whether or not the title of the incumbent to the position or office is specifically covered by the phrase 'professional employees' in the statute." *Smith, supra,* 388 Pa. at 309-10, 130 A.2d at 666 (footnote omitted).

Section 1101(1) of the School Code[5] provides:

> "(1) The term 'professional employe' shall include those who are certificated as teachers, supervisors, supervising principals, principals, assistant principals, vice-principals, directors of vocational education, dental hygienists, visiting teachers, home and school visitors, school counselors, child nutrition program specialists, school librarians, school secretaries the selection of whom is on the basis of merit as determined by eligibility lists and school nurses."

The argument of the Board is that, since the title "reading supervisor" is not specifically mentioned in the statute, it is "nonmandated". The Board then relies on *Smith, supra,* for the proposition that "by implication, at least, an interpretation of the statute has arisen to the effect that a professional employee may be assigned from an abolished position or office of the so-called 'non-mandated' group without effecting a demotion. . . . " 388 Pa. at 310, 130 A.2d at 667.

The Board maintains, therefore, that no demotion has taken place. We cannot agree.

---

5. 24 P.S. § 11-1101(1).

The distinction between "mandated" and "nonmandated" positions is not relevant to the necessity for a hearing on the threshold issue of *whether or not a demotion has taken place.*

A demotion is, by its nature, relative. A change in the title of one's job may have no bearing on one's authority, prestige, or responsibility in any given organizational structure. It may be very difficult for persons outside the system to assess the "pecking order" accurately. For this reason, in cases where a demotion in type of position is alleged, the reviewing body requires a complete record in which testimony as to the relative standing of the old and new positions in the hierarchy is developed. We therefore hold that a professional employee who claims that he or she has been demoted, whether from a "mandated" or "nonmandated" position is entitled to a hearing as provided in Section 1127 of the School Code to determine initially whether or not a demotion has, in fact, occurred.

In this case, the Secretary has determined that the position of remedial reading supervisor is clearly a position of higher authority than that of teacher. While we have no reason to find that the Secretary is in error on this point, a full hearing before the Board would have provided the Secretary with a more adequate record of testimony regarding the relative positions of remedial reading supervisor and teacher *in the Charleroi district.*

The Board next argues that, because Miss McCormick's salary was partially paid from federal funds, she was not entitled to a hearing. The Board asks us to follow *Anthony* v. *Conemaugh Township Area School District,* 29 Somerset Legal Journal 309 (1974), on this point. The Department of Education, on the other hand, requests us to overrule the same case on that exact point. We are not satisfied that either party has correctly stated the holding in that case; however, we find the case inapposite. *Anthony* did not involve a claim of demotion; plaintiff in the *Anthony* case was hired under a letter contract specifically stating that it was not intended that he become a professional employee. In addition, his *entire* salary was paid from federal funds. These facts distinguish *Anthony* from the case at bar.

We are compelled by the provisions of the School Code to find on this record that Eleanor McCormick was entitled to a full hearing, pursuant to the School Code, on the issue of her alleged demotion. However, we must consider whether the Secretary of Education erred in reinstating Miss McCormick to the position of remedial reading supervisor rather than returning the matter to the Board for the purpose of holding the hearing to which she was entitled, We conclude, on the basis of our holding in *Shellem* v. *Springfeld School District,* 6 Pa.Cmwlth. 515, 297 A.2d 182 (1972), that the Secretary did err in reinstating Miss McCormick. . . .

James v. Board of Education of Central District No. 1 of the Towns of Addison, et al.

461 F.2d 566 (2d Cir. 1972)

IRVING R. KAUFMAN, Circuit Judge.

The first amendment proscription against any law abridging freedom of expression, perhaps more than any other constitutional guarantee, frequently brings into sharp focus the inexorable tension between enduring concerns for individual freedom and the authority required to preserve the democracy so crucial to realizing that freedom. For several decades, the courts have struggled with principles and concepts necessary to strike a functional balance between protected speech and the government's legitimate interest in protecting our democracy.

The Supreme Court has more than once instructed that "[t]he vigilant protection of constitutional freedoms is nowhere more vital than in the community of American schools." . . . Appellant is quick to agree that we cannot tolerate undisciplined, coercive, intimidating or disruptive activities on the part of teachers or students which threaten the essential functions of our schools, and that such conduct requires a disciplinary response. But, the issue in this case is whether, in assuming the role of judge and disciplinarian, a Board of Education may forbid a teacher to express a political opinion, however benign or noncoercive the manner of expression. We are asked to decide whether a Board of Education, without transgressing the first amendment, may discharge an 1 lth grade English teacher who did no more than wear a black armband in class in symbolic protest against the Vietnam War, although it is agreed that the armband did not disrupt classroom activities, and as far as we know did not have any influence on any students and did not engender protest from any student, teacher or parent. We hold that the Board may not take such action.

The facts essential to a resolution of the conflicting interests are undisputed. On June 7, 1969, Charles James was employed as an 11th grade English teacher at Addison High School, located near Elmira, New York. He previously had taught in the New York City public schools. . . .

When November 14 and December 12, 1969, were designated as "moratorium" days by the opponents of the Vietnam War, the Elmira Meeting determined to observe the two days by wearing black armbands. On November 14 James affixed one of the armbands, which had been prepared by the Meeting, to the sleeve of his jacket. He since has stated that he "resolved to wear one of the black armbands as an expression of [his] religious aversion to war in any form and as a sign of [his] regret over the loss of life in Vietnam."

Shortly after school began that day, Carl Pillard, the Principal, entered James's homeroom, noticed the armband, but made no comment. Pillard waited until midway through the second period when James was teaching poetry, apparently without any incident or discussion whatsoever relating to Vietnam or the armband, to summon James to his office and to request him to remove the armband. When James refused to remove it, Pillard sent him to the District Principal, Edward J. Brown. Brown ordered James to remove the armband or risk suspension or dismissal because the armband constituted a symbolic expression of his political views. In addition, Brown feared that "wearing the armband would tend to be disruptive and would possibly encourage pupils to engage in disruptive demonstrations." When James again refused to remove the armband, Brown summarily suspended him and ordered James to leave the school at once.

The following day James received a letter from the Board of Education of Central District No. 1, reinstating him on "the understanding that [he] engage in no political activities while in the school." James resumed his teaching duties, but, steadfastly abiding by his principles, whether religious (Quakers are doctrinally opposed to war) or political in nature, he came to school wearing an armband on December 12, the second moratorium day. He was summarily suspended as soon as Brown learned that James again had worn an armband. Here, too, the record is barren of a scintilla of evidence indicating that there were any incidents or threats to school discipline, that any students or teachers had complained of or were offended by James's first or second symbolic protest, or that the armband constituted more than a silent expression of James's own feelings. On January 13, however, without affording James a hearing, the Board of Education of Central District No. 1 discharged him from his teaching position in accordance with § 3013(1) of the Education Law of New York, McKinney's Consol. Laws, c. 16.

James appealed his dismissal to the New York State Commissioner of Education, Ewald B. Nyquist, asserting that his dismissal infringed upon his first amendment rights and deprived him of due process of law. The "hearing" before the Commissioner, as we were informed at the argument of this appeal, was no more than an informal roundtable discussion between the Commissioner, the parties and their attorneys. No transcript of the proceedings was made. On September 23, 1970, Commissioner Nyquist filed his decision. Although he recognized that a board of education does not have unfettered discretion to dismiss a probationary teacher, he concluded that James had violated "sound educational principles" and that his actions "were not constitutionally protected." In addition, he reaffirmed the Board of Education's absolute right to dismiss a probationary teacher without affording the teacher a hearing or explaining the basis of the discharge. . . .

I

At the outset we are presented with the contention that the claims asserted below are *res judicata.* We consider this to be wholly without merit. Appellees argue that James, at his own choosing, was given the full opportunity to litigate his claims before the Commissioner of Education, a "judicial officer" of the State, and therefore that James should be bound by the Commissioner's decision. Judge Burke buttressed their position with a pointed reference to James's failure to appeal the Commissioner's decision to the New York courts.

It is no longer open to dispute that a plaintiff with a claim for relief under the Civil Rights Act, 42 U.S.C. § 1983, is not required to exhaust state judicial remedies. . . . It is still the law in this Circuit, however, that a Civil Rights plaintiff must exhaust state administrative remedies. *Eisen* v. *Eastman,* 421 F.2d 560 (2d Cir. 1969), cert. denied, 400 U.S. 841, 91 S.Ct. 82, 27 L.Ed.2d 75 (1970). It hardly can be suggested that a plaintiff having followed the course laid out by *Eisen,* was to be barred henceforth from pressing his claim to final judicial review or to be deprived of his opportunity to litigate his constitutional claims in the judicial forum of his choice. To adopt the full implication of appellees' argument would be to effect a judicial repeal of 42 U.S.C. § 1983 and strike down the Supreme Court's decision in *Monroe* v. *Pape, supra.* James would be placed in the paradoxical position of being barred from the federal courts if he had not exhausted administrative remedies and barred if he had.

II

We come now to the crucial issue we must decide—did the Board of Education infringe James's first amendment right to freedom of speech?

Any meaningful discussion of a teacher's first amendment right to wear a black armband in a classroom as a symbolic protest against this nation's involvement in the Vietnam War must begin with a close examination of the case which dealt with this question as it applied to a student. *Tinker* v. *Des Moines Independent Community School District, supra.* Mary Beth Tinker, a junior high school student, her older brother and his friend, both high school students, were suspended from school for wearing black armbands in school to publicize their opposition to the war in Vietnam. Noting that neither students nor teachers "shed their constitutional rights to freedom of speech or expression at the schoolhouse gate," 393 U.S. at 506, 89 S.Ct. at 736, the Supreme Court held that a school cannot bar or penalize students' exercise of primary first amendment rights akin to "pure speech" without "a showing that the students' activities would materially and substantially disrupt the work and discipline of the school." *Id.* at 513, 89 S.Ct. at 740.

With respect to both teacher and student, the responsibility of school authorities to maintain order and discipline in the schools remains the same. The ultimate goal of school officials is to insure that the discipline necessary to the proper functioning of the school is maintained among both teachers and students. Any limitation on the exercise of constitutional rights can be justified only by a conclusion, based upon reasonable inferences flowing from concrete facts and not abstractions, that the interests of discipline or sound education are materially and substantially jeopardized, whether the danger stems initially from the conduct of students or teachers. Although it is not unreasonable to assume that the views of a teacher occupying a position of authority may carry more influence with a student than would those of students *inter sese,* that assumption merely weighs upon the inferences which may be drawn. It does not relieve the school of the necessity to show a reasonable basis for its regulatory policies. As the Court has instructed in discussing the state's power to dismiss a teacher for engaging in conduct ordinarily protected by the first amendment: "The problem in any case is to arrive at a balance between the interests of the teacher, as a citizen, in commenting upon matters of public concern and the interest of the State, as an employer, in promoting the efficiency of the public services it performs through its employees." *Pickering* v. *Board of Education,* 391 U.S. 563, 568, 88 S.Ct. 1731, 1734, 20 L.Ed.2d 811 (1968).

It is to be noted that in this case, the Board of Education has made no showing whatsoever at any stage of the proceedings that Charles James, by wearing a black armband, threatened to disrupt classroom activities or created any disruption in the school. Nor does the record demonstrate any facts "which might reasonably have led school authorities to forecast substantial disruption of or material interference with school activities. . . . " *Tinker* v. *Des Moines Independent Community School District,* 393 U.S. at 514, 89 S.Ct. at 740. All we can learn from the record is that in the opinion of Edward Brown, the District Principal, "wearing the armband would tend to be disruptive and would possibly encourage pupils to engage in disruptive demonstrations." "But," the Supreme Court warned in *Tinker,* "in our system, undifferentiated fear or apprehension of disturbance is not enough to overcome the right to freedom of expression." *Id.* at 508, 89 S.Ct. at 737.

Appellees urge us not to conclude that schools must wait until disruption is on the doorstep before they may take protective action. We do not suggest this course, but if anything is clear from the tortuous development of the first amendment right, freedom of expression demands breathing room. To preserve the "marketplace of ideas" so essential to our system of democracy, we must be willing to assume the risk of argument and lawful disagreement. *Id.* at 508-509; *Terminiello* v. *Chicago,* 337 U.S. 1, 69 S.Ct. 894, 93 L.Ed. 1131 (1949). This is entirely different, however, from saying that the school must await open rebellion, violence or extensive disruption before it acts. *Compare Burnside* v. *Byars,* 363 F.2d 744 (5th Cir. 1966), *with Blackwell* v. *Issaquena County Board of Education,* 363 F.2d 749 (5th Cir. 1966).

III

That does not end our inquiry, however. The interest of the state in promoting the efficient operation of its schools extends beyond merely securing an orderly classroom. Although the pros and cons of progressive education are debated heatedly, a principal function of all elementary and secondary education is indoctrinative—whether it be to teach the ABC's or multiplication tables or to transmit the basic values of the community. "[S]ome measure of public regulation is inherent in the very provision of public education." Note, *Developments in the Law—Academic Freedom,* 81 HAR.L.REV. 1045, 1053 (1968). Accordingly, courts consistently have affirmed that curriculum controls belong to the political process and local school authorities. "Courts do not and cannot intervene in the resolution of conflicts which arise in the daily operation of school systems and which do not directly and sharply implicate constitutional values." *Epperson* v. *Arkansas,* 393 U.S. 97, 104, 89 S.Ct. 266, 270, 21 L.Ed.2d 228 (1968).

Appellees argue that this broad power extends to controlling a teacher's speech in public schools, that "assumptions of the 'free marketplace of ideas' on which freedom of speech rests do not apply to school-aged children, especially in the classroom where the word of the teacher may carry great authority." Note, *Developments in the Law-Academic Freedom,* 81 HAR.L.REV. at 1053. Certainly there must be some restraints because the students are a "captive" group. But to state the proposition without qualification is to uncover its fallacy. More than a decade of Supreme Court precedent leaves no doubt that we cannot countenance school authorities arbitrarily censoring a teacher's speech merely because they do not agree with the teacher's political philosophies or leanings. This is particularly so when that speech does not interfere in any way with the teacher's obligations to teach, is not coercive and does not arbitrarily inculcate doctrinaire views in the minds of the students. *Cf. Keyishian* v. *Board of Regents, supra.*

As we have indicated, there is merit to appellees' argument that *Tinker* does not control this case, because a teacher may have a far more pervasive influence over a student than would one student over another. Although sound discussions of ideas are the beams and buttresses of the first amendment, teachers cannot be allowed to patrol the precincts of radical thought with the unrelenting goal of indoctrination, a goal compatible with totalitarianism and not democracy. When a teacher is only content if he persuades his students that his values and only his values ought to be their values, then it is not unreasonable to expect the state to protect impressionable children from such dogmatism. But, just as clearly, those charged with overseeing the day-to-day interchange between teacher and student must exercise that degree of restraint necessary to protect first amendment rights. The question we must ask in every first amendment case is whether the regulatory policy is drawn as narrowly as possible to achieve the social interests that justify it, or whether it exceeds permissible bounds by unduly restricting protected speech to an extent "greater than is essential to the furtherance of" those interests. . . . Thus, when a teacher presents a colorable claim that school authorities have infringed on his first amendment rights and arbitrarily transgressed on these transcendent values, school authorities must demonstrate a reasonable basis for concluding that the teacher's conduct threatens to impair their legitimate interests in regulating the school curriculum. What we require, then, is only that rules formulated by school officials be reasonably related to the needs of the educational process and that any disciplinary action taken pursuant to those rules have a basis in fact.

Several factors present here compel the conclusion that Board of Education arbitrarily and unjustifiably discharged James for wearing the black armband. Clearly, there was no attempt by James to proselytize his students. It does not appear from the record that any student believed the armband to be anything more than a benign symbolic expression of the teacher's personal views. Moreover, we cannot ignore the fact that James was teaching 11th grade (high school) English. His students were approximately 16 or 17 years of age, thus more mature than those junior high school students in *Tinker*.

Recently, this country enfranchised 18-year-olds. It would be foolhardy to shield our children from political debate and issues until the eve of their first venture into the voting booth. Schools must play a central role in preparing their students to think and analyze and to recognize the demagogue. Under the circumstances present here, there was a greater danger that the school, by power of example, would appear to the students to be sanctioning the very "pall of orthodoxy," condemned in *Keyishian*, which chokes freedom of dissent.

Finally, James was first removed from class while he was teaching poetry. There is no suggestion whatsoever that his armband interfered with his teaching functions, or, for that matter, that his teaching ever had been deficient in any respect.

IV

We emphasize that we do not question the broad discretion of local school authorities in setting classroom standards, nor do we question their expertise in evaluating the effects of classroom conduct in light of the special characteristics of the school environment.

The federal courts, however, cannot allow unfettered discretion to violate fundamental constitutional rights. Professor Jaffe put it aptly in an analogous area of the federal courts' review power: " . . . expertness is not a magic wand which can be indiscriminately waved over the corpus of an agency's findings to preserve them from review." L. JAFFE, JUDICIAL CONTROL OF ADMINISTRATIVE ACTION 613 (1965). We cannot abdicate our responsibility to form our own conclusions when, having thoroughly searched the records, we find no sound constitutional basis for the Board's or the Commissioner's conclusions.

The dangers of unrestrained discretion are readily apparent. Under the guise of beneficient concern for the welfare of school children, school authorities, albeit unwittingly, might permit prejudices of the community to prevail. It is in such a situation that the will of the transient majority can prove devastating to freedom of expression. Indeed, James has alleged in his complaint that another teacher, "without incurring any disciplinary sanction, prominently displayed the slogan 'Peace with Honor' on a bulletin board in his classroom." This slogan has been associated with our foreign policy. If the allegation is true, and we must assume that it is in light of the summary dismissal of the complaint, it exemplifies the concern we have expressed. The Board's actions under such circumstances would indicate that its regulation against political activity in the classroom may be no more than the fulcrum to censor only that expression with which it disagrees. . . .

By requiring the Board of Education to justify its actions when there is a colorable claim of deprivation of first amendment rights, we establish a prophylactic procedure that automatically tempers abuse of properly vested discretion.

It is characteristic of resolutions of first amendment cases, where the price of freedom of expression is so high and the horizons of conflict between countervailing interests seemingly infinite, that they do not yield simplistic formulas or handy scales for weighing competing values. "The best one can hope for is to discern lines of analysis and advance formulations sufficient to bridge past decisions with new facts. One must be satisfied with such present solutions and cannot expect a clear view of the terrain beyond the periphery of the immediate case." *Eisner* v. *Stamford Board of Education,* 440 F.2d 803, 804 n. 1 (2d Cir. 1971).

It is appropriate, however, lest our decision today (which is based on the total absence of any facts justifying the Board of Education's actions) be misunderstood, that we disclaim any intent to condone partisan political activities in the public schools which reasonably may be expected to interfere with the educational process.

Accordingly, we conclude that the district court erred. The judgment of the district court is reversed and the case remanded for proceedings not inconsistent with this opinion.

Connick v. Myers

461 U.S. 138 (1983)

Justice WHITE delivered the opinion of the Court.

[1a] In Pickering v Board of Education, 391 US 563, 20 L Ed 2d 811, 88 S Ct 1731 (1968), we stated that a public employee does not relinquish First Amendment rights to comment on matters of public interest by virtue of government employment. We also recognized that the State's interests as an employer in regulating the speech of its employees "differ significantly from those it possesses in connection with regulation of the speech of the citizenry in general." Id., at 568, 20 L Ed 2d 811, 88 S Ct 1731. The problem, we thought, was arriving "at a balance between the interests of the [employee], as a citizen, in commenting upon matters of public concern and the interest of the State, as an employer, in promoting the efficiency of the public services it performs through its employees." Ibid. We return to this problem today and consider whether the First and Fourteenth Amendments prevent the discharge of a state employee for circulating a questionnaire concerning internal office affairs.

I

The respondent, Sheila Myers, was employed as an Assistant District Attorney in New Orleans for five and a half years. She served at the pleasure of petitioner Harry Connick, the District Attorney for Orleans Parish. During this period Myers competently performed her responsibilities of trying criminal cases.

In the early part of October, 1980, Myers was informed that she would be transferred to prosecute cases in a different section of the criminal court. Myers was strongly opposed to the proposed transfer. . . .

Myers again spoke with Dennis Waldron, one of the first assistant district attorneys, expressing her reluctance to accept the transfer. A number of other office matters were discussed and Myers later testified that, in response to Waldron's suggestion that her concerns were not shared by others in the office, she informed him that she would do some research on the matter.

That night Myers prepared a questionnaire soliciting the views of her fellow staff members concerning office transfer policy, office morale, the need for a grievance committee, the level of confidence in supervisors, and whether employees felt pressured to work in political campaigns. Early the following morning, Myers typed and copied the questionnaire. She also met with Connick who urged her to accept the transfer. She said she would "consider" it. Connick then left the office. Myers then distributed the questionnaire to 15 assistant district attorneys. Shortly after noon, Dennis Waldron learned that Myers was creating a "mini-insurrection" within the office. Connick returned to the office and told Myers that she was being terminated because of her refusal to accept the transfer. She was also told that her distribution of the questionnaire was considered an act of insubordination. Connick particularly objected to the question which inquired whether employees "had confidence in and would rely on the word" of various superiors in the office, and to a question concerning pressure to work in political campaigns which he felt would be damaging if discovered by the press.

Myers filed suit under 42 USC § 1983 [42 USCS § 1983], contending that her employment was wrongfully terminated because she had exercised her constitutionally-protected right of free speech. The District Court agreed, ordered Myers reinstated, and awarded backpay, damages, and attorney's fees. 507 F Supp 752 (ED La 1981). The District Court found that although Connick informed Myers that she was being fired because of her refusal to accept a transfer, the facts showed that the questionnaire was the real reason for her termination. The court then proceeded to hold that Myer's questionnaire involved matters of public concern and that the state had not "clearly demonstrated" that the survey "substantially interfered" with the operations of the District Attorney's office.

Connick appealed to the United States Court of Appeals for the Fifth Circuit, which affirmed on the basis of the District Court's opinion. 654 F2d 719 (1981). Connick then sought review in this Court by way of certiorari, which we granted. 455 US 999, 71 L Ed 2d 865, 102 S Ct 1629 (1982).

For at least 15 years, it has been settled that a state cannot condition public employment on a basis that infringes the employee's constitutionally protected interest in freedom of expression.

Our task, as we defined it in Pickering, is to seek "a balance between the interests of the [employee], as a citizen, in commenting upon matters of public concern and the interest of the State, as an employer, in promoting the efficiency of the public services it performs through its employees." 391 US, at 568, 20 L Ed 2d 811, 88 S Ct 1731. The District Court, and thus the Court of Appeals as well, misapplied our decision in Pickering and consequently, in our view, erred in striking the balance for respondent.

A

The District Court got off on the wrong foot in this case by initially finding that, "[t]aken as a whole, the issues presented in the questionnaire relate to the effective functioning of the District Attorney's Office and are matters of public importance and concern." 507 F Supp, at 758. Connick contends at the outset that no balancing of interests is required in this case because Myer's questionnaire concerned only internal office matters and that such speech is not upon a matter of "public concern," as the term was used in Pickering. Although we do not agree that Myer's communication in this case was wholly without First Amendment protection, there is much force to Connick's submission. The repeated emphasis in Pickering on the right of a public employee "as a citizen, in commenting upon matters of public concern," was not accidental. This language, reiterated in all of Pickering's progeny, reflects both the historical evolvement of the rights of public employees, and the common sense realization that government offices could not function if every employment decision became a constitutional matter.

For most of this century, the unchallenged dogma was that a public employee had no right to object to conditions placed upon the terms of employment—including those which restricted the exercise of constitutional rights. The classic formulation of this position was Justice Holmes', who, when sitting on the Supreme Judicial Court of Massachusetts, observed: "A policeman may have a constitutional right to talk politics, but he has no constitutional right to be a policeman." McAuliffe v Mayor of New

Bedford, 155 Mass 216, 220, 29 NE 517, 517 (1892). For many years, Holmes' epigram expressed this Court's law. . . .

The Court cast new light on the matter in a series of cases arising from the widespread efforts in the 1950s and early 1960s to require public employees, particularly teachers, to swear oaths of loyalty to the state and reveal the groups with which they associated. In Wieman v. Updegraff, 344 US 183, 97 L Ed 216, 73 S Ct 215 (1952), the Court held that a State could not require its employees to establish their loyalty by extracting an oath denying past affiliation with Communists. In Cafeteria Workers v McElroy, 367 US 886, 6 L Ed 2d 1230, 81 S Ct 1743 (1961), the Court recognized that the government could not deny employment because of previous membership in a particular party.

. . . By the time Sherbert v Verner, 374 US 398, 10 L Ed 2d 965, 83 S Ct 1790 (1963), was decided, it was already "too late in the day to doubt that the liberties of religion and expression may be infringed by the denial of or placing of conditions upon a benefit or privilege." Id., at 404, 10 L Ed 2d 965, 83 S Ct 1790.

. . . In all of these cases, . . . the invalidated statutes and actions sought to suppress the rights of public employees to participate in public affairs. The issue was whether government employees could be prevented or "chilled" by the fear of discharge from joining political parties and other associations that certain public officials might find "subversive." . . .

"[S]peech concerning public affairs is more than self-expression; it is the essence of self-government." Garrison v Louisiana, 379 US 64, 74-75, 13 L Ed 2d 125, 85 S Ct 209 (1964). Accordingly, the Court has frequently reaffirmed that speech on public issues occupies the "highest rung of the heirarchy of First Amendment values," and is entitled to special protection. NAACP v Claiborne Hardware Co., _____US_____, , 73 L Ed 2d 1215, 102 S Ct 3409 (1982); Carey v Brown, 447 US 455, 467, 65 L Ed 2d 263, 100 S Ct 2286 (1980).

Pickering v Board of Education, supra, followed from this understanding of the First Amendment. In Pickering, the Court held impermissible under the First Amendment the dismissal of a high school teacher for openly criticizing the Board of Education on its allocation of school funds between athletics and education and its methods of informing taxpayers about the need for additional revenue. Pickering's subject was "a matter of legitimate public concern" upon which "free and open debate is vital to informed decisionmaking by the electorate." 391 US at 571-572, 20 L Ed 2d 811, 88 S Ct 1731.

Our cases following Pickering also involved safeguarding speech on matters of public concern. The controversy in Perry v Sindermann, 408 US 593, 33 L Ed 2d 570, 92 S Ct 2694 (1972), arose from the failure to rehire a teacher in the state college system who had testified before committees of the Texas legislature and had become involved in public disagreement over whether the college should be elevated to four-year status—a change opposed by the Regents. In Mt. Healthy City Board of Ed. v Doyle, 429 US 274, 50 L Ed 2d 471, 97 S Ct 568 (1977), a public school teacher was not rehired because, allegedly, he had relayed to a radio station the substance of a memorandum relating to teacher dress and appearance that the school principal had circulated to various teachers. The memorandum was apparently prompted by the view of some in the administration that there was a relationship between teacher appearance and public support for bond issues, and indeed, the radio station promptly announced the adoption of the dress code as a news item. Most recently, in Givhan v Western Line Consolidated School District, 439 US 410, 58 L Ed 2d 619, 99 S Ct 693 (1979), we held that First Amendment protection applies when a public employee arranges to communicate privately with his employer rather than to express his views publicly. Although the subject-matter of Mrs. Givhan's statements were not the issue before the Court, it is clear that her statements concerning the school district's allegedly racially discriminatory policies involved a matter of public concern.

Pickering, its antecedents and progeny, lead us to conclude that if Myer's questionnaire cannot be fairly characterized as constituting speech on a matter of public concern, it is unnecessary for us to scrutinize the reasons for her discharge. When employee expression cannot be fairly considered as relating to any matter of political, social, or other concern to the community, government officials should enjoy wide latitude in managing their offices, without intrusive oversight by the judiciary in the name of the First Amendment. Perhaps the government employer's dismissal of the worker may not be fair, but ordinary dismissals from government service which violate no fixed tenure or applicable statute or regulation are not subject to judicial review even if the reasons for the dismissal are alleged to be mistaken or unreasonable. . . .

We do not suggest, however, that Myers' speech, even if not touching upon a matter of public concern, is totally beyond the protection of the First Amendment. "The First Amendment does not protect speech and assembly only to the extent that it can be characterized as political. 'Great secular causes, with smaller ones, are guarded.'" . . .

We in no sense suggest that speech on private matters falls into one of the narrow and well-defined classes of expression which carries so little social value, such as obscenity, that the state can prohibit and punish such expression by all persons in its jurisdiction. . . .

We hold only that when a public employee speaks not as a citizen upon matters of public concern, but instead as an employee upon matters only of personal interest, absent the most unusual circumstances, a federal court is not the appropriate forum in which to review the wisdom of a personnel decision taken by a public agency allegedly in reaction to the employee's behavior. Cf. Bishop v Wood, 426 US 341, 349-350, 48 L Ed 2d 684, 96 S Ct 2074 (1976). Our responsibility is to ensure that citizens are not deprived of fundamental rights by virtue of working for the government; this does not require a grant of immunity for employee grievances not afforded by the First Amendment to those who do not work for the state.

Whether an employee's speech addresses a matter of public concern must be determined by the content, form, and context of a given statement, as revealed by the whole record. In this case, with but one exception, the questions posed by Myers to her coworkers do not fall under the rubric of matters of "public concern." We view the questions pertaining to the confidence and trust that Myer's coworkers possess in various supervisors, the level of office morale, and the need for a grievance committee as mere extensions of Myer's dispute over her transfer to another section of the criminal court. Unlike the dissent, post. . . . we do not believe these questions are of public import in evaluating the performance of the District Attorney as an elected official. Myers did not seek to inform the public that the District Attorney's office was not discharging its governmental responsibilities. . . . Nor did Myers seek to bring to light actual or potential wrongdoing or breach of public trust on the part of Connick and others. Indeed, the questionnaire, if released to the public, would convey no information at all other than the fact that a single employee is upset with the status quo. While discipline and morale in the workplace are related to an agency's efficient performance of its duties, the focus of Myer's questions is not to evaluate the performance of the office but rather to gather ammunition for another round of controversy with her superiors. These questions reflect one employee's dissatisfaction with a transfer and an attempt to turn that displeasure into a cause celèbre.

To presume that all matters which transpire within a government office are of public concern would mean that virtually every remark—and certainly every criticism directed at a public official—would plant the seed of a constitutional case. While as a matter of good judgement, public officials should be receptive to constructive criticism offered by their employees, the First Amendment does not require a public office to be run as a roundtable for employee complaints over internal office affairs.

One question in Myers' questionnaire, however, does touch upon a matter of public concern. Question 11 inquires if assistant district attorneys "ever feel pressured to work in political campaigns on behalf of office supported candidates." We have recently noted that official pressure upon employees to work for political candidates not of the worker's own choice constitutes a coercion of belief in violation of fundamental constitutional rights. Branti v Finkel, 445 US 507, 515–516, 63 L Ed 2d 574, 100 S Ct 1287 (1980); Elrod v Burns, 427 US 347, 49 L Ed 2d 547, 96 S Ct 2673 (1976). In addition, there is a demonstrated interest in this country that government service should depend upon meritorious performance rather than political service. CSC v Letter Carriers, 413 US 548, 37 L Ed 2d 796, 93 S Ct 2880 (1973); United Public Workers v Mitchell, 330 US 75, 91 L Ed 754, 67 S Ct 556 (1947). Given this history, we believe it apparent that the issue of whether assistant district attorneys are pressured to work in political campaigns is a matter of interest to the community upon which it is essential that public employees be able to speak out freely without fear of retaliatory dismissal.

B

Because one of the questions in Myers' survey touched upon a matter of public concern, and contributed to her discharge we must determine whether Connick was justified in discharging Myers. Here the District Court again erred in imposing an unduly onerous burden on the state to justify Myers' discharge. The District Court viewed the issue of whether Myers' speech was upon a matter of "public concern" as a threshold inquiry, after which it became the government's burden to "clearly demonstrate" that the speech involved "substantially interfered" with official responsibilities. Yet Pickering unmistakably states, and respondent agrees, that the state's burden in justifying a particular discharge varies depending upon the nature of the employee's expression. Although such particularized balancing is difficult, the courts must reach the most appropriate possible balance of the competing interests.

C

The Pickering balance requires full consideration of the government's interest in the effective and efficient fulfillment of its responsibilities to the public. . . .

Connick's judgement, and apparently also that of his first assistant Dennis Waldron, who characterized Myers' actions as causing a "mini-insurrection", was that Myers' questionnaire was an act of insubordination which interfered with working relationships. When close working relationships are essential to fulfilling public responsibilities, a wide degree of deference to the employer's judgment is appropriate. Furthermore, we do not see the necessity for an employer to allow events to unfold to the extent that the disruption of the office and the destruction of working relationships is manifest before taking action. We caution that a stronger showing may be necessary if the employee's speech more substantially involved matters of public concern.

The District Court rejected Connick's position because "unlike a statement of fact which might be deemed critical of one's superiors, [Myers'] questionnaire was not a statement of fact, but the presentation and soliciation of ideas and opinions," which are entitled to greater constitutional protection because "under the First Amendment there is no such thing as a false idea." 507 F Supp, at 759. This approach. . . . bears no logical relationship to the issue of whether the questionnaire undermined office relationships. Questions, no less than forcefully stated opinions and facts, carry messages and it requires no unusual insight to conclude that the purpose, if not the likely result, of the questionnaire is to seek to precipitate a vote of no confidence in Connick and his supervisors. Thus, Question 10 . . . is a statement that carries the clear potential for undermining office relations. Also relevant is the manner, time, and place in which the questionnaire was distributed.

Finally, the context in which the dispute arose is also significant. This is not a case where an employee, out of purely academic interest, circulated a questionnaire so as to obtain useful research. Myers acknowledges that it is no coincidence that the questionnaire followed upon the heels of the transfer notice. When employee speech concerning office policy arises from an employment dispute concerning the very application of that policy to the speaker, additional weight must be given to the supervisor's view that the employee has threatened the authority of the employer to run the office. . . .

Myers' questionnaire touched upon matters of public concern in only a most limited sense; her survey, in our view, is most accurately characterized as an employee grievance concerning internal office policy. The limited First Amendment interest involved here does not require that Connick tolerate action which he reasonably believed would disrupt the office, undermine his authority, and destroy close working relationships. Myers' discharge therefore did not offend the First Amendment. We reiterate, however, the caveat we expressed in Pickering, supra, at 569, 20 L Ed 2d 811, 88 S Ct 1731: "Because of the enormous variety of fact situations in which critical statements by . . . public employees may be thought by their superiors . . . to furnish grounds for dismissal, we do not deem it either appropriate or feasible to lay down a general standard against which all such statements may be judged."

Our holding today is grounded in our long-standing recognition that the First Amendment's primary aim is the full protection of speech upon issues of public concern, as well as the practical realities involved in the administration of a government office. Although today the balance is struck for the government, this is no defeat for the First Amendment. For it would indeed be a Pyrrhic victory for the great principles of free expression if the Amendment's safeguarding of a public employee's right, as a citizen, to participate in discussions concerning public affairs were confused with the attempt to constitutionalize the employee grievance that we see presented here. The judgement of the Court of Appeals is reversed.

Perry Education Ass'n. v. Perry Local Educators' Ass'n.

460 U.S. 37 (1983).

[Suit by Perry Local Educators Association (PLEA) against Perry Education Assn (PEA) and Perry Township School Board to challenge denial to PLEA of access to use of school mail system and school mailboxes, pursuant to collective bargaining agreement between the school board and PEA, on constitutional grounds.]

Justice WHITE delivered the opinion of the Court.

Perry Education Association is the duly elected exclusive bargaining representative for the teachers of the Metroplitan School District of Perry Township, Indiana. A collective bargaining agreement with the Board of Education provided that Perry Education Association, but no other union, would have access to the interschool mail system and teacher mailboxes in the Perry Township schools. . . .

[The] exclusive access policy applies only to use of the mailboxes and school mail system. PLEA is not prevented from using other school facilities to communicate with teachers. PLEA may post notices on school bulletin boards; may hold meetings on school property after school hours; and may, with approval of the building principals, make announcements on the public address system. Of course, PLEA also may communicate with teacher by word of mouth, telephone, or the United States mail. Moreover, under Indiana law, the preferential access of the bargaining agent may continue only while its status as exclusive representative is insulated from challenge. While a representation contest is in progress, unions must be afforded equal access to such communication facilities. . . .

The primary question presented is whether the First Amendment is violated when a union that has been elected by public school teachers as their exclusive bargaining representative is granted access to certain means of communication, while such access is denied to a rival union. There is no question that constitutional interests are implicated by denying PLEA use of the interschool mail system. . . .

A. In places which by long tradition or by government fiat have been devoted to assembly and debate, the rights of the state to limit expressive activity are sharply circumscribed. At one end of the spectrum are streets and parks . . . In these quintessential public forums, the government may not prohibit all communicative activity. For the state to enforce a content-based exclusion it must show that its regulation is necessary to serve a compelling state interest and that it is narrowly drawn to achieve that end. Carey v. Brown. The state may also enforce regulations of the time, place, and manner of expression which are content-neutral, are narrowly tailored to serve a significant government interest, and leave open ample alternative channels of communication. [United States Postal Service v. Council of Greenburgh; Consolidated Edison Co. v. Public Service Comm'n.]

A second category consists of public property which the state has opened for use by the public as a place for expressive activity. The Constitution forbids a state to enforce certain exclusions from a forum generally open to the public even if it was not required to create the forum in the first place. [Widmar v. Vincent.][1] . . .

Public property which is not by tradition or designation a forum for public communication is governed by different standards. We have recognized that the "First Amendment does not guarantee access to property simply because it is owned or controlled by the government." United States Postal Service v. Greenburgh Civic Ass'n. In addition to time, place, and manner regulations, the state may reserve the forum for its intended purposes, communicative or otherwise, as long as the regulation on speech is reasonable and not an effort to suppress expression merely because public officials oppose the speaker's view. As we have stated on several occasions, "the State, no less than a private owner of property, has power to preserve the property under its control for the use to which it is lawfully dedicated." Id. [Greer; Adderley.]

The school mail facilities at issue here fall within this third category. [Perry] School District's interschool mail system is not a traditional public forum. . . . The internal mail system [is] not held open to the general public. It is instead PLEA's position that the school mail facilities have become a "limited public forum" from which it may not be excluded because of the periodic use of the system by private non-school connected groups, and PLEA's own unrestricted access to the system prior to PEA's certification as exclusive representative.

Neither of these arguments is persuasive. The use of the internal school mail by groups not affiliated with the schools is no doubt a relevant consideration. If by policy or by practice the Perry School District has opened its mail system for indiscriminate use by the general public, then PLEA could justifiably argue a public forum has been created. This, however, is not the case. [There] is no indication [that] the school mailboxes and interschool delivery system are open for use by the general public. Permission to sue the system to communicate with teachers must be secured from the individual building principal. There is no [evidence] [that] this permission has been granted as a matter of course to all who seek to distribute material. We can only conclude that the schools do allow some outside organizations such as the YMCA, Cub Scouts, and other civic and church organizations to use the facilities. This type of selective access does not transform government property into a public forum. [Greer; Lehman v. Shaker Heights.]

Moreover, even if we assume that by granting access to the Cub Scouts, YMCAs, and parochial schools, the school district has created a "limited" public forum, the constitutional right of access would in any event extend only to other entities of similar

---

1. A public forum may be created for a limited purpose such as use by certain groups, e.g., Widmar v. Vincent (student groups), or for the discussion of certain subjects, e.g., City of Madison Joint School District v. Wisconsin Public Employment Relations Comm'n 429 U.S. 167 (1976) (school board business). [Footnote by Justice White.]

character. While the school mail facilities thus might be a forum generally open for use by the Girl Scouts, the local boys' club and other organizations that engage in activites of interest and educational relevance to students, they would not as a consequence be open to an organization such as PLEA, which is concerned with the terms and conditions of teacher employment.

PLEA also points to its ability to use the school mailboxes and delivery system on an equal footing with PEA prior to the collective bargaining agreement signed in 1978. . . . Prior to 1977, there was no exclusive representative for the Perry school district teachers. PEA and PLEA each represented its own members. Therefore the school district's policy of allowing both organizations to use the school mail facilities simply reflected the fact that both unions represented the teachers and had legitimate reasons for use of the system. PLEA's previous access was consistent with the school district's preservation of the facilities for school-related business, and did not constitute creation of a public forum in any broader sense.

Because the school mail system is not a public forum, the School District had no [constitutional obligation to let any organization use the school mail boxes.] In the Court of Appeals' view, however, the access policy adopted by the Perry schools favors a particular viewpoint, that of the PEA, on labor relations, and consequently must be strictly scrutinized regardless of whether a public forum is involved. There is, however, no indication that the school board intended to discourage one viewpoint and advance another. We believe it is more accurate to characterize the access policy as based on the *status* of the respective unions rather than their views. Implicit in the concept of the nonpublic forum is the right to make distinctions in access on the basis of subject matter and speaker identity. These distinctions may be impermissible in a public forum but are inherent and inescapable in the process of limiting a nonpublic forum to activities compatible with the intended purpose of the property. . . .

The differential access provided PEA and PLEA is reasonable because it is wholly consistent with the district's legitimate interest in [preserving the property for the use to which it is lawfully dedicated.] Use of school mail facilities enables PEA to perform effectively its obligations as exclusive representative of all Perry Township teachers. Conversely, PLEA does not have any official responsibility in connection with the school district and need not be entitled to the same rights of access to school mailboxes. [Moreover,] exclusion of the rival union may reasonably be considered a means of insuring labor-peace within the schools. The policy "serves to prevent the District's schools from becoming a battlefield for inter-union squabbles." . . .

Finally, the reasonableness of the limitations on PLEA's access to the school mail system is also supported by the substantial alternative channels that remain open for union-teacher communication to take place. These means range from bulletin boards to meeting facilities to the United States mail. During election periods, PLEA is assured of equal access to all modes of communication. There is no showing here that PLEA's ability to communicate with teachers is seriously impinged by the restricted access to the internal mail system. . . .

IV. The Court of Appeals also held that the differential access provided the rival unions constituted impermissible content discrimination in violation of the Equal Protection Clause of the Fourteenth Amendment. We have rejected this contention when cast as a First Amendment argument, and it fares no better in equal protection garb. As we have explained above, PLEA did not have a First Amendment or other right of access to the interschool mail system. The grant of such access to PEA, therefore, does not burden a fundamental right of the PLEA. Thus, the decision to grant such privileges to the PEA need not be tested by the strict scrutiny applied when government action impinges upon a fundamental right protected by the Constitution. See [San Antonio v. Rodriguez.] The school district's policy need only rationally further a legitimate state purpose. That purpose is clearly found in the special responsibilities of an exclusive bargaining representative. . . .

When speakers and subjects are similarly situated, the state may not pick and choose. Conversely on government property that has not been made a public forum, not all speech is equally situated, and the state may draw distinctions which relate to the special purpose for which the property is used. As we have explained above, for a school mail facility, the difference in status between the exclusive bargaining representative and its rival is such a distinction. . . .

Justice BRENNAN, with whom *Justice* MARSHALL, *Justice* POWELL, and *Justice* STEVENS join, dissenting.

Ellis v. Railway Clerks

466 U.S. 85 (1984)

Justice WHITE delivered the opinion of the Court.

In 1951, Congress amended the Railway Labor Act (the Act or RLA) to permit what it had previously prohibited—the union shop. Section 2, Eleventh of the Act permits a union and an employer to require all employees in the relevant bargaining unit to join the union as a condition of continued employment. . . .

In Machinists v Street, 367 US 740, 6 L Ed 2d 1141, 81 S Ct 1784 (1960), the Court held that the Act does not authorize a union to spend an objecting employee's money to support political causes. The use of employee funds for such ends is unrelated to Congress' desire to eliminate "free riders" and the resentment they provoked. . . .

The Court did not express a view as to "expenditures for activities in the area between the costs which led directly to the complaints as to 'free riders,' and the expenditures to support union political activities." . . . Petitioners challenge just such expenditures.

In 1971, respondent . . . (the union or BRAC) and Western Airlines implemented a previously negotiated agreement requiring that all Western's clerical employees join the union within 60 days of commencing employment. As the agreement has been interpreted, employees need not become formal members of the union, but must pay agency fees equal to members' dues. Petitioners are present or former clerical employees of Western who objected to the use of their compelled dues for specified union activities. They do not contest the legality of the union shop as such. . . . They do contend, however, that they can be compelled to contribute no more than their pro rata share of the expenses of negotiating agreements and settling grievances with Western Airlines.

Respondents . . . concede that the statutory authorization of the union shop does not permit the use of petitioners' contributions for union political or ideological activities . . . and have adopted a rebate program covering such expenditures. The parties disagree about the adequacy of the rebate scheme, and about the legality of burdening objecting employees with six specific union expenses that fall between the extremes identified in Hanson and Street: the quadrennial Grand Lodge convention, litigation not involving the negotiation of agreements or settlement of grievances, union publications, social activities, death benefits for employees, and general organizing efforts. . . . Turning to the question of permissible expenditures, the Court of Appeals framed "the relevant inquiry [a]s whether a particular challenged expenditure is germane to the union's work in the realm of collective bargaining. . . .

The court found that each of the challenged activities strengthened the union as a whole and helped it to run more smoothly, thus making it better able to negotiate and administer agreements. . . .

We hold that the union's rebate scheme was inadequate and that the Court of Appeals erred in finding that the RLA authorizes a union to spend compelled dues for its general litigation and organizing efforts. . . .

As the Court of Appeals pointed out, there is language in this Court's cases to support the validity of a rebate program. . . . On the other hand, we suggested a more precise advance reduction scheme in Railway Clerks v Allen, 373 US 113, 122, 10 L Ed 2d 235, 83 S Ct 1158 (1963), where we described a "practical decree" comprising a refund of exacted funds in the proportion that union political expenditures bore to total union expenditures and the reduction of future exactions by the same proportion. Those opinions did not, nor did they purport to, pass upon the statutory or constitutional adequacy of the suggested remedies. Doing so now, we hold that the pure rebate approach is inadequate.

By exacting and using full dues, then refunding months later the portion that it was not allowed to exact in the first place, the union effectively charges the employees for activities that are outside the scope of the statutory authorization. The cost to the employee is, of course, much less than if the money was never returned, but this is a difference of degree only. The harm would be reduced were the union to pay interest on the amount refunded, but respondents did not do so. Even then the union obtains an involuntary loan for purposes to which the employee objects.

The only justification for this union borrowing would be administrative convenience. But there are readily available alternatives, such as advance reduction of dues and/or interest-bearing escrow accounts, that place only the slightest additional burden, if any, on the union. Given the existence of acceptable alternatives, the union cannot be allowed to commit dissenters' funds to improper uses even temporarily. A rebate scheme reduces but does not eliminate the statutory violation.

Petitioners' primary submission is that the use of their fees to finance the challenged activities violated the First Amendment. This argument assumes that the Act allows these allegedly unconstitutional exactions. When the constitutionality of a statute is challenged, this Court first ascertains whether the statute can be reasonably construed to avoid the constitutional difficulty . . . we therefore first inquire whether the statute permits the union to charge petitioners for any of the challenged expenditures. . . .

Railway Clerks v Allen, 373 US 113, 10 L Ed 2d 235, 83 S Ct 1158 (1963), reaffirmed the approach taken in Street, and described the union expenditures that could fairly be charged to all employees as those "germane to collective bargaining." Id., at 121, 122, 10 L Ed 2d 235, 83 S Ct 1158. Still later, in Abood v Board of Education, 431 US 209, 52 L Ed 2d 261, 97 S Ct 1782 (1977), we found no constitutional barrier to an agency shop agreement between a municipality and a teachers' union insofar as the agreement required every employee in the unit to pay a service fee to defray the costs of collective bargaining, contract administration, and grievance adjustment. The union, however, could not, consistently with the Constitution, collect from dissenting employees any sums for the support of ideological causes not germane to its duties as collective-bargaining agent. In neither Allen nor Abood, however, did the Court find it necessary further to define the line between union expenditures that all employees must help defray and those that are not sufficiently related to collective bargaining to justify their being imposed on dissenters.

We remain convinced that Congress' essential justification for authorizing the union shop was the desire to eliminate free riders—employees in the bargaining unit on whose behalf the union was obliged to perform its statutory functions, but who refused to contribute to the cost thereof. . . . Under this standard, objecting employees may be compelled to pay their fair share of not only the direct costs of negotiating and administering a collective-bargaining contract and of settling grievances and disputes, but also the expenses of activities or undertakings normally or reasonably employed to implement or effectuate the duties of the union as exclusive representative of the employees in the bargaining unit.

With these considerations in mind, we turn to the particular expenditures for which petitioners insist they may not be charged.

V

1. *Conventions.* Every four years, BRAC holds a national convention at which the members elect officers, establish bargaining goals and priorities, and formulate overall union policy. We have very little trouble in holding that petitioners must help defray the costs of these conventions. Surely if a union is to perform its statutory functions, it must maintain its corporate or associational existence, must elect officers to manage and carry on its affairs, and may consult its members about overall bargaining goals and policy. . . .

2. *Social Activities.* Approximately .7% of Grand Lodge expenditures go toward purchasing refreshments for union business meetings and occasional social activities. 685 F2d, at 1074. These activities are formally open to nonmember employees. While these affairs are not central to collective bargaining, they are sufficiently related to it to be charged to all employees. . . .

We cannot say that these de minimus expenses are beyond the scope of the Act. Like conventions, social activities at union meetings are a standard feature of union operations. . . .

3. *Publications.* The Grand Lodge puts out a monthly magazine, the Railway Clerk/interchange, paid for out of the union treasury. The magazine's contents are varied and include articles about negotiations, contract demands, strikes, unemployment and

health benefits, proposed or recently enacted legislation, general news, products the union is boycotting, and recreational and social activities. . . .

Under the union's rebate policy, objecting employees are not charged for that portion of the magazine devoted to "political causes." . . . The rebate is figured by calculating the number of lines that are devoted to political issues as a proportion of the total number of lines.

The union must have a channel for communicating with the employees, including the objecting ones, about its activities. Congress can be assumed to have known that union funds go toward union publications; it is an accepted and basic union activity. . . . By the same token, the Act surely allows it to charge objecting employees for reporting to them about those activities it can charge them for doing.

4. *Organizing.* The Court of Appeals found that organizing expenses could be charged to objecting employees because organizing efforts are aimed toward a stronger union, which in turn would be more successful at the bargaining table. Despite this attenuated connection with collective bargaining, we think such expenditures are outside Congress' authorization. . . .

5. *Litigation.* The expenses of litigation incident to negotiating and administering the contract or to settling grievances and disputes arising in the bargaining unit are clearly chargeable to petitioners as a normal incident of the duties of the exclusive representative. The same is true of fair representation litigation arising within the unit, of jurisdictional disputes with other unions, and of any other litigation before agencies or in the courts that concerns bargaining unit employees and is normally conducted by the exclusive representative. The expenses of litigation not having such a connection with the bargaining unit are not to be charged to objecting employees. Contrary to the view of the Court of Appeals, therefore, unless the Western Airlines bargaining unit is directly concerned, objecting employees need not share the costs of the union's challenge to the legality of the airline industry mutual aid pact; of litigation seeking to protect the rights of airline employees generally during bankruptcy proceedings; or of defending suits alleging violation of the non-discrimination requirements of Title VII.

6. *Death benefits.* BRAC pays from its general funds a $300 death benefit to the designated beneficiary of any member or nonmember required to pay dues to the union. . . . Petitioners, of course, press the view that death benefits have no connection with collective bargaining at all, let alone one that would warrant forcing them to participate in the system.

We find it unnecessary to rule on this question. Because the union is no longer the exclusive bargaining agent and petitioners are no longer involved in the death benefits system, the only issue is whether petitioners are entitled to a refund of their past contributions. We think that they are not so entitled, even if they had the right to an injunction to prevent future collections from them for death benefits. Although they objected to the use of their funds to support the benefits plan, they remained entitled to the benefits of the plan as long as they paid their dues; they thus enjoyed a form of insurance for which the union collected a premium. We doubt that the equities call for a refund of those payments.

Petitioners' primary argument is that for the union to compel their financial support of these six activities violates the First Amendment. We need only address this contention with regard to the three activities for which, we have held, the RLA allows the union to use their contributions. We perceive no constitutional barrier. . . .

Petitioners do not explicitly contend that union social activities implicate serious First Amendment interests. We need not determine whether contributing money to such affairs is an act triggering First Amendment protection. . . .

The First Amendment concerns with regard to publications and conventions are more serious; both have direct communicative content and involve the expression of ideas. Nonetheless, we perceive little additional infringement of First Amendment rights beyond that already accepted, and none that is not justified by the governmental interests behind the union shop itself.

Chicago Teachers Union v. Hudson

________U.S.________, 106 S.Ct.1066, 89 L Ed. 2d 232 (1986)

[Appeal on challenge by nonunion employees to union procedure for assessing and reviewing challenges to agency shop fees]

STEVENS, J.

In this case, we must determine whether the challenged Chicago Teachers Union procedure survives First Amendment scrutiny, . . .

The procedure that was initially adopted by the Union and considered by the District Court contained three fundamental flaws. First, as in Ellis, a remedy which merely offers dissenters the possibility of a rebate does not avoid the risk that dissenters' funds may be used temporarily for an improper purpose. . . . A forced exaction followed by a rebate equal to the amount improperly expended is thus not a permissible response to the nonunion employees' objections.

Second, the "advance reduction of dues" was inadequate because it provided nonmembers with inadequate information about the basis for the proportionate share. . . . Basic considerations of fairness, as well as concern for the First Amendment rights at stake, also dictate that the potential objectors be given sufficient information to gauge the propriety of the union's fee. . . . Instead of identifying the expenditures for collective bargaining and contract administration that had been provided for the benefit of nonmembers as well as members—and for which nonmembers as well as members can fairly be charged a fee—the Union identified the amount that it admittedly had expended for purposes that did not benefit dissenting nonmembers. An acknowledgment that nonmembers would not be required to pay any part of 5% of the Union's total annual expenditures was not an adequate disclosure of the reasons why they were required to pay their share of 95%.

Finally, the original Union procedure was also defective because it did not provide for a reasonably prompt decision by an impartial decisionmaker. Although we have not so specified in the past, we now conclude that such a requirement is necessary. . . . The Union's procedure does not meet this requirement. As the Seventh Circuit observed, the "most conspicuous feature of the procedure is that from start to finish it is entirely controlled by the union, which is an interested party, since it is the recipient of the agency fees paid by the dissenting employees." . . .

We need not hold, however, that a 100% escrow is constitutionally required. . . . If, for example, the original disclosure by the Union had included a certified public accountant's verified breakdown of expenditures, including some categories that no dissenter could reasonably challenge, there would be no reason to escrow the portion of the nonmember's fees that would be represented by those categories.

We hold today that the constitutional requirements for the Union's collection of agency fees include an adequate explanation of the basis for the fee, a reasonably prompt opportunity to challenge the amount of the fee before an impartial decisionmaker, and an escrow for the amounts reasonably in dispute while such challenges are pending. . . .

Board of Education of Long Beach Unified School District of Los Angeles County v. Jack M.

566 P.2d 602 (Cal. 1977)

TOBRINER, *Justice.*

On October 19, 1972, defendant was arrested for an alleged homosexual solicitation in a public restroom. Although no charges were ever filed against him, plaintiff school board initiated proceedings in the superior court to establish its right to discharge defendant from his tenured teaching position. The superior court, however, resolved conflicting evidence in defendant's favor and found that his conduct did not demonstrate unfitness to teach. The board appeals from the judgment in favor of defendant.

In accord with the unquestioned principle that trial court findings supported by substantial evidence will be upheld on appeal, we affirm the judgment below. The board's attempt to escape . . . this principle of appellate review by claiming that defendant's conduct in itself proves unfitness to teach must fail, since neither statute nor decisional authority has applied a rule of per se unfitness to persons who were not convicted of specified sex offenses. The board's argument, moreover, conflicts with legislation enacted in 1976 that grants even to a person convicted of a specified sex offense the right to a fitness hearing; consistent with the purpose of that legislation we cannot hold the commission of such acts demonstrates unfitness per se.

1. *Proceedings in the trial court*

Defendant has been continuously employed for 16 years as a permanently certificated teacher for elementary schools. Until the incident of October 19, 1972, he was recognized as a teacher of fitness, ability and unimpeached moral character. . . .

The only two witnesses to the incident were defendant and the arresting officer. The officer testified to the following sequence of events. Entering a department store restroom equipped with five doorless stalls, he occupied the stall furthest from the door. Defendant entered the adjoining stall, bent down and looked up at the officer from under the partition separating the stalls. The officer dressed and, looking into defendant's stall, observed defendant masturbating. Defendant then beckoned to the officer, saying "come here. You will like this." The officer thereupon arrested defendant for lewd conduct in a public place. (Pen. Code, § 647, subd. (a).) Defendant testified that he had not masturbated or solicited the officer, but the trial court upheld the officer's version.

The remaining testimony concerned defendant's fitness to teach. The board presented the testimony of Mrs. White, defendant's principal, and Mr. Lepic, an experienced school principal who did not know defendant but testified as an expert on teaching qualifications. Defendant countered with testimony from Dr. Davis, a psychiatrist who was experienced in examining persons convicted of sexual offenses.

Mrs. White testified that defendant was fit and competent in all respects as a teacher; that she knew that he was under heavy emotional stress at the time in question but that nevertheless she felt that the charged conduct demonstrated "unusual judgment and improper reaction to stress and pressure." She stated that she had no reason to believe that he could not now perform his specific duties as a certified teacher but that she was not willing to take the chance that the incident might recur and that, therefore, she felt that defendant was unfit to teach.

Mr. Lepic testified as to the essential qualifications of an elementary school teacher—adequate professional training and development of a close relationship with students, parents and staff. In response to a hypothetical question premised upon the account given by the arresting officer, he gave his opinion that defendant was unfit to teach. As reasons for his opinion he testified that defendant could not provide a behavioral example to students and that his conduct would create uneasiness and an erosion of confidence in those with whom he was in association, such as students, parents and staff. He was unaware of any knowledge by those groups of such conduct or any attendant publicity, but was disturbed by the possibility of recurrence, depending upon the tensions and pressures to which defendant might be subjected in the future.

Dr. Davis's background indicated that he was well experienced as a psychiatrist in the examination and treatment of sexual deviates. He concluded from the history of defendant and his clinical examination of defendant that defendant was not a homosexual; that if the arresting officer's version were true, this account would indicate to the doctor an isolated act of aggressive behavior by one of an otherwise passive sexual disposition precipitated by an unusual accumulation of pressure and stress stemming from his mother's serious illness; that it would be most unusual for an individual with a predisposition to aggressive homosexual behavior to reach middle age without some prior antisocial conduct reflected in a police record, and here there was none; and that even if the incident happened, he believed there was no danger of recurrence because of the trauma to defendant from this arrest and the trial proceedings. He believed that there was no danger to pupils or associates, and no possibility of recurrence, and because of a medically recognized proclivity of sexual deviates to follow a specific pattern, the conduct attributed to defendant would not be consistent with acts endangering children or associates.

The trial court resolved the conflicting testimony on the issue of fitness in favor of defendant. Finding that defendant's conduct did not demonstrate an unfitness to teach, the court entered judgment ordering his reinstatement with back pay.

2. Substantial evidence supports the trial court's finding that defendant's conduct does not demonstrate his unfitness to teach.

Defendant's fitness to teach was the factual issue which faced the trial court. Although defendant was charged with "immoral or unprofessional conduct" . . . we have previously held that the determinative test was fitness to teach; the terms "immoral" or "unprofessional conduct" are so broad and vague that, standing alone, they could be constitutionally infirm; hence the proper criteria is fitness to teach. (*Morrison* v. *State Board of Education* (1969) 1 Cal.3d 214, 82 Cal. Rptr. 175, 461 P.2d 375.) Observing that a statute can constitutionally bar a person from practicing a lawful profession only for reasons related to his fitness to practice that profession . . . we concluded in *Morrison* that the board cannot "abstractly characterize the conduct in this case as 'immoral,' 'unprofessional,' or 'involving moral turpitude' within the meaning of section 13202 . . . unless that conduct indicates that petitioner is unfit to teach." . . . If appellate scrutiny reveals that substantial evidence supports the trial court's findings and conclusions, the judgment must be affirmed.

Relying upon the foregoing authorities, the trial court accordingly framed the following findings in terms of fitness to teach, and those facts which bear on the subject of fitness: "¶6. Defendant's conduct did not come to the attention of the public, students, parents, fellow teachers, and other staff members other than to defendant's immediate superior to whom he reported the incident. ¶ 7. Defendant's conduct was an isolated act precipitated by an unusual accumulation of pressure and stress. There is no danger that defendant will repeat the conduct. ¶ 8. Defendant does not represent a threat to students or fellow teachers. ¶ 9. Defendant's conduct does not demonstrate an unfitness to teach."

Review of the record reveals ample evidence to support those findings. . . .

In challenging the trial court's findings, the board argues that students, viewing their teacher "in the light of an exemplar" (*Board of Education* v. *Swan* (1953) 41 Cal.2d 546, 552, 261 P.2d 261, 265), may emulate defendant's act; that defendant may be unable to fulfill his duty "to impress . . . and to instruct [his students] in manners and morals" (Ed. Code, § 13556.5); and that defendant's conduct evidenced a lack of judgment and discretion. But these arguments are really no more than disputable inferences which the trial court rejected in favor of other inferences more favorable to defendant. The courts uniformly hold that "where two or more inferences reasonably can be drawn from the facts, an appellate court is without power to substitute its deductions for those of the trial court." (*Slater* v. *Alpha Beta Acme Markets, Inc.* (1975) 44 Cal.App.3d 274, 278, 118 Cal.Rptr. 561, 563.)

Moreover, the evidentiary record provides reasonable grounds to justify the trial court in rejecting the inferences drawn by the board. Proof that defendant's act was unknown to his students, testimony that he would not repeat such conduct, the absence of evidence that he had by word or example influenced students to engage in improper activity all combine to indicate the insubstantiality of any risk that students would imitate his conduct.[1]

---

1. . . . In any event, the fear that students will emulate immoral or illegal conduct of their teachers becomes realistic only under two conditions. First, the teacher's conduct must be sufficiently notorious that the students know or are likely to learn of it. (See *Andrews* v. *Drew Municipal Separate School District* (5th Cir. 1975) 507 F.2d 611, 616-617; *Comings* v. *State Bd. of Education*, supra, 23 Cal.App.3d 95, 104-106, 100 Cal.Rptr. 73; Comment (1973) 61 Cal. L.Rev. 1442, 1451, 1458; Comment, 1973 Utah L.Rev. 797, 806 fn. 66.) Second, the teacher must continue to model his past conduct (as in *Watson* v. *State Bd. of Education* (1971) 22

The board presented no evidence to show that defendant, in 16 years of teaching, had failed to impress and instruct his students in manners and morals . . . And although defendant's actions on October 19, 1972, may suggest a lack of judgment and discretion, the trial court found that this particular conduct "was an isolated act precipitated by an unusual accumulation of pressure and stress. . . . "

3. *The fact that defendant may have committed public sexual offense does not authorize an appellate court to disregard contrary trial court findings and declare him unfit to teach per se.*

Confronting the adverse findings of fact by the trial court, the board shifts its ground and contends that proof that defendant committed a public sexual offense demonstrates unfitness to teach per se. As we shall explain, the pre-1976 statutes in effect at the time of trial of this case carefully distinguished between persons convicted of listed sex offenses, who were subject to automatic sanctions, and those not convicted, who were entitled to a fitness hearing. The board's assertion that a teacher not convicted of a listed offense is unfit per se undermines that statutory distinction. . . . And as we shall further explain, the 1976 statutes, which govern the appeal of this case, grant even some persons *convicted* of listed sex crimes a fitness hearing; the board's claim that commission of such a crime demonstrates unfitness per se cannot be reconciled with that legislation. . . .

Cases interpreting the pre-1976 statutes conform to this distinction between persons convicted of listed crimes and those not convicted. Those three decisions that have denied teachers a fitness hearing involved teachers who were convicted of a listed crime. (*Di Genova* v. *State Board of Education* (1955) 45 Cal.2d 255, 288 P.2d 862; *Purifoy* v. *State Board of Education* (1973) 30 Cal.App.3d 187, 106 Cal.Rptr. 201; *Vogulkin* v. *State Board of Education* (1961) 194 Cal.App.2d 424, 15 Cal. Rptr. 335.) Distinguishing the case of one convicted of a listed crime, our decision in *Morrison* v. *State Board of Education* supra, 1 Cal.3d 214, 82 Cal.Rptr. 175, 461 P.2d 375 established the right of a person not so convicted to a fitness hearing. . . .

Our listing in *Morrison* of the factors to be considered in evaluating fitness made it clear that the hearing could not be limited to the single question whether the teacher committed the charged act. . . .

We now turn to the effect of the 1976 legislation amending Education Code section 12910. That legislation, by severely narrowing the list of persons who can be deemed unfit per se, further undermines the board's position.

Effective as of January 1, 1977, section 12910 now provides that "Notwithstanding any other provision of this code, no person shall be denied a hearing solely on the basis that he has been convicted of a crime if he has obtained a certificate of rehabilitation under Section 4852.01 and following of the Penal Code, and if his probation has been terminated and the information or accusation has been dismissed

---

Cal. App.3d 559, 99 Cal.Rptr. 468); the teacher who committed an indiscretion, paid the penalty, and now seeks to discourage his students from committing similar acts may well be a more effective supporter of legal and moral standards than the one who has never been found to violate those standards. (See WILLEMSEN, SEX AND THE SCHOOL TEACHER (1975) 14 Santa Clara Law. 839, 855.) Since these conditions will vary from case to case, proof that one has at some past time committed a crime should not in itself suffice to demonstrate that he is not now and never will be a suitable behavior model for his students.

pursuant to Section 1203.4 of the Penal Code." The term "crime" in this section is plainly intended to encompass the specific sex crimes listed in section 12912, many of which require public conduct or solicitation as an element of the crime. But if some persons convicted of public sex offenses are entitled to fitness hearings, as the statute now provides, it cannot logically be maintained that all persons who commit such offenses are unfit as a matter of law; acceptance of the board's proposition would render the right to a hearing granted by the Legislature a meaningless formality. . . .

4. *Conclusion.*

Substantial evidence supports the trial court's finding that defendant's conduct did not demonstrate his unfitness to teach. . . . Since substantial evidence supports the trial court findings of fact and conclusions of law, we affirm its judgment directing reinstatement of defendant to his teaching position with back pay.

Hortonville Dist. v. Hortonville Ed. Asso.

426 U.S. 482 (1976)

Mr. *Chief Justice BURGER* delivered the opinion of the Court.

We granted *certiorari* in this case to determine whether School Board members, . . . could, consistent with the Due Process Clause of the Fourteenth Amendment, dismiss teachers engaged in a strike prohibited by state law.

I

The petitioners are a Wisconsin school district, the seven members of its School Board, and three administrative employees of the district. Respondents are teachers suing on behalf of all teachers in the district and the Hortonville Education Association (HEA), the collective-bargaining agent for the district's teachers.

During the 1972–1973 school year Hortonville teachers worked under a master collective-bargaining agreement; negotiations were conducted for renewal of the contract, but no agreement was reached. . . . On March 18, 1974, the members of the teachers' union went on strike, in direct violation of Wisconsin law. On March 20, the district superintendent sent all teachers a letter inviting them to return to work; a few did so. On March 23, he sent another letter, asking the 86 teachers still on strike to return, and reminding them that strikes by public employees were illegal; none of these teachers returned to work. After conducting classes with substitute teachers on March 26 and 27, the Board decided to conduct disciplinary hearings for each of the teachers on strike. Individual notices were sent to each teacher setting hearings for April 1, 2, and 3.

On April 1, most of the striking teachers appeared before the Board with counsel. Their attorney indicated that the teachers did not want individual hearings, but preferred to be treated as a group. Although counsel agreed that the teachers were on strike, he raised several procedural objections to the hearings. He also argued that the Board was not sufficiently impartial to exercise discipline over the striking teachers and that the Due Process Clause of the Fourteenth Amendment required an independent, unbiased decisionmaker. An offer of proof was tendered to demonstrate that the strike had been provoked by the Board's failure to meet teachers' demands, and respondents' counsel asked to cross-examine Board members individually. The Board rejected the request, but permitted counsel to make the offer of proof, aimed at showing that the Board's contract offers were unsatisfactory, that the Board used coercive and illegal bargaining tactics, and that teachers in the district had been locked out by the Board.

On April 2, the Board voted to terminate the employment of striking teachers, and advised them by letter to that effect. However, the same letter invited all teachers on strike to reapply for teaching positions. One teacher accepted the invitation and returned to work; the Board hired replacements to fill the remaining positions.

Respondents then filed suit . . . alleging, among other things, that the notice and hearing provided them by the Board were inadequate to comply with due process requirements. . . .

II

The Hortonville School District is a common school district under Wisconsin law, financed by local property taxes and state school aid and governed by an elected seven-member School Board. . . . . . . The Board is the only body vested by statute with the power to employ and dismiss teachers. § 118.22(2).

The sole issue in this case is whether the Due Process Clause of the Fourteenth Amendment prohibits this School Board from making the decision to dismiss teachers admittedly engaged in a strike and persistently refusing to return to their duties. The Wisconsin Supreme Court held that state law prohibited the strike and that termination of the striking teachers' employment was within the Board's statutory authority. 66 Wis. 2d, at 479-481, 225 N.W.2d, at 663-665. We are, of course, bound to accept the interpretation of Wisconsin law by the highest court of the State. . . .

A.

Respondents argue, and the Wisconsin Supreme Court held, that the choice presented for the Board's decision is analogous to that involved in revocation of parole . . . that the decision could be made only by an impartial decisionmaker, and that the Board was not impartial. . . . The Board cannot make a "reasonable" decision on this issue, the Wisconsin Supreme Court held and respondents argue, because its members are biased in some fashion that the due process guarantees of the Fourteenth Amendment prohibit. A school board is not to be equated with the parole officer as an arresting officer; the school board is more like the parole board, for it has ultimate plenary authority to make its decisions derived from the state legislature. General language about due process in a holding concerning revocation of parole is not a reliable basis for dealing with the School Board's power as an employer to dismiss teachers for cause. We must focus more clearly on, first, the nature of the bias respondents attribute to the Board, and, second, the nature of the interests at stake in this case.

B.

Respondents' argument rests in part on doctrines that have no application to this case. They seem to argue that the Board members had some personal or official stake in the decision whether the teachers should be dismissed, . . . and that the Board has manifested some personal bitterness toward the teachers, aroused by teacher criticism of the Board during the strike. . . . Even assuming that those cases state the governing standards when the decisionmaker is a public employer dealing with employees, the teachers did not show, and the Wisconsin courts did not find, that the Board members had the kind of personal or financial stake in the decision that might create a conflict of interest, and there is nothing in the record to support charges of personal animosity. The Wisconsin Supreme Court was careful "not to suggest . . . that the board members were anything but dedicated public servants, trying to provide the district with quality education . . . within its limited budget." 66 Wis. 2d, at 494, 225 N.W.2d, at 671. That court's analysis would seem to be confirmed by the Board's repeated invitations for striking teachers to return to work, the final invitation being contained in the letter that notified them of their discharge.

The only other factor suggested to support the claim of bias is that the School Board was involved in the negotiations that preceded and precipitated the striking teachers' discharge. Participation in those negotiations was a statutory duty of the Board. The Wisconsin Supreme Court held that this involvement, without more, disqualified the Board from deciding whether the teachers should be dismissed. . . .

Mere familiarity with the facts of a case gained by an agency in the performance of its statutory role does not, however, disqualify a decisionmaker. *Withrow* v. *Larkin,* 421 U.S. 35, 47, 43 L.Ed.2d 712, 95 S.Ct. 1456 (1975); *F.T.C.* v. *Cement Institute,* 333 U.S. 683, 700-703, 92 L.Ed. 1010, 68 S.Ct. 793 (1948). Nor is a decisionmaker disqualified simply because he has taken a position, even in public, on a policy issue related to the dispute, in the absence of a showing that he is not "capable of judging a particular controversy fairly on the basis of its own circumstances." *United States* v. *Morgan,* 313 U.S. 409, 421, 85 L.Ed. 1429, 61 S.Ct. 999 (1941); see also *F.T.C.* v. *Cement Institute,* supra, at 701, 92 L.Ed. 1010, 68 S.Ct. 793. . . .

C.

Due process, as this Court has repeatedly held, is a term that "negates any concept of inflexible procedures universally applicable to every imaginable situation." *Cafeteria Workers* v. *McElroy,* 367 U.S. 886, 895, 6 L.Ed.2d 1230, 81 S.Ct. 1743 (1961). Determining what process is due in a given setting requires the Court to take into account the individual's stake in the decision at issue as well as the State's interest in a particular procedure for making it. . . . Our assessment of the interests of the parties in this case leads to the conclusion that this is a very different case from *Morrissey* v. *Brewer,* and that the Board's prior role as negotiator does not disqualify it to decide that the public interest in maintaining uninterrupted classroom work required that teachers striking in violation of state law be discharged.

The teachers' interest in these proceedings is, of course, self-evident. . . . Since the teachers admitted that they were engaged in a work stoppage, there was no possibility of an erroneous factual determination on this critical threshold issue. Moreover, what the teachers claim as a property right was the expectation that the jobs they had left to go and remain on strike in violation of law would remain open to them. The Wisconsin court accepted at least the essence of that claim in defining the property right under state law, and we do not quarrel with its conclusion. But even if the property interest claimed here is to be compared with the liberty interest at stake in Morrissey, we note that both "the risk of an erroneous deprivation" and "the degree of potential deprivation" differ in a qualitative sense and in degree from those in *Morrissey*. *Matthews* v. *Eldridge*, supra, at 341, 47 L.Ed.2d 18, 96 S.Ct. 893.

The governmental interests at stake in this case also differ significantly from the interests at stake in *Morrissey*. The Board's decision whether to dismiss striking teachers involves broad considerations, and does not in the main turn on the Board's view of the "seriousness" of the teachers' conduct or the factors they urge mitigated their violation of state law. It was not an adjudicative decision, for the Board had an obligation to make a decision based on its own answer to an important question of policy: What choice among the alternative responses to the teachers' strike will best serve the interests of the school system, the interests of the parents and children who depend on the system, and the interests of the citizens whose taxes support it? The Board's decision was only incidentally a disciplinary decision; it had significant governmental and public policy dimensions as well. See SUMMERS, *Public Employee Bargaining: A Political Perspective*, 83 YALE L.J. 1156 (1974).

State law vests the governmental, or policymaking, function exclusively in the School Board and the State has two interests in keeping it there. . . . Second, the state legislature has given to the Board the power to employ and dismiss teachers, as a part of the balance it has struck in the area of municipal labor relations; altering those statutory powers as a matter of federal due process clearly changes that balance. Permitting the Board to make the decision at issue here preserves its control over school district affairs, leaves the balance of power in labor relations where the state legislature struck it, and assures that the decision whether to dismiss the teachers will be made by the body responsible for that decision under state law.

III

Respondents have failed to demonstrate that the decision to terminate their employment was infected by the sort of bias that we have held to disqualify other decisionmakers as a matter of federal due process. A showing that the Board was "involved" in the events preceding this decision . . . is not enough to overcome the presumption of honesty and integrity in policymakers with decision making power. *Cf. Withrow* v. *Larkin*, 421 U.S., at 47, 43 L.Ed.2d 712, 95 S.Ct. 1456. Accordingly, we hold that the Due Process Clause of the Fourteenth Amendment did not guarantee respondents that the decision to terminate their employment would be made or reviewed by a body other than the School Board.

The judgment of the Wisconsin Supreme Court is reversed, and the case is remanded for further proceedings not inconsistent with this opinion.

Reversed and remanded.

Mr. Justice STEWART, with whom *Mr. Justice BRENNAN* and *Mr. Justice MARSHALL* join, dissenting.

CHAPTER 6

CHAPTER OUTLINE

A. Procedural due process
   1. Constitutional requirements
      a. Notice and hearing
      b. Published regulations—vagueness and overbreadth
      c. Impartial tribunal
      d. Right of confrontation
      e. Right to counsel
      f. Right to a hearing record and appeal
      g. Waiver and cure of procedural defects
   2. Statutory procedures
B. Substantive rights
   1. General fundamental rights
   2. First Amendment freedom of expression
      a. Individual speech
      b. Symbolic expression
      c. Student literature
      d. Student appearance
   3. Rights of privacy
      a. Search and seizure
      b. Married and pregnant students
      c. Student records
      d. Confidentiality
      e. Rights of separated parents
      f. Student associations and clubs
      g. Student rights against physical punishments and restraints

Student Rights and Discipline

TABLE OF CASES FOR CHAPTER 6

Goss v. Lopez, 419 U.S. 565 (1975), 340.
Gonzales v. McEuen, 435 F. Supp. 460 (1977), 344.
New Jersey v. T.L.O., 469 U.S. ________(1985) 105 S.Ct. 733, 350.

The law dealing with discriminatory treatment of students, based upon their group characteristics, is treated in Chapter 7. This chapter deals with the discipline and civil rights of individual students, irrespective of their group identification. Civil rights law is largely concerned with two distinct branches of constitutional "due process," namely, *procedural due process* and *substantive due process.* Procedural due process concerns the method or procedure by which decisions are made. Its core element is fairness. Substantive due process identifies constitutional *rights* that school authorities may not penalize or abridge without substantial justification. Student rights are not absolute. They are limited in the public school context by the counterbalancing state interests in maintaining necessary order and discipline. The following materials indicate how the balance of student and public school interests is struck.

A. Procedural Due Process

Justice Frankfurter once observed that "The history of liberty has largely been the history of observance of procedural safeguards."[1] Many disciplinary actions are overturned solely for denial of procedural due process, even though the student was in fact guilty of serious misconduct.[2] Constitutional due process under the Fourteenth Amendment is distinct from procedural requirements of individual state statutes.

1. Constitutional Requirements

The Fourteenth Amendment protects all persons, including school students, from governmental infringements; hence the principles of procedural due process with regard to teachers are equally applicable to students. (Review pp.219–229.)

Procedural due process claims raise two issues: is the party entitled to Fourteenth Amendment due process, and, if so, what measure of process is due in particular situations? Unless a person can show that he or she is deprived of a "property" or "liberty" interest, there is no right to due process. For example, denial of kindergarten education where none is required by state law or exclusion from first grade of children below the statutory minimum admission age can be effected without due process hearings because children are not deprived of any protected property or liberty interest.[3]

A student who is found to be entitled to constitutional process is not entitled automatically to the full range of procedures associated with formal judicial due process.[4]

The first three traditional elements of due process—notice, hearing, and impartial tribunal—are almost always indispensible. But the right to any of the other elements will depend upon whether the particular charge and facts in the case warrant the additional

---

1. *See* McNabb v. United States, 318 U.S. 332, 347 (1943).

2. *See* Eisner v. Stamford Bd. of Education, 440 F.2d 803 (2d Cir. 1971); Quarterman v. Byrd, 453 F.2d 54 (4th Cir. 1971).

3. *See* O'Leary v. Wisecup, 364 A.2d 770 (Pa. 1976); Hammond v. Marx, 406 F.Supp. 853 (D. Me. 1975).

4. *See* Boykins v. Fairchild Bd. of Education, 492 F.2d 697, 701 (5th Cir. 1974); Linwood v. Bd. of Education 462 F.2d at 770 (7th Cir. 1972); deJesus v. Penberthey, 334 F.Supp. 70 (D. Conn. 1972).

steps.[5] The *Gonzales* case (reproduced at the end of this chapter) contains a good discussion of constitutional requirements for the additional elements.

a. Notice and Hearing. Prior to 1975, procedural due process for students was ill defined. Lower courts disagreed about whether student disciplinary decisions implicated any constitutional right to procedural due process.[6] In *Goss* v. *Lopez*, the United States Supreme Court ruled by a five to four vote that public school students who were suspended for periods up to 10 days did have a sufficient "property interest" (entitlement under state statutes to public education) and a sufficient "liberty interest" (in their reputation as it affected their future development opportunities) to command at least minimal due process.[7] In overturning the suspension and the state statute that authorized short-term suspension without a hearing, the majority ruled that the brevity of the suspensions was not relevant to the question of a *right* to due process, though it was relevant to the question of *how much* procedural process was due.

The Court recognized that some student interests might be so insubstantial (*de minimus*) as not to require any constitutional due process, but it concluded that the interest in avoiding even brief suspension was not *de minimus.*

On the question of the process to be required, the Court declared that there must always be *some* kind of notice and hearing, but that its timing and formality "will depend upon appropriate accommodation of the competing interests of reasonable student protection with no unreasonable burden on school objectives."[8] The Court concluded that oral notice to the student of the reason for short suspensions, together with an immediate informal hearing by a faculty member (including a disciplinarian), without any involvement of attorneys or former trial type proceedings would suffice for brief suspensions.

So long as the suspended student was advised of the charge, and given an opportunity to respond, due process would be satisfied.

Accordingly, courts have held that informal conferences in a principal's office providing a fair discussion of the grounds for short suspensions meet the due process standard of *Goss*.[9]

---

5. The Fifth Amendment privilege against compulsion to give self-incriminating evidence is not strictly applicable to school disciplinary hearings. Such hearings are not criminal in nature, and any compelled testimony in school hearings would not be admissible in criminal proceedings where the Fifth Amendment could be pleaded. *See* Garrity v. New Jersey, 385 U.S. 493 (1967); Furutani v. Ewigleben, 297 F.Supp. 1163 (N.D. Cal. 1969); Johnson v. Bd., 310 N.Y.S.2d 429 (1970). *But see* Caldwell v. Cannady, 348 F.Supp. 835, 841 (N.D. Tex. 1972).

6. *See* Murray v. W. Baton Rouge Sch. Bd., 472 F.2d 438, 442 (5th Cir. 1973) and the authorities there cited.

7. See the Goss opinion at the end of this chapter.

8. Constitutional due process has been repeatedly described as "an elusive concept" involving "differing rules of fair play" that vary "according to specific factual contexts." *See* Hannah v. Larche, 363 U.S. 420, 442 (1960); *accord:* Farrell v. Joel, 437 F.2d 160 (2d Cir. 1961).

9. Hillman v. Elliott, 436 F.Supp. 812 (W.D.Va. 1977); Coffman v. Kuehler, 409 F.Supp. 546 (N.D. Tex. 1976); Boynton v. Casey, 543 F.Supp. 995 (D.ME. 1982); Walker v. Bradley, 320 N.W.2d 900 (Neb. 1982); Reinman v. Valley View School District, 527 F.Supp. 661, 665 (N.D.Ill. 1981). Some courts have additionally held that where a student is briefly suspended after an informal conference, any extension of suspension, or subsequent expulsion for the same conduct, would require a second, more formal notice and hearing. *Cf.* Montoya v. Sanger Unified School District 502 F.Supp. 209 (E.D.Cal. 1980); Garcia v. Los Angeles County Board of Education, 177 Cal. Rptr. 29 (1981).

The form or the timing of hearing notices is not fixed. Oral notice was upheld as fair in some cases but not in others. Similarly, the extent of information required to give fair notice of the charge will also vary with the gravity and complexity of the charge.[10]

In *Goss,* the court refused to specify what procedures would be required in all circumstances, but it indicated that additional procedural safeguards are required as the severity of charges or penalties increases. Lower courts had held that notice in an expulsion case must be in writing, reasonably specific in describing the charge, and must be given sufficiently in advance of a hearing to allow the student time to prepare a defense.[11]

The *Goss* Court also noted an important exception to the requirement of presuspension hearings: students could be immediately removed from school without hearing when their presence would pose a continuing danger to person or property or of disrupting the academic process. Even in such cases, however, hearing would be required as soon as practicable after student exclusion. On this reasoning, emergency suspensions have been upheld.[12]

Lower courts before and after *Goss* have considered brief *in-school* sanctions too insubstantial to require prepunishment hearings."Certainly . . . measures such as after-school detention, restriction to classroom during free periods, reprimand or admonition do not per se involve matters rising to the dignity of constitutional magnitude."[13] Notwithstanding some student loss of regular class time and some stigmatization, these punishments were considered "de minimus," i.e., too trivial to require due process.

The *Goss* ruling was limited by two later Supreme Court cases (also decided by 5 to 4 votes) that found no right to constitutional due process for students subjected to corporal punishment or discharged for academic failure. In *Ingraham* v. *Wright,* the majority held that *Goss* did not apply because corporal punishment did not interrupt the student's education.[14] Regarding indisputable "liberty" interest in avoiding unwarranted physical beating, the majority reasoned that this interest did not require constitutional protection for two reasons. First, the common law tort remedy for improper corporal punishment provided an adequate deterrent to unlawful punishment; and second, the state's interest in prompt, successful discipline would be defeated by mandatory prepunishment hearings. In the second case, the court held that a third-year medical

---

10. Jenkins v. La. State Bd. of Education, 506 F.2d 992 (5th Cir. 1975). *See* Davis v. Ann Arbor Public Schools, 313 F. Supp. 1217 (E.D.Mich. 1970); (timely telephone notice to parent held sufficient); *but see* Vought v. Van Buren Pub. Schools, 306 F.Supp. 1388 (E.D.Mich. 1969) (five days' notice required for expulsion hearings); Graham v. Knutzen, 362 F.Supp. 881 (D.Neb. 1973) (school must inform student of his procedural rights in advance of the hearing).

11. *See* Texarkana Ind. Sch. District v. Lewis, 470 S.W.2d 727, 737 (Tex. 1971); *cf.* Knight v. Bd. of Education, 48 F.R.D. 108 (E.D.N.Y. 1969) (mass expulsions).

12. McClain v. Lafayette Cty. Bd. of Ed., 673 F.2d 106 (5th Cir. 1982) (carrying a deadly weapon to school); Gardenshire v. Chalmers, 326 F.Supp. 1200 (D.Ky. 1971) (college student carrying firearms); Rose v. Nasua Bd. of Ed., 679 F.2d 279 (1st Cir. 1982) (bus route suspension); *cf.* Sweets v. Childs, 581 F.2d 320 (5th Cir. 1975) (radio suspension of student (suspension by radio of student who left school to conduct a protest march).

13. Linwood v. Bd. of Education, 463 F.2d 763, 769 (7th Cir. 1972).

14. 430 U.S. 651 (1977).

student was not constitutionally entitled to a hearing on the school's decision to dismiss her for poor academic and clinical performance. This higher education case clearly governs academic decisions in public schools. It resolved earlier conflicts among lower courts regarding student demands for hearings on academic failures.[15]

The irony of requiring hearings for brief suspensions, but not for corporal punishment or academic sanctions, is explained by the Court's view that academic judgments of educators should not be subjected to outside oversight or interference unless, of course, the challenger were to allege and prove fraud or bad faith by the school authorities.

The close division among the justices in the three preceding cases forecasts still more lawsuits to determine what process is due for other forms of student discipline. Whether hearings are required for exclusion from athletic or other extracurricular activity will depend upon the perceived importance of the activity. Some courts required prior hearing for talented athletes who would suffer loss of career potential by disciplinary exclusion from varsity sports, but most courts have treated participation in interscholastic athletics as a privilege and not a right protected by constitutional due process.[16] In their view, public school students could be disqualified from sports activity for disciplinary reasons without any prior hearing.

Nondisciplinary (i.e., administrative) transfers of students between schools of comparable quality in the same school district were recently treated as having the same effect as a short-term suspension, though not intended to punish the student, and thus to require the same informal notice and hearing that was prescribed in *Goss.*[17] Transfers to less desirable schools and classes have even greater impact on student interests and require a hearing.[18]

The student's right to demand an *open hearing* is not settled. The policy of protecting the reputation of involved parties was held to justify denial of an open hearing, but in a few other cases executive sessions to decide the outcome of disciplinary hearings were disapproved as procedurally deficient.[19]

---

15. Bd. of Curators v. Horowitz, 435 U.S. 78 (1978). *Compare* Gaspar v. Bruton, 513 F.2d 843 (10th Cir. 1975); Keys v. Sawyet, 353 F.Supp. 936 (S.D.Tex. 1973) (failing grades in law school), *with* Hagopian v. Knowlton, 470 F.2d 201 (2d Cir. 1972) (discharge from service academy for academic demerits); Greenville v. Bailey, 519 F.2d 5 (8th Cir. 1975) (medical school student entitled to predischarge hearing on issue of "intellectual ability").

16. *Prior hearing required:* Regents of U. of Minn. v. NCAA, 422 F.Supp 1158 (D.Mich. 1976). O,Connor v. Bd. of Education, 316 N.Y.S.2d 799 (1970) (hearing required on retraction of student athletic letter). *Prior hearing not required:* Hamilton v. Tenn. Secondary Sch. Ath. Assn., 552 F.2d 681 (6th Cir. 1976); Albach v. Odle, 531 F.2d 983 (10th Cir. 1976); Dallam v. Cumberland Valley Sch. District, 391 F.Supp. 358 (M.D.Pa. 1975).

17. Everett v. Marcase, 426 F.Supp. 397 (E.D.Pa. 1977); *but see* Madera v. Board of Education, 386 F.2d 778 (2d Cir. 1967).

18. See the Mills and PARC cases, fn. 41.

19. *Closed hearing upheld:* Racine Un. Sch. District v. Thomas, 321 N.W.2d 334, 338 (Wis. 1982) (noting statutory right of student to have closed hearing); Pierce v. Sch. Comm. of New Bedford, 322 F.Supp. 957 (D.Mass. 1971); Linwood v. Bd. of Education, fn. 13. *Executive session disapproved:* de Jesus v. Penberthey, 334 F.Supp. 70–77 (D.Conn. 1972). *Cf.* Canney v. Bd. of Public Instruction, 278 So.2d 260 (Fla. 1973) (violation of state "sunshine law"); *cf.* the Mills case, (student option of open or closed hearing), fn. 41. *See also* Palladium Publishing Co. v. River Valley School District 321 N.W.2d 705 (Mich. 1982) (construing open-meeting statute to require school board to list in board minutes the names of suspended students by student name and not by student number).

b. Published Regulations—Vagueness and Overbreadth. The *notice* element of fairness is also expressed in doctrines dealing with vagueness and overbreadth of published regulations. These doctrines require written regulations to be sufficiently clear and specific to apprise students of ordinary intelligence of the conduct and the penalties covered by each regulation. The Constitution does not require schools to publish advance regulations for every conceivable offense or penalty. Where conduct is patently wrongful and disruptive, students cannot complain because they received no formal notice of the obvious.[20] However, advance notice by published regulations has been required where disciplinary penalties are severe or where school rules impinge upon speech-related activity.[21]

> "'[P]recision of regulation must be the touchstone in an area so clearly touching our most precious freedoms.' . . . Because First Amendment freedoms need breathing room to survive, government may regulate in the area only with narrow specificity. . . . The danger of that chilling effect upon the exercise of vital First Amendment rights must be guarded against by sensitive tools which clearly inform teachers [students] what is being proscribed."[22]

Vagueness is fatal if the regulation fails to give fair warning as to what conduct is proscribed. An overbroad regulation is void if it covers (and thereby deters) conduct that is constitutionally protected along with conduct that may be lawfully controlled. In most instances, the vice of vagueness also involves overbreadth.

> "[E]ven though the governmental purpose be legitimate and substantial, that purpose cannot be pursued by means that broadly stifle fundamental personal liberties when the end can be more narrowly achieved." *Shelton* v. *Tucker,* 364 U.S. at 488 (1960).

There is no fixed formula to identify particular language that suffices to avoid the barriers of vagueness or overbreadth. Courts make judgments on the facts of each case, but they stress that the strict standards of vagueness that govern criminal cases do not apply to school regulations. Such terms as *willful disobedience, intentional disruption, student walkouts, boycott, incorrigible behavior, profanity, excessive absenteeism,* and *vulgarity* have been held not to be unduly vague in school regulations.[23]

Whether particular words will be found clear or vague also depends upon the particular history and environment of the school where they are used. The word *misconduct* has been held unconstitutionally vague in some discipline cases, but not in

20. Pierce v. Sch. Committee of New Bedford, 322 F.Supp. 957 (D. Mass. 1971); Shanley v. Northeast Ind. Sch. Dist., 462 F.2d 960, 970–1 (5th Cir. 1972).

21. *See* Leibner v. Sharbaugh, 429 F.Supp. 744 (D.Va. 1977); Nitzberg v. Parks, 525 F.2d 378 (4th Cir. 1975).

22. *See* Keyishian v. Bd. of Regents, 385 U.S. 589, 603–604 (1967); Shanley v. Northeast Ind. Sch. District, 462 F.2d 960, 975–977 (5th Cir. 1972).

23. Williams v. Bd. of Education, 626 S.W.2d 361 (Ark. 1982). *See also* Murray v. W. Baton Rouge Sch. Bd., 472 F.2d 438 (5th Cir. 1973); Rumler v. Bd. of Sch. Trustees, 327 F.Supp. 729 (D.S.Car. 1971); Baker v. Downey City Bd. of Education, 307 F.Supp 517 (D.C.Cal. 1969); Alex v. Allen, 409 F.Supp. 379 (W.D.Pa. 1976); Fielder v. Bd. of Education, fn.33; *cf.* Grayned v. City of Rockford, 408 U.S. 104 (1972) (antinoise ordinance to protect school from distraction—upheld). See Addendum on p. 662.

others.[24] The statutory criterion for expulsion in Colorado—"behavior . . . inimical to the welfare, safety or morals of other pupils"—was upheld as not unduly vague or overbroad.[25]

The failure to define by specific criteria the meaning of *substantial disruption* in regulations governing student publications or to provide procedures for determination of disruptive literature has been held by some courts to render those regulations void.[26] However, in the area of speech regulation and censorship, some courts take an extremely strict view of regulatory language in applying the vagueness and overbreadth doctrines.

c. Impartial Tribunal. An impartial hearing body is indispensible to due process, but the Supreme Court has ruled that school authorities are presumptively impartial with respect to hearings resulting in dismissal of teachers conducting an illegal strike. The *Hortonville* opinion extended earlier lower court decisions that upheld student suspensions pursuant to hearings by superintendents, board-appointed hearing panels, and school boards, though the hearings were prosecuted by a school board solicitor.[27] An interesting gambit on the bias theme was ventured by a student who called the hearing panel "fascist pigs" and thereafter sought to overturn the panel's decision on the ground that it had to be biased by his conduct. In upholding the board, the court added that a student could not defeat the hearing merely by attempting to stir up bias.[28]

Impartiality was negated, however, where a teacher acted as both an accusing witness and as a member of the judging panel in a student hearing.[29] Courts have disagreed on whether impartiality is destroyed where the school solicitor plays a double role, that is, as prosecutor as well as advisor or member of the hearing panel.[30]

d. Right of Confrontation. Opportunity to refute adverse evidence required both access to that evidence *prior* to hearing and the right to challenge and cross-examine documents and witnesses *at* the hearing. Some courts hesitate to recognize a right to obtain adverse evidence in school files, even in expulsion cases.[31] Others considered notification of such evidence to be essential in cases of serious charges and heavy penalties.[32] One court placed upon the board the burden of producing adverse witnesses at the hearing, even though the student's attorney failed to request their presence.[33]

---

24. *Vague*: Soglin v. Kaufmann, 418 F.2d 163 (7th Cir. 1969); *cf.* Veasgy v. Bd. of Public Instruction, 247 So.2d 80 (Fla. 1971). *Not vague*: Whitfield v. Simpson, 312 F.Supp. 889 (E.D.Ill. 1970); Linwood v. Bd. of Education, 463 F.2d 763 (7th Cir. 1972).

25. People in the interest of K.P., 514 P.2d 1131 (Colo. 1973).

26. *See* Cintron v. State Bd. of Education, 384 F.Supp. 674 (D.Puerto Rico 1974).

27. Murray v. W. Baton Rouge Sch. Bd., fn. 23. (superintendent held impartial); Alex v. Allan,409 F.Supp. 379 (W.D.Pa. 1976) (school board held impartial, notwithstanding participation by its counsel as prosecutor).

28. *See* Pierce v. Sch. Committee of New Bedford, 322 F.Supp. 957, at 962 (D. Mass. 1971).

29. Warren v. Nat'l Assn. of Secondary Sch. Principals, 375 F.Supp. 1043 (N.D.Tex. 1974).

30. See the Gonzales opinion reproduced at the end of this chapter; Harrall v. Wilson County Schools, 293 S.E.2d 687 (No.Car. 1932); *contra*: Allex v. Allen, 409 F.Supp. 379 (W.D.Pa. 1976).

31. Texarkana Ind. Sch. District v. Lewis, 470 S.W.2d at 736, and cases there cited.

32. *See, e.g.*, Graham v. Knutzen, 362 F.Supp. 881 (D.Neb. 1973); Williams v. Dade County Sch. Bd., 441 F.2d 299 (5th Cir. 1971).

33. *See* Fielder v. Bd. of Education, 346 F.Supp. at 730 (D.Neb. 1972). Contra: Greene v. Moore, 373 F.Supp 1194 (N.D.Tex. 1974).

As noted in *Goss*, cross examination is not always required. In grave cases such as expulsion, cross examination would be indispensible, especially if the outcome could turn on the credibility of conflicting witnesses.[34] The use of cross examination does not, however, imply that technical rules of evidence must be observed.
Rules barring "hearsay" evidence in courts, though closely related to the right of confrontation, do not always disqualify hearsay testimony before the school board:[35]

> "There are a number of federal cases which have addressed the question of the admissibility of hearsay at a disciplinary hearing, but many are distinguishable on their facts, and, in any case, their holdings are mixed."[36]
>
> "This court is particularly persuaded by the rationale in favor of admitting hearsay as presented in *Boykins* v. *Fairfield Board of Education*, 492 F.2d 697 (5th Cir. 1974), *cert. denied*, 420 U.S. 962, 95 S.Ct. 1350, 43 L.Ed.2d 438 (1975)."[37]

e. Right to Counsel. Discovery of evidence and cross examination of witnesses are best accomplished by an attorney. Hence the right to counsel will usually exist where the right to confrontation is given. Here, also, the right depends upon the nature of the hearing:

> "Other federal courts are divided on the issue of confrontation and cross-examination. Some have held that a hearing incorporating that safeguard must be afforded in school expulsion proceedings. (*Black Coalition* v. *Portland School District No. 1* (9th Cir.) 484 F.2d 1040, 1045; *Mills* v. *Board of Education of District of Columbia* (D.D.C.) 348 F.Supp. 866, 882–883; *DeJesus* v. *Penberthy* (D.Conn.) 344 F.Supp. 70, 75–76; *Buttny* v. *Smiley* (D.Colo.) 281 F.Supp 280, 288; *Esteban* v. *Central Missouri State College*, 277 F.2d 649, 652.) Others have declined to accord that right. In *Boykins* v. *Fairfield Board of Education*. 492 F.2d 697, the Fifth Circuit declined to extend its decision in the landmark case of *Dixon* v. *Alabama State Board of Education* (5th Cir.) 294 F.2d 150 [cert. den. 368 U.S. 930, 82 S.Ct. 368, 7 L.Ed.2d 193], to require confrontation and cross-examination in school expulsion cases. *Boykins*, however, was decided before *Goss*. *Whiteside* v. *Kay* (W.D.La.) 446 F.Supp. 716, 720–711, interpreted *Goss* as not anticipating confrontation and cross-examination in

---

34. deJesus v. Penberthey, 334 F.Supp. 70 (D.Conn. 1972); *accord*: Fielder v. Bd. of Education, 346 F.Supp. 722 (D.Neb. 1972). *See also* Winnick v. Manning, 460 F.2d 545, 549 (2d Cir. 1972).

35. Boykins v. Fairfield Bd. of Education, 492 F.2d 697 (5th Cir. 1974). *See* Gonzales, fn. 30, on when the hearsay rule may be enforced to avoid unfairness.

36. [Court's footnote—renumbered] *Tasby* v. *Estes*, 643 F.2d 1103 (5th cir. 1981) (hearsay allowed in hearings for serious student offenses); *Boykins* v. *Fairfield Bd. of Educ.*, 492 F.2d. 697 (5th cir. 1974), *cert. denied*, 420 U.S. 962, 95 S.Ct. 1350, 43 L.Ed.2d 438 (1975) (hearsay allowed in suspension/expulsion hearings); *Linwood* v. *Bd. of Educ.*, 463 F.2d 763 (7th Cir.), *cert. denied*, 409 U.S. 1027, 93 S.Ct. 475, 34 L.Ed.2d 320 (1972) (hearsay allowed by implication in expulsion hearing); *Whiteside* v. *Kay*, 446 F.Supp. 716 (W.D.La. 1978) (hearsay allowed by implication at expulsion hearing); *Fielder* v. *Bd. of Educ.*, 346. F.Supp. 722 (D.Neb. 1972) (hearsay not allowed by implication at expulsion hearing); *DeJesus* v. *Penberthy*, 344 F.Supp. 70 (D.Conn. 1972) (hearsay not allowed in hearing for thirty-day suspension).

37. [Court's footnote—renumbered] Even though this case predates the United States Supreme Court holding in *Goss* v. *Lopez*. 419 U.S. 565, 95, S.Ct. 729, 42 L.Ed.2d 725 (1975), the hearsay principles set forth in it have been recently reaffirmed by the Fifth Circuit in *Tasby* v. *Estes*, 643 F.2d 1103 (5th Cir. 1981). *See* Racine Unified Dist. v. Thompson, 321 N.W.2d 334, 337 (Wis. 1982).

expulsion cases, relying in part on *Board of Curators, Univ. of Mo.* v. *Horowitz, supra,* 435 U.S. 78, 98 S.Ct. 948, 55 L.Ed.2d 124, where the court held that due process did not require a hearing for an academic dismissal from medical school. . . .

"In *Dillon* v. *Pulaski City Special Sch. Dist.* (E.D.Ark.) 468 F. Supp. 54, 58, the court held that a student not permitted to confront and cross-examine teachers or administrators who accused him of wrongdoing was denied due process, but stated in dicta that confrontation and cross-examination of student accusers might be disallowed consistent with due process if reprisals were likely." See *Aguirre* v. *San Bernardino City Unified School,* 170 Cal. Rptr. 206, 215 (1981).

"The requirement of counsel as an ingredient of fairness is a function of all of the other aspects of the hearing. Where the proceeding is non-criminal in nature, where the hearing is investigative and not adversarial and the government does not proceed through counsel, where the individual concerned is mature and educated, where his knowledge of the events . . . should enable him to develop the facts adequately through available sources, and where the other aspects of the hearing taken as a whole are fair, due process does not require representation by counsel. It is significant that . . . where the balancing of government and private interests favored the individual far more than here, the court did not suggest that a student must be represented by counsel in an expulsion proceeding." See *Wasson* v. *Trowbridge,* 382 F.2d 807, 812 (2d Cir. 1967).

The presence or absence of school board counsel is a factor to be considered in determining a student's need for legal representation. No right to counsel was found where school counsel was not present or where the hearing was considered to be advisory and not adversary in nature.[38] But disqualification of a student from taking scholarship examinations because of cheating was overturned where the accused student was denied the right to legal counsel.[39] Counsel was even afforded by one court in connection with suspension hearings.[40] Where there is heightened concern for specially disadvantaged groups, the courts have gone further and *required* school authorities to advise the students of their right to legal counsel.[41]

f. Right to a Hearing Record and Appeal. Stenographic or mechanical recordings of school hearings are not universally required for due process, but a court can always require a record if it considers one necessary to ensure fairness to all parties.[42] At present, there are no firm legal criteria for knowing when a hearing record is essential for due process in student disciplinary hearings. A right of appeal from a disciplinary decision to a court must be founded in state law, and may even be barred by state law.[43] Where a

---

38. *School council not present*: Texarkana case, fn. 31. *Advisory hearing*: Madera v. Bd. of Education, 380 F.2d 778 (2nd Cir. 1967).

39. *Re* Goldwyn, 281 N.Y.S.2d 199 (1967).

40. Givens v. Poe, 346 F.Supp. 202 (W.D.No.Car. 1972).

41. Mills v. Bd. of Education, 348 F.Supp. 866 (D.Dist. of Col. 1972); Pa. Assn. for Retarded Children v. Commonwealth, 343 F.Supp. 279 (E.D.Pa. 1972).

42. *Compare* Mills v. Bd. of Education 348 F.Supp. 866 (D.D.C. 1972) (record required) *with* S. v. Bd. of Education, 97 Cal. Rptr, 422 (1971).

43. *Compare, e.g.,* Mason v. Thetford Sch. Bd., 457 A.2d 647, 649 (Vt. 1982) (denying any right of appeal) *with* cases finding a right of appeal under state statutes: Racine Un. Sch. District v. Thompson, *supra,* 321 N.W.2d at p. 339 (board minutes of hearing); Ross v. Disare, *supra,* 500 F.Supp. at p. 931 (hearing record, but no stenographic transcript record of hearing). *See also* Gonzales v. McEuen, *supra,* 435 F.Supp. at p. 463 (statutory right of appeal).

right of appeal is provided by law, however, some kind of hearing record is usually required, either expressly by law, or by due process principles, since an appeal without a record for review would not comport with procedural fairness.[44]

g. Waiver and Cure of Procedural Defects. Due process rights may be waived voluntarily by failure to follow available procedures. A waiver requires "an intentional relinquishment or abandonment of a known right or privilege."[45] Hence, school authorities may only rely on waivers that are freely and intelligently made. Hearing deficiencies can also be cured by affording timely corrective procedures.[46]

2. Statutory Procedures

Many statutes require special procedures. School authorities are bound to comply with those statutes as well as with the Constitution. Some examples are statutes dealing with student dismissals,[47] with sex discrimination and with the handicapped. Under New York law, students assigned to home-bound instruction must be given a hearing.[48] Hearing requirements are also commonplace under state codes for other placement and disciplinary decisions.

Central state agencies are authorized under the statutes of some states to regulate disciplinary hearing procedures by school boards. Where the state's code vests disciplinary jurisdiction in local school boards, the state board's authority may be challenged, as was recently done in Pennsylvania. There the court ruled that the state board had concurrent jurisdiction over student disciplinary matters and that the state board's Code of Student Rights and Responsibilities was lawful.[49] Local board regulations that conflict with statutory procedures for student suspensions have been struck down.[50]

B. Substantive Rights

Substantive rights under the Due Process Clause of the Fourteenth Amendment extend to all persons. As previously noted, the phrase "substantive due process" has several meanings. First, it expresses a general principle that government agencies may not impose restraints upon individuals without a rational justification. Second, it refers to basic liberties that are not enumerated in the Constitution but are derived from tradition,

---

44. *Idem.*

45. *See* Johnson v. Zerbst, 304 U.S. 458, 464 (1938).

46. *See* Pervis v. LaMarque Ind. Sch. District, 328 F.Supp. 638, 645 (S.D. Tex. 1971).

47. *See* Minn. Pupil Fair Dismissal Act, Minn. Gen. Stat. § 127.30 (1974); Conn. Gen. Stat. Ann. § 4(c) 1975 (exclusion of students from school); Wash. Ad. Code ch. 180–40 (1972).

48. Johnson v. Bd. of Education, 393 N.Y.S.2d 510 (1977).

49. Girard Sch. District v. Pittinger, 392 A.2d 261 (Pa. 1978).

50. Dorsey v. Bale, 521 S.E.2d 76 (Ky. 1975); Garcia v. Los Angeles County Board of Education, 177 Cal. Rptr. 29 (1981); Ross v. Disare, 500 F.Supp. 418 (D.Minn. 1979) (construing school statute as limiting suspension power to school principal and voiding suspension by other school authorities).

such as the right to marry and to beget children. Third, and most frequently, it covers a body of rights specified in the Bill of Rights.

1. General Fundamental Rights

Student discipline in government (i.e., public) school involves personal restraint and must, therefore, (1) have a rational, school-connected *purpose*[51] and (2) employ rational means to achieve the purposes to be served. The school cannot prohibit or punish conduct, however reprehensible, that poses no harm to public education. Neither can it impose punishments that are excessive or unreasonable. This "reasonable nexus" standard is necessarily contextual, because the rationality of particular restraints or penalties necessarily depends on actual circumstances. The judicial yardsticks are, therefore, limited to the specific situations covered in the cases.

Decisions limiting student freedom, such as placement of truants in a custodial school, are impermissible unless the district proves that the remedy is *educationally sound* and is the *least restrictive* means of assuring educational objectives.[52] Expulsion and suspension for drug usage inside the school clearly satisfy this test.[53] Out-of-school misconduct may be punished when it threatens school or student welfare (out-of-school assaults on other students, sale of drugs to other students away from school).[54]

Courts differ on the proofs required to establish punishable conduct. One held that arrest for drug possession, without independent findings of fact, would not support a suspension sanction.[55] Others upheld school punishment of students for out-of-school drinking of alcoholic beverages.[56] Proof that a student was with other students in a car that contained alcoholic beverages was held not sufficient to justify punishment.[57] A clear violation of the rational nexus test occurred where the school board expelled a student because his parent assaulted a board member.[58]

The legality of imposing academic penalities for misconduct unrelated to a course of study is questionable. Nevertheless, a few courts have sustained forfeiture of semester credits where students were suspended for serious misconduct.[59] However, even if a penalty meets constitutional standards, it must still comply with state law. For example, grade penalties to discipline students were overturned as unauthorized in several states,

---

51. *See* Woods v. Wright, 334 F.2d 369 (5th Cir. 1964) (punishment for out of school arrest for nonschool related conduct held unlawful). The overlap of different sources of substantive and procedural rights is noted in Brookhart v. Ill. Bd. of Ed., 697 F.2d 179, 186 (7th Cir. 1983).

52. Braesch v. DePasquale, 265 N.W.2d 842 (Neb. 1978); Chicago Bd. of Trust v. Terrille, 361 N.E.2d 778 (Ill. 1977).

53. Giles v. Marple Newtown S.D. Bd. of Directors, 367 A.2d 399 (Pa. 1976); Fisher v. Burkburnett Ind. Sch. District, 419 F.Supp. 1200 (N.D.Tex. 1976); Rondol v. Newberg P.S. Bd., 542 P.2d 938 (Ore. 1975).

54. For a recent collection of cases on discipline for conduct away from school, see Annotation, *Discipline of Pupil for Non-School Conduct* 53 A.L.R.3d 1124 (1973). *See also* Fortman v. Texarkana Sch. District, 514 S.W.2d 720 (Ark. 1974); Boykins v. Fairfield Bd. of Education, 492 F.2d 697 (5th Cir. 1974).

55. Howard v. Clark, 299 N.Y.S.2d 65 (1969).

56. *Cf.* O'Connor v. Bd. of Education, 316 N.Y.S.2d 799 (1970).

57. Bunger v. Iowa H.S. Athletic Assn., 197 N.W.2d 555 (Iowa 1972).

58. St. Ann v. Palisi, 495 F.2d 423 (5th Cir. 1974).

59. *See* Fisher v. Burkburnett Ind. Sch. District, fn. 53.

and a school board's power to suspend a student was qualified by a New York statute requiring the board to provide alternative instruction to suspended students.[60]

School laws and regulations that specify automatic penalties for defined misconduct have been challenged as unreasonable on the ground that they disallowed consideration of mitigating circumstances that might justify less severe sanctions. However, in the few decided cases the automatic penalties were upheld.[61] As the following section will show, courts use stricter standards in reviewing disciplinary punishments that affect First Amendment rights.

2. First Amendment Freedom of Expression

As noted in Chapter 5, the special needs of the schools render them only "limited" pubic forums for First Amendment purposes, so that greater official control of expression in that locale may be lawfully exercised for the purposes of maintaining order, discipline, and educational functions. Corollary to that proposition is the oft-mentioned observation that the First Amendment rights of students are not coextensive with those of adult members of the school community.

> "It is . . . clear that students do have rights which are protected by the federal and California state constitutions and that they do not shed them at the schoolhouse gate. . . . However, it must be recognized that a student may be subject to far more stringent regulations than an adult outside a school environment due to his immaturity and status as a student in a school environment where disciplinary and health problems and considerations relating to safety of minors take on special significance." . . . where there is an invasion of protected freedoms "the power of the state to control the conduct of children reaches beyond the scope of its authority over adults." . . . We specifically reject appellant's contention that a student is in the same position as an adult not in a school environment. The courts have universally recognized the difference, including those situations where First Amendment rights admittedly are involved." *See Montalvo* v. *Madera Unified Sch. Dist. Bd. of Education,* 98 Cal. Rptr. 593 (1971).

Tinker v. *Des Moines Independent Community School District* is the leading authority on student rights of expression in public schools.[62] The Supreme Court there held that students had a constitutional right to wear arm bands in school as a form of symbolic speech to protest the Vietnam War. The Court's ruling was simple, but its reasoning is rather complex.

> "First Amendment rights applied in the light of the special characteristics of the school environment, are available to teachers and students. It can hardly be argued that either students or teachers shed their constitutional rights to freedom of speech or expression at the school house gate. . . . On the other hand, the Court has repeatedly emphasized the need

---

60. Dorsey v. Bale, 521 S.W.2d 76 (Ky. 1975); Hamer v. Bd. of Education, 383 N.E.2d 231 (Ill. 1978); Guitirrez v. Sch. District R-1, 585 P.2d 935 (Colo. 1978); Turner v. Kowalski, 374 N.Y.S.2d 133 (1975).

61. Fisher v. Burkburnett Ind. Sch. District, fn.53; Dunn v. Tyler Ind. Sch. District, 460 F.2d 137 (5th Cir. 1972).

62. 393 U.S. 503 (1969).

> for affirming the comprehensive authority of the States and of school authorities, consistent with fundamental constitutional safeguards, to prescribe and control conduct in the schools. . . . In order for the State in the person of school officials to justify prohibition of particular expression of opinion, it must be able to show that its action was caused by something more than a mere desire to avoid the discomfort and unpleasantness that always accompany an unpopular viewpoint. Certainly where there is no finding and no showing that the exercise of the forbidden right would "materially and substantially interfere with the requirements of appropriate discipline in the operation of the school," the prohibition cannot be sustained."[63]

The Court expressly limited the decision to its finding that the passive use of arm bands in *that particular school* was not disruptive of school operations. It cited with approval a pair of cases that held that symbolic insignia could be constitutionally barred where they disrupted the school; but could not be barred in another school, absent proof of disruption.[64] Since the *Tinker* record "did not concern aggressive, disruptive action or even group demonstrations," it raised the same problem discussed in the teacher expression cases: What kinds and levels of physical or psychological upset or interference establish that degree of "disruption" that justifies limitation of expression? The countervailing interests in maintaining school discipline and preserving student liberty must be balanced, but as one court trenchantly noted, the "mere articulation of a well-intentioned but abstract principle does not always provide the pragmatic and just answer."[65]

The spectrum of protected expression includes oral and written speech, expression by nonverbal signs, by dress and grooming, and by group demonstration. These categories of expression trigger differentiated analysis, and courts have a manifest tendency to afford higher protection to some forms of expression (e.g., student publications) than to others (e.g., student dress and grooming). Practical guidance must, therefore, be sought in cases dealing with like classes of speech-related activity by students of comparable age and maturity. First Amendment freedoms for minors and precollege students are not coextensive with those of adults or college level students, but this fact does not relieve school authorities of the burden of justifying restraints on expression.[66]

a. Individual Speech. No one has an unfettered right to commandeer school property or an audience and thus intrude upon the rights of others. Reasonable regulation of the time, place, and manner of speech for orderly scheduling and housekeeping purposes and not for the purpose of censoring ideas is clearly constitutional.[67]

School authorities may confine student rallies to reasonably prescribed times and places, and they may punish speech activity that is bracketed with disruptive physical

---

63. 393 U.S. at 506, 507, 509.

64. *Compare* Burnside v. Byars, 363 F.2d 744 (5th Cir. 1966) *with* Blackwell v. Issaquena County Bd. of Education, 363 F.2d 749 (5th Cir. 1966) cited at 393 U.S. 511 and 513, respectively.

65. *See* Zanders v. Bd. of Education, 381 F.Supp. 747, 757 (W.D.La. 1968).

66. Quarterman v. Byrd, 453 F.2d 54, 57–58 (4th Cir. 1971); Eisner v. Bd. of Education, 440 F.2d 803, 808 n.5 (2d Cir. 1971); Shanley v. Northeast Ind. Sch. District, 462 F.2d 960 (5th Cir. 1972).

67. *See* Sullivan v. School District, 307 F.Supp. 1322 (S.D.Tex. 1969); Lipkis v. Caveney, 96 Cal. Rptr. 779 (1971); *see also* Shanley v. Northeast Ind. School District, 462 F.2d 960 (5th Cir. 1972); Grayned v. City of Rockford, 408 U.S. 104 (1972).

conduct.[68] The fact that students intended to express ideas does not immunize them from punishment for occupation or obstruction of facilities that are assigned to other school uses.[69]

Freedom of speech includes the right to criticize and protest school policies in a nondisruptive manner, but it does not include the use of "fighting" words or the abuse of school superiors with profane and vulgar speech.[70] Speech that incites to disruptive action, such as a call for a student strike or for a takeover of school buildings, is not protected by the First Amendment.[71]

b. Symbolic Expression. *Tinker* established that the First Amendment protects nonverbal expression inside the school, but just as pure speech may lose protection when it incites to unlawful conduct, so unlawful conduct gains no protection by a plea of symbolic speech. "[W]hen speech and non-speech elements are combined in the same course of conduct, a sufficiently important governmental interest in regulating the non-speech element can justify incidental limitation of First Amendment freedoms."[72] Courts have, accordingly, upheld school bans on use of symbols and insignias that threaten substantial disorder in the school.[73]

Student refusal to participate in patriotic exercises, as a sign of political protest, has been considered to be constitutionally protected. On this view, school regulations and statutes requiring students to either stand or leave the room if unwilling to participate during the flag salute ceremonies were held unconstitutional.[74] On the other hand, courts rejected the defense of symbolic expression by students who boycotted school classes or programs, instigated walkouts during regular sessions, and conducted sit-ins in areas assigned for other class activity.[75]

c. Student Literature. As an exercise of freedom of the press, student literature enjoys constitutional protection regardless of its sponsorship, authorship, or place of

---

68. *See* Lipkis case, prior fn.; United States v. O'Brien, 391 U.S. 367 (1968); *but see* Dorn v. Bd. of Billings Sch. Dist., 661 P.2d 426 (Mont. 1983) (regulations barring all demonstrations, where many students had free time during study periods, held to be unreasonable).

69. *Cf.* Evans v. Bd. of Agriculture, 325 F.Supp. 1353 (D.Colo. 1971).

70. *See* Hatter v. L.A. City H.S. District, 452 F.2d 673 (9th Cir. 1971) (peaceful protest against school dress code); Scoville v. Bd. of Education, 425 F.2d 10 (7th Cir. 1970) (criticism of school policies); *compare* Fenton v. Steor, 423 F.Supp. 767 (W.D.Pa. 1976). See Addendum on p. 662.

71. *Compare* Williams v. Spencer, 622 F.2d 1206 (4th Cir. 1980); Lake Park Education Association v. Lake Park High School District, 526 F.Supp 719 (N.D.Ill 1981); Ring v. Reorganized School District, 609 S.W.2d 241 (Mo. 1980); Schwartz v. Schuker, 298 F.Supp. 238 (E.D.N.Y. 1969).

72. *See* U.S. v. O'Brien, 391 U.S. 367, 376 (1968).

73. *See* Hill v. Lewis, 323 F.Supp. 55 (E.D.N.C. 1971) (ban on antiwar armbands upheld); Melton v. Young, 465 F.2d 1332 (6th Cir. 1972) (prohibition of Confederate flag patches upheld in racially tense school); *but see* Butts v. Sch. District, 436 F.2d 728, 731–32 (5th Cir. 1961) (where authorities failed to prove student armbands threatened disruption, and, therefore, could not punish them).

74. Sheldon v. Fannin, 221 F.Supp. 766 (Ariz. 1963). *Compare* Caldwell v. Craighead, 432 F.2d 213 (6th Cir. 1970); *with* Frain v. Barron, 307 F.Supp. 27 (E.D.N.Y. 1969).

75. Sapp v. Renpoe, 511 F.2d 172 (5th Cir. 1975) (stay-out); *cf.* Hobson v. Bailey, 309 F.Supp. 1393 (W.D.Tenn. 1970); Rhyne v. Childs, 359 F.Supp. 1085 (N.D.Fla. 1973) (student walkout); Tate v. Bd. of Education, 453 F.2d 975 (8th Cir. 1972) (black student walkout to protest use of "Dixie" as the school song); Washington v. State, 190 S.E.2d 138 (Ga. 1972) (attempt to organize student walkout protest regarding specific incident); Gebert v. Hoffman, 336 F.Supp. 694 (E.D.Pa. 1972) (sit-in).

publication.[76] School authorities may reasonably control the time, place, and manner of literature distribution for noncensorial purposes; but they may not use such regulations as a guise to suppress or censor the content of student writings.

Student literature content may be suppressed or partially censored only if the authorities can show that the suppressed content does or will create a substantial threat of school disruption.[77] What remains to be clarified by court decisions are those practical determinations of the circumstances and proofs that justify censorship or penalties for particular writings.

Courts have repeatedly noted that the interests of public schools and their students are not coextensive with those of colleges and college students, hence decisions on university leafletting are not reliable guides for public schools.[78]

Where school authorities practice "prior censorship" and require submission of student literature for administrative review and approval prior to actual publication, special rules apply. "Prior restraints" are presumed invalid, unless school authorities can prove that prepublication controls are fair in operation as well as necessary to maintain school order.[79] The courts do not agree altogether on what specific procedures are constitutionally required. The 4th, 5th, and 7th Circuit Courts of Appeals have listed several prerequisites:

1. Schools must issue clear and narrowly drawn regulations in advance to notify students of what is required.
2. School procedures must ensure prompt decision by school authorities on submitted materials.
3. Timely and fair (informal) hearings and a prompt appeal to higher authority on decisions to censor must be ensured.[80]

The 2nd Circuit Court of Appeals espoused the requirement of fair and expeditious procedures for prepublication review, but denied the need for published written regulations before school authorities may act to ban or punish disruptive literature.[81]

The courts that required advance written regulations also subjected those regulations to severe, perhaps prohibitive, demands under the vagueness and overbreadth doctrines. Examples of judicial zeal to dissect commonly understood words for possible

---

76. Nitzberg v. Park, 525 F.2d 378 (4th Cir. 1975); Jacobs v. Bd. of Sch. Commissioners, 490 F.2d 601 (7th Cir. 1973); Shanley v. Northeast Ind. Sch. District, 462 F.2d 960 (5th Cir. 1972). See generally Huffman and Trauth, *High School Student's Publications,* 10 J. of LAW & ED. 484 (1981).

77. Eisner v. Stanford Bd. of Education, 440 F.2d 803 (2d Cir. 1971); Riseman v. Sch. Committee of Quincy, 439 F.2d 148 (1st Cir. 1971).

78. Egner v. Texas City Ind. Sch. District, 338 F.Supp. 931 (D.Tex. 1972). *Cf.* Papish v. Bd. of Curators, U. of Mo., 410 U.S. 667 (1973); Nicholson v. Bd. of Ed., 682 F.2d 858, 863 n. 4 (9th Cir. 1982).

79. See the Nitzberg, Jacobs, Shanley, Eisner and Riseman cases, *supra*; *cf.* Bright v. L.A. Un. Sch. District, 124 Cal. Rptr. 59 (1975) (state statute barring prior censorship of student newspaper).

80. *See* the Nitzberg, Jacobs, and Shanley cases, *supra*; Leibner v. Sharbaugh, 429 F.Supp. 744 (D.Va. 1977).

81. *See* Eisner v. Stamford Bd. of Education, fn. 77, n. 4.

unconstitutional ambiguities are found in student literature decisions of the 4th and 7th Circuit Courts of Appeal. Those circuits voided, as vague and overbroad, school regulations that were drafted almost directly from the Supreme Court opinion in the *Tinker* case. Their attitude is summarized in the following excerpt:

> "A crucial flaw exists in this directive since it gives no guidance whatsoever as to what amounts to a 'substantial disruption or material intereference with' school activities; and equally fatal, it fails to detail the criteria by which an administrator might reasonably predict the occurrence of such a disruption. Though the language comes directly from the opinion in Tinker, we agree with Judge Fairchild's remark in *Jacobs* v. *Bd. of Sch. Comm'rs,* 490 F.2d 610 (7th Cir. 1973), vacated as moot, 420 U.S. 128 . . . (1975) that: 'It does not at all follow that the phrasing of a constitutional standard by which to decide whether a regulation infringes upon rights protected by the first amendment is sufficiently specific in a regulation to convey notice to students or people in general of what is prohibited.' "[82]

Although the 4th and 7th Circuit Courts require a greater, though undefined, degree of linguistic clarity than was supplied by the Supreme Court itself (or by any other court),[83] the 2nd Circuit Court of Appeals found that similar language tailored from the *Tinker* opinion was not unconstitutionally vague or overbroad.[84] Federal courts in Maryland and Texas found the following language to be unconstitutionally vague: "advocacy of illegal action and gross insult to a group or individual" and "illegal action or disobedience to published rules."[85]

Prior censorship raises the question whether students must obey censorship orders and thereafter challenge them or whether they may disobey orders they believe to be unlawful without first resorting to available channels of appeal. Some courts have held that students must obey their superiors even though the order later proves to be invalid. Others would overturn penalties for disobedience if it were shown that the punishment were directed to the expression rather than to the act of disobedience and the material was not in fact censorable.[86]

School bans against distribution of partisan political literature have also come under constitutional attack. The 2nd Circuit Court of Appeals upheld such a ban where

---

82. *See* Nitzberg v. Parks, 525 F.2d at 383. The strict view of vagueness in the Nitzberg case is rendered questionable by the United States Supreme Court decision to review the Jacobs case, which Nitzberg relied upon. This action suggested that the Jacobs standard was at least open to question. Before the Supreme Court could decide the Jacobs appeal, the student graduated, and the Supreme Court therefore mooted the entire case, which had the effect of vacating the judgment of the Court of Appeal and leaving in effect the school regulations that the lower court thought unconstitutional. *See* 420 U.S. 128 (1975); *cf.* Oxfelt v. N.J. Bd. of Education, 344 A.2d 769 (N.J. 1975).

83. After noting that it was striking down the third attempt of the same district to forge regulations to the court's satisfaction, the opinion in Nitzberg v. Parks, *supra,* added: "We have both compassion and understanding of the difficulties facing school administrators, but we cannot permit those conditions to suppress the First Amendment rights of individual students." 525 F.2d at 384.

84. Eisner v. Stamford Bd. of Education, fn. 77.

85. Baughman v. Feienmuth 343 F.Supp. 487 (D.Md. 1972); Sullivan v. Houston Ind. Sch. District, 333 F.Supp. 1149 (D.Tex. 1971).

86. *Compare* Graham v. Houston Ind. Sch. District, 335 F.Supp. 1164 (D.Tex. 1970); Baker v. Downey City Bd. of Education, 307 F.Supp. 517 (D.Cal. 1969); *with* Scoville v. Bd. of Education, 425 F.2d 10 (7th Cir. 1970).

students solicited other students to contribute funds for antiwar activists.[87] Another court took a contrary view in similar circumstances on the ground that the school's interest in shielding students from outside political pressures did not outweigh the students' freedom of speech.[88] Regulation of commercial communications inside school grounds is equally unsettled. A Nebraska court ruled that a school board could not lawfully ban all commercial solicitation, including the sale of newspapers, unless it could show that the prohibition was necessary to avoid interference with school work and discipline.[89] But the 7th Circuit Court of Appeals appeared to distinguish between publications produced by students and those produced by outside parties indicating that school authorities might prohibit commerical news sales by outsiders, but could not forbid sales of private student newspapers without the showing of material disruption.[90] Prohibitions against political advertisements in student papers have also proven to be constitutional.[91]

School-sponsored newspapers are subjected to greater school control on the grounds that they are publicly subsidized and are directed to a captive audience of students. School authorities have further argued that student editors have no right to defeat school board decisions regarding exclusion of particular subjects from the school curriculum by using school newspapers to influence or educate the student body on such matters. These latter arguments have not been fully canvassed by the courts, but they have not been favored in the cases decided to date.[92]

In 1975, the 2nd Circuit Court of Appeals affirmed *without opinion* a lower court decision that school newspaper editors had a constitutional right to publish a sex supplement that contained seriously written articles on contraception and abortion. The court also ruled that the school authorities could not seize or ban distribution on their view that the material was not fit for high school students.[93] However, in 1977 the same Court ruled in a written opinion that high school administrators could ban school newspaper editors from conducting and publishing a student poll that sought "personal and frank" information regarding their sexual experiences and attitudes. The voluntary questionnaire was not vulgar or obscene, but the court found that the state's interest in preventing psychological harm to immature students sufficed to override the liberty claims of students. The school authorities there established a substantial basis, (including expert testimony) to support their judgment that the sex poll threatened emotional upset and confusion among immature students.[94] In an apparent warning against judicial second-guessing of educators' opinions, the court stressed that judges are not to substitute

87. Katz v. McAuley, 438 F.2d 1058 (2d Cir. 1971), cert. denied, 405 U.S. 993 (1972). *Accord:* Hernandez v. Hanson, 430 F.Supp. 1154 (D.Neb. 1977).

88. Cintron v. St. Bd. of Education, 384 F.Supp. 674 (D.Puerto Rico 1974). The balance clearly tilts in favor of student activists in a college setting. *See* New Left Ed. Project v. Bd. of Regents, 326 F.Supp. 158 (W.D.Tex. 1970).

89. Peterson v. Bd. of Education, 370 F.Supp. 1208 (D.Neb. 1973).

90. *See* Jacobs v. Bd. of Commissioners, fn. 76.

91. Riseman v. Sch. Committee of Quincy, fn. 77. Zucker v. Panitz, 299 F.Supp. 102 (E.D.N.Y.1969).

92. *See* Gambino v. Fairfax City Sch. Bd., 429 F. Supp. 731, 734 (E.D.Va. 1977), aff'd. 564 F.2d 157 (4th Cir. 1977) and case authorities therein cited.

93. Bayer v. Kinzler, 343 F.Supp. 1164 (E.D.N.Y. 1974) aff'd. 515 F.2d 504 (2d Cir. 1975).

94. Kuhlmeier v. Hazlewood Sch. Distr. 578 F.Supp. 1286 (E.D.Mo. 1984); Trachtman v. Anker, 563 F.2d 512 (2d Cir. 1977) cert. denied, 435 U.S. 925 (1978); *cf.* Mercer v. Michigan State Bd. of Education, 379 F.Supp. 580, affd. 419 U.S. 1081 (1974).

their opinions for those of school authorities so long as those opinions are supported by substantial evidence. The 4th Circuit Court of Appeals later declined to follow the 2nd Circuit in a similar case involving school suppression of an article entitled "Sexually Active Students Fail to Use Contraception," which reported results of a student-conducted poll. The trial court had declined to invalidate the school newspaper regulations, but found that the authorities failed to justify their application of the regulation. The 4th Circuit summarily affirmed that decision.[95] Although the two circuit cases are distinguishable in terms of evidence presented, the opinions in these cases reveal a fundamental conflict of views on what is censorable content. The Virginia court evinces a radically lower regard for arguments concerning the captive audience, parental and community opinion: " . . . the material is not suppressible by reason of its objectionability to the sensibilities of the School Board *or its constituents.*"[96] (Emphasis supplied.)

To be distinguished from school control of student newspapers is the issue of school control of school-sponsored plays. A lead case (involving the play *Pippin*) viewed the presentation of a school play as more akin to curriculum control, and upheld the schools authorities' decision to cancel the play's production, over the students' objections, because of its sexual content and sexually explicit scenes.[97]

Censorship of vulgarity and indecent speech in high school publications has not been extensively litigated. While some cases upheld student punishment for use of vulgar and profane language, at least one court indicated that language must be more than offensive and must threaten disorder, before it can be censored.[98] The college press cases are much more tolerant of indecent speech in state university publications, but their application to public schools is doubtful.[99]

Obscenity, as distinguished from offensive or vulgar speech, is not entitled to First Amendment protection. For more than 20 years, the United States Supreme Court struggled unsuccessfully to satisfactorily define the elusive concept of obscenity. It has recognized variable definitions of obscenity for adults and minors and between panderers and serious publishers. At present, the standard of obscenity for minors poses a fact question. It must be determined by a jury applying contemporary local community standards (1) whether or not, to the average person, a literary work taken as a whole appeals to the prurient interest of minors in a patently offensive way, by reference to specific sexual conduct; *and* (2) whether the work lacks serious literary, artistic, political, or scientific value.[100] (The tortuous language of the preceding sentence is not the author's, and is required to fit the cases.) The Supreme Court has not had occasion to apply its latest obscenity standards to student publications, and it is doubtful whether adolescent students, no less educated adults, can be clearly advised of its operation in the

95. Gambino v. Fairfax Cty. Sch. Bd., fn. 92.

96. 429 F.Supp. at 736.

97. Seyfried v. Walton, 668 F.2d 214 (3d Cir. 1981). See Addendum on p. 662.

98. *See* Graham v. Houston Ind. Sch. District; Scoville v. Bd. of Education, fn. 86.

99. *See* Nicholson v. Bd. of Education, 682 F.2d 858 (9th Cir. 1982); Papish v. Bd. of Curators, U. of Mo., 410 U.S. 667 (1973).

100. *See* Miller v. California, 413 U.S. 15 (1973) (adult standard); Ginsberg v. New York, 390 U.S. 629 (1968) (standard for minors).

"captive audience" school context.[101] For these reasons, administrators and courts may prefer to consider titillating sexual material in terms of psychological harm to students, rather than abstract definitions of "obscenity."

Similar conceptual difficulties attend censorship of libelous (defamatory) content in student literature. Libel is censorable, but difficult to define. Further, the constitutional defenses created by the Supreme Court to protect freedom of the press limit official control, even of defamatory material. In the case of "public officials" or "public figures" punishment for libel is limited to false statements that are intentionally or recklessly made.[102] In 1984 the Supreme Court added a further unique point of libel law, namely, that appellate judges must find in their own independent judgment that the evidence shows malice, "with convincing clarity," a standard that is considerable higher than the usual norm of substantial and preponderant evidence. These new accretions of constitutional law, and even newer state "shield" statutes were not fashioned with an eye to student publications or to the special needs of the public school context. While their extension to public schools cannot be ruled out, their concern with monetary penalties and not with matters of school discipline may well render them inappropriate for student publications.

How these developments will affect the school setting is neither explained by courts nor realistically explainable to students. Like obscenity law, libel law may be modified for minors and specially tailored for student publications.[103]

As one court indicated, there is ground to wonder whether libel law should be modified and specially tailored to the public school context—and to distinguish higher education student publications from public school publication controls:

> "Plaintiff's final argument with respect to the libel implications of Exhibit "B" focuses upon John's position as vice-president of the student government. From this, plaintiffs argue that John was a "public figure" . . . and that since there is no suggestion of malice, there could be no libel. As important as an unrestrained press may be to the furtherance of our democratic government and society, the "public figure" exception to libel liability ought not to be extended to the level of a high school newspaper editor's comments about a fellow student. Significant here is the educational function, not only of the school newspaper, but also of the student government and every other activity carried on in the school. Part of the educational process is to learn in a protected environment where one's mistakes do not have damaging or irrevocable consequences. For the law to place a high school member of the student government organization in the same withering spotlight of the press as it does our publicly elected officials, would serve neither the policies of the First Amendment nor the democratic principles it seeks to further. Even if the *New York Times* v. *Sullivan* principle were to be applied here, thereby insulating the individual defendants, the school district, and the editorial staff from a possible damage judgment for publishing Exhibit "B", Andrews'

---

101. "This Court has recognized that the States have a legitimate interest in prohibiting dissemination or exhibition of obscene material when the mode of dissemination carries with it a significant danger of . . . exposure to juveniles." *See* Miller v. California, *supra* 413 U.S. at p. 418, 419. See generally Nichols, Vulgarity and Obscenity in the Student Press, 10 J. OF LAW & ED. 207 (1981).

102. *See* New York Times Co. v. Sullivan, 376 U.S. 254 (1964); *Tort Liability of a University for Libelous Material in a Student Publication,* 71 MICH. L. REV. 1061 (1973).

103. *See* Nicholson v. Bd. of Education, 682 F.2d 858, 863 (9th Cir. 1982) (justifications for libel controls).

suppression of the article under the circumstances that faced him on June 15, 1978, knowing the harm that would be done without any reasonable opportunity to mitigate or correct it if wrong, was a rational, reasonable decision made on the basis of substantial evidence before him at the time."[104]

Should the goals of training students in responsible journalism be deemed sufficiently weighty, courts may permit censorship of student press material that unfairly exposes others to defamation. Such a position would restore the policy of the common law of libel: to deter negligent as well as intentional falsehoods that tend to uphold a person to hatred, contempt, or ridicule, or cause him or her to be shunned.

Another question that remains to be settled is whether school authorities can ban any literature that does not identify the author or publisher. The right of anonymous publication has been constitutionally protected for public-street leafletting, but only one case has been found to indicate a similar right in the school setting, and that case is of questionable authority.[105]

d. Student Appearance. Student resistance to appearance regulations has centered on male hair regulations and on dress. Most of the challenges rely upon constitutional claim of freedom to determine one's appearance. To date, the United States Supreme Court has declined to address this issue, even though the Circuit Courts of Appeal remain divided on the question.

Hair Style. As of this writing, five of the federal Circuit Courts of Appeals (3rd, 5th, 6th, 9th, and 10th) have sustained the authority of public schools to regulate hair styles of male students (the 3rd and 5th Circuit Courts of Appeals reversed their prior rulings).[106] Four federal circuits (1st, 4th, 7th and 8th) have overturned such regulations.[107] The 4th Circuit recognized that schools may constitutionally limit student hair style in special circumstances (football players during the football season).[108] Significantly, all of the circuit courts refused to treat hair style as a form of symbolic speech, which would implicate the test of the Tinker case.[109] One lower court did rule that the

---

104. *See* Frasca v. Andrews, 463 F.Supp. 1043, 1052 (E.D.N.Y. 1977).

105. Talley v. California, 362 U.S. 60 (1960). See discussion of Jacobs v. Bd. of Sch. Commn'rs., fn. 76. Compare the Healey and Eisen cases, discussed at pp. 289–290, this text.

106. For a review of the law in various circuits, *see* Zeller v. Donagel Sch. District Bd. of Education, 517 F.2d 600 (3d Cir. 1975); rev'g Stull v. Sch. Bd. of Western Beaver Jr.-Sr. H.S., 459 F.2d 339 (3d Cir. 1972); Murray v. W. Baton Rouge Parish Sch. Bd., 472 F.2d 438, (5th Cir. 1973); Ferrel v. Dallas Ind. Sch. District, 392 F.2d 697 (6th Cir. 1968), cert. denied, 393 U.S. 856 (1968); Gfell v. Rickelman, 441 F.2d 444 (6th Cir. 1971); Olff v. East Side H.S. District, 445 F.2d 932 (9th Cir. 1971); Hatch v. Goerke, 502 F.2d 1189 (10th Cir. 1974); Freeman v. Flake, 448 F.2d 258 (10th Cir. 1971).

107. Richards v. Thurston, 424 F.2d 128 (1st Cir. 1970); Long v. Zopp, 476 F.2d 180 (4th Cir. 1973); Holsapple v. Woods, 500 F.2d 49 (7th Cir. 1974); Torvik v. Deborah Community Schools, 453 F.2d 779 (8th Cir. 1972).

108. *See* Long v. Zopp, prior fn. *But see* Dostert v. Berthold Pub. Sch. District No. 54, 391 F.Supp. 876 (D.N.D. 1975) (hair regulation overturned as not shown to be "necessary.)"

109. *See* Gfell v. Rickelman, fn. 106; Olff v. E. Side Un. H.S., *supra*; Richards v. Thursten, fn. 107; Hatch v. Goerke, fn. 106; Davis v. Ferment, 408 F.2d 1189 (5th Cir. 1968); New Rider v. Bd. of Education, 480 F.2d 693 (10th Cir. 1973) (Indian braided hair style not protected by First Amendment).

student's hair style was a symbolic expression to protest the Vietnam war, but that decision is contrary to the weight of authority.[110]

Three federal circuit courts have refused to recognize a sufficient liberty interest in hair style to entitle students to any hearing or right to challenge hair regulations.[111] Six other circuits recognized some student interest, but disagreed on its weight or on the reasonableness of school regulations as a constitutional means of assuring successful school operations.[112] Though divided on theory, the majority of the federal circuits that upheld school hair regulation expressed a common concern over judicial intrusion into educational administration and a "trivialization" of the Constitution.

Attempt to overturn hair regulations that are limited to boys on the claim of sex discrimination under a state equal rights amendment and under a federal civil rights statute have been rejected on findings that those laws did not apply to school hair standards.[113] However, hair regulations have been overturned in Alaska as violations of student rights under the Alaska state constitution and in Ohio and Oregon as not authorized by the school codes of these states.[114]

Dress Codes. School regulations of everyday attire raise a broader set of problems than those dealing with expressive symbols (arm band, flag patches, buttons) or with attire for special occasions (graduation, gym, field trips). Student interest in ordinary dress does not rank high among the forms of expression, but the very recognition of a constitutional interest implies limits upon the school authority to regulate student dress. Dress may always be regulated to protect student health, safety, and school discipline.[115] A minority of courts still reject the idea that students have any constitutional right in their choice of dress.[116] However, the majority cases recognize such a right, either as a general liberty interest or as a specific right of expression.[117] Accordingly, school regulations that abridge that right by being unduly vague or overbroad or by lacking any clear connection to disruption or interference with school operations will be overturned.[118] Courts have not always agreed on the justification for particular regulations. School bans on wearing of jeans by girls were upheld in Kentucky, but overturned in Idaho and New

---

110. Church v. Bd. of Education, 339 F.Supp, 538 (E.D. Mich. 1972). *Compare* New Rider v. Bd. of Education, 480 F.2d 693 (10th Cir. 1973), cert. denied, 414 U.S. 1097 (1974); Royer v. Bd. of Education, 365 N.E.2d 888 (Ohio 1977).

111. *See* Zeller and Freeman cases, fn. 106.

112. *See* Gfell v. Rickelman, and Olff v. E. Side Un. H.S., fn. 106.

113. Mercer v. Bd. of Trustees, N. Forest Independent Sch. District, 538 S.W.2d 201 (Tex. 1976) (state law); Trent v. Perritt, 391 F. Supp. 171 (S.D. Miss. 1975) (Federal statute).

114. Breese v. Smith, 502 P.2d 159 (Alaska 1972); Jacobs v. Benedict, 316 N.E.2d 898 (Ohio 1974); Neuhaus v. Federico, 505 P.2d 939 (Ore. 1972).

115. Stromberg v. French, 236 N.W.477 (N. Dak. 1931) (ban on steel plated shoes); Jones v. Day, 89 S. 906 (Miss. 1921) (school uniform requirement); Pugsley v. Sellmeyer, 250 S.W. 538 (Ark. 1923) (regulation barring cosmetics).

116. Press v. Pasadena Ind. Sch. District, 326 F.Supp. 550 (S.D. Tex. 1971); *see also* Dunkerson v. Russell, 502 S.W.2d (Kan. 1973).

117. Johnson v. Jt. Sch. District No. 60, 508 P.2d 547 (Idaho 1973); Wallace v. Ford, 346 F.Supp. 156 (E.D. Ark. 1972); Crossen v. Fatsi, 309 F.Supp. 114 (D. Conn. 1970); Miller v. Gillis, 315 F.Supp. 94 (N.D. Ill. 1969); Cott v. Bd. of Education, 305 N.Y.S.2d 601 (1969).

118. Crossen v. Fatsi, *supra* (vague); Bannister, 316 F.Supp. 185 (D.N.H. 1970); Wallace v. Ford, *supra.* (disruptive).

Hampshire.[119] In Arkansas,the wearing of tight skirts, pants, or short skirts (more than six inches above the knee) was found to be sufficiently immodest to justify prohibition.[120] The case variations may well reflect different community mores and diverse environments of the affected school district than any conflict in legal theory.

3. Rights of Privacy

a. Search and Seizure. The introduction of drugs and other contraband into high schools has increased the occasions for student search and for student claims of immunity from search without a warrant (court order) under the Fourth Amendment. This conflict between official interests and student privacy involves more than the abstract power to search.

To the extent that a student search by public school authorities violates student constitutional rights under the Fourth Amendment, it exposes the school authorities and the school district to possible civil liability under civil rights statutes,[121] as well as suppression of illegally seized evidence in any subsequent proceeding. While the legality of "searches" vis à vis "seizures" sometimes involves special considerations, the following discussions will not explore the unique elements of seizure law. The reason for the continuing confusion over the proper interpretation of the Fourth Amendment in the school context is evidence from the Amendment's own inconclusive language:

> "The right of the people to be secure in their persons, houses, papers, and effects, against unreasonable searches and seizures, shall not be violated, and no warrants shall issue, but upon probable cause, supported by oath or affirmation, and particularly describing the place to be searched, and the persons or things to be seized."

Lower courts have been severely divided on the operation of the Fourth Amendment in public schools, as is indicated by the following observation of the United States Supreme Court as of 1985:

"State and federal courts considering these questions have struggled to accommodate the interests protected by the Fourth Amendment and the interest of the States in providing a safe environment conducive to education in the public schools. Some courts have resolved the tension between these interests by giving full force to one or the other side of the balance. Thus, in a number of cases courts have held that school officials conducting in-school searches of students are private parties acting *in loco parentis* and are therefore not subject to the constraints of the Fourth Amendment. See, *e.g.*, *D.R.C.* v. *State,* 646 P.2d 252 (Alaska App. 1982); *In re* G., 11 Cal. App. 3d 1193, 90 Cal. Rptr. 361 (1970); *In re Donaldson,* 269 Cal. App. 2d 509, 75 Cal. Rptr. 220 (1969); R.C.M.

---

119. *Compare* Dunkerson v. Russell, 502 S.W.2d 64 (Ky. 1973): *with* Murphy v. Pocatello Sch. District, 480 P.2d 878 (Idaho 1971); Bannister v. Paradis, 316 F. Supp. 185. (D.N.H. 1970).

120. Wallace v. Ford, fn. 117. *See also* Graber v. Kniola, 216 N.W.2d 925 (Mich. 1974) (re bikinis). *See also* Fowler v. Williams, 251, S.E.2d 889 (N.Car. 1979) (dress pants required for graduation ceremonies—upheld).

121. Picha v. Wiedgos, 410 F.Supp. 1214 (N.D.Ill. 1976); *contra,* M. v. Bd. of Education, 429 F.Supp. 288 (S.D.Ill. 1977).

v. State, 660 S. W. 2d 552 (Tex. App. 1983); *Mercer* v. *State,* 450 S. W. 2d 715 (Tex. Civ. App. 1970). At least one court has held, on the other hand, that the Fourth Amendment applies in full to in-school searches by school officials and that a search conducted without probable cause is unreasonable, see *State* v. *Mora,* 307 So. 2d 317 (La.), vacated, 423 U.S. 809 (1975), on remand, 330 So. 2d 900 (La. 1976); others have held or suggested that the probable-cause standard is applicable at least where the police are involved in a search, see M. v. *Board of Ed. Ball-Chatham Community Unit School Dist. No. 5,* 429 F. Supp. 288, 292 (SD Ill. 1977); *Picha* v. *Wilgos,* 410 F. Supp. 1214, 1219–1221 (ND Ill. 1976); *State* v. *Young,* 234 Ga. 488, 498, 216 S. E. 2d 586, 594 (1975); or where the search is highly intrusive, see M. M. v. *Anker,* 607 F. 2d 588, 589 (CA2 1979).

"The majority of courts that have addressed the issue of the Fourth Amendment in the schools have, like the Supreme Court of New Jersey in this case, reached a middle position: the Fourth Amendment applies to searches conducted by school authorities, but the special needs of the school environment require assessment of the legality of such searches against a standard less exacting than that of probable cause. These courts have, by and large, upheld warrantless searches by school authorities provided that they are supported by a reasonable suspicion that the search will uncover evidence of an infraction of school disciplinary rules or a violation of the law. See, *e.g., Tarter* v. *Raybuck,* No. 83–3174 (CA6, Aug. 31, 1984); *Bilbrey* v. *Brown,* 738 F.2d 1462 (CA9 1984); *Horton* v. *Goose Creek Independent School Dist.,* 690 F.2d 470 (CA5 1982); *Bellnier* v. *Lund,* 438 F.Supp. 47 (NDNY 1977); M. v. *Board of Ed. Ball-Chatham Community Unit School Dist. No. 5, supra; In re W.,* 29 Cal. App. 3d 777, 105 Cal. Rptr. 775 (1973); *State* v. *Baccino* 282 A.2d 869 (Del. Super. 1971); *State* v. *D.T.W.,* 425 So. 2d 1383 (Fla. Dist. Ct. App. 1983); *State* v. *Young, supra; In re* J.A., 85 Ill. App.3d 567, 406 N.E.2d 958 (1980); *People* v. *Ward,* 62 Mich. App. 46, 233 N.W.2d 180 (1975); *Doe* v. *State,* 88 N.M. 827, 540 P.2d 827 (App. 1975); *People* v. *D.,* 34 N.Y.2d 483, 358 N.Y.S.2d 403, 315 N.E.2d 466 (1974); *State* v. *McKinnon,* 88 Wash.2d 75, 558 P. 2d 781 (1977); *In re L.L.,* 90 wis. 2d 585, 280 N.W.2d 343 (App. 1979).

Although few have considered the matter, courts have also split over whether the exclusionary rule is an appropriate remedy for Fourth Amendment violations committed by school authorities. The Georgia courts have held that although the Fourth Amendment applies to the schools, the exclusionary rule does not. See, *e.g., State v. Young, supra; State* v. *Lamb,* 137 Ga. App. 437, 224 S. E. 2d 51 (1976). Other jurisdictions have applied the rule to exclude the fruits of unlawful school searches from criminal trials and delinquency proceedings. See *State* v. *Mora, supra; People* v. *D., supra.*"[122]

As recently as November 1984, the courts of California were still continuing to refine their rulings on student searches; for example, by holding that the Fourth Amendment would apply to exclude evidence from illegal student searches in criminal or juvenile delinquency prosecutions, but not in school disciplinary proceedings.[123]

---

122. *See* New Jersey v. T.L.O. 469 U.S. ________, 105 S.Ct. 733 (1985). *See also* Comm. v. Dingfelt, 323 A. 2d 145 (Pa. 1974); State in Interest of G.C., 296 A.2d 102 (N.J. 1972); Kenney v. Rodgers, 316 F.Supp. 217 (D.Me. 1970); Annot: *Searches by School Officials—Validity,* 49 A.L.R.3d 978 (1973).

123. *E.g.,* Gordon J. v. Santa Ana Un. Sch. Dist., 208 Cal. Rptr. 657 (1984). *Accord:* Bellnier v. Lund, 438 F.Supp. 437 (N.D.N.Y. 1977); Morale v. Grigel, 422 F.Supp. 988 (D.N.H. 1976).

The foregoing conflicts and variations were partially but not totally resolved by the United States Supreme Court in *New Jersey* v. *T.L.O.*,[124] which is excerpted at the end of this chapter. There, the Court affirmed the majority view of lower courts, that the Fourth Amendment provides some constitutional protection of student privacy in public school searches of the student's person or personal effects. However, the Court declined to comment on the question whether the Amendment also applied to cover school searches of lockers, desks, or other school property for the storage of school supplies,[125] or whether a different Fourth Amendment standard would apply to searches undertaken by school authorities jointly with, or at the request of, law enforcement officials.[126] Equally significant is the Court's refusal to decide whether, assuming an unconstitutional search had taken place, the evidence produced by the search would be subject to the "exclusionary rule" whereby illegally seized evidence could not be introduced in proceedings against the student:

> "In holding that the search of T.L.O.'s purse did not violate the Fourth Amendment, we do not implicitly determine that the exclusionary rule applies to the fruits of unlawful searches conducted by school authorities. The question whether evidence should be excluded from a criminal proceeding involves two discrete inquiries: whether the evidence was seized in violation of the Fourth Amendment, and whether the exclusionary rule is the appropriate

---

124. 469 U.S. ________, 105 S.Ct. 733 (1985).

125. "We do not address the question, not presented by this case, whether a schoolchild has a legitimate expectation of privacy in lockers, desks, or other school property provided for the storage of school supplies. Nor do we express any opinion on the standards (if any) governing searches of such areas by school officials or by other public authorities acting at the request of school officials. Compare *Zamora* v. *Pomeroy*, 639 F.2d 662, 670 (CA10 1981) ("Inasmuch as the school had assumed joint control of the locker it cannot be successfully maintained that the school did not have a right to inspect it."), and *People* v. *Overton*, 24 N.Y.2d 522, 249 N.E.2d 366 (1969) (school administrators have power to consent to search of a student's locker), with *State* v. *Engerud*, 94 N.J. 331, 348, 463 A.2d 934, 943 (1983) ("We are satisfied that in the context of this case the student had an expectation of privacy in the contents of his locker. . . . For the four years of high school, the school locker is a home away from home. In it the student stores the kind of personal 'effects' protected by the Fourth Amendment")." *Id.* In accord with Overton, *see also* State v. Stein, 456 P.2d 1 (Kan. 1969); Moore v. Student Affairs Comm., 284 F.Supp. 725 (M.D.Ala. 1968)

126. "We here consider only searches carried out by school authorities acting alone and on their own authority. This case does not present the question of the appropriate standard for assessing the legality of searches conducted by school officials in conjunction with or at the behest of law enforcement agencies, and we express no opinion on that question. Cf. *Picha* v. *Wilgos*, 410 F.Supp. 1214, 1219–1221 (ND Ill. 1976) (holding probable cause standard applicable to searches involving the police).

"We do not decide whether individualized suspicion is an essential element of the reasonableness standard we adopt for searches by school authorities. In other contexts, however, we have held that although 'some quantum of individualized suspicion is usually a prerequisite to a constitutional search or seizure[, . . . the Fourth Amendment imposes no irreducible requirement of such suspicion.' *United States* v. *Martinez-Fuerte*, 428 U.S. 543, 560–561 (1976). See also *Camara* v. *Municipal Court*, 387 U.S. 523 (1967). Exceptions to the requirement of individualized suspicion are generally appropriate only where the privacy interests implicated by a search are minimal and where "other safeguards" are available 'to assure that the individual's reasonable expectation of privacy is not 'subject to the discretion of the official in the field.'" *Delaware* v. *Prouse*, 440 U.S. 648, 654–655 (1979) (citation omitted). Because the search of T.L.O.'s purse was based upon an individualized suspicion that she had violated school rules, see *infra*, at 16–20, we need not consider the circumstances that might justify school authorities in conducting searches unsupported by individualized suspicion." New Jersey v. T.L.O., supra.

The above dicta skirts the question whether searches by school security officers are subject to stricter rules than teacher searches. *Compare, e.g.*, People v. Bowers, 356 N.Y.S.2d 432 (1974) (requiring "probable cause" for search by school security officer), *with* Keene v. Rodgers, 316 F.Supp. 217 (D.Me. 1970), which rejected that view.

> remedy for the violation. Neither question is logically antecedent to the other, for a negative answer to either question is sufficient to dispose of the case. Thus, our determination that the search at issue in this case did not violate the Fourth Amendment implies no particular resolution of the question of the applicability of the exclusionary rule."[127]

It is thus evident that the *T.L.O.* case is as important for the points that it raised without resolving as it is for the fundamental questions that it did settle. Briefly, the Court ruled, that, to be constitutional, searches of students' persons and effects must be based upon "reasonable suspicion" of illegal activity *or* a violation of school rules. In so ruling, the Supreme Court affirmed the majority view of the lower courts that the constitutional standard for a valid search is "reasonable suspicion" and not "probable cause," which would require a much higher degree of proof of actual threatened illegal activity. The *T.L.O.* ruling went further than the lower courts, however, in holding that school authorities could constitutionally search not only for reasonable suspicion of illegal activity, but also for reasonable suspicion of violation of school rules that do not implicate illegal or criminal activity. As to the latter ruling, the majority of Justices made clear that the constitutionality of a search did not depend on the importance of the school rule and that courts should not substitute their judgment as to the importance or wisdom of such rules:

> "Our reference to the nature of the infraction is not intended as an endorsement of JUSTICE STEVENS' suggestion that some rules regarding student conduct are by nature too "trivial" to justify a search based upon reasonable suspicion. See *post,* at 7–12. We are unwilling to adopt a standard under which the legality of a search is dependent upon a judge's evaluation of the relative importance of various school rules. The maintenance of discipline in the schools requires not only that students be restrained from assaulting one another, abusing drugs and alcohol, and committing other crimes, but also that students conform themselves to the standards of conduct prescribed by school authorities. . . .
>
> "The promulgation of a rule forbidding specified conduct presumably reflects a judgment on the part of school officials that such conduct is destructive of school order or of a proper educational environment. Absent any suggestion that the rule violates some substantive constitutional guarantee, the courts should, as a general matter, defer to that judgment and refrain from attempting to distinguish between rules that are important to the preservation of order in the schools and rules that are not."[128]

The *T.L.O.* decision in setting a Fourth Amendment standard for searches by school authorities of students' persons and personal effects expressly noted that states are still free to impose stricter search requirements under their own statutes and constitutions.[129] It clearly refutes the view espoused by some courts and by some academic commentators that courts should require a high level of proof of justification for school searches and should substitute their independent judgment for the discretion of the

---

127. New Jersey v. T.L.O., *supra.*

128. 105 S.Ct. at 744, n. 9.

129. Of course, New Jersey may insist on a more demanding standard under its own Constitution or statutes. In that case, its courts would not purport to be applying the Fourth Amendment when they invalidate a search. *Id.* at 745, no. 10.

school authorities in the maintenance of school discipline, at least as far as student searches are concerned. To that degree, *T.L.O.* would appear to support decisions that have held the following grounds to justify a search: (1) information from student informers, (2) police tips, (3) anonymous callers, (4) unusual conduct by the searched student (secretive movements), (5) fleeing an instructor when called, and (6) tips from outside callers and personnel.[130]

Inasmuch as the court in *T.L.O.* declined to comment upon the operation of the "exclusionary rule" in public schools or upon potential variations in constitutional standards for student locker searches or for searches conducted in collaboration with police authorities, the various views taken by the different state jurisdictions and federal circuits, as cited above, remain in effect in those jurisdictions.

The scope of student personal searches is still constitutionally confined in two respects. First, the *zone* of the search cannot reasonably intrude into areas not indicated by reasonable suspicion as containing evidence of violations of law or of school rules. As *T.L.O.* decided, however, the lawful zone of an original search may be expanded by discovery of evidence causing further reasonable suspicion that still new areas may contain evidence of such violations. Second, while the Supreme Court has not addressed the issue, the lower courts have uniformly required higher quanta of proof to meet the "reasonable suspicion" test for highly intrusive searches of the student's body. Thus, strip searches—even by faculty members of the same sex—are so potentially embarrassing and injurious to the student that they should not be undertaken without the clearest evidence of serious need for such a search. The cases evoking the greatest judicial sympathy to student damage suits for illegal searches have involved strip searches.[131] The heightened constitutional protection heretofore extended to searches that closely impinged upon the person of a student is evident in the recent Fifth Circuit Court of Appeals ruling that followed two other Circuit Courts in holding that exploratory dog sniffs of student lockers and cars do not constitute a "search" under the Fourth Amendment,[132] but that such sniffs in close proximity of a student's body indicate such a degree of personal intrusiveness as to constitute a "search."[133]

The Court further ruled that canine sniffing of a student's person, in close proximity, would not be "reasonable" in the absence of facts to support an "individual-

---

130. (1) *E.g.*, M. v. Board of Education, 425 F.Supp. 288 (S.D.Ill. 1977); *In re* W, 105 Cal. Rptr. 775 (1973); In re Donaldson, 75 Cal. Rptr. 220 (1969); Cmwlth v. Dingfelt, 323 A.2d 145 (Pa. 1974); (2) State v. McKinnon, 558 P.2d 781 (Wash. 1977); (3) In re State in Interest of G.C., 296 A.2d 102 (N.J. 1972); (4) Doe v. State, 540 P.2d 827 (N. Mex. 1975), Ranninger v. State, 460 S.W.2d 181 (Tex. 1970); *but see* Waters v. United States, 311 A.2d 835 (D.C. Cir. 1973); (5) People v. Jackson, 319 N.Y.S.2d 731 (1971); (6) People v. Ward, 233 N.W.2d 180 (Mich. 1975). Not every unusual or secretive action by a student will give rise to a "reasonable suspicion." *Cf.* People v. D., 315 N.E.2d 466 (N.Y. 1974); State v. Mora, 330 So.2d 900 (La. 1976).

131. *See* M.M. v. Anker, 607 F.2d 588 (2d Cir. 1979); Doe v. Renfrow, 475 F.Supp. 1012 (N.D.Ind. 1979); Picha v. Widgos, *supra*; Potts v. Wright, 357 F.Supp. 215 (E.D. Pa. 1973); *cf.* Bellnier v. Lund, 438 F.Supp. 47 (N.D.N.Y. 1977).

132. *See* Horton v. Goose Creek Independent Sch. Dist., 690 F.2d 470, 475–77 (5th Cir. 1982); Zamora v. Pomeroy, 639 F.2d 662 (10th Cir. 1981); Doe v. Renfrow, 631 F.2d 91 (7th Cir. 1980). *Accord:* People v. Mayberry, 644 P.2d 810 (Cal. 1982); State v. Morrow, 625 P.2d 898 (Ariz. 1981); State v. Wolohan, 598 P.2d 421 (Wash. 1979).

133. *See* Horton v. Goose Creek Independent Sch. Dist., *supra*, 690 F.2d at p. 479.

ized" suspicion of the sniffed student.[134] It is clear, therefore, that strip or personal sniff searches of the foregoing type call for a different balancing of school and student privacy interests in determining what is "reasonable."

There are several well-recognized exceptions to the constitutional requirement that a search or seizure without a warrant be based upon "reasonable suspicion": (1) searches to which a student knowingly and voluntarily consents, (2) seizure of contraband material that is in "plain view" of the searcher, (3) emergency searches to preserve school property or personal safety, (4) searches by police authorities that are incident to the lawful arrest of the student, (5) searches of lost property undertaken to ascertain its lawful owner and to make record thereof.[135] An additional exception involves searches classified as "administrative" and not as "investigatory" has been recognized in some jurisdictions, but not in others.[136]

These exceptions obviously give rise to fact issues that may later be disputed between the student and the searching authority. For example, the "consent" defense may be challenged by claims that the student's consent was coerced or pressured, or was given without full appreciation of its import or of the full scope of the ensuing search.[137] Nor have courts developed clear guidelines to differentiate between administrative searches routinely undertaken to inspect and preserve school property, on one hand, and investigatory searches—an issue that the Supreme Court in the *T.L.O.* case indirectly noted, without clarifying comment.[138]

As the Supreme Court noted in *T.L.O.*, the Fourth Amendment does not prevent the imposition of stricter search requirements under the constitutions or statutes of individual states, but the cases decided to date indicate that only a small minority of states have imposed greater restrictions on official searches under state law than are imposed by the Constitution.[139]

b. Married and Pregnant Students. Public school rules and regulations intended to discourage teenage marriage and pregnancy by denying such students admission to regular school studies or to extracurricular activities have come under increasing constitutional attack. Although there is no constitutional right to public education, nor

---

134. *Id.* at pp. 481–82. The later Supreme Court decision in *T.L.O.* avoided any ruling on the question whether "individualized suspicion" of a searched student would be required in any or all circumstances. See fn. 126, supra.

135. (1) Consent: *See, e.g.,* Jones v. Latexo Ind. Sch. Dist., 449 F.Supp. 223, 236–37 (E.D. Tex. 1980); Carter v. Raybuck, 742 F.2d 977 (6th Cir. 1984); State v. Stein, 456 P.2d 1 (Kans. 1969). (2) "*Plain view*" *exception*: State v. D.T.W., 425 So.2d 1383 (Fla. 1983); semble: Speake v. Grantham, 440 F.2d 1351 (4th Cir. 1971); People v. Lanthier, 488 P.2d 625 (Cal. 1971) (plain view exposure following emergency search). (3) *cf.* People v. Lanthier, *supra.* (4) *Police search incident to arrest*: State v. Kimball, 503 P.2d 176 (Haw. 1972) (student loitering on school grounds); *cf.* United States v. Robinson, 414 U.S. 218 (1973). (5) *Identification or preservation of lost property*: State v. Johnson, 530 P.2d 911 (Ariz. 1975) (lost purse of junior college student). Cf. Illinois v. Lafayette, 462 U.S. 640 (1983) (upholding warrantless inventory search by police).

136. The authorities are divided on the exceptional classification for administrative searches. *Compare* In re C, 102 Cal. Rptr. 682 (1972) (personal search); *In re* Donaldson, 75 Cal. Rptr. 220 (1969) (locker search); *with* Picha v. Wiegos, 410 F. Supp. 1214 (N.D. Ill. 1976); People v. Bowers, 356 N.Y.S.2d 432 (1974). See Annot: *Searches by School Officials—Validity, 49 A.L.R.3d 978 (1973) for other case authorities).*

137. See fn. 135 (1) *supra.*

138. See fn. 125, *supra.*

139. See fn. 129, *supra.*

to extracurricular activities, the government may not impose unconstitutional conditions on student participation or penalize the exercise of constitutional rights. The right to marry and to beget children is granted under the due process clause and the right to be free from discriminatory classifications is granted under the equal protection clause. The state must, therefore, justify disqualifying conditions by proving that educational need requires such conditions. These principles have a stricter application where the penalty for marriage or pregnancy is exclusion from school than where it is only exclusion from extracurricular activities.[140]

Most modern cases hold that schools may not exclude students solely on the basis of their marriage or pregnancy unless the school proves at an adversary hearing that the student's moral deficiency is so great as to taint the education of other students or that the exclusion is necessary for the health and safety of the pregnant student.[141] Similar results have been achieved under state law (findings that suspension of a married couple was an abuse of discretion and that their presence in school did not adversely affect other students).[142]

Prior to 1970, several state courts upheld school rules that barred married students from extracurricular activities.[143] But the courts have since consistently invalidated such regulations as violations of substantive due process rights, or of equal protection, or both.[144] The fact that marriage involves greater outside responsibilities and reduction of available time for studies has not been considered sufficient to satisfy the constitutional standard. Nor has the statistically unproven argument that teenage marriages induce early dropouts.[145]

Finally the HEW regulations on sex discrimination under Title IX of the Federal Education Amendments of 1972 forbid any school recipient of federal funds from discriminating against any student in any school program on the basis of pregnancy-related conditions, unless the student requests leave or excusal.[146] The federal regulations do not preclude school rules that are required for student welfare, but they clearly restrict the school's discretion to cases of demonstrable necessity.

c. Student Records. Claims of privacy in school records rest almost exclusively upon nonconstitutional grounds. Emerging concepts of constitutional privacy have not

---

140. *See* Indiana H.S. Athletic Assn. v. Raike, 329 N.E.2d 66 (Ind. 1975) for a good survey of the modern cases in this area.

141. *Cases involving unwed mothers*: Shull v. Columbus Mun. Separate Sch. District, 338 F.Supp. 1376 (N.D. Miss. 1972); Ordway v. Hargraves, 323 F.Supp. 1155 (D. Mass. 1971); Alvin Ind. Sch. District v. Cooper, 404 S.W. 2d 76 (Tex. 1966). *Compare* State ex rel. Idle v. Chamberlain, 175 N.E.2d 539 (Ohio 1961) (exclusion of pregnant student for safety of student without loss of school assignments).

142. Carrollton-Farmers Branch Independent Sch. Dist. v. Knight, 418 S.W.2d 535 (Tex. 1967); Bd. of Education v. Bentley, 383 S.W. 2d 677 (Ky. 1964); *contra*: State ex rel. Thompson v. Marien City Bd. of Education, 302 S.W.2d 57 (Tenn. 1957).

143. *E.g.*, Estay v. LaFourche Parish Sch. Bd., 230 So.2d 443 (La. 1969); Bd. of Directors of Ind. Sch. District v. Green, 147 N.W.2d 854 (Iowa 1967); Starkey v. Bd. of Education, 381 P.2d 718 (Utah 1963).

144. Beeson v. Kiowa City Sch. District, 567 P.2d 801 (Colo. 1977); Bell v. Lone Oak Independent Sch. Dist., 507 S.W.2d 636 (Tex. 1974); Holt v. Shelton, 341 F.Supp. 821 (M.D. Tenn. 1972); Davis v. Meek, 344 F.Supp. 298 (N.D. Ohio 1972).

145. *See* Bell v. Lone Oak Ind. Sch. Dist., *supra.*

146. See 45 C.F.R. § 83.37.

been extended to student records, but future developments may evolve to in constitutional rights, particularly on sensitive information. Claims to right sure of student records were recently discounted by a federal court:

> "Virtually every governmental action interferes with personal privacy to some degree." *Katz* v. *United States,* 389 U.S. at 350 n.5, 88 S.Ct. at 510 n.5. Courts called upon to balance virtually every government action against the corresponding intrusion on individual privacy may be able to give all privacy interests only cursory protection. . . .
>
> "Inferring very broad 'constitutional' rights where the Constitution itself does not express them is an activity not appropriate to the judiciary. . . .
>
> "For all of the foregoing reasons we conclude that the Constitution does not encompass a general right to nondisclosure of private information. We agree with those courts that have restricted the right of privacy to its boundaries as established in *Paul* v. *Davis, supra,* and *Roe* v. *Wade,* 410 U.S. at 152, 93 S.Ct. at 726—those personal rights that can be deemed 'fundamental' or 'implicit in the concept of ordered liberty' . . . ('rights under the ninth amendment are only those 'so basic and fundamental and so deeprooted in our society' to be truly 'essential rights,' and which nevertheless, cannot find direct support elsewhere in the Constitution'). . . .
>
> The interest asserted by appellant class in nondisclosure of juvenile court records, like the interest in nondisclosure at issue in *Paul* v. *Davis,* is 'far afield' from those privacy rights that are 'fundamental' or 'implicit in the concept of ordered liberty.' . . .
>
> "Our opinion does not mean that we attach little significance to the right of privacy, or that there is no constitutional right to nondisclosure of private information. . . .
>
> "Our opinion simply holds that not all rights of privacy or interests in nondisclosure of private information are of constitutional dimension, so as to require balancing government action against individual privacy."[147]

The law on management and control of student records has developed piecemeal and is still uncoordinated and incomplete. State public records statutes seek to assure records access by officials and citizens to promote public knowledge and accountability of government functions. Student records statutes seek to restrict public access in the interest of protecting the privacy and reputations of students and their families. These statutes must be applied consistently with each other, but as shown in Table 6–1, there is no prevailing pattern among the statutes of the sister states. A leading case authority has refused to take an either-or approach to classifying student records as private or public in nature. It adopted the common law test that the right of access to a student's records applies only to persons with a "sufficient interest" to the particular information being sought.[148] Thus, in the absence of specific legislative rules, courts must decide who has a sufficient interest in each case.

---

147. *See* J.P. v. DeSanti, 653 F.2d 1080, 1090–1091 (6th Cir. 1981)

148. Van Allen v. McCleary, 211 N.Y.S.2d 501 (1961) (parent entitled to inspect child's records); *cf.* Young v. Armstrong Sch. District, 344 A.2d 738 (Pa. 1975) (citizen held entitled to copy names and addresses of school parents to petition them regarding district proposal on school session changes); Hendricks v. Bd. of Trustees, 525 S.W.2d 930 (Tex. 1975) (taxpayer entitled to reproduce at his cost voluminous financial records of school district). *See generally* Butler, Moran, and Vanderpool, Legal Aspects of Student Records (1972), which, however, does not cover the later 1974 federal records act hereafter discussed.

TABLE 6-1. Summary of state laws on pupil records *

STATES	ACCESS TO RECORDS							PERMANENCE OF RECORDS				
	DISCRETION OF:											
	Local School	Parent	Student	All Interested Persons	Professional Staff	Law Enforcement Agency	Confiden-tiality Provision	Mandatory Up Dating	Provisions for Correction	Copy of Records Transfered	Files Destroyed	Kept Indefinitely
ALABAMA								X		X		X
ALASKA	X				X			X		X		X
ARIZONA												
ARKANSAS												
CALIFORNIA		A	AX		X	X	X		X	X		X
COLORADO	X		A			X	X					
CONNECTICUT			A									
DELAWARE			A		X		X			X		
FLORIDA										X		
GEORGIA												
HAWAII	X	X					X			X	X	
IDAHO			A		X			X				
ILLINOIS		X	X		X		X					
INDIANA			A						X			
IOWA	X				X		X			X		
KANSAS										X		
KENTUCKY					X		X			X		
LOUISIANA												
MAINE		AX	AX		X		X	X		X		
MARYLAND			A				X				X	
MASSACHUSETTS			A									
MICHIGAN		X	X				X					
MINNESOTA			A						X		X	
MISSISSIPPI												
MISSOURI				X							X	
MONTANA												
NEBRASKA		A	A		X			X			X	
NEVADA												
NEW HAMPSHIRE												
NEW JERSEY					X	X	X					
NEW MEXICO	X	A	A		X		X					
NEW YORK		A	AX				X		X		X	
NORTH CAROLINA			X			X						
NORTH DAKOTA							X					
OHIO		A	A									
OKLAHOMA		A	A									
OREGON		AX	AX		X		X			X		
PENNSLYVANIA		X	X				X		X		X	
RHODE ISLAND												
SOUTH CAROLINA								X		X		
SOUTH DAKOTA												
TENNESSEE		X	X									
TEXAS		X	X									
UTAH							X					
VERMONT												
VIRGINIA		A	A		X			X			X	X
WASHINGTON		A										X
WEST VIRGINIA												
WISCONSIN				X							X	
WYOMING		A	A									

SOURCE: National Institute of Education

*All data tables must be updated for possible changes in each state since 1979.

TABLE 6-1. Summary of state laws on pupil records (*cont.*)

STATUTE	REGULATION	CONTENTS OF RECORDS					CUSTODIAN OF RECORDS	
		Biographical	Attendance	Testing	Health	Local Discretion	District Officer	Local School
S	R	X	X			X		
	R	X	X		X	X		
S	R	X	X			X		X
S				X	X		X	
S								
	R	X						X
	R							X
S			X					X
	R						X	X
	R							X
	R	X	X	X				
S								
S	R					X		X
S		X	X					X
S		X	X	X	X		X	X
S	R	X						
S	R		X					X
	R							
S								
	R		X			X	X	
S			X	X	X			
S						X	X	
	R						X	X
S	R		X		X		X	X
	R	X				X		X
	R	X	X			X		
S	R					X		
	R	X	X					X
S	R							X
S		X	X					
	R	X	X	X	X	X		
S		X	X	X	X		X	
	R							
S	R							X
S		X	X	X	X			
	R	X	X				X	X
	R		X					
S	R							
	R							
	R	X	X	X	X	X		
	R	X	X	X	X	X		X
S		X	X	X				X
S			X					
S								
S			X					

Many elements of state records law have been displaced, indeed nationalized, by congressional legislation known as the Family Educational Rights and Privacy Act of 1974 (hereafter called *FERPA*) and by federal regulations thereunder.[149] Noncompliance with that act would forfeit most federal education aid. Hence state legislatures, courts, and public schools may be expected to fit their laws and practices to the federal requirements. FERPA regulates methods of record administration, not content, and merely imposes *minimum* requirements. It does not, therefore, prevent individual states from adopting more rigorous rules on student records.[150] The act generally governs "educational records" (any record "directly related to a student" who is or was actually admitted to the school, except for certain records of law enforcement agencies, treating physicians, and other professionals).[151] Its principal themes are to guarantee access to records by the covered student or eligible parent or guardian and to prevent disclosure of personal information without their consent, subject again to very limited exceptions specified in the law.[152]

In brief, the federal law creates a right in "eligible students" (over 18 years of age) and in parents of ineligible students to see, inspect, reproduce, and challenge the accuracy of their educational records;[153] and a right to control disclosure of personally identifiable record information to nonprivileged parties, by requiring advance written authorization by such student or parent for each release of record information.[154] Written waiver of access to such records by the affected student or parent is permitted by the law, but schools are prohibited from demanding any waiver. Further, waivers of access given by parents may be revoked by their student ward when the student reaches the age of 18.

The federal restriction on disclosure (written or oral) of record information is confined to "personally identifiable" information (that which "includes any reference that would make the reader . . . reasonably certain of the identity of the student").[155] The release of statistical nonpersonal data from student records as now permitted or required by state law remains largely unaffected by the federal Act.[156] The federal law permits disclosure without student or parental consent of even personally identifiable

---

149. 20 U.S.C. § 1232(g); 45 Code of Federal Regulations Part 99 (1976). For an excellent summary of the law, *see Student Records, 22 Inequality in Education* (Center for Law and Education, Cambridge, Mass. 02138 (1977)).

150. *See, e.g., Regulations Pertaining to Student Records,* promulgated by Massachusetts State Board of Education.

151. The federal definition of educational records does not include records of applicants who never attended the school, personal teacher notes that are not filed or discussed with others, records of treating physicians, or certain law enforcement agency records.

152. Exceptions from student access include the financial records or data of their parents, doctor's records, and information on which they validly waived the right of access.

153. Expungement of student records under state law usually required formal court proceeding. *Cf.* Stewart v. Reng, 321 F.Supp. 618 (D. Ark. 1970); Sims v. Colfax Community Sch. Dist., 307 F. Supp. 485 (D. Iowa 1970); Howard v. Clark, 299 N.Y.S.2d 65 (1965). Federal law provides for administrative hearings and simplifies the process.

154. Each authorization for release and waiver of access must be specific as to content, recipient, and purpose of the authorization or waiver. Each disclosure is subject to the same requirements.

155. See 45 C.F.R. Part 99 (1976).

156. Many state statutes entitle interested citizens to nonpersonal statistical information. *See* Pooler v. Nyquist, 392 N.Y.S.2d 948 (1976) (consumer agency entitled to school statistics on dropout rates); Young v. Armstrong Sch. District, fn. 148; Citizens for Better Education v. Bd. of Education, 308 A.2d 35 (N.J. 1973) (civic association entitled to standardized test results).

records to specified parties who have legitimate educational and governmental interests in requested data (such as members of a school board).[157]

The federal law does not address, and leaves state law intact on, many incidents of record administration, such as the content, form, classification, and preservation of various student records. For example, the only federal restriction against destruction of student records is that they cannot be destroyed while a valid request of inspection or release remains to be processed. To the extent that state laws are more strict than the new federal law, they must be observed. State laws forbidding release of confidential information to third parties remain in effect.[158] Neither does the federal law repeal rights of privacy that are protected by the constitution or by other laws.[159]

FERPA resolves problems of record requests by a separated parent who is not the custodial parent or guardian by permitting school authorities to presume that a natural parent has status to demand access unless they receive evidence of a state law or court order that removes any such right. The release of record information under a court order is a safe course, but schools cannot practicably demand that every parent request be accompanied by a court order.[160]

Where a custodial parent or guardian asks them not to disclose student record information to the noncustodial parent on the ground that the other parent has no legal rights, the school authorities may demand documentary proof to that effect. A father with visitation rights was held entitled to trace the forwarding address of his child from school records under New York law.[161] However, a noncustodial father seeking the address of his children from school records prior to the enactment of FERPA was held to lack the right to such disclosure in the same state.[162] School administrators must, therefore, seek counsel on whether their prevailing state law concerning the rights of separated parents has been superseded by FERPA.

The potential for conflict between FERPA, which deals explicitly with student records, and federal or state Freedom of Information Acts has not been tested by litigation. The federal Freedom of Information Act would appear to apply only to federal records, and therefore have only minimal impact upon the operation of FERPA in state public schools. More serious problems may be anticipated, however, in states that have

---

157. This follows prior state law. King v. Ambellon, 173 N.Y.S.2d 98 (1958). Release of records under court order, in an emergency to protect public safety, to a parent of dependent student, certain government officials, and to teachers and principals for their work with the student are examples of the exemptions from the consent requirements. *See also* Palladium Publishing Co. v. River Valley Sch. Dist., 321 N.W.2d 705 (Mich. 1982) (ordering school board to record names of suspended students on official minutes and release minutes to public press as a public record).

158. *See* Elder v. Anderson, 23 Cal. Rptr. 48 (1962) (disclosure of adverse personal student information to unprivileged parties held unlawful under California statutes).

159. Merriken v. Cressman, 364 F.Supp. 913, 916 (E.D. Pa. 1973) (intensely personal student questionnaire about family, enjoined as invasion of privacy).

160. State law is in accord. *See* In re Irene F, 366 N.Y.S.2d 423 (1975) (order to permit record inspection and copies of school records in court cases regarding foster parent status); Johnson v. Bd. of Education, 220 N.Y.S.2d 362 (1961) (order to produce student records in aid of student tort action); Marmo v. N.Y. City Bd. of Education, 289 N.Y.S.2d 51 (1968) (defendant in criminal case entitled to names and addresses of classmates in aid of his court defense).

161. Dachs v. Bd. of Education, 277 N.Y.S.2d 449 (1967).

162. Marquesano v. Bd. of Education, 199 N.Y.S.2d 713 (1959). *But see* Young v. Armstrong Sch. District, fn. 148.

Freedom of Information Acts that must be reconciled with or else superseded by, FERPA to the extent that they are inconsistent.[163]

d. Confidentiality. Closely related to the foregoing problems is this question: What information may be safely withheld from a student's records? Should damaging information be wrongfully inserted into a student's file to which the student or parent has access, the author would be exposed to a possible tort suit on a theory of defamation or breach of confidentiality and privacy. Conversely, should material be withheld from the records on the mistaken view that it is confidential and privileged, the informed professional could be subject to charges of default in job responsibilities. This dilemma is not adequately resolved either by the common law testimonial privilege of maintaining confidentiality, which extends only to ministers, doctors, and lawyers, or by extant statutes, most of which do not cover many of the problem situations.[164] The initial question facing a recipient of information is: What communications are "confidential" in a legal sense? Even if the information is deemed confidential by professional ethical standards, two legal problems remain. Does statute law cover the particular profession involved (psychologist, counselor, nurse, or social worker)?[165] Does it protect the particular information that is received? For example, nontherapeutic counseling is not generally considered a protected confidential activity; and information concerning child abuse or social diseases, by whomsoever received, are required by the law of most states to be reported to proper state authorities. Yet, other statutes authorize doctors and treating agencies to render medical assistance without parental notification or consent to minors who are pregnant, or suffering from venereal disease or drug-related illnesses.[166]

In the absence of specific legislative guidance, school employees in allied health professions face a perplexing gap between their professional standards and their legal obligations regarding received student information. Instructors are even more vulnerable since they generally lack any legal status to claim a privilege of confidentiality.

Many school employees have chosen the course of not placing disparaging or confidential information in student files, but the failure to report dangerous student tendencies (to protect threatened victims) still raises the risk of tort liability. In two recent celebrated decisions state courts held that psychotherapists' failure to warn victims against violent threats of their patients could constitute a tort cause of action, notwithstanding the conflicting duties of keeping patient information confidential and of warning the known victim. The cases suggested that the public interest in safety from violent assault could outweigh the breach of trust in revealing the confidential

---

163. *See, e.g.*, Palladium Publishing Co. v. River Valley School Dist., fn. 157; F. Rosenfeld, *The Freedom of Information Act's Privacy Exemption and the Privacy Act of 1974*, 11 Harv. Civil Rights Civil Liberties L. Rev. 596 (1976); McClung, *Student Records*, 22 Inequality in Education (Center for Law and Education, Cambridge, MA 1977).

164. *Testimonial privilege*: A privilege of nondisclosure was recently extended for criminal trials to cover a psychiatric social worker operating under the supervision of a psychiatrist, with respect to the patient's self-incriminating statements. Allred v. State, 554 P.2d 411 (Alaska 1976).

165. See Pa. Stat. Ann. tit. 24, § 13–1319 (limited to guidance counselor, school nurse, and school psychologist).

166. See Pa. Stat. Ann., tit. 35 § 10103; tit. 71, § 1690.112; 16 McKinney's Cons. L. N.Y., § 3028-a.

communication.[167] While there is very little law in this area, the California decision poses a warning that the privilege of maintaining confidentiality may not apply in dire emergencies.

e. Rights of Separated Parents. The respective rights of separated parents regarding access to student records, educational decisions, and custody, have not been specifically addressed by the above mentioned statutes, and they are not subject to any uniform common law among the state jurisdictions. Those issues are compounded by rising rates of divorce and separation as well as a trend toward the award of split or shared custody under court decrees and under private separation agreements.

With respect to records access and disclosure, the above-discussed FERPA and its implementing regulations presumptively entitle each parent to its protections regarding records access and disclosure.[168] Whether FERPA will be construed to incorporate state law limitations on individual parental rights remains to be seen, but a strong argument can be made that it is not intended to supersede the state law governing parental status, especially "decrees that are entered in the 'best interest' of the child."[169]

With respect to participation in educational decisions and the exercise of physical custody of the child, much will depend upon the terms of individual court orders and separation agreements. Absent a controlling order or agreement, both parents retain their normal general rights. In the event of disagreement between separated spouses, a majority of jurisdictions hold that the educational decisions of the parent having lawful sole custody would control.[170] In cases of shared or split custody, or in other doubtful cases, the answers to the foregoing problems would have to be worked out by the courts on the basis of individual case facts. Since the variable affecting interests of the child and of the child's parents are too multifarious to subject to any single rule, school authorities should, in doubtful cases, consult legal counsel regarding the respective rights of parents who had not agreed or consented to each other's respective authority over their child's education and custody.

e. Student Associations and Clubs. Students have a constitutional right of association, to form and join lawful groups to pursue common purposes. As to organizations that are not school centered and that do not affect the school, their rights are clear.[171]

---

167. Hedlund v. Superior Court, 34 Cal.3d 695 (1982); McIntosh v. Milano, 403 A.2d 500 (N.J. 1979); Tarasoff v. Regents of the Univ. of California, 551 P.2d 334 (Cal. 1976).

168. The FERPA regulations (34 C.F.R., part 99) state that educational agencies may presume that a parent has the authority to exercise rights under the act, unless the agency or institution is provided with evidence by state law, court order, or other binding instrument providing to the contrary. Regulation 99.3. *Accord*: Page v. Rotterdam-Mohonasen, etc., 441 N.Y.S.2d 323 (1981).

169. Strosnider v. Strosnider, 686 P.2d 981 (Ariz. 1984); *Idem*; Pa. Stat. Annot, tit. 23, §101; 1981–82 Report of Attorney General, South Dakota, p. 41. See generally Annotation: *Non-custodial Parent Rights re Education of Child,* 36 A.L.R.3d 1093 (1971).

170. *See, e.g.*, Mills v. Phillips, 407 So.2d 302 (Fla. 1981); Morris v. Morris, 412 A.2d 139 (Pa. 1979); Mester v. Mester, 296 N.Y.S.2d 193 (1969); Fanning v. Warfield, 248 A.2d 890 (Md. 1969); Jenks v. Jenks, 385 S.W.2d 370 (Mo. 1964); Lerner v. Superior Court, 242 P. 2d 321 (Cal. 1952).

171. Wilson v. Aboline Ind. Sch. District, 190 S.W.2d 406 (Tex. 1945); *see* Burkitt v. Sch. District No. 1, 246 P.2d 566, 578 (Ore. 1952).

Within the school, however, the public interest of promoting equality and nondiscrimination and in avoiding the tensions, divisiveness, and elitism among students has been held to outweigh student associational interests in joining secret or separatist fraternities, sororities, or clubs.[172] For like reasons, the need for school information to supervise school-related activities can outweigh claims of associational privacy, and regulations that require disclosure of student organization officers and bylaws have been approved in court opinions.[173] Courts have also drawn the line between protected association and unprotected group conduct. Members of an officially recognized school club could not, therefore, escape punishment for subjecting new student candidates to injurious hazing practices, such as belt beatings and having hot pepper sauce rubbed into their faces.[174]

g. Student Rights against Physical Punishments and Restraints. Traditional school discipline by means of corporal punishment or in-school detentions may implicate student constitutional rights of bodily security and freedom of movement, and parental constitutional rights to control the treatment of their children. Those rights, however, have been subordinated to the rights of public school educators to maintain discipline in the school, so long as the need and degree of such discipline are "reasonable."[175] That constitutional balance may be altered where the positive laws of individual states either forbid the imposition of such punishments or condition their use upon prior parental notification or consent.[176]

In upholding the constitutionality of the use of corporal punishment, the United States Supreme Court declined to decide "whether and under what circumstances corporal punishment of a public school child may give rise to an independent federal cause of action to vindicate substantive rights under the due process clause."[177] It thus remains possible that a court might find the constitutional right of the student to be free from "severe" corporal punishment, but on this point, a conflict of judicial opinion exists.[178] While most state courts have for their own state laws and constitutions adopted the federal view that corporal punishment does not per se violate rights to bodily security and is not a form of "cruel and unusual punishment," a recent West Virginia case did construe the state constitution differently.[179]

---

172. *See, e.g.*, Passel v. Ft. Worth Ind. Sch. District, 453 S.W.2d 888 (Tex. 1970). For collection of the statutes and case authorities in more than 25 states, *see* Robinson v. Sacramento Uni. Sch. District, 53 Cal. Rptr. 781, 788–789 (1966); the only contrary authority reported by the Robinson opinion is Wright v. Bd. of Education, 246 S.W. 43 (Mo. 1922).

173. *Cf.* Healy v. James, 408 U.S. 169 (1972); Eisen v. Regents, U. of California, 75 Cal. Rptr. 45 (1969).

174. McNaughton v. Circleville Bd. of Education, 345 N.E.2d 649 (C.D. Ohio 1974).

175. Ingraham v. Wright, 430 U.S. 651 (1977); Hall v. Tawney, 631 F.2d 607, 610 (4th Cir. 1980).

176. The laws of the individual states are canvassed in Smith v. W. Virginia Board of Ed., 295 S.E.2d 680, 685–88 (W.Va. 1982); and in Ingraham v. Wright, *supra,* at nn. 24 & 25; Annot: *Corporal Punishment,* 25 A.L.R. Fed. 431 (1975).

177. Ingraham v. Wright, *supra,* 430 U.S. at 679, n. 47.

178. *Compare, e.g.*, Hall v. Tawney, *supra,* 621 F.2d at pp. 610–15 (appearing to accept the constitutional thesis); *with* Woodard v. Los Fresnos Ind. School Dist., 732 F.2d 1243 (5th Cir. 1984), and Hall v. Pringle, 562 F.Supp. 598 (M.D. Ala. 1983) (which indicates disfavor of the substantive right argument).

179. Smith v. W. Virginia Bd. of Ed., 295 S.E.2d 680 (W.Va. 1982) (finding student due process rights to limit corporal punishment under the state constitution).

While there are some borderline variations on the constitutionality of corporal punishments or physical restraints, all authorities agree that public school students are entitled to be free from arbitrary or excessive corporal punishment, as a matter of common law or positive state law; and are entitled to such prepunishment notice, hearings, or other procedures that are enacted for their benefit by state statute. Students would have causes of action in tort for excessive corporal punishment, as noted in Chapter 8; and possibly a special monetary claim for deprivation of civil rights, although decisions on the latter point are still incomplete and in conflict.[180]

With regard to disciplinary detention during or after school hours, the cases have viewed the temporary loss of free movement and incidental stigmatization as too minimal to rise to the dignity of a constitutional injury.[181]

In addition, where protected associational activities are coupled with symbolic First Amendment expression rights, a Court may utilize the stricter level of scrutiny found in the *Tinker* case. This can be illustrated by a Rhode Island case where a male student wanted to take a male friend to the school prom. The Rhode Island court applied *Tinker's* "disruption" test and found insufficient evidence of unavoidable disruption that outweighed the student's right of expression.[182]

---

180. *Compare, e.g.*, cases rejecting civil rights statutes claims: Rhodus v. Dunmiller, 552 F.Supp. 425 (M.D.La. 1982); Hall v. Pringle, 562 F.Supp. 598 (M.D.Ala. 1983); *cf.* Streeter v. Hundley, 580 S.W.2d 283 (Mo. 1979); with Hall v. Tawney, fn. 175, *supra.*

181. *See, e.g,* Fenton v. Stear, 523 F.Supp. 767 (W.D. Pa. 1976); Linwood v. Bd. of Ed., 563 F.2d 763, 769 (7th Cir. 1972); Fitzpatrick v. Bd. of Ed., 284 N.Y.S.2d 590 (1967).

182. Fricke v. Lynch, 491 F.Supp. 381 (D.R.I. 1980).

CASES

Goss v. Lopez

419 U.S. 565 (1975)

WHITE, Justice.

This appeal by various administrators of the Columbus, Ohio, Public School System (CPSS) challenges the judgment of a three-judge federal court, declaring that appellees—various high school students in the CPSS—were denied due process of law contrary to . . . the Fourteenth Amendment in that they were temporarily suspended from their high schools without a hearing either prior to suspension or within a reasonable time thereafter. . . .

Ohio law, Rev. Code Ann. § 3313.64 (1972), provides for free education to all children between the ages of six and 21. Section 3313.66 of the Code empowers the principal of an Ohio public School to suspend a pupil for misconduct for up to 10 days or to expel him. . . .

A pupil who is expelled, or his parents, may appeal the decision to the Board of Education and in connection therewith shall be permitted to be heard at the board meeting. . . .

The nine named appellees, each of whom alleged that he or she had been suspended . . . for up to 10 days without a hearing . . . filed an action under 42 U.S.C. § 1983. . . .

The proof below established that the suspensions arose out of a period of widespread student unrest . . . Six of the named plaintiffs . . . were each suspended for 10 days on account of disruptive or disobedient conduct committed in the presence of the school administrator who ordered the suspension. One of these, Tyrone Washington, was among a group of students demonstrating in the school auditorium while a class was being conducted there. . . .

Rudolph Sutton . . . physically attacked a police officer who was attempting to remove Tyrone Washington from the auditorium. . . . The other four . . . students were suspended for similar conduct. None was given a hearing to determine the operative facts underlying the suspension, but each together with his or her parents was offered the opportunity to attend a conference, subsequent to the effective date of the suspension, to discuss the student's future.

Two named plaintiffs, Dwight Lopez and Betty Crome, were students. . . . The former was suspended in connection with a disturbance in the lunchroom which involved some physical damage to school property. . . . He also testified below that he was not a party to the destructive conduct but was instead an innocent bystander. Because no one from the school testified with regard to this incident, there is no evidence . . . indicating the official basis for concluding otherwise. Lopez never had a hearing.

Betty Crome was present at a demonstration at a high school other than the one she was attending. There she was arrested together with others. . . . Before she went to school on the following day, she was notified that she had been suspended for a 10-day period. Because no one from the school testified with respect to this incident, the record does not disclose how the McGuffey Junior High School principal went about making the decision to suspend Crome, nor does it disclose on what information the decision was based. . . .

There was no testimony with respect to the suspension of the ninth named plaintiff, Carl Smith. The school files were also silent as to his suspension. . . .

On the basis of this evidence, the three judge court declared that plaintiffs were denied due process of law because they were "suspended without hearing prior to suspension or within a reasonable time thereafter," and that Ohio Rev. Code Ann. § 3313.66 (1972) and regulations issued pursuant thereto were unconstitutional in permitting such suspensions. It was ordered that all references to plaintiffs' suspensions be removed from school files. . . .

At the outset, appellants contend that because there is no constitutional right to an education at public expense, the Due Process Clause does not protect against expulsions from the public school system. This position misconceives the nature of the issue. . . . The Fourteenth Amendment forbids the State to deprive any person of life, liberty, or property without due process of law. Protected interests in property are normally "not created by the Constitution. Rather, they are created and their dimensions are defined" by an independent source such as state statutes or rules entitling the citizen to certain benefits. *Board of Regents* v. *Roth,* 408 U.S. 564, 577, 92 S.Ct. 2701, 2709, 33 L. Ed.2d 548 (1972). . . .

Here, on the basis of state law, appellees plainly had legitimate claims of entitlement to a public education. Ohio Rev. Code Ann. §§ 3313.48 and 3313.64 (1972 and Supp. 1973) direct local authorities to provide a free education to all residents between five and 21 years of age, and a compulsory-attendance law requires attendance for a school year of not less than 32 weeks. Ohio Rev. Code Ann. § 3321.04 (1972). It is true that § 3313.66 of the Code permits school principals to suspend students for up to 10 days; but suspensions may not be imposed without any grounds whatsoever. . . . Having chosen to extend the right to an education to people of appellees' class generally. Ohio may not withdraw that right on grounds of misconduct absent, fundamentally fair procedures to determine whether the midconduct has occurred. . . .

Although Ohio may not be constitutionally obligated to establish and maintain a public school system, it has nevertheless done so and has required its children to attend. . . . The authority possessed by the State to prescribe and enforce standards of conduct in its schools, although concededly very broad, must be exercised consistently with constitutional safeguards. Among other things, the State is constrained to recognize a student's legitimate entitlement to a public education as a property interest which is protected by the Due Process Clause and which may not be taken away for misconduct without adherence to the minimum procedures required by that Clause. . . .

Appellants proceed to argue that even if there is a right to a public education protected by the Due Process Clause generally, the Clause comes into play only when the State subjects a student to a "severe detriment or grievous loss." The loss of 10 days it is said, is neither severe nor grievous. . . . Appellants' argument is again refuted by our prior decisions; for in determining "whether due process requirements apply in the first place, we must look not to the 'weight' but to the *nature* of the interest at stake." *Board of Regents* v. *Roth,* supra at 570–571, 92 S. Ct. 1 at 2705–2706. . . .

A 10-day suspension from school is not de minimis in our view and may not be imposed in complete disregard of the Due Process Clause.

A short suspension is, of course, a far milder deprivation than expulsion. But, "education is perhaps the most important function of state and local governments," *Brown* v. *Board of Education,* 347 U.S. 483, 493, 74 S.Ct. 686, 691, 98 L. Ed. 873 (1954), and the total exclusion from the educational process for more than a trivial period . . . is a serious event in the life of the suspended child. Neither the property interest in educational benefits temporarily denied nor the liberty interest in reputation, which is also implicated, is so insubstantial that suspensions may constitutionally be imposed by any procedure the school chooses, no matter how arbitrary.

"Once it is determined that due process applies, the question remains what process is due." *Morrissey* v. *Brewer,* 408 U.S. at 481, 92 S.Ct., at 2600. We turn to that question, fully realizing as our cases regularly do that the interpretation and application of the Due Process Clause are intensely practical matters and that "[t]he very nature of due process negates any concept of inflexible procedures universally applicable to every imaginable situation." Cafeteria Workers v. McElroy, 367 U.S. 886, 895, 81 S.Ct. 1743, 1748, 6 L.Ed.2d 1230 (1961). We are also mindful of our own admonition:

> "Judicial interposition in the operation of the public school system of the Nation raises problems requiring care and restraint. . . . By and large, public education in our Nation is committed to the control of state and local authorities." *Epperson* v. *Arkansas,* 393 U.S. 97, 104, 89 S.Ct. 266, 270, 21 L.Ed.2d 228 (1968).

. . . "The fundamental requisite of due process of law is the opportunity to be heard." . . . At the very minimum, therefore, students facing suspension and the consequent interference with a protected property interest must be given *some* kind of notice and afforded *some* kind of hearing. . . .

It also appears from our cases that the timing and content of the notice and the nature of the hearing will depend on appropriate accommodation of the competing interests involved. . . . The student's interest is to avoid unfair or mistaken exclusion from the educational process, with all of its unfortunate consequences. The Due Process Clause will not shield him from suspensions properly imposed, but it disserves both his interest and the interest of the State if his suspension is in fact unwarranted. . . .

The risk of error is not at all trivial, and it should be guarded against if that may be done without prohibitive cost or interference with the educational process.

The difficulty is that our schools are vast and complex. Some modicum of discipline and order is essential. . . . Events calling for discipline are frequent occurrences and sometimes require immediate, effective action. Suspension is considered not only to be a necessary tool to maintain order but a valuable educational device. The prospect of imposing elaborate hearing requirements in every suspension case is viewed with great concern, and many school authorities may well prefer the untrammeled power to act unilaterally, unhampered by rules about notice and hearing. But it would be a strange disciplinary system in an educational institution if no communication was sought by the disciplinarian with the student in an effort to . . . inform him of his dereliction and to let him tell his side of the story in order to make sure that an injustice is not done. . . .

We do not believe that school authorities must be totally free from notice and hearing requirements. . . . Students facing temporary suspension have interests qualifying for protection of the Due Process Clause, and due process requires, in connection with a suspension of 10 days or less, that the student be given oral or written notice of the charges against him and, if he denies them, an explanation of the evidence the authorities have and an opportunity to present his side of the story. The Clause requires at least these rudimentary precautions against unfair or mistaken findings of misconduct and arbitrary exclusion from school.

There need be no delay between the time "notice" is given and the time of hearing. In the great majority of cases the disciplinarian may informally discuss the alleged misconduct with the student minutes after it has occurred. We hold only that, in being given an opportunity to explain his version of the facts at this discussion, the student first be told what he is accused of doing and what the basis of the accusation is. Lower courts . . . in short suspension cases have reached the same conclusion. *Tate* v. *Board of Education,* 453 F.2d 975, 979 (CA8 1972); *Vail* v. *Board of Education,* 354 F.Supp. 592, 603 (NH 1973). Since the hearing may occur almost immediately following the misconduct, it follows that as a general rule notice and hearing should precede removal of the student from school. We agree with the District Court, however, that there are recurring situations in which prior notice and hearing cannot be insisted upon. Students whose presence poses a continuing danger to persons or property or an ongoing threat of disrupting the academic process may be immediately removed from school. In such cases, the necessary notice and rudimentary hearing should follow as soon as practicable, as the District Court indicated.

In holding as we do, we do not believe that we have imposed procedures on school disciplinarians which are inappropriate in a classroom setting. Instead we have imposed requirements which are, if anything, less than a fair-minded school principal would impose upon himself in order to avoid unfair suspensions. . . .

We stop short of construing the Due Process Clause to require, countrywide, that hearings in connection with short suspensions must afford the student the opportunity to secure counsel, to confront and cross-examine witnesses supporting the charge, or to call his own witnesses to verify his version of the incident. Brief disciplinary suspensions are almost countless. To impose in each such case even truncated trial-type procedures might well overwhelm administrative facilities in many places and, by diverting resources, cost more than it would save in educational effectiveness. Moreover, further formalizing the suspension process and escalating its formality and adversary nature may not only make it too costly as a regular disciplinary tool but also destroy its effectiveness as part of the teaching process.

On the other hand, requiring effective notice and informal hearing permitting the student to give his version of the events will provide a meaningful hedge against erroneous action. At least the disciplinarian will be alerted to the existence of disputes about facts and arguments about cause and effect. He may then determine himself to . . . permit cross-examination, and allow the student to present his own witnesses. In more difficult cases, he may permit counsel. In any event, his discretion will be more informed and we think the risk of error substantially reduced.

Requiring that there be at least an informal, give-and-take between student and disciplinarian, preferably prior to the suspension, will add little to the factfinding function where the disciplinarian himself has witnessed the conduct forming the basis for the charge. But things are not always as they seem to be, and the student will at least have the opportunity to characterize his conduct and put it in what he deems the proper context.

We should also make it clear that we have addressed ourselves solely to the short suspension, not exceeding 10 days. Longer suspensions or expulsions for the remainder of the school term, or permanently, may require more formal procedures. Nor do we put aside the possibility that in unusual situations, although involving only a short suspension, something more than the rudimentary procedures will be required. . . .

The District Court found each of the suspensions involved here to have occurred without a hearing, either before or after the suspension, and that each suspension was therefore invalid and the statute unconstitutional insofar as it permits such suspensions without notice or hearing. Accordingly, the judgment is Affirmed.

Mr. Justice POWELL, with whom *THE CHIEF JUSTICE, Mr. Justice BLACKMUN,* and *Mr. Justice REHNQUIST* join, dissenting.

Gonzales v. McEuen

435 E.Supp. 460 (1977)

TAKASUGI, District Judge.

Eleven high school students, by their next friends, have brought this action under the Civil Rights Act, 42 U.S.C. § 1983, and the Due Process Clause of the Fourteenth Amendment of the Constitution of the United States. The case stems from the suspension and expulsion of the named plaintiffs from Oxnard Union High School following a period of student unrest on campus during October 14–15, 1976. The plaintiffs were charged with having committed certain acts which, it was alleged, led to a riot at Oxnard High School.

The complaint was filed on November 11, 1976. . . .

On November 12, 1976, this Court entered a Temporary Restraining Order directing the Superintendent and the District to reinstate nine students, the original named plaintiffs, and to permit them to make up work they had missed during their involuntary suspension, pending a hearing on their proposed expulsion before the Board. . . . [I]t was the opinion of this Court that the notices given to the plaintiffs and their parents concerning the expulsion proceedings were constitutionally inadequate and denied the plaintiffs due process of law as suggested by the United States Supreme Court in *Goss* v. *Lopez,* 419 U.S. 565, 95 S.Ct. 729, 42 L.Ed.2d 725 (1975).

Subsequently, corrected notices were sent by the District to each of the plaintiffs . . . specifying the charges against each plaintiff and also setting forth the rights of the plaintiffs as required by § 10608(d) of the California Education Code. Hearings were conducted by the Board of Trustees. . . . Because the charges against some of the plaintiffs grew out of the same incidents, hearings were consolidated for some plaintiffs. Individual hearings were set for the other plaintiffs. The Board sustained the charges against all the students and found that there was just cause for expulsion. The students were expelled for the remainder of the 1976–1977 school year.

Pursuant to California Education Code § 10609, plaintiffs have the right to appeal their expulsions to the Ventura County Board of Education, and they have declared their intention to pursue such appeals. However, plaintiffs contend that their expulsions were violative of due process and they seek a preliminary injunction directing their reinstatement at Oxnard High School pending trial or, alternatively, pending hearing and determination by the Ventura County Board of Education.

Common Issues

California Education Code Section 10605. Plaintiffs contend that their rights to due process have been violated by the defendants' failure to attempt milder measures of correction before imposing the harsher penalty of expulsion. California Education Code, § 10605, reads as follows:

> "The governing Board of any school district shall suspend or expel pupils for misconduct when other means or correction fail to bring about proper conduct."

. . . Defendants, on the other hand, point to numerous other sections of the Education Code which unequivocably authorize expulsions and suspensions and contain no reference to other corrective and less harsh action. . . .

The court need not, and does not, reach this issue of statutory interpretation, Plaintiffs' theory is that the failure to follow the quoted provisions of § 10605 of the California Education Code constitutes a violation of due process. The court disagrees. Not every violation of state statute or a school board's procedural requirement is a denial of due process. *Winnick* v. *Manning,* 460 F.2d 545 (2d Cir. 1970). The defendants' failure to follow the procedure suggested by the plaintiffs would be a violation of state law only. Plaintiffs are not thereby deprived of any federal right. Title 42, U.S.C. § 1983 is not concerned with violations of state law unless such violations result in an infringement of a federally protected right. . . .

Impartiality of the Board. Plaintiffs' strongest and most serious challenge is to the impartiality of the Board. They contend that they were denied their right to an impartial hearing before an independent fact-finder. The basis for this claim is, first, overfamiliarity of the Board with the case; second, the multiple role played by defendants' counsel; and, third, the involvement of the Superintendent of the District, Mr. McEuen, with the Board of Trustees during the hearings.

No one doubts that a student charged with misconduct has a right to an impartial tribunal, see *Wasson* v. *Trowbridge,* 382 F.2d 807, 813 (2d Cir. 1967); *Esteban* v. *Central Missouri State College,* 277 F.Supp. 649, 651 (D.C.W.D.Mo. 1967). There is doubt, however, as to what this means. Various situations have been identified in which experience teaches that the probability of actual bias on the part of the judge or decisionmaker is too high to be constitutionally tolerable. Bias is presumed to exist, for example, in cases in which the adjudicator has a pecuniary interest in the outcome; . . . or in which he has been the target of personal attack or criticism from the person before him. . . . The decisionmaker may also have such prior involvement with the case so as to acquire a disqualifying bias. *Wasson* v. *Trowbridge,* supra. The question before the Court is not whether the Board was actually biased, but whether, under the circumstances, there existed probability that the decisionmaker would be tempted to decide the issues with partiality to one party or the other. It is with this view that the plaintiffs' claims must be considered.

Overfamiliarity. Much has been made of "The Red Book" which, it is claimed, contained information about the academic and disciplinary records of plaintiffs. It is alleged that the Board had access to this material from twenty to thirty days before the expulsion hearings. Depositions submitted to the court show that the members of the Board met with school officials prior to the hearings. Plaintiffs contend that this prior involvement by the Board deprived plaintiffs of the opportunity for a fair hearing. The court rejects this contention. Exposure to evidence presented in a nonadversary investigative procedure is insufficient in itself to inpugn the fairness of the Board members at a later adversary hearing. *Withrow* v. *Larkin,* 421 U.S. 35, 47, 95 S.Ct. 1456,45 L.Ed.2d 712 (1975). Nor is a limited combination of investigatory and adjudicatory functions in an administrative body necessarily unfair, absent a showing of other circumstances such as malice or personal interest in the outcome. *Withrow,* supra, at 47, 95 S.Ct. 1456; *Jones* v, *Board of Educ.*, 279 F.Supp. 190, 200 (D.C., 1968). A school board would be amiss in its duties if it did not make some inquiry to know what was going on in the district for which it is responsible. Some familiarity with the facts of the case gained by an agency in the performance of its statutory role does not disqualify a decisionmaker. *Hortonville Dist.* v. *Hortonville Ed. Assoc.*, 426 U.S. 482, 491, 96 S.Ct. 2308, 2314, 49 L.Ed.2d 1, 9 (1976).

Multiple Roles of Counsel. Turning now to the issue of the multiple roles performed by defendants' counsel, the court notes that the Board members are defendants in this pending related action and may thereby become subject to personal liability.

It is undisputed that attorneys for the District who prosecuted the charges against the plaintiffs in the expulsion proceedings, also represent the Board members in this action. Plaintiffs claim that the attorneys acted in dual roles at the expulsion hearings: as prosecutors for the Administration and as legal advisors to the Board. Counsel for defendants admit that they advised the Board prior to the hearings with respect to its obligations regarding these expulsions, but they deny that they advised the Board during the proceedings themselves.

A reading of the transcripts reveals how difficult it was to separate the two roles. Special mention should be made of the fact that the Board enjoys no legal expertise and must rely heavily upon its counsel. This places defendants' attorneys in a position of intolerable prominence and influence.

It is the opinion of this court that the confidential relationship between the attorneys for the District and the members of the Board, reinforced by the advisory role played by the attorneys for the Board, created an unacceptable risk of bias. Bearing in mind also that the Board members are subject to personal liability in this action, the court concludes that bias can be presumed to exist.

Involvement of Superintendent McEuen. Superintendent McEuen sat with the Board members during the expulsion hearings; he acted as Secretary to the Board on at least one occasion. By statute, Mr. McEuen is the chief advisor to the Board. The fact remains, however, that he is also the chief of the "prosecution" team, to wit, the District.

It is clear from the record that at least on one occasion, at the joint hearing of plaintiffs, Flores, Chavez and Rodriguez, Superintendent McEuen was present with the Board for approximately forty-five minutes during its deliberations on the issue of expelling these plaintiffs. The plaintiffs contend that their due process rights were violated by this involvement of Mr. McEuen with the Board. This court agrees.

Defendants' counsel maintain that Mr. McEuen did not participate in the deliberations and did no more, perhaps, than serve cookies and coffee to the Board members. Whether he did or did not participate, his presence to some extent might operate as an inhibiting restraint upon the freedom of action and expression of the Board. Defendants argue that there is no evidence that Mr. McEuen influenced or biased the Board. Proof of subjective reasoning processes are incapable of corroboration or disproval. Plaintiffs should not be forced to rely upon the memory or sense of fairness of Superintendent McEuen or the Board as to what occurred there. Perhaps Mr. McEuen's physical presence in deliberation becomes more offensive because of the pre-hearing comments which showed something less than impartiality.

The court concludes that the process utilized by the Board was fundamentally unfair. This raises a presumption of bias. In view of the alternatives for the selection of an impartial hearing body under California Education Code Section 10608, it would have been more reasonable to provide procedures that insured not only that justice was done, but also that it appeared to have been done.

In the ordinary case, the scope of judicial review of an administrative board's determination is limited to the question whether there is substantial evidence in the record to support the Board's findings. . . . However, in light of this court's holding that there was a presumption of bias in this hearing, plaintiffs are entitled to this court's review of the evidence under the standard of "clear and convincing" proof.

Discussion of Individual Students

David Barrington and Charles Munden Notice. Plaintiffs Barrington and Munden were expelled at a meeting of the Board on November 10, 1976. Neither Barrington nor Munden was present; neither was represented by either parent or counsel.

On October 29, 1976, letters had been sent to the parents advising them that the principal was recommending expulsion of the students. The letters contained a specific statement of the charges. . . . The letters contained no notice to the student or parent of the student's right to be present at the hearing, to be represented by counsel, and to present evidence. This was a clear violation of § 10608 of the California Education Code. . . .

Attorneys for Munden and Barrington, on November 19 and 20, respectively, requested that the Board set aside their expulsions on account of alleged inadequacy of the notices given to the plaintiffs. They asked for new hearings at which the plaintiffs could be present to defend themselves. . . . The defendants maintain that the notices sent to Barrington and Munden complied, at least, with *federal* due process. . . . They contend that since a hearing was held and there was notice to the parents of the charges against the student, the requisites of procedural due process were satisfied. The court disagrees.

The precise question concerning the content of the notice to be given in expulsion proceedings will depend on the nature of the proceeding that is required. . . .

The question here is common to almost every case in which it is claimed due process has been violated: "Once it is determined that due process applies, the question remains what process is due?" *Goss,* supra, 419 U.S. at 577, 95 S.Ct. at 738; *Morrissey* v. *Brewer,* 408 U.S. 471 at 481, 92 S.Ct. 2593, 33 L.Ed.2d 484.

The requirements of due process are flexible and different cases may require different procedural safeguards. If the possible penalties are mild, quite informal procedures may be sufficient. More formal proceedings may be required where severe penalties may attach. See *Goss* v. *Lopez,* supra. Where the cutoff is between a "severe" and a "mild" penalty is not clear; what is clear is that expulsion is by far the most severe. . . .

Goss clearly anticipates that where the student is faced with the severe penalty of expulsion he shall have the right to be represented by and through counsel, to present evidence on his own behalf, and to confront and cross-examine adverse witnesses.

Other courts have held that a hearing incorporating these safeguards must be held before or shortly after a child is suspended for a prolonged or indefinite period. *Black Coalition* v. *Portland School District* No. 1, 484 F.2d 1040, 1045 (9th Cir. 1973); *Esteban* v. *Central Missouri State College,* 277 F.Supp. 649 (W.D.Mo. 1967). This court agrees.

Notice to be adequate must communicate to the recipient the nature of the proceeding. In an expulsion hearing, the notice given to the student must include a statement not only of the specific charge, but also the basic rights to be afforded the student: to be represented by counsel, to present evidence, and to confront and cross-examine adverse witnesses. Section 10608 of the California Education Code provides, inter alia, for notice to the student and the parent of the specific charge, of the right to be represented by counsel, and of the right to present evidence. Federal due process requires no less.

Defendants next argue that even if the notice was defective, the court must still determine whether the plaintiffs were given a fair and impartial hearing. Defendants misapprehend the meaning of notice. It is not "fair" if the student does not know, and is not told, that he has certain rights which he may exercise at the hearing.

The court, in any event, has held that there was a presumption of bias and that plaintiffs did not have a fair and impartial hearing. . . .

It follows that their expulsions were improper.

Angel Flores, Jerry Chavez and Jerry Rodriguez. The combined hearing of plaintiffs Rodriguez, Flores and Chavez was held on November 20, December 1, and 2. All charges against these three students were sustained. They were expelled for the balance of the 1976–77 school year. . . .

These three students were involved in a fracas on October 14, 1976, with two white, adult males who climbed over a fence to enter the school yard. The evidence was that the two trespassers appeared to be intoxicated and that one of them had a large flashlight which he waved around. The intruders confronted several Chicano students who were eating lunch. Eventually, words led to fisticuffs. The three students were charged with battery of Keysworth, one of the trespassers. . . .

Failure to Produce Percipient Witnesses. Plaintiffs contend that the defendants' failure to produce Smith and Keysworth as witnesses at the hearing effectively deprived them of due process in that plaintiffs were unable to confront and cross-examine these witnesses.

It is questionable whether the hearsay statement of Smith was properly admissible since Chavez was unable to confront and cross-examine one of his accusers whose statements were being used against him. See *Fielder* v. *Board of Education of Winnebago, Neb.*, 346 F.Supp. 722 (D.C.Neb. 1972). But it is difficult to see how Chavez was prejudiced in this case. Chavez, by his own admission, travelled over 20 to 21 feet to join the fray. This, together with the eyewitness testimony of teachers who saw Chavez striking Smith is more than sufficient to support the charge against him.

As to the trespasser, Keysworth, the court does not believe that the prosecution was obligated to call any witnesses. Even in criminal cases, a defendant has no right to confront a "witness" who provides no evidence at trial. Nor, is the government required to call all of the witnesses to a crime. *United States* v. *Heck,* 499 F.2d 778 (9th Cir. 1974). . . .

Amendment of Charges Against Rodriguez. It is clear that the District failed to prove the charge that Rodriguez had committed a battery upon Craig Smith. The charge was amended only after the District rested its case and had failed to prove the original charge. . . . Examination of the record, however, reveals that Rodriguez had an opportunity for continuance or new hearing on the amended charge, but chose to proceed. The court concludes, therefore, that the defect was waived by plaintiff Rodriguez. . . .

Wayne Berry. The alleged victim, Munden, refused to testify for either the District or the students. . . . Defendants claim that this hearsay is admissible as a spontaneous statement and admissible under California Evidence Code § 1240. . . .

The strongest reason, of course, for not permitting these hearsay statements is that the accused student is deprived of his constitutional right to confront and cross-examine his accuser. Although strict adherence to common law rules of evidence is not required in school disciplinary proceedings, where the student is faced with the severe sanction of expulsion, due process does not permit admission of *ex parte* evidence given by witnesses not under oath, and not subject to examination by the accused student.

The Board's own rules provide that hearsay cannot be the sole basis for decision. . . .

Steve Gonzales. The expulsion of Steve Gonzales holds many of the same infirmities as Berry's. Vice-principal Hernandez testified again with respect to the hearsay statements of Berry and Munden, implicating Gonzales. For the reasons stated above, the court holds that admission of these hearsay statements without opportunity to cross-examine the declarant, in student expulsion proceedings, deprived the accused student of his rights of confrontation. . . . The court finds that the charges against Gonzales are not supported by clear and convincing evidence.

Failure to Testify. At the hearing, on the advice of counsel, both Berry and Gonzales declined to testify. . . . The court holds that comment by counsel on the students' refusal to testify, and arguments that guilt could be inferred from such refusal was a violation of the students' Fifth Amendment rights.

Lillian Castellanos. The charge was that Lillian Castellanos battered another female student and a male teacher on October 15, 1976. At the hearing, there was testimony by the student-victim and teachers concerning the attack. Two teachers testified that Castellanos kicked a male teacher "in the *gluteous maximus.*" The court can find no defense and concludes that the District did sustain its burden of proof. . . .

New Jersey v. T.L.O.

469 U.S. 000, 105 S.Ct. 733 (1985)

[A teacher at a New Jersey high school, upon discovering . . . a 14-year-old freshman, and her companion smoking cigarettes . . . in violation of a school rule, took them to the Principal's office. . . . When respondent . . . denied that she had been smoking and claimed that she did not smoke at all, the Assistant Vice Principal demanded to see her purse. Upon opening the purse, he found a pack of cigarettes and also noticed a package of cigarette rolling papers that are commonly associated with the use of marihuana. He then proceeded to search thoroughly and found some marihuana, a pipe, plastic bags, a fairly substantial amount of money, an index card containing a list of students who owed respondent money, and two letters that implicated her in marihuana dealing. Thereafter, the State brought delinquency charges against respondent in the Juvenile Court, which, ruled . . . that the search in question was a reasonable one, and adjudged respondent to be a delinquent. . . . The New Jersey Supreme Court reversed and ordered the suppression of the evidence found in respondent's purse, holding that the search of the purse was unreasonable. The United States Supreme Court reversed the New Jersey Supreme Court, and upheld the search as constitutional.]

Justice WHITE delivered the opinion of the Court.

We granted certiorari in this case to examine the appropriateness of the exclusionary rule as a remedy for searches carried out in violation of the Fourth Amendment by public school authorities. Our consideration . . . has led us to conclude that the search that gave rise to the case now before us did not violate the Fourth Amendment. Accordingly, we here address only the questions of the proper standard for assessing the legality of searches conducted by public school officials and the application of that standard to the facts of this case. . . .

In determining whether the search at issue in this case violated the Fourth Amendment, we are faced initially with the question whether that Amendment's prohibition on unreasonable searches and seizures applies to searches conducted by public school officials. We hold that it does. . . .

. . . On reargument, however, the State of New Jersey has argued that the history of the Fourth Amendment indicates that the Amendment was intended to regulate only searches and seizures carried out by law enforcement officers; accordingly, although public school officials are concededly state agents for purposes of the Fourteenth Amendment, the Fourth Amendment creates no rights enforceable against them.

It may well be true that the evil toward which the Fourth Amendment was primarily directed was the resurrection of the pre-Revolutionary practice of using general warrants or "writs of assistance" to authorize searches for contraband by officers of the Crown. See *United States* v. *Chadwick,* 433 U.S. 1, 7–8 (1977); *Boyd* v. *United States,* 116 U.S. 616, 624–629 (1886). But this Court has never limited the Amendment's prohibition on unreasonable searches and seizures to operations conducted by the police. . . . Accordingly, we have held the Fourth Amendment applicable to the activities of civil as well as criminal authorities. . . .

Notwithstanding the general applicability of the Fourth Amendment a few courts have concluded that school officials are exempt from the dictates of the Fourth Amendment by virtue of the special nature of their authority over schoolchildren. See, *e.g., R.C.M.* v. *State,* 660 S.W. 2d 552 (Tex. App. 1983). . . .

Such reasoning is in tension with contemporary reality and the teachings of this Court. We have held school officials subject to the commands of the First Amendment, see *Tinker* v. *Des Moines Independent Community School District,* 393 U.S. 503 (1969), and the Due Process Clause of the Fourteenth Amendment, see *Goss* v. *Lopez,* 419 U.S. 565 (1975). If school authorities are state actors for purposes of the constitutional guarantees of freedom of expression and due process, it is difficult to understand why they should be deemed to be exercising parental rather than public authority when conducting searches of their students. . . . In carrying out searches and other disciplinary functions pursuant to such policies, school officials act as representatives of the State . . . and they cannot claim the parents' immunity from the strictures of the Fourth Amendment.

To hold that the Fourth Amendment applies to searches conducted by school authorities is only to begin the inquiry into the standards governing such searches. Although the underlying command of the Fourth Amendment is always that searches and seizures be reasonable, what is reasonable depends on the context within which a search takes place. The determination of the standard of reasonableness . . . requires "balancing the need to search against the invasion which the search entails." *Camara* v.

Municipal Court, supra, at 536–537. . . . A search of a child's person or of a closed purse or other bag carried on her person, no less than a similar search carried out on an adult, is undoubtedly a severe violation of subjective expectations of privacy.

Of course, the Fourth Amendment does not protect subjective expectations of privacy that are unreasonable or otherwise "illegitimate." See, *e.g., Hudson* v. *Palmer,* 468 U.S. ______(1984); *Rawlings* v. *Kentucky,* 448 U.S. 98 (1980). To receive the protection of the Fourth Amendment, an expectation of privacy must be one that society is "prepared to recognize as legitimate." *Hudson* v. *Palmer, supra,* at ______. . . .

Against the child's interest in privacy must be set the substantial interest of teachers and administrators in maintaining discipline in the classroom and on the school grounds. Maintaining order in the classroom has never been easy, but in recent years, school disorder has often taken particularly ugly forms: drug use and violent crime in the schools have become major social problems. . . .

. . . It is evident that the school setting requires some easing of the restrictions to which searches by public authorities are ordinarily subject. The warrant requirement, in particular, is unsuited to the school environment: requiring a teacher to obtain a warrant before searching a child suspected of an infraction of school rules (or of the criminal law) would unduly interfere with the maintenance of the swift and informal disciplinary procedures needed in the schools. Just as we have in other cases dispensed with the warrant requirement when "the burden of obtaining a warrant is likely to frustrate the governmental purpose behind the search," *Camara* v. *Municipal Court,* 387 U.S., 532–533, we hold today that school officials need not obtain a warrant before searching a student who is under their authority.

The school setting also requires some modification of the level of suspicion of illicit acitivity needed to justify a search. Ordinarily, a search . . . must be based upon "probable cause" to believe that a violation of the law has occurred. . . . However, "probable cause" is not an irreducible requirement of a valid search. . . .

Thus, we have in a number of cases recognized the legality of searches and seizures based on suspicions that, although "reasonable," do not rise to the level of probable cause. . . .

We join the majority of courts that have examined this issue in concluding that the accommodation of the privacy interests of schoolchildren with the substantial need of teachers and administrators for freedom to maintain order in the schools does not require strict adherence to the requirement that searches be based on probable cause to believe that the subject of the search has violated or is violating the law. Rather, the legality of a search of a student should depend simply on the reasonableness, under all the circumstances, of the search. Determining the reasonableness of any search involves a twofold inquiry. . . .

Under ordinary circumstances, a search of a student by a teacher or other school official will be "justified at its inception" when there are reasonable grounds for suspecting that the search will turn up evidence that the student has violated or is violating either the law or the rules of the school. Such a search will be permissible in its scope when the measures adopted are reasonably related to the objectives of the search and not excessively intrusive in light of the age and sex of the student and the nature of the infraction.

This standard will, we trust, neither unduly burden efforts of school authorities to maintain order in their schools nor authorize unrestrained intrusions upon the privacy of schoolchildren. By focusing attention on the question of reasonableness, the standard will spare teachers and school administrators the necessity of schooling themselves in the niceties of probable cause and permit them to regulate their conduct according to the dictates of reason and common sense. At the same time, the reasonableness standard should ensure that the interests of students will be invaded no more than is necessary to achieve the legitimate end of preserving order in the schools.

There remains the question of the legality of the search in this case. . . . Our review of the facts surrounding the search leads us to conclude that the search was in no sense unreasonable for Fourth Amendment purposes.

The incident that gave rise to this case actually involved two separate searches, with the first—the search for cigarettes—providing the suspicion that gave rise to the second—the search for marihuana. Although it is the fruits of the second search that are at issue here, the validity of the search for marihuana must depend on the reasonableness of the initial search for cigarettes, as there would have been no reason to suspect that T.L.O. possessed marihuana had the first search not taken place. Accordingly, it is to the search for cigarettes that we first turn our attention. . . . The relevance of T.L.O.'s possession of cigarettes to the question whether she had been smoking and to the credibility of her denial . . . supplied the necessary "nexus" between the item searched for and the infraction under investigation. See *Warden* v. *Hayden,* 387 U.S. 294, 306–307 (1967). Thus, if Mr. Choplick in fact had a reasonable suspicion that T.L.O. had cigarettes in her purse, the search was justified despite the fact that cigarettes, if found, would constitute "mere evidence" of a violation. *Ibid.*

. . . A teacher had reported that T.L.O. was smoking in the lavatory. Certainly this report gave Mr. Choplick reason to suspect that T.L.O. was carrying cigarettes with her; and if she did have cigarettes, her purse was the obvious place in which to find them. Mr. Choplick's suspicion that there were cigarettes in the purse was not an "inchoate and unparticularized suspicion or 'hunch,'" *Terry* v. *Ohio,* 392 U.S., at 27; rather, it was the sort of "common-sense conclusio[n] about human behavior" upon which "practical people"—including government officials—are entitled to rely. *United States* v. *Cortez,* 449 U.S. 411, 418 (1981). Of course, even if the teacher's report were true, T.L.O. *might* not have had a pack of cigarettes with her; she might have borrowed a cigarette from someone else or have been sharing a cigarette with another student. But the requirement of reasonable suspicion is not a requirement of absolute certainty: "sufficient probability, not certainty, is the touchstone of reasonableness under the Fourth Amendment. . . ." *Hill* v. *California,* 401 U.S. 797, 804 (1971). Because the hypothesis that T.L.O. was carrying cigarettes in her purse was itself not unreasonable, it is irrelevant that other hypotheses were also consistent with the teacher's accusation. Accordingly, it cannot be said that Mr. Choplick acted unreasonably when he examined T.L.O.'s purse to see if it contained cigarettes.

Our conclusion that Mr. Choplick's decision to open T.L.O.'s purse was reasonable brings us to the question of the further search for marihuana once the pack of cigarettes was located. . . . Although T.L.O. does not dispute the reasonableness of Mr. Choplick's belief that rolling papers indicated the presence of marihuana, she does contend that the scope of the search . . . exceeded permissible bounds when he seized and read certain letters that implicated T.L.O. in drug dealing. This argument, too, is unpersuasive. The discovery of the rolling papers concededly gave rise to a reasonable suspicion that T.L.O. was carrying marihuana . . . This suspicion justified further exploration of T.L.O.'s purse, which turned up more evidence of drug-related activities: a pipe, a number of plastic bags of the type commonly used to store marihuana, a small quantity of marihuana, and a fairly substantial amount of money. Under these circumstances, it was not unreasonable to extend the search to a separate zippered compartment of the purse; and when a search of that compartment revealed an index card containing a list of "people who owe me money" as well as two letters, the inference that T.L.O. was involved in marihuana trafficking was substantial enough to justify Mr. Choplick in examining the letters to determine whether they contained any further evidence. In short, we cannot conclude that the search for marihuana was unreasonable in any respect.

Because the search resulting in the discovery of the evidence of marihuana dealing by T.L.O. was reasonable, the New Jersey Supreme Court's decision to exclude that evidence from T.L.O.'s juvenile delinquency proceedings on Fourth Amendment grounds was erroneous. Accordingly, the judgment of the Supreme Court of New Jersey is *reversed.*

CHAPTER 7

CHAPTER OUTLINE

A. Introduction
  1. Constitutional safeguards against official discrimination
  2. Statutory remedies
B. Racial and ethnic discrimination
  1. State-sponsored segregation
  2. Intradistrict segregation
    a. School sites and attendance zones
    b. Open transfers
    c. Problems in testing and placement
  3. Interdistrict segregation
  4. Affirmative action and reverse discrimination
    a. Termination of constitutional oversight
  5. Antidiscrimination statutes
    a. Federal laws
    b. State laws
C. Sex discrimination
  1. Student classifications and treatment
    a. Academic courses and admissions
    b. Nonacademic activities
  2. Teacher classifications and treatment
    a. Teacher pregnancy
    b. Compensation and fringe benefits
    c. Improper treatment
    d. Affirmative action
D. Handicapped and gifted
  1. Handicapped students
    a. The appropriate public education requirement
    b. Procedural and noninstructional requirements
    c. The interaction of E.H.A. and § 504

Equal Opportunity in Public Education

        d. Supplemental state support of handicapped children
    2. Gifted children
    3. Handicapped teachers
E. Age discrimination
F. Religious discrimination
G. Poverty groups
H. Aliens
    1. Alien children
    2. Alien teachers and employees

TABLE OF CASES FOR CHAPTER 7

Milliken v. Bradley, 418 U.S. 717 (1974), 394.
Firefighters Local v. Stotts, 467 U.S. 561 (1984), 395.
Wygant v. Jackson Board of Education, ______U.S. ______, 54 U.S.L.W. 4479(1986), 396.
Hendrick Hudson Dist. Bd. of Ed. v. Rowley, 458 U.S. 176 (1982), 405.
Smith v. Robinson, 468 U.S. 992, 104 S.Ct. 3457 (1984), 409.
Stuart v. Nappi, 443 F.Supp. 1235 (D. Conn. 1978), 413.

FEDERAL CIVIL RIGHTS STATUTES, 418–423
A. 42 U.S.C. § 1981—Civil Rights Acts of 1866, 1870
B. 42 U.S.C. § 1983—The Civil Rights Act of 1871
C. 42 U.S.C. §§ 1985 and 1986—The Civil Rights Act of 1871
D. 42 U.S.C. § 1988—Civil Rights Acts of 1866, 1870
E. 42 U.S.C. § 2000(d)—Civil Rights Act of 1964, Title VI
F. 42 U.S.C. § 2000(e)—Civil Rights Act of 1964, Title VII

G. 20 U.S.C. § 1681—Education Amendments of 1972, Title IX
H. 29 U.S.C. § 206(d)—Equal Pay Act
I. 29 U.S.C. § 621—Age Discrimination Act (§ 623)
J. 20 U.S.C. § 1703—Equal Education Opportunities Act
K. 29 U.S.C. § 794—Rehabilitation Act of 1973 (§ 504)
L. 20 U.S.C. § 1401—The Education of the Handicapped Act (§ 1412)

A. Introduction

The modern law on equal opportunity in education was spurred by the landmark racial segregation decisions that set the stage for many new laws designed to protect disadvantaged minorities. Discrimination based upon sex, handicap, age, race, religion, or national origin is now covered by federal and state statutes that go beyond the bare minimums of constitutional protection. Antidiscrimination law primarily is concerned with the *status* of persons based upon group characteristics, rather than with individual conduct. Though group discrimination law ultimately affects individuals, it focuses upon how school authorities *classify* students and teachers.

The right to be free from class discrimination rested initially upon the principles of the Constitution's equal protection clause; individuals' rights that exist independently of group characteristics rest primarily, though not exclusively, upon the due process clause, which was reviewed in the prior chapters.

The concern with group needs often creates tension between legal and educational roles,[1] but confusion is minimized by a candid recognition that the ideal achievement of both individual and group needs is not always feasible. For example, students' needs may warrant assignment to a special school, course, or "track." But a series of such assignments may remove large identifiable groups (whether by race, sex, or handicap) from the educational "mainstream" with adverse group or community consequences that might outweigh the intended benefit to particular individuals. Further, there are different yardsticks of educational opportunity, e.g., selective remedial treatment or access to richer academic programs. Group tensions arise regardless of the choice made, and they are reflected in the code slogans—"affirmative action" and its contrary, "reverse discrimination."

Development of classification methods to accommodate both individualized and group needs remains an unfinished task for educators and lawmakers.

1. Constitutional Safeguards against Official Discrimination

The principal constitutional safeguard against group discrimination is found in the equal protection clause of the Fourteenth Amendment, which guarantees not absolute equality of treatment, but freedom from official "discrimination," or adverse treatment that is not justified by a proper government interest.[2] In deciding what group classifications or assignments are justified, the Supreme Court has fashioned three different constitutional tests, each one of which applies exclusively to particular groups. For classifications deemed not to infringe fundamental rights or target protected minorities, the Court applies a "rationality" test, under which the law will be held constitutional if it serves a reasonable government purpose by means that reasonably achieve that purpose, notwithstanding incidental disadvantage to any particular group or citizen. Legal classifications

---

1. See KIRP, *Schools as Sorters: The Constitutional and Policy Implications of Student Classification,* 124 U. Pa. L. Rev. 705 (1973).

2. The same protection against federal government discrimination is provided by the due process clause of the Fifth Amendment. *See* Bolling v. Sharpe, 347 U.S. 497 (1954).

based upon race or that abridge fundamental rights or interests are deemed by the Court as "suspect," and the Court applies "strict scrutiny." Suspect classifications are presumptively unconstitutional and will be invalidated unless the government can prove that the classification is required by a "compelling" state interest and employs the least infringing means possible to achieve that "compelling" interest. The strict scrutiny test has proven to be nigh impossible to satisfy. For a third type of legal classification, namely "gender" based treatment, the Court has adopted an "intermediate scrutiny" standard that falls between the extremes of rationality deference and suspect scrutiny. Under this mid-tier test, a government action that is challenged as sexually discriminatory "must serve important government objectives and must be substantially related to those objectives," though not necessary to meet a "compelling" state need.[3]

Given these different tests for different branches of "equality" protection, federal constitutional law must be studied specifically with reference to particular minority groups. The constitutional and statute law of most states parallel the antidiscrimination principles of the Constitution, but, as will be shown later, there is no legal prohibition against each state enacting its own antidiscrimination laws to provide even stricter protection against group disadvantage than is furnished by the Constitution.

2. Statutory Remedies

The Fourteenth Amendment deals only with "official" discrimination, and it does not govern purely private discrimination. This limitation of scope has special importance for private schools. (See Chapter 10.) Further, the relief for constitutional violations is only corrective and not compensatory because the Constitution itself does not authorize individuals to sue for money damages against offending officials. Congress and the states have accordingly enacted statutes to broaden the legal protection from discrimination by providing stronger legal remedies, such as damage recovery by injured parties against violators of those statutes. These federal civil rights statutes withstood challenges that they invaded rights reserved to the states under the Tenth Amendment of the Constitution,[4] since other parts of the Constitution empower Congress to promote commerce and the national welfare, as well as the goal of equal protection.[5] The major federal civil rights statutes were enacted in two unrelated series, at distant points in time—following the Civil War, and then following World War II. Hence they do not present any consistent or common scheme of procedures and remedies. Indeed, the failure of Congress to integrate or coordinate the provisions of its various civil rights statutes has resulted in some collision between the laws seeking to remedy racial and sexual discrimination and statutory requirements of affirmative action, on one hand; and

---

3. Craig v. Boren, 429 U.S. 190, 197 (1976).

4. "The powers not delegated to the United States by the Constitution, nor prohibited by it to the states, are reserved to the states respectively, or to the people."

5. *See, e.g.*, Usery v. Bettendorf Comm. Sch. District, 423 F.Supp. 637 (S.D. Iowa 1976) (upholding Title VII and the Equal Pay Act); Fitzpatrick v. Bitzer, 427 U.S. 445 (1976); Remmick v. Barnes County, 435 F.Supp. 914 (D. No. Dak. 1977); Usery v. Bd. of Education of Salt Lake City, F.Supp. 718 (D. Utah 1976) (upholding Age Discrimination in Employment Act). The majority and minority line of cases are reported in the Remmick case, *supra*.

laws preserving seniority rights on the other. See the opinion in *Firefighters Local Union v. Stotts* at the end of this chapter. The major statutes are compared and catalogued at p. 388, et seq., *infra.*

Many state civil rights statutes supplement federal law. Members of protected minorities may thus have several federal or state avenues of relief in seeking to vindicate their civil rights.[6]

B. Racial and Ethnic Discrimination

1. State-Sponsored Segregation

The Equal Protection Clause covers only "state action," and prohibits only state-fostered discrimination.[7] Racial or ethnic segregation that is derived from the influence of law is called *de jure* segregation and is unconstitutional; but segregation or imbalance created by social forces, independently of government sponsorship, is called *de facto* segregation and is not unconstitutional.[8] The following elements must exist for de jure segregation:

1. It must have been initiated or supported by government action;
2. With the intent or motive to discriminate; and
3. The action must actually create or increase segregation.[9]

Despite powerful criticisms, the Supreme Court has repeatedly approved the de jure-de facto distinction in ruling that public school authorities have no constitutional obligation to eliminate de facto segregation.[10] Given the difficulty of proving unconstitutional purpose as well as segregative effect, the distinction has proven critical in recent Supreme Court cases.[11] "Our cases have not embraced the proposition that a law or other official act . . . is unconstitutional *solely* because it has racially disproportionate impact."[12] The difficulty of determining what kind and degree of proofs are required to establish unconstitutional purpose has been recognized, but not resolved by, the Supreme Court.[13] Some lower courts accept statistical evidence of racial concentrations as

---

6. The remedies provided by these statutes are reviewed in Chapter 8, as an aspect of tort liability.

7. Similar discrimination by the federal government is, however, barred by the Fifth Amendment.

8. Legislative (as distinguished from constitutional) remedies for de facto segregation are treated later in this chapter.

9. Alexander v. Youngstown Bd. of Education, 675 F.2d 787, 791 (6th Cir. 1982); *see* Oliber v. Mich. State Bd. of Education, 508 F.2d 178, 182 (6th Cir. 1974).

10. *See* Keyes v. Sch. District No. 1, Denver, 413 U.S. 189, 202, 203 (1973).

11. Austin Ind. Sch. District v. United States, 429 U.S. 990 (1977); Sch. District of Omaha v. U.S., 433 U.S. 667 (1977).

12. Sch. District of Omaha v. U.S., 433 U.S. 667, at p. 668 (1977).

13. *See* Dayton Bd. of Education v. Brinkman, 433 U.S. 406 (1977). The Court recognized that the proof of intent requirements under federal statutes are less stringent than under the constitution. *See also* Buford v. Morgantown City Bd. of Education, 244 F.Supp. 437 (W.D. N.C. 1965).

sufficient proof of segregative intent or purpose.[14] The Supreme Court has stated that "discriminatory purpose may often be inferred from the totality of the relevant facts" including a law's disproportionate impact on one race only.[15] It has, nevertheless, rejected the position that disproportionately adverse impact of official actions alone (viz. from employment screening tests) is inherently unconstitutional.[16]

Unconstitutional (de jure) segregation is not subject to a fixed definition:

> "What is or is not a segregated school will necessarily depend on the facts of each particular case. In addition to the . . . composition of a school's student body, other factors, such as the racial and ethnic composition of faculty and staff and the community and administration attitudes toward the school must be taken into consideration." *Keyes* v. *Sch. District No. 1, Denver,* 413 U.S. 189, 196 (1973).

Although states are constitutionally free to tolerate de facto segregation, they are also constitutionally free to attack it as a matter of educational policy (such voluntary actions are considered in a later section).

In 1954 the Supreme Court struck down state laws that *required* public schools to be racially segregated. This ruling was later extended to cover ethnic minorities (Hispanos, Indians), northern states, and federal enclaves that practiced de jure segregation.[17]

Official segregation of school faculty and staff and official discrimination in the hiring and treatment of minority teachers and administrators equally violate the equal protection rights of teachers.[18]

The constitutional *remedy* for de jure segregation was first pronounced in the second *Brown* case (*Brown II*) where the Court ordered public school authorities to take immediate action toward desegregating their schools under the continuing supervision of the lower federal courts.[19] *Brown II* failed to set any time deadline for completing the desegregation process and merely instructed the lower courts *to proceed with all deliberate speed.* The dragging pace of desegregation through the ensuing decade prompted the

---

14. U.S. v. Midland Ind. Sch. District, 519 F.2d 60 (5th Cir. 1975); U.S. v. Missouri, 515 F.2d 1365 (8th Cir. 1975). The lines of lower court cases are listed in fn. 12 of the Supreme Court's opinion in Washington v. Davis, cited in the following footnote.

15. *See* Washington v. Davis, 426 U.S. 229 at p. 242 (1976); Sweeney Ind. Sch. District v. Harkness, noted at p. 368 this text; *cf.* Arthur v. Nyquist, 573 F.2d 134 (2d Cir. 1978); *cert. denied,* Manch v. Arthur, 439 U.S. 860 (1978) (using natural, probable and forseeable result test); United States v. Board of School Commissioners of the City of Indianapolis, 573 F.2d 400 (7th Cir. 1978), *cert. denied,* Bowen v. U.S., 439 U.S. 824 (1978).

16. *Re* race, see prior footnote; *re* sex, see National Educational Assn. v. So. Carolina, 434 U.S. 1026 (1978).

17. Brown v. Bd. of Education, 347 U.S. 483 (1954); Keyes v. Sch. Dist. No. 1, Denver, 413 U.S. 189 (1973); Natonabah v. Board of Education, 355 F.Supp. 716 (D.N.M. 1973); Hernandez v. Texas, 347 U.S. 475 (1954); Bolling v. Sharpe, 347 U.S. 497 (1954) (de jure segregation in the District of Columbia, violates the Fifth Amendment).

18. *Re* segregated assignments, *see, e.g.,* Bradley v. School Board, 382 U.S. 103 (1965); Rogers v. Paul, 382 U.S. 198 (1965); Singleton v. Jackson Municipal Separate School Dist., 419 F.2d 1211 (5th Cir. 1970), cert. den. 396 U.S. 1032 (1970); No. Carolina Teachers Ass'n. v. Asheboro City Bd. of Educ., 393 F.2d 736 (4th Cir. 1968). *Re* discriminatory treatment, *see* Lee v. Washington County Bd. of Education, 682 F.2d 894, 895 (11th Cir. 1982).

19. Brown v. Bd. of Education (Brown II), 349 U.S. 294 (1955).

Court in 1964 to declare that: "The time for mere 'deliberate speed' has run out, and that phrase can no longer justify denying . . . school children their constitutional rights. . . . " *Griffin* v. *School Board,* 377 U.S. 218, 234 (1964).

Court-ordered desegregation was stalled by numerous evasionary devices, which required further decrees. When state authorities closed public schools in Little Rock, Arkansas, and in Prince Edward County, Virginia, the courts held such action unconstitutional in that it frustrated and defeated court-ordered desegregation.[20] State encouragement of private school segregation by providing state funding or leasing public school buildings to segregated private schools was held equally unconstitutional.[21] In the latter cases, the Supreme Court stressed that state aid to private education was not per se unconstitutional, but was unlawful when used to avoid and defeat outstanding desegregation orders.

Other unlawful actions to defeat desegregation included school district reorganization that resegregated schools.[22]

School authorities must also avoid discrimination in the methods used to desegregate schools. Casting the entire burden of travel and relocation only on black students where less burdensome alternatives were available was held impermissible, as was the closing of a black school in the belief that white students would not go to that school.[23] Where the closing of a black school without cross transfers was made to provide students with better resources in a newer school, however, the court found no discrimination by reason of the incidental burdens on black students.[24]

2. Intradistrict Segregation

a. School Sites and Attendance Zones. School boards may not create racially identifiable schools in the guise of fixing school locations or of drawing attendance boundaries.[25] Where board action produced unlawful segregation in only part of the city, however, the Supreme Court ruled that the constitutional remedy was limited to that

---

20. Griffin v. County Sch. Bd. of Prince Edward County, 377 U.S. 218 (1964); Aaron v. McKinley, 173 F.Supp. 944 (E.D. Ark.), aff'd 361 U.S. 197 (1959).

21. Norwood v. Harrison 413 U.S. 455 (1973); Poindexter v. La. Financial Assistance Comm., 296 F.Supp. 686 (E.D. La., affd. sub nom. La. Education Comm. v. Poindexter, 393 U.S. 17 (1968)); Brown v. So. Carolina State Board of Education, 296 F. Supp. 199 (D.S.C., aff'd. 393 U.S.222 (1968)). *See also* Wright v. Baker City Bd. of Education, 501 F.2d 131 (5th Cir. 1974); U.S. v. State of Mississippi, 499 F.2d 425 (5th Cir. 1974).

22. United States v. Scotland Neck City Board of Education, 407 U.S.484 (1972); Wright v. Council of City of Emporia, 407 U.S. 451 (1972).

23. United States v. Texas Ed. Agency, 467 F.2d 848, 871-72 (5th Cir. 1972); Gordon v. Jefferson Davis Parish School, 330 F. Supp. 1119 (W.D. La. 1971); Bell v. West Point Mun. Separate Sch. District, 446 F.2d 1362 (5th Cir. 1971); Brice v. Landis, 314 F.Supp. 974 (N.D. Cal. 1969).

24. Higgins v. Grand Rapids Bd. of Education, 508 F.2d 779, 793-95 (6th Cir. 1974); Norwalk CORE v. Norwalk Bd. of Education,423 F.2d 121 (2d Cir. 1970); Moss v. Stamford Bd. of Education, 356 F. Supp. 675 (D. Conn. 1973).

25. *Segregative site selections*: Lee v. Autanga County Bd. of Education, 514 F.2d 646 (5th Cir. 1975); Akron Bd. of Education v. State Bd. of Education, 490 F.2d 1285 (6th Cir. 1974). *Segregated attendance zones*: *See* Milliken v. Bradley (Milliken I), 418 U.S. 717 (1974); Keyes v. School District No. 1, Denver, 413 U.S. 189 (1973). The impact of segregation law upon the practice of student grouping by standardized aptitude tests requires separate analysis. Ability grouping is taken up in the context of exceptional children at p. 364 et seq.

part of the city in which the board fostered de jure segregation.[26] While the Court recognized that segregation in one part of the city could in certain cases have citywide impact as to justify citywide desegregation, it insisted that the constitutional remedy must be confined to territory actually affected by unconstitutional action. In addition to ordering reassignments of teachers and students, courts may remedy the adverse *effects* of past segregation by ordering offending states and districts to initiate and fund special education programs (remedial speech and reading, in-service teacher training) for the injured minority group.[27]

The cases have been divided on whether changes in student assignment plans of predecessor boards that were intended to eliminate de facto segregation could amount to intentional de jure segregation.[28]

b. Open Transfers. School districts cannot avoid desegregation orders by allowing students to elect any school they wish to attend. A "minority-to-majority" transfer plan permitted a student to transfer from a school where he was in the racial minority to a school where he would be in the racial majority. The plan, which resegregated the schools, was unanimously struck down.[29] "Freedom of choice" plans met the same fate when they operated to block a desegregation decree:

> "The burden on a school board today is to come forward with a plan that promises realistically to work, . . . *now.* We do not hold that 'freedom-of-choice' plan might of itself be unconstitutional. . . . Rather, all we decide today is that a plan utilizing 'freedom of choice' is not an end in itself. . . . 'If the means prove effective, it is acceptable, but if it fails to undo segregation, other means must be used. . . . '" *Green* v. *County School Board,* 391 U.S. 430, 439-40 (1968).

> "The only school desegregation plan that meets constitutional standards is one that works." *United States* v. *Jefferson County Bd. of Education,* 372 F.2d 836, 847 (5th Cir. 1966).

c. Problems in Testing and Placement. The practice of grouping students according to aptitudes derived from standardized tests deprives many students of diverse peer association and has been attacked as elitist or stigmatizing. The underlying test methods have been challenged as unreliable, at best, and biased and discriminatory, at worst. The measures taken to avoid cultural segregation—mixing different students in some activities of the same school and retesting periodically to assure mobility between course tracks—have not quelled attacks on testing for homogenous grouping that produces racially disparate school and course assignments. The legality of such practices has turned upon specific proofs in each case and not upon any blanket principle that

---

26. Dayton Bd. of Education v. Brinkman, 433 U.S. 406 (1977).

27. Milliken v. Bradley (Milliken II), 433 U.S. 267 (1977). Unlike Milliken I, *supra,* the state was found to have officially been involved in the segregation remedied by Millken II.

28. *Compare* NAACP v. Lansing Bd. of Education, 429 F.Supp. 583 (W.D. Mich. 1977), aff'd. 559 F.2d 1042 (6th Cir. 1973), cert. denied 434 U.S. 997 (1978); *with* the Dayton case, supra.

29. Goss v. Board of Education, 373 U.S. 683 (1963).

covers all situations. In overturning a student testing and tracking system of the public schools in the District of Columbia, the court pointed to the problem of measuring ability through language skills and social perspectives, which disadvantaged children lack: "If a student has had little or no opportunity to acquire and develop the requisite verbal and nonverbal skills, he obviously cannot score well on the tests." The Court of Appeals approved the court's overturning of the tests in question but refused to adopt the principle that all tests producing racial segregation are per se unlawful. It held instead that courts would outlaw only tests that were proven to be unfair.[30] Disproportionate racial impact of student grouping has drawn uneven lower court responses even where the minority could point to past discrimination as the cause of poor group performance, but since the Supreme Court decision upholding police testing that disproportionately eliminated black candidates, the burden of proving test unreliability appears to remain with the challengers.[31]

The validity of tests that result in lower evaluation and lower-level student or teacher placement of blacks or other minorities depends in part upon the school district's record of de jure segregation. For districts undergoing desegregation with a duty to eliminate the effects of past segregation, courts nullified tests that produced racially imbalanced classes for underachievers or learning disabled since the tests themselves tended to perpetuate unlawful segregation.[32] For nonsegregated districts, however, there is no foursquare Supreme Court decision to resolve the conflict in lower court cases.[33]

Children whose sole or primary language is not English are peculiarly disadvantaged by normal English instruction, but their claims of *constitutional right* to special (bilingual or bicultural) education have generally been turned aside.[34] Exceptions have occurred in cases where their linguistic deficiency was traceable to de jure segregation and was thus considered remediable as part of a desegregation order.[35] The right to special language education has, however, been supplied by federal and state statutes.

In *Lau* v. *United States,* the court found that denial of special English instruction to a large community of linguistically handicapped Chinese-Americans violated Title VI of the 1964 Civil Rights and the California Education Code, which required instruction

30. Smuck v. Hobson, 408 F.2d 175 (D.C. Cir. 1969).

31. *See* Washington v. Davis, discussed at p. 367, n. 45.

32. McNeal v. Tate County Sch. District, 508 F.2d 1017 (5th Cir. 1975); *cf.* Moses v. Washington Par. Sch. Bd., 456 F.2d 1285 (5th Cir. 1972).

33. *Compare* Murray v. W. Baton Rouge Sch. Bd., 472 F.2d 438 (5th Cir. 1973); Copeland v. Sch. Bd., City of Portsmouth, 464 F.2d 932 (4th Cir. 1972); *with* Hobson v. Hensen, 269 F.Supp. 401 (D.D.C. 1967) aff'd sub nom. Hobsen v. Smuck, 408 F.2d 175 (D.C.Cir. 1969); Larry P. v. Riles, 343 F.Supp. 1306 (N.D. Cal. 1972) (holding standardized tests unconstitutional because of racial overrepresentation in EMR classes). Also unresolved is the question of what degree of racial imbalance is needed to support an inference of racial discrimination. *See* Morales v. Shannon, 516 F.2d 411 (5th Cir. 1975) (statistical results not so unusual as to require judicial review under civil rights statutes). Consent decrees save time and expense, but they do not stand as firm precedent. *See* Pa. Asso. of Retarded Children (PARC) v. Pennsylvania, 334 F.Supp. 1257 (E.D. Pa. 1971); LeBanks v. Spears, 60 F.R.D. 135 (E.D. La. 1973).

34. *See* Guadulupe Organization, Inc. v. Tempe Elementary Sch. Dist. 587 F.2d 1022 (9th Cir. 1978) (no duty under Title VI or the Equal Educational Opportunity Act of 1974 to provide bilingual-bicultural education to non-English-speaking students).

35. United States v. Texas, 466 F.2d. 519 (5th Cir. 1976); *Re* present school district discrimination, *see* Cisneros v. Corpus Christi Ind. Sch. District, 467 F.2d 142 (5th Cir. 1972).

and proficiency in the English language. Similar decisions were made with respect to Spanish-speaking minorities in other states.[37]

In the *Lau* case, the Supreme Court upheld the affirmative action requirements of federal regulations, which provided in part that " . . . the district must take affirmative steps to rectify the language deficiency in order to open its instructional program to these students. . . . Any ability grouping or tracking system employed . . . to deal with the special language skill needs of national-origin-minority-group children must be designed to meet such language skill needs . . . and must not operate as an educational deadend or permanent track."[38]

In 1967, Congress amended the 1965 Education law by the Bilingual Education Act, which provides federal grants to assist states in bilingual education programs in public and private schools.[39] A growing number of states have special statutes for bilingual education.[40] In the absence of explicit state guidelines, however, the school district's obligations to provide language remediation is determined by a rule of reason. Courts have referred to such factors as (1) the number of students involved, (2) the degree of their linguistic deficiency, (3) the perceived utility of bicultural content as well as bilingual communication to motivate cultural minorities, (4) the availability of instructors who are facile with the primary ethnic language. Thus, Chicanos seeking bilingual-bicultural special education in Colorado failed because the court found that the number of linguistically handicapped children was not large and that there was no showing of school district disregard of individual student-language problems.[41] The powers to fashion remedies appropriate to circumstances is illustrated by a federal court order that required bilingual education only for those Spanish-speaking students whose English test scores fell below the 20th percentile of the statistical norm for English-speaking students and whose tests in Spanish scored higher than the 20th percentile of the statistical norm of Spanish-speaking students. Conceding that its formula was inexact, the court observed that Spanish-speaking students who scored better in English testing than one-fifth of their English-speaking peers could reasonably be considered not so uniquely disadvantaged as to require special education. Another court ordered retesting of thousands of Mexican-American children in EMR classes to be given in their native language because a grossly disproportionate number of that group were placed in EMR classes on the basis of English IQ testing.[42]

Whether public schools are bound under the Equal Education Opportunities Act of 1974 to take action to overcome language barriers that are based on social factors

---

36. Lau v. United States 414 U.S. 563 (1974). *See* 35 Fed. Reg. 11595, App. 26a (1970).

37. Aspira v. Bd. of Education, 394 F.Supp. 1161 (S.D. N.Y. 1975) (consent decree); Serna v. Portales Mun. Schools, 499 F.2d 1147 (10th Cir. 1975) (under Title VI).

38. 35 Fed. Reg. 11595 (1970).

39. 20 U.S.C. § 880(b).

40. Bilingual Education Programs are mandated by state statute in Alaska, Massachusetts, and Michigan; and are authorized by state statute in Arizona, Arkansas, California, Colorado, Illinois, Iowa, Maine, New Mexico, New York, Oregon, Pennsylvania, Rhode Island, and Texas, among others.

41. Otero v. Mesa County Valley Sch. District No. 51, 408 F.Supp 162 (D. Colo. 1975). Note, *Bilingual Education—A Problem of Substantial Numbers,* V FORDHAM L. REV. 561 (1977). *See also* Morales v. Shannon, 516 F.2d 411 (5th Cir. 1975).

42. Diana v. State Bd. of Education, Cir. No. 7037 R.F.P. (N.D. Cal. 1970) (consent decree).

rather than ethnic origin was considered recently in a suit by black students whose "Black English" was so alien to standard English as to impair their ability to learn. The court decided that the act placed no limit on the source of language deficiencies and ruled that the plaintiffs stated a good claim under that statute.[43] Although most linguistic problems appear in poverty groups, other children are also entitled to the benefits of the above laws.[44]

Disproportionate racial impact of teacher employment tests does not automatically establish unconstitutional discrimination. In a 1976 decision, the Supreme Court overturned many lower court cases by holding that statistical evidence of disproportionate exclusion of black job applicants under police department examinations was not sufficient to prove intentional discrimination or to render the test practice unconstitutional.[45] In so ruling, the Court noted that the burden of proving purposive discrimination under the Constitution is heavier than that required to show a violation of employment discrimination statutes. While recognizing that statistical evidence may be relevant for both purposes, the Court noted that the weight of such evidence is very much a matter of case-by-case analysis: "Statistics . . . come in an infinite variety . . . [T]heir usefulness depends on all of the surrounding facts and circumstances."[46]

In public schools the legal effect of disparate impact of employment tests has been complicated by the lack of dominant, objective standards to validate testing procedures: "It appears beyond doubt by now that there is no single method of appropriately validating employment tests for their relationship to job performance." *Washington* v. *Davis* 426 U.S. 229, 247 (1976).

In 1978 the Supreme Court again considered a challenge, under both the constitution and Title VII (employment discrimination) of the 1964 Civil Rights Act, to the National Teachers Examination, which was used to determine teacher certification and rate of pay in South Carolina. The plaintiffs charged the test was discriminatory because it resulted in excluding 83 percent of the black applicants against 17.5 percent of the white applicants and produced a white/black ratio of 96/1 in the newly certified teachers. Since the plaintiff did not prove discriminatory *intent* in selecting the test and the state established that the test was objectively valid, the trial court found no illegality. The United States Supreme Court summarily affirmed this decision.[47]

The importance of statistical impacts was also limited by safety factors. In a Title VII case, the Supreme Court found no employment discrimination where an employer, in order to assure safety in a hazardous project, passed over three qualified black firebrick artisans to employ more experienced white artisans. Since other, experienced blacks were not systematically excluded, the Supreme Court sustained the defense, notwithstanding

---

43. Martin Luther King. Jr. El'y. Sch. Children v. Michigan Bd. of Education, 413 F.Supp. 1371 (E.D. Mich. 1979).

44. Deerfield Hutterian Assn. v. Ipswich Bd. of Education, 444 F.Supp. 159 (S.D. 1978).

45. Washington v. Davis, 426 U.S. 229 (1976). *Cf.* United States v. Midland Ind. Sch. District 519 F.2d 60 (5th Cir. 1975). On the kinds of evidence needed to prove discriminatory intent, *see* Arlington Heights v. Metropolitan Housing Corp. 429 U.S. 252 (1977).

46. *See* Hazelwood Sch. District v. United States, 433 U.S. 267, 312 (1977).

47. National Education Assn. v. South Carolina; United States v. South Carolina, both reported at 434 U.S. 1026 (1978). See Addendum on p. 662.

possible disproportionate racial impact.[48] How these rulings will apply to the school context in a district found not to have violated the constitution remains to be seen.

The *American Bar Association Journal* summarized the changes and rapid development in the law of employment discrimination as of March, 1978:

> "Cases deal with a variety of issues, ranging from housing to the classroom, and those that have gained review have sometimes been hard to distinguish from those that have not. Comparing lower court decisions that the Justices have not taken on petitions or appeals may be even more bewildering. Decisions that have been allowed to stand often have supported conflicting approaches to discrimination law. . . . School-desegregation problems have prompted the largest number of requests for review, but so far the Court has not granted any. Its failure to step into the area leave standing such decisions as the imposition of a plan welding the Wilmington (Delaware) School District and several suburban ones . . . without specific findings of discriminatory intent (77-131, *Delaware State Board of Education* v. *Evans*), but the Court allowed to stand the use of 'natural and foreseeable consequences' as a test for intent in a school desegration case from the Sixth Circuit, . . . (77-600, *Lansing Board of Education* v. *NAACP*) . . . In a teacher employment case, denied review, there was a conclusion by the Fifth Circuit that the discriminatory intent could be presumed from the firing of seventeen black teachers after different criteria were employed to evaluate black and white teachers (77-392, *Sweeney Independent School District* v. *Harkness*). On the other hand, the Justices summarily affirmed a ruling . . . that found intentional bias was lacking in school certification and evaluation procedures. . . . (77-422, *National Education Association* v. *South Carolina*). In the employment sphere in general, the significance of statistics appears to be the greatest area of uncertainty. . . . Although the Court appears to be moving cautiously in the discrimination area, it is moving, developing what may be new lines in social philosophies. And if there is anything that can be said with certainty about the balance of interests of racial groups or other classes of citizens, it is that the questions will never be settled for all time."[49]

Title VI of the 1964 Act generally prohibits racial (but not sex) discrimination in any federally aided program or activity (see appendix 7-A), Conflicting interpretations of that title by the courts leave its impact uncertain. (See the discussion of the *Bakke* case at p. 370, *infra.*)

3. Interdistrict Segregation

Federal courts have no authority to order one school district to cross-assign or cross-bus its students or teachers into another district unless both districts or their parent state fostered segregation between districts. (See *Milliken* v. *Bradley* at the end of this chapter.) The lack of jurisdiction to remedy de facto interdistrict racial imbalance has been

---

48. Furnco Construction Corp. v. Waters 438 U.S. 567 (1978). Where no past hiring discrimination was proven, seniority layoff systems (last hired-first fired) were upheld. *See* Chance v. Bd. of Examiners and Bd. of Education, 534 F.2d 993, 997 (2nd Cir. 1976). However, where hiring discrimination occurred *after* the passage of the federal Civil Rights Act the Supreme Court approved the granting of constructive seniority to minority employees. International Brotherhood of Teamsters v. United States, 431 U.S. 324 (1977).

49. 64 American Bar Association Journal 309, 311 (1978).

confirmed by the Supreme Court in later cases.[50] However, where adjoining school districts or the parent state fostered interdistrict segregation, the Supreme Court sustained interdistrict desegregation orders because they matched the scope of de jure segregation found to exist in those districts.[51] It is possible to find intentional de jure segregation where officials act to *freeze* existing de facto segregation by prohibiting natural changes that would undo such segregation.[52]

4. Affirmative Action and Reverse Discrimination

The use of racial standards, goals, or quotas, benignly described as affirmative action and perjoratively condemned as reverse discrimination, has different implications in different fact settings. Where an official finding of past unconstitutional discrimination exists the law is clear:

> "Just as the race of students and teachers must be considered in determining whether a constitutional violation has occurred, so also must race be considered in formulating a remedy. To forbid this . . . would deprive school authorities of the one tool absolutely essential to fulfillment of their constitutional obligation to eliminate existing dual school systems." *North Carolina State Bd. of Education* v. *Swann,* 402 U.S. 43 (1971).

State and federal lawmakers may not prohibit race-conscious court remedies through antibusing statutes that would frustrate court-ordered desegregation, nor can state statutes be enforced where such action would undercut the constitutional power of federal courts to use busing as a tool to undo unconstitutional segregation.[53]

Where there is no *official* determination of past unconstitutional discrimination, the legal limits of minority preference are not the same for all forms of affirmative action. The ambiguous phrase *affirmative action* can mean very different things. If a program seeks to improve the lot of a minority by special efforts that do not deprive other groups of their rights or of fair treatment (e.g., special training programs), little difficulty is encountered. If, however, the means used to help a minority take away other groups' rights, major difficulties are presented. The law regarding affirmative action by school districts to redress de facto racial disparities (i.e., when such is not required by court decree or legislation) is still incomplete and developing. Recent trends in that law are provided by the Supreme Court opinions in *Wygant* v. *Jackson Board of Education* and in *Firefighters Local* v. *Stotts,* both of which are reproduced at the end of this chapter, and which should be read at this point. The fact that even these decisions remain subject to conflicting

---

50. Berry v. Sch. District, 698 F.2d 813 (2d Cir. 1983); Metropolitan Sch. District of Perry Twp. v. Buckley; School Town of Speedway v. Buckley; Metropolitan School District of Lawrence Twp. v. Buckley; Bd. of School Commissioners of Indianapolis v. Buckley—all reported at 429 U.S. 1068 (1977).

51. The history of the Delaware segregation cases and their relation to Milliken v. Bradley, *supra,* is reported in Evans v. Buchanan, 555 F.2d 373 (3d Cir. 1977) from which the Supreme Court, by 4 to 3 vote, denied cert. *See* Dela. State Bd. of Education v. Evans, and related cases, reported at 434 U.S. 880, 994, (1977); *see also* United States v. State of Missouri, 515 F.2d 1365 (8th Cir. 1975).

52. See prior footnote; Lee v. Nyquist, 318 F.Supp. 710 (W.D. N.Y. 1970) aff'd, 402 U.S. 935 (1971); *cf.* San Francisco Unified School Dist. v. Johnson, 479 P.2d 669 (Cal. 1971).

53. See the North Carolina case in the text; Chance v. Bd. of Examiners, 534 F.2d 993, 997, n. 7 (2d Cir. 1976); Vulcan Soc. of N.Y. City Fire Dept. Inc. v. Civil Serv. Comm., 490 F.2d 387 (2d Cir. 1973).

interpretation[54] points up the uncertain and varied legal bounds of affirmative minority racial preferences in different student and teacher programs.

Racial preference in teacher promotion that is not tied to permissible remediation may violate equal protection, as well as Title VI and Title VII of the 1964 Act, which proscribe antiwhite as well as anti-black discrimination.[55] But a school board's preference of black candidates who were best able to identify with a predominantly black student body was held nondiscriminatory since whites were not excluded from consideration.[56] A similar preference standard (ability to identify with a predominantly white student body) was found discriminatory in a different setting.[57] Minority preference as a matter of administrative discretion was upheld as compensatory in one case, but condemned as reverse discrimination in another.[58] These case variations may rest more on differences in fact interpretation than on constitutional principle.

Prior to the milestone case of *Regents, U. of California* v. *Bakke,* the lower courts did not agree on whether public administrators could, on their own initiative (without judicial, statutory, or executive authority), adopt minority preference admission programs.[59] In *Bakke,* the Supreme Court Justices split 4-1-4 on the legality of minority quotas for admission to a state medical school. Five justices held the practice unlawful, and four voted to sustain it. Four of the five-man majority held that fixed minority preference amounted to unlawful discrimination under Title VI of the 1964 Act (see Appendix 7-A, Section E.) The fifth concluded that Title VI was no stricter than the federal constitution and voted that the use of race as an *exclusive* test of admission was unconstitutional. This crucial "swing" opinion of Mr. Justice Powell significantly made no reference to the slogan terms "affirmative action" and "reverse discrimination." He stressed that race may be a relevant, but not exclusive, consideration in admitting students to a professional school because "diversity" of student bodies enhances the educational process.

---

54. See, e.g., Local No. 98, International Assn. of Firefighters v. City of Cleveland. 54 U.S.—L.W. 5005 (1986), wherein the Supreme Court, in a suit charging unconstitutional discrimination, held that an affirmative action consent decree on minority *promotions* did not violate the Title VII rights of white firemen. Compare, Kromnick v. School District of Philadelphia, 739 F.2d 894 (3d Cir. 1984) with Stotts and Wygant, pp. 395 and 396, supra. Kromnick upheld a practice of involuntary transfers of senior teachers as a means of improving the quality of all schools through improved racial balance in teaching staffs of each school. It found Stotts, which voided preferential retention of black teachers over more senior white teachers in layoffs, not to govern transfer affirmative action. Deveraux v. Geary, 596 F.Supp. 1487 (D.Mass. 1984) (upholding affirmative action promotional preference of black candidate over white candidates with higher test scores).

55. Anderson v. S. Francisco Un. Sch. District, 357 F.Supp. 248 (N.D. Cal. 1972) (equal protection); McDonald v. Santa Fe Trans. Co., 427 U.S. 273 (1976) (Title VII).

56. Council of Supervisory Ass'ns. v. Bd. of Educ., 245 N.E.2d 204 (N.Y. 1969); Porcelli v. Titus, 431 F.2d 1254 (3d Cir. 1970), cert. denied 402 U.S. 944 (1971). *Cf.* Morton v. Mancari, 417 U.S. 535 (1974) (employment preference of Indians in U.S. Bureau of Indian Affairs held constitutional). *But see* Auerbach v. African-American Teachers Assn., 356 F. Supp. 1046 (E.D. N.Y. 1973).

57. Compare NAACP v. Allen, 493 F.2d 614 (5th Cir. 1974).

58. *Compensatory*: Smith v. Bd. of Education, 365 F.2d 770 (8th Cir. 1966). *Reverse discrimination*: Legg v. Fair Emp. Pract. Comm'n, 329 N.E.2d 486 (Ill. 1975) (transfer of white teacher to end de facto segregation). *See also* fns. 54, 55 *supra.*

59. 438 U.S. 912 (1978); *compare* Germann v. Kipp, 429 F. Supp. 1323 (W.D. Mo. 1977) *with* Brunetti v. City of Berkeley, 12 FEP 937 (N.D. Cal. 1976). For a review of the checkered case law, *see* Annotation: *Sex Discrimination in Employment,* 26 A.L.R. Fed. 27, 100-113 (1976).

The *Bakke* limitation on racial quotas was confined to its facts, i.e., admission policy, by the later Supreme Court decision in *United Steelworkers of America* v. *Weber.*[60] The Court there sustained an employment training program set up by company-union agreement that assigned a fixed ratio of openings to minority races. The *Bakke* and *Weber* opinions made clear that not all racial preferences for beneficent purposes will be upheld and thus anticipated the later Supreme Court decision in Wygant (reproduced at the end of this chapter), which struck down affirmative action preference on layoffs for black teachers over white teachers with greater seniority. The *Wygant* decision leaves unanswered the legality of other untested forms of affirmative action.

a. Termination of Constitutional Oversight. The Supreme Court has limited the power of federal courts in several ways. As previously stated, their jurisdiction is limited to de jure violations. They may not act arbitrarily: "Remedial judicial authority does not put judges automatically in the shoes of school authorities . . . judicial authority enters only when local authority defaults. . . . No fixed, or even substantially fixed, guidelines can be established as to how far a court can go, but it must be recognized there are limits." *Swann* v. *Charlotte-Mecklenberg Bd. of Education,* 402 U.S. II (1971) at p. 16, 28.

Considerations, such as child welfare, educational efficiency, financial resources, demography, and the geography of involved districts, must be weighed in deciding the propriety of particular desegregation plans. The Supreme Court stated that even one-race schools could be justified in special circumstances.

Once de jure segregation is eliminated, the court's constitutional jurisdiction terminates, and it cannot be revived unless a new suit is brought to establish new de jure violations. Thus a court order to compel a previously desegregated school district to eliminate de facto racial imbalances arising from later population shifts was reversed by the United States Supreme Court.[61] As noted in the prior section and elsewhere, however, broader jurisdiction to remedy discrimination may be provided by civil rights statutes that expand the remedial powers of the courts.

5. Antidiscrimination Statutes

a. Federal Laws. The federal statutes have hastened school desegregation by providing federal aid for desegregation expenses; by authorizing federal agency regulations and supervision of desegregation plans; and by authorizing court action by the Attorney General to complete desegregation.[62] The combination of fiscal incentives and enforcement advanced desegregation without displacing the power of federal courts to act

---

60. 443 U.S. 93 (1979), *re* fixed minority employment quotas required of government contractors, the conflict in lower court decisions may be resolved by the Supreme Court which recently agreed to review an appeal on that issue. Fullilove v. Kreps, 584 F.2d 600, cert. granted, 99 S.Ct. 2403 (1979).

61. Pasadena City Bd. of Education v. Spangler 427 U.S. 424 (1976). *Accord:* Cousin v. Bd. of Trustees, Houston Mun. Sep. Sch. District, 726 F.2d 262 (5th Cir. 1984). See also Riddick v. School Board, 627 F.2d 814 (E.D.Va. 1984).

62. *Board of Public Instruction of Taylor County v. Finch,* 414 F.2d 1068 (5th Cir. 1969); Comment, The Courts, HEW, and Southern School Desegregation, 77 Yale L.J. 311 (1967-68).

directly under the Fourteenth Amendment.[63] Additional private remedies under the civil rights statutes are discussed in Chapter 8. The federal statutes allow the courts broad discretion in fashioning relief. For example, courts may deny advanced seniority status to a victim of discrimination where other remedies will make that victim "whole" without injuring the interests of other employees.[64]

b. State Laws. The "floor" requirements of federal laws do not disable individual states from adopting more stringent antidiscrimination rules under their own constitutions and statutes. (See Appendix 7-A for a sample listing of state laws.)[65] Several courts held that their state constitutional provisions were violated by tax laws that produced materially disproportionate per pupil expenditures in the school districts, notwithstanding the Supreme Court's decision that such tax schemes did not violate the federal constitution. (See p. 392, this text.)

Under their general welfare powers, states may outlaw discrimination in private as well as public schools, establish compensatory education programs for disadvantaged minorities even though no de jure segregation exists; and fix racial balance ratios for public school students and staff, regardless of the causes of such imbalance.[66] The rule against arbitrary action will still operate, however, to stay a racial balance scheme that unfairly burdens a particular racial group.[67]

Reasonable measures to achieve racial balance by out-of-neighborhood busing are within the state's police power, but a state is not bound to elect such an approach. Thus a California constitutional amendment to prohibit court ordered busing to alleviate de facto racial imbalance of students in schools was held constitutional by the Supreme Court; and an Illinois statute to prohibit teacher transfers to alleviate de facto racial imbalance in school teaching staffs was also upheld.[68]

---

63. Swan v. Charlotte-Mecklenberg Bd. of Education, 402 U.S. 1(1971); Drummond v. Acree, 409 U.S. 1228 (1972).

64. "We are not to be understood as holding that an award of seniority status is requisite in all circumstances. The fashioning of appropriate remedies invokes the sound equitable discretion of the district courts." *See* Franks v. Bowman, 424 U.S. 747, 770 (1976).

65. *See also* Ill. Rev. Stat. ch. 122, § 34-18 (7) (1965); Burns Ind. Stat. Ann., Tit. 30, 30-8.1-2-2) (1975); Guilderland Central Sch. Dist. v. N.Y. State Hum. Rights Appeal Bd., 461 N.Y.S.2d 599 (1983).

66. *Re compensatory programs*: *See generally* National Association of Inter-Group Relations Officials (NAIRO), Public School Segregation and Integration in the North, 75-91 (1963); Kaplan, Equal Justice in an Unequal World: Equality for the Negro—The Problem of Special Treatment, 61 N.W.U. L. Rev. 363, 398 (1966-67). *Re racial balance ratios*: Piscataway Twp. Bd. of Education v. Burke, 386 A.2d 439 (N.J. 1978); Pa. Human Relations Commission v. Uniontown Area School Dist., 313 A.2d 156 (Pa. 1973); Darville v. Dade County Sch. Bd., 497 F.2d 1002 (5th Cir. 1974); Citizens Against Mandatory Bussing v. Palmason, 495 P.2d 657 (Wash. 1972). *Contra*: Londerholm v. Unified School Dist. No. 500, 430 P.2d 188 (Kan. 1967). *Cf.* Johnson v. Chicago Bd. of Education, 604 F.2d 504 (7th Cir. 1979).

67. Brice v. Landis, 314 F. Supp. 974 (N.D. Cal. 1969).

68. Crawford v. Los Angeles Bd. of Education, 458 U.S. 527 (1982); Legg v. Ill. Fair Employ. Practice Com'n., 329 N.E. 2d 486 (Ill. 1975) (dictum); *cf.* Bustop, Inc. v. Board of Education of the City of Los Angeles, 439 U.S. 1384, (1978).

C. Sex Discrimination

The law on sex discrimination provides many parallels to the law on racial discrimination, but there are significant differences. As noted above, the test for sex discrimination under the federal constitution is fairly new. "To withstand constitutional challenge, . . . classifications by gender must serve important governmental objectives and must be substantially related to achievement of those objectives."[69] Litigants have placed increasing reliance upon new sex discrimination statutes, but they are also subject of conflicting decisions. Finally, equal rights amendments to state constitutions add an entirely new dimension to sex discrimination law in the minority of states that have heretofore had such ERAs.

1. Student Classifications and Treatment

a. Academic Courses and Admissions. While the Supreme Court has not decisively ruled on the constitutionality of segregating public school students by sex, its recent decision striking down sex segregation of students in state universities[70] lends support to the view that a system-wide segregation of students by sex would be constitutionally vulnerable. The only public school case reaching the Supreme Court on this issue involved a special situation in which a large urban district that enrolled more than 90% of its students in coeducational schools maintained two sex-segregated schools for high-achievement students, one for boys and one for girls. The Supreme Court divided 4-4 on the constitutionality of these special-purpose, single-sex schools,[71] but that decision may be limited to its special facts. It would appear that the state, through its public school administration, may not segregate students on a system-wide basis. The high court of New York, to preserve a gender-restricted trust setting up special scholarships on the basis of sex, recently approved the removal of the trust from state agencies to private trustees, thus indicating that state involvement in the administration of the sex-segregated educational trust would have been unconstitutional.[72] Unconstitutional discrimination was found where a public school set higher grade requirements for girls' admission than for boys' and allocated fewer places to girls than to boys.[73]

Title IX of the Education Amendments of 1972 prohibits sex discrimination in federally aided educational programs, but expressly exempts admission practices from its coverage. (See Appendix 7-A, section G.) Nevertheless, the federal (HEW) regulations

---

69. Craig v. Boren, 429 U.S. 190 (1976).

70. Missouri Univ. for Women v. Hogan, 458 U.S. 718 (1982); *cf.* Williams v. McNair, 316 F.Supp. 134 (D.S.Car. 1970), *aff'd,* 401 U.S. 952 (1971).

71. Vorcheimer v. Sch. District of Philadelphia, 430 U.S. 703 (1977), *aff'd,* 532 F.2d 880 (3d cir. 1976). *Compare,* however, Newberg v. Bd. of Ed., 26 Pa. D.&C.2d 682 (Pa. 1983), which held the same two sex-segregated schools to be unconstitutional under both state law and federal grounds, and distinguished Vorcheimer on the basis of new additional fact findings of discriminatory resource allocation between the boys' and girls' special school.

72. Matter of Estate of Wilson, 465 N.Y.S.2d 900 (1983).

73. Berkelman v. San Francisco Un. Sch. District, 501 F.2d 1264 (9th Cir. 1974); Bray v. Lee, 337 F.Supp. 934 (D. Mass. 1972).

under Title IX purport to bar sex discrimination in admissions standards.[74] Federally aided schools cannot discriminate between male and female students or teachers, either under Title IX or other related laws.[75] There is ample room for argument as to what practices are in fact discriminatory.

a. Nonacademic Activities. The law on student discrimination in nonacademic activities, especially in sports, is burgeoning.[76] The remedies under federal and state statutes for sex discrimination render reliance upon constitutional doctrines unnecessary in most cases.

Sex discrimination is readily found where school districts do not provide comparable resources or programs for girls and boys.[77] Where comparable resources and programs are provided, courts have disagreed on the legality of separating the students by sex. A minority of courts found sex separation in sports to be rational, and therefore lawful on the view that, in particular sports, sexually separated teams accommodate the physical and psychological differences between the sexes and avoid untoward male dominance.[78] In noncontact sports, however, a majority of courts rejected this view and held sex-based exclusion either unconstitutional or a violation of Title IX.[79]

Single-sex competition in contact sports has also been contested. There is no consensus on what activities qualify as "contact sports," or on girls' rights to compete with boys in admitted contact sports.[80] The federal regulations avoided these questions—first, by failing to venture a full list of "contact" sports, and second, by authorizing single-sex "contact" competition in ambiguous language.[81] To the extent that the federal

74. 45 C.F.R. § 86 (1984).

75. *See* U.S. v. Crisp County Bd. of Education, (M.D. Ga. 1976) (consent order to eliminate student sex segregation in grades 5-8); United States v. Hinds, 560 F.2d 619 (5th Cir. 1977) (Equal Educational Opportunities Act of 1974); North Haven Board of Education v. Bell, 456 U.S. 512 (1982) (teacher sex discrimination).

76. For extensive review of the state and federal authorities in this area, *see, e.g.*, Force v. Pierce City R-VI Sch. Dist., 570 F.Supp. 1020 (W.D.Mo. 1983); Attorney General v. Massachusetts Interscholastic Assn., 393 N.E.2d 284 (Mass. 1979); Note, *The Application of Title IX to School Athletic Programs,* 68 Cornell L. Rev. 222 (1983). See also annotations in the following footnote.

77. Hoover v. Meiklejohn, 430 F. Supp. 164 (Colo. 1977) (Soccer); Cape v. Tenn. Sec. Sch. Athletic Assn., 424 F.Supp. 732 (D. Tenn. 1976) (basketball); Brenden v. Minnesota State H.S. League, 477 F.2d 1292 (8th Cir. 1973) (tennis, cross-country skiing and running); Haas v. S. Bend Community School Corp., 289 N.E. 2d 495 (Ind. 1972). Under state ERAs: Comm. v. Pa. Interscholastic Athletic Assn., 334 A.2d 839 (Pa. 1975); *accord*: Darrin v. Gould, 540 P.2d 882 (Wash. 1975). Case authorities on sex discrimination in athletics are collected in Annotation: 66 A.L.R. 3d 1262 (1975); 23 A.L.R. Fed. 664 (1975).

78. Clark v. Ariz. Interscholastic Assn., 695 F.2d 1126 (9th Cir. 1982); Ruman v. Eskew, 343 N.E. 2d 806 (Ind. 1976) (tennis); Ritacco v. Norwin School Dist., 361 F.Supp. 930 (W.D.Pa. 1973) (general sports); Bucha v. Ill. High School Assn., 351 F.Supp. 69 (N.D.Ill. 1972) (swimming).

79. Morris v. Michigan State Bd. of Education, 472 F.2d 1207 (6th Cir. 1973) (tennis); Bednar v. Neb. Sch. Activities Assn., 531 F.2d 922 (8th Cir. 1976); Gilpin v. Kansas State H.S. Activities Assn., Inc., 377 F.Supp. 1233 (D. Kans. 1973) (cross country).

80. *Compare* Magill v. Avondale Baseball Conference 364 F.Supp. 1212 (W.D.Pa. 1973) (dictum) *with* the Carne case, fn. 83, *infra.* In 1985 the New Jersey State Commissioner of Education ruled that a high school must permit a girl to try out for the varsity football team. One year later, he ruled that a high school need not permit a boy to play on the girl's field hockey team. *New York Times,* 5-22-86, p. B-7.

81. "86.41 Athletics: (a) *General.* No person shall, on the basis of sex, be excluded from participation in, be denied the benefits of, . . . or otherwise be discriminated against in any interscholastic, . . . club or intramural athletics. . . . (b) *Separate teams.* Notwithstanding . . . paragraph (a) . . . a recipient may operate or sponsor separate teams for members of each sex where selection for such teams is based upon

law may exempt contact sports, the question remains whether such sex separation still violates the higher constitutional law. Thus an equal protection challenge was successfully raised to nullify school rules that limited girls to "half-court" basketball while allowing boys to play full-court basketball.[82]

The Sixth Circuit Court of Appeals upheld sex segregation in contact sports, but other federal and state courts found it unlawful.[83] Until the law is clarified, school authorities are faced with a catch-22 situation of potential liability for sex discrimination in establishing single-sex teams, on one hand, and of tort liability for mismatching boys and girls in risky sports activity, on the other. Under the optimistic rulings in the four states where "competent" girls must be given football tryouts with boys, administrators, like Odysseus, must steer between Scylla and Charybdis, only without the visible forewarnings of a whirlpool and a hard rock.[84]

The impact of new equal rights amendments to state constitutions must also await clarification by the courts.

2. Teacher Classifications and Treatment

The protection provided against gender-discrimination by federal and state employment discrimination statutes (particularly Titles VII and IX of the Federal Civil Rights Act, as amended) extends to all public school employees and protects male as well as female professionals from gender discrimination.[85] Under one or more of the statutes above and hereafter mentioned, employees may obtain affirmative relief from employment practices that discriminate by gender in matters of hiring, promotions, compensation (including fringe benefits such as hospitalization, vacations, and pension plans) and adverse treatment regarding working facilities or personal relationships at the work place. The range and quantum of incidents of sexually discriminating employment practices, both recorded and potential, is too large to explore here; the following materials merely illustrate the kinds of adverse treatment that constitute unlawful denial of employment opportunities by reason of sexual discrimination. It should be noted first that the principal federal statute (Title VII) covers only biological sex discrimination, not individual sex preference. Thus employers' refusals to hire an effeminate male or to renew the contract of a self-declared lesbian teacher have been held not to violate Title VII.[86]

---

competitive skill or . . . is a contact sport. However, where a recipient operates . . . a team in a particular sport for . . . one sex but . . . no such team for . . . the other sex, . . . members of the excluded sex must be allowed to try out for the team offered unless the sport involved . . . contact. . . . For the purposes of this part, contact sports include boxing, wrestling, rugby, ice hockey, football, basketball and other sports the purpose of major activity of which involves bodily contact." 45 C.F.R. § 86.41 (1984).

82. Dodson v. Arkansas Activities Ass'n 468 F. Supp. 394 (E.D. Ark. 1979) (slip opinion).

83. *Compare* Morris v. Michigan State Bd. of Education, fn. 79, with Cape v. Tenn. Sec. Sch. Athletic Assn., fn. 77; Carne v. Tenn. Sec. School Athletic Assn., 415 F.Supp. 569 (E.D. Tenn. 1976); *see also* Leffel v. Wis. Interscholastic Ath. Assn., 444 F.Supp 1117 (E.D. Wis. 1978).

84. *See* Force v. Pierce City, etc., fn. 76, *supra*; Yellow Springs Ex. Vill. Sch. District Bd. of Ed. v. Ohio H.S. Ath. Assn., 443 F.Supp. 753 (S.D. Ohio 1978); Darrin v. Gould, 540 P.2d 882 (Wash. 1975) (State ERA ruling); Opinion of the Justices, 371 N.E.2d 426 (Mass. 1977) (state ERA ruling).

85. United Teachers v. Bd. of Education, 712 F.2d 1349 (9th Cir. 1983)

86. Smith v. Liberty Mutual Life Ins. Co., 569 F.2d 325 (5th Cir. 1978) (effeminate male); Rowland v. Mad River Local School Dist., 730 F.2d 444 (6th Cir. 1984) (self-announced lesbian).

In discrimination claims under Title VII, the employee must prove that he or she is qualified for the contested position or benefit, and then rebut any defense that a bona fide school need justified sex preference.[87] For example, a school decision to hire a male teacher without a master's degree over a female teacher with a master's degree was upheld because the male applicant could be hired at a lower salary and also perform supplemental coaching duties.[88] Payment of a lower salary for a female coach of girls' tennis than that paid a male coach of boys' tennis was also upheld under state law on evidence that the boys' team had a heavier schedule and greater coaching burdens than the girls' team.[89] Where, however, the district fails to justify gender discrimination, the victim may recover equal pay for the same work, including back pay and placement in the position from which he or she was improperly excluded.[90] Thus, a female instructor who was denied comparable offices and instructional facilities without justification was awarded for differential damages under Title VII.[91]

In 1978, the Supreme Court ruled on the clouded question as to what proofs would suffice to justify gender preference. It held that the employer need only articulate some legitimate nondiscriminatory reason and need not disprove any presumption of discriminatory motive.[92] The ruling thus cast upon the complainant the heavy burden of proving that the asserted justification was a pretext or untrue. Substantially the same rules apply to discharge decisions that are challenged as sexually discriminatory, placing upon the employee the burden of disproving any articulated nondiscriminatory reason for the challenged decision and for showing that "but for" sex bias the employee would not have been discharged.[93]

As with race, sexual discrimination under Title VII may be shown by statistical evidence that a particular employment practice operated to disadvantage only one of the sexes. But, as previously noted, the validity and sufficiency of statistical evidence is determined case by case.[94]

---

87. Anderson v. City of Bessemer, 717 F.2d 149 (5th Cir. 1983); Dothard v. Rawlinson, 433 U.S. 321 (1977); Peters v. Middlebury College, 409 F.Supp. 857 (Vt. 1976); Stieler v. Spokane Sch. District No. 81, 558 P.2d 198 (Wash. 1977).

88. Shenefield v. Sheridan Co. Sch. District 1, 544 P.2d 870 (Wyo. 1976). *See also* Meier v. Evansville-Vanderberg Sch. Corp., 416 F.Supp. 748 (S.D. Ind. 1975); Eckroth v. Flasher Pub. Sch. District, 436 F. Supp. 942 (D. No. Dak. 1977) (educational qualifications held evidence but not conclusive proof of superior ability for particular position).

89. Sch. District, Twp. of Millcreek v. Cmwlth. Hum. Rel. Comm., 368 A.2d 901 (Pa. 1977).

90. *See, e.g.*, Schoneberg v. Grundy County Bd. of Education, 385 N.E.2d 351 (Ill. 1979) (unconstitutional exclusion from appointment); Marshall v. Kirkland, 602 F.2d 1282 (8th Cir. 1979) (unconstitutional denial of promotion); Tyler v. Bd. of Education, 519 F.Supp. 834 (D.Del. 1981) (Title VII violation); Danzel v. North St. Paul-Maplewood-Oakdale Independent School Dist., 706 F.2d 813 (8th Cir. 1982); Caufield v. Bd. of Ed., 632 F.2d 999 (2d Cir. 1980) (Title IX ruling). Burkey v. Marshall County Bd. of Ed., 513 F.Supp. 1084 (N.D.W.VA. 1981); Usery v. A & M Cons. Ind. Sch. District, No. 74-H-1532 (S.D. Tex. 1976); United States v. Wattsburg Area Sch. District, 429 F.Supp. 1370 (W.D. Pa. 1977). *But see* Katz v. Sch. District of Clayton, 411 F.Supp. 1140 (E.D. Mo. 1976) (teacher volunteering extra work cannot recover though others are paid for similar work).

91. Harrington v. Vandalia-Butler Bd. of Education, 418 F.Supp. 603 (S.D. Ohio 1976).

92. Bd. of Trustees of Keene State College v. Sweeney, 439 U.S. 24 (1978).

93. *See, e.g.*, Verniero v. Air Force Academy School District, 705 F.2d 388 (10th Cir. 1983); Avery v. Holmewood City Bd. of Ed., 674 F.2d 337 (5th Cir. 1982); Parker v. Bd. of School Commissioners, 558 F.Supp. 680 (S.D. Ind. 1983).

94. Dothard v. Rawlinson, fn. 87.

a. Teacher Pregnancy. As with race, sex identification first gained protection from discrimination under the Equal Protection Clause of the 14th Amendment. In *Cleveland Bd. of Education* v. *LaFleur,* the Supreme Court struck down the board policy of forcing all pregnant teachers to take mandatory maternity leave at fixed periods before and following the pregnancy term, without regard to the ability of different women to continue to work through different stages of pregnancy or recovery.[95] Similar rigid regulations were overturned under federal and state sex discrimination statutes, and these rulings were extended to untenured, as well as to unmarried teachers.[96] Teachers wrongfully laid off under unlawful pregnancy regulations could recover back pay for lost time as well as reinstatement.[97]

The law does not bar all maternity leave regulations. School boards may reasonably regulate pregnancy situations to ensure continuity of instructional services by requiring teachers to give advance notice of their pregnant condition, and even by declining to renew a pregnant probationer's contract at year end.[98] A mandatory ninth-month pregnancy leave policy was upheld as a reasonable business necessity.[99] Similar public interests justified a requirement that maternity leave be taken at the beginning of a new semester.[100] The reasonableness and legality of a regulation may thus depend upon the available resources and special needs in a given school district. A teacher who was terminated for failure to obtain her master's degree within the period required by her contract could not excuse her breach merely because she elected to take an extended (five year) voluntary maternity leave.[101]

b. Compensation and Fringe Benefits. Disqualification of pregnancy-related conditions for sick leave, disability benefits, and seniority increments have been challenged as discriminatory since only females are burdened by the pregnancy classification. Differentials in male and female pension costs and benefits under employer retirement plans are also contested, but different fringe benefits present special problems that require separate analysis.

Exclusion of pregnancy conditions from sick leave or disability coverage were originally upheld by the Supreme Court under the Constitution and under Title VII,[102] but in 1978 Congress amended Title VII to require employers to treat pregnancy-related

---

95. 414 U.S. 632 (1974) (also covering companion case of Cohen v. Chesterfield County Sch. Bd.).

96. Fabian v. Ind. Sch. District, 409 F.Supp. 94 (W.D. Okla. 1976); Black v. Sch. Committee of Malden. 341 N.E.2d 896 (Mass. 1976); see U.S. Dept. HEW Title Vll Regulations, 37 Fed. Reg. 6837 (4/5/72),Jinks v. Mays, 332 F.Supp. 254 (N.D. Ga. 1971) (untenured teacher); Leechburg Area Sch. District, v. Pa Hum. Rel. Comm., 335 A.2d 873 (Pa. 1975) (unmarried teacher).

97. Paxman v. Wilkerson, 390 F.Supp. 442 (E.D. Va. 1975).

98. *See* Cleveland Bd. of Education v. LaFleur, 414 U.S. at 642; Bradley v. Cathern, 384 F.Supp. 1216 (E.D. Tex. 1975); *cf.* Kornblum v. Newark Un. Sch. District, 112 Cal. Rptr.457 (1974); Mitchell v. Bd. of Trustees 15 F.E.P. 338 (D. So. Car. 1977).

99. deLaurier v. San Diego Unified Sch. Dist., 588 F.2d 674 (9th Cir. 1979).

100. Richards v. Omaha Public Schools, 232 N.W.2d 29 (Neb. 1975).

101. N.Y. City Bd. of Education v. N.Y. Hum. Rts. App. Bd., 387 N.Y.S.2d 873 (1976).

102. Nashville Gas Co. v. Satty, 434 U.S. 136 (1977); General Electric Co. v. Gilbert, 429 U.S. 125 (1976). *Accord*: Geduldig v. Aiello, 417 U.S. 484 (1975). Geduldig nullified earlier lower court decisions to the contrary.

illness or disability no differently than other disabling conditions under employee benefit plans.[103]

Where *all* leave periods are excluded from measuring a probationary period, Title VII does not require an exception for maternity leave. It does, however, prohibit employers from treating maternity leave as a discontinuance of seniority rank.[104]

Pregnant teachers receive even greater protection under the state sex discrimination laws in Iowa, Massachusetts, New Jersey, New York, and Pennsylvania.[105] In a few states, local laws expressly require school districts to pay fringe benefits for pregnancy-related disability.[106] A male teacher, however, was denied paid maternity leave even though he was needed at home to care for a disabled pregnant wife.[107]

Pension plans that require female employees to pay a higher monthly contribution than male employees for the same monthly benefits have been held to violate Title VII, even though women, as a class, generally live longer than men after retirement and thus receive more pension benefits.[108] Five years later, the Supreme Court further held that Title VII prohibited retirement pension payments to be calculated separately for male and female employees under gender-based actuarial tables and that unisex tables must be used for all employees.[109]

Employer plans that give lower-cost family benefit coverage to heads of households were upheld under Title VII, but the denial of similar privileges to women who are not heads of households remains questionable under Title VII and was disapproved under Pennsylvania law.[110]

Other forms of prohibited discrimination in compensation—particularly under Title VII, the Equal Pay Act, or Title IX—include the setting of unequal pay for the same work,[111] but the question of what constitutes "equal work" is a point of contention that depends largely on the analysis of work burdens and duties. Thus a coach of a boys' team who works longer and different hours than the coach of a girls' team may lawfully receive higher pay, so long as qualified employees of both sexes are not excluded from holding the higher-paying position.[112]

---

103. P.L. 95-555, 95th Cong. (1978). For a review of this legislation, *see* Clanton v. Orleans Parish Sch. Bd., 649 F.2d 1084, 1094 (5th Cir. 1981); Schwabenbauer v. Bd. of Ed., 667 F.2d 305, 310 (2d Cir. 1981).

104. Nashville Gas Co. v. Satty, fn. 102.

105. *See* Quaker Oats Co. v. Cedar Rapids Human Rts. Comm., 268 N.W.2d 862 (Iowa 1978). Contra: Narragansett Elec. Co. v. Rhode Island Comm. Human Rts., 374 A.2d 1022 (1977); Tawney v. Bd. of Education, 426 F.Supp. 528 (S.D. W. Va. 1977).

106. Lewis v. L.A. City Un. Sch. District, 429 F.Supp. 935 (Cal. 1977); Taylor Fed. Teachers v. Bd. of Ed. 249 N.W. 2d 399 (Mich. 1976).

107. Ackerman v. Bd. of Education, 287 F.Supp. 76 (S.D. N.Y. 1974).

108. Los Angeles v. Manhart, 435 U.S. 702 (1978).

109. Norris v. Arizona Governing Committee, 463 U.S. 1073 (1983). This ruling was made retroactive in Spirt v. TIAA-CREF, 735 F.2d 23 (2d Cir. 1984), cert. denied, ________U.S. ________105 S.Ct. 247 (1984). *Cf.* Reilley v. Robertson, 360 N.E.2d 171 (Ind. 1977) (state law ground).

110. *Upheld:* Willett v. Emory & Henry College, 427 F.Supp. 631 (W.D. Va. 1977). *Disapproved:* Canon-McMillan Sch. District v. Hum. Rel. Comm. 372 A.2d 498 (Pa. 1977) *Compare* State Division of Hum. Rts. v. Bd. of Education, 381 N.Y.S.2d 544 (1976); *with* Matter of Bd. of Education v. State Division of Hum. Rts., 319 N.E.2d 203 (N.Y. 1974).

111. Danielson v. DuPage Area Voc. Educational Authority, 595 F.Supp. 27 (N.D.Ill. 1984); County of Washington v. Gunther, 452 U.S. 161 (1981); *cf.* Pittman v. Hattiesburg Municipal Separate School Dist., 644 F.2d 1071 (5th Cir. 1981).

112. Erikson v. Bd. of Education, 458 N.E.2d 84 (Ill. 1983); Kennew v. Hampton Twp. Sch. Dist., 438 F.Supp. 575 (W.D.Pa. 1977).

Determining what constitutes equal work in the school context where persons are employed as teachers for similar positions, on a salaried basis, but which involve different "work load" hours, can be troublesome. Thus, in a recent case a federal court held that a female professor who carried twice the number of teaching hours as male professors could not recover under the Equal Pay Act, since her complaint was of "workload discrimination," which is not covered by the act. The court went on to say by way of dicta, however, that she might be entitled to some relief under Title VII, based upon a claim of sexual discrimination in work assignments.[113]

The theory of "comparable worth" of different positions as a ground of sex discrimination claims recently appeared, but has indeterminate parameters. That theory, which has yet to find place in the law, raises a number of economic and legal issues that are far from settled.

c. Improper Treatment. It is now settled that Title VII and Title IX protect employees from gender-based hostility, harassment, or demeaning treatment in the workplace.[114] As the federal regulations recognize, however, the issue of hostile, demeaning, or exploitive conduct must be made case-by-case on the basis of particularized facts.[115] While most sexual harassment cases involve female victims, the law's protection extends as well to male employees.[116]

d. Affirmative Action. Programs to improve female employment opportunities raise the same reverse discrimination issues that were previously discussed in connection with race. Male candidates successfully challenged female preference for teaching positions under a state executive order as a violation of the Fourteenth Amendment and of Title VII.[117] The law may place limits on the forms of affirmative action, even where sex discrimination has existed. Thus, where male university employees proved they were being paid less than women for equal work, the court nullified the pay differential aspect of the affirmative action plan as a violation of the Equal Pay Act.[118]

D. The Handicapped and the Gifted

Teachers and students who are exceptionally gifted or handicapped do not, in constitutional law, comprise any special class (such as race or sex) that is entitled to special constitutional protection. As a matter of constitutional law, public schools are neither required to optimize the special talents of the gifted by special arrangements, nor to eliminate the peculiar educational disadvantages that burden the handicapped. Prior

113. Berry v. Bd. of Supervisors, 715 F.2d 971 (5th Cir. 1983).

114. *E.g.*, Harrington v. Vandalia-Butler Bd. of Ed., 418 F.Supp. 603 (S.D. Ohio 1976) (Title VII violation in provision of less desirable working conditions); Alexander v. Yale Univ., 631 F.2d 178 (2d Cir. 1980) (Title IX). *Re* sexual harassment, see, e.g., 29 C.F.R. § 1604.11; Annot: *Sex Advances—Sex Discrimination*, 46 A.L.R. Fed. 224 (1980).

115. EEOC Guidelines, 29 C.F.R. § 1604.11.

116. *Cf.* Huebschen v. Dept. of Health and Human Services, 547 F.Supp. 1168 (W.D.Wis. 1982).

117. Cramer v. Va. Comm. U.,415 F.Supp. 673 (E.D. Va. 1976).

118. Bd. of Regents U. of Nebraska v. Dawes, 522 F.2d 380 (8th Cir. 1975).

to enactment of recent reform legislation, the protection of the handicapped was largely limited to situations that amounted to actual physical exclusion from schools or to functional deprivation of reasonable educational benefits to children.[119] The prime sources of equal opportunity law for exceptional persons are found in recent federal statutes and in modern state special education statutes that were enacted to satisfy those federal statutes.

As to gifted students, what little legislation exists is found in individual state laws. The bulk of special education legislation at the federal and state levels deals with the handicapped. The principal federal statutes are the Rehabilitation Act of 1973 (hereafter called § 504) which applies to all handicapped persons and The Education for All Handicapped Children Act of 1975 (hereafter called EHA) which applies specifically to handicapped students.[120] The scope and occasional overlap of these statutes was recently summarized by the Supreme Court as follows:

> "Section 504 and EHA are different substantive statutes. While the EHA guarantees a right to a free appropriate public education, § 504 simply prevents discrimination on the basis of handicap. But while the EHA is limited to handicapped children seeking access to public education, § 504 protects handicapped persons of all ages from discrimination in a variety of programs and activities receiving federal financial assistance.
>
> "Because both statutes are built around fundamental notions of equal access to state programs and facilities, their substantive requirements, as applied to the right of a handicapped child to a public education, have been interpreted to be strikingly similar. . . .
>
> "On the other hand, although both statutes begin with an equal protection premise that handicapped children must be given access to public education, it does not follow that the affirmative requirements imposed by the two statutes are the same. The significant difference between the two, as applied to special education claims, is that the substantive and procedural rights assumed to be guaranteed by both statutes are specifically required only by the EHA. . . .
>
> "In *Southeastern Community College* v. *Davis,* 442 U.S. 397, 99 S.Ct. 2361, 60 L.Ed.2d 980 (1979), the Court emphasized that § 504 does not require affirmative action on behalf of handicapped persons, but only the absence of discrimination against those persons. 442 U.S., at 411-412, 99 S.Ct., at 2369-2370.
>
> "In the EHA, on the other hand, Congress specified the affirmative obligations imposed on States to ensure that equal access to a public education is not an empty guarantee, but offers some benefit to a handicapped child."[121]

---

119. *Re physical exclusion: see* Frederick L. v. Thomas, 557 F.2d 373 (3d Cir. 1977); *in re* Stella, 367 N.Y.S.2d 946 (1975); Harrison v. Michigan, 350 F.Supp. 846 (E.D. Mich. 1972); in re G.H., 218 N.W.2d 441 (N. Dak. 1974). *Contra*: Cuyahoga County Assn. for Retarded Children v. Essex, 411 F.Supp. 46 (N.D. Ohio 1976). *Re functional deprivation: see* Society for Autistic Children v. Tidewater Bd. of Education, No. 426-72-N (E.D. Va. 1972). *But see* Martin Luther King, Jr., El'y School Children v. Michigan Bd. of Education, 451 F.Supp. 1324 (E.D. Mich. 1979) (denying constitutional right of underpriviledged children to special education).

120. *See* 29 U.S.C. § 794 (§504); 20 U.S.C. §1401 (EHA). Other federal statutes that affect the handicapped, but that have minimal or rare application to public schools, *e.g.*, the Developmentally Disabled Assistance Act, are not covered in this text. *See, e.g.*, Hurry v. Jones, 560 F.Supp. 500, 504 (D.R.I. 1983); *cf.* Youngsberg v. Romeo, 457 U.S. 307 (1982) (rights of confined state wards to minimal "habilitation" training).

121. *See* Smith v. Robinson, 468 U.S. 992, 104 S.Ct. 3457 (1984).

The foregoing statutes provide the framework for antidiscrimination principles discussed hereafter. They are reviewed in further detail in the two Supreme Court opinions (*Rowley* and *Robinson*) reproduced at the end of this chapter.

1. Handicapped Students

Specification of educational arrangements that are reasonable and appropriate for particular classes of handicapped students no longer depends upon judicial rulings under the Constitution. They have been clarified in express terms by federal statutes and regulations and by state special education statutes.[122] Broadly stated, these federal and state statutes require school agencies to (1) identify handicapped children, (2) evaluate their respective educational needs, and (3) assign them to appropriate schools, classes, or supportive services. Federal and state laws also provide for procedural due process by requiring timely notices, hearing, and participation by affected parents or guardians in the process of student evaluation and assignment. The prevailing statutory schemes generally mirror the following requirements of the EHA, as summarized by the Supreme Court:

"The Education of the Handicapped Act (Act), 84 Stat. 175, as amended, 20 U.S.C. § 1401 *et seq.* (1976 ed. and Supp. IV), provides federal money to assist state and local agencies in educating handicapped children, and conditions such funding upon a State's compliance with extensive goals and procedures. The Act represents an ambitious federal effort to promote the education of handicapped children. . . .

"In order to qualify for federal financial assistance under the Act, a State must demonstrate that it 'has in effect a policy that assures all handicapped children the right to a free appropriate public education.' 20 U.S.C. § 1412(1). That policy must be reflected in a state plan submitted to and approved by the Secretary of Education, § 1413, which describes in detail the goals, programs, and timetables under which the State intends to educate handicapped children within its borders. §§ 1412, 1413. States receiving money under the Act must provide education to the handicapped by priority, first "to handicapped children who are not receiving an education" and second "to handicapped children . . . with the most severe handicaps who are receiving an inadequate education," § 1412(3), and "to the maximum extent appropriate" must educate handicapped children "with children who are not handicapped." § 1412(5). The Act broadly defines "handicapped children" to include "mentally retarded, hard of hearing, deaf, speech impaired, visually handicapped, seriously emotionally disturbed, orthopedically impaired, [and] other health impaired children, [and] children with specific learning disabilities." § 1401(1).

"The "free appropriate public education" required by the Act is tailored to the unique needs of the handicapped child by means of an "individualized educational

---

122. Summaries of state laws on special education are contained in Sen. Rep. No. 168, 94 Cong., 1st sess., 20-21,table 2 (1975); Nolpe, Contemporary Legal Problems in Education, pp. 189, 190 (1975). Under federal law, a person is handicapped if his or her physical or mental impairment "substantially limits" a major life activity. See 45 C.F.R. § 84.3 (1984). See also Frederick L. v. Thomas, 419 F.Supp. 960 (E.D. Pa. 1976); Harrison v. State of Michigan, 350 Supp. 846 (E.D. Mich. 1972).

program" (IEP). § 1401(18). The IEP, which is prepared at a meeting between a qualified representative of the local educational agency, the child's teacher, the child's parents or guardian, and, where appropriate, the child, consists of a written document containing

> '(A) a statement of the present levels of educational performance of such child, (B) a statement of annual goals, including short-term instructional objectives, (C) a statement of the specific educational services to be provided to such child, and the extent to which such child will be able to participate in regular educational programs, (D) the projected date for initiation and anticipated duration of such services, and (E) appropriate objective criteria and evaluation procedures and schedules for determining, on at least an annual basis, whether instructional objectives are being achieved.' § 1401(19).

Local or regional educational agencies must review, and where appropriate revise, each child's IEP at least annually. § 1414(a)(5). See also § 1413(a)(11).

"In addition . . . the Act imposes extensive procedural requirements upon States receiving federal funds under its provisions. Parents or guardians of handicapped children must be notified of any proposed change in "the identification, evaluation, or educational placement of the child or the provision of a free appropriate public education to such child," and must be permitted to bring a complaint about "any matter relating to" such evaluation and education. §§ 1415(b)(1)(D) and (E). Complaints brought by parents or guardians must be resolved at "an impartial due process hearing," and appeal to the State educational agency must be provided if the initial hearing is held at the local or regional level. §§ 1415(b)(2) and (c). Thereafter, '[a]ny party aggrieved by the findings and decision' of the state administrative hearing has "the right to bring a civil action with respect to the complaint . . . in any State court of competent jurisdiction or in a district court of the United States. . . .

" . . . Compliance is assured by provisions permitting the withholding of federal funds upon determination that a participating state or local agency has failed to satisfy the requirements of the Act. . . . At present, all States except New Mexico receive federal funds under the portions of the Act at issue today. . . . "[123]

The E.H.A. presents two basic elements, one substantive, the other procedural. First, the state must provide a "free appropriate public education"; second, it must follow E.H.A. procedures that are designed to ensure substantive goals.

a. The "Appropriate Public Education" Requirement. In the Courts' words[124] this does not require the state to "maximize the potential of each handicapped child. . . . Desirable though that goal might be, it is not the standard that Congress imposes upon states. . . . " Rather, if the state "complied with the procedures set forth in the Act" and they are "reasonably calculated to enable the child to receive educational benefits," "the courts can require no more under the EHA." Since states must educate a wide spectrum of handicapped children, "from the marginally hearing impaired to the profoundly

---

123. *See* Hendrick Hudson Bd. of Education v. Rowley, 458 U.S. 176–184 (1982).

124. The quotations in the text are from the *Rowley* opinion of the United States Supreme Court, which appears at the end of this chapter.

retarded," the Court recognized that educational benefits required by the Act will vary. It declined to venture "any one test for determining the adequacy of educational benefits conferred upon all children. . . . "

The foregoing statements indicate that the state will have met E.H.A. requirements of affording "basic floor of opportunity" to achieve educational benefits if it makes reasonable efforts to follow E.H.A. guidelines to develop and implement an appropriate "individualized educational program" and to provide "related services" for the handicapped child.

Applying these standards, the Supreme Court ruled that Amy Rowley, who performed better than the average student in her regular public school class, was not entitled to have a publicly paid sign language interpreter assist her, even though that service would have enabled her to achieve even better grades. That decision undercut prior lower court cases that interpreted E.H.A. to require some fixed level of educational achievement; conversely, it validated contrary cases that required that handicapped children receive only an *opportunity* to acquire skills consistent with their capabilities, however limited they might be.[125] The Supreme Court opinion language in *Rowley* further suggests that E.H.A. does not require a special education program for all handicapped children, but only for those whose evaluated handicap indicated a need for the same.[126] Nevertheless, the opinion recognizes that in appropriate circumstances of need, courts could find that provision of an interpreter as a "related service" would be required under E.H.A. to enable a particular child to obtain the benefits of a free public education and a later case so held.[127]

The view that E.H.A. imposes limited effort obligations and not achievement goals is indirectly expressed in cases that refused to exempt handicapped students from the passage of competency tests as a requirement of a high school diploma. The fact that some students could not pass such a test by reason of their handicap—and consequent denial of a diploma for failure to pass the competency test—neither denied handicapped students of E.H.A. rights to receive a free appropriate public education,[128] nor constituted discrimination against the handicapped under § 504 of the Rehabilitation Act.[129] Since § 504 prohibits only discrimination against "otherwise qualified" handicapped persons, its requirement is one of "accommodation" to "qualified" persons and not one of "affirmative action."[130]

The finding that Congress relied upon compliance with E.H.A. procedures (particularly the IEP process) as an index of appropriate public education, rather than

---

125. *See, e.g.*, Rettig v. Kent City Sch. Dist., 539 F.Supp. 768, 777 (N.D.Ohio 1981); Campbell v. Talledega County Bd. of Ed., 518 F.Supp. 47 (N.D.Ala. 1981).

126. *See, e.g.*, Shanenberg v. Cmwlth Sec. of Ed., 426 A.2d 232 (Pa. 1981) (paraplegic student entitled to physical therapy, but not to special education program). *Cf.* Akers v. Bolton, 531 F.Supp. 300 (D.Kans. 1981) (denying class action relief where not all members of handicapped class had identified need for special education).

127. Woolcott v. St. Bd. of Ed., 351 N.W.2d 601 (Mich. 1984).

128. *See* Brookhart v. Illinois State Bd. of Ed., 697 F.2d 179, 1983 (7th Cir. 1983); Bd. of Ed. v. Ambach, 458 N.Y.S.2d 680, 684-5 (1982) (confirming that EHA does not require specific results, but only access to educational services.

129. *Idem. See also* Anderson v. Banks, 520 F.Supp. 472, 511 (S.D.Ga. 1981).

130. *See* Southeastern Community College v. Davis, 442 U.S. 397, 411-412 (1979).

achievement levels, apparently rests upon the dearth of reliable educational measures. Courts are reluctant to mediate conflicting educational theories and opinions: "[I]t is almost impossible to accurately determine what his potential is,. . . . The plaintiffs' own experts have presented conflicting opinions as to what they believe an appropriate education for Tom entails."[131] As the Supreme Court itself warned: "Courts must be careful to avoid imposing their view of preferable education or methods on the state. . . . "[132]

Lower courts have, however, imposed a negative achievement standard with respect to those handicapped children who suffer achievement regression due to inadequate duration or discontinuity of instruction. Where the normal school hours, term, or calendar are inappropriate to enable a handicapped child to maintain their progress, courts have required public school authorities to adopt special class schedules beyond the normal school day, week, or year to prevent significant educational regression.[133] For similar reason, where an appropriate public facility is not available to serve reasonable educational needs of a handicapped child, E.H.A. has been held to require placement of the child in an appropriate "private" facility, at public expense.[134]

The federal E.H.A. regulations, and a few decided cases, require that extracurricular activity must be provided to a handicapped child who needs or can benefit from an I.E.P. component of extracurricular activity.[135] Other nonacademic services that may be required, under the heading of "educationally related services," are discussed in a later section.

b. Procedural and Noninstructional Requirements. The opinion in *Stuart* v. *Nappi*, p. 383, *infra*, provides a helpful review of points hereafter discussed. As a case of first impression, *Stuart* surveyed the E.H.A. procedures to afford "due process" to parents who dispute the decisional methods of school authorities regarding any phase of their child's education.

At the threshold stage of handicap identification and evaluation, parents may challenge the validity of official classifications in terms of handicap diagnoses (physical, functional, emotional) and its severity. Later they may challenge proposed educational plans (IEPs) as to content and placement. The burden of proving errors by the school authorities, however, generally lies with challenging parents, but that issue is not free

---

131. *See* Rettig v. Kent City Sch. Dist., *supra*, 539 F.Supp. at p. 777.

132. *See* Rowley opinion, *infra*, at p. 379.

133. Yaris v. Special Sch. Dist., 728 F.2d 1005 (8th Cir. 1984); Crawford v. Pittman, 708 F.2d 1028 (5th Cir. 1983); Georgia Assn. of Retarded Citizens v. McDaniel, 511 F.Supp. 1263 (N.D.Ga. 1981); (all requiring extended school year). *See also* Abrahamson v. Hershman, 701 F.2d 233 (1st Cir. 1983) (round-the-clock training for severely retarded child); semble: Stacy G. v. Pasadena School Dist., 547 F.Supp. 61 (S.D.Tex. 1981); Birmingham & Lamphere Sch. Districts v. Sup't of Public Inst., 228 N.W.2d 59 (Mich. 1982). *But see* Bales v. Clarke, 523 F.Supp. 1366 (E.D.Va. 1981).

134. *See* discussion of placement issues, *infra*.

135. *See* Rettig v. Kansas City Sch. Dist., *supra*, 720 F.2d at pp. 466-67. The regulations covering the handicapped also bar exclusion of qualified handicapped students from extracurricular activities. 45 C.F.R. § 84.37 (1984).

from doubt.[136] As indicated above, the validity of testing and remedial methods is often open to reasonable differences in opinion. This is especially true regarding the choice of alternative placements (i.e., between a regular public school or a special education facility between school district facilities, or in facilities beyond the district or at private institutions).

Placement Issues. the statutory requirement that handicapped children be placed in "the least restrictive" environment adopts "mainstreaming" as an ideal, but it does not resolve the key questions whether or when mainstreaming is (1) appropriate for a particular child,[137] and (2) reasonable in light of the district's physical, professional, and financial resources. On each question, courts must decide what is "reasonable" under the specific circumstances. While the heavier cost of mainstreaming is not per se a ground to deny regular school placement, neither is cost irrelevant. Courts have rejected the view that E.H.A. requires regular public school classroom placement "at all cost."[138]

So long as a child is placed in an appropriate facility, parents may not demand alternative placements that are more beneficial to the child,[139] nor may a parent overturn a district's decision to place a child in district facilities, rather than in a superior outside facility.[140] Where, however, school authorities default in their duty to place a child in an appropriate facility, parents who are forced to do so by that default may recover reimbursement of their placement expenses.[141]

Placement issues are compounded by the E.H.A. requirement of periodic reevaluation of each I.E.P. in light of the child's condition and progress; reevaluation may lead to proposals for a change in placement. Where a district or parent objects to a placement change, the "stay put" provisions of E.H.A. prohibit placement changes until the E.H.A. procedures for resolving placement disputes are exhausted (i.e., by final administrative or judicial ruling). The E.H.A. hearing and appeal provisions can be a trap for unwary parents. Their failure to pursue those channels may foreclose any right to obtain public payment for new placement unless, as noted above, a court finds an inexcusable default by public school authorities in their duty to seek an appropriate placement as contemplated by E.H.A.[142] The "stay put" requirements have the virtue of

---

136. *See* Johnston by Johnston v. Ann Arbor Public School, 569 F.Supp. 1502, 1507-8 (E.D.Mich. 1983); Sch. Committee of Brookline v. Bureau of Special Education, 452 N.E.2d 476, 481-2 (Mass. 1983). *See also* Aspira v. Bd. of Education, 394 F.Supp. 1161 (S.D.N.Y. 1975) (consent decree); Serna v. Portales Mun. Schools, 499 F.2d 1147 (10th Cir. 1975) (under Title VI).

137. *See, e.g.*, Springdale Sch. Dist. v. Grace, 693 F.2d 41, 43 (8th Cir. 1982) (requiring only part-time mainstreaming to meet child's needs).

138. *Compare, e.g.*, Espino v. Besteiro, 520 *F.Supp.* 905 (S.D.Tex. 1981), rev'd solely on issue of attorney's fees, 708 F.2d 1002 (5th Cir. 1983) wherein court required mainstreaming of child, even though that required air conditioning an entire classroom, *with* Pinkerton v. Moye, 509 F.Supp. *107*, 112-114 (W.D.Pa. 1981).

139. Wilson v. Marana Un. Sch. Dist., 735 F.2d 1178 (9th Cir. 1984); Hessler v. St. Bd. of Ed., 700 F.2d 134 (4th Cir. 1983). *See also* Age v. Bullitt County Pub. Schools, 673 F.2d 141, 143 (6th Cir. 1982).

140. *Idem.*; Clevenger v. Oakridge Sch. Bd., 573 F.Supp. 349 (E.D.Tenn. 1983); Marvin H. v. Boston Ind. Sch. Dist., 714 F.2d 1348 (5th cir. 1983). *See also* Sch. Committee v. Commissioner of Ed., 462 N.E.2d 338 (Mass. 1984).

141. Burlington School Committee v. Dept. of Education, ________U.S. 105 S.Ct. 1996 (1985).

142. *Compare, e.g.*, Marvin H. v. Austin Ind. Sch. Dist., *supra*, 714 F.2d at p. 1356 and authorities there cited; Willim S. v. Gill, 572 F.Supp. 509, 516 (N.D.Ill. 1983); M.R. v. Milwaukee Public Schools, 584 F.Supp. 767 (E.D.Wisc. 1984); Doe v. Anrig, 728 F.2d 30 (1st Cir. 1984); Quackenbush v. Johnson City Sch.

certainty, but they can, as illustrated by the *Stuart* case, p. 383, *infra,* permit placement delays that harm a child in ways that cannot adequately be cured or compensated by monetary damages.

"Related Services." As used in the E.H.A., "related service" includes "Transportation, developmental, corrective and other supportive services . . . that are required to enable a handicapped child to benefit from special education." These include "speech pathology and audiology, psychological services, physical and occupational therapy, recreation and medical and counseling services, except that such medical services shall be for diagnostic and evaluation purposes only."[143] The fact that a service is related to a child's physical and medical condition does not automatically disqualify it as an educationally related service. The test appears to be whether the service or treatment in question is (1) necessary to enable a child to benefit from public education, (2) must be provided at school if the child is to benefit educationally therefrom, and (3) whether it can be rendered safely and competently at school by one other than a licensed physician. Applying those tests, the Supreme court recently ruled that, under E.H.A., a school district must arrange for clean intermittent catheterization "(CIC) of a handicapped student at school."

> "It is clear on this record that without having CIC services available during the school day, Amber cannot attend school and thereby "benefit from special education." CIC services therefore fall squarely within the definition of a supportive service. . . .
>
> "CIC services in this case qualify as a 'supportive service . . . required to assist a handicapped child to benefit from special education.'
>
> "We also agree . . . that provision of CIC is not a 'medical' service which a school is required to provide only for purposes of diagnosis or evaluation."[144]

Supportive services thus bear upon the child's access to and benefit from the educational program.

Related services of a nonmedical nature include special transportation arrangements and facilities modifications to accommodate the physically handicapped.[145]

School Discipline of the Handicapped. School punishment for handicapped students' misbehavior is not outlawed by E.H.A. or § 504, but those laws (and comparable state

---

Dist., 716 F.2d 141 (2d Cir. 1983) (denying recovery for failure to "stay put"); *with* Parks v. Pavkovic, 557 F.Supp. 1280 (N.D.Ill. 1983) (gross district disregard of statutory obligations); Anderson v. Thompson, *supra,* 658 F.2d at pp. 1213–14 (emergency unilateral change of placement); Christopher N. v. McDaniel, *supra,* 569 F.Supp. at p. 294; Burlington School Committee v. Dept. of Education, n. 141, *supra.*

143. *See* Board of Education v. Rowley, *supra* 458 U.S. at p. 188. McKenzie v. Jefferson, 566 F.Supp. 404 (D.D.C. 1983) (psychiatric hospital treatment held medical and not a "related" service); semble: Darlene L. v. Ill. Dept. of Education, 568 F.Supp. 1340 (N.D.Ill. 1983).

144. Irving Ind. Sch. District v. Tatro, 468 U.S. 883, 104 S.Ct. 3371 (1984); Tokarcik v. Forest Hills Sch. District, 665 F.2d 443 (3d Cir. 1981).

145. Dubois v. Connecticut State Board of Education, 727 F.2d 44 (2nd Cir. 1984) (transportation services); Hurry v. Jones 734 F.2d 829 (1st Cir. 1984) (transportation services); Hawaii Department of Education v. Kathryn D., 727 F.2d 809 (9th Cir. 1983) (transportation). Facilities modifications (ramps, doorways, and equipment) are required by the regulations under both EHA and § 504. 34 C.F.R. § 104.22; § 300.13(b)(13).

laws) do qualify disciplinary authority over the handicapped. Punishment for misbehavior caused by a student's handicap would defeat both the educational purpose of the E.H.A. and the nondiscriminatory command of § 504. In determining whether misbehavior is attributable to a handicapped condition, the courts have bemoaned the lack of clear statutory direction.[146] They appear to qualify disciplinary authority by requiring a showing that the student's misconduct was not attributable to his or her handicap, and is within the reasonable control of such child.[147] For disciplinary punishments that involve interruptions of a child's education (transfers, suspension, or expulsion) the E.H.A. due process procedures for a change of placement, or change of program, must be followed before such discipline is administered, notwithstanding any state law to the contrary.[148] Further, should sanctions less burdensome than disruption of the child's program be reasonably adequate for disciplinary purposes, courts require the less restrictive sanction to be employed.[149] E.H.A. procedural restrictions on discipline would not, of course, apply to students who, notwithstanding their handicap, do not require individualized special education programs.[150]

c. The Interaction of E.H.A. and § 504. Prior to the Supreme Court's decision in *Smith* v. *Robinson,* reported at p. 379, *infra,* there was confusion in lower court decisions on the application of § 504 to students who were also covered by E.H.A. In *Smith,* the Court resolved the conflicts by ruling that available relief under E.H.A. is exclusive and preempts any § 504 application with one possible exception, namely, "where § 504 guarantees substantive rights greater than those available under the E.H.A." The door was thus left ajar for limited operation of § 504 to handicapped student issues, in the rare instance where E.H.A. did not provide adequate relief.[151] To that extent, the § 504 principles (hereafter discussed with relation to handicapped teachers) may prove relevant to handicapped students.

d. Supplemental State Support of Handicapped Children. While all states that receive federal funds under E.H.A. must comply with E.H.A. standards, some go further to alleviate the financial burdens of local districts in maintaining children with severe handicaps, especially those who require full-time institutional care. State law coverage sometimes depends upon the classification of a child as a ward of the state, under state welfare laws; and sometimes upon the law's classification of a particular handicap. Thus New York courts have upheld as rational and constitutional different state subsidies for different classes of handicapped children.[152]

---

146. *See* S-1 v. Turlington, 635 F.2d 342, 347 (5th Cir. 1981).

147. *See* Kaelin v. Grubbs, 682 F.2d 595 (6th Cir. 1982) and cases there cited.

148. S-1 v. Turlington, *supra,* at pp. 347–348; Vogel v. Sch. District, 491 F.Supp. 989 (W.D.Mo. 1980)

149. Sch. District v. Dept. of Pub. Instruction, 284 N.W.2d 173 (Iowa 1979). *See* Stuart v. Nappi opinion, p. 383, *infra.*

150. Mrs. A.J. v. Special School District, 478 F.Supp. 418, 432 (Minn. 1979).

151. *E.g.,* New York State Assn. for Retarded Children v. Carey, 612 F.2d 644 (2d Cir. 1979) the court held that school quarantining of a handicapped child with mildly contagious hepatitis violated § 504 in the absence of showing that the threat of contagion was substantial). *See also* Community H.S. Dist. v. Denz, 463 N.E.2d 998 (Ill. 1984).

152. *Schools: See* Matter of Jessup, 379 N.Y.S.2d 629 (1975). Grants have been made for special education

2. Gifted Children

Like the handicapped, gifted children have no constitutional right to education that is specifically tailored to optimize their talents or potential. After initial attempts to provide incentive funds for special programs for gifted students (e.g., The Equal Educational Opportunities Act and Education Amendments of 1974), federal efforts largely expired. State statutory programs for gifted children are very sporadic and limited.[153] The provision of special schools for the academically talented has been upheld, however, even in school districts undergoing desegregation, though such programs incidentally produce some racial imbalances.[154]

3. Handicapped Teachers

Employment exclusion of handicapped individuals as a class has survived constitutional challenge, where the exclusion was found to be "rational."[155] Such class-based exclusion is forbidden by § 504 of the Rehabilitation Act. That act applied to any federally aided employer[156] and thus to all public schools. Victims of § 504 discrimination by public schools may institute private suits against the district for damage and injunctive relief.[157] The prohibitions of § 504 extend to all phases of the employment process—from recruiting and screening; through hiring, promotion, and dismissal; through provision of benefits or privileges regarding working terms and conditions.[158]

A person is considered handicapped under § 504 if his or her physical or mental impairment is such as to "substantially limit" a major life activity[159] The act prohibits discrimination based solely on the existence of a handicap, but unless the individual is "otherwise qualified," it does not require employment or retention of a person whose handicap disables him or her from properly performing the particular position.[160] A person will not be considered unqualified, however, merely because the handicap makes performance more difficult. If with "reasonable" employer support, he or she can fulfill the job duties involved, the employer must provide reasonable support. The act stops short, however, of requiring employers to undertake "affirmative action" beyond

---

out of the district. *In re* Davis, 370 N.Y.S.2d 357 (1975); Lisbon Reg. Sch. District v. Landaff Sch. District, 327 A.2d 727 (N.H. 1974). *Maintenance*: In re G.H., 218 N.W.2d 441 (N.Dak. 1974). *See also* Matter of Levy, 38 N.Y.2d 653 (1976); Matter of Saberg, 386 N.Y.S.2d 593 (1976) (differential subsidies); In re Claire, 335 N.Y.S.2d 399 (1975); In re Logel, 356 N.Y.S.2d 775 (1974) (parental contribution); Doe v. Colburg, 555 P.2d 753 (Mont. 1976).

153. *See* Hart v. Community School Board of Education, 512 F.2d 37, 54 (2nd Cir. 1975); Stout v. Jefferson County Board of Education, 483 F.2d 84, 85 (5th Cir. 1973); *cf.* Vorcheimer v. School District of Philadelphia, fn. 71.

154. 20 U.S.C. §§1141(k); 1713(f); 1863. *See* California Education Code § 52200 (West 1976); Illinois Ann. Stat. ch. 122, § 14A; Mich. Comp. Laws Ann. § 388.1147; Pa. Stat. Ann., tit. 71, § 369.

155. New York City Transit Authority v. Beazer, 438 U.S. 904 (1979).

156. *See* text of § 504 p. 393, *infra.*

157. Consolidated Rail Corp. v. Darrone, 465 U.S. 624 (1984).

158. 34 C.F.R. § 104.11(b) Doe v. Syracuse Sch. Dist., 508 F.Supp. 333 (N.D.N.Y. 1981).

159. 34 C.F.R. § 104.3(j). *See also* Pittsburgh Fed. of Teachers v. Langer, 546 F.Supp. 434 (W.D.Pa. 1982).

160. *E.g.*, Anonymous v. Bd. of Examiners, 318 N.Y.S.2d 163 (1970) (decertification of drug-addicted teacher).

reasonable accommodation to allow individuals to overcome work handicaps.[161] In close cases, therefore, parties encounter nice questions about whether a particular degree of support demanded amounts to "reasonable" accommodation or nonrequired affirmative action.[162]

On the issue of qualification, the grievant has the burden of proving that he or she is qualified for the position in question,[163] while the employer has the burden of proving that necessary arrangements to enable the grievant to do the work would be "unreasonable" either in costs or in operating arrangements.[164]

The importance of focusing upon the consequences of a handicap in relation to a particular job, rather than upon the handicap itself, is illustrated by cases involving blind applicants for teaching positions. Where a school district refused to consider the applicant because of her blindness, the court held that it violated § 504. In another case, however, where a blind applicant was denied employment on finding that her blindness disqualified her from proper performance of supervisory duties, the district was held not to violate the Act.[165] Similarly, decertification of a drug addict and subsequent dismissal was not considered discriminatory, although drug addiction has been held to fall within § 504 definition of a handicap.[166] In many cases, the effect of a particular handicap upon the victim's ability to perform work safely and efficiently will depend upon a court's judgment rather than upon objective criteria. In making such judgments, the nature of the particular handicap in relation to the demands and risks of a particular job will be the central factors. Some physical impairments that would not seriously impede a classroom teacher would seriously impede the work of a security officer or bus driver.

While the foregoing observations primarily involve the employment interests of teachers and other full-time school employees, they apply as well to part-time or special school employment of students either directly or under specially funded employment programs.

E. Age Discrimination

In the school context, age discrimination primarily involves teacher employment.[167] The forced retirement of teachers at a specified age was attacked on constitutional grounds,

---

161. *See* Southeastern Community College v. Davis, 442 U.S. 397, 407-12 (1979); Coleman v. Casey County Bd. of Ed., 510 F.Supp. 301, 303 (W.D.Ky. 1980).

162. *Compare* Southeastern Community College v. Davis, *supra* (holding provision of lip-reader interpreter not required by § 504) *with* Strathie v. Dept. of Transportation, 716 F.2d 227 (3d Cir. 1983) (suggesting that provision of hearing aid to applicant for school bus driver's license might be required "support" under § 504).

163. Strathie v. Dept. of Transportation, *supra*; Hart v. Moyer & City Council, 624 F.2d 13 (4th Cir. 1980).

164. *E.g.*, Nelson v. Thornburgh, 567 F.Supp. 369, 379 (E.D.Pa. 1983).

165. *Compare* Gurmankin v. Constanzo, 556 F.2d 184 (3d Cir. 1977) (presumptive disqualification of blind person from reaching consideration—disapproved); *with* Upshur v. Love, 474 F.Supp. 332 (N.D.Cal. 1979) (refusal to hire blind administrator as lacking ability to supervise others—upheld).

166. *See* Anonymous v. Bd. of Examiners, fn. 160, *supra*. The Rehabilitation Act was amended in 1978 to exclude certain types of drug and alcohol abuse in employment cases, where such conditions would pose a risk to property or persons at the work place.

167. As reported in Chapter 3, age limits for student admission to public schools have been regularly upheld.

with mixed results. The United States Supreme Court sustained mandatory retirement ages for police officers, but the Seventh Circuit Court of Appeal held that decision not applicable to forced retirement of teachers at age 65.[168] It found the connection of age to work duties significantly different for police officers than for teachers, and held the teacher retirement age to be unconstitutional because there was no justification to assume that all teachers at age 65 lacked the intellectual or physical vigor to teach well.

The open constitutional issue is rendered largely academic by the federal Age Discrimination in Employment Act of 1967, as amended in 1978. These acts prohibit forced retirement of employees before age 70 and also ban age-based discrimination in other employment terms and conditions. They cover teachers and other public employees.[169] Like other discrimination statutes, they do not prevent dismissal or discipline based upon inadequate skill and performance, even though the age of an employee may contribute to the level of work efficiency. Since the condition of the individual, rather than his or her age, must justify the employment decision, a uniform age qualification for all individuals within a protected age group will not satisfy the law.[170]

The federal statutes do not bar a state legislature from fixing a higher minimum retirement age than age 70 or from outlawing any fixed retirement age, as was done in Alaska.[171] At least 26 states have age-discrimination statutes similar to the federal act, but their specific coverage, exemptions, and enforcement provisions vary.[172] A graphic comparison of federal and state age discrimination laws will be found in a recent study by Kovarsk and Kovarsky—*Economic, Medical, and Legal Aspects of Age Discrimination Law in Employment.*[173] Thus, a school district may not set a retirement age that conflicts with either the federal or its state statutes.[174]

The age discrimination statutes do not specify whether or when they prevent a school board from declining to renew a nontenured teacher's contract. If nonrenewal is based on factors other than age, it will not be defeated merely because of the probationer's age. In many cases, however, parties can be expected to dispute the facts underlying nonrenewal decisions. One court recently held that a policy of nonrenewal

---

168. Mass. Bd. of Retirement v. Murgia, 427 U.S. 307 (1976); Weisbrod v. Lynn, 383 F.Supp. 933 (D. D.C. 1974) aff'd. 420 U.S. 940 (1975); lower courts upheld teacher retirement laws: Frantz v. Baldwin Whitehall Sch. District, 331 A.2d 484 (Pa. 1975); Harren v. Middle Island Central Sch. District No. 12, 373 N.Y.S.2d 20 (1975); Kennedy v. Community Un. Sch. District No. 7,319 N.E. 2d 243 (Ill. 1974); Lewis v. Tucson Sch. District No. 1,531 P.2d 199 (Ariz. 1975); Weiss v. Walsh, 324 F.Supp. 75 (S.D. N.Y. 1971), aff'd. 461 F.2d 846 (2d Cir. 1972) cert. denied, 409 U.S. 1129 (1973). *But see* Nelson v. Niva, 546 P.2d 1005 (Haw. 1976), for a contrary view under a peculiar state statutory scheme. *Contra*: Gault v. Garrison, 569 F.2d 993 (7th Cir. 1977).

169. 29 U.S.C. §§621-634. Usery v. Bd. of Education of Salt Lake City, 421 F. Supp. 718 (D. Utah 1976); Kuhar v. Greensburg-Salem Sch. District, 466 F.Supp. 806 (W.D.Pa. 1979).

170. *Compare* Usery v. Tamiami Trial Tours Inc., 531 F.2d 224 (5th Cir. 1976) (upholding refusal to hire persons over 40 as bus drivers); *with* Hodgson v. First Federal Savings & Loan Assn., 455 F.2d 818 (5th Cir. 1972) (disapproving refusal to hire 47-year-old woman as bank teller).

171. *See* Simpson v. Alaska State Comm. for Human Rights, 423 F.Supp. 552 (D.Alaska 1976).

172. *See, e.g.*, Iowa Civil Rights Act, I.C.A. §601 A.1; N.Y. Exec. Law § 296; Pa. Human Relations Act, Pa. Stat. Ann., tit. 43, § 951.

173. Published in 27 Vanderbilt L. Rev. 839 (1974).

174. Cole v. Town of Hartford Sch. District, 306 A.2d 101 (Vt. 1973); Herzig v. Bd. of Education, 204 A.2d 827 (Conn. 1964); *cf.* Monnier v. Todd County Ind. Sch. District, 245 N.W.2d 503 (S. Dak. 1976).

based on the age of an experienced nontenured teacher was lawful.[175] But if nonrenewal were based *solely* on age, the validity of that decision would be questionable.

F. Religious Discrimination

The constitutional safeguards against government preference for—or interference with—particular religions or religious beliefs, as reviewed in Chapter 4, and the equal protection principle discussed in the beginning of this chapter, operate to prohibit official discrimination against the individual, teacher, or student, on the basis of religion. Victims of religious discrimination may sue under those constitutional provisions and obtain court decrees to terminate such discrimination. They may also seek monetary recovery under remedial federal statutes (§§ 1983, 1988) which are discussed in the next chapter.

In the field of employment discrimination, Congress has included religious discrimination as one of the proscriptions of Title VII (p. 390, *infra*). The monetary remedies and equitable relief provided by Title VII are discussed in the next chapter. Religious discrimination is also addressed and remedied in various ways by state laws dealing with human rights and employment opportunity.

The Constitutional and statute claims are most commonly tested in public schools where religious interests and claims of teachers and students conflict with the operational schedules of the school. Thus, where a school limit on student- or teacher-excused absences or leaves that are taken for religious observance is too short to meet their religious obligations, courts have voided such limits as abridgements of the free exercise of religion.

Those rulings have occurred where the state's interest in maintaining school schedules was not found to be sufficiently compelling to override the constitutionally protected free exercise of religion.[176] The right of religious accommodation in public school employment is fortified by Title VII, which has been construed to require employers to provide reasonable religious accommodations to their employees so long as such accommodation does not cause undue hardship. One court recently construed the reasonable accommodation duty, where both the employee's proposed accommodation and a different employer's proposed accommodation are reasonable. In such instance, it held that the employee's preferred "reasonable" accommodation must be provided in the absence of hardship to the school employer.[177]

G. Poverty Groups

The gross disparity of per-pupil expenditures between affluent and poor public school districts was the basis for constitutional challenges by poverty groups to laws that require

175. King v. Cockran, 419 F.Supp. 54 (W.D.Ark. 1976).

176. Church of God Worldwide v. Amarillo, 511 F.Supp. 613 (N.D.Tex. 1981) (student): Niederhuber v. Camden County Vo-Tech. Sch. District Bd. of Education, 495 F.Supp. 273 (D.N.J. 1980)

177. Philbrook v. Ansonia Bd. of Education, 757 F.2d 476 (2d Cir. 1985) citing to Pinsker v. Jt. District, 735 F.2d 388 (10th Cir. 1984). The state may not, however, absolutely require employer accommodation of employees' religion in all circumstances. See ch. 10, fn. 561, *infra*.

school districts to rely upon local property taxes for their funds. These challenges under the Constitution failed, but they generated a trend of state reforms to develop other revenue sources for poorly funded districts.

In upholding state systems of educational finance, the Supreme Court ruled that public education is not a "fundamental interest" under the Constitution and that district tax wealth is not a "suspect classification" that would require strict scrutiny of equal protection.[178] The states need not show a compelling state interest to justify their tax laws, and interdistrict fiscal disparities were held not to be unconstitutional or discriminatory.

Similar poverty-based challenges under state constitutions have met with mixed success. Several state courts adopted the reasoning of the United States Supreme Court as equally valid under their state constitutions.[179] Others ruled that their school finance laws violated either the state constitutional equal protection provision or the state constitutional requirement that the legislature establish a "thorough and efficient" system of public education.[180] It bears repeating that constitutional cases do not prevent any state, as a matter of voluntary educational policy, to equalize educational funding. They only answer the question of what the state lawmakers *must* (not may) do under the federal or state constitutions.[181]

H. Aliens

In 1983, the Supreme Court held that an alien, whether lawfully or unlawfully present in the United States, is a "person" within the protection of the Fourteenth Amendment[182] and that state law governing an alien's right to education or employment in the public school system is subject to federal constitutional limits. Constitutional standards for alien classification have developed along different lines with respect to alien students and to alien teachers and employees.

1. Alien Children.

It is clear that lawfully resident alien children have a constitutional right to receive public education on equal terms with citizen students. The more difficult question is whether children who unlawfully enter this country may be barred from attending a state public school. In the landmark case of *Plyler* v. *Doe*,[183] the Supreme Court held that Texas

---

178. San Antonio Ind. Sch. District, v. Rodriguez, 411 U.S. 1 (1973) reproduced at the end of Chapter 9.

179. Thompson v. Engelking, 537 P.2d 635 (Idaho 1975); Olsen v. State, 554 P.2d 139 (Ore. 1976); North Shore Sch. District No. 147 v. Kinnear, 530 P.2d 178 (Wash. 1974); Shofstall v. Hollins, 515 P.2d 590 (Ariz. 1973); Milliken v. Green, 212 N.W.2d 711 (Mich. 1973), rev'd. 203 N.W.2d 457 (Mich. 1972); *cf.* Hootch v. Alaska State Operated Sch. System, 536 P.2d 793 (Alaska 1975).

180. Bd. of Education v. Nyquist, 408 N.Y.S.2d 606 (1978); Serrano v. Priest (II) 557 P.2d 929 (Cal. 1976); Robinson v. Cahill, 303 A.2d 273 (N.J. 1973); 358 A.2d 457 (N.J. 1976).

181. See also Chapter 9 or "School Finance" for related discussion.

182. Plyler v. Doe, 457 U.S. 202, 210 (1982).

183. *Idem.*

could not deny public education to Mexican children who had illegally entered the country because the state had not demonstrated that the exclusion of these children furthered a "substantial state interest". In reaching its decision, the *Plyler* Court applied a "heightened scrutiny" test that fell somewhere between strict scrutiny applied to racial discrimination and the deferential scrutiny applied to business regulations. A year after the *Plyler* decision, the Supreme Court held that a state law requiring bona fide residence within the educating district could be constitutionally applied to deny admission to the district's public schools of an alien child who was sent across the border by his Mexican parents to live with an aunt, solely for the purpose of securing a free public education.[184]

2. Alien Teachers and Employees.

In 1979, the Supreme Court ruled that lawfully admitted aliens who are eligible for—but refuse to seek—naturalized citizenship may be denied employment as public school teachers, on the view that the teaching position involved an important governmental function justifying a citizenship requirement.[185] Thus, in contrast to children who are illegally taken into the country by their parents, the Court applied a looser constitutional test of equal protection to would-be teachers. The rationale of the foregoing decision raises the question of which other professional or quasiprofessional positions could be constitutionally limited to citizens or intended citizens. It would appear that public school positions not involving essentially educational functions (viz. bus drivers, maintenance workers, cafeteria workers, etc.) could still avoid the above case by declaring that citizenship status is not a rational need of the public for those positions. Nevertheless, given the Supreme Court's uncertain meanderings in dealing with different access claims by aliens to different positions of public or governmental importance, the constitutional issue must be considered open for many public school employment positions.

---

184. Martinez v. Bynum, 461 U.S. 321 (1983).
185. Ambach v. Norwick, 441 U.S. 68 (1979).

CASES

Milliken v. Bradley

418 U.S. 717 (1974)

Mr. *Chief Justice Burger* delivered the opinion of the Court.

We granted certiorari in these consolidated cases to determine whether a federal court may impose a multidistrict, areawide remedy to a single district *de jure* segregation problem absent any finding that the other included school districts have failed to operate unitary school systems within their districts, absent any claim or finding that the boundary lines of any affected school district were established with the purpose of fostering racial segregation in public schools, absent any finding that the included districts committed acts which effected segregation within the other districts, and absent a meaningful opportunity for the included neighboring school districts to present evidence or be heard on the propriety of a multidistrict remedy or on the question of constitutional violations by those neighboring districts. . . . A federal remedial power may be exercised "only on the basis of a constitutional violation" and, "[a]s with any equity case, the nature of the violation determines the scope of the remedy." . . . [W]e first note that in the District Court the complainants sought a remedy aimed at the *condition* alleged to offend the Constitution—the segregation within the Detroit City school district.

Viewing the record as a whole, it seems clear that the District Court and the Court of Appeals shifted the primary focus from a Detroit remedy to the metropolitan area only because of their conclusion that total desegregation of Detroit would not produce the racial balance which they perceived as desirable. . . .

Boundary lines may be bridged where there has been a constitutional violation calling for inter-district relief, but, the notion that school district lines may be casually ignored or treated as a mere administrative convenience is contrary to the history of public education in our country. . . .

The metropolitan remedy would require, in effect, consolidation of 54 independent school districts historically administered as separate units into a vast new super school district. . . .

The controlling principle consistently expounded in our holdings is that the scope of the remedy is determined by the nature and extent of the constitutional violation. *Swann, supra,* 402 U.S., at 16, 91 S.Ct., at 1276. Before the boundaries of separate and autonomous school districts may be set aside by consolidating the separate units for remedial purposes or by imposing a cross-district remedy, it *must first be shown that there has been a constitutional violation within one district that produces a significant segregative effect in another district. Specifically it must be shown that racially discriminatory acts of the state or local school districts, or of a single school district have been a substantial cause of inter-district segregation.* Thus an inter-district remedy might be in order where the racially discriminatory acts of one or more school districts caused racial segregation in an adjacent district, or where district lines have been deliberately drawn on the basis of race. . . .

Conversely, without an inter-district violation and inter-district effect, there is no constitutional wrong calling for an inter-district remedy.

The record before us, voluminous as it is, contains evidence of *de jure* segregated conditions only in the Detroit schools, . . . To approve the remedy ordered by the court would impose on the outlying districts, not shown to have committed any constitutional violation, a wholly impermissible remedy based on a standard not hinted at in *Brown I* and *II* or any holding of this Court. . . .

Mr. *Justice White,* with whom Mr. *Justice* DOUGLAS, Mr. *Justice* BRENNAN, and Mr. *Justice* MARSHALL join, dissenting. . . .

Firefighters v. Stotts

467 U.S. 561 (1984)

[After city was sued for employment discrimination under Title VII and entered into a consent decree to implement an affirmative action program to hire more black applicants, and after increasing the number of black employees through new hirings, it was required to reduce its work force due to lack of funds. When it attempted to do so on the bases of seniority per its collective bargaining agreement (which the Supreme Court found to be bona fide), the minority employees who were hired and promoted in accordance with the prior consent decree sought to enjoin the seniority-based layoffs as a violation of the employment ratios contemplated by the consent decree. The lower court order prohibiting layoff by seniority was reversed by the United States Supreme Court on the following reasoning.]

Justice White delivered the opinion of the Court.

. . . The issue at the heart of this case is whether the District Court exceeded its powers in entering an injunction requiring white employees to be laid off, when the otherwise applicable seniority system would have called for the layoff of black employees with less seniority. We are convinced that the Court of Appeals erred in resolving this issue and in affirming the District Court. . . .

As our cases have made clear, however, . . . Title VII protects bona fide seniority systems, and it is inappropriate to deny an innocent employee the benefits of his seniority in order to provide a remedy in a pattern or practice suit such as this. We thus have no doubt that the City considered its system to be valid and that it had no intention of departing from it when it agreed to the 1980 decree.

Finally, it must be remembered that neither the Union nor the non-minority employees were parties to the suit when the 1980 decree was entered. Hence the entry of that decree cannot be said to indicate any agreement by them to any of its terms. Absent the presence of the Union or the non-minority employees and an opportunity for them to agree or disagree with any provisions of the decree that might encroach on their rights, it seems highly unlikely that the City would purport to bargain away non-minority rights under the then-existing seniority system. We therefore conclude that the injunction does not merely enforce the agreement of the parties as reflected in the consent decree. If the injunction is to stand, it must be justified on some other basis.

The Court of Appeals held that even if the injunction is not viewed as compelling compliance with the terms of the decree, it was still properly entered because the District Court had inherent authority to modify the decree when an economic crisis unexpectedly required layoffs which, if carried out as the City proposed, would undermine the affirmative action outlined in the decree and impose an undue hardship on respondents. This was true, the court held, even though the modification conflicted with a bona fide seniority system adopted by the City. The Court of Appeals erred in reaching this conclusion. . . .

If individual members of a plaintiff class demonstrate that they have been actual victims of the discriminatory practice, they may be awarded competitive seniority and given their rightful place on the seniority roster. This much is clear from Franks v Bowman Transportation Co. 424 US 747, 47 L Ed 2d 444, 96 S Ct 1251 (1976) and Teamsters v United States, 431 US 324, 52 L Ed 2d 396, 97 S Ct 1843 (1977). Teamsters, however, also made clear that mere membership in the disadvantaged class is insufficient to warrant a seniority award; each individual must prove that the discriminatory practice had an impact on him. 431 US, at 367-371, 52 L Ed 2d 396, 97 S Ct 1843. Even when an individual shows that the discriminatory practice has had an impact on him, he is not automatically entitled to have a non-minority employee laid off to make room for him. He may have to wait until a vacancy occurs, and if there are non-minority employees on layoff, the Court must balance the equities in determining who is entitled to the job. Teamsters, supra, 431 US, at 371-376, 52 L Ed 2d 396, 97 S Ct 1843. See also Ford Motor Co. v EEOC, 458 US 219, 236-240, 73 L Ed 2d 721, 102 S Ct 3057 (1982). Here, there was no finding that any of the blacks protected from layoff had been victim of discrimination and no award of competitive seniority to any of them. Nor had the parties in formulating the consent decree purported to identify any specific employee entitled to particular relief other than those listed in the exhibits attached to the decree. It therefore seems to us that in light of Teamsters, the Court of Appeals imposed on the parties as an adjunct of settlement something that could not have been ordered had the case gone to trial and the plaintiffs proved that a pattern or practice of discrimination existed. . . . Finally, the Court of Appeals was of the view that the District Court ordered no more than that which the City unilaterally could have done by way of adopting an affirmative action program. Whether the City, a public employer, could have taken this course without violating the law is an issue we need not decide. The fact is that in this case the City took no such action and that the modification of the decree was imposed over its objection.

We thus are unable to agree either that the order entered by the District Court was a justifiable effort to enforce the terms of the decree to which the city had agreed or that it was a legitimate modification of the decree that could be imposed on the City without its consent. Accordingly, the judgment of the Court of Appeals is reversed.

Wygant v. Jackson Board of Education

________U.S. ________54 U.S.L.W. 4479 (1986)

Justice POWELL announced the judgment of the Court.

This case presents the question whether a school board, consistent with the Equal

Protection Clause, may extend preferential protection against layoffs to some of its employees because of their race or national origin.

I

In 1972 the Jackson Board of Education, because of racial tension in the community that extended to its schools, considered adding a layoff provision to the Collective Bargaining Agreement (CBA) between the Board and the Jackson Education Association (the Union) that would protect employees who were members of certain minority groups against layoffs. The Board and the Union eventually approved a new provision, Article XII. . . . It stated:

> "In the event that it becomes necessary to reduce the number of teachers through layoff . . . teachers with the most seniority in the district shall be retained, except that at no time will there be a greater percentage of minority personnel laid off than the current percentage of minority personnel employed at the time of the layoff. In no event will the number given notice of possible layoff be greater than the number of positions to be eliminated. Each teacher so affected will be called back in reverse order for positions for which he is certified maintaining the above minority balance."

When layoffs became necessary in 1974, it was evident that adherence to the CBA would result in the layoff of tenured nonminority teachers while minority teachers on probationary status were retained. Rather than complying with Article XII, the Board retained the tenured teachers and laid off probationary minority teachers, thus failing to maintain the percentage of minority personnel that existed at the time of the layoff. The Union, together with two minority teachers who had been laid off, brought suit in federal court, claiming that the Board's failure to adhere to the layoff provision violated the Equal Protection Clause of the Fourteenth Amendment and Title VII of the Civil Rights Act of 1964. They also urged the District Court to take pendent jurisdiction over state law contract claims. In its answer the Board denied any prior employment discrimination and argued that the layoff provision conflicted with the Michigan Teacher Tenure Act. App. 33. Following trial, the District Court *sua sponte* concluded that it lacked jurisdiction over the case, in part because there was insufficient evidence to support the plaintiffs' claim that the Board had engaged in discriminatory hiring practices prior to 1972, . . . and in part because the plaintiffs had not fulfilled the jurisdictional prerequisite to a Title VII claim by filing discrimination charges with the Equal Employment Opportunity Commission. After dismissing the federal claims, the District Court declined to exercise pendent jurisdiction over the state law contract claims.

Rather than taking an appeal, the plaintiffs instituted a suit in state court, . . . (*Jackson II*), raising in essence the same claims that had been raised in *Jackson I*. In entering judgment for the plaintiffs, the state court found that the Board had breached its contract with the plaintiffs and that Article XII did not violate the Michigan Teacher Tenure Act. In rejecting the Board's argument that the layoff provision violated the Civil Rights Act of 1964, the state court found that it "ha[d] not been established that the board had discriminated against minorities in its hiring practices. . . . " The state court also found that "[t]here is no history of overt past discrimination by the parties to this contract." . . . Nevertheless, the court held that Article XII was permissible, despite its discriminatory effect on nonminority teachers, as an attempt to remedy the effects of societal discrimination.

After *Jackson II*, the Board adhered to Article XII. As a result, . . . nonminority teachers were laid off, while minority teachers with less seniority were retained. The displaced nonminority teachers, petitioners here, brought suit . . . alleging violations of the Equal Protection Clause, Title VII, 42 U.S.C. § 1983, and other federal and state statutes. On cross motions for summary judgment, the District Court dismissed all of petitioners' claims. The Court of Appeals for the Sixth Circuit affirmed. . . . We granted certiorari, 471 U.S. ________(1985), to resolve the important issue of the constitutionality of race-based layoffs by public employers. We now reverse.

II

Petitioners' central claim is that they were laid off because of their race in violation of the Equal Protection Clause of the Fourteenth Amendment. Decisions by faculties and administrators of public schools based on race or ethnic origin are reviewable under the Fourteenth Amendment. This Court has "consistently repudiated '[d]istinctions between citizens solely based of their ancestry'. . . . "Racial and ethnic distinctions of any sort are inherently suspect and thus call for the most exacting judicial examination." *Regents of University of California* v. *Bakke,* 438 U.S. 265, 291 (1978) (opinion of *POWELL, J.*, joined by *WHITE, J.*)

The Court has recognized that the level of scrutiny does not change merely because the challenged classification operates against a group that historically has not been subject to governmental discrimination. *Mississippi University for Women* v. *Hogan,* 458 U.S. 718, 724 n. 9 (1982); *Bakke,* 438 U.S., at 291-299;. . . . In this case, Article XII of the CBA operates against whites and in favor of certain minorities, and therefore constitutes a classification based on race. "Any preference based on racial or ethnic criteria must necessarily receive a most searching examination to make sure that it does not conflict with constitutional guarantees." *Fullilove* v. *Klutznick,* 448 U.S. 448, 491 (1980) (opinion of *BURGER, C.J.*). There are two prongs to this examination. First, any racial classification "must be justified by a compelling governmental interest." . . . Second, the means chosen by the State to effectuate its purpose must be "narrowly tailored to the achievement of that goal." *Fullilove,* 448 U.S. at 480. We must decide whether the layoff provision is supported by a compelling state purpose and whether the means chosen to accomplish that purpose are narrowly tailored.

• • •

The Court of Appeals, relying on the reasoning and language of the District Court's opinion, held that the Board's interest in providing minority role models for its minority students, as an attempt to alleviate the effects of societal discrimination, was sufficiently important to justify the racial classification embodied in the layoff provision. . . . The court discerned a need for more minority faculty role models by finding that the percentage of minority teachers was less than the percentage of minority students.

This Court never has held that societal discrimination alone is sufficient to justify a racial classification. Rather, the Court has insisted upon some showing of prior discrimination by the governmental unit involved before allowing limited use of racial classification in order to remedy such discrimination. . . . In *Hazelwood* the Court concluded that, absent employment discrimination by the school board, "'nondiscriminatory hiring practices will in time result in a work force more or less representative of the racial and ethnic composition of the population in the community from which the employees are hired.'" . . . *Hazelwood* demonstrates this Court's focus on prior discrimination as the justification for, and the limitation on, a State's adoption of race-based remedies. . . .

Unlike the analysis in *Hazelwood,* the role model theory employed by the District Court has no logical stopping point. The role model theory allows the Board to engage in discriminatory hiring and layoff practices long past the point required by any legitimate remedial purpose. Indeed, by tying the required percentage of minority teachers to the percentage of minority students, it requires just the sort of year-to-year calibration the Court stated was unnecessary in *Swann,* 402 U.S., at 31-32:

• • •

Moreover, because the role model theory does not necessarily bear a relationship to the harm caused by prior discriminatory hiring practices, it actually could be used to escape the obligation to remedy such practices by justifying the small percentage of black teachers by reference to the small percentage of black students. . . . Carried to its logical extreme, the idea that black students are better off with black teachers could lead to the very system the Court rejected in *Brown* v. *Board of Education,* 347 U.S. 483 (1954) (*Brown I*).

Societal discrimination, without more, is too amorphous a basis for imposing a racially classified remedy. . . . There are numerous explanations for a disparity between the percentage of minority students and the percentage of minority faculty, many of them completely unrelated to discrimination of any kind. In fact, there is no apparent connection between the two groups.

. . . No one doubts that there has been serious racial discrimination in this country. But as the basis for imposing discriminatory *legal* remedies that work against innocent people, societal discrimination is insufficient and over expansive. . . .

Respondents also now argue that their purpose in adopting the layoff provision was to remedy prior discrimination against minorities by the Jackson School District in hiring teachers. . . .

Evidentiary support for the conclusion that remedial action is warranted becomes crucial when the remedial program is challenged in court by nonminority employees. . . . In such a case, the trial court must make a factual determination that the employer had a strong basis in evidence for its conclusion that remedial action was necessary. The ultimate burden remains with the employees to demonstrate the unconstitutionality of an affirmative action program. But unless such a determination is made, an appellate court reviewing a challenge to remedial action by nonminority employees cannot determine whether the race-based action is justified as a remedy for prior discrimination.

Despite the fact that Article XII has spawned years of litigation and three separate lawsuits, no such determination ever has been made. . . . The Board now contends that, given another opportunity, it could establish the existence of prior discrimination. Although this argument seems belated at this point in the proceedings, we need not consider the question since we conclude below that the layoff provision was not a legally appropriate means of achieving even a compelling purpose.

The Court of Appeals examined the means chosen to accomplish the Board's race-conscious purposes under a test of "reasonableness." That standard has no support in the decisions of this Court. As demonstrated in Part II above, our decisions always have employed a more stringent standard. . . . See *e.g.*, *Palmore,* 466 U.S., at 432 ("to pass constitutional muster, [racial classifications] must be necessary . . . to the accomplishment of their legitimate purpose"). . . . Under strict scrutiny the means chosen to accomplish the State's asserted purpose must be specifically and narrowly framed to accomplish that purpose. . . .

We have recognized, however, that in order to remedy the effects of prior discrimination, it may be necessary to take race into account. . . . "When effectuating a limited and properly tailored remedy to cure the effects of prior discrimination, such a 'sharing of the burden' by innocent parties is not permissible." *Id.*, at 484, quoting *Franks* v. *Bowman Transportation Co.*, 424 U.S. 747 (1976). In *Fullilove,* the challenged statute required at least 10 percent of federal public works funds to be used in contracts with minority-owned business enterprises. This requirement was found to be within the remedial powers of Congress in part because the "actual burden shouldered by nonminority firms is relatively light." 448 U.S., at 484.

Significantly, none of these cases discussed above involved layoffs. Here, by contrast, the means chosen to achieve the Board's asserted purposes is that of laying off nonminority teachers with greater seniority in order to retain minority teachers with less seniority. We have previously expressed concern over the burden that a preferential layoffs scheme imposes on innocent parties. See *Firefighters* v. *Stotts.* 467 U.S. 561, 574-576, 578-579 (1984): . . . In cases involving valid *hiring* goals, the burden to be borne by innocent individuals is diffused to a considerable extent among society generally. Though hiring goals may burden some innocent individuals, they simply do not impose the same kind of injury that layoffs impose. Denial of a future employment opportunity is not as intrusive as loss of an existing job.

Many of our cases involve union seniority plans with employees who are typically heavily dependent on wages for their day-to-day living. . . . Layoffs disrupt these settled expectations in a way that general hiring goals do not.

While hiring goals impose a diffuse burden, often foreclosing only one of several opportunities, layoffs impose the entire burden of achieving racial equality on particular individuals, often resulting in serious disruption of their lives. That burden is too intrusive. We therefore hold that, as a means of accomplishing purposes that otherwise may be legitimate, the Board's layoff plan is not sufficiently narrowly tailored. Other, less intrusive means of accomplishing similar purposes—such as the adoption of hiring goals—are available. For these reasons, the Board's selection of layoffs as the means to accomplish even a valid purpose cannot satisfy the demands of the Equal Protection Clause.

We accordingly reverse the judgment of the Court of appeals for the Sixth Circuit.

Justice O'CONNOR, concurring in part and concurring in the judgment.

• • •

There is no issue here of the interpretation and application of Title VII of the Civil Rights Act; accordingly, we have only the constitutional issue to resolve.

• • •

Although *Justice POWELL'S* formulation may be viewed as more stringent than that suggested by *Justices BRENNAN, WHITE, MARSHALL,* and *BLACKMUN*, the disparities between the two tests do not preclude a fair measure of consensus. . . . The Court is in agreement that, whatever the formulation employed, remedying past or present racial discrimination by a state actor is a sufficiently weighty state interest to warrant the remedial use of a carefully constructed affirmative action program.

It appears, then, that the true source of disagreement on the Court lies not so much in defining the state interests which may support affirmative action efforts as in defining the degree to which the means employed must "fit" the ends pusued to meet constitutional standards. . . .

Ultimately, the Court is at least in accord in believing that a public employer, consistent with the Constitution, may undertake an affirmative action program which is designed to further a legitimate remedial purpose and which implements that purpose by means that do not impose disproportionate harm on the interests, or unnecessarily trammel the rights, of innocent individuals directly and adversely affected by a plan's racial preference.

In sum, I do not think that the layoff provision was constitutionally infirm simply because the School Board, the Commission or a court had not made particularized findings of discrimination at the time the provision was agreed upon. But when the plan was challenged, the District Court and the Court of Appeals did not make the proper inquiry into the legitimacy of the Board's asserted remedial purpose; instead, they relied upon governmental purposes that we have deemed insufficient to withstand strict scrutiny, and therefore failed to isolate a sufficiently important governmental purpose that could support the challenged provision.

There is, however, no need to inquire whether the provision actually had a legitimate remedial purpose based on the record, such as it is, because the judgment is vulnerable. . . .

Petitioners have met their burden of establishing that this layoff provision is not "narrowly tailored" to achieve its asserted remedial purpose. . . .

Although the constitutionality of the hiring goal as such is not before us, it is impossible to evaluate the necessity of the layoff provision as a remedy for the apparent prior employment discrimination absent reference to that goal. . . . In this case, the hiring goal that the layoff provision was designed to safeguard was tied to the percentage of minority students in the school district, not to the percentage of qualified minority teachers within the relevant labor pool. The disparity between the percentage of minorities on the teaching staff and the percentage of minorities in the student body is not probative of employment discrimination. . . . Because the layoff provision here acts to maintain levels of minority hiring that have no relation to remedying employment discrimination, it cannot be adjudged "narrowly tailored" to effectuate its asserted remedial purpose.

I therefore . . . concur in the judgment.

Justice WHITE, concurring in the judgment.

. . . None of the interests asserted by the board, singly or together, justify this racially discriminatory layoff policy and save it from the strictures of the Equal Protection Clause. Whatever the legitimacy of hiring goals or quotas may be, the discharge of white teachers to make room for blacks, none of whom has been shown to be a victim of any racial discrimination, is quite a different matter. I cannot believe that in order to integrate a work force, it would be permissible to discharge whites and hire blacks until the latter comprised a suitable percentage of the work force. None of our cases suggest that this would be permissible under the Equal Protection Clause. . . . I agree with the plurality that this official policy is unconstitutional and hence concur in the judgment.

Justice MARSHALL, with whom *Justice* BRENNAN and *Justice* BLACKMUN join, dissenting.

• • •

I, too, believe that layoffs are unfair. But unfairness ought not be confused with constitutional injury. Paying no heed to the true circumstances of petitioners' plight, the plurality would nullify years of negotiation and compromise designed to solve serious educational problems in the public schools of Jackson, Michigan. Because I believe that a public employer, with the full agreement of its employees, should be permitted to preserve the benefits of a legitimate and constitutional affirmative-action hiring plan even while reducing its work force, I dissent.

The record and extra-record materials that we have before us persuasively suggest that the plurality has too quickly assumed the absence of a legitimate factual predicate, . . . for affirmative action in the Jackson schools.

• • •

From the outset, it is useful to bear in mind what this case is not. There has been no court order to achieve racial balance. . . .

There is also no occasion here to resolve whether a white worker may be required to give up his or her job in order to be replaced by a black worker. . . .

Nor are we asked to order parties to suffer the consequences of an agreement that they had no role in adopting. . . .

Moreover, this is not a case in which a party to a collective-bargaining agreement has attempted unilaterally to achieve racial balance by refusing to comply with a contractual, seniority-based layoff provision. . . .

The sole question posed by this case is whether the Constitution prohibits a union and a local school board from developing a collective- bargaining agreement that apportions layoffs between two racially determined groups as a means of preserving the effects of an affirmative hiring policy, the constitutionality of which is unchallenged.

• • •

Despite the Court's inability to agree on a route, we have reached a common destination in sustaining affirmative action against constitutional attack. In *Bakke,* we determined that a state institution may take race into account as a factor in its decisions, 438 U.S., at 326, and in *Fullilove,* the Court upheld a congressional preference for minority contractors because the measure was legitimately designed to ameliorate the present effects of past discrimination, 448 U.S., at 520.

In this case it should not matter which test the Court applies. What is most important, under any approach to the constitutional analysis, is that a reviewing court genuinely consider the circumstances of the provision at issue. The history and application of Article XII, assuming verification upon a proper record, demonstrate that this provision would pass constitutional muster, no matter which standard the Court should adopt.

• • •

Moreover, under the apparent circumstances of this case, we need not rely on any general awareness of "societal discrimination" to conclude that the Board's purpose is of sufficient importance to justify its limited remedial efforts. There are allegations that the imperative to integrate the public schools was urgent. Racially motivated violence had erupted at the schools, interfering with all educational objectives. We are told that, having found apparent violations of the law and a substantial underrepresentation of minority teachers, the state agency responsible for ensuring equality of treatment for all citizens of Michigan had instituted a settlement that required the Board to adopt affirmative hiring practices in lieu of further enforcement proceedings. That agency, . . . still stands fully behind the solution that the Board and the Union adopted in Article XII, viewing it as a measure necessary to attainment of stability and educational quality in the public schools. . . . Surely, if properly presented to the District Court, this would supply the "[e]vidientiary support for the conclusion that remedial action is warranted" that the plurality purports to seek, ... Since the District Court did not permit submission of this evidentiary support, I am at a loss as to why *Justice POWELL* so glibly rejects the obvious solution of remanding for the factfinding he appears to recognize is necessary.

Were I satisfied with the record before us, I would hold that the state purpose of preserving the integrity of a valid hiring policy—which in turn sought to achieve diversity and stability for the benefit of *all* students—was sufficient, in this case, to satisfy the demands of the Constitution.

V

The second part of any constitutional assessment of the disputed plan requires us to examine the means chosen to achieve the state purpose.

Under *Justice POWELL'S* approach, the community of Jackson, having painfully watched the hard-won benefits of its integration efforts vanish as a result of massive layoffs, would be informed today, simply, that preferential layoff protection is never permissible because hiring policies serve the same purpose at a lesser cost. . . . As a matter of logic as well as fact, a hiring policy achieves no purpose at all if it is eviscerated by layoffs.

• • •

The general practice of basing employment decisions on relative seniority may be upset for the sake of other public policies. For example, a court may displace innocent workers by granting retroactive seniority to victims of employment discrimination. *Franks v. Bowman Transportation Co.*, 424 U.S. 747, 775 (1976). . . .

Article XII is a narrow provision because it allocates the impact of an unavoidable burden proportionately between two racial groups. It places no absolute burden or benefit on one race, and, within the confines of constant minority proportions, it preserves the hierarchy of seniority in the selection of individuals for layoff. Race is a factor, along with seniority, in determining which individuals the school system will lose; it is not alone dispositive of any individual's fate. . . .

The Board's goal of preserving minority proportions could have been achieved, perhaps, in a different way. For example, if layoffs had been determined by lottery, the ultimate effect would have been retention of current racial percentages. A random system, however, would place every teacher in equal jeopardy, working a much greater upheaval of the seniority hierarchy. . . . Another possible approach would have been a freeze on layoffs of minority teachers. This measure, too, would have been substantially more burdensome than Article XII, ... Indeed, neither petitioners nor any Justice of this Court has suggested an alternative to Article XII that would have attained the stated goal in any narrower or more equitable a fashion. Nor can I conceive of one.

• • •

The concerns that have prompted some Members of this Court to call for narrowly tailored, perhaps court-ordered, means of achieving racial balance spring from a legitimate fear that racial distinctions will again be used as a means to persecute individuals, while couched in benign phraseology. That fear has given rise to mistrust of those who profess to take remedial action, and concern that any such action "work the least harm possible to other innocent persons competing for the benefit."

The collective-bargaining process is a legitimate and powerful vehicle for the resolution of thorny problems, . . . The best evidence that Article XII is a narrow means to serve important interests is that representatives of all affected persons, starting from diametrically opposed perspectives, have agreed to it—not once, but six times since 1972.

The narrow question presented by this case, if indeed we proceed to the merits, offers no occasion for the Court to issue broad proclamations of public policy concerning the controversial issue of affirmative action. . . . When an elected school board and a teachers' union collectively bargain a layoff provision designed to preserve the effects of a valid minority recruitment plan by apportioning layoffs between two racial groups, as a result of a settlement achieved under the auspices of a supervisory state agency charged with protecting the civil rights of all citizens, that provision should not be upset by this Court on constitutional grounds. . . . I would vacate the judgment of the Court of Appeals and remand with instructions that the case be remanded to the District Court for further proceedings consistent with the views I have expressed.

Justice STEVENS, dissenting.
In my opinion, it is not necessary to find that the Board of Education has been guilty of racial discrimination in the past to support the conclusion that it has a legitimate interest in employing more black teachers in the future. . . .

• • •

In the context of public education, it is quite obvious that a school board may reasonably conclude that an integrated faculty will be able to provide benefits to the student body that could not be provided by an all white, or nearly all white, faculty. . . .

• • •

. . . Our ultimate goal must, of course, be "to eliminate entirely from governmental decisionmaking such irrelevant factors as a human being's race." In this case, however, I am persuaded that the decision to include more minority teachers in the Jackson, Michigan, school system served a valid public purpose, that it was adopted with fair procedures and given a narrow breadth, that it transcends the harm to petitioners, and that it is a step toward that ultimate goal of eliminating entirely from governmental decisionmaking such irrelevant factors as a human being's race. I would therefore affirm the judgment of the Court of Appeals.

Hendrick Hudson Dist. Bd. of Ed. v. Rowley

458 U.S. 176 (1982)

[In suit by parents of hearing-impaired child claiming right to have school district provide a sign language instructor for the child in all her academic classes, at public expense, under the federal Education of the Handicapped Act, the Court held that such a resource, on the facts presented, was not necessary for a "free, appropriate public education" as those terms are used in the federal act.]

Justice REHNQUIST delivered the opinion of the Court.
This case presents a question of statutory interpretation. Petitioners contend that the

Court of Appeals and the District Court misconstrued the requirements imposed by Congress upon States which receive federal funds under the Education of the Handicapped Act. We agree and reverse the judgment of the Court of Appeals.

This case arose in connection with the education of Amy Rowley, a deaf student at the Furnace Woods School in the Hendrick Hudson Central School District, Peekskill, N.Y. Amy has minimal residual hearing and is an excellent lipreader. . . .

As required by the Act, an IEP was prepared for Amy during the fall of her first-grade year. . . . The Rowleys agreed with parts of the IEP but insisted that Amy also be provided a qualified sign-language interpreter in all her academic classes in lieu of the assistance proposed in other parts of the IEP. Such an interpreter had been placed in Amy's kindergarten class for a 2-week experimental period, but the interpreter had reported that Amy did not need his services at that time. The school administrators likewise concluded that Amy did not need such an interpreter in her first-grade classroom. . . .

When their request for an interpreter was denied, the Rowleys demanded and received a hearing before an independent examiner. . . . Pursuant to the Act's provision for judicial review, the Rowleys then brought an action in the United States District Court . . . claiming that the administrators' denial of the sign-language interpreter constituted a denial of the "free appropriate public education" guaranteed by the Act.

The District Court found that Amy "is a remarkably well-adjusted child" who interacts and communicates well with her classmates and has "developed an extraordinary rapport" with her teacher. 483 F.Supp. 528, 531 (1980). It also found that "she performs better than the average child in her class and is advancing easily from grade to grade," *id.*, at 534, but "that she understands considerably less of what goes on in class than she could if she were not deaf" and thus "is not learning as much, or performing as well academically, as she would without her handicap," *id.*, at 532. This disparity between Amy's achievement and her potential led the court to decide that she was not receiving a "free appropriate public education". . . .

This is the first case in which this Court has been called upon to interpret any provision of the Act. As noted previously, the District Court and the Court of Appeals concluded that "[t]he Act itself does not define 'appropriate education,'" 483 F.Supp., at 533, but leaves "to the courts and the hearing officers" the responsibility of "giv[ing] content to the requirement of an 'appropriate education.'" . . .

We are loath to conclude that Congress failed to offer any assistance in defining the meaning of the principal substantive phrase used in the Act. It is beyond dispute that, contrary to the conclusions of the courts below, the Act does expressly define "free appropriate public education":

> "The term 'free appropriate public education' means *special education* and *related services* which (A) have been provided at public expense, under public supervision and direction, and without charge, (B) meet the standards of the State educational agency, (C) include an appropriate preschool, elementary, or secondary school education in the State involved, and (D) are provided in conformity with the individualized education program required under section 1414(a)(5) of this title." § 1401(18) (emphasis added).

"Special education," as referred to in this definition, mean "specially designed instruction, at no cost to parents or guardians, to meet the unique needs of a handicapped child, including classroom instruction, instruction in physical education, home instruction, and instruction in hospitals and institutions." § 1401(16). "Related services" are defined as "transportation, and such developmental, corrective, and other supportive services . . . as may be required to assist a handicapped child to benefit from special education." § 1401(17).[1]

According to the definitions contained in the Act, a "free appropriate public education" consists of educational instruction specially designed to meet the unique needs of the handicapped child, supported by such services as are necessary to permit the child "to benefit" from the instruction. . . . Thus, if personalized instruction is being provided with sufficient services to permit the child to benefit from the instruction, and the other items on the definitional checklist are satisfied, the child is receiving a "free appropriate education" as defined by the Act.

Noticeably absent from the language of the statute is any substantive standard prescribing the level of education to be accorded handicapped children. Certainly the language of the statute contains no requirement like the one imposed by the lower courts—that States maximize the potential of handicapped children "commensurate with the opportunity provided to other children." 483 F.Supp., at 534. . . .

It is evident from the legislative history that the characterization of handicapped children as "served" referred to children who were receiving some form of specialized educational services. . . .

Respondents contend that "the goal of the Act is to provide each handicapped child with an equal educational opportunity." Brief for Respondents 35. We think, however, that the requirement that a State provide specialized educational services to handicapped children generates no additional requirement that the services so provided be sufficient to maximize each child's potential "commensurate with the opportunity provided other children." . . .

. . . The theme of the Act is "free appropriate public education," a phrase which is too complex to be captured by the word "equal" whether one is speaking of opportunities or services.

The District Court and the Court of Appeals thus erred when they held that the Act requires New York to maximize the potential of each handicapped child commensurate with the opportunity provided nonhandicapped children. Desirable though that goal might be, it is not the standard that congress imposed upon States which receive funding under the Act. . . .

Implicit in the congressional purpose of providing access to a "free appropriate public education" is the requirement that the education to which access is provided be sufficient to confer some educational benefit upon the handicapped child. . . . The statutory definition of "free appropriate public education," in addition to requiring that States provide each child with "specially designed instruction," expressly requires the

1. Examples of "related services" identified in the Act are "speech pathology and audiology, psychological services, physical and occupational therapy, recreation, and medical and counseling services, except that such medical services shall be for diagnostic and evaluation purposes only." § 148 1401(17).

provision of "such . . . supportive services . . . as may be required to assist a handicapped child to *benefit* from special education." § 1401(17) (emphasis added). We therefore conclude that the "basic floor of opportunity" provided by the Act consists of access to specialized instruction and related services which are individually designed to provide educational benefit to the handicapped child. The determination of when handicapped children are receiving sufficient educational benefits to satisfy the requirements of the Act presents a more difficult problem. The Act requires participating States to educate a wide spectrum of handicapped children, from the marginally hearing-impaired to the profoundly retarded and palsied. It is clear that the benefits obtainable by the children at one end of the spectrum will differ dramatically from those obtainable by children at the other end, with infinite variations in between. . . . We do not attempt today to establish any one test for determining the adequacy of educational benefits conferred upon all children covered by the Act. Because in this case we are presented with a handicapped child who is receiving substantial specialized instruction and related services, and who is performing above average in the regular classrooms of a public school system, we confine our analysis to that situation.

When the language of the Act and its legislative history are considered together, the requirements imposed by Congress become tolerably clear. Insofar as a State is required to provide a handicapped child with a "free appropriate public education," we held that it satisfies this requirement by providing personalized instruction with sufficient support services to permit the child to benefit educationally from that instruction. Such instruction and services must be provided at public expense, must meet the State's educational standards, must approximate the grade levels used in the State's regular education, and must comport with the child's IEP. In addition, the IEP, and therefore the personalized instruction, should be formulated in accordance with the requirements of the Act and, if the child is being educated in the regular classrooms of the public education system, should be reasonably calculated to enable the child to achieve passing marks and advance from grade to grade.

. . . In reviewing the complaint, the Act provides that a court "shall receive the record of the [state] administrative proceedings, shall hear additional evidence at the request of a party, and, basing its decision on the preponderance of the evidence, shall grant such relief as the court determines is appropriate." § 1415(e)(2).

The parties disagree sharply over the meaning of these provisions, petitioners contending that courts are given only limited authority to review for state compliance with the Act's procedural requirements and no power to review the substance of the state program, and respondents contending that the Act requires courts to exercise *de novo* review over state educational decisions and policies. . . .

Thus the provision that a reviewing court base its decision on the "preponderance of the evidence" is by no means an invitation to the courts to substitute their own notions of sound educational policy for those of the school authorities which they review. . . .

Therefore, a court's inquiry in suits brought under § 1415(e)(2) is two fold. First, has the State complied with the procedures set forth in the Act? And second, is the individualized educational program developed through the Act's procedures reasonably calculated to enable the child to receive educational benefits? If these requirements are met, the State has complied with the obligations imposed by Congress and the courts can require no more.

In assuring that the requirements of the Act have been met, courts must be careful to avoid imposing their view of preferable educational methods upon the States. . . .

Entrusting a child's education to state and local agencies does not leave the child without protection. . . . As this very case demonstrates, parents and guardians will not lack ardor in seeking to ensure that handicapped children receive all of the benefits to which they are entitled by the Act.

Smith v. Robinson

468 U.S. 992, 104 S.Ct. 3457 (1984)

[Because local school authorities refused to fund special education placement of a handicapped child, the parents sued local and state education officials on several different counts for alleged violations of Fourteenth Amendment due process and equal protection clauses, and of three federal statutes (Education of the Handicapped Act, § 504 of the Rehabilitation Act, and the Civil Rights Act of 1871). After receiving substantive relief as to the child's placement at public expense, the parents pressed their claim under the Federal Attorney's Fees Awards Act of 1976, with respect to legal fees during various stages of the prolonged litigation. The Court's disposition of their fee claims, which follows, also reveals the complex interaction of the substantive statutes, both with each other and with the fee-awards statute.]

Justice BLACKMUN delivered the opinion of the Court.

This case presents questions regarding the award of attorney's fees in a proceeding to secure a "free appropriate public education" for a handicapped child. At various stages in the proceeding, petitioners asserted claims for relief based on state law, on the Education of the Handicapped Act (EHA), . . . on § 504 of the Rehabilitation Act of 1973, . . . and on the Due Process and Equal Protection Clauses of the Fourteenth Amendment to the United States Constitution. The United States Court of Appeals for the First Circuit concluded that because the proceeding, in essence, was one to enforce the provisions of the EHA, a statute that does not provide for the payment of attorney's fees, petitioners were not entitled to such fees. *Smith* v. *Cumberland School Committee,* 703 F.2d 4 (1983). Petitioners insist that this Court's decision in Maher v. Gagne, 448 U.S. 122, 100 S.Ct. 2570, 65 L.Ed.2d 653 (1980), compels a different conclusion.

I

The procedural history of the case is complicated, but it is significant to the resolution of the issues. Petitioner Thomas F. Smith, III (Tommy), suffers from cerebral palsy and a variety of physical and emotional handicaps. When this proceeding began in November 1976, Tommy was 8 years old. In the preceding December, the Cumberland School Committee had agreed to place Tommy in a day program at Emma Pendleton Bradley Hospital in East Providence, R.I., and Tommy began attending that program. In November 1976, however, the Superintendent of Schools informed Tommy's parents, who are the other petitioners here, that the School Committee no longer would fund

Tommy's placement because, as it construed Rhode Island law, the responsibility for educating an emotionally disturbed child lay with the State's Division of Mental Health, Retardation and Hospitals [MHRH]. App. 25-26.

Petitioners took an appeal from the decision of the Superintendent to the School Committee. In addition, petitioners filed a complaint under 42 U.S.C. § 1983. . . .

On May 10, 1978, petitioners filed a First Amended Complaint. . . . By that time, petitioners had completed the state administrative process. . . .

All the state officers agreed that, under R.I.Gen.Laws, Tit. 40, ch. 7 (1977), the responsibility for educating Tommy lay with MHRH. The Associate Commissioner acknowledged petitioners' argument that since § 40.1-7-8 would require them to pay a portion of the cost of services provided to Tommy, the statute conflicted with the EHA, but concluded that the problem was not within his jurisdiction to resolve.

In their First Amended Complaint, petitioners added as defendants the Commissioner of Education, the Associate Commissioner of Education, the Board of Regents for Education, and the Director of MHRH. They also specifically relied for the first time on EHA. . . .

In the First Count of their Amended Complaint, petitioners challenged the fact that both the hearing before the School Committee and the hearing before the Associate Commissioner were conducted before examiners who were employees of the local or state education agency. They sought a declaratory judgment that the procedural safeguards . . . in Article IX of the Regulations did not comply with the Due Process Clause of the Fourteenth Amendment or with the requirements of the EHA, 20 U.S.C. § 1415, and its accompanying regulations. . . . Finally, they sought reasonable attorney's fees and costs.

In the Second Count of their Amended Complaint, petitioners challenged the substance of the Associate Commissioner's decision. . . . They sought an injunction requiring the School Committee to provide Tommy such an education. They also asked for reasonable attorney's fees and costs. . . .

On May 29, 1979, the District Court granted partial summary judgment for the defendants on petitioners' claim that they were denied due process by the requirement of the Regulations that they submit their dispute to the School Committee and by the Associate State Commissioner's refusal to recuse himself. . . .

Petitioners thereafter filed their Second Amended and Supplemental complaint. App. 152. In it they added to Count II claims for relief under the Equal Protection Clause of the Fourteenth Amendment and under § 504 of the Rehabilitation Act of 1973, as amended, 29 U.S.C. § 794. They also requested attorney's fees under 42 U.S.C. § 1988 and what was then 31 U.S.C. § 1244(e) (1976 ed.). . . .

Because of confusion in the circuits over the proper interplay among the various statutory and constitutional bases for relief in cases of this nature, and over the effect of that interplay on the provision of attorney's fees, we granted certiorari, _____U.S. , 104 S.Ct. 334, 78 L.Ed.2d 304 (1983). . . .

As the legislative history illustrates and as this Court has recognized, § 1988 is a broad grant of authority to courts to award attorney's fees to plaintiffs seeking to vindicate federal constitutional and statutory rights. *Maine* v. *Thiboutot,* 448 U.S. 1, 9, 100 S.Ct. 2502, 2506 (1980) . . . (a prevailing plaintiff "'should ordinarily recover an attorney's fee unless special circumstances would render such an award unjust,'" quoting *Newman* v. *Piggie Park Enterprises, Inc.*, 390 U.S. 400 402, 88 S.Ct. 964, 966, 19 L.Ed.2d 1263 (1968)). Congress did not intend to have that authority extinguished by the fact that the case was settled or resolved on a nonconstitutional ground. *Maher* v. *Gagne,* 448 U.S., at 132, 100 S.Ct., at 2576. As the Court also has recognized, however, the authority to award fees in a case where the plaintiff prevails on substantial constitutional claims is not without qualification. Due regard must be paid, not only to the fact that a plaintiff "prevailed," but also to the relationship between the claims on which effort was expended and the ultimate relief obtained. *Hensley* v. *Eckerhart,* 461 U.S. 424, 103 S.Ct. 1933, 76 L.Ed.2d 40 (1983); *Blum* v. *Stenson,* ____U.S. ____, 104 S.Ct. 1541, 79 L.Ed.2d 891 (1984). Thus, for example, fees are not properly awarded for work done on a claim on which a plaintiff did not prevail and which involved distinctly different facts and legal theories from the claims on the basis of which relief was awarded. . . . The fact that constitutional claims are made does not render automatic an award of fees for the entire proceeding. . . .

Besides making a claim under the EHA, petitioners asserted at two different points in the proceedings that procedures employed by state officials denied them due process. They also claimed that Tommy was being discriminated against on the basis of his handicapping condition, in violation of the Equal Protection Clause of the Fourteenth Amendment.

The first due process claim may be disposed of briefly. Petitioners challenged the refusal of the School Board to grant them a full hearing before terminating Tommy's funding. Petitioners were awarded fees against the School Board for their efforts in obtaining an injunction to prevent that due process deprivation. The award was not challenged on appeal and we therefore assume that it was proper.

The fact that petitioners prevailed on their initial due process claim, however, by itself does not entitle them to fees for the subsequent administrative and judicial proceedings. . . . Petitioners' initial due process claim is not sufficiently related to their ultimate success to support an award of fees for the entire proceeding. We turn, therefore, to petitioners' other § 1983 claims.

As petitioners emphasize, their § 1983 claims were not based on alleged violations of the EHA, but on independent claims of constitutional deprivations. As the Court of Appeals recognized, however, petitioners' constitutional claims . . . are virtually identical to their EHA claims. The question to be asked, therefore, is whether Congress intended that the EHA be the exclusive avenue through which a plaintiff may assert those claims.

We have little difficulty concluding that Congress intended the EHA to be the exclusive avenue through which a plaintiff may assert an equal protection claim to a publicly financed special education. The EHA is a comprehensive scheme set up by Congress to aid the States . . .

In the statement of findings with which the EHA begins, Congress noted that there were more than 8,000,000 handicapped children in the country, the special education needs of most of whom were not being fully met. . . . The EHA was an attempt to relieve the fiscal burden placed on States and localities. . . . At the same time, however, Congress made clear that the EHA is not simply a funding statute. . . .

And the Act establishes an enforceable substantive right to a free appropriate public education. See *Board of Education* v. *Rowley,* 458 U.S. 176, 102 S.Ct. 3034, 73 L.Ed.2d 690 (1982). . . .

In light of the comprehensive nature of the procedures and the guarantees set out in the EHA and Congress' express efforts to place on local and state educational agencies the primary responsibility for developing a plan to accommodate the needs of each individual handicapped child, we find it difficult to believe that Congress also meant to leave undisturbed the ability of a handicapped child to go directly to court with an equal protection claim to a free appropriate education. Not only would such a result render superfluous most of the detailed procedural protections outlined in the statute, but, more important, it would run counter to Congress' view that the needs of the handicapped children are best accommodated by having the parents and the local education agency work together. . . . No federal district court presented with a constitutional claim to a public education can duplicate that process.

We do not lightly conclude that Congress intended to preclude reliance on § 1983 as a remedy for a substantial equal protection claim. . . . Nevertheless, § 1983 is a statutory remedy and Congress retains the authority to repeal it or replace it with an alternative remedy. . . . We conclude, therefore, that where the EHA is available to handicapped child asserting a right to a free appropriate public education, based either on the EHA or on the Equal Protection Clause of the Fourteenth Amendment, the EHA is the exclusive avenue through which the child and his parents or guardian can pursue their claim. . . .

We conclude that where, as here, petitioners have presented distinctly different claims for different relief, based on different facts and legal theories, and have prevailed only on a non-fee claim, they are not entitled to a fee award simply because the other claim was a constitutional claim that could be asserted through § 1983. See *Hensley* v. *Eckhart,* 461 U.S., at ____, 103 S.Ct., at 1945. We note that a contrary conclusion would mean that every EHA plaintiff who seeks judicial review . . . could ensure a fee award for successful judicial efforts simply by including in his substantive challenge a claim that the administrative process was unfair. If the court ignored the due process claim but granted substantive relief, the due process claim could be considered a substantial unaddressed constitutional claim and the plaintiff would be entitled to fees. It is unlikely that Congress intended such a result.

We turn, finally, to petitioners' claim that they were entitled to fees under § 505 of the Rehabilitation Act, because they asserted a substantial claim for relief under § 504 of that Act.

Much of our analysis of petitioners' equal protection claim is applicable here. . . . We also concluded that Congress did not intend to have the EHA scheme circumvented by resort to the more general provisions of § 1983. We reach the same conclusion regarding petitioners' § 504 claim. The relationship between the EHA and § 504, however, requires a slightly different analysis from that required by petitioners' equal protection claim. . . .

We need not decide the extent of the guarantee of a free appropriate public education Congress intended to impose under § 504. . . . Even assuming that the reach of § 504 is coextensive with that of the EHA, there is no doubt that the remedies, rights, and procedures Congress set out in the EHA are the ones it intended to apply to a handicapped child's claim to a free appropriate public education. We are satisfied that Congress did not intend a handicapped child to be able to circumvent the requirements or supplement the remedies of the EHA by resort to the general antidiscrimination provision of § 504.

There is no suggestion that § 504 adds anything to petitioners' substantive right to a free appropriate public education. The only elements added by § 504 are the possibility of circumventing EHA administrative procedures and going straight to court with a § 504 claim, the possibility of a damages award in cases where no such award is available under the EHA, and attorney's fees. As discussed above, Congress' intent to place on local and state educational agencies the responsibility for determining the most appropriate educational plan for a handicapped child is clear. To the extent § 504 otherwise would allow a plaintiff to circumvent that state procedure, we are satisfied that the remedy conflicts with Congress' intent in the EHA. . . .

Where § 504 adds nothing to the substantive rights of a handicapped child, we cannot believe that Congress intended to have the careful balance struck in the EHA upset by reliance on § 504 for otherwise unavailable damages or for an award of attorney's fees.

We emphasize the narrowness of our holding. We do not address a situation where the EHA is not available or where § 504 guarantees substantive rights greater than those available under the EHA. We hold only that where, as here, whatever remedy might be provided under § 504 is provided with more clarity and precision under the EHA, a plaintiff may not circumvent or enlarge on the remedies available under the EHA by resort to § 504. . . .

Stuart v. Nappi

443 F.Supp. 1235 (D. Conn. 1978)

DALY, District Judge.

Plaintiff seeks a preliminary injunction of an expulsion hearing to be held by the Danbury Board of Education. She claims that she has been denied rights afforded her by the Handicapped Act. Her claims raise novel issues concerning the impact of recent regulations to the Handicapped Act on the disciplinary process of local schools. . . .

. . . State eligibility for federal funding under the Handicapped Act is made contingent upon the implementation of a detailed state plan and upon compliance with certain procedural safeguards. See 20 U.S.C. §§ 1413, 1415. The state plan must require all public schools within the state to provide educational programs which meet the unique needs of handicapped children. . . . As a handicapped student in a recipient state, plaintiff is entitled to a special education program that is responsive to her needs and may insist on compliance with the procedural safeguards contained in the Handicapped Act. . . .

The events leading to the present controversy began in 1975 when one of plaintiff's teachers reported to the school guidance counselor that plaintiff was "academically unable to achieve success in his class." As a result of this report and corroboration from her other teachers, it was suggested that plaintiff be given a psychological evaluation and that she be referred to a Planning and Placement Team (PPT). . . . The PPT's functions are to identify children requiring special education, to prescribe special education programs, and to evaluate these programs.

A meeting of the PPT was held in February of 1975, at which plaintiff was diagnosed as having a major learning disability. The PPT recommended that plaintiff be scheduled on a trial basis in the special education program for remediating learning disabilities and that she be given a psychological evaluation. Although the PPT report specifically stated that the psychological evaluation be given "at the earliest feasible time", no such evaluation was administered.

A second PPT meeting was held in May in order to give plaintiff the annual review mandated by Conn.Reg. § 10-76b-7(b). . . . A psychological evaluation was again recommended. . . .

When school commenced in September of 1975, the PPT requested an immediate psychological evaluation. . . .

For reasons which have not been explained to the Court, the psychological evaluation was not administered for some time, and the clinical psychologist's report of the evaluation was not completed until January 22, 1976. The report stated that plaintiff had severe learning disabilities derived from either a minimal brain dysfunction or an organically rooted perceptual disorder. It recommended her continued participation in the special education program and concluded: "I can only imagine that someone with such deficit and lack of development must feel utterly lost and humiliated at this point in adolescence in a public school where other students . . . are performing in such contrast to her." The report of plaintiff's psychological evaluation was reviewed at a March, 1976 PPT meeting. The PPT noted that plaintiff was responding remarkably well to the intensive one-to-one teaching she received in the special education program, and recommended that she continue the program until the close of the 1975-1976 school year.

The first indication that the special education program was no longer appropriate came in May of 1976. At that time plaintiff's special education teacher reported that plaintiff had all but stopped attending the program. The teacher requested a PPT meeting to consider whether plaintiff's primary handicap was an emotional disability rather than a learning disability. Despite this request, plaintiff's schedule was not changed nor was a PPT meeting held to review her program before the close of the school year.

At the beginning of the 1976-1977 school year, plaintiff was scheduled to participate in a learning disability program on a part-time basis. . . . By late fall she had completely stopped attending her special education classes and had begun to spend this time wandering the school corridors with her friends. Although she was encouraged to participate in the special education classes, the PPT meeting concerning plaintiff's program, which had been requested at the end of the previous school year, was not conducted in the fall of 1976.

In December of 1976 plaintiff was involved in several incidents which resulted in a series of disciplinary conferences between her mother and school authorities. These conferences were followed by a temporary improvement in plaintiff's attendance and behavior. In light of these improvements, the annual PPT review held in March of 1977 concluded that plaintiff should continue to participate in the special education program on a part-time basis for the remaining three months of the school year. . . . The PPT report stated that it was of primary importance for plaintiff to be given a program of study in the 1977-1978 school year which was based on a realistic assessment of her abilities and interests.

Despite the PPT recommendation, plaintiff has not been attending any learning disability program this school year. It is unclear whether this resulted from the school's failure to schedule plaintiff properly or from plaintiff's refusal to attend the program. Regardless of the reason, the school authorities were on notice in the early part of September that the program prescribed by the PPT in March of 1977 was not being administered. In fact, a member of the school staff who was familiar with plaintiff requested that a new PPT review be conducted. This review has never been undertaken.

On September 14, 1977 plaintiff was involved in school-wide disturbances which erupted at Danbury High School. As a result of her complicity in these disturbances, she received a ten-day disciplinary suspension and was scheduled to appear at a disciplinary hearing on November 30, 1977. The Superintendent of Danbury Schools recommended to the Danbury Board of Education that plaintiff be expelled for the remainder of the 1977-1978 school year at this hearing.

Plaintiff's counsel made a written request on November 16, 1977 to the Danbury Board of Education for a hearing and a review of plaintiff's special education program in accordance with Conn. Gen. Stat, § 10-76h, On November 29, 1977 plaintiff obtained a temporary restraining order from this Court which enjoined the defendants from conducting the disciplinary hearing. This order was continued on December 12, 1977 at the conclusion of the preliminary injunction hearing. Between the time the first temporary restraining order was issued and the preliminary injunction hearing was held plaintiff was given a psychological evaluation. However, the results of this evaluation were unavailable at the time of the hearing. A PPT review of plaintiff's program has not been conducted since March of 1977, nor has the school developed a new special education program for plaintiff. Furthermore, there was no showing at the hearing that plaintiff's attendance at Danbury High School would endanger her or others.

Plaintiff is entitled to a preliminary injunction enjoining Danbury Board of Education from conducting a hearing to expel her. . . .

Plaintiff has made a persuasive showing of possible irreparable injury. It is important to note that the issuance of a preliminary injunction is contingent upon *possible* injury. . . . If plaintiff is expelled, she will be without any educational program from the date of her expulsion until such time as another PPT review is held and an appropriate educational program is developed. . . . The second irreparable injury to which plaintiff will be subjected derives from the fact that her expulsion will preclude her from taking part in any special education programs offered at Danbury High School. If plaintiff is expelled, she will be restricted to placement in a private school or to homebound tutoring. Regardless of whether these two alternatives are responsive to plaintiff's needs, the PPT will be limited to their use in fashioning a new special education program for plaintiff. Of particular concern to the Court is the possibility that an appropriate private placement will be unavailable and plaintiff's education will be reduced to some type of homebound tutoring. Such a result can only serve to hinder plaintiff's social development and to perpetuate the vicious cycle in which she is caught. See *Hairston* v. *Drosick,* 423 F.Supp. 180, 183 (S.D. W.Va. 1973) (holding that it is "imperative that every child receive an education with his or her peers insofar as it is at all possible "). . . .

The Court cannot disregard the possibility that Danbury High School's handling of plaintiff may have contributed to her disruptive behavior. The existence of a causal relationship between plaintiff's academic program and her anti-social behavior was supported by expert testimony introduced at the preliminary injunction hearing. Cf. *Frederick* v. *Thomas,* 408 F.Supp. 832, 835 (E.D. Pa. 1976) (argument that inappropriate educational placement caused anti-social behavior is raised). . . .

The Court is not making a final determination of whether plaintiff has been afforded an appropriate education. The resolution of this question is beyond the scope of the present inquiry. In order to sustain a preliminary injunction plaintiff need only demonstrate probable success on the merits of her claim. She has satisfied this standard.

Plaintiff also claims that her expulsion prior to the resolution of her special education complaint would be in violation of 20 U.S.C. § 1415(e)(3). The subsection of the Handicapped Act states: "During the pendency of any proceedings conducted pursuant to this section, unless the state or local educational agency and the parents or guardian otherwise agree, the child shall remain in the then current educational placement of such child . . . until all such proceedings have been completed." Plaintiff qualifies for the protection that this subsection provides. . . .

Moreover, there has been no agreement to leave her present special education placement voluntarily. Thus, plaintiff has a right to remain in this placement until her complaint is resolved. The novel issue raised by plaintiff arises from the fact that the right to remain in her present placement directly conflicts with Danbury High School's disciplinary process. If the high school expels plaintiff during the pendency of her special education complaint, then her placement will be changed in contravention of 20 U.S.C. § 1415(e)(3). The Court must determine whether this subsection of the Handicapped Act prohibits the expulsion of handicapped children during the pendency of a special education complaint.

This is a case of first impression. Although there are no decisions in which the relation between the special education processes and disciplinary procedures is discussed, the regulations promulgated under the new law are helpful. The Department of Health, Education and Welfare (HEW) released regulations in August of this year that are aimed at facilitating the implementation of the Handicapped Act. . . . Contained therein is a comment addressing the conflict between 20 U.S.C. § 1415(e)(3) and the disciplinary procedures of public schools. The comment reiterates the rule that after a complaint proceeding has been initiated, a change in a child's placement is prohibited. It then states: "While the placement may not be changed, this does not preclude a school from using its normal procedures for dealing with children who are endangering themselves or others," . . . This somewhat cryptic statement suggests that subsection 1415 (e)(3) prohibits disciplinary measures which have the effect of changing a child's placement, while permitting the type of procedures necessary for dealing with a student who appears to be dangerous. . . . There is no indication in either the regulations or the comments thereto that schools should be permitted to expel a handicapped child while a special education complaint is pending.

The Court concurs with HEW's reading of subsection 1415(e)(3). . . . Furthermore, school authorities can deal with emergencies by suspending handicapped children. Suspension will permit the child to remain in his or her present placement, but will allow schools in Connecticut to exclude a student for up to ten consecutive school days. . . . Therefore, plaintiff's expulsion prior to the resolution of her complaint would violate the Handicapped Act.

Plaintiff makes a third claim that the Handicapped Act prohibits her expulsion even after her complaint proceedings have terminated. She bases this claim on her right to an education in the "least restrictive environment" and on the overall design of the Handicapped Act. An important feature of the Handicapped Act is its requirement that children be educated in the "least restrictive environment." The right of handicapped children to an education in the "least restrictive environment" is implemented, in part, by requiring schools to provide a continuum of alternative placements. . . .

By providing handicapped children with a range of placements, the Handicapped Act attempts to insure that each child receives an education which is responsive to his or her individual needs while maximizing the child's opportunity to learn with nonhandicapped peers. . . .

An expulsion has the effect not only of changing a student's placement, but also of restricting the availability of alternative placements. . . .

The expulsion of handicapped children not only jeopardizes their right to an education in the least restrictive environment, but is inconsistent with the procedures established by the Handicapped Act for changing the placement of disruptive children. . . . The responsibility for changing a handicapped child's placement is allocated to professional teams, such as Connecticut's PPTs. See 42 Fed. Reg. 42,473, 42,497 (1977) (to be codified in 45 C.F.R. § 121a.533(a)(3)). Furthermore, parents of handicapped children are entitled to participate in and to appeal from these placement decisions. See 42 Fed.Reg, 42,473, 42,490 (1977) (to be codified in 45 C.F.R. § 121a.345); 20 U.S.C. § 1415(b)(1)(C), (c). Thus, the use of expulsion proceedings as a means of changing the placement of a disruptive handicapped child contravenes the procedures of the Handicapped Act. After considerable reflection the Court is persuaded that any changes in plaintiff's placement must be made by a PPT after considering the range of available placement and plaintiff's particular needs. . . .

Handicapped children are neither immune from a school's disciplinary process nor are they entitled to participate in programs when their behavior impairs the education of other children in the program. First, school authorities can take swift disciplinary measures, such as suspension, against disruptive handicapped children. Secondly, a PPT can request a change in the placement of handicapped children who have demonstrated that their present placement is inappropriate by disrupting the education of other children. The Handicapped Act thereby affords schools with both short-term and long-term methods of dealing with handicapped children who are behavioral problems.

Defendants contend that their disciplinary procedures are beyond the purview of this Court. They are mistaken. It has long been fundamental to our federalism that public education is under the control of state and local authorities. . . . Although there is little doubt that the judgment of state and local school authorities is entitled to considerable deference, it is equally clear that even a school's disciplinary procedures are subject to the scrutiny of the federal judiciary.

Defendants' principle objection to the issuance of a preliminary injunction is that the procedures for securing a special education are distinct from disciplinary procedures and therefore one process should not interfere with the other. This contention is based on a non sequitur. The inference that the special education and disciplinary procedures cannot conflict, does not follow from the premise that these are separate processes. Defendants are really asking the Court to refuse to resolve an obvious conflict between these procedures. This Court will not oblige them.

Danbury Board of Education is HEREBY ORDERED to require an immediate PPT review of plaintiff's special education program and is preliminarily enjoined from conducting a hearing to expel her. Furthermore, any changes in her placement must be effectuated through the proper special education procedures until the final resolution of plaintiff's claims.

APPENDIX 7-A

Principal Federal Laws Affecting Equal Opportunity in Schools

Early (Civil War) Statutes:

Acts of 1866, 1870 (race) 42 U.S.C. §§ 1981, 1988
Act of 1871 (Injury under color of law) 42 U.S.C. § 1983
Act of 1871 (Conspiracy) 42 U.S.C. § 1985

Modern Statutes and Executive Orders:

Equal Pay Act of 1963, 29 U.S.C. 206(d) (sex discrimination in pay)
Civil Rights Act of 1964, 42 U.S.C. § 2000. Title VI (general prohibition—§ 2000 (d)); Title VII (employment discrimination—§ 2000 (e))
Education Amendments of 1972 (Title IX), 20 U.S.C. § 1681 (discrimination in education programs)
Age Discrimination in Employment Act of 1967, as amended 1978 (92 Stat. 189), 29 U.S.C.§621
Equal Employment Opportunity Act of 1972 (amending Title VII, *supra*) 42 U.S.C. § 2000(e)
Equal Educational Opportunities Act of 1974, 20 U.S.C. § 1701
Rehabilitation Acts of 1973, 29 U.S.C. § 794 (discrimination against the handicapped)
Education for All Handicapped Children Act of 1975, 20 U.S.C. § 1401 (federal funds to provide educational opportunities for handicapped)
Education of Gifted and Talented Children, Education Amendments of 1974, 20 U.S.C. § 1863
Bilingual Education Act of 1974, (20 U.S.C. § 880(b))

State and Local Assistance Act, 31 U.S.C. § 1242 (antidiscrimination conditions in federal revenue sharing)
Presidential Executive Orders (barring discrimination by all federal contractors on same grounds as Civil Rights Act of 1964, as amended: 10925 (1961); 11246 (1965); 11375 (1967)

A. 42 U.S.C. § 1981—Civil Rights Acts of 1866, 1870

Section 1981 provides: "All persons within the jurisdiction of the United States shall have the same right . . . to make and enforce contracts, to sue, be parties, give evidence, and to the full and equal benefit of all laws and proceedings for the security of persons and property as is enjoyed by white citizens, and shall be subject to like punishments, pains, penalties, taxes, licenses, and exactions of every kind, and to no other."

B. 42 U.S.C. § 1983–The Civil Rights Act of 1871

Section 1983 provides: "Every person who, under color of any statute, ordinance, regulation, custom or usage, of any State or Territory, subjects, or causes to be subjected, any citizen of the United States or other person within the jurisdiction thereof to the deprivation of any rights, privileges or immunities secured by the Constitution and laws, shall be liable to the party injured in an action at law, suit in equity, or other proper proceeding for redress."

C. 42 U.S.C. §§ 1985 and 1986—The Civil Rights Act of 1871

Section 1985(3) provides: "If two or more persons in any State or Territory conspire or go in disguise on the highway or on the premises of another, for the purpose of depriving, either directly or indirectly, any person or class of persons of the equal protection of the laws, or of equal privileges and immunities under the laws: or for the purpose of preventing or hindering the constituted authorities of any State or Territory from giving or securing to all persons within such State or Territory the equal protection of the laws . . . : in any case of conspiracy set forth in this section, if one or more persons engaged therein do, or cause to be done, any act in furtherance of the object of such conspiracy, whereby another is injured in his person or property, or deprived of having and exercising any right or privilege of a citizen of the United States, the party so injured or deprived may have an action for the recovery of damages, occasioned by such injury or deprivation, against any one or more of the conspirators."

Section 1986 provides: "Every person who, having knowledge that any of the wrongs conspired to be done, and mentioned in Section 1985 of this title, are about to be committed, and having the power to prevent or aid in preventing the commission of the same, neglects or refuses so to do, if such wrongful act be committed, shall be liable to the party injured, or his legal representatives, for all damages caused by such wrongful act, which such person by reasonable diligence could have prevented; and such damages may be recovered in an action on the case; and any number of persons guilty of such wrongful neglect or refusal may be joined as defendants in the action. . . . "

D. 42 U.S.C. § 1988–Civil Rights Acts of 1866, 1870

As amended 1976, § 1988 provides:

Proceedings in Vindication of Civil Rights. The jurisdiction in civil and criminal matters conferred on the district courts by the provisions of this chapter and Title 18, for the protection of all persons in the United States in their civil rights, and for their vindication, shall be exercised and enforced in conformity with the laws of the United States, so far as such laws are suitable to carry the same into effect; but in all cases where they are not adapted to the object, or are deficient in the provisions necessary to furnish suitable remedies and punish offenses against law, the common law, as modified and changed by the constitution and statutes of the State wherein the court having jurisdiction of such civil or criminal cause is held, so far as the same is not inconsistent with the Constitution and laws of the United States, shall be extended to and govern the said courts in the trial and disposition of the cause, and, if it is of a criminal nature, in the infliction of punishment on the party found guilty. In any action or proceeding to enforce a provision of sections 1981, 1982, 1983, 1985, and 1986 of this title, title IX of Public Law 92-318, or in any civil action or proceeding, by or on behalf of the United States of America, to enforce, or charging a violation of, a provision of the United States Internal Revenue Code, or title VI of the Civil Rights Act of 1964, the court, in its discretion, may allow the prevailing party, other than the United States, a reasonable attorney's fee as part of the costs. As amended Pub.L. 94-559, § 2, Oct. 19, 1976, 90 Stat. 2641.

E. 42 U.S.C. § 2000(d)—Civil Rights Act of 1964, Title VI

Section 601 of Title VI provides: "No person in the United States shall, on the ground of race, color, or national origin, be excluded from participation in, be denied the benefits of, or be subjected to discrimination under any program or activity receiving Federal financial assistance."

F. 42 U.S.C. § 2000(e) Civil Rights Act of 1964, Title VII

Section 702 of Title VII provides: "This title shall not apply to . . . a religious corporation, association, educational institution, or society with respect to the employment of individuals of a particular religion to perform work connected with the carrying on by such corporation, association, educational institution, or society of its activities."

Section 703(a) provides in part that: "It shall be an unlawful employment practice for an employer—(1) . . . to discriminate against any individual with respect to his compensation, terms, conditions, or privileges of employment, because of such individual's race, color, religion, sex, or national origin; or (2) to limit, segregate, or classify his employees . . . in any way which would deprive or tend to deprive any individual of employment opportunities or otherwise adversely affect his status as an employee, because of such individual's race, color, religion, sex, or national origin."

Section 703(e) provides: "Notwithstanding any other provision of this [title], (1) it shall not be an unlawful employment practice for an employer to hire and employ employees, for an employment agency to classify or refer for employment any individual, for a labor organization to classify its membership or to classify or refer for employment any individual, or for an employer, labor organization, or joint labor-management committee controlling apprenticeship or other training or retraining programs to admit or employ any individual in any such program, on the basis of his religion, sex, or national origin *in those certain instances where religion, sex, or national origin is a bona fide occupational qualification reasonably necessary to the normal operation of that particular business or enterprise*. . . . " (Emphasis supplied.)

Section 703(h) reads in relevant part: "Notwithstanding any other provision of this title, it shall not be an unlawful employment practice for an employer to apply different standards of compensation, or different terms, conditions, or privileges of employment *pursuant to a bona fide seniority or merit system,* . . . provided that such differences are not the result of an intention to discriminate because of race, color, religion, sex, or national origin. . . . " (Emphasis supplied.)

G. 20 U.S.C. § 1681—Education Amendments of 1972, Title IX

Section 901 of Title IX provides in part:

SEC. 901. (A) No person in the United States shall, on the basis of sex, be excluded from participation in, be denied the benefits of, or be subjected to discrimination under any education program or activity receiving Federal financial assistance, except that: (1) in regard to admissions to educational institutions, this section shall apply only to institutions of vocational education, professional education, and graduate higher education, and to public institutions of undergraduate higher education. . . . (3) this section shall not apply to an educational institution which is controlled by a religious organization if the application of this subsection would not be consistent with the religious tenets of such organization. . . . (5) in regard to admissions this section shall not apply to any public institution of undergraduate higher education which is an institution that traditionally and continually from its establishment has had a policy of admitting only students of one sex.

H. 29 U.S.C. § 206(d)—Equal Pay Act

§ 206 provides: "No employer having employees subject to [the minimum wage provisions of the FLSA] shall discriminate, within any establishment . . . , between employees on the basis of sex by paying wages to employees in such establishment at a rate less than the rate at which he pays wages to employees of the opposite sex in such establishment for equal work on jobs the performance of which requires equal skill, effort, and responsibility, and which are performed under similar working conditions. . . . " The Act nevertheless permits differences in wages if paid pursuant to: "(i) a seniority system; (ii) a merit system; (iii) a system which measures earnings by quantity or quality of production; or (iv) a differential based on any factor other than sex. . . . "

I. 29 U.S.C. § 621—Age Discrimination Act (§ 623)

(a) It shall be unlawful for an employer—

(1) to fail or refuse to hire or to discharge any individual or otherwise discriminate against any individual with respect to his compensation, terms, conditions, or privileges of employment, because of such individual's age. . . .

(c) It shall be unlawful for a labor organization—

(1) to exclude or to expel from its membership, or otherwise to discriminate against, any individual because of his age. . . .

(3) to cause or attempt to cause an employer to discriminate against an individual in violation of this section. . . .

(f) It shall not be unlawful for an employer, employment agency, or labor organization—

(1) to take any action otherwise prohibited under subsections (a), (b), (c),or (e) of this section where age is a bona fide occupational qualification reasonably necessary to the normal operation of the particular business, or where the differentiation is based on reasonable factors other than age. . . .

(3) to discharge or otherwise discipline an individual for good cause. . . .

J. 20 U.S.C. § 1703—Equal Education Opportunities Act

§ 1703 provides: No State shall deny equal educational opportunity to an individual on account of his or her race, color, sex, or national origin, by—

(a) the deliberate segregation by an educational agency of students on the basis of race, color, or national origin among or within schools. . . .

(c) the assignment by an educational agency of a student to a school, other than the one closest to his or her place of residence within the school district in which he or she resides, if the assignment results in a greater degree of segregation of students on the basis of race, color, sex, or national origin. . . .

(d) discrimination by an educational agency on the basis of race, color, or national origin in the employment, employment conditions, or assignment to schools of its faculty or staff, except to fulfill the purposes of subsection (f) below. . . .

(e) the transfer by an educational agency, whether voluntary or otherwise, of a student from one school to another if the purpose and effect of such transfer is to increase segregation of students on the basis of race, color, or national origin among the schools of such agency; or

(f) the failure by an educational agency to take appropriate action to overcome language barriers that impede equal participation by its students in its instructional programs.

K. 29 U.S.C. § 794—Rehabilitation Act of 1973 (§ 504)

The Act provides in part: "No otherwise qualified handicapped individual . . . shall, solely by reason of his handicap, be excluded from the participation in, be denied the benefits of, or be subjected to discrimination under any program or activity receiving Federal financial assistance."

L. 20 U.S.C. § 1401—The Education of The Handicapped Act (§ 1412)

The Act provides in part: "In order to qualify for assistance under this subchapter in any fiscal year, a State shall demonstrate to the Secretary that the following conditions are met:

(1) The State has in effect a policy that assures all handicapped children the right to a free appropriate public education.

(2) The State has developed a plan pursuant to section 1413(b) of this title . . . which will be amended so as to comply with the provisions of this paragraph."

Sample state antidiscrimination laws[1]

State	*Law*
Illinois	Ill. Ann. Stat. §§ 654, 669 (Supp. 1963)
Indiana	Ind. Rev. Stat. §§ 40-2307 to 40-2317 (Supp. 1964)
Kansas	Gen. Stat. Kans. Ann. § 21-2424 (1959)
Kentucky	Regulation BS-1, 8 RACE REL. L. REP. 272 (1963)[2]
Massachusetts	Mass. Gen. Laws ch. 151C, § 1-5 (1959)
Minnesota	Minn. Stat. Ann. §§ 127.07, 127.08 (1960); § 137.16 (Supp. 1963); § 155.11 (as amended through 1963)
New Jersey	N.J. Stat. Ann. §§ 18-25-1 to 18-25-28 (Supp. 1963)
New York	N.Y. Education Law § 313 (1964); N.Y. Exec. Law (1961)[3]
Pennsylvania	Pa. Stat. Ann. tit. 24, §§ 5001-5010 (1962)
Washington	Rev. Code Wash. § 9.91.010.

NOTES:

1. The table summarizes existing state legislation as of 1967, which affects private as well as public schools. All data tables must be updated for possible changes in each state since 1979.
2. The Kentucky State Board of Business Schools has a regulation prohibiting discrimination in business schools on account of race, creed, color, or ethnic origin.
3. New York has recently amended its Civil Rights Law to include education as a civil right, ch. 851, § 219(2), *1965 Acts of the New York Legislature*, 10 RACE REL. L. REP. 1350.

* Ten states have statutes prohibiting discrimination in all or some private schools. Those that are starred have comprehensive fair education acts, enforced by commissions.

CHAPTER 8

CHAPTER OUTLINE

A. General principles of tort law
   1. Duty of care
   2. Proximate cause
   3. Special defenses
   4. Written waivers of tort claims
B. Tort liability under state law
   1. Liability of teachers and other employees
      a. Corporal punishment
      b. Premises liability
      c. Duties of supervision
      d. Libel and slander
      e. Educational malpractice
   2. School district liability
      a. Governmental tort immunity
      b. Procedural prerequisites
      c. Dollar limits on recovery
   3. Liability of school officers
C. Tort liability under federal civil rights statutes
   1. Section 1983
   2. Titles VI, VII, and IX
   3. Statutes governing the handicapped
   4. Other civil rights statutes
   5. Tort immunity under federal statutes
D. Tort liability under state civil rights statutes

Tort Liability

TABLE OF CASES FOR CHAPTER 8

Cirillo v. City of Milwaukee, 150 N.W. 2d 460 (Wis. 1967), 459.
Grant v. Lake Oswego School District No. 7, 515 P.2d 947 (Ore. 1973), 461.
Ingraham v. Wright, 430 U.S. 651 (1977), 464.
Ayala v. Philadelphia Board of Public Education, 305 A.2d 877 (Pa. 1973), 467.
Carey v. Piphus, 435 U.S. 247 (1978), 471.
Monell v. Department of Social Services of the City of New York, 436 U.S. 658 (1978), 474.

Under tort law, a person who causes injury to another through violation of some legal duty is answerable to the injured party in money damages. This law applies to school officers and employees. Although the risk of monetary losses through tort claims has been mollified by group insurance (and in some states by statutes that indemnify school officers and employees who incur liability in the course of their duties), the burdens of defending a law suit and preserving one's professional image are incentive enough to avoid tort claims. In recent decades, tort liability has expanded under civil rights statutes that have created new grounds of recovery. The following materials are sequenced to cover first the general tort law of the states, and then the overlay of special statutory torts.

A. General Principles of Tort Law

Technically defined, *a tort is a civil* (as distinguished from criminal) *wrong arising out of a breach of duty that is imposed by law* and not by contract. There is no public school implied *contract* to protect students from harm,[1] hence the importance of tort law. Tort duties are not voluntarily assumed by agreement, and unlike crimes, they are not prosecuted or punished by the state. It is possible for the same act to be both a tort and a crime (e.g., assault), but many torts are not crimes, and proof of tort does not require criminal intent or proof beyond a reasonable doubt.[2]

Tort law is primarily judge-made (common law), and it is predominantly grounded in the concept of *fault*. We cannot overemphasize that persons are not liable in tort for every accidental injury. Only if a person intentionally or negligently causes injury will that person be held liable in tort.[3] Instances of intentional injury by school employees (viz. physical assaults against persons or property) are rare and will not be pursued in this text.[4]

These general principles leave important questions to be answered, namely: What duty of care does the law require of individuals in particular situations? When is the duty of care lawfully met or breached? If breached, was it a sufficient cause of the claimed injury? What special defenses, privileges and immunities may limit or defeat an otherwise valid tort claim? Finally, what role do judges and juries play in answering the foregoing questions and in assessing the amount of damages to be paid to the injured party?

---

1. Brown v. Calhoun County Bd. of Ed., 432 So.2d 230 (Ala. 1983).

2. *See* People v. DeCaro, 308 N.E.2d 196 (Ill. 1974); State v. Lutz, 113 N.E.2d 757 (Ohio 1953); People v. Mummert, 50 N.Y.S.2d 699 (1944).

3. In very limited instances, not commonplace to schools, tort law does impose "strict liability" for accidents, irrespective of wrongful intent or fault. These are not covered in this text. ". . . [A] school district is not the insurer of complete safety of school children, nor is it strictly liable for any injuries which may occur to them." *See* Benton v. School Bd. of Broward County, 386 So.2d 831, 834 (Fla. App. 1980); *accord:* District of Columbia v. Connelly, 465 A.2d 395, 398 (D.C. Cir. 1983); Vann v. Bd. of Education, 464 A.2d 684 (Pa. 1983).

4. See Annot: *Liability of Governmental Unit for Intentional Assault,* 17 A.L.R. 4th 881 (1982): Scott v. Abilene Ind. Sch. Dist., 438 F.Supp. 594 (N.D.Tex. 1977).

1. Duty of Care

Whether a person owes any duty of care to another is a question of law to be decided by courts.[5] In practice, the jury is often permitted, under court instructions, to decide the outcome because the answer may depend on conflicting evidence and variations in juries' judgments.[6]

In all states except Illinois the duty of care required to avoid tort liability is that which a reasonable person of ordinary prudence would exercise for the safety of others, in the same circumstances. As explained later, the duty can be lowered by statute, as in Illinois, to impose liability only for willful or wanton misconduct.[7] The prevailing test looks to what the particular individuals should have reasonably foreseen and done—"the risk reasonably to be perceived defines the duty to be obeyed."[8] The law does not require that the specific risk of injury be foreseeable; only that risks of that general type were foreseeable.[9] Nor does tort law require a person to assume impractical and unreasonable burdens to prevent all possible harm. Rather, it only requires what can reasonably be done to avoid probable (not all possible) harm.

> "Failure to take *every* precaution against *all* foreseeable injury to another does not *necessarily* constitute negligence. That would amount to making one an insurer of the other's safety. The risk involved must be both foreseeable and *unreasonable.* And failure to perform any given act to guard against injury to another in connection with the risk constitutes negligence only when it appears that the performance of such act would have been undertaken, under the circumstances, by the reasonably prudent person. . . . The risk of foreseeable harm to others is *unreasonable* . . . if the magnitude of the risk created outweighs the utility or social value of the conduct creating it; in this respect consideration is given, inter alia, to the probability or extent of the harm to others threatened by the risk." *Turner* v. *Caddo Par. Sch. Bd.*, 214 So. 2d 153 (156-157 (La. 1968)).

Since there is no set measure of due care for the limitless variety of risk relationships in a school, the reasonable man standard allows courts and juries to adopt community judgments of reasonableness as they change from time to time or place to place. The age, relationship, and physical characteristics of the parties involved; the gravity and probability of danger presented; and the necessity and utility of the actor's conduct must all be weighed and balanced to determine the issue of foreseeability, the level of care that is reasonably required, and whether such care could have prevented the harm.

As previously stated, courts first determine whether the evidence is sufficient to permit a finding of negligence. Only if such evidence exists do they permit the jury to

---

5. Barrett v. Phillips, 223 S.E.2d 918 (N.C. 1976).

6. The adequacy of supervising arrangements is often referred to the jury. District of Columbia v. Connelly, *supra*; Hunt v. Bd. of Education, 352 N.Y.S.2d 237 (1974).

7. *See* Pomrehn v. Crete-Monee S. Dist., 427 N.E.2d 1887 (Ill. 1981); Landers v. Sch. District No 203, 383 N.E.2d 645 (Ill. 1978). See Annotation: *Public Schools—Torts—Supervision,* 38 A.L.R.3d 30 (1971); Annotation: *Public Schools—Torts—Student Activity,* 36 A.L.R.3d 330 (1970).

8. Cardozo, J., in Palsgraf v. Long Island R.R. Co., 162 N.E. 99, 100 (N.Y. 1928).

9. Beck v. San Francisco Un. Sch. District, 37 Cal. Rptr. 471 (1964) (student assaulted by other students at school carnival).

pass upon the question. The diverse results of seemingly similar tort cases stem from diverse fact findings of different juries rather than from conflicts of law. Courts have the power, however, to preclude or correct improper jury verdicts by dismissing the case without submitting it to the jury; by directing the jury to enter a verdict for a particular party; by reversing a verdict that is manifestly against the law or the evidence; by reducing an excessive verdict; or by granting a new trial.[10]

2. Proximate Cause

To recover in tort, a plaintiff must prove that defendant's fault was the "proximate cause" of the plaintiff's harm. To be proximate, a cause need not be the immediate, or even the primary, cause of injury; but it must be a *material* and *substantial* factor in producing the harm, "but for" which the harm would not have occurred.[11]

Proximate cause is a common defense to negligent supervision claims where the immediate cause of injury was some intervening act of an unsupervised student. In such cases, the court or jury must decide whether or not proper supervision could have prevented or deterred the student conduct that immediately caused the injury.[12] When a student was killed in a slap fight during lunch recess, one court ruled that the jury should decide the question of proximate cause.[13] But in another case the court indicated that misconduct by other students during recess removed any possibility of treating teacher negligence as the proximate cause of the victim's harm.[14] Thus, proximate cause, like negligence, is a generalized standard whose operation may turn critically upon particular circumstances in each case. For example, the negligent failure of a principal and teacher to report the unauthorized absence of a 13-year-old girl (who was later found murdered) was held not sufficient to establish their liability.[15] The lack of evidence as to how and when the crime occurred prevented any inference that a prompt report would have prevented the crime. It would be foolhardy, however, to conclude that failure to note an absence might not be actionable negligence in other circumstances.

3. Special Defenses

The common law shielded school districts and officials from tort liability by vesting them with immunity from suit. Only a few states have statutes extending limited tort immunity

---

10. *E.g.*, Passaforo v. Bd. of Education, 353 N.Y.S.2d 178 (1974).

11. This "but for" test is generally reliable, but not universal. For example, proximate cause may be found where the tort and an unrelated third force both cause the same harm that would have occurred if either cause were solely involved.

12. *Compare* Lauricella v. Bd. of Education, 381 N.Y.S.2d 566 (1976) (whether failure to supervise student group was proximate cause of injury to student attacked by other students); *with* Collins v. Wilson, 331 So.2d 603 (La. 1976) (injury held not preventable by proper supervision, by ruling of the court). *See generally* Ehlinger v. Bd. of Education, 465 N.Y.S.2d 378 (1983); Dibartolo v. Metropolitan Sch. Dist., 440 N.E.2d 506 (Ind. 1982); Ankers v. District Sch. Bd., 406 So.2d 72 (Fla. 1981).

13. Daily v. L.A. Un. Sch. District, 470 P.2d 360 (Cal. 1970).

14. Fagan v. Summers, 498 P.2d 1227 (Wyo. 1972) (dictum); *but see* Lauricella v. Bd. of Education, fn. 12.

15. Levandoski v. Jackson City Sch. District, 328 So.2d 339 (Miss. 1976).

to teachers, even though a parent, in whose place teachers act (*in loco parentis*), generally could not be sued by his or her child in tort.[16]

Tort law does, however, extend certain "privileges" to teachers and administrators for actions that would otherwise be tortious, for example, administering reasonable corporal punishment and using necessary force in self-defense. Such privileges, unlike immunity from suit, are based not upon general relationships, but upon proof of special facts. Other special statutory defenses of a technical, procedural nature (i.e., short statutes of limitations and notice of claim statutes) are discussed later in this chapter.

A party may commonly avoid tort or limit liability by showing that the harm resulted from the action of the injured party. A student who knowingly assumed the risk that caused the injury[17] or whose own negligence contributed to the harm may be denied tort recovery. An increasing number of states, however, have modified by statute or decision the doctrine that any degree of contributory negligence or risk assumption would absolutely bar any tort recovery, and have adopted a doctrine of comparative negligence whereby the victim's fault reduces, but does not prevent, recovery of damages for the defendant's negligence.[18]

However, assumption of risk or contributory negligence can only be attributed to a party sufficiently mature to be cognizant of the risks incurred: "A child is not held to the same degree of care as an adult. Rather, the test is whether the particular child, considering his age, background, and inherent intelligence, indulged in gross disregard of his own safety in face of known, understood, and perceived danger."[19] "A defense of assumption of risk is, however, narrowly . . . restricted by requirements that a party must have full knowledge and appreciation of the danger, yet voluntarily expose himself to the risks and embrace the known danger."[20] Teachers may not confidently rely on these defenses especially in dealing with very young school children. Consider the following examples: (1) a kindergarten child who wandered off school grounds into a busy street was found not to be contributorily negligent; (2) a student injured by an explosion in preparing a science project was found not to have assumed the risk that the project involved; (3) a 13-year-old was found not contributorily negligent as a matter of law in placing his hand inside a door jamb; but (4) a 17-year-old who ran around a darkened

---

16. *See* Barr v. Bernhard, 562 S.W.2d 844 (Tex. 1978); Morrison v. Comm'y. Anita Sch. District, 358 N.E.2d 389 (Ill. 1976). *See* the new Pennsylvania Act 330 of 1978; Re parental immunity from suit by child: Baird v. Hosmer, 347 N.E.2d 533 (Ohio, 1976); Lovitt v. Concord Sch. District, 228 N.W.2d 479 (Mich. 1975); Numerous authorities from other states are cited in Baird v. Hosmer, *supra*.

17. Berman by Berman v. Philadelphia Bd. of Education, 456 A.2d 545 (Pa. 1983); Vendrell v. Sch. District, 376 P.2d 406 (Ore. 1962) (junior high school student assumed the risk of injury in varsity football); Becker v. Beaverton Sch. District, 551 P.2d 498 (Ore. 1976) (student violation of school rule); Levin v. Bd. of Ed., 388 N.Y.S.2d 645 (1976).

18. See Annot: *Effect of Comparative Negligence in Assumption of Risk,* 16 A.L.R. 4th 700 (1982); Annot: *Modern Trends in Contributory Negligence,* 32 A.L.R.4th 56 (1984); Viveiros v. State, 513 P.2d 487 (Haw. 1973); Pa. Stat. Ann. tit. 17, § 2101-02; N.J.S.A. tit. 17, § 2101. The little-used doctrine known as "last clear chance," which is allowed in marginal situations in some states to relieve a plaintiff of contributory negligence, is not covered in this text. *See* Whorley v. Brewer, 315 So.2d 511 (Fla. 1975).

19. *See* Simmons v. Beauregard Par. Sch. Bd., 315 So.2d 883, 888 (La. 1975); Mitchell v. Guilford County Bd. of Education, 161 S.E.2d 645 (N.Car. 1968) (11-year-old found incapable of contributory negligence).

20. *Idem.*, Brown v. Oakland, 124 P.2d 369 (Cal. 1942) (child playing in high school yard sandpit, cut by submerged broken glass).

school stage when the lights went out (and fell into a hatchway) was held contributorily negligent, as was (5) a visitor who elected to cut across an unlit portion of open school grounds to enter the school and (6) a strong high school student athlete who challenged a coach to a wrestling match was held to have assumed the risk of injury.[21] Knowing violation of a safety rule by an injured student was also held contributory negligence to bar recovery.[22] As with negligence, contributory negligence will usually be left to jury determination.[23] Judicial exposition of all of foregoing general principles is provided by the *Cirillo* and *Grant* opinions at the end of this chapter.

4. Written Waivers of Tort Claims

Form slips for parental consent to student participation in special activities such as field trips and athletic competitions often include a provision that the parent releases the school and its personnel from all legal responsibility for any injury the child may sustain in the described activity. Such release language has limited, if any, legal effect under the law, even though it may psychologically disincline parents to bring tort suits. First, many courts consider release of possible future tort liability to be contrary to public policy and void.[24] The scarcity of cases wherein school authorities relied upon such releases as a defense to a suit may also indicate their unreliability.[25] Second, it is generally recognized that even if a parent could surrender his or her own possible future tort claim, the parent could not legally surrender the independent claim of the minor child (i.e., for pain and suffering and or any loss of future earning power beyond age of majority).[26] Since minors lack the legal capacity to make binding agreements, their signature on a release form would be equally unenforceable. Third, a release is, by definition, an "intentional" abandonment of a "known" right, hence a release form is always subject to possible nullification as having been procured or executed without full disclosure and knowledge of the facts regarding the risks involved in the school activity or the nature of rights being waived.

---

21. (1) Ballard v. Polly, 387 F.Supp.895 (D.D.C. 1975). See generally cases collected in Annotation: *Contributory Negligence of Children*, 77 A.L.R.2d 917 (1961); (2) Simmons v. Beauregard Par. Sch. Bd., fn. 19; *see also* Kush v. City of Buffalo, 462 N.Y.S.2d 831 (1983) (injuries caused by unsecured stolen chemicals); (3) Robinson v. City of New York, 377 N.Y.S.2d 576 (1975); (4) Tannenbaum v. Bd. of Education, 214 N.E.2d 378 (N.Y. 1966); (5) Shannon v. Addison Trail H. School, 339 N.E.2d 372 (Ill. 1972); (6) Kluka v. Livingston Parish Sch. Board, 433 So.2d 302 (La. 1983).

22. Swartley v. Seattle Sch. District, 421 P.2d 1009 (Wash. 1966).

23. See fn. 21, *supra.*

24. Restatement of Contracts 2d § 512; Williston on Contracts, 3d ed. § 1750A (1961); Whittington v. Sowela Technical Inst., 438 So.2d 236 (La. 1983) (waiver by adult student on field trip, for credit—held not fully voluntary and contra public policy).

25. *See* 175 A.L.R. 3d, at p. 75 (1946); Haynes v. County of Missoula, 517 P.2d 370 (Mont. 1973) (voiding waiver by adult for property damage in a nonschool situation); 59 Am. Jur. (parent and child) § 49; 66 Am. Jur.2d (release) § 14.

26. Fedor v. Mauwehu Council of Boy Scouts, 143 A.2d 466 (Conn. 1958); A.L.I. Restatements, Torts § 575.

B. Tort Liability Under State Law

1. Liability of Teachers and Other Employees

a. Corporal Punishment. The conflict among courts on the constitutionality of corporal punishment was finally resolved by the United States Supreme Court in 1977 in the case of *Ingraham* v. *Wright,* which is reported at the end of this chapter. The *Ingraham* opinion provides a useful historical review of the law of corporal punishment in the various states. It also established that states may *constitutionally* authorize corporal punishment without prior hearing or notice and without consent by the student's parents. It recognized that any state may elect, as a matter of policy, to prohibit or limit the use of corporal punishment.

The common law rule on corporal punishment still prevails in most states.[27] Under that rule, teachers and educators have a legal privilege to administer reasonable corporal punishment.[28] Other school employees do not have that privilege. Bus drivers lack the privilege except in situations where force is necessary to preserve the safety of transported students.[29] The so-called in loco parentis privilege of teachers is limited to teaching responsibilities and is not coextensive with that of natural parents.[30] As reported in *Ingraham,* Massachusetts and New Jersey statutes prohibit disciplinary corporal punishment, and the California statute requires parental consent.[31]

School boards are usually authorized to regulate the specific grounds, methods, and procedures for administering corporal punishment. With increased sensitivity to student rights, a trend of administrative regulation has developed to restrict the occasions, nature, and manner of administering corporal punishment. Many districts require the school principal, rather than individual teachers, to determine whether, when, and how such punishment shall be administered; and require the presence of another adult under conditions calculated to avoid unnecessary abuse or embarrassment of students.[32]

Only a few courts have allowed corporal punishment for purely instructional purposes (e.g., in coaching sports or other physical education exercises).[33] In any event, such punishment must be reasonable as to the purpose served, methods employed, and degree of force. Thus, courts have disapproved the use of a cattle prod or a broken paddle

---

27. *See* Roberts v. Way, 398 F.Supp. 856 (Vt. 1975). See also N.Y. Penal Law § 35.10(1) (McKinney 1975); Nev. Rev. Stat. § 382.465 (1971).

28. Indiana St. Personnel Bd. v Jackson, 192 N.E.2d 740 (Ind. 1963); Suits v Glover, 71 So.2d 49 (Ala. 1954).

29. Allen v. LaSalle Par. Sch. Bd., 341 So.2d 73 (La. 1977) (school bus driver dismissed for administering corporal punishment).

30. Axtell v. LaPenna, 323 F.Supp. 1077 (W.D. Pa. 1971).

31. *Re* these legislative changes and the Montana notification statute, see the Supreme Court's footnote number 24 to the Ingraham opinion, p. 464, this text.

32. *See* Glaser v. Marietta, 351 F.Supp. 555 (W.D.Pa. 1972).

33. *See* Hogenson v. Williams, 542 S.W.2d 456 (Tex. 1976). The Hogenson case involved helmet slapping on a student by a football coach. The opinion reports on the case authorities on the use of corporal punishment for instructional purposes. *Id.* at 460, note 1.

regardless of the degree of force used and have held teachers liable where the purpose of punishment was itself unreasonable.[34]

The burden of establishing that corporal punishment is unprivileged rests upon the child or parent.[35] This issue often turns on disputed facts that are resolved by the jury.[36] Since "reasonableness" reflects local community attitudes, its measure will vary in different regions. Typical factors include the nature of the infraction; the student's past record, age, sex, mental and physical condition; and the suitability of the instrument and force employed. A student's intent (e.g., mistake) and the teacher's motive for the child's good or for personal malice are also relevant.[37] Parental objection will not render punishment tortious unless state law or board regulations expressly make parental consent a precondition of the general privilege.[38]

In addition to the use of corporal punishment, the law recognizes another privilege not confined to teachers: to use reasonable force to defend oneself or others who are the legitimate objects of the actor's care. This privilege of defense applies to persons who have a reasonable, though mistaken, belief of danger from attack. In stressful circumstances, a person of ordinary prudence may act with less detachment and control than he or she should under normal circumstances. The greater the threatened peril, the greater will be the justification for quick and strong reaction. Even the use of a "sneeze gun" to ward off student attack was held justified where the accosted teacher thought it necessary to protect herself.[39] The privilege of defense is also limited to reasonable force. Vindictive or excessive retailiation, though provoked by student assault, would be tortious.[40] A teacher was held liable for using excessive force in subduing an emotionally upset, mentally retarded student.[41]

The fact that punishment produces pain or minor bruises does not automatically constitute excessive force.[42] The use of considerable force was held reasonable in dealing with chronically unruly students.[43] But corporal punishment that produces physical dislocations (bleeding, deep bruises, sprains, or fractures) is more likely to be considered tortiously excessive.[44] No liability follows, however, where a teacher could not reasonably anticipate that normal corporal punishment would produce serious injury due

---

34. *Cf.* Rolando v. Sch. Directors, 358 N.E.2d 945 (Ill. 1976) (tenured teacher dismissed for using cattle prod); Johnson v. Horace Mann Mut. Ins. Co., 241 So.2d 588 (La. 1970) (use of broken paddle). *Cf.* Berry v. Arnold Sch. Dist., 137 S.W.2d 256 (Ark. 1940); Morrow v. Wood, 35 Wis. 59 (1874) (S.Ct. Wis.) (beating child for following parents' objection); *cf.* Johnson v. Horace Mann Mut. Ins. Co., prior fn. (beating child for false start in a foot race).

35. Drake v. Thomas, 33 N.E.2d 889 (Ill 1941); Haycraft v. Grigsby, 88 Mo. App. 354 (1901).

36. Carr v. Wright, 423 S.W.2d 521 (Ky. 1968).

37. Tinkham v. Kole, 110 N.W.2d 258 (Iowa 1961); Suits v. Glover, 71 So.2d 49 (Ala. 1954).

38. *See* Baker v. Owen, 395 F.Supp. 294 (M.D.N.C. 1975), aff'd. 423 U.S.907 (1975); Ingraham opinion at the end of this chapter.

39. Owen v. Comm. of Kentucky, 473 S.W.2d 827 (Ky. 1971). *See also* Small v. Bd. of Education, 450 N.Y.S.2d 987 (1982).

40. Frank v. Orleans Par. Sch. Bd., 195 So.2d 451 (La. 1967).

41. Williams v. Cotton, 346 So.2d 1039 (Fla. 1977).

42. Roy v. Continental Ins. Co., 313 So.2d 349 (La. App. 1975).

43. Simms v. Sch. District, No. 1, 508 P.2d 236 (Or. 1973); Andreozzi v. Rubano, 141 A.2d 639 (Conn. 1958).

44. *E.g.*, People v. Smith, 335 N.E.2d 125 (Ill. 1975) (bleeding nose and severely swollen eye). *But see* prior footnote.

to a child's latent medical conditions.[45] Therefore, much will depend on what the teacher knows or should know about the student's condition.

A teacher who beat a boy with a broken paddle for improperly lining up for a foot race–resulting in bruises to the boy's head, shoulder, buttocks, and thigh—was held subject to a jury finding of liability.[46] Excessive force could also be found where a 190-pound principal sat upon a disobedient 10-year-old student and where a teacher struck an 8-year-old with sufficient force to puncture an eardrum.[47] In lesser injury claims, courts held that spanking and paddling of healthy students was privileged.[48] The foregoing cases highlight the practical difficulty, as well as legal necessity, of deciding how much force may be safely employed in any particular situation and of the need for erring on the side of caution. It would further appear that the privilege of bodily restraint for proper school purposes extends to school detentions of school children.[49]

b. Premises Liability. The owners and possessors of land and buildings have a duty to their invitees to keep the premises in reasonably safe condition. Students and persons who are invited to school performances and functions may recover for injuries caused by negligent failure to make the premises reasonably safe.[50] This duty does not require school authorities to *ensure* the premises' safety at all times and for all persons. If reasonable measures are followed, such as periodic inspections and repairs, unforeseeable and unexplained accidents will not sustain recovery.[51] Under the evidence rule of *res ipsa loquitur* ("the thing speaks for itself") negligence may be inferred from circumstantial evidence. The jury is often required to decide the sufficiency of such evidence.[52] Negligence has been shown where school personnel carelessly created the hazard or permitted it to continue after it became known or failed to discover and correct a hazard after it could have been discovered by due diligence.[53] However, school authorities are

45. *Cf.* Kerby v. Elk Grove Un. Sch. District, 36 P.2d 431 (Cal. 1934).

46. *See* Johnson v. Horace Mann Mut. Ins. Co., fn. 34.

47. Calway v. Williamson, 36 A.2d 377 (Conn. 1944); Tinkham v. Kole, fn. 37.

48. Suits v. Glover and Indiana St. Personnel Bd. v. Jackson, fn. 28.

49. See *Small,* fn. 39.

50. For extensive collections of premises liability cases, *see* Annotations: *Public School Premises Liability,* 37 A.L.R.3d 712, 738 (1971); 34 A.L.R.3d 1166 (1970); Smith v. Broken Arrow Pub. School, 655 P.2d 858 (Okla. 1983) (patron at school supper). Guilford v. University, 23 A.2d 917 (Conn. 1942) (injury to invitee to class reunion). *Compare* Stevens v. Central Sch. Dist., 235 N.E.2d 448 (N.Y. 1966) (recovery for unsafe use of glass door panel); *with* Cabell v. State, 430 P.2d 34 (Cal. 1967) (recovery for faulty design barred by statute).

51. Narcisse v. Continental Ins. Co., 419 So.2d 13 (La. 1983) (no duty to install door closures); Chimerofsky v. Sch. District, 257 N.E.2d 480 (Ill. 1970) (fall on nondefective slide); Kass v. Bd. of Education, 193 N.E.2d 643 (N.Y. 1963) (stage screen falling on student); *cf.* Vreeland v. State Bd. of Regents, 449 P.2d 78 (Ariz. 1969).

52. *E.g.*, Douglas v. Bd. of Ed., 468 N.E.2d 473 (Ill. 1984); Watts v. Town of Homer, 301 So.2d 729 (La. 1974) (collapsing schoolyard slide); Raffa v. Central Sch. District, 227 N.Y.S.2d 723 (1962) (collapsing chair).

53. Gurule v. Salt Lake City Bd. of Ed., 661 P.2d 957 (Utah 1983) (iced school sidewalks); semble: Lostumbo v. Bd. of Ed., 418 A.2d 949 (Conn. 1980); Kidwell v. Sch. District, 335 P.2d 805 (Wash. 1959); Dawson v. Tulare Un. H.S. Dist., 276 P.424 (Cal. 1929) (unstable piano); District of Columbia v. Washington, 332 A.2d 347 (D.C. App. 1975) (ragged edge on sliding board); Freund v. Oakland Bd. of Education, 82 P.2d 197 (Cal. 1938) (unstable lockers); Kingsley v. Ind. District No. 2, 251 N.W.2d 634 (Minn. 1977) (ragged edge of metal locker).

not required to discover or correct instantly every defect that is not of their own creation.[54]

No duty to keep a lookout or make premises safe is owed to unknown trespassers. The law imposes only limited duties to *discovered* trespassers and (uninvited) licensees, namely to warn them of known but concealed hazards and to avoid any affirmative action that unreasonably imperils them.[55] An exception to the trespasser rule is made for children where the landowner should have known that its facilities would attract children to trespass and pursue dangerous play. Under this doctrine (originally called attractive nuisance) child trespassers are in effect treated as invitees.

However, even where an attractive nuisance is present, the school authorities are not obliged to do the impossible or to expend prohibitive resources to ensure child safety. Railroad and electric utility stations and construction sites are the most commonly cited attractive nuisances, but the doctrine has been applied sparingly to school grounds since they do not normally present grave foreseeable risks to children. For example, a district was held not liable when a 12-year-old used a ladder hanging from the side of a school to climb to the building's roof.[56]

Recovery has been allowed for injuries to students that were caused by foreseeably dangerous conditions: slippery walkways; defective bleachers, handrails, gates, and doors; defective lighting in darkened passageways; unstable and unsecured lockers, furniture, equipment, or stacked materials; and by building protusions in play areas against which children were likely to fall.[57]

School districts and school boards are the usual targets of suits for premises liability, but school principals and teachers with supervisory duties may also be held liable.[58]

---

54. *See* Jackson v. Cartwright Sch. Dist., 607 P.2d 975 (Ariz. 1980) (no constructive notice of fairly fresh hazard); Quigley v. Sch. District, 446 P.2d 177 (Ore. 1968) (no recovery when recently delivered gym equipment fell); Duncan v. Bd. of Education, 159 N.Y.S.2d 745 (1957) (broken door-check); Dausend v. Bd. of Education, 138 N.Y.S.2d 633 (1955) (clean-up of wet floor at reasonable intervals); Nunez v. Isadore Newman H.S., 306 So.2d 457 (La. 1975) (fresh slippery condition). *But see* Sansonni v. Jefferson Par. Sch. Bd., 344 So.2d 42 (La. 1977) (liability for food sauce on school floor).

55. Slovin v. Gauger, 200 A.2d 565 (Del. 1964) (no liability to visitor falling from stage exit); Gauss v. State, 142 N.Y.S.2d 870 (1955) (no liability for visitor fall due to uneven steps).

56. Heva v. Seattle Sch. District, 188 P.776 (Wash. 1920); *see also* Jackson v. Bd. of Education, 441 N.E.2d 120 (Ill. 1982) (attractive nuisance theory limited to negligence, and not a ground to avoid governmental immunity). *But see* Yeske v. Avon Old Farm School, Inc., 470 A.2d 704, 710-11 (Conn. 1984); Fitzgerald v. Montgomery County Bd. of Education, fn. 67.

57. *E.g.*, Tieman v. Ind. Sch. Dist., 331 N.W.2d 259 (Minn. 1983) (gym horse without handles); Hampton v. Orleans Parish Sch. Board, 422 So.2d 202 (La. 1982) (citing case examples of building hazards); Bessette v. Enderlin Sch. Dist., 310 N.W.2d 79 (N.Dak. 1981) (defective slide in playground); Bd. of Education v. Fredericks, 147 S.E.2d 789 (Ga. 1966) (hazardous stadium seats); Lorenz v. Santa Monica City H.S. District, 124 P.2d 846 (Cal. 1942) (slippery floor); Wiener v. Bd. of Education, 369 N.Y.S.2d 207 (1975) (loose handrail); Smith v. Clintondale Sch. District, 165 N.W.2d 332 (Mich. 1968) (unsecured door); Murphy v. Bd. of Education, 209 N.E.2d 284 (N.Y. 1963) (unlit walkway); Freund v. Oakland Bd. of Education, supra (unsecured lockers); Dawson v. Tulare Un. H.S. District, supra (unstable piano); Cappel v. Bd. of Education, 337 N.Y.S.2d 836 (1972) (five-year-old injured while lifting field hockey cage that was not anchored). *See also* Watts and Raffa cases, fn. 52.

58. Caltavuturo v. City of Passaic, 307 A.2d 115 (N.J. 1973) (school principal liable for injury to student going through hole in chain link fence).

c. Duties of Supervision. Most school-related torts involve negligent supervision. The failure to instruct or warn students; to inspect, report, and correct unsafe situations; to arrange student activity in a safe manner; or to aid stricken students all relate to the essential issue of what is proper supervision in particular circumstances. The cases raise two basic questions: (1) Was there any duty to supervise under the presented facts; and if so, (2) did the defendant breach that duty?

Unless there is a reasonable ground to anticipate the need for particular supervision, no duty arises to support a claim of negligence. However, if a party undertakes to protect a student, he or she is held to the same duty as one who has an original legal obligation to act in the situation.[59] In determining how far one must go to satisfy prudent supervision, a number of factors must be considered, namely, the activity and location involved, the number and ages of the students, and the practicability and expense of affording particular supervision. *The law demands only what is reasonable and practicable.*[60]

Supervision has two aspects, namely, care not to create danger by one's own conduct (e.g., by issuing commands requiring unsafe acts)[61] and care to avoid foreseeable perils that are created by others. The dangerous-machinery cases illustrate how both of these duties can arise concurrently. While educators share a general obligation of care for student safety, the specific responsibility of any particular teacher or principal is defined by his or her job duties.

In the absence of some basis to anticipate particular student disobedience, the issuance of adequate safety rules and procedures will normally relieve educators of liability for injuries caused by violation of such rules.[62] Since teachers cannot be expected to observe every movement of every child, courts do not require special, direct supervision unless circumstances indicate a need for such supervision. "The duty of reasonable supervision entails general supervision . . . unless specific needs, or a dangerous or likely to be dangerous situation calls for specific supervision." In so stating, the court found no negligence when a girl leaving school grounds was struck by a rock thrown by other students.[63] But where students were known to gather and engage in rough horseplay at specific times and places, the failure to provide direct supervision gave rise to tort liability.[64]

---

59. See the Guerreri case, fn. 123 (voluntary, negligent operation of street crossing signal); Padgett v. Sch. Bd., 295 So.2d 504 (Fla. 1981).

60. Raymond v. Paradise, fn. 65.

61. *See* Verduce v. Bd. of Higher Ed., 168 N.E.2d 838 (N.Y. 1960) (instructor's order to student not to look down despite 20-inch drop at end of stage).

62. Schuyler v. Bd. of Education, 205 N.E.2d 311 (N.Y. 1965); Morris v. Ortiz, 437 P.2d 652 (Ariz. 1968). *But see* Hoyem v. Manhattan Beach City Sch. District, 150 Cal. Rptr. 1 (1978).

63. "General supervision is required in situations where students are engaged in many activities which are not usually dangerous. Specific supervision is required when activities are unusually dangerous or the supervisor is instructing an activity with which students are not familiar." *See note, School Liability for Athletic Injuries,* 21 Washburn L.J. 315, 321 n. 52 (1982); Miller v. Yoshimoto, 536 P.2d 1195, 1199 (Hawaii 1975). *See also* Hunter v. Evergreen Presbyterian Voc. School, 338 So.2d 164 (La. 1976) (no negligence where student fell into pool and drowned); Barrett v. Phillips, 223 S.E.2d 918 (N.C. 1976) (no negligence for failure to anticipate resumption of student fight after teacher broke it up). *But see* Justus v. Jefferson Co. School Dist., 683 P.2d 805 (Colo. 1984) (school, by its rules and regulations, assumed duty to prevent first grader from leaving school grounds).

64. *See* Titus v. Lindberg, 228 A.2d 65 (N.J. 1967) (schoolyard before start of classes); semble: Cianci v.

The proximate cause requirement is particularly thorny where one student is injured by action of other students. If such action was not reasonably foreseeable, there can be no negligence, but if it was foreseeable, the question–whether proper supervision could have prevented the injury–becomes crucial. This is a fact question for the jury and one on which juries often differ.[65]

General Student Activities. There is no fixed time or territorial limit for school supervisory duties. The nature of student activity, rather than its location or time of day, will determine whether supervision rests with the school, with parents, or with other authorities.

School Grounds. Beyond the duty to supervise school grounds during normal operating hours, supervision may be required before and after class hours when students are known to congregate on school grounds.[66] Liability has been imposed for playground injuries before the opening of school, whether caused by regular play, by other students' misconduct, by unsafe conditions on the grounds, or by scuffling at school bus stops.[67] A stronger case for liability arises where supervision is explicitly required by school rules.[68] Absent special rules, however, school authorities are not required to supervise dismissed children who remained on school grounds to await private transportation to another nonschool activity.[69]

The nature of adequate supervision when school is in session varies. Failure to provide special direct supervision over normal playground games is generally held not to be negligence.[70] Failure to provide supervisors to prevent ordinary snowball fights where school rules prohibited such activity was not negligent.[71] But a duty of direct supervision,

---

Bd. of Education, 238 N.Y.S.2d 547 (1963) (failure to supervise play area during recess); Silverman v. Bd. of Education, 225 N.Y.S.2d 77 (1962) (brutal assault and lack of sufficient supervisors).

65. *Compare* Raymond v. Paradise Un. Sch. District, 31 Cal. Rptr, 847 (1963) (whether duty existed held a question of law for the court); *with* Sch. Bd. v. Anderson, 411 So.2d 940 (Fla. 1982); Cianci v. Bd. of Education, fn.64 (issue of duty left to jury on the evidence). *Compare* the Cianci and Titus cases, *supra, with* Nash v. Rapides Par. Sch. Bd., 188 So.2d 508 (La. 1966) (injury by other students held not preventable by presence of a supervisor); Woodsmall v. Mt. Diablo Un. Sch. District, 10 Cal. Rptr. 447 (1961). For a good review of the case law dealing with supervision issues, see Annotation: *Public Schools—Torts—Supervision,* 38 A.L.R.3d 30 (1971); Annotation: *Public Schools—Torts—Student Activity,* 36 A.L.R.3d 330 (1970).

66. Ulm v. Gitz, 286 So.2d 720 (La. 1973) (after-school playground accident); Crossen v. Bd. of Education, 359 N.Y.S.2d 316 (1974); Miller v. Yoshimoto, fn. 63 and related text; Richard v. St. Landry Par. Sch. Bd., 344 So. 2d 1116 (La. 1977) (boys left in classroom after school hours).

67. *Regular play*: Tymkowicz v. San Jose Un. Sch. District, 312 P.2d 388 (Cal. 1957) (10-year-old injured shortly before school hours in game of "black-out"). *Student misconduct*: Titus v. Lindberg and Cianci v. Bd. of Education, fn. 64; *but see* Nash v. Rapides Parish Sch. Bd., fn. 65; Sly v. Bd. of Education, 516 P.2d 895 (Kans. 1973) (no notice of prior misconduct). *Unsafe conditions*: Rice v. Sch. District, 248 P. 388 (Wash. 1926) (student burned by electric shock on radio aerial recently installed by janitor); *but see contra*: Fitzgerald v. Montgomery Co. Bd. of Education, 336 A.2d 795 (Md. 1975) (exposed wire). *Scuffling at bus stop*: Raymond v. Paradise (school bus exchange point) fn. 65; Taylor v. Oakland Scavenger Co., 110 P.2d 1044 (Cal. 1941).

68. Raymond v. Paradise, *supra*; Briscoe v. Sch. District, 201 P.2d 697 (Wash. 1949) (teacher permitting football game in playground contrary to school rules).

69. Lee v. Sch. District, 324 N.W.2d 632 (Mich. 1982); Hill v. Bd. of Education, 237 N.Y.S.2d 404 (1963).

70. *See* Gordon v. Deer Park Sch. District, 426 P.2d 824 (Wash. 1967) (student spectator struck by bat); to like effect, *see* Nestor v. New York, 211 N.Y.S.2d 975 (1961).

71. Lawes v. Bd. of Education, 16 N.Y.2d 302 (1965).

and liability, was found where school authorities had notice that students were throwing iceballs and attacking isolated children in the yard.[72]

Once supervision is undertaken, it must be adequate both in numbers and in the manner of its exercise.[73] One court recently upheld a jury finding of insufficient supervision where some 23 teachers were assigned to supervise a heavily attended school carnival.[74]

Where the school is used by outside groups for nonschool activities, the duty of supervision shifts to the outside party so that liability does not attach to the school personnel unless they affirmatively created the dangerous condition.[75]

Classrooms and Corridors. Teacher supervision need not be perfect. Temporary absence or distraction from class or from the locus of an accident does not automatically create a tort. Whether such absence is reasonable or negligent will depend upon the reason and duration of the absence, the distance the teacher was removed from his or her charges, the makeup of the class, and the activities assigned to the students during a teacher's absence. A kindergarten music teacher who momentarily looked down to his piano before a child suffered a fall was held not negligent.[76] Nor can a teacher shepherding children into class while standing outside the door be held negligent for failing to anticipate and prevent an assault inside the classroom.[77] Negligence could be found, however, where a teacher left her class of mentally retarded adolescents unsupervised for almost half an hour, during which time one student was seriously injured.[78]

The uncertainty of jury reactions to particular circumstances is indicated by two Louisiana cases. In one, a teacher was held liable for a brief absence from a normal class; in the other, the teacher of a special education class was absolved when she left the class unattended for a five-minute coffee break.[79] If the absence from class is brief and for school purposes and if the class has a good behavior record, most courts would consider brief absences to be consistent with prudent supervision.[80]

The tolerance of general supervision is evident in cases that exonerate teachers for

---

72. Cioffi v. Bd. of Education, 278 N.Y.S.2d 249 (1967).

73. *Adequate in number*: Decker v. Dundee Central Sch. District, 151 N.E.2d 866 (N.Y. 1958) (child injured in fall from bleachers, 1000 feet away from the sole playground supervisor); Charronat v. San Francisco Un. Sch. District, 133 P.2d 643 (Cal. 1943) (failure to assign more than one supervisor to playground). *Adequate in manner*: Buzzard v. Eastlake Sch. District, 93 P.2d 233 (Cal. 1939) (teacher permitting students to ride bicycles among small pupils engaged in play).

74. Beck v. San Francisco Un. Sch. District, 37 Cal. Rptr. 471 (1964). *See also* Gibbons v. Orleans Parish Sch. Board, 391 So.2d 976 (La. 1980) (one teacher to supervise several hundred children held clearly inadequate for general supervision).

75. Brand v. Sertoma Club of Springfield, 349 N.E.2d 502 (Ill. 1976) (no school liability for injurious activity); Sims v. Etowah City Bd. of Education, 337 So.2d 1310 (Ala. 1976) (liability for defective bleachers).

76. Barbato v. Bd. of Education, 182 N.Y.S.2d 875 (1959).

77. Bertola v. Bd. of Education, 150 N.Y.S.2d 831 (1956). *See also* Swaitkowski v. Bd. of Education, 319 N.Y.S.2d 783 (1971) (teacher briefly absent from class to aid another teacher held not liable for unforeseeable injurious prank by one student upon another).

78. Gonzales v. Mackler, 241 N.Y.S.2d 254 (1963).

79. *Liable for absence*: Schnell v. Travelers Ins. Co., 260 So.2d 346 (La. 1972). *Not liable:* Banks v. Terrebone Parish Sch. Bd., fn. 89.

80. *See* James for James v. Charlotte-Mecklenburg Bd. of Education, 300 S.E.2d 21 (N.Car. 1983); Ohman v. Bd. of Education, 93 N.E.2nd 927 (N.Y. 1950); semble, Segerman v. Jones, 259 A.2d 794 (Md. 1969).

injuries resulting from student jostling in corridors and lines of marches.[81] Knowledge of special danger, however, is a basis of requiring special care and is an important element in tort claims. Thus, failure to closely supervise students with known violent tendencies, including failure to warn a substitute teacher of such students, has resulted in tort liability of principals and teachers.[82]

Special Activities.

Athletics and Physical Education. Physical exercises are common occasions of negligent supervision. The following are grounds for tort liability: (1) dangerous placement of gym equipment, (2) mismatching of contestants, (3) imprudent inducement to perform exercises for which pupils are not physically or psychologically prepared, and (4) dangerous placement of games in congested areas.[83]

As negligence depends upon a combination of factors, liability does not necessarily result from any single one. A football player did not prove negligence simply because he was tackled by a much larger lineman.[84] The mere act of permitting adjoining games in a gym did not alone prove to be unreasonable. Nor are instructors liable for unknown risks, such as a student's unreported medical condition, which made him abnormally vulnerable to physical strain.[85] Instructor violation of school safety rules raises a strong inference of negligence.[86] A high school football player could recover for head injury attributable to an ill-fitting, inadequate helmet that was supplied by the district.[87]

---

81. Lewis v. St. Bernard Par. School Bd., 350 So.2d 1256 (La. 1977); Woodsmall v. Mt. Diablo Un. School District, 10 Cal. Rptr. 447 (1961); *cf.* Sanchick v. Bd. of Education, 172 N.Y.S.2d 748 (1958) (no negligence for corridor disorder injury, while instructor was talking to another teacher).

82. Ferraro v. Bd. of Education, 221 N.Y.S.2d 279 (1961) (principal's failure to warn substitute teacher of problem student); Korenak v. Curative Work Shop Adult Rehabilitation Center, 237 N.W.2d 43 (Wis. 1976) (exposing student to person with criminal tendencies); Lauricella v. Bd. of Education, 52 A.D.2d 710 (N.Y. 1976) (racially troubled school).

83. (1) Grant v. Lake Oswego Sch. District, reported at the end of this chapter; (2) See Brooks v. Bd. of Education, 189 N.E. 2d 497 (N.Y. 1963) (kickball competition); (3) Morris v. Union H. S. District, 294 P. 998 (Wash. 1931) (engaging unfit student in football game); Summers v. Milwaukee Un. H.S. District, 481 P.2d 369 (Ore. 1971) (girl with history of falls directed to attempt risky exercise); to like effect, *see* Cherney v. Bd. of Education, 297 N.Y.S.2d 668 (1969); Rodriguez v. Seattle Sch. District, 401 P.2d 326 (Wash. 1965). *But see* Mancini v. Bd. of Education, 25 N.Y.S.2d 1014 (1941) (board not liable for collapse of student with a known heart condition). (4) Bauer v. Bd. of Education, 140 N.Y.S.2d 167 (1955) (48 boys playing, in three-man teams, on eight adjoining areas in the gym); Dobbins v. Bd. of Education, 335 A.2d 23 (N.J. 1975) (racing students over macadam surface); Domino v. Mercurio, 193 N.E.2d 893 (N.Y. 1963) (allowing spectators to crowd baseball catcher); Wright v. San Bernardino H.S. District, 263 P.2d 25 (Cal. 1953) (no liability for student running into line of play).

84. *Football player: See* Vendrell v. Sch. District, fn. 17.

85. *Adjoining games*: See the Wright case, *supra.* Unreported medical condition: Kerby v. Elk Grove Un. Sch. District, 36 P.2d 431 (Cal. 1934) (student with undetected aneurism killed by head blow). *Cf.* Rodrigues v. San Jose Un. Sch. District, 322 P.2d 70 (Cal. 1958) (fall and death of child with cerebral palsy and heart disease where parent advised school that child could take care of himself).

86. Armlin v. Bd. of Education, 320 N.Y.S.2d 402 (1971) (violation of safety rules in gym exercises); Brown v. Bd. of Education, 326 N.Y.S.2d 9 (1971) (drowning case); Germond v. Bd. of Education, 197 N.Y.S.2d 548 (1960) (sending young children to play in school yard without supervision); Kefesee v. Bd. of Education, 235 N.Y.S.2d 300 (1962) (placing inexperienced girls into soccer game).

87. Gerrity v. Beatty, 373 N.E.2d 1323 (Ill. 1977).

Courts recognize that certain risks are reasonably incidental to physical exercises, especially for mature and properly trained students.[88] General supervision will normally satisfy the duty of care, so long as circumstances do not dictate a need for special supervision.[89] Examples of such circumstances include ordering a seven-year-old child to climb a cargo net and monitoring of a wrestling match.[90] Leaving gym classes unsupervised for a long period constitutes negligence for which school principals, as well as instructors, may be held liable.[91]

The foregoing parameters of supervision and risk assumption apply as well to spectators at school athletic events. Adult spectators who ventured into the zone of play assumed the risk of injury, regardless of the negligence of field managers.[92]

Laboratory and Shop Work.[93] The supervision of laboratory and shop work courses must be appropriate to the hazards in those classes. Tort claims typically rest upon instructor negligence in handling dangerous chemicals or equipment and in failing to instruct and warn students on their use.[94] The defenses of student contributory negligence or assumption of risk will often be unavailable because the uninformed students could not appreciate the peril of their actions.[95] However, contributory negligence did bar recovery by students who took chemicals from storage without permission and conducted unauthorized experiments.[96]

---

88. For an extensive review of cases involving injuries in organized sports competition, *see* Annotation: *Schools—Liability—Athletic Events,* 35 A.L.R.3d 627 (1971); Annotation: *Schools—Liability—Physical Training,* 36 A.L.R.3d 361 (1970) *Compare* Berman by Berman v. Philadelphia Bd. of Education, 456 A.2d 545 (Pa. 1983) (negligence re 11-year-old student injured in hockey play); *with* Smith v. Vernon Parish Sch. Board, 442 So.2d 1319 (La. 1983) (no negligence re 15-year-old injured on trampoline). Fosselman v. Waterloo Sch. District 229 N.W.2d 280 (Iowa 1975) (gym game of "bombardment"); Read v. Sch. District, 110 P.2d 179 (Wash. 1941) (touch football); Passantino v. Bd. of Education, 395 N.Y.S.2d 628 (1977) (baseball contest).

89. Banks v. Terrebonne Par. Sch. Bd., 339 So.2d 1295 (La. 1976) (no liability for absence during gym recess); Seda v. Bd. of Education, 152 N.Y.S.2d 356 (1956) (student falling from horizontal bar).

90. Tardiff v. Shoreline Sch. District, 411 P.2d 889 (Wash. 1966); Carabba v. Anacortes Sch. District, 435 P.2d 936 (Wash. 1967).

91. See the Cirillo case at the end of this chapter.

92. Perry v. Seattle Sch. District, 405 P.2d 589 (Wash. 1965) (67- year-old lady); Cadieux v. Bd. of Education, 266 N.Y.S.2d 895 (1966); Colclough v. Orleans Parish Bd., 166 So.2d 647 (La. 1964); *cf.* Turner v. Caddo Par. Sch. Bd., 214 So.2d 153 (La. 1968).

93. Shop and laboratory cases are collected in Annotation: *Schools—Tort Liability—Shop Training,* 35 A.L.R.3rd 728 (1971).

94. Nielson v. Comm'y. Unit Sch. District, 412 N.E.2d 1177 (Ill. 1980) (mislabelled container) Connett v. Fremont Co. Sch. District, 581 P.2d 1097 (Wyo. 1978); Bush v. Oscoda Area Schools, 250 N.W.2d 759 (Mich. 1977) (explosion from science experiment); Mastrangelo v. W.Side Un. H.S. District, 42 P.2d 634 (Cal. 1935) (gunpowder experiments); Simmons v. Beauregard Par. Sch. Bd., 315 So.2d 883 (La. 1975) (student work with explosives without proper supervision); Calandri v. Ione Un. Sch. District, 33 Cal. Rptr. 333 (1963) (student use of shop-made toy cannon).

95. Lemelle v. State through Bd. of Secondary and Elem. Ed., 435 So.2d 1162 (La. 1983) (sheet of steel in welding shop); Isard v. Hickory City Bd. of Education, 315 S.E.2d 765 (N.Car. 1984 (power saw); Reagh v. San Francisco Un. Sch. District, 259 P.2d 43 (Cal. 1943) (student improper mix of chemicals). *But see* LaPorte v. Bd. of Education, 395 N.Y.S.2d 262 (1977) (no negligence where student upset bottle of acid; *cf.* Bottorf v. Waltz, 369 A.2d 332 (Pa. 1976) (negligence for jury where candle mold fell onto student); Severson v. Beloit, 167 N.W.2d 258 (Wis. 1969) (running grinding wheel at improper high speed).

96. Hutchison v. Toews, 476 P.2d 811 (Or. 1970) (15-year-old); Frace v. Long Beach City H.S. District, 137 P.2d 60 (Cal. 1943) (17-year-old student); Wilhem v. Bd. of Education, 189 N.E.2d 503 (N.Y. 1962) (13-year-old student). *But see* Kush v. City of Buffalo, 59 N.Y.S.2d 831 (1983)

School use of equipment that violates state safety statutes may be held to be negligence per se (i.e., without further proof of carelessness).[97] Improperly guarded equipment (power presses, grinders, saws, and other cutting equipment) or unreliable safety devices (faulty pressure gauges or goggles) are likely to result in a finding of negligence.[98] Even in the absence of safety statutes, a failure to establish safety rules in dangerous situations could constitute negligence, as would an instructor's failure to stop such dangerous horseplay as tossing metal scraps in the shop class.[99]

No liability attaches where shop injuries are caused by sudden, unauthorized actions of students that could not have been reasonably anticipated or prevented. Such rulings were made where a student threw a power switch after the close of shop class, without any warning, and caused injury to a student who was cleaning the energized tool and where a student injured a classmate by disobeying express instructor orders to drop, rather than throw, nails into the trash box.[100]

Student Transportation. Public schools have no obligation to provide or supervise student transportation between the school and the homes of students unless required by statute.[101] Where school transportation is provided, the standard of care varies among the states. Most states apply the general standard of reasonable care, but a small minority adopt the rule applied to public common carriers, namely, a duty of extraordinary care, and some courts apply a special rule of automatic (i.e., absolute) liability for accidents that are caused by defective equipment that violates the requirements of special safety statutes.[102] No liability will attach where the accident is unavoidable, such as where the driver lost control due to a severe bee sting to his neck.[103]

Transportation-related torts most often rest on one of three principal grounds: unsafe equipment, negligent bus operation, and negligent supervision of students at bus stops.[104] The following materials provide typical illustrations. A tort basis was found

---

97. Lehmann v. Los Angeles Bd. of Education, 316 P.2d 55 (Cal. 1957) (unguarded printing press).

98. Matteucci v. H.S. District, 281 N.E.2d 383 (Ill. 1972); Ayala v. Phila. Pub. Bd. of Education, 305 A.2d 877 (Pa. 1973); Meade v. Oakland H.S. District, 298 P.987 (Cal. 1931) (defective pressure gauge); Ross v. San Francisco Un. H.S. District, 260 P.2d 663 (Cal. 1953) (failure to supply safety goggles). *But see* Joseph v. Monroe, 419 A.2d 927 (Del. 1980) (school handbook did not carry force and effect of state law, and violation thereof did not constitute negligence per se).

99. *Absence of safety rules*: Govel v. Bd. of Education, 60 N.E.2d 133 (N.Y. 1944) (shop repair of loaded gun); Steffani v. Baker, 387 N.Y.S.2d 355 (1976) (unsupervised car lift in school shop). *Horseplay*: Lilienthall v. San Leandro Un. Sch. District, 293 P.2d 889 (Cal. 1956).

100. Meyer v. Bd. of Education, 86 A.2d 761 (N.J. 1952); Ressle v. Bd. of Education, 395 N.Y.S.2d 263 (1977); Hammond v. Scott, 232 S.E.2d 336 (So. Car. 1977); Morris v. Ortiz, 437 P.2d 652 (Ariz. 1968).

101. Plesnicav v. Kovach, 430 N.E.2d 648 (Ill. 1981); Hoyem v. Manhattan Beach Co. Sch. District, 139 Cal. Rptr. 769 (1977); Oglesby v. Seminole City Bd. of Instr., 328 So.2d 515 (Fla. 1976); Lunsford v. Bd. of Education, 374 A.2d 1162 (Md. 1972).

102. *Reasonable care*: *See* Mitchell v. Guilford Cnty. Bd. of Education, 161 S.E.2d 645 (N.C. 1968); Hawkins County v. Davis, 391 S.W.2d 658 (Tenn. 1965); Enlow v. Ill. Central R. Co., 243 N.E.2d 847 (Ill. 1968). *Extraordinary care*: Norris v. American Casualty Co., 178 So.2d 662 (La. 1965); Burke County Bd. of Education v. Raley, 123 S.E.2d 272 (Ca. 1961). *Safety Statutes*: *see* Van Gaasbeck v. Webatuck Central Sch. District, 243 N.E.2d 253 (N.Y. 1967) (failure to use bus light signals while child crossing street); State Use of Parr v. Bd. of County Commissioners, 113 A.2d 397 (Md. 1955) (defective emergency door).

103. Schultz v. Cheney Sch. District, 371 P.2d 59 (Wash. 1962).

104. For an extensive review of the case authorities in this field, *see* Annotation: *Schools—Transportation—Student Injury*, 34 A.L.R.3d 1210 (1970).

where a defective tire blew out, resulting in a collision.[105] Failure to provide bus supervision may be actionable where school authorities had reason to anticipate assaults between student passengers, but not where they had no reason to expect student attacks on the busses.[106]

Cases of negligent bus operation are numerous. Examples include (1) driving too fast on school grounds, (2) causing children to fall by sudden stops and starts, or (3) sudden turning at high speed.[107] Drivers and their superiors have been held liable for failing to flash the warning lights until children cleared street crossings and for parking in unsafe places while a child was leaving the bus.[108]

The potential for mishap to children of tender age is perhaps greatest at bus stops away from school. Although courts have not ventured any precise formula of care, they have stressed the need for special caution at bus stops. Children can be expected to run after and alongside a moving bus, and failure to guard against these perils will support tort recovery.[109] Boarding accidents are not self-evident proof of negligence. Driver negligence must be shown or liability will be denied.[110] Similarly, where student injury was precipitated by an unforeseeable act of another student, the driver was absolved of negligence.[111]

In disembarking cases, bus drivers are duty-bound to guard children from the hazards of approaching traffic. Negligence was found where bus drivers observed but failed to warn crossing students of approaching traffic.[112] Allowing a student to act as "flagman" without safety instructions and failure to check clearance of disembarking children also resulted in liability.[113]

In establishing bus-stop locations, the only duty of school authorities is to select points that are reasonably safe. The fact that other locations might have been safer is not sufficient to prove lack of care.[114]

In the absence of any statutory requirement, school authorities (1) have no duty to provide safety patrols for students who walk between home and school, but (2)

---

105. Durr v. Alfred Jacobshagen Co., 139 So.2d 853 (Miss. 1962).

106. *Reason to expect assault: see* Blair v. Bd. of Education, 448 N.Y.S.2d 556 (1982); Jackson v. Hankinson, fn. 136. *No reason to expect assault*: Huff v. Northampton County Bd. of Education, 130 S.E.2d 26 (N.C. 1963); Garza v. McAllen Ind. Sch. Dist., 613 S.W.2d 526 (Tex. 1981).

107. (1) Crawford v. Wayne County Bd. of Education, 168 S.E.2d 33 (N.C. 1968); (2) Coral Gables v. Patty, 162 So.2d 530 (Fla. 1964); (3) Croghan v. Hart City Bd. of Education, 549 S.W.2d 306 (Ky. 1977); Slade v. New Hanover Co. Bd. of Education, 179 S.E.2d 453 (N.C. 1971); *cf.* Sparrow v. Forsyth Co. Bd. of Education, 198 S.E.2d 762 (N.C. 1973) (swerving in reaction to snowball thrown at bus windshield—held not negligent).

108. *Warning lights*: County Sch. Bd. v. Thomas, 112 S.E.2d 877 (Va. 1960); VanGaasbeck v. Webatuck Central Sch. District, fn. 102. *Unsafe parking*: Scott v. Thompson, 363 N.E.2d 295 (Mass. 1977).

109. *See* Mitchell v. Guilford Cnty. Bd. of Education, fn. 102; Webb v. Seattle, 157 P.2d 312 (Wash. 1945).

110. Bailey v. Gallatin Cnty Bd. of Education, 383 S.W.2d 363 (Ky. 1964) (student shoved out of stationary bus); Norris v. American Casualty Co. 176 So.2d 677 (La. 1965) (student pushed or fell under bus).

111. Powers v. Jt. Sch. District, 87 N.W.2d 275 (Wis. 1958) (small student running after bus).

112. Anderson v. Ohm. 258 N.W.2d 114 (Minn. 1977); Slade v. New Hanover Bd. of Education, 178 S.E.2d 316 (N.Car. 1971); Shannon v. Central-Gaither Union Sch. District, 23 P.2d 769 (Cal. 1933). *See also* Van Gaasbeck case fn. 102, and Croghan case, fn. 107.

113. Greene v. Mitchell Cnty Bd. of Education, 75 S.E.2d 129 (N.C. 1953).

114. Pratt v. Robinson, 360 N.Y.S.2d 349 (1974); Sanderlin v. Central Sch. District, 487 P.2d 1399 (Ore. 1971).

supervision must be provided for student pedestrians who remain in the custody of the school, such as those moving between classes that are separated by a public highway.[115]

Other Activities. There is no general duty to supervise off-campus activities that are not school sponsored, but a duty extends to all school-sponsored activity, whether on or off campus.[116] Moderators who failed to supervise school club initiations have been held liable for resulting injuries.[117] Special care is required for field trips to unfamiliar and hazardous places. A child who was injured on a seashore outing after the teacher abandoned supervision to pursue other interests was entitled to have the claim submitted to the jury.[118] The field trip environment determines the required degree of supervision. The fact that a teacher permitted a student to wander out of her presence during a class visit to a museum did not establish tort liability for an assault upon that student by strangers.[119]

Recovery for unexplained drownings in a supervised swimming pool was denied on several occasions either because the facts did not support a finding of negligence or because the drownings could have occurred from unforeseen or unpreventable medical conditions.[120]

The duty to render first aid to students arises only when the need is reasonably indicated, but not when there are no circumstances to alert school superiors to that need.[121] Coaches who aggravated the known condition of stricken athletes (e.g., by refusing to excuse heat stroke victims or by having an injured player negligently moved by fellow students) have been held liable.[122] When teachers volunteer medical assistance to students, the fact that they had no initial duty to do so will not relieve them from liability for negligence in rendering such aid.[123]

d. Libel and Slander. A leading text on tort law describes defamation as follows:

> "Defamation is made up of the twin torts of libel and slander—the one being, in general written, while the other in general is oral. . . . In either form, defamation is an invasion of

115. (1) Gilbert v. Sacramento Un. Sch. District, 65 Cal. Rptr. 913 (1968). Some states authorize the use of safety patrols within legislative guidelines. See Pa. Stat. Ann., titl. 24, § 5-510. (2) Whorley v. Brewer, 315 So.2d 511 (Fla. 1975); Satariano v. Sleight, 129 P.2d 35 (Cal. 1942).

116. Coates v. Tacoma Sch. District, 347 P.2d 1093 (Wash. 1960).

117. Chappel v. Franklin Pierce Sch. District, 426 P.2d 471 (Wash. 1967) (failure to provide substitute for absent instructor); DeGooyer v. Harkness, 13 N.W.2d 815 (S.D. 1944).

118. Morris v. Douglas County School, 403 P.2d 775 (Ore. 1965); Williamson v. Bd. of Education, 375 N.Y.S.2d 221 (1975).

119. Mancha v. Field Museum of Natural History, 283 N.E.2d 899 (Ill. 1972). *See also* Arnold v. Hafling, 474 P.2d 638 (Colo. 1970) (no duty to supervise high school lettermen at mountain camp).

120. Wong v. Waterloo Community Sch. District, 232 N.W.2d 865 (Iowa 1975) (11-year-old); Stephens v. Shelbyville Central Schools, 318 N.E.2d 590 (Ind. 1974) (14-year-old).

121. Applebaum v. Nemon, 678 S.W.2d 533 (Tex. 1984) (no duty to provide life-saving aid to child that required special training to acquire); Peck v. Bd. of Education, 319 N.Y.S.2d 919 (1970) (gym student kicked in the head); Pirkle v. Oakdale Un. Sch. District, 253 P.2d 1 (Cal. 1953); Duda v. Caines, 79 A.2d 695 (N.J. 1951).

122. *Heat stroke*: Lovitt v. Concord Sch. District, 228 N.W.2d 479 (Mich. 1975); Peck v. Bd. of Education 30 N.Y.2d 700 (1972); Mogabgab v. Orleans Par. Sch. Bd., 239 So.2d 456 (La. 1970). *Negligent moving of injured student*: Welch v. Dunsmuir Jt. Union H.S. District, 326 P.2d 633 (Cal. 1958).

123. Guerrieri v. Tyson, 24 A.2d 468 (Pa. 1942).

the interests in reputation and good name. . . . Consequently defamation requires that something be communicated to a third person that may affect that opinion. Derogatory words and insults directed to the plaintiff himself may afford ground for . . . infliction of mental suffering, but unless they are communicated to another the action cannot be one for defamation. . . . Defamation is rather that which tends to injure 'reputation' in the popular sense; to diminish the esteem, respect, good will or competence in which the plaintiff is held, or to excite adverse, derogatory or unpleasant feelings or opinions against him."[124]

Not every unpleasant criticism is defamatory. Defamation may be committed indirectly by inuendo if the words are capable of imputing a defamatory charge in a particular context. A person who republishes or repeats a defamatory statement by others may also be guilty of the tort of libel or slander.

To summarize, defamation at common law requires unprivileged communication to a third person of a false or misleading statement that damages the victim's reputation, whether made intentionally or negligently. If the speaker did not intend or could not reasonably anticipate that his statement would reach anyone other than the victim or that it were untrue and defamatory, he would not be liable.

There are several special defenses against defamation claims. Truth of the statement is always a defense. Further, the law extends conditional privileges in the school context where the author is properly interested in making the statement for protection of public interests.[125] Courts reason that the damage to an individual's reputation is outweighed in such circumstances by the public need for candid communications concerning school welfare. A typical occasion for the privilege involves official hearings or discussions of a teacher's fitness in which adverse comments are made by board members, superintendents, or even parents, provided the statements are made without malice and in connection with official consideration of a teacher's competence.[126] A similar conditional privilege attaches to comments made by teachers about students, in appropriate circumstances.

Beginning in 1964, the Supreme Court developed a special constitutional defense against defamation liability for news agencies when reporting on public proceedings or discussing "public officials" or "public figures."[127] In the interest of protecting freedom of the press, the Court ruled that news agencies were immune from liability for negligent

---

124. See W. Prosser, Law of Torts (4th ed.) 737, 739.

125. Parties who are obligated by child-abuse reporting statutes would appear to be clothed with a strong privilege defense to defamation suits. See generally Annot: *Child Abuse—Failure to Diagnose and Report,* 97 A.L.R.2d 338 (1980). Absolute privilege is confined to certain high officers (i.e., courts, legislatures, prosecutors). See Imbler v. Pachtman, 424 U.S. 409 (1976); Abercrombie v. McClung, 525 P.2d 594 (Hawaii 1974).

126. *Board members*: Mancuso v. Oceanside Un. Sch. Dist., 200 Cal. Rptr. 535 (1984); Brubaker v. Bd. of Education, 502 F.2d 973 (7th Cir. 1974); *but see* Lipman v. Brisbane Elementary Sch., 359 P.2d 465 (Cal. 1961) (no immunity for statements made to the press). *See generally* Annotation: *Libel and Slander—School Bd. Members Privilege* 85 A.L.R.3d 1137 (1978). *Superintendents*: Williams v. School District, 447 S.W.2d 256 (Mo. 1969); *cf.* McLaughlin v. Tilendis, 253 N.E.2d 85 (Ill. 1969) (superintendent evaluation report). *Parents*: Martin v. Kearney, 124 Cal. Rptr. 281 (1975); Schulze v. Coykendall, 545 P.2d 392 (Kan. 1976); *but see* Everett v. Cal. Teachers Asso. 25 Cal. Rptr. 120 (1962) (liability for knowingly false statement).

127. *See* New York Times Co. v. Sullivan, 376 U.S. 254 (1964); Curtis Pub. Co. v. Butts, 388 U.S. 130 (1967). *Cf.* Franklin v. Elks Lodge, 97 C.A.3d 915 (1979) (teachers held *not* "public figures"). Neither are students. Jones v. Maness, 648 S.W.2d 629 (Mo. 1983).

publications of falsehoods and that they could be held liable only if the plaintiff could prove that the publication were made maliciously–with knowledge that it was false or with reckless disregard for its truth. The courts have yet to clarify some questions raised by this new doctrine: Who is a "public official" or a "public figure?" What conduct is "reckless" rather than "negligent?" and how does the consitutional immunity apply to newspapers and other writings in public schools? Since the constitutional limitation on defamation recovery is narrowly limited to "public figures" and the foregoing circumstances, the general common law rule—that utterance of defamation is a tort—still prevails in most cases.[128]

e. Educational Malpractice. The occasional references in legal texts to "educational malpractice" tend to confuse three possible tort claims that are very different from each other, namely:

1. failure of school authorities to exercise due care in the testing, evaluation, and placement of any particular student, with consequent injury to the student's development;
2. the failure of a school generally to bring a student up to satisfactory levels of achievement in learning basic courses, especially English, with similar injurious consequences; and
3. failure to warn intended victims of grave threats made by an assailant who previously disclosed such threats in confidence to the party charged with the tort.

As to the first two types of "malpractice" claims, courts have shied away from imposing upon educators any liability in tort, largely because of the difficulty of structuring an objective standard of care upon which to hold educators negligently liable.[129] Those cases do not, however, foreclose the possibility that in appropriately

---

128. *See, e.g.*, Jones v. Maness, *supra.*

129. 1) *Failure to achieve satisfactory educational levels: see* Donohue v. Copiague Union Free Sch. Dist., 391 N.E.2d 1352 (N.Y. 1979) (no cause of action for failure to educate); Peter W. v. San Francisco Un. Sch. Dist., 131 Cal. Rptr. 854 (1976) (no cause of action in tort for failure to educate adequately and no cause of action for violation of certain enactments of educational code); Aubrey v. Sch. Dist. of Philadelphia, 437 A.2d 1306 (Pa. 1981) (student failure to pass health examination that included sex education materials, objected to by his parents, held not actionable); *cf.* Carroll v. Lucas, 313 N.E.2d 864 (Ohio 1974) (no cause of action for assigning book that presented group sexual practices, as causing emotional injuries). (2) *Failure to properly test, evaluate, and place student* (court rejection of any claim of cause of action): *see* Daniel B. v. Wis. Dept. of Pub. Inst'n, 581 F.Supp. 585 (E.D.Wis. 1984); Tubell v. Dade County Public Sch., 419 So.2d 388 (Fla. 1982) (misclassification and misplacement in special educational program); Doe v. Bd. of Education, 453 A.2d 814 (Md. 1982) (misclassification and misplacement of child as brain injured and retarded); D.S.W. v. Fairbanks North Star Borough Sch. Dist., 628 P.2d 554 (Alaska 1981) (misclassification and misplacement of students suffering from dyslexia); Hoffman v. Bd. of Education, 400 N.E.2d 317 (N.Y. 1979) (misclassification of student as retarded); Smith v. Alameda County Social Services, 153 Cal.Rptr. 712 (1979) (misclassification of student as retarded). *But see contra*: B.M. v. State, 649 P.2d 425 (Mont. 1982) (misclassification and misplacement of student, as retarded); *cf.* Snow v. State of New York, *infra* (misclassification and misplacement in state institution). See generally Annot: *Tort Liability—Educational Malpractice,* 1 A.L.R.4th 1339 (1980); *note, Nonliability for Negligence in the Public Schools—Educational Malpractice,* 55 NOTRE DAME L. REV. 814 (1980).

egregious or clear cases, gross negligence or wanton misconduct in failing properly to test and evaluate a child might be held actionable in tort. Certainly, with respect to the handicapped, specific relief under the Education for the Handicapped Act (p. 381, *supra*) would be available, if not monetary damages. As to the third type of malpractice claim, the two decided cases have been confined to medical professionals, but their rationale of a duty to warn a party who is clearly at risk, notwithstanding the duty of maintaining doctor-patient confidentiality,[130] would appear to apply with even greater force to public school teachers and administrators, who are under no such confidentiality restraint or privilege.

To be distinguished from "educational" malpractice is the more familiar tort of medical negligence, whether committed by school authorities or by medical professionals working on behalf of the school.[131]

2. School District Liability

The liability of school districts is necessarily vicarious since the district, as a fictional person, can only act through persons whose conduct is imputable to it. Generally speaking, four possible defenses have been asserted: that the district's officer or employee did not commit the tort; that the tort committed was not done within the scope of their authority or employment by the district; that the individual actor was personally immune from tort liability, hence the district's liability could rise no higher than the immunized individual; or that the district itself has governmental immunity from tort liabilty. As will be seen shortly, the validity of these defenses depends in part upon the nature of the presented claim and in part upon variations in the tort law of each state.[132] Generally speaking, a school district will be liable for the negligence of any individual who was under the direction or control of the district when the tort was committed.[133]

The common law principle of "respondeat superior" holds a master responsible only for *authorized* acts of its servants or agents. Under that rule the tort of an agent or employee could be imputed to the district only so long as their conduct fell within the

---

130. Tarasoff v. Regents, U. of California, 551 P.2d 334 (Cal. 1976); McIntosh v. Milano, 403 A.2d 500 (N.J. 1979); *cf.* Lipari v. Sears Roebuck & Co., 497 F.Supp. 185 (D.Neb. 1980). *See generally* Annotation: *Liability of One Treating Mentally Afflicted Patients for Failure to Warn or Protect Third Persons Threatened by Patient*, 83 A.L.R.3rd 1201 (1978). *See also* Estate of Mathes v. Ireland, 419 N.E.2d 782 (Ind. 1981). *But see contra* Cole v. Taylor, 301 N.W.2d 766 (Iowa 1981). Durflinger v. Artiles, 673 P.2d 86 (Kan. 1983); Sherrill v. Wilson, 653 S.W.2d 661 (Mo. 1983) (there is no duty to warn the general public, and some courts require proof that the victim was the fairly identified object of the executed threat). Doyle v. U.S., 530 F.Supp. 1278 (C.D. Cal. 1982); Leedy v. Hartnet, 510 F.Supp. 1125 (M.D. Pa. 1981); Thompson v. County of Alameda, 614 P.2d 728 (Cal. 1980); Shaw v. Glickman, 415 A.2d 625 (Md. 1980).

131. *Re* cause of action for medical negligence, which is held actionable, *see, e.g.*, Snow v. State of New York, 469 N.Y.S.2d 959 (1983); *cf.* Doe v. Bd. of Education, *supra*, 453 A.2d at p. 820 et seq. (dissenting opinion). *But see* Peck v. Bd. of Education, 317 N.Y.S.2d 919 (1970) (proximate cause not proven on delay in rushing injured student to hospital).

132. The states are divided on the question whether the school district may avoid liability on the basis of the personal immunity of its servants. *See* Carter v. Carlson, 447 F.Supp. 358, 367 (D.D.C. 1971).

133. *E.g.*, Gaston v. Becker, 314 N.W.2d 728, 731-732 (Mich. 1982). Conversely, there is no vicarious district liability for the acts of independent contractors who, while doing work for the district, are not under its direct supervision or control. *See* Hunter v. Bd. of Education, 439 A.2d 582, 587 n. 8 (Md. 1982) and the authorities there cited.

scope of their authority or employment. This threshold issue of scope of authority or employment raises difficult questions of fact because the point at which a continuous course of individual conduct crosses from private action to officially authorized action cannot be defined in the abstract. Like negligence, scope of employment questions are resolved on the basis of case facts.[134] Where an individual commits a willful or intentional tort, the courts are in conflict as to whether a board could in law be said to have the power to authorize the same.[135] Earlier cases drew a distinction between active wrongdoing (misfeasance) and passive wrongdoing (nonfeasance) in determining vicarious liability, but that distinction has not proven workable in most courts.[136]

a. Governmental Tort Immunity. From early common law times, courts created governmental tort immunity for municipalities and later for school districts.[137] Although the doctrine discriminates between victims of public and private wrongdoers, it has been upheld against constitutional challenge.[138]

The courts excepted from the immunity rule torts arising from a "nuisance" or a "proprietary activity." Some courts also disallowed the immunity defense where the government agency was held to "waive" immunity by taking out liability insurance.[139] The nonliability rule was further eroded by modern statutes that authorize school districts to indemnify (pay for) tort judgments against their officers and employees who incurred liability in the course of their school district duties.[140] A growing list of states have abandoned the governmental immunity doctrine in uneven stages, but a minority of states still adheres to the common law rule. These developments are canvassed in the *Ayala* opinion at the end of this chapter. Notwithstanding judicial abandonment of tort immunity, it was restored by legislative action in Arkansas and partially restored in other states.[141]

The progressive erosion of school district immunity continues to this date.[142] It is well expressed in an Illinois case which notes that a child who is injured on a defective playground slide may recover fully in tort, if the city owned the playground, but only in

134. Withers v. Charlotte-Mecklenburg Bd. of Education, 231 S.E.2d 276 (N.C. 1976) (board not liable for collision by school bus being driven by unauthorized student); *see also* Sumter County v. Pritchett, 186 S.E.2d 798 (Ga. 1971) (district held not liable); *cf.* Rosser v. Meriwether County, 186 S.E.2d 788 (Ga. 1971).

135. *Compare* Galli v. Kirkeby, 248 N.W.2d 149 (Mich. 1977); Bedrock Foundations, Inc., v. G. E. Brewster & Son, 155 A.2d 536, 545 (N.J. 1955); *with* Adams v. Tatsch, 362 P.2d 984 (N. Mex. 1961). See generally Annotation: *Vicarious Liability for Intentional Assault,* 17 A.L.R. 4th 870 (1982).

136. Picard v. Greisinger, 138 N.W.2d 508 (Mich. 1965); Jackson v. Hankinson, 238 A.2d 685 (N.J. 1968). *But see* Desmarais v. Wachesett Reg. Sch. District 276 N.E.2d 691 (Mass. 1971) (lab teacher held not liable for inaction nonfeasance).

137. The sovereign immunity of the state itself, and the 11th Amendment barriers to suit against the state, as distinguished from its subdivisions, are not covered in this text. *See* Mt. Healthy Sch. District v. Doyle, 429 U.S. 274 (1977), on the difference between state sovereign immunity and local government immunity.

138. *See* Rohrabaugh v. Huron-Clinton Metro Inc., 256 N.W.2d 240 (Mich. 1977); Dairyland Ins. Co. v. Bd. Co. Commrs., 538 P.2d 1201 (N.M. 1975); Krause v. Ohio 285 N.E.2d 736 (Ohio 1972).

139. Clary v. Alexander City Bd. of Education, 212 S.E.2d 160 (N.C. 1975) (waiver by insurance). *But see contra,* Bernhard v. Kerrville Ind. Sch. District, 547 S.W.2d 685 (Tex. 1977).

140. *See* Ill. Stat. Ann. 122: 10-20.20; Mich. Comp. Laws §§ 691, 1408 (1964); Minn. Stat. Ann. 20A § 466.07 (1963); W.Va. Code Ann. § 8-12-7(b) (1969); Pa. Act 330 of 1978.

141. *See* Ark. Stat. Ann. § 12-2901 (Supp. 1973); Colo. Rev. Stat. §§ 130-11-6, 130-11-8 (Supp. 1971).

142. *See* Pittman v. City of Taylor, 247 N.W.2d 512 (Mich. 1976); Annotation: *Schools—Torts—Sovereign Immunity,* 33 A.L.R.3d 703 (1970).

certain circumstances if the school district owned the playground, and not at all if a park district owned the site.[143] It remains true, nevertheless, that many states continue to carry forward some elements of versions of common law governmental tort immunity, albeit on a reduced or selective basis.[144]

Nuisances. In states where the rule of nonliability survives, school districts nevertheless remain liable for nuisances:[145]

> "A municipal corporation has no more right to create and maintain a nuisance than does a private person. To constitute a nuisance . . . the condition must in some way constitute an unlawful invasion of the property rights of others. And it has been said that the invasion . . . must be inherent in the thing or condition itself, beyond that merely from its negligent or improper use."[146]

Under this dominant conception of nuisance, as a tort against *property*, school districts retain immunity from tort claims for personal injuries (even though they are caused by property conditions) and from claims arising from negligent use rather than from defects in school property.[147] Once a nuisance is found, however, it is not material whether it was created in the course of governmental or of proprietary activity.[148]

The case law from different states is very confused as to what conditions amount to a nuisance, but the following examples are illustrative: (1) maintenance of a school district sewage lagoon to the injury of an adjoining dairy farm; (2) construction of a wall that diverted natural surface drainage from the school onto neighboring land; and (3) location of school building beyond setback limits allowed by zoning laws, which caused students continually to trespass and litter upon the adjoining property.[149]

Proprietary Activities. Courts have equal difficulty in agreeing upon the elements of "proprietary" activity. Broadly speaking, activities that are more like commercial enterprise than governmental service may be considered proprietary and thus exempt from the immunity defense. This vague distinction produces hopeless inconsistency in

---

143. *See* Harvey v. Clyde Park District, 203 N.E.2d 573, 577 (Ill. 1964).

144. *See, e.g.*, Bankston v. Pulaski County Sch. Bd., 665 S.W.2d 859 (Ark. 1984); McManus v. Anahuac Ind. Sch. District 667 S.W.2d 275 (Tex. 1984); Bodano v. Wayne-Westland Comm'y School, 318 N.W.2d 613 (Mich 1982).

145. Grames v. King, 332 N.W.2d 615 (Mich. 1983); Stein v. Highland Park Ind. Sch. District, 540 S.W.2d 551 (Tex. 1976); Kreiner v. Turkey Val. Comm. Sch. District, 212 N.W.2d 526 (Iowa 1973) Rose v. Bd. of Education, 337 P.2d 652 (Kans. 1959); *contra*: Kellam v. Bd. of Education, 117 S.E.2d 96 (Va. 1960).

146. *See* Stein case, prior fn., at p. 553.

147. *Property conditions*: Williams v. Primary Sch. District, 142 N.W.2d 894 (Mich. 1966) (playground equipment);, Sly v. Bd. of Education, fn. 67 (negligent supervision held not a nuisance); Jones v. Kansas City, 271 P.2d 803 (Kans. 1954) (negligent maintenance of wash basin held not a nuisance). *But see* Bush v. Norwalk, 189 A.608 (Conn. 1937) (slippery balance beam could be a nuisance). *Negligent use*: Sheley v. Bd. of Public Education, 212 S.E.2d 627 (Ga. 1975) (uncovered septic tank).

148. See the Kreiner case and the Rose case, fn. 145.

149. (1) See the Kreiner case, fn. 145; semble: Watson v. New Milford, 45 A. 167 (Conn. 1900). (2) Sturges v. Sch. District, 33 Pa. D. & C. 525 (1938). (3) *See* the Stein case, fn. 145.

the case law.[150] As activity is more clearly education-related, the likelihood increases that it will be considered governmental.[151] A minority of courts consider the factor of free versus paid admission to school events significant in distinguishing governmental from proprietary activities.[152] However, courts found no proprietary activity in allowing community uses of the school at nominal charge.[153]

Ministerial-Discretionary Actions. Even where governmental immunity no longer prevails, school districts in some states may still avoid liability where the negligent actor has personal tort immunity by reason of his or her office.[154] As hereafter explained, board members are school officials and given immunity in most states for their discretionary, but not for their ministerial, actions. The distinction between ministerial and discretionary conduct thus becomes significant to school districts as well as to their officials.[155]

The reason for official tort immunity is to encourage public officials to exercise policymaking responsibilities without fear of tort consequences. This reason is lost once the policy judgments have been made. Hence, law does not license officials to act wrongfully in carrying out policy decisions. Negligent or willful failure to maintain safe school premises as required by law or discharge of a teacher in violation of tenure laws[156] have been held to be ministerial duties that are not covered by official immunity. The fuzzy discretionary-ministerial distinction admittedly defies neat conceptual analysis: "The expression, discretionary function, is clearly a standard, requiring measured judgment in its application, and its meaning cannot be reduced to a set of specific rules."[157] Many courts refuse to adopt a semantic delineation of where discretionary powers end and ministerial acts begin and prefer to be guided by the public purposes of granting or denying immunity in deciding specific cases.[158]

Safety Statute Violations. Where injuries are caused by safety statute violations, the conflict between the legislative policy of promoting safety (by imposing tort liability) and the policy of governmental immunity must be resolved. Many state courts elect to impose liability upon school districts for such violations.[159]

---

150. Examples are provided in Rohrobaugh v. Huron-Clinton Metro, Inc., 256 N.W.2d 240, 242 (Mich. 1977).

151. Lovitt v. Concord Sch. District, 228 N.W.2d 479 (Mich. 1975) (school games); Rennie v. Belleview Sch. District, 521 S.W.2d 423 (Mo. 1975); Coleman v. Beaumont Ind. Sch. District, 496 S.W.2d 245 (Tex. 1973) (playground maintenance); McNees v. Scholley, 208 N.W.2d 643 (Mich. 1973) (laying out bus stops and routes).

152. Sawaya v. Tuscon H.S. District, 281 P.2d 105 (Ariz. 1955) (lease of school stadium to another school district). *Contra*: Watson v. Sch. District, 36 N.W.2d 195 (Mich. 1949).

153. Smith v. Bd. of Education, 464 P.2d 571 (Kans. 1970).

154. *Cf.* McCorkle v. City of Los Angeles, 449 P.2d 453 (Cal. 1969); Arnolt v. City of Highland Park, 282 N.E.2d 144 (Ill. 1972).

155. *See* Tietz and Lipman cases, fn. 132.

156. *Failure to maintain safe premises*: Elgin v. District of Columbia, 337 F.2d 152 (D.C. Cir. 1964); Whitt v. Reed, 239 S.W.2d 489 (Ky. 1951). *Discharge of a teacher*: Babb v. Moore, 374 S.W.2d 516 (Ky. 1964); Bronaugh v. Murray, 172 S.W.2d 591 (Ky. 1951).

157. Restatement of Law 2d, Torts, § 895 D, Comment b (Tent. Draft No. 19-1973).

158. *See* Lipman v. Brisbane Elementary Sch. District, fn. 132.

159. *Cf.* Scott v. Independent Sch. District, 256 N.W.2d 485 (Minn. 1977).

b. Procedural Prerequisites. Where tort recovery against school districts is not barred state statutes raise other obstacles on the manner, methods, and limits under which recoveries may be effected.

Notice of claim statutes prohibit suit against a school district unless timely written notice of the tort claim, usually within three to six months of the injury, is given to the district in the form and to the officials specified by statute.[160] These statutes are intended to protect the public by affording government agencies a fair opportunity to verify the legitimacy of tort claims, to cure noticed conditions and avoid additional tort claims; and to budget sufficient funds to pay valid claims. Notice statutes have withstood due process challenges and have been upheld in all save a few states.[161]

Nevertheless, many courts construe those statutes loosely in order to avoid harsh results on purely technical grounds. Looking to the reason rather than the letter of the notice rule, courts have held such statutes to be satisfied on proof that: the defendant agency was not prejudiced by the absence of statutory notice (had adequate notice from other sources); that the claim notice substantially, though not fully, met with the statutory requirement; that certain conditions prevented and thus excused the giving of required notice (due to physical or mental incapacity); that the plaintiff lacked the legal capacity to understand the notice requirement (a minor); that the defendant agency waived the right to notice; or that there was some other good cause for not applying the statute.[162]

A second obstacle to suit is raised by short statutes of limitations that bar any suits against school districts unless suit is filed within a brief period, usually one year from the date of injury.

c. Dollar Limits on Recovery. A number of state legislatures have substituted dollar limitation of school district tort liability for the abrogated defense of immunity. The ceiling recovery for various types of torts varies among the states and ranges from a

---

160. *See, e.g.*, Prof'l Detail Service, Inc. v. Bd. of Education, 479 N.Y.S.2d 40 (1984) (notice to wrong source); Parochial Bus Systems v. Bd. of Education, 470 N.Y.S.2d 564, 567–68 (1983); Shearer v. Perry Comm. Sch. District, 236 N.W.2d 688 (Iowa 1975).

161. SENA School Bus Co. v. Bd. of Ed., 677 P.2d 639 (N. Mex. 1984); Brown v. Portland Sch. Dist., 617 P.2d 665 (Ore. 1980). See generally Annotation: *Notice of Tort Claims Against Municipality,* 59 A.L.R. 3d 93 (1974); Newlan v. State, 535 P.2d 1348 (Idaho 1975) Michigan, Nevada, and Washington courts found short notice statutes to be unconstitutional. Hunter v. North Mason H.S., 539 P.2d 845 (Wash. 1974); Friedman v. Farmington Twp. Sch. District, 198 N.W.2d 785 (Mich. 1972); Turner v. Staggs, 510 P.2d 879 (Nev. 1973).

162. *Lacking capacity to understand notice*: *Re* waiver of notice requirement, *see* Flandera v. Jamesville-Dewitt Cent. Schools, 369 N.Y.S.2d 920 (1975); *re* excuse for infancy, *see* Welsh v. Berne-Knox-Westerlo Cent. Sch. Dist., 479 N.Y.S.2d 567 (1984); Hunter v. No. Mason H.S., 529 P.2d 898 (Wash. 1974); *re* excuse for substantial compliance, *see* Jenkins v. Bd. of Education, 228 N.W.2d 265 (Minn. 1975); *but see* Johns v. Wynnewood Sch. Bd., 656 P.2d 248 (Okla. 1984); Scarborough v. Granite Sch. District, 531 P.2d 480 (Utah 1975). Variations in case law are recorded in Annotations: *Municipality—Notice of Injury—Waiver,* 65 A.L.R.2d 1278 (1959); *Infancy or Incapacity as Affecting Notice,* 34 A.L.R.2d 725 (1954). *Other good cause*: Valiquette v. City Sch. District, 391 N.Y.S.2d 23 (1977). See generally Annotations: *Tort Claims Against Public Entity—Notice,* 44 A.L.R.3d 1108 (1976); *Municipality—Notice of Injury,* 65 A.L.R.2d 1278 (1958); *Claims Against City—Notice,* 63 A.L.R.2d 863, 911 (1958).

ceiling of several thousand dollars in one state to a ceiling of several hundreds of thousand dollars in another.[163]

3. Liability of School Officers

Both state and federal tort laws distinguish between governmental immunity, which applies to school districts, and official immunity, which applies only to individual "officers" such as board members. A further distinction is made between "officers" who enjoy official immunity in appropriate circumstances and "employees" such as the superintendent and teachers who in most states do not qualify for official immunity.[164] There is, however, a growing trend among the states to extend by statute personal immunity to teachers and supervisors for their acts or omissions taken in the course of their employment, but the scope of this new immunity varies from state to state.[165] Official immunity attaches to the officer, not to the board as a corporate body. As the personification of the school district, the board, as a board, may assert governmental immunity where that defense is still recognized.

The distinction between governmental and personal immunity is more than academic. In some circumstances these doctrines could result in school district and school board liability, without individual board member liability. Official immunity is not absolute. It does not extend to ministerial actions, but only to discretionary actions. Where officers act maliciously or intentionally to injure another, the courts are in conflict as to whether or not official immunity applies.[166] Immunity defenses under state tort law do not operate with equal effect against tort claims under federal statutes.[167]

Where a tort claimant invokes the doctrine of *respondeat superior,* liability may attach only to the school district and the school board as a corporate body since it, and not the individual board members, is the employer in law.[168] Only if the board member lost official immunity by some unauthorized or ministerial act may he or she be subjected to vicarious liability.

In addition to clothing certain officers and employees with selective tort immunity, modern tort claims statutes often include provision for indemnification of

---

163. See generally GREENHILL and MURTO. *Governmental Immunity,* 49 TEX. L. REV. (1971); Doe v. Bd. of Education, 453 A.2d 814, 822 (Md. 1982); *cf.* Thompson v. Sanford, 603 S.W.2d 932 (Ark. 1984); Packard v. Jt. Sch. District, 661 P.2d 770 (Idaho 1983).

164. See Annotation: *Libel—School Board Members Privilege,* 85 A.L.R.3d 1137 (1978), Stein v. Highland Park Ind. Sch. District, 540 S.W.2d 551 (Tex. 1976). The absolute immunity of high government officials, viz. judges, legislators and prosecutors does not apply to school district officials. *See* Imbler v. Pachtman, 424 U.S. 409 (1976).

165. *E.g.,* Vitale v. Lentine, 358 N.W.2d 2 (Mich. 1984). The variations on teacher immunity by state are reported in Annotation: *Student Injury—Teacher Liability,* 34 A.L.R. 4th 228, 234–46 (1984). Reckless, unauthorized or unlawful acts are often excluded from such immunity. Holman v. Wheeler, 677 P.2d 645 (Okla. 1983).

166. *Compare* Bedrock Foundations, Inc., v. Geo. E. Brewster & Son, 155 A.2d 536, 545 (N.J. 1959) *with* Adams v. Tatsch, 362 P.2d 984 (N.M. 1961). *See* Barr v. Matteo, 360 U.S. 564, 569 (1959).

167. *See* Wood v. Strickland, 420 U.S. 308 (1975); Picha v. Wieglos, 410 F.Supp. 1214 (N.D. Ill. 1976). State statutes of limitation may, however, bar federal tort suits in the absence of a federal limitations statute. Chambers v. Omaha P. Sch. District, 536 F.2d 222 (8th Cir. 1976).

168. *See* Wood v. Bd. of Education, 412 S.W.2d 877 (Ky. 1967); Annotation: *School Officers—Negligence—Liability,* 32 A.L.R.2d 1163 (1953).

individual officers and employees who are held liable for torts committed in the course of their public school duties.[169]

C. Tort Liability Under Federal Civil Rights Statutes

Tort liability in public schools has been dramatically expanded under old (Civil War) and new federal civil rights statutes that support a broad range of tort remedies that were unknown to prior law. Further, under the supremacy of federal law, those torts are not automatically subject to defenses created by state law. The potential for tort litigation under federal civil rights laws can hardly be overstated.

Special forms of affirmative relief such as injunctions, reinstatement or appointment to positions, affirmative action to redress past discrimination, and cutoff of federal aid to programs are afforded by most federal statutes. However, the following discussion deals solely with the right of individuals (primarily teachers and students) to collect *money damages* for injuries that flow from civil rights violations. Not all of the federal statutes authorize money recovery; hence it is necessary to outline the peculiar recoveries and defenses that pertain to each major statute. "Because a claim of discrimination can be framed to assert rights under such a variety of sources, the interrelationship of these rights and sources is a matter of extreme concern to potential claimants and respondents."[170]

Unfortunately, the different Congresses that passed each civil rights statute did so without any attempt to dovetail each new law with the operation of preceding statutes or to develop uniform policies and standards of liability. Most of the case law on civil rights torts is less than 20 years old. Current conflicts in the lower courts can only be resolved by appeals to the Supreme Court. Although it is neither possible nor appropriate to canvass all open questions under the major civil rights statutes, their looming importance for tort liability in the schools warrants study of their main features. The core provisions and comparisons of these statutes in appendix 7-A (Chapter 7) provide a convenient point of basic reference for the following discussion. It should be emphasized that the following materials merely sketch some of the more prominent tort features of the statutes under discussion; the law on federal statutory torts for civil rights infringements is still in the early stages of development.

1. Section 1983

The significance of § 1983 was forecast in 1972 by the United States Supreme Court:

> "Section 1983 opened the federal courts to private citizens, offering a uniquely federal remedy against the incursions [of their civil rights] under the claimed authority of state law."[171]

---

169. Annotation: *Indemnification of Public Officer or Employee,* 71 A.L.R.3d §§ 25,26 (1076).

170. *See* SCHLEI and GROSSMAN, EMPLOYMENT DISCRIMINATION LAW. p. 943 (1976), and 1979 supplement thereto.

171. Mitchum v. Foster, 407 U.S. 225, 238-39 (1972). See also W. Valente, *Federal Tort Liability for Civil Rights Deprivations in Public Schools,* 5 WEST ED. L. REP. 701 (1982).

The expanded operation of § 1983 to public school districts is discussed in the *Monell* case, p. 474, *infra*, which provides a convenient background discussion of that law.

Unlike the more specialized modern civil rights statutes that speak to discrimination against specific disadvantaged classes, § 1983 creates a "cause of action" for invasion of rights protected by federal law (constitutional or statutory). It does not create substantive federal rights, but vindicates them by its remedies.[172] Those federal rights must be found either in the federal constitution or in other federal statutes.

It is important to recognize those grievances that § 1983 does *not* cover. It does not convert *every* act of negligence by public authorities into a federal civil rights tort, even though that conduct may amount to a state law tort.[173] Nor does it render school districts vicariously liable for all civil rights abridgements caused by public school employees, since there must be an official policy or custom by the district under which such deprivation occurred for there to be a requisite "state action" to render the school district liable.[174] This is so even though district officers or employees who deprive an individual of a federal civil right (in the absence of a school district policy or custom) may still be held liable under § 1983, because individuals can act "under color of law" even in the absence of official directive.[175] In addition, there are three other grounds to deny § 1983 coverage: (1) if the federal statute invoked by the plaintiff is not intended to create an individually enforceable right, (2) where an alleged due process injury is cured by state law which provides adequate due process to prevent any such deprivation, (3) where Congress, in creating a federal right by statute, also enacts remedies under that particular statute that are intended to be exclusive of, any other (including § 1983) remedies.[176] In most cases, however, § 1983 remedies are available, either because the substantive right statute does not speak to the question of remedy, or if it does, it is deemed to be an alternative to § 1983 remedies.[177]

The attractiveness of § 1983 action lies not only in its authorization of monetary recovery. In most cases the preconditions to suit, procedures, and recovery limits under § 1983 are less burdensome and restrictive than those provided by other federal statutes.[178] In granting private tort recoveries under § 1983, federal courts have adopted

---

172. *See* Fields v. Bd. of Higher Education, 463 N.Y.S.2d 785, 788 (1983); Davis v. Passman, 442 U.S. 228, 239 (1979).

173. *E.g.*, Daniels v. Williams, ______U.S.______, 106 S.Ct. 662 (1986); Davidson v. Cannon, ______U.S.______, 106 S.Ct. 668 (1986); Enright v. Bd. of School Directors, 346 N.W.2d 771 (Wis. 1984); Leite v. City of Providence, 463 F.Supp. 585 (D. R.I. 1978). J. Horner & K. Frels, *The Death Knell to the Negligence Cause of Action. Deprivation of Liability Interests Under 42 U.S.C. § 1983,* 31 West Ed. L. Rep. 1 (1986).

174. *Idem. See also* Rendell-Baker v. Kohn, 454 U.S. 891 (1982); Polk County v. Dodson, 454 U.S. 312 (1981); Annotation: *Vicarious Liability of Superiors . . . for Subordinate's Acts in Deprivations of Civil Rights,* 51 A.L.R. Fed. 285 (1981).

175. *See* Monroe v. Pape, 365 U.S. 167,172 (1981)

176. (1) *E.g.*, Day v. Wayne County Bd. of Auditors, 749 F.2d 1199 (6th Cir. 1984) (no § 1983 "action" for a Title VII violation); Stevenson v. Bd. of Education, 426 F.2d 1154 (5th Cir. 1970). (2) Sutton v. Mariana Sch. District, 573 F.Supp. 159 (E.D.Ark. 1983); Carder v. Michigan City Sch. Corp., 552 F.Supp. 869 (N.D. Ind. 1982) both citing to Paratt v. Taylor, 451 U.S. 527 (1981). (3) *See* Smith v. Robinson, p. 379, *supra*; Note, Preclusion of §1983 Causes of Action by Comprehensive Statutory Remedial Schemes, 83 Columbia L. Rev. 1183 (1982), W. Valente, *Smith v. Robinson-Confusion Clarified,* 22 West Ed. L. Rep. 693 (1985).

177. Doe v. New York U., 442 F.Supp. 522 (S.D.N.Y. 1978).

178. Patsy v. Bd. of Regents, 457 U.S. 496 (1982) (Exhaustion of state remedies not generally required for §1983 action). *Accord:* Britt v. Simi Valley Un. Sch. District, 696 F.2d 644 (9th Cir. 1982); Hockman v. Bd. of Education, 534 F.2d 1094 (3d Cir. 1976).

some state tort-law principles, while rejecting others they deemed inconsistent with the policy goals of § 1983. For example, they have (subject to exceptions above and hereafter noted) awarded plaintiffs "compensatory" damages for both tangible (out-of-pocket expenses) and intangible (emotional injuries) harms that are caused by a federal civil rights injury.[179] On the other hand, the Supreme Court has denied recovery of "penal" or exemplary damages under § 1983 against a local government entity, notwithstanding wanton or willfull misconduct by public servants, on the view that punishing local governments and school districts is not necessary to further the intent of § 1983.[180] However, there is no such policy barrier to the imposition of penal damages under § 1983 upon individuals, that is, school officers and employees who intentionally or wantonly interfere with protected civil rights.[181] In contrast to § 1983, the employment discrimination statutes (Title VII, Equal Pay Act, Age Discrimination Act) allow damages only for tangible losses such as reduction of wages.

The Supreme Court has stressed that § 1983 damages will not be *presumed* from the bare fact of a civil rights violation. In the absence of any proof, it limited the successful plaintiff's recovery to $1 as nominal damages. See the Supreme Court opinion in *Carey* v. *Piphus,* reproduced at the end of this chapter, for a fuller discussion of the foregoing points.

2. Titles VI, VII, and IX

The provisions of Title VI (p. 390, *supra*) and Title IX (p. 391, *supra*) contain closely parallel language and have received parallel construction from the courts, even though the former title deals with race and national origin, while the latter title deals with sex discrimination in education. Both statutes operate only upon conduct in a federally aided program or activity. Title IX has been authoritatively construed to cover any participant in the aided program even though that individual was not the primary, intended beneficiary thereof.[182] As to what particular activities will be deemed to be embraced by a federally aided activity, there remain many unanswered questions.[183]

Suits may be brought directly under either of those statutes to obtain specific relief, (i.e., injunctions to reverse or prohibit actions that interfere with the protected

179. See the *Carey* case, p. 471, *infra*; Simineo v. Sch. District, 594 F.2d 1353 (10th Cir. 1979); Flores v. Edinburg Cons. Ind. Sch. Dist., 547 F.Supp. 974 (S.D. Tex. 1983); Needleman v. Bohlen, 386 F.Supp. 741 (D. Mass. 1974) (alleged interference with speech activities); *cf.* Bates v. Dause, 502 F.2d 865 (6th Cir. 1974); Williams v. Albemarle Cty. Bd. of Education, 508 F.2d 1242 (4th Cir. 1974) (alleged racial discrimination); Strickland v. Inlow, 519 F.2d 744 (8th Cir. 1975) (due process).

180. City of Newport v. Fact Concerts, Inc., 453 U.S. 247 (1981); Keson v. Tolley Sch. Dist., 570 F.Supp. 408 (D.N.D. 1983).

181. *See* City of Newport v. Fact Concerts, Inc., *supra,* 453 U.S. at p. 269. *See also* Wells v. Haico Ind. Sch. District, 736 F.2d 243, 259 (5th Cir. 1984) and the authorities there cited.

182. North Haven Bd. of Education v. Bell, 456 U.S. 512 (1982) (teachers in federally funded program for student benefit—held covered by Title IX); Annotation: *Application of Title IX to Sex Discrimination in Educational Employment,* 54 A.L.R. Fed. 522 (1981). A private party who is neither participant nor beneficiary of the aided program lacks standing to sue under Title IX. Murphy v. Middletown Twp. Enlarged Sch. Dist., 525 F.Supp. 678 (S.D.N.Y. 1981).

183. *See* Grove City College v. Bell, 465 U.S. 555 (1984).

statutory rights);[184] and (by government agency) to cut off federal funding to violators of those rights.[185] The right of individuals to sue directly under either of those statutes for money damages (rather than under § 1983) remains somewhat confused. The latest Supreme Court pronouncement under Title VI would seem to indicate that Title VI *alone* does not provide a private right to recover monetary damages, at least for unintentional deprivations.[186] That ruling may well be extended to Title IX actions. It is possible for courts to hold that deprivation of rights under either of those statutes would support a private action for monetary damages in a § 1983 suit,[187] but that question has not been fully considered by the courts at this writing.

Title VII (p. 390, *supra*) expressly entitles employment discrimination victims to recover lost wages and other employment benefits in addition to specific injunctions to protect their employment status, but it imposes preconditions to private suit, principally exhaustion of prior administrative remedies. Title VII exhaustion requirements may be tolled for good reason, however.[188] One procedure not required by Title VII is the pursuit of grievance arbitration under employer-union agreements.[189]

Title VII, like the Equal Pay Act and the Age Discrimination Act, also authorizes equitable relief to restore lost employment opportunities caused by prohibited discrimination; but it limits monetary recovery to lost wages and other employment benefits. All three of the foregoing acts require exhaustion of the prescribed administrative remedies before instituting suit.[190]

Unlike § 1983, Title VII does not authorize recovery for intangible injury, or for punitive damages.[191] Like the Equal Pay and Age Discrimination Acts, Title VII damages are limited to wage losses attributable to unlawful discrimination. Unlike the Equal Pay Act and the Age Discrimination Act, Title VII does not provide for special (double) damages over the amount of the base recovery.[192] Together with the Equal Pay Act and the Age Discrimination Act, Title VII actions may result in the award of attorneys' fees, which are discussed shortly.

3. Statutes Governing the Handicapped

As noted in Chapter 7, the Education for the Handicapped Children Act (EHA) does not support a private action to recover monetary "damages," either directly or via § 1983,

184. North Haven Bd. of Education v. Bell, fn. 182, *supra*; Cannon v. U. of Chicago and Northwestern U., 441 U.S. 677 (1979) (sex discrimination in teacher employment).

185. Grove City College v. Bell, *supra.*

186. Guardians Assn. v. Civil Service Comm'n, 463 U.S. 582 (1983); Drayden v. Leedville Ind. Sch. District, 642 F.2d 119, 133 (5th Cir. 1981)

187. Strong v. Demapolis City Bd. of Education, 515 F.Supp. 730 (D.D.C. 1981).

188. Whately v. Dept. of Education, 673 F.2d 873 (5th Cir. 1982); White v. Dallas Ind. Sch. District, 566 F.2d 906 (5th Cir. 1978); *cf.* EEOC v. Union Bank, 408 F.2d 867 (9th Cir. 1969).

189. Alexander v. Gardner-Denver Co., 415 U.S. 36 (1974).

190. *See* Oscar Meyer & Co. v. Evans, 441 U.S. 750, 757 (1979).

191. *See* Lorillard v. Pons, 434 U.S. 575 (1978); *re* age discrimination there is considerable case confusion. *Compare* Brennan v. Ace Hardware Corp., 495 F.2d 368 (8th Cir. 1974); *with* Dean v. American Security Ins. Co., 559 F.2d 1036, 564 F.2d 97 (5th Cir. 1977).

192. See EEOC v. Detroit Edison Co., 515 F.2d 301 (6th Cir. 1975); Annotation: *Award of Back Pay Under Title VII,* 21 A.L.R. Fed. 472 (1975).

but the Supreme Court has construed the EHA to authorize recovery of certain reimbursement expenses, as hereafter explained, on the view that such a recovery is not a matter of "damages" but of statutory right. Thus where state education agencies fail to provide appropriate placement at state expense, as required by the EHA, it must reimburse parents for the expenses incurred in making an appropriate placement.[193] Where that act provides adequate nonmonetary relief for discrimination against handicapped students, it also precludes monetary recovery under the Rehabilitation Act. Where the EHA does not provide adequate redress to a handicapped student victim, the availability of monetary remedy under the Rehabilitation Act was left undecided by the Supreme Court, notwithstanding uncertainty and conflicts among the lower courts on the availability of § 504 damages.[194] At this stage of case development, one can only venture an opinion that the courts will allow § 504 monetary relief, either directly under § 504 or via § 1983 where no alternative, exclusive relief is available under the EHA to victims of handicap discrimination, be they students or teachers.

4. Other Civil Rights Statutes

The civil rights statutes codified as §§ 1981, 1982, and 1985, (pp. 389, *supra*) provide independent bases for suit against a private party who did not act under "color of law," and, therefore, was beyond the coverage of § 1983.[195]

Of particular import is the Civil Rights Attorney's Fee Award Act of 1976, as amended (codified as § 1988, p. 390, *infra*). In the absence of such a statute, attorney's fees would not be recoverable under the traditional U.S. rule that denies to a successful party any attorney fee recovery, unless authorized by statute or unless a court found that the losing party acted "in bad faith."[196] While § 1988 merely authorizes, and does not require, the award of attorney's fees, in the discretion of the trial court,[197] the Supreme Court has promulgated the prevailing rule governing the exercise of judicial discretion on attorney's fees awards. That rule indicates that successful complainants should be awarded fees "unless special circumstances would remedy such an award unjust," while attorney's fees should not normally be awarded to successful defendants, unless the plaintiff's suit were found to be "frivolous, unreasonable and without foundation."[198] The

---

193. Burlington School Committee v. Dept. of Education, ________U.S. ________(1985).

194. Smith v. Robinson, p. 379, *supra*;Marvin H. v. Austin Ind. School Dist., 414 F.2d 1348, 291, 296 (N.D.Ga. 1983); David H. v. Spring Branch Ind. Sch. Dist., 569 F.Supp. 1324, 1331 (S.D.Tex. 1983), and the authorities there reviewed.

195. These sections supported private suits for private racial discrimination in Jones v. Alfred H. Mayer Co., 392 U.S. 409 (1978), Johnson v. REA, 421 U.S. 454 (1975), but also apply to public employers: District of Columbia v. Carter, 409 U.S. 418 (1973). *Re* § 1985 limitations, *see* Novotny v. Great American S. & L. Assn., 584 F.2d 1235 (3d Cir. 1978), Rev'd 442 U.S. 366 (1979).

196. *See* Alyeska Pipeline Service Co. v. The Wilderness Society, 421 U.S. 240, 258-59 (1975).

197. Skehan v. Bd. of Trustees, 436 F.Supp. 657 (M.D. Pa. 1977); Annotation: *Civil Rights Act—Attorneys Fees,* 16 A.L.R. Fed 621 (1973).

198. *See* Christiansburg Garment Co. v. EEOC, 434 U.S. 412 (1978). "A party 'prevails' within the meaning of § 1988 and § 794a(b) if his or her lawsuit is a substantial factor or significant catalyst in achieving the primary relief sought. *Robinson* v. *Kimbrough,* 652 F.2d 458, 465 (5th Cir. 1981). The fact that a party prevails through settlement rather than through full litigation does not prevent the awarding of fees. *Maher* v. *Gagne,* 448 U.S. 122, 129, 100 S.Ct. 2570, 2575, 65 L.Ed.2d 653 (1980)." *See* Teresa Diane P. v. Alief Ind. Sch. District, 744 F.2d 484, 488 (5th Cir. 1984).

Court's justification for this double standard of statutory interpretation lies in its finding that § 1988 was enacted to encourage discrimination of victims to sue; and that that incentive would be defeated if good faith plaintiffs were fearful of the risk of having to pay the defendant's attorney's fees if they lost the suit.

While the statutes codified as §§ 1982 and 1985 have relatively rare operation in the public schools, the Civil Rights Act codified as § 1981 has been regularly litigated and been construed to support monetary damage recovery for tangible as well as intangible injuries, and even for punitive damages.[199] Section 1981 has also been held to be an independent alternative source for racially animated employment discrimination; so that it is not barred by the fact that a Title VII action could also be brought for the same conduct.[200] The only effect of the overlapping statutes would be to prevent a double recovery.[201] Hence § 1981 damages are not limited to the damages specified by Title VII,[202] and it supports recovery of attorney's fees under § 1988.[203]

5. Tort Immunity Under Federal Statutes

The scope of school district and individual immunity from monetary liability under the various federal civil rights statutes is clearly not coextensive with the immunity standards created by state law for state torts. In *Monell* (p. 474, *infra*), the United States Supreme Court held that local governments and school boards do not enjoy governmental tort immunity under § 1983, and that Congress did not intend to grant universal tort immunity for civil rights deprivations.[204] It further held that § 1983 does not make school districts liable for all civil rights violations, but only for those committed pursuant to an official policy or custom.[205] Since school district liability turns upon an abridging official policy or custom, the Supreme Court further held that school districts cannot assert as a

---

199. "An individual who establishes a cause of action under § 1981 is entitled to both equitable and legal relief, including compensatory and, under certain circumstances, punitive damages." *See* Johnson v. Railway Express Agency, 421 U.S. 454, 460 (1974). *Tangible injuries: see, e.g.*, Lee v. Washington County Bd. of Education, 625 F.2d 1235 (5th Cir. 1980) (back pay); accord: Campbell v. Gadsden, 534 F.2d 650 (5th Cir. 1976); Sethy v. Alameda. 545 F.2d 1157 (9th Cir. 1976). *Intangible injuries: see, e.g.*, Runyan v. McCrary, 427 U.S. 160 (1976) (humiliation and embarrassment). *Accord*: Gonzales v. Fairfax Brewster Sch., Inc., 515 F.2d 1082 (4th Cir. 1975). *Punitive damages against individuals: see, e.g.*, Boyd v. Shawnee Mission Public School District, 522 F.Supp. 1185 (D. Kans. 1981); Heritage Homes v. Seekonk Water District, 648 F.2d 761 (1st Cir. 1981). The Supreme Court bar to punitive damages against local governments in § 1983 actions fn. 180, supra, would probably apply as well to § 1981 claims.

200. *See, e.g.*, Johnson v. Rwy. Express Agency, Inc., *supra*, 421 U.S. at p. 460; Campbell v. Gadsden Sch. District, *supra.*

201. Guerra v. Manchester Terminal Corp., 498 F.2d 641 (5th Cir. 1974).

202. *See* Johnson v. Railway Express Agency, Inc., *supra*, 421 U.S. at p. 460

203. Espinosa v. Hillwood Sq. Mutual Assn., 532 F.Supp. 440 (D.Va. 1982).

204. *See* the Monell case, p. 474, *infra*; Stoddard v. School District, 590 F.2d 829 (10th Cir. 1979); Kingsville v. Ind. School District, 611 F.2d 1109 (5th Cir. 1978). Nor can school districts claim Eleventh Amendment immunity against federal civil rights actions. *See, e.g.*, Smith v. New Castle County Vo-Tech School Dist., 574 F.Supp. 813, 819 (D.Del. 1983); Boyd v. Shawnee Mission Public Schools, 522 F.Supp. 1115 (D.Kans. 1981); Mark R. v. Board of Education, 546 F.Supp. 1027, 1033 (N.D.Ill. 1982).

205. *See* Monell v. Dept. of Social Services, *supra*, 406 U.S. at p. 701: Stoddard v. School District, *supra*; Moore v. Tangipahoa Par. School Board, 594 F.2d 489 (5th Cir. 1979).

defense any personal immunity that may be attached to its officers and employees who, in carrying out official policy or custom, had no reason to know that they were violating civil rights.[206] In sum, § 1983 renders the official entity absolutely liable for official rules that infringe federal civil rights.

By way of contrast, however, the Supreme Court has held that officials, such as school board members, are clothed with a qualified immunity from federal tort liability to the following extent:

> "We therefore hold that government officials performing discretionary functions generally are shielded from liability for civil damages insofar as their conduct does not violate clearly established statutory or constitutional rights of which a reasonable person would have known. . . . Reliance on the objective reasonableness of an official's conduct, as measured by reference to clearly established law, should avoid excessive disruption of government. . . . "[207]

While superintendents, principals, and school supervisors are not technically officers, the above-qualified immunity has also been extended to them for their discretionary acts.[208] The above ruling eliminated the subjective "good faith" test of qualified immunity, leaving only the objective standard of "reason to know" that the action in question was unlawful. This renders official "honesty" or lack of malice on civil rights mistakes largely irrelevant. If the mistake were "reasonable," immunity attaches; but if the mistake were unreasonable (i.e., the actor had "reason to know" that civil rights were being infringed), no immunity attaches. The *Monell* case was invoked by the 8th Circut to hold a school district liable for back pay to a teacher whose constitutional right was abridged when the board denied renewal in retaliation for her exercise of the right to criticize its policies.[209]

D. Tort Liability Under State Civil Rights Statutes

The scope and protection of civil rights that is offered by federal law has been supplemented and, to some degree, expanded by state constitutions and modern state civil rights statutes. Such laws are generally considered consistent with and not preempted by the federal laws.[210] They are usually found in different statutory sources, rather than in a single code, but the more typical modern statutes create state commissions to investigate and redress violations of covered civil rights by injunctive or affirmative action orders. The law in the individual states on the allowance of monetary

---

206. Owen v. City of Independence, 445 U.S. 622 (1980).

207. *See* Harlow v. Fitzgerald, 457 U.S. 800, 817–19 (1982).

208. Roman v. Appelby, 558 F.Supp 449 (E.D.Pa. 1983); Flores v. Edinburgh Cons. Ind. School Dist., 544 F.Supp. 974 (S.D.Tex. 1983); Curran v. Portland Supervising Sch. Comm., 435 F.Supp. 1063 (D.Me. 1977); Wagle v. Murray, 546 F.2d 1329 (9th Cir. 1976), vacated on other grounds, 431 U.S. 935 (1977).

209. Zoll v. Eastern Allamakee Community Sch. Dist., 588 F.2d 246 (8th Cir. 1978).

210. *See, e.g.*, Right to Choose v. Byrne,, 450 A.2d 925, 931 (N.J. 1982); Simpson v. Alaska State Commission for Human Rights, 423 F.Supp. 552 (D.Alaska 1976), 608 F.2d 1171 (9th Cir. 1979); Brennan, *State Constitutions and the Protection of Individual Rights*, 90 HARV. L. REV. 489 (1977).

damages, to individuals injured by a violation of state civil rights laws, is still developing and incomplete. In some states a complainant may recover monetary compensation for economic losses resulting from a state civil rights violation, but the ability to recover such compensation, or to recover intangible damages (viz. for emotional distress), has not been uniformly settled and will depend upon the particular wording and construction of the governing statutes in each state.[211] Since there is no common statutory pattern among the states, either as to the types of civil rights or the specific minorities covered; or as to governing procedures and remedies thereunder; the laws of each state must be consulted. A sampling of state law authorities and compilations on specific discrimination subjects is listed in the margin.[212]

---

211. See Annotation: *Recovery of Damages as Remedy for Wrongful Discrimination under State or Local Civil Rights Provisions*, 85 A.L.R.3d 351 (1978); Hinfey v. Matawan Regional Board of Education, 317 A.2d 78 (N.J. 1977); Danielson v. DuPage Area Vocational Education Authority, 595 F.Supp. 27 (N.D.Ill. 1984); Guilderland Central School v. New York State Human Rights Appeal Board, 461 N.Y.S.2d 599 (1983). See also 24 Pa. Stat. § 5002.

212. *Age discrimination*: see generally *Age Discrimination Problems*, pp. 33-47 (Practicing Law Institute 1983) (list of age discrimination statutes in some 40 states); Annotation: *Application of State Law to Age Discrimination*, 90 A.L.R.3d 195 (1980); Bd. of Ed'n v. State Div. of Human Rights, 486 N.Y.S.2d 469 (1985); Zimmerman v. Bd. of Ed'n, 597 F.Supp. 72 (D. Conn. 1984); Kelly v. American Standard, 640 F.2d 974 (9th Cir. 1981); Wells v. Franklin Broadcasting Corp., 403 A.2d 771 (Me. 1979); Kelly v. Albuquerque, 509 P.2d 1329 (N.M. 1973). *Retirement age standards and exceptions: see, e.g.*, Ten Hoeve v. Board of Education, 478 N.E.2d 200 (N.Y. 1985); Dolan v. School District, 636 P.2d 825 (Mont. 1981); Gross v. New York State Human Rights Appeal Board, 436 N.Y.S.2d 376 (1981); Loras College v. Iowa Civil Rights Commission, 285 N.W.2d 143 (Iowa 1979); Monnier v. Todd County Independent School District, 245 N.W.2d 503 (S.D. 1976); Clark County School District v. Beebe, 533 P.2d 161 (Nev. 1975); Kennedy v. Community Unit School District, 319 N.E.2d 243 (Ill. 1974); Cole v. Town of Hartford School District, 306 A.2d 101 (Vt. 1973); Herzig v. Board of Education, 204 A.2d 827 (Conn. 1964). *Race discrimination: see generally* Discussion of state statutes in Alaska, Arizona, Arkansas, California, Colorado, Illinois, Iowa, Maine, Massachusetts, Michigan, New York, Oregon, Pennsylvania, Rhode Island, and Texas, in ZIRKEL, *Spanish-Speaking Students*, 5 NOLPE School L.J. 34 (1975); Crawford v. Board of Education, 187 Cal. Rptr. 646 (1982); NAACP v. San Bernardino Unified School District, 187 Cal. Rptr. 646 (1982). A later amendment to the California Constitution undercut the foregoing authority. *See* Crawford v. Los Angeles Board of Education, 458 U.S. 527 (1982); Piscataway Twp. Bd. of Education v. Burke, 386 A.2d 439 (N.J. 1978); Pennsylvania Human Relations Commission v. Uniontown Area School District, 390 A.2d 1238 (Pa. 1978); Legg v. Illinois Fair Employment Practice Commission, 329 N.E.2d 486 (Ill. 1975); Darville v. Dade County School Board, 497 F.2d 1002 (5th Cir. 1974); Citizens Against Mandatory Bussing v. Palmason, 495 P.2d 657 (Wash. 1972); Brice v. Landis, 314 F.Supp. 974 (N.D. Cal. 1969); Brice v. Landis, 314 F.Supp. 974 (N.D. Cal. 1969); Tometz v. Board of Education, 237 N.E.2d 498 (Ill. 1968); Londerholm v. Unified School District No. 500, 430 P.2d 188 (Kan. 1967). Sex discrimination: See generally Annotation: *Sexual Harassment, State Civil Rights Laws*, 18 A.L.R.4th 328 (1982); Annotation: *State Laws—Sex Discrimination in Employment*, 84 A.L.R.3d 93 (1978); Annotation: *State Laws—Sex Discrimination in Advertising*, 66 A.L.R.3d 1237 (1975) Annotation: *State Equal Rights Amendments*, 90 A.L.R.3d 158 (1979). ERAs have been adopted in Colorado, Maryland, Massachusetts, New Hampshire, New Mexico, Pennsylvania, Texas and Washington. Utah and Wyoming have provisions on sex discrimination in their main constitutions, but those provisions have not been actively applied. See Illinois Constitution 1970, art. I, § 18; Erickson v. Board of Education, 458 N.E.2d 84 (Ill. 1984). *Male preference: see, e.g.*, Board of Education v. McCall, 485 N.Y.S.2d 357 (1985); Planchet v. New Hampshire Hospital, 341 A.2d 267 (N.H. 1975). *Discrimination in compensation: see, e.g.*, Board of Education v. Ohio Civil Rights Commission, 421 N.E.2d 511 (Ohio 1981); Jones v. Tracy School District, 611 P.2d 441 (Cal. 1980); Pennsylvania Human Relations Commission v. School District of Township of Millcreek, 377 A.2d 156 (Pa. 1977); *cf.* Schoneberg v. Grundy County Special Education Cooperative, 385 N.E.2d 351 (Ill. 1979); (differential based upon work load differences—upheld); *accord*: Kings Park Central School District, v. State Division of Human Rights, 424 N.Y.S.2d 293 (1980). *Pregnancy discrimination: see, e.g.*, Cedar Rapids County School District v. Parr, 227 N.W.2d 486 (Iowa 1975); School District v. Nilsen, 534 P.2d 1135 (Oreg. 1975); Leechburg Area School District v. Commonwealth, Human Relations Commission, 339 A.2d 850 (Pa. 1975); Board of Education v. New York State Division of Human Rights, 319 N.E.2d 202 (N.Y. 1973). Proof of discrimination: *see* Civil Rights Division v. Amphitheater Unif. School District, 693 P.2d 342 (Ariz. 1983); Thompson v. Board of Education, 526 F.Supp. 1035 (W.D. Mich. 1981); School Committee of Brockton v.

CASES

Cirillo v. City of Milwaukee

150 N.W.2d 460 (Wis. 1967)

WILKIE, Justice.

. . . *Grosso* v. *Wittemann* this court recognized that " . . . [a] teacher in the public schools is liable for injury to the pupils in his charge caused by his negligence or failure to use reasonable care." The question presented on this appeal is whether Paul Sherry's conduct on January 20, 1965, as a matter of law, was reasonable. The trial court came to this conclusion based upon its determination that Sherry " . . . could not have foreseen any risk or harm to plaintiff Donald Cirillo, or any other student in his class, as a probable consequence of his conduct."

This court has often stated that "harm must be reasonably foreseen as probable by a person of ordinary prudence under the circumstances, if conduct resulting in such harm is to constitute negligence." There is no necessity, however, that the actual harm that resulted from the conduct be foreseen. . . .

The controlling factor to the trial court was the nature of the conduct in which Cirillo was engaged when he was injured—the fact that Cirillo was participating in rowdyism. The trial court stated it would have been a different situation.

" . . . had the plaintiff minor been sitting at a table or desk in thc classroom and had been

---

Massachusetts Committee Against Discrimination, 386 N.E.2d 1240 (Mass. 1979). Union discrimination: *see* United Teachers of Seaford v. New York State Human Rights Appeal Board. 396 N.E.2d 207 (N.Y. 1979). *Defenses of bona fide employment qualifications, see* Harrisburg School District v. Commonwealth, Pennsylvania Human Relations Commission, 466 A.2d 760 (Pa. 1983); Board of Education v. Fair Employment Practices Commission, 398 N.E.2d 619 (Ill. 1979); School District v. Nilsen, *supra*; *cf.* Philadelphia v. Pennsylvania Human Relations Commission, 300 A.2d 97 (Pa. 1973). *Defenses of business needs: see, e.g.*, Roslyn Union Free School District v. State Division of Human Rights, 421 N.Y.S.2d 915 (1979); Gilchrist v. Board of Education, 382 A.2d 946 (N.J. 1978). *Handicapped Discrimination*: see generally Annotation: *State Legislation—Job Discrimination on Account of Physical Handicap*, 98 A.L.R.3d 393 (1979); In re State Div. of Human Rights v. Xerox, 65 N.Y.2d 213 (1985) (obesity discrimination covered by state law); D.S. v. East Brunswick Township Board of Education, 458 A.2d 129 (N.J. 1983); State Division of Human Rights v. Averill Park Central School District, 388 N.E.2d 729 (N.Y. 1979). *State law maintenance subsidies for different classes of handicapped children: see, e.g.*, New York City Board of Education v. Ambach, 452 N.Y.S.2d 731 (1982); Matter of Levy, 345 N.E.2d 556 (N.Y. 1976); Matter of Saberg, 386 N.Y.S.2d 592 (1976); Doe v. Colburg, 555 P.2d 753 (Mont. 1976); Matter of Jessup, 379 N.Y.S.2d 626 (1975); In re Davis, 370 N.Y.S.2d 351 (1975); Lisbon Regional School District v. Landaff School District, 327 A.2d 727 (N.H. 1974); *cf.* In re G.H. 218 N.W.2d 441 (N.D. 1974); In re Claire, 355 N.Y.S.2d 399 (1974); McMillan v. Board of Education, 430 F.2d 1145 (2d Cir. 1970). *Religious discrimination*: see generally Annotation: *State Legislation—Religious Discrimination in Employment*, 91 A.L.R.3d 155 (1979). *Proof of religious bias, see* State Division of Human Rights v. Gorton, 254 N.E.2d 911 (N.Y. 1969); Sowers v. Ohio Civil Rights Commission, 252 N.E.2d 463 (Ohio 1969); Hollon v. Pierce, 64 Cal. Rptr. 808 (1967). *Accommodation of religion: see* Maine Human Rights Commission v. Local 1361, 383 A.2d 369 (Me. 1978); Umberfield v. School District, 522 P.2d 730 (Colo. 1974); State Division of Human Rights v. Carnation Co., 366 N.E.2d 869 (N.Y. 1977).

minding his own business and thereafter sustained an injury as a result of a commotion instituted by other classmates during the period when the teacher had left the room. . . . "

• • •

Under the theory of the *Shilling case*, however, if Sherry could foresee harm to some students in the class arising from rowdyism as a result of his absence, it is immaterial that the harm actually resulting was not that foreseen by Sherry.

The principal difficulty in this case is, therefore, the nature of the activity in which Donald Cirillo and his friends engaged after Sherry left the room. . . . In *Ohman* the plaintiff student was struck in the eye by a pencil thrown by a fellow student while the teacher was absent from the room putting supplies away in a closet down the hall. The New York court held this was an unforeseen act of a third party which could as well have happened if the teacher had been present. In *Guyten* the plaintiff was in a class for defectives and incorrigibles and was struck in the eye by a milk bottle thrown by another student while the teacher was gossiping in another room. The Ohio court held the proximate cause of the injury was the sudden and unwarranted assault, and there was nothing to show the same thing would not have happened if the teacher had been present. . . .

In the instant case a jury could find that Sherry acted unreasonably in leaving his class unsupervised for a period of twenty-five minutes. That a group of almost 50 adolescents left unsupervised in a gymnasium for this period of time contains within it at least the seeds of unruliness is perhaps not a proper object of judicial notice. However, the least that can be said is "Boys will be boys." . . .

It is not unreasonable to consider there may be circumstances in which a teacher could anticipate even the type of conduct in which Donald Cirillo was engaged in this case. Furthermore, it is not unreasonable to consider the very presence of the teacher in the classroom might have discouraged the throwing of the milk bottle in *Guyten,* supra, or the pencil in *Ohman,* supra, or the pushing and tripping in the instant case. One of the participants in the rowdyism, Roger Kenny, indicated they were watching for Sherry while playing the game "Because we started playing rougher and rougher but we thought Mr. Sherry might yell at us or stop us." Kenny also indicated that if Sherry had looked in on the class the game would have been stopped "Because we were playing rough." This testimony, before a jury, would permit an inference that Sherry's absence was *sine qua non* to the injury in this case, even if it is accepted that the injuries in *Ohman* and *Guyten,* supra, might have happened even if the teacher had been present. . . .

. . . This should not, of course, mean that a teacher who absents himself from a room is negligent as a matter of law. As this court said in *Grosso* v. *Wittemann,* the teacher's duty is to use "reasonable care." What this means must depend upon the circumstances under which the teacher absented himself from the room. Perhaps relevant considerations would be the activity in which the students are engaged, the instrumentalities with which they are working (band saws, dangerous chemicals), the age and composition of the class, the teacher's past experience with the class and its propensities, and the reason for and duration of the teacher's absence. Even if the teacher is found to be negligent, when the injury is the result of rowdyism or intentional conduct, the question of intervening and superseding cause arises, as does apportionment of negligence. The question will be whether, under all the circumstances, the teacher acted reasonably. The trial court also found that even if the conduct of Paul Sherry created a jury question on negligence, the conduct of Donald Cirillo was such that it constituted 50 percent or more of the negligence as a matter of law, thus precluding a recovery for the plaintiff and rendering a trial futile. . . .

The question is, therefore, whether the affidavits in support of defendants' motion for summary judgment establish as a matter of law that this is one of those rare cases where the comparison of negligence question is to be assumed by the court. We conclude that the apportionment of negligence in the instant case is a jury question.

Summary judgment is a poor device for deciding questions of comparative negligence. What is contemplated by our comparative negligence statute, sec. 895.045, is that the totality of the casual negligence present in the case will be examined to determine the contribution each party has made to that whole. It is the "respective contributions to the result" which determine who is most negligent, and by how much. A comparison, of course, assumes the things to be compared are known, and can be placed on the scales. If a defendant, on summary judgment, is to be permitted to set forth in his affidavits the conduct of the plaintiff, and seek summary judgment on the ground the plaintiff's negligence outweighs his own as a matter of law, the only recourse to the plaintiff is to set forth in his counteraffidavits all of the conduct of the defendant. The upshot is a trial on affidavits, with the trial court ultimately deciding what is peculiarly a jury question. Our summary judgment statute does not authorize a trial by affidavits. The granting of summary judgment on this ground cannot be sustained. . . .

Finally, it is contended on behalf of the defendants that to permit a recovery by plaintiffs under these circumstances would be to constitute the defendants the insurer of the safety of Milwaukee school children. . . . To permit a recovery where the defendant is found to be negligent is not to render that defendant an insurer.

Judgment reversed.

Grant v. Lake Oswego School District No. 7

515 P.2d 947 (Ore. 1973)

LANGTRY, Judge

. . . Plaintiff Carol Grant, a child, by her guardian ad litem Marian Grant, her mother, brought this action against defendants for personal injuries sustained in an accident that occurred during a physical education class on January 4, 1971. Plaintiff was a 12-year-old seventh grade student at the time of the accident. Defendants are the School District and Toni Berke, the physical education teacher in charge of the class. The injury occurred when plaintiff jumped off a springboard and struck her head on the low doorway beam.

Plaintiff alleged that defendants were negligent:

> "1. In placing a springboard under a low ceiling and doorway. 2. In failing to turn the springboard on its side or otherwise making it harmless. 3. In failing to warn the students

> of the danger of hitting the low ceiling and/ or doorway. 4. In failing to supervise the students in the use of dangerous exercise equipment."

Defendants School District and Berke alleged that the plaintiff was contributorily negligent in jumping on the board without permission at a time and place when and where it was not supposed to be used, in using the springboard with too much force, and in failing to maintain a proper lookout. Evidence showed that on January 4, 1971 a class of 17 seventh grade girls was having its first instruction in gymnastics in a school "exercise room" with a high ceiling. When class began, a springboard was in place on a mat in the center of the room. Defendant Toni Berke was in charge of the class, aided by two eighth grade student assistants. . . . Near the end of the class plaintiff and three other girls, on instruction of defendant Toni Berke, dragged the springboard from the middle of the exercise room to an entrance alcove where the springboard was normally stored. The alcove had a low ceiling and was separated from the exercise room by a doorway that had a seven-foot clearance. . . .

After instructing the girls to move the springboard, defendant Toni Berke turned her attention elsewhere in the exercise room. She was standing in a position where she had no view into the entrance alcove. Plaintiff and the others testified that they dragged the springboard into the alcove and left it there upright. . . . Plaintiff then jumped off the springboard. She felt that she would propel herself into the exercise room. The lighting was good and she was aware of the low clearance of the doorway. She struck her head on the beam above the door and fell, injured. Another girl was standing behind her intending to jump into the exercise room after plaintiff. . . . The jury returned a verdict for plaintiff and awarded her $10,500 in damages. Upon motion by defendants the trial judge granted judgment notwithstanding the verdict on the grounds that its denial of the motion for a directed verdict had been improper since the evidence was insufficient to support any of plaintiff's allegations of negligence and that plaintiff was guilty of contributory negligence as a matter of law. . . .

The issues on appeal are: (1) whether the court erred in concluding that the evidence showed that plaintiff was guilty of contributory negligence as a matter of law; (2) whether the court erred in holding that the evidence failed to support any of plaintiff's allegations of negligence; and (3) if we conclude that the court erred on both issues, (1) and (2) above, was the evidence insufficient to support at least one of plaintiff's allegations so that defendants are entitled to a new trial on the remaining specifications of negligence.

(1) The child was not barred from recovery by contributory negligence as a matter of law. A child may be, under proper evidence, so barred. . . .

> "Whether the question of a child's contributory negligence is regarded as one of capacity, standard of care, or compliance with that standard, the courts are in substantial agreement that normally, if not always, a question of fact for the jury is presented, rather than one of law for the court. This conclusion seems to follow almost necessarily from the consideration that the answers to the relevant questions involve an investigation of the child's actual development, that is, of his age, intelligence, and experience or education; the formulation

> of a fictional child having the same or similar capacities; and then the determination as to whether the plaintiffs actual conduct under the circumstances, often itself a matter of dispute, comes up to the standard which is expected of his fictional counterpart." (Footnote omitted.) Annotation, 77 A.L.R.2d 917, 932 (1961).

This rule appears to apply in Oregon because, in those cases we have cited where the court held contributory negligence barred jury verdicts for the plaintiffs, there was positive testimony by the child plaintiffs that they knew they were engaging in dangerous courses of conduct. . . .

The court in *Nikkila* v. *Niemi,* supra, also stated:

> "A party's youth . . . does not excuse his embarking on a course of knowingly dangerous conduct." 248 Or. at 598, 433 P.2d at 827.

In the case at bar there is no testimony to the effect that plaintiff knowingly embarked on a course of dangerous conduct. Her contributory negligence, if any, was in her failure to appreciate the danger of her act, not in her failure to perceive the source of her danger. She knew the beam was there but jumped anyway, thinking she would miss it. If she should have known this was dangerous and did it anyway, then she would be guilty of negligence. . . . However, the question of what she should have known (absent testimony that she actually knew) is a question that depends upon what a hypothetical child of like age, intelligence, and experience should have known given similar circumstances. From the evidence presented in this case, that this was plaintiff's first experience with the use of a springboard and the apparent absence of in- depth instruction in its use and characteristics, a reasonable jury could have concluded that a similar child would not have appreciated the danger. . . .

Plaintiff has alleged that defendants were negligent in four particulars, supra. Defendant School Board's negligence is predicated on a finding that its servant Toni Berke was negligent. School District No. 26C et al., 226 Or. 263, 60 P.2d 282 (1961).

Plaintiff's first two specifications of negligence—(1)"In placing a springboard under a low ceiling and doorway; (2) In failing to turn the springboard on its side or otherwise making it harmless"—are interrelated.

The evidence presented a conflict as to whether Toni Berke told the girls to "just drag [the springboard] over here" or to put the springboard away and "tip it on its side." . . .

In *Allen* v. *Shiroma (Leathers)*, 97 Or. Adv.Sh. 1665, 1667, 514 P.2d 545 (1973), the court said:

> " . . . The jury determines whether the injury is foreseeable unless the court is of the opinion that there is insufficient evidence to support a finding that the injury was foreseeable."

Here there was sufficient evidence to support a jury finding that the injury suffered was foreseeable. Toni Berke testified that inexperienced students should not use the springboard. The question of plaintiff's experience was as we have noted above a jury question.

Plaintiff's second two specifications of negligence—"(3) in failing to warn the students of the danger of hitting the low ceiling and/or doorway; (4) in failing to supervise the students in the use of dangerous exercise equipment"—are also interrelated. Failure to warn can be viewed as a specific instance of failure to supervise.

A teacher's duty of care and supervision does not extend to unforeseeable harm. . . .

However, the facts of this case indicate that it can reasonably be found that proper supervision could have prevented this accident for the teacher would have noticed that the springboard was not being stored properly before plaintiff jumped off and struck her head on the beam. A quick admonition could have prevented her injury.

(3) We have concluded under issues (1) and (2) that there was a jury question presented on all four specifications of negligence. This is contrary to the trial court's conclusion. . . . It follows that the ruling below must be reversed and remanded with instructions to reinstate the jury verdict, so the order for a new trial must be set aside.

Reversed and remanded.

Ingraham v. Wright

430 U.S. 651(1977)

Mr. *Justice POWELL* delivered the opinion of the Court.

This case presents questions concerning the use of corporal punishment in public schools: first, whether the paddling of students as a means of maintaining school discipline constitutes cruel and unusual punishment in violation of the Eighth Amendment; and second, to the extent that paddling is constitutionally permissible, whether the Due Process Clause of the Fourteenth Amendment requires prior notice and an opportunity to be heard.

I

Petitioners James Ingraham and Roosevelt Andrews filed the complaint in this case on January 7, 1971. . . . At the time both were enrolled in the Charles R. Drew Junior High School in Dade County, Fla. . . . The complaint contained three counts, each alleging a separate cause of action for deprivation of constitutional rights, under 42 U.S.C. §§ 1981-1988. Counts one and two were individual damage actions by Ingraham and Andrews based on paddling incidents that allegedly occurred in October 1970 at Drew Junior High School. Count three was a class action for declaratory and injunctive relief filed on behalf of all students in the Dade County schools.

We granted certiorari, limited to the questions of cruel and unusual punishment and procedural due process. 425 U.S. 990. . . .

The use of corporal punishment in this country as a means of disciplining school children dates back to the colonial period. . . . the practice continues to play a role in the public education of schoolchildren in most parts of the country. Professional and public opinion is sharply divided on the practice, and has been for more than a century. Yet we can discern no trend toward its elimination. . . .

The prevalent rule in this country today privileges such force as a teacher or administrator "reasonably believes to be necessary for [the child's] proper control, training, or education." Restatement (Second) of Torts § 147(2); see id., 153(2). To the extent that the force is excessive or unreasonable, the educator in virtually all States is subject to possible civil and criminal liability.

Although the early cases viewed the authority of the teacher as deriving from the parents, the concept of parental delegation has been replaced by the view . . . that the State itself may impose such corporal punishment as is reasonably necessary "for the proper education of the child and for the maintenance of group discipline." I.F. HARPER & F. JAMES, THE LAW OF TORTS 292. . . .

Of the 23 States that have addressed the problem through legislation, 21 have authorized the moderate use of corporal punishment in public schools.[1] Of these States only a few have elaborated on the common law test of reasonableness, typically providing for approval or notification of the child's parents,[2] or for infliction of punishment only by the principal or in the presence of an adult witness. Only two States, Massachusetts and New Jersey, have prohibited all corporal punishment in their public schools. Where the legislatures have not acted, the state courts have uniformly preserved the common law rule permitting teachers to use reasonable force in disciplining children in their charge.[3]

Against this background . . . we turn to the constitutional questions before us. . . . We adhere to this long-standing limitation and hold that the Eighth Amendment does not apply to the paddling of children as a means of maintaining discipline in public schools. . . .

The Americans who adopted the language of this part of the English Bill of Rights in framing their own state and federal constitutions 100 years later feared the imposition of torture and other cruel punishments not only by judges acting beyond their lawful authority, but also by legislatures engaged in making the laws by which judicial authority would be measured. . . .

In light of this history, it is not surprising to find that every decision of this Court

---

1. Cal. Education D Code, §§ 49000-49001 (1976): Del. Code Ann. Tit. 14. § 701 (1976 Supp.); Fla. Stat. Ann. § 232.27 (1977); Geo. Code Ann. §§ 32-835, 32-836 (1976); Haw. Rev. Stat. §§ 298-16 (1975 Supp.) 703-309 (2) (1975); Ill. Ann. Stat., c. 122, §§ 24-24, 34-84a (1977 Supp.); Ind. Code Ann. § 20-8. 1-5-2 (1975); Md. Educ. Code Ann., Art. 77, § 98B (1975) (in specified counties); Mich. Comp. Laws Ann., § 340.756 (1976); Mont. Rev. Codes Ann., § 75-6109 (1947); Nev. Rev. Stat., § 392-465 (1973); N.C. Gen. Stat. § 115-146 (1975); Ohio Rev. Code Ann., § 3319.41 (1972); Okla. Stat. Ann., Tit. 70, § 6-114 (1972); Penn. Cons. Stat. Ann., Tit. 24, § 13-1317 (1976-1977 Supp.); S.C. Code § 21- 776 (1975 Supp.); S.D. Comp. Laws Ann. § 13-32-2 (1975); Vt. Stat. Ann., Tit. 16, § 1161 (1974); Va. Code Ann. § 22-231.1 (1950); W. Va. Code, § 18A-5-1 (1977); Wyo. Stat. § 21.1-64 (1975 Supp.).

2. Cal. Education Code, § 49001 (1976) (requiring prior parental approval in writing); Fla. Stat. Ann. § 232.27 (3) (1977) requiring a written explanation on request); Mont. Rev. Codes Ann., § 75-6109 (1947) (requiring prior parental notification).

3. E.g., Suits v. Glover, 260 Ala. 449, 71 So.2d 49 (1954); La Frentz v. Gallagher, 105 Ariz. 255, 462 P.2d 804 (1969). Berry v. Arnold School District, 199 Ark. 1118, 137 S. W. 256 (1940); Andreozzi v. Rubano, 145 Conn. 280, 141 A. 2d 639 (1958); Tinkham v. Kole, 252 Iowa 1303, 110 N.W. 2d 258 (1961); Carr v. Wright, 423 S. W. 2d 521 (Ky. 1968); Christman v. Hickman, 225 Mo. App. 828, 37 S. W. 2d 672 (1931).

considering whether a punishment is "cruel and unusual" within the meaning of the Eighth and Fourteenth Amendments has dealt with a criminal punishment. . . .

Petitioners acknowledge that the original design of the Cruel and Unusual Punishments Clause was to limit criminal punishments, but urge nonetheless that the prohibition should be extended to ban the paddling of school children. Observing that the Framers of the Eighth Amendment could not have envisioned our present system of public and compulsory education, with its opportunities for noncriminal punishments, petitioners contend that extension of the prohibition against cruel punishments is necessary lest we afford greater protection to criminals than to school children. . . .

Whatever force this logic may have in other settings, we find it an inadequate basis for wrenching the Eighth Amendment from its historical context and extending it to traditional disciplinary practices in the public schools. . . .

The schoolchild has little need for the protection of the Eighth Amendment. . . .

The openness of the public school and its supervision by the community afford significant safeguards against the kinds of abuses from which the Eighth Amendment protects the prisoner. In virtually every community where corporal punishment is permitted in the schools, these safeguards are reinforced by the legal constraints of the common law. Public school teachers and administrators are privileged at common law to inflict only such corporal punishment as is reasonably necessary for the proper education and discipline of the child; any punishment going beyond the privilege may result in both civil and criminal liability. . . .

We conclude that when public school teachers or administrators impose disciplinary corporal punishment, the Eighth Amendment is inapplicable. The pertinent constitutional question is whether the imposition is consonant with the requirements of due process.

IV

The Fourteenth Amendment prohibits any State deprivation of life, liberty or property without due process of law. Application of this prohibition requires the familiar two-stage analysis; we must first ask whether the asserted individual interests are encompassed within the Fourteenth Amendment's protection of "life, liberty or property"; if protected interests are implicated, we then must decide what procedures constitute "due process of law." . . . Following that analysis here, we find that corporal punishment in public school implicates a constitutionally protected liberty interest, but we hold that the traditional common law remedies are fully adequate to afford due process. . . .

There is, of course, a *de minimis* level of imposition with which the Constitution is not concerned. But at least where school authorities, acting under color of state law, deliberately decide to punish a child for misconduct by restraining the child and inflicting appreciable physical pain, we hold that Fourteenth Amendment liberty interests are implicated.[4]

---

4. Unlike Goss v. Lopez, 419 U.S. 565 (1975), this case does not involve the state-created property interest in public education. The purpose of corporal punishment is to correct a child's behavior without interrupting his education . . . Nor does this case involve any state-created interest in liberty going beyond the Fourteenth Amendment's protection of freedom from bodily restraint and corporal punishment.

"[T]he question remains what process is due." . . . Were it not for the common law privilege permitting teachers to inflict reasonable corporal punishment on children in their care, and the availability of the traditional remedies for abuse, the case for requiring advance procedural safeguards would be strong indeed. But here we deal with a punishment—paddling—within that tradition, and the question is whether the common law remedies are adequate to afford due process. . . .

Under that longstanding accommodation of interests, there can be no deprivation of substantive rights as long as disciplinary corporal punishment is within the limits of the common law privilege . . .

. . . We have found frequently that some kind of prior hearing is necessary to guard against arbitrary impositions on interests protected by the Fourteenth Amendment. . . . But where the State has preserved what "has always been the law of the land, the case for administrative safeguards is significantly less compelling." . . .

But even if the need for advance procedural safeguards were clear, the question would remain whether the incremental benefit could justify the cost. . . .

Such a universal constitutional requirement would significantly burden the use of corporal punishment as a disciplinary measure. Hearings—even informal hearings—require time, personnel, and a diversion of attention from normal school pursuits. School authorities may well choose to abandon corporal punishment rather than incur the burdens of complying with the procedural requirements. . . .

"At some point the benefit of an additional safeguard to the individual affected . . . and to society in terms of increased assurance that the action is just, may be outweighed by the cost." *Mathews* v. *Eldridge,* 424 U.S. at 348. . . .

We conclude that the Due Process clause does not require notice and a hearing prior to the imposition of corporal punishment in the public schools, as that practice is authorized and limited by the common law. . . .

[*Justices BRENNAN, MARSHALL, STEVENS* and *WHITE* dissented from the foregoing decision and opinion.]

Ayala v. Philadelphia Board of Public Education

305 A.2d 877 (Pa. 1973)

ROBERTS, Justice.

Appellants, William Ayala and William Ayala, Jr., instituted this action to recover damages for injuries suffered by William, Jr., when his arm was caught in a shredding machine in the upholstery class of the Carrol School in Philadelphia. As a result of these injuries, the 15 year old student's arm was amputated.

Appellants alleged that appellee school district, through its employees, was negligent in failing to supervise the upholstery class, in supplying the machine for use without a proper safety device, in maintaining the machine in a dangerous and defective condition, and in failing to warn the children of the dangerous condition. Appellee, the Philadelphia Board of Public Education, interposed preliminary objections asserting the defense of governmental immunity. These objections were sustained and the Superior Court affirmed in a per curiam order. *Ayala* v. *Philadelphia Board of Public Education,* 223 Pa.Super. 171, 297 A.2d 495 (1972). We granted allocatur.

We now hold that the doctrine of governmental immunity—long since devoid of any valid justification—is abolished in this Commonwealth. In so doing, we join the ever-increasing number of jurisdictions which have judicially abandoned this antiquated doctrine. See, e.g., *Spencer* v. *General Hospital of District of Columbia,* 138 U.S. App.D.C. 48-425 F.2d 479 (1969); *Campbell* v. *State,* 284 N.E.2d 733 (Ind. 1972) (citing with approval *Klepinger* v. *Board of Commissioners,* 143 Ind. App. 155, 239 N.E.2d 160 (1968) and *Brinkman* v. *City of Indianapolis,* 141 Ind. App. 662, 231 N.E.2d 169 (1967)); *Evans* v. *Board of County Commissioners,* 174 Colo. 97, 482 P.2d 968 (1971); *Flournoy* v. *School District No. 1,* 174 Colo. 110, 482 P.2d 966 (1971); *Smith* v. *State* 93 Idaho 795, 473 P.2d 937 (1970); *Willis* v. *Department of Conservation* and Econ. Dev., 55 N.J. 534, 264 A.2d 34 (1970); Becker v. Beaudoin, 106 R.I. 562, 261 A.2d 896 (1970); *Johnson* v. *Municipal University of Omaha* 184 Neb. 512. 169 N.W.2d 286 (1969); *Brown* v. *City of Omaha,* 183 Neb. 430, 160 N.W.2d 805 (1968); *Parish* v. *Pitts,* 244 Ark. 1239, 429 S.W.2d 45 (1968); *Veach* v. *City of Phoenix,* 102 Ariz. 195, 427 P.2d 335 (1967) (relying on *Stone* v. *Arizona Highway Commission,* 93 Ariz. 384, 381 P.2d 107 (1963)); *Haney* v. *City of Lexington* 386 S.W.2d 738 (Ky. 1964); *Sherbutte* v. *Marine City,* 374 Mich. 48, 130 N.W.2d 920 (1964); *Rice* v. *Clark County,* 79 Nev. 253, 382 P.2d 605 (1963); *Scheele* v. *City of Anchorage,* 385 P.2d 582 (Alaska 1963); *City of Fairbanks* v. *Schaible,* 375 P.2d 201 (Alaska 1962); *Spanel* v. *Mounds View School District No. 621,* 264 Minn. 279, 118 N.W.2d 795 (1962); *Holytz* v. *City of Milwaukee,* 17 Wis.2d 26, 115 N.W.2d 618 (1962); *Muskopf* v. *Corning Hospital District,* 55 Cal.2d 211, 11 Cal.Rptr. 89, 359 P.2d 457 (1961); Williams v. City of Detroit, 364 Mich. 231, 111 N.W.2d 1 (1961); *Molitor* v. *Kaneland Community Unit District No. 302,* 18 Ill.2d 11, 163 N.E.2d 89 (1959); *Hargrove* v. *Town of Cocoa Beach,* 96 So.2d 130 (Fla. 1957). (See Case table at the end of this case.)

I

It is generally agreed that the historical roots of the governmental immunity doctrine are found in the English case of *Russell* v. *Men of Devon,* 2 T.R. 667, 100 Eng.Rep. 359 (1788). . . . There, the court, in extending immunity to an unincorporated county, expressed the fear that if suits against such political subdivisions were permitted, there would be "an infinity of actions." *Russell* v. *Men of Devon,* supra at 672, 100 Eng.Rep. at 362. That court was also influenced by the absence of a fund "out of which satisfaction is to be made." *Id.* Finally, Justice Ashurst, expressing the eighteenth century societal evaluation of the individual and local governmental interests, observed that "it is better that an individual should sustain an injury than that the public should suffer an inconvenience." *Id.*

While some attribute the immunity of municipal corporations and quasi-corporations to an extension of the theory that "the King can do no wrong", it has been noted that in *Russell* v. *Men of Devon* there is no intention of that phrase. . . .

Whatever may have been the actual basis for *Russell* v. *Men of Devon,* the doctrine it advanced was soon applied in the United States. . . .

Although the English courts abandoned the doctrine and permitted suits against municipalities and school districts, this Commonwealth continued to deny recovery. . . .

Thus, until the present action, we have retained the archaic and artificial distinction between tortious conduct arising out of the exercise of a proprietary function and tortious conduct arising out of exercise of a governmental function.

II

Today we conclude that no reasons whatsoever exist for continuing to adhere to the doctrine of governmental immunity. . . .

Moreover, we are unwilling to perpetuate the notion that "it is better that an individual should sustain an injury than that the public should suffer an inconvenience." Russell v. Men of Devon, supra at 673, 100 Eng. Rep. at 362. . . .

We must also reject the fear of excessive litigation as a justication for the immunity doctrine. Empirically, there is little support for the concern that the courts will be flooded with litigation if the doctrine is abandoned. . . .

Equally unpersuasive is the argument advanced in *Russell* v. *Men of Devon,* and *Ford* v. *School District* that immunity is required because governmental units lack funds from which claims could be paid. . . . Initially, we note our disagreement with the assumption that the payment of claims is not a proper governmental function. . . .

Additionally, the empirical data does not support the fear that governmental functions would be curtailed as a result of liability for tortious conduct. . . . . . . Moreover, the distinction between governmental and proprietary functions "is probably one of the most unsatisfactory known to the law, for it has caused confusion not only among the various jurisdictions but almost always within each jurisdiction." Davis, *Administrative Law Treatise* § 25.07 at 460 (1958). . . .

Imposition of tort liability will, thus, be more responsive to current concepts of justice. Claims will be treated as a cost of administration and losses will be spread among all those benefited by governmental action. . . .

III

. . . Indeed, appellee does not attempt to justify retention of immunity on policy grounds. Rather, it contends that abrogation, if it is to be achieved, should be accomplished by legislative direction rather than by judicial determination.

In response to arguments that the Court should defer to legislative action, we stated in *Flagiello* v. *Pennsylvania Hospital,* supra, 417, Pa. at 503, 208 A.2d at 202: "[T]he controverted rule [charitable immunity] is not the creation of the Legislature. *This Court fashioned it, and, what it put together, it can dismantle.*" (Emphasis added.). . . .

Similarly, here, the doctrine of governmental immunity—judicially imposed—may be judicially terminated. . . .

On prior occasions, we recognized that errors of "history, logic and policy" were responsible for the development of the governmental immunity doctrine. *Morris* v. *Mount Lebanon Township School District,* supra, 393 Pa. at 635, 144 A.2d at 738. See also *Dillon* v. *York City School District,* supra. Nevertheless we suggested that the legislature should undertake the abrogation of governmental immunity. *Id.* These suggestions do not preclude our Court from now abolishing this judicially created doctrine. In so doing, we join numerous other jurisdictions which similarly, by judicial decision, have abandoned governmental immunity notwithstanding prior deference to legislative action. . . .

IV

Appellee urges that abrogation of the immunity doctrine disturbs the principle of *stare decisis*. . . .

This Court has repeatedly recognized that the principle of stare decisis is not a "confining phenomenon." We are mindful of the observation of Mr. Justice Schaefer of the Supreme Court of Illinois:

> "Precedent speaks for the past; policy for the present and the future. The goal which we seek is a blend which takes into account in due proportion the widsom of the past and the needs of the present." SCHAEFER, *Precedent and Policy*, 34 U.CHI.L.REV. 3, 24 (1966). . . .

The cases are numerous in which this Court has rejected principles which were "out of accord with modern conditions of life." . . .

V

Finally, it is suggested that if we abolish governmental immunity, our decision to do so should not apply to the instant case. We refused to adopt that suggestion in *Falco* v. *Pados*, supra, as well as numerous other cases. . . . On the basis of these decisions, appellee's argument that we do not apply our newly adopted rule to the facts of this case must be rejected.

Having concluded that local governmental units—municipal corporations and quasi-corporations—are no longer immune from tort liability, the order sustaining appellee's preliminary objections is reversed and the record remanded for proceedings consistent with this opinion.

CASE TABLE. Position of states with regard to Doctrine of Governmental Immunity[1] *

Judicially abrogated	Statutorily abrogated	Modified	Insurance-waiver theory	Common law
Alaska	Hawaii	Connecticut	Georgia	Alabama
Arizona	Iowa	South Carolina	Kansas	Arkansas[2]
California	New York	Texas	Maine	Delaware
Colorado	Oklahoma		Mississippi	Maryland
Florida	Oregon		Missouri	Massachusetts
Idaho	Utah		Montana	Pennsylvania[3]
Illinois	Washington		N. Hampshire	South Dakota
Indiana			New Mexico	Virginia
Kentucky			North Carolina	
Louisiana			North Dakota	
Michigan			Ohio	
Minnesota			Tennessee	
Nebraska			Vermont	
Nevada			West Virginia	

Judicially abrogated	Statutorily abrogated	Modified	Insurance-waiver theory	Common law
New Jersey Rhode Island Wisconsin District of Columbia			Wyoming	

NOTES: 1. This compilation is based on material presented in Restatement, Second, Torts § 895A 12-20 (Tentative Draft, March 30, 1973).
2. Judicially abolished but statutorily reinstated.
3. Until today Pennsylvania retained the common-law immunity.

AUTHOR'S NOTE: The foregoing tabulation is no longer totally accurate. Since 1973, school district immunity has been disapproved in Massachusetts, Missouri, and Iowa. See Whitney v. City of Worcester, 366 N.E.2d 1210 (Mass. 1977); Prewitt v. Parkway Sch. District, 557 S.W.2d 232 (Mo. 1977); Anderson v. Calamus Comm. Sch. District, 174 N.W.2d 643 (Iowa 1900). Conversely, Kentucky adheres to school district immunity, while Florida retains governmental immunity for any claim in excess of available insurance. Knott City Bd. of Education v. Mullins, 553 S.W.2d 852 (Ky. 1977); Surette v. Galiardo, 323 So.2d 53 (Fla. 1975).

*All data tables must be updated for possible changes in each state since 1979.

Carey v. Piphus

435 U.S. 247 (1978)

Mr. *Justice* POWELL delivered the opinion of the Court.

In this case, brought under 42 U.S.C. 1983, we consider the elements and prerequisites for recovery of damages by students who were suspended from public elementary and secondary schools without procedural due process. The Court of Appeals for the Seventh Circuit held that the students are entitled to recover substantial nonpunitive damages even if their suspensions were justified, and even if they do not prove that any other actual injury was caused by the denial of procedural due process. We disagree, and hold that in the absence of proof of actual injury, the students are entitled to recover only nominal damages.

I

Respondent Jarius Piphus was a freshman at Chicago Vocational High School. . . . On January 23, 1974, during school hours, the school principal saw Piphus and another student standing outdoors on school property passing back and forth what the principal described as an irregularly shaped cigarette. The principal approached the students unnoticed and smelled what he believed was the strong odor of burning marihuana. . . . When the students became aware of the principal's presence, they threw the cigarette into a nearby hedge.

The principal took the students to the school's disciplinary office and directed the assistant principal to impose the "usual" 20-day suspension for violation of the school rule against the use of drugs. The students protested that they had not been smoking marihuana, but to no avail. . . .

A suspension notice was sent to Piphus' mother, and a few days later two meetings were arranged among Piphus, his mother, his sister, school officials, and representatives from a Legal Aid Clinic. The purpose of the meetings was not to determine whether Piphus had been smoking marihuana, but rather to explain the reasons for the suspension. . . . The complaint sought declaratory and injunctive relief, together with actual and punitive damages in the amount of $3,000. . . .

Respondent Silas Brisco was in the sixth grade at Clara Barton Elementary School in Chicago during the 1973-1974 school year. On September 11, 1973, Brisco came to school wearing one small earring. The previous school year the school principal had issued a rule against the wearing of earrings by male students because he believed that this practice denoted membership in certain street gangs and increased the likelihood that gang members would terrorize other students. Brisco was reminded of this rule, but he refused to remove the earring asserting that it was a symbol of black pride, not of gang membership.

The assistant principal talked to Brisco's mother, advising her that her son would be suspended for 20 days if he did not remove the earring. Brisco's mother supported her son's position, and a 20-day suspension was imposed. Brisco and his mother, as guardian *ad litem*, filed suit in Federal District Court under 42 U.S.C. § 1983 . . . charging that Brisco had been suspended without due process of law in violation of the Fourteenth Amendment. . . .

Piphus' and Brisco's cases were consolidated for trial and submitted on stipulated records. The District Court held that both students had been suspended without procedural due process. It also held that petitioners were not entitled to qualified immunity from damages . . . because they "should have known that a lengthy suspension without any adjudicative hearing of any type" would violate procedural due process. . . . Despite these holdings, the District Court declined to award damages because:

> "Plaintiffs put no evidence in the record to quantify their damages, and the record is completely devoid of any evidence which could even form the basis of a speculative inference measuring the extent of their injuries. Plaintiffs' claims for damages therefore fail for complete lack of proof." *Ibid.* . . .

On respondents' appeal, the Court of Appeals reversed and remanded. 545 F.2d 30 (CA7 1976). . . .

. . . [T]he Court of Appeals held that even if the District Court found on remand that respondents' suspensions were justified, they would be entitled to recover substantial "nonpunitive" damages simply because they had been denied procedural due process. . . . We granted *certiorari* to consider whether, in an action under § 1983 for the deprivation of procedural due process, a plaintiff must prove that he actually was injured by the deprivation before he may recover substantial "nonpunitive" damages. . . .

The legislative history of § 1983, elsewhere detailed . . . demonstrates that it was intended to "create a species of tort liability" in favor of persons who are deprived of "rights, privileges, or immunities secured" to them by the Constitution. . . .

Petitioners contend that the elements and prerequisites for recovery of damages under this "species of tort liability" should parallel those for recovery of damages under the common law of torts. . . . Unless respondents prove that they actually were injured by the deprivation of procedural due process, petitioners argue, they are entitled at most to nominal damages.

Respondents seem to make two different arguments. . . . First, they contend that substantial damages should be awarded under § 1983 . . . *whether or not* any injury was caused by the deprivation. This, they say, is appropriate both because constitutional rights are valuable in and of themselves, and because of the need to deter violations of constitutional rights. . . .

Second, respondents argue that even if the purpose of a § 1983 damages award is, as petitioners contend, primarily to compensate persons for injuries that are caused by the deprivation of constitutional rights, every deprivation of procedural due process may be presumed to cause some injury. This presumption, they say, should relieve them from the necessity of proving that injury actually was caused.

A

Insofar as petitioners contend that the basic purpose of a § 1983 damages award should be to compensate persons for injuries caused by the deprivation of constitutional rights, they have the better of the argument. Rights, constitutional and otherwise, do not exist in a vacuum. . . .

To the extent that Congress intended that awards under § 1983 should deter the deprivation of constitutional rights, there is no evidence that it meant to establish a deterrent more formidable than that inherent in the award of compensatory damages. . . .

In this case, the Court of Appeals held that if petitioners can prove on remand that "[respondents] would have been suspended even if a proper hearing had been held." 545 F.2d at 32, then respondents will not be entitled to recover damages. . . .

The court suggested that in such circumstances, an award of damages for injuries caused by the suspensions would constitute a windfall, rather than compensation, to respondents. . . . We do not understand the parties to disagree with this conclusion. Nor do we.

The parties do disagree as to the further holding of the Court of Appeals that respondents are entitled to recover substantial—although unspecified—damages to compensate them for "the injury which is 'inherent in the nature of the wrong,'" 545 F.2d. at 31, even if their suspensions were justified. . . . Respondents, . . . submit that the holding is correct because injury fairly may be "presumed" to flow from every denial of procedural due process. . . .

Petitioners' argument is the more limited one that such injury cannot be presumed to occur, and that plaintiffs at least should be put to their proof on the issue, as plaintiffs are in most tort actions.

We agree with petitioners in this respect. . . . First, it is not reasonable to assume that every departure from procedural due process, no matter what the circumstances or how minor, inherently is as likely to cause distress. . . . Where the deprivation of a protected interest is substantively justified but procedures are deficient in some respect, there may well be those who suffer no distress over the procedural irregularities. . . .

Finally, we foresee no particular difficulty in producing evidence that mental and emotional distress actually was caused by the denial of procedural due process itself. Distress is a personal injury familiar to the law, customarily proved by showing the nature and the circumstances of the wrong and its effect on the plaintiff. In sum, then, although mental and emotional distress caused by the denial of procedural due process itself is compensable under § 1983, we hold that neither the likelihood of such injury nor the difficulty of proving it is so great as to justify awarding compensatory damages without proof that such injury actually was caused.

Common-law courts traditionally have vindicated deprivations of certain "absolute" rights that are not shown to have caused actual injury through the award of a nominal sum of money. By making the deprivation of such rights actionable for nominal damages without proof of actual injury, the law recognizes the importance to organized society that those rights be scrupulously observed; but at the same time, it remains true to the principle that substantial damages should be awarded only to compensate actual injury or, in the case of exemplary or punitive damages, to deter or punish malicious deprivations of rights.

Because the right to procedural due process is "absolute" in the sense that it does not depend upon the merits of a claimant's substantive assertions, and because of the importance to organized society that procedural due process be observed, . . . we believe that the denial of procedural due process should be actionable for nominal damages without proof of actual injury. We therefore hold that if, upon remand, the District Court determines that respondents' suspensions were justified, respondents nevertheless will be entitled to recover nominal damages not to exceed one dollar from petitioners.

The judgment of the Court of Appeals is reversed, and the case is remanded for further proceedings consistent with this opinion. . . .

Monell v. Department of Social Services of the City of New York

436 U.S. 658 (1978)

Mr. *Justice* BRENNAN delivered the opinion of the Court.

Petitioners, a class of female employees of the Department of Social Services and the Board of Education of the City of New York, commenced this action under 42 U.S.C. § 1983. . . . The gravamen of the complaint was that the Board and the Department had as a matter of official policy compelled pregnant employees to take unpaid leaves of absence before such leaves were required for medical reasons. . . .

The suit sought injunctive relief and back pay for periods of unlawful forced leave. Named as defendants in the action were the Department and its Commissioner, the Board and its Chancellor, and the city of New York and its Mayor. In each case, the individual defendants were sued solely in their official capacities. . . .

Nonetheless plaintiff's prayers for back pay were denied because any such damages would come ultimately from the City of New York and, therefore, to hold otherwise would be to "circumvent" the immunity conferred on municipalities by *Monroe* v. *Pape,* 365 U.S. 167 (1961). . . .

Although . . . we have decided the merits of over a score of cases brought under § 1983 in which the principal defendant was a school board—and, indeed, in some of which § 1983 . . . provided the only basis for jurisdiction—we indicated in *Mt. Healthy City Board of Ed.* v. *Doyle,* 429 U.S. 274, 279 (1977), last Term that the question presented here was open and would be decided "another day." That other day has come and we now overrule *Monroe* v. *Pape,* supra, insofar as it holds that local governments are wholly immune from suit under § 1983. . . . [1]

II

Our analysis of the legislative history of the Civil Rights Act of 1871 compels the conclusion that Congress *did* intend municipalities and other local government units to be included among those persons to whom § 1983 applies. Local governing bodies, therefore, can be sued directly under § 1983 for monetary, declaratory, or injunctive relief where, as here, the action that is alleged to be unconstitutional implements or executes a policy statement, ordinance, regulation, or decision officially adopted and promulgated by that body's officers. Moreover, although the touchstone of the § 1983 action against a government body is an allegation that official policy is responsible for a deprivation of rights protected by the Constitution, local governments, like every other § 1983 "person," by the very terms of the statute, may be sued for constitutional deprivations visited pursuant to governmental "custom" even though such a custom has not received formal approval through the body's official decisionmaking channels. As Mr. Justice Harlan, writing for the Court, said in *Adickes* v. *S. H. Kress & Co.* 398 U.S. 144, 167-168 (1970): "Congress included custom and usage [in § 1983] because of persistent and widespread discriminatory practices of State officials. . . . Although not authorized by written law, such practices of state officials could well be so permanent and well settled as to constitute a 'custom or usage' with the force of law."

On the other hand, the language of § 1983, read against the background of the same legislative history, compels the conclusions that Congress did not intend municipalities to be held liable unless action pursuant to official municipal policy of some nature caused a constitutional tort. In particular, we conclude that a municipality cannot be held liable *solely* because it employs a tortfeasor—or, in other words, a municipality cannot be held liable under § 1983 on a *respondeat superior* theory. . . .

Equally important, creation of a federal law of *respondeat superior* would have raised all the constitutional problems associated with the obligation to keep the peace, an obligation Congress chose not to impose because it thought imposition of such an obligation unconstitutional. . . .

We conclude, therefore, that a local government may not be sued for an injury inflicted solely by its employees or agents. Instead, it is when execution of a government's policy or custom, whether made by its lawmakers or by those whose edicts or acts may fairly be said to represent official policy, inflicts the injury that the government as an entity is responsible under § 1983. Since this case unquestionably involves official policy as the moving force of the constitutional violation found by the District Court, see pp.

---

1. However, we do affirm Monroe v. Pape, 365 U.S. 167 (1961), insofar as it holds that the doctrine of *respondeat superior* is not a basis for rendering municipalities liable under § 1983 for the constitutional torts of their employees. See Part II, infra.

1-2, and n. 2, supra, we must reverse the judgment below. *In so doing, we have no occasion to address, and do not address, what the full contours of municipal liability under § 1983 may be.* We have attempted only to sketch so much of the § 1983 cause of action against a local government as is apparent from the history of the 1871 Act and our prior cases and *we expressly leave further development of this action to another day.* . . .

CHAPTER 9

CHAPTER OUTLINE

A. Introduction
  1. Budgets and appropriations
  2. Accounting checks
B. Public school revenues
  1. Local school taxes
  2. Borrowed funds
    a. Short-term loans
    b. Long-term debt
    c. Debt calculation
    d. Exemptions from "debt"
    e. Statutory procedures
    f. Indirect borrowing
    g. Bondholder's remedies
  3. Fees and charges
    a. Tuition, matriculation, and registration fees
    b. Textbooks and school supplies
    c. Special activity fees
    d. Special events
    e. Federal and private grants
C. Expenditure controls
  1. Centrally administered funds
  2. Controls on the making of public contracts
  3. Competitive bidding
  4. Unlawful devices to eliminate bidding
  5. Contract amendments
  6. Exempt products and services
  7. Bidder qualification
  8. Withdrawal of bids
  9. Right to reject bids
  10. Remedies following award of improperly bid contracts
  11. Individual school funds

Financing Public Education

TABLE OF CASES FOR CHAPTER 9

San Antonio Independent School District v. Rodriguez, 411 U.S. 1 (1973), 507.
Hartzell v. Connell, 679 P.2d 35 (Cal. 1984), 514.
Cardiff v. Bismarck Public School Dist., 263 N.W. 2d 105 (N. Dak. 1978), 518,
Secrist v. Diedrich, 430 P. 2d 448 (Ariz. 1967), 524.
Boise Junior College District v. Mattefs Const. Co., 450 P. 2d 604 (Idaho 1969), 526.
Gerzof v. Sweeney, 239 N.E. 2d 521 (N. Y. 1968), 530.

A. Introduction

With the exception of Hawaii, public education is financed by a combination of state grants, local school district taxes, and federal aid. Contemporary educational costs have increased to the point where they command a major portion of state government budgets, as well as local school taxes and borrowing. These rival in sum the taxes received by municipalities and counties. (See Figures 9–1 and 9–2.) As in other matters, school boards have no inherent legal fiscal powers and can only exercise those that are delegated to them by state law. The delegation doctrines discussed in Chapter 2 have peculiar force in educational finance. The state may relieve local school districts of responsibility to finance all or part of its functions and may even require funds raised by taxes in one school district to be transferred to another district for the purpose of equalizing educational resources.[1] The fiscal powers of local school districts and school boards thus remain subject to the pervasive control of state legislatures. Fiscal restrictions are also imposed by the general law of contracts and, in the case of private federal grants, by the law of trusts.

Therefore, it is necessary for school authorities to observe the foregoing legal controls in determining what financing options are available to achieve particular educational goals. The following materials outline the principal arrangements governing public school finances. As will be seen, the law governing financing procedures and

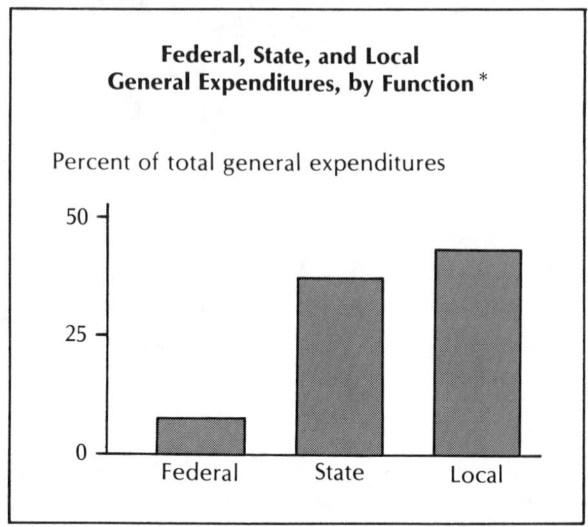

SOURCE: *The Condition of Education* Vol. 3, Part I, p. 127 (National Center for Educational Statistics: HEW, 1977).
*All data tables must be updated for possible changes in each state since 1979.
NOTE: Public education constitutes the largest single item of expenditures for either State or local governments. Education accounted for 39 percent of all State government and 45 percent of all local government expenditures in 1974–75.

FIGURE 9-1. Federal, state, and local expenditure for education

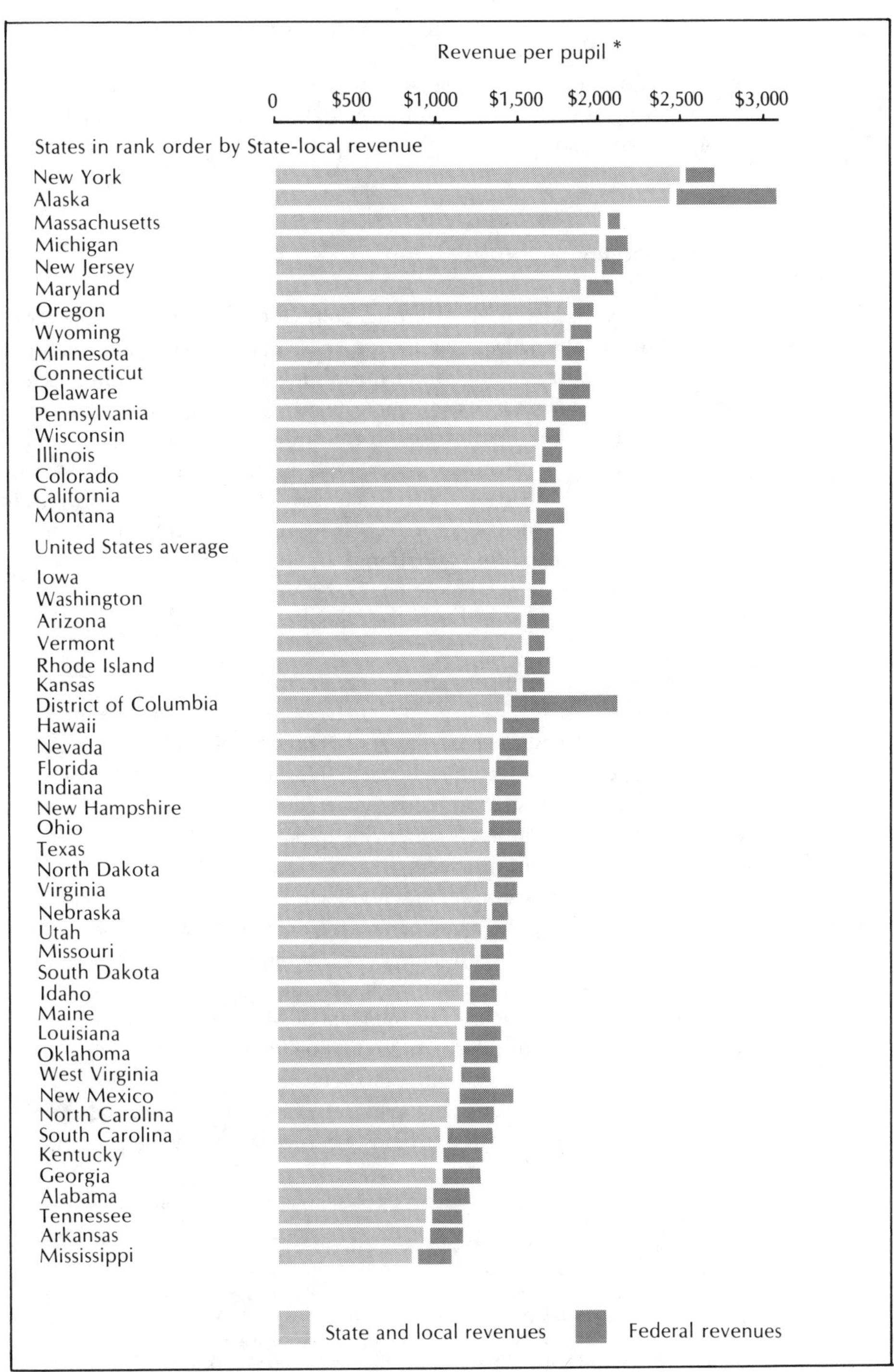

SOURCE: *The Condition of Education* (National Center for Educational Statistics: HEW, 1978).

*All data tables must be updated for possible changes in each state since 1979.

NOTE: States vary considerably in the amounts of funds they allocate to public elementary and secondary education. Federal funding helps to reduce these interstate disparities because the poorest States tend to receive somewhat greater shares than the wealthier ones.

FIGURE 9-2. Per-pupil revenue for elementary and secondary education by source

methods is often critical to the substantive power to collect and dispense funds. The pertinent constitutions and statutes of each state vary considerably; hence financing questions must always be carefully checked against the current law of the governing state.

1. Budgets and Appropriations

The operating budget is the starting point and basic legal framework of all public finance.[2] In law, the budget is an instrument of control as well as of planning. In addition to estimating probable receipt and expenditures, the budget confines school board fiscal authority. Budget law seeks to promote fiscal stability, official accountability, taxpayer protection, and citizen information on educational priorities and costs. For example, the power to levy local school taxes is generally limited to the amount required to fund the current budget. The budget also restricts district expenditures to the subjects and the amounts specified in the budget. Given these strictures, the time periods and procedures for budget development and adoption are particularly significant. Budget formats and procedures vary in detail, but financing statutes generally determine when and how budgets must be proposed, amended, publicized, submitted to public hearing, and adopted.

State laws only require reasonable, and not impossibly precise, budget forecasts of sums that will actually be needed, received, and expended. Courts tend to construe budget statutes liberally to enable school boards to meet special or emergency situations not anticipated in the original budget. This is usually done by special amendment provisions and by transferring funds budgeted for certain items to other underbudgeted items, so long as the transfer is reasonable in purpose and amount and so long as the total budget ceilings are not breached.[3]

The discretionary power of school boards to determine reasonably how to allocate available funds among the many competing demands within a school system is settled.[4] School boards may not intentionally levy taxes in excess of current budgeted expenses to build up an excessive surplus, but the budgeting of a reasonable surplus for contingencies is generally upheld as lawful.[5] On the issue of what levies are unreasonably excessive in relation to current need, the courts are inclined to uphold school board judgments in the absence of convincing proof by the challengers.[6]

It is equally settled that public funds may not be expended unless there is an official "appropriation" of those funds for the designated purpose. In most states the

2. Specialized law on "capital budgets" for planning and financing long-term capital improvements is not reviewed in this text.

3. *See* Raffalone v. Pearsall 333 N.Y.S.2d 316 (1972); Ashley v. Rye Sch. District, 274 A.2d 795 (N.H. 1971); Isley v. Sch. District, 305 P.2d 432 (Ariz. 1956).

4. *E.g.*, Bd. of Selectmen of Pittsfield v. School Bd., 311 A.2d 124 (N.H. 1973).

5. Aiken County Bd. of Education v. Knotts, 262 S.E.2d 14 (S.Car. 1980) (a statute rule that school district not levy taxes in excess of needs for current year); Kissinger v. Sch. District, 77 N.W.2d 767 (Neb. 1956) (excess surplus); Bd. of Education v. Mayor and Council of Borough of Fair Lawn 362 A.2d 1270 (N.J. 1976) (permissible contingency fund).

6. Watkins v. Jackson, 179 S.E.2d 747 (Ga. 1971); cf. Sweet v. Cent. Ill. Publ. Serv. Co., 268 N.E.2d 404 (Ill. 1971).

official adoption of the budget is itself considered to be the act of appropriation.[7] However, where governing law distinguishes between prior authorization and actual appropriation, a separate act of appropriation is required to permit the expenditure. Thus, payment of appropriated funds may be enforced by suit, but payment funds that are authorized by law or contract, but not appropriated, could not be so enforced.[8] Where insufficient funds are appropriated for designated programs, they may be prorated to the eligible school districts at the reduced level required by the shortfall of appropriations. The impact of appropriation requirements was dramatically illustrated by a recent decision. A teacher collective bargaining agreement for wage increases in the year following its execution was held void on the ground that the board of education could not incur liability under that contract when it did not make the necessary appropriation in the following year.[9] New public employee labor statutes that authorize arbitration of wage disputes may, however, have the effect of modifying prior appropriations law, depending upon a court's construction of the legislative intention of the interacting statutes. Thus a Pennsylvania court recently upheld an arbitrator's award for payment of wages in excess of the annual salaries fixed in the teachers' contracts by invoking a code provision that permitted the board to grant temporary or emergency salary increases.[10]

2. Accounting Checks

Compliance with budget limits is best assured by maintaining accounts showing the balance of budgeted funds that have not been expended or encumbered for the budgeted items. This pre-audit check assures the availability of funds for required expenditures. Following exhaustion of appropriated funds, a "postaudit" review may also be made as a double check both on compliance with the law and on the proper receipt of the services or materials for which payment was made.

In addition to the foregoing monitoring devices, certain funds or receipts are legislatively or constitutionally earmarked as "special funds" that can only be put to specified uses. Earmarked funds, unlike general budgeted funds, are not subject to discretionary allocation or transfers by the school board and must be separately accounted. Whether created by state laws, federal grant, or private grant, special funds are normally considered to be trust funds, imposing a fiduciary obligation on the district to use them exclusively for the purposes for which they were created. Such funds may not, therefore, be commingled or used interchangeably with other funds.[11]

---

7. *E.g.*, Bd. of Sch. Trustees v. Benner, 24 S.E.2d 259 (N.C. 1943).

8. Town of Lexington v. Comm'r of Education, 473 N.E.2d 673 (Mass. 1985); Carter County Board of Education v. Am. Fed. of Teachers, 609 So. 2d 512 (Tenn. 1980); *compare* Bd. of Education of Iron Mountain v. Voelker, 259 N.W. 891 (Mich. 1935) (funds appropriated) *with* Bd. of Education v. Porter, 221 N.W.2d 345 (Mich. 1974); Kosa v. Treasurer, 259 N.W.2d 463 (Mich. 1977) (teacher retirement fund claim); Murphy v. City of Brockton, 305 N.E.2d 103 (Mass. 1973) (valid contract) (funds not appropriated); Bd. of Education of Oakland Schools v. Supt. Pub. Instr., 257 N.W.2d 73 (Mich. 1977).

9. Bd. of Education v. Chicago Teachers Union, 326 N.E.2d 158 (Ill. 1975).

10. Northampton Area Bd. of Education v. Zehner, 360 A.2d 793 (Pa. 1976).

11. Calloway v. Ouachita Parish Sch. Bd., 158 So.2d 360 (La. 1963).

B. Public School Revenues

State constitutions oblige state legislatures to establish and maintain public schools but do not require state governments to provide the school funds exclusively from the state treasury.[12] The constitutional duty may be met by state laws requiring local school districts or municipalities to raise needed funds by local taxation. More typically, state legislatures adopt a mixed system whereby both state public school subsidies and local district taxation are employed to fund the schools. State reliance upon local property taxes has been legally challenged on the ground that such taxes result in substantial disparities of per pupil revenues and expenditures between school districts that have high and low taxable property sources. These challenges failed under the Fourteenth Amendment and met with only partial success in some states under state constitutional provisions. (See San Antonio Ind. Sch. District v. Rodriguez p. 507 infra.) The need for stronger school revenue sources has, however, generated an ongoing trend of legislative reforms to improve school finance.[13]

Legal challenges have also been made to the formulae for allocating state subsidies among school districts. Apportionment of state funds to school districts need only be fair and rational to withstand legal challenge.[14] The use of multiple variable factors, including that of "need," in distribution formulae has gained increasing judicial, as well as political, acceptance.

1. Local School Taxes

School districts may levy only those taxes expressly authorized by state law, and local taxing power will not be implied from the general obligation to provide public education.[15] Within constitutional limits, state legislatures may delegate different taxing

---

12. *Cf.* Cronin v. Lindberg, 360 N.E.2d 360 (Ill. 1977) (state withdrawal of aid for noncompliance with state law—no violation of constitutional duty to establish public schools).

13. For a brief summary of state legislative reforms to enhance school revenues, see *The Condition of Education*—1977, Vol. 3, Part I (National Center for Educational Statistics, HEW) at p. 138.

14. "'Every state appellate court which has considered the question since *Rodriquez* was decided has held that the state's school finance system does not offend the federal equal protection clause.' *See* Pauley v. Kelly, 255 S.E.2d 895 (W.Va. 1979); Horton v. Meskill, 172 Conn. 615 376 A.2d 359 (1977); Illinois v. Adams, 40 Ill. App. 3d 189, 350 N.E.2d 767 (1976); Serrano v. Priest, 135 Cal. Rptr. 345, 557 P.2d 929 (1976), cert. denied, 432 U.S. 907 (1977); Thompson v. Engelking, 96 Idaho 793, 537 P.2d 635 (1975); Northshire School District v. Kinnear, 84 Wash.2d 685, 530 P.2d 178 (1974), overruled on other grounds, Seattle School District v. State, 90 Wash.2d 476, 585 P.2d 71 (1978); Milliken v. Green, 390 Mich. 389, 212 N.W.2d 711 (1973); Shofstall v. Hollins, 110 Ariz. 88, 515 P.2d 590 (1973); Robinson v. Cahill, 62 N.J. 473, 303 A.2d 273, cert. denied, 414 U.S. 976 (1973); Lujan v. Colorado State Bd. of Educ., Colo., 649 P.2d 1005 (1982); Board of Educ., Levittown, Etc. v. Nyquist, 57 N.Y.2d 27, 439 N.E.2d 359, 453 N.Y.S.2d 643 (1982)." *See* Hornbeck v. Somerset County Bd. of Education, 458 A.2d 758, 783 (Md. 1983). Bd. of Educ. v. Superintendent of Public Instr., 257 N.W.2d 73 (Mich. 1977); Scarnato v. Parker, 415 F. Supp. 272 (M.D.La. 1976); Northwestern Sch. District v. Pittinger, 397 F.Supp. 975 (W.D.Pa. 1975). But see Buse v. Smith, 247 N.W.2d 141 (Wis. 1976) for equalization scheme that violated state law on uniformity of taxation.

15. Manges v. Freer Ind. School District, 653 S.W.2d 553 (Tex. 1983); School District of Pittsburgh v. City, 443 A.2d 1206 (Pa. 1982) (tax rate limit); Aikens County Bd. of Education v. Knotts, fn. 5, *supra*; *E.g.*, Blue v. Stockton, 355 P.2d 395 (Alaska 1960); Idaho Power Co. v. Three Creek Good Roads District, 390 P.2d 960 (Idaho 1964) (voiding local tax as *ultra vires*). *But see* Hankins v. District Boundary Bd.,502 P.2d 368 (Wyo. 1972) (tax upheld as levied under color of law by de facto officer).

authority to different classes of school districts.[16] Though levied and collected locally, in legal contemplation, school taxes are state taxes. Thus, a state legislature need not use school districts as the vehicle for levying taxes on district residents.[17] In recent years, limits on school tax levies and expenditures have been subjected to cap statutes and state constitutional amendments, as part of the taxpayers' revolt. Such limits have been judicially upheld, except where special court orders required levies or expenditures in excess of the lawful ceiling.[18]

Even where taxing power is properly delegated, its exercise may be defeated on procedural grounds. Thus, if a procedure required by statute for a tax levy is ignored, the tax may be nullified.[19] The earlier discussion of judicial construction of statutory provision as being mandatory and directory thus takes on particular significance in tax protest cases. As there noted, courts are prone to uphold taxes notwithstanding procedural errors by treating the tax statutes as "directory" where enforcement of the procedure would seriously disrupt school income and operations.[20]

When, for whatever reasons, a school tax is found to be unlawful, the remedies of the taxpayer will depend upon whether and how the taxes were paid. No problem arises where legislation specifically authorizes tax refunds or recovery of unlawful taxes that were paid under protest, or by mistaken billing of the school district.[21] Courts generally rule that taxes voluntarily paid are not recoverable if they are later declared unlawful.[22] In the absence of legislation, most courts conclude that the public interest in stable government justifies denial of taxpayer relief. For like reasons courts generally refuse to overturn taxes of a plaintiff because some other parties were not properly taxed. Though such errors probably overburden remaining taxpayers, courts place a nearly impossible requirement of proof that the complaining taxpayer incurred actual and substantial economic loss.[23] In the absence of a statutory protest and recovery procedure,

---

16. Sims v. Town of Baldwin, 290 S.E.2d 433 (Ga. 1982); Pirrone v. City of Boston, 305 N.E.2d 96 (Mass. 1973); Shofstall v. Hollins, 515 P.2d 590 (Ariz. 1973); Northshore Sch. District v. Kinnear, 530 P.2d 178 (Wash. 1975).

17. Opinion of the Justices, 246 A.2d 90 (Del. 1968); Bd. of Trustees v. Bd. of County Comm'rs., 359 P.2d 635 (Idaho 1961). *Cf* Ind. Sch. District v. Glass, 639 P.2d 1233 (Okla. 1982) (state alteration of local taxing authority).

18. *See, e.g.*, Hot Springs Sch. District v. Wells, 663 S.W.2d 733 (Ark. 1984) (cap statute); N.J.S.A. 40 A:4-45.3; Amador Valley Jt. Union H.S. District v. State Bd. of Equalization, 583 P.2d 1281 (Cal. 1978) (state constitutional amendment). *Exception for compliance with judicial decree: see, e.g.*, Corey v. Poway Un. Sch. District, 195 Cal. Rptr. 586 (1983).

19. Wingate v. Whitney Ind. Sch. District, 129 S.W.2d 385 (Tex. 1939).

20. *See* Wilson v. School Bd. of Marion County, 424 So.2d 16, 19-21 (Fla. 1982); Greenberg v. Lower Marion Sch. District, 462 A.2d 972 (Pa. 1983); Blumer v. Sch. Bd. of Beresford Ind. Sch. District 250 N.W.2d 282 (S.D. 1977).

21. Bd. of Directors of N. Pocono Sch. District v. Gouldsboro Taxpayers Ass'n, 466 A.2d 299 (Pa. 1983) Bethlehem Steel v. Bd. of Education 378 N.E.2d 115 (N.Y. 1978); Union Electric Co. v. Collector, 562 S.W. 2d 370 (Mo. 1978). McDonough v Aylward 500 S.W.2d 721 (Mo. 1973); McGinnes v. Dept. of Finance, 377 A.2d 16 (Del. 1977).

22. Gindel v. Dept. of Education 396 So.2d 1105, 1106 (Fla. 1981); Cornell v. Bd. of Education, 3 N.E.2d 717 (Ill. 1936); *cf.* Arnold v. Crockett Ind. Sch. District, 389 S.W.2d 608 (Tex. 1965).

23. *See generally* Bynum v. Alto Ind. Sch. District, 521 S.W.2d 656 (Tex. 1975); Superior Oil Co. v. Sinton Ind. Sch. District, 431 S.W.2d 383 (Tex. 1973).

most courts conclude that the taxpayer's remedy is to bring suit to enjoin the initial collection of taxes and that the failure to seek such prior relief bars later refund claims.[24]

2. Borrowed Funds

The *cash flow* requirements of schools nearly always outstrip the funds in the district's possession. The heavy cost of new construction or alteration of permanent facilities can only be met by large loans, with repayment made by installments over a term of years. Further, current operations often require cash at a time before the current year's taxes are fully collected. In such cases, school expenses must be financed by borrowing. Loans are subject to varied legal controls, depending upon term, purpose, and form.

a. Short-Term Loans. School districts are generally authorized to borrow funds needed for current operations. In effect, such loans are treated as a current expense to be repaid from current income. The dominant legal principle in short-term borrowing is "pay as you go": "Some confusion has arisen in the cases as to the extent of the right to anticipate the collection of taxes. We think, however, it is fairly well settled that, as applied to ordinary revenues, that right undoubtedly does not extend beyond the current year, nor can it be exercised as to such revenues for any purpose beyond the payment of ordinary expense. . . . "[25] State statutes commonly require that short-term loans must mature and be redeemed in the fiscal year of their creation or soon thereafter, out of revenues that are currently due or collectible for that year.[26] The New York legislature liberalized the general rule to permit repayment of short-term borrowings over the following budget year.[27] Short-term loans are often secured by a pledge of taxes coming due to repay them. Hence the custom of issuing "tax anticipation" notes or warrants.

The abuse of short-term borrowing by postponing repayment to future years is disguised deficit financing and is well illustrated by the fiscal plight of the City of New York in recent years. That plight was anticipated in a report of the United States Advisory Committee on Intergovernmental Relations:

> "The inability to repay several years accumulation of short-term operating loans has been the most important single factor in throwing a city [school district] into a financial crisis. Cities [school districts] may find it tempting to 'roll over' short term debt from year to year in ever increasing amounts. . . . The Commission recommends, therefore, that the States enact legislation to regulate the use of short-term operating debt that carries beyond the end of the fiscal year. At a minimum such laws should require that a short-term operating debt remaining unliquidated at the end of the fiscal year should be charged against general debt limits and provision for its retirement be automatically included in the next year's budget."[28]

---

24. Del Valle Ind. Sch. District Bd. of Equalization v. Hackett, 563 S.W.2d 338 (Tex. 1978); Pittsburgh Coal Co. v. Sch. District, 78 A.2d 253 (Pa. 1951) Gulesian v. Dade Co. Sch. Bd., 281 So.2d 325 (Fla. 1973); Nelson v. Blanco Ind. Sch. District, 386 S.W.2d 636 (Tex. 1965).
25. *See* Swanson v. City of Ottumwa, 91 N.W. 1048, 1056–57 (1902).
26. *E.g.*, Pa. Stat. Annotated tit. 53, § 6780-201.
27. *See N.Y. Local Finance Law*, MC KINNEY'S CONS. LAWS OF N.Y. tit. §§ 33 24:00, 25:00.
28. A.C.I.R., CITY FINANCIAL EMERGENCIES, p. 5 (1973).

It is clear that state legislatures may impose whatever limitations on school district borrowings that they deem prudent and that school districts have no implied powers to raise funds by short-term or long-term borrowing.[29]

The legal controls that are imposed on short-term borrowing are not as rigorous as those affecting long-term debts. For example, short-term loans are limited to anticipated revenues, but are not subject to the dollar limits fixed by debt limitations statutes that govern long-term notes and bonds. Further, the need for strict procedural measures is not so strong since the annual budget and tax limits provide some protection against abuses of short-term financing. Thus, the procedural conditions that commonly limit long-term borrowing (advertising the nature, purpose, and amount of the loan; clearance of bond forms and terms; and prior voter approval) are not usually required for short-term loans. Where procedural requirements are imposed by law, however, a failure to observe them will render the short-term loan transaction void, unless the error is excused on a finding that the statutory requirement was merely "directory."

b. Long-Term Debt. Most government units, including school districts, must resort to long-term loans to finance school construction and other capital improvements. These loans are regulated in great detail by state constitutions and statutes both as to the substance of the loans and the form and procedures of the contracts covering them.[30] The term *bonds* only refers to a special type of contract or promissory note that sets forth the contract terms under which loans and monies advanced in exchange of the bonds are to be repaid. Descriptive terms such as *general obligation bonds, revenue bonds,* and *sinking fund bonds* merely indicate what sources of repayment or security are pledged by the borrower to pay off the loan.

The principal substantive control is the fixing of an absolute "debt" ceiling by "debt limitation" laws. The purpose of such laws was well expressed in an old case:

> "[T]he framers had in mind the great and ever growing evil to which the municipalities of the state were subjected by the creation of a debt in one year, which debt was not, and was not expected to be paid out of the revenue of that year, but was carried on into the next year increasing like a rolling snowball as it went until the weight of it became almost unbearable upon the taxpayers. It was to prevent this abuse that the constitutional provision was enacted."[31]

Debt limit statutes are often supplemented by additional statutory requirements to secure available funds to repay long term debts. The creation of sinking funds to meet future debt payments by providing payments from current revenues is a typical means of assuring debt liquidation.

Numerous ways have been devised to avoid ceilings. They generally take two forms: (1) the exclusion of particular obligations that are directly incurred by school districts from the calculation of their "debt" as that term is construed under debt limit

29. *See* In re Advisory Opinion, 211 N.W.2d 28 (Mich. 1963).

30. For variations in statutes and case law of different states see VALENTE, LOCAL GOVERNMENT LAW, ch. V. (1975). See generally BOWMAR. *The Anachronism Called Debt Limitation,* 52 IOWA L. REV. 863 (1967).

31. McBean v. Fresno, 112 Cal. 159, 164, 44 P. 358, 359 (1896).

laws; and (2) not considering indirect financing by outside sources as "debt" by the school district. These avoidance techniques are briefly described by the following illustrations.

c. Debt Calculation. In ascertaining the present level of school district indebtedness in relation to the legal debt ceiling, only the "net" outstanding "debt" applies so that certain kinds of obligations are excluded. "Involuntary" obligations are excluded on the rationale that the purpose of debt limitation law—to prevent official abuse—is not affected by the existence of involuntary obligations. Thus a court judgment against the district to pay sums created by a district's tort liability and a state legislative mandate that a district raise funds to construct a particular building at a particular time, which can only be achieved by long-term financing, are not counted as debt for limitations purposes.[32] Deductions from past debt by the amount of funds presently set aside to meet those debts are also allowed.[33] Thus "refunding" loans or bonds that produce funds to pay off outstanding loans do not increase the net indebtedness,[34] except to the extent of any increase in interest and service costs.

The time for calculating outstanding debt can be critical. Debt is normally calculated as of the time when new obligation is incurred, that is, when the bonds are issued and not when they are authorized, though this rule is not universally followed.[35] Thus, if existing debt plus the proposed loans do not exceed the debt limit when the bonds are issued, the bonds are lawful, even though at the time of their authorization the existing debt leaves insufficient room for the additional loans and has to be reduced by payments in the interval between the authorization and issuance of the new bonds.[36]

Most government units, including school districts, fail to set aside adequate revenues under public employee pensions as reserves to cover pension obligations that are vested (ripened) though not to be paid until the future. This failure raises the question whether the pension fund reserve deficiency amounts to "debt" for debt limitation purposes. The question has not been extensively litigated, but one court ruled that no debt was created by underfunded long-term pension liabilities.[37] A related but different question is posed by suits to force public authorities to set aside additional funds in order to comply with their duty to maintain an "actuarially sound" pension system.[38]

d. Exemptions from "Debt." Long-term leases and installment contracts for materials or services and for the use of real estate are also favored instruments to avoid technical debt creation. On the view that such obligations merely create a succession of separate obligations in the nature of current expenses to be paid when due from current revenues, most courts allow their exclusion from the amount of debt that is subject to

---

32. *Tort liability:* Brown v. Jefferson County, 406 S.W.2d 185 (Tex. 1966). *Legislative mandate*: Los Angeles County v. Byram, 227 P.2d 4 (Cal. 1951); 15 Mc Quillin, Mun. Corps, 41.28 (1970 rev. ed.).

33. Halldorson v. State Sch. Constr. Fund, 224 N.W.2d 814 (N.D. 1974).

34. Ex Park Progresso Ind. Sch. District, 650 S.W.2d 158 (Tex. 1983); Florida v. Bd. of Pub. Instr., 164 So.2d 6 (Fla. 1964).

35. *Compare* Baker v. Un. Sch. District, 480 P.2d 409 (Kan. 1971) *with* Bilardi Const. Co. v. Spencer, 86 Cal. Rptr. 406 (1970).

36. Torres v. Laramie Co. Sch. District, 506 P.2d 817 (Wyo. 1973).

37. Rochlin v. State, 540 P.2d 643 (Ariz. 1975).

38. Dombrowski v. City of Phila., 245 A.2d 238 (Pa. 1968).

debt ceilings. Some, but not all, state courts have indulged this fiction even where a long-term lease is patently an installment purchase contract to acquire real estate.[39]

Loans that are not "guaranteed" by the assets, general revenues, or credit of the school district but are repayable only from other sources are considered not to be debt for limitation purposes. *Self-liquidating* projects that are repayable *solely* from revenues generated by new construction (such as a stadium) are exempt as *nonguaranteed debt.* Since lenders can only collect from the "special fund" created by project revenues, courts hold that no general debt is created. The bonds issued in such cases are thus called *revenue* bonds.

The laws of many states also permit electorally approved debt to be exempt from debt-ceiling limits. Under such laws, the only checks on accumulation of electoral debt are the lack of voter support and the lack of bond purchasers who will risk making such loans. The use of electoral debt has become more difficult in recent years as increasing numbers of voters and lending sources reject proposals for new electoral borrowings. However, when voters approve a particular financing scheme, courts are reluctant to overturn their decision.[40] They are inclined to uphold bond approval elections notwithstanding noncompliance with some election procedure if the election results are not shown to be materially effected by the noncompliance.[41]

e. Statutory Procedures. The procedures for issuing of long-term bonds are specified in considerable detail by state laws. As previously noted, the effect of a failure to observe statutory procedures will depend upon whether courts treat procedural errors as material or insubstantial and whether the procedure requirements are directory or mandatory. If not excused as insubstantial or directory in nature, noncompliance with statutory procedures will render the bond obligation void and legally unenforceable.

To avoid such miscalculations, modern bond legislation authorizes or requires local government officials, including school boards, to *prevalidate* proposed bond borrowings by submitting specified reports or petitions to designated courts or supervising state agencies for their official clearance. Such prevalidation statutes provide advance and conclusive assurance that particular bond issues are valid and enhance the market for bond sales, as well as taxpayer and investor protection.[42] The law may also permit postissuance validations of bonds that were unlawfully issued, whether for procedural defects or as having exceeded statutory debt limits. Statutory ratification and approval of issued bonds, where the legislature was constitutionally empowered to authorize them in the first place, is generally upheld.[43] A good state-by-state summary of state laws for state supervision of local bonding practices is presented in the report of the U.S. Advisory

---

39. *See* City of Phoenix v. Phoenix Civil Auditorium and Convention Center Assn., 408 P.2d 818 (Ariz. 1965); *cf.* Schull Constr. Co. v. Webster Ind. Sch. District, 198 N.W.2d 512 (S.D. 1972).

40. For a review of Supreme Court authorities on constitutional issues of voter qualifications and classifications, *see* Ex Parte Progresso Ind., fn. 34, *supra. See* Butsche v. Coon Rapids Community Sch. Dist., 255 N.W.2d 337 (Iowa 1977).

41. *See* cases cited in Chapter 2.

42. *See* Pa. Local Government Unit Debt Act, Pa. Stat. Ann. tit. 53 §§ 6780: 351-60; Mich. Comp. Laws Ann. § 600.2942; Fla. Stat. Ann. § 75.01; Hamilton County v. Cloud, 236 N.E.2d 803 (Ohio 1967); Cox v. Ga. Educ. Authority, 170 S.E.2d 240 (Ga. 1969).

43. Osage National Bank v. Oakes Special Sch. District, 7 N.W.2d 920 (N.D. 1943).

Commission on Intergovernmental Relations, *City Financial Emergencies,* 164 et seq, (1973).

f. Indirect Borrowing. School districts that have exhausted their debt limits and electoral or credit support have still another avenue to finance capital construction. Many states statutes authorize other government entities (such as state or local school building authorities) to finance and construct public schools for long-term rental to underlying school districts. Since each such authority has a separate fiscal base and debt limit, this "tapping" into their credit by school districts is not considered to create school district debt.[44] The use of this type of *overlying debt* by fiscally pressed school districts probably represents the largest legal loophole to avoid school district debt limits.

g. Bondholder's Remedies. If a court declares bonds unlawful after they are issued and paid for, the rights of the bondholders to claim refunds of the monies advanced in exchange for the bonds come into question. Though the bond contracts are themselves unenforceable at law, courts in equity always have the power to order restitution of monies received, under the principle of *preventing unjust enrichment.* However, the courts are divided on the propriety of such equitable relief, and the cases cannot be neatly summarized. Some cases deny any relief on the view that restitution would undermine the public policy of discouraging unlawful bond practices. Other courts permit restitution on a case-by-case basis where the circumstances indicate that restitution would not result in any actual substantial public harm. Courts are more likely to allow restitution to bondholders where they are without fault and where the funds have not been spent or irrevocably committed by the district. Other courts draw technical distinctions between bonds that are only *voidable* because the legal defect goes only to the *manner* of their issuance and bonds that are totally *void* because the school district never had the legal authority to issue the bonds, irrespective of the procedures used. In practical terms, the timing of the lawsuit and the particular case circumstances critically affect individual decisions as to whether purchasers of unlawfully issued bonds can recover their monies.[45]

3. Fees and Charges

Under the pressure of revenue shortages, a growing number of school districts have resorted to student fees to fund certain services and activities. These fees are often challenged as contrary to laws that make public schools "free" and "open to all" district residents. An assortment of legal tests as to what fees may be charged appears in the cases, based partly upon peculiar wording of individual state statutes and partly upon diverse judicial opinion as to what activities should be included in free public education.

A good survey of the diverse views taken by different state jurisdictions is presented by the *Hartzell* case, p. 514, infra, wherein the California Supreme Court ruled

---

44. Mercure v. Bd. of Education, 361 N.E.2d 273 (Ohio 1976); *cf.* Dortch v. Lugar, 266 N.E.2d 25 (Ind. 1971).

45. *See* Johns-Manville Corp. v. Village of DeKalb, 439 F.2d 656 (8th Cir. 1971).

that the California state constitution prohibited and nullified *all* school fees.[46] Many jurisdictions, however, treat different classes of fees differently. While many fees do not fit neatly into the major fee classifications, such charges generally fall into three categories; namely, instructional fees, fees for books and supplies, and student activity fees. Further subclassifications under these headings may also be made to distinguish lawful from unlawful fees.[47]

a. Tuition, Matriculation, and Registration Fees. Pupils residing within a school district may not be subjected to general charges for admission to the public school during the normal school year. It makes little difference whether the charge is labeled as *tuition, matriculation, or registration fee.*[48] It is equally settled that, in the absence of special statutes covering a special situation, school districts are not obliged to admit students who are not residents of the district.[49] Residency, unlike domicile, depends upon bona fide physical habitation within a district with intention to remain there for an indefinite period of time, even though the residence is not the child's ultimate and permanent home place.[50] Residency will not be deemed bona fide if the sole purpose of locating within a school district is to gain tuition-free admission to its schools.[51] School districts are normally permitted by state law to charge tuition to students who are not residents of the district and to resident students who are wards of other states.[52]

The amount of admission charges to nonresidents may be set by statutory formula, the calculation of which may be left to a central state agency or to the local district.[53] Where the nonresident student is being sent by another public school district that lacks the required school facility, the sending district will normally be assessed with the charge under statutory guidelines.[54] Otherwise the responsibility for tuition would be upon the parents or custodians of the nonresident student.[55]

With respect to admission charges for summer school programs, the states are not

---

46. See generally Annotation: *Validity of Public School Fees*, 41 A.L.R.3d 752 (1972) and current pocket part thereto.

47. Excluded from this discussion are charges to special schools or activities that are not a normal part of general public education.

48. *Tuition: see* Bd. of Education v. Sinclair, 222 N.W.2d 143 (Wis. 1974); Chandler v. So. Bend Comm. Sch. Corp., 312 N.E.2d 915 (Ind. 1974); Grange v. Cascade Co. Sch. District, 499 P.2d 780 (Mont. 1972); and cases in Annotation, fn. 46. *General and matriculation fee: see* Vandevender v. Cassell, 208 S.E.2d 436 (W. Va. 1974); Dowell v. Sch. District, 250 S.W.2d 127 (Ark. 1952); *contra:* Vincent v. County Bd. of Ed., 131 So.2d 893 (Ala. 1931) (matriculation fee upheld).

49. Jeter v. Ellenville Central Sch. District, fn. 1.

50. State ex rel. Doe v. Kingery, 203 S.E.2d 385 (W.Va. 1974).

51. Turner v. Bd. of Education, 294 N.E.2d 264 (Ill. 1973).

52. Board of Education v. Board of Education, 445 N.E.2d 464 (Ill. 1983); School Board v. Ehrlich, 421 So.2d 18 (Fla. 1982); Oracle School District v. Mammoth High School District, 633 P.2d 450 (Ariz. 1981); Jackson v. Wald Independent School District, 629 S.W.2d 201 (Tex. 1982); Walker v. Lockland City School District Board of Education, 429 N.E.2d 1179 (Ohio 1980). See, e.g., Union Free H.S. District v. Jt. Sch. District, 117 N.W.2d 273 (Wis. 1962); E. Texas Guidance and Achievement Ctr. v. Brockette, 431 F. Supp. 231 (E.D. Tex. 1977).

53. Warrensburg School District v. Johnson County School District, 624 S.W.2d 170 (Mo. 1981).

54. *Idem.*

55. Jackson v. Wald Independent School Dist., 629 S.W.2d 201 (Tex. 1982); Spriggs v. Altheimer Arkansas School District, 384 F.2d 254, 259 (8th Cir. 1967); Union Free H.S. Dist. v. Joint School Dist., 117 N.W.2d 273 (Wisc. 1962).

in agreement.[56] Where the question is not clearly addressed by state law, courts must decide whether the summer school session is to be viewed as part of the state system of free education. Two state courts have concluded that they are not and permitted summer sessions to be conducted on a tuition-paying basis.[57]

The courts are divided on the validity of fees for nonrequired courses. Under a strict reading of "free" education, the courts of Missouri appear to have barred any course fee, but course fees were allowed for elective subjects in New Mexico.[58] A middle ground has been followed in other states where free public education was construed to forbid fees for any courses (whether required or elective) if the courses either qualified for credit toward graduation, were approved by the state board of education, or were reasonably related to a recognized academic and educational goal of the school.[59] The Montana test of *reasonable relationship to recognized educational goals* has the virtue of flexibility. It empowers school districts to define their own educational goals and to decide what courses qualify for fee charges; but it also invites dispute as to what is a recognized goal or is "reasonably related" to that goal. In the few states where the right to public education is fixed by statute and not by the state constitution, the legislature can authorize the imposition of fees in the state schools.[60]

b. Textbooks and School Supplies. Although school facilities and faculty must be provided without charge, the authorities are divided on the question whether students may be charged for particular instructional materials. The opinion in *Cardiff v. Bismark P.S. District* (at the end of this chapter) reviews the divergent cases from 12 states.[61] Idaho, Michigan, and Montana cases apply the same legal test to textbooks and school supplies (e.g., workbooks, stationery, pens, pencils, and maps) to determine what charges are permissible and consistent with free public education. If those materials are necessary elements of public school activity or reasonably related to the general educational goals of the school, they must be furnished without fee. Conversely, charges may be made for materials in areas that are not considered essential elements of schooling.[62] While these authorities do not specify which particular items go into these categories, they do indicate activities that fall outside the normal academic program, such as extracurricular activities. The Idaho court indicated that fees could be lawfully charged, but a Montana court ruled the opposite. Thus even where courts adopt similar

---

56. *E.g.*, California Teachers Assn. v. Bd. of Education, 167 Cal. Rptr. 429 (1980) (summer session tuition held impermissible).

57. Washington by and through Washington v. Salisbury, 306 S.E.2d 600 (1983); Crim v. McWhorter, 252 S.E.2d 421 (Ga. 1979).

58. Concerned Parents v. Caruthersville Sch. D., 548 S.W.2d 554 (Mo. 1977); Norton v. Bd. of Education, 553 P.2d 1277 (N.M. 1976).

59. Grange v. Cascade Sch. District, fn. 48 (involving music, driver education and summer school courses); Bd. of Education v. Sinclair, fn. 48 (dictum re courses for credit); Vandevender v. Cassell, fn. 48 (re state approved curriculum courses).

60. *See* O'Leary v. Wisecup, 364 A.2d 770, 773 (Pa. 1976); Holler v. Rock Hill Sch. District, 38 S.E.220 (So. Car. 1901).

61. *See also* Union Free Sch. District v. Jackson, 403 N.Y.S.2d 621 (1978) (disallowing charges for instructional supplies).

62. Paulson v. Minidoka Co. Sch. District, 463 P.2d 935 (Idaho 1970); Grange case, fn. 48; Bond v. Ann Arbor Sch. District, 178 N.W.2d 484 (Mich. 1970).

legal tests they may differ on specific applications. Many other states decline to adopt a single test for all students. They are stricter with respect to needy students whose parents cannot pay normal school fees for materials that are needed to complete public education.[63]

A growing majority of state courts have upheld reasonable school fees (tied to actual cost) for textbooks and school supplies.[64] An Arizona court recently held that the state law mandated free textbooks only for elementary school students but not for high school students.[65] As to supplies unrelated to general academic courses such as musical instruments and gym supplies (swim suits, towels) the few decided cases are in conflict.[66] Courts also differentiate between fees for supplies and fees for nonconsumable equipment, such as microfilm readers and electronic display or communications devices, in holding the equipment to be part of the required facilities that public schools must furnish free of charge.[67]

State legislatures may always specify that particular items may or may not be supplied free of charge, hence the law of each state must be consulted. For example, a new Illinois statute differentiated between textbooks and other supplies and disallowed any right to free maps, magazines, and workbooks.[68] The legality of various school fees has not been expressly passed upon in many states. Fee questions are thus often left to administrative interpretation and the advice of legal counsel.

School requirements of student deposits to ensure proper handling and return of reusable books and supplies are not the same as fees. Cases involving deposits are rare, but the view seems sound that a school can reasonably encourage preservation of reusable school books by holding financially able students accountable for their damage.[69]

c. Special Activity Fees. Special activity fees present the same two-part problem affecting other fees: Are they consistent with the state constitutional requirement of free public education; and if so, were they authorized by state statutes? Most of the case law on activity or incidental fees appeared decades ago and may not be persuasive in contemporary education. It would seem that if special activities fees are imposed as a condition of general admission to the school, they would be vulnerable as a disguised form of registration fee.[70] The cases furnish no clear answer for all states. If fees only affect admission to student activities that are not required or for credit, they would more likely survive challenge.

---

63. *See* Marshall v. Sch. District RE #3, 553 P.2d 784 (Colo. 1976); Vandevender v. Cassell, fn. 48; Hamer v. Bd. of Education, 292 N.E.2d 569 (Ill. 1973); Chandler v. So. Bend Comm. Sch. Corp., fn.48. Some courts may rest the distinction on the constitutional ground of equal protection, viz., Bd. of Education of Freeport v. Nyquist, 399 N.Y.S.2d 844 (1977); *but see* Carpio v. Tucson H.S. District, 524 P.2d 948 (Ariz. 1976).

64. Marshall v. Sch. District, *supra*; Chandler v. So. Bend Comm. Sch. Corp., *supra*; Bd. of Education v. Sinclair, fn. 48; Hamer v. Bd. of Education, *supra*.

65. Carpio v. Tucson H.S. District, fn. 63.

66. *Compare* Bd. of Education v. Sinclair, fn. 48 (upholding charges for swim suits and musical instruments), *with* Grange v. Cascade County Sch. District, fn. 48 (holding such charges impermissible).

67. *See* Bd. of Education v. Sinclair, *supra*.

68. Beck v. Bd. of Education, 344 N.E.2d 440 (Ill. 1976).

69. *See* Segar v. Bd. of Education, 148 N.E. 289 (Ill. 1925).

70. *See* Morris v. Vandiver, 145 So. 228 (Miss. 1933).

The divergent state authorities on activities fees were recently reviewed by the California Supreme Court in *Hartzell v. Connell*, which is reported at p. 514, *infra;* and which should be read as part of this text. As the court there noted, individual states have pursued one of several possible positions under their respective constitutions and statutes; namely, that all activity fee charges are unlawful, that uniform general activities fees not tied to student participation or need are unlawful, or that the validity of any particular activity fee would depend upon several factors, such as its relation to course credits and to the school's educational program. Obviously, a particular state court decision will turn upon its construction of the intent of its own constitution and statute.[71] The judicial power to refine fee classifications is illustrated by an Idaho decision that indicated that a school could not charge a fee for an original student transcript but could do so for additional transcripts.[72]

d. Special Events. Admission fees for special events to which the public is invited are not seriously questioned today.[73] Similarly, the legal authority of school boards to allow outside use of school facilities when not required for school purposes at reasonable charges or rentals is equally settled. (See Chapter 3.)

e. Federal and Private Grants. No modern case has been found that denies general school district authority to accept grants for public education purposes from the federal government or from private sources. Such authority may be withdrawn by the parent state, but it is commonly granted by state school codes.[74] The power of school districts to accept or ignore the conditions and restrictions on the use of such grants raises more serious issues of expenditure control, and these are reviewed in the following section.

C. Expenditure Controls

1. Centrally Administered Funds

The main substantive checks on school spending rest on the rule that school district funds are held in trust to be used only for purposes that are authorized by law.[75]

While school boards may act upon implied powers and purposes to justify expenditures, courts will not imply powers that contradict the expressed aims and

71. *Compare, e.g.*, Paulson v. Minidoka County School District, 463 P.2d 935 (Idaho 1970) (voiding uniform activity fees irrespective of student participation in school activities) *with* Sneed v. Greensboro City Board of Education, 264 S.E.2d 106 (N.C. 1980) (upholding legality of uniform activity fees). *See also* Michigan Attorney General Op. No. 5974 (9-3-81) interpreting state law to deny school board authority to charge interscholastic athletic fees.

72. *See* the dictum in the Paulson case, *supra*, 463 P.2d 935 at 939.

73. *Cf.* Board of Education v. Calvert, 321 S.W.2d 413 (Ky. 1959); Petition Auditors of Hatfield Twp. Sch. District, 54 A.2d 833 (Pa. 1947).

74. Vestal v. Pickering, 267 P. 821 (Ore. 1928).

75. *E.g.*, Ingraham v. Boone, 458 N.Y.S.2d 671 (1983); Missoula H.S. Legal Defense Assn. v. Supt. of Public Instruction, 637 P.2d 1188 (Mont. 1981); Barth v. Board of Education, 322 N.W.2d 694 (Wis. 1982) (sinking fund); Mahrenholtz v. County Board of School Trustees, 466 N.E.2d 322 (Ill. 1984) (restricted private grant). See also discussion of individual school funds. p. 505, *infra*.

obligations of statutes or common law. Thus, a school board cannot spend special education subsidies for psychological therapy where those subsidies were restricted by law to other purposes.[76] Where there is a factual disagreement as to whether a particular use falls within the purposes of earmarked funds, the courts are inclined to defer to the judgment of the board. For example, a school board announced that the purpose of a bond proposal was raising money to construct elementary and high schools. After electoral approval of the bonds the board found that unanticipated building costs made the bond proceeds only sufficient to build a high school. The court rejected a suit to prorate the bonds between elementary and high school construction. It reasoned that the construction of only a high school was within the announced general purpose of school construction and that the board's discretion as to efficient use of funds should not be overturned by a strict construction of the bonds' purposes.[77]

While courts tend to respect school board discretion as to what are public purposes for which school funds may be expended, they will not permit expenditures for improper purposes. For example, a school board may not lawfully use school funds for partisan political purposes. Such a case arose where a referendum proposal would, if approved, amend the Colorado constitution to limit public spending. The school board opposed the proposal as harmful to public education and authorized the use of school funds and facilities to persuade voters to defeat the amendment. A federal court held that the board lacked authority under state law to use school funds for that purpose and that even if state law permitted such use it would be unconstitutional. The court reasoned that the right of citizens freely to alter their form of government was constitutionally protected by the First Amendment against undue influence or interference by government officials. It added that the federal guarantee to each state of a republican form of government (Article IV, § 4, U.S. Constitution) might also require a federal court injunction against any attempt by government agencies to so influence the electoral process.[78]

The foregoing situation of partisan involvement by electioneering or lobbying with government assets is to be distinguished, however, from activity designed merely to provide civic information regarding important public matters or to encourage citizens to participate in the processes of government, such as encouraging citizens to register and vote in public elections. It is not always easy to determine whether or when a public information and good citizenship campaign becomes a political propaganda campaign to serve partisan purposes. Such difficult judgments must ultimately rest with a judge or a jury and with the particular background circumstances of individual cases.[79]

The purpose limitations imposed by federal grants are more strictly applied. In one

---

76. Doe v. Colburg, 555 P.2d 753 (Mont. 1976).

77. Ricker v. Board of Education, 396 P.2d 416 (Utah 1964). *Cf.* Louisiana Association of Education v. St. Tammany Parish Sch. Board, 430 So.2d 1144 (La. 1983) (school board interpretation of ordinance as not allocating specific portion of tax receipts for teacher salaries—upheld). *See also* Richland Parish Bus Drivers Assn. v. Richland Parish School Board, 420 So.2d 696 (La. 1982) (tax receipts that were earmarked for employees' salaries held subject to school board discretion to allocate them, 80% to certified personnel and 20% to noncertified employees).

78. Mountain States Legal Foundation v. Denver Sch. District, 459 F. Supp. 357 (D. Colo, 1978). *See also* Campbell v. St. School District, 704 F.2d 501 (10th Cir. 1983). *but see* Phillips v. Maurer, 486 N.Y.S.2d 804 (1985) (upholding board expenditure to advertise in support of school budget and bond election).

79. *See, e.g.*, Mitchell v. No.Car. Ind. Dev. Financing Authority, 159 S.E.2d 745, 750 (N.Car. 1968)

case the federal statute required federal grants to be used for both public and parochial schools, and the Missouri constitution was construed to prohibit state officers to so use the grant. The Supreme Court held that, although Congress could not force a state to act contrary to its charter, neither could that state violate the federal statute.[80] In such conflict of law situations, the only safe legal course would be for the state to decline the federal funds. Where federal law required federal grants to be used only for "supplementary" purposes and required states to independently fund existing state programs, to avoid substitution of federal funds for state expenditures, the federal restriction was enforced by injunction where the state sought to reduce its own fiscal commitment by substitution of the federal funds.[81]

2. Controls on the Making of Public Contracts

By definition, a contract is not any agreement or promise, but only one that is *legally enforceable.* Common law imposed a number of requirements for private contracts that also apply to public contracts: that there be competent parties, legality of subject matter, proper offers that are properly accepted with a sufficient' "consideration" (bargained-for exchange between the parties), and in certain circumstances, a writing to prove the agreement. The presence of these technical requirements will be assumed in the following discussion of special statutory requirements of legally effective public contracts, including school district contracts. Since citizens as well as school officials have legal standing to bring suit to block or recover expenditures under unlawful contracts, and since ignorance of the law is no defense or excuse for statutory violations, the law of public contracts is a substantial deterrent to contract abuse by school officials and parties contracting with them.

Proper school board authorization of contracts is almost universally made a prerequisite of an enforceable contract obligation. Where the board never approved the contract or attempted to do so in an unauthorized manner (such as in executive session), attempted to authorize an agreement beyond its delegated power (e.g., letting out work that must be done in-house), or failed to reduce an oral agreement to writing, as required by statute, the resulting agreements have been held to be unlawful and unenforceable.[82]

As indicated in Chapter 2, the lack of proper procedure of board approval may be cured retroactively by postagreement ratification by the board if, but only if, the

80. *Compare* Wheeler v. Barrera, 417 U.S. 402 (1974); *with* Mallory v. Barrera, 544 S.W.2d 556 (Mo. 1976).

81. Shepheard v. Godwin, 280 F. Supp. 869 (E.D.Va. 1968) (impact aid); semble, Hergenreter v. Hayden, 295 F. Supp. 251 (D. Kan. 1968).

82. State ex. rel. School Dist. of Springfield v. Wickliffe, 650 S.W.2d 623 (Mo. 1983) (*ultra vires* contract because school board lacked authority over contract subject matter); Community Projects for Students, Inc. v. Wilder, 299 S.E.2d 434 (N.Car. 1982); Responsive Env. Corp. v. Pulaksi Co. Spe. Sch. District, 366 F.Supp. 241 (E.D. Ark. 1973); Grippo v. Dunmore Sch. Bd., 365 A.2d 678 (Pa. 1976); Big Sandy Sch. District v. Carroll, 433 P.2d 325 (Colo. 1967) (improper delegation of authority to superintendent); Achenbach v. Sch. District, 491 P.2d 57 (Colo. 1971) (*ultra vires* contract); California School Employees Asso. v. Willits Un. Sch. District, 52 Cal. Rptr. 765 (1966) (unlawful contracting out of work required to be done by employees); Santa Monica Sch. District v. Persh, 85 Cal. Rptr. 463 (1970) (contract unlawfully authorized by executive session); Panther Oil and Grease Mfg. Co. v. Blount Co. Bd. of Education, 134 So.2d 220 (Ala. 1961) (contract not authorized by school board).

agreement was within the board's authority and is ratified by proper board action with full notice of all relevant facts and without fraud or unfairness to other parties.[83] Thus where a contract for steel used in a school building was let without compliance with the bidding statutes, the supplier was denied contract recovery on the ground that the school board lacked authority to ratify a nonbid contract of that order.[84]

Even where a board duly approves an agreement authorized by law, courts retain the power to deny enforcement if they find the agreement to be contrary to public policy.[85] The common law doctrine that contracts against public policy are void ensures continuing judicial oversight and gives courts broad leeway to determine what transactions are unworthy of enforcement in ever-changing circumstances. Agreements of unreasonable duration, though made in good faith, are generally denied legal effect because their enforcement would thwart the managerial powers of future school boards and invite political abuses by incumbent or lame-duck school boards.[86] Not all long-term contracts are condemned as unreasonable, however, since practical necessity may well render such a contract reasonable (e.g., a multiyear contract for architectural services in connection with construction projects).[87]

At common law and under the statutes of most states, a person may not make a public contract that poses a conflict between his or her public obligations and personal interests. Unfortunately this broad principle has not been diligently applied or clarified either by legislatures or by courts. State courts have split on the proper tests of a legal conflict of interests.[88] Many hold that only a showing of direct and pecuniary personal interest of a public official in a public contract amounts to unlawful conflict. Others adopt a strict view that any personal interest, however indirect, renders the contract unlawful. Still other courts look to the facts of each case to determine whether the official's personal interest in a public contract is sufficiently immediate or too remote to taint that agreement. These case variations are due in part to considerable differences among the statutes of sister states.[89] Courts are also in disarray on whether and when a contract tainted by conflict of interest is totally void or merely voidable under appropriate circumstances. A clear example of a direct pecuniary conflict of interest that invalidates a district contract is provided by a Kentucky case. The school board member was the principal stockholder of a soft drink company that sold soft drinks through vending machines in the public schools.[90]

An indirect pecuniary interest may invalidate a school district contract,[91] but an indirect interest was considered too remote where a board member was part owner of a

---

83. Kennedy v. Ringgold Sch. District, 309 A.2d 269 (Pa. 1973).

84. St. Paul Foundry Co. v. Burnstad Sch. District, 269 N.W. 738 (N.D. 1963).

85. Coalition to Preserve Education v. School District, 649 S.W.2d 533 (Mo. 1983) (contract requiring opening of new school).

86. Thomas v. Bd. of Education, 215 A.2d 35 (N.J. 1965); Sch. Dist. v. Pennington, 165 N.W. 209 (Iowa 1917); *Cf.* Reinken v. Keller, 280 N.Y.S.2d 253 (1967); Bd. of Education of Pendleton Co. v. Gulick, 398 S.W.2d 483 (Ky. 1966).

87. *See Bd.* of Education v. Finne, Lyman and Finne, 210 A.2d 794 (N.J. 1965).

88. EISENBERG, *Conflict of Interests Situations and Remedies,* 13 RUTGERS L. REV. 666 (1959).

89. *Compare* Stroud v. Pulaski Co. Public Sch. District, 424 S.W.2d 141 (Ark. 1968); *with* People v. Darby, 250 P.2d 743 (Cal. 1952).

90. Commonwealth v. Collins, 379 S.W.2d 436 (Ky. 1964).

91. Thompson v. Sch. District, 233 N.W. 439 (Mich. 1930).

trucking company that received a subcontract from the company that received the school district contract.[92] A looser standard of sufficient pecuniary conflict is whether the interest of the official in the business and welfare of the contracting party would naturally tend to affect the official's judgment on the merits of the contract.[93] School district contracts with a spouse of a board member have been upheld and disapproved for conflict of interest by different courts.[94] Nepotism cases reveal similar disparities in the case law.[95]

3. Competitive Bidding

The requirement of public competitive bidding by outside independent contractors doing business with school districts did not exist at common law, but has been created by statutes in most states. Such legislation seeks to prevent fraud, collusion, favoritism, and improvidence in contract administration and to ensure that public schools and agencies receive the best products and services at the lowest available price. Bid statutes vary in their particulars, but they generally apply only to contracts above a stated dollar amount, with exemption for certain kinds of contract procurement. Further, they require awards only to the lowest "responsible" bidder. The foregoing requirements and exemptions necessarily vest considerable discretion in school boards as to: (1) what bid is actually lowest in net cost, (2) who is a "qualified" or "responsible" bidder, and (3) what special needs, services, or materials are so unique or so urgently needed, as to justify negotiated, nonbid procurement regardless of contract amount. The application of these statutes thus requires an assessment of whether a school board exercised its discretion reasonably in particular circumstances.

4. Unlawful Devices to Eliminate Bidding

To ensure fair and open competition in biddable contracts, certain practices are required or forbidden by law. Advertisements for bids must give sufficient facts to enable bidders to submit intelligent bids, to avoid giving any bidder an advantage from undisclosed facts, and to avoid disqualification for not complying with the board's intended requirements. "[A]n invitation to bid must be as definite, precise and full as practicable in view of the character of the work, the quality and quantity of the materials to be furnished. . . . The specifications must furnish the same information to all prospective bidders, . . . "[96] Nor may a school board evade bid statutes by artificially splitting work or materials into small contracts solely to drop the contract price below the dollar requirement for bidding. In many instances courts lack clear guidelines to determine whether a particular job was split for the unlawful purpose of evading competitive bidding or for purposes of public convenience and economy. The *Secrist* case (reproduced at the end of this chapter)

---

92. *See* Stroud v. Pulaski Co. Public Sch. District, fn. 89; State ex rel Corrigan v. Hensel, 206 N.E.2d 563 (Ohio 1965) (board member operation of teacher employment agency).

93. Brown v. Kirk, 342 N.E.2d 137 (Ill. 1975).

94. See the nepotism cases at p. 187, et seq.

95. *Compare* Githins v. Butler Co., 165 S.W.2d 650 (Mo. 1942); *with* Nucklos v. Lyle, 70 P.401 (Idaho 1902).

96. *See* J. Petrozello Co. v. Chatham Twp., 182 A.2d 572, 575 (N.J. 1962).

explains this problem. Courts tend to accept board discretion as to when and how much work may be ordered by contract. The award of separate contracts for distinct items to the same supplier was upheld in Kentucky, even though the ordered items, if combined in one contract, would have a dollar amount that required competitive bidding.[97] Similarly, where a school project was split to permit cost-saving installation by the school board's own employees, while procuring other materials and services by outside contract, the action was upheld as a reasonable exercise of discretion.[98] But where the circumstances indicated a deliberate intent to avoid bid statutes by splitting a continuous service into small successive contracts, the court condemned the action as unlawful.[99]

Broad discretion is also permitted to school authorities when inviting "alternative" bids—a series of separate bid proposals, each of which may serve the same general end. So long as the contract is awarded to the lowest bid within the same alternative bid package it may be upheld, even though bids in other alternative packages might have been lower.[100]

The practice of excluding bidders by rigging the specifications to eliminate competing bidders is disapproved by courts as a violation of bid statutes. Specifications that are drawn to match the product or services exclusively of one or a few suppliers, without apparent justification, may be invalidated as unlawful evasion of bid statutes.[101] Cases do arise where bid-confining specifications are demonstrably justified to meet a special need. In such cases, courts have upheld the specifications. (See the later discussion on exempt products and services.)

Where specification restrictions are directed not to subject matter, but to bidder practices, the authorities are mixed. For example, the requirement that all bidders pay minimum wages conflicts with the policy of obtaining public work at lowest possible cost. The courts are divided on how to resolve such policy conflicts.[102] An Alabama court held the minimum wage provision in a public contract to be a violation of the state bidding law, but where a Maryland statute required bidders to pay prevailing wage rates, the application of that statute was upheld.[103] To the extent that federal funds are used in school district contracts, the federal law and regulations concerning minimum wages cannot be ignored since federal law cannot be superseded by state law.

Other performance standards of bidders, such as the requirement of union labor, have been disapproved as undermining competitive bidding in some states, but this rule

---

97. Board of Education v. Hall, 353 S.W.2d 194 (Ky. 1962). See Generally Annotation: Public Contracts—Competitive Bidding, 33 A.L.R.3d 397 (1970).

98. Utah Plumbing and Heating Contractors Association v. Bd. of Education, 429 P.2d 49 (Utah 1967); National Electrical Contractors Association v. Seattle Sch. District, 400 P.2d 778 (Wash. 1965).

99. *See* Bd. of Education v. Hoek, 183 A.2d 633, 647 (N.J. 1962); In re Audit of School District of Scranton, 47 A.2d 288 (Pa. 1946).

100. *Cf.* Paul Goodman, Inc. v. Burns, 283 A.2d 673 (Rhode Island 1971) (award of bid covering higher bracket automobile models sustained).

101. *See* Resco Equipment and Supply Corporation v. City Council of Watertown, 313 N.Y.S.2d 74 (1970); Gamewell Co. v. City of Phoenix, 216 F.2d 928 (9th Cir. 1954); Gerzof v. Sweeney, 239 N.E.2d 521 (N.Y. 1968).

102. See the opinion and authorities reviewed in Parish Council of East Baton Rouge v. Louisiana Highway, etc. Association General Contractors, Inc., 131 So.2d 272 (La. App. 1961).

103. Wallace v. Bd. of Education, 197 So.2d 428 (Ala. 1967); Demory Bros., Inc.,v. Bd. of Public Works, 329 A.2d 674 (Md. 1974).

is not universally followed.[104] It would appear, however, that bid regulations on employment discrimination are not subject to serious challenge as being inconsistent with bidding statutes.[105]

5. Contract Amendments

Changes in previously awarded contracts raise the question of whether rebidding is required. The answer depends upon the nature and scope of the contract changes: "We recognize that a generally accepted rule is that where a statute requires that a contract . . . be let to the lowest responsible bidder, municipal corporations . . . cannot evade the law by making a substantial change in the contract after it had been awarded pursuant to the law. If the deviations . . . vary so substantially from the original plan as to constitute a new undertaking, the contract could be let only by competitive bidding. However, in order to render the contract void because of the changes or deviations, the same must be substantial."[106] The contingent operation of the foregoing principle is seen in the following examples. An amendment was not resubmitted to bidding although it eliminated large items from a $2 million construction contract with a resulting reduction of about 15% in the original price. Even though the amendment was necessitated by a shortage of funds, it was held impermissible.[107] The cases also indicate that courts will not hold school districts to impractical burdens by requiring resubmission of work in the course of projects that cannot readily be divided between different contractors. For this reason, awarded contracts that allow for alteration and addition of work will be upheld as consistent with bid policy if administered reasonably and in good faith.

6. Exempt Products and Services

Even in the absence of express legislative exemption, courts exclude many specialty service and material contracts from the operation of bidding statutes, but the discretion permitted to public officials to opt for negotiated contracts is limited,[108] Exemptions rest upon the fact that some materials and services are not susceptible to objective comparison or are not readily obtained from reliable, competing sources. The public interest would be defeated by insistence upon competitive bidding in such cases. Examples of permissible sole-source procurement include expert professional services, such as real estate appraisals, certain architectural or engineering services, experimental procurement (especially where frontier technology is involved), and the purchases of products of proven reliability or special interchangeability with existing inventory.[109] The foregoing exemptions are

---

104. *Performance standards disapproved:* Upchurch v. Adelsberger, 332 S.W.2d 242 (Ark. 1960); Van Campen v. Building and Construction Trades Council, 195 A.2d 134 (Pa. 1963). *Performance standards approved:* Pallas v. Johnson, 68 P.2d 559 (Colo. 1937).

105. Weiner v. Cuyahoga Community College District, 249 N.E.2d 907 (Ohio 1969).

106. *See* City of Crockett v. Murdock, 440 S.W.2d 864, 867 (Tex. 1969).

107. Hanna v. Bd. of Education, 87 A.2d 846 (Md. 1952); *but see* Seim v. Ind. District of Monroe, 17 N.W.2d 342 (S. Dak. 1945).

108. See the case authorities in Annotation: *Public Contracts—Personal Service,* 15 A.L.R.3d 733 (1967).

109. See the prior footnote; Cobb v. Pasadena City Bd. of Ed., 285 P.2d 41 (Cal. 1955); Parker v. Panama City, 151 So.2d 469 (Fla. 1963); Marino v. Town of Ramapo, 326 N.Y.S.2d 162 (1971); Hylton v. Mayor and

not absolute, however, because much depends upon the showing of public need or convenience to justify exemption in each case.

7. Bidder Qualification

Bid statutes also permit public authorities to disqualify any bids that do not comply with the preconditions and specifications of bid invitations and to eliminate even low bidders who are not "qualified" or "responsible."[110] Courts recognize the discretionary authority of public officials to make qualification decisions, but they overturn capricious or fraudulent disqualification decisions. Unfortunately, the criteria for administrative discretion in these cases is seldom stipulated in statute law.

Bids failing to meet *material* conditions of bid invitations may be disqualified, but courts do not consider insubstantial variations, which give no advantage or benefit to any bidders, to be a ground for disqualification.[111]

The cases on the standards for a "responsible" bidder suggest inconsistent interpretation of bid statutes. Some courts require award to the lowest monetary bidder unless the bidder is found not to be responsible, without reference to the *relative superiority* of higher bidders. Other courts permit relative superiority to be considered as a ground to disqualify the low monetary bidder as not being the lowest "responsible" bidder. In such courts, a low bidder of marginal performance capability may be passed over to favor a higher bidder of much stronger performance capability.[112] Among the variables recognized by some courts as pertinent to the question of "responsibility" are moral integrity (disqualification of bidders who are indicted, convicted, or previously barred for violating antibribery regulations) and bidder unreliability in terms of financial soundness, business resources or skill, and past performance of public contracts.[113]

Thus an award of a gasoline supply contract by a Mississippi school district to the second lowest bidder because the low bidder lacked adequate storage capacity to ensure reliable deliveries was upheld, as was the award of a Connecticut construction contract to a second-low bidder who could ensure earlier completion of the project than the low bidder.[114]

A compromise rule on bidder responsibility and qualification was expressed in a lead case as follows: "Where more than one bid is received from a responsible bidder, . . . the council has no discretion but to accept the low bid. . . . Where the thing

---

City Council of Baltimore, 300 A.2d 656 (Md. 1972); Rewco, Inc., v. City of Cleveland, 183 N.E.2d 646 (Ohio 1961); Hodge and Hammond, Inc., v. Burns, 202 N.Y.S.2d 133 (1960).

110. Capital City Office Machines, Metropolitan Bd. of Education, 632 S.W.2d 142 (Tenn. 1982).

111. Failing to meet material conditions: Parks & Sons v. City of Pocatello, 419 P.2d 683 (Idaho 1966); Claus v. Babiarz, 185 A.2d 283 (Del. 1962). *Insubstantial variations:* Duffy v. Village of Princeton, 60 N.W.2d 27 (Minn. 1953); Gil-Bern Construction Corp. v. City of Brockton, 233 N.E.2d 197 (Mass. 1968).

112. See Commercial Cleaning Corporation v. Sullivan, 222 A.2d 4 (N.J. 1966); Jerry's Rides, Inc. v. City Council of Baltimore, 172 A.2d 487 (Md. 1961).

113. *Barred for bribery: See* Trap Rock Industries, Inc., v. Kohl, 284 A.2d 161 (N.J. 1971); Caristo Construction Corp. v. Rubin, 180 N.E.2d 794 (N.Y. 1962); Kayfield Construction Corporation v. Morris, 225 N.Y.S.2d 507 (1962). *Bidder Unreliable:* J. N. Futia Co. v. Office of General Services, 332 N.Y.S.2d 261 (1972); Raymond v. Fresno City Un. Sch. Dist., 267 P.2d 69 (Cal. 1954). *See also* fn. 110, *supra.*

114. Walley v. Bd. of Trustees of Richton Mun. Sep. Sch. District, 241 So. 2d 644 (Miss. 1970); Vellaco v. City of Derby, 232 A.2d 335 (Conn. 1966).

sought to be purchased . . . is not entirely subject to exact specification . . . the officer should consider the quality and utility of the thing offered. . . . In determining . . . who is the lowest bidder, the quality . . . as well as the price therefore is to be taken into consideration. . . . "[115]

8. Withdrawal of Bids

Under traditional contract law, a bid is treated as an offer that may be revoked at any time prior to acceptance. Under public contract law, the rule may be changed by statute, school board regulations, and terms of the invitation to bid. In many jurisdictions, once a public bid is submitted it creates option rights in the district and cannot be withdrawn.[116] Nevertheless, relief from the normal rules of contract law may be granted, as a matter of equity law, where strict enforcement of the bid would produce gross hardship and injustice. The power of equity to prevent unconscionable bargains is in no way lessened by the fact that a statute or invitation to bid expressly prohibits withdrawal of submitted bids.[117] Although the case law of sister states is not uniform, the principal considerations that affect the enforcement or excusal of submitted bids are discussed in the *Boise Jr. College District* case at the end of this chapter.[118]

The equitable grounds for permitting withdrawal of an unaccepted bid are essentially the same, whether the mistake is uncovered before or after the bids are open; but it is easier to allow withdrawal before bid openings since the dangers of fraud are not as great at that time.

The grounds for relieving a bidder have been expressed differently by different courts. As a matter of contract theory, one may argue that no one has the right to snap up an offer which contains such a major error that it could not have reasonably been intended to be made in those terms. As a matter of equity law, such unconscionable bargains will not be favored. Thus, even where the mistake is discovered after the bids are opened for official consideration, equitable relief has been granted if (1) the mistake is so substantial that it would be unconscionable to enforce the contract; (2) the mistake relates to a material feature of the contract (price, quantity, or quality of materials); (3) the mistake was "excusable" (not due to fraud or culpable negligence); and (4) the school district can be restored to its prior status and will not suffer irreparable injury by relieving the bidder from the mistaken bid.[119] The same principles have been applied to allow rescission of a contract where the bid mistake was discovered shortly after the bid was accepted.[120] Some courts have, however, refused to subordinate the strict protection of

---

115. Otter Tail Power Co. v. Village of Elbow Lake, 49 N.W.2d 197, 201 (Minn. 1951).

116. *See* Cataldo Const. Co. v. County of Essex, 265 A.2d 842 (N.J. 1970); *cf.* Hotel China & Glass Co. v. Bd. of Pub. Instruction, 130 So.2d 78 (Fla. 1961).

117. Balaban-Gordon Co. v. Brighton Sewer Dist., 342 N.Y.S.2d 435 (1973).

118. Boise Jr. College District v. Mattef's Construction Co., at end of this chapter; Fraser Public School District v. Kolon, 193 N.W.2d 64 (Mich. 1971). See also cases collected in Annotation: Bid for *Public Contract—Mistake,* 52 A.L.R.2d 792 (1957).

119. James T. Taylor & Son, Inc. v. Arlington Ind. Sch. District, 335 S.W.2d 371 (Tex. 1960); Elsinore Un. Elementary Sch. Dist. v. Kastorff, 353 P.2d 713 (Cal. 1960). *But see* Bd. of Education v. Sever-Williams Co., 258 N.E.2d 605 (Ohio 1970).

120. Union Free Sch. District v. Gumbs, 191 N.Y.S.2d 183 (1958); Sch. District of Scottsbluff v. Olson

bid statutes to considerations of fairness and have required strict compliance with a submitted bid, notwithstanding timely disclosure of serious errors.[121]

9. Right to Reject Bids

Once a school board formally accepts a valid low bid, it cannot thereafter seek other bids for the same work.[122] Since invitations to bid are generally considered to be requests for offers, the bid submission constitutes an offer and not an acceptance of a school board proposal. An exception to this rule appears under a Washington statute that was construed to treat a bid invitation as an offer so that the submitted low bid effected a binding acceptance.[123] Under that law the bidder was entitled to recover damages for an unjustified refusal by the school district to allow it to perform the work.

The right to reject all bids often exists by statute, charter law, or by the terms of the invitation to bid in many states. In those situations a school board may reject all bids, however low or qualified, so long it does so in good faith.[124] However, where a board rejects a qualified low bid in bad faith or without reasonable basis, courts have overturned the rejection as subverting the purposes of mandatory competitive bidding.[125] Even in the absence of an express reservation of the right to reject all bids, a few courts have recognized such a right, subject only to exercising it reasonably and in good faith.[126]

Obviously, a board is under no obligation to consider any bid that fails to comply with the requirements and terms of its invitation to bid. Low-bid rejections have been upheld for bidder's (1) failure to attach the financial statement called for in the invitation; (2) failure to include the statement of warranty required by the invitation; (3) improperly endorsed certified check,; and (4) omission of signature on the bid.[127]

Courts generally hold that bid statutes are intended to protect the public and not to create any rights for bidders in the absence of express provisions to that effect. Hence, a disappointed low bidder may not sue for damages from a wrongful denial of a contract award.[128] The courts are not in agreement, however, on whether a bidder has a right to a hearing before being disqualified from consideration.[129] Nor is there unanimous

---

Constr. Co., 45 N.W.2d 164 (Neb. 1950).

121. *See* Bd. Of Education v. Sever-Williams Co., 258 N.E.2d 605 (1970); A.J. Colella Inc. v. Allegheny County, 137 A.2d 265 (Pa. 1958).

122. Foti v. Orleans Parish Sch. Bd., 358 So.2d 353 (La. 1978).

123. Butler v. Federal Way School District, 562 P.2d 271 (Wash. 1977).

124. LaMar Construction Corp. v. Holt County, R-II School District, 542 S.W.2d 568 (Mo. 1976), Joseph Rugo, Inc. v. Henson, 171 A.2d 409 (Conn. 1961).

125. *Cf.* American Asphalt Distributors, Inc. v. County of Otsego, 334 N.Y.S.2d 465 (1972).

126. *Cf.* Electronics Unlimited, Inc. v. Burnsville, 182 N.W.2d 679 (Minn. 1971).

127. **(1)** Albert F. Ruehl Co. v. Bd. of Trustees of Schools, 203 A2d 410 (N.J. 1964); **(2)** New Mexico Bus Sales v. Michael, 360 P.2d 639 (N.M. 1961); **(3)** Menke v. Bd. of Education, 211 N.W.2d 601 (Iowa 1973); **(4)** A.A.B. Elec. Inc. v. Stevenson Pub. Sch. District, 491 P.2d 684 (Wash. 1971).

128. R. S. Noonan Inc. v. Sch. District, 162 A.2d 623 (Pa. 1968).

129. *Compare* Willett Motor Coach Co. v. Bd. of Educ., 431 N.E.2d 1190 (Ill. 1981); M. A. Stephen Constr. Co. v. Borough of Rumson, 288 A.2d 873 (N.J. 1972); Seacoast Constr. Corp. v. Lockport Urban Renewal Agency, 339 N.Y.S.2d 188 (1972); *with* Arglo Painting Corp. v. Bd. of Education, 263 N.Y.S.2d 124 (1965).

agreement that a disgruntled bidder may sue to overturn an illegal contract award to another bidder, in the interest of preserving the public policy of the bid statutes, but that view is gaining favor.[130]

Constitutional claims to due process hearings by dissatisfied bidders may arise in the special situation where the bid disqualification is based primarily on an unconstitutional motive—to punish the bidder for exercising a Fifth Amendment right to remain silent in government investigations under a plea of self-incrimination.[131] In the absence of such special infringements, however, there is no general constitutional interest in bidding on public contracts that necessitates due process hearings.[132]

The right to predisqualification hearing may be conferred by statutes, and at least one court has found that denial of a hearing on bidder responsibility could amount to an arbitrary and capricious abuse of administrative discretion in certain circumstances.[133]

10. Remedies Following Award of Improperly Bid Contracts

Where the parties have not irrevocably altered their precontract position before a violation is discovered or where all parties can be restored to their previous position without loss, the courts readily declare the agreement to be void.

However, where nonrestorable benefits have passed between parties through nonremovable work, nonrecoverable supplies and materials, or school district payments that have been spent in turn by the contractor, courts are forced to mediate two inconsistent lines of cases. On one hand, the enforcement of the policy of bidding statutes would require denying the contractor any recovery or right to retain payments made under the unlawful agreement. On the other hand, the equity principle of avoiding unjust enrichment would prohibit unconscionable retention of benefits by the district without paying their fair value to the contractor. The problem is one of policy, not of technical doctrine. A court can easily state that the absence of a lawful express contract does not prevent a court of equity from granting recovery for fair value (*quantum meruit*) under its own doctrine of quasi contract (a contract implied-in-law). The difficulty is in harmonizing the policy of bidding statutes with the policy against forfeitures or unjust enrichment.

In deciding such cases, the equitable discretion of courts is guided by the same basic considerations discussed above on bid withdrawal: the nature and size of the mistake, the degree of fault or lack thereof in either party, the extent of the loss that may be borne by either party or by innocent third parties under a particular allowance of recovery. As seen in the *Gerzof* opinion (at the end of this chapter), the courts are not in accord on the application of equity principles in relief of unlawful contracts. The majority of courts limit recovery to the value of benefits conferred. They preserve some of the protection of bidding statutes because such recovery usually covers costs actually

---

130. *Compare* the Stephen and Seacoast cases in prior footnote *with* Kelley Co. v. City of Cleveland, 290 N.E.2d 562 (Ohio 1972); Austin v. Housing Auth'y., 122 A.2d 399 (Conn. 1956).

131. Lefkowitz v. Turley, 414 U.S. 70 (1973).

132. *Cf.* Goldberg v. Kelly, 397 U.S. 254, 263-4 n. 10 (1970).

133. *See* Coast Construction Corp. v. Lockport Urban Renewal Agency, 339 N.Y.S.2d 188 (1972).

expended by the contractor without the benefit of the contract price or profits, and thus leaves the contractor in no better position than before the contract was awarded. Such recovery avoids absolute forfeiture and loss by the contractor. The measure of fair value damages adopted in different states varies considerably.[134] Some authorities deny any recovery to the contractor under improper bid contracts, even though the school district retains benefits at the expense of the contractor.

When there is fraud or culpable negligence, courts may deny any equitable relief, notwithstanding the harsh loss to the bidder. Judicial opinion on these issues is divided and must be traced through the case law of each state.[135]

11. Individual School Funds

Funds that are raised to benefit a particular school remain subject to school board authority unless the control over such funds has been vested in the school principal or organization by the terms of a private trust, by legislation, or by school board resolution. The bare fact that funds are generated by the efforts of individual classes, clubs, or organizations does not authorize the school principal, faculty, or local group to control them if they were raised with school resources and sponsorship.

Outside parties may always raise funds without involvement of school resources or sponsorship and make gifts to the district on condition that they be used for local school purposes. In such cases, the school board retains the ultimate power of decision to accept or reject the restricted gift.

In states where local administration of individual school funds is authorized by state law or by school board regulations, the school authorities must observe the specific legal guidelines. For example, the Pennsylvania statute empowers individual schools and school groups to raise, retain, and expend their own funds. It declares such funds to be the property of the local organizations or school, and not of the school district; but it still subjects each school fund to statutory audit and accounting procedures under the supervision of the school board.[136] Further, individual principals, faculty members, or school organizations are bound by trust law to use particular funds only for the purposes for which they were raised.[137] Should anyone divert special funds to foreign uses, he or she may be held personally liable to replace the misused funds.

School principals are often faced with the problem of how to free restricted school funds that have remained long unused or ignored by the controlling school organization. The temptation is strong to mingle or redirect earmarked school funds in order to put them to some pressing school need, but the only safe course would be to obtain legal authorization from the owner group to apply surplus funds for other general or specific school purposes. For example, unused funds raised as a class fund by a graduated class may be made transferable as a gift to a general, unrestricted school fund. The transfer may be

134. Edwards v. City of Renton, 409 P.2d 153 (Wash. 1965).

135. See Annotation: *Municipality—Quasi Contract Liability,* 33 A.L.R.3d 1164 (1970); Annotation: *Competitive Bid—Violation—Recovery,* 33 A.L.R.3d 397 (1970).

136. See Pa. Stat. Ann., tit. 24, §5-511(d).

137. Petition of Auditors of Hatfield Township School District, 54 A.2d 833 (Pa. 1974).

made automatically after a certain period of time or expressly upon resolution of the elected officers of that class, if such authority is created by the class organization bylaws. Similar rules or bylaws could be fashioned and adopted by each school club or organization to meet its own goals. At any rate, such forethought in creating special school funds will deter misappropriation of restricted funds by organization leaders or school personnel and prevent such funds from being technically locked into a condition of disuse.

CASES

San Antonio Independent School District v. Rodriguez

411 U.S. 1 (1973)

Mr. *Justice* POWELL delivered the opinion of the Court.

This suit attacking the Texas system of financing public education was initiated by Mexican-American parents whose children attend the elementary and secondary schools in the Edgewood Independent School District, an urban school district in San Antonio, Texas. . . . They brought a class action on behalf of school children throughout the State who are members of minority groups or who are poor and reside in school districts having a low property tax base. Named as defendants were the State Board of Education, the Commissioner of Education, the State Attorney General, and the Bexar County (San Antonio) Board of Trustees. . . . In December 1971 the panel rendered its judgment in a per curiam opinion holding the Texas school finance system unconstitutional under the Equal Protection Clause of the Fourteenth Amendment. The State appealed, and we noted probable jurisdiction to consider the far-reaching constitutional questions presented. . . . For the reasons stated in this opinion, we reverse the decision of the District Court. . . .

Early in its history, Texas adopted a dual approach to the financing of its schools, relying on mutual participation by the local school districts and the State. . . .

Until recent times, Texas was a predominantly rural State and its population and property wealth were spread relatively evenly across the State. Sizable differences in the value of assessable property between local school districts became increasingly evident as the State became more industrialized and as rural-to-urban population shifts became more pronounced. The location of commercial and industrial property began to play a significant role in determining the amount of tax resources available to each school district. These growing disparities in population and taxable property between districts were responsible in part for increasingly notable differences in levels of local expenditure for education. . . .

Recognizing the need for increased state funding to help offset disparities in local spending and to meet Texas' changing educational requirements, the state legislature in the late 1940s undertook a thorough evaluation of public education. . . . In 1947, an 18-member committee . . . was appointed. The Committee's efforts led to the passage of the Gilmer-Aikin bills, . . . establishing the Texas Minimum Foundation School Program. Today, this Program accounts for approximately half of the total educational expenditures in Texas.

The Program calls for state and local contributions to a fund earmarked specifically for teacher salaries, operating expenses, and transportation costs. The State, . . . finances approximately 80% of the Program, and the school districts are responsible—as a unit—for providing the remaining 20%. The districts' share, known as the Local Fund Assignment, is apportioned among the school districts under a formula designed to reflect each district's relative taxpaying ability. . . . The district, in turn, finances its share of the Assignment out of revenues from local property taxation.

The design of this complex system was twofold. First, it was an attempt to assure that the Foundation Program would have an equalizing influence on expenditure levels between school districts by placing the heaviest burden on the school districts most capable of paying. Second, the Program's architects sought to establish a Local Fund Assignment that would force every school district to contribute to the education of its children but that would not by itself exhaust any district's resources. Today every school district does impose a property tax from which it derives locally expendable funds in excess of the amount necessary to satisfy its Local Fund Assignment under the Foundation Program. . . .

The school district in which appellees reside, the Edgewood Independent School District, has been compared throughout this litigation with the Alamo Heights Independent School District. This comparison between the least and most affluent districts in the San Antonio area serves to illustrate the manner in which the dual system of finance operates and to indicate the extent to which substantial disparities exist despite the State's impressive progress in recent years. Edgewood is one of seven public school districts in the metropolitan area. The district is situated in the core city sector of San Antonio in a residential neighborhood that has little commercial or industrial property. The residents are predominantly of Mexican-American descent: approximately 90% of the student population is Mexican-American and over 6% is Negro. The average assessed property value per pupil is $5,960—the lowest in the metropolitan area—and the median family income ($4,686) is also the lowest. . . .

Alamo Heights is the most affluent school district in San Antonio. The school population is predominantly "Anglo," having only 18% Mexican-Americans and less than 1% Negroes. The assessed property value per pupil exceeds $49,000, and the median family income is $8,001. . . .

Despite . . . recent increases, substantial interdistrict disparities in school expenditures found by the District Court to prevail in San Antonio and in varying degrees throughout the State still exist. And it was these disparities, largely attributable to differences in the amounts of money collected through local property taxation, that led the District Court to conclude that Texas' dual system of public school financing violated the Equal Protection Clause. The District Court held that the Texas system discriminates on the basis of wealth in the manner in which education is provided for its people. 337 F. Supp., at 282. Finding that wealth is a "suspect" classification and that education is a "fundamental" interest, the District Court held that the Texas system could be sustained only if the State could show that it was premised upon some compelling state interest. Id., at 282-284. . . .

Texas virtually concedes that its historically rooted dual system of financing education could not withstand the strict judicial scrutiny that this Court has found appropriate in reviewing legislative judgments that interfere with fundamental constitutional rights or that involve suspect classifications. If, strict scrutiny means that the State's system is not entitled to the usual presumption of validity, that the State . . . must carry a "heavy burden of justification," that the State must demonstrate that its educational system has been structured with "precision," and is "tailored" narrowly to serve legitimate objectives and that it has selected the "less drastic means" for effectuating its objectives, the Texas financing system and its counterpart in virtually every other State will not pass muster. . . .

This, then, establishes the framework for our analysis. We must decide, first, whether the Texas system of financing public education operates to the disadvantage of some suspect class or impinges upon a fundamental right explicitly or implicitly protected by the Constitution, thereby requiring strict judicial scrutiny. If so, the judgment of the District Court should be affirmed. If not, the Texas scheme must still be examined to determine whether it rationally furthers some legitimate, articulated state purpose and therefore does not constitute an invidious discrimination in violation of the Equal Protection Clause of the Fourteenth Amendment.

The District Court's opinion does not reflect the novelty and complexity of the constitutional questions posed. . . . In concluding that strict judicial scrutiny was required, that court relied on decisions dealing with the rights of indigents to equal treatment in the criminal trial and appellate processes, and on cases disapproving wealth restrictions on the right to vote. Those cases, the District Court concluded, established wealth as a suspect classification. . . . It then reasoned, that there is a fundamental right to education and that, absent some compelling state justification, the Texas system could not stand. . . . We are unable to agree that this case, which in significant aspects is *sui generis,* may be so neatly fitted into the conventional mosaic of constitutional analysis under the Equal Protection Clause. Indeed we find neither the suspect classification nor the fundamental interest analysis persuasive.

The wealth discrimination discovered by the District Court in this case is quite unlike any of the forms of wealth discrimination heretofore reviewed by this Court. Rather than focusing on the unique features of the alleged discrimination, the courts in these cases have virtually assumed their findings of a suspect classification through a simplistic process of analysis. . . . This approach largely ignores the hard threshold questions, including whether it makes a difference . . . that the class of disadvantaged "poor" cannot be identified or defined, whether the relative—rather than absolute—nature of the asserted deprivation is of significant consequence. . . . The individuals, or groups of individuals, who constituted the class discriminated against in our prior cases shared two distinguishing characteristics: because of their impecunity they were completely unable to pay for some desired benefit, and as a consequence, they sustained an absolute deprivation of a meaningful opportunity to enjoy that benefit. . . .

Even a cursory examination, however, demonstrates that neither of the two distinguishing characteristics of wealth classifications can be found here. First, . . . appellees have made no effort to demonstrate that it operates to the peculiar disadvantage of any class fairly definable as indigent, or as composed of persons whose incomes are beneath any designated poverty level. Indeed, there is reason to believe that the poorest families are not necessarily clustered in the poorest property districts. A recent and exhaustive study of school districts in Connecticut concluded that "[i]t is clearly incorrect . . . to contend that the 'poor' live in 'poor' districts. . . . Thus, the major factual assumption of Serrano—that the educational financing system discriminates against the 'poor'—is simply false in Connecticut." . . . [T]he Connecticut study found, not surprisingly, that the poor were clustered around commercial and industrial areas—those same areas that provide the most attractive sources of property tax income for school districts. Whether a similar pattern would be discovered in Texas is not known, but there is no basis on the record in this case for assuming that the poorest people—defined by reference to any level of absolute impecunity—are concentrated in the poorest districts.

Second, neither appellees nor the District Court addressed the fact that . . . lack of personal resources has not occasioned an absolute deprivation of the desired benefit. The argument here is not that the children in districts having relatively low assessable property values are receiving no public education; rather, it is that they are receiving a poorer quality education. . . . Apart from the unsettled and disputed question whether the quality of education may be determined by the amount of money expended for it, a sufficient answer . . . [is] that, at least where wealth is involved, the Equal Protection Clause does not require absolute equality or precisely equal advantages. By providing 12 years of free public-school education, and by assuring teachers, books, transportation, and operating funds, the Texas Legislature has endeavored to "guarantee" for the welfare of the state as a whole, that all people shall have at least an adequate program of education. . . . No proof was offered at trial persuasively discrediting or refuting the State's assertion.

For these two reasons—the absence of any evidence that the financing system discriminates against any definable category of "poor" people or that it results in the absolute deprivation of education—the disadvantaged class is not susceptible of identification in traditional terms.

The principal evidence adduced in support of this comparative-discrimination claim is an affidavit submitted by Professor Joel S. Berke of Syracuse University's Educational Finance Policy Institute. . . .

His findings . . . show only . . . that the wealthiest few districts in the sample have the highest median family incomes and spend the most on education, and that the several poorest districts have the lowest family incomes and devote the least amount of money to education. For the remainder of the districts—96 districts composing almost 90% of the sample—the correlation is inverted, i.e., the districts that spend next to the most money on education are populated by families having next to the lowest median family incomes while the districts spending the least have the highest median family incomes. It is evident that, even if the conceptual questions were answered favorably to appellees, no factual basis exists upon which to found a claim of comparative wealth discrimination.

This brings us, then, to the third way in which the classification scheme might be defined—*district* wealth discrimination. Since the only correlation indicated by the evidence is between district property wealth and expenditures, it may be argued that discrimination might be found without regard to the individual income characteristics of district residents. Assuming a perfect correlation between district property wealth and expenditures from top to bottom, the disadvantaged class might be viewed as encompassing every child in every district except the district that has the most assessable wealth and spends the most on education. Alternatively, . . . the class might be defined more restrictively to include children in districts with assessable property which falls below the statewide average, or median, or below some other artificially defined level. . . .

However described, it is clear that appellees' suit asks this Court to extend its most exacting scrutiny to review a system that allegedly discriminates against a large, diverse, and amorphous class, unified only by the common factor of residence in districts that happen to have less taxable wealth than other districts. The system of alleged discrimination and the class it defines have none of the traditional indicia of suspectness. . . .

We thus conclude that the Texas system does not operate to the peculiar disadvantage of any suspect class.

But appellees have not relied solely on this contention. They also assert that the State's system impermissibly interferes with the exercise of a "fundamental" right and that accordingly the prior decisions of this Court require the application of the strict standard of judicial review. It is this question—whether education is a fundamental right, in the sense that it is among the rights and liberties protected by the Constitution—which has so consumed the attention of courts and commentators in recent years.

In *Brown* v. *Board of Education,* 347 U.S. 483 (1954), a unanimous Court recognized that "education is perhaps the most important function of state and local governments." . . . What was said there in the context of racial discrimination has lost none of its vitality with the passage of time. . . . Nothing this Court holds today in any way detracts from our historic dedication to public education. . . . But the importance of a service performed by the State does not determine whether it must be regarded as fundamental for purposes of examination under the Equal Protection Clause. Mr. Justice Harlan, dissenting from the court's application of strict scrutiny to a law impinging upon the right of interstate travel, admonished that "[v]irtually every state statute affects important rights." . . . In his view, if the degree of judicial scrutiny of state legislation fluctuated depending on a majority's view of the importance of the interest affected, we would have gone "far toward making this Court a 'super-legislature.'" We would, indeed, then be assuming a legislative role and one for which the Court lacks both authority and competence. . . .

Thus, the key to discovering whether education is "fundamental" is not to be found in comparisons of the relative societal significance of education as opposed to subsistence or housing. Nor is it to be found by weighing whether education is as important as the right to travel. Rather, the answer lies in assessing whether there is a right to education explicitly or implicitly guaranteed by the Constitution. . . .

Education, of course, is not among the rights afforded explicit protection under our Federal Constitution. Nor do we find any basis for saying it is implicitly so protected. As we have said, the undisputed importance of education will not alone cause this Court to depart from the usual standard for reviewing a State's social and economic legislation. It is appellees' contention, however, that education is distinguishable from other services and benefits. . . . Specifically, they insist that education is itself a fundamental personal right because it is essential to the effective exercise of First Amendment freedoms and to intelligent utilization of the right to vote. In asserting a nexus between speech and education, appellees urge that the right to speak is meaningless unless the speaker is capable of articulating his thoughts intelligently and persuasively. The "marketplace of ideas" is an empty forum for those lacking basic communicative tools. Likewise, they argue that the corollary right to receive information becomes little more than a hollow privilege when the recipient has not been taught to read, assimilate, and utilize available knowledge.

A similar line of reasoning is pursued with respect to the right to vote. Exercise of the franchise, it is contended, cannot be divorced from the educational foundation.

We need not dispute any of these propositions. Yet we have never presumed to possess either the ability or the authority to guarantee to the citizenry the most *effective* speech or the most *informed* electoral choice. That these may be desirable goals of a system of freedom of expression and of a representative form of government is not to be doubted. . . .

But they are not values to be implemented by judicial intrusion into otherwise legitimate state activities.

Even if it were conceded . . . we have no indication that the present levels of educational expenditure in Texas provide an education that falls short. Whatever merit appellees' argument might have if a State's financing system occasioned an absolute denial of educational opportunities to any of its children, that argument provides no basis for finding an interference with fundamental rights where only relative differences in spending levels are involved and where—as is true in the present case—no charge fairly could be made that the system fails to provide each child with an opportunity to acquire the basic minimal skills necessary for the enjoyment of the rights of speech and of full participation in the political process. . . . In one further respect we find this a particularly inappropriate case in which to subject state action to strict judicial scrutiny. The present case . . . is significantly different from any of the cases in which the Court has applied strict scrutiny to state or federal legislation. . . . Each of our prior cases involved legislation which "deprived," "infringed," or "interfered" with the free exercise of some such fundamental personal right or liberty. . . . A critical distinction between those cases and the one now before us lies in what Texas is endeavoring to do with respect to education. . . .

Every step leading to . . . the system Texas utilizes today— . . . was implemented in an effort to *extend* public education and to improve its quality. Of course, every reform that benefits some more than others may be criticized for what it fails to accomplish. But we think it plain that . . . the thrust of the Texas system is affirmative and reformatory and, therefore, should be scrutinized under judicial principles sensitive to the nature of the State's efforts and to the rights reserved to the States under the Constitution.

We need not rest our decision . . . solely on the inappropriateness of the strict-scrutiny test. A century of Supreme Court adjudication . . . affirmatively supports the application of the traditional standard of review, which requires only that the State's system be shown to bear some rational relationship to legitimate state purposes. . . .

This Court has often admonished against such interferences with the State's fiscal policies under the Equal Protection Clause: . . .

No scheme of taxation, whether the tax is imposed on property, income, or purchases of goods and services, has yet been devised which is free of all discriminatory impact. In such a complex arena in which no perfect alternatives exist, the Court does well not to impose too rigorous a standard of scrutiny lest all local fiscal schemes become subjects of criticism under the Equal Protection Clause. . . .

Related to the questioned relationship between cost and quality is the equally unsettled controversy as to the proper goals of a system of public education. And the question regarding the most effective relationship between state boards of education and local school boards, in terms of their respective responsibilities and degrees of control, is now undergoing searching re-examination. The ultimate wisdom as to these and related problems of education is not likely to be divined for all time even by the scholars who now so earnestly debate the issues. In such circumstances, the judiciary is well advised to refrain from imposing on the States inflexible constitutional restraints. . . .

The foregoing considerations buttress our conclusion that Texas' system of public school finance is an inappropriate candidate for strict judicial scrutiny. These same considerations are relevant to the determination whether that system, with its conceded imperfections, nevertheless bears some rational relationship to a legitimate state purpose. It is to this question that we next turn our attention. . . . The District Court found that the State had failed even "to establish a reasonable basis" for a system that results in different levels of per pupil expenditure . . .

We disagree.

In its reliance on state as well as local resources, the Texas system is comparable to the systems employed in virtually every other State. . . .

Appellees further urge that the Texas system is unconstitutionally arbitrary because it allows the availability of local taxable resources to turn on "happenstance." . . . But any scheme of local taxation . . . requires the establishment of jurisdictional boundaries that are inevitably arbitrary. It has simply never been within the constitutional prerogative of this Court to nullify statewide measures for financing public services merely because the burdens or benefits thereof fall unevenly depending upon the relative wealth of the political subdivisions in which citizens live.

In sum, to the extent that the Texas system of school financing results in unequal expenditures between children who happen to reside in different districts, we cannot say that such disparities are the product of a system that is so irrational as to be invidiously discriminatory.

It certainly is not the product of purposeful discrimination against any group or class. . . . The constitutional standard under the Equal Protection Clause is whether the challenged state action rationally furthers a legitimate state purpose or interest. . . . We hold that the Texas plan abundantly satisfies this standard. . . .

In light of the considerable attention that has focused on the District Court opinion in this case and on its California predecessor, *Serrano* v. *Priest,* 5 Cal. 3d 584, 487 P.2d 1241 (1971), a cautionary postscript seems appropriate. . . .

These practical considerations, of course, play no role in the adjudication of the constitutional issues presented here. But they serve to highlight the wisdom of the traditional limitations on this Court's function. . . . Those who have devoted the most thoughtful attention to the practical ramifications of these cases have found no clear or dependable answers and their scholarship reflects no such unqualified confidence in the desirability of completely uprooting the existing system. . . .

We hardly need add that this Court's action today is not to be viewed as placing its judicial imprimatur on the status quo. The need is apparent for reform in tax systems which may well have relied too long and too heavily on the local property tax. And certainly innovative thinking . . . is necessary to assure both a higher level of quality and greater uniformity of opportunity. These matters merit the continued attention of the scholars who already have contributed much by their challenges. But the ultimate solutions must come from the lawmakers and from the democratic pressures of those who elect them.

Reversed.

Hartzell v. Connell

679 P.2d 35 (Cal. 1984)

BIRD, Chief Justice.

May a public high school district charge fees for educational programs simply because they have been denominated "extracurricular"?

I.

The Santa Barbara High School District (District) offers a wide variety of extracurricular activities, ranging from cheerleading to madrigal singing, and from archery to football. Many of these activities are of relatively recent origin. For example, in 1956, Santa Barbara High School fielded six athletic teams while today there are thirty-eight.

Prior to the 1980–1981 school year, any student could participate in these activities free of charge. . . .

In the spring of 1980, the District school board (Board) decided to cut its budget by $1.1 million. This decision reflected a drop in revenues due to the combined effects of inflation, declining enrollment, and the adoption of Proposition 13. . . .

The Board considered two plans for adapting the programs to fit its reduced budget. The first plan called for a major cut in interscholastic athletic competition,. . . . Under this plan, the surviving programs were to remain open to all students free of charge.

The second plan provided for a less extensive cut in athletic competition—elimination of the ninth grade program only. To make up the difference, it proposed to raise money by charging students fees for participation in dramatic productions, musical performances, and athletic competition.

The Board chose the second option. Under the plan finally adopted, students are required to pay $25 for *each* athletic team in which they wish to participate, and $25 per category for any or all activities in *each* of the following four categories: (1) dramatic productions (e.g., plays, dance performances, and musicals); (2) vocal music groups (e.g., choir and madrigal groups); (3) instrumental groups (e.g., orchestra, marching band, and related groups such as the drill team and flag twirlers); and (4) cheerleading groups.

Thus, a student who desires to play football in the fall and tennis in the spring, in addition to participating in a dramatic production, must pay $75. A more musically inclined student, who plays an instrument, sings in a group, and performs in a musical, also pays $75.

None of the affected activities yield any credit toward graduation. However, each is connected to a credit course. . . . The teachers of the credit courses also supervise the noncredit performances. District policy prohibits them from considering the performances in calculating grades. . . .

. . . The teachers are compensated by one of two methods: extra pay (in the form of a "stipend") or "release time." The stipends are paid partly from general school revenues (derived mostly from taxes) and partly from fees. Under the "release time" policy, teachers are "released" from one hour of regular teaching duties for each hour spent supervising extracurricular activities. . . .

In an attempt to ensure that the fees would not prevent any students from participating, the District has implemented a fee-waiver program. Upon a showing of financial need, a student may obtain a "scholarship" to participate without paying the fee. The standard of need is similar to that of the free lunch program.

The fee waiver policy has been supplemented with an outreach program. Teachers and coaches are asked to inform their principals of any students who, though expected to participate in an activity, do not do so. These students are then interviewed by the principal to determine whether the fee prevented them from participating. . . . There was no evidence that any student was prevented from participating because of the fees.

Shortly before the start of the 1980–1981 school year, Barbara Hartzell, a taxpayer with two children in the public schools, and the Coalition Opposing Student Fees, a grouping of community organizations, filed this taxpayers' action against the District, various school officials, and the members of the Board. Plaintiffs sought declaratory and injunctive relief, claiming that defendants' fee program violates the "free school" and equal protection guarantees of the California Constitution (Cal. Const., arts. IX, § 5, IV, § 16, I, § 7), that it is barred by title 5, section 350, of the California Administrative Code, and that it is preempted by state law. . . .

II.

The California Constitution requires the Legislature to "provide for a system of common schools by which a *free school* shall be kept up and supported in each district. . . . " (Cal. Const., art. IX, § 5, emphasis added.) This provision entitles "the youth of the State . . . to be educated at the public expense." (*Ward v. Flood* (1874) 48 Cal. 36, 51.). . . .

The first question raised by plaintiffs' challenge is whether extracurricular activities fall within the free education guaranteed by section 5. California courts have not yet addressed this issue. The reported decisions from other jurisdictions reveal two distinct approaches.

One approach restricts the free school guarantee to programs that are "essential to the prescribed curriculum." (*Smith v. Crim* (1977) 240 Ga. 390, 391, 240 S.E.2d 884; see also *Paulson v. Minidoka County School District No. 331* (1970) 93 Idaho 469, 472, 463 P.2d 935.) Under this view, the right to an education does not extend to activities that are "outside of or in addition to the regular academic courses or curriculum of a school." (*Paulson, ibid.*, fn. omitted.) Accordingly, it has been held that students have no right to participate in extracurricular activities. (*Smith v. Crim, supra*, 240 Ga. at p. 391, 240

S.E.2d 884; see also *Granger et al. v. Cascade Co. Sch. Dist.* (1972) 159 Mont. 516, 499 P.2d 780.[1])

The second approach holds that the free school guarantee extends to all activities which constitute an "an integral fundamental part of the elementary and secondary education" or which amount to "'necessary elements of any school's activity.'" (*Bond v. Ann Arbor School District* (1970) 383 Mich. 693, 702, 178 N.W.2d 484; see also *Moran v. School District #7, Yellowstone County* (D.Mont. 1972) 350 F.Supp. 1180, 1184.) Courts applying this approach have held that "the right to attend school includes the right to participate in extracurricular activities." (*Moran, ibid.*) In particular, courts have struck down extracurricular activities fees as unconstitutional. (See *Bond v. Ann Arbor School District, supra,* 383 Mich. at p. 698, 178 N.W.2d 484; *Pacheco v. Sch. Dist. No. 11* (1973) 183 Colo. 270, 516 P.2d 629.[2])

To determine which, if either, of these approaches is consistent with California's free school guarantee, this court must examine the role played by education in the overall constitutional scheme. Because the nature of the free school concept has rarely been addressed by the courts, it will be necessary to explore its underpinnings in some depth. . . .

Finally, education serves as a "unifying social force" among our varied population, promoting cohesion based upon democratic values. (*Serrano I, supra,* 5 Cal.3d at p. 608, 96 Cal. Rptr. 601, 487 P.2d 1241; see also *Ambach v. Norwick* (1979) 441 U.S. 68, 77, 99 S.Ct. 1589, 1594, 60 L.Ed.2d 49.) The public schools bring together members of different racial and cultural groups and, hopefully, help them to live together "'in harmony and mutual respect.'" (*Washington v. Seattle School Dist. No. 1* (1982) 458 U.S. 457, 473, 102 S.Ct. 3187, 3196, 73 L.Ed.2d 896.)

Viewed in light of these constitutionally recognized purposes, the first of the two tests described above is insufficient to ensure compliance with California's free school

---

1. *Granger,* cited by both parties, appears to straddle the two approaches identified here. The trial court had enjoined fees for "required" activities, but not for "optional or extracurricular" activities. (*Id.,* at pp. 526-527, 499 P.2d 780.) The Montana Supreme Court altered the standard to encompass all courses and activities "reasonably related to a recognized academic and educational goal of the particular school system." (*Id.,* at p. 527, 499 P.2d 780.) This alteration of the standard appears to have been grounded in the court's desire to include optional, credit courses within the guarantee. (*Ibid.*)

As this court interprets the *Granger* standard, it would prohibit the defendants' fee program because each of the performance activities involved is "reasonably related" to an optional, credit course. Indeed, preparation for performances appears to be a major function of the credit courses.

However, nothing in the *Granger* standard would prevent local districts from evading the free school guarantee by the simple expedient of offering the underlying courses on an "extracurricular" basis. Nor would *Granger* prevent a district from offering any number of courses, for example advanced algebra or computer science, on a noncredit basis for a fee. Hence, *Granger,* in spite of its broadly stated holding, does not fundamentally depart from the "prescribed curriculum" standard.

2. In *Bond,* the trial court had held interscholastic athletic fees to be unconstitutional and had issued a permanent injunction barring their future collection. (383 Mich. at p. 698, 178 N.W.2d 484.) Neither party raised the constitutionality of the fees before the Michigan Supreme Court, which let the injunction stand.

In *Pacheco,* the trial court had held that a school policy requiring the purchase of an activities card as a precondition for participating in extracurricular activities such as athletic contests, dances, plays, and concerts, violated the free school guarantee as applied to children of indigent parents. (183 Colo. at pp. 272–273, 516 P.2d 629.) The Colorado Supreme Court upheld the trial court's action without ruling on the constitutionality of such fees as applied to children of nonindigent parents. (*Id.,* at pp. 273–275, 516 P.2d 629.)

Justice Kelley dissented from the court's refusal to reach this issue, reasoning that "the entire educational program is required to be provided to all students 'gratuitously.'" (*Id.,* at p. 280, 516 P.2d 629.)

guarantee. That approach determines whether a given program falls within the guarantee not by assessing its actual educational value, but by deferring to a school board's decision on whether or not to offer it for formal, academic credit.[3] Under this test, a for-credit program would fall within the guarantee, while a noncredit program with identical content—and equal value in fulfilling the constitutionally recognized purposes of education—could be offered for a fee.[4]

The second approach, on the other hand, does not sever the concept of education from its purposes. It focuses not upon the formalities of credit, but upon the educational character of the activities in question. . . .

Accordingly, this court holds that all educational activities—curricular or "extracurricular"—offered to students by school districts fall within the free school guarantee of article IX, section 5. Since it is not disputed that the programs involved in this case are "educational" in character, they fall within that guarantee.[5]

Defendants argue, however, that the fee-waiver policy for needy students satisfies the requirements of the free school guarantee. They suggest that the right "to be educated at the public expense" (*Ward v. Flood, supra*, 48 Cal. at p. 51) amounts merely to a right *not to be financially prevented* from enjoying educational opportunities. This argument contradicts the plain language of the Constitution.

In guaranteeing "free" public schools, article IX, section 5 fixes the precise extent of the financial burden which may be imposed on the right to an education—none. . . . A school which conditions a student's participation in educational activities upon the payment of a fee clearly is *not* a "free school."

The free school guarantee reflects the people's judgment that a child's public education is too important to be left to the budgetary circumstances and decisions of individual families. It makes no distinction between needy and nonneedy families. . . .

Nor may a student's participation be conditioned upon application for a special waiver. The stigma that results from recording some students as needy was recognized early in the struggle for free schools. . . .

Finally, defendants warn that, if the fees are invalidated, many school districts may be forced to drop some extracurricular activities. They argue that invalidation would—in the name of the free school guarantee—produce the anomalous result of reducing the number of educational opportunities available to students.

This court recognizes that, due to legal limitations on taxation and spending . . . school districts do indeed operate under difficult financial constraints. However, financial hardship is no defense to a violation of the free school guarantee. . . .

Perhaps, in the view of some, public education could be more efficiently financed

---

3. This is not to suggest that a school board's decision to offer a program for credit is irrelevant as a measure of its educational value. However, as indicated by the numerous authorities cited below (*post*, at pp. 607–609 of 201 Cal. Rptr., at pp. 41–43 of 679 P.2d), the fact that some activities are less suited to a formal, graded program does not mean that they are less essential to the goals of public education.

4. Under this standard, the Constitution would not prevent a school board from evading the constitutional guarantee by the simple expedient of labeling courses "extracurricular" and offering them for no credit. In addition to the performances involved in the present case, metal working courses, computer instruction, language laboratories, or even advanced algebra could be offered for a fee.

5. Educational activities are to be distinguished from activities which are purely recreational in character. Examples of the latter might include attending weekend dances or athletic events.

by peddling it on the open market. Under the California Constitution, however, access to public education is a right enjoyed by all—not a commodity for sale. Educational opportunities must be provided to all students without regard to their families' ability or willingness to pay fees or request special waivers. This fundamental feature of public education is not contingent upon the inevitably fluctuating financial health of local school districts. A solution to those financial difficulties must be found elsewhere—for example, through the political process.

In conclusion, this court holds that the imposition of fees for educational activities offered by public high school districts violates the free school guarantee. The constitutional defect in such fees can neither be corrected by providing waivers to indigent students, nor justified by pleading financial hardship.

Cardiff v. Bismarck Public School Dist.

263 N.W. 2d 105 (N. Dak. 1978)

SAND, Justice.

Gary Cardiff and other parents of school children attending elementary schools in the Bismarck Public School District brought an action in Burleigh County district court challenging the authority of the school district to charge rental fees for the use of necessary school textbooks. . . .

The basic issue for our resolution is whether or not § 148 of the North Dakota Constitution provides for free textbooks and prohibits the Legislature from authorizing school districts to charge for textbooks. The parents contend the constitutional provision prohibits charging for textbooks, and the school district contends it merely prohibits charging tuition. . . .

To resolve the first issue we must examine and construe the provisions of § 148 of the North Dakota Constitution. . . .

In 1968 this section was amended as follows:

> "The legislative assembly shall provide for a uniform system of free public schools throughout the state, beginning with the primary and extending through all grades up to and including schools of higher education, except that the legislative assembly may authorize tuition, fees and service charges to assist in the financing of public schools of higher education."

In construing a written constitution we must make every effort to determine the intent of the people adopting it. . . .

We must examine the whole instrument in order to determine the true intention of every part so as to give effect to each section and clause. If different portions seem to be in conflict, we must make a true effort to harmonize them if practicable.

In interpreting clauses in a constitution we must presume that words have been employed in their natural and ordinary meaning. . . .

In 1895 the North Dakota Legislature enacted chapter 109, the title of which provides as follows: "AN ACT to Provide for Free Text Books and School Supplies for the Use of the Pupils in the Public Schools of North Dakota." The body of the Act, however, conditions the free textbooks upon a favorable election by a majority of qualified electors of the district. . . . The title of the Act is misleading when compared to the body of the Act. . . .

From this examination we are left with a firm conviction that the legislative acts referred to do not lend any significant comfort or aid to the resolution of the basic question under consideration, namely, what does the term "uniform system of free public schools" mean? Contemporaneous construction in this instance is not helpful to either party. The Journal entries of the constitutional convention are not very helpful in determining the meaning of the language, "free public schools."

The first item relating to public schools introduced at the North Dakota Constitutional Convention, as found in the Journal, was File No. 47 §2, which provided, in part: "It shall be the duty of the legislature to establish and maintain a system of free public schools, adequate for education of all children in the state between the ages of six and eighteen years, inclusive, in the common branches of knowledge, and in virtue and Christian morality." File No. 17 was referred to the Committee of the Whole, where its provisions were restructured, given section numbers 150 through 156, and placed under Article VIII.

In the final revision, § 151 became § 148 as it was actually adopted. . . .

From this brief review it is clear that the framers consistently had in mind a free public school.

A short survey of the constitutional provisions of other states and their case law will shed some light on our question.

ARIZONA: "The Legislature shall provide for a system on common schools by which a free school shall be established." Constitution, Article XI, § 6.

In *Carpio* v. *Tucson High School District No. I of Pima County,* 111 Ariz, 127, 524 P.2d 948 (1974), cert. denied 420 U.S. 982, 95 S.Ct. 1412, 13 L.Ed.2d 664, the court had under consideration Article XI, § 6, of the Arizona Constitution. The court held that textbooks were not required to be furnished to high school students. However, the court referred to an earlier decision, *Shoftstall* v. *Hollins,* 110 Ariz. 88, 515 P.2d 590 (1973), where the court held that these constitutional provisions had been satisfied when the legislature provided for the means of establishing required courses, qualifications of teachers, textbooks to be used in common schools, etc. Considering this statement and the statement in *Carpio* that "textbooks have not been provided free in high schools as they have been in the common schools" leaves the impression that under the constitutional provisions of Arizona, textbooks in common schools were provided free of charge.

COLORADO: "The general assembly shall provide for the establishment and maintenance of a thorough and uniform system of free public schools. . . ." Constitution, Article IX, § 2.

In *Marshall* v. *School District RE #3 Morgan County,* 553 P.2d 784 (Colo. 1976), the court held that the school district was not required to furnish books free of charge to all students.

INDIANA: "[I]t shall be the duty of the General Assembly to . . . provide by law, for a general and uniform system of Common Schools, wherein tuition shall be without charge, and equally open to all." Constitution, Article 8, § 1.

In *Chandler* v. *South Bend Community School Corporation,* 160 Ind. App. 592, 312 N.E.2d 915 (1974), the court held that this constitutional provision did not require textbooks to be provided free, but merely to provide a system of common schools where tuition would be without charge.

ILLINOIS: "Education in public schools through the secondary level shall be free." Constitution, Article X, § 1.

In *Beck* v. *Board of Education of Harlem Consolidated School District No. 122,* 63 Ill. 2d 10, 344 N.E.2d 440 (1976), the court held that workbooks, and other educational material were not textbooks so as to come within the statutory provision of free textbooks, and as such it did not preclude the school board from charging the parents a fee for supplying the students with such material.

Earlier, in *Hamer* v. *Board of Education of School District No. 109,* . . . , 265 N.E.2d 616 (1970), the court was specifically concerned with the constitutional provision and held that under its provisions the school board was not prohibited from purchasing textbooks and renting them to pupils. It further held that the legislature had the power to direct the district school boards to issue textbooks to students free of charge but the constitution did not require it. In a related case entitled *Hamer* v. *Board of Education of School District No. 109, County of Lake,* 9 Ill. App. 3d 663, 292 N.E.2d 569 (1973), the court in effect reaffirmed its earlier decision in the *Hamer* case.

WISCONSIN: "The legislature shall provide for . . . district schools and such schools shall be free and without charge for tuition. . . . " Constitution, Article X, § 3.

The court in *Board of Education* v. *Sinclair,* 65 Wis.2d 179, 222 N.W.2d 143 (1974), held that the schools may charge a fee for the use of textbooks and items of similar nature authorized by statute and that such did not violate the constitutional provision commanding that schools shall be free without charge for tuition for all children. It basically held that the term "free" referred to school buildings and equipment and what is normally understood by the term "tuition."

IDAHO: " . . . it shall be the duty of the legislature of Idaho to establish and maintain a general, uniform and thorough system of public, free common schools." Constitution, Article 9, § 1.

In *Paulson* v. *Minidoka County School District No. 331,* 93 Idaho 469, 463 P.2d 935 (1970), the court held that school districts could not charge students for textbooks under the state constitutional provision. It also held that public high schools in Idaho are "common schools."

MICHIGAN: "The legislature shall maintain and support a system of free public elementary and secondary schools. . . . " Constitution, Article 8, § 2.

In 1908 the Michigan Constitution, Article 11, § 9 in part provided: "The legislature shall continue a system of primary schools, whereby every school district in the state shall provide for the education of its pupils without charge for tuition . . . "

The Michigan court in *Bond* v. *Public Schools of Ann Arbor School District,* 383 Mich. 693, 178 N.W.2d 484 (1970), held that the 1963 constitutional provision meant that books and school supplies were an essential part of the system of free public elementary and secondary schools and that the schools should not charge for such items. We note that the 1908 Constitution provided "without charge for tuition," whereas the 1963 Constitution provides for a system of "free public elementary and secondary schools."

MONTANA: "It shall be the duty of the legislative assembly of Montana to establish and maintain a general, uniform and thorough system of public, free, common schools." Constitution, Article XI, § 1.

In *Granger* v. *Cascade County School District No. 1,* 159 Mont. 516, 499 P.2d 780 (1972), the school district, as the school district here, contended that the pertinent language simply meant "tuition-free" as far as required courses were concerned and did not prohibit fees and charges for optional extra-curricular or elective courses and activities. The Montana parents, however, contended that the schools could not impose fees or charges for anything, whether elective or required, that is encompassed in the constitutional requirement of a "thorough system of public, free, common schools." The fees involved more than just charges for workbooks and textbooks, as in this case. The Montana Supreme Court answered the question in the following manner:

> "We believe that the controlling principle or test should be stated in this manner: Is a given course or activity reasonably related to a recognized academic and educational goal of a particular school system? If it is, it constitutes part of the free, public school system commanded by Art. XI, Sec. 1 of the Montana Constitution and additional fees or charges cannot be levied, directly or indirectly, against the student or his parents. If it is not, reasonable fees or charges may be imposed."

The court, however, pointed out that its decision does not apply to supplementary instruction offered by the school district on a private basis during the summer recess or at special times. It should be observed that the school district in the *Granger* case, as well as in the instant case, argued that they had a system of waivers and charges for welfare recipients and other cases of economic hardship. The court rejected this argument.

NEW MEXICO: "A uniform system of free public schools sufficient for the education of, and open to, all children of school age in the state shall be established and maintained." Constitution, Article XII, § 1.

The court, in *Norton* v. *Board of Education of School District No. 16,* 89 N.M. 470, 553 P.2d 1277 (1976), held that under this constitutional provision courses required of every student shall be without charge to the student. However, reasonable fees may be charged for elective courses. The court also recognized that the board of education shall define what are required or elective courses in the educational system of New Mexico.

SOUTH DAKOTA: " . . . it shall be the duty of the legislature to establish and maintain a general and uniform system of public schools wherein tuition shall be without charge." Constitution adopted 1889, Article VIII, § 1.

We have found no South Dakota case law on the question of tuition or textbooks.

WEST VIRGINIA: "The legislature shall provide by general law, for a thorough and efficient system of free schools." Constitution, Article XII, § 1.

The court in *Vandevender* v. *Cassell,* 208 S.E.2d 436 (W. Va. 1974), held that furnishing textbooks free to needy students satisfied the constitutional requirement. But two of the five judges, in a concurring opinion, stated that they did not interpret "free" as pertaining only to indigent pupils. They further stated: "It is clear to me [us], however, that where state constitutions contain language providing for free schools, such as Article XIII, Section 1 of the West Virginia Constitution, that this means free schools for students of all economic classes."

MISSOURI: " . . . A general diffusion of knowledge and intelligence being essential to the preservation of the rights and liberties of the people, the general assembly shall establish and maintain free public schools for the gratuitous instruction of all persons in this state within ages not in excess of twenty-one years as prescribed by law. . . . " Constitution Article IX, § 1(a), Source Constitution of 1875, Article XI, §§ 1 and 3.

The court held in *Concerned Parents* v. *Caruthersville School District No. 18,* 548 S.W.2d 554 (Mo. 1977), that under this constitutional provision school districts were prohibited from charging registration fees or course fees in connection with courses for which academic credit was given.

WASHINGTON: "The Legislature shall provide for a general and uniform system of public schools. The public school system shall include common schools, and such high schools, normal schools, and technical schools as may hereafter be established." Constitution, Article 9, § 2.

The Supreme Court of the State of Washington, in *Litchman* v. *Shannon,* 90 Wash. 186, 155 P.783 (1916), said: "Public schools are usually defined as schools established under the laws of the state, usually regulated in matters of detail by local authorities in the various districts, towns, or counties, and maintained at the public expense by taxation, and open without charge to the children of all the residents of the town or other district." . . .

From this study we have concluded that the courts have consistently construed the language "without payment of tuition" or "wherein tuition shall be without charge" or such similar language to mean that a school is prohibited from charging a fee for a pupil attending school. This language has also been construed as not prohibiting the charging of fees for textbooks.

However, as to constitutions containing language such as "free public schools" or "free common schools" or similar language, the courts have generally held, with a few exceptions, that this language contemplates furnishing textbooks free of charge, at least to the elementary schools. The exceptions have generally relied upon extrinsic material such as contemporary construction, history, or practices, as well as the language itself. Although the cases involving language similar to that contained in the North Dakota Constitution are not in themselves conclusive, they nevertheless are helpful, if not persuasive.

A comparison of the key constitutional provisions and existing case law of states which entered the Union at the same time and under similar conditions as North Dakota will be very helpful and valuable in determining the intent of the people of North Dakota in adopting § 148 of the North Dakota Constitution. . . .

The key language in the constitutional provisions of the four States are as follows:

> Montana: " . . . thorough system of public, free common schools."
> South Dakota: " . . . uniform system of public schools wherein tuition shall be without charge,"
> North Dakota: " . . . uniform system of free public schools throughout the state. . . . "
> Washington: " . . . uniform system of public schools. . . . "

We are impressed with the different language employed in the constitutions of the four states, Montana, South Dakota, North Dakota, and Washington, which came into the Union at the same time and under the same Enabling Act. . . .

It is significant to note that Montana and North Dakota adopted the "free common schools" and the "free public schools" concept, whereas South Dakota adopted the "public schools wherein tuition shall be without charge" concept, and Washington merely provided for a "uniform system of public schools."

. . . If the framers of the North Dakota Constitution and the people of North Dakota had in mind only to provide public schools without charging tuition they could have, and probably would have, used the language "without payment of tuition" or "wherein tuition shall be without charge," rather than the language "free public schools." We must assume that the framers of the constitution made a deliberate choice of words which reflected or expressed thoughts. The term "free public schools" without any other modification must necessarily mean and include those items which are essential to education.

It is difficult to envision a meaningful educational system without textbooks. . . .

We cannot overlook the fact that attendance at school between certain ages was compulsory from the very beginning under penalty of law. This lends support to the contention that textbooks were to be included in the phrase "free public schools."

We have also examined the North Dakota constitutional debates but have not been able to uncover any helpful information. We must therefore resolve the basic question primarily on the language found in the North Dakota constitutional provision.

The word 'free' takes on its true and full meaning from the context in which it is used, . . . Books and school supplies are a part of the education system. This is true whether we apply the necessary elements of the school's activities test or the integral part of the educational system test.

After a review of the case law and constitutional provisions of other states, . . . we have come to the conclusion that the term "free public schools" means and includes textbooks, and not merely "free from tuition."

However, our conclusion must necessarily apply only to the elementary schools, as they are the only ones covered in this action. The action in district court was not a class action and factually involved only students enrolled in the elementary schools. The briefs, arguments, and whatever practices were involved relate only to elementary schools. This opinion therefore is limited to textbooks used in elementary schools in the required subjects, as set out in § 15-38-07, North Dakota Century Code.

Sections 15-43-07, 15-43-08, 15-43-09, 15-13-10, and 15-13-12, North Dakota Century Code, to the extent that they apply to elementary textbooks, are in conflict with § 148 of the North Dakota Constitution and are therefore invalid and unconstitutional as to elementary school textbooks. . . .

Secrist v. Diedrich

430 P.2d 448 (Ariz. 1967)

MOLLOY, *Judge.*

Appellants, members of the School Board of Tucson School District No. 1, appeal from a declaratory judgment in which the appellants were held to be violating statutory law (A.R.S. § 34-201) in performing landscaping work at new school buildings without advertising for competitive bids.

It was admitted . . . that, in connection with the construction of each of three new schools, it had performed site improvements at a cost in excess of $2500. This work was contemplated at the time of the letting of the school construction contract but was not included therein. According to the opening brief, . . . "plans and specifications for the work in question were prepared by regular employees of the school board." It was established at the trial that the school board employed a full-time architect.

The judgment rendered below is attacked on appeal on three bases. The first is that the plaintiffs established no standing to bring an action for declaratory judgment for the reason that only a taxpayer's interest was established without any showing of special damage as to any of the plaintiffs. Though there is authority to the contrary, we believe the weight of authority and the better view to be that a taxpayer has sufficient standing to question in an appropriate action illegal expenditures made or threatened by a public agency. . . . We hold that the plaintiffs, taxpayers within the defendant school district, had sufficient standing to maintain the subject action. . . .

The fact that the landscaping work in question was contemplated when the contract for the new school building was let is not determinative of the question before us. The applicable law appears to be that a residuum of discretion is reposed by bidding statutes such as the one under consideration in the public agency in control of the work. The division of work into separate units for purposes of execution, when not done for the purpose of avoiding the bidding statutes, should be upheld if such division has any reasonable basis:

> "When it is apparent that the work has been split up for the purpose of evading the statute, the courts have generally held the contracts to be invalid. On the other hand, if the public officials responsible for letting the contract appear to have acted in good faith, multiple contracts may be upheld even though the total involved in them in the aggregate is greater than the amount specified in the statute." 53 A.L.R.2d Anno: Public Contract—Competitive Bidding § 2, p. 499.

Here, there appears to be a reasonable basis for separating the landscaping work from the new school construction, in that the landscaping work could be performed by regular employees of the school district, with a possible saving in cost to the school district. Landscaping is not such an integral part of a school building as to suggest bad faith in separating its performance from the construction of the building itself. In the absence of showing of such bad faith, the judgment of the school board in this regard should be upheld. Cf. *Sulphur Springs Val. Elec. Coop.* v. *City of Tombstone,* 1 Ariz. App. 268, 401 P.2d 753 (1965).

We now reach the question of statutory construction. The plaintiffs contend that the expenditures in question were in violation of A.R.S. § 34-201, subsecs. A and C, reading as follows:

> "A. Every agent shall, upon acceptance and approval of the working drawings and specifications, publish a notice to contractors of intention to receive bids and contract for the proposed work. . . .
>
> "C. If the agent believes the work can be done more advantageously by day work or force account, any building, structure, addition or alteration not exceeding twenty-five hundred dollars in total cost, may be constructed without advertising for bids."
>
> The school board argues that these provisions must be read in connection with other sections of our code, and particularly the following: "§ 34-102.
>
> "A. When authority is given by law to an agent to construct a state, county or other building or structure, or additions to or alterations of existing buildings or structures, an architect or engineer or both, as warranted by the type of construction, shall be employed by the agent *if the work is deemed of a nature warranting such employment.*" (Emphasis supplied) 11 A.R.S. "§34-103.
>
> "A. The employment of an architect shall be by direct selection or by public competition." 11 A.R.S. "§34-104.
>
> "A. The architect employed shall execute with the agent a contract to prepare *working drawings and details and specifications* for the proposed project, and to supervise its construction unless the agent does not employ the architect to supervise the work." (Emphasis supplied) 11 A.R.S.

We agree with the appellants that A.R.S. § 34-201 must be construed along with the provisions of A.R.S. § 34-101 et seq., in order to derive the true meaning of that section. . . .

But, we reject the school board's contention that because plans and specifications have been prepared by other than an architect or engineer specially employed for that purpose, the board has thus avoided the competitive bidding statute. The law cannot so easily be evaded. We believe the following to be applicable:

> "Since they are based upon public economy and are of great importance to the taxpayers, laws requiring competitive bidding as a condition precedent to the letting of public contacts ought not to be frittered away by exceptions, but, on the contrary, should receive a construction always which will fully, fairly, and reasonably effectuate and advance their true intent and purpose, and which will avoid the likelihood of their being circumvented, evaded, or defeated. Stern insistence upon positive obedience to such provisions is necessary to maintain the policy which they uphold." 43 Am. Jur. Public Works and Contracts § 26 p. 768.

See also 10 McQuillin, Municipal Corporations § 29.29, p. 266. In passing the subject competitive bidding statute, we believe the legislature was intending to affect all contracts for the construction of buildings and structures, or alterations thereto, which are of such substance as to require working drawings and specifications when the total cost is to be in excess of $2500, and that it would be a circumvention of this intent to permit construction of this type to be performed without competitive bidding merely because the plans and specifications are prepared by full-time employees of the public agency.

We do not pass upon whether the "landscaping" work here performed constitutes the construction of a " . . . building or structure, or additions to or alterations of existing buildings or structures . . . " so as to come within the purview of the subject statutory provisions. Both in the lower court and in the briefs filed in this court, it has been assumed that this work does fall within the subject statute, and we leave this record as we find it. . . .

Boise Junior College District v. Mattefs Const. Co.

450 P.2d 604 (Idaho 1969)

SPEAR, Justice.

The issue presented is whether, under the circumstances of this case, a contractor is entitled to the equitable relief of rescission when it has submitted a bid which contains a material clerical mistake. We conclude that such relief is available.

Mattefs Construction Company (hereinafter termed respondent) was one of ten bidders on a construction contract to be let by Boise Junior College District (hereinafter referred to as appellant). Along with its bid respondent submitted the customary bid bond containing a promise to pay the difference between its bid and the next higher bid actually accepted if respondent refused to enter into a contract with appellant. Contract specifications also provided that the bid could not be withdrawn for 45 days after it was opened.

The architect's estimate of costs on the building project was $150,000, but when the bids were opened seven of them ran in excess of $155,000 while three of them were less than $150,000. Fulton Construction Company bid $134,896. The respondent bid $141,048. The third bid by Cain and Hardy, Inc., was $148,915. When Fulton refused to sign a contract it was tendered to respondent who likewise refused to sign it. Ultimately the contract was awarded to Cain and Hardy, Inc., the third lowest bidder and appellant proceeded to attempt collection on respondent's bid bond.

One who errs in preparing a bid for a public works contract is entitled to the equitable relief of rescission if he can establish the following conditions: (1) the mistake is material; (2) enforcement of a contract pursuant to the terms of the erroneous bid would be unconscionable; (3) the mistake did not result from violation of a positive legal duty or from culpable negligence; (4) the party to whom the bid is submitted will not be prejudiced except by the loss of his bargain; and (5) prompt notice of the error is given. These principles are established by substantial authority, i.e., Annot., 52 A.L.R.2d 792, § III; *City of Baltimore* v. *De Luca-Davis Construction Co.*, 210 Md. 518, 124 A.2d 557 (1956). . . .

Therefore, we shall consider each of these conditions necessary for equitable relief, in the context of the objections raised.

I

Appellant contends that the trial court erred in determining that omission of the glass bid was a material mistake. The trial court found: "This was the second largest sub bid item in the whole contract, only the mechanical sub bid being larger. It amounted to about 14% of the contract and was thus a material item." . . . We have no difficulty in reaching the conclusion that omission of an item representing 14% of the total bid submitted is substantial and material. Appellant cites a number of cases, wherein courts have directly or indirectly determined that material error was not involved, in spite of mistakes which ranged up to 50%, i.e., *Modany Bros.* v. *State Public School Building Authority,* 417 Pa. 39, 208 A.2d 276 (1965); *Tony Amodeo Company* v. *Town of Woodward,* 192 Iowa 535, 185 N.W. 94 (1921); *A. J. Collella, Inc.* v. *County of Allegheny,* 391 Pa. 103, 137 A.2d 265 (1958); *Gregory Ferend Company* v. *State,* 251 App. Div. 13, 295 N.Y.S. 715 (1937). However, we are persuaded we should adopt a rule which is not so harsh and turn instead to authority such as *Elsinore Union Elementary School Dist.* v. *Kastorff,* 54 Cal.2d 380, 6 Cal. Rptr. 1, 353 P.2d 713 (1960), in which the court stated:

> "Plaintiff suggests that in any event the amount of the plumbing bid omitted from the total was immaterial. The bid as submitted was in the sum of $89,994, and whether the sum for the omitted plumbing was $6,500 or $9,285 (the two sub bids),the omission of such a sum is plainly material to the total. In *Lemoge (Lemoge Electric* v. *County of San Mateo*(1965), supra, 46 Cal.2d 659, 661-662, 297 P.2d 638) the error which it was declared would have entitled plaintiff to rescind was the listing of the cost of certain materials as $104.52, rather

than $10,452, in a total bid of $172,421. Thus the percentage of error here was larger than in *Lemoge,* and was plainly material."

II

An error in the computation of a bid may be material, representing a large percentage of the total bid submitted, and yet requiring compliance with the bid may not be unconscionable. Thus, omission of a $25,000 item in a $100,000 bid would be material, but if the $100,000 bid included $50,000 in profit, no hardship would be created by requiring the contractor to comply with the terms of his bid.

This does not represent the case at bar. Here the record reveals that if respondent were forced to comply with the terms of its bid it would lose at least $10,000. Respondent's costs including the omitted item, would be roughly $151,000 while the total amount of its bid was only $141,000. Enforcement of the bid is deemed unconscionable as working a substantial hardship on the bidder where it appears he would incur a substantial pecuniary loss. *Donaldson* v *Abraham,* 68 Wash. 208, 122 .P 1003 (1912). This is particularly so where, as here, no injury is caused by withdrawal of the bid. . . .

III

One who seeks equitable relief from error must establish that such error does not result from violation of a positive legal duty or from culpable negligence. . . .

In several of its assignments appellant contends that the trial court erred in not finding that respondent was negligent to the point of being grossly negligent. . . .

On the basis of this and other evidence in the record, the trial court found:

> " . . . Defendant Mattefs' bid was compiled in its office and was completed by Mr. Howie, defendant's superintendent, on rough work sheets at about 1:00 P.M. on October 5, 1965. Last minute bids from subcontractors came in until said time. In compiling the work sheet, Mr. Howie failed to insert the amount of any subcontractor's bid for 'Window walls—glass and glazing.' Mattefs' company had received four bids for this work, the lowest of which was $19,741.00. . . .
>
> "Immediately thereafter the figures on the work sheet were totaled by the defendant's office manager, but she did not check to see whether all bid items were on the work sheet. Mr. Mattefs, after 1:00 P.M. of the same day, looked over the work sheets and also failed to catch this omission. Thereafter the formal bid . . . was prepared and was taken to plaintiffs office by defendant's president. This was after 1:30 P.M. the day of the bid opening. At approximately 1:55 P.M. defendant's office manager discovered the omission on the work sheet. She attempted to call Mr. Mattefs at plaintiff's office, but before she could get connected to the proper office . . . it was after 2:00 P.M. and the bid opening had commenced. . . . "

On the basis of these facts the trial court concluded:

> "There was no willful or even negligent act by plaintiff's agents which prevented knowledge of the error from reaching Mr. Mattefs prior to the opening. In preparing the bid Mattefs

> Construction Company proceeded in the usual way and under the same last minute pressures that are experienced by all general contractors bidding on bids of this kind. Under the evidence I conclude that it was using ordinary care in its methods of bid preparation; that is, the same care that other contractors in the area use in making bids of the kind here involved. There was no evidence of any gross negligence or fraudulent or willful intent to omit this item for the purpose of obtaining any advantage in the bidding."

It is appellant's contention that the trial court erred in making these findings. It has long been the rule of this court that:

> "Where the findings of the trial court are supported by substantial and competent, though conflicting evidence, such findings will not be disturbed on appeal."

. . . Thus, the finding of the trial court that the mistake of respondent was not due to the required type of negligence must be affirmed. . . .

IV

It is well settled by the authorities that a bid may not be withdrawn if such withdrawal would work a substantial hardship on the offeree. Many situations can be hypothesized where such a hardship would result. However, none appears here, nor has appellant attempted to prove any hardship. Appellant expected to pay $150,000 for the work it solicited. Its actual cost will be $149,000. It complains because it cannot have the work done for $141,000. Thus, appellant's injury consists of a failure to save $9,000 on its construction rather than saving $1,000:

> " . . . [T]he city will not be heard to complain that it cannot be placed in statu quo because it will not have the benefit of an inequitable bargain. [citations]" . . . *Kemper Const. Co.*, supra, at page 11. See also *Kutsche* v. *Ford*, 222 Mich. 442, 192 N.W. 714, 717 (Mich. 1923).

The most appellant can argue is that its damage is presumed by the requirement of a bid bond . . . and that release of a bidder whenever he makes a mistake will impair the purposes for which a bid bond is required. First of all, as previously pointed out, not all mistakes entitle a bidder to equitable rescission, and second, withdrawal of a bid under proper circumstances will not destroy the irrevocability of bids. . . .

V

The final element of the right to equitable relief raised by appellant is actually an adjunct of the previous question of whether the offeree will be damaged by withdrawal of the bid. . . .

The bids were opened on October 5, 1965. The lowest bidder immediately indicated that it might not accept the contract. At that time respondent's president, who was present at the bidding, did not have actual knowledge that respondent's bid was incorrect. When respondent's president returned to the office he was informed of the mistake. That evening appellant's secretary was informed, on an informal basis, that respondent had made an error in preparation of its bid, according to the testimony of respondent's president. Appellant's secretary admitted on cross-examination that such might have been the case. In any event, the next morning the nature of the mistake was explained in detail to appellant's secretary. . . .

Relief from mistaken bids is consistently allowed where the acceptor has actual notice of the error prior to its attempted acceptance and the other elements necessary for equitable relief are present. M. F. *Kemper Const. Co.*, 235 P.2d at page 10. We see no reason to deviate from this rule where, as here, the party opposing the grant of equitable relief can show no damage other than loss of benefit of an inequitable bargain. . . .

Judgment affirmed. . . .

Gerzof v. Sweeney

239 N.E.2d 521 (N.Y. 1968)

FULD, Chief Judge.

On this appeal . . . we are concerned only with the question of remedies. However, to place the issues in proper perspective, it will be helpful to summarize the facts. . . .

The Village of Freeport . . . advertised for bids for the purchase and installation of . . . an engine. In early 1961, two bids were received, one from Enterprise Engineering Co. and the other from Nordberg Manufacturing Co. Enterprise's bid was $615,685, while Nordberg's, higher by some $58,000, was $673,840. The Village Water and Light Commission . . . urged the Board of Trustees to accept Enterprise's lower bid. However, before further action was taken, a new Mayor and two new trustees were elected and, upon the request of the former, the matter was deferred.

When, a short time later, the reconstituted Board of Trustees met, it summarily dismissed the members of the Water and Light Commission, accepted Nordberg's higher bid and awarded the contract to that company. Enterprise thereupon brought suit to rescind the award and succeeded in having the contract set aside. Then, despite the court's direction that it "award the contract as provided by Law," The Board of Trustees arranged, over the objection of a majority of the Water and Light Commission, for the drawing up of new specifications for a larger generator of 5,000 kilowatts. These specifications, as we noted in our earlier opinion (16 N.Y.2d, at pp. 210, 212, 264 N.Y.S.2d, at pp. 380, 381, 211 N.E. 2d, at pp. 828-829), were prepared "with the active assistance of a representative of the defendant Nordberg" and were "so slanted as to make impossible a bid on the second contract by any other manufacturer."

As had been anticipated, Nordberg was the only bidder. Its bid, of $757,625, was accepted and it was awarded the contract.

These were substantially the facts which led us to hold in 1965 that there was such "unlawful manipulation" . . . as to render the contract illegal (16 N.Y.2d, at p. 209, 264 N.Y.S.2d, at p. 379, 211 N.E.2d, at p. 827). We remitted the case for rendition of a judgment in favor of the plaintiff. The trial court, after a hearing, held that the Village should retain the generator, which was installed and in full operation, and should, in addition, recover from Nordberg the purchase price of $757,625 which it had paid. . . .

On cross appeals by all parties, the Appellate Division modified the judgment by providing that, while Nordberg was to pay back the purchase price of the generator, it could retake the machine upon posting a bond of $350,000 to secure the Village against any damages stemming from the removal and replacement of the equipment. . . .

Both the plaintiff and the defendant Nordberg have appealed to us from the Appellate Division's order of modification.

We have not previously been called upon to fashion a remedy appropriate to a case such as this, where an illegal and void contract for public work, entered into in defiance of the competitive bidding statute (General Municipal Law, Consol. Laws, c. 24, § 103) has performed in full on both sides. We have, however, dealt with the situation, one step removed, in which the municipality has consumed or had the full benefit of illegally purchased goods or services but the vendor or supplier has not been paid. We have repeatedly refused, in such cases, to allow the sellers to recover payment either for the price agreed upon or in quasi-contract. . . . If we were to sanction payment of the fair and reasonable value of items sold in contravention of the bidding requirements, the vendor, having little to lose, would be encouraged to risk evasion of the statute; by the same token, if public officials were free to make such payments, the way would be open to them to accomplish by indirection what they are forbidden to do directly. . . .

There should, logically, be no difference in ultimate consequence between the case where a vendor has been paid under an illegal contract and the one in which payment has not yet been made. If, in the latter case, he is denied payment, he should, in the former, be required to return the payment unlawfully received—and he should not be excused from making this refund simply because it is impossible or intolerably difficult for the municipality to restore the illegally purchased goods or services to the vendor. In neither case can the usual concern of equity to prevent unjust enrichment be allowed to overcome and extinguish the special safeguards which the Legislature has provided for the public treasury. Although this court has not had occasion to pass on the question, appellate courts of at least two other states have so decided, holding that the vendor must pay back the amount received from the purchaser even though the items sold are not capable of being returned (see *County of Shasta* v. *Moody,* 90 Cal. App. 519, 523-524, 265 P. 1032; *McKay* v. *Town of Lowell,* 41 Ind. App. 627, 638, 84 N.E. 778),[1] and we strongly favor this view. Only thus can the practical effectiveness and vigor of the bidding statutes be maintained.

There was, therefore, justification—and precedent—for Special Term's decision directing Nordberg to repay the full purchase price of $757,625 and allowing the Village to retain the machinery which had been installed and was in operation. We conclude, nevertheless, though the patently illegal conduct of the defendants entitles them to little consideration, that the amount to be awarded should be less than that. We may adopt this course, in the unusual circumstances of the present case, without disturbing the salutary rationale and policy underlying such decisions as *Albany Supply & Equip. Co.* v.

---

1. The courts of several other jurisdictions have reached a contrary result. (See Vincennes Bridge Co. v. Board of County Comrs. 8 Cir. 248 F. 93, 98-102. Grady v. City of Livingston 115 Mont. 47, 141 P.2d 346: Scott Twp. School Dist. Auth. v. Branna Constr. Corp., 409 Pa. 136, 185 A.2d 320.)

City of Cohoes, 18 N.Y.2d 968, 224 N.E.2d 716, affg. 25 A.D.2d 700, supra, 268 N.Y.S.2d 42. The sheer magnitude of the forfeiture that would be suffered by the defendant Nordberg, as well as the corresponding enrichment that would enure to the Village of Freeport, under Special Term's determination adds an element to this case not to be found in any of those in which the principles we have been discussing have been applied.

Ordinarily, the application of the law to particular cases may not, of course, vary with the sums involved. But we must recognize that the rule with which we are concerned has unique aspects that make it appropriate for us to take into account the severity of its impact in cases as extreme as the present one. The purposes of our competitive bidding statutes may be fully vindicated here without our rendering so Draconian a decree as to subject the defendant Nordberg to a judgment for over three quarters of a million dollars. Justice demands that even the burdens and penalties resulting from disregard of the law be not so disproportionately heavy as to offend conscience. We must regard the machinery as unreturnable, as were the goods or services for which payment was denied in the cases cited above. . . .

A more appropriate alternate remedy is available on the record before us, a remedy which takes into account both the wrong done to the village by the defendants' callous disregard of the competitive bidding statutes and our policy of depriving sellers of any incentive to participate in such a violation. In point of fact, the remedy, lying well within the domain of equity, impresses us as one uniquely suited to the circumstances of this case.

The Board of Trustees, it is to be noted, had originally decided that a 3,500 kilowatt generator—such as the one for which specifications had been prepared—met the Village's reasonable needs, and bona fide competitive bidding established that such an engine could be purchased for the sum of $615,685. The Village was diverted from that purchase by the persistent efforts of Nordberg to persuade the trustees, to rewrite the specifications in a way that would prevent any other manufacturer from submitting a competing bid.

We may estimate the ensuing loss to the Village by taking the difference between the $757,625 paid to Nordberg and the $615,685 which the Village would have paid if it had accepted the low bid of Enterprise for the 3,500 kilowatt engine the village had earlier set out to procure. That difference is $141,940. To the sum just mentioned we should add the difference between what it cost the Village to install the Nordberg machine and what it would have cost it to install the one offered by Enterprise. . . . The defendant Nordberg itself introduced into evidence the expert opinion of qualified engineers that the cost of installing its engine was $36,696 greater than the amount the Village would have had to expend for installing the Enterprise machine, and no one else testified to a lesser figure. . . . The total of the two items mentioned is $178,636, and the judgment against the defendant Nordberg should be modified so as to direct payment of this sum to the Village, together with interest at the rate of 3% per annum. . . .

The order appealed from should be modified, without costs, in accordance with this opinion and, as so modified, affirmed. . . .

CHAPTER 10

CHAPTER OUTLINE

- A. Private education in the legal structure
- B. State regulation of private education
  - 1. Constitutional considerations
  - 2. Statutory and regulatory requirements
    - a. Home instruction
    - b. Burden of proof in compulsory attendance prosecutions
    - c. School sites and construction
    - d. Admission standards
- C. Teacher status and rights
  - 1. Introductory note
  - 2. Contract rights and duties
  - 3. Collective labor-management relations
    - a. Voluntary negotiations
    - b. Statutory negotiations
- D. Student status and rights
  - 1. Contract rights
  - 2. Student discipline
  - 3. Student records and confidentiality
- E. Antidiscrimination law in private schools
  - 1. Racial and ethnic discrimination
    - a. Constitutional considerations
    - b. Statutory considerations
  - 2. Sex discrimination
    - a. Constitutional considerations
    - b. Statutory considerations
  - 3. Handicapped and gifted
  - 4. Age discrimination
  - 5. Religious discrimination
  - 6. State antidiscrimination laws
- F. Tort liability
  - 1. Introductory note

Private Education

2. Liability of the private school
    a. Tort immunity and limitations of liability
    b. Premises liability
    c. Duties of supervision
    d. Affirmative defenses
    e. Defamation liability
    f. Educational malpractice
    g. Statutory torts—discrimination

G. Private school finance
  1. In general
  2. Government financial assistance
  3. Direct aid to nonpublic schools
  4. Assistance directed to students and parents
    a. School transportation
    b. Tuition reimbursement
    c. Books, instructional materials, and equipment
    d. Diagnostic, remedial, and therapeutic services
    e. Tax relief to parents
    f. Dual enrollment schemes

TABLE OF CASES FOR CHAPTER 10

The State of Ohio v. Whisner, 351 N.E. 2d 750 (Ohio 1976), 584.

State of New Jersey v. Massa, 231 A.2d 252 (N.J. 1967), 589.

National Labor Relations Board v. The Catholic Bishop of Chicago, et al, 440. U.S. 490 (1979), 592.

Wolman v. Walter, 433 U.S. 229 (1977), 598.

Geraci v. St. Xavier High School, 3 Ohio Op. 3d 146 (1978), 608.

Aguilar v. Felton, ______U.S. ______105 S.Ct. 3232 (1985), 611.

Grand Rapids School District v. Ball, ______U.S. ______105 S.Ct. 3216 (1985), 621.

A. Private Education in the Legal Structure

Private education at home or in nonpublic schools is of increasing concern to public authorities as well as private educators. Public administrators are often required to supervise and serve particular aspects of private education under compulsory educational laws and under government aid programs. Such intersystem administration requires public and private school authorities to know each other's rights and obligations. This chapter will identify the principal areas of private education wherein the law differs markedly from the law discussed in previous chapters.

Private schools receive different legal treatment than public schools in some areas, but in others, they are subject to the same laws that govern public schools. This chapter will emphasize the law that is unique to private education, but will also refer back to preceding chapters wherein the law applies to private as well as public schools.

As used in this chapter, the term "private education" includes education in the nonschool setting (home instruction) as well as in private schools. For purposes of this text, the following definition of a private school suffices:

> "A school which is controlled by an individual or by an agency other that a State, a subdivision of a State, or the federal government, usually which is supported primarily by other than public funds, and the operation of whose programs rests with other than publicly elected or appointed officials."[1]

As of 1975, nonpublic school enrollment comprised about 10 percent of the total elementary school population in the nation, and between 6 and 7 percent of the total high school population, with little apparent variation in recent years.[2] The church-related or religious schools are, by far, the largest component of private education, accounting for more than 90 percent of the total nonpublic school enrollment.[3] The concentration and socio-economic characteristics of private schools vary drastically in different regions of the country. The largest private systems are concentrated in the urban-suburban metropolitan areas and thus change and influence the fiscal and social problems of our major urban centers. The mix of church schools is undergoing significant changes. The total number of church schools has increased in recent years, while the number of the dominant system (Catholic schools) has decreased.[4]

The historic background of American education is indispensible to an appreciation of the legal status of private schools. All schools were private following the American Revolution, until the 1830s when public schools were first created. The states made no serious attempts to regulate private schools until the 1920s when the federal government (in Hawaii) and the state of Nebraska attempted to outlaw the use of foreign languages in private schools and when the state of Oregon enacted a law to force all

---

1. See *The Condition of Education* (1982 ed.), (National Center for Education Statistics, U.S. Dept. of Education) at p. 248.

2. See *The Condition of Education* (1977 ed.), (National Center for Education Statistics, U.S. Dept. of Education), Vol. 3, Part I, pp. 74, 77, 127. See also 1979 edition of same study, Table 2.3, p. 54.

3. See *Report of the President's Panel on Nonpublic Education*, p. 7 (1972).

4. *See* fn. 1, *supra*, at p. 39.

children to attend public schools. In each of these cases, the Supreme Court struck down the laws as unconstitutional infringements of the substantive rights of parents and of the school operators, which were found to be aspects of the "liberty" protected by the Fifth and Fourteenth Amendments.[5] These cases have been repeatedly approved in recent times.[6] It is often forgotten that they had nothing to do with religion claims under the First Amendment. They dealt with nonsectarian as well as sectarian private schools and were decided before the religion clauses of the First Amendment were applied to the states in 1940.[7] In upholding parental rights, however, the Court stressed that even those rights are subject to "reasonable" regulation by the state, since the state also has an interest in child education.

State regulation of private education was subjected to a second constitutional restriction in 1976—the First Amendment protection of free exercise of religion. State regulation may not infringe religious practice *unless* the state can prove a "compelling" interest that requires such infringement. In *Wisconsin* v. *Yoder* (reproduced at the end of Chapter 3), the Supreme Court applied this rule to hold that Wisconsin could not require the Amish, contrary to their religion, to send their children to school after grade 8. The *Yoder* ruling was narrowed to cases of religious necessity and could not apply to mere dissatisfaction or philosophical disagreement with the public schools.[8] It left to future litigation how the free exercise clause might affect other state controls over sectarian education. The Supreme Court did not venture any specific guidelines to indicate what regulations would be "reasonable" or "sufficiently compelling" to override parental or religious prerogatives. Some of the more typical problems of balancing state and private interests appear in the following discussion.

B. State Regulation of Private Education

The principal alternatives to total public education are private schools, home education, and dual enrollment. The legal practical problems associated with dual enrollment (noted in part G, *infra,* and in Chapter 4) make it a little-used option. Home education is permitted by law in about 31 states, but it has rarely been pursued.[9] All states allow education at an approved private school, but their approval standards vary widely. Some states' standards for private schools are separate and distinct from those adopted for special categories of private education (e.g., schools for the handicapped, private academies, church-related schools, and home education).[10]

---

5. Meyer v. Nebraska, 262 U.S. 390 (1923); Pierce v. Society of Sisters; Pierce v. Hill Military Academy, both reported at 268 U.S. 510 (1925); Farrington v. Tokushige, 273 U.S. 284 (1927).

6. *See* Runyon v. McCrary, 427 U.S. 160, 179 (1976).

7. *Compare* Barron v. Mayor and City Council of Baltimore, 32 U.S. 243 (1833); *with* Cantwell v. Connecticut, 310 U.S. 296 (1940).

8. *See* Scoma v. Chicago Board of Education, 391 F.Supp. 452 (N.D.Ill. 1974); F. v. Duval Cty., 273 So.2d 15 (Fla. 1973); Re Shinn, 16 Cal. Rptr. 165 (1961); State v. Kasuboski, 275 N.W. 2d 101 (Wis. 1978).

9. *See* People v. Turner, 98 N.Y.S.2d 886, 888 (1950).

10. Grigg v. Comm., 297 S.E.2d 799 (Va. 1982) and cases there cited; Wiley House v. Scanlon, 465 A.2d 995 (Pa. 1983) (private schools for handicapped); Glenmore Academy v. State Bd. of Private Academic Schools, 385 A.2d 1049 (Pa. 1978) (separate licensure of private academies); DelConte v. State, 308 S.E.2d

Until recent years, state regulation of private schools was minimal, but with declining public school enrollments and increasing proliferation of private schools, a number of states have begun to impose stricter requirements for their approval. These developments sparked a wave of litigation on the legality of new state controls.

Where state statutes refer only to "school" attendance, the sufficiency of individualized or home instruction to qualify as a "school" depends upon court interpretations. Some courts held that home instruction is not a school within the meaning of their statutes.[11] The majority of states accept home instruction either as falling within the word "school" or within legislation that expressly allows home instruction.[12] In these cases, the criteria for acceptable alternative education must still be settled. Courts commonly refer to "equivalent" or "qualified" education, but the terms mean different things to different judges depending upon the wording of the particular statute. Approval disputes focus on two basic questions:

1. Is the state limited (by parental rights) to setting only "floor" standards that ensure minimally adequate education; or may it set higher, though more expensive, standards that reflect the secular aspirations of public education?
2. May the state require private schools to furnish comparable teacher qualifications and instructional resources, or is the state interest limited to requiring acceptable student achievement, irrespective of the school's educational resources?

In answering these questions, each court must decide what school goals are sufficiently relevant to state goals, to justify state regulation. For example, may a state require private schools to hire only state certified teachers? To provide comparable extracurricular or community action programs? To provide enrichment curricula beyond core-mandated subjects?

1. Constitutional Considerations

Most extant cases on private school regulation predated the modern constitutional decisions on parental and religious rights. Those cases provide a necessary backdrop to evaluate later legal developments.

The *Yoder* case represents the lead constitutional authority on compulsory education. Though it did not cover elementary education, its rationale of parental and religious liberty has influenced state cases dealing with private schools.[13] Under *Yoder*,

---

898, 901-2 (N.Car. 1983) (legislative differentiation between church-related and nonsectarian private schools). Annotation: *Attendance at Private or Parochial Schools*, 65 A.L.R.3d 1222 (1975); H.Punke, *Home Instruction and Compulsory School Attendance*, 5 NOLPE L.J. (1975).

11. The various meanings given to "school," as used under unclear statutes in various states, are discussed in *DelConte* v. *State*, *supra*, and *Grigg* v. *Commonwealth*, *supra*. *See also* P. Lines & J. Bray, *What Is a School?* 16 WEST ED. L. REP. 371 (1984); State v. Hoyt, 146 A.170 (N.H.38 (1929)); State v. Counart, 124 P. 910 (Wash. 1912); State v. Lowry, 383 P.2d 962 (Kan. 1963), People v. Turner, 263 P.2d 685 (Calif. 1953).

12. People v. Levisen, 90 N.E.2d 213 (Ill. 1950); State v. Peterman, 70 N.E. 550 (Ind. 1904).

13. The Yoder decision overrules prior state decisions to the contrary, such as State v. Garber, 419 P.2d 896 (Kan. 1966); Knox v. O'Brien, 72 A.2d 389 (N.J. 1950).

courts still uphold reasonable state grounds to deny approval to private schools and sustain prosecution for enrollment of children in unapproved schools.[14] Where parents were required to seek prior approval of state authorities for home education programs, their failure to do so rendered them liable to prosecution, even though the home education would have been acceptable, had approval been sought.[15]

State courts recently considered the extent to which Fourteenth and First Amendment liberty limit state approval regulations. These decisions are not binding on other states and some are contrary to pre-*Yoder* state cases, but they could influence future legal developments.

In 1978, the Ohio court in *Whisner* v. *State Bd. of Education* (reported at the end of this chapter), adopted the view that a state may not require equivalence or comparability between private and public educational resources, programs, and goals; but may require only standards to assure basic citizen training for economic self-support and social responsibility as measured by adequate training and achievement in essential courses. The court there reversed truancy convictions of 10 parents affilitated with a Christian Bible school that refused to seek a state charter or state approval because such action would express their acquiescence in the state's detailed education standards. The minority judges reasoned that the state's approval regulations were unconstitutionally vague, but the majority rested decision on substantive rulings that the state regulations on teacher certification, instructional time allocation, educational philosophy, community involvement, and comparability to public school programs infringed the liberties of the defending parents under the Ohio and Federal constitutions. By resting its decision partly upon the state constitution, the Ohio court foreclosed any reversal by the federal courts, since federal courts cannot overturn state court decisions that are based on valid state laws.

Whisner was later followed in Kentucky and, to a limited degree, in North Carolina.[16] The Kentucky trial court echoed the *Whisner* theme on

> "irreconcilable philosophical differences between their educational concepts, notions of textbook and curriculum content and teacher qualification. The differences . . . having a foundation in firmly held religious belief. Expert testimony in this case certainly established that there is not the slightest connection between teacher certification and enhanced educational quality. . . . The state is unable to demonstrate that its regulatory scheme applied to public schools has any reasonable relationship to the supposed objective of advancing educational quality; . . . plaintiffs, on the other hand, have shown that without benefit of the state's ministrations their educational product is at least equal to if not somewhat better than that of the public schools, in purely secular competence."

---

14. State v. Vietto, 247 S.E.2d 298 (N.C. 1978); Scoma v. Chicago Board of Education, 391 F.Supp. 452 (N.D. Ill. 1974); Application of Auster, 100 N.Y.S.2d 60 (1951).

15. *Compare* State ex rel. Shoreline School District v. Superior Court, 346 P.2d 999 (Wash. 1959); Rice v. Commonwealth, 49 S.E.2d 342 (Va. 1948) (prosecutions upheld for lack of prior state approval); *with* People v. Levisen, 90 N.E.2d 213 (Ill. 1950) (prosecution dismissed) and the Whisner case, at the end of this chapter.

16. Hinton v. Kentucky State Bd. of Education, Civil Action No. 88314, Franklin Cir. Ct. (Ky. 1978), aff'd sub nom. Kentucky St. Bd. Of Elementary and Secondary Education v. Rudasill, 589 S.W.2d 877 (Ky. 1979); State of No. Carolina v. Columbus Christian Academy, Sup. Ct., Div. No.78 CUS 1678 (N.C. 1978).

On appeal, however, the Kentucky Supreme Court limited ruling in favor of the private schools on the peculiar provisions of the Kentucky State Constitution expressly protecting parental choice of schools.[17]

In the absence of any finding of unnecessary excessiveness or oppression (viz. regulations requiring equivalence of resources or educational philosophy between public and private schools), the majority of modern decisions uphold state regulations that are reasonably related to the state's interest in ensuring minimally adequate education to all students. Such regulations cannot be defeated by allegations that state approval requirements are religiously offensive or economically burdensome. The party claiming religious exemption must prove that the approval requisite is truly religiously offensive and not merely philosophically distasteful;[18] and that, if so, no reasonable educational alternative satisfies the state conditions.[19]

Most modern decisions also reject the claim that state school regulations interfere with individual constitutional rights of contract, association, or privacy, unless those claims are anchored in constitutionally protected parental or religious rights.[20] The current case trend is equally unsympathetic to claims that school approval statutes, regulations, or approval criteria are unconstitutionally vague or overbroad.[21] Nor may the regulated party object to the application of school approval criteria as discriminatory (viz. as a form of selective prosecution) without strong proof that the enforcing authorities are acting with malice or unlawful motive.[22]

The power of states to enforce normal education standards under the compulsory

---

17. Section 5 of the Kentucky Constitution provides in part "nor shall any man be compelled to send his child to any school to which he may be conscientiously opposed."

18. *Requirement of sincere religious belief*: *see, e.g.*, State v. Calvary Academy, 348 N.W.2d 898 (Neb. 1984); State v. Andrews, 651 P.2d 473 (Haw. 1982); Hill v. State, 410 So.2d 431 (Ala. 1981); Jernigan v. State, 412 So.2d 1242, 1246 (Ala. 1982); State ex rel. Nagle v. Olin, 415 N.E.2d 279 (Ohio 1980); State v. Kasuboski, 275 N.W.2d 101 (Wis. 1978) (defendant's church did not require rejection of public schools); F. v. DuVal County, 273 So.2d 15 (Fla. 1973) (objection not shown to be truly "religious"). Semble: DelConte v. State, 308 S.E.2d 898 (N. Car. 1983); Brown v. Dade Christian Schools Inc., 556 F.2d 310 (5th Cir. 1977). But "Men may believe what they cannot prove. They may not be put to the proof of their religious doctrine." *See* United States v. Ballard, 322 U.S. 78, 86 (1977).

19. *E.g.*, State ex. rel Nagle v. Olin, *supra.*

20. *See, e.g.*, Attorney General v. Bailey, 436 N.E.2d 139 (Mass. 1982); Jernigan v. State, *supra*; State v. McDonough, 448 A.2d 977, 979 (Me. 1983). *But see* State v. Nuss, 114 N.W.2d 633 (S. Dak. 1962) (statute prohibiting schools from collecting advance tuition, held unconstitutional as an interference with freedom of contract).

21. *Re* vagueness, *see* Bangor Baptist Church v. State, 549 F.Supp. 1208 (D.Me. 1982) (standard of "equivalent" education held not vague); State v. Moorehead, 308 N.W.2d 60 (Iowa 1981) ("equivalent instruction" and "certified teacher," not unconstitutionally vague); semble: Scoma v. Chicago Bd. of Education, fn. 8, *supra. But see contra*: State v. Popanz, 332 N.W.2d 750 (Wis. 1983) (term "private school" held impermissibly vague, as applied to prosecution); Roemhild v. State, 308 S.E.2d 154 (Ga. 1983). Compare DelConte v. State, fn. 18, *supra,* where the court gave the term "school" a narrow (constitutional) construction. *Overbreadth: compare* Bangor Baptist Church v. State, *supra*; Jernigan v. State, 412 So.2d 1242, 1247 (Ala. 1982) (rejecting overbreadth challenges); *with* State ex rel. Nagle v. Olin, 415 N.E.2d 279 (Ohio 1980); State v. Whisner, 351 N.E.2d 750 (Ohio 1976); *cf.* Surinach v. Pasquere deBusquets, 460 F.Supp. 121 (D. Puerto Rico 1978) (recognizing overbreadth challenges).

22. Attorney General v. Bailey, *supra*; State v. Edgington, 663 P.2d 74 (N. Mex. 1983); State ex rel. Nagle v. Olin, *supra*; State v. Bowman, 653 P.2d 254 (Ore. 1982) (denying equal protection challenges to state approval laws and prosecutions). *But see* Milwaukee Montessori School v. Percy, 473 F.Supp. 1358 (W.D. Wis. 1979) (different licensing requirements for different classes of private schools—held irrational and a violation of equal protection).

education laws has been held to include the power to require even unapproved schools to report and identify children in attendance at such schools.[23]

In mounting constitutional objections to private school regulations, the development of evidence, often through expert witnesses, is critical. For example, whether a parent's objections truly rest upon religious claims or merely upon personal preferences is primarily an issue of fact. (See the following section on "Burden of Proof.")

2. Statutory and Regulatory Requirements

Under the *ultra vires* doctrine, education administrators may not exceed the scope of their statutory authority. A court accordingly overturned a state board's attempt to supervise the activities and management of private schools where the statute only authorized it to approve the school's instructional program.[24] Challenges to the *statutory authority* of state agencies to regulate private schools have failed more often than they succeeded. The bare statutory authorization of state approval was found to be a standardless and unlawful delegation in North Carolina, but held sufficient in several states.[25]

As shown by Table 10–1, relatively few states before the 1970s adopted approval standards for private schools beyond those relating to health, safety, core curriculum, and school calendar. Since that time, however, a growing minority of states has continued to

TABLE 10–1. State statutes on qualifications for teachers in private schools *

Requirement	State
Require teachers to be certified	California (Re Shinn, 16 Cal. Rptr. 165 (1965); Kentucky (Ky. Rev. Stat. 161-030); Michigan (Michigan Comp. Laws 388.553); Mississippi (Miss. Code § 37-17-7); Nebraska (79 Neb. Rev. Stat. § 1701); North Carolina (State of No. Carolina v. Columbus Christian Academy, p. 459); South Dakota (So. Dak. Comp. Laws § 13-4-2); Washington (State ex rel. Shoreline Sch. District v. Superior Court, 346 P.2d 999 (Wash. 1965).
Requires teachers to be qualified, but not certified	Indiana (Indiana Stat. 2-1-19-10); Ohio (Ohio Rev. Code 3301.071 (nullified in Whisner v. St. Bd. of Education, p. 458); Oregon (Oregon Rev. Stat. § 345.525).
Require certification if public funds are provided for tuition at private schools	Maine (Me. Rev. Stat. Ann. § 1751).

*All data tables must be updated for possible changes in each state since 1979.

23. Attorney General v. Bailey, *supra.*

24. Santa Fe Comm. School v. N. Mexico State Bd. of Education, 581 P.2d 272 (N. Mex. 1977).

25. *Compare* cases in fn. 21, *supra*; People v. Turner, 263 P.2d 685 (Cal. 1953) (upholding broad statute authorizations); *with* State v. Williams, 117 S.E.2d 444 (N. Car. 1960).

promulgate laws and regulations imposing more detailed approval criteria. These range from formal requirements of teacher certification and courses of instruction, to informal guidelines that vest broad discretion in approval agencies. This evolving law in the states often differentiates approval criteria for formal schooling from that of home instruction.[26] The trend toward greater state regulation of private education is not universal. Recent studies reveal that a few states have consciously deregulated private schools and expressly limited the authority of state agencies to promulgate approval requirements for private schools. The diverse approval schemes taken by individual states are indicated by the following comment from a recent study by the Education Commission of the States:

"Acceptable ways of meeting the schooling requirement vary widely among states. Some states require certification of teachers and schools, some only approval and some only minimal evidence that schooling takes place. States like Alabama, Iowa, Nebraska, North Dakota, West Virginia and Wisconsin are at one end of the spectrum. They have obtained state court approval of at least some aspects of the state's power to regulate private educational alternatives. Ohio provided even more detailed regulation, but its high court has curbed the state's regulatory system as applied to religious schools. States with more lenient requirements will probably experience less litigation. Such states include, for example, Connecticut, which provides a broad exception to the school attendance requirement. Parents who do not send their children to public school must educate or "cause" their children to be educated in specific subjects. Other states following this model include Delaware, Idaho, New Jersey, South Dakota and Vermont. These states do not specify who must be the teacher or where instruction is to take place. Instruction apparently can be by anyone and anywhere so long as it is equivalent to that taking place in public schools. Some states, such as Alaska, Arizona, Georgia and Ohio give state and local school officials wide discretionary authority to excuse a child from the compulsory attendance requirement. Virginia and Kentucky expressly permit exemption from compulsory school attendance where the parent has conscientious objections to such attendance. In other states, in certain cases, courts have interpreted federal or state constitutional provisions in a way that permits individuals or churches to operate schools despite the state compulsory attendance law. California and Alabama permit home instruction but require the tutor to be certified by the state.

Some states have consciously deregulated their private schools. These states expressly limit state administrative authority to promulgate regulations. Tennessee, for example, provides: "The state board of education and local boards of education are prohibited from regulating the selection of faculty or textbooks or the establishment of a curriculum in church related schools." The law contains no hint as to whether the state can impose even minimal reporting requirements. However, private schools in Tennessee still have the option of seeking state approval. North Carolina presents a somewhat similar option, with two 1979 laws that deregulate all private schools. . . .

"Under the new law, North Carolina has minimal requirements for recordkeeping (pupil attendance and disease immunization) and requires that the schools select and administer a nationally standardized test to students each year. . . . Washington, like Tennessee and North Carolina, has consciously limited the extent to which the state

26. People v. Turner, *supra.*

board can regulate private schools. The Washington law provides for stricter requirements for these schools, relative to Tennessee or North Carolina. It sets minimum standards as to school year, length of day and subjects to be taught. It expressly provides that these minimum standards shall not be altered by state agencies. However, the Washington law continues to require teacher certification . . . This requirement is a sore point with fundamentalist Christian schools and a stumbling block to many other private education alternatives. However, Washington law allows teaching by a person of "unusual competence," if supervised by a certified teacher. In practice the state may allow more flexibility than would initially appear.

Mississippi, like Tennessee and North Carolina, adopts a laissez faire attitude, . . . It has since enacted a new compulsory education law with no sanctions and a "sunset" date of July 1984."[27]

Recent test cases have upheld state requirements of teacher certification[28] and course approval[29] for private schools, subject to the above-noted constitutional limits.

a. Home Instruction. The range of home education law in the sister states is reviewed in the case of *State* v. *Massa* (reproduced at the end of this chapter). They vary considerably, but generally fall into several classes. A small minority of cases holds that no form of home education may satisfy the compulsory education statute because the statute is silent on home education and the term "school" is not construed to cover it; or because home education lacks peer learning experience that a court deems necessary for proper education.[30] In the majority of states, home education may satisfy state

---

27. See P. Lines, *Private Education Alternatives and State Regulation,* pp. 3-4 (March 1982, Education Commission of the States). Footnotes to the above excerpt follow. (1) State v. Faith Baptist Church, 301 N.W.2d 571 (Neb. 1981); State v. Shaver, 294 N.W.2d 883 (N.D. 1980); State v. Kasuboski, 275 N.W.2d 101 (Wis. 1978); Hill v. State, 381 So.2d 91 (Ala. 1979); State v. Riddle, 285 S.E.2d 359 (W. Va. 1981). (2) Del. Code Ann. tit. 14, §2703 (1981); Idaho Code § 33-202 (1981); N.J. Stat. Ann. §§18(a); 38-25 (West 1968); South Dakota Comp. Laws Ann. §13-27-3 (Supp. 1981). (3) Ga. Code Ann. §32-2106(b) (1980); Ohio Rev. Code Ann. §3321.04(C) (1980). See also Alaska Stat. §14.30.010(b)(8) (1981); Ariz. Rev. Stat. Ann. §15-802(B)(5) (Supp. 1981); Some states provide for broad exemption within certain age brackets. *E.g.*, N.M. Stat. Ann. §22-12-2(4) (1981 Supp.). (4) Ky. Const. §5. *See also* Va. Const. Art. VIII §1. (5) Ala. Code §16-28-3, 16-28-5 (1975); Cal. Educ. Code §48224 (West 1978). (6) Tenn. Stat. Ann. §49 5201-5204 (1970). (7) N.Car. Gen. Stat. §155C-547 to 555 (Cum. Supp. 1981). (8) Wash. Rev. Code §§28.02.201 et seq.; 28.A27.010. (9) Miss. Code Ann. §37-13-95 (1981 Cum. Supp.). See also Note, *State Regulation of Private Religious Schools,* 25 ARIZ. L. REV. 123 (1983); *Comment, The State and Sectarian Education: Regulation to Deregulation,* 1980 DUKE L. J. 801; P. Lines, *State Regulation of Private Education,* 1982 PHI DELTA KAPPAN 119; Annotations; *Validity of State Regulation of Curriculum* and *Instruction in Private and Parochial Schools,* 18 A.L.R.4th 649 (1982); *Attendance at "Private or Parochial Schools,* 65 A.L.R.3d 1222 (1975).

28. *See, e.g.*, Sheridan Baptist Church v. Dept. of Education, 348 N.W.2d 263 (Mich. 1984); State ex rel. Douglas v. Morrow, 343 N.W.2d 903 (Neb. 1984); Bangor Baptist Church v. State, *supra;* State v. Rivinius, 328 N.W.2d 220 (N.D. 1982); State v. Faith Baptist Church, 301 N.W.2d 571 (Neb. 1981); State v. Moorehead, 308 N.W.2d 60 (Iowa 1981); Hill v. State, 410 So.2d 431 (Ala. 1981); State v. Riddle, 285 S.E.2d 359 (W.Va. 1981); State v. Shaver, 294 N.W.2d 883 (N.D. 1980); State ex rel. Shoreline School District v. Superior Court, 346 P.2d 999 (Wash. 1959). *See also* State ex rel. Nagle v. Olin, *supra;* Lanner v. Winmer, 662 F.2d 1349 (10th Cir. 1981); Paladino v. Adelphi University, 454 N.Y.S.2d 868, 872 (1982); State v. Andrews, 651 P.2d 473 (Haw. 1982).

29. State v. Shaver, *supra;* State v. Lowry, 383 P.2d 962 (Kan. 1963); In re Shinn, 16 Cal. Rptr. 165 (1961).

30. State v. Edgington, 663 P.2d 74 (N. Mex. 1983); DelConte v. State, 308 S.E.2d 898 (N. Car. 1983); State v. Hoyt, 146 A. 170 (N.H. 1929).

educational requirements if it meets appropriate criteria (i.e. that it is "sufficient," equivalent," or "comparable" to that received in approved schools). Under these standards, the question remains whether the adequacy of home education is to be measured by satisfactory achievement and educational "output," or by the quantum and quality of resource "input." The states are divided on the application of these standards where the statute is not specific on the approval criteria.[31]

Illinois, New Jersey, and New York courts allowed home education by uncertified but adequate teachers, but the laws of California, Florida, Maine, Ohio, Virginia, and Washington were held to require home instruction by state-qualified teachers.[32] The earlier home-education cases must be reevaluated under current statutes, since more and more states are enacting statutes that elevate professional qualification standards for home education. That the states may, if they choose, impose improved education requirements—that instruction be given only by state certified teachers and include specified courses, that a minimum instruction time be met, and that state-prescribed testing and reporting be supplied—is not open to serious challenge. The more serious questions under elevated legal standards involve the limits placed upon the *degree* of state oversight by parental and religious constitutional rights. However, it is unlikely, save in special fact situations, that a parent's rights will supersede the state's power to demand adequate citizen education.

b. Burden of Proof in Compulsory Attendance Prosecutions. State prosecutions of parents who reject state standards can turn on rules of evidence and burden of proof, rather than on the inadequacy of a particular program.[33] For example, if the state fails to produce evidence of a violation, the prosecution may be dismissed even though the parent was in fact violating the law. Conversely, a parent who failed to prove excuse would be held guilty, even if in fact he or she was providing lawful education. Placing of burden of proof on each opposing party may thus be crucial.

States that follow the view that compulsory education prosecutions are criminal or quasicriminal in nature are governed by the traditional criminal law that a defendant is presumed innocent until proven guilty by the state. Under this view, the state must prove beyond a reasonable doubt all elements of the offense—that the parent was not providing adequate private education and was not excused on health grounds.[34]

---

31. "Laws in about half the states permit instruction at home by a parent. Other states permit instruction at home by a certified teacher or parent. Usually the certification requirements preclude most parents from qualifying. In some states, opinions from courts or attorneys general have authorized home instruction by ruling that the home can qualify as a school if it meets all of the requirements of a private school. (This general rule would seem to apply to any state, even if no ruling exists.) In some states, such as Ohio, Oregon and South Dakota, this home instruction may be done by a parent or a qualified person. In Arizona, home instruction must be by a 'competent teacher'. In Nevada and Utah, home instruction must be equivalent to that taking place in the public schools." See P. Lines, fn. 27, *supra,* at p. 5.

32. *Compare* State v. Massa (at end of this chapter); People v. Turner, 98 N.Y.S.2d 886 (1950); People v. Levison, 90 N.E.2d 213 (Ill. 1950); *with* In re Shinn, 16 Cal. Rptr. 165 (1965); State v. M., 407 So.2d 987 (Fla. 1981); State v. McDonough, 468 A.2d 977 (Me. 1983); State v. Hershberger, 144 N.E.2d 693 (Ohio 1955); Grigg v. Commonwealth, 297 S.E.2d 799 (Va. 1982); State ex rel. Shoreline School District v. Superior Court, 346 P.2d 999 (Wash. 1959).

33. See the excellent treatment of this question by Professor Punke, fn. 10.

34. *See* State v. Mass. (at end of this chapter); In re Monnig, 638 S.W.2d 782 (Mo. 1982); *cf.* In re Interest of Sawyer, 672 P.2d 1093 (Ky. 1983) (requiring proof of "clear and convincing evidence"). State of

A number of states have taken the opposite view, namely, that parents are prima facie guilty unless *they* can prove that they are entitled to a statutory exemption, as a matter of affirmative defense.[35] In a few states, the burden of proof is expressly fixed by statute. Thus, under New York law, a parent whose child is not attending a recognized school must prove that the child is receiving alternative education that meets state standards.[36] Further, if the statute requires a parent to obtain *prior* official approval of a home education program, the failure to obtain such approval will alone support prosecution, even though the unapproved program might in fact satisfy state standards.[37]

The differences among the states may turn either on the way a state statute is worded, or on the way in which a court classifies a particular enforcement proceeding, i.e., as criminal or civil in nature. Where the proceedings involve an attempt to remove a child from a parent, and strip away parental rights, all courts are bound by the constitutional ruling of the United States Supreme Court—that to justify divestiture of parental rights, the state has the burden of proof, by "clear and convincing" evidence, that such removal is necessary to meet the child's basic needs.[38]

c. School Sites and Construction. The laws affecting the location and construction of private schools are not identical to those reviewed in Chapter 3 with respect to public schools. Private schools are generally subject to municipal zoning and building codes, but there are some recognized limits to the public authority.[39] Whether cast in constitutional terms of deprivation of rights (due process), discriminatory treatment (equal protection), or abuse of discretion, land-use restrictions that have no substantial relation to the public interest in health, safety, or welfare are unlawful. The root issue, therefore, is whether building and use regulations are reasonable exercises of government power. Fair zoning restrictions on parochial school location cannot be said to infringe upon religious liberty.[40] As the following materials show, the law often turns on the degree or extent of burden that zoning laws place upon private schools.

Restrictions effecting total or near-total exclusion of private schools from the entire municipality have been universally overturned, as have oppressive requirements (e.g., that the private school site cover 50 acres of land).[41] But exclusion of both private

---

Vermont v. LaBarge, 136 Vermont 276 (1976); Sheppard v. State, 306 P.2d 346 (Okla. 1957); State v. Cheney, 305 S.W.2d 892 (Mo. 1957); State v. Pilkinton, 310 S.W.2d 304 (Missouri 1958); Parr v. State, 157 N.E. 555 (Ohio 1927). *Cf.* In re Contempt of Liles, 349 N.W.2d 377 (Neb. 1984).

35. State v. Shaver, fn. 28, *supra*; Scoma v. Chicago Bd. of Education, fn. 14; State v. Lowry, fn. 28; Cooper v. State, 47 Ind. 61 (1874).

36. In re H., 357 N.Y.S.2d 384 (1974); In re Conlin, 130 N.Y.S.2d 811 (1954).

37. Commonwealth v. Renfrow, 126 N.E.2d 109 (Mass. 1955); Rice v. Commonwealth, fn. 15.

38. Santosky v. Kremer, 450 U.S. 993 (1982); semble: In re Interest of Sawyer, fn. 34, *supra.*

39. Seward Chapel, Inc. v. City of Seward, 655 P. 2d 1293, 1297-98 (Alaska 1982); City of Sumner v. First Baptist Church, 639 P.2d 1358, 1363 (Wash. 1982); Johnson & Wales College v. DiPrete, 448 A.2d 1271, 1279 (R.I. 1982); St. John's Roman Catholic Church Corp. v. Town of Darien, 184 A.2d 42 (Conn. 1962); State Bd. of Elementary & Secondary Education v. Rudesill, 589 S.W.2d 877, 879 (Ky. 1979). See generally Annotation: *Zoning Regulations—Private Schools,* 74 A.L.R.3d 14 (1976).

40. St. John's Roman Catholic Church Corp. v. Darien, 184 A.2d 42 (Conn. 1962); *see* Lakewood, Ohio Cong. of Jehovah's Witnesses Inc. v. City of Lakewood, 699 F2d 303, 305 (6th Cir. 1983).

41. *Exclusion from the municipality*: Brookville v. Paulgene Realty Corp.,180 N.E.2d 905 (N.Y. 1960); Roman Cath. Welfare Corp. v. Piedmont, 289 P.2d 438 (Cal. 1955); Mooney v. Orchard Lake, 53 N.W.2d 308 (Mich. 1952). *Oppressive requirements*: Westbury Hebrew Cong'n. Inc. v. Downer, 302 N.Y.S.2d 923 (1969).

and public schools from *selected* residential districts has been upheld.[42] Where a zoning law is more restrictive for only certain kinds of schools (between nursery and elementary schools or between profit and nonprofit private schools) the courts have split on their validity.[43] Exclusion of private nursery schools from zones open to public nursery schools was nullified as discriminatory.[44] For like reasons a court condemned zoning exclusion of nonsectarian private schools from areas where public and parochial schools were allowed to locate.[45]

Although the majority of cases have struck down laws and regulations that excluded private schools from residential zones in which public schools were allowed, a few courts have sustained the practice, either because the public schools were not subject to municipal regulation or because of perceived differences in the benefits and burdens visited by public and private schools upon residential areas.[46] The rule prohibiting zoning discrimination between public and private schools was enacted into statute law in New Jersey and partially adopted in a Massachusetts statute and a city ordinance that forbade local governments from limiting land use for religious purposes, including a parochial school.[47] In the rare instance when municipal authorities attempted to impose restrictions that were not authorized by statute by requiring consent of unauthorized officials, their action was overturned as *ultra vires*.[48]

Although absolute exclusion of schools is generally disfavored, the imposition of special use conditions and review requirements—to ensure consistency of school use with public planning—has been upheld.[49] However, where the courts found no substantial evidence to support the denial of school use petitions, they have ordered public authorities to grant the petitions.[50]

The imposition of reasonable conditions on grants of special exceptions or zoning variances (special setback, parking, or occupancy limitations) is lawful.[51] However,

---

42. Roman Cath. Diocese v. Ho-Ho-Kus, 220 A.2d 97 (N.J. 1966).

43. *Compare* Rockefeller v. Pynchon, 244 N.Y.S.2d 978 (1963); Three L. Corp. v. Bd. of Adj't., 288 A.2d 312 (N.J. 1972) (held valid); *with* Chicago v. Sachs, 115 N.E.2d 762 (Ill. 1953).

44. Merrick Comm'y. Nursery School v. Young, 171 N.Y.S.2d 522 (1958).

45. State v. Northwestern Preparatory School, 37 N.W.2d 370 (Minn. 1949); Lumpkin v. Twp. Committee, 48 A.2d 798 (N.J. 1946).

46. *Zoning exclusion voided:* Diocese of Rochester v. Planning Bd., 136 N.E.2d 827 (N.Y. 1956); Phillips v. Homewood, 50 So.2d 267 (Ala. 1951); Catholic Bishop of Chicago v. Kingery, 20 N.E.2d 583 (Ill. 1939); City of Miami Beach v. State ex rel Lear, 175 So.537 (Fla. 1937). *Exclusion sustained:* Tustin Heights Assn. v. Bd. of Supervisors, 339 P.2d 914 (Cal. 1954); Great Neck Comm'y School v. Dick. 158 N.Y.S.2d 379 (1955); State v. Sinar, 65 N.W.2d 43 (Wis. 1954).

47. *See* St. Cassian's Catholic Church v. Allen, 190 A.2d 667 (N.J. 1963); Attorney General v. Dover, 100 N.E.2d 1 (Mass. 1951); *Accord:* City of Concord v. New Testament Baptist Church, 382 A.2d 377 (N.H. 1978).

48. Congregation Temple Israel v. Creve Coeur, 320 S.W.2d 451 (Mo. 1959); Saddle River Country Day School v. Saddle River, 144 A.2d 425, aff'd. per curiam, 150 A.2d 34 (N.J. 1959).

49. Creative Country Day School v. Montgomery County Bd. of Appeals, 219 A.2d 789 (Md. 1966); Archdiocese of Portland v. County of Washington, 458 P.2d 682 (Ore. 1969); Rockefeller v. Pynchon, 244 N.Y.S.2d 978 (1963); State ex rel. Hacharedi v. Baxter, 74 N.E.2d 242 (Ohio 1947).

50. *See* Re Creative Country Day School v. Burns, 238 N.Y.S.2d 348 (1963); Trinity Ev. Lutheran Church v. Bd. of Adjustment, 179 A.2d 45 (N.J. 1962); Bd. of Zoning Appeals v. Schulte, 172 N.E.2d 39 (Ind. 1961); Appeal of O'Hara, 131 A.2d 587 (Pa. 1957).

51. First Assembly of God v. City of Alexandria, 739 F.2d 942 (4th Cir. 1984); St. Cassian's Catholic Church v. Allen, 190 A.2d 667 (N.J. 1963).

arbitrary rulings, such as denying use of onsite water, are overturned as abuses of discretion.[52]

Public restrictions on private school uses of property frequently present issues of legislative interpretation, rather than of constitutional law. For example, where a zoning law or ordinance is unclear as to what uses are covered by the terms "school" or "educational institution" and what educational activities are permitted as "accessory uses" to other permitted institutional uses (i.e. churches) courts must decide whether the presented use falls within the intended scope of those terms.[53] Since land use classification terms are not controlled by the meaning given to them under school statutes,[54] the construction of building and zoning laws may well vary from one state or municipality to another. A state or municipal legislature can, of course, always clarify legislation to remove ambiguities,[55] but even when such clarification is made by new restrictions, courts must decide whether a prior use falls within the new restriction, or qualifies as an exception thereto:

> "On remand to the trial court, the zoning ordinance issue in this case reduces to whether Washington Christian Academy *is* "church" use, inseparable in a sense sufficient to bring it within the excepted prior use. The church maintains that since the school is an integral and inseparable part of their religious faith, the use for church and school are one and the same. The City views the uses as separable. Since there was no evidence on this issue produced by either side, we decline to decide this.[56]

In the absence of any constitutional or statutory objection, private schools may overturn a use restriction in cases where the order rests upon administrative discretion in the application of zoning laws and where the agency acted arbitrarily and capriciously.[57] In such instances, the challenger bears a heavy burden of proof in the abuse of discretion issue.

---

52. West Goshen Twp. v. Bible Baptist Church, 313 A.2d 177 (Pa. 1973).

53. Allegheney West Civil Council, Inc. v. Zoning Board of Adjustment, 446 A.2d 334 (Pa. 1982) (meaning of "educational institution"); Fountain Gate Ministries v. City of Plano, 654 S.W.2d 841 (Tex. 1983) (particular use in church complex, classified as "college," and not as church, rectory, or school); Damascus Community Church v. Clackamas County, 610 P.2d 273 (Ore. 1980) (different ordinance classification of "church" and "parochial school"). *Compare* Concord v. New Testament Baptist Church Heritage Christian School, 382 A.2d 377 (N.H. 1978) (zoning exception for "church" held to include school as part of practice of religion).

54. *See, e.g.*, Livingston v. Davis, 50 N.W.2d 592 (Iowa 1951)

55. "The zoning ordinance permitted churches and accessory uses and did not specifically address the question of parochial schools; several courts have held that parochial schools are accessory uses within the meaning of zoning ordinances which permit accessory uses to churches. *See, e.g., City of Concord v. New Testament Baptist Church,* 118 N.H. 56, 382 A.2d 377 (1978) (five day per week school is a facility "usually connected with a church"). Nonetheless, in this case the possibility that a parochial school might be considered an accessory use to the church was foreclosed when the zoning ordinance was amended to address specifically the question of parochial schools, thus removing such schools from the general classification of accessory uses. *See infra* note 10 and accompanying text; *Damascus Comm. Church* v. *Clackamas County,* 45 Or.App. 1065, 610 P.2d 273 (1980), *appeal dismissed,* 450 U.S. 902, 101 S.Ct. 1336, 67 L.Ed.2d 326 (1981)." *See* Seward Chapel Inc. v. City of Seward, *supra,* 655 P.2d at p. 1295, n. 4. *Accord:* First Assembly of God v. City of Alexandria, 739 F.2d 942 (4th Cir. 1984)

56. *See* City of Sumner v. First Baptist Church, 639 P.2d 1358, 1365 (Wash. 1982).

57. *See* Johnson & Wales College v. DiPrete, 448 A.2d 1271, 1280-1282 (R.I. 1982).

The law on *private* use restrictions created by private owners of land is distinct from public zoning law. In one of the few cases on this issue, a New York court upheld a privately created deed covenant that prohibited the use of a particular parcel of land for a religious school.[58]

Of increasing current interest are the zoning classifications of residential private schools that combine housing or treating facilities with education of handicapped children. The petitions of such institutions for zoning permits were opposed on the ground that they did not qualify as private schools or educational centers under local zoning laws. The court of New York recently ruled that such facilities were more in the nature of treatment centers than private schools and that they were not entitled to locate in school zones, but Massachusetts and New Jersey courts ruled that a facility that is rehabilitative as well as educational does not diminish its status as a school.[59] Since each cases gave particular attention to the specific features of each center, it is too early to draw any generalizations from them.

Though private schools perform quasi-public services, they generally are not immune from being taken by government condemnation for other public uses, subject to their right to fair compensation.[60]

d. Admission Standards. Private schools are free to set their own standards of admission and to cater to selected social or religious groups, except in the limited situations where they are controlled by antidiscrimination statutes (See chapter 7 and section E in this chapter.)

C. Teacher Status and Rights

1. Introductory Note

The most crucial and often overlooked fact distinguishing the legal relations of private schools with their staff and students is that, unlike public schools, they are not governed by many statutes and provisions of the federal and state constitutions that extend special rights and protections to public school teachers and students. The significant procedural and substantive civil rights guaranteed by the First, Fourth, Fifth and Fourteenth Amendments, for example, do not apply to private actors, and private school activity is seldom linked sufficiently to government action to establish the requisite ground for constitutional protections.

Thus, a teacher who is offended by private school orders that suppress speech, invade privacy, or impose disciplinary sanctions without notice or hearings must look

58. Ginsburg v. Yeshiva of Far Rockaway, 358 N.Y.S.2d 477 (1974).

59. *Compare* Brandt v. Zoning Bd. of Appeals of New Castle, 393 N.Y.S.2d 264 (1977); *with* Harbor Schools v. Bd. of Appeals of Haverhill, 366 N.E.2d 764, 767-69 (Mass. 1977); Areba School Corp. v. Mayor and Council of Twp. of Randolph, 376 A.2d 1273 (N.J. 1977).

60. See generally Annotation: *Eminent Domain: Right to Condemn Property Owned or Used by Private Educational, Charitable or Religious Organization,* 80 A.L.R.3d 833 (1977).

elsewhere than to constitutional doctrines for legal relief, except in the unusual situation where the private school is considered to be engaged in official government action.

Since state school codes are, for the most part, directed exclusively to public education, their provisions regarding employment eligibility, collective bargaining, job security (renewal, tenure, and demotion), and retirement do not affect private school teachers. For these reasons, the legal rights of private school teachers must be traced primarily to their individual contracts with the schools. The following materials outline the more prominent elements of contract law that affect private school teachers. The special civil rights statutes that may reach them are considered later in this chapter.

2. Contract Rights and Duties

Teachers as well as employers are protected from unlawful breach by contract law. When a private school in breach of its contract terminates a teacher before the end of the contract period, the teacher may recover the salary for the full contract term.[61] If the teacher breaches his or her contract, that breach justifies immediate termination by the school.[62] Since contract disputes turn upon interpretation of specific agreements, both with regard to the express terms and with regard to obligations to be implied therefrom, the role of courts in interpreting contract obligations is crucial.[63] For example, the discharge of a Catholic school teacher for marrying a Catholic priest (contrary to Church law and contrary to an official policy of the school board) was overturned in a recent case. It was not overturned because the school could not impose a condition of employment that Catholic teachers not violate church law, but because the written contract required her to abide by school board policies that were "promulgated." Since the school board had failed to "promulgate" its policy, the court held that the teacher was not bound to observe it.[64] Thus, private schools could avoid contracts where the covered teacher in applying for the position intentionally withheld facts material to his or her acceptance (viz. a recent dismissal by another private school employer, or remarriage by the applicant, contrary to the teaching of the school-sponsoring church).[65] Generally speaking, courts will interpret the words of a private school contract to meet the fair expectations of the parties as disclosed by the nature, rules, and customs of the particular school. A court upheld a contract nonrenewal of a Catholic school teacher who remarried following divorce without obtaining a Church annulment of the prior marriage.[66] The reasoning of the foregoing cases is not peculiar to Catholic schools. In the absence of a contrary express contract term, the implication of an obligation not to contradict by public action the religious teachings of the school may apply to any religious school, and it is settled that secular courts will not question the validity of

---

61. Dunn v. Bessie F. Heirn School, Inc., 209 So.2d 538 (La. 1968).
62. Story v. San Rafaele Military Academy, 3 Cal. Rptr. 847 (1960).
63. See Chapter 5, part 2, regarding implied duties of teachers.
64. Wiethoff v. St. Veronica's School, 210 N.W.2d 108 (Mich. 1973).
65. Ostrolenk v. Louise S. McGhee School, 402 So.2d 237 (La. 1981) (failure to disclose termination of employment by another private school); Bischoff v. Brothers of Sacred Heart, 416 So.2d 348 (La. 1982) (applicant to teach religion intentionally concealed remarriage contrary to teaching of sponsoring church).
66. Steeber v. Benilde-St. Margaret's High School, No. D.C. 739 378, Hennepin County, Minnesota (1978).

religious precepts of any church (but only their sincerity) since any judicial review of church doctrine would violate the religion clauses of the First Amendment.[67] The implication of a contract duty not to undermine the goals or value orientation of the private school employer has been applied as well to nonreligious schools.[68]

In making contracts, the parties may expressly incorporate, by reference, the regulations and rulings of school authorities and of sponsoring institutions. For example, an informal collective labor agreement between church-sponsored high schools and the teachers' association in the Philadelphia Catholic Archdiocese contained a clause known as the "Cardinal's Clause." The clause stipulated that teachers could be dismissed for publicly contradicting, by word or action, the moral precepts of the sponsoring church.

Contract agreements concerning procedural rights of teachers will be enforced, even though the employer private school had no initial obligation to provide such procedures,[69] but the nature of the enforcement (i.e. damage recovery or injunction) may be determined by positive state law[70] or at the discretion of the court. Hence, individual contract interpretation provides a possible avenue of legal relief in cases where constitutions or labor law may not be applicable to particular private schools. For this reason, increasing care and attention is being given by private schools to the written terms of their employment contracts, to avoid any miscalculation concerning any express or implied obligations to observe procedures that are deemed to be matters of right in public schools.

3. Collective Labor-Management Relations

a. Voluntary Negotiations. Where not compelled by law, employers may voluntarily negotiate collectively with teachers on working terms and conditions. The terms and procedures for voluntary collective negotiations could be set by the school administration alone or by agreement with the teachers. Voluntary bargaining occurs in many private schools not subject to statutory bargaining under federal or state law.

b. Statutory Negotiations. The labor-relations laws governing private school employment are still somewhat confused due to the following history of federal and state labor legislation. The National Labor Relations Act (hereafter NLRA)[71] authorized the National Labor Relations Board (hereafter NLRB) to oversee collective bargaining and enforce its terms for nongovernment employers. However, the NLRB until 1974 elected not to apply its jurisdiction over private schools and since then has elected to enforce the NLRA only against private school employers whose annual gross revenues amount to $1 million, a figure that clearly excludes the overwhelming majority of private schools. Even

---

67. *See* Presbyterian Church v. Mary E. Blue Hull Memorial Presbyterian Church, 393 U.S. 440 (1969).

68. Martin v. Coral Gables Academy, 369 So.2d 255 (La. 1979) (teacher discharge for opposing school's disciplinary policy).

69. Reardon v. Lemoyne, 454 A.2d 428 (N.H. 1982); *cf.* Toussaint v. Blue Cross, 292 N.W.2d 880 (Mich. 1980).

70. Schauer v. Jamestown College, 323 N.W.2d 114 (N.D. 1982) (state statute prohibiting injunctive orders to reinstate teachers).

71. 29 U.S.C. §151.

for large church school systems that might meet that jurisdictional amount, serious questions on the applicability of the NLRA to church schools, discussed hereafter, have arisen. With respect to state labor laws that might apply to private schools not falling within NLRB jurisdiction, there persist constitutional questions of government involvement with religious schools that are not fully resolved. Because the operation of the federal and state labor laws may be different for religious and nonreligious private schools, they will be discussed separately with respect to each of these classes of private school.

Church-Sponsored Schools. In 1979, the United States Supreme Court was called upon to decide whether the NLRA applied to teacher negotiation by church-sponsored schools. In the obvious desire to avoid any ruling on the constitutional question whether such application would violate the religion clauses of the First Amendment (due to excessive government entanglement and interference with religious school practices), the Court decided, by 5-4 vote, that Congress did not intend the NLRA to apply to bargaining between church-related schools and their teachers. That landmark opinion (*NLRB* v. *Catholic Bishop of Chicago*) is digested at the end of this chapter. It left unresolved three independently important questions, namely, whether the NLRA was intended to cover church school employees *other than* those engaged in sensitive teaching positions (viz. janitors); whether if it were construed to cover nonteachers, such coverage would still infringe the establishment or free exercise clauses of the First Amendment; and, assuming, for any nonconstitutional reason, that the NLRA did not reach private school employees, whether any labor relations statutes of an individual state could constitutionally apply to them.

With respect to the first two questions, serious fact issues may arise as to what is a "religious" school and what class of employees within such a school would be considered involved in its religious mission. These questions, which were avoided by the Supreme Court's holding in the above case, later resurfaced under the New York State labor relations law in a case involving unfair labor charges by a teacher union against admittedly religious high schools.

In *Catholic High School Assn.* v. *Culvert,*[72] the Second Circuit Court of Appeals, contrary to prior holding of the Seventh Circuit Court of Appeals in *Catholic Bishop,* held that the New York State labor law did not violate the religion clauses of the First Amendment because, as read by the Second Circuit, the New York law only required collective bargaining and state agency review of employment practices on *secular* work issues and would not apply to labor disputes that affected the *religious* doctrine or motivation of church-sponsored schools. Whether that ruling will be deemed consistent with the Supreme Court dicta in *Catholic Bishop,* or survive future review by the Supreme Court of the United States, cannot be determined at this writing. The *Culvert* opinion does not, for example, explain how state oversight of labor disputes can avoid administrative entanglement in the very process of determining whether or not a particular labor dispute involves purely secular or substantial religious questions. These

72. Catholic High School Assn. v. Culvert, 753 F.2d 1161 (2d Cir. 1985).

questions were also avoided under Pennsylvania labor statute by a lower court holding that the Pennsylvania statute did not cover private religious schools.[73]

Nonsectarian Schools. The federal labor law, to the extent it applies to nonsectarian schools, would preempt and supersede state labor laws. Where such schools meet the jurisdictional amount set by the NLRB, there is no question. But where the NLRB declines jurisdiction over schools that do not meet its prescribed annual revenues, a technical question remains as to whether the NLRA still preempts the field as to exclude state labor law. The preemption argument has not been decisively settled, but takes its color from the fact that the NLRB has exercised jurisdiction over private schools[74] and unlike its elective jurisdiction (based upon annual revenues), the issue of preemption is one of congressional intent and not one of the NLRB discretion.

However the federal or state labor statutes may apply, the case law dealing with nonprofit private schools is sparse. The basic legal concepts on collective negotiations and bargaining, union representation, union security, and methods of dispute resolution are well developed and were largely copied in public employee labor laws. Therefore, many of the issues and concepts reviewed in Chapter 5 regarding public school teachers will generally operate in parallel, though not identical, fashion in the private school sector. Under the NLRA, labor law rulings are tailored to the needs and practices of particular enterprises. For this reason, many new rulings will be sought to test whether particular negotiations, grievances, and disciplinary practices will be required, permitted, or prohibited for private school employees and employers. Until that law is better developed, private school teachers and administrators would do well to rely upon the opinions of labor law specialists, rather than speculate on the extent to which the commercial and industrial labor practice will affect the private school law.

In the area of dispute resolution, private employers and employees have greater leeway in selecting the forms of arbitration (e.g. for negotiation deadlocks and for performance grievances) than is allowed public employees. Similarly, the right to strike by private-school teachers may be less restricted than the strike privileges given public school employees under state public employee labor statutes. Here also the undecided applicability of federal or state labor laws will have a material bearing on the labor relations practices of private schools. It should be recognized, however, that any greater legal freedom to strike is counterbalanced in many small private schools by the weaker economic and political bargaining position of many private-school teachers.

---

73. Pennsylvania Labor Relations Board v. Beth Jacob Schools, 301 A.2d 715 (Pa. 1973).

74. "As a threshhold matter, we must decide whether the National Labor Relations Act preempts the State Board's jurisdiction. We hold that it does not. If *Catholic Bishop* had held that teachers are within the jurisdiction granted by the NLRA but are not "employees" within the meaning of the Act, the State Board would plainly be preempted from exercising jurisdiction. . . . But *Catholic Bishop* held merely that the NLRB did not have jurisdiction over lay teachers because there was no clear statement that Congress had intended to cover them. 440 U.S. at 506-07. . . . Thus, this case is unlike *Committee of Interns and Residents* in which the NLRB retained jurisdiction over the employer, but deemed residents and interns not to be employees within the meaning of the Act." *See* Catholic High School Assn. v. Culvert, *supra,* 753 F.2d at p. 1165, n. 2.

D. Student Status and Rights

1. Contract Rights

What has been said of school-teacher relations at the beginning of the prior section applies as well to school-student relations. The rights, both substantive and procedural, that the Constitution guarantees to individuals with respect to *government* action, do not apply to individual grievances against *private* action. Hence the constitutional rights of public school students that apply to the state agencies operating those schools do not exist for private school students vis-à-vis the private operators of their schools, except in the relatively rare instance where the private school may be deemed to be acting as a government agent and therefore involved in "state action," which is necessary to render the Constitution applicable. It is well settled, however, that state regulation of private schools and incidental financial aid to them do not suffice to create "state action" subject to constitutional constraints.[75] "The state must be involved not simply with some activity of the school, but with *the* activity that caused the injury."[76]

But for special statutes, such as those governing student records, the rights of private school students and their parents are largely defined by the express and implied terms of their contract with the private school. Student enrollment in a private school generally connotes a good faith agreement to abide by school catalogues, regulations, handbooks, and properly announced directives or generally understood customs of the school. Where the school adopts certain grievance procedures, such as appeal hearings or arbitration, these will be considered binding upon the school as well as the students.

The central role and reliance placed upon contract terms in disputes between parents and private schools is evident in the fact that lawsuits often involve disagreements as to the intent of the contract of admission, and as to existence or propriety of "implied" understandings that are drawn from the history and background of the involved school. Those disagreements most commonly arise in disputes concerning tuition and tuition refund, academic credits, and disciplinary punishment of students.

With regard to tuition, a parent's liability is governed by contract terms, unless they are deemed to be unconscionable or against public policy.[77] For example, where the agreement is interpreted to require payment of full tuition, without refund, notwithstanding a student's failure or inability to complete the covered semester, through no fault of the school, the parent remained liable for the full tuition. Such was the case even where the student's withdrawal took place pursuant to powers reserved to the school to request the same for stated reasons.[78] Where a parent defaults on a contract obligation to pay agreed tuition and charges, that breach will also relieve the school of any contract

---

75. *See* Wisch v. Sanford School, Inc., 420 F. Supp 1310 (D. Del. 1976); Flint v. St. Augustine H.S., 323 So.2d 229 (La. 1975); Oefelein v. Msgr. Farrell H.S., 353 N.Y.S.2d 674 (1974); Bright v. Isenbarger, 445 F.2d 412 (7th Cir. 1971). *See also* Rendell-Baker v. Kohn, 457 U.S. 830 (1982).

76. *Idem.*

77. King v. Dramatic Arts, 102 Misc. 2d 1111 (N.Y. 1980) (contract permitting student dismissal without justification while tuition retained by school—voided as unconscionable). See also Annot: *School Tuition or Board,* 20 A.L.R.4th 303 (1983).

78. Leo Foundation, Inc. v. Kiernan, 240 A.2d 218 (Conn. 1967); Wentworth Military Academy v. Marshall, 283 S.W.2d 868 (Ark. 1955). But see fn. 77, *supra.*

obligations, including any duty to prepare and release academic records of the students.[79] Conversely, school breaches of contract duties (for example, failing to keep educational records required by the state to license the student to practice the skills taught at a vocational school) will preclude recovery of unpaid tuition because of its own breach of implied contract duty.[80] Courts will not review school decisions regarding academic standards, performance, or competence, but they can always remedy a bad faith breach by a private school.[81] Courts are particularly loathe to find a contract violation in the administration of academic grading. The First Circuit upheld the private college dean's decision to retain the failing grade in a required course that was occasioned by excessive student absences, notwithstanding the recommendation of a grade appeals committee to modify the grade to *incomplete*.[82] It noted that the commercial contract law was not to be rigidly applied to private school relationships and that the school rules on committee recommendation would not be interpreted to bind the dean, where the rules did not so specify. A good summary of the constitutional and contract law pertaining to private school students is presented by the *Geraci* case at the end of this chapter.

2. Student Discipline

Since constitutional protection regarding freedom of speech, privacy, due process, and equal protection do not apply to private schools,[83] the legal controls over student discipline and punishment are to be found primarily in the contract understandings of the party, and only rarely in governing state statute. Where those understandings are unclear on a disputed point, a court can, of course, "interpret" the agreement of the parties to favor a particular policy (e.g., to discourage racial discrimination).[84] Further, while private schools are not bound by constitutional due process requirements, a court may construe the contract, or exercise its equitable powers, to disapprove discretionary procedures that the court considers unfair.[85] Nevertheless, courts regularly uphold student punishments for violation of school rules, oral or written,[86] as they are not inclined to challenge the legality of private schools' standards of student conduct, especially when they are tied to religious teachings. Thus, prohibition of student conduct that is "immoral" or "detrimental" to the school or its interests has been upheld as within the fair contemplation and understanding of the parties, even though the use of such terms in a public school would be subject to constitutional challenge on grounds of

---

79. Girardier v. Webster College, 563 F.2d 1267 (8th Cir. 1977); Fayman v. Trustees of Burlington College, 247 A.2d 688 (N.J. 1968).

80. Sciortino v. Leech, 242 So.2d 269 (La. 1971).

81. Village Community School v. Adler, 478 N.Y.S.2d 546 (1984) (suit to recover tuition met by counterclaim that school misrepresented and breached its contract); Paladino v. Adelphia University, 454 N.Y.S.2d 246 (1980) (claim of contract breach based on failure to provide a quality education— rejected).

82. Lyons v. Salve Regina College, 565 F.2d 200 (1st Cir. 1977).

83. See fn. 75, *supra.*

84. *Cf.* Fiedler v. Marumsco Christian School, 631 F.2d 1144 (4th Cir. 1980) (ordering reinstatement of student expelled for interracial dating).

85. "Although . . . such [private] schools have broad discretion . . . a court will intervene where such discretion is abused or the proceedings do not comport with fundamental fairness." *See* Geraci v. St. Xavier H.S., *supra,* 13 O.P.3d at p. 149.

86. See fn. 75, *supra.*

vagueness.[87] Courts are likely to subject private school student penalties to greater scrutiny where those penalties are very heavy (e.g., expulsion) and to remedy excessive penalties as a contract violation.[88]

3. Student Records and Confidentiality

The fact that the Constitution may not apply to confer substantive rights (viz., free speech and association, student dress and grooming, or freedom from search in private schools) does not preclude the creation of special rights by statute. An example is found in the federal Family Education Rights and Privacy Act of 1974, which governs any school that receives federal financial assistance and which is discussed in detail in Chapter 6. Under that act, federally aided private schools, regardless of state action, are bound to observe the privacy and record maintenance conditions of the statute. Similar controls to protect student privacy may be imposed by state statutes.

In the absence of any governing statute, it is uncertain whether courts will imply a contract duty by private schools to keep student information confidential. No cases have been found that speak to that possibility. The prospect of a court implying such a term in appropriate circumstances is not, however, so unlikely that private school administrators should ignore all student privacy interests. In this respect, the discussion in Chapter 6 regarding confidentiality obligations of public schools provides safe-side guidelines for private school practice.

The major noncontractual sources of student rights in private schools is found in the class discrimination statutes discussed in the following section.

E. Antidiscrimination Law in Private Schools

The statutes governing class discrimination in public schools (reviewed in Chapters 7 and 8) do not always apply to the same extent or in the same fashion in private schools. For example, the much-used statute § 1983 only applies to action taken "under color of law" and generally cannot reach private schools in the absence of the same "state action" precondition. Civil rights statutes that do not require "state action" often provide express exclusion or exemptions for private schools. Thus, Title VII of the 1964 Civil Rights Act, which bars employment discrimination, exempts employers with fewer than 15 employees. Title VII, along with Title IX of the 1972 Education Amendments (sex discrimination), also exempts religiously based sex discrimination in church-sponsored schools that would otherwise be unlawful. (See Appendix 7–A.) These latter exemptions reflect the desire, or perhaps constitutional necessity, of avoiding excessive government interference or entanglement with religion in the private schools.

---

87. Compare cases in fn. 75, *supra,* with cases in Ch. 6, Part A, *supra.*

88. Bloch v. Hillel Torah Northern Sub. Day School, 426 N.E.2d 976 (Ill. 1981); *cf.* Aronson v. No. Park College, 418 N.E.2d 776 (Ill. 1981) (damages for wrongful expulsion).

1. Racial and Ethnic Discrimination

a. Constitutional Considerations. The degree of connection between private schools and the state required to subject them to the Fourteenth Amendment has been very loosely described by the courts. There must be a "significant involvement" or "substantial connection" linking the state to the school activity. These descriptions take concrete meaning only on a case-by-case basis, as many state-school contacts are not sufficient to create "state action." Private schools are not brought into Fourteenth Amendment "state action" merely because they are incorporated, licensed, and regulated by the state.[89]

The classic illustration of a private school engaged in state action arose in the *Girard College* cases. Girard College, actually a nondenominational primary and secondary school, was built and maintained under the will of Stephen Girard. The will limited school admissions to "white male orphans" only. As a prerequisite to his gift, the will required the State of Pennsylvania and City of Philadelphia to make certain public grants and to enact certain laws regarding the operation of the school by a city board of trusts. This was done over the better part of a century, but the racial exclusion of blacks was ultimately found to be prohibited by the Fourteenth Amendment because there was sufficient state action.[90]

The receipt of government financial assistance may involve a private school in state action, but only if the aid is sufficient in amount and proximity to the challenged practice to involve the government in the school's policy. Suits by private school students to overturn their expulsions on constitutional grounds (denial of due process) were dismissed where the state aid to those schools was found insufficient to create the state action foundation for constitutional protection.[91] But government financial aid that ties directly to discrimination may link the school to state action sufficiently to render the state aid itself to be unconstitutional.[92]

b. Statutory Considerations. In the absence of unconstitutional state action, private racial discrimination may still be subject to statutory control. The Act of 1866 (known as § 1981) was passed to protect newly freed slaves from deprivation of the right to make contracts on account of race. It was cited in 1976 to enjoin a private school from excluding qualified black applicants who responded to the school's public advertisements.[93] In that case, the Supreme Court did not indicate whether § 1981 law would apply if the school did not seek public patronage. It later avoided the question whether racial exclusion on the basis of religious belief would be protected by the First Amendment guarantee of free exercise of religion by finding that the school's racial

---

89. *Cf.* Jackson v. Metropolitan Edison Co., 419 U.S. 345 (1974).

90. Pennsylvania v. Brown, 270 F. Supp. 782 (E.D. Pa. 1967), aff'd. 392 F.2d 120 (3rd Cir. 1968).

91. Huff v. Notre Dame High School, 456 F.Supp. 1145 (D. Conn. 1978); Family Forum v. Archdiocese of Detroit, 347 F.Supp. 1167 (E.D. Mich. 1972); Wisch v. Stanford School Inc., 420 F.Supp. 1310 (D. Del. 1976); Bright v. Isenbarger, 314 F.Supp. 1382 (N.D. Ind. 1970). *See also* Rendell-Baker v. Kohn, fn. 75, *supra.*

92. Lodge v. Buxton, 639 F.2d 1358 (5th Cir. 1981); Norwood v. Harrison, 413 U.S. 455, 469-70 (1973); Gilmore v. City of Montgomery, 417 U.S. 556 (1974); Bishop v. Starkville Academy, 442 F.Supp. 1176 (N.D. Miss. 1977).

93. Runyon v. McCrary, 427 U.S. 160 (1976).

exclusion was in fact not religion based.[94] Two lower courts have held that expulsions from religious schools for interracial dating between students, when based on religious tenets, was lawful,[95] but a different question is presented where the religion belief underlying racial discrimination is asserted, not to resist a government order against that religious practice, but to claim a constitutionally based right to a government benefit. In the lead case of *Bob Jones University* v. *United States*,[96] the Supreme Court upheld as constitutional the denial of tax exemption to the University because its admittedly religious practice prohibiting interracial dating of students violated the tax exemption prerequisites of the Internal Revenue Code. In constitutional law, therefore, the distinction between immunity from conduct prohibitions and access to government benefits remains significant.

The statutory sanctions for private school racial discrimination includes loss of tax exemption, cutoff of any existing federal financial assistance,[97] and possible court actions by government agencies or injured individuals, in appropriate cases. The operation of Titles VI, VII, and IX (see Appendix 7–A at the end of Chapter 7) with respect to private school racial discrimination will depend upon the judicial construction of each of those statutes.

Title VII, which applies only to employment discrimination, and therefore is of little interest to students, has broad impact upon teachers and other employees in that it is not dependent upon "state action" or "federal aid" but operates upon all private schools that hire more than 15 employees. The discussion of Title VII in Chapter 7 is, therefore, equally relevant to private schools, with the sole exception that Title VII does provide for certain religion-based exemptions that are particularly relevant to religious private schools.[98] For example, a church-sponsored private school whose religious tenets require it to make racial or sexual preferences in employment is by the terms of Title VII, exempt from its prohibitions. It appears, however, that not every church affiliation will remove a private school from Title VII. Unless the school is in substantial part supported or controlled by a religious association, it may be denied the religious-tenet defense. Thus, some private schools have been held not to fall within the foregoing exception.[99] The case law is still incomplete on the question of the degree of religious support or control that will entitle a private school to claim the religious preference exemption. Even if a

---

94. *Cf.* Brown v. Dade Christian Schools, Inc., 556 F.2d 310 (5th Cir. 1977); cert. denied 434 U.S. 1063 (1978). *See also* Riley v. Adirondack Southern School for Girls, 541 F.2d 1124 (5th Cir. 1976).

95. Fiedler v. Marumsco Baptist Church, 631 E.2d 1144 (4th Cir. 1980); *semble,* Bob Jones University v. United States, 468 F.S. 890 (D.So.Car. 1978), rev'd., 461 U.S. 574 (1983).

96. 461 U.S. 574 (1983).

97. Grove City College v. Bell, 465 U.S. 555 (1984).

98. "Notwithstanding any other provision of this subchapter, it shall not be an unlawful employment practice for an employer to hire and employ employees . . . on the basis of his religion . . . in those certain instances where religion . . . is a bona fide occupational qualification reasonably necessary to the normal operation of that particular business or enterprise. . . . " 42 U.S.C. § 703(e) 2. "It shall not be an unlawful employment practice for a school, college, university, or other educational institution or institution of learning to hire and employ employees of a particular religion if such school, college, university, or other educational institution or institution of learning is, in whole or in substantial part, owned, supported, controlled, or managed by a particular religion or by a particular religious corporation, association, or society. . . . " 42 U.S.C. § 703(e)1.

99. Dolter v. Ahlert High School, 483 F.Supp. 266 (N.D.Iowa 1980); Pime v. Loyola Univ. of Chicago, 585 F.Supp. 435 (N.D.Ill. 1984).

private school has the necessary religious coloration, courts will also have to decide what employment positions are of sufficient religious significance to justify the religious preference.

The Title VI prohibition against racial discrimination in "any program or activity receiving federal financial assistance" would appear to cover any federal aid to private school students as well as teachers and operators. This is so because Title IX, whose language parallels Title VI, has been so construed by the United States Supreme Court.[100] In such case, however, the remedy of cutting off the federal funding would be limited to the private school "program" deemed to involve prohibited discrimination. Dissatisfaction with that decision has led to proposed legislation that would cut off federal aid in all activities of any institution that, in any way, violates the Title VI discrimination prohibition. At this writing, those proposals have not been enacted, but legislative developments should be followed, since those proposals have substantial support in Congress.

State statutes have a different, often longer, reach over private discrimination than do the federal laws. The provisions of individual state statutes are too varied to permit any summary generalizations, and school administrators in each state must ascertain the particulars of their own state law.

2. Sex Discrimination

a. Constitutional Considerations. The constitutional principles (discussed in Chapter 7) regarding sex discrimination would pertain only to private schools whose activity meets the "state action" requirements for constitutional protection. Even where state action might be present, the application of the Equal Protection clause to church-related schools could be complicated by the First Amendment's guarantee of free exercise of religion. To the extent that sex distinctions or preferences are based upon religious grounds, a possible conflict might arise between the religious guarantees of the First Amendment and the antidiscrimination guarantees of the Fourteenth Amendment. This possible conflict has not been squarely joined in any case to date, and may not arise with any frequency in the future.

b. Statutory Considerations. Since Title VII protects gender as well as racial groups from employment discrimination, the preceding discussion of Title VII applies as well here. Title IX bars sex discrimination only in federally aided activities. It is subject to the same interpretive problems raised in the preceding section.

While Title IX is limited to sex discrimination, it significantly does not cover private school admissions practices, except in vocational, graduate, and professional education; it also exempts religiously dictated sex preferences.[101]

The Equal Pay Act (see Appendix 7-A), like Title VII, is not limited to federally aided programs, but like Title IX is limited to sex-based discrimination. It does cover

---

100. See Grove City College v. Bell, fn. 97, *supra.*
101. 20 U.S.C. § 1681(a)(1), (3).

private schools,[102] and therefore remedies private school discrimination wherein employees doing the same work do not receive the same pay based upon sex differentiation. Equal pay act cases in the private schools are, however, relatively rare, and the law remains undeveloped in that area. The question whether particular sex preferences are religion based has not been illuminated by the scant case law and will have to be decided case by case, on the basis of specific facts.

With respect to students, federally aided private schools are subject to the same Title IX obligations discussed in Chapter 7, with the above-noted exception for religiously dictated practices. Here, also, courts face the difficult question whether private school sex separation or disparities in class composition, resource allocations, and course assignments are sufficiently "rooted in religious belief" to qualify for the exemption.

If state statutes do not specify any religion-based exemption, they may be challenged as unconstitutional. Such a conflict was recently presented in a case that upheld a teacher's dismissal from a Catholic school because the teacher remarried after divorce, contrary to the law of the Catholic Church.[103] Though the state statute barred teacher discrimination based on marital status, the court obviously thought it constitutionally necessary to avoid interference with the school's religious judgment that the teacher's life style would defeat the religious mission of the school. The mentioned case is not directly in point since the school rule would have applied equally to a female as well as male teacher, but it illustrates the principle that discrimination statutes cannot operate to abridge freedom of religion. Under the supremacy clause of the Constitution, even a state's equal rights amendment banning private sex discrimination would be inoperative to the extent that it violated the First Amendment.[104] Unlike some state ERAs, however, the proposed federal Equal Rights Amendment was worded to apply only to government-sponsored action and not to purely private religiously motivated conduct.

3. Handicapped and Gifted

To date, the handicapped, unlike racial and gender groups, have not commanded any special constitutional protection, even in public schools. Handicapped classifications have not been deemed to be so "suspect" as to require "strict scrutiny" under the equal protection clause of the Fourteenth Amendment.[105] Thus, even in the relatively rare private school where "state action" might be found, the constitutional protection of the handicapped is no greater than that afforded to ordinary students and teachers. While private schools are not required to admit and serve handicapped students, if they do so and receive federal or state funds for their services to the handicapped, they are subject

---

102. EEOC v. Fremont Christian School, 101 Labor Cases (CCH) ¶34,565 (N.D. Cal. Civ. Action C-88-2619; 4/13/84) (Title VII application to religious school); Horner v. Mary Institute, 613 F.2d 706, 713 (8th Cir. 1980) (application of Equal Pay Act to private school). Not all circuits are in accord on the application of the Equal Pay Act. *Compare, e.g.,* Russell v. Belmont College, 554 F.Supp. 667 (M.D.Tenn. 1982); *with* Ritter v. Mt. St. Mary's College, 495 F.Supp. 724 (D.Md. 1980).

103. Steeber v. Benilde-St. Margaret's H.S., No. DC 739378 (Hennepin Co. Ct. Minn. 1978).

104. Bishop v. Starkville Academy, 442 F.Supp 1176 (N.D.Miss. 1977).

105. City of Cleburne, Tex. v. Cleburne Living Center, ________U.S. ________, 105 S.Ct. 3249 (1985).

to the same obligations noted in Chapter 7 (for public schools) under the Education For All Handicapped Children Act. Further, with respect to teachers as well as students, private schools that participate in a federally aided program must also comply with the antidiscrimination provisions of the federal Rehabilitation Act, which are also reviewed in Chapter 7. As noted in Chapter 7, schools covered by the above statutes have certain affirmative obligations to accommodate student and teacher handicaps as well as negative obligations to refrain from discriminatory denials of educational or employment opportunities.

Many states impose parallel obligations. Since many specialized schools for the education of the handicapped are private institutions, the federal regulations require that public authorities include nonpublic schools among the institutions that are eligible to participate in federally assisted programs.[106] One court has suggested that a private school employee whose termination violated the Rehabilitation Act might be entitled to personal relief (over and above federal fund cutoff).[107]

The Supreme Court in *Southeastern Community College* v. *Davis*[108] denied that the Rehabilitation Act requires affirmative action that is unreasonably burdensome upon a school and denied that HEW had the authority to issue regulations requiring undue affirmative action. The problem of what accommodations are reasonable is summarized in the court's statement, "We do not suggest that the line between a lawful refusal to extend affirmative action and illegal discrimination against handicapped persons will always be clear."[109]

In accepting students subject to the Education for the Handicapped Act, private schools must accept the same limitations placed by said Act upon the public schools. Thus, a private school cannot dispute salary ceilings placed by state law for state-funded teachers of handicapped children;[110] nor ignore reimbursement conditions and ceilings placed by federal and state law on educational expenses of the handicapped.[111] Where a handicapped child is placed in a private school, without official authorization, the private school assumes the risk that payment of its tuition and charges will be made by the parent, whether or not the parent succeeds in obtaining reimbursement under the Education for All Handicapped Children Act.[112]

4. Age Discrimination

The federal and state statutes barring age discrimination in employment are not restricted to schools that are sponsored or subsidized by government. The discussion of age

106. 45 C.F.R., part 121.

107. Ross v. Allen, 515 F.Supp. 972 (S.D.N.Y. 1981); *cf.* Cain v. Archdiocese of Kansas City, 508 F.Supp. 1021 (D.Kans. 1981) (parochial school teacher).

108. 442 U.S. 397 (1979).

109. *Id.* at p. 412.

110. Organization to Assure Services v. Ambach, 434 N.E.2d 1329 (N.Y. 1982).

111. *Idem.* See, e.g., N.J. Stat. Anno., tit. 18A, §§46-19.1 et seq.

112. *E.g.*, Newport-Mesa Unified Sch. District v. Hubert, 183 Cal. Rptr. 334 (1982).

discrimination in Chapter 7 is, therefore, equally pertinent to private school employment.

5. Religious Discrimination

The constitutional prohibitions against religious discrimination under the establishment and free exercises clauses, as reviewed in Chapter 4, have no application, for lack of the requisite "state action" in the overwhelming majority of private schools. In the rare and limited situation where a private school does engage in "state action," it would be subject to the religious clauses of the First Amendment.

The only major federal statute that covers religious discrimination in private schools, namely, Title VII, involves employment discrimination. Under Title VII, the private schools, both religious and nonreligious, would be subject to the principles discussed in the prior sections on race and sex discrimination, but the exemptions for religious necessity under Title VII would apply with special force to religiously affiliated schools.

The delineation of Title VII duties to afford reasonable accommodation for employees' religious observance is even less developed in private school cases than in public school cases. The decisions, discussed in Chapter 7, Section F, afford some general guidance on the key questions as to what employee claims for religious accommodation are "reasonable," and what circumstances justify employer refusal of religious accommodation, based upon business necessity or undue hardship. The attempt to avoid that balancing problem, by state statute that imposed an absolute employer duty to accommodate employees' religion, with no exception, was struck down by the United States Supreme Court as an unconstitutional aid to religion in violation of the Establishment Clause.[113] Finding the proper balance between the duty of reasonable accommodation of religion under Title VII and employer rights in covered private schools is even more complicated in religious private schools, since in addition to their constitutional right of free exercise of religion they are expressly exempted by Title VII from the duty of religious accommodation, if such would contravene the religious tenets of the employer school.

6. State Antidiscrimination Laws

As noted in Chapter 7, Section B-5(b), state antidiscrimination laws in many ways parallel federal laws,[114] but they sometimes reach private schools and practices not covered by federal laws (viz. state equal rights amendments).[115] In their application to religious schools, however, the antidiscrimination provisions of state constitutions and

113. Estate of Thornton v. Caldor, 105 S.Ct. 2914 (1985).

114. *E.g.*, VanScoyk v. St. Mary's Assumption Parochial School, 580 P.2d 1315 (Kans. 1978) (state antidiscrimination law exemption for religion-based religious preferences).

115. *See, e.g.*, Marchioro v. Chaney, 582 P.2d 487 (Wash. 1978) (adopting expansive interpretation of Washington ERA and reviewing state constitutional equal rights amendments from Pennsylvania and Massachusetts). *Cf.* Henderson v. Henderson, 327 A.2d 60 (Pa. 1974); Lowell v. Kowalski, 405 N.E.2d 135 (Mass. 1980).

statutes are still subject to the limitations imposed by the federal constitution, particularly with respect to prohibitions against establishment of religion and interference with free exercise of religion.[116]

E. Tort Liability

1. Introductory Note

The general law of torts draws no sharp distinction between public and private schools save for a few limited exceptions that will be hereafter explained. Whether a private school is profit making or nonprofit is not legally significant in those states where the defense of charitable immunity is no longer recognized. Tort law binds all private school employees, and the particular responsibilities of school teachers and administrators subject them to the same standards of care and to the same limited privilege of administering reasonable corporal punishment to maintain student discipline, as those previously discussed with respect to public school teachers.[117] The discussion of tort principles in Chapter 8 applies, but will not be repeated in this chapter, save by way of illustrative cases.

2. Liability of the Private School

a. Tort Immunity and Limitations of Liability. At common law, charitable organizations were held immune from tort liability. Nonprofit private schools are treated as charitable organizations, even though they may earn income incidental to their educational programs. Schools classified as operating for profit are not entitled to charitable tort immunity. A growing number of state courts and legislatures have, however, abrogated or reduced the charitable tort immunity of nonprofit schools.[118] In those states, private schools are subject to vicarious liability for the torts of their agents or employees under the same principles and conditions of the doctrine of *respondeat superior*.

---

116. See, e.g., fn. 113, *supra*; Bishop v. Starkville Academy, 422 F.Supp. 1176 (N.D.Miss. 1977) (Mississippi ERA could not be constitutionally applied to situations where its application would violate First Amendment rights under the federal Constitution).

117. *See, e.g.*, Smith, etc. v. Archbishop of St. Louis, 632 S.W.2d 516, 521-22 (Mo. 1982) (applying public school negligence standards to private schools); *semble*: Brown v. N. Carolina Wesleyan College, 309 S.E.2d 701, 702–03 (N.Car. 1983); Baikie v. Luther H.S. South, 366 N.E.2d 542 (Ill. 1977) (corporal punishment).

118. The varied treatment of charitable immunity for private schools in the sister states is seen in the cases collected in Annotations: *Tort Immunity—Nongovernmental Charities*, 25 A.L.R.4th 517 (1983); *Tort Immunity—Private Schools*, 38 A.L.R.3d 480 (1971). States that have abrogated private school tort immunity, in whole or in part, include Arizona, California, District of Columbia, Idaho, Illinois, Indiana, Iowa, Kansas, Kentucky, Louisiana, Massachusetts, Minnesota, Missouri, New Jersey, New York, Ohio, Oklahoma, Pennsylvania, Rhode Island, South Carolina, Texas, Utah, Vermont, Washington, and Wisconsin. Some of these states have substituted limited or partial immunity for general common law immunity, as have the following states: Arkansas, Connecticut, Colorado, Maryland, Nebraska, Nevada, Tennessee, and Virginia. Since tort immunity law is continually being modified by both court decisions and legislation, it cannot be assumed that the foregoing listing of individual state positions will remain unchanged.

The kinds and degrees of charitable immunity extended to private schools vary considerably from state to state. Private schools must, therefore, consult the law in their home state. Illinois law creates a peculiar limitation of tort liability by holding public and private schools and their teachers liable only for willful and wanton injuries, but not for mere negligence.[119]

There is some authority to the effect that charitable tort immunity, like governmental tort immunity, does not apply to injuries caused by nuisance conditions in the maintenance of school property.[120] Several states have also held that private schools, though immune from tort liability in carrying out their educational functions, are not immune for torts arising out of activities that are proprietary or commercial in nature.[121] Others deny immunity for injuries caused by reckless or wanton misconduct.[122]

A state legislature may limit the amount of money damages recoverable from a charitable organization, including private schools (viz. to the sum provided by outstanding liability insurance or to a sum specified in the state statute).[123] The high court of Illinois, however, recently held such a limitation statute unconstitutional on the ground that the statute irrationally discriminated in favor of school defendants, vis-à-vis other nonschool charities.[124]

The tort immunity extended to private schools, as corporate entities (hereafter designated "entity immunity") is to be distinguished from any claim of personal immunity by individual proprietors, superiors, or employees (hereafter designated as "personal immunity"). Personal tort immunity did not exist at common law, but it may be created by legislation. Statutory personal immunity has only recently been enacted in a small number of states. Even there, personal immunity has been limited to particular circumstances. While personal immunity is the exception rather than the rule in private schools, its recent creation by modern state tort statutes may signal a trend that will grow in the foreseeable future.

In view of the selective applications of immunity doctrines by different states and of the general trend to abrogate charitable tort immunity, private schools and their personnel are well-advised to conduct their affairs as though no such immunity existed.

b. Premises Liability. Nonimmune schools are liable to invitees, including students and business visitors, for injuries due to hazardous conditions of buildings, equipment, or outside premises that could have been prevented by reasonable care in inspection and

---

119. Cotton v. Catholic Bishop of Chicago, 351 N.E.2d 247 (Ill. 1976); Merrill v. Catholic Bishop of Chicago, 290 N.E.2d 259 (Ill. 1972).

120. *See* Love v. Nashville A. and Normal Institute, 243 S.W.304 (Tenn. 1922); discussion of nuisances in Ch. 8.

121. Kasten v. YMCA, 412 A.2d 1346 (N.J. 1980) (no immunity for injury to fee-paying members); Grueninger v. President and Fellows of Harvard College, 178 N.E.2d 917 (Mass. 1961); Miller v. Concordia Teachers College, 296 F.2d 100 (8th Cir. 1961) (applying Nebraska law). *See also* Mason v. Southern New England Conference Assn., 696 F.2d 135 (1st Cir. 1980) (immunity statute applied to noncharitable use of school room, let without charge).

122. Bernesak v. Catholic Bishop, 409 N.E.2d 287 (Ill. 1980).

123. *Statutory waiver of immunity to extent of available liability insurance coverage*; see, e.g., Maine Rev. Stat. Ann. tit. 14, § 158 (1980); Kobylanski v. Chicago Bd. of Education, 347 N.E.2d 705, 709 (Ill. 1976).

124. Haymes v. Catholic Bishop of Chicago, 243 N.E.2d 203 (Ill. 1968).

maintenance.[125] However, the duty of care extends only to the specific physical areas to which students or other persons are invited. Otherwise, the persons are considered mere *licensees* to whom the school owes a duty to refrain from intentional wrongs or from failure to warn of known latent dangers. Thus an invitee to a school concert who strayed from the parts of the school to which he was not invited became a licensee and could not recover for consequent injury for defects in the premises.[126]

An exception to the rule on licensees is provided by the doctrine of *attractive nuisance* whereby a dangerous condition, known to attract unwitting children into hazardous play, will render the school liable to such injured children, even though they are technically trespassers.[127]

The question of what conditions of building, equipment, or grounds show actionable negligence turns on the facts in each case—the foreseeability of danger and the existence of a sufficient time period prior to injury to permit reasonable opportunity for the school to discover and remedy the dangerous condition.[128] The *lack-of-notice* defense does not apply where the private school actively created the dangerous condition, as by using glass panels rather than thick plate glass in a school door.[129] In many cases, questions regarding the foreseeability of timely notice of the danger are left to jury determination as questions of fact. Examples of conditions for which private schools may be held liable in negligence include slippery floors, unstable equipment or furnishings, defective elevators, unsafe machinery, ramps, fire extinguishers, and inadequate lighting in walkways and parking lots.[130]

Private schools, especially boarding schools, also have a duty to provide reasonable security arrangements to protect students from criminal acts and assaults. Failure to do so has rendered them liable for injuries to student victims of criminal acts.[131]

c. Duties of Supervision. The school is only responsible for the acts of its employees where those acts occur within the scope of their authority and employment. There is, therefore, no *respondeat superior* liability for a school doctor's negligent medical treatment that represents his own discretion and not that of the school.[132] Neither is a school liable for negligence of its bus driver who without authority ranged far from his

---

125. Perbost v. San Marino Hall-School for Girls, 199 P.2d 710 (Cal. 1949); Eberle v. Benedictine Sisters, 385 P.2d 765 (Ore. 1963). See generally Annotation: *Colleges—Premises Tort Liability,* 35 A.L.R.3d 975 (1971).

126. *See* Cortright v. Trustees of Rutgers College, 198 A. 837 (N.J. 1938).

127. Yeske v. Aron Old Farm Schools, 470 A.2d 705 (Conn. 1984) (child trespasser injured by cable across trail); Saul v. Roman Catholic Church, 402 P.2d 48 (N. M. 1965) (10-year-old boy falling into excavation on school grounds). *But see contra:* Siver v. Atlantic Union College, 154 N.E.2d 360 (Mass. 1958).

128. Velez v. Our Lady of Victory Church, 486 N.Y.S.2d 302 (1985).

129. Wilkinson v. Hartford Acc. & Ind. Co., 411 So.2d 22 (La. 1982); Eberle v. Benedictine Sisters, 385 P.2d 765 (Oreg. 1963).

130. Garofoli v. Salesianum School, Inc., 208 A.2d 308 (De. 1965); and case authorities collected in 68 Am. Jur. 2d §324; and in Annotation cited at fn. 125.

131. Kim v. State, 616 P.2d 1376 (Haw. 1980) (duty to prevent criminal assault between students); *semble*: James v. Charlette-Mecklenburg Bd. of Education, 300 S.E.2d 21, 24 (N.Car. 1983); Chavez v. Tolleson El. Sch. District, 595 P.2d 1017 (Ariz. 1979). *See also* Schultz v. Gould Academy, 332 A.2d 368 (Me. 1975) (failure to warn students of known intruder rendered boarding school liable for injury to students by said intruder).

132. Cramer v. Hoffman, 390 F.2d 19 (2d Cir. 1968).

directed route before causing an accident.[133] However, it would clearly be liable for negligence of its drivers who did not depart from their assigned duties.[134]

The school's vicarious liability for the conduct of persons under its control has been extended to unpaid volunteer workers.[135] Its duty to provide reasonable supervision includes a duty of care in the selection of persons to whom the supervision of its students is entrusted. Negligent hiring practices may, therefore, render a school liable for injuries caused by incompetent personnel.[136] The school is not held to ensure the competence of all employees, whose future conduct is often not reasonably ascertainable, but it is held to act reasonably in the selection of such employees.

The discussion of supervisory duties in public schools (Chapter 8) applies as well to private schools, in the absence of affirmative defenses or charitable immunity. The distinctions in tort law between the duty of general and special supervision were recently outlined in a private school tort case in which a second grade student suffered severe burns when her holiday school costume was ignited by a nearby candle:

> "Negligent supervision, like any other tort, involves a breach of a duty defendant owes plaintiff which causes plaintiff to suffer damages. . . . To recover, plaintiff need not show that the very injury resulting from defendant's negligence was foreseeable, but merely that a reasonable person could have foreseen that injuries of the type suffered would be likely to occur under the circumstances. . . . In Missouri the scope of Ms. Wiegand's duty to supervise plaintiff is narrow. The defendant is not an insurer of plaintiff's safety, . . . nor is defendant required to maintain a constant vigil over each member of the class by keeping every student within eyesight. . . . The duty of defendant, or in this case Ms. Wiegand, was merely to exercise reasonable or ordinary care in the supervision of plaintiff. . . . The exercise of ordinary care where children are involved, however, requires more vigilance and caution than might the exercise of ordinary care where adults are concerned. . . . This is particularly true when a potentially dangerous condition exists and the supervisor is or should be aware of it."[137]

A student injured by discharge of a firearm in the presence of a supervising teacher was granted recovery upon a jury finding of negligent supervision.[138] Recovery was also allowed on circumstantial evidence of negligence, under the doctrine of *res ipsa loquitur,* where a private nursery school student was found by her mother to have a brain concussion at the end of the school day and the school failed to explain what had occurred.[139]

---

133. Malmquist v. Hellenic Community, 203 N.W. 420 (Minn. 1925).

134. St. Mary's Academy v. Solomon, 238 P.25 (Colo. 1925).

135. See Annot: *Liability of Charitable Organization for Tort of Unpaid Volunteer,* 82 A.L.R.3d 1213 (1978).

136. *See, e.g.,* Schultz v. Roman Catholic Archdiocese of Newark, 472 A.2d 531 (N.J. 1984) for a discussion of administrative negligence by alleged failure to use care in hiring school personnel having charge of students.

137. *See* Smith v. Archbishop of St. Louis, 632 S.W.2d 516, 521, 522 (Mo. 1982).

138. Noland v. Colorado School of Trades, Inc., 386 P.2d 358 (Colo. 1963).

139. Fowler v. Seaton, 394 P.2d 697 (Cal. 1964). On the limited duty of school authorities to provide reasonable first aid to stricken students, but not to undertake emergency procedures that require special training, *see* Stineman v. Fontbonne College, 664 F.2d 1082 (8th Cir. 1981), and the authorities there cited from other state jurisdictions; Applebaum v. Nemon, 678 S.W.2d 533 (Tex. 1984) (no duty to provide CPR treatment).

As with public schools, private school personnel are not required to provide special immediate supervision over students at all times and places. General supervision has been held to constitute due care, sufficient to defeat tort claims for out-of-class injuries caused by student violations of school rules where the school had no reason to anticipate such violations. Thus injuries by students driving bicycles across school grounds in violation of regularly enforced school rules did not give rise to school negligence.[140] A student who returned to school during the lunch hour before he was directed to do so and was injured in playing on a snow-covered bush had no cause of action.[141] Similarly, students placed on disciplinary assignment (to pull weeds) who engaged in football play could not hold the school liable for negligent lack of supervision.[142] As with the public schoolyard cases, however, a private school may be held liable for injuries during class recess where it had notice of dangerous student activities (viz. students throwing pebbles at each other).[143]

Schools will not be liable for unavoidable accidents, notwithstanding the lack of immediate supervision, for example, where a child spectator at a school baseball game was struck by a bat that slipped from the hands of a player.[144] The cases are not consistent on school liability for failure of supervising coaches to provide proper safety equipment in athletic games.[145]

The need for proof that a supervising teacher should have foreseen the risk of harm as a precondition of tort liability is starkly presented by a case in which a young retarded student at a private school was drowned in a pond on a 50-acre rural campus. The court held that since the child had been at the school for some weeks and had often walked near the pond, there was no indication of any duty to provide continuous immediate supervision or to enclose the pond.[146]

The difficult question of when temporary absence of a teacher/supervisor supports liability for injuries of one student by another student was also reviewed in Chapter 8. In such cases, the question whether the teacher's absence was a proximate cause (i.e., that the teacher's presence would have prevented the injury) often turns upon particular facts. A school was held liable for student injury in a classroom assault where the teacher was 25 minutes late in reporting to class.[147] Other schools were held not liable for lack of supervision in cases of schoolyard and cafeteria student misconduct.[148] Where schoolyard

---

140. Selleck v. Ins.Co. of North America, 182 So.2d 547 (La. 1966). *See also* Conley v. Martin, 42 A.2d 26 (R I. 1945).

141. Shanahan v. St James' R.C. Church, 223 N.Y.S.2d 519 (1960).

142. Martin v. Roman Catholic Archbishop, 322 P.2d 31 (Cal. 1958). *See also* Bernesak v. Catholic Bishop, 409 N.E.2d 287 (Ill. 1980) (permitting children to play "crack the whip" during class recess).

143. Sheehan v. St. Peter's Catholic School, 188 N.W.2d 868 (Minn. 1971); *compare* Titus v. Lindberg, 288A.2d 65 (N.J. 1967).

144. Benedetto v. Travelers Ins. Co., 172 So.2d 354 (La. 1965).

145. *Compare* Brackman v. Adrian, 472 S.W.2d 735 (Tenn. 1971) (no liability for coach's failure to require catcher's mask in softball game); *with* Everett v. Sch. District, 380 N.E.2d 653 (Mass. 1978) (liability for use of defective hockey helmets).

146. Hunter v. Evergreen Presbyterian Vocational School, 338 So.2d 164 (La. 1976).

147. Christofides v. Hellenic Eastern Orthodox Christian Church, 227 N.Y.S.2d 946 (1962). *But see* Kim v. State 161 P.2d 137 (Haw. 1980) (female teacher not negligent in leaving class to seek help to stop fight between large boys).

148. Kos v. Catholic Bishop of Chicago, 45 N.E.2d 1006 (Ill. 1942) (student struck by brush thrown by another student); Benedetto v. Travelers Ins. Co., 172 So.2d 354 (La. 1965) (student struck by slipped bat

supervision could prevent injury (i.e., in discus throwing practice) a jury could find actionable negligence with respect to a student in the path of the hurled discus.[149]

In determining questions of negligence and proximate cause, courts and juries must take into consideration all of the circumstances and factors: the nature of the activity, the age and past conduct history of the students, and the practicability and probable effect of general or special supervision. Thus, a jury could find a school negligent for injury to a young child falling off a schoolyard merry-go-round.[150] One state court dismissed a tort suit for a child who was injured while unsupervised in a fall from monkey bars in the schoolyard, while a different state court found that a child's fall from a four-foot railing in the schoolyard stated a basis for a negligence suit and trial.[151] With respect to nonhazardous after-school activities by high school students, a private school was held as a matter of law to have no duty of supervision.[152]

The duty of supervision clearly attaches where a student is directed by a school superior to perform a potentially dangerous task. Thus where a student was directed to obtain driveway fill with a tractor from a mine, liability for his injury by a falling rock was held to be a jury question.[153]

As with public schools, private schools have the duty to supervise school-sponsored activities away from school grounds. Where the school superior authorized an off-duty employee to drive a student to join an organized school field trip, the school was held liable for the student's injuries caused by the driver's negligence.[154]

d. Affirmative Defenses. An injured party who is guilty of contributory negligence or assumption of the risk may be barred from recovering for another's negligence, but the burden of proving these defenses is upon the defendants (see Chapter 8). Like negligence, these issues commonly involve inferences from a variety of circumstances and are often sufficiently close judgments to be left for jury decision. A high school freshman who was admitted to chemistry lab unsupervised for the purpose of preparing equipment could not recover for injuries following his unauthorized attempt to concoct gunpowder from stored materials.[155] Even where an instructor actively ordered an adolescent student to climb a tree to gather pecans, a jury was entitled to deny recovery on a finding that the student was negligent in putting his weight on a shaky branch.[156] The jury was also permitted to find contributory negligence to bar recovery where a student attempted to board a school vehicle by stepping on the side wheel just before it started up.[157] However,

---

while watching softball game in school yard); Townsend by Benavente, 339 F.2d 421 (9th Cir. 1964) (student struck by nut thrown by another student during noon recess).

149. Marques v. Riverside Military Academy, 73 So.E.2d 574 (Ga. 1952).

150. R.C. Church v. Keenan 243 P.2d 455 (Ariz. 1952).

151. Hillman v. Greater Miami Hebrew Academy, 72 So.2d 668 (Fla. 1954) (case dismissed); Mlynarski v. St. Rita's Congregation, 142 N.W.2d 207 (1966) (trial granted).

152. *See* the Martin case, fn. 142.

153. McMullen v. Ursuline Order of Sisters, 246 P.2d 1052 (N. Mex. 1952).

154. Brokaw v. Black-Foxe Military Inst,, 231 P.2d 816 (Cal. 1951). *See also* Sharpe v. Quality Educ. Inc., 296 S.E.2d 661 (N.Car. 1982).

155. Moore v. Order Minor Conventuals, 267 F.2d 296 (4th Cir. 1959).

156. Bryant v. Thunderbird Academy, 439 P.2d 818 (Ariz. 1968).

157. Beardsell v. Tilton School, 200 A. 783 (N.H. 1938).

few courts would have overruled a contrary finding by a jury since so much depends on the inferences to be drawn from specific circumstances.

In the majority states that have altered the common law rule to permit recovery based on the degree of comparative negligence (see Chapter 8), a school may be liable for injuries in the proportion that *its* negligence contributed to the injury.[158]

e. Defamation Liability. The tort law of defamation (see Chapter 8) is equally applicable to private schools and their employees.

f. Educational Malpractice. As indicated by the few decided authorities involving public schools, the courts have refused to recognize a general tort duty to ensure adequate educational achievement unless special circumstances give rise to a special duty.[159] It is, therefore, doubtful that any court will interpret the contract between parents and private schools as a special ground to find a duty to ensure adequate educational achievement, unless the language of that contract clearly so specifies. In the absence of such language, the likelihood is that the courts will apply the same rule applied in the public school cases, to require merely a reasonable "best efforts" performance of the teaching function and not a guaranteed level of educational achievement.[160]

g. Statutory Torts—Discrimination. The broadest and most favored avenue of federal tort relief in public schools is § 1983, but that provision is limited to "state action" torts and will not apply to private schools except in the uncommon circumstance where the private school conduct can be linked to state action.[161] A second category of federal statutes includes those based upon and covering only activities that receive federal financial assistance (e.g., Title VI, Title IX, and the Rehabilitation Act). These statutes apply only to those private schools whose activity can be said to be federally assisted. To the extent that the foregoing statutes may apply, the specific remedies discussed in Chapter 8 will be available in the absence of an express statutory exemption, such as those allowed for preferences or exclusions of particular individuals that are dictated by religious needs or beliefs.

The third category of federal statutes, which provides monetary relief for specified discrimination, requires neither state action nor federal financial assistance to support recovery (e.g., the employment discrimination statutes—Title VII, Equal Pay Act, Age Discrimination Act) and those Civil War Reconstruction Statutes that reach private action (§§ 1981, 1982, 1985). The remedies provided by these statutes (discussed in Chapter 8) would also apply to private school employment.

The tort remedies provided by state discrimination statutes are too varied to permit any generalization, but most state statutes limit discrimination remedies to agency investigation and corrective orders to eliminate discriminatory practices. It is, therefore,

---

158. *See* Faber v. Roelofs, 212 N.W.2d 856 (Minn. 1973).

159. Helm v. Professional Childrens School, 431 N.Y.S.2d 246 (1980).

160. *See* Pietro v. St. Joseph's School, N.Y. Sup. Ct., Suffolk County (1979) reported at 48 U.S.L.W. 2229.

161. *See* Powe v. Miles, 407 F.2d 73 (2d Cir. 1968) and the discussion of tort relief under federal statutes in Chapter 8 and in this chapter under the topic "Antidiscrimination Law in Private Schools."

necessary on any given form of discrimination to ascertain whether and what kind of tort relief is provided by the law of the home state.

G. Private School Finance

1. In General

Private education in the United States is predominantly financed by nongovernmental sources: tuition and fee charges, private grants, and personal donations. For this reason, the general laws on public finance reviewed in Chapter 9 do not apply to private schools. To the limited extent that governmental funds are employed in aid of private schools, government controls on the disposition of public funds must be observed. Examples of such controls are noted in Section E of this chapter. Even in the absence of public financing, private school expenditures are subject to limited public controls under certain tax and public welfare legislation (e.g., employer contributions for social security, unemployment compensation, workers' compensation, and employer obligations regarding the payment of minimum statutory wages and maintenance of certain employee benefit and pension funds).[162]

But for the foregoing peripheral areas, private schools are free to select their own fiscal policies regarding receipts, borrowing, and expenditures. However, they are bound as any other private party by the law of contracts regarding their agreements, and by the laws governing fiduciaries regarding the receipts of restricted private grants. The major legal controversies regarding private educational finance relate to the legality, under both federal and state constitutions, of various forms of governmental financial aids to private

---

162. *Minimum wage law coverage of private schools: see, e.g.*, Donovan v. Shenandoah Baptist Church, 573 F.Supp. 320 (W.D.Va. 1983); Donovan v. Central Baptist Church, 25 BNA Wage and Hour Cases 815, 816 (S.D. Tex. 1982); Marshall v. First Baptist Church, 82 CCH Labor Cases ¶33,548 (D. S. Car. 1977). *See also* Tony and Susan Alamo Foundation v. Sec'y. of Labor, 105 S.Ct. 1953 (1985). *Workers' compensation law coverage of private schools: see, e.g.*, Victory Baptist Temple v. Industrial Comm'n, 442 N.E.2d 819 (Ohio 1982). In LARSON, WORKMEN'S COMPENSATION LAW, V. 1C, §§ 50.40-.44(a) (1983), the author reports six states (Alaska, Arkansas, Georgia, Idaho, Mississippi, and North Dakota) as excluding charitable and religious employers from workers' compensation obligations to some degree; with one state, Illinois, expressly including them. *Social security coverage: see, e.g.*, United States v. Lee, 455 U.S. 252 (1982). *Unemployment compensation coverage and exemptions for religious and nonreligious private schools: see, e.g.*, St Martin's Evangelical Lutheran Church and Northwestern Lutheran Academy v. South Dakota, 451 U.S. 772 (1981); California v. Grace Brethren Church, 457 U.S. 393, 403 (1982); Salem College and Academy v. Employment Div., *supra* (interdenominational School); Hollis Hills Jewish Center, 461 N.Y.S.2d 555 (1983) (nursery school); Community Lutheran School, etc. v. Iowa Dept. of Job Service, 326 N.W.2d 286 (Iowa 1982) (association of church schools affiliated with the Lutheran Church); Begley v. Employment Security Comm., 274 S.E.2d 370 (N.Car. 1981) (Catholic schools); Ursuline Academy v. Director of Division of Employment Security, 420 N.E.2d 326 (Mass. 1981); Christian School Association v. Commonwealth Dept. of Labor & Indus., 423 A.2d 1340 (Pa. 1980); Grace Lutheran Church v. North Dakota Employment Security Bureau, 294 N.W.2d 767 (N. Dak. 1980); Employment Division v. Archdiocese of Portland, 600 P.2d 926 (Ore. 1979); Sant Bani Ashram, Inc. v. New Hampshire Employment Security, 426 A.2d 34 (N.H. 1981). *See also* Hickey v. Dist. of Columbia Dept. of Employment Services, 448 A.2d 871 (D. Col. 1982) (Catholic schools). Exempt private schools can elect to participate in state unemployment compensation programs. *See, e.g.*, Holy Name School v. Dept. of Industry, 326 N.W.2d 121 (Wis. 1982)

schools, and particularly to religious private schools. These problems are taken up in the following section.

2. Government Financial Assistance

The law concerning government assistance to various elements in private education is primarily concerned with federal and state constitutional restrictions against the use of public funds either for private purposes or for aid to religion. That law is complicated by the fact that the constitutions of individual states are different from each other and from the federal Constitution. As later noted, some aid forms that satisfy the federal Constitution may be struck down under some state constitutions but not under other state constitutions. Moreover, legal distinctions are made between public aid to nonsectarian schools and to church-sponsored schools, and between higher and lower levels of education. For example, direct grants or loans by government to private colleges, including church-related institutions, for the construction of permanent academic facilities have been upheld under both federal and state constitutions, whereas such grants to parochial schools have been struck down as unconstitutional aids to religion.[163] Furthermore, scholarship grants and student loans by the federal and state governments to all college institutions were held to be constitutional, though tuition reimbursement grants to parents of parochial school students were previously held to be unconstitutional.[164] As between nonsectarian and church-related schools, the state authorities are in conflict on whether state aid is barred only to church-sponsored schools on religious grounds or also to nonsectarian schools on the issue whether the spending serves a public or only a private purpose.[165]

This welter of federal and state law on private educational assistance is best disentangled and explained by separating for individual analysis the different forms of governmental assistance under the federal law and respective laws of individual states. Before doing so, it is well to recognize that the legal guidelines provided by the United States Supreme Court are more like flickering signals than clear beacons. A majority of the Justices employs a three-part test of constitutionality of aid to nonpublic schools, but they do not agreed as to what forms of aid do or do not satisfy the constitutional tests. The continuing divisions among the justices on the legality of different aid forms is well-illustrated by that Court's decisions as late as 1985, which appear at the end of this chapter. Those opinions, which furnish an excellent view of the Constitutional case law and indicate the range of government-religion tests espoused by different justices, should be read with care as essential background to the following materials.

Before appraising individual cases, the Supreme Court's description of its

163. *Upheld:* Tilton v. Richardson, 403 U.S. 672 (1971); Hunt v. McNair, 413 U.S. 736 (1973); Roemer v. Maryland Public Works Board, 426 U.S. 734 (1976). *Struck down:* Committee for Public Education and Religious Liberty v. Nyquist, 413 U.S. 756 (1973).

164. *Grants and loans, constitutional:* Americans United for Separation of Church and State v. Blanton, 434 U.S. 803 (1977), aff'g 433 F.Supp 97 (M.D. Tenn. 1977); Americans United for Separation of Church and State v. Bubb, 379 F.Supp. 872 (D. Kan. 1974). *Reimbursement, unconstitutional: See* Nyquist, prior fn.; Sloan v. Lemon, 413 U.S. 825 (1973).

165. *See* Minnesota Civil Liberties Union v. Roemer, 452 F.Supp. 1316 (D. Minn. 1978); Commonwealth Dept. of Ed. v. First School, 370 A.2d 702 (Pa. 1977).

constitutional criteria should be noted: "First, the statute must have a secular legislative purpose. . . . Second, it must have a 'primary effect' that neither advances nor inhibits religion. . . . Third, the statute and its administration must avoid excessive government entanglement with religion."[166] The Court has for the most part accepted the secularity of purpose in challenged legislation and has focused upon the issues of primary effect and of excessive entanglement.

While some Supreme Court opinions referred to "political" entanglement arising from public controversy over government aid to religious private schools, the political entanglement thesis, as distinguished from the administrative entanglement test, has not been consistently embraced by a clear majority of Supreme Court justices through the latest cases, as to constitute a firm independent constitutional test. The fact that a test of political entanglement would, in practical effect, deny or devalue First Amendment civil rights of freedom of speech and freedom to petition the government, on the part of proponents of private school aid, may explain why a number of Justices have more lately expressly rejected that thesis.[167]

The stated tests are not absolute and self-applying. To quote the court:

> "It is well to emphasize, however, that the tests must not be viewed as setting the precise limits to the necessary constitutional inquiry, but serve only as guidelines with which to identify instances in which the objectives of the Establishment Clause have been impaired. . . . Primary among the evils against which the Establishment Clause protects 'have been sponsorship, financial support, and active involvement of the sovereign in religious activity.' . . . But it is clear that not all legislative programs that provide indirect or incidental benefit to a religious institution are prohibited by the Constitution."[168]

Since these standards are tentative, their application requires the Court to make specific judgments as to particular forms of aid.

3. Direct Aid to NonPublic Schools

Direct government grants of *funds* to church-related private schools, whether for building maintenance in poverty areas or for instructional expenses in state prescribed secular courses have been held unconstitutional.[169] The Supreme Court has upheld direct government grants to colleges for construction of academic buildings,[170] a ruling that it refused to apply to lower education. It has also held that taxpayer citizens cannot challenge grants of federal surplus property disposition.[171] It therefore remains possible for the federal government to make surplus property grants to church-related schools, unless the Supreme Court should in the future depart from the foregoing ruling.

---

166. *See* Meek v. Pittenger, 421 U.S. 349, 358 (1975).

167. See opinions of the various Justices in Wallace v. Jaffree, 105 S.Ct. 2479 (1985).

168. Meek v. Pittenger, *supra,* at 358–359 (1975).

169. Comm. for Public Education v. Nyquist, 413 U.S. 756 (1973) (facilities maintenance expenses); Lemon v. Kurtzman, 403 U.S. 602 (1971) (instructional expense reimbursement).

170. Tilton v. Richardson, fn. 163, *supra.*

171. Valley Forge Christian College v. Americans United For Separation of Church and State, 454 U.S. 464 (1982).

While the Supreme Court has squarely nullified direct government subsidy of religious school instruction in secular courses, no serious challenges to government purchase of service contracts with private schools for the special treatment of the handicapped have been raised, and none has been considered by the Supreme Court. This is true even though many religious institutions receive such contracts for orphans, court wards, and special educational services.[172] A few lower courts that have addressed this issue have upheld such assistance programs as not violating the federal constitution.[173] It is, of course, possible for a court to hold that, even if such purchase of services result in aid to religion, it would be excepted from the general rule because it is necessary to achieve a "compelling" state interest.

Another form of direct aid to schools that triggers constitutional challenge arose under statutes that authorized state reimbursement to private schools for expenses incurred in conducting and reporting to state agencies general standardized tests of student achievement, as required by state law. In a first test case, the Supreme Court struck down a New York statute providing for such reimbursement on the ground that the student tests were prepared by and administered by religious-school teachers and "no means are available to assure that internally prepared tests are free of religious instruction."[174] In 1977, however, the same Court upheld the Ohio statute that provided similar cost reimbursement even though the tests were still administered by private school teachers. The fact that state employees controlled the content and scoring of the tests in Ohio proved to be crucial.[175] After that decision, a later New York reimbursement statute covering testing and record-keeping expenses was upheld even though it permitted scoring by the parochial school teachers, and not by state officials.[176] The Supreme Court reasoned that because the New York tests were almost totally objective, there was little risk of religious influence in the government-financed activity.

The validity of favorable tax treatment given by governments to private schools (e.g., exemptions from state and local property taxes or from federal income taxes), will depend in part upon each particular tax scheme. It is clear, however, that the establishment clause does not automatically render all forms of favorable tax treatment unconstitutional as aids to religion, for in the words of the United States Supreme Court: "There is no genuine nexus between tax exemption and establishment of religion."[177] Conversely, the free exercise clause and the principle against government entanglement with religion do not mandate the opposite result, namely that the government must exempt religious private schools from taxation. In the twin landmark decisions of *Bob Jones University* v. *United States* and *Goldsboro Christian Schools, Inc.* v. *United States,*[178]

---

172. *See, e.g.*, Rendell-Baker v. Cohn, fn. 75, *supra.*

173. *Compare* Opinion of Justices, 258 N.E.2d 779 (Mass. 1970) (voiding general state purchases of educational services); *with* Commonwealth v. School Comm. of Springfield, 417 N.E.2d 408 (Mass. 1981) (upholding purchase of special educational services from private schools for the handicapped). *See also* State ex. rel. Warren v. Nussbaum, 219 N.W.2d 577 (Wis. 1974).

174. *See* Levitt v. Committee for Public Education, 413 U.S. 472, 480 (1973).

175. See Part IV of the Wolman opinion at the end of this chapter.

176. Committee for Public Education v. Regan, 444 U.S. 646 (1980).

177. *See* Walz v. Tax Commission, 397 U.S. 664, 674 (1970).

178. 461 U.S. 574 (1983). *Semble:* Green v. Regan, 731 F.2d 995 (D.C. Cir. 1983), cert. denied, 105 S.Ct. 125, (1984).

the Supreme Court of the United States, while recognizing the constitutional authority of government to grant tax exemptions to nonprofit private schools, as public charities, also held that the government could deny such exemptions to racially discriminatory schools, even where the racial discrimination was religiously dictated. In balancing the government's interest in discouraging racial discrimination with the religious claims of the involved schools, the Court found that the government's interest was sufficiently "compelling" to override the religious claims of the schools. These decisions leave unanswered, however, the questions about what other government public policy interests would justify denial of tax benefits to private schools by reason of their religious practices.

With respect to the prevailing state law patterns of exempting nonprofit private schools from state property taxes, as part of the exempt class of educational charities, no serious constitutional barrier appears to exist, in light of the Supreme Court's decision that sustained property tax exemption on houses of worship.[179]

As noted above, no serious constitutional barrier exists to the imposition of employer levies by government under income security statutes.[180]

The constitutionality of favorable tax treatment of educational institutions is to be distinguished from the much more commonplace issues of statutory construction (i.e., whether particular tax statutes, federal or state, should be interpreted to cover or exclude particular properties, activities, or revenues of individual private schools).[181] Thus, even though particular taxation or exemption would be constitutional, judicial construction of the scope of tax statutes is equally important to their application.

State constitutional limitations on government aid to private schools become critical only where the aid in question is either unchallenged or upheld under the federal constitution.[182] Government aids that are invalid under the federal Constitution cannot be made valid by state law or state considerations. Tax relief and benefits to parents of nonpublic school children are taken up later.

4. Assistance Directed to Students and Parents

Government aid includes a wide range of financial assistance to particular programs in both public and nonpublic schools, including student lunches, special educational services, books for school libraries, and special educational projects in poverty areas. (See Table 10–2.) Many statutes have gone unchallenged, but the reported decisions indicate that the form and degree of financial assistance and of government administrative involvement in such programs are crucial to determining whether particular student or parental aids are constitutional. The fact that the Supreme Court, beginning in 1947 and continuing to 1985, has been closely and constantly divided in adjudicating each form of

---

179. See fn. 177, *supra*.

180. See text at fn. 162, *supra*.

181. *E.g.*, Bd. of Appraisal Review v. Protestant Episcopal Church Council, 676 S.W.2d 616 (Tex. 1984) finding that 185 acres of 392-acre tract was "reasonably necessary" for the operation of the school within the meaning of the governing tax statute. *Compare* Summit U. Methodist Church v. Kinney, 7 Ohio St.3d 13 (1983) (church educational unit not entitled to property tax exemption when other part of same building was rented for use as a day care center).

182. See, e.g., variant federal and state constitutional rulings on publicly provided school bus transportation, *infra*.

TABLE 10-2. Nonpublic school participation in federal assistance programs *

Affiliation	Total number of schools	Program participation: One or more — Number	One or more — Percent	ESEA — Number	ESEA — Percent	Food and milk — Number	Food and milk — Percent
All schools	14,757	12,083	81.9	11,154	75.6	8,564	58.0
Not affiliated	2,210	1,129	51.1	900	40.7	588	26.6
Affiliated	12,547	10,954	87.3	10,254	81.7	7,976	63.6
Baptist	310	49	15.8	36	11.6	19	6.1
Calvinist	182	167	91.8	159	87.4	158	86.8
Roman Catholic	8.986	8.846	98.4	8,567	95.3	6,313	70.3
Episcopal	304	187	61.5	156	51.3	105	34.5
Jewish	264	240	90.9	210	79.5	187	70.8
Lutheran	1,366	1,055	77.2	850	62.2	920	67.3
Seventh Day Adventist	517	111	21.5	41	7.9	90	17.4
Other	618	299	48.4	235	38.0	184	29.8

SOURCE: U.S. Department of Health, Education, and Welfare, National Center for Education Statistics, *Nonpublic School Statistics, 1976–77, Advance Report.*

*All data tables must be updated for possible changes in each state since 1979.

aid bespeaks the inexact nature of so-called constitutional tests and the lack of solid consensus among the Justices as to what those tests should be. In terms of result, however, the decision on each form of aid is clear and binding unless and until further shifts of opinion develop within the Court. The safe course is to take as law the result on each aid form and to discount the argumentative rhetoric of contending Justices.

a. School Transportation. The operation of the federal Constitution upon public funding of student transportation to and from nonpublic schools, including religious schools, was well summarized as follows:

> ". . . this and other Supreme Court and federal cases [which] have indicated that the Fourteenth Amendment *permits,* but does not *require,* expenditure of government funds on parochial students. *Meek* v. *Pittenger,* 421 U.S. 349, 364, 95 S.Ct. 1753, 1763, 44 L.Ed.2d 217, 231 (1975). . . . "[183]

183. *See* Janasiewicz v. Bd. of Education, 299 S.E.2d 34, 37 (W.Va. 1982): "Many states have specific statutes mentioning transportation of non-public school students: Alaska Stat. § 14.09.020 (regular bus routes); Cal. [Educ.] Code § 39808 (West) (regular routes, no stipends); Conn.Gen.Stat.Ann. § 10-281 (West) (regular services not to exceed twice last year's public student transportation cost); Del.Code Ann., (tit. 14) § 2905 (same as public school transportation); Ill.Ann.Stat. ch. 122 § 29-4 (Smith-Hurd) (regular routes or separate routes); Ind.Code Ann. § 20-9.1-7-1 (Burns) (regular routes); Iowa Code Ann. § 285.2 (West) (reimbursement); Kan.Stat.Ann. § 72-8306 (regular routes); Louisiana Rev.Stat.Ann. § 17:158 (West) (any student attending approved school within district); Mass.Gen.Laws Ann., ch. 76, § 1 (West) (same as public students); Mich.Comp.Laws Ann. § 380.1321 and 1322 (West) (regular routes; stipends); Mont.Code Ann. § 20-10-123 (nonpublic student must pay, get permit and can be denied if seating unavailable); Neb.Rev.Stat.

Ever since the landmark decision in *Everson* v. *Board of Education*,[184] the Supreme Court has adhered to that position as to *school* transportation. However, in 1975, the same Court, by a 5-4 majority, held that state funding of field trip transportation for nonpublic school students under the supervision of religious school teachers would constitute an aid to religion in violation of the federal Constitution. (See the *Wolman* opinion at the end of this chapter.) Presumably, state funding of educational field trips not organized, supervised, or controlled by religious school authorities would fall within the *Everson*, rather than the *Wolman*, decision, but that question has not been addressed by the Supreme Court.

The broad claim that denial of comparable publicly funded transportation to nonpublic school children would be unconstitutional discrimination—a denial of their rights under the equal protection clause and an infringement of free exercise of religion—has been rejected.[185] Where the state undertakes to provide nonpublic school bus transportation confined to transportation within school district lines, Courts found no unconstitutional discrimination against nonpublic school children under the federal or state constitutions.[186] Courts have considered statutes to be facially neutral and valid where they authorized interdistrict transportation to both public and nonpublic school students, even though nonpublic school students made much greater use of interdistrict transportation.[187] Where, however, school transportation on its face permits interdistrict transportation only to nonpublic school students, the courts of Iowa and Rhode Island held them to be void and unconstitutional.[188]

Even where the law itself is facially neutral toward public and nonpublic school students, administrative discrimination in providing such transportation may give rise to an equal protection claim by the victims of such discrimination.[189] Where the validity of private school transportation is tested not under the equal protection clause, but under the establishment clause, a separate issue arises, namely, the extent to which public authorities may compare or investigate the religious aspects of schools without themselves

---

§ 79-487 (regular routes and times within district); N.H.Rev.Stat.Ann. § 189:9 (same as public students); N.J.Stat.Ann. § 18A:39-1 (West) (nonpublic students allowed statutory maximum amount for school bus transportation costs or stipend to parents); N.M.Stat.Ann. § 22-16-7 (regular routes; stipends allowed); N.Y.Educ.Law § 3635 (McKinney) (nonpublic school children transported from pick-up points at public schools); N.D.Cent. Code § 15-34.2-16 (established times and routes when space available); Ohio Rev. Ann. § 3327.01 (Page) (stipend allowed); Or.Rev.Stat. § 332.415 (same as public students); Pa.Stat.Ann., titl 24, § 13-1361 (Purdon) (nonprofit within district); R.I. Gen. Laws § 16-21-1 (nonprofit); Wash. Rev.Code Ann. § 28A.24.065 (same routes if seats available; private students must pay); Wisc.Stat.Ann. § 121.54(2)(b) (West) (regular routes within district or five miles beyond school district)." *Id.* at p. 38.

184. 330 U.S. 1 (1947).

185. Luetkemeyer v. Kaufmann, 364 F.Supp. 376 (W.D. Mo.); aff'd. 419 U.S. 888 (1974); *accord:* Cook v. Griffin, 364 N.Y.S.2d 632 (1975).

186. *See, e.g.*, Reed v. Attorney General, 478 A.2d 788 (N.J. 1984); Attorney General v. School Committee of Essex, 439 N.E.2d 770 (Mass. 1982).

187. Members of the Jamestown Sch. Committee v. Schmidt, 669 F.2d 1 (1st Cir. 1983); Springfield Sch. District v. Pennsylvania Dept. of Ed., 397 A.2d 1154, appeal dismissed for want of a substantial federal question sub nom., School District of Pittsburgh v. Pennsylvania Dept. of Ed., 443 U.S. 901 (1979). *See also* McKeesport Area Sch. Dist. v. Pennsylvania Dept. of Ed., 392 A.2d 912, appeal dismissed for want of a substantial question, 446 U.S. 970 (1980).

188. Members of Jamestown School Committee v. Schmidt, 427 F.Supp. 1338 (D.R.I. 1977); Americans United for Separation of Church and State v. Benton,413 F. Supp.955 (S.D. Iowa 1975).

189. *See* Young v. Bd. of Education, 246 N.W.2d 230 (Wis. 1976).

becoming unconstitutionally involved in government entanglement with religion. A few courts have disapproved of statutes authorizing religious investigations, beyond objective evidence of the school's official policy or pronouncements in the school's charter documents.[190]

A third possible constitutional objection to private school transportation laws rests upon the doctrine against impermissible delegation of legislative authority, discussed in Chapter 2, part B-1. A court invalidated a bus authorization statute as a standardless invalid delegation,[191] but courts can avoid that result by construing an otherwise vague statute to mean nonpublic school transportation "to the same extent" as that authorized for public school students.[192]

In the absence of a federal constitutional bar, publicly paid private school transportation may still be challenged under the state constitutions. State constitutional prohibitions vary in their wording and scope, and have been invoked in only about half of the states, with the majority line of decisions upholding such aids.[193] Such transportation statutes and practices remain in effect in states where they have not been challenged by test litigation.[194]

Where a state constitution does not absolutely prohibit such transportation, objections may still be raised to particular arrangements (viz. on minimum distance allowances, bus routings, and geographic limits of transportation). To the extent that such arrangements discriminate for or against students in particular schools, they must also be justified under state as well as federal constitutions.

A variation on the bus subsidy controversy arises where the agency charged with a statutory duty to provide private school transportation elects, in lieu of providing direct

---

190. *See, e.g.*, Members of Jamestown Sch. Committee v. Schmidt, *supra*, 699 F.2d at p. 13, (nullified and severed from the transportation statute, a provision that would require the state commissioner to compare sectarian schools.) *See also* Holy Trinity Community School, Inc. v. Kahl, 262 N.W.2d 210 (Wis. 1978) (barring public school superintendent's investigation into religious nature of school beyond looking to its charter and bylaws).

191. Jennings v. Exeter-West Greenwich Regional School District, 352 A.2d 634 (R.I. 1976).

192. *See, e.g.*, Attorney General v. Sch. Comm. of Essex, fn. 186, *supra* (providing saving construction to the phrase "to the same extent"); Janasiewicz v. Bd. of Education, fn. 183, *supra* (construing the phrase "adequate means").

193. The following jurisdictions have upheld the transportation of children attending private schools: Bowker v. Baker, 167 P.2d 256 (Cal. 1946); Snyder v. Town of Newtown, 161 A.2d 770 (Conn. 1960); Board of Education v. Bakalis, 299 N.E.2d 737 (Ill. 1973); Nichols v. Henry, 191 S.W.2d 930 (Ky. 1945); Board of Education of Baltimore County v. Wheat, 199 A. 628 (Md. 1938); Bloom v. School Committee, 379 N.E.2d 578 (Mass. 1978); Alexander v. Bartlett, 165 N.W.2d 445 (Mich. 1968); Americans United, Inc., as Protestants v. Independent School District, No. 622, 179 N.W.2d 146 (Minn. 1970); West Morris Regional Board of Education v. Sills, 279A.2d609 (N.J. 1971); Bd. of Education of Central School District No. 1 v. Allen, 228 N.E.2d 791 (N.Y. 1967); Honohan v. Holt, 244 N.E.2d 537 (Ohio 1968); Springfield School District v. Dept. of Education, 397 A.2d 1154 (Pa. 1979); Members of Jamestown School Committee v. Schmidt, 405 A.2d 16 (R.I. 1979); Janasiewicz v. Board of Educ., Etc., 299 S.E.2d 34 (W.V. 1982). Prior decisions in New York and Wisconsin against such assistance were superseded by later state constitutional amendments. *See* Bd. of Educ. of Central Sch. District v. Allen, 228 N.E.2d 791 (N.Y. 1967); O'Connell v. Kniskern, 484 F.Supp. 896, 899 (E.D. Wis. 1980). The following jurisdictions have ruled against the transportation of children to private schools: Matthews v. Quinton, 362 P.2d 932 (Alaska 1961); Opinion of the Justices, 216 A.2d 668 (Del. 1966); Spears v. Honda, 449 P.2d 130 (Haw. 1968); Epeldi v. Engelking, 488 P.2d 860 (Idaho 1971); Mallory v. Barrera, 544 S.W.2d 556 (Mo. 1976); Board of Education v. Antone, 384 P.2d 911 (Okla. 1963); Visser v. Nooksack Valley School District, No. 506, 207 P.2d 198 (Wash. 1949).

194. See generally Annotation: *Private Schools—Public Aid—Bus Service,* 41 A.L.R.3d 344 (1972).

bus service, to pay to parents a sum of money to cover the cost of alternative mass transit or private transportation between the student's home and school. The trend of reported cases has been to interpret enabling statutes as authorizing that practice, especially where it is less costly to do so,[195] and as long as that alternative is not unreasonable or discriminatory.[196] Where a statute expressly requires nonpublic school transportation, state administrators have no discretion to deny the same,[197] but parents may not demand transportation to points more distant than those required by the statute.[198] On the other hand, even where discretion as to transportation arrangements is vested in state education authorities, they may not exercise that discretion arbitrarily to deny transportation services to nonpublic school students.[199] The burden of acting reasonably under a bus authorization law applies to parents as well as public school authorities. The failure to make timely application for such transportation with provider school districts has been held to justify discretionary denial of such service by the school district.[200]

As with public school transportation, the duties and discretion of local authorities are defined by the specific terms of transportation statutes. School administrators are bound by specific statutory restrictions under the same administrative law doctrines that were reviewed in Chapter 3. Thus, a school district may not provide transportation to private school children unless expressly authorized to do so by state law.[201] Where the statute vests discretion to provide such transportation in the local school district, an arbitrary exercise of that discretion can be judicially overturned. When a school board declined to transport a child to his private school because it lay 400 feet beyond the district boundary, a Wisconsin federal court reversed the board decision as an arbitrary denial of equal protection of the law—even though the state law gave the board the option to grant or withhold cross-district busing service.[202] Where, however, a statute limited the authority of the State Commissioner to order bus transportation for parochial school students to "the nearest available public school," parents could not insist on state transportation of children to a more distant parochial school of the same denomination.[203]

b. Tuition Reimbursement. The Supreme Court has consistently held that partial state reimbursement of tuition costs incurred by parents for their children in church-sponsored schools is an unconstitutional form of aid to the religious mission of those

---

195. *See, e.g.*, St. John Vianney School v. Board of Education, 336 N.W.2d 387 (Wis. 1983) (public school board not required to transport nonpublic students by any one mode of transportation, but could use mass transit); Janasiewicz v. Board of Education, fn. 188, *supra* (monetary stipends to parents of parochial school children to pay for their transportation, as well as permission to ride school district buses, held *intra vires* the statute, and constitutional).

196. *See* Young v. Board of Education, 246 N.W.2d 230 (Wis. 1976).

197. *E.g.*, O'Connell v. Kniskern, 484 F.Supp. 896 (E.D. Wis. 1980); Cook v. Griffin, 364 N.W.S.2d 632 (1975); *cf.* Dickinson Public School Dist. v. Scott, 252 N.W.2d 216 (N.D. 1977).

198. Rickmyer v. Gates-Chili Central School District, 368 N.Y.S.2d 636 (1975).

199. Deutsch v. Teel, 400 F.Supp. 598, 600 (E.D. Wis. 1975).

200. Bd. of Education, Hauppauge Union Free School District v. Ambach, 462 N.Y.S.2d 294 (1983).

201. See fn. 186, Cook v. Griffin, fn. 185; Dickinson P.S. District No. 1 v. Scott 252 N.W. 2d 216 (N. Dak. 1977).

202. Deutsch v. Teel, fn. 199.

203. Rackmyer v. Gates-Chili Cent. Sch. District, 368 N.Y.S.2d 636 (1975).

schools and therefore impermissible.[204] While for elementary and secondary schools the Court employed the religious enterprise theory and treated the parents as "conduits" of funds to the schools, it has rejected that rationale in upholding state tuition subsidies of students in church-sponsored colleges.[205] However, it has not been called upon to consider whether contracts of reimbursement for the education of the handicapped at state expense at church-sponsored schools would be considered an exception to the tuition reimbursement cases. It is also not settled, for lack of a test law or test case, whether various proposals for state payment of tuition vouchers to all parents, regardless of school attended, would escape the prohibitions of the above-mentioned tuition cases. If such vouchers were confined exclusively to nonpublic school students, they would contradict the prohibitory precedents unless extended to all parents to use a school of their choice. Since these proposals have not been enacted, their validity remains a matter of speculation. They are, however, to be distinguished from the financial benefits of tax deductions and credits, considered in a later section of this chapter.

Since tuition voucher schemes have not been enacted, their validity under state constitutional provisions is also a matter of academic opinion. Given the disparate treatment under different state constitutions to other forms of aid to nonpublic education, one may opine that any voucher scheme permitted under federal law might still encounter acceptance in some states and rejection in others.

c. Books, Instructional Materials, and Equipment. In 1930, the United States Supreme Court ruled that state loan of secular textbooks to nonpublic school children served a public purpose and did not violate the federal constitutional ban on public expenditures for private purposes.[206] In 1968, that Court also upheld the loan of secular textbooks to parochial schoolchildren on the ground that such loans did not aid religion in violation of the establishment clause.[207] To date, the Supreme Court has not been called upon to consider any challenge to the public provision of textbooks for nonpublic school libraries, as is provided under the federal Elementary and Secondary Education Act.

As with school bus transportation, however, the public provision of secular textbooks to children in nonpublic schools has been disallowed under the constitutions of some states (Massachusetts, Kentucky, California, Michigan, Missouri, Nebraska, Oregon, and South Dakota), and upheld under the constitutions of other states (New York, Pennsylvania and Ohio).[208]

---

204. Committee for Public Education and Religious Liberty v. Nyquist, 413 U.S. 756 (1973); Sloan v. Lemon, 413 U.S. 825 (1973) (voiding state tuition subsidies to parents of children in church-related primary and secondary schools).

205. Americans United for the Separation of Church and State v. Blanton, 434 U.S. 803 (1977), aff'd. 433 F.Supp., 97 (M.D. Tenn. 1977). (upholding state scholarship subsidies to students in higher education, including church-related colleges).

206. Cochran v. Louisiana Bd. of Ed., 281 U.S. 913 (1930).

207. *See* Wolman case at end of this chapter.; Bd. of Education v. Allen, 392 U.S. 236 (1968).

208. California Teachers Assn. v. Riles, 172 Cal. Rptr. 300 (1981); Fannin v. Williams, 655 S.W2d 480 (Ky. 1983); Bloom v. School Committee, 379 N.E.2d 578 (Mass. 1978); McDonald v. Sch. Bd. of Yankton, 246 N.W.2d 93 (S. Dak. 1976); Paste v. Tussey, 512 S.W.2d 97 (Mo. 1974); Gaffney v. St. Dept. of Ed., 220 N.W.2d 550 (Neb. 1974); In re Advisory Opinion, 228 N.W.2d 772 (Mich. 1975); Dickman v. Sch. District No. 62C, 366 P.2d 533 (Ore. 1961).

In the *Wolman* decision (discussed at the end of this chapter), however, the United States Supreme Court did draw a significant distinction under the federal Constitution between provision of textbooks and provision of instructional materials. It voided, as unconstitutional, government loans of instructional materials and equipment for student use in religious schools. Though not directly given to the school, the Court concluded that, unlike textbooks, instructional materials and equipment constituted aids to the "religious role of the schools" and were less separable from religious functions of church-sponsored schools. While these refinements as to what constitutes indirect aid to the school's "religious enterprise" invited criticisms by several Justices, they do prohibit states from furnishing instructional materials to nonpublic school children unless ways can be found to ensure that such materials will be classified as student and not institutional benefits.

d. Diagnostic, Remedial, and Therapeutic Services. The United States Supreme Court decided three cases between 1975 and 1985 on the constitutionality of government-funded "auxiliary services" to children attending religious schools. In *Meek* v. *Pittinger,*[209] the Court voided a Pennsylvania statute that authorized publicly employed professionals to enter parochial schools and to there render to needful individual students specified counseling, diagnostic, therapeutic, and remedial services (psychological, speech, and hearing therapy). The Justices split three ways, with one bloc arguing that such child benefits were valid in all circumstances, another bloc holding that such services were invalid in all circumstances, and the third bloc concluding that some diagnostic and health services could be validly provided, but that the Pennsylvania statutory arrangement of providing remedial services *inside* parochial schools rendered the law invalid. A few years later, in *Wolman* v. *Walter,* reproduced hereafter, a different majority line of judges upheld state provision of *diagnostic* services with respect to speech, hearing, and psychological testing though taking place in private and church-related schools, when rendered by state employees. The view was that such child benefits, like medical and nursing services, pose no threat to aiding religion or fostering excessive government-religion entanglements. The Court further decided that the provision of *therapeutic,* guidance, and remedial services by state employees could only be provided to such children at "neutral" locations (i.e., away from the religious schools) because on-site therapy, unlike diagnosis, might pose a risk of religious influence or entanglement of government and religious considerations. These distinctions explain why the Pennsylvania law that placed public school therapists *inside* the normal school environment of the treated child was nullified, while a similar Ohio law, which placed the therapist and child in a meeting place *outside* the church school premises, was upheld. Whether such isolation of children in need of treatment makes sense as a matter of administrative logistics, or as a matter of stigmatizing the child or of effective remedial practice was apparently not considered by the majority Justices to be constitutionally relevant. Splitting diagnostic functions from therapeutic functions, however, will require state authorities to revise their remedial practices.[210]

---

209. 421 U.S. 349 (1975).

210. *See* Filler v. Pt. Washington Un. Free Sch. District, 436 F.Supp. 1231 (E.D.N.Y. 1977).

Most recently, in *Aguilar* v. *Felton,* also reproduced at the end of this chapter, a still different lineup of Justices voted 5–4 to strike down Title I of the federal Elementary and Secondary Education Act as applied to children at religious schools. The five Justices concluded that, notwithstanding the act's secular purpose, the use of state-employed specialists and the lack of any claim or proof of diversion of remedial services to religious uses, the law fostered an excessive entanglement of government with religion by way of the state administrative cooperation and oversight of those services inside church schools. Justice Powell, who voted with the majority, also concluded that Title I aided religion in violation of the establishment clause. It would appear that none of the Justices in *Aguilar* abandoned the rationale of the *Wolman* case that the unconstitutional ingredient lay not in state provision of remedial services to children, but in providing such services on the premises of religious schools. The case thus appears to leave intact the application of Title I providing remedial services by state-employed specialists to children at "neutral sites" away from religious school premises, however logistically difficult that arrangement might be.[211]

Even assuming, per *Wolman,* that the federal Constitution permits on-site diagnostic services to parochial school children, and off-site remedial services to them, there remains the issue whether such services would pass muster under individual state constitutions. A Missouri case held that even student services permitted under the federal constitution were barred by state law. It invalidated speech therapy services to parochial school students by school districts, whether at or outside the parochial school, as contrary to state law. Unless state rulings are found to violate superior federal law, such as constitutional rights of students, they also bind educational authorities.[212]

e. Tax Relief to Parents. A search for acceptable means of government financial assistance to nonpublic education has, in recent years, produced new proposals and some enactments for special relief to taxpayers who incur educational expenses in elementary and secondary schools. The traditional allowance of "deductions" for contributions to public charities, including nonprofit educational institutions, applies to all citizens and not merely parents and poses no serious problems. Where, however, payments to nonprofit schools are made to meet an obligation for educational services to the contributors' children, such payments have not been considered to be deductible

---

211. "Today's ruling does not spell the end of the Title I program of remedial education for disadvantaged children. . . . Impoverished children who attend parochial schools may also continue to benefit from Title I programs offered off the premises of their schools—possibly in portable classrooms just over the edge of the school property." (O'Connor, J., dissenting in Aguilar v. Felton, *supra.*) "If, for example, Congress could fashion a program of evenhanded financial assistance to both public and private schools that could be administred, without governmental supervision in the private schools, so as to prevent the diversion of the aid from secular purposes, we would be presented with a different question." (Powell, J., concurring in Aguilar v. Felton, *supra.*)

212. "The Court recognized, however, that in certain states, statutory and constitutional restrictions on church-state involvement in education might be so severe as to rule out any parochial school program that would be comparable in quality to on-the-premises instruction in the public schools." *Wheeler* v. *Barrera, supra,* 417 U.S. at 423-25. *See* Barrera v. Wheeler, 531 F.2d 402, 406 (8th Cir. 1976). *See also* Special District for Education and Training of Handicapped Children v. Wheeler, 408 S.W.2d 60 (Mo. 1966); Filler v. Port Washington Un. Free School District, 436 F.Supp. 1231 (E.D.N.Y. 1977).

charitable contributions, but more in the way of legal obligations.[213]

Congress has not to date enacted any of the proposals for income tax credits or deductions for expenses incurred by parents of elementary and secondary school children.[214] With respect to state legislation that provides tax relief against private education expenses, only a half dozen cases have been reported and their results have been mixed, since each of the challenged laws provided different forms and schemes of tax relief. Since the constitutional validity of the tax benefits may be materially affected by the form which it takes, the law remains somewhat incomplete.

The first question to be resolved is whether the subject statute is a true tax measure or merely a disguised device to provide tuition reimbursement, which has been held unconstitutional. A complex New York statute provided tuition reimbursement to low income families only, but provided a different benefit to middle and high income families by way of state tax relief, on the basis of their private school costs. It did not survive constitutional challenge because the Supreme Court found that the tax relief provision was really an alternative adjunct to the main statutory scheme of tuition reimbursement and a disguised form of tuition reimbursement.[215] In its ruling, the Court made clear that tax relief is not inherently or universally unconstitutional: "It is equally well-established, however, that not every law that confers an indirect, remote or incidental benefit upon religious institutions is, for that reason alone, constitutionally invalid."[216] The Court cited with approval its decision upholding state property tax exemption of houses of worship as not violating the establishment clause.[217] Much then will depend on the specific incidents and impact of particular tax relief.

A later New Jersey law providing tax credits in a fixed amount ($1000) to all nonpublic school parents, irrespective of their individual school expenses, was also struck down as unconstitutional, as were income tax deduction statutes in California, Ohio, and Minnesota.[218] The potential significance of the design of tax legislation is indicated by the latest Supreme Court decision in this area. After a prior Minnesota tax relief law was invalidated, Minnesota enacted a new state income tax law that allowed all parents a deduction against taxable income of expenses actually incurred for child education, up to an annual limit of $700. The tax deduction was available to parents of public as well as nonpublic school children. In *Mueller* v. *Allen*,[219] the Supreme Court, again by close 5-4 vote, upheld the statute as constitutional, even though its benefits would redound primarily and to a much greater extent to parents of private and religious school students. The Court had little difficulty finding that the law satisfied the secular purpose and

---

213. Gotlieb v. Commissioner of Taxation, 245 N.W.2d 244 (Minn. 1976).

214. See "Tax Treatment of Tuition Expenses," hearings before Committee on Ways and Means, House of Representatives, 95th Congress, 2d Session, February 14–21, 1978 (Serial 95-56).

215. Committee for Public Education and Religious Liberty v. Nyquist, 413 U.S. 756 (1973).

216. *Idem.* at p. 771.

217. Walz v. Tax Commission, 397 U.S. 664 (1970).

218. Public Funds for Public Schools of New Jersey v. Byrne, 444 F.Supp. 1228 (D. N.J. 1978); Franchise Tax Bd. of United Americans for Public Schools, 419 U.S. 890 (1974) (judgment aff'd. without opinion, not reported below); Kosydar v. Wolman, 353 F.Supp. 744 (S.D. Ohio 1972); aff'd. sub nom. Grit v. Wolman, 413 U.S. 901 (1973); Minnesota Civil Liberties Union v. State, 224 N.W.2d 344 (1974), cert. den. 421 U.S. 988 (1975).

219. 463 U.S. 388 (1983).

nonexcessive entanglement prongs of the test for nonestablishment. The major issue of "primary effect"—whether the law impermissibly aided the religious purposes of nonpublic schools, however indirectly—turned on the Court's analysis of the specific scheme of tax relief. In upholding the law, the Court stressed certain features of the law that distinguished it from tax benefit laws that it had previously held unconstitutional, principally the facial neutrality of the law with respect to parents in both public and nonpublic schools:

> "Other characterists of § 290.09(22) argue equally strongly for the provision's constitutionality. Most importantly, the deduction is available for educational expenses incurred by *all* parents, including those whose children attend public schools and those whose children attend non-sectarian private schools or sectarian private schools. . . . In this respect, as well as others, this case is vitally different from the scheme struck down in *Nyquist.* There, public assistance amounting to tuition grants, was provided only to parents of children in *nonpublic* schools. [Moreover,] we intimated that 'public assistance (e.g., scholarships) made available generally without regard to the sectarian-nonsectarian or public-nonpublic nature of the institution benefited,' might not offend the Establishment Clause. We think the tax deduction adopted by Minnesota is more similar to this latter type of program than it is to the arrangement struck down in *Nyquist.* [As] *Widmar* and our other decisions indicate, a program, like § 290.09(22), that neutrally provides state assistance to a broad spectrum of citizens is not readily subject to challenge under the Establishment Clause."[220]

The *Mueller* decision resolved prior case conflicts on the nature and validity of state tax deductions for specified school expenses,[221] but of even greater significance is its recognition that governments could constitutionally employ tax policy to lessen the financial burden of private as well as public education, and thus to advance government interests in "assuring the continued financial health of private schools, both sectarian and nonsectarian."[222] The majority in *Mueller* also rejected the objection that the challenged law promoted "political divisiveness" species of entanglement because of the dominance of certain sects in the operation of nonpublic schools. Its confinement of the political divisiveness argument to cases of "direct" aid to schools may portend further attenuation of the political divisiveness theme:

> "The Court's language in *Lemon I* respecting political divisiveness was made in the context of . . . statutes which provided for either direct payments of or reimbursement of, a proportion of teachers' salaries in parochial schools. We think, in the light of the treatment of the point in later cases discussed above, the language must be regarded as confined to cases where direct financial subsidies are paid to parochial schools or to teachers in parochial schools."[223]

---

220. *Id.* at pp. 397, 398.

221. "Because this question was reserved in *Committee for Public Education* v. *Nyquist,* 413 U.S. 756, 93 S.Ct. 2955, 37 L.Ed.2d 948 (1973), and because of a conflict between the decision of the Court of Appeals for the Eighth Circuit and that of the Court of Appeals for the First Circuit in *Rhode Island Federation of Teachers* v. *Norberg,* 630 F.2d 855 (CA1 1980), we granted certiorari." *Id.* at pp. 390, 391.

222. *Id.* at p. 395.

223. *Id.* at p. 403, n.11.

As with other forms of indirect aid to private and religious education, tax benefit or relief laws that pass muster under the federal Constitution may still be challenged under state constitutions. In this area, state constitutional law remains undeveloped.

f. Dual Enrollment Schemes. As indicated in the discussion of dual enrollment in Chapter 4, Part A-7, the validity of part-time instruction of private school students by publicly paid instructors will depend upon the specific shared time arrangements. The recent Supreme Court decisions in *Aguilar* v. *Felton* and *Grand Rapids School District* v. *Ball* outlaw dual enrollment arrangements that serve religious school children at public expense inside the premises of the religious school. Those opinions are reproduced in the following section and should be read carefully, not only for their outcome, but for their presentation of the diverse views of the individual majority and dissenting Justices as to the types of cooperative state-religious school arrangements that might satisfy the federal Constitution.

CASES

The State of Ohio v. Whisner

351 N.E.2d 750 (Ohio 1976)

[Defendants were convicted of failing to send their children to school. . . . Defendants appealed. The Supreme Court held that the State Board of Education's minimum standards relating to the operation of schools infringed the free exercise of religion of parents of students attending a nonpublic religious school, where the religious beliefs of the parents were truly held, the parents adequately demonstrated the manner in which the minimum standards infringe on their federal and state constitutional right to the free exercise of religion, and the state failed to establish an interest of sufficient magnitude to override the claim. It further held that where the minimum standards were so comprehensive in scope and effect as to eradicate the distinction between public and nonpublic education, application of those minimum standards to parents of children attending a nonpublic religious school abrogated their fundamental freedom, protected by the liberty clause of the Fourteenth Amendment, to direct the upbringing and education, secular or religious, of their children.]

CELEBREZZE, *Justice.*

This cause presents sensitive issues of paramount importance involving the power of the state to impose extensive regulations upon the structure and government of nonpublic education, and conversely, upon the right of these appellants to freely exercise their professed religious beliefs in the context of providing an education to their children. Because both the Court of Appeals and the Court of Common Pleas fundamentally misconstrued the principles of law applicable to resolution of the instant cause, and because the issues presented herein are apparently questions of first impression in Ohio, a thorough examination of the relevant decisional law, as expressed by the Supreme Court of the United States, and of the applicable constitutional and statutory provisions, both federal and state, is required.

At the outset we recognize that appellants do not facially attack the compulsory school attendance laws of this state. . . .

Nor do the appellants maintain that the state is devoid of all power to promulgate and enforce *reasonable* regulations affecting the operation of nonpublic schools. Numerous decisions of the Supreme Court of the United States over the years have clearly sounded the death knell with respect to any such assertion. . . .

Appellants do contend, however, that application of Ohio's compulsory attendance laws as to them, through the medium of the Minimum Standards for Ohio Elementary Schools, prescribed by the State Board of Education pursuant to the express legislative command contained in R. C. 3321.03, infringes upon their free exercise of religion as guaranteed by the First and Fourteenth Amendments to the Constitution of the United States, and by Section 7, Article I of the Ohio Constitution.

With regard to appellants' assertion . . . both the Court of Appeals and the

Court of Common Pleas committed error in failing to accord the requisite judicial deference to the veracity of those beliefs. Indeed, both courts *questioned* whether appellants' beliefs were founded upon religious principles. . . .

However, at this date and time in the history of our nation, it is crystal clear that neither the validity of what a person believes nor the reasons for so believing may be contested by an arm of the government. As stated in *United States* v. *Ballard* (1944), 322 U.S. 78, 86, 64 S.Ct. 882, 886, 88 L.Ed. 1148:"Men may believe what they cannot prove. They may not be put to the proof of their religious doctrines or beliefs." . . . The applicable test was enunciated in *United States* v. *Seeger* (1965), 380 U.S. 163, 185, 85 S.Ct. 850, 863, 13 L.Ed.2d 733, in these words:" . . . that while the 'truth' of a belief is not open to question, there remains the significant question whether it is 'truly held.' This is the threshold question of sincerity which must be resolved in every case. It is, of course, a question of fact. . . . "

Based upon the extensive record before us, there can be no doubt but that appellants' religious beliefs are "truly held." Rev. Whisner's testimony clearly reveals that the religion in which he believes is a historical religion consisting of "born-again" Christians, who adhere to a life of separation from worldliness, and who strictly structure their lives upon a subjective interpretation of Biblical language. . . .

However, the fact that appellants' religious beliefs are "truly held" does not end, but rather serves only to begin, our inquiry. . . .

In the instant cause, therefore, it was incumbent upon appellants to demonstrate the manner in which the state's "minimum standards" infringed upon their free exercise of religious liberty.

Through the testimony of Rev. Whisner, appellants voiced religious objections to four of the state's denominated "minimum standards." Those standards, and appellants' objections thereto, are set forth herein as follows:

1. EDb-401-02(E)(6)—"A charter shall be granted after an inspection which determines that all standards have been met." (Appellants do not desire a charter, because acceptance of same would constitute their agreement to comply with all standards, and thereby effectively remove their ability to control the direction of the school by reposing vast powers in the hands of the state.)
2. EDb-401-02(G)—"Based on a minimum five-hour school day or one of greater length, the total instructional time allocation per week shall be: . . . (Appellants complain that this standard does not expressly allot time in which Biblical and spiritual training may be given, and, therefore, is inimicable to the fundamental purpose of a religious school in that it severely restricts the ability of the school to incorporate its religious teachings.)
3. EDb-401-02(O)—" . . . All activities shall conform to policies adopted by the board of education." (The contention is advanced by appellants that this standard virtually provides a blank check to the public authorities to control the entire operation of their school.)
4. EDb-401-07—"Efforts toward providing quality education by the school . . . shall be achieved through cooperation and interaction between the school

> and the community. . . . "(A) The elementary principal and staff in keeping with administrative or board of education policies shall provide evidence, through written materials and informational meetings, of a continuous effort to give professional interpretation of the school's policies, program, purposes, planning, strengths and needs. "(B) Each elementary school shall demonstrate, through school-community activities, evidence of cooperative assessment of community needs to determine the purposes, program and planning for future educational improvement." (Appellants maintain that a Christian school cannot seek its direction from the world or from the community it serves.)

. . . Our review of the particular "minimum standards" objected to by appellants discloses that the language utilized in those standards is facially neutral. . . .

However, as required by *Wisconsin* v. *Yoder,* supra, 406 U.S. 205, at page 220, 92 S.Ct. 1526, at page 1536, 32 L.Ed.2d 15, we must also determine whether "a regulation neutral on its face may, in its application, nonetheless offend the constitutional requirement for governmental neutrality . . . because it unduly burdens the free exercise of religion." . . .

In this regard, we must conclude that the compendium of "minimum standards" promulgated by the State Board of Education, taken as a whole, "unduly burdens the free exercise of [appellants'] religion." *Wisconsin* v. *Yoder,* supra.

To begin with, although admittedly an admirable effort to extol the secular aims of the state in assuring that each child educated in this state obtains a quality education, we believe that these "minimum standards" overstep the boundary of reasonable regulation as applied to a non-public religious school.

It must be remembered that one of the "minimum standards" requires compliance will all such standards before a charter can be granted. See EDb-401-02(E)(6). This is so despite the fact that the statutes upon which the "minimum standards" are based, R.C. 3301.07 and 3301.16, do not expressly require such absolute compliance.

Moreover, certain of the "minimum standards" at least indirectly hamper the right of appellants to freely exercise their religious beliefs through the medium of the educational institution they have established expressly for that purpose.

We refer, first, to EDb-401-02 (G), which allocates instructional time in the comprehensive curriculum . . . almost to the minute. R.C. 3313.48 and 3313.60, although requiring a school day of a defined length, and effectively controlling the courses of study taught non-public school children, do not further impede the ability of a religious school to incorporate the tenets of its particular faith into its required courses. We think that EDb-401-02(G) "unduly burdens the free exercise of religion" and interferes "with the rights of conscience," by requiring a set amount of time to be devoted to subjects which, by their very nature, may not easily lend themselves to the teaching of religious principles (e.g., mathematics). We do not mean to imply that the subjects contained within EDb-401-02(G), or those contained within R.C. 3313.60, are not helpful in preparing nonpublic, as well as public, school children for the obligations which will eventually arise in the process of maturing into adulthood. We only emphasize that the reasonableness of the requirements contained within "minimum standard"

EDb-401-02(G) wanes in the face of an attack premised upon a violation of the constitutional right of appellants to the free exercise of their chosen religion.

Secondly, in our view, EDb-401-02(O), which requires "all activities" of a nonpublic school to conform to policies adopted by the board of education, plainly violates appellants' right to the free exercise of their religion. If the state is to discharge its duty of remaining strictly neutral, pursuant to the establishment clause of the First Amendment, with respect to religion, how can the state constitutionally require *all activities* of a non-public religious school, which, of necessity, must include *religious activities,* to conform to the policies of a purportedly "neutral" board? . . .

Viewed in the above light, the inconsistency inherent in EDb-401-02(O), and the concomitant unconstitutional interference with, and infringement upon, appellants' rights to freely pursue their religious beliefs, is apparent to a majority of this court.

Finally, EDb-401-07(B), which requires a nonpublic religious school to cooperate with elements of the community in which it exists, infringes upon the rights of these appellants, consistent with their religious beliefs, to engage in complete, or nearly complete, separation from community affairs. As Rev. Whisner testified, these appellants religiously adhere to the literal Biblical command that they "[b]e not conformed to this world. . . . " Upon the face of the record before us, the state may not require the contrary.

In light of the foregoing, we conclude that appellants have sustained their burden of establishing that the "minimum standards" infringe upon the right guaranteed them by the First Amendment to the Constitution of the United States, and by Section 7, Article I of the Ohio Constitution, to the free exercise of their religion. . . .

There is an additional, independent reason . . . that compels upholding appellants' attack upon the state's "minimum standards." In our view, these standards are so pervasive and all-encompassing that total compliance with each and every standard by a non-public school would effectively eradicate the distinction between public and non-public education, and thereby deprive these appellants of their traditional interest as parents to direct the upbringing and education of their children.

In three early cases, *Farrington* v. *Tokushige* (1927), 273 U.S. 284, 47 S.Ct. 406, 71 L.Ed. 646, *Pierce* v. *Society of Sisters* (1925), 268 U.S. 510, 45 S.Ct. 571, 69 L.Ed. 1070, and *Meyer* v. *Nebraska,* supra, 262 U.S. 390, 43 S.Ct. 625, 67 L.Ed. 1042, the court utilized the "liberty" concept embodied within the due process clause of the Fourteenth Amendment to invalidate legislation that interfered with the right of a parent to direct the education, religious or secular, of his or her children. Thus, it has long been recognized that the right of a parent to guide the education, including the religious education, of his or her children is indeed a "fundamental right" guaranteed by the due process clause of the Fourteenth Amendment.

The principle espoused in *Farrington, Pierce* and *Meyer* was recognized as contemporarily valid in *Wisconsin* v. *Yoder,* supra, 406 U.S. 205, at page 232, 92 S.Ct. 1526, at page 1541, 32 L.Ed.2d 15, where the court stated:

> "The fundamental theory of liberty upon which all governments in this Union repose excludes any general power of the State to standardize its children by forcing them to accept instruction from public teachers only. The child is not the mere creature of the State; those

who nurture him and direct his destiny have the right, coupled with the high duty, to recognize and prepare him for additional obligations. 268 U.S., at 534-535, 45 S.Ct. [571], at 573.

"The duty to prepare the child for 'additional obligations,' referred to by the Court, must be read to include the inculcation of moral standards, religious beliefs, and elements of good citizenship. *Pierce,* of course, recognized that where nothing more than the general interest of the parent in the nurture and education of his children is involved, it is beyond dispute that the State acts 'reasonably' and constitutionally in requiring education to age 16 in some public or private school meeting the standards prescribed by the State.

"However read, the Court's holding in *Pierce* stands as a charter of the rights of parents to direct the religious upbringing of their children. . . . "

The "minimum standards" under attack herein effectively repose power in the state Department of Education to control the essential elements of nonpublic education in this state. The expert testimony received in this regard unequivocably demonstrates the absolute suffocation of independent thought and educational policy, and the effective retardation of religious philosophy engendered by application of these "minimum standards" to nonpublic educational institutions. . . .

Under the facts of this case, the right of appellants to direct the upbringing and education of their children in a manner in which they deem advisable, indeed essential, and which we cannot say is harmful, has been denied by application of the state's "minimum standards" as to them. . . .

In the opinion of a majority of this court, a "general education of a high quality" can be achieved by means other than the comprehensive regimentation of *all* academic centers in this state. . . .

Having demonstrated that application of the "minimum standards" to appellants violates their constitutional rights in two different ways, we turn, now, to the question of whether those standards may yet be sustained by the state. . . . What is required is a finding "that there is a state interest of sufficient magnitude to override the interest claiming protection under the Free Exercise Clause." . . . Moreover, even if the state can establish the requisite degree of interest, it must yet demonstrate that such interests cannot otherwise be served in order to overbalance legitimate claims to the free exercise of religion. . . .

The state did not, either in this court or in the lower courts, attempt to justify its interest in enforcing the "minimum standards" as applied to a nonpublic religious school. In the face of the record before us, and in light of the expert testimony summarized in the statement of the case herein, it is difficult to imagine " . . . a state interest of sufficient magnitude to override the interest claiming protection under the Free Exercise Clause." *Wisconsin* v. *Yoder,* supra, 406 U.S. at page 214, 92 S.Ct. at page 1532. And, equally difficult to imagine, is a state interest sufficiently substantial to sanction abrogation of appellants' liberty to direct the education of their children. . . .

For the foregoing reasons, the judgment of the Court of Appeals is reversed and the defendants are ordered discharged.

Judgment reversed and defendants discharged.

State of New Jersey v. Massa

231 A.2d 252 (N.J. 1967)

COLLINS, J.C.C.

. . . Defendants were charged and convicted with failing to cause their daughter Barbara, age 12, regularly to attend the public schools of the district and further for failing to either send Barbara to a private school or provide an equivalent education elsewhere than at school, contrary to the provisions of N.J.S.A. 18: 14–14. The municipal magistrate imposed a fine of $2490 for both defendants. . . .

The State presented two witnesses who testified that Barbara had been registered in the Pequannock Township School but failed to attend the 6th grade class from April 25, 1966 to June 1966 and the following school year from September 8, 1966 to November 16, 1966—a total consecutive absence of 84 days.

Mrs. Massa testified that she had taught Barbara at home for two years before September 1965. Barbara returned to school in September 1965, but began receiving her education at home again on April 25, 1966.

Mrs. Massa said her motive was that she desired the pleasure of seeing her daughter's mind develop. . . . She also maintained that in school much time was wasted and that at home a student can make better use of her time.

Mrs. Massa is a high school graduate. Her husband is an interior decorator. Neither holds a teacher's certificate. However, the State stipulated that a child may be taught at home and also that Mr. and Mrs. Massa need not be certified by the State of New Jersey to so teach. The sole issue in this case is one of equivalency. Have defendants provided their daughter with an education equivalent to that provided by the Pequannock Township School System?

Mrs. Massa introduced into evidence 19 exhibits. Five of these exhibits, in booklet form, are condensations of basic subjects, are concise and seem to contain all the basic subject material for the respective subjects. Mrs. Massa also introduced textbooks which are used as supplements to her own compilations as well as for test material and written problems.

Mrs. Massa introduced English, spelling and mathematics tests taken by her daughter at the Pequannock School after she had been taught for two years at home. The lowest mark on these tests was a B.

Other exhibits included one of over 100 geography booklets prepared by Mrs. Massa from National Geographic Magazine, each containing articles and maps concerning the topography and societies of a particular part of the world; a 1' wide and 30' long scroll depicting the evolution of life on earth commencing five billion years ago and continuing to the present, which appears to be a good visual aid not merely for children but adults as well; a series of 27 maps for study and memorization; textbooks used to supplement defendant's material; examples of books used as either references or historical reading, and photographs to show that the Massa family lives a normal, active, wholesome life. The family consists of the parents, three sons (Marshall, age 16 and Michael, age 15, both attend high school; and William, age 6), and daughter Barbara.

There is also a report by an independent testing service of Barbara's scores on standard achievement tests. They show that she is considerably higher than the national median except in arithmetic.

Mrs. Massa satisfied this court that she has an established program of teaching and studying. There are definite times each day for the various subjects and recreation. She evaluates Barbara's progress through testing. If Barbara has not learned something which has been taught, Mrs. Massa then reviews that particular area.

Barbara takes violin lessons and attends dancing school. She also is taught art by her father, who has taught this subject in various schools.

Mrs. Massa called Margaret Cordasco as a witness. She had been Barbara's teacher from September 1965 to April 1966. She testified basically that Barbara was bright, well behaved and not different from the average child her age except for some trouble adjusting socially.

The State called as a witness David MacMurray, the Assistant Superintendent of Pequannock Schools. . . .

Leslie Rear, the Morris County Superintendent of Schools, then testified for the State. His testimony, like that of MacMurray, dealt primarily with social development of the child and Mrs. Massa's qualifications. . . .

N.J.S.A. 18:14-14 provides:

> "Every parent, guardian or other person having custody and control of a child between the ages of 6 and 16 years shall cause such child regularly to attend the public schools of the district or a day school in which there is given instruction equivalent to that provided in the public schools for children of similar grades and attainments *or to receive equivalent instruction elsewhere than at school.*" (Emphasis added.)

State v. *Vaughn,* 44 N.J. 142, 207 A. 2d 537 (1965), interpreted the above statute to permit the parent having charge and control of the child to elect to substitute one of the alternatives for public school. It is then incumbent upon the parent to introduce evidence showing one of the alternatives is being substituted. "If there is such evidence in the case, then the ultimate burden of persuasion remains with the State," (at p. 147, 207 A.2d at p. 540).

N.J.S.A. 18:14-39 provides for the penalty for violation of N.J.S.A. 18:14-14: .. The statute subjects the defendants to conviction as a disorderly person, a quasicriminal offense. In quasicriminal proceedings the burden of proof is beyond a reasonable doubt. *State* v. *Cestone,* 38 N.J. Super. 139, 148, 118 A.2d 416 (App. Div. 1955).

This case presents two questions on the issue of equivalency for determination. What does the word "equivalent" mean in the context of N.J.S.A. 18:14-14? And, has the State carried the required burden of proof to convict defendants?

In *Knox* v. *O'Brien,* 7 N.J. Super. 608, 72 A.2d 389 (1950), the County Court interpreted the work "equivalent" to include not only academic equivalency but also the equivalency of social development. This interpretation appears untenable in the face of the language of our own statute and also the decisions in other jurisdictions.

If the interpretation in *Knox,* were followed, it would not be possible to have children educated outside of school. . . .

The Legislature must have contemplated that a child could be educated alone provided the education was equivalent to the public schools. . . .

The court in *State* v. *Counort,* 69 Wash. 361, 124 P.910, 41 L.R.A., N.S., 95 (Wash. Sup.Ct. 1912), held that defendant had not complied with the state law on compulsory school attendance. The Washington statute, however, provided that parents must cause their child to attend public school or private school, or obtain an excuse from the superintendent. . . . The conviction was upheld because of the failure of the parents to obtain permission from the superintendent.

In discussing the nature of schools the court said, "This provision of the law [concerning what constitutes a private school] is not to be determined by the place where the school is maintained, *nor the individuality or number of pupils who attend it.*" (124 P. at p. 912, emphasis added) The court further said that the evidence of the state was to the effect that defendant maintained no school at his home. This is not the case here. Mrs. Massa was certainly teaching Barbara something.

The court in *State* v. *Peterman,* 32 Ind. App. 665, 70 N.E. 550, 551 (Ind.App.Ct. 1904), also commented on the nature of a school, stating, "We do not think that the number of persons whether one or many, makes a place where instruction is imparted any less or more a school." That case held that a child attending the home of a private tutor was attending a private school within the meaning of the Indiana statute.

This court agrees with the above decisions. . . .

A different form of legislative intention is illustrated by the case of *People* v. *Turner,* 121 Cal.App.2d Supp. 861, 263 P.2d 685 (Cal.Super.Ct.1953). The California statute provided that parents must send their children to public school or a private school meeting certain prescribed conditions, or that the children be instructed by a private tutor or other person possessing a *valid state credential for the grade taught.* Defendants were convicted for failure to have such state credentials.

Other similar statutes are discussed in *Rice* v. *Commonwealth,* 188 Va. 224, 49 S.E.2d 342 (Sup.Ct. 1948), where the Virginia law required certification of teachers in the home and specified the number of hours and days that the child was to be taught each year; *Parr* v. *State,* 117 Ohio St. 23, 15 N.E. 555 (Ohio Sup.Ct. 1927), where the Ohio statute provided that a child would be exempted if he is being instructed at home by a *qualified* person in the subjects required by law.

Perhaps the New Jersey Legislature intended the word "equivalent" to mean taught by a certified teacher elsewhere than at school. However, I believe there are teachers today teaching in various schools in New Jersey who are not certified. The prosecutor stipulated, as stated above, that the State's position is that a child may be taught at home and that a person teaching at home is not required to be certified as a teacher by the State for the purpose of teaching his own children. Had the Legislature intended such a requirement, it would have so provided.

The other type of statute is that which allows *only* public school or private school education without additional alternatives. See *People* v. *Levisen,* 404 Ill. 574, 90 N.E.2d 213, 14 A.L.R.2d 1364 (Sup.Ct. 1950); *State* v. *Hoyt,* 84 N.H. 38, 146A. 170 (N.H.Sup.Ct. 1929), and *State* v. *Peterman,* supra. Even in this situation, home education has been upheld as constituting a private school. *People* v. *Levisen* and *State* v. *Peterman,* supra.

The case of *Commonwealth* v. *Roberts,* 159 Mass. 372, 34 N.E. 402 (Mass.-Sup.Jud.Ct. 1893), dealt with a statute similar to New Jersey's. The Massachusetts statute permitted instruction . . . by the parents themselves provided it is given in good faith and is sufficient in extent. The court stated that under this statute the parents may show that the child has been sufficiently and properly instructed. The object of the statute was stated to be that all children shall be educated, not that they shall be educated in a particular way.

It is in this sense that this court feels the present case should be decided. The purpose of the law is to insure the education of all children. . . . . . . Having determined the intent of the Legislature as requiring only equivalent academic instruction, the only remaining question is whether the defendants provided their daughter with an education equivalent to that available in the public schools. After reviewing the evidence presented by both the State and the defendants, this court finds that the State has not shown beyond a reasonable doubt that defendants failed to provide their daughter with an equivalent education.

The majority of testimony of the State's witnesses dealt with the lack of social development.

The other point pressed by the State was Mrs. Massa's lack of teaching ability and techniques based upon her limited education and experience. However, this court finds this testimony to be inapposite to the actual issue of equivalency under the New Jersey statute and the stipulations of the State. In any case, . . . I am satisfied that Mrs. Massa is self-educated and well qualified to teach her daughter the basic subjects from grades one through eight.

The remainder of the testimony of the State's witnesses dealt primarily with the child's deficiency in mathematics. This alone, however, does not establish an educational program unequivalent to that in the public schools in the face of the evidence presented by defendants. . . .

The evidence of the State which was actually directed toward the issue of equivalency in this case fell short of the required burden of proof.

The Massa family, all of whom were present at each of the hearings, appeared to be a normal, well-adjusted family. The behavior of the four Massa children in the courtroom evidenced an exemplary upbringing.

It is the opinion of this court that defendants' daughter has received and is receiving an education equivalent to that available in the Pequannock public schools. There is no indication of bad faith or improper motive on defendants' part. Under a more definite statute with sufficient guidelines or a lesser burden of proof, this might not necessarily be the case. However, within the framework of the existing law and the nature of the stipulations by the State, this court finds the defendant not guilty and reverses the municipal court conviction. . . .

National Labor Relations Board v. The Catholic Bishop of Chicago, et al.

440 U.S. 490 (1979)

Mr. *Chief Justice BURGER* delivered the opinion of the Court.

This case arises out of the National Labor Relations Board's exercise of jurisdiction over lay faculty members at two groups of Catholic high schools. We granted certiorari to consider two questions: (a) Whether teachers in schools operated by a church to teach both religious and secular subjects are within the jurisdiction granted by the National Labor Relations Act; and (b) If the Act authorizes such jurisdiction, does its exercise violate the guarantees of the Religion Clauses of the First Amendment? 434 U.S. 1061 (1978).

I

One group of schools [Quigley Schools] is operated by the Catholic Bishop of Chicago, a corporation sole; the other group is operated by the Diocese of Fort Wayne-South Bend, Inc. . . .

The Diocese of Fort Wayne-South Bend, Inc., has five high schools. Unlike the Quigley schools, the special recommendation of a priest is not a prerequisite for admission. Like the Quigley schools, however, these high schools seek to provide a traditional secular education but oriented to the tenets of the Roman Catholic faith; religious training is also mandatory. These schools are similarly certified by the State.

In 1974 and 1975, separate representation petitions were filed with the Board by interested union organizations for both the Quigley and the Fort Wayne-South Bend schools; representation was sought only for lay teachers. The schools challenged the assertion of jurisdiction on two grounds: (a) that they do not fall within the Board's discretionary jurisdictional criteria; and (b) that the Religion Clauses of the First Amendment preclude the Board's jurisdiction. The Board rejected the jurisdictional arguments on the basis of its decision in *Roman Catholic Archdiocese of Baltimore,* 216 N.L.R.B. 249 (1975). There the Board explained that its policy was to decline jurisdiction over religiously sponsored organizations "only when they are completely religious, not just religiously associated." *Id.*, at 250, Because neither group of schools was found to fall within the Board's "completely religious" category, the Board ordered elections. . . .

In the Board-supervised election at the Quigley schools, the Quigley Education Alliance, a union affiliated with the Illinois Education Association, prevailed and was certified as the exclusive bargaining representative for 46 lay teachers. In the Diocese of Fort Wayne-South Bend, the Community Alliance for Teachers of Catholic High Schools, a similar union organization, prevailed and was certified as the representative for the approximately 180 lay teachers. Norwithstanding the Board's order, the schools declined to recognize the unions or to bargain. The unions filed unfair labor practice complaints with the Board under § 8 (a) (1) and (5) of the National Labor Relations Act, 29 U.S.C. § 158 (a) (1) and (5). The schools opposed the General Counsel's motion for summary judgment, again challenging the Board's exercise of jurisdiction over religious schools on both statutory and constitutional grounds. . . . The Board concluded that the schools had violated the Act and ordered that they cease their unfair labor practices and that they bargain collectively with unions. . . .

II

The schools challenged the Board's orders in petitions to the Court of Appeals for the Seventh Circuit. That court denied enforcement of the Board's orders. *Catholic Bishop of Chicago, A Corporation Sole* v. *NLRB,* 559 F.2d 1112 (CA7 1977). . . .

It concluded that the Board had not properly exercised its discretion, because the Board's distinction between "completely religious" and "merely religiously associated" failed to provide a workable guide for the exercise of discretion. . . .

The Court of Appeals recognized that the rejection of the Board's policy as to church-operated schools meant that the Board would extend its jurisdiction to all church-operated schools. The court therefore turned to the question of whether the Board could exercise that jurisdiction, consistent with constitutional limitations. It concluded that both the Free Exercise Clause and the Establishment Clause of the First Amendment foreclosed the Board's jurisdiction. It reasoned that from the initial act of certifying a union as the bargaining agent for lay teachers the Board's action would impinge upon the freedom of church authorities to shape and direct teaching in accord with the requirements of their religion. . . .

The court distinguished local regulations which required fire inspections or state laws mandating attendance, reasoning that they did not "have the clear inhibiting potential upon the relationship between teachers and employers with which the present Board order is directly concerned." *Ibid.* The court held that interference with management prerogatives, found acceptable in an ordinary commercial setting, was not acceptable in an area protected by the First Amendment. "The real difficulty is found in the chilling aspect that the requirement of bargaining will impose on the exercise of the bishops' control of the religious mission of the schools." *Id.*, at 1124.

III

The Board's assertion of jurisdiction over private schools is, as we noted earlier, a relatively recent development. Indeed, in 1951 the Board indicated that it would not exercise jurisdiction over nonprofit, educational institutions because to do so would not effectuate the purposes of the Act. *The Trustees of Columbia University in the City of New York,* 97 N.L.R.B. 424 (1951). In 1970, however, the Board pointed to what it saw as an increased involvement in commerce by educational institutions and concluded that this required a different position on jurisdiction. In Cornell University, 183 N.L.R.B. 329 (1970), the Board overruled its *Columbia University* decision. *Cornell University* was followed by the assertion of jurisdiction over nonprofit, private secondary schools. *Shattuck School,* 189 N.L.R.B. 886 (1971). See also *Judson School,* 209 N.L.R.B. 677 (1974). The Board now asserts jurisdiction over all private, nonprofit, educational institutions with gross annual revenues that meet its jurisdictional requirements whether they are secular or religious. 29 CFR § 103.1 (1977). See, e.g., *Academia San Jorge,* 234 N.L.R.B. No. 183 (1978) (advisory opinion stating that Board would not assert jurisdiction over Catholic educational institution which did not meet jurisdictional standards); *The Windsor School, Inc.*, 199 N.L.R.B. 457, 200 N.L.R.B. 991 (1972) (declining jurisdiction where private proprietary school did not meet jurisdictional amounts).

That broad assertion of jurisdiction has not gone unchallenged. But the Board has rejected the contention that the Religion Clauses of the First Amendment bar the extension of its jurisdiction to church-operated schools. Where the Board has declined to exercise jurisdiction, it has done so only on the grounds of the employer's minimal impact on commerce. Thus, in *Association of Hebrew Teachers of Metropolitan Detroit,* 210 N.L.R.B. 1053 (1974), the Board did not assert jurisdiction over the Association which offered courses in Jewish culture in after-school classes, a nursery school and a college. The Board termed the Association an "isolated instance of [an] atypical employer." *Id.*, at 1058-1059. It explained that "[w]hether an employer falls within a given 'class' of enterprise depends upon those of its activities which are predominant and give the employing activity its character. . . . [T]he fact that an employer's activity . . . is dedicated to a sectarian religious purpose is not a sufficient reason for the Board to refrain from asserting jurisdiction." Id., at 1058. Cf. *Board of Jewish Education of Greater Washington, D.C.*, 210 N.L.R.B. 1037 (1974). In the same year the Board asserted jurisdiction over an association chartered by the State of New York to operate diocesan high schools. *Henry M. Hald High School Association,* 213 N.L.R.B. 415 (1974). It rejected the argument that its assertion of jurisdiction would produce excessive governmental entanglement with religion. In the Board's view, the Association had chosen to entangle itself with the secular world when it decided to hire lay teachers. *Id.*, at 418 n. 7.

When it ordered an election for the lay professional employees at five parochial high schools in Baltimore in 1975, the Board reiterated its belief that exercise of its jurisdiction is not contrary to the First Amendment. . . . The Board also rejected the First Amendment claims in *Cardinal Timothy Manning, Roman Catholic Archbishop of the Archdiocese of Los Angeles, A Corporation Sole* 223 N.L.R.B. 1218, (1976); "Regulation of labor relations does not violate the First Amendment when it involves a minimal intrusion on religious conduct and is necessary to obtain that [the Act's] objective." (Emphasis added.)

The Board thus recognizes that its assertion of jurisdiction over teachers in religious schools constitutes some degree of intrusion into the administration of the affairs of church-operated schools. Implicit in the Board's distinction between schools that are "completely religious" and those "religiously associated" is also an acknowledgement of some degree of entanglement. Because that distinction was measured by a school's involvement with commerce, however, and not by its religious association, it is clear that the Board never envisioned any sort of religious litmus test for determining when to assert jurisdiction. Nevertheless, . . . the Board has plainly recognized that intrusion into this area could run afoul of the Religion Clauses and hence preclude jurisdiction on constitutional grounds.

IV

That there are constitutional limitations on the Board's actions has been repeatedly recognized by this Court even while acknowledging the broad scope of the grant of jurisdiction. The First Amendment, of course, is a limitation on the power of Congress. Thus, if we were to conclude that the Act granted the challenged jurisdiction over these teachers we would be required to decide whether that was constitutionally permissible under the Religion Clauses of the First Amendment.

Although the respondents press their claims under the Religion Clauses, the question we consider first is whether Congress intended the Board to have jurisdiction over teachers in church-operated schools. In a number of cases the Court has heeded the essence of Chief Justice Marshall's admonition in *The Charming Betsy,* 2 Cranch (6 U.S.) 64, 118 (1804), by holding that an Act of Congress ought not be construed to violate the Constitution if any other possible construction remains available. . . .

V

In recent decisions involving aid to parochial schools we have recognized the critical and unique role of the teacher in fulfilling the mission of a church-operated school. What was said of the schools in *Lemon* v. *Kurtzman,* 403 U.S. 602, 617 (1971), is true of the schools in this case: "Religious authority necessarily pervades the school system." . . .

Only recently we again noted the importance of the teacher's function in a church school: "Whether the subject is 'remedial reading,' 'advanced reading,' or simply 'reading,' a teacher remains a teacher, and the danger that religious doctrine will become intertwined with secular instruction persists." Meek v. Pittinger, 421 U.S. 349, 370 (1975). Cf. *Wolman* v. *Walter,* 433 U.S. 229, 244 (1977). Good intentions by government—or third parties—can surely no more avoid entanglement with the religious mission of the school . . . than in the well motivated legislative efforts consented by the church-operated schools which we found unacceptable in *Lemon, Meek,* and *Wolman.*

The Board argues that it can avoid excessive entanglement since it will resolve only factual issues such as whether an anti-union animus motivated an employer's action. But at this stage of our consideration we are not compelled to determine whether the entanglement is excessive as we would were we considering the constitutional issue. Rather, we make a narrow inquiry whether the exercise of the Board's jurisdiction presents a significant risk that the First Amendment will be infringed.

Moreover, it is already clear that the Board's actions will go beyond resolving factual issues. The Court of Appeals' opinion refers to charges of unfair labor practices filed against religious schools. 559 F.2d, at 1125, 1126. The court observed that in those cases the schools had responded that their challenged actions were mandated by their religious creeds. The resolution of such charges by the Board, in many instances, will necessarily involve inquiry into the good faith of the position asserted by the clergy-administrators and its relationship to the school's religious mission. It is not only the conclusions that may be reached by the Board which may impinge on rights guaranteed by the Religion Clauses, but the very process of inquiry leading to findings and conclusions.

The Board's exercise of jurisdiction will have at least one other impact on church-operated schools. The Board will be called upon to decide what are "terms and conditions of employment" and therefore mandatory subjects of bargaining. See 29 U.S.C. § 158 (d). Although the Board has not interpreted that phrase as it relates to educational institutions, similar state provisions provide insight into the effect of mandatory bargaining. The Oregon Court of Appeals noted, "nearly everything that goes on in the schools affects teachers and is therefore arguably a 'condition of employment'." *Springfield Education Association* v. *Springfield School District No. 19,* 24 Ore. App. 751, 759, 547 P.2d 647, 650 (1976).

The Pennsylvania Supreme Court aptly summarized the effect of mandatory bargaining when it observed that "the introduction of a concept of mandatory collective bargaining, regardless of how narrowly the scope of negotiations is defined, necessarily represents an encroachment upon the former autonomous position of management." *Pennsylvania Labor Relations Board* v. *State College Area School District,* 461 Pa. 494, 504, 337 A. 2d 262, 267 (1975). Cf. *Clark County School District* v. *Local Government Employee Management Relations Board,* 530 P.2d 114, 117-18 (Nev. 1974). . . .

The church-teacher relationship in a church-operated school differs from the employment relationship in a public or other non-religious school. We see no escape from conflicts flowing from the Board's exercise of jurisdiction over teachers in church-operated schools and the consequent serious First Amendment questions that would follow. We therefore turn to an examination of the National Labor Relations Act to decide whether it must be read to confer jurisdiction that would in turn require a decision on the constitutional claims raised by respondents.

VI

There is no clear expression of an affirmative intention of Congress that teachers in church-operated schools should be covered by the Act. Admittedly, Congress defined the Board's jurisdiction in very broad terms; we must therefore examine the legislative history of the Act to determine whether Congress contemplated that the grant of jurisdiction would include teachers in such schools.

In enacting the National Labor Relations Act in 1935, Congress sought to protect the right of American workers to bargain collectively. . . . But congressional attention focused on employment in private industry and on industrial recovery. . . .

Our examination of the statute and its legislative history indicates that Congress simply gave no consideration to church-operated schools. It is not without significance, however, that the Senate Committee on Education and Labor chose a college professor's dispute with the college as an example of employer-employee relations *not* covered by the Act. S.Rep. No. 573, 74th Cong., 1st Sess., 7, 2 N.L.R.B., Legislative History of the National Labor Relations Act 1935, p. 2307.

Congress' next major consideration of the jurisdiction of the Board came during the passage of the Labor Management Relations Act of 1947—the Taft-Hartley Act. In that Act Congress amended the definition of "employer" in § 2 of the original Act to exclude nonprofit hospitals. 61 Stat. 136, 29 U.S.C. § 152 (2) (1970 ed.). . . .

The most recent significant amendment to the Act was passed in 1974, removing the exemption of nonprofit hospitals. Pub. L. No. 93-360, 88 Stat. 395. The Board relies upon that amendment as showing that Congress approved the Board's exercise of jurisdiction over church-operated schools. A close examination of that legislative history, however, reveals nothing to indicate an affirmative intention that such schools be within the Board's jurisdiction. Since the Board did not assert jurisdiction over teachers in a church-operated school until after the 1974 amendment nothing in the history of the amendment can be read as reflecting Congress' tacit approval of the Board's action. . . . The absence of an "affirmative intention of the Congress clearly expressed" fortifies our conclusion that Congress did not contemplate that the Board would require church-operated schools to grant recognition to unions as bargaining agents for their teachers. . . .

Accordingly, in the absence of a clear expression of Congress' intent to bring teachers in church-operated schools within the jurisdiction of the Board, we decline to construe the Act in a manner that could in turn call upon the Court to resolve difficult and sensitive questions arising out of the guarantees of the First Amendment Religion Clauses.

Affirmed. . . .

Mr. *Justice* BRENNAN, with whom Mr. *Justice* WHITE, Mr. *Justice* MARSHALL, and Mr. *Justice* BLACKMUN join, dissenting.

The Court today holds that coverage of the National Labor Relations Act does not extend to lay teachers employed by church-operated schools. That construction is plainly wrong in light of the Act's language, its legislative history, and this Court's precedents. It is justified solely on the basis of a canon of statutory construction seemingly invented by the Court for the purpose of deciding this case. I dissent. . . .

Thus, the available authority indicates that Congress intended to include—not exclude—lay teachers of church-operated schools. . . .

III

Under my view that the NLRA includes within its coverage lay teachers employed by church-operated schools, the constitutional questions presented would have to be reached. I do not now do so only because the Court does not. See *Sierra Club* v. *Morton,* 405 U.S. 727, 755 (1972) (*BRENNAN, J.*, dissenting). I repeat for emphasis, however, that while the resolution of the constitutional question is not without difficulty, it is irresponsible to avoid it by a cavalier exercise in statutory interpretation which succeeds only in defying congressional intent. . . .

Wolman v. Walter

433 U.S. 229 (1977)

Mr. *Justice* BLACKMUN delivered the opinion of the Court (Parts I, V, VI, VII, and VIII), together with an opinion (Parts II, III, and IV), in which *The Chief Justice,* Mr. *Justice* STEWART, and Mr. *Justice* POWELL joined.

This is still another case presenting the recurrent issue of the limitations imposed by the Establishment Clause of the First Amendment, made applicable to the States by the Fourteenth Amendment, *Meek* v. *Pittenger,* 421 U.S. 349, 351 (1975), on state aid to pupils in church-related elementary and secondary schools. Appellants are citizens and taxpayers of Ohio. They challenge all but one of the provisions of Ohio Rev. Code § 3317.06 (Supp. 1976) which authorize various forms of aid. . . .

I

Section 3317.06 was enacted after this Court's May 1975 decision in *Meek* v. *Pittenger*, supra, and obviously is an attempt to conform to the teachings of that decision. . . . In broad outline, the statute authorizes the State to provide nonpublic school pupils with books, instructional materials and equipment, standardized testing and scoring, diagnostic services, therapeutic services, and field trip transportation. . . . All disbursements made with respect to nonpublic schools have their equivalents in disbursements for public schools, and the amount expended per pupil in nonpublic schools may not exceed the amount expended per pupil in the public schools.

The parties stipulated that during the 1974-1975 school year there were 720 chartered nonpublic schools in Ohio. Of these, all but 29 were sectarian. More than 96% of the nonpublic enrollment attended sectarian schools, and more than 92% attended Catholic schools. . . . It was also stipulated that, if they were called, officials of representative Catholic schools would testify that such schools operate under the general supervision of the Bishop of the Diocese; that most principals are members of a religious order within the Catholic Church; that a little less than one-third of the teachers are members of such religious orders; that "in all probability a majority of the teachers are members of the Catholic faith"; and that many of the rooms and hallways in these schools are decorated with a Christian symbol. . . . All such schools teach the secular subjects required to meet the State's minimum standards. The state-mandated five-hour day is expanded to include, usually, one-half hour of religious instruction. Pupils who are not members of the Catholic faith are not required to attend religion classes or to participate in religious exercises or activities, and no teacher is required to teach religious doctrine as a part of the secular courses taught in the schools. . . .

The parties also stipulated that nonpublic school officials, if called, would testify that none of the schools covered by the statute discriminate in the admission of pupils or in the hiring of teachers on the basis of race, creed, color, or national origin. . . .

The District Court concluded: "Although the stipulations of the parties evidence several significant points of distinction, the character of these schools is substantially comparable to that of the schools involved in *Lemon* v. *Kurtzman*, 403 U.S. 602, 615-618 . . . (1971)." 417 F.Supp., at 1116.

II

The mode of analysis for Establishment Clause questions is defined by the three-part test that has emerged from the Court's decisions. In order to pass muster, a statute must have a secular legislative purpose, must have a principal or primary effect that neither advances nor inhibits religion, and must not foster an excessive government entanglement with religion. . . .

In the present case we have no difficulty with the first prong of this three-part test. We are satisfied that the challenged statute reflects Ohio's legitimate interest in protecting the health of its youth and in providing a fertile educational environment for all the school children of the State.[224] As is usual in our cases, the analytical difficulty has to do with the effect and entanglement criteria.

We have acknowledged before, and we do so again here, that the wall of separation that must be maintained between church and state "is a blurred, indistinct, and variable barrier depending on all the circumstances of a particular relationship." *Lemon*, 403 U.S., at 614. Nonetheless, the Court's numerous precedents "have become firmly rooted," *Nyquist*, 413 U.S., at 761, and now provide substantial guidance. We therefore turn to the task of applying the rules derived from our decisions to the respective provisions of the statute at issue.

III

Textbooks

Section 3317.06 authorizes the expenditure of funds:

> "(A) To purchase such secular textbooks as have been approved by the superintendent of public instruction for use in public schools in the state and to loan such textbooks to pupils attending nonpublic schools within the district or to their parents. Such loans shall be based upon individual requests submitted by such nonpublic school pupils or parents. . . . As used in this section, 'textbook' means any book or book substitute which a pupil uses as a text or text substitute in a particular class or program in the school he regularly attends."

The parties' stipulations reflect operation of the textbook program in accord with the dictates of the statute. In addition, it was stipulated:

> "The secular textbooks used in nonpublic schools will be the same as the textbooks used in the public schools of the state. Common suppliers will be used to supply books to both public and nonpublic school pupils. . . . "

This system for the loan of textbooks to individual students bears a striking resemblance to the systems approved in *Board of Education* v. *Allen*, 392 U.S. 236 (1968), and in *Meek* v. *Pittenger*, supra. Indeed, the only distinction offered by appellants is that the challenged statute defines "textbook" as "any book or book substitute." Appellants argue that a "book substitute" might include auxiliary equipment and materials that, they assert, may not constitutionally be loaned. See Part VII, infra. We find this argument untenable in light of the statute's separate treatment of instructional materials and equipment in its subsections (B) and (C), and in light of the stipulation defining textbooks as "limited to books, reusable workbooks, or manuals." . . . As read, the statute provides the same protections against abuse as were provided in the textbook programs under consideration in *Allen* and in *Meek*.

In the alternative, appellants urge that we overrule *Allen* and *Meek*. This we decline to do. Accordingly, we conclude that § 3317.06 (A) is constitutional.

---

1. Section 3317.06 explicitly provides: "No school district shall provide services, materials, or equipment for use in religious courses, devotional exercises, religious training, or any other religious activity."

IV

Testing and Scoring

Section 3317.06 authorizes expenditure of funds "(J) To supply for use by pupils attending nonpublic schools within the district such standardized tests and scoring services as are in use in the public schools of the state." These tests "are used to measure the progress of students in secular subjects." App.48. Nonpublic school personnel are not involved in either the drafting or scoring of the tests. 417 F.Supp., at 1124. The statute does not authorize any payment to nonpublic school personnel for the costs of administering the tests.

In *Levitt* v. *Committee for Public Education,* 413 U.S. 472 (1973), this Court invalidated a New York statutory scheme for reimbursement of church-sponsored schools for the expenses of teacher-prepared testing. The reasoning behind that decision was straightforward. The system was held unconstitutional because "no means are available to assure that internally prepared tests are free of religious instruction." *Id.* at 480.

There is no question that the State has a substantial and legitimate interest in insuring that its youth receive an adequate secular education. *Id.*, at 479-480, n. 7. The State may require that schools that are utilized to fulfill the State's compulsory education requirement meet certain standards of instruction. *Allen,* 392 U.S., at 245-246, and n. 7, and may examine both teachers and pupils to ensure that the State's legitimate interest is being fulfilled. *Levitt,* 413 U.S., at 479-480, n. 7; Lemon, 403 U.S., at 614. See App. 28. Cf. *Pierce* v. *Society of Sisters,* 268 U.S. 510, 534 (1925). Under the section at issue, the State provides both the schools and the school district with the means of ensuring that the minimum standards are met. The nonpublic school does not control the content of the test or its result. This serves to prevent the use of the test as a part of religious teaching, and thus avoids that kind of direct aid to religion found present in *Levitt.* Similarly, the inability of the school to control the test eliminates the need for the supervision that gives rise to excessive entanglement. We therefore agree with the District Court's conclusion that § 3317.06 (J) is constitutional.

V

Diagnostic Services

Section 3317.06 authorizes expenditures of funds

> "(D) To provide speech and hearing diagnostic services to pupils attending nonpublic schools within the district. Such service shall be provided in the nonpublic school attended by the pupil receiving the service. . . . "(F) To provide diagnostic psychological services to pupils attending nonpublic schools within the district. Such services shall be provided in the school attended by the pupil receiving the service."

It will be observed that these speech and hearing and psychological diagnostic services are to be provided within the nonpublic school. It is stipulated, however, that the personnel (with the exception of physicians) who perform the services are employees of the local board of education; that physicians may be hired on a contract basis; that the purpose of these services is to determine the pupil's deficiency or need of assistance; and that treatment of any defect so found would take place off the nonpublic school premises. App. 37-38. See Part VI, infra.

Appellants assert that the funding of these services is constitutionally impermissible. They argue that the speech and hearing staff might engage in unrestricted conversation with the pupil and, on occasion, might fail to separate religious instruction from secular responsibilities. They further assert that the communication between the psychological diagnostician and the pupil will provide an impermissible opportunity for the intrusion of religious influence.

The District Court found these dangers so insubstantial as not to render the statute unconstitutional. 417 F.Supp., at 1121-1122. We agree. This Court's decisions contain a common thread to the effect that the provision of health services to all school children—public and nonpublic—does not have the primary effect of aiding religion. . . .

Indeed, appellants recognize this fact in not challenging subsection (E) of the statute that authorizes publicly funded physician, nursing, dental, and optometric services in nonpublic schools. We perceive no basis for drawing a different conclusion with respect to diagnostic speech and hearing services and diagnostic psychological services.

In *Meek* the Court did hold unconstitutional a portion of a Pennsylvania statute at issue there that authorized certain auxiliary services—"remedial and accelerated instruction, guidance counseling and testing, speech and hearing services"—on nonpublic school premises. 421 U.S., at 367. The Court noted that the teacher or guidance counselor might "fail on occasion to separate religious instruction and the advancement of religious beliefs from his secular educational responsibilities." *Id.*, at 371. The Court was of the view that the publicly employed teacher or guidance counselor might depart from religious neutrality because he was "performing important educational services in schools in which education is an integral part of the dominant sectarian mission and in which an atmosphere dedicated to the advancement of religious belief is constantly maintained." . . . The statute was held unconstitutional on entanglement grounds, namely, that in order to insure that the auxiliary teachers and guidance counselors remained neutral, the State would have to engage in continuing surveillance on the school premises. . . . The Court in *Meek* explicitly stated, however, that the provision of diagnostic speech and hearing services by Pennsylvania seemed "to fall within that class of general welfare services for children that may be provided by the State regardless of the incidental benefit that accrues to church-related schools." 421 U.S., at 371 n. 21. The provision of such services was invalidated only because it was found unseverable from the unconstitutional portions of the statute. . . .

The reason for considering diagnostic services to be different from teaching or counseling is readily apparent. First, diagnostic services, unlike teaching or counseling, have little or no educational content and are not closely associated with the educational mission of the nonpublic school. Accordingly, any pressure on the public diagnostician to allow the intrusion of sectarian views is greatly reduced. Second, the diagnostician has only limited contact with the child, and that contact involves chiefly the use of objective and professional testing methods to detect students in need of treatment. The nature of the relationship between the diagnostician and the pupil does not provide the same opportunity for the transmission of sectarian views as attends the relationship between teacher and student or that between counselor and student.

We conclude that providing diagnostic services on the nonpublic school premises will not create an impermissible risk of the fostering of ideological views. It follows that there is no need for excessive surveillance, and there will not be impermissible entanglement. We therefore hold that §§ 3317.06 (D) and (F) are constitutional.

VI

Therapeutic Services

Sections 3317.06 (G), (H), (I), and (K) authorize expenditures of funds for certain therapeutic, guidance, and remedial services for students who have been identified as having a need for specialized attention. Personnel providing the services must be employees of the local board of education or under contract with the State Department of Health. The services are to be performed only in public schools, in public centers, or in mobile units located off the nonpublic school premises. . . . The parties have stipulated: "The determination as to whether these programs would be offered in the public school, public center, or mobile unit will depend on the distance between the public and nonpublic school, the safety factors involved in travel, and the adequacy of accommodations in public schools and public centers." . . .

Appellants concede that the provision of remedial, therapeutic, and guidance services in public schools, public centers, or mobile units is constitutional if both public and nonpublic school students are served simultaneously. Brief for Appellants 41-42, 46. Their challenge is limited to the situation where a facility is used to service only nonpublic school students. They argue that any program that isolates the sectarian pupils is impermissible because the public employee providing the service might tailor his approach to reflect and reinforce the ideological view of the sectarian school attended by the children. Such action by the employee, it is claimed, renders direct aid to the sectarian institution. Appellants express particular concern over mobile units because they perceive a danger that such a unit might operate merely as an annex of the school or schools it services.

At the outset, we note that in its present posture the case does not properly present any issue concerning the use of a public facility as an adjunct of a sectarian educational enterprise. The District Court construed the statute, as do we, to authorize services only on sites that are "neither physically nor educationally identified with the functions of the nonpublic school." . . . Thus, the services are to be offered under circumstances that reflect their religious neutrality. . . .

The fact that a unit on a neutral site on occasion may serve only sectarian pupils does not provoke the same concerns that troubled the Court in *Meek.* The influence on a therapist's behavior that is exerted by the fact that he serves a sectarian pupil is qualitatively different from the influence of the pervasive atmosphere of a religious institution. . . .

Accordingly, we hold that providing therapeutic and remedial services at a neutral site off the premises of the nonpublic schools will not have the impermissible effect of advancing religion. Neither will there be any excessive entanglement arising from supervision of public employees to insure that they maintain a neutral stance. It can hardly be said that the supervision of public employees performing public functions on public property creates an excessive entanglement between church and state. Sections 3317.06 (G), (H), (I), and (K) are constitutional.

VII

Instructional Materials and Equipment

Sections 3317.06 (B) and (C) authorize expenditures of funds for the purchase and loan to pupils or their parents upon individual request of instructional materials and instructional equipment of the kind in use in the public schools within the district and which is "incapable of diversion to religious use." Section 3717.06 also provides that the materials and equipment may be stored on the premises of a nonpublic school and that publicly hired personnel who administer the lending program may perform their services upon the nonpublic school premises when necessary "for efficient implementation of the lending program."

Although the exact nature of the material and equipment is not clearly revealed, the parties have stipulated: "It is expected that materials and equipment loaned to pupils or parents under the new law will be similar to such former materials and equipment except that to the extent that the law requires that materials and equipment capable of diversion to religious issues will not be supplied." App. 36. Equipment provided under the predecessor statute, invalidated as set forth in n. 1, supra, included projectors, tape recorders, record players, maps and globes, science kits, weather forecasting charts, and the like. The District Court . . . found the new statute, as now limited, constitutional because the Court could not distinguish the loan of material and equipment from the textbook provisions upheld in *Meek,* 421 U.S., at 359-362, and in *Allen,* 392 U.S., at 248.

In *Meek,* however, the Court considered the constitutional validity of a direct loan to nonpublic schools of instructional material and equipment, and, despite the apparent secular nature of the goods, held the loan impermissible. *Mr. Justice STEWART,* in writing for the Court, stated:

> "The very purpose of many of those schools is to provide an integrated secular and religious education; the teaching process is, to a large extent, devoted to the inculcation of religious values and belief. See *Lemon* v. *Kurtzman,* 403 U.S., at 616-617. Substantial aid to the educational function of such schools, accordingly, necessarily results in aid to the sectarian school enterprise as a whole. '[T]he secular education those schools provide goes hand in hand with the religious mission that is the only reason for the schools' existence. Within the institution, the two are inextricably intertwined.' *Id.,* at 657 (opinion of *BRENNAN, J.*)." 421 U.S., at 366.

Thus, even though the loan ostensibly was limited to neutral and secular instructional material and equipment, it inescapably had the primary effect of providing a direct and substantial advancement of the sectarian enterprise.

Appellees seek to avoid *Meek* by emphasizing that it involved a program of direct loans to nonpublic schools. In contrast, the material and equipment at issue under the Ohio statute are loaned to the pupil or his parent. In our view, however, it would exalt form over substance if this distinction were found to justify a result different from that in *Meek*. . . .

If a grant in cash to parents is impermissible, we fail to see how a grant in kind of goods furthering the religious enterprise can fare any better. Accordingly, we hold §§ 3316.06 (B) and (C) to be unconstitutional.

VIII

Field Trips

Section 3316.06 also authorizes expenditures of funds:

> "(L) To provide such field trip transportation and services to nonpublic school students as are provided to public school students in the district. School districts may contract with commercial transportation companies for such transportation service if school district busses are unavailable."

There is no restriction on the timing of field trips; the only restriction on number lies in the parallel the statute draws to field trips provided to public school students in the district. The parties have stipulated that the trips "would consist of visits to governmental, industrial, cultural, and scientific centers designed to enrich the secular studies of students." . . . The choice of destination, however, will be made by the nonpublic school teacher from a wide range of locations.

The District Court . . . held this feature to be constitutionally indistinguishable from that with which the Court was concerned in *Everson* v. *Board of Education,* 330 U.S. 1 (1947). We do not agree. In *Everson* the Court approved a system under which a New Jersey board of education reimbursed parents for the cost of sending their children to and from school, public or parochial, by public carrier. The Court analogized the reimbursement to situations where a municipal common carrier is ordered to carry all school children at a reduced rate, or where the police force is ordered to protect all children on their way to and from school. *Id.*, at 17. The critical factors in these examples . . . are that the school has no control over the expenditure of the funds and the effect of the expenditure is unrelated to the content of the education provided. . . .

The Ohio situation is in sharp contrast. First, the nonpublic school controls the timing of the trips and, within a certain range, their frequency and destinations. Thus, the schools, rather than the children, truly are the recipients of the service and, as this Court has recognized, this fact alone may be sufficient to invalidate the program as impermissible direct aid. See *Lemon* v. *Kurtzman*, 403 U.S., at 621. Second, although a trip may be to a location that would be of interest to those in public schools, it is the individual teacher who makes a field trip meaningful. The experience begins with the study and discussion of the place to be visited; it continues on location with the teacher pointing out items of interest and stimulating the imagination; and it ends with a discussion of the experience. The field trips are an integral part of the educational experience, and where the teacher works within and for a sectarian institution, an unacceptable risk of fostering of religion is an inevitable byproduct. See *Meek* v. *Pittenger*, 421 U.S., at 366. In *Lemon* the Court stated:

> "We need not and do not assume that teachers in parochial schools will be guilty of bad faith or any conscious design to evade the limitations imposed by the statute and the First Amendment. We simply recognize that a dedicated religious person, teaching in a school affiliated with his or her faith and operated to inculcate its tenets, will inevitably experience great difficulty in remaining religiously neutral." 403 U.S., at 618. . . .

We hold § 3317.06 (L) to be unconstitutional.

IX

In summary, we hold constitutional those portions of the Ohio statute authorizing the State to provide nonpublic school pupils with books, standardized testing and scoring, diagnostic services, and therapeutic and remedial services. We hold unconstitutional those portions relating to instructional materials and equipment and field trip services.

The judgment of the District Court is therefore affirmed in part and reversed in part.

It is so ordered.

The Chief Justice dissents from Parts VII and VIII of the Court's opinion. . . . Mr. *Justice WHITE* and Mr. *Justice REHNQUIST* concur in the judgment with respect to textbooks, testing, and scoring, and diagnostic and therapeutic services (Parts III, IV, V and VI of the opinion) and dissent from the judgment with respect to instructional materials and equipment and field trips (Parts VII and VIII of the opinion).

Mr. *Justice BRENNAN,* concurring and dissenting.

I join Parts I, VII, and VIII of the Court's opinion, and the reversal of the District Court's judgment insofar as that judgment upheld the constitutionality of § 3317.06 (B), (C), and (L).

I dissent however from Parts II, III, IV, V, and VI of the opinion and the affirmance of the District Court's judgment insofar as it sustained the constitutionality of § 3317.06 (A), (D), (F), (G), (H), (I), (J), and (K). . . .

Mr. *Justice MARSHALL,* concurring and dissenting.

I join Parts I, V, VII, and VIII of the Court's opinion. For the reasons stated below, however, I am unable to join the remainder of the Court's opinion or its judgment upholding the constitutionality of § 3317.06 (A), (G), (H), (I), (J), and (K).

The Court upholds the textbook loan provision, § 3317.06 (A), on the precedent of *Board of Education* v. *Allen*, 392 U.S. 236 (1968). *Ante,* at 5-7. It also recognizes, however, that there is "a tension" between Allen and the reasoning of the Court in *Meek* v. *Pittenger*, 421 U.S. 349 (1975). I would resolve that tension by overruling *Allen*. . . .

Mr. *Justice POWELL,* concurring in part and dissenting in part.

Our decisions in this troubling area draw lines that often must seem arbitrary. No doubt we could achieve greater analytical tidiness if we were to accept the broadest implications of the observation in *Meek* v. *Pittenger*, 421 U.S. 349, 366 (1975), that "[s]ubstantial aid to the educational function of [sectarian] schools . . . necessarily results in aid to the sectarian enterprise as a whole." If we took that course, it would become impossible to sustain state aid of any kind—even if the aid is wholly secular in character and is supplied to the pupils rather than the institutions. *Meek* itself would have to be overruled, along with *Board of Education* v. *Allen*, 392 U.S. 236 (1968), and even perhaps *Everson* v. *Board of Education*, 330 U.S. 1 (1947). The persistent desire of a number of States to find proper means of helping sectarian education to survive would be doomed. This Court has not yet thought that such a harsh result is required by the Establishment Clause. Certainly few would consider it in the public interest. Parochial schools, quite apart from their sectarian purpose, have provided an educational alternative for millions of young Americans; they often afford wholesome competition with our public schools; and in some States they relieve substantially the tax burden incident to the operation of public schools. The State has, moreover, a legitimate interest in facilitating education of the highest quality for all children within its boundaries, whatever school their parents have chosen for them.

It is important to keep these issues in perspective. At this point in the 20th century we are quite far removed from the dangers that prompted the Framers to include the Establishment Clause in the Bill of Rights. See *Walz* v. *Tax Commission*, 397 U.S. 664, 668 (1970). The risk of significant religious or denominational control over our democratic processes—or even of deep political division along religious lines—is remote, and when viewed against the positive contributions of sectarian schools, any such risk seems entirely tolerable in light of the continuing oversight of this Court. Our decisions have sought to establish principles that preserve the cherished safeguard of the Establishment Clause without resort to blind absolutism. If this endeavor means a loss of some analytical tidiness, then that too is entirely tolerable. Most of the Court's decision today follows in this tradition, and I join Parts I through VI of its opinion.

With respect to Part VII, I concur only in the judgment. I am not persuaded, nor did *Meek* hold, that all loans of secular instructional material and equipment "inescapably have the primary effect of providing a direct and substantial advancement of the sectarian enterprise." *Ante,* at 18. . . . Here the statute is expressly limited to materials incapable of diversion. Therefore the relevant question is whether the materials are such that they are "furnished for the use of individual students and at their request." *Allen,* 392 U.S., at 244 n. 6 (emphasis added).

The Ohio statute includes some materials such as wall maps, charts and other classroom paraphernalia for which the concept of a loan to individuals is a transparent fiction. A loan of these items is indistinguishable from forbidden "direct aid" to the sectarian institution itself, whoever the technical bailee. See *Meek,* 421 U.S., at 362-366. Since the provision makes no attempt to separate these instructional materials from others meaningfully lent to individuals, I agree with the Court that it cannot be sustained under our precedents. But I would find no constitutional defect in a properly limited provision lending to the individuals themselves only appropriate instructional materials and equipment similar to that customarily used in public schools.

I dissent as to Part VIII, concerning field trip transportation. The Court writes as though the statute funded the salary of the teacher who takes the students on the outing. In fact only the bus and driver are provided for the limited purpose of physical movement between the school and the secular destination of the field trip. As I find this aid indistinguishable in principle from that upheld in *Everson*, supra, I would sustain the District Court's judgment approving this part of the Ohio statute.

Mr. *Justice* STEVENS, concurring in part and dissenting in part.

The distinction between the religious and secular is a fundamental one. . . .

The line drawn by the Establishment Clause of the First Amendment must also have a fundamental character. It should not differentiate between direct and indirect subsidies, or between instructional materials like globes and maps on the one hand and instructional materials like textbooks on the other. For that reason, rather than the three-part test described in Part II of the Court's opinion, I would adhere to the test enunciated for the Court by Mr. Justice Black: "No tax in any amount, large or small, can be levied to support any religious activites or institutions, whatever they may be called, or whatever form they may adopt to teach or practice religion." *Everson* v. *Board of Education*, 330 U.S. 1, 16.

Under that test, a state subsidy of sectarian schools is invalid regardless of the form it takes. The financing of buildings, field trips, instructional materials, educational tests, and school books are all equally invalid. For all give aid to the school's educational mission, which at heart is religious. On the other hand, I am not prepared to exclude the possibility that some parts of the statute before us may be administered in a constitutional manner. The State can plainly provide public health services to children attending nonpublic schools. The diagnostic and therapeutic services described in Parts V and VI of the Court's opinion may fall into this category. Although I have some misgivings on this point, I am not prepared to hold this part of the statute invalid on its face. . . .

Geraci v. St. Xavier High School

3 Ohio Op. 3d 146 (1978)

BETTMAN, J. Appellants, Mark Geraci and his father, brought this action . . . seeking to have Mark reinstated as a student in good standing in said high school. St. Xavier is a private, parochial, college preparatory school operated by the Society of Jesus. . . . Mark was a student from his freshman year (9th grade) until his expulsion on June 2, 1978, the end of his junior year. This appeal raises basically two issues. First, whether appellants' constitutional right to due process has application to the conduct of disciplinary proceedings by a private school. Secondly, whether appellees' handling of Mark's expulsion was arbitrary and unreasonable and therefore a breach of appellants' contract of enrollment.

Appellants' first assignment of error complains that the trial court erred in holding that St. Xavier's disciplinary proceedings are not controlled by Fourteenth Amendment due process requirements. . . .

The due process requirements of the Fourteenth Amendment are only applicable to situations involving "state action." The basic issue raised by this assignment is therefore whether St. Xavier's disciplinary proceedings constitute state action. . . . A determination of whether the actions of a "private" school constitute state action requires an analysis of all the facts and circumstances of the case. . . .

Where, as in this case, the enterprise in question is regulated by the state, state action will be found if there is "a sufficiently close nexus between the State and the challenged action of the regulated entity so that the action of the latter may be fairly treated as that of the State itself." . . . This mode of analysis would here focus on the specific action of expulsion from St. Xavier. The state regulation of St. Xavier is relatively minimal. Our attention has been directed to nothing indicating state involvement in St. Xavier's disciplinary process. To the extent that appellant may be correct in asserting that a private school's decision to suspend or expel a student is sanctioned by R.C. § 3321.04 (C), this still does not involve the state in the decision-making process.

Even without state involvement in the disciplinary proceedings, state action may still be found if the state is so entwined with the administration and operation of the school that a "symbiotic relationship" has developed. . . . Determining whether a symbiotic relationship has developed requires an analysis of all the facts and circumstances of the state's involvement with St. Xavier.

St. Xavier is approved by the state as a high school. It files annual reports with the state dealing with its curriculum, class loads, number of teachers, etc. The teachers at St. Xavier all have state certificates of qualification. The state provides, on loan, certain standard textbooks and furnishes transportation to students. The school is exempted from state taxation. However, other than ascertaining that the school meets minimum state standards for a high school, the state exercises no control over the school whatsoever. This is certainly not the sort of pervasive state involvement required for a finding of a symbiotic state action. See *Powe* v. *Miles,* 407 F.2d 73 (2d Cir. 1968); *Rackin* v. *Univ. of Pa.*, 386 F.Supp. 992 (E.D. Pa. 1974).

Our conclusion that there is no state action in the disciplinary proceedings of a private high school such as St. Xavier is supported by *Wisch* v. *Sanford School, Inc.*, 420 F.Supp. 1310 (D.C. Del. 1976); *Bright* v. *Isenbarger,* 314 F.Supp. 1382 (N.D. Ind. 1970); and a long line of federal cases involving private universities. The assignment is, accordingly, overruled.

Appellants' assignments of error . . . maintain that the trial court erred in finding that the contract between the parties was breached by Mark's conduct and not by the procedures used by appellees in determining to expel him.

Mr. Geraci had paid Mark's tuition for his junior year and made the required deposit toward the senior year tuition. The parties are in agreement that this gave rise to a contract that St. Xavier would continue to provide education to Mark so long as he met its academic and disciplinary standards. They are further in agreement that the catalogue, describing St. Xavier High School's academic program and its standards and requirements constituted a part of the terms and conditions of such contract. The catalogue (Exhibit 1) provides in pertinent parts:

> "By the act of registering at St. Xavier High School, a student and his parents (or guardians) understand and agree to pursue the educational objectives and practices as stated in this catalogue and to observe the disciplinary code of the school. . . .
>
> "Disciplinary Norms
>
> "The St. Xavier norms of conduct are predicated on two premises: first, that every student has the right to certain situations (such as the protection of his personal property, the physical integrity of the facilities, an atmosphere conducive to personal growth and development) and, second, that every student has the duty to preserve these rights for others. . . . Since no list of norms can cover every situation, the administration presumes that common sense, mature judgment, and Christian charity are the guides by which every St. Xavier student should measure his actions.
>
> The assistant principal is in charge of all matters of discipline. . . .
>
> "Expulsion The following offenses are grounds for expulsion:
>
> "1. conduct detrimental to the reputation of the school. . . .
>
> "8. immorality in talk or action."

Appellants understood that Xavier maintained high standards of deportment. The evidence before the trial court was as follows. On the final day of the school year Tom McKenna, a student at Moeller High School, entered St. Xavier High School, went to the classroom where Mark Geraci and his classmates were taking a final test and threw a meringue pie in the face of Mr. Downie, the teacher. Pandemonium ensued involving teachers and students. By Mark's own testimony, several weeks before he and some fellow students had decided it would be a "funny prank" to get McKenna to "pie" Mr. Downie. "I called Tom . . . and he said he would go along with it." The original plan was that Mark would collect $50.00 from the group to pay McKenna. He did not, however, collect any money. Nevertheless, the evening preceding the last day of school, when Mark called McKenna to ask him to a party, McKenna asked "whatever happened about the pie throwing." Geraci told him he had not collected any money and McKenna said "he might come over and do it anyway." Mark made no response to this statement. On McKenna's inquiry Geraci told him the room number of the class where Mr. Downie would be teaching and, on further inquiry, which door of the building to enter. At McKenna's request, Geraci called another Moeller student to arrange for transportation for McKenna.

The very recital of the above facts makes abundantly clear that Geraci aided and abetted McKenna's throwing of the pie in the face of his teacher, Mr. Downie, an act patently "immoral," "detrimental to the reputation of the school" and violative of Geraci's acknowledged duty to exercise "common sense, mature judgment, and Christian charity." The trial court's finding that Geraci's acts constituted a breach of the contract with St. Xavier is, therefore, fully supported by the evidence.

Although, as hereinbefore discussed, a private school's disciplinary proceedings are not controlled by the due process clause, and accordingly such schools have broad discretion in making rules and setting up procedures for their enforcement, nevertheless, under its broad equitable powers a court will intervene where such discretion is abused or the proceedings do not comport with fundamental fairness. *Schoppelrei* v. *Franklin University*, 11 Ohio App.2d 60, 228 N.E.2d 334, 40 O.O.2d 228 (10th Dist. 1967); *Koblitz* v. *Western Reserve*, 11 O.C.D. 515, 21 O.C.C. 144 (8th Dist. 1901).

The record shows that Mr. Meyer, the Assistant Principal of Xavier in charge of discipline, called Mark to his office several hours after the event. At that time Mark, though protesting that he did not really expect McKenna to go through with it, admitted substantially all the elements of his involvement, herein before set out. Meyer forthwith advised him that he was expelled. The transcript further shows that before this decision was finalized Mr. Meyer, Mr. Trainor, the Principal, and Father Borgmann, President of St. Xavier, all discussed and considered the matter; that Meyer discussed it with Mr. Geraci; that Trainor discussed it with Mr. Geraci and that Father Borgmann discussed it with both father and son. The testimony as to these discussions shows an appreciation and consideration by appellees of Mark's previously unblemished disciplinary record and his academic excellence, an understanding of how much Xavier meant to appellants and a genuine human concern for them. On the basis of the record we cannot say that appellees abused their discretion nor that the procedures were unfair.

The trial court did not err in holding that Mark's expulsion was just, proper, and in accordance with the contract between the parties and did not constitute an abuse of discretion. . . .

The judgment of the trial court must accordingly be affirmed.

Aguilar v. Felton

________U.S. ________, 105 S.Ct. 3232 (1985)

Justice BRENNAN delivered the opinions of the Court.

The City of New York uses federal funds to pay the salaries of public employees who teach in parochial schools. In this companion case to *School District of Grand Rapids* v. *Ball, ante,* p. _____, we determine whether this practice violates the Establishment Clause of the First Amendment.

The program at issue in this case, originally enacted as Title I of the Elementary and Secondary Education Act of 1965, authorizes the Secretary of Education to distribute financial assistance to local educational institutions to meet the needs of educationally deprived children from low-income families. . . .

The proposed programs must also meet the following statutory requirements: the children involved in the program must be educationally deprived, § 3804(a), the children must reside in areas comprising a high concentration of low-income families, § 3805(b), and the programs must supplement, not supplant, programs that would exist absent funding under Title I. § 3807(b).

Since 1966, the City of New York has provided instructional services funded by Title I to parochial school students on the premises of parochial schools. Of those students eligible to receive funds in 1981–1982, 13.2% were enrolled in private schools. Of that group, 84% were enrolled in Hebrew day schools. With respect to the religious atmosphere of these schools, the Court of Appeals concluded that "the picture that emerges is of a system in which religious considerations play a key role in the selection of students and teachers, and which has as its substantial purpose the inculcation of religious values." 739 F.2d 48, 68 (1984).

The programs conducted at these schools include remedial reading, reading skills, remedial mathematics, English as a second language, and guidance services. These programs are carried out by regular employees of the public schools (teachers, guidance counselors, psychologists, psychiatrists and social workers) who have volunteered to teach in the parochial schools. The amount of time that each professional spends in the parochial school is determined by the number of students in the particular program and the needs of these students.

The City's Bureau of Nonpublic School Reimbursement makes teacher assignments, and the instructors are supervised by field personnel, who attempt to pay at least one unannounced visit per month. The field supervisors, in turn, report to program coordinators, who also pay occasional unannounced supervisory visits to monitor Title I classes in the parochial schools. The professionals involved in the program are directed to avoid involvement with religious activities that are conducted within the private schools and to bar religious materials in their classrooms. All material and equipment used in the programs funded under Title I are supplied by the Government and are used only in those programs. The professional personnel are solely responsible for the selection of the students. Additionally, the professionals are informed that contact with private school personnel should be kept to a minimum. Finally, the administrators of the parochial schools are required to clear the classrooms used by the public school personnel of all religious symbols.

B

In 1978, six taxpayers commenced this action in the District Court for the Eastern District of New York, alleging that the Title I program administered by the city of New York violates the Establishment Clause. . . . The District court granted the appellants' motion for summary judgment. . . .

A unanimous panel of the Court of Appeals for the Second Circuit reversed, holding that

> "[t]he Establishment Clause, as it has been interpreted by the Supreme Court in *Public Funds for Public Schools* v. *Marburger,* 358 F.Supp. 29 (D NJ 1973), *aff'd mem.,* 417 U.S. 961 (1974); *Meek* v. *Pittenger,* 421 U.S. 349 (1975) (particularly Part V, pp. 367–372); and *Wolman* v. *Walter,* 433 U.S. 229 (1977), constitutes an insurmountable barrier to the use of federal funds to send public school teachers and other professionals into religious schools to carry on instruction, remedial or otherwise, or to provide clinical and guidance services of the sort at issue here." 739 F.2d at 49–50.

. . . In *School Districts of the City of Grand Rapids* v. *Ball, ante,* p. _____, the Court has today held unconstitutional under the Establishment Clause two remedial and enhancement programs operated by the Grand Rapids Public School District, in which classes were provided to private school children at public expense in classrooms located in and leased from the local private schools. The New York programs challenged in this case are very similar to the programs we examined in *Ball.* In both cases, publicly funded instructors teach classes composed exclusively of private school students in private school buildings. In both cases, an overwhelming number of the participating private schools are religiously affiliated. In both cases, the publicly funded instructors teach classes composed exclusively of private school students in private school buildings. In both cases, the publicly funded programs provide not only professional personnel, but also all materials and supplies necessary for the operation of the programs. Finally, the instructors in both cases are told that they are public school employees under the sole control of the public schools system.

The appellants attempt to distinguish this case on the ground that the City of New York, unlike the Grand Rapids Public School District, has adopted a system for monitoring the religious content of publicly funded Title I classes in the religious schools. At best, the supervision in this case would assist in preventing the Title I program from being used, intentionally or unwittingly, to inculcate the religious beliefs of the surrounding parochial school. But appellants' argument fails in any event, because the supervisory system established by the City of New York inevitably results in the excessive entanglement of church and state, an Establishment Clause concern distinct from that addressed by the effects doctrine. Even where state aid to parochial institutions does not have the primary effect of advancing religion, the provision of such aid may nonetheless violate the Establishment Clause owing to the nature of the interaction of church and state in the administration of that aid. . . .

In *Lemon* v. *Kurtzman,* 403 U.S. 602 (1971), the Court held that the supervision necessary to ensure that teachers in parochial schools were not conveying religious messages to their students would constitute the excessive entanglement of church and state. . . .

In *Roemer* v. *Maryland Public Works Board,* 426 U.S. 736 (1976), the Court sustained state programs of aid to religiously affiliated institutions of higher learning. The state allowed the grants to be used for any nonsectarian purpose. The Court upheld the grants on the ground that the institutions were not "'pervasively sectarian,'" *id.*, at 758–759, and therefore a system of supervision was unnecessary to ensure that the grants were not being used to effect a religious end. In so holding, the Court identified "what is crucial to a nonentangling aid program: the ability of the State to identify and subsidize separate secular functions carried out at the school, without on-the-site inspections being necessary to prevent diversion of the funds to sectarian purposes." *Id.*, at 765. similarly, in *Tilton* v. *Richardson,* 403 U.S. 672 (1971), the Court upheld one-time grants to sectarian institutions because ongoing supervision was not required. See also *Hunt* v. *McNair*, 413 U.S. 734 (1973).

As the Court of Appeals recognized, the elementary and secondary schools here are far different from the colleges at issue in *Roemer, Hunt,* and *Tilton.* 739 R.2d, at 68–70. Unlike the colleges, which were found not to be "pervasively sectarian," many of the schools involved in this case are the same sectarian schools which had "'as a substantial purpose the inculcation of religious values'" in *Committee for Public Education* v. *Nyquist,* 413 U.S. 756, 768 (1973), quoting *Committee for Public Education* v. *Nyquist,* 350 F.Supp. 655 663 (SDNY 1972). . . .

The critical elements of the entanglement proscribed in *Lemon* are thus present in this case. First, as noted above, the aid is provided in a pervasively sectarian environment. Second, because assistance is provided in the form of teachers, ongoing inspection is required to ensure the absence of a religious message. Cf. *Lemon,* 403 U.S., at 619, with *Tilton, supra,* at 668, and *Roemer, supra,* at 765. In short, the scope and duration of New York's Title I program would require a permanent and pervasive State presence in the sectarian schools receiving aid.

This pervasive monitoring by public authorities in the sectarian schools infringes precisely those Establishment Clause Values at the root of the prohibition of excessive entanglement. . . .

The administrative cooperation that is required to maintain the educational program at issue here entangles Church and State in still another way that infringes interests at the heart of the Establishment Clause. Administrative personnel of the public and parochial school systems must work together in resolving matters related to schedules, classroom assignments, problems that arise in the implementation of the program, requests for additional services, and the dissemination of information regarding the program. Furthermore, the program necessitates "frequent contacts between the regular and the remedial teachers (or other professionals), in which each side reports on individual student needs, problems encountered, and results achieved." 739 F.2d at 65. . . .

III

Despite the well-intentioned efforts taken by the City of New York, the program remains constitutionally flawed owing to the nature of the aid, to the institution receiving the aid, and to the constitutional principles that they implicate—that neither the State nor Federal Government shall promote or hinder a particular faith or faith generally through the advancement of benefits or through the excessive entanglement of church and state in the administration of those benefits. *Affirmed.*

Justice POWELL, concurring.

I concur in the Court's opinions and judgments today in this case and in *Grand Rapids School District* v. *Ball, ante.* . . . I write to emphasize additional reasons why precedents of this court require us to invalidate these two educational programs that concededly have "done so much good and little, if any, detectable harm." . . .

Regrettaby, however, the Title I and Grand Rapids programs do not survive the scrutiny required by our Establishment Clause cases.

I agree with the Court that in this case the Establishment Clause is violated because there is too great a risk of government entanglement in the administration of the religious schools. . . . Our cases have noted that "'[t]he State must be *certain,* given the Religion Clauses, that subsidized teachers do not inculcate religion.'" *Meek* v. *Pittenger,* 421 U.S. 349, 371 (1975) (emphasis added) (quoting *Lemon* v. *Kurtzman,* 403 U.S. 602, 619 (1971)). . . .

The risk of entanglement is compounded by the additional risk of political divisiveness stemming from the aid to religion at issue here. I do not suggest that at this point in our history the Title I program or similar parochial aid plans could result in the establishment of a state religion. There likewise is small chance that these programs would result in significant religious or denominational control over our democratic processes. See *Wolman* v. *Walter, supra,* at 263 (*POWELL, J.,* concurring in part, concurring in the judgment in part, and dissenting in part). Nonetheless, there remains a considerable risk of continuing political strife over the propriety of direct aid to religious schools and the proper allocation of limited governmental resources. . . . Although the Court's opinion does not discuss it at any length, see *ante,* at 11, the potential for such divisiveness is a strong additional reason for holding that the Title I and Grand Rapids programs are invalid on entanglement grounds.

The Title I program at issue in this case also would be invalid under the "effects" prong of the test adopted in *Lemon* v. *Kurtzman, supra.* . . . Rather, by directly assuming part of the parochial schools' education function, the effect of the Title I aid in "inevitably . . . to subsidize and advance the religious mission of [the] sectarian schools," *id.*, at 779–780, even though the program provides that only secular subjects will be taught. . . .

I recognize the difficult dilemma in which governments are placed by the interaction of the "effects" and entanglement prongs of the *Lemon* test. Our decisions require governments extending aid to parochial schools to tread an extremely narrow line between being certain that the "principal or primary effect" of the aid is not to advance religion, *Lemon* v. *Kurtzman, supra,* at 612, and avoiding excessive entanglement. Nonetheless, the Court has never foreclosed the possibility that some types of aid to parochial schools could be valid under the Establishment Clause. *Mueller* v. *Allen, supra,* at _____. Our cases have upheld evenhanded secular assistance to both parochial and public school children in some areas . . . I do not read the Court's opinion as precluding these types of indirect aid to parochial schools. . . . The constitutional defect in the Title I program, as indicated above, is that it provides a direct financial subsidy to be administered in significant part by public school teachers within parochial schools—resulting in both the advancement of religion and forbidden entanglement. If, for example, Congress could fashion a program of evenhanded financial assistance to both public and private schools that could be administered, without governmental supervision in the private schools, so as to prevent the diversion of the aid from secular purposes, we would be presented with a different question.

I join the opinions and judgments of the Court.

Chief Justice BURGER, dissenting.

Under the guise of protecting Americans from the evils of an Established Church such as those of the Eighteenth Century and earlier times, today's decision will deny countless schoolchildren desperately needed remedial teaching services funded under Title I. The program at issue covers remedial reading, reading skills, remedial mathematics, English as a second language, and assistance for children needing special help in the learning process. The "remedial reading" portion of this program, for example, reaches children who suffer from dyslexia, a disease known to be difficult to diagnose and treat. Many of these children now will not receive the special training they need, simply because their parents desire that they attend religiously affiliated schools.

What is disconcerting about the result reached today is that, in the face of the human cost entailed by this decision, the Court does not even attempt to identify any threat to religious liberty posed by the operation of Title I. I share *Justice WHITE'S* concern that the Court's obsession with the criteria identified in *Lemon* v. *Kurtzman,* 403

U.S. 602 (1971), has led to results that are "contrary to the long-range interests of the country," post, at 2. As I wrote in *Wallace* v. *Jaffree*, ____U.S. ____, ____(1985) (dissenting opinion), "our responsibility is not to apply tidy formulas by rote; our duty is to determine whether the statute or practice at issue is a step toward establishing a state religion." Federal programs designed to prevent a generation of children from growing up without being able to read effectively are not remotely steps in that direction. It borders on paranoia to perceive the Archbishop of Canterbury or the Bishop of Rome lurking behind programs that are just as vital to the nation's school children as textbooks, . . . transportation to and from school, . . . and school nursing services. . . . We have frequently recognized that some interaction between church and state is unavoidable, and that an attempt to eliminate all contact between the two would be both futile and undesirable. Justice Douglas, writing for the Court in *Zorach* v. *Clauson*, 343 U.S. 306, 312 (1952), stated:

> The First Amendment . . . does not say that in every and all respects there shall be a separation of Church and State. . . . Otherwise the state and religion would be aliens to each other—hostile, suspicious, and even unfriendly."

The Court today fails to demonstrate how the interaction occasioned by the program at issue presents any threat to the values underlying the Establishment Clause.

I cannot join in striking down a program that, in the words of the Court of Appeals, "has done so much good and little, if any, detectable harm." 739 F.2d 48, 72 (CA2 1984). The notion that denying these services to students in religious schools is a neutral act to protect us from an Established Church has no support in logic, experience, or history. Rather than showing the neutrality the Court boasts of, it exhibits nothing less than hostility toward religion and the children who attend church-sponsored schools.

Justice WHITE, dissenting.

As evidenced by my dissenting opinions in *Lemon* v. *Kurtzman,* 403 U.S. 602, 661 (1971) and *Committee for Public Education* v. *Nyquist,* 413 U.S. 756, 813 (1973), I have long disagreed with the Court's interpretation and application of the Establishment Clause in the context of state aid to private schools. For the reasons stated in those dissents, I am firmly of the belief that the Court's decisions in these cases, like its decisions in *Lemon* and *Nyquist,* are "not required by the First Amendment and [are] contrary to the long- range interests of the country." 413 U.S., at 820. For those same reasons, I am satisfied that what the States have sought to do in these cases is well within their authority and is not forbidden by the Establishment Clause. Hence, I dissent and would reverse the judgment in each of these cases.

Justice REHNQUIST, dissenting.

I dissent for the reasons stated in my dissenting opinion in *Wallace* v. *Jaffree,* Nos. 83–812, 83–929. In *Aguilar* v. *Felton* the Court takes advantage of the "Catch-22" paradox of its own creation . . . whereby aid must be supervised to ensure no entanglement but the supervision itself is held to cause an entanglement. The Court in *Aguilar* strikes down nondiscriminatory nonsectarian aid to educationally deprived children from low-income families. The Establishment Clause does not prohibit such sorely needed assistance; we have indeed travelled far afield from the concerns which prompted the adoption of the First Amendment when we rely on gossamer abstractions to invalidate a law which obviously meets an entirely secular need. I would reverse.

Justice O'CONNOR, with whom *Justice REHNQUIST* joins as to Parts II and III, dissenting.

Today the Court affirms the holding of the Court of Appeals that public schoolteachers can offer remedial instruction to disadvantaged students who attend religious schools "only if such instruction . . . [is] afforded at a neutral site off the premises of the religious school." 739 F.2d 48, 64 (CA2 1984). This holding rests on the theory, enunciated in Part V of the Court's opinion in *Meek* v. *Pittenger,* 421 U.S. 349, 367–373 (1975), that public schoolteachers who set foot on parochial school premises are likely to bring religion into their classes, and that the supervision necessary to prevent religious teaching would unduly entangle church and state. Even if this theory were valid in the abstract, it cannot validly be applied to New York City's 19-year-old Title I program. . . . Under *Lemon* and its progeny, direct state aid to parochial schools that has the purpose or effect of furthering the religious mission of the schools is unconstitutional. I agree with that principle. According to the Court, however, the New York Title I program is defective not because of any improper purpose or effect, but rather because it fails the third part of the *Lemon* test: the Title I program allegedly fosters excessive government entanglement with religion. I disagree with the Court's analysis of entanglement and I question the utility of entanglement as a separate Establishment Clause standard in most cases. . . .

The purpose of Title I is to provide special educational assistance to disadvantaged children who would not otherwise receive it. Congress recognized that poor academic performance by disadvantaged children is part of the cycle of poverty. S. Rep. No. 146, 89th Cong., 1st Sess., 4 (1965). Congress sought to break the cycle by providing classes in remedial reading, mathematics, and English to disadvantaged children in parochial as well as public schools, for public schools enjoy no monopoly on education in low income areas.

After reviewing the text of the statute and its legislative history, the District Court concluded that Title I serves a secular purpose of aiding needy children regardless of where they attend school. . . . The Court of Appeals did not dispute this finding, and no party in this Court contends that the purpose of the statute or of the New York City Title I program is to advance or endorse religion. Indeed, the record demonstrates that New York City public schoolteachers offer Title I classes on the premises of parochial schools solely because alternative means to reach the disadvantaged parochial school students—such as instruction for parochial school students at the nearest public school, either after or during regular school hours—were unsuccessful. *PEARL,* 489 F.Supp., at 1255. . . . Whether one looks to the face of the statute or to its implementation, the Title I program is undeniably animated by a legitimate secular purpose.

The Court's discussion of the effect of the New York City Title I program is even more perfunctory than its analysis of the program's purpose. . . .

One need not delve too deeply in the record to understand why the Court does not belabor the effect of the Title I program. The abstract theories explaining why on-premises instruction might possibly advance religion dissolve in the face of experience in New York. . . . Indeed, in 19 years there has never been a single incident in which a Title I instructor "subtly or overtly" attempted to "indoctrinate the students in particular religious tenets at public expense." *Grand Rapids, ante,* at _____.

Common sense suggests a plausible explanation for this unblemished record. New York City's public Title I instructors are professional educators who can and do follow instructions not to inculcate religion in their classes. They are unlikely to be influenced by the sectarian nature of the parochial schools where they teach, not only because they are carefully supervised by public officials, but also because the vast majority of them visit several different schools each week and are not of the same religion as their parochial students.* In light of the ample record, an objective observer of the implementation of the Title I program in New York would hardly view it as endorsing the tenets of the participating parochial schools. . . .

Our Establishment Clause decisions have not barred remedial assistance to parochial school children, but rather remedial assistance *on the premises of the parochial school* . . . Yet it is difficult to understand why a remedial reading class offered on parochial school premises is any more likely to supplant the secular course offerings of the parochial school than the same class offered in a portable classroom next door to the school. Unless *Wolman* was wrongly decided, the defect in the Title I program cannot lie in the risk that it will supplant secular course offerings.

II

Recognizing the weakness of any claim of an improper purpose or effect, the Court today relies entirely on the entanglement prong of *Lemon* to invalidate the New York City Title I program. The Court holds that the occasional presence of peripatetic public schoolteachers on parochial school grounds threatens undue entanglement of church and state. . . .

This analysis of entanglement, I acknowledge, finds support in some of this Court's precedents. . . .

I would accord these decisions the appropriate deference commanded by the doctrine of *stare decisis* if I could discern logical support for their analysis. But experience has demonstrated that the analysis in Part V of the *Meek* opinion is flawed. At the time *Meek* was decided, thoughtful dissents pointed out the absence of any record support for the notion that public school teachers would attempt to inculcate religion simply because they temporarily occupied a parochial school classroom, or that such instruction would produce political divisiveness. . . . Experience has given greater force to the arguments of the dissenting opinions in *Meek.* It is not intuitively obvious that a dedicated public school teacher will tend to disobey instructions and commence proselytizing students at public expense merely because the classroom is within a parochial school. *Meek* is correct

* It is undisputed that 78% of Title I instructors who teach in parochial schools visit more than one school each week. Almost three-quarters of the instructors do not share the religious affiliation of any school they teach in. App. 49

in asserting that a teacher of remedial reading "remains a teacher," but surely it is significant that the teacher involved is a professional, full-time public school employee who is unaccustomed to bringing religion into the classroom. Given that not a single incident of religious indoctrination has been identified as occurring in the thousands of classes offered in Grand Rapids and New York over the past two decades, it is time to acknowledge that the risk identified in *Meek* was greatly exaggerated.

Just as the risk that public schoolteachers in parochial classrooms will inculcate religion has been exaggerated, so has the degree of supervision required to manage that risk. In this respect the New York Title I program is instructive. What supervision has been necessary in New York to enable public school teachers to held disadvantaged children for 19 years without once proselytizing? Public officials have prepared careful instructions warning public schoolteachers of their exclusively secular mission, and have required Title I teachers to study and observe them. App. 50–51. Under the rules, Title I teachers are not accountable to parochial or private school officials; they have sole responsibility for selecting the students who participate in their class, must administer their own tests for determining eligibility, cannot engage in team teaching or cooperative activities with parochial school teachers, must make sure that all materials and equipment they use are not otherwise used by the parochial school, and must not participate in religious activities in the schools or introduce any religious matter into their teaching. To ensure compliance with the rules, a field supervisor and a program coordinator, who are full-time public school employees, make unannounced visits to each teacher's classroom at least once a month. *Id.*, at 53.

The Court concludes that this degree of supervision of public school employees by other public school employees constitutes excessive entanglement of church and state. I cannot agree.

. . . *Justice POWELL* suggests that the required supervision is extensive because the State must be *certain* that public schoolteachers do not inculcate religion. *Ante,* at——. That reasoning would require us to close our public schools, for there is always some chance that a public schoolteacher will bring religion into the classroom regardless of its location. See *Wallace* v. *Jaffree,* 472 U.S. _____, _____, n. 23 (1985). Even if I remained confident of the usefulness of entanglement as an Establishment Clause test, I would conclude that New York's efforts to prevent religious indoctrination in title I classes have been adequate and have not caused excessive institutional entanglement of church and state.

The Court's reliance on the potential for political divisiveness as evidence of undue entanglement is also unpersuasive. There is little record support for the proposition that New York's admirable Title I program has ignited any controversy other than this litigation. . . .

I adhere to the doubts about the entanglement test that were expressed in *Lynch.* It is curious indeed to base our interpretation of the Constitution on speculation as to the likelihood of a phenomenon which the parties may crease merely by prosecuting a lawsuit. My reservations about the entanglement test, however, have come to encompass its institutional aspects as well. As *Justice REHNQUIST* has pointed, many of the inconsistencies in our Establishment Clause decisions can be ascribed to our insistence that parochial aid programs with a valid purpose and effect may still be invalid by virtue of undue entanglement. *Wallace* v. *Jaffree, supra,* at _____–_____. For example, we permit a State to pay for bus transportation to a parochial school, *Everson* v. *Board of Education,* 330 U.S. 1 (1947), but precludes States from providing buses for parochial school field trips, on the theory such trips involve excessive state supervision of the parochial officials who lead them. *Wolman,* 433 U.S., at 254. To a great extent, the anomalous results in our Establishment Clause cases are "attributable to [the] 'entanglement' prong." Choper, The Religion Clauses of the First Amendment: Reconciling the Conflict, 41 U. Pitt. L. Rev. 673, 681 (1980).

Pervasive institutional involvement of church and state may remain relevant in deciding the *effect* of a statute which is alleged to violate the Establishment Clause, *Walz* v. *Tax Commission,* 397 U.S. 664 (1970), but state efforts to ensure that public resources are used only for nonsectarian ends should not in themselves serve to invalidate an otherwise valid statute. The State requires sectarian organizations to cooperate on a whole range of matters without thereby advancing religion or giving the impression that the government endorses religion. *Wallace* v. *Jaffree, supra,* at _____(dissenting opinion of *REHNQUIST, J.*) (noting that State educational agencies impose myriad curriculum, attendance, certificance, fire, and safety regulations on sectarian schools). If a statute lacks a purpose or effect of advancing or endorsing religion, I would not invalidate it merely because it requires some ongoing cooperation between church and state or some state supervision to ensure that state funds do not advance religion.

III

Today's ruling does not spell the end of the Title I program of remedial education for disadvantaged children. . . . Impoverished children who attend parochial schools may also continue to benefit from Title I programs offered off the premises of their schools—possibly in portable classrooms just over the edge of school property. The only disadvantaged children who lose under the Court's holding are those in cities where it is not economically and logistically feasible to provide public facilities for remedial education adjacent to the parochial school. But this subset is significant, for it includes more than 20,000 New York City schoolchildren and uncounted others elsewhere in the country.

For these children, the Court's decision is tragic. The Court deprives them of a program that offers a meaningful chance at success in life, and it does so on the untenable theory that public schoolteachers (most of whom are of different faiths than their students) are likely to start teaching religion merely because they have walked across the threshold of a parochial school. I reject this theory and the analysis in *Meek* v. *Pittenger* on which it is based. I cannot close my eyes to the fact that, over almost two decades, New York's public schoolteachers have helped thousands of impoverished parochial schoolchildren to overcome educational disadvantages without once attempting to inculcate religion. Their praiseworthy efforts have not eroded and do not threaten the religious liberty assured by the Establishment Clause. The contrary judgment of the Court of Appeals should be reversed.

I respectfully dissent.

Grand Rapids School District of the City of Grand Rapids, et al., Petitioners v. Phyllis Ball et al.

________U.S. ________, 105 S.Ct. 3216 (1985)

Justice BRENNAN delivered the opinion of the Court.

The School District of Grand Rapids, Michigan, adopted two programs in which classes for nonpublic school students are financed by the public school system, taught by teachers hired by the public school system, and conducted in "leased" classrooms in the nonpublic schools. Most of the nonpublic schools involved in the programs are sectarian religious schools. This case raises the question whether these programs impermissibly involve the government in the support of sectarian religious activities and thus violate the Establishment Clause of the First Amendment. . . .

The Shared Time program offers classes during the regular school day that are intended to be supplementary to the "core curriculum" courses that the State of Michigan requires as a part of an accredited school program. Among the subjects offered are "remedial" and "enrichment" mathematics, "remedial" and "enrichment" reading, art, music, and physical education. A typical nonpublic school student attends these classes for one or two class periods per week; approximately "ten percent of any given nonpublic school student's time during the academic year would consist of Shared Time instruction." *Americans United for Separation of Church and State* v. *School Dist. of Grand Rapids,* 46 F.Supp. 1071, 1079 (WD Mich. 1982). Although Shared Time itself is a program offered only in the nonpublic schools, there was testimony that the courses included in that program are offered, albeit perhaps in a somewhat different form, in the public schools as well. All of the classes that are the subject of this case are taught in elementary schools, with the exception of Math Topics, a remedial math course taught in the secondary schools.

The Shared Time teachers are full-time employees of the public schools, who often move from classroom to classroom during the course of the school day. A "significant portion" of the teachers (approximately 10%) "previously taught in nonpublic schools, and many of those had been assigned to the same nonpublic school where they were previously employed." *Id.*, at 1078. The School District of Grand Rapids hires Shared Time teachers in accordance with its ordinary hiring procedures. *Ibid.* The public school system apparently provides all of the supplies, materials, and equipment used in connection with Shared Time instruction. See App. 341.

. . . The classes at issue here are taught in the nonpublic elementary schools and commence at the conclusion of the regular school day. Among the courses offered are Arts and Crafts, Home Economics, Spanish, Gymnastics, Yearbook Production, Christmas Arts and Crafts, Drama, Newspaper, Humanities, Chess, Model Building, and Nature Appreciation. . . .

Community Education teachers are part-time public school employees. Community Education courses are completely voluntary and are offered only if 12 or more students enroll. Because a well-known teacher is necessary to attract the requisite number of students, the School District accords a preference in hiring to instructors already teaching within the school. Thus, "virtually every Community Education course conducted on facilities leased from nonpublic schools has an instructor otherwise employed full time by the same nonpublic school." *Ibid.*

Both programs are administered similarly. The Director of the program, a public school employee, sends packets of course listings to the participating nonpublic schools before the school year begins. the nonpublic school administrators then decide which courses they want to offer. The Director works out an academic schedule for each school, taking into account, *inter alia,* the varying religious holidays celebrated by the schools of different denominations.

Nonpublic school administrators decide which classrooms will be used for the programs, and the Director then inspects the facilities and consults with Shared Time teachers to make sure the facilities are satisfactory. The public school system pays the nonpublic schools for the use of the necessary classroom space by entering into "leases" at the rate of $6 per classroom per week. The "leases," however, contain no mention of the particular room, space, or facility leased and teachers' rooms, libraries, lavatories, and similar facilities are made available at no additional charge. *Id.*, at 1077. Each room used in the programs has to be free of any crucifix, religious symbol, or artifact, although such religious symbols can be present in the adjoining hallways, corridors, and other facilities used in connection with the program. During the time that a given classroom is being used in the programs, the teacher is required to post a sign stating that it is a "public school classroom." However, there are no signs posted outside the school buildings indicating that public school courses are conducted inside or that the facilities are being used as a public school annex.

Although petitioners label the Shared Time and Community Education students as "part-time public school students," the students attending Shared Time and Community Education courses in facilities leased from a nonpublic school are the same students who attend that particular school otherwise. *Id.*, *;ro at 1078. There is no evidence that any public school student has ever attended a Shared Time or Community Education class in a nonpublic school. Id.*, at 1097. . . .

. . . The schools of course vary from one another, but substantial evidence suggests that they share deep religious purposes. . . . the District Court found that the schools are "pervasively sectarian," *id.*, at 1096, n. 13, and concluded "without hesitation that the purposes of these schools is to advance their particular religions," *id.*, at 1096, and that "a substantial portion of their functions are subsumed in the religious mission." *Id.*, at 1084.

Since *Everson* made clear that the guarantees of the Establishment Clause apply to the States, we have often grappled with the problem of state aid to nonpublic, religious schools. In all of these cases, our goal has been to give meaning to the sparse language and broad purposes of the Clause, while not unduly infringing on the ability of the States to provide for the welfare of their people in accordance with their own particular circumstances. Providing for the education of schoolchildren is surely a praiseworthy purpose. But our cases have consistently recognized that even such a praiseworthy, secular purpose cannot validate government aid to parochial schools when the aid has the effect of promoting a single religion or religion generally or when the aid unduly entangles the government in matters religious. . . .

We have noted that the three-part test first articulated in *Lemon* v. *Kurtzman,* at

612–613, guides "[t]he general nature of our inquiry in this area," *Mueller* v. *Allen,* 463 U.S. 388, 394 (1983). . . .

These tests "must not be viewed as setting the precise limits to the necessary constitutional inquiry, but serve only as guidelines with which to identify instances in which the objectives of the Establishment Clause have been impaired." *Meek* v. *Pittenger,* 421 U.S. 349, 359 (1975). . . . The *Lemon* test concentrates attention on the issues—purposes, effect, entanglement—that determine whether a particular state action is an improper "law respecting an establishment of religion." We therefore reaffirm that state action alleged to violate the Establishment Clause should be measured against the *Lemon* criteria.

As has often been true in school aid cases, there is no dispute as to the first test. Both the District Court and the Court of Appeals found that the purpose of the Community Education and Shared Time programs was "manifestly secular." 546 F.Supp., at 1085; see also 718 F.2d, at 1398. We find no reason to disagree with this holding, and therefore go on to consider whether the primary or principal effect of the challenged programs is to advance or inhibit religion. . . .

Given that 40 of the 41 schools in this case are thus "pervasively sectarian," the challenged public-school programs operating in the religious schools may impermissibly advance religion in three different ways. First, the teachers participating in the programs may become involved in intentionally or inadvertently inculcating particular religious tenets or beliefs. Second, the programs may provide a crucial symbolic link between government and religion, thereby enlisting—at least in the eyes of impressionable youngsters—the powers of government to the support of the religious denomination operating the school. Third, the programs may have the effect of directly promoting religion by impermissibly providing a subsidy to the primary religious mission of the institutions affected. . . .

The programs before us today share the defect that we identified in *Meek.* With respect to the Community Education Program, the District Court found that "virtually every Community Education course conducted on facilities leased from nonpublic schools has an instructor otherwise employed full time by the same nonpublic school." 546 F.Supp.. at 1079. These instructors . . . are expected during the regular school day to inculcate their students with the tenets and beliefs of their particular religious faiths. . . . Nonetheless, as petitioners themselves asserted, Community Education classes are not specifically monitored for religious content. App. 353.

We do not question that the dedicated and professional religious school teachers employed by the Community Education program will attempt in good faith to perform their secular mission conscientiously. Cf. *Lemon,* 403 U.S., at 618–619. Nonetheless, there is a substantial risk that, overtly or subtly, the religious message they are expected to convey during the regular school day will infuse the supposedly secular classes they teach after school. The danger arises "not because the public employee [is] likely deliberately to subvert his task to the service of religion, but rather because the pressures of the environment might alter his behavior from its normal course." *Wolman* v. *Walter,* 433 U.S. 229, 247 (1977). . . .

The Shared Time program, though structured somewhat differently, nonetheless also poses a substantial risk of state-sponsored indoctrination. The most important difference between the programs is that most of the instructors in the Shared Time program are full-time teachers hired by the public schools. Moreover, although "virtually every" Community Education instructor is a full-time religious school teacher, 546 F.Supp., at 1079, only "[a] significant portion" of the Shared Time instructors previously worked in the religious schools. *Id.*, at 1078. Nonetheless, as with the Community Education program, no attempt is made to monitor the Shared Time courses for religious content. App. 330.

Thus, despite these differences between the two programs, our holding in *Meek* controls the inquiry with respect to Shared Time, as well as Community Education. . . .

The Court of Appeals of course recognized that respondents adduced no evidence of specific incidents of religious indoctrination in this case. 718 F.2d, at 1404. But the absence of proof of specific incidents is not dispositive. When conducting a supposedly secular class in the pervasively sectarian environment of a religious school, a teacher may knowingly or unwillingly tailor the content of the course to fit the school's announced goals. If so, there is no reason to believe that this kind of ideological influence would be detected or reported by students, by their parents, or by the school system itself. . . . And the public school system itself has no incentive to detect or report any specific incidents of improper state-sponsored indoctrination. Thus, the lack of evidence of specific incidents of indoctrination is of little significance.

(2)

Our cases have recognized that the Establishment Clause guards against more than direct, state-funded efforts to indoctrinate youngsters in specific religious beliefs. Government promotes religion as effectively when it fosters a close identification of its powers and responsibilities with those of any—or all—religious denominations as when it attempts to inculcate specific religious doctrines. If this identification conveys a message of government endorsement or disapproval of religion, a core purpose of the Establishment clause is violated. . . .

In the programs challenged in this case, the religious school students spend their typical school day moving between religious-school and "public-school" classes. Both types of classes take place in the same religious-school building and both are largely composed of students who are adherents of the same denomination. In this environment, the students would be unlikely to discern the crucial difference between the religious-school classes and the "public-school" classes, even if the latter were successfully kept free of religious indoctrination. . . . This effect—the symbolic union of government and religion in one sectarian enterprise—is an impermissible effect under the Establishment Clause.

. . . With but one exception, our subsequent cases have struck down attempts by States to make payments out of public tax dollars directly to primary or secondary religious educational institutions. See, *e.g.*, *Committee for Public Education* v. *Nyquist,* 413 U.S., at 774-781 (reimbursement for maintenance and repair expenses); *Levitt* v. *Committee for Public Education,* 413 U.S. 472 (1973) (reimbursement for teacher-prepared tests); *Lemon* v. *Kurtzman,* 403 U.S. 602 (1971) (salary supplements for nonpublic school teachers). But see *Committee for Public Education* v. *Regan,* 444 U.S.

646 (1980) (permitting public subsidy for certain routinized recordkeeping and testing services performed by nonpublic schools but required by state law).

Aside from cash payments, the Court has distinguished between two categories of programs. . . . In the first category, the Court has noted that it is "well established . . . that not every law that confers an 'indirect,' 'remote,' or 'incidental' benefit upon religious institutions is, for that reason alone, constitutionally invalid." *Committee for Public Education* v. *Nyquist, supra,* at 771; *Roemer* v. *Maryland Public Works Board,* 426 U.S. 736, 747 (1976); *Hunt* v. *McNair,* 413 U.S., at 742-743. In such "indirect" aid cases, the government has used primarily secular means to accomplish a primarily secular end, and no "primary effect" of advancing religion has thus been found. On this rationale, the Court has upheld programs providing for loans of secular textbooks to nonpublic school students, *Board of Education* v. *Allen,* 392 U.S. 236 (1968); see also *Wolman* v. *Walter,* 433 U.S., at 236-238; *Meek* v. *Pittenger,* 421 U.S., at 359–362, and programs providing bus transportation for nonpublic school children, *Everson* v. *Board of Education, supra.*

In the second category of cases, the Court has relied on the Establishment Clause prohibition of forms of aid that provide "direct and substantial advancement of the sectarian enterprise." *Wolman* v. *Walter, supra,* at 250. In such "direct aid" cases, the government, although acting for a secular purpose, has done so by directly supporting a religious institution. Under this rationale, the Court has struck down state schemes providing for tuition grants and tax benefits for parents whose children attend religious school, see *Sloan* v. *Lemon,* 413 U.S. 825 (1973); *Committee for Public Education* v. *Nyquist, supra,* at 780–794, and programs providing for "loan" of instructional materials to be used in religious schools, see *Wolman* v. *Walter, supra,* at 248–251; *Meek* v. *Pittenger, supra,* at 365. In *Sloan* and *Nyquist,* the aid was formally given to parents and not directly to the religious schools, while in *Wolman* and *Meek,* the aid was in-kind assistance rather than the direct contribution of public funds. Nonetheless, these differences in form were insufficient to save programs whose effect was indistinguishable from that of a direct subsidy to the religious school. . . .

The question in each case must be whether the effect of the proffered aid is "direct and substantial," *Committee for Public Education* v. *Nyquist, supra,* at 784–785, n. 39, or indirect and incidental. "The problem, like many problems in constitutional law, is one of degree." *Zorach* v. *Clauson,* 343 U.S., at 314. . . . This kind of direct aid to the educational function of the religious school is indistinguishable from the provision of a direct cash subsidy to the religious school that is most clearly prohibited under the Establishment Clause. . . .

We conclude that the challenged programs have the effect of promoting religion in three ways. The state-paid instructors, influenced by the pervasively sectarian nature of the religious schools in which they work, may subtly or overtly indoctrinate the students in particular religious tenets at public expense. The symbolic union of church and state inherent in the provision of secular, state-provided instruction in the religious school buildings threatens to convey a message of state support for religion to students and to the general public. Finally, the programs in effect subsidize the religious functions of the parochial schools by taking over a substantial portion of their responsibility for teaching secular subjects. For these reasons, the conclusion is inescapable that the Community Education and Shared Time programs have the "primary or principal" effect of advancing religion, and therefore violate the dictates of the Establishment Clause of the First Amendment.

Chief Justice BURGER, concurring in the judgment in part and dissenting in part.

I agree with the Court that, under our decisions in *Lemon* v. *Kurtzman*, 403 U.S. 602 (1971), and *Earley* v. *DiCenso*, 403 U.S. 602 (1971), the Grand Rapids Community Education program violates the Establishment Clause. As to the Shared Time program, I dissent for the reasons stated in my dissenting opinion in *Aguilar* v. *Felton*, _____U.S. _____(1985).

Justice O'CONNOR, concurring in the judgment in part and dissenting in part.

For the reasons stated in my dissenting opinion in *Aguilar* v. *Felton*, _____U.S. _____, _____(1985), I dissent from the Court's holding that the Grand Rapids Shared Time program impermissibly advances religion. . . .

I agree with the Court, however, that the Community Education program violates the Establishment Clause. . . .

Justice WHITE, dissenting.

As evidenced by my dissenting opinions in *Lemon* v. *Kurtzman*, 403 U.S. 602, 661 (1971) and *Committee for Public Education* v. *Nyquist*, 413 U.S. 756, 813 (1973), I have long disagreed with the Court's interpretation and application of the Establishment Clause in the context of state aid to private schools. For the reasons stated in those dissents, I am firmly of the belief that the Court's decisions in these cases, like its decisions in *Lemon* and *Nyquist*, are "not required by the First Amendment and [are] contrary to the long-range interests of the country." 413 U.S., at 820. For those same reasons, I am satisfied that what the States have sought to do in these cases is well within their authority and is not forbidden by the Establishment Clause. Hence, I dissent and would reverse the judgment in each of these cases.

Justice REHNQUIST, dissenting.

I dissent for the reasons stated in my dissenting opinion in *Wallace* v. *Jaffree*, Nos. 83-812 and 83-929, _____U.S. _____. . . .

The Court today attempts to give content to the "effects" prong of the *Lemon* test by holding that a "symbolic link between government and religion" creates an impermissible effect. *Post*, at _____, slip op. at 11. But one wonders how the teaching of "Math Topics," "Spanish," and "Gymnastics," which is struck down today, creates a greater "symbolic link" than the municipal creche upheld in *Lynch* v. *Donelly*, 465 U.S. _____, or the legislative chaplain upheld in *Marsh* v. *Chambers*, 463 U.S. 783 (1983).

A most unfortunate result of *Grand Rapids* is that to support its holding the Court, despite its disclaimers, impugns the integrity of public school teachers. . . . Not one instance of attempted religious inculcation exists in the records of the school aid cases decided today, even though both the Grand Rapids and New York programs have been in operation for a number of years. I would reverse.

GLOSSARY

This glossary briefly explains selected legal terms of art not defined in the text itself, which are commonly used as shorthand references to describe legal principles and proceedings. The first part of the glossary lists terms derived from early English usage of Latin and Old French. The second part lists English words and phrases that have peculiar meaning in the law. For words not here listed, but that are defined in the text, the Index may provide a quick page reference. Since no glossary can pretend to cover the extensive lexicon of the law, even as condensed in abridged legal dictionaries, the lists here seek to cover only those terms most frequently encountered in this book.

Legal Phrases Drawn from Latin and French

Ab initio. From the very beginning.

Ad valorem. To the value. The phrase is used to describe property taxes based upon assessed value.

Amicus curiae. Friend of the court. Refers to one, not a party to the litigation, who submits a brief to direct the court's attention to particular arguments.

Arguendo. For the sake of argument.

Assumpsit. Suit on a contract.

Bona fide. In good faith. Refers to action taken innocently and without notice of legal deficiencies or adverse third party rights.

Caveat. A warning to take care.

Certiorari. One of the writs for gaining review by a higher court.

De facto. Derived from practice, not created by law. Used in contrast to "de jure."

De jure. Derived from law, i.e. founded in official authority or action.

De minimis. A matter of minimal importance, i.e., insufficient to command judicial relief.

De novo. A new legal proceeding, independent of prior findings.

Dicta (obiter). Remarks in court opinions not essential to the decision, and therefore not binding.

Ejusdem generis. A rule of statutory construction, whereby general words following a list of specific items are confined to matters of the same nature and kind as the specified items.

En banc. By the full bench, i.e. hearing by all of the judges of a particular court, rather than an individual or panel of judges selected from the full body.

Et al. And others.

Et seq. And the following. Usually refers to pages following a referenced page.

Ex officio. By reason of holding a public office.

Ex parte. From one party only. Refers to proceeding brought without notice to an adverse party.

Ex rel. Out of relation. Refers to proceeding instigated by an individual that is brought in the name of the state.

Ibid. In the same place.

Idem. The very same. Refers to a prior citation, to avoid repetition.

Inclusio unius est exclusio alterius. A rule of construction whereby coverage or authorization of one matter is deemed to exclude other matters.

Infra. Below—usually referring to later text or citation.

In loco parentis. In the place of the parent.

In pari materia. On like subject matter.

In re. In the matter of.

Inter alia. Among other things.

Ipsi dixit. He or it speaks for himself or itself.

Ipso facto. By reason of the fact itself.

Mandamus. Action to compel official to perform a ministerial duty.

Modus operandi. The mode or method of accomplishing a result.

Non sequitur. It does not follow. A fallacy in logic.

N.O.V. [non obstante verdicto]. Notwithstanding the verdict. A judgment N.O.V. reverses the jury verdict as unsupported by fact or law.

Nunc pro tunc. Now for then. A retroactive ruling.

Per curiam. By the court—usually signifying an unsigned judicial opinion.

Per se. By itself; not requiring further support.

Prima facie. On its face. A case sufficient at first view. A prima facie finding is rebuttable by additional proofs.

Quantum meruit. The amount that is deserved. Recovery of reasonable value to avoid unjust enrichment.

Quasi. Nearly, but not quite, like.

Quo warranto. By what authority. Name of writ to test office.

Ratio decidendi. The rationale of a judicial decision.

Res ipsa loquitur. The thing speaks for itself. A rule of proof.

Res judicata. Adjudicated matter which bars subsequent litigation by the same parties on the same subject.

Respondeat superior. Let the master answer (for the acts of his servant). A tort doctrine.

Scienter. Knowledge (of operative facts).

Sine die. Without day. A public session adjournment without appointing a future day for reassembly.

Stare decisis. To stand by the decision. The basis of relying upon prior decisions (precedents).

Sua sponte. Of its own volition; on its own motion.

Subpoena. Court order to appear at a designated time and place, to produce testimony or records.

Supra. Above; referring to preceding text or cases.

Ultra vires. Beyond (in excess of) official authority.

Vel non. Or not.

Volenti non fit injuria. A volunteer may not claim injury arising from his or her volunteered conduct.

English Terminology Having Special Meaning in the Law

Abandonment. Knowing relinquishment of one's right to property or position.

Abatement. Reduction, suspension or termination of a legal obligation or proceeding.

Abridge. To shorten. In constitutional law, to interfere with.

Abuse of discretion. Basis for overturning an administrative agency ruling, by a court.

Action (at law). A lawsuit.

Affidavit. A written declaration under oath.

Affirmative Action. Intentional preference of disadvantaged minorities as a remedy for past disadvantage.

Agency shop. Employment situations wherein employees are by law required to pay service fees to the union that is the exclusive bargaining representative of employees.

Appearance. Entry of a party in a legal proceeding.

Appellant. A party who appeals a trial decision to a higher court.

Appellee. A party against whom an appeal is taken.

Arbitrator. A person chosen to resolve a dispute.

Assault. An offer or threat to inflict physical harm.

Assignment. A transfer.

Battery. Unlawful contact with the person of another.

Bond. A written promise containing guarantees or security for performance.

Brief. Written argument presented by lawyers to a court.

Cause of action. Basis for a legal claim or lawsuit.

Class action. A suit brought on behalf of a large class of individuals by one or more representative members of that class.

Cohabitation. A living together by members of the opposite sex, usually involving sexual intercourse.

Color of law. Under the appearance or aegis of legal authority.

Common law. Law developed by courts through case decisions, independently of written statutes or constitutions.

Complaint. The pleading by a party instituting a lawsuit that alleges the grievance and request for relief.

Complainant. See plaintiff.

Consideration. In contract law, the bargained for value given in exchange for another's promise.

Contempt of court. Conduct that interferes with or disobeys court order or proceedings.

Contract. A legally enforceable promise or set of promises.

Corporation. A fictional entity or person that is created by law, but does not exist in nature.

Counterclaim. A demand by a defendant against a plaintiff.

Covenant. An agreement or promise.

Damages. Monetary compensation to redress a legal injury.

Defendant. The party against whom a legal proceeding is brought.

Delegation. The transfer of authority.

Demurrer. Objection to a pleading as legally insufficient.

Deposition. Record of written testimony under oath, not taken at trial.

Directory. A legal instruction that is not "mandatory."

Discretion. An exercise of judgment and choice.

Duress. Unlawful coercion.

Emancipation. Legal release from another's control, e.g., of a married child from parents.

Eminent domain. The sovereign power of government to take private property for public use.

Enjoin. To order forebearance or action.

Estoppel. Equitable doctrine to preclude assertion or denial of a fact or promise.

Excise. A tax on a privilege.

Executory. An incomplete transaction or interest.

Expunge. Delete completely, e.g., from a court record.

Felony. A class of serious crimes, as distinguished from lesser offenses called misdemeanors.

Fornication. Sexual intercourse between unmarried persons.

Forum. The court or place where disputes are heard.

Grievance. A claim of injury. In collective bargaining a procedure to resolve disputes.

Holding. A court's decision.

Hung jury. A jury whose members cannot agree on a verdict.

Immunity. Exemption from legal obligations or liability, based upon legal status.

Implied. Not expressed, but inferred.

Infancy. The age below that of legal majority.

Invitee. A visitor by invitation, as distinguished from a trespasser.

Judgment. The final finding in a legal proceeding.

Jurisdiction. The lawful authority to manage or decide particular activities or disputes.

Latent defect. A defect not reasonably ascertainable by normal observation.

Libel. An unprivileged defamatory publication.

Licensee. In tort law, a party permitted to enter property for his own purposes—not an invitee.

Mandate. A legal command.

Ministerial. A directed act that does not involve discretionary decision.

Minority. Not of legal age.

Misdemeanor. See felony.

Mitigation of damages. Duty of injured person to minimize losses caused by another's breach of obligation.

Motion. A request for a court ruling.

Opinion. A court's essay explaining its decision.

Petitioner. Party asking for relief by a trial or appeals court.

Plagiarism. Use of the composition of another as one's own product.

Plaintiff. The party who brings a law suit.

Police power. The inherent power of government to promote public welfare.

Privilege. An advantage accorded by law to a particular class of persons.

Probative. Having evidentiary value.

Quorum. The number of members required for lawful action by an official assembly.

Remand. A return of a case, for further proceedings, to the tribunal from which it was appealed.

Respondent. The party answering a complaint or petition.

Restitution. The restoration of value received, in kind or money, to make good another's loss.

Review. Judicial reconsideration of a decision by an administrative agency or a lower court.

Slander. Defamation by oral communication; as distinguished from libel.

Syllabus. An abridged statement of a court's decision that precedes the full court opinion.

Tender. An offer to perform a particular act.

Trespass. An unlawful interference with another's person or property. In pleading, a form of action to recover damages for such interference.

Unilateral. Action taken by one party only.

Venue. A place selected for trial.

Verdict. The finding of a jury.

Vested. Complete and fixed; not contingent.

Vicarious. A party's right or obligation imputed from the actions of another. See, e.g., respondeat superior.

Void. Without any legal force.

Voidable. Capable of being voided under certain circumstances.

Waiver. A voluntary and knowing surrender of particular rights or immunities.

Writ. Official order of a court or tribunal commanding a response or action.

Zoning. Legislative restrictions on locality, uses and construction of particular classes of real property.

TABLE OF CASES

The cases in bold type represent Supreme Court decisions and cases reproduced at the end of each chapter. All other cases are cited in the footnotes on the indicated pages.

A.A.B. Elec. Inc. *v.* Stevenson Public School District, 503
Aaron *v.* McKinley, 363
Abbott *v.* Board of Educ., 221
ABC League *v.* Missouri H.S. Activities Assn., 92
Abercrombie *v.* McClung, 443
Aberdeen Educ. Assn. *v.* Aberdeen Board of Educ., 246, 248
Abood *v.* Detroit Board of Educ., 245, 249
Abraham *v.* Wallenpaupak Area School District, 73
Abrahamson *v.* Hershman, 384
Abrams *v.* Ambach, 196
Acanfora *v.* Board of Educ., 216
Achenbach *v.* School District, 496
Ackerman *v.* Board of Educ., 378
Ackerman *v.* Rubin, 81
Adamek *v.* Pennsylvania Interscholastic Athletic Assn., 93
Adams *v.* Tasche, 446, 450
Adcock *v.* Board of Educ., 198, 234
Adelt *v.* Richmond School District, 198
AFSCME, AFL-CIO *v.* Woodward, 240
Aquilar v. Felton, 611–620
Ahern *v.* Board of Educ., 211
Aiken County Board of Educ. *v.* Knotts, 482, 484
Ajluni *v.* Board of Educ., 221
Akers *v.* Bolton, 383
Akron Board of Educ. *v.* State Board of Educ., 363
Alex *v.* Allen, 308, 309
Alexander *v.* Gardner-Denver Co., 454
Alexander *v.* Phillips, 69, 82
Alexander *v.* School District No. 17, 224
Alexander *v.* Yale Univ., 379
Alexander *v.* Youngstown Board of Educ., 361
Alford *v.* Dept. of Educ., 181
Allegheny West Civil Council, Inc. *v.* Zoning Board of Adj., 547
Allen *v.* Hickel, 132
Allen *v.* LaSalle Par. School Board, 431
Allen *v.* Morton, 132
Allred *v.* State, 336
Alvin Ind. School District *v.* Cooper, 330
Alyeska Pipeline Service Co. *v.* The Wilderness Society, 455
Amador *v.* New Mexico State Board of Educ., 189
Amato *v.* Oxford Area Comm. School District, 199
Ambach *v.* Norwick, 185
Ambrose *v.* Comm. School Board, 184
Amburgey *v.* Cassady, 212, 234
American Asphalt Distributors Inc. *v.* County of Otsego, 503
American Civil Liberties Union of So. California *v.* Board of Educ. of Los Angeles, 100
American Federation of Teachers *v.* Oakland Unified School District, 198
Americans United for Separation of Church and State *v.* Blanton, 570, 575, 577
Americans United for Separation of Church and State *v.* Bubb, 570
Americans United for Separation of Church and State *v.* Paire, 134, 135
Americans United, Inc. *v.* Ind. School District, 576
Anderson *v.* Banks, 95, 383
Anderson *v.* City of Bessemer, 376
Anderson *v.* Ind. School District, 211
Anderson *v.* Salt Lake City, 132
Anderson *v.* San Francisco Un. School District, 370
Anderson *v.* So. Dakota H.S. Activities, 92
Andreozzi *v.* Rubano, 432
Andreson *v.* Ohm, 441
Andrews *v.* Drew Mun. Separate School District, 209, 215
Angwin *v.* City of Manchester, 186
Ankers *v.* District School Board, 428
Anonymous *v.* Board of Educ., 211
Anonymous *v.* Board of Examiners (N.Y.S.), 181
Appeal of Flannery, 213
Appeal of Ganaposki, 193
Applebaum *v.* Nemon, 442, 565
Application of Auster, 539
Application of Bay *v.* State Board of Educ., 183
Archdiocese of Portland *v.* County of Washington, 546
Areba School Corp. *v.* Mayor and Council of Twp. of Randolph, 548
Arglo Painting Corp. *v.* Board of Educ., 503
Arlington Heights *v.* Metropolitan Housing Corp., 367
Arlington Ind. Sch. District *v.* Weekley, 192
Armlin *v.* Board of Educ., 438
Arnett *v.* Kennedy, 228
Arnold *v.* Crockett Ind. School District, 485
Arnold *v.* Hafling, 442
Arnolt *v.* City of Highland Park, 448
Aronson *v.* No. Pork College, 555
Art Gaines Baseball Camp, Inc. *v.* Houston, 90
Arthur *v.* Nyquist, 362
Ashley *v.* Rye School District, 482
Aspira *v.* Board of Educ., 366
Atherton *v.* Superior Court of San Mateo County, 68–69
Atkins *v.* City of Charlotte, 240
Attorney General *v.* Bailey, 540, 541
Attorney General *v.* Dover, 546
Attorney General *v.* Massachusetts Interscholastic Assn., 374
Attorney General *v.* School Committee of Northhampton, 53
Aubrey *v.* School District of Phila., 444
Aubuchon *v.* Gasconade, R-1 School District, 226, 228
Auerbach *v.* African-American Teachers Assn., 370
Aulwurm *v.* Board of Educ., 211
Austin Ind. School District *v.* United States, 361
Austin Ind. School District *v.* Morris, 30
Austin Ind. School District *v.* Sunset Valley, 68
Austin *v.* Housing Auth'y, 504
Avard *v.* Dupuis, 29, 30, 138
Avery *v.* Homewood City Board of Educ., 215, 376
Avon *v.* Old Farm School, 434
Axtell *v.* LaPenna, 431
Ayala v. Philadelphia Public Board of Educ., 440, 467–470
Ayers *v.* Lincoln County School District, 226
Ayres *v.* Junek, 47

B.M. *v.* State, 444
Babb *v.* Moore, 448
Backman *v.* Bateman, 188
Baer *v.* Nyquist, 32, 203
Baikie *v.* Luther H.S. South, 562

Bailey *v.* Gallatin County Board of Educ., 441
Baird *v.* Hosmer, 429
Baker *v.* Downey City Board of Educ., 308, 318
Baker *v.* Owen, 432
Baker *v.* Un. School District No. 346, 68, 488
Bakke Case, 370–371
Balaban-Gordon Co. *v.* Brighton Sewer District, 502
Bales *v.* Clarke, 384
Ball *v.* Bunch, 182
Ball *v.* Kerriville Ind. School District, 236
Ballard *v.* Gregory, 42
Ballard *v.* Polly, 430
Baltic Ind. School District *v.* So. Dakota H.S. Activities Assn., 93
Bangor Baptist Church *v.* State, 540, 543
Banks *v.* Comm. School Board No. 29, 199
Banks *v.* Terrebone Parish School Board, 437, 439
Bankston *v.* Pulaski County School Board, 447
Bannister *v.* Paradis, 323, 324
Barbato *v.* Board of Educ., 437
Barnes *v.* Fair Dismissal Board, 211
Barnhardt Ind. School District *v.* Mertzon Ind. School District, 49
Baron *v.* Mackreth, 203
Barr *v.* Bernhard, 429
Barr *v.* Matteo, 450
Barrett *v.* E. Iowa Community College District, 225
Barrett *v.* Phillips, 427, 435
Barrington School Committee *v.* Rhode Island State Labor Relations Board, 247
Barron *v.* Mayor and City Council of Baltimore, 537
Barth *v.* Board of Education, 494
Barth *v.* Philadelphia School District, 21
Bartlett *v.* Board of Trustees, 79
Barton *v.* Governing Board of Middletown Un. School District, 201
Bassett *v.* Braddock, 51
Bates *v.* Dause, 202, 257, 453
Bates *v.* Hinds, 182, 183, 221, 225, 227
Bauch *v.* City of New York, 251
Bauer *v.* Board of Educ., 438
Baughman *v.* Feienmuth, 318
Bay *v.* State Board of Educ., 181
Bayer *v.* Kinzler, 319
Beard *v.* Board of Educ., 73, 98
Beardsell *v.* Tilton School, 567
Beattie *v.* Roberts, 36
Beaudeof *v.* State Board of Educ., 240
Beck *v.* Board of Educ., 493
Beck *v.* San Francisco Un. School District, 427, 437
Becker *v.* Beaverton School District, 429
Becket *v.* Roderick, 205
Bednar *v.* Nebraska School Activities Assn., 374
Bedrock Foundations, Inc. *v.* G.E. Brewster & Son, 446, 450
Beeson *v.* Kiowa City School District, 330
Begich *v.* Jefferson, 189
Beilan *v.* Board of Public Education, 209, 210, 217
Belanger *v.* Matteson, 254
Belcher *v.* Mansi, 52
Bell *v.* Lone Oak Independent School District, 330
Bell *v.* West Point Mun. Separate School District, 363
Bellnier *v.* Lund, 325, 328
Bender *v.* Williamsport Area School Dist., 162–168, 217
Benedetto *v.* Travelers Ins. Co., 566
Benton *v.* School Board of Broward County, 426
Berg *v.* Berger, 222
Berkelman *v.* San Francisco Un. School District, 373
Berman *v.* Philadelphia Board of Educ., 429, 439
Bernasconi *v.* Tempe Elementary School District No. 3, 234
Bernerd *v.* Shelburne, 94
Bernesak *v.* Catholic Bishop, 563, 566
Bernhard *v.* Kerrville Ind. School District, 446
Berry *v.* Arnold School District, 432
Berry *v.* Board of Supervisors, 379
Bertola *v.* Board of Education, 437
Bertot *v.* School District No. 1, 220, 230, 234
Bessler *v.* Board of Chartered School District, 207
Bethlehem Steel *v.* Board of Educ., 485
Betterson *v.* Stewart, 213
Beverlin *v.* Board of Educ., 33, 212
Biancardi *v.* Waldwick Board of Educ., 195
Bicknell *v.* Vergennes Union H.S. Board, 88, 208
Bierman *v.* Campbell, 23
Big Sandy District *v.* Carroll, 48, 496
Biklen *v.* Syracuse Board of Education, 185, 224
Bilardi Const. Co. *v.* Spencer, 488
Bilbrey *v.* Brown, 325
Bilby, State ex rel. *v.* Brooks, 46
Birdwell *v.* Hazelwood School District, 211
Birmingham & Lamphere School Districts *v.* Sup't of Public Inst., 384
Bischoff *v.* Brothers of Sacred Heart, 549
Bishop *v.* Starkville Academy, 556, 559, 562
Bishop *v.* Wood, 34, 220, 222
Black *v.* School Committee of Malden, 377
Black *v.* Wyalusing Area School Dist., 201
Blackburn *v.* Board of Educ., 225
Blackmore *v.* Jasper City Comm. Un. School District No. 1, 206
Blackwell *v.* Issaquena County Board of Educ., 315
Blair *v.* Board of Educ., 441
Blair *v.* Robstown Ind. School District, 193, 226
Blanchet *v.* Vermilion Parish School Board, 236
Bloch *v.* Hillel Torah Northern Sub. Day School, 555
Bloomburgh-Dubin *v.* Board of Educ., 184
Blue *v.* Stockton, 484
Bluemer *v.* Turner, 30
Blumer *v.* School Board of Beresford Ind. School District, 485
Blunt *v.* State Board of Educ., 209
Board of Curators *v.* Horowitz, 307
Board of Directors of Ind. School District *v.* Green, 330
Board of Directors of N. Pocono Sch. District *v.* Gouldsboro Taxpayers Ass'n, 485
Board of Directors *v.* Merrymeeting Educ. Assn., 254
Board of Educ. of Charles County *v.* Crawford, 224
Board of Educ. of City of Lincoln Park *v.* Board of Educ. of Detroit, 44
Board of Educ. of Freeport *v.* Nyquist, 493
Board of Educ. of Iron Mountain *v.* Voelker, 483
Board of Educ. of Long Beach *v.* Unified School District, 184, 213–214, 294–298
Board of Educ. of Mountain Lakes *v.* Mass., 138
Board of Educ. of Oakland Schools *v.* Supt. Pub. Instr., 483
Board of Educ. of Okay Ind. School District *v.* Carrol, 86
Board of Educ. of Pendleton Co. *v.* Gulick, 497
Board of Educ. of W. Orange *v.* W. Orange Educ. Assn., 247
Board of Educ. *v.* Akers, 182
Board of Educ. *v.* Allen, 576, 578
Board of Educ. *v.* Ambach, 95, 383
Board of Educ. *v.* Antone, 576
Board of Educ. *v.* Areman, 248, 253
Board of Educ. *v.* Bellemore-Merrick Soc. Teachers, 254
Board of Educ. *v.* Bentley, 330
Board of Educ. *v.* Burkett, 227

Board of Educ. *v.* Calvert, 494
Board of Educ. *v.* Chicago Teachers Union, 253, 483
Board of Educ. *v.* Detroit Fed. of Teachers, 257
Board of Educ. *v.* Englewood Teachers Assn., 254
Board of Educ. *v.* Finne, Lyman and Finne, 497
Board of Educ. *v.* Fredericks, 434
Board of Educ. *v.* Greenburgh Teachers Educ., 254
Board of Educ. *v.* Hall, 499
Board of Educ. *v.* Harrison Assn. of Teachers, 254
Board of Educ. *v.* Hoek, 499
Board of Educ. *v.* Jennings, 214
Board of Educ. *v.* Johnson, 241
Board of Educ. *v.* Kankakee Fed. of Teachers, 256
Board of Educ. *v.* Mayor and Council of Borough of Fair Lawn, 482
Board of Educ. *v.* Messer, 175
Board of Educ. *v.* Metskas, 217
Board of Educ. *v.* Millette, 214
Board of Educ. *v.* National Gay Task Force, 215
Board of Educ. *v.* Newark Teachers Union, 256
Board of Educ. *v.* Niagara Wheatfield Teachers, 254
Board of Educ. *v.* North Bergen Fed. of Teachers, 246, 253
Board of Educ. *v.* Nyquist, 197
Board of Educ. *v.* Ohio Educ. Assn., 256
Board of Educ. *v.* Oklahoma School Board of Educ., 79
Board of Educ. *v.* Park District of Minot, 70
Board of Educ. *v.* Peoria Educ. Assn., 256
Board of Educ. *v.* Philadelphia Federation of Teachers, 186, 254
Board of Educ. *v.* Phillips, 71
Board of Educ. *v.* Pico, 213
Board of Educ. *v.* Porter, 483
Board of Educ. *v.* Poughkeepsie P.S. Teachers Assn., 247
Board of Educ. *v.* Presque Island County Board of Educ., 30
Board of Educ. *v.* Rockaway Twp. Educ. Assn., 31, 47
Board of Educ. *v.* Rockford Education Assn., 31, 47, 241
Board of Educ. *v.* Sever-Williams Co., 502, 503
Board of Educ. *v.* Shank, 211
Board of Educ. *v.* Shanker, 255
Board of Educ. *v.* Sinclair, 224, 491, 492, 493
Board of Educ. *v.* State Bd. of Education (N.M.), 52
Board of Educ. *v.* State Board of Education (Ohio), 21
Board of Educ. *v.* State Division of Human Rts. (N.Y.), 378
Board of Educ. *v.* Superintendent of Public Instr. (Mich.), 484
Board of Educ. *v.* Wheat, 576
Board of Educ. *v.* Williams, 198, 200, 202
Board of Educ. *v.* Wis. Employment Relations Comm., 251
Board of Educ. *v.* Yonkers Fed. of Teachers, 247
Board of Educ., Borough of Union Beach *v.* N.J. Educ. Assn., 255
Board of Educ., Island Tree Union Free District *v.* Pico, 88–89
Board of Educ., Levittown, etc. *v.* Nyquist, 484
Board of Educ., School District V *v.* Bakalis, 30, 576
Board of Educ., Town of Huntington *v.* Assn. Teachers of Hunt., 253
Board of Education of Long Beach Un. Sch. District of Los Angeles County *v.* Jack, 294–298
Board of Education *v.* Board of Education, 491
Board of Education *v.* Common Council, 68
Board of Education *v.* Pico, 89, 114–120
Board of Education, Union Free School District No. 3 *v.* NEA, 255
Board of Public Educ. *v.* Intille, 229
Board of Public Instruction *v.* Soler, 210
Board of Public Instruction of Taylor County *v.* Finch, 371
Board of Regents U. of Nebraska *v.* Dawes, 379
Board of Regents *v.* City of Tempe, 71
Board of Regents *v.* Roth, 220, 221, 222
Board of Regents *v.* U.P.W.A., 241
Board of School Commissioners of Indianapolis *v.* Buckley, 369
Board of School Directors *v.* Dock, 79
Board of School Directors *v.* Pittinger, 201
Board of School Directors *v.* Wis. Employment Relations Comm., 251
Board of School Trustees *v.* Brenner, 483
Board of School Trustees *v.* O'Brien, 204
Board of Selectment of Pittsfield *v.* School Board, 482
Board of Trustees of Keene State College *v.* Sweeney, 376
Board of Trustees *v.* Board of County Comm'rs., 485
Board of Trustees *v.* Cook Cty. College Teachers Union, 254
Board of Trustees *v.* Perini, 181, 186
Board of Trustees *v.* Spiegel, 225
Board of Trustees *v.* Stubblefield, 209, 213
Board of Zoning Appeals *v.* Schulte, 546
Bob Jones University *v.* United States, 557
Bodano *v.* Wayne-Westland Comm. School, 447
Boise Junior College District *v.* Mattefs Construction Co., 502, 526–530
Bolling *v.* Sharpe, 359, 362
Bond *v.* Ann Arbor School District, 492
Bonner *v.* Lyons School Committee, 99
Borg *v.* Kolmorgen, 132
Borough *v.* Governing Board of El Segundo Un. School District, 86
Boston Teachers Union *v.* School Committee, 248
Bott *v.* Board of Educ., 33
Bottorf *v.* Waltz, 439
Bovino *v.* Board of School Directors, 209
Bowen *v.* U.S., 362
Boyce *v.* Alexis I. duPont School District, 31
Boyce *v.* Board of Educ., 204
Boyd *v.* Mary E. Dill School District, 31
Boykins *v.* Fairfield Board of Educ., 304, 310, 313
Boynton *v.* Casey, 305
Brackman *v.* Adrian, 566
Bradford Cent. Sch. District *v.* Ambach, 180
Bradford *v.* Board of Education, 90
Bradford *v.* School District No. 20, 213, 217
Bradley *v.* Cathern, 377
Bradley *v.* School Board, 362
Braesch *v.* DePasquale, 313
Brand *v.* Sertoma Club of Springfield, 437
Brandon *v.* Board of Educ. of Guilderland Central School Dist., 127
Brandon Valley Ind. School District *v.* Minnehaha County Board of Educ., 32
Brandt *v.* Zoning Board of Appeals of New Castle, 548
Branti *v.* Finkel, 234
Brantley *v.* Surles, 235
Braxton *v.* Board of Public Instruction, 235
Breese *v.* Smith, 323
Brenden *v.* Minnesota State H.S. League, 93, 374
Brennan *v.* Ace Hardware Corp., 454
Brice *v.* Landis, 363, 372
Bright *v.* Isenbarger, 554, 556
Bright *v.* L.A. Un. School District, 317
Briscoe *v.* School District, 436
Barth *v.* Philadelphia School District, 21
Bristol Twp. Educ. Assn. *v.* School District of Bristol Twp., 256
Brodie *v.* School Committee, 195

Brokaw *v.* Black-Foxe Military Inst., 567
Bromley *v.* Wilks, 188
Bronaugh *v.* Murray, 448
Bronestine *v.* Geinsendorfer, 79
Broolhart *v.* Illinois State Board, 95
Brooks *v.* Board of Educ., 438
Brooks *v.* School Board of Brevard County, 35
Brookville *v.* Paulgene Realty Corp., 545
Brophy *v.* School Committee, 195
Brough *v.* Board of Education, 198
Brown *v.* Bathke, 215
Brown *v.* Board of Educ., 195, 218, 362, 438
Brown *v.* Calhoun County, 426
Brown *v.* Dade Christian Schools, Inc. 557
Brown *v.* Heller, 135
Brown *v.* Houston Ind. School District, 129
Brown *v.* Jefferson County, 488
Brown *v.* Kirk, 498
Brown *v.* N. Carolina Wesleyan College, 562
Brown *v.* Oakland, 429
Brown *v.* Patterson, 47
Brown *v.* Portland School District, 449
Brown *v.* Portsmouth School District, 210
Brown *v.* South Carolina State Board of Educ., 363
Brown *v.* Stone, 78
Brownsville Area School District *v.* Lucostic, 202
Brubaker *v.* Board of Educ., 212, 226, 443
Brunetti *v.* City of Berkeley, 370
Bryant *v.* St. Helena Par. School Board, 230
Bryant *v.* Thunderbird Academy, 567
Bucha *v.* Illinois High School Assn., 374
Buck *v.* Board of Educ., 224
Buford *v.* Morgantown City Board of Educ., 361
Buford *v.* Southeast Dubois County School Corp., 133, 136
Buhr *v.* Buffalo Public School District No. 38, 206, 222
Bunger *v.* Iowa High School Athletic Assn., 23, 92, 313
Bunsen *v.* County Board of School Trustees, 50–51
Burke County Board of Educ. *v.* Raley, 440
Burkey *v.* Marshall County Board of Educ., 376
Burkitt *v.* School District, 337
Burnside *v.* Byars, 315
Burton *v.* Cascade School District Union H.S. No. 5, 209, 213, 216
Burton *v.* Wilmington Parking Authority, 99
Burtt *v.* Nassau County Athletic Assn., 93
Buse *v.* Smith, 484
Bush *v.* Norwalk, 447
Bush *v.* Oscoda Area Schools, 439
Busker *v.* Board of Educ., 230
Bustop, Inc. *v.* Board of Education of the City of Los Angeles, 372
Butler *v.* Federal Way School District, 503
Butsche *v.* Coon Rapids Community School Dist., 36, 489
Butts *v.* School District, 316
Buzzard *v.* Eastlake School District, 437
Bynum *v.* Alto Ind. School District, 485

Cabell *v.* State, 433
Cadieux *v.* Board of Educ., 439
Cain *v.* Archdiocese of Kansas City, 560
Calandri *v.* Ione Un. School District, 439
Caldwell *v.* Cannady, 305
Caldwell *v.* Craighead, 316
Calhoun *v.* Cassidy, 198, 201, 233
California School Employees Assn. *v.* Board of Trustees, 138, 247
California School Employees Assn. *v.* Sequoia Union H.S. Dist., 126
California School Employees Assn. *v.* Willits Un. Sch. District, 496
California Teachers Assn. *v.* Board of Education, 492
Calloway *v.* Ouachita Parish School Board, 483
Caltavuturo *v.* City of Passaic, 434
Calvin *v.* Rupp, 212
Calway *v.* Williamson, 433
Camara *v.* Municipal Court, 326
Camardo *v.* Bd. of Educ. of City School District, 44
Camden City Voc. *v.* Cam/Voc Teachers, 246
Campbell Elementary Teachers Assn., Inc. *v.* Abbott, 86
Campbell *v.* St. School District, 495
Campbell *v.* Talledega County Board of Education, 383
Canal National Bank *v.* School Administrative District, 44
Candelari *v.* Board of Educ., 200
Canney *v.* Board of Public Instruction, 307
Cannon *v.* U. of Chicago and Northwestern U., 454
Canon-McMillan School Board *v.* Commonwealth, 247
Canon-McMillan School District *v.* Hum. Rel. Comm., 378
Canter *v.* Lake City Baseball Club, 98
Cantwell *v.* Connecticut, 139, 537
Cape *v.* Tenn. Sec. School Athletic Assn., 374, 375
Cappel *v.* Board of Educ., 434
Carabba *v.* Anacortes School District, 439
Caravello *v.* Board of Educ., 213
Cardiff *v.* Bismarck Public School District, 518–524
Carey *v.* Piphus, 471–474
Caristo Construction Corp. *v.* Rubin, 501
Carl S. *v.* Comm. for Teacher Preparation, 183
Carl *v.* So. San Antonio Ind. School District, 206
Carne *v.* Tenn. Sec. School Athletic Assn., 375
Carpenter *v.* City of Greenfield School District, 222
Carpio *v.* Tucson H.S. District, 493
Carr *v.* Wright, 432
Carrao *v.* Board of Educ., 212
Carroll *v.* Lucas, 129, 444
Carrollton-Farmers Branch Independent School District *v.* Knight, 330
Carson *v.* State, 68
Carter County Board of Educ. *v.* Am. Fed. of Teachers, 483
Carter *v.* Allen, 32
Carter *v.* Carlson, 445
Cartwright *v.* Sharpe, 74
Cary *v.* Board of Educ., 88, 237, 238
Cataldo Const. Co. *v.* County of Essex, 502
Catholic Bishop of Chicago *v.* Kingery, 546
Catholic High School Assn. *v.* Culvert, 551, 552
Caufield *v.* Board of Educ., 376
Cedar Rapids Comm. School District *v.* City of Cedar Rapids, 69
Cedar *v.* Commissioner of Education, 219
Celestine *v.* Lafayette Parish School Board, 210, 239
Central Pt. School District *v.* Emp. Rel. Board, 254
Chamberlain *v.* Dade County Board of Public Instruction, 133
Chambers *v.* Board of Educ., Lisbon Cent. School District, 86
Chambers *v.* Omaha P. School District, 450
Chance *v.* Board of Examiners and Board of Educ., 368, 369
Chandler *v.* So. Bend Comm. School Corp., 491, 493
Channel No. 10, Inc. *v.* Ind. School District, 51, 58–62
Chappel *v.* Franklin Pierce School District, 442
Charles Co. Supp. Services Emp. Local Union 301 *v.* Board of Educ., 244
Charronat *v.* San Francisco Un. School District, 437

Chartiers Valley Jt. Schools *v.* County Board of School Directors, 21, 44
Chatham Assn. of Educ. *v.* Board of Public Educ., 32, 248
Chatham *v.* Johnson, 189
Chaves *v.* School Committee of Town of Middletown, 73
Chavez *v.* Tolleson El. School District, 564
Chavich *v.* Board of Educ. of City of New York, 197
Chavick *v.* Board of Examiners, 181
Cheney *v.* Strasburger, 70
Cherney *v.* Board of Educ., 438
Chester School District Audit, 48
Chicago Teachers Union *v.* Hudson, 293–294
Chicago *v.* Sachs, 546
Child Welfare Society of Flint *v.* Kennedy School District, 20, 21
Chimerofsky *v.* School District, 433
Chippewa Valley Schools *v.* Hill, 254
Choal *v.* Lyman Ind. School District, 79
Christian Brothers Institute *v.* No. N.J. Int. League, 93
Christofides *v.* Hellenic Eastern Orthodox Christian Church, 566
Christopherson *v.* Spring Valley Elem. Sch. District, 211
Church (R.C.) *v.* Keenan, 567
Church of God Worldwide Texas Region *v.* Amarillo, 126
Church *v.* Board of Educ., 323
Cianci *v.* Board of Educ., 435–436
Cintron *v.* State Board of Educ., 309, 319
Cioffi *v.* Board of Educ., 437
Cipu *v.* No. Haven Board of Educ., 191
Cirillo *v.* City of Milwaukee, 459–461
Cisneros *v.* Corpus Christi Ind. School District, 365
Citizens Against Mandatory Bussing *v.* Palmason, 372
Citizens for Parental Rights *v.* San Mateo Board of Educ., 131, 148–156
Citizens to Advance Public Education *v.* Porter, 135
City of Beloit *v.* WERC and Beloit Educ. Assn., 247
City of Biddeford *v.* Biddeford Teachers Assn., 253
City of Bloomfield *v.* Davis County Community School District, 69
City of Concord *v.* New Testament Baptist Church, 546
City of Crockett *v.* Murdock, 500
City of Dallas *v.* Mosely, 82
City of Eastlake *v.* Forest City Enterprises, Inc., 23
City of Grand Rapids *v.* Ball, 135
City of Madison Jt. School District No. 8 *v.* Wisconsin Employment Relations Comm., 252
City of Miami Beach *v.* State ex rel. Lear, 546
City of New Rochelle *v.* New Rochelle Federation of Teachers, 247
City of Phoenix *v.* Phoenix Civil Auditorium and Convention Center Assn., 489
City of Rockford *v.* Local 113, IAF, 256
City of San Diego *v.* AFSCME, Local 127, 240
City of Summer *v.* First Baptist Church, 545, 547
City University *v.* Board of Higher Education, 195
Civil Service Comm. *v.* National Assn. of Letter Carriers, 189
Clanton *v.* Orleans Parish School Board, 378
Clark City School District *v.* Local Govt. Relations Board, 246
Clark Co. Classroom Teachers Assn. *v.* Clark Co. School Distr., 251
Clark *v.* Ariz. Interscholastic Assn., 374
Clark *v.* Arizona Interscholastic Assn., 93
Clark *v.* Mt. Greylock Regional H.S. District, 201
Clark, In re, 78, 138
Clary *v.* Alexander City Board of Educ., 446
Claus *v.* Babiarz, 501
Clayton *v.* Board of Educ., 210, 212
Clear Creek School District RE-1 *v.* Holmes, 70
Cleveland Board of Education *v.* LaFleur, 377
Close *v.* Lederle, 237
Coalition to Preserve Education *v.* School District, 496
Coates *v.* Ambach, 195
Coates *v.* Tacoma School District, 442
Cobb *v.* Pasadena City Board of Educ., 500
Cochran *v.* Louisiana Board of Educ., 577
Codd *v.* Velger, 222
Coe *v.* Bogart, 181, 198
Coen *v.* Boulder Valley School District, 222
Coffman *v.* Kuehler, 305
Cohen *v.* Chesterfield County School Board, 377
Cohen *v.* State, 21
Cohoes City School District *v.* Cohoes Teachers' Assn., 246
Colclough *v.* Orleans Parish Board, 439
Cole *v.* Richardson, 185
Cole *v.* Taylor, 445
Colella (A.J.) Inc. *v.* Allegheny County, 503
Coleman *v.* Beaumont Ind. School District, 448
Collins *v.* Chandler Union School District, 127
Collins *v.* Wakonda Ind. Sch. District, 198
Collins *v.* Wilson, 428
Collinsville Comm. Unit. School District No. 10 *v.* White, 51
Columbus Education Assn. *v.* Columbus School System, 229
Comeaux *v.* School Employees Retirement System, 37
Comings *v.* State Board of Education, 184
Comm. ex rel. School District *v.* Ross, 76
Comm. *v.* Coatney, 47
Comm. *v.* Dingfelt, 325
Comm. *v.* Doran, 49
Commercial Cleaning Corporation *v.* Sullivan, 501
Committee for Public Education and Religious Freedom *v.* Nyquist, 570, 571, 578, 581, 582
Commonwealth Dept. of Educ. *v.* First School, 570
Commonwealth Dept. of Educ. *v.* Great Valley Sch. District, 182, 183
Commonwealth Dept. of Educ. *v.* Oxford Area School District, 227
Commonwealth of Pennsylvania *v.* Charleroi Area School District, 202, 271–273
Commonwealth *v.* Bey, 126
Commonwealth *v.* Collins, 47, 497
Commonwealth *v.* County Board of Arlington County, 241
Commonwealth *v.* Dingfelt, 328
Commonwealth *v.* Pennsylvania Interscholastic Athletics Assn., 93, 374
Commonwealth *v.* Renfrow, 545
Commonwealth *v.* Ressler, 47
Commonwealth *v.* Ryan, 256, 257
Commonwealth *v.* Tate, 90
Commonwealth *v.* Tekavec, 189
Communist Party of Indiana *v.* Whitcomb, 47
Community Projects for Students, Inc. *v.* Wilder, 496
Conard *v.* Goolsby, 235, 236
Concerned Citizens for Neighborhood Schools *v.* Board of Educ., 75
Concerned Parents *v.* Cauthersville School District, 492
Concord *v.* New Testament Baptist Church Heritage Christian School, 547
Conecuh County Board of Educ. *v.* Campbell, 72
Congregation Temple Israel *v.* Creve Coeur, 546
Conley *v.* Martin, 566
Conn. State Fed. Teachers *v.* Board of Educ. Members, 251

Connecticut State Fed. Teachers *v.* Board of Educ. Members, 251
Connell *v.* Higginbotham, 185
Connett *v.* Fremont Co. School District, 439
Connick *v.* Myers, 280–286
Conover *v.* Board of Educ. of Nebo School District, 53, 63–65
Conover *v.* Board of Examiners, 181
Cons. School District of Glidden *v.* Griffith, 49
Conte *v.* School Committee, 207
Cook *v.* Griffin, 575, 577
Cook *v.* Hudson, 235
Cooley *v.* Board of Education, 210, 223, 232
Cooper *v.* County School Board, 136
Cooper *v.* Curry, 222
Cooper *v.* Fair Dismissal Appeals Board, 86
Copeland *v.* School Board, City of Portsmouth, 365
Copella *v.* Board of Educ., 195
Coral Gables *v.* Patty, 441
Corbin *v.* Special School District of Fort Smith, 187, 188
Cord-Charlotte School District *v.* Independence Co. Board of Educ., 77
Cords *v.* Window Rock School District, 218, 224
Corey *v.* Poway Un. Sch. District, 485
Cornell *v.* Board of Education, 485
Cornwell *v.* State Board of Education, 131
Corrigan, State ex rel. *v.* Hensel, 498
Cortright *v.* Trustees of Rutgers College, 564
Cott *v.* Board of Education, 323
Cotton *v.* Catholic Bishop of Chicago, 563
Coughlin *v.* Seattle School District, 36
Coulter *v.* Board of Educ., 188
Council of Directors and Supervisors *v.* Los Angeles Un. School District, 200
Council of Supervisory Assn. *v.* Board of Educ. (N.Y.), 370
County Hills Christian Church *v.* Un. School District, 137
County School Board of Spottsylvania County *v.* McConnell, 229
County School Board *v.* Thomas, 441
Cousin *v.* Board of Trustees, 371
Crabtree *v.* Board of Educ., Wellston City School District, 53
Craig *v.* Boren, 360, 373
Cramer *v.* Hoffman, 564
Cramer *v.* Va. Comm., 379
Crandall *v.* N. Dakota H.S. Activities Assn., 92
Cranston Teachers Assn. *v.* Cranston School Committee, 180
Crawford *v.* Board of Educ., 372
Crawford *v.* Pittman, 384
Crawford *v.* Wayne County Board of Educ., 441
Creative Country Day School *v.* Burns, 546
Creative Country Day School *v.* Montgomery County Board of Appeals, 546
Crim *v.* McWhorter, 492
Crockett *v.* Sorensen, 130
Crofts *v.* Board of Educ., 188
Croghan *v.* Hart City Board of Educ., 441
Cronacher *v.* Scribner, 206
Cronin *v.* Lindberg, 484
Crossen *v.* Board of Educ., 436
Crossen *v.* Fatsi, 323
Cude *v.* State, 138
Cullum *v.* Board of Education, 49
Cumberland Valley Educ. Assn. *v.* Cumberland Valley School District, 253
Currence, In re, 126
Curtis Pub. Co. *v.* Butts, 443
Cuyahoga County Assn. for Retarded Children *v.* Essex, 380

Dachs *v.* Board of Education, 355
Daily Gazette Co. *v.* North Colonie Board of Educ., 51
Daily *v.* L.A. Un. School District, 428
Dairyland Ins. Co. *v.* Board Co. Commrs., 446
Dallam *v.* Cumberland Valley Sch. District, 307
Dalli *v.* Board of Educ., 138
Damascus Community Church *v.* Clackamas County, 547
Daniel B. *v.* Wis. Dept. of Pub. Inst'n, 444
Daniel *v.* Waters, 129
Danielson *v.* DuPage Voc. Educational Authority, 378
Danskin *v.* San Diego Un. Sch. District, 100
Danville Board of School Directors *v.* Fifield, 247, 253, 254
Danzel *v.* North St. Paul-Maplewood-Oakdale Ind. School District, 376
Darrin *v.* Gould, 374, 375
Darville *v.* Dade County School Board, 372
Dauphin Co. Tech. School Educ. Assn. *v.* School Board, 248
Dausend *v.* Board of Educ., 434
Davis *v.* Ann Arbor Public Schools, 306
Davis *v.* Board of Educ., 241
Davis *v.* Fentress County Board of Educ., 74
Davis *v.* Ferment, 322
Davis *v.* Page, 129, 130
Dawson *v.* Iowa Merit Employment Commission, 35
Dawson *v.* Tulare Un. H.S. Dist., 433
Dayton Board of Education *v.* Brinkman, 361, 364
Dayton Classroom Teachers Assn. *v.* Dayton Board of Educ., 32, 253
Dean *v.* American Security Ins. Co., 454
Debra P. *v.* Turlington, 95
Decker *v.* Dundee Central School District, 437
Deerfield Hutterian Assn. *v.* Ipswich Board of Educ., 367
DeGooyer *v.* Harkness, 442
deGroat *v.* Newark Un. School District, 216
deJesus *v.* Penberthy, 304, 307, 310
Del Prete *v.* Board of Selectmen, 53
Del Valle Ind. School District Board of Equalization, 486
deLaurier *v.* San Diego Unified School District, 377
Delaware State Board of Educ. *v.* Evans, 369
Delaware State Board of Education *v.* Evans, 368
Delaware *v.* Prouse, 326
DelConte *v.* State, 537, 540, 543
DeLeon *v.* Harlingen Con. Ind. School District, 77
DeLozier *v.* Tyrone Area School Board, 45
Demory Bros. Inc. *v.* Board of Public Works, 499
Dennis *v.* United States, 217
Denton *v.* South Kitsap School District No. 402, 209, 213
Denville *v.* Board of Educ., 69
Department of Educ. *v.* Charleroi Area School District, 201
Department of Educ. *v.* Jersey Shore Area School District, 37, 191
Department of Educ. *v.* Kauffman, 200
Desmarais *v.* Wachesett Reg. School District, 446
DeSpain *v.* DeKalb Co. Comm. School District, 127
Detroit Police Officers Association *v.* City of Detroit, 186
Deutsch *v.* Teel, 577
Devereaux *v.* Geary, 370
di Leo *v.* Greenfield, 210
Dibartolo *v.* Metropolitan School District, 428
Dicken *v.* Kentucky State Board of Educ., 30
Dickinson P.S. District No. 1 *v.* Scott, 577

Dickman *v.* School District, No. 62C, 578
Diefenderfer *v.* Budd, 248
Diocese of Rochester *v.* Planning Board, 546
District of Columbia *v.* Connelly, 426, 427
District 300 Educ. Assn. *v.* Board of Educ., 193, 194
District of Columbia *v.* Carter, 455
District of Columbia *v.* Washington, 433
District *v.* Lollar, 195
Dix, State ex rel. *v.* Board of Educ., 32
Dixon *v.* Carroll County Board of Educ., 71
Dixon *v.* Love, 225
Dobbins *v.* Board of Education, 438
Dobler *v.* Mincemoyer, 189
Dobrovolny *v.* Reinhardt, 21, 51, 52
Dodge *v.* Board of Educ., 200
Dodson *v.* Arkansas Activities Assn., 375
Doe *v.* Board of Educ., 444, 445, 450
Doe *v.* Colburg, 495
Doe *v.* Commonwealth's Attorney, 215
Doe *v.* New York, 452
Doe *v.* Renfrow, 328
Doe *v.* State, 325, 328
Doe, State ex rel. *v.* Kingery, 491
Doherty *v.* Wilson, 215
Dolter *v.* Ahlert High School, 557
Dombrowski *v.* City of Philadelphia, 488
Domico *v.* Rapides Par. School Board, 235
Domino *v.* Mercurio, 438
Don Wilson Builders *v.* City of Torrance, 100
Donaldson, In re, 324, 328
Donnelly *v.* City of Manchester, 186
Donohue *v.* Copiague Union Free School District, 444
Doran *v.* Board of Educ., 226
Dorn *v.* Board of Billings School District, 316
Dornacker *v.* Olson, 480
Dorsey *v.* Bale, 312, 314
Dostert *v.* Berthold Pub. School District No. 54, 321
Dothard *v.* Rawlinson, 376
Dougherty County *v.* White, 190
Douglas *v.* Board of Education, 433
Douglas, State ex rel. *v.* Morrow, 543
Dowell *v.* School District, 491
Downey *v.* School Committee of Lowell, 202
Downs *v.* Conway School District, 234
Doyle *v.* U.S., 445
Drake *v.* Covington County Board of Educ., 215
Drake *v.* Thomas, 432
D.R.C. *v.* State, 324
Dreyfuss *v.* Board of Educ., 195
Drummond *v.* Acree, 372
Dryden *v.* Marcellus Comm. Schools, 51, 207
D.S.W. *v.* Fairbanks North Star Borough School District, 444
Duda *v.* Caines, 442
Duffley *v.* New Hampshire Interscholastic Athletic Assn., 93
Duffy *v.* Village of Princeton, 501
Dugan *v.* Bollman, 48
Duke *v.* No. Texas St. Univ., 227
Dumex *v.* Louisiana H.S. Athletic Assn., 92
Duncan *v.* Board of Education, 434
Dunellen Board of Educ. *v.* Dunellen Educ. Assn., 246
Dunkerson *v.* Russell, 323, 324
Dunkle *v.* Elkins, 100
Dunn *v.* Bessie F. Heirn School Inc., 549
Dunn *v.* Tyler Ind. Sch. District, 314
DuPont–Fort Lewis School District *v.* Bruno, 71
Durand *v.* Board of Coop. Educational Assn., 68
Durant *v.* Dept. of Education, 480
Durflinger *v.* Artiles, 445
Durr *v.* Alfred Jacobshagen Co., 441
Dusanek *v.* Hannon, 211
Dworken *v.* Cleveland Board of Educ., 34

E. Detroit Fed. of Teachers *v.* Board of Educ., 203, 204
E. Hartford Educ. Assn. *v.* Board of Educ., 236
E. Texas Guidance and Achievement Ctr. *v.* Brockette, 491
East Meadow Comm. Concerts Assn. *v.* Board of Educ., 99
Eastbrook Community School Corp. *v.* Indiana Ed. Employment Relations Board, 246
Easthampton *v.* County Commissioners of Hampshire, 70
Eberle *v.* Benedictine Sisters, 564
Eckroth *v.* Flasher Pub. School District, 376
Edmonds Sch. District *v.* City of Mountain Lake Terrace, 71
Edwards *v.* City of Renton, 505
Edwards *v.* Mettler, 50
Edwards *v.* School Board, 126
EEOC *v.* Detroit Edison Co., 454
EEOC *v.* Fremont Christian School, 559
EEOC *v.* Union Bank, 454
Egner *v.* Texas City Ind. Sch. District, 317
Ehlinger *v.* Board of Educ., 428
Eisen *v.* Regents, U. of California, 338
Eisner *v.* Board of Educ., 304, 315, 317, 318, 322
Elder *v.* Anderson, 335
Electronics Unlimited Inc. *v.* Burnsville, 503
Elfbrandt *v.* Russell, 185
Elgin *v.* District of Columbia, 448
Elisofon *v.* Board of Education, 196
Elk Point Ind. School District No. 3 *v.* State Commission of Elementary and Secondary Educ., 32, 42
Elliot *v.* School District No. 64-JT, 52
Ellis v. Railway Clerks, 289–293
Ellis *v.* Board of Educ., 98, 101
Elroy Kendall Winton Schools *v.* Coop. Educ. Service Agency D, 32
Embrey *v.* Hampton, 226
Emerson *v.* Bible, 35
Endeavor-Oxford Union Free H.S. District *v.* Walters, 50
Engle *v.* Vitale, 126
English *v.* Northeast Board of Educ., 227
Enlow *v.* Ill. Central R. Co., 440
Epeldi *v.* Engelking, 576
Epperson *v.* Arkansas, 6, 128–129, 237
Erb *v.* Iowa State Board of Public Instruction, 215
Erie R. Co. *v.* Tompkins, 15
Erikson *v.* Board of Educ., 379
Estay *v.* LaFourche Parish School Board, 330
Eugene Sand and Gravel, Inc. *v.* City of Eugene, 132
Evans *v.* Board of Agriculture, 316
Evans *v.* Buchanan, 369
Evans *v.* Mount View School, 204
Evans *v.* Page, 211
Everett *v.* Cal. Teachers Assoc., 443
Everett *v.* Marcase, 307
Everett *v.* School District, 566
Excise Board of Lincoln County *v.* St. Louis S.F. Ry., 43

F. *v.* Duval County, 537, 540
Faber *v.* Roelofs, 568
Fabian *v.* Ind. School District, 377
Fagan *v.* Summers, 428
Family Forum *v.* Archdiocese of Detroit, 556
Fanning *v.* Warfield, 337
Farrell *v.* Joel, 305
Farrelly *v.* Timberlake Reg. School District, 227, 257

Farrington *v.* Tokushige, 537
Fatscher *v.* Board of School Directors, 204
Fayette Co. Educ. Assn. *v.* Hardy, 241, 244
Fayman *v.* Trustees of Burlington College, 554
Fedele *v.* Board of Educ. of Town of Branford, 204
Federated Conservationists *v.* Reed, 68
Federation of Delaware Teachers *v.* DeLaWarr Board of Educ., 251
Fedor *v.* Mauwehu Council of Boy Scouts, 430
Felton *v.* Aquilar, 135
Fender *v.* School District No. 25, 210
Fenton *v.* Steor, 316, 339
Ferguson *v.* Board of Trustees, 224
Ferndale *v.* City of Ellsworth Sup'g School District, 211, 212
Ferraro *v.* Board of Educ., 438
Ferrel *v.* Dallas Ind. School District, 322
Fiedler *v.* Marumsco Baptist Church, 554, 557
Fiedler *v.* Board of Educ., 223, 308, 309, 310
Filler *v.* Pt. Washington Un. Free School District, 579, 580
Finot *v.* Pasadena City Board of Educ., 198, 235
Firefighters Local *v.* Stotts, 395–396
First Assembly of God *v.* City of Alexandria, 546, 547
Fisher *v.* Burkburnett Ind. School District, 313, 314
Fisher *v.* Clackamas Cty. School District, 135, 136
Fisher *v.* Ind. School District No. 118, 206
Fisher *v.* Snyder, 215, 235
Fitzpatrick *v.* Board of Educ., 339
Fitzgerald *v.* Montgomery Co. Board of Educ., 434, 436
Fitzpatrick *v.* Bitzer, 360
Flandera *v.* Jamesville-Dewitt Cent. Schools, 449
Flast *v.* Cohen, 5
Fleming *v.* Concordia Parish School Board, 224
Flint *v.* St. Augustine H.S., 553
Florey *v.* Sioux Falls School District, 132
Florida *v.* Board of Pub. Instr., 488
Flowers *v.* Ind. School of Tama, 73
Flowing Wells School District *v.* Stewart, 35
Floyd County Board of Educ. *v.* Slone, 182
Foesch *v.* Ind. School District No. 646, 204
Fogel *v.* Board of Educ., 221, 228
Force *v.* Pierce City R-VII Sch. Dist., 374, 375
Fortman *v.* Texarkana School District, 313
Fosselman *v.* Waterloo School District, 439
Foster, 76
Foti *v.* Orleans Parish School Board, 503
Fountain Gate Ministries *v.* City of Plano, 547
Fowler *v.* Seaton, 565
Fowler *v.* Williams, 324
Fowler *v.* Williamson, 97
Fox *v.* Board of Educ., 193
Fox *v.* City of Los Angeles, 132
Frace *v.* Long Beach City H.S. District, 439
Frain *v.* Barron, 137, 316
Franchise Tax Board of United Americans for Public Schools, 581
Francisco *v.* Board of Directors, 229
Frank *v.* Arapahoe County School District, 201
Frank *v.* Orleans Par. School Board, 432
Franklin *v.* Elks Lodge, 443
Franks *v.* Bowman Trans. Co., Inc., 35, 372
Fraser Public School District *v.* Kolon, 502
Frasier, State ex rel. *v.* Whaley, 78
Frederick L. *v.* Thomas, 380, 381
Fredericks *v.* School Board of Monroe Co., 253
Freeman *v.* Flake, 322, 323
Freund *v.* Oakland Board of Educ., 433, 434
Fricke *v.* Lynch, 339
Friedman *v.* Farmington Twp. School District, 449
Friedman *v.* Union Free School District No. 1, 232, 251
Frost *v.* Yerozunis, 79
Fuentas *v.* Board of Educ., 203
Fuentes *v.* Rohr, 36
Fuller *v.* N. Kansas City Sch. Dist., 196
Fullilove *v.* Kreps, 371
Furnco Construction Corp. *v.* Walters, 368
Furutani *v.* Ewingleben, 304
Futia (J.N.) Co. *v.* Office of General Services, 501

G.H., In re, 380
Gabriel *v.* Trinity Area School District, 33, 206
Gaffney *v.* St. Dept. of Educ., 578
Gaines *v.* Anderson, 128
Galli *v.* Kirkeby, 446
Gambese *v.* Board of Educ., 187
Gambino *v.* Fairfax City School Board, 319, 320
Gamewell Co. *v.* City of Phoenix, 499
Gann *v.* Harrisburg, Community Unit. School District, 55
Garcia *v.* Los Angeles Co. Board of Educ., 305–306, 312
Gardenshire *v.* Chalmers, 306
Gardner *v.* Hollifield, 218
Garofoli *v.* Salesainum School, Inc., 564
Garrity *v.* New Jersey, 304
Gary Teachers Union *v.* School City, 213, 217
Garza *v.* McAllen Ind. School District, 449
Gaspar *v.* Bruton, 307
Gassman *v.* Gov'g. Board of Rincon Valley School District, 203
Gaston *v.* Becker, 445
Gauss *v.* State, 434
Gaylord *v.* Tacoma School District, 214, 215, 216
Geduldig *v.* Board of Educ., 204
Gedulgig *v.* Aiello, 377
General Electric Co. *v.* Gilbert, 377
George *v.* Comm. Dept. of Educ., 191
George *v.* Union Area High School, 199
Georgia Assn. of Retarded Citizens *v.* McDaniel, 384
Geraci *v.* St. Xavier H.S., 554, 608–611
Gerbert *v.* Hoffman, 316
Germann *v.* Kipp, 370
Germond *v.* Board of Educ., 438
Gerrity *v.* Beatty, 438
Gerry *v.* Board of Educ., 34
Gerzof *v.* Sweeney, 499, 530–532
Gfell *v.* Rickelman, 322, 323
Gibbons *v.* Orleans Parish School Board, 437
Gibson *v.* Butler, 206
Gieringer *v.* Central School District, 233
Gil-Bern Construction Corp. *v.* City of Brockton, 501
Gilbert *v.* Sacramento Un. School District, 442
Gilbertson *v.* McAlister, 211, 234
Giles *v.* Marple Newtown S.D. Board of Directors, 313
Gill *v.* Duchess County Board of Coop. Educ. Services, 205
Gillard *v.* Schmidt, 239
Gilliland *v.* Board of Educ., 211
Gilmore *v.* City of Montgomery, 556
Gilpin *v.* Kansas State H.S. Activities Assn., Inc., 374
Gindel *v.* Dept. of Education, 485
Ginsberg *v.* New York, 320
Ginsberg *v.* Yeshiva of Far Rockaway, 548
Girard School District of Pittinger, 312
Girardier *v.* Webster College, 554
Gish *v.* Board of Educ., 197
Gitkins *v.* Butler Co., 498
Givens *v.* Poe, 311
Givhan *v.* Western Line Cons. School District, 198, 203
Glaser *v.* Marietta, 431

Glenmore Academy *v.* State Board of Private Academic Schools, 537
Glennon *v.* School Committee of Boston, 200
Glowacki *v.* Ambach, 180
Golanka *v.* State Board of Educ., 180
Goldberg *v.* Kelly, 504
Goldin *v.* Board of Central School District No. 1, 214
Goldin *v.* Board of Education, 212
Goldsmith *v.* Board of Educ., 208, 212
Gonzales *v.* Mackler, 437
Gonzales *v.* McEuen, 309, 310, 312, 344–350
Gonzales *v.* Shenker, 36
Goodman *v.* Board of Educ., 99
Goodwin *v.* Bennett County H.S. Ind. School District, 197
Goodwin *v.* Cross County School District, 127, 128, 133
Gordon J. *v.* Santa Ana Un. School District, 325
Gordon *v.* Deer Park School District, 436
Gordon *v.* Jefferson Davis Parish School, 363
Goss *v.* Board of Education, 364
Goss *v.* Lopez, 220, 223, 225, 310, 340–344
Gotlieb *v.* Commissioner of Taxation, 581
Gov'g Board of Nicasio School District, 214
Govel *v.* Board of Educ., 440
Governing Board of Mountainview School District *v.* Metcalf, 216, 239
Governing Board of Palo Verde Peninsula Un. School District *v.* Felt, 207
Graber *v.* Kniola, 324
Graham *v.* Houston Ind. School District, 318, 320
Graham *v.* Knutzen, 306, 309
Grames *v.* King, 447
Grams *v.* Melrose-Mindoro Jt. School District, 180
Grand Rapids School District of the City of Grand Rapids, et al., Petitioners *v.* Phyllis Ball, et al., 621–626
Grange *v.* Cascade Co. School District, 491, 492
Grant *v.* Lake Oswego School District No. 7, 438, 461–464
Gray *v.* Union County Intermediate Educ. District, 222, 230, 233
Grayned *v.* City of Rockford, 100, 308, 315
Great Neck Comm. School *v.* Dick, 546
Greenberg *v.* Lower Marion Sch. District, 485
Greene *v.* County Board of Educ., 201
Greene *v.* Mitchell County Board of Educ., 441
Greene *v.* Moore, 309
Greenville *v.* Bailey, 307
Griffin *v.* County School Board of Prince Edward County, 363
Griffith *v.* Board of Educ., 196
Grigg *v.* Commonwealth, 537, 538, 544
Grippo *v.* Dunmore School Board, 37, 496
Griswold *v.* Mt. Diablo Un. School District, 35, 52
Grit *v.* Wolman, 581
Groopman *v.* Community School Board, 224
Grossburg *v.* Deusebio, 133
Grossman, N. Ray, 216
Grove City College *v.* Bell, 557, 558
Grueninger *v.* President and Fellows of Harvard College, 563
Guadalupe Organization, Inc. *v.* Tempe El. School District, 365
Guerra *v.* Roma Ind. School District, 233
Guerrieri *v.* Tyson, 435, 442
Guilderland Central Sch. Dist. *v.* N.Y. State Hum. Rights Appeal Bd., 372
Guilford *v.* University, 433
Guitirrez *v.* School District, 314
Gulesian *v.* Dade Co. School Board, 486
Gurule *v.* Salt Lake City Board of Educ., 433
Guthrie *v.* Board of Educ., 210
Guthrie *v.* Taylor, 23, 181

Haas *v.* So. Bend Community School Corp., 93, 374
Hacharedi, State ex rel. *v.* Baxter, 546
Hagopian *v.* Knowlton, 307
Hall *v.* City of Taft, 71
Hall *v.* Pringle, 338, 339
Hall *v.* Shelby County Board of Educ., 98, 101
Hall *v.* Tawney, 338, 339
Halldorson *v.* State School Constr. Fund, 488
Halsey *v.* Board of Educ. of Garrett County, 191, 195
Hamer *v.* Board of Educ., 314, 493
Hamilton County *v.* Cloud, 489
Hamilton *v.* State Board of Education, 42
Hamilton *v.* Tenn. Secondary School Ath. Assn., 307
Hammond *v.* Marx, 77, 304
Hammond *v.* Scott, 440
Hampton *v.* Orleans Parish School Board, 434
Hankins *v.* District Boundary Board, 484
Hankla *v.* Governing Board of Roseland School District, 210
Hanna *v.* Board of Educ., 500
Hannah *v.* Larche, 220, 305
Hanover Twp. Fed. of Teachers *v.* Hanover Comm., 208
Hanover *v.* Northrup, 137, 231
Hanson *v.* Unified School District No. 500, 186
Harbe *v.* Hazelwood School District, 195
Harbor Schools *v.* Board of Appeals of Haverhill, 548
Hardwick *v.* Board of School Trustees, 137
Harrall *v.* Wilson County Schools, 309
Harrington *v.* Vandalia-Butler Board of Educ., 376, 379
Harris *v.* Mechanicsville Central School District, 211, 238
Harrisburg R-VIII School District *v.* O'Brien, 181, 198
Harrison Cent. School District *v.* Nyquist, 191
Harrison *v.* State of Michigan, 380, 381
Hart *v.* School Board of Wahalla County, 218
Hartford Union H.S. *v.* City of Hartford, 71
Harvey *v.* Clyde Park District, 447
Haschke *v.* School District, 32
Haskins *v.* State, 47
Hatch *v.* Board of Education, Ithaca City School District, 74
Hatch *v.* Goerke, 76, 322
Hatter *v.* L.A. City H.S. District, 316
Hawaii Public Employee Relations Bd. Decision, 246
Hawkins Co. *v.* Davis, 440
Hawkins *v.* Linn County School District No. 14, 263–265
Haycraft *v.* Grigsby, 432
Hayes *v.* Cape Henlopen School District, 35, 224, 225
Hayes *v.* Orleans Parish School Board, 195
Haymes *v.* Catholic Bishop of Chicago, 563
Haynes *v.* County of Missoula, 430
Hazelwood School District *v.* United States, 367
Head *v.* Spec. School District No. 1, 257
Healy *v.* James, 100, 338
Hebert *v.* Lafayette Parish School Board, 210
Hector County Ind. Sch. District *v.* Hopkins, 35
Hedlund *v.* Superior Court, 337
Heifner *v.* Board of Educ., 197
Heine *v.* School District No. 271, 191
Helm *v.* Professional Childrens School, 568
Hempel *v.* School District No. 329, 98
Henderson *v.* Henderson, 561
Henderson *v.* Los Angeles Board of Educ., 51
Hendrick Hudson Board of Educ. *v.* Rowley, 382, 405–409

Hendricks *v.* Board of Trustees, 331
Hennessey *v.* Ind. School District No. 4, Lincoln County, 99
Henry George School of Social Science *v.* San Diego Un. School, 101
Hensley *v.* State Board of Educ., 205
Hentschke *v.* Sink, 198
Herbert *v.* Nyquist, 218
Hergenreter *v.* Hayden, 496
Hernandez *v.* Hanson, 319
Hernandez *v.* Texas, 362
Herscher Comm. Unit. School District *v.* Kankakee School Dist., 77
Heva *v.* Seattle School District, 434
Hickey *v.* Board of School Directors, 35, 211, 224
Hiers *v.* Brownell, 79
Higgins *v.* Grand Rapids Board of Educ., 363
Hill *v.* Board of Educ., 436
Hill *v.* Dayton School District, 35, 207
Hill *v.* Lewis, 316
Hill *v.* State, 540, 543
Hillman *v.* Elliott, 305
Hillman *v.* Greater Miami Hebrew Academy, 567
Hillsborough Classroom Teachers Assn. *v.* School Board, 246
Hinek *v.* Bowman Public School District No. 1, 188
Hinton *v.* Kentucky State Board of Educ., 539
Hobolth *v.* Greenway, 131
Hobsen *v.* Smuck, 365
Hobson *v.* Bailey, 316
Hobson *v.* Hensen, 365
Hodge and Hammond, Inc. *v.* Burns, 501
Hodgkins *v.* Central School District No. 1, 226
Hoefer *v.* Hardin County Board of Educ., 74
Hoffman *v.* Board of Educ., 444
Hoffman *v.* Jannarone, 211, 223, 227
Hogenson *v.* Williams, 431
Holland *v.* Board of Educ., 199
Hollenbaugh *v.* Carnegie Free Library, 214, 235
Holler *v.* Rock Hill School District, 492
Hollister *v.* North, 187
Holman *v.* Wheeler, 450
Holsapple *v.* Woods, 321
Holt *v.* Shelton, 330
Hootch *v.* Alaska State Operated School System, 68
Hoover *v.* Meikle John, 374
Hopkins *v.* Board of Educ., 130
Hopp *v.* Oroville School District, 191
Hornbeck *v.* Somerset County Board of Educ., 484
Horton *v.* Goose Creek Independent School District, 325, 328
Horton *v.* Meskill, 484
Hortonville Ed. Assn. *v.* Hortonville School Dist., 255
Hortonville Jt. School District No. 1 *v.* Hortonville Educ. Assn., 235, 257, 298–301
Hosford *v.* Board of Educ., 218
Hoskins *v.* Walker, 188, 189
Hostrop *v.* Board of Jr. College District No. 515, 237
Hot Springs School District *v.* Wells, 485
Hotel China & Glass Co. *v.* Board of Pub. Instruction, 502
Howard *v.* Bogart, 175
Howard *v.* Clark, 313, 334
Howell *v.* Winn Parish School Board, 212
Hoyem *v.* Manhattan Beach City School District, 435, 440
Huebschen *v.* Dept. of Health and Human Services, 379
Huff *v.* Harlan County Board of Educ., 202
Huff *v.* Northampton Co. Board of Educ., 441
Huff *v.* Notre Dame High School, 556
Human Rights Party *v.* Secretary of State, 47
Hunt *v.* Board of Educ., 427
Hunt *v.* McNair, 570
Hunt *v.* Board of Educ., 127
Hunter *v.* Board of Educ., 445
Hunter *v.* Evergreen Presbyterian Vocational School, 435, 566
Hunter *v.* North Mason H.S., 449
Hunter *v.* Pittsburgh, 20
Hunter *v.* Board of Dir. of Inchelium School District, 207, 224
Hunterden Central H.S. Board of Educ. *v.* Hunterden H.S. Teachers Assn., 126
Huntley *v.* Comm. School Board of Brooklyn, 226
Huntley *v.* No. Carolina State Board of Educ., 183, 220
Hurry *v.* Jones, 380
Hutchison *v.* Toews, 439
Hyde *v.* Willpinit Sch. Dist., 196
Hyland *v.* Smollack, 210
Hylton *v.* Mayor and City Council of Baltimore, 500–501
Hysong *v.* Sch. District, 133

Idaho Power Co. *v.* Three Creek Good Roads District, 484
Idle, State ex rel. *v.* Chamberlain, 330
Illinois Educ. Assn. *v.* Board of Educ., 218, 247
Illinois *v.* Adams, 484
Illinois *v.* Lafayette, 329
Imbler *v.* Pachtman, 443, 450
Ind. School District *v.* Glass, 485
Indiana H.S. Athletic Assn. *v.* Raike, 92, 330
Indiana High School Athletic Assn. *v.* Blanche, 35
Indiana St. Personnel Board *v.* Jackson, 431, 433
Indian Oasis School District No. 40 *v.* Zambrano, 208
Ingraham *v.* Boone, 494
Ingraham *v.* Wright, 220, 223, 338, 431, 432, 464–467
International Board of Firemen *v.* School District of Phila., 253
International Brotherhood of Teamsters *v.* United States, 368
Irby *v.* McGowan, 222
Irene F., In re, 335
Isard *v.* Hickory City Board of Educ., 439
Isley *v.* School District, 482

Jackson *v.* Board of Educ., 434
Jackson *v.* Cartwright School District, 434
Jackson *v.* Hankinson, 441, 446
Jackson *v.* Metropolitan Edison Co., 556
Jackson *v.* Wald Ind. School District, 491
Jacob *v.* Board of Regents, 50, 206
Jacobs *v.* Benedict, 323
Jacobs *v.* Board of School Commissioners, 317, 318, 319, 322
Jacobson *v.* Commonwealth of Massachusetts, 78, 138
Jadick *v.* Board of Educ., 202, 205
James *v.* Board of Educ. of Central District No. 1 of the Towns of Addison, et al., 230, 232, 242, 274–79
James *v.* Charlotte-Mecklenburg Board of Educ., 437, 564
Jamestown School Committee *v.* Schmidt, 575, 576
Jantzen *v.* School Committee of Chelmsford, 201, 205
Jarrett *v.* Good, 82
Jarvella *v.* Willoughby-Eastlake City School District Board of Educ., 216
Jenkins *v.* Board of Educ., 449
Jenkins *v.* Louisiana State Board of Educ., 306
Jenks *v.* Jenks, 337
Jennings *v.* Caddo Parish School Board, 197

Jennings v. Exeter–West Greenwich Regional School District, 576
Jernigan v. State, 540
Jerry v. Board of Educ., 211
Jerry's Rides, Inc. v. City Council of Baltimore, 501
Jessup, Matter of, 387
Jeter v. Ellenville Central School District, 480, 491
Jewell v. Board of Educ., 51
Jinkerson v. Lane City School District, 207
Jinks v. Mays, 377
Joanou v. Board of Educ., 207
Johns v. Wynnewood School Board, 449
Johns-Manville Corp. v. Village of DeKalb, 490
Johnson & Wales College v. Diprete, 545, 547
Johnson v. Board (1970), 305
Johnson v. Board of Educ. (1961), 335
Johnson v. Board of Educ. (1977), 312
Johnson v. Board of Educ., District of Riveredge, 204, 220
Johnson v. Board of Elementary and Secondary Educ., 181
Johnson v. Branch, 232
Johnson v. Chicago Board of Educ., 372
Johnson v. Dixon, 186
Johnson v. Horace Mann Mut. Ins. Co., 432, 433
Johnson v. Nyquist, 248
Johnson v. REA Express, 455, 456
Johnson v. School Committee, 82
Johnson v. School District No. 3, 182
Johnson v. School District No. 60, 323
Johnson v. Sullivan, 94
Johnson v. United States District Jt. School Board, 193
Johnson v. Zerbst, 312
Joint School District No. 1 of Village of Cedar Grove v. Unified Sch. District No. 1 of the Village of Belgium and Fredonia, 46
Jones v. Alfred H. Mayer Co., 455
Jones v. Battles, 234
Jones v. Day, 323
Jones v. Grand Ledge Public Schools, 77
Jones v. Kansas City, 447
Jones v. Latexo Ind. School Dist., 329
Jones v. Maness, 443, 444
Jordahl v. Ind. School District No. 129, 203
Joseph Rugo, Inc. v. Henson, 503
Joseph v. Monroe, 440
Jt. School District No. 1 v. Wisconsin Rapids Educ. Assn., 256, 257
Jt. School District No. 8 v. Wis. Employees' Relation Board, 246
Justus v. Jefferson Co. School District, 435

Kaleva-Norman-Dickson School District No. 6 v. Kaleva-Norman-Dickson Sch. Teachers Assn., 253, 254
Kamjathy v. Board of Educ., 227
Kaplan v. School Committee of Melrose, 202
Karbach v. Board of Educ., 203, 204
Karen B. v. Treen, 127, 128
Karstetter v. Evans, 224
Kass v. Board of Educ., 433
Kasten v. YMCA, 563
Katz v. McAuley, 319
Katz v. School District of Clayton, 376
Kaufman v. Pannuccio, 189
Kayfield Construction Corporation v. Morris, 501
Kearns v. Lower Merion School District, 219
Keckeisen v. Independent School District, 612
Keefe v. Geanakos, 237, 238
Keeling v. Public Utility Dist. No. 1 of Clapham Cy., 22
Keene v. Rodgers, 325, 326
Kefesee v. Board of Educ., 438
Keith v. Community School District, 227
Kellam v. Board of Educ., 447
Kelley Co. v. City of Cleveland, 504
Kelley v. Johnson, 236
Kelley v. Metropolitan County Board of Educ., 93
Kenai Pen. Borough School District v. Kenai Pen. Educ. Assn., 246, 247
Kenaston v. School Admin. District No. 40, 200
Kennedy v. Ringgold School District, 497
Kent v. Commissioner of Education, 127, 128
Kentucky Educ. Public Affairs Council v. Kentucky Registry of Finance, 250
Kentucky St. Board of Elementary and Secondary Education v. Rudasill, 539
Kerby v. Elk Grove Un. School District, 433, 438
Keyes v. Class B School District, 50
Keyes v. School District No. 1, Denver, 361, 362, 363
Keyishian v. Board of Regents, 217, 228, 237, 308
Keys v. Swayet, 307
Kidwell v. School District, 433
Kies v. Lowry, 43
Kim v. State, 564, 566
King v. Ambellon, 335
King v. Caesar Rodney School District, 227
King v. Dramatic Arts, 553
King v. Farmer, Matter of, 75
King-Smith v. Aaron, 186, 197
Kingsley v. Ind. District No. 2, 433
Kinsel v. Rettinger, 79
Kinsella v. Board of Education, 226
Kirkpatrick v. Wright, 228
Kite v. Marshall, 92
Kleid v. Board of Education, 138
Kluka v. Livingston Parish School Board, 430
Knarr v. Board of School Trustees, 232
Knauff v. Board of Education, 74
Knight v. Board of Education, 306
Knox County Board of Education v. Willis, 225
Knox v. O'Brien, 538
Kobylanski v. Chicago Board of Educ., 563
Kobylski v. Board of Educ., 181
Konovalchik v. School Comm. of Salem, 48
Korenak v. Curative Work Shop Adult Rehabilitation Center, 438
Kornblum v. Newark Un. School District, 377
Kos v. Catholic Bishop of Chicago, 566
Kosa v. Treasurer, 483
Kosmicki v. Kowalski, 21
Kosydar v. Wolman, 581
Kotan v. School District No. 110C, 202
Kraft v. Board of Education, 48
Kramer v. Union Free School District No. 15, 45
Krause v. Ohio, 446
Kreiner v. Turkey Val. Comm. Sch. District, 447
Krolopp v. So. Range Local School District Board of Educ., 180
Kromnick v. School District of Philadelphia, 370
Kruse v. Board of Directors, 206, 221, 228
Krzewinski v. Kruger, 186
Kubriszyn v. Alabama H.S. Athletic Assn., 93
Kudasik v. Board of Directors, 199
Kuhlmeier v. Hazlewood School District, 319
Kuntz v. Benz, 79
Kurlander v. School Committee, 212
Kush v. City of Buffalo, 430, 439

La Buhn v. White, 189
LaBarr v. Board of Educ., 196
LaBorde v. Franklin Parish School Board, 196

Lach *v.* Defigio, 188
Lacy *v.* Richmond Union School District, 203
Ladsen *v.* Board of Education, 95, 97
Lake Mich. College Federation of Teachers *v.* Lake Mich. Community College, 257
Lake Park Educ. Assn. *v.* Lake Park H.S. District, 316
Lakewood Cong. of Jehovah's Witnesses Inc. *v.* City of Lakewood, 545
Landers *v.* School District, 427
Lane *v.* Board of Educ., 200
Lanner *v.* Wimmer, 125, 543
Lansing Board of Educ. *v.* NAACP, 368
Lanza *v.* Wagner, 21
Lapolla *v.* Dullaghan, 99
LaPorte *v.* Board of Educ., 439
LaRocca *v.* Board of Educ., 128
Larry P. *v.* Riles, 365
Last *v.* Board of Educ., 181, 197
Lau *v.* United States, 365–366
Laurence *v.* Buckmueller, 132
Lauricella *v.* Board of Educ., 428, 438
Lavin *v.* Board of Educ., 222
Lawes *v.* Board of Educ., 436
Lawrence U. Bicentennial Comm. *v.* City of Appleton, 99
Lea Foundation, Inc. *v.* Kiernan, 553
Leach *v.* Board of Educ., 226
LeBanks *v.* Spears, 365
Ledew *v.* School Board, 218
Lee *v.* Autanga County Board of Education, 363
Lee *v.* Macon County Board of Education, 197, 200, 202
Lee *v.* Nyquist, 369
Lee *v.* Pickens County School Systems, 200
Lee *v.* School District, 436
Lee *v.* Washington County Board of Educ., 362
Leechburg Area School District *v.* Pennsylvania Hum. Rel. Comm., 377
Leedy *v.* Hartnet, 445
Leetham *v.* McGinn, 183
Leffel *v.* Wisconsin Interscholastic Athletic Assn., 93, 375
Lefkowitz *v.* Turley, 504
Legg *v.* Ill. Fair Employ. Practice Comm'n., 370, 372
Lehman *v.* Board of Educ., 183
Lehmann *v.* Los Angeles Board of Educ., 440
Leibner *v.* Sharbaugh, 308
Leithliter *v.* Board of Trustees, 219
LeMar Construction Corp. *v.* Holt County, R-11 School District, 503
Lemelle *v.* State through Board of Sec. and Elem. Educ., 439
Lemke *v.* Black, 133
Lemon *v.* Kurtzman, 124, 571
Leone *v.* Hunter, 44
Lerner *v.* L.A. City Board of Education, 183
Lerner *v.* Superior Court, 337
Leslie *v.* Oxford Area School District, 213
Levandoski *v.* Jackson City School District, 428
Levin *v.* Board of Educ., 429
Levitt *v.* Committee for Public Education, 572
Lewis *v.* Board of Education of Johnson County, 53, 137
Lewis *v.* L.A. City Un. School District, 378
Lewis *v.* Mandeville, 136
Lewis *v.* St. Bernard Par. School Board, 438
Lezette *v.* Board of Educ., 205
Libertyville Educ. Assn. *v.* Libertyville Board of Educ., 241
Lilienthall *v.* San Leandro Un. School District, 440
Lincoln *v.* Page, 133
Linden School District *v.* Porter, 53
Lindros *v.* Gov'g Board of Tarrance Un. School District, 239
Linwood *v.* Board of Educ., 310
Linwood *v.* Board of Educ., 339
Linwood *v.* Board of Education, 304, 306, 307, 309, 310, 339
Lipan *v.* Board of Educ., 199
Lipari *v.* Sears Roebuck & Co., 445
Lipkis *v.* Caveney, 315, 316
Lipman *v.* Brisbane Elementary School District, 443, 448
Lipp *v.* Morris, 137
Little *v.* Alto Ind. School District, 36
Livingston *v.* Davis, 547
Local 858 of AFT *v.* School District, 251
Lockport Area Sp. Educ. Coop. *v.* Lockport Area Sp. Educ. Coop. Assn., 207
Lombard *v.* Board of Educ., 223
Lombardo *v.* Board of Educ., 213
Londerholm *v.* Unified School District No. 500, 372
Long *v.* Zopp, 322
Longarzo *v.* Anker, 199
Looney *v.* Cons. School District, 48
Lorenz *v.* Santa Monica City H.S. District, 434
Los Angeles *v.* Manhart, 378
Los Angeles County *v.* Byram, 488
Louisiana Assn. of Education *v.* St. Tammany Par. School Board, 495
Louisiana Education Comm. *v.* Poindexter, 363
Love *v.* Nashville A. and Normal Institute, 563
Lovitt *v.* Concord School District, 429, 442, 448
Lowell *v.* Kowalski, 561
Lubbock Civil Liberties Union *v.* Lubbock Ind. School District, 127
Lucciola *v.* Comm. of Pennsylvania, 211
Lucia *v.* Duggan, 236
Luetkemeyer *v.* Kaufman, 575
Lujan *v.* Colorado Bd. of Educ., 484
Lukac *v.* Acocks, 220
Lund *v.* Schrader, 46
Lunsford *v.* Board of Educ., 440
Luoma *v.* Union School District of Keene, 77, 78
Luse *v.* Waco Community School District, 219
Lusk *v.* Estes, 206
Luz *v.* School Committee of Lowell, 181, 182
Lynch v. Donnelly, 132, 156–162
Lyons *v.* Salve Regina College, 554

M. *v.* Board of Ed. Ball-Chatham Community Unit. School Dist., 324, 325, 328
M.M. *v.* Anker, 328
Madera *v.* Board of Educ., 307, 311
Madison County Board of Educ. *v.* Grantham, 73
Magabgab *v.* Orleans Par. School Board, 442
Magill *v.* Avondale Baseball Conference, 374
Mahan *v.* Agee, 93
Mahrenholtz *v.* County Board of School Trustees, 494
Maier *v.* Besser, 138
Mailloux *v.* Kiley, 237, 238
Mallory *v.* Barrera, 134, 496
Malmquist *v.* Hellenic Community, 565
Malnak *v.* Yogi, 128
Manch *v.* Arthur, 362
Mancha *v.* Field Museum of Natural History, 442
Mancini *v.* Board of Educ., 438
Mandel *v.* Hodges, 126
Manges *v.* Freer Ind. School District, 484
Mangold *v.* Albert Gallatin Sch. District, 126
Manjares *v.* Newton, 73
Mans *v.* Lebanon School Board, 53
Marchioro *v.* Chaney, 561

Marino *v.* Town of Ramapo, 500
Marland *v.* Ambach, 218
Marmo *v.* N.Y. City Board of Educ., 335
Marques *v.* Riverside Military Academy, 567
Marquesano *v.* Board of Educ., 335
Marsh *v.* St. Vrain School District, 246
Marshall *v.* Kirkland, 376
Marshall *v.* School District RE #3, 493
Martin Luther King Jr. El. Sch. Children *v.* Michigan Board of Educ., 367, 380
Martin *v.* Coral Gables Academy, 550
Martin *v.* Harrah Ind. School District, 35, 221
Martin *v.* Roman Catholic Archbishop, 566, 567
Mason *v.* Southern New England Conference Assn., 563
Mason *v.* Thetford School Board, 311
Mass. *v.* Board of Educ. of San Francisco Unified School District, 182
Mastrangelo *v.* W. Side Un. H.S. District, 439
Mathes, Estate of *v.* Ireland, 445
Mathews *v.* Eldridge, 224, 225
Mathews *v.* Quinton, 576
Matter of Baer, 184
Matter of Baum, 76
Matter of Election of D. Bayless, 188
Matter of McMillan, 75, 76
Matter of Montcrieffe, 77
Matter of Proios, 78
Matter of Washoe Co. School District, 246
Matteson *v.* State Board of Educ., 199
Matteucci *v.* H.S. District, 440
Matthews *v.* Board of Education, 175, 191, 198
McBean *v.* Fresno, 487
McCarthy *v.* Philadelphia Civil Service Commission, 185
McCartney *v.* Austin, 138
McClain *v.* Lafayette Cty. Board of Educ., 306
McClean *v.* Arkansas Board of Educ., 129
McCollum *v.* Board of Education, 125
McConnell *v.* Anderson, 216
McCorkle *v.* City of Los Angeles, 448
McCown *v.* Patagonia Union School District, 51
McCoy *v.* McConnell, 198, 200
McCoy *v.* Tanginpahoa Parish School Board, 200, 202
McCreary *v.* Stone, 132
McCullough *v.* Cashmere School District, 218
McDaniel *v.* Patty, 133
McDonald *v.* Santa Fe Trans. Co., 370
McDonald *v.* School Board of Yankton, 578
McDonough *v.* Aylward, 485
McDonough *v.* Kelley, 224, 225
McGinnes *v.* Dept. of Finance, 485
McGrath *v.* Burkhard, 192, 193, 259–263
McIntosh *v.* Milano, 337, 445
McKelvey *v.* Colonial School District, 35, 206, 208, 223
McKittrick, State ex rel. *v.* Whittle, 188
McKnight *v.* Board of Educ., 137
McLaughlin *v.* Tilendis, 240
McManus *v.* Anahuac Ind. Sch. District, 447
McManus *v.* Ind. School District, 204
McMullen *v.* Dist. School Board, 202
McMullen *v.* Ursuline Order of Sisters, 567
McNabb *v.* United States, 304
McNamara *v.* Board of Education, 195
McNaughton *v.* Circleville Board of Educ., 338
McNeal *v.* Tate County School District, 101, 365
McNees *v.* Scholley, 448
Meade *v.* Oakland H.S. District, 440
Mead School District *v.* Mead Educ. Assn., 49, 257
Medeiros *v.* Kiyosaki, 131
Meek *v.* Pittenger, 571
Meier *v.* Evansville-Vanderburgh School Corp., 188, 376
Meliti *v.* Nyquist, 183
Melton *v.* Young, 316
Meltzer *v.* Bd. of Pub. Instruction, etc., 126, 128
Memphis A.F.T. *v.* Board of Educ., 251
Mencke *v.* Board of Educ., 503
Menke *v.* Ohio H.S. Athletic Assn., 92
Mercer *v.* Board of Trustees, N. Forest Independent School District, 323
Mercer *v.* Michigan State Board of Education, 89, 145–148, 319
Mercer *v.* State, 325
Mercure *v.* Board of Educ., 490
Merrick Comm. Nursery School *v.* Young, 546
Merriken *v.* Cressman, 335
Merrill *v.* Catholic Bishop of Chicago, 563
Merritt *v.* West Mifflin Area School District, 35
Mester *v.* Mester, 337
Metropolitan School District of Lawrence Twp. *v.* Buckley, 369
Metropolitan School District of Perry Twp. *v.* Buckley, 369
Meyer Board of Educ., 440
Meyer *v.* Nebraska, 537
Meyer *v.* Oklahoma, 132
Meyers *v.* Newport Cons. School District, 185
Meyr *v.* Board of Educ., 220, 221
Middough *v.* Board of Trustees, 35
Milberry *v.* Board of Educ., 254
Miller *v.* B.C. Board of Educ., 217
Miller *v.* Board of Educ., 227
Miller *v.* California, 320
Miller *v.* Concordia Teachers College, 563
Miller *v.* Gillis, 323
Miller *v.* Noe, 218
Miller *v.* School District No. 167, 206, 220, 235, 236
Miller *v.* Yoshimoto, 435, 436
Miller, State ex rel. *v.* Board of Educ., 47
Milliken *v.* Board of Directors, 237
Milliken *v.* Bradley, 363, 364, 369, 394–395
Milliken *v.* Green, 484
Mills *v.* Board of Educ., 307, 311
Mills *v.* Phillips, 337
Milwaukee Montessori School *v.* Percy, 540
Mims *v.* W. Baton Rouge Parish School District, 210
Minarcini *v.* Strongsville City School District, 88
Minnesota Assn. of Public Schools *v.* Hanson, 42, 206
Minnesota Civil Liberties Union *v.* Roemer, 570
Minnesota Civil Liberties Union *v.* State, 581
Minnesota Fed. Teachers *v.* Minn. Sp. School District, 246, 247
Missoula H.S. Legal Defense Assn. *v.* Supt. of Public Instruction, 494
Missouri Univ. for Women *v.* Hogan, 373
Mitchell *v.* Board of Educ., 204
Mitchell *v.* Board of Trustees, 202, 377
Mitchell *v.* Garrett, 202
Mitchell *v.* Guilford Co. Board of Educ., 440, 441, 429
Mitchell *v.* McCall, 137
Mitchell *v.* No. Car. Ind. Dev. Financing Authority, 495
Mitchum *v.* Foster, 451
Mlynarski *v.* St. Rita's Congregation, 567
Moffett *v.* Calcasieu Parish School Board, 233
Mogle *v.* Sevier Co. School Board, 185
Mohr *v.* Dade County School Board, 202
Monaghan *v.* School District No. 1, 189
Monell *v.* Department of Social Services of the City of New York, 456, 474–476
Monnig, In re, 544
Montalvo *v.* Madera Un. School District Board of Educ., 314

Montoya *v.* Sanger Unified School District, 305
Mooney *v.* Orchard Lake, 545
Moore *v.* Board of Education, 125, 133
Moore *v.* Knowles, 206
Moore *v.* Order Minor Conventuals, 567
Moore *v.* School Board of Gulf County, 239
Moore *v.* Student Affairs Comm., 326
Morale *v.* Grigel, 325
Morales *v.* Shannon, 365, 366
Moranek *v.* Davenport Community School District, 247
Morelli *v.* Board of Educ., 212
Morgan *v.* Board of Educ., 81, 86
Morris Cent. School District *v.* Morris Educ. Assn., 254
Morris *v.* Board of Educ., 223
Morris *v.* Douglas County School, 442
Morris *v.* Michigan State Board of Educ., 374, 375
Morris *v.* Morris, 337
Morris *v.* Ortiz, 435, 440
Morris *v.* Union H.S. District, 438
Morris *v.* Vandiver, 493
Morrisette *v.* De Zonia, 74
Morrison *v.* Comm. Anita School District, 429
Morrison *v.* Hamilton County Board of Educ., 235, 236
Morrison *v.* State Board of Educ., 213, 214
Morrow *v.* Wood, 432
Morse *v.* Wozniak, 196, 199
Morton *v.* Board of Educ., 135
Morton *v.* Mancari, 370
Mortweet *v.* Ethan Board of Educ., 210
Moser *v.* State Board of Educ., 182
Moses Lake School District No. 161 *v.* Big Bend Community College, 43
Moses *v.* Washington Par. School Board, 365
Mosier *v.* Baron County Board of Health, 138
Moss *v.* Stamford Board of Educ., 363
Mountain States Legal Foundation *v.* Denver School District, 495
Mouras *v.* Jefferson Parish School Board, 202
Mt. Healthy City School District Board of Educ. *v.* Doyle, 208, 222, 230, 446
Mugavin *v.* Nyquist, 196
Muka *v.* Cornell, 5, 36
Mullally *v.* Board of Educ., 224
Mullen *v.* Board of School Directors of Dubois Area S. District, 56–58
Mullins *v.* Eveland, 50
Munro *v.* Elk Rapids School, 206
Murphy *v.* Board of Educ., 434
Murphy *v.* City of Brockton, 483
Murphy *v.* Pocatello School District, 323
Murray *v.* W. Baton Rouge Parish School, 305, 308, 309, 322, 365
Myers *v.* Board of Educ., 225
Myers *v.* Orleans Parish School Board, 212

NAACP *v.* Alabama, 99, 370
NAACP *v.* Lansing Board of Educ., 364
Nagle, State ex rel. *v.* Olin, 540, 543
Nagy *v.* Board of Educ., 195
Narcisse *v.* Continental Ins. Co., 433
Narragansett Elec. Co. *v.* Rhode Island Comm. Human Rts., 378
Nash *v.* Rapides School Board, 436
Nashville Gas Co. *v.* Satty, 377, 378
Nat'l. Educ. Assn. of Shawnee Mission, Inc. *v.* Board of Educ., 246
National Educ. Assn. *v.* Lee County Board of Instruction, 235
National Educ. Assn. *v.* So. Carolina, 362, 367
National Educ. Assn. *v.* Unified School Dist., 250
National Electrical Contractors Assoc. *v.* Seattle School District, 499
National Labor Relations Board *v.* The Catholic Bishop of Chicago, et al., 592–598
National Socialist White People's Party *v.* Ringers, 99
Natonabah *v.* Board of Educ., 362
Neal *v.* Bryant, 183
Needleman *v.* Bohlen, 453
Nelson *v.* Blanco Ind. School District, 486
Nelson *v.* Tuscarora Intermediate Unit, 78
Nestor *v.* New York, 436
Nethercutt *v.* Pulaski County Special School District, 47
Nevens *v.* City of Chino, 52
Newberg *v.* Board of Educ., 373
New Castle Area School District *v.* Bair, 210
New Castle County School District *v.* State, 43, 100
Newcastle-Gunning-Bedford Educ. Assn. *v.* Board of Educ., 221
New Jersey *v.* T.L.O., 325, 326, 327, 328, 329, 350–354
Newkirk *v.* School District of Philadelphia, 248
Newlan *v.* State, 449
New Left Educ. Project *v.* Board of Regents, 319
Newman *v.* Board of Educ., 206, 246, 253, 297
New Mexico Bus Sales *v.* Michael, 503
New Mexico St. Board of Educ. *v.* Stoudt, 215
Newport-Mesa Unified Sch. District *v.* Hubert, 560
New Rider *v.* Board of Educ., 322, 323
News & Observer Pub. *v.* Interim Board of Educ., 49
New York City Board of Educ. *v.* N.Y. Human Rts. App. Board, 377
New York Times Co. *v.* Sullivan, 321
Nichols *v.* Bolding, 241
Nichols *v.* Henry, 576
Nicholson *v.* Board of Educ., 320
Nicholson *v.* Board of Educ., 321
Niederhuber *v.* Camden Co. Voc. Tech. School District Board of Educ., 126
Nielson *v.* Comm. Unit. School District, 439
Nistad *v.* Board of Educ., 99, 231
Nitzberg *v.* Parks, 308, 317, 318
Noe *v.* Edmonds School District, 31
Noland *v.* Colorado School of Trades, Inc., 565
Noonan (R.S.) Inc. *v.* School District, 503
Norbeck *v.* Davenport Comm. School District, 235
Norris *v.* American Casualty Co., 440, 441
Norris *v.* Arizon Governing Committee, 378
North Carolina State Board of Educ. *v.* Swann, 369
North Carolina Teachers Assn. *v.* Asheboro City Board of Educ., 362
North Haven Board of Educ. *v.* Bell, 374
North Shore School District No. 147 *v.* Kinnear, 484, 485
Northwestern School District *v.* Pittinger, 485
Norton *v.* Board of Educ., 492
Norwalk CORE *v.* Norwalk Board of Educ., 363
Norwin School District *v.* Chlodney, 200
Norwood *v.* Harrison, 363, 556
Novotny *v.* Great American S. & L. Assn., 455
Nucklos *v.* Lyle, 498
Nunez *v.* Isadore Newman H.S., 434
Nutter *v.* School Com. of Lowell, 228

Oak Harbor School District *v.* Oak Harbor Educ. Assn., 195, 248
O'Connell (Dennis J.) H.S. *v.* Virginia H.S. League, 92, 93
O'Connor *v.* Board of Educ., 307, 313
O'Connor *v.* Hendrick, 133, 134
O'Hara, Appeal of, 546

O'Leary *v.* Wisecup, 77, 304, 492
O'Melia *v.* Sweetwater County School District, 185–6
O'Neil *v.* School District No. 15, 74
Odorizzi *v.* Bloomfield School District, 218
Oefelein *v.* Msgr. Farrell H.S., 553
Oglesby *v.* Seminole City Board of Instr., 440
Ohio Assn. of Public School Employees *v.* Bexley City School District Board of Educ., 245
Ohman *v.* Board of Educ., 437
Older *v.* Board of Educ., 34
Oldham *v.* Drummond Board of Educ., 50, 51
Olff *v.* East Side H.S. District, 322
Oliber *v.* Mich. State Board of Educ., 361
Olin *v.* Fair Emp. Practices Comm'n., 126
Oliveri *v.* Carlstatd E. Rutherford Reg. School Board of Educ., 224
Oneal *v.* Colton Cons. School District No. 396, 211
Opinion of the Justices, 375, 485, 576
Oracle School District *v.* Mammoth High School District, 491
Ordway *v.* Hargraves, 325
Orford Teachers Association *v.* Watson, 51, 53
Orr *v.* Thorpe, 240
Osage National Bank *v.* Oakes Special School District, 489
Osborne *v.* Bullitt County Board of Educ., 229
Ostrolenk *v.* Louise S. McGhee School, 549
Otero *v.* Mesa County Valley School District No. 51, 366
Ott *v.* Board of Educ. of Hamilton Twp., 226
Otter Tail Power Co. *v.* Village of Elbow Lake, 502
Owen *v.* Comm. of Kentucky, 432

Packard *v.* Jt. School District, 450
Paladino *v.* Adelphi University, 543, 554
Palladium Publishing Co. *v.* River Valley School Dist., 306, 307, 335
Pallas *v.* Johnson, 500
Palmer *v.* Board of Educ., 137, 231
Palo Verde Un. School District *v.* Hensey, 239
Palone *v.* Jefferson Parish School District, 201, 203, 204
Palsgraf *v.* Long Island R.R. Co., 427
Panlillio *v.* Dallas Ind. Sch. District, 180
Panther Oil and Grease Mfg. Co. *v.* Blount Co. Board of Educ., 496
Paolus *v.* Board of Trustees, 175
Papish *v.* Board of Curators, U. of Mo., 317, 320
Paqua *v.* LaForche Paris Sch. Bd., 196
Parducci *v.* Rutland, 238
Parish Council of East Baton Rouge *v.* Louisiana Highway, etc., Association General Contractors, etc., 499
Park Progresso Ind. School District, 488
Park *v.* Lansing, 185
Parker *v.* Board of Educ., 238
Parker *v.* Board of School Commissioners, 376
Parker *v.* Letson, 224
Parks & Sons *v.* City of Pocatello, 501
Parochial Bus Systems *v.* Board of Educ., 449
Parolisi *v.* Board of Educ., 181, 185
Parr *v.* State, 545
Parrish *v.* Moss, 193
Passaforo *v.* Board of Educ., 428
Passantino *v.* Board of Educ., 439
Passel *v.* Ft. Worth Ind. School District, 90, 338
Paste *v.* Tussey, 578
Paul Goodman, Inc. *v.* Burns, 499
Paul *v.* Dade County, 132
Paul *v.* Davis, 331
Pauley *v.* Kelly, 484
Paulson *v.* Minidoka Co. School District, 492, 494
Paxman *v.* Wilkerson, 377
Payroll Guarantee Assn. Inc. *v.* Board of Educ. of San Francisco Un. School District, 100
Pease *v.* Mill Creek Twp. School District, 193
Peck *v.* Board of Educ., 442, 445
Pelisek *v.* Trevor State Graded School District, 222, 224
Pell *v.* Board of Educ., 211
Penasco Ind. School District No. 4 *v.* Lucero, 205
Penn Delco School District *v.* URSO, 213, 214, 217
Pennell *v.* Pond Un. School District, 219
Pennsylvania Assn. for Retarded Children *v.* Commonwealth, 311
Pennsylvania Assn. of Retarded Children (PARC) *v.* Pennsylvania, 365
Pennsylvania Human Relations Commission *v.* Uniontown Area School District, 372
Pennsylvania Labor Relations Board *v.* Beth Jacob Schools, 552
Pennsylvania Labor Relations Board *v.* Mars Area School District, 247
Pennsylvania Labor Relations Board *v.* State College Area School District, 246
Pennsylvania *v.* Brown, 556
Penzenstadler *v.* Avonworth School District, 86
People ex rel. Schuldt *v.* Schimanski, 73
People *v.* Bowers, 326
People *v.* D., 325, 328
People *v.* Darby, 497
People *v.* DeCaro, 426
People *v.* Jackson, 328
People *v.* Kapp, 195
People *v.* Lanthier, 329
People *v.* Levisen, 538, 539, 543
People *v.* Mayberry, 328
People *v.* Mummert, 426
People *v.* Overton, 326
People *v.* Smith, 432
People *v.* Turner, 537, 538, 541, 542, 544
People *v.* Ward, 325, 328
People *v.* Willard, 188
PERB *v.* Hawaii St. Teacher Assn., 256
Perbost *v.* San Marino Hall-School for Girls, 564
Perker *v.* Panama City, 500
Perry Education Ass'n *v.* Perry Local Educators' Ass'n, 286–288
Perry *v.* Seattle School District, 439
Perry *v.* Sindermann, 183, 207, 221, 222
Pervis *v.* LaMarque Ind. School District, 312
Peter W. *v.* San Francisco Un. Sch. Dist., 444
Peters *v.* Board of Educ., 205
Peters *v.* Health & Hospital Gov'g Comm., 241
Peters *v.* Middlebury College, 376
Petersburg Educ. Assn. *v.* Petersburg School District No. 14, 208
Peterson *v.* Board of Education, 90, 319
Petition of Davenport, 211, 227, 232
Pettit *v.* State Board of Educ., 216
Phila. Fed'n. of Teachers *v.* Board of Education, 180
Philbrook *v.* Ansonia Board of Educ., 126
Phillippi *v.* School District, 204
Phillips *v.* Board of Educ., 210
Phillips *v.* Homewood, 546
Phillips *v.* Maure, 495
Phoenix *v.* Kolodziejski, 45
Picard *v.* Greisinger, 446
Picha *v.* Wiedgos, 324, 325, 326, 329, 450
Pickering *v.* Board of Educ., 230, 231
Pickings *v.* Bruce, 99

Pierce *v.* Hill Military Academy, 537
Pierce *v.* School Comm. of New Bedford, 307, 308, 309
Pierce *v.* Society of Sisters, 537
Pietro *v.* St. Joseph's School, 568
Pietrunti *v.* Board of Educ., 234, 238
Pime *v.* Loyola Univ. of Chicago, 557
Piper *v.* Board of Trustees, 218
Pirkle *v.* Oakdale Un. Sch. District, 442
Pirrone *v.* City of Boston, 485
Piscataway Twp. Board of Educ. *v.* Burke, 372
Pittman *v.* Hattiesburg Municipal Separate School Dist., 378
Pittsburgh Coal Co. *v.* School District, 486
Pittsburgh Fed'n. of Teachers *v.* Aaron, 186
Placerville Un. School District *v.* Porini, 197
Plainview Old Bethpage Cong. of Teachers *v.* Board of Educ., 257
Plesnicer *v.* Kovach, 73, 440
Poindexter *v.* La. Financial Assistance Comm., 363
Pointek *v.* Elk Lake School District, 182
Police Dept. of Chicago *v.* Mosley, 98
Pomrehn *v.* Crete-Monee S. District, 427
Pooler *v.* Nyquist, 334
Porcelli *v.* Titus, 370
Pordom *v.* Board of Regents of State of New York, 183, 225
Port Arthur Independent School District *v.* City of Groves, 102–104
Port Jefferson Station Teachers Assn. *v.* Brookhaven Comsewogue School District, 253
Portage Area School District *v.* Portage Area School Assn., 205
Potter *v.* Richland School District, 210
Potter *v.* School Directors, 79
Potts *v.* Gibson, 201, 224
Potts *v.* Wright, 328
Poulos *v.* Board of Trustees, 191, 192, 195
Pounder *v.* Harper Woods Board of Educ., 226
Powe *v.* Miles, 568
Powell *v.* Young, 210
Powers *v.* Jt. School District, 441
Pratt *v.* Arizona Board of Regents, 136
Pratt *v.* Independent School District No. 831, 88
Pratt *v.* Robinson, 441
Presbyterian Church *v.* Mary E. Blue, Hull Memorial Presbyterian Church, 550
Prescott Community Hospital Commission *v.* Prescott School District, 101
President's Council, District 25 *v.* Community School Board, 238
Presley *v.* Vernon Parish Board of Educ., 100
Press *v.* Pasadena Ind. School District, 323
Princeton University *v.* Schmid, 90
Prof'l. Detail Service, Inc. *v.* Board of Educ., 449
Proposal C, In re, 135
Protest of Mo. Keno-Tex. R. Co., 42
Pruzan *v.* Board of Educ., 255
Public Funds for Public Schools of New Jersey *v.* Byrne, 581
Puglisi *v.* School Committee of Whitman, 51
Pugsley *v.* Sellmeyer, 323
Purifoy *v.* State Board of Educ., 209
Pyle *v.* Wash. Co. School Board, 224

Quaker Oats Co. *v.* Cedar Rapids Human Rts. Comm., 378
Quarterman *v.* Byrd, 304, 315
Quast *v.* Knudson, 50
Qunigley *v.* School District, 434

Racine Un. School District *v.* Thomas, 307, 311
Raffa *v.* Central School District, 433, 434
Raffalone *v.* Pearsall, 482
Ramirez *v.* Flores, 47
Ramsey *v.* Hopkins, 236
Randle *v.* Indianola Sep. School District, 235
Randolph *v.* School Unit 201, 73
Rankin *v.* Commission on Professional Competence, 126, 138
Ranninger *v.* State, 328
Rapp *v.* Bethel Tate Cons. School District, 46
Ratchford *v.* Gay Lib., 215
Rawlings *v.* Butler, 133
Raymond *v.* Fresno City Un. School District, 501
Raymond *v.* Paradise, 435, 436
Read *v.* School District, 439
Reagh *v.* San Francisco Un. School District, 439
Reardon *v.* Lemoyne, 550
Reassignment of Hayes, 79, 86
Red Bank Board of Educ. *v.* Warrington, 254
Redcay *v.* State Board of Educ., 210
Reed *v.* Board of Educ., 211
Reeves *v.* Orleans Parish School Board, 51, 52
Regents of U. of Minnesota *v.* NCAA, 93, 307
Regents, U. of California *v.* Bakke, 370–371
Reilley *v.* Robertson, 378
Reinhardt *v.* Board of Educ., 215
Reinken *v.* Keller, 497
Reinman *v.* Valley View School District, 305
Remmick *v.* Barnes County, 360
Rendell-Baker *v.* Kohn, 553, 556
Rennie *v.* Belleview School District, 448
Rensselear Co. Ed. Local *v.* Newman, 186
Resco Equipment and Supply Corporation *v.* City Council of Watertown, 499
Resnick *v.* E. Brunswick Twp. Board of Educ., 136, 137
Responsive Env. Corp. *v.* Pulaski Co. Spe. School District, 496
Ressle *v.* Board of Educ., 440
Rettig *v.* Kansas City School District, 384
Rettig *v.* Kent City School District, 383, 384
Rewco, Inc. *v.* City of Cleveland, 501
Reynolds School District *v.* Oregon School Employment Assn., 245
Rhee *v.* Allegheny Intermediate Unit No. 3, 195
Rhodus *v.* Dunmiller, 339
Rhyne *v.* Childes, 316
Rible *v.* Hughes, 197
Rice *v.* Commonwealth, 6
Rice *v.* School District, 436
Richard *v.* St. Landry Par. School Board, 436
Richards *v.* Omaha Public Schools, 377
Richards *v.* Thursten, 322
Richland Par. Bus Drivers Assn. *v.* Richland Par. Sch. Board, 495
Richmond Educ. Assn. *v.* Crocksford, 240
Ricker *v.* Board of Educ., 495
Riddick *v.* School Board, 370
Ridenour *v.* Board of Educ., City of Dearborn, 51
Ridgefield Park Educ. Assn. *v.* Ridgefield Park Board of Educ., 247, 254
Right to Read Defense Committee *v.* School Committee, 88
Riley *v.* Adirondack Southern School for Girls, 557
Riley *v.* School District, 24, 181
Ring *v.* Grand Forks, 132
Riseman *v.* School Committee of Quincy, 317, 319
Ritacco *v.* Norwin School District, 374
Ritter *v.* Mt. St. Mary's College, 559
Rive *v.* Commonwealth, 539

Roane *v.* Callisburg Ind. School District, 221
Robb *v.* School District No. RE50(J), 50
Roberts *v.* Lake Central School District, 205, 233
Roberts *v.* Way, 431
Robinson *v.* Cahill, 20, 484
Robinson *v.* City of New York, 430
Robinson *v.* Sacramento City Un. School District, 90, 92, 338
Rochlin *v.* State, 488
Rockefeller *v.* Pynchon, 546
Rockey *v.* School District No. 11, 198, 241
Rockville Center Teachers Assn. *v.* Board of Educ., 254
Rockwell *v.* Board of Educ., 219, 256, 257
Rockwell *v.* Crestwood District Board of Educ., 194
Rodrigues *v.* San Jose Un. School District, 438
Rodriguez *v.* Seattle School District, 438
Roe *v.* Wade, 331
Roemer *v.* Maryland Public Works Board, 570
Rogers *v.* Board of Educ., 92
Rogers *v.* Paul, 362
Rohrabaugh *v.* Huron-Clinton Metro Inc., 446
Roland *v.* School Directors, 211, 216, 432
Roller *v.* Young, 210
Roman Catholic Diocese *v.* Ho-Ho-Kus, 546
Roman Catholic Welfare Corp. *v.* Piedmont, 545
Rondol *v.* Newberg, 313
Ronish, State ex rel. *v.* School District, 80
Rose *v.* Board of Educ., 447
Rosenburg *v.* Board of Educ., 88, 195
Rosenstein *v.* North Penn School District, 79
Rosenstock *v.* Scaringe, 47
Rosenthal *v.* Orleans Parish School Board, 198, 200
Ross *v.* Allen, 560
Ross *v.* San Francisco Un. H.S. District, 440
Rosser *v.* Meriwether County, 446
Rost *v.* Horky, 224
Roth *v.* Board of Regents, 208
Roy *v.* Continental Ins. Co., 432
Royer *v.* Board of Educ., 323
Ruehl, (Albert F.) Co. *v.* Board of Trustees of Schools, 503
Ruman *v.* Eskew, 374
Rumler *v.* Board of School Trustees, 267, 308
Rumora *v.* Board of Educ., 212
Rumph *v.* Wayne Community School District, 218
Runyon *v.* McCrary, 537, 556
Russ *v.* White, 237
Russell *v.* Belmont College, 559
Russo *v.* Central School District, 137, 202, 231
Rutgers State University *v.* Piluso, 69
Ryan *v.* Aurora City Board of Educ., 206, 220, 221, 266–271
Ryan *v.* Board of Educ., 97
Rylke *v.* Portage Area School District, 253

S. *v.* Board of Educ., 220, 223, 311
Sabin *v.* La. State Board of Educ., 37
Saddle River County Day School *v.* Saddle River, 546
Sageser *v.* Ledbetter, 95
Sailors *v.* Board of Educ., 45
Salvail *v.* Nassua Board of Educ., 88
San Antonio Ind. School District *v.* Rodriguez, 21, 484, 507–514
San Francisco Unified School District *v.* Johnson, 369
San Lorenzo Educ. Assn. *v.* Wilson, 251
Sanchick *v.* Board of Educ., 438
Sanderlin *v.* Central School District, 441
Sanders *v.* Board of Educ., 209
Sandlin *v.* Johnson, 80
Sansonni *v.* Jefferson Par. School Board, 434
Santa Clara *v.* Santa Clara Unified School District, 69
Santa Fe Comm. School District *v.* New Mexico State Board of Educ., 541
Santa Monica School District *v.* Persh, 496
Santee's Appeal, 200
Santosky *v.* Kremer, 75, 545
Sapp *v.* Renpoe, 316
Sarro *v.* N.Y.C. Board of Educ., 208
Satariano *v.* Sleight, 441
Satterfield *v.* Edenton-Chowan Board of Educ., 206
Saul *v.* Roman Catholic Church, 564
Savino *v.* Bradford Central School Dist. Board of Educ., 47
Sawaya *v.* Tucson H.S. District, 448
Scales *v.* United States, 217
Scarborough *v.* Granite School District, 449
Scarnato *v.* Parker, 484, 485
Schauer *v.* Jamestown College, 550
Scheelhaase *v.* Woodbury Cent. Comm. School District, 222, 229
Schmidt *v.* Blair, 72
Schmidt *v.* Payne, 74
Schnell *v.* Travelers Ins. Co., 437
Schoneberg *v.* Grundy County Board of Educ., 376
School Board District No. 18 *v.* Thompson, 83
School Board of Escombia County *v.* PERB, 250
School Board *v.* Anderson, 436
School Board *v.* Ehrlich, 491
School Board *v.* Goodson, 48
School Board *v.* Parham, 20
School City of E. Chicago *v.* Sigler, 189
School Committee of Hanover *v.* Curry, 247, 253
School Comm. of Danvers *v.* Tyman, 254
School Comm. of New Bedford *v.* Commissioner of Education, 30
School Committee of Boston *v.* Board of Educ., 34
School Committee of W. Springfield *v.* Korbut, 254
School Directors *v.* Toll, 100
School Dist. of Chester Twp. *v.* School Dist. of City of Chester, 77
School District 12 *v.* Hughes, 20
School District 12 *v.* Hughes, 47
School District 14 *v.* School District 21, 46
School District City of Lansing *v.* State Board of Education, 46
School District City of Pittsburgh *v.* Zebra, 76
School District City of Royal Oak *v.* Schulman, 51
School District No. 1 *v.* Lohr, 47
School District No. 3 of Maricopa County *v.* Dailey, 78
School District No. 8 *v.* Board of Educ. (Neb.), 30
School District No. 22 *v.* Castell, 49
School District No. 47 of Hall County *v.* School District of City of Grand Island, 46
School District No. 50 *v.* Witthaus, 48
School District of Abington Twp. *v.* Schempp, 124, 126, 130
School District of Omaha *v.* U.S., 361
School District of Philadelphia *v.* Zoning Board of Adjustment, 69, 71
School District of Pittsburgh *v.* City, 484
School District of Pittsburgh *v.* Commonwealth, 73
School District of Scottsbluff *v.* Olson Constr. Co., 502–503
School District of Seward Educ. Assn. *v.* School District of Seward, 246, 253
School District of Springfield, State ex rel. *v.* Wickliffe, 496
School District *v.* Moeller, 53
School District *v.* Norwood, 197

School District *v.* Pennington, 497
School District *v.* Zoning Board (Pa.), 69
School District, Twp. of Millcreek *v.* Commonwealth, 376
School District No. 1 Multnomah Cty. *v.* Teachers' Retirement Fund Ass'n., 197
School Town of Speedway *v.* Buckley, 369
Schull Constr. Co. *v.* Webster Ind. School District, 489
Schults *v.* Board of Educ., 51–52
Schultz *v.* Cheney School District, 440
Schultz *v.* Gould Academy, 564
Schultz *v.* Roman Catholic Archdiocese of Newark, 565
Schulze *v.* Coykendall, 443
Schuyler *v.* Board of Educ., 435
Schwabenauer *v.* Board of Educ., 378
Schwan, etc. *v.* Board of Educ., etc., 80
Schware *v.* Board of Bar Examiners, 213
Schwartz *v.* Board of Educ., 218
Schwartz *v.* Bogen, 183
Schwartz *v.* Schuker, 316
Sciotino *v.* Leech, 554
Scoma *v.* Chicago Board of Educ., 537, 539, 540, 545
Scoma *v.* Illinois, 75
Scott *v.* Board of Educ., 213
Scott *v.* Independent School District, 448
Scott *v.* Thompson, 441
Scotts *v.* Wygant, 370
Scottsdale Sch. District *v.* Clark, 198
Scoville *v.* Board of Educ., 316, 318
Scranton School Board *v.* Scranton Fed. of Teachers, 247, 254
Seacoast Constr. Corp. *v.* Lockport Urban Renewal Agency, 503, 504
Seattle School District *v.* State, 484
Secrist *v.* Diedrich, 524–526
Seda *v.* Board of Educ., 439
Sedule *v.* Capitol School District, 214
Seger *v.* Board of Educ., 493
Segerman *v.* Jones, 437
Seim *v.* Ind. District of Monroe, 500
Selleck *v.* Ins. Co. of North America, 566
Seloover *v.* Columbia County Admin. School District, 100
SENA School Bus Co. *v.* Board of Educ., 449
Serna *v.* Portales Mun. Schools, 366
Serrano *v.* Priest, 484
Severson *v.* Beloit, 439
Seward Chapel, Inc. *v.* City of Seward, 545, 547
Seyfried *v.* Walton, 320
Shanahan *v.* St. James R.C. Church, 566
Shanenberg *v.* Commonwealth Sec. of Ed., 383
Shanley *v.* Northeast Ind. School District, 308, 315, 317
Shannon *v.* Addison Trail H. School, 430
Shannon *v.* Central-Gaither Union Sch. District, 441
Shapiro *v.* Thompson, 186
Sharp *v.* Huron Valley Board of Educ., 86
Sharpe *v.* Quality Education, Inc., 567
Shaw *v.* Glickman, 445
Shearer *v.* Perry Comm. School District, 449
Sheck *v.* Baileyville School Committee, 88
Sheehan *v.* St. Peter's Catholic Church, 566
Sheldon *v.* Fannin, 316
Sheley *v.* Board of Public Educ., 447
Shelton *v.* Tucker, 228, 308
Shenefield *v.* Sheridan Co. School District, 376
Shepheard *v.* Godwin, 496
Sheppard *v.* State, 545
Sherbert *v.* Verner, 138
Sherefield *v.* Sheridan County School District, 34
Sheridan Baptist Church *v.* Dept. of Education, 543
Sherman *v.* Board of Educ., 218
Sherrill *v.* Wilson, 445
Shiffen *v.* Board of Educ., 219
Shinn, In re, 543, 544
Shirley *v.* School Board, 45
Shofstall *v.* Hollins, 484
Shoreline School District, State ex rel. *v.* Superior Court, 75, 76, 539, 543, 544
Shoresman *v.* Burgess, 188
Shrewsbury et al. *v.* Board of Education, 73
Shull *v.* Columbus Mun. Separate School District, 330
Siegel *v.* Allen, 71
Siegel, Matter of, 32
Siglin *v.* Kayenta Un. School District, 211
Sigmon *v.* Poe, 227
Siler *v.* Brady Ind. School District, 220, 221
Silverberg *v.* Board of Educ., 79
Silverman *v.* Board of Educ., 436
Simard *v.* Groton, 227
Simcox *v.* Board of Educ., 208, 210
Simmons *v.* Beauregard Par. School Board, 429, 430, 439
Simms *v.* Roosevelt Union Free School District, 78
Simms *v.* School District No. 1, 432
Simon *v.* Jefferson Davis Parish School Board, 217, 239
Sims *v.* Colfax Community School District, 334
Sims *v.* Etowah City Board of Educ., 437
Sims *v.* Town of Baldwin, 485
Singleton *v.* Iberville Parish School District, 210
Singleton *v.* Jackson Mun. Sep. School District, 202, 362
Siver *v.* Atlantic Union College, 564
Skeim *v.* Ind. School District, 257
Skidmore *v.* Shamrock Ind. School District, 220
Slade *v.* New Hanover Co. Board of Educ., 441
Slattery *v.* Comm. of Cranston, 181
Sloan *v.* Lemon, 570, 578
Slovin *v.* Gauger, 434
Sly *v.* Board of Educ., 447
Small *v.* Board of Educ., 432
Smith Lab *v.* Chester Co. School Board, 48
Smith *v.* Alameda County Social Services, 444
Smith *v.* Archbishop of St. Louis, 565
Smith *v.* Board of Educ., 370
Smith *v.* Board of Educ. (Kans.), 448
Smith *v.* Board of School Directors, 199, 204, 205
Smith *v.* Broken Arrow Pub. School, 433
Smith *v.* Clintondale School District, 434
Smith *v.* Liberty Mutual Life Ins., 375
Smith *v.* Ricci, 131
Smith *v.* Robinson, 381, 409–413
Smith *v.* Siders, 34
Smith *v.* Smith, 125
Smith *v.* Vernon Parish School Board, 439
Smith *v.* W. Virginia Board of Educ., 338
Smith, etc. *v.* Archbishop of St. Louis, 562
Sneed *v.* Greensboro City Board of Education, 494
Snell *v.* Brothers, 197
Snider *v.* Kit Carson School District, 207
Snipes *v.* McAndrew, 196
Snow *v.* State of New York, 444
Snyder *v.* Charlotte Public School District, 135
Snyder *v.* Newtown, 576
Socialist Workers Party *v.* Hardy, 47
Society For Autistic Children *v.* Tidewater Board of Educ., 380
Soglin *v.* Kaufmann, 309
Soni *v.* Board of Trustees, 221
Sorenson *v.* School District No. 28, 182
South Side Estates Baptist Church *v.* Board of Trustees Tax District No. 1, 136

Southeastern Community College *v.* Davis, 380, 383
Southern Pacific Co. *v.* Maricopa County, 43
Spann *v.* Joint Boards of School Directors, 53, 68
Spano *v.* School District of Brentwood, 210
Sparrow *v.* Forsyth Co. Board of Educ., 441
Sparrow *v.* Gill, 74
Speake *v.* Grantham, 329
Spears *v.* Honda, 576
Special District for Educ. and Training Handicapped Children *v.* Wheeler, 580
Spencer *v.* Laconia School District, 210
Spriggs *v.* Altheimer Arkansas School District, 491
Springfield School District *v.* Dept. of Educ., 124
Springfield School District *v.* Shellem, 226
St. Ann *v.* Palisi, 313
St. Cassian's Catholic Church *v.* Allen, 546–547
St. John's Roman Catholic Church Corps. *v.* Darien, 545
St. Joseph Stockyards Co. *v.* United States, 15
St. Mary's Academy *v.* Solomon, 565
St. Paul Foundary Co. *v.* Brunstad School District, 497
Stacy G. *v.* Pasadena School Dist., 384
Stahelin *v.* Board of Educ., 13
Stang *v.* Ind. School District, 195
Stapp *v.* Awoyelles Par. School Board, 221
Starkey *v.* Board of Educ., 330
State Bd. of Elementary Educ. *v.* Rudesill, 545
State Board of Educ. *v.* Anthony, 35
State Division of Human Relations *v.* Board of Educ. (N.Y.S.), 378
State in Interest of G.C., In re, 328
State of Missouri *v.* Schoenlaub, 34
State of New Jersey *v.* Massa, 589–592
State of No. Carolina *v.* Columbus Christian Academy, 539
State of Ohio *v.* Whisner, 584–588
State of Vermont *v.* LaBarge, 545
State Use of Parr *v.* Board of Cty. Commissioners, 440
State *v.* Andrews, 540, 543
State *v.* Baccino, 325
State *v.* Berger, 198
State *v.* Board of Directors (Wisc.), 239
State *v.* Board of Educ. (Minn.), 210, 211
State *v.* Board of Educ. (Ohio), 182, 198
State *v.* Board of Educ. (W. Va.), 201
State *v.* Board of Educ. of Bath-Richfield Local School District, 53
State *v.* Board of School Directors, 197
State *v.* Calvary Academy, 540
State *v.* Cheney, 545
State *v.* Cons. School District No. 3, 48
State *v.* Counart, 538
State *v.* D.T.W., 325, 329
State *v.* Delaware Educ. Assn., 256
State *v.* Edgington, 540, 543
State *v.* Faith Baptist Church, 543
State *v.* Ferguson, 83
State *v.* Garber, 538
State *v.* Gloist, 80
State *v.* Grand Coulee Dam School District, 73, 74
State *v.* Hatley, 218
State *v.* Haworth, 20, 21
State *v.* Hensel, 47
State *v.* Hershberger, 544
State *v.* Hoyt, 538
State *v.* Ind. School District No. 695, 204
State *v.* Jefferson Parish School Board, 226
State *v.* Johnson, 329
State *v.* Judges of the Court of Common Pleas, 92
State *v.* Kasuboski, 537, 540
State *v.* Kimball, 329
State *v.* Kinnear, 22
State *v.* Lamb, 325
State *v.* Lowry, 538, 543
State *v.* Lutz, 426
State *v.* M., 544
State *v.* M.M., 75
State *v.* Mass., 544
State *v.* McDonough, 540, 544
State *v.* McKinnon, 72, 325, 328
State *v.* Miday, 138
State *v.* Moorehead, 540, 543
State *v.* Mora, 325
State *v.* Morrow, 328
State *v.* Nebraska State Board of Educ., 135, 136
State *v.* Northwestern Preparatory School, 546
State *v.* Nuss, 540
State *v.* Peterman, 538
State *v.* Peterson, 210
State *v.* Pilkinton, 545
State *v.* Redman, 195
State *v.* Riddle, 543
State *v.* School District No. 10, 135
State *v.* Shaver, 543, 545
State *v.* Sinar, 546
State *v.* Stein, 329
State *v.* Stojack, 70, 104–105
State *v.* Taylor, 134, 136
State *v.* Thomas, 47
State *v.* Thompson, 125
State *v.* Vanosdal, 51
State *v.* Vietto, 539
State *v.* Weber, 86
State *v.* Williams, 541
State *v.* Wilson (Mo.), 95
State *v.* Wilson (Tenn.), 198
State *v.* Young, 325
Staton *v.* Mayes, 227
Steeber *v.* Benilde–St. Margaret's H.S., 549, 559
Steele *v.* Board of Educ. of City of N.Y., 184
Steele *v.* Board of Educ. of Valhalla Union Free School District, 180
Steele *v.* Waters, 129
Steffani *v.* Baker, 440
Steiler *v.* Spokane School District, 202
Stein *v.* Highland Park Ind. School District, 450, 477
Stein *v.* Oshinsky, 127
Stella, In re, 380
Stephen, (M.A.) Constr. Co. *v.* Borough of Rumson, 503
Stephens *v.* Shelbyville Central Schools, 442
Sterzing *v.* So. Bend Ind. School District, 238
Stevens *v.* Central School District, 433
Stewart *v.* E. Baton Rouge Parish School Board, 183, 215
Stewart *v.* Pearce, 181
Stewart *v.* Reng, 334
Stieler *v.* Spokane School District No. 81, 376
Stineman *v.* Fontbonne College, 565
Sto-Rox School District *v.* Horgan, 204
Stone *v.* Graham, 132
Stough *v.* Crenshaw County Board of Educ., 235
Street *v.* Board of Educ., 200
Street *v.* Cobb Co. School District, 77
Streeter *v.* Hundley, 339
Strickland *v.* Inlow, 453
Stromberg *v.* French, 323
Strong *v.* Ind. School District, 194
Strosnider *v.* Strosnider, 337
Stroud *v.* Pulaski Co. Public School District, 497

Stroy *v.* San Rafael Military Academy, 549
Stuart *v.* Nappi, 413–418
Student Members of the Playcrafters *v.* Board of Educ. of the Twp. of Teaneck, 125
Studley *v.* Allen, 74
Sturges *v.* School District, 447
Sturgis *v.* Allegan County, 21
Suits *v.* Glover, 431, 432, 433
Sullivan *v.* Brown, 202
Sullivan *v.* Houston Ind. School District, 318
Sullivan *v.* Meade County Ind. School District No. 101, 214
Sullivan *v.* School District, 315
Summers *v.* Milwaukee Un. H.S. District, 438
Sumter County *v.* Pritchett, 446
Sup. School Committee *v.* Portland Teachers Assn., 253
Superior Oil Co. *v.* Sinton Ind. School District, 485
Surinach *v.* Pasquare deBusquets, 540
Susq. Valley C. School District *v.* Susq. Valley Teachers Assn., 246
Sutherby *v.* Board of Educ., 211
Sutherland Educ. Assn. *v.* Sutherland School District, 246
Swaitkowski *v.* Board of Educ., 437
Swann *v.* Charlotte-Mecklenberg Board of Educ., 371, 372
Swanson *v.* City of Ottumwa, 486
Swartley *v.* Seattle School District, 430
Sweeney Independent School District *v.* Harkness, 362, 368
Sweet *v.* Cent. Ill. Public Serv. Co., 482
Sweets *v.* Childs, 306
Swilley *v.* Alexander, 234
Syska *v.* Montgomery County Board of Educ., 78

Taggert *v.* Board of Directors of Cannon-MacMillan Jt. School System, 175
Talley *v.* California, 322
Tannenbaum *v.* Board of Educ., 430
Tarasoff *v.* Regents of the Univ. of California, 337, 445
Tardif *v.* Quinn, 236
Tardiff *v.* Shoreline School District, 439
Tarter *v.* Raybuck, 325
Tasby *v.* Estes, 310
Tate *v.* Board of Educ., 316
Tawney *v.* Board of Educ., 378
Taylor Fed. Teachers *v.* Board of Educ., 378
Taylor *v.* Oakland Scavenger Co., 436
Taylor, James I. & Son *v.* Arlington Ind. School District, 502
Taylor, State ex rel. *v.* Lease, 46
Tecumseh School District No. 7 *v.* Throckmorton, 23
Tennessee Secondary School Athletic Assn. *v.* Cox, 93
Tenure Comm. *v.* Anniston City Board of Educ., 198
Texarkana Ind. School District *v.* Lewis, 306, 311
Thichenor *v.* Orleans Parish School Board, 210
Thomas *v.* Board of Educ., 193, 497
Thomas *v.* Schmidt, 135, 136
Thomas *v.* Ward, 221
Thompson, State ex rel. *v.* Marien City Board of Educ., 330
Thompson *v.* County of Alameda, 445
Thompson *v.* E. Baton Rouge Parish School Board, 195
Thompson *v.* Engleking, 484
Thompson *v.* School District (Mich.), 497
Thompson *v.* School District (Ore.), 195
Thompson *v.* Southeast School District, 214
Thornton, Estate of *v.* Caldor, 561
Three L. Corp. *v.* Board of Adj't., 546
Tieman *v.* Ind. School District, 434
Tilton *v.* Richardson, 570, 571
Timberlane Regional School District *v.* Timberlane Regional Educ. Assn., 256
Tindal *v.* Byers, 44
Tinker *v.* Des Moines Ind. Community School District, 314
Tinkham *v.* Kole, 432, 433
Titus *v.* Lindberg, 435, 566
Todd *v.* Rochester Comm. Schools, 129
Tomerlin *v.* Dade County School Board, 215
Torcaso *v.* Watkins, 129
Torres *v.* Laramie Co. School District, 488
Torvik *v.* Deborah Community Schools, 321
Toups *v.* Authement, 212
Toussaint *v.* Blue Cross, 550
Town of Lexington *v.* Comm'r of Education, 483
Town of Waterford *v.* Connecticut State Board of Educ., 73
Town of Winchester *v.* Cox, 43
Townsend by Benavente, 567
Toyah Ind. School District *v.* Pecos-Barstow Ind. School Dist., 52
Trabox *v.* Greensborough Central School District, 34
Trachtman *v.* Anker, 319
Trans World Airlines *v.* Hardison, 139
Trap Rock Industries, Inc. *v.* Kohl, 501
Trent *v.* Perritt, 323
Trinity Ev. Lutheran Church *v.* Board of Adjustment, 546
Tripp *v.* Board of Examiners, 184
Tsakiris *v.* Phoenix Union High School System, 207
Tubell *v.* Dade County Public Schools, 444
Tucker *v.* San Francisco Un. School District, 210
Tudor *v.* Board of Educ., 128
Turner *v.* Board of Educ., 491
Turner *v.* Board of Trustees (Cal. 1975), 207
Turner *v.* Board of Trustees (Cal. 1976), 229
Turner *v.* Caddo Par. School Board, 427, 439
Turner *v.* Kowalski, 314
Turner *v.* Staggs, 449
Tustin Heights Assn. *v.* Board of Supervisors, 546
Twp. Board of Educ. *v.* Maurice River Twp. Teachers Assn., 52
Tyler *v.* Board of Educ., 376
Tyler *v.* Jefferson City–DuBoise Area Voc. Tec., 199
Tymkowicz *v.* San Jose U. School District, 436
Tyrone Area Educ. Assn. *v.* Tyrone Area School District, 192
Tyska *v.* Board of Educ., 31, 33

Ulm *v.* Gitz, 436
Unified Sch. District No. 255 *v.* Unified Sch. District No. 254, 46
Unified School District *v.* State Board of Educ. (Kan.), 42
Unified School District *v.* Wisconsin Emp. Relations Comm., 247
Union Electric Co. *v.* Collector, 485
Union Free H.S. District *v.* Jt. School District, 491
Union Free School District No. 6 *v.* N.Y. Human Rights App. Bd., 248
Union Free School District *v.* Gumbs, 502
Union Free School District *v.* Hewlett Bay Park, 68
Union Free School District *v.* Jackson, 492
United States ex rel. Missouri State High School, In re, 93, 111–114
United States Trust Co. *v.* New Jersey, 44, 45
United States *v.* Choctaw County Board of Educ., 95

United States *v.* Crisp County Board of Education, 374
United States *v.* Hinds, 374
United States *v.* Jefferson County Board of Educ., 364
United States *v.* Martinez-Fuerte, 326
United States *v.* Midland Ind. School District, 362, 367
United States *v.* O'Brien, 316
United States *v.* Robinson, 329
United States *v.* Scotland Neck City Board of Educ., 363
United States *v.* Seeger, 138
United States *v.* South Carolina, 367
United States *v.* State of Mississippi, 101, 363
United States *v.* State of Missouri, 362, 369
United States *v.* Texas, 365
United States *v.* Texas Educ. Agency, 363
United States *v.* Wattsburg Area School District, 376
United Steelworkers of America *v.* Weber, 371
United Teachers *v.* Board of Educ., 375
University Center, Inc. *v.* Ann Arbor Public Schools, 78
Upchurch *v.* Adelsberger, 500
Usery *v.* A & M Cons. Ind. School District, No. 74-H-1532, 376
Usery *v.* Bettendorf Comm. School District, 360
Usery *v.* Board of Educ. of Salt Lake City, 360
Utah Plumbing and Heating Contractors Association *v.* Board of Educ., 499

Valencio *v.* Blue Hen Conference, 93
Valent *v.* New Jersey Board of Educ., 131
Valiquette *v.* City School District, 449
Van Allen *v.* McCleary, 331
Van Buren P. School District *v.* Wayne Cty. Cir. Judge, 247
Van Campen *v.* Building and Construction Trades Council, 500
Vandevender *v.* Cassell, 491, 492, 493
VanGaasbeck *v.* Webatuck Central School District, 440, 441
VanScoyk *v.* St. Mary's Assumption Parochial School, 561
Vaughn *v.* Reed, 131
Veasgy *v.* Board of Public Instruction, 309
Vela, Al J., & Assoc., Inc. *v.* Glendora Un. School District, 100
Velez *v.* Our Lady of Victory Church, 564
Vellaco *v.* City of Derby, 501
Vendrell *v.* School District, 429, 438
Venes *v.* Comm. School Board, 207
Verduce *v.* Board of Higher Educ., 435
Verniero *v.* Air Force Academy School District, 376
Verrett *v.* Calcasieu Parish School Board, 202
Vestal *v.* Pickering, 494
Viemeister *v.* Board of Educ., 203
Village Community School *v.* Adler, 554
Village of Baline *v.* Indep. School District No. 12, 69
Vincent *v.* County Board of Educ., 491
Visser *v.* Nooksack Valley School District, 576
Vitale *v.* Lentine, 450
Viveiros *v.* State, 429
Vogulkin *v.* State Board of Educ., 183
Vorcheimer *v.* School District of Philadelpia, 373
Vought *v.* Van Buren Pub. Schools, 306
Vreeland *v.* State Board of Regents, 433
Vulcan Soc. of N.Y. City Fire Dept. Inc. *v.* Civil Service Comm., 369

W., In re, 325, 328
Wagle *v.* Murray, 233
Wagner *v.* Little Rock School District, 225
Walker *v.* Board of Educ., 205
Walker *v.* Board of Educ. of Olean City School District, 38
Walker *v.* Bradley, 305
Walker *v.* Lockland City School District Board of Educ., 491
Wallace *v.* Board of Educ., 499
Wallace *v.* Ford, 323, 324
Wallace *v.* Jaffree, 124–125, 128, 140–145
Walley *v.* Board of Trustees of Richton Mun. Sep. School District, 501
Walsh *v.* Louisiana H.S. Athletic Assn., 93
Walton *v.* Turlington, 184
Waltz *v.* Board of Education, 196
Walz *v.* Tax Commissioner, 572, 581
Ward *v.* Nyquist, 204
Wardwell *v.* Board of Educ., 185
Warren Educ. Assn. *v.* Adams, 256
Warren *v.* Nat'l. Assn. of Secondary School Principals, 309
Warrensburg School District *v.* Johnson County School District, 491
Washington School District *v.* Superior Ct., 51
Washington *v.* Board of Educ., 234
Washington *v.* Davis, 362, 367
Washington *v.* Salisbury, 492
Washington *v.* State, 316
Watkins *v.* Jackson, 482
Watson *v.* New Milford, 447
Watts *v.* Seward School Board, 233
Watts *v.* Town of Homer, 433
Wayman *v.* Board of Educ., 69
Wayne County Civil Service Comm. *v.* Board of Supervisors, 248
Weathers *v.* W. Yuma County School District, 208
Webb *v.* Lake Mills School District, 228
Webb *v.* Seattle, 441
Wecherly *v.* Board of Educ., 47
Weinberger *v.* Salfi, 35
Weiner *v.* Board of Educ., 434
Weiner *v.* Cuyahoga Community College District, 500
Weissbaum *v.* Hannon, 215
Weissman *v.* Board of Educ., 213, 227
Weist *v.* Mt. Lebanon School District, 132–3
Welch *v.* Dunsmuir Jt. Union H.S. District, 442
Welling *v.* Board of Educ., 79
Welo *v.* District School Board, 207
Welsh *v.* Berne-Knox-Westerlo Cent. Sch. Dist., 449
Welsh *v.* United States, 78
Wentworth Military Academy *v.* Marshall, 553
Wertz *v.* Southern Cloud Unified School District, 208, 221, 223
Wesclin Education Assn. *v.* Board of Educ., 241
Wesley *v.* Board of Educ., 50, 51
Westbury Hebrew Cong'n. Ind. *v.* Downer, 546
West Goshen Twp. *v.* Bible Baptist Church, 547
West Hartford Educ. Assn. *v.* deCourcey, 246
West Irandequoit Teachers Assn. *v.* Helsby, 246
Westlin Area Spec. Educ. Coop. *v.* Lockport Spec. Educ. Coop., 247
West Morris Regional Board of Educ. *v.* Sills, 576
Westtown Educ. Assn. *v.* Westtown Pub. School Board of Educ., 247
West Virginia Board of Educ. *v.* Barnett, 82, 124, 137
Whalen *v.* Minn. Special School District, 48
Whateley *v.* Leonia Board of Educ., 187, 188
Wheeler *v.* Barrera, 134, 496
Wheeler *v.* School District No. 20, 181, 198, 202
Whisner *v.* State Board of Educ., 539
White *v.* Banks, 200
White *v.* Battaglia, 52

White *v.* Board of Educ., 227
White *v.* Dallas Independent School District, 454
Whitehill *v.* Elkins, 228
Whiteside *v.* Kay, 310
Whitfield *v.* Simpson, 309
Whitsel *v.* Southeast Local School District, 211
Whitt *v.* Reed, 448
Whittington *v.* Sowela Technical Institute, 430
Whorley *v.* Brewer, 429, 442
Widmar *v.* Vincent, 137, 168–170
Wieman *v.* Updegraff, 185
Wiest *v.* Mt. Lebanon Sch. District, 132–133
Wiethoff *v.* St. Veronica's School, 549
Wiley House *v.* Scanlon, 537, 538
Wiley *v.* Franklin, 130
Wilhelm *v.* Board of Educ., 439
Wiljamaa *v.* Board of Educ., 218
Wilkinson *v.* Hartford Acc. & Ind. Co., 564
Willett *v.* Emory & Henry College, 378
Williams *v.* Arblemarle Cty. Board of Educ., 453
Williams *v.* Board of Educ., 89, 308
Williams *v.* Board of Educ. (Kans.), 76
Williams *v.* Board of Educ. (Mo.), 196
Williams *v.* Board of Educ. (W. Va.), 81, 88, 129
Williams *v.* Cody, 201, 224
Williams *v.* Cotton, 432
Williams *v.* Dade County School Board, 309
Williams *v.* McNair, 373
Williams *v.* Primary Sch. District, 447
Williams *v.* School District, 443
Williams *v.* School District of Springfield, 234
Williams *v.* Spencer, 316
Williamson *v.* Board of Educ., 442
Willis *v.* School District, 211
Williston on Contracts, 430
Wilson *v.* Aboline Ind. School Dist., 337
Wilson *v.* Board of Educ., 34
Wilson *v.* Chancellor, 99, 231, 232
Wilson *v.* School Board of Marion County, 485
Wilson, Matter of Estate of, 373
Wilt *v.* Flannigan, 196
Windsor Park Baptist Church, Inc. *v.* Arkansas Activities Assn., 93
Wingate *v.* Whitney Ind. School District, 485
Winnick *v.* Manning, 310
Winston-Salem/Forsythe Co. Unit, No. Car. Assn. of Educ'rs. *v.* Phillips, 240
Wisch *v.* Stanford School Inc., 553, 556
Wisconsin State Employees Assn. *v.* Wisconsin Natural Resources Board, 189
Wisconsin *v.* Yoder, 76, 106–111, 137, 538
Wishart *v.* McDonald, 209, 212, 214, 216
Withers *v.* Charlotte-Mecklenburg Board of Educ., 446
Withrow *v.* Larkin, 226, 227
Wolman *v.* Walter, 572, 578, 598–608
Wondzell *v.* Alaska Wood Products, Inc., 126
Wong *v.* Waterloo Comm. School District, 442
Wood *v.* Board of Educ., 450
Wood *v.* Goodman, 212
Wood *v.* School District No. 65, 99
Wood *v.* Strickland, 450
Woodahl, State ex rel. *v.* Straub, 480
Woodrum *v.* Rolling Hills Board of Educ., 182
Woods *v.* Wright, 313
Woodsmall *v.* Mt. Diablo Un. School District, 436, 438
Woodward *v.* Los Fresnos Ind. School District, 338
Woolcott *v.* St. Board of Educ., 383
Wooten *v.* Alabama Tenure Commission, 196
Woracheck *v.* Stephenson Town School District, 182
Worchester Vocational Teachers Assn. *v.* City of Worchester, 86
Wright *v.* Board of Educ., 338
Wright *v.* Council of Emporia, 363
Wright *v.* Houston Ind. School District, 129
Wright *v.* San Bernardino H.S. District, 438
Wright *v.* Superintending Committee, 33
Wygant *v.* Jackson Board of Education, 396–405

Yang *v.* Special Charter School District, 213
Yaris *v.* Special School District, 384
Yellow Springs Ex. Vill. School District Board of Educ. *v.* Ohio H.S. Athl. Assn., 375
Yeske *v.* Aron Old Farm Schools, 564
Yorktown Faculty Asn. *v.* Yorktown Central School District, 246
Young *v.* Armstrong School District, 331, 334, 355
Young *v.* Board of Educ., 203, 204, 575, 577
Youngsberg *v.* Romeo, 380
Yuen *v.* Board of Educ., 227, 257

Zamora *v.* Pomeroy, 328
Zanders *v.* Board of Educ., 315
Zeller *v.* Donagel School District Board of Educ., 322, 323
Zellers *v.* Huff, 134, 136
Zeluck *v.* Board of Educ., 240
Zevin *v.* School District No. 11, 37, 182
Zimmerman *v.* Minot State College, 204
Zoll *v.* Anker, 79
Zoll *v.* Eastern Allamakee Community School District, 234
Zorach *v.* Clauson, 125
Zucht *v.* King, 78
Zucker *v.* Panitz, 319
Zweifel *v.* Jt. District No. 1, Belleville, 78
Zykan *v.* Warsaw Community School Corp., 88

INDEX

Abandonment. *See* Resignation
Ability grouping. *See* Tests
Abolition, 203
Abuse of discretion, 33, 34
Academic freedom, 237–239
Academic penalties, 313, 314
Accreditation, 21, 538
Administrative law, 13, 14
Admissions. *See* Tests 77–78, 548
Affirmative action. *See* Discrimination
Age. *See* Discrimination
Agency Shop. *See* Labor relations
Aliens, 392, 393
Appearance
  Students, 322–324
  Teachers, 235, 236
Abritration. *See* Labor relations
Associations and clubs. *See also* Interscholastic associations
  Students, 337–338
  Teachers, 234, 240
Assumption of risk. *See* Torts
Athletics, 92–93
Attendance. *See* Compulsory education

Bargaining. *See* Labor relations
Bibles. *See* Religion
Bidding. *See* Contracts
Bilingual education, 365–367
Boards of education. (*See also* Intermediate units; School districts)
  Local school boards, 46
    Appointments, election, and removal, 47
    Meetings, procedures, and requirements, 48–53
    Powers in general, 45
    Records, 51–53
  State boards, 38, 39
Bonds. *See* School finance
Books, 86–92, 115, 237–239
Borrowing. *See* School finance
Budgets. *See* School finance
Busing. *See* Discrimination; Transportation

Cause. *See* Termination for cause
Certification. (*See also* Tests)
  Private school teachers, 542
  Public school teachers, 180–184
Chief state school officers, 38
Church-state relations. *See* Religion
Citizenship requirements
  Students, 392
  Teachers, 184, 185, 393
Civil rights. *See* Discrimination; Due process
  Federal statutes, Excerpts, 388–393
  In general
Common law, 8, 13, 45
Comparative negligence. *See* Torts, Defenses
Competency. *See* Termination for cause; Tests, Competency
Compulsory education (*See also* Home education)
  In general, 75–76
Confidentiality, 336–337
Conflict of interest. *See* Dual loyalty
Constitution
  Excerpts, ix, x
  Federal
    Contract obligations clause, 43–45
    Fifth amendment, 229, 239
    First amendment, 75, 87, 88, 90, 124, 308, 314–322
    Fourteenth amendment, 43, 45, 54, 75, 324, 556
    Fourth amendment, 229, 239, 324–329
    In general, 6, 8, 54
    Separation of powers, 23
    Supremacy clause, 7
    Tenth amendment, 5
  States, 5, 42
Contracts (*See also* School finance, Contracts)
  Contract renewal, 206–208
Contributory negligence (*See also* Torts, Defenses)
Corporal punishment, 306, 338–339, 431
Courts, 14–17, 33
Curriculum (*See also* Books; Extracurricular activities; Graduation; Special education)
  In general, 7, 82–86

Damages. *See* Remedies
De facto–de jure distinctions. *See* Discrimination, Race
Debts. *See* School finance
Defamation. *See* Torts
Delegation, 22, 23, 30–32, 46
Demotion, 200–203
Detention, 339
Diploma. *See* Graduation
Directory, Mandatory distinctions, 36
Discharge. *See* Termination
Discipline. *See* Students; Teachers
Discrimination. (*See also* Tests)
  Private schools, 556–562
  Public schools, 359–361
    Affirmative action, 369–371, 379
    Age, 389–391, 560
    Aliens, 392, 393
    Gifted, 388
    Handicapped, 379–389, 559, 560
    Linguistic, 365–367
    Race, 361–371, 556–558
    Religion, 391, 561
    Sex, 373–379, 558, 559

Statutes (antidiscrimination)
Federal, 371, 388–393, 556–558
State, 372, 561
Testing and placement, 364–368
Transportation, 74
Dress. *See* Appearance
Dual enrollment, 134, 135, 537
Dual loyalty (Conflict of interest, Incompatible offices, Nepotism), 187–190, 497
Due process. (*See also* Freedom of speech and expression)
Procedural rights
Students, 304–312
Teachers, 219–229, 309
Substantive rights. *See* Freedom of speech and expression

Educational malpractice. *See* Torts
Elections, 36, 45
Eminent domain, 70. 548
Employment. *See* Teachers
Equal opportunity. *See* Discrimination
Equity. *See also* Estoppel; Restitution
In general, 13
Estoppel, 196
Exceptional children. *See* Handicapped; Gifted students
Executive sessions. *See* Boards of education
Exhaustion of administrative remedies, 359
Explusion, 306, 307
Extracurricular activities, 90–92

Federal law. *See* Civil rights
Jurisdiction in education, 6, 7
Supremacy over state law, 7
Fees and charges. *See* School finance (Tuition, fees, and charges)
Field trips, 72, 73, 442
Finance. *See* School finance
First aid. *See* Torts
Flag salute, 137, 231, 316
Freedom of speech and expression. *See also* Appearance, Associations, Flag salute
In general
Students, 314–324, 337
Teachers, 229–235
Fourteenth amendment. *See* Constitution (Fourteenth amendment)
Funds. *See* School finance

Gifted students, 388
Government aid. *See* School finance
Grading, 79, 80, 554
Graduation. *See* Tests (Competency) 93–97, 554

Hairstyle. *See* Appearance
Handicapped
Students, 381–387, 559, 560
Teachers, 388, 389, 560
Health, 186
Hearings. *See* Due process
Home education, 543, 545
Homosexuality, 215, 216

Immorality, 213–216
Immunity. *See* Torts
Immunization, 78
Impartial tribunal. *See* Due process (Procedural rights)
Implied duties and powers, of teachers, 192–194
Incapacity, 211
Incompetence, 210, 211
Indemnity. *See* Torts
Injunction. *See* Equity, 13, 256
In loco parentis, 324, 429, 431
Insubordination, 211, 212
Intermediate units, 39
Interscholastic associations, 92–93
Invitees, 433, 564

Judicial review, 33–35
Jurisdiction, 7

Labor relations
Private schools, 550–552
Public schools, 240–258
Arbitration, 252–254
Bargaining and negotiations, 241, 244–249
Picketing, 258
Strikes, 254–258
Union security
Dues and fees, 249–251
Exclusive use of school facilities, 251
Layoff, 205
Legislative authority, 20–22
Liability. *See* Contracts; Torts
Libel. *See* Torts
Liberty interests, 222, 223
Licensee, 434, 564
Limitations. *See* Torts (Defenses)
Lobbying. *See* Political activity
Loyalty oaths, 184, 185

Malpractice. *See* Torts
Mandatory statute and duties, 36, 46
Marriage, students, 329–330
Maternity. *See* Discrimination (Sex)
Mediation. *See* Labor relations (Bargaining)
Meditation. *See* Religion
Meet and discuss. *See* Labor relations (Bargaining)
Meetings. *See* Boards of education
Ministerial functions, 22

National teacher examination, 367
Negligence. *See* Torts
Nepotism. *See* Dual loyalty
Nonpublic schools. *See* Private schools
Nuisance. *See* Torts

Officers, 450
Open meeting laws. *See* Boards of education (Meetings)

Parents rights
  In general, 45, 337, 553
Parochial schools. *See* Private schools
Picketing. *See* Labor relations (Picketing)
Placement and transfers
  Students, 79–81, 93–97
  Teachers, 197, 198
Political activity
  Board members, 99
  Lobbying, 495
  Relations to law and education, 4
  Teachers, 232
Poverty groups, 391–392
Prayer. *See* Religion (Public schools)
Pregnancy, 329–330, 337
Privacy. *See* Marriage; Pregnancy; Records; Search and seizure
  In general, 239
Private schools. *See* Home education
  Admissions, 548
  Approval criteria, 537–543
  Dual enrollment, 134, 135, 579, 580, 583
  Government aids to, 570–583
  In general, 536, 537
  Labor relations, 550–552
  Records, 555
  School property regulations. *See* School property
  Student rights and discipline. *See* Discrimination
  Teacher rights and discipline. *See* Discrimination
    Certification, 542
    Civil rights, 548, 549
    Contracts, 549
    Tenure, 549
  Transportation, 574–577
Privilege, 429, 432, 443
Probationers. *See* Contracts (Renewal)
Procedural rights. *See* Due process
Promotion, 93–97
Property. *See* School finance (Taxation)
Property interests, 220, 221
Punishment (Excessive), 313

Quorum, 50

Race. *See* Discrimination (Race)
Ratification, 36, 37, 496, 497
Records. *See* Boards of education (Records)
  Students, 330–336, 555
  Teachers, 239, 248
Reductions in force, 203–206
Released time. *See* Religion and education
Religion and education. *See also* Private schools (Government aid)
  First amendment religion clauses, 124–126, 137–139
  Public schools
    Baccalaureate services, 132, 133
    Bible readings and studies, 126–128, 130
    Evolution and creation science, 128–130
    Flag salute, 137
    Holiday displays, 131, 132
    Invocations, meditation and prayer, 132, 133
    Religious garb, 133
    Religious holidays, leaves, released time, 125, 126, 391
    Religious literature, 128
    Religious objections to activities, courses, texts and reading assignments, 128–130, 137–139
    Sex education, 130, 131
    Use of church property for public school purposes, 135
    Use of public school by religious groups, 127, 136
Remedies
  Damages, 217
Res ipsa loquitur, 433, 565
Residence, 77, 185
  Board members, 47
  Students, 77, 92, 491
  Teachers, 185
Resignation and abandonment, 217–219
Respondeat superior. *See* Torts
Restitution, 490, 502–504
Retirement, 217, 218, 390

School boards. *See* Boards of education
School buildings. *See* School property
School closing, 79
School codes, 9–12
School construction, 70, 71
School districts
  Classes, formation and reorganization, 39–42
School finance
  Private schools
    Government aid, 570–583
    In general, 553–554, 569
  Public schools
    Borrowed funds, 486–490
    Budget controls, 482
    Contracts, 496–505
    Grants, 495
    School funds, 505, 506
    Taxation, 484
    Tuition, fees and charges, 490–494
School newspapers, 316–322

School property
Private schools, 545–548
Public schools
Acquisition and construction, 68–71, 545–548
Non-school uses, 97–100
Disposition (Sale, lease, etc.) 100–101
Search and seizure
Students, 324–329
Teachers, 239
Segregation. *See* Discriminaion (Race, Sex)
Seniority, 204
Separation of church and state. *See* Religion
Sex classifications. *See* Discrimination (Sex)
Sex education. *See* Religion (Public schools)
Shared time. *See* Dual enrollment
Special education. *See also* Handicapped (students)
In general, 97
Standing to sue, 5, 36, 496
State aid. *See* School finance
State education agencies. *See* Boards of education
Statutes
In general, 8
Stigmatization, 222
Strikes. *See* Labor relations (Strikes)
Students. *See also* Admissions, Appearance, Association, Discrimination, Due process, Immunization, Graduation, Privacy, Records, Residence, School newspapers, Search and seizure, Substantive rights, Suspensions, Tests, Transportation
Assignment and Placement, 78–81
Substantial evidence rule, 33, 34
Substantive rights. *See* Appearance, Association, Civil rights, Constitution, Freedom of speech and expression, Privacy, Religion
Supervision. *See* Torts (Supervision)
Suspension
Students, 305
Teachers, 203–205

Taxes. *See* School Finance
Teachers. *See also* Academic freedom, Appearance, Associations, Certification, Citizenship, Civil rights, Demotion, Discrimnation, Dual loyalty, Due process, Flag salute, Health, Homosexuality, Labor relations, Layoff, Loyalty oaths, Placement, Political activity, Pregnancy, Privacy, Probationers, Promotion, Records, Reductions in force, Residence, Resignation, Retirement, Search and seizure, Seniority, Substantive rights, Suspension, Tenure, Termination for cause, Tests, Torts
In general, 175
Performance rating, 199
Tenure, 194–197
Termination for cause, 208–217
Tests
Ability grouping, 364–366
Competency tests, 94, 95
Textbooks. *See* Books
Torts
Federal torts—Injury to civil rights, 451–457
State law torts, 426–430
Corporal punishment, 429, 431–433, 562
Defamation (Libel and slander), 442–444, 568
Defenses to liability (Assumption of risk, Comparative negligence, Contributory negligence, Immunity, Lack of proximate cause, Limitations on amount of recovery, Limitations on suit, Privilege), 428–431, 449, 450, 562, 563, 567, 568
Field trips, 72, 73, 442
Immunity doctrines, 445–448, 450, 451, 562, 563
Indemnity, 450, 451
Malpractice, 444, 445, 568
Negligence claims, 433–442, 562–567
Nuisance, 446, 447, 563, 564
Releases and waivers of tort claims, 430
Respondeat superior, 445, 562, 564
State civil rights statutes, 457–458, 568
Supervision duties, 435–442
Transportation, 440–442
Tracking. *See* Tests (Ability grouping)
Transcripts, 553, 554
Transportation. *See* Private schools (Transportation); Torts (Transportation), 71–74
Trespassers, 434
Truancy, 75
Tuition. *See* School finance

Ultra vires actions, 31
Unions. *See* Labor relations
Unprofessional conduct, 212–216

Voting. *See* Boards of education
Vouchers, 578

Waivers. *See* Torts

Zoning, 6
Private schools, 545–548
Public schools, 68, 69

ADDENDUM

As this book was going to press, the United States Supreme Court issued two major decisions that affect its content.

p. 215, n. 246. The Supreme Court ruled that a state may criminally punish private consensual homosexual conduct. *Bowers v. Hardwick,* 106 S. Ct. ______ (1986). The potential effect of that decision on teacher discharge for homosexual conduct is the subject of current debate but remains unsettled.

p. 308, n. 23. The Supreme Court ruled that a school rule against student use of obscenity provided sufficient due process notice that lewd and indecent speech would also be punishable. *Bethel School District v. Fraser,* 106 S. Ct. ______ (1986). This case suggests a looser notice standard than that previously adopted by lower courts.

p. 316, n. 70. In the Bethel decision the Supreme Court also limited prior lower court protection of vulgar student speech, by upholding the constitutionality of school suspension of a student for an address to his high school assembly that was lewdly suggestive.